ADVANCES IN

NEURAL INFORMATION PROCESSING SYSTEMS 5

OTHER TITLES OF INTEREST FROM MORGAN KAUFMANN PUBLISHERS

NIPS-4-
Advances in Neural Information Processing Systems
Proceedings of the 1991 Conference
Edited by John E. Moody, Stephen J. Hanson, and Richard P. Lippmann

NIPS-3-
Advances in Neural Information Processing Systems
Proceedings of the 1990 Conference
Edited by Richard P. Lippmann, John E. Moody, and David S. Touretzky

NIPS-2-
Advances in Neural Information Processing Systems
Proceedings of the 1989 Conference
Edited by David S. Touretzky

NIPS-1-
Advances in Neural Information Processing Systems
Proceedings of the 1988 Conference
Edited by David S. Touretzky

Computer Systems That Learn: Classification and Prediction Methods from Statistics, Neural Nets, Machine Learning, and Expert Systems
By Sholom M. Weiss and Casimir A. Kulikowski

Learning Machines
By Nils J. Nilsson, with an Introduction by Terrence J. Sejnowski and Halbert White

Foundations of Genetic Algorithms–2
Edited by L. Darrell Whitley

Foundations of Genetic Algorithms
Edited by Gregory J. E. Rawlins

Genetic Algorithms: Proceedings of the Fourth International Conference
Edited by Rick Belew and Lashon Booker

Genetic Algorithms: Proceedings of the Third International Conference
Edited by David Schaffer

ADVANCES IN

NEURAL INFORMATION PROCESSING SYSTEMS 5

EDITED BY

STEPHEN JOSÉ HANSON
SIEMENS RESEARCH CENTER

JACK D. COWAN
UNIVERSITY OF CHICAGO

C. LEE GILES
NEC RESEARCH INSTITUTE

MORGAN KAUFMANN PUBLISHERS
2929 CAMPUS DRIVE
SUITE 260
SAN MATEO CALIFORNIA 94403

Senior Editor *Bruce M. Spatz*
Production Manager *Yonie Overton*
Composition *BookMasters, Inc.*
Cover Design *Jo Jackson*
Printer *R. R. Donnelley & Sons*

MORGAN KAUFMANN PUBLISHERS, INC.
Editorial Office:
2929 Campus Drive, Suite 260
San Mateo, CA 94403
(415)578-9911

97 96 95 94 93 5 4 3 2 1

Library of Congress Cataloging in Publication Data
is available for this book.

ISSN 1049-5258
ISBN 1-55860-274-7

CONTENTS

Part I LEARNING AND GENERALIZATION

Part II ARCHITECTURES AND ALGORITHMS

Part III CONTROL, NAVIGATION, AND PLANNING

Part IV VISUAL PROCESSING

Part V STOCHASTIC LEARNING AND ANALYSIS

Part VI NETWORK DYNAMICS AND CHAOS

Part VII THEORY AND ANALYSIS

Part VIII SPEECH AND SIGNAL PROCESSING

Part IX APPLICATIONS

Part X IMPLEMENTATIONS

Part XI COGNITIVE SCIENCE

Part XII COMPUTATIONAL AND THEORETICAL NEUROBIOLOGY

PREFACE

This volume contains the collected papers summarizing the talks and posters presented at the sixth annual NIPS conference (short for Neural Information Processing Systems—Natural and Synthetic), held in Denver, Colorado, from 30 November to 3 December, 1992.

NIPS began initially as a small workshop in the early 1980s (see last year's Preface) at Caltech with an interface between physics and computation. In particular, the associative and memory storage capabilities of a system of simplified computing elements interacting in a network architecture led to an investigation of how the general properties of systems of neurons in the brain might be analogous to the system level properties of computational networks. Computational, mathematical, biological, and psychological implications of such networks were hotly debated and discussed.

At some point in these early days, we could say the "Decade of Neural Networks" began. We are roughly halfway through this maturation process and, although the size, diversity, and scope of the meetings have transformed the field many times now, the basic belief that a network of simplified computing elements can have important consequences across a multidisciplinary landscape is still at the heart of the NIPS meeting in its sixth year.

The NIPS technical program, while highly selective, has always tried to be inclusive. "Neural networks" were to be defined more from the bottom up by the quality of the submissions than by a single unifying vision of what was or was not deemed a neural network. This year sees an even greater expansion of trends begun in past conferences in the interface between neural networks, statistics, complexity theory, AI, neurobiology, and cognitive science.

The breadth of work and topics in both theory and application, draws comments from repeat attendees of how the field is beginning to transform to cover what might be better called "Machine Intelligence"—something akin to a reconstituted AI, with a stronger identity and broader intellectual roots. In any case, a brief review of the program will impress one with the vitality and strength of this field as it moves towards its "middle age." As usual, there were many exciting talks on various learning and architectural topics, including hybrid systems that exploit connections with HMMS, projection pursuit, and principal component analysis. Application work was even more varied than in previous years, including neural networks applied to clinical decision making (Baxt), sleep EEG (Tarassenko), regulation of glucose in diabetics (Tresp), fingerprint matching (Baldi), steering a van on the open highway at high speeds (Pomerleau), and cursive handwriting recognition (Schenkel). Finally, within the neurobiological track, there were some computational accounts of hippocampal function with regard to navigation (Burgess) and conditioning and memory (Gluck).

The workshops this year were held at Vail and chaired by Gerry Tesauro. As the attendees have known for many years now, these workshops are very special and provide a forum for further discussion, new results, and future directions in the field. Against a background of some of the best skiing in years, the workshops covered theory and applications in which new trends in learning theory were framed and state-of-the-art methods for various applications areas were discussed, including robot learning, character recognition, neural network training algorithms, time series prediction, hidden unit interpretation, and many more.

In January 1992, the NIPS foundation was formed. As announced at this meeting, the NIPS Foundation was formed to provide continuity and stability for future NIPS conferences. As a nonprofit organization, its main activity is general long-term policy for the NIPS programs and administration and financial stability of the conference in future years. Ed Posner was elected as first president of the Foundation, Terry Sejnowski as secretary, and John Moody as Treasurer. Other members of the foundation include previous general chairs Scott Kirkpatrick; Richard Lippmann; Stephen Hanson; Jack Cowan; IEEE representative Terry Fine; and general legal counsel, Philip Sotel. General chairs and program chairs of future conferences have complete responsibility for the implementation of policy and all administrative and program-related decisions for that year.

At its present size, the NIPS conference requires the contributions and efforts of a committed, highly altruistic group of volunteers. We would first like to thank all the other members of the 1992 program and organizing committees who helped make this conference possible. (They are listed in the following sections.) In particular, we thank Chuck Anderson for unflagging efforts at local arrangements and all the wonderful student volunteers from Colorado State and from UC Bolder; Davi Geiger for the fantastic poster and extensive publicity this year; Karin Cermele of Siemens for her extensive work throughout the year as the conference secretary; and both Karin and Denise Hall of Colorado State for running the conference desk so smoothly. Finally, we thank everyone who attended and submitted papers and the 130 referees who carefully read and reviewed the 500 + papers we received this year.

Stephen J. Hanson, Siemens

Jack D. Cowan, University of Chicago

C. Lee Giles, NEC

January, 1993

NIPS-92 Organizing Committee

General Chair	Stephen J. Hanson, Siemens
Program Chair	Jack Cowan, University of Chicago
Workshop Chair	Gerry Tesauro, IBM
Publicity Chair	Davi Geiger, Siemens
Publications Chair	Lee Giles, NEC Research Institute
Treasurer	Bob Allen, Bellcore
Government/Corporate Liaison	Lee Giles, NEC Research Institute
Local Arrangements Chair	Chuck Anderson, Colorado State University
IEEE Liaison	Terrence Fine, Cornell University
Tutorials Chair	Stephen J. Hanson, Siemens

NIPS-92 Publicity Committee

Publicity Chair	Davi Geiger, Siemens
Overseas Liaison (Japan)	Mitsuo Kawato, ATR Research Laboratories
Overseas Liaison (Australia, India, Singapore)	Marwan Jabri, University of Sydney
Overseas Liaison (United Kingdom)	John Bridle, RSRE
Overseas Liaison (Europe)	Benny Lautrup, Niels Bohr Institute
Overseas Liaison (South America)	Andreas Meier, Simon Bolivar University

NIPS-92 Program Committee

Program Chair	Jack Cowan, University of Chicago
Program CoChairs	Andy Barto, University of Massachusetts
	Jim Burr, Stanford University
	David Haussler, UCSC
	Alan Lapedes, Los Alamos
	Bruce McNaughton, University of Arizona
	Bartlett Mel, JPL
	Mike Mozer, University of Colorado
	John Pearson, SRI
	Terry Sejnowski, Salk Institute
	David Touretzky, CMU
	Alex Waibel, CMU
	Halbert White, UCSD
	Alan Yuille, Harvard University

NIPS Foundation Board Members

Ed Posner, President
Scott Kirkpatrick
Terry Sejnowski
Richard Lippmann
John Moody
Stephen J. Hanson
Terrence Fine, IEEE Representative 1992–93
Philip K. Sotel, Attorney

NIPS-92 REFEREES

Yasar Abu-Mostafa, Caltech
Subutai Ahmad, Siemens AG
Robert Allen, Bellcore
Thomas Anastasio, USC
Martin Anthony, London School of Economics
Joseph Atick, Institute for Advanced Study
Christopher Atkeson, MIT
Jonathan Bachrach
Pierre Baldi, JPL
Chris Barnes, Los Alamos
Andy Barto, University of Massachusetts
Eric Baum, NEC Research Institute
Sue Becker, University of Queensland
William Bialek, NEC Research Institute
A. B. Bonds, Vanderbilt University
Lyle Borg-Graham, MIT
James Bower, Caltech
Leo Breiman, UC Berkeley
Thomas Brown, Yale University
Joe Bryngleson, Los Alamos
David Burr, Bellcore
Jim Burr, Stanford
Marc Cohen, NIH National Eye Institute
Gary Cottrell, UCSD
Chris Darken, Yale University
Bert de Vries, David Sarnoff Research Center
Bradley Dickinson, Princeton University
Diane Duffy, Bellcore 445
Scott Fahlman, CMU
Frank Fallside, Cambridge University
Meir Feder, Tel Aviv University
Terrence Fine, Cornell University
Judy Franklin, GTE Laboratories
Mark Gluck, Rutgers University
Norberto Grzywacz, The Smith-Kettlewell Eye Institute
Vijaykumar Gullipalli, University of Massachusetts
Patrick Haffner, Centre National d'Etudes des Telecommunications
David Haussler, UCSC
Robert Hecht-Nielsen, HNC
John Hertz, NORDITA
Geoff Hinton, University of Toronto
Kurt Hornik, Technische Universitt
Nathan Intrator, Brown University
Larry Jackel, AT&T Bell Labs
Robert Jacobs, Harvard University
Michael Jordan, MIT
Stephen Judd, Siemens
Dan Kersten, University of Minnesota Minneapolis
David Kirk, Caltech
Christof Koch, Caltech
Alan Kramer, UC Berkeley
Anders Krogh, UCSC
Chung Ming Kuan, University of Illinois
Gary Kuhn, CCRP-IDA
Stephen Lane, Robicon Systems
Alan Lapedes, Los Alamos
John Lazzaro, UC Berkeley
William B. Levy, University of Virginia
Richard Lippmann, MIT Lincoln Labs
James Little, University of British Columbia
Michael Littman, Bellcore
Shawn Lockery, Salk Institute
Bruce McNaughton, University of Arizona
Jitendra Malik, UC Berkeley
Lina Massone, Northwestern University
Bartlett Mel, Caltech
Risto Miikkulainen, University of Texas
Kenneth Miller, Caltech
Andy Moore, Caltech

Nelson Morgan, ICS Institute
Mike Mozer, University of Colorado
Paul Munro, University of Pittsburgh
Michiel Noordewier, Rutgers University
Steven Nowlan, Salk Institute
Stephen Omohundro, ICS Institute
Art Owen, Stanford University
Barak Pearlmutter, Yale University
John C. Pearson, David Sarnoff Research
Pietro Perona, Caltech
James K. Peterson, Clemson University
Tom Petsche, Siemens
John Platt, Synaptics
David Plaut, CMU
Mark Plutowski, UCSD
Dean Pomerleau, CMU
K. Venkatesh Prasad, Caltech
Lori Pratt, Colorado School of Mines
Jose Principe, University of Florida
David Rogers
Juergen Schmidhuber, University of Colorado
Daniel Seligson, Intel Corp
Terry Sejnowski, Salk Institute
Patricia Sharp, Yale University
Jude Shavlik, University of Wisconsin
Gordon Shepherd, Yale University
Patrice Simard, AT&T Bell Labs
Paul Smolensky, University of Colorado
Max Stinchcombe, UCSD
Paul Stolorz, Los Alamos
Richard Sutton, GTE Laboratories
Richard Szeliski, Digital Equipment Corporation
Joe Tebelskis, CMU
James Theiler, Los Alamos
Sebastian Thrun, CMU
Naftali Tishby, AT&T Bell Labs
David Touretzky, CMU
Roger Traub, IBM TJ Watson Research Center
Alessandro Treves, Oxford University
David van Essen, Caltech
Kelvin Wagner, University of Colorado
Alex Waibel, CMU
Raymond Watrous, Siemens
Andreas Weigend, Xerox Corporation
Halbert White, UCSD
Matt Wilson, University of Arizona
David Wolpert, Santa Fe Institute
Lei Xu, Harvard University
Ben Yuhas, Bellcore
Alan Yuille, Harvard University
Richard Zemel, University of Toronto

PART I

LEARNING AND GENERALIZATION

On the Use of Projection Pursuit Constraints for Training Neural Networks

Nathan Intrator*
Computer Science Department
Tel-Aviv University
Ramat-Aviv, 69978 ISRAEL
and
Institute for Brain and Neural Systems,
Brown University
nin@math.tau.ac.il

Abstract

We present a novel classification and regression method that combines exploratory projection pursuit (unsupervised training) with projection pursuit regression (supervised training), to yield a new family of cost/complexity penalty terms. Some improved generalization properties are demonstrated on real world problems.

1 Introduction

Parameter estimation becomes difficult in high-dimensional spaces due to the increasing sparseness of the data. Therefore, when a low dimensional representation is embedded in the data, dimensionality reduction methods become useful. One such method – projection pursuit regression (Friedman and Stuetzle, 1981) (PPR) is capable of performing dimensionality reduction by composition, namely, it constructs an approximation to the desired response function using a composition of lower dimensional smooth functions. These functions depend on low dimensional projections through the data.

*Research was supported by the National Science Foundation, the Army Research Office, and the Office of Naval Research.

When the dimensionality of the problem is in the thousands, even projection pursuit methods are almost always over-parametrized, therefore, additional smoothing is needed for low variance estimation. Exploratory Projection Pursuit (Friedman and Tukey, 1974; Friedman, 1987) (EPP) may be useful for that. It searches in a high dimensional space for structure in the form of (semi) linear projections with constraints characterized by a projection index. The projection index may be considered as a universal prior for a large class of problems, or may be tailored to a specific problem based on prior knowledge.

In this paper, the general form of exploratory projection pursuit is formulated to be an additional constraint for projection pursuit regression. In particular, a hybrid combination of supervised and unsupervised artificial neural network (ANN) is described as a special case. In addition, a specific projection index that is particularly useful for classification (Intrator, 1990; Intrator and Cooper, 1992) is introduced in this context. A more detailed discussion appears in Intrator (1993).

2 Brief Description of Projection Pursuit Regression

Let (X, Y) be a pair of random variables, $X \in R^d$, and $Y \in R$. The problem is to approximate the d dimensional surface

$$f(x) = E[Y|X = x]$$

from n observations $(x_1, y_1), \ldots, (x_n, y_n)$.

PPR tries to approximate a function f by a sum of ridge functions (functions that are constant along lines)

$$f(x) \simeq \sum_{j=1}^{m} g_j(a_j^T x).$$

The fitting procedure alternates between an estimation of a direction $\hat{a}$ and an estimation of a smooth function g, such that at iteration j, the square average of the residuals

$$r_{ij}(x_i) = r_{ij-1} - \hat{g}_j(\hat{a}_j^T x_i)$$

is minimized. This process is initialized by setting $r_{i0} = y_i$. Usually, the initial values of a_j are taken to be the first few principal components of the data.

Estimation of the ridge functions can be achieved by various nonparametric smoothing techniques such as locally linear functions (Friedman and Stuetzle, 1981), k-nearest neighbors (Hall, 1989b), splines or variable degree polynomials. The smoothness constraint imposed on g, implies that the actual projection pursuit is achieved by minimizing at iteration j, the sum

$$\sum_{i=1}^{n} r_{ij}^2(x_i) + C(\hat{g}_j),$$

for some smoothness measure C.

Although PPR converges to the desired response function (Jones, 1987), the use of non-parametric function estimation is likely to lead to overfitting. Recent results (Hornik, 1991) suggest that a feed forward network architecture with a single hidden layer and a rather general fixed activation function is a universal approximator. Therefore, the use of a non-parametric single ridge function estimation can be avoided. It is thus appropriate to concentrate on the estimation of good projections. In the next section we present a general framework of PPR architecture, and in section 4 we restrict it to a feed-forward architecture with sigmoidal hidden units.

3 Estimating The Projections Using Exploratory Projection Pursuit

Exploratory projection pursuit is based on seeking *interesting* projections of high dimensional data points (Kruskal, 1969; Switzer, 1970; Kruskal, 1972; Friedman and Tukey, 1974; Friedman, 1987; Jones and Sibson, 1987; Hall, 1988; Huber, 1985, for review). The notion of interesting projections is motivated by an observation that for most high-dimensional data clouds, most low-dimensional projections are approximately normal (Diaconis and Freedman, 1984). This finding suggests that the important information in the data is conveyed in those directions whose single dimensional projected distribution is far from Gaussian. Various projection indices (measures for the goodness of a projection) differ on the assumptions about the nature of deviation from normality, and in their computational efficiency. They can be considered as different priors motivated by specific assumptions on the underlying model.

To partially decouple the search for a projection vector from the search for a non-parametric ridge function, we propose to add a penalty term, which is based on a projection index, to the energy minimization associated with the estimation of the ridge functions and the projections. Specifically, let $\rho(a)$ be a projection index which is minimized for projections with a certain deviation from normality; At the j'th iteration, we minimize the sum

$$\sum_i r_j^2(x_i) + C(g_j) + \rho(a_j).$$

When a concurrent minimization over several projections/functions is practical, we get a penalty term of the form

$$B(\hat{f}) = \sum_j [C(g_j) + \rho(a_j)].$$

Since C and ρ may not be linear, the more general measure that does not assume a stepwise approach, but instead seeks l projections and ridge functions concurrently, is given by

$$B(\hat{f}) = C(g_1, \ldots, g_l) + \rho(a_1, \ldots, a_l),$$

In practice, ρ depends implicitly on the training data, (the empirical density) and is therefore replaced by its empirical measure $\hat{\rho}$.

3.1 Some Possible Measures

Some applicable projection indices are discussed in (Huber, 1985; Jones and Sibson, 1987; Friedman, 1987; Hall, 1989a; Intrator, 1990). Probably, all the possible measures should emphasize some form of deviation from normality but the specific type may depend on the problem at hand. For example, a measure based on the Karhunen Loève expansion (Mougeot et al., 1991) may be useful for image compression with autoassociative networks, since in this case one is interested in minimizing the L^2 norm of the distance between the reconstructed image and the original one, and under mild conditions, the Karhunen Loève expansion gives the optimal solution.

A different type of prior knowledge is required for classification problems. The underlying assumption then is that the data is clustered (when projecting in the right directions) and that the classification may be achieved by some (nonlinear) mapping of these clusters. In such a case, the projection index should emphasize multi-modality as a specific deviation from normality. A projection index that emphasizes multimodalities in the projected distribution (without relying on the class labels) has recently been introduced (Intrator, 1990) and implemented efficiently using a variant of a biologically motivated unsupervised network (Intrator and Cooper, 1992). Its integration into a back-propagation classifier will be discussed below.

3.2 Adding EPP constraints to back-propagation network

One way of adding some prior knowledge into the architecture is by minimizing the effective number of parameters using weight sharing, in which a single weight is shared among many connections in the network (Waibel et al., 1989; Le Cun et al., 1989). An extension of this idea is the "soft weight sharing" which favors irregularities in the weight distribution in the form of multimodality (Nowlan and Hinton, 1992). This penalty improved generalization results obtained by weight elimination penalty. Both these methods make an explicit assumption about the structure of the weight space, but with no regard to the structure of the input space.

As described in the context of projection pursuit regression, a penalty term may be added to the energy functional minimized by error back propagation, for the purpose of measuring directly the goodness of the projections sought by the network. Since our main interest is in reducing overfitting for high dimensional problems, our underlying assumption is that the surface function to be estimated can be faithfully represented using a low dimensional composition of sigmoidal functions, namely, using a back-propagation network in which the number of hidden units is *much smaller* than the number of input units. Therefore, the penalty term may be added only to the hidden layer. The synaptic modification equations of the hidden units' weights become

$$\begin{aligned}\frac{\partial w_{ij}}{\partial t} &= -\epsilon \Big[\frac{\partial \mathcal{E}(w,x)}{\partial w_{ij}} \\ &\quad + \frac{\partial \rho(w_1,\ldots,w_n)}{\partial w_{ij}} \\ &\quad + (\text{Contribution of cost/complexity terms})\Big].\end{aligned}$$

An approach of this type has been used in image compression, with a penalty aimed at minimizing the entropy of the projected distribution (Bichsel and Seitz, 1989). This penalty certainly measures deviation from normality, since entropy is maximized for a Gaussian distribution.

4 Projection Index for Classification: The Unsupervised BCM Neuron

Intrator (1990) has recently shown that a variant of the Bienenstock, Cooper and Munro neuron (Bienenstock et al., 1982) performs exploratory projection pursuit using a projection index that measures multi-modality. This neuron version allows theoretical analysis of some visual deprivation experiments (Intrator and Cooper, 1992), and is in agreement with the vast experimental results on visual cortical plasticity (Clothiaux et al., 1991). A network implementation which can find several projections in parallel while retaining its computational efficiency, was found to be applicable for extracting features from very high dimensional vector spaces (Intrator and Gold, 1993; Intrator et al., 1991; Intrator, 1992)

The activity of neuron k in the network is $c_k = \sum_i x_i w_{ik} + w_{0k}$. The *inhibited* activity and threshold of the k'th neuron is given by

$$\tilde{c}_k = \sigma(c_k - \eta \sum_{j \neq k} c_j), \qquad \tilde{\Theta}_m^k = E[\tilde{c}_k^2].$$

The threshold $\tilde{\Theta}_m^k$ is the point at which the modification function ϕ changes sign (see Intrator and Cooper, 1992 for further details). The function ϕ is given by

$$\phi(c, \Theta_m) = c(c - \Theta_m).$$

The risk (projection index) for a single neuron is given by

$$R(w_k) = -\{\frac{1}{3}E[\tilde{c}_k^3] - \frac{1}{4}E^2[\tilde{c}_k^2]\}.$$

The total risk is the sum of each local risk. The negative gradient of the risk that leads to the synaptic modification equations is given by

$$\frac{\partial w_{ij}}{\partial t} = E[\phi(\tilde{c}_j, {\Theta_m}^j)\sigma'(\tilde{c}_j)x_i - \eta \sum_{k \neq j} \phi(\tilde{c}_k, \tilde{\Theta}_m^k)\sigma'(\tilde{c}_k)x_i].$$

This last equation is an additional penalty to the energy minimization of the supervised network. Note that there is an interaction between adjacent neurons in the hidden layer. In practice, the stochastic version of the differential equation can be used as the learning rule.

5 Applications

We have applied this hybrid classification method to various speech and image recognition problems in high dimensional space. In one speech application we used voiceless stop consonants extracted from the TIMIT database as training tokens (Intrator and Tajchman, 1991). A detailed biologically motivated speech representation was produced by Lyon's cochlear model (Lyon, 1982; Slaney, 1988). This representation produced 5040 dimensions (84 channels $\times$ 60 time slices). In addition to an initial voiceless stop, each token contained a final vowel from the set [aa, ao, er, iy]. Classification of the voiceless stop consonants using a test set that included 7 vowels [uh, ih, eh, ae, ah, uw, ow] produced an average error of 18.8%

while on the same task classification using back-propagation network produced an average error of 20.9% (a significant difference, $P < .0013$). Additional experiments on vowel tokens appear in Tajchman and Intrator (1992).

Another application is in the area of face recognition from gray level pixels (Intrator et al., 1992). After aligning and normalizing the images, the input was set to 37 $\times$ 62 pixels (total of 2294 dimensions). The recognition performance was tested on a subset of the MIT Media Lab database of face images made available by Turk and Pentland (1991) which contained 27 face images of each of 16 different persons. The images were taken under varying illumination and camera location. Of the 27 images available, 17 randomly chosen ones served for training and the remaining 10 were used for testing. Using an ensemble average of hybrid networks (Lincoln and Skrzypek, 1990; Pearlmutter and Rosenfeld, 1991; Perrone and Cooper, 1992) we obtained an error rate of 0.62% as opposed to 1.2% using a similar ensemble of back-prop networks. A single back-prop network achieves an error between 2.5% to 6% on this data. The experiments were done using 8 hidden units.

6 Summary

A penalty that allows the incorporation of additional prior information on the underlying model was presented. This prior was introduced in the context of projection pursuit regression, classification, and in the context of back-propagation network. It achieves partial decoupling of estimation of the ridge functions (in PPR) or the regression function in back-propagation net from the estimation of the projections. Thus it is potentially useful in reducing problems associated with overfitting which are more pronounced in high dimensional data.

Some possible projection indices were discussed and a specific projection index that is particularly useful for classification was presented in this context. This measure that emphasizes multi-modality in the projected distribution, was found useful in several very high dimensional problems.

6.1 Acknowledgments

I wish to thank Leon Cooper, Stu Geman and Michael Perrone for many fruitful conversations and to the referee for helpful comments. The speech experiments were performed using the computational facilities of the Cognitive Science Department at Brown University. Research was supported by the National Science Foundation, the Army Research Office, and the Office of Naval Research.

References

Bichsel, M. and Seitz, P. (1989). Minimum class entropy: A maximum information approach to layered netowrks. *Neural Networks*, 2:133–141.

Bienenstock, E. L., Cooper, L. N., and Munro, P. W. (1982). Theory for the development of neuron selectivity: orientation specificity and binocular interaction in visual cortex. *Journal Neuroscience*, 2:32–48.

Clothiaux, E. E., Cooper, L. N., and Bear, M. F. (1991). Synaptic plasticity in visual cortex: Comparison of theory with experiment. *Journal of Neurophysiology*, 66:1785–1804.

Diaconis, P. and Freedman, D. (1984). Asymptotics of graphical projection pursuit. *Annals of Statistics*, 12:793–815.

Friedman, J. H. (1987). Exploratory projection pursuit. *Journal of the American Statistical Association*, 82:249–266.

Friedman, J. H. and Stuetzle, W. (1981). Projection pursuit regression. *Journal of the American Statistical Association*, 76:817–823.

Friedman, J. H. and Tukey, J. W. (1974). A projection pursuit algorithm for exploratory data analysis. *IEEE Transactions on Computers*, C(23):881–889.

Hall, P. (1988). Estimating the direction in which data set is most interesting. *Probab. Theory Rel. Fields*, 80:51–78.

Hall, P. (1989a). On polynomial-based projection indices for exploratory projection pursuit. *The Annals of Statistics*, 17:589–605.

Hall, P. (1989b). On projection pursuit regression. *The Annals of Statistics*, 17:573–588.

Hornik, K. (1991). Approximation capabilities of multilayer feedforward networks. *Neural Networks*, 4:251–257.

Huber, P. J. (1985). Projection pursuit. (with discussion). *The Annals of Statistics*, 13:435–475.

Intrator, N. (1990). Feature extraction using an unsupervised neural network. In Touretzky, D. S., Ellman, J. L., Sejnowski, T. J., and Hinton, G. E., editors, *Proceedings of the 1990 Connectionist Models Summer School*, pages 310–318. Morgan Kaufmann, San Mateo, CA.

Intrator, N. (1992). Feature extraction using an unsupervised neural network. *Neural Computation*, 4:98–107.

Intrator, N. (1993). Combining exploratory projection pursuit and projection pursuit regression with application to neural networks. *Neural Computation*. In press.

Intrator, N. and Cooper, L. N. (1992). Objective function formulation of the BCM theory of visual cortical plasticity: Statistical connections, stability conditions. *Neural Networks*, 5:3–17.

Intrator, N. and Gold, J. I. (1993). Three-dimensional object recognition of gray level images: The usefulness of distinguishing features. *Neural Computation*. In press.

Intrator, N., Gold, J. I., Bülthoff, H. H., and Edelman, S. (1991). Three-dimensional object recognition using an unsupervised neural network: Understanding the distinguishing features. In Feldman, Y. and Bruckstein, A., editors, *Proceedings of the 8th Israeli Conference on AICV*, pages 113–123. Elsevier.

Intrator, N., Reisfeld, D., and Yeshurun, Y. (1992). Face recognition using a hybrid supervised/unsupervised neural network. Preprint.

Intrator, N. and Tajchman, G. (1991). Supervised and unsupervised feature extraction from a cochlear model for speech recognition. In Juang, B. H., Kung, S. Y., and Kamm, C. A., editors, *Neural Networks for Signal Processing – Proceedings of the 1991 IEEE Workshop*, pages 460–469. IEEE Press, New York, NY.

Jones, L. (1987). On a conjecture of huber concerning the convergence of projection pursuit regression. *Annals of Statistics*, 15:880–882.

Jones, M. C. and Sibson, R. (1987). What is projection pursuit? (with discussion). *J. Roy. Statist. Soc.*, Ser. A(150):1–36.

Kruskal, J. B. (1969). Toward a practical method which helps uncover the structure of the set of multivariate observations by finding the linear transformation which optimizes a new 'index of condensation'. In Milton, R. C. and Nelder, J. A., editors, *Statistical Computation*, pages 427–440. Academic Press, New York.

Kruskal, J. B. (1972). Linear transformation of multivariate data to reveal clustering. In Shepard, R. N., Romney, A. K., and Nerlove, S. B., editors, *Multidimensional Scaling: Theory and Application in the Behavioral Sciences, I, Theory*, pages 179–191. Seminar Press, New York and London.

Le Cun, Y., Boser, B., Denker, J., Henderson, D., Howard, R., Hubbard, W., and Jackel, L. (1989). Backpropagation applied to handwritten zip code recognition. *Neural Computation*, 1:541–551.

Lincoln, W. P. and Skrzypek, J. (1990). Synergy of clustering multiple back-propagation networks. In Touretzky, D. S. and Lippmann, R. P., editors, *Advances in Neural Information Processing Systems*, volume 2, pages 650–657. Morgan Kaufmann, San Mateo, CA.

Lyon, R. F. (1982). A computational model of filtering, detection, and compression in the cochlea. In *Proceedings IEEE International Conference on Acoustics, Speech, and Signal Processing*, Paris, France.

Mougeot, M., Azencott, R., and Angeniol, B. (1991). Image compression with back propagation: Improvement of the visual restoration using different cost functions. *Neural Networks*, 4:467–476.

Nowlan, S. J. and Hinton, G. E. (1992). Simplifying neural networks by soft weight-sharing. *Neural Computation*. In press.

Pearlmutter, B. A. and Rosenfeld, R. (1991). Chaitin-kolmogorov complexity and generalization in neural networks. In Lippmann, R. P., Moody, J. E., and Touretzky, D. S., editors, *Advances in Neural Information Processing Systems*, volume 3, pages 925–931. Morgan Kaufmann, San Mateo, CA.

Perrone, M. P. and Cooper, L. N. (1992). When networks disagree: Generalized ensemble method for neural networks. In Mammone, R. J. and Zeevi, Y., editors, *Neural Networks: Theory and Applications*, volume 2. Academic Press.

Slaney, M. (1988). Lyon's cochlear model. Technical report, Apple Corporate Library, Cupertino, CA 95014.

Switzer, P. (1970). Numerical classification. In Barnett, V., editor, *Geostatistics*. Plenum Press, New York.

Tajchman, G. N. and Intrator, N. (1992). Phonetic classification of TIMIT segments preprocessed with lyon's cochlear model using a supervised/unsupervised hybrid neural network. In *Proceedings International Conference on Spoken Language Processing*, Banff, Alberta, Canada.

Turk, M. and Pentland, A. (1991). Eigenfaces for recognition. *J. of Cognitive Neuroscience*, 3:71–86.

Waibel, A., Hanazawa, T., Hinton, G., Shikano, K., and Lang, K. (1989). Phoneme recognition using time-delay neural networks. *IEEE Transactions on ASSP*, 37:328–339.

Hidden Markov Model Induction by Bayesian Model Merging

Andreas Stolcke[*,**]
[*]Computer Science Division
University of California
Berkeley, CA 94720
stolcke@icsi.berkeley.edu

Stephen Omohundro[**]
[**]International Computer Science Institute
1947 Center Street, Suite 600
Berkeley, CA 94704
om@icsi.berkeley.edu

Abstract

This paper describes a technique for learning both the number of states and the topology of Hidden Markov Models from examples. The induction process starts with the most specific model consistent with the training data and generalizes by successively merging states. Both the choice of states to merge and the stopping criterion are guided by the Bayesian posterior probability. We compare our algorithm with the Baum-Welch method of estimating fixed-size models, and find that it can induce minimal HMMs from data in cases where fixed estimation does not converge or requires redundant parameters to converge.

1 INTRODUCTION AND OVERVIEW

Hidden Markov Models (HMMs) are a well-studied approach to the modelling of sequence data. HMMs can be viewed as a stochastic generalization of finite-state automata, where both the transitions between states and the generation of output symbols are governed by probability distributions. HMMs have been important in speech recognition (Rabiner & Juang, 1986), cryptography, and more recently in other areas such as protein classification and alignment (Haussler, Krogh, Mian & Sjölander, 1992; Baldi, Chauvin, Hunkapiller & McClure, 1993).

Practitioners have typically chosen the HMM topology by hand, so that learning the HMM from sample data means estimating only a fixed number of model parameters. The standard approach is to find a maximum likelihood (ML) or maximum *a posteriori* probability (MAP) estimate of the HMM parameters. The Baum-Welch algorithm uses dynamic programming to approximate these estimates (Baum, Petrie, Soules & Weiss, 1970).

A more general problem is to additionally find the best HMM topology. This includes both the number of states and the connectivity (the non-zero transitions and emissions). One could exhaustively search the model space using the Baum-Welch algorithm on fully connected models of varying sizes, picking the model size and topology with the highest posterior probability. (Maximum likelihood estimation is not useful for this comparison since larger models usually fit the data better.) This approach is very costly and Baum-Welch may get stuck at sub-optimal local maxima. Our comparative results later in the paper show that this often occurs in practice. The problem can be somewhat alleviated by sampling from several initial conditions, but at a further increase in computational cost.

The HMM induction method proposed in this paper tackles the structure learning problem in an incremental way. Rather than estimating a fixed-size model from scratch for various sizes, the model size is adjusted as new evidence arrives. There are two opposing tendencies in adjusting the model size and structure. Initially new data adds to the model size, because the HMM has to be augmented to accommodate the new samples. If enough data of a similar structure is available, however, the algorithm collapses the shared structure, decreasing the model size. The merging of structure is also what drives generalization, i.e., creates HMMs that generate data not seen during training.

Beyond being incremental, our algorithm is data-driven, in that the samples themselves completely determine the initial model shape. Baum-Welch estimation, by comparison, uses an initially random set of parameters for a given-sized HMM and iteratively updates them until a point is found at which the sample likelihood is locally maximal. What seems intuitively troublesome with this approach is that the initial model is completely uninformed by the data. The sample data directs the model formation process only in an indirect manner as the model approaches a meaningful shape.

2 HIDDEN MARKOV MODELS

For lack of space we cannot give a full introduction to HMMs here; see Rabiner & Juang (1986) for details. Briefly, an HMM consists of states and transitions like a Markov chain. In the discrete version considered here, it generates strings by performing random walks between an initial and a final state, outputting symbols at every state in between. The probability $P(x|M)$ that a model M generates a string x is determined by the conditional probabilities of making a transition from one state to another and the probability of emitting each symbol from each state. Once these are given, the probability of a particular path through the model generating the string can be computed as the product of all transition and emission probabilities along the path. The probability of a string x is the sum of the probabilities of all paths generating x.

For example, the model M_3 in Figure 1 generates the strings $ab, abab, ababab, \ldots$ with probabilities $\frac{2}{3}, \frac{2}{3^2}, \frac{2}{3^3}, \ldots$, respectively.

3 HMM INDUCTION BY STATE MERGING

3.1 MODEL MERGING

Omohundro (1992) has proposed an approach to statistical model inference in which initial models simply replicate the data and generalize by similarity. As more data is received, component models are fit from more complex model spaces. This allows the formation of arbitrarily complex models without overfitting along the way. The elementary step used in modifying the overall model is a *merging* of sub-models, collapsing the sample sets for the corresponding sample regions. The search for sub-models to merge is guided by an attempt to sacrifice as little of the sample likelihood as possible as a result of the merging process. This search can be done very efficiently if (a) a greedy search strategy can be used, and (b) likelihood computations can be done locally for each sub-model and don't require global recomputation on each model update.

3.2 STATE MERGING IN HMMS

We have applied this general approach to the HMM learning task. We describe the algorithm here mostly by presenting an example. The details are available in Stolcke & Omohundro (1993).

To obtain an initial model from the data, we first construct an HMM which produces exactly the input strings. The start state has as many outgoing transitions as there are strings and each string is represented by a unique path with one state per sample symbol. The probability of entering these paths from the start state is uniformly distributed. Within each path there is a unique transition arc whose probability is 1. The emission probabilities are 1 for each state to produce the corresponding symbol.

As an example, consider the regular language $(ab)^+$ and two samples drawn from it, the strings *ab* and *abab*. The algorithm constructs the initial model M_0 depicted in Figure 1. This is the most specific model accounting for the observed data. It assigns each sample a probability equal to its relative frequency, and is therefore a maximum likelihood model for the data.

Learning from the sample data means generalizing from it. This implies trading off model likelihood against some sort of bias towards 'simpler' models, expressed by a prior probability distribution over HMMs. Bayesian analysis provides a formal basis for this tradeoff. Bayes' rule tells us that the posterior model probability $P(M|x)$ is proportional to the product of the model prior $P(M)$ and the likelihood of the data $P(x|M)$. Smaller or simpler models will have a higher prior and this can outweigh the drop in likelihood as long as the generalization is conservative and keeps the model close to the data. The choice of model priors is discussed in the next section.

The fundamental idea exploited here is that the initial model M_0 can be gradually transformed into the generating model by repeatedly *merging states*. The intuition for this heuristic comes from the fact that if we take the paths that generate the samples in an actual generating HMM M and 'unroll' them to make them completely disjoint, we obtain M_0. The iterative merging process, then, is an attempt to undo the unrolling, tracing a search through the model space back to the generating model.

Merging two states q_1 and q_2 in this context means replacing q_1 and q_2 by a new state r with a transition distribution that is a weighted mixture of the transition probabilities of q_1, q_2, and with a similar mixture distribution for the emissions. Transition probabilities into q_1 or q_2 are added up and redirected to r. The weights used in forming the mixture distributions are the relative frequencies with which q_1 and q_2 are visited in the current model.

Repeatedly performing such merging operations yields a sequence of models M_0, M_1,

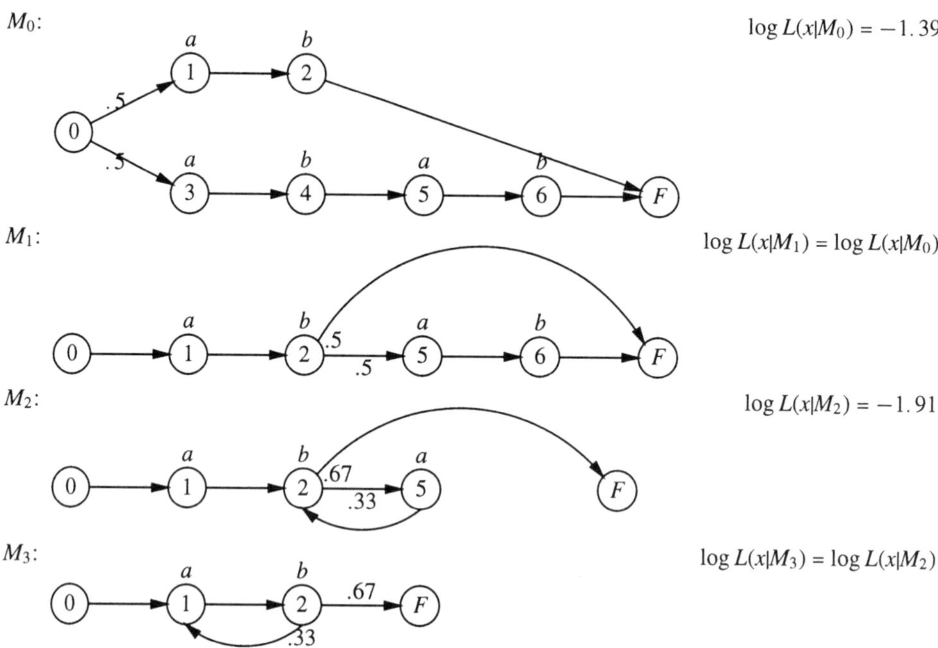

Figure 1: Sequence of models obtained by merging samples $\{ab, abab\}$. All transitions without special annotations have probability 1; Output symbols appear above their respective states and also carry an implicit probability of 1. For each model the log likelihood is given.

M_2, ..., along which we can search for the MAP model. To make the search for M efficient, we use a greedy strategy: given M_i, choose a pair of states for merging that maximizes $P(M_{i+1}|X)$.

Continuing with the previous example, we find that states 1 and 3 in M_0 can be merged without penalizing the likelihood. This is because they have identical outputs and the loss due to merging the outgoing transitions is compensated by the merging of the incoming transitions. The .5/.5 split is simply transferred to outgoing transitions of the merged state. The same situation obtains for states 2 and 4 once 1 and 3 are merged. From these two first merges we get model M_1 in Figure 1. By convention we reuse the smaller of two state indices to denote the merged state.

At this point the best merge turns out to be between states 2 and 6, giving model M_2. However, there is a penalty in likelihood, which decreases to about .59 of its previous value. Under all the reasonable priors we considered (see below), the posterior model probability still increases due to an increase in the prior. Note that the transition probability ratio at state 2 is now 2/1, since two samples make use of the first transition, whereas only one takes the second transition.

Finally, states 1 and 5 can be merged without penalty to give M_3, the minimal model that generates $(ab)^+$. Further merging at this point would reduce the likelihood by three orders of magnitude. The resulting decrease in the posterior probability tells the algorithm to stop at this point.

3.3 MODEL PRIORS

As noted previously, the likelihoods $P(X|M_i)$ along the sequence of models considered by the algorithm is monotonically decreasing. The prior $P(M)$ must account for an overall increase in posterior probability, and is therefore the driving force behind generalization.

As in the work on Bayesian learning of classification trees by Buntine (1992), we can split the prior $P(M)$ into a term accounting for the model structure, $P(M_s)$, and a term for the adjustable parameters in a fixed structure $P(M_p|M_s)$.

We initially relied on the structural prior only, incorporating an explicit bias towards smaller models. Size here is some function of the number of states and/or transitions, $|M|$. Such a prior can be obtained by making $P(M_s) \propto e^{-|M|}$, and can be viewed as a *description length prior* that penalizes models according to their coding length (Rissanen, 1983; Wallace & Freeman, 1987). The constants in this "MDL" term had to be adjusted by hand from examples of 'desirable' generalization.

For the parameter prior $P(M_p|M_s)$, it is standard practice to apply some sort of smoothing or regularizing prior to avoid overfitting the model parameters. Since both the transition and the emission probabilities are given by multinomial distributions it is natural to use a Dirichlet conjugate prior in this case (Berger, 1985). The effect of this prior is equivalent to having a number of 'virtual' samples for each of the possible transitions and emissions which are added to the actual samples when it comes to estimating the most likely parameter settings. In our case, the virtual samples made equal use of all potential transitions and emissions, adding bias towards uniform transition and emission probabilities.

We found that the Dirichlet priors by themselves produce an implicit bias towards smaller models, a phenomenon that can be explained as follows. The prior alone results in a model with uniform, flat distributions. Adding actual samples has the effect of putting bumps into the posterior distributions, so as to fit the data. The more samples are available, the more peaked the posteriors will get around the maximum likelihood estimates of the parameters, increasing the MAP value. In estimating HMM parameters, what counts is not the total number of samples, but the number of samples *per state*, since transition and emission distributions are local to each state. As we merge states, the available evidence gets shared by fewer states, thus allowing the remaining states to produce a better fit to the data.

This phenomenon is similar, but not identical, to the Bayesian 'Occam factors' that prefer models with fewer parameter (MacKay, 1992). Occam factors are a result of integrating the posterior over the parameter space, something which we do not do because of the computational complications it introduces in HMMs (see below).

3.4 APPROXIMATIONS

At each iteration step, our algorithm evaluates the posterior resulting from every possible merge in the current HMM. To keep this procedure feasible, a number of approximations are incorporated in the implementation that don't seem to affect its qualitative properties.

- For the purpose of likelihood computation, we consider only the most likely path through the model for a given sample string (the Viterbi path). This allows us to express the likelihood in product form, computable from sufficient statistics for each transition and emission.

- We assume the Viterbi paths are preserved by the merging operation, that is, the paths previously passing through the merged states now go through the resulting new state. This allows us to update the sufficient statistics incrementally, and means only O(number of states) likelihood terms need to be recomputed.
- The posterior probability of the model structure is approximated by the posterior of the MAP estimates for the model parameters. Rigorously integrating over all parameter values is not feasible since varying even a single parameter could change the paths of all samples through the HMM.
- Finally, it has to be kept in mind that our search procedure along the sequence of merged models finds only local optima, since we stop as soon as the posterior starts to decrease. A full search of the space would be much more costly. However, we found a *best-first look-ahead* strategy to be sufficient in rare cases where a local maximum caused a problem. In those cases we continue merging along the best-first path for a fixed number of steps (typically one) to check whether the posterior has undergone just a temporary decrease.

4 EXPERIMENTS

We have used various artificial finite-state languages to test our algorithm and compare its performance to the standard Baum-Welch algorithm.

Table 1 summarizes the results on the two sample languages $ac^*a \cup bc^*b$ and $a^+b^+a^+b^+$. The first of these contains a contingency between initial and final symbols that can be hard for learning algorithms to uncover.

We used no explicit model size prior in our experiments after we found that thc Dirichlet prior was very robust in giving just the the right amount of bias toward smaller models.[1] Summarizing the results, we found that merging very reliably found the generating model structure from a very small number of samples. The parameter values are determined by the sample set statistics.

The Baum-Welch algorithm, much like a backpropagation network, may be sensitive to its random initial parameter settings. We therefore sampled from a number of initial conditions. Interestingly, we found that Baum-Welch has a good chance of settling into a suboptimal HMM structure, especially if the number of states is the minimal number required for the target language. It proved much easier to estimate correct language models when extra states were provided. Also, increasing the sample size helped it converge to the target model.

5 RELATED WORK

Our approach is related to several other approaches in the literature.

The concept of state merging is implicit in the notion of state equivalence classes, which is fundamental to much of automata theory (Hopcroft & Ullman, 1979) and has been applied

[1]The number of ‘virtual’ samples per transition/emission was held constant at 0.1 throughout.

(a)

Method	Sample	Entropy	Cross-entropy	Language	n
Merging	8 m.p.	2.295	2.188 ± .020	$ac^*a \cup bc^*b$	6
Merging	20 random	2.087	2.158 ± .033	$ac^*a \cup bc^*b$	6
Baum-Welch	8 m.p.	2.087	2.894 ± .023 (best)	$(a \cup b)c^*(a \cup b)$	6
(10 trials)		2.773	4.291 ± .228 (worst)	$(a \cup b)c^*(a \cup b)$	6
Baum-Welch	20 random	2.087	2.105 ± .031 (best)	$ac^*a \cup bc^*b$	6
(10 trials)		2.775	2.825 ± .031 (worst)	$(a \cup b)c^*(a \cup b)$	6
Baum-Welch	8 m.p.	2.384	3.914 ± .271	$ac^*a \cup bc^*b$	10
Baum-Welch	20 random	2.085	2.155 ± .032	$ac^*a \cup bc^*b$	10

(b)

Method	Sample	Entropy	Cross-entropy	Language	n
Merging	5 m.p.	2.163	7.678 ± .158	$a^+b^+a^+b^+$	4
Baum-Welch	5 m.p.	3.545	8.963 ± .161 (best)	$(a^+b^+)^+$	4
(3 trials)		3.287	59.663 ± .007 (worst)	$(a^+b^+)^+$	4
Merging	10 random	5.009	5.623 ± .074	$a^+b^+a^+b^+$	4
Baum-Welch	10 random	5.009	5.688 ± .076 (best)	$a^+b^+a^+b^+$	4
(3 trials)		6.109	8.395 ± .137 (worst)	$(a^+b^+)^+$	4

Table 1: Results for merging and Baum-Welch on two regular languages: (a) $ac^*a \cup bc^*b$ and (b) $a^+b^+a^+b^+$. Samples were either the top most probable (m.p.) ones from the target language, or a set of randomly generated ones. 'Entropy' is the average negative log probability on the training set, whereas 'cross-entropy' refers to the empirical cross-entropy between the induced model and the generating model (the lower, the better generalization). n denotes the final number of model states for merging, or the fixed model size for Baum-Welch. For Baum-Welch, both best and worst performance over several initial conditions is listed.

to automata learning as well (Angluin & Smith, 1983).

Tomita (1982) is an example of finite-state model space search guided by a (non-probabilistic) goodness measure.

Horning (1969) describes a Bayesian grammar induction procedure that searches the model space exhaustively for the MAP model. The procedure provably finds the globally optimal grammar in finite time, but is infeasible in practice because of its enumerative character.

The incremental augmentation of the HMM by merging in new samples has some of the flavor of the algorithm used by Porat & Feldman (1991) to induce a finite-state model from positive-only, ordered examples.

Haussler et al. (1992) use limited HMM 'surgery' (insertions and deletions in a linear HMM) to adjust the model size to the data, while keeping the topology unchanged.

6 FURTHER RESEARCH

We are investigating several real-world applications for our method. One task is the construction of unified multiple-pronunciation word models for speech recognition. This is currently being carried out in collaboration with Chuck Wooters at ICSI, and it appears that our merging algorithm is able to produce linguistically adequate phonetic models.

Another direction involves an extension of the model space to stochastic context-free grammars, for which a standard estimation method analogous to Baum-Welch exists (Lari

& Young, 1990). The notions of sample incorporation and merging carry over to this domain (with merging now involving the non-terminals of the CFG), but need to be complemented with a mechanism that adds new non-terminals to create hierarchical structure (which we call chunking).

Acknowledgements

We would like to thank Peter Cheeseman, Wray Buntine, David Stoutamire, and Jerry Feldman for helpful discussions of the issues in this paper.

References

Angluin, D. & Smith, C. H. (1983), 'Inductive inference: Theory and methods', *ACM Computing Surveys* **15**(3), 237–269.

Baldi, P., Chauvin, Y., Hunkapiller, T. & McClure, M. A. (1993), 'Hidden Markov Models in molecular biology: New algorithms and applications', this volume.

Baum, L. E., Petrie, T., Soules, G. & Weiss, N. (1970), 'A maximization technique occuring in the statistical analysis of probabilistic functions in Markov chains', *The Annals of Mathematical Statistics* **41**(1), 164–171.

Berger, J. O. (1985), *Statistical Decision Theory and Bayesian Analysis*, Springer Verlag, New York.

Buntine, W. (1992), Learning classification trees, *in* D. J. Hand, ed., 'Artificial Intelligence Frontiers in Statistics: AI and Statistics III', Chapman & Hall.

Haussler, D., Krogh, A., Mian, I. S. & Sjölander, K. (1992), Protein modeling using hidden Markov models: Analysis of globins, Technical Report UCSC-CRL-92-23, Computer and Information Sciences, University of California, Santa Cruz, Ca. Revised Sept. 1992.

Hopcroft, J. E. & Ullman, J. D. (1979), *Introduction to Automata Theory, Languages, and Computation*, Addison-Wesley, Reading, Mass.

Horning, J. J. (1969), A study of grammatical inference, Technical Report CS 139, Computer Science Department, Stanford University, Stanford, Ca.

Lari, K. & Young, S. J. (1990), 'The estimation of stochastic context-free grammars using the Inside-Outside algorithm', *Computer Speech and Language* **4**, 35–56.

MacKay, D. J. C. (1992), 'Bayesian interpolation', *Neural Computation* **4**, 415–447.

Omohundro, S. M. (1992), Best-first model merging for dynamic learning and recognition, Technical Report TR-92-004, International Computer Science Institute, Berkeley, Ca.

Porat, S. & Feldman, J. A. (1991), 'Learning automata from ordered examples', *Machine Learning* **7**, 109–138.

Rabiner, L. R. & Juang, B. H. (1986), 'An introduction to Hidden Markov Models', *IEEE ASSP Magazine* **3**(1), 4–16.

Rissanen, J. (1983), 'A universal prior for integers and estimation by minimum description length', *The Annals of Statistics* **11**(2), 416–431.

Stolcke, A. & Omohundro, S. (1993), Best-first model merging for Hidden Markov Model induction, Technical Report TR-93-003, International Computer Science Institute, Berkeley, Ca.

Tomita, M. (1982), Dynamic construction of finite automata from examples using hill-climbing, *in* 'Proceedings of the 4th Annual Conference of the Cognitive Science Society', Ann Arbor, Mich., pp. 105–108.

Wallace, C. S. & Freeman, P. R. (1987), 'Estimation and inference by compact coding', *Journal of the Royal Statistical Society, Series B* **49**(3), 240–265.

Computing with Almost Optimal Size Neural Networks

Kai-Yeung Siu
Dept. of Electrical & Comp. Engineering
University of California, Irvine
Irvine, CA 92717

Vwani Roychowdhury
School of Electrical Engineering
Purdue University
West Lafayette, IN 47907

Thomas Kailath
Information Systems Laboratory
Stanford University
Stanford, CA 94305

Abstract

Artificial neural networks are comprised of an interconnected collection of certain nonlinear devices; examples of commonly used devices include linear threshold elements, sigmoidal elements and radial-basis elements. We employ results from harmonic analysis and the theory of rational approximation to obtain almost tight lower bounds on the size (i.e. number of elements) of neural networks. The class of neural networks to which our techniques can be applied is quite general; it includes any feedforward network in which each element can be piecewise approximated by a low degree rational function. For example, we prove that any depth-$(d+1)$ network of sigmoidal units or linear threshold elements computing the parity function of n variables must have $\Omega(dn^{1/d-\epsilon})$ size, for any fixed $\epsilon > 0$. In addition, we prove that this lower bound is almost tight by showing that the parity function can be computed with $O(dn^{1/d})$ sigmoidal units or linear threshold elements in a depth-$(d+1)$ network. These almost tight bounds are the first known complexity results on the size of neural networks with depth more than two. Our lower bound techniques yield a unified approach to the complexity analysis of various models of neural networks with feedforward structures. Moreover, our results indicate that in the context of computing highly oscillating symmetric Boolean functions, networks of continuous-output units such as sigmoidal elements do not offer significant reduction in size compared with networks of linear threshold elements of binary outputs.

1 Introduction

Recently, artificial neural networks have found wide applications in many areas that require solutions to nonlinear problems. One reason for such success is the existence of good "learning" or "training" algorithms such as Backpropagation [13] that provide solutions to many problems for which traditional attacks have failed. At a more fundamental level, the computational power of neural networks comes from the fact that each basic processing element computes a nonlinear function of its inputs. Networks of these nonlinear elements can yield solutions to highly complex and nonlinear problems. On the other hand, because of the nonlinear features, it is very difficult to study the fundamental limitations and capabilities of neural networks. Undoubtedly, any significant progress in the applications of neural networks must require a deeper understanding of their computational properties.

We employ classical tools such as harmonic analysis and rational approximation to derive new results on the computational complexity of neural networks. The class of neural networks to which our techniques can be applied is quite large; it includes feedforward networks of sigmoidal elements, linear threshold elements, and more generally, elements that can be piecewise approximated by low degree rational functions.

1.1 Background, Related Work and Definitions

A widely accepted model of neural networks is the feedforward multilayer network in which the basic processing element is a *sigmoidal element.* A sigmoidal element computes a function $f(X)$ of its input variables $X = (x_1, \ldots, x_n)$ such that

$$f(X) = \sigma(F(X)) = \frac{2}{1+e^{-F(X)}} - 1 = \frac{1-e^{-F(X)}}{1+e^{-F(X)}}$$

where

$$F(X) = \sum_{i=1}^{S} w_i \cdot x_i + w_0.$$

The real valued coefficients w_i are commonly referred to as the *weights* of the sigmoidal function. The case that is of most interest to us is when the inputs are binary, i.e., $X \in \{1, -1\}^n$. We shall refer to this model as *sigmoidal network.*

Another common feedforward multilayer model is one in which each basic processing unit computes a binary *linear threshold function* $sgn(F(X))$, where $F(X)$ is the same as above, and

$$sgn(F(X)) = \begin{cases} 1 & \text{if } F(X) \geq 0 \\ -1 & \text{if } F(X) < 0 \end{cases}$$

This model is often called the *threshold circuit* in the literature and recently has been studied intensively in the field of computer science.

The *size* of a network/circuit is the number of elements. The *depth* of a network/circuit is the longest path from any input gate to the output gates. We can arrange the gates in layers so that all gates in the same layer compute concurrently. (A single element can be considered as a one-layer network.) Each layer costs a unit delay in the computation. The depth of the network (which is the number of layers) can therefore be interpreted as the time for (parallel) computation.

It has been established that threshold circuit is a very powerful model of computation. Many functions of common interest such as multiplication, division and sorting can be computed in polynomial-size threshold circuits of small constant depth [19, 18, 21]. While many upper bound results for threshold circuits are known in the literature, lower bound results have only been established for restricted cases of threshold circuits. Most of the existing lower bound techniques [10, 17, 16] apply only to depth-2 threshold circuits. In [16], novel techniques which utilized analytical tools from the theory of rational approximation were developed to obtain lower bounds on the size of depth-2 threshold circuits that compute the parity function. In [20], we generalized the methods of rational approximation and our earlier techniques based on harmonic analysis to obtain the first known almost tight lower bounds on the size of threshold circuits with depth more than two. In this paper, the techniques are further generalized to yield almost tight lower bounds on the size of a more general class of neural networks in which each element computes a continuous function.

The presentation of this paper will be divided into two parts. In the first part, we shall focus on results concerning threshold circuits. In the second part, the lower bound results presented in the first part are generalized and shown to be valid even when the elements of the networks can assume continuous output values. The class of networks for which such techniques can be applied include networks of sigmoidal elements and radial basis elements. Due to space limitations, we shall only state some of the important results; further results and detailed proofs will appear in an extended paper.

Before we present our main results, we shall give formal definitions of the neural network models and introduce some of the Boolean functions, which will be used to explore the computational power of the various networks. To present our results in a coherent fashion, we define throughout this paper a *Boolean function* as $f : \{1,-1\}^n \rightarrow \{1,-1\}$, instead of using the usual $\{0,1\}$ notation.

Definition 1 A *threshold circuit* is a Boolean circuit in which every gate computes a linear threshold function with an additional property: *the weights are integers all bounded by a polynomial in n.* □

Remark 1 The assumption that the weights in the threshold circuits are integers bounded by a polynomial is common in the literature. In fact, the best known lower bound result on depth-2 threshold circuit [10] does not apply to the case where exponentially large weights are allowed. On the other hand, such assumption does not pose any restriction as far as constant-depth and polynomial-size is concerned. In other words, the class of constant-depth polynomial-size threshold circuits (TC^o) remains the same when the weights are allowed to be arbitrary. This result was implicit in [4] and was improved in [18] by showing that any depth-d threshold circuit with arbitrary weights can be simulated by a depth-$(2d + 1)$ threshold circuit of polynomially bounded weights at the expense of a polynomial increase in size. More recently, it has been shown that any polynomial-size depth-d threshold circuit with arbitrary weights can be simulated by a polynomial-size depth-$(2d + 1)$ threshold circuit. □

In addition to Boolean circuits, we shall also be interested in the computation of Boolean functions by networks of continuous-valued elements. To formalize this notion, we adopt the following definitions [12]:

Definition 2 Let $\gamma : \mathbf{R} \to \mathbf{R}$. A γ element with weights $w_1, \ldots, w_m \in \mathbf{R}$ and threshold t is defined to be an element that computes the function $\gamma(\sum_{i=1}^{m} w_i x_i - t)$ where $(x_1, \ldots, x_m)$ is the input. A γ-network is a feedforward network of γ elements with an additional property: *the weights w_i are all bounded by a polynomial in n.* □

For example, when γ is the sigmoidal function $\sigma(x)$, then we have a sigmoidal network, a common model of neural network. In fact, a threshold circuit can also be viewed as a special case of γ network where γ is the *sgn* function.

Definition 3 A γ-network C is said to compute a Boolean function $f : \{1, -1\}^n \to \{1, -1\}$ with separation $\epsilon > 0$ if there is some $t_C \in \mathbf{R}$ such that for any input $X = (x_1, \ldots, x_m)$ to the network C, the output element of C outputs a value $C(X)$ with the following property: If $f(X) = 1$, then $C(X) \geq t_C + \epsilon$. If $f(X) = -1$, then $C(X) \leq t_C - \epsilon$. □

Remark 2 As pointed out in [12], computing with γ networks without separation at the output element is less interesting because an infinitesimal change in the output of any γ element may change the output bit. In this paper, we shall be mainly interested in computations on γ networks C_n with separation at least $\Omega(n^{-k})$ for some fixed $k > 0$. This together with the assumption of polynomially bounded weights makes the complexity class of constant-depth polynomial-size γ networks quite *robust* and more interesting to study from a theoretical point of view (see [12]). □

Definition 4 The PARITY function of $X = (x_1, x_2, \ldots, x_n) \in \{1, -1\}^n$ is defined to be -1 if the number of -1 in the variables $x_1, \ldots, x_n$ is odd and $+1$ otherwise. Note that this function can be represented as the product $\prod_{i=1}^{n} x_i$. □

Definition 5 The Complete Quadratic (CQ) function [3] is defined to be the following:

$$CQ(X) = (x_1 \wedge x_2) \oplus (x_1 \wedge x_3) \oplus \ldots \oplus (x_{n-1} \wedge x_n)$$

i.e. $CQ(X)$ is the sum modulo 2 of all AND's between the $\binom{n}{2}$ pairs of distinct variables. Note that it is also a symmetric function. □

2 Results for Threshold Circuits

For the lower bound results on threshold circuits, a central idea of our proof is the use of a result from the theory of rational approximation which states the following

[9]: *the function $sgn(x)$ can be approximated with an error of $O(e^{-ck/\log(1/\epsilon)})$ by a rational function of degree k for $0 < \epsilon < |x| < 1$.* (In [16], they apply an equivalent result [15] that gives an approximation to the function $|x|$ instead of $sgn(x)$.) This result allows us to approximate several layers of threshold gates by a rational function of low (i.e. logarithmic) degree when the size of the circuit is small. Then by upper bounding the degree of the rational function that approximates the PARITY function, we give a lower bound on the size of the circuit. We also give similar lower bound on the Complete Quadratic (CQ) function using the same degree argument. By generalizing the 'telescoping' techniques in [14], we show an almost matching upper bound on the size of the circuits computing the PARITY and the CQ functions. We also examine circuits in which additional gates other than the threshold gates are allowed and generalize the lower bound results in this model. For this purpose, we introduce tools from harmonic analysis of Boolean functions [11, 3, 18, 17]. We define the class of functions called $\widetilde{SP}$ such that every function in $\widetilde{SP}$ can be closely approximated by a *sparse polynomial* for all inputs. For example, it can be shown that [18] the class $\widetilde{SP}$ contains functions AND, OR, COMPARISON and ADDITION, and more generally, functions that have polynomially bounded spectral norms.

The main results on threshold circuits can be summarized by the following theorems. First we present an explicit construction for implementing PARITY. This construction applies to any 'periodic' symmetric function, such as the CQ function.

Theorem 1 For every $d < \log n$, there exists a depth-$(d+1)$ threshold circuit with $O(dn^{1/d})$ gates that computes the PARITY function. □

We next show that any depth-$(d+1)$ threshold circuit computing the PARITY function or the CQ function must have size $\Omega(dn^{1/d-\epsilon})$ for any fixed $\epsilon > 0$. This result also holds for any function that has strong degree $\Omega(n)$.

Theorem 2 Any depth-$(d+1)$ threshold circuit computing the PARITY (CQ) function must have size $\Omega(dn^{1/d}/\log^2 n)$. □

We also consider threshold circuits that *approximate* the PARITY and the CQ functions when we have *random* inputs which are uniformly distributed. We derive *almost tight* upper and lower bounds on the size of the approximating threshold circuits.

We next consider threshold circuits with additional gates and prove the following result.

Theorem 3 Suppose in addition to threshold gates, we have polynomially many gates $\in \widetilde{SP}$ in the first layer of a depth-2 threshold circuit that computes the CQ function. Then the number of threshold gates required in the circuit is $\Omega(n/\log^2 n)$. □

This result can be extended to higher depth circuits when additional gates that have *low degree polynomial approximations* are allowed.

Remark 3 Recently Beigel [2], using techniques similar to ours and the fact that the PARITY function cannot be computed in polynomial-size constant-depth circuits of AND, OR gates [7], has shown that any constant-depth threshold circuit with $(2^{n^{o(1)}})$ AND, OR gates but only $o(\log n)$ threshold gates cannot compute the *PARITY* function of n variables. □

3 Results for γ-Networks

In the second part of the paper, we consider the computational power of networks of continuous-output elements. A celebrated result in this area was obtained by Cybenko [5]. It was shown in [5] that any continuous function over a compact domain can be closely approximated by sigmoidal networks with two layers. More recently, Barron [1] has significantly strengthened this result by showing that a wide class of functions can be approximated with mean squared error of $O(n^{-1})$ by two-layer sigmoidal networks of only n elements. Here we are interested in networks of continuous-output elements computing Boolean functions instead of continuous functions. See Section 1.1 for a precise definition of computation of Boolean functions by a γ-network.

While quite a few techniques have been developed for deriving lower bound results on the complexity of threshold circuits, an understanding of the power and the limitation of networks of continuous elements such as sigmoidal networks, especially as compared to threshold circuits, have not been explored. For example, we would like to answer questions such as: how much added computational power does one gain by using sigmoidal elements or other continuous elements to compute *Boolean* functions? Can the size of the network be reduced by using sigmoidal elements instead of threshold elements?

It was shown in [12] when the depth of the network is restricted to be two, then there is a Boolean function of n variables that can be computed in a depth-2 sigmoidal network with a fixed number of elements, but requires a depth-2 threshold circuit with size that increases at least logarithmic in n. In other words, in the restricted case of depth-2 network, one can reduce the size of the network *at least* a logarithmic factor by using continuous elements such as the sigmoidal elements instead of threshold elements with binary output values. This result has been recently improved in [6], where it is shown that there exists an explicit function that can be computed using only a constant number of sigmoidal gates, and that *any* threshold circuit (irrespective of the depth) computing it must have size $\Omega(\log n)$.

These results motivate the following question: Can we characterize a class of functions for which the threshold circuits computing the functions have sizes *at most* a logarithmic factor larger than the sizes of the sigmoidal networks computing them? Because of the monotonicity of the sigmoidal functions, we do not expect that there is substantial gain in the computational power over the threshold elements for computing the class of highly oscillating functions.

It is natural to extend our techniques to sigmoidal networks by approximating sigmoidal functions with rational functions. We derive a key lemma that yields a single low degree rational approximation to any function that can be *piecewise approximated* by low degree rational functions.

Lemma 1 Let f be a continuous function over $\Delta = [a, b]$. Let $\Delta_1 = [a, c]$ and $\Delta_2 = [c, b]$, $a < c < b$. Denote $\| g \|_{\Delta_i} = \sup_{x \in \Delta_i} |g(x)|$. Suppose there are rational functions r_1 and r_2 such that

$$\| f - r_i \|_{\Delta_i} \leq \epsilon$$

where $\epsilon > 0$. Then for each $\tilde{\epsilon} > 0$ and $\delta > 0$, there is a rational function r such that

$$\| f - r \|_{\Delta} \leq \epsilon + \tilde{\epsilon} + \omega(f; \delta)_{\Delta}$$

$$\deg r \leq 2 \deg r_1 + 2 \deg r_2 + C_1 \log(e + \frac{b-a}{\delta}) \log(e + \frac{\| f \|_{\Delta}}{\tilde{\epsilon}}) \quad (1)$$

where $\omega(f; \delta)_{\Delta}$ is the modulus of continuity of f over Δ, C_1 is a constant. □

The above lemma is applied to show that both sigmoidal functions and radial basis functions can be closely approximated by low degree rational functions. In fact the above lemma can be generalized to show that if a continuous function can be piecewise approximated by low degree rational functions over $k = \log^{O(1)} n$ consecutive intervals, then it can be approximated by a *single* low degree rational function over the union of these intervals.

These generalized approximation results enable us to show that many of our lower bound results on threshold circuits can be carried over to sigmoidal networks. Prior to our work, there was no nontrivial lower bound on the size of sigmoidal networks with depth more than two. In fact, we can generalize our results to neural networks whose elements can be *piecewise approximated* by low degree rational functions. We show in this paper that for symmetric Boolean functions of large strong degree (e.g. the parity function), any depth-d network whose elements can be piecewise approximated by low degree rational functions requires almost the same size as a depth-d threshold circuit computing the function.

In particular, if $\tilde{R}$ is the class of polynomially bounded functions that are piecewise continuous and can be piecewise approximated with low degree rational functions, then we prove the following theorem.

Theorem 4 Let W be any depth-$(d+1)$ neural network in which each element v_j computes a function $f^j(\sum_i w_i x_i)$ where $f^j \in \tilde{R}$ and $\sum_i |w_i| \leq n^{O(1)}$ for each element. If the network W computes the PARITY function of n variables with separation δ, where $0 < \delta = \Omega(n^{-k})$ for some $k > 0$, then for any fixed $\epsilon > 0$, W must have size $\Omega(dn^{1/d-\epsilon})$. □

References

[1] A. Barron. Universal Approximation Bounds for Superpositions of a Sigmoidal Function . *IEEE Transactions on Information Theory*, to appear.

[2] R. Beigel. Polylog(n) Majority or $O(\log \log n)$ Symmetric Gates are Equivalent to One. ACM Symposium on Theory of Computing (STOC), 1992.

[3] J. Bruck. Harmonic Analysis of Polynomial Threshold Functions . *SIAM Journal on Discrete Mathematics*, pages 168–177, May 1990.

[4] A. K. Chandra, L. Stockmeyer, and U. Vishkin. Constant depth reducibility. *Siam J. Comput.*, 13:423–439, 1984.

[5] G. Cybenko. Approximations by superpositions of a sigmoidal function. *Math. Control, Signals, Systems*, vol. 2, pages 303–314, 1989.

[6] B. Dasgupta and G. Schnitger. Efficient Approximation with Neural Networks: A Comparison of Gate Functions. In 5th Annual Conference on Neural Information Processing Systems - Natural and Synthetic (NIPS'92), 1992.

[7] M. Furst, J. B. Saxe, and M. Sipser. Parity, Circuits and the Polynomial-Time Hierarchy. *IEEE Symp. Found. Comp. Sci.*, 22:260–270, 1981.

[8] M. Goldmann, J. Håstad, and A. Razborov. Majority Gates vs. General Weighted Threshold Gates. *Seventh Annual Conference on Structure in Complexity Theory, 1992.*

[9] A. A. Gončar. On the rapidity of rational approximation of continuous functions with characteristic singularities. *Mat. Sbornik*, 2(4):561–568, 1967.

[10] A. Hajnal, W. Maass, P. Pudlak, M. Szegedy, and G. Turan. Threshold circuits of bounded depth. *IEEE Symp. Found. Comp. Sci.*, 28:99–110, 1987.

[11] R. J. Lechner. *Harmonic analysis of switching functions.* In A. Mukhopadhyay, editor, Recent Development in Switching Theory. Academic Press, 1971.

[12] W. Maass, G. Schnitger, and E. Sontag. On the computational power of sigmoid versus boolean threshold circuits. IEEE Symp. Found. Comp. Sci., October 1991.

[13] J. L. McClelland D. E. Rumelhart and the PDP Research Group. *Parallel Distributed Processing: Explorations in the Microstructure of Cognition, vol. 1.* MIT Press, 1986.

[14] R. Minnick. Linear-Input Logic. *IEEE Trans. on Electronic Computers*, EC 10, 1961.

[15] D. J. Newman. Rational Approximation to $|x|$. *Michigan Math. Journal*, 11:11–14, 1964.

[16] R. Paturi and M. Saks. On Threshold Circuits for Parity. IEEE Symp. Found. Comp. Sci., October 1990.

[17] V. P. Roychowdhury, K. Y. Siu, A. Orlitsky, and T. Kailath. A Geometric Approach to Threshold Circuit Complexity . Workshop on Computational Learning Theory (Colt'91), pp. 97–111, 1991.

[18] K. Y. Siu and J. Bruck. On the Power of Threshold Circuits with Small Weights . SIAM J. Discrete Math, pp. 423-435, August 1991.

[19] K. Y. Siu and J. Bruck. Neural Computation of Arithmetic Functions. Proceedings of the IEEE, Special Issue on Neural Networks, pp. 1669–1675, October 1990.

[20] K. Y. Siu, V. P. Roychowdhury, and T. Kailath. Computing with Almost Optimal Size Threshold Circuits . *IEEE International Symposium on Information Theory, Budapest, Hungary*, June 1991.

[21] K.-Y. Siu, J. Bruck, T. Kailath, and T. Hofmeister. Depth-Efficient Neural Networks for Division and Related Problems . to appear in *IEEE Trans. Information Theory*, 1993.

Intersecting regions: The key to combinatorial structure in hidden unit space

Janet Wiles
Depts of Psychology and
Computer Science,
University of Queensland
QLD 4072 Australia.
janetw@cs.uq.oz.au

Mark Ollila,
Vision Lab, CITRI
Dept of Computer Science,
University of Melbourne,
Vic 3052 Australia
molly@vis.citri.edu.au

Abstract

Hidden units in multi-layer networks form a representation space in which each region can be identified with a class of equivalent outputs (Elman, 1989) or a logical state in a finite state machine (Cleeremans, Servan-Schreiber & McClelland, 1989; Giles, Sun, Chen, Lee, & Chen, 1990). We extend the analysis of the spatial structure of hidden unit space to a combinatorial task, based on binding features together in a visual scene. The logical structure requires a combinatorial number of states to represent all valid scenes. On analysing our networks, we find that the high dimensionality of hidden unit space is exploited by using the intersection of neighboring regions to represent conjunctions of features. These results show how combinatorial structure can be based on the spatial nature of networks, and not just on their emulation of logical structure.

1 TECHNIQUES FOR ANALYSING THE SPATIAL AND LOGICAL STRUCTURE OF HIDDEN UNIT SPACE

In multi-layer networks, regions of hidden unit space can be identified with classes of equivalent outputs. For example, Elman (1989) showed that the hidden unit patterns for words in simple grammatical sentences cluster into regions, with similar patterns representing similar grammatical entities. For example, different tokens of the same word are clustered tightly, indicating that they are represented within a small region. These regions can be grouped into larger regions, reflecting a hierarchical structure. The largest groups represent the abstract categories, nouns and verbs. Elman used cluster analysis to demonstrate this hierarchical grouping, and principal component analysis (*PCA*) to show dimensions of variation in the representation in hidden unit space.

An alternative approach to Elman's hierarchical clustering is to identify each region with a functional state. By tracing the trajectories of sequences through the different regions, an equivalent finite state machine (*FSM*) can be constructed. This approach has been described using Reber grammars with simple recurrent networks (Cleeremans, Servan-Schreiber & McClelland, 1989) and higher-order networks (Giles, Sun, Chen, Lee, & Chen, 1990). Giles et al. showed that the logical structure of the grammars is embedded in hidden unit space by identifying each regions with a state, extracting the equivalent finite state machine from the set of states, and then reducing it to the minimal FSM.

Clustering and FSM extraction demonstrate different aspects of representations in hidden unit space. Elman showed that regions can be grouped hierarchically and that dimensions of variation can be identified using PCA, emphasizing how the functionality is reflected in the spatial structure. Giles et al. extracted the logical structure of the finite state machine in a way that represented the logical states independently of their spatial embedding. There is an inherent trade off between the spatial and logical analyses: In one sense, the FSM is the idealized version of a grammar, and indeed for the Reber grammars, Giles et al. found improved performance on the extracted FSMs over the trained networks. However, the states of the FSM increase combinatorially with the size of the input. If there is information encoded in the hierarchical grouping of regions or relative spatial arrangement of clusters, the extracted FSM cannot exploit it.

The basis of the logical equivalence of a FSM and the hidden unit representations is that disjoint regions of hidden unit space represent separate logical states. In previous work, we reversed the process of identifying clusters with states of a FSM, by using prior knowledge of the minimal FSM to label hidden unit patterns from a network trained on sequences from three temporal functions (Wiles & Bloesch, 1992). Canonical discriminant analysis (*CDA*, Cliff, 1987) was then used to view the hidden unit patterns clustered into regions that corresponded to the six states of the minimal FSM.

In this paper we explore an alternative interpretation of regions. Instead of considering disjoint regions, we view each region as a sub-component lying at the *intersection* of two or more larger regions. For example, in the three-function simulations, the six clusters can be interpreted in terms of three large regions that identify the three possible temporal functions, overlapping with two large regions that identify the output of the network (see Figure 1). The six states can then be seen as combinations of the three function and two output classes (i.e, 5 large overlapping regions instead of 6 smaller disjoint ones). While the three-function simulation does provide a clear demonstration of the intersecting structure of regions, nonetheless, only six states are required to represent the minimal FSM and harder tasks are needed to demonstrate combinatorial representations.

2 SIMULATIONS OF THE CONJUNCTION OF COLOR, SHAPE AND LOCATION

The representation of combinatorial structure is an important aspect of any computational task because of the drastic implications of combinatorial explosion for scaling. The intersection of regions is a concise way to represent all possible combinations of different items. We demonstrate this idea applied to the analysis of a hidden unit space

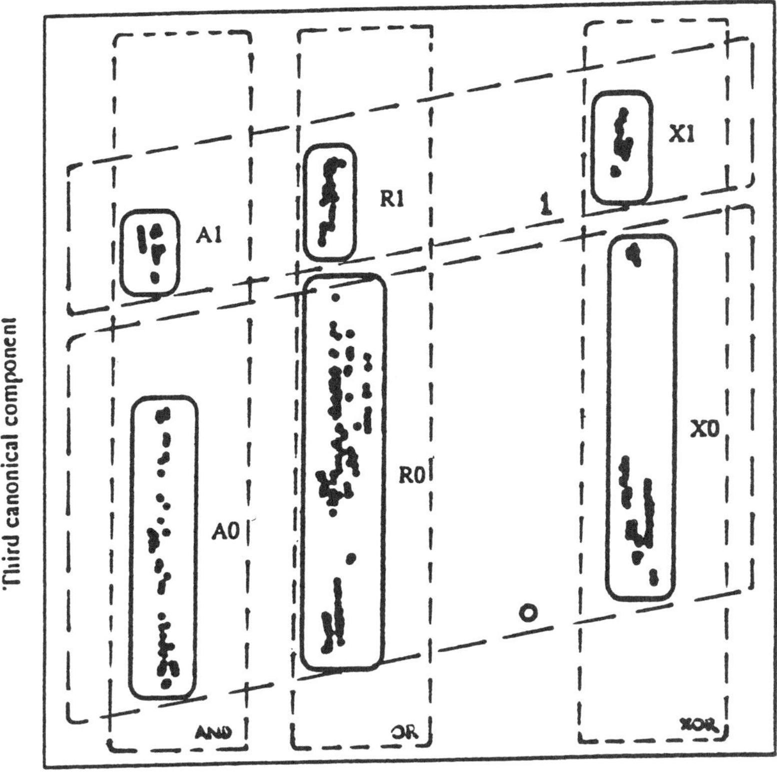

Figure 1. Intersecting regions in hidden unit space. Hidden unit patterns from the three-function task of Wiles and Bloesch (1992) are shown projected onto the first and third canonical components. Each temporal function, XOR, AND and OR is represented by a vertical region, separated along the first canonical component. The possible outputs, 0 and 1 are represented by horizontal regions, separated down the third canonical component. The states of the finite state machine are represented by the regions in the intersections of the vertical and horizontal regions. (Adapted from Wiles & Bloesch, 1992, Figure 1b.)

representation of conjunctions of colors, shapes and locations. In our task, a *scene* consists of zero or more objects, each object identified by its color, shape and location. The number of scenes, C, is given by $C = (sf+1)^l$ where s, f, and l are the numbers of shapes, features and locations respectively. This problem illustrates several important components: There is no unique representation of an object in the input or output – each object is represented only by the presence of a shape and color at a given location. The task of the network is to create hidden unit representations for all possible scenes, each containing the features themselves, and the binding of features to position.

The simulations involved two locations, three possible shapes and three colors (100 legitimate scenes). A 12–20–12 encoder network was trained on the entire set of scenes and the hidden unit patterns for each scene were recorded. Analysis using CDA with 10 groups designating all possible combinations of zero, one or two colors showed that the hidden unit space was partitioned into intersecting regions corresponding to the three colors or no color (see Figure 2a). CDA was repeated using groups designating all combinations of shapes, which showed an alternative partitioning into four intersecting regions related to the component shapes (see Figure 2b). Figures 2a and 2b show alternate two-dimensional projections of the 20-dimensional space. The analyses showed that each hidden unit pattern was contained in many different groupings, such as all objects that are red, all triangles, or all red triangles. In linguistic terms, each hidden unit pattern corresponds to a *token* of a feature, and the region containing all tokens of a given group corresponds to its abstract *type*. The interesting aspect of this representation is that the network had learnt not only how to separate the groups, but also to use overlapping regions. Thus given a region that represents a circle and one representing a triangle, the intersection of the two regions implies a scene that has both a circle and a triangle.

Given suitable groups, the perspectives provided by CDA show many different abstract types within the hidden unit space. For example, scenes can be grouped according to the number of objects in a scene, or the number of squares in a scene. We were initially surprised that contiguous regions exist for representing scenes with zero, one and two objects, since the output units only require representations of individual features, such as square or circle, and not the abstraction to "any shape", or even more abstract, "any object". It seems plausible that the separation of these regions is due to the high dimensionality provided by 12–20–12 mappings. The excess degrees of freedom in hidden unit space can encode variation in the inputs that is not necessarily required to complete the task. With fewer hidden units, we would expect that variation in the input patterns that is not required for completing the task would be compressed or lost under the competing requirement of maximally separating functionally useful groups in the hidden unit space. This explanation found support in a second simulation, using a 12–8–12 encoder network. Whereas analysis of the 12–20–12 network showed separation of patterns into disjoint regions by number of objects, the smaller 12–8–12 network did not. Over all, our analyses showed that as the number of dimensions increases, additional aspects of scenes may be represented, even if those aspects are not required for the task that the network is learning.

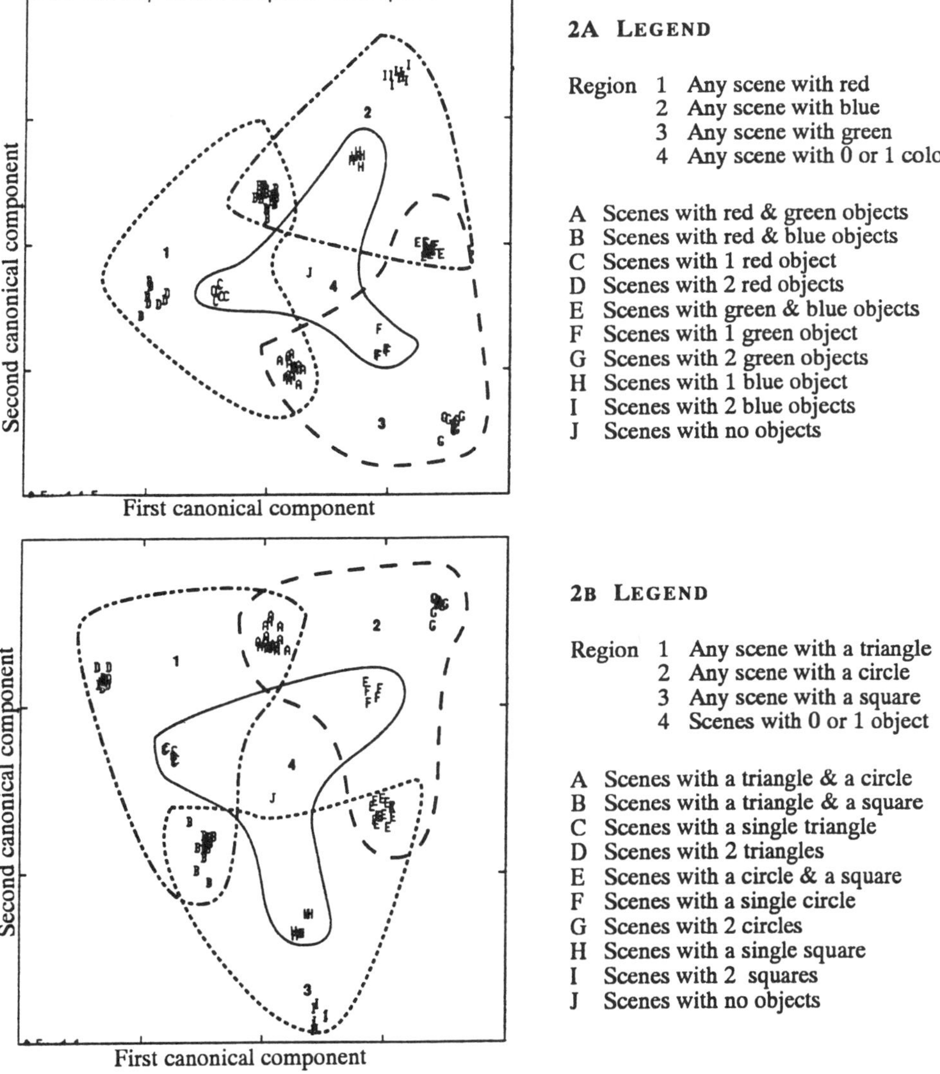

Figure 2. CDA plots showing the representations of features in a scene. A scene consists of zero, one or two objects, represented in terms of color, shape and location. *2a. Patterns labelled by color:* Hidden unit patterns form ten distinct clusters, which have been grouped into four intersecting regions, 1-4. For example, the hidden unit patterns within region 1 all contain at least one red object, those in regions 2 contain at least one blue one, and those in the intersection of regions 1 and 2 contain one red and one blue object. *2b. Patterns labelled by shape:* Again the hidden unit patterns form ten distinct clusters, which have been grouped into four intersecting regions, however, these regions represent scenes with the same shape. 2a and 2b show alternate groupings of the same hidden unit space, projected onto different canonical components. The two projections can be combined in the mind's eye (albeit with some difficulty) to form a four dimensional representation of the spatial structure of intersecting regions of both color and shape.

3 THE SPATIAL STRUCTURE OF HIDDEN UNIT SPACE IS ISOMORPHIC TO THE COMBINATORIAL STRUCTURE OF THE VISUAL MAPPING TASK

In conclusion, the simulations demonstrate how combinatorial structure can be embedded in the spatial nature of networks in a way that is isomorphic to the combinatorial structure of the task, rather than by emulation of logical structure. In our approach, the representation of intersecting regions is the key to providing combinatorial representations. If the visual mapping task were extended by including a feature specifying the color of the background scene (e.g., blue or green) the number of possible scenes would double, as would the number of states in a FSM. By contrast, in the hidden unit representation, the additional feature would involve adding two more overlapping regions to those currently supported by the spatial structure. This could be implemented by dividing hidden unit space along an unused dimension, orthogonal to the current groups.

The task presented in this case study is extremely simplified, in order to expose the intrinsic combinatorial structure required in binding. Despite the simplifications, it does contain elements of tasks that face real cognitive systems. In the simulations above, individual objects can be clustered by their shape or color, or whole scenes by other properties, such as the number of squares in the scene. These representations provide a concise and easily accessible structure that solves the combinatorial problem of binding several features to one object, in such a way as to represent the individual object, and yet also allow efficient access to its component features. The flexibility of such access processes is one of the main motivations for tensor models of human memory (Humphreys, Bain & Pike, 1989) and analogical reasoning (Halford et al., in press). Our analysis of spatial structure in terms of intersecting regions has a straightforward interpretation in terms of tensors, and provides a basis for future work on network implementations of the tensor memory and analogical reasoning models.

Acknowledgements

We thank Simon Dennis and Steven Phillips for their canonical discriminant program. This work was supported by grants from the Australian Research Council.

References

Cleeremans, A., Servan-Schreiber, D., and McClelland, J.L. (1989). Finite state automata and simple recurrent networks, *Neural Computation*, 1, 372-381.

Cliff, N. (1987). *Analyzing Multivariate Data.* Harcourt Brace Jovanovich, Orlando, Florida.

Elman, J. (1989). Representation and structure in connectionist models. CRL Technical Report 8903, Center for Research in Language, University of California, San Diego, 26pp.

Giles, C. L., Sun, G. Z., Chen, H. H., Lee, Y. C., and Chen, D. (1990). Higher Order Recurrent Networks. In D.S. Touretzky (ed.) *Advances in Neural Information Processing Systems 2*, Morgan-Kaufmann, San Mateo, Ca., 380-387.

Halford, G.S., Wilson, W.H., Guo, J., Wiles, J. and Stewart, J.E.M. Connectionist implications for processing capacity limitations in analogies. To appear in K.J. Holyoak & J. Barnden (Eds.), *Advances in Connectionist and Neural Computation Theory, Vol 2: Analogical Connections*. Norwood, NJ: Ablex, in press.

Humphreys, M.S., Bain, J.D., and Pike, R. (1989). Different ways to cue a coherent memory system: A theory of episodic, semantic and procedural tasks, *Psychological Review, 96* (2), 208-233.

Wiles, J. and Bloesch, A. (1992). Operators and curried functions: Training and analysis of simple recurrent networks. In J. E. Moody, S. J. Hanson, and R. P. Lippmann (Eds.) *Advances in Neural Information Processing Systems 4*, Morgan-Kaufmann, San Mateo, Ca.

Holographic Recurrent Networks

Tony A. Plate
Department of Computer Science
University of Toronto
Toronto, M5S 1A4 Canada

Abstract

Holographic Recurrent Networks (HRNs) are recurrent networks which incorporate associative memory techniques for storing sequential structure. HRNs can be easily and quickly trained using gradient descent techniques to generate sequences of discrete outputs and trajectories through continuous space. The performance of HRNs is found to be superior to that of ordinary recurrent networks on these sequence generation tasks.

1 INTRODUCTION

The representation and processing of data with complex structure in neural networks remains a challenge. In a previous paper [Plate, 1991b] I described Holographic Reduced Representations (HRRs) which use circular-convolution associative-memory to embody sequential and recursive structure in fixed-width distributed representations. This paper introduces Holographic Recurrent Networks (HRNs), which are recurrent nets that incorporate these techniques for generating sequences of symbols or trajectories through continuous space. The recurrent component of these networks uses convolution operations rather than the logistic-of-matrix-vector-product traditionally used in simple recurrent networks (SRNs) [Elman, 1991, Cleeremans *et al.*, 1991].

The goals of this work are threefold: (1) to investigate the use of circular-convolution associative memory techniques in networks trained by gradient descent; (2) to see whether adapting representations can improve the capacity of HRRs; and (3) to compare performance of HRNs with SRNs.

1.1 RECURRENT NETWORKS & SEQUENTIAL PROCESSING

SRNs have been used successfully to process sequential input and induce finite state grammars [Elman, 1991, Cleeremans *et al.*, 1991]. However, training times were extremely long, even for very simple grammars. This appeared to be due to the difficulty of finding a recurrent operation that preserved sufficient context [Maskara and Noetzel, 1992]. In the work reported in this paper the task is reversed to be one of generating sequential output. Furthermore, in order to focus on the context retention aspect, no grammar induction is required.

1.2 CIRCULAR CONVOLUTION

Circular convolution is an associative memory operator. The role of convolution in holographic memories is analogous to the role of the outer product operation in matrix style associative memories (e.g., Hopfield nets). Circular convolution can be viewed as a vector multiplication operator which maps pairs of vectors to a vector (just as matrix multiplication maps pairs of matrices to a matrix). It is defined as $\mathbf{z} = \mathbf{x} \circledast \mathbf{y} : z_j = \sum_{k=0}^{n-1} y_k x_{j-k}$, where $\circledast$ denotes circular convolution, $\mathbf{x}$, $\mathbf{y}$, and $\mathbf{z}$ are vectors of dimension n , x_i etc. are their elements, and subscripts are modulo-n (so that $x_{-2} \equiv x_{n-2}$). Circular convolution can be computed in $O(n \log n)$ using Fast Fourier Transforms (FFTs). Algebraically, convolution behaves like scalar multiplication: it is commutative, associative, and distributes over addition. The identity vector for convolution ($\mathbf{I}$) is the "impulse" vector: its zero'th element is 1 and all other elements are zero. Most vectors have an inverse under convolution, i.e., for most vectors $\mathbf{x}$ there exists a unique vector $\mathbf{y}$ ($=\mathbf{x}^{-1}$) such that $\mathbf{x} \circledast \mathbf{y} = \mathbf{I}$. For vectors with identically and independently distributed zero mean elements and an expected Euclidean length of 1 there is a numerically stable and simply derived approximate inverse. The approximate inverse of $\mathbf{x}$ is denoted by $\mathbf{x}^*$ and is defined by the relation $x_j^* = x_{n-j}$.

Vector pairs can be associated by circular convolution. Multiple associations can be summed. The result can be decoded by convolving with the exact inverse or approximate inverse, though the latter generally gives more stable results.

Holographic Reduced Representations [Plate, 1991a, Plate, 1991b] use circular convolution for associating elements of a structure in a way that can embody hierarchical structure. The key property of circular convolution that makes it useful for representing hierarchical structure is that the circular convolution of two vectors is another vector of the same dimension, which can be used in further associations.

Among associative memories, holographic memories have been regarded as inferior because they produce very noisy results and have poor error correcting properties. However, when used in Holographic Reduced Representations the noisy results can be cleaned up with conventional error correcting associative memories. This gives the best of both worlds – the ability to represent sequential and recursive structure and clean output vectors.

2 TRAJECTORY-ASSOCIATION

A simple method for storing sequences using circular convolution is to associate elements of the sequence with points along a predetermined trajectory. This is akin to the memory aid called the method of loci which instructs us to remember a list of items by associating each term with a distinctive location along a familiar path.

2.1 STORING SEQUENCES BY TRAJECTORY-ASSOCIATION

Elements of the sequence and loci (points) on the trajectory are all represented by n-dimensional vectors. The loci are derived from a single vector $\mathbf{k}$ – they are its successive convolutive powers: $\mathbf{k}^0$, $\mathbf{k}^1$, $\mathbf{k}^2$, etc. The convolutive power is defined in the obvious way: $\mathbf{k}^0$ is the identity vector and $\mathbf{k}^{i+1} = \mathbf{k}^i \circledast \mathbf{k}$.

The vector $\mathbf{k}$ must be chosen so that it does not blow up or disappear when raised to high powers, i.e., so that $||\mathbf{k}^p|| = 1 \ \forall \ p$. The class of vectors which satisfy this constraint is easily identified in the frequency domain (the range of the discrete Fourier transform). They are the vectors for which the magnitude of the power of each frequency component is equal to one. This class of vectors is identical to the class for which the approximate inverse is equal to the exact inverse.

Thus, the trajectory-association representation for the sequence "abc" is

$$\mathbf{s}_{abc} = \mathbf{a} + \mathbf{b} \circledast \mathbf{k} + \mathbf{c} \circledast \mathbf{k}^2.$$

2.2 DECODING TRAJECTORY-ASSOCIATED SEQUENCES

Trajectory-associated sequences can be decoded by repeatedly convolving with the inverse of the vector that generated the encoding loci. The results of decoding summed convolution products are very noisy. Consequently, to decode trajectory associated sequences, we must have all the possible sequence elements stored in an error correcting associative memory. I call this memory the "clean up" memory.

For example, to retrieve the third element of the sequence $\mathbf{s}_{abc}$ we convolve twice with $\mathbf{k}^{-1}$, which expands to $\mathbf{a} \circledast \mathbf{k}^{-2} + \mathbf{b} \circledast \mathbf{k}^{-1} + \mathbf{c}$. The two terms involving powers of $\mathbf{k}$ are unlikely to be correlated with anything in the clean up memory. The most similar item in clean up memory will probably be $\mathbf{c}$. The clean up memory should recognize this and output the clean version of $\mathbf{c}$.

2.3 CAPACITY OF TRAJECTORY-ASSOCIATION

In [Plate, 1991a] the capacity of circular-convolution based associative memory was calculated. It was assumed that the elements of all vectors (dimension n) were chosen randomly from a gaussian distribution with mean zero and variance $1/n$ (giving an expected Euclidean length of 1.0). Quite high dimensional vectors were required to ensure a low probability of error in decoding. For example, with 512 element vectors and 1000 items in the clean up memory, 5 pairs can be stored with a 1% chance of an error in decoding. The scaling is nearly linear in n: with 1024 element vectors 10 pairs can be stored with about a 1% chance of error. This works out to a information capacity of about 0.1 bits per element. The elements are real numbers, but high precision is not required.

These capacity calculations are roughly applicable to the trajectory-association method. They slightly underestimate its capacity because the restriction that the encoding loci have unity power in all frequencies results in lower decoding noise. Nonetheless this figure provides a useful benchmark against which to compare the capacity of HRNs which adapt vectors using gradient descent.

3 TRAJECTORY ASSOCIATION & RECURRENT NETS

HRNs incorporate the trajectory-association scheme in recurrent networks. HRNs are very similar to SRNs, such as those used by [Elman, 1991] and [Cleeremans *et al.*, 1991]. However, the task used in this paper is different: the generation of target sequences at the output units, with inputs that do not vary in time.

In order to understand the relationship between HRNs and SRNs both were tested on the sequence generation task. Several different unit activation functions were tried for the SRN: symmetric (tanh) and non-symmetric sigmoid ($1/(1+e^{-x})$) for the hidden units, and softmax and normalized RBF for the output units. The best combination was symmetric sigmoid with softmax outputs.

3.1 ARCHITECTURE

The HRN and the SRN used in the experiments described here are shown in Figure 1. In the HRN the key layer $\mathbf{y}$ contains the generator for the inverse loci (corresponding to $\mathbf{k}^{-1}$ in Section 2). The hidden to output nodes implement the clean-up memory: the output representation is local and the weights on the links to an output unit form the vector that represents the symbol corresponding to that unit. The softmax function serves to give maximum activation to the output unit whose weights are most similar to the activation at the hidden layer.

The input representation is also local, and input activations do not change during the generation of one sequence. Thus the weights from a single input unit determine the activations at the code layer. Nets are reset at the beginning of each sequence.

The HRN computes the following functions. Time superscripts are omitted where all are the same. See Figure 1 for symbols. The parameter g is an adaptable input gain shared by all output units.

Code units:		$c_j = \sum_k i_k w^c_{jk}$	
Hidden units:	(first time step)	$h_j = c_j$	
	(subsequent steps)	$h_j = \sum_k p_k y_{j-k}$	($\mathbf{h} = \mathbf{p} \circledast \mathbf{y}$)
Context units:		$p_j^{t+1} = p_j^t$	
Output units:	(total input)	$x_j = g \sum_k h_k w^o_{jk}$	
	(output)	$o_j = \frac{e^{x_j}}{\sum_k e^{x_k}}$	(softmax)

In the SRN the only difference is in the recurrence operation, i.e., the computation of the activations of the hidden units which is, where b_j is a bias:

$$h_j = \tanh(c_j + \textstyle\sum_k w^r_{jk} p_k + b_j).$$

The objective function of the network is the asymmetric divergence between the activations of the output units (o_j^{st}) and the targets (t_j^{st}) summed over cases s and timesteps t, plus two weight penalty terms (n is the number of hidden units):

$$E = -\left(\sum_{stj} t_j^{st} \log \frac{o_j^{st}}{t_j^{st}}\right) + \frac{0.0001}{n}\left(\sum_{jk} w^{r}_{jk} + \sum_{jk} w^{c}_{jk}\right) + \sum_j \left(1 - \sum_k {w^o_{jk}}^2\right)^2$$

The first weight penalty term is a standard weight cost designed to penalize large

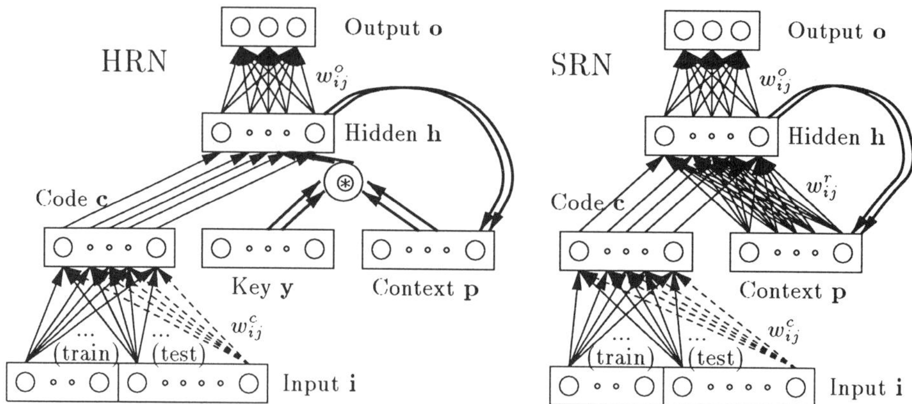

Figure 1: Holographic Recurrent Network (HRN) and Simple Recurrent Network (SRN). The backwards curved arrows denote a copy of activations to the next time step. In the HRN the code layer is active only at the first time step and the context layer is active only after the first time step. The hidden, code, context, and key layers all have the same number of units. Some input units are used only during training, others only during testing.

weights. The second weight penalty term was designed to force the Euclidean length of the weight vector on each output unit to be one. This penalty term helped the HRN considerably but did not noticeably improve the performance of the SRN.

The partial derivatives for the activations were computed by the unfolding in time method [Rumelhart *et al.*, 1986]. The partial derivatives for the activations of the context units in the HRN are:

$$\frac{\partial E}{\partial p_j} = \sum_k \frac{\partial E}{\partial h_j} y_{k-j} \qquad (\equiv \nabla_{\mathbf{p}} E = \nabla_{\mathbf{h}} \circledast \mathbf{y}^*)$$

When there are a large number of hidden units it is more efficient to compute this derivative via FFTs as the convolution expression on the right.

On all sequences the net was cycled for as many time steps as required to produce the target sequence. The outputs did not indicate when the net had reached the end of the sequence, however, other experiments have shown that it is a simple matter to add an output to indicate this.

3.2 TRAINING AND GENERATIVE CAPACITY RESULTS

One of the motivations for this work was to find recurrent networks with high generative capacity, i.e., networks which after training on just a few sequences could generate many other sequences without further modification of recurrent or output weights. The only thing in the network that changes to produce a different sequence is the activation on the codes units. To have high generative capacity the function of the output weights and recurrent weights (if they exist) must generalize to the production of novel sequences. At each step the recurrent operation must update and retain information about the current position in the sequence. It was expected that this would be a difficult task for SRNs, given the reported difficulties with getting SRNs to retain context, and Simard and LeCun's [1992] report of being unable to train a type of recurrent network to generate more than one trajectory through continuous space. However, it turned out that HRNs, and to a lesser extent SRNs, could be easily trained to perform the sequence generation task well.

The generative capacity of HRNs and SRNs was tested using randomly chosen sequences over 3 symbols (a, b, and c). The training data was (in all but one case) 12 sequences of length 4, e.g., "abac", and "bacb". Networks were trained on this data using the conjugate gradient method until all sequences were correctly generated. A symbol was judged to be correct when the activation of the correct output unit exceeded 0.5 and exceeded twice any other output unit activation.

After the network had been trained, all the weights and parameters were frozen, except for the weights on the input to code links. Then the network was trained on a test set of novel sequences of lengths 3 to 16 (32 sequences of each length). This training could be done one sequence at a time since the generation of each sequence involved an exclusive set of modifiable weights, as only one input unit was active for any sequence. The search for code weights for the test sequences was a conjugate gradient search limited to 100 iterations.

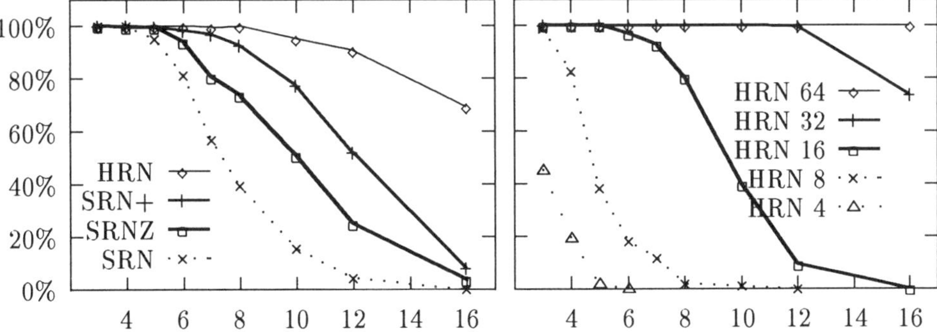

Figure 2: Percentage of novel sequences that can be generated versus length.

The graph on the left in Figure 2 shows how the performance varies with sequence length for various networks with 16 hidden units. The points on this graph are the average of 5 runs; each run began with a randomization of all weights. The worst performance was produced by the SRN. The HRN gave the best performance: it was able to produce around 90% of all sequences up to length 12. Interestingly, a SRN (SRNZ in Figure 2) with frozen random recurrent weights from a suitable distribution performed significantly better than the unconstrained SRN.

To some extent, the poor performance of the SRN was due to overtraining. This was verified by training a SRN on 48 sequences of length 8 (8 times as much data). The performance improved greatly (SRN+ in Figure 2), but was still not as good that of the HRN trained on the lesser amount of data. This suggests that the extra parameters provided by the recurrent links in the SRN serve little useful purpose: the net does well with fixed random values for those parameters and a HRN does better without modifying any parameters in this operation. It appears that all that is required in the recurrent operation is some stable random map.

The scaling performance of the HRN with respect to the number of hidden units is good. The graph on the right in Figure 2 shows the performance of HRNs with 8 output units and varying numbers of hidden units (averages of 5 runs). As the number of hidden units increases from 4 to 64 the generative capacity increases steadily. The scaling of sequence length with number of outputs (not shown) is also good: it is over 1 bit per hidden unit. This compares very will with the 0.1 bit per element achieved by random vector circular-convolution (Section 2.3).

The training times for both the HRNs and the SRNs were very short. Both required around 30 passes through the training data to train the output and recurrent weights. Finding a code for test sequence of length 8 took the HRN an average of 14 passes. The SRN took an average of 57 passes (44 with frozen weights). The SRN trained on more data took much longer for the initial training (average 281 passes) but the code search was shorter (average 31 passes).

4 TRAJECTORIES IN CONTINUOUS SPACE

HRNs can also be used to generate trajectories through continuous space. Only two modifications need be made: (a) change the function on the output units to sigmoid and add biases, and (b) use a fractional power for the key vector. A fractional power vector $\mathbf{f}$ can be generated by taking a random unity-power vector $\mathbf{k}$ and multiplying the phase angle of each frequency component by some fraction α, i.e., $\mathbf{f} = \mathbf{k}^{\alpha}$. The result is that $\mathbf{f}^i$ is similar to $\mathbf{f}^j$ when the difference between i and j is less than $1/\alpha$, and the similarity is greater for closer i and j. The output at the hidden layer will be similar at successive time steps. If desired, the speed at which the trajectory is traversed can be altered by changing α.

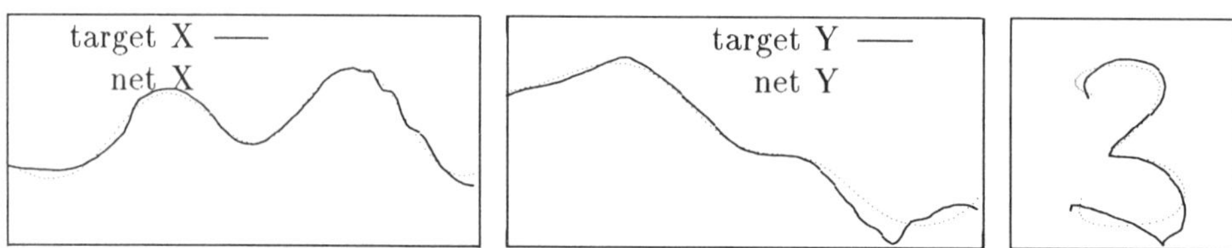

Figure 3: Targets and outputs of a HRN trained to generate trajectories through continuous space. X and Y are plotted against time.

A trajectory generating HRN with 16 hidden units and a key vector $\mathbf{k}^{0.06}$ was trained to produce pen trajectories (100 steps) for 20 instances of handwritten digits (two of each). This is the same task that Simard and Le Cun [1992] used. The target trajectories and the output of the network for one instance are shown in Figure 3.

5 DISCUSSION

One issue in processing sequential data with neural networks is how to present the inputs to the network. One approach has been to use a fixed window on the sequence, e.g., as in NETtalk [Sejnowski and Rosenberg, 1986]. A disadvantage of this is any fixed size of window may not be large enough in some situations. Another approach is to use a recurrent net to retain information about previous inputs. A disadvantage of this is the difficulty that recurrent nets have in retaining information over many time steps. Generative networks offer another approach: use the codes that generate a sequence as input rather than the raw sequence. This would allow a fixed size network to take sequences of variable length as inputs (as long as they were finite), without having to use multiple input blocks or windows.

The main attraction of circular convolution as an associative memory operator is its affordance of the representation of hierarchical structure. A hierarchical HRN, which takes advantage of this to represent sequences in chunks, has been built. However, it remains to be seen if it can be trained by gradient descent.

6 CONCLUSION

The circular convolution operation can be effectively incorporated into recurrent nets and the resulting nets (HRNs) can be easily trained using gradient descent to generate sequences and trajectories. HRNs appear to be more suited to this task than SRNs, though SRNs did surprisingly well. The relatively high generative capacity of HRNs shows that the capacity of circular convolution associative memory [Plate, 1991a] can be greatly improved by adapting representations of vectors.

References

[Cleeremans *et al.*, 1991] A. Cleeremans, D. Servan-Schreiber, and J. L. McClelland. Graded state machines: The representation of temporal contingencies in simple recurrent networks. *Machine Learning*, 7(2/3):161–194, 1991.

[Elman, 1991] J. Elman. Distributed representations, simple recurrent networks and grammatical structure. *Machine Learning*, 7(2/3):195–226, 1991.

[Maskara and Noetzel, 1992] Arun Maskara and Andrew Noetzel. Forcing simple recurrent neural networks to encode context. In *Proceedings of the 1992 Long Island Conference on Artificial Intelligence and Computer Graphics*, 1992.

[Plate, 1991a] T. A. Plate. Holographic Reduced Representations. Technical Report CRG-TR-91-1, Department of Computer Science, University of Toronto, 1991.

[Plate, 1991b] T. A. Plate. Holographic Reduced Representations: Convolution algebra for compositional distributed representations. In *Proceedings of the 12th International Joint Conference on Artificial Intelligence*, pages 30–35, Sydney, Australia, 1991.

[Rumelhart *et al.*, 1986] D. E. Rumelhart, G. E. Hinton, and Williams R. J. Learning internal representations by error propagation. In *Parallel distributed processing: Explorations in the microstructure of cognition*, volume 1, chapter 8, pages 318–362. Bradford Books, Cambridge, MA, 1986.

[Sejnowski and Rosenberg, 1986] T. J. Sejnowski and C. R. Rosenberg. *NETtalk: A parallel network that learns to read aloud.* Technical report 86-01, Department of Electrical Engineering and Computer Science, Johns Hopkins University, Baltimore, MD., 1986.

[Simard and LeCun, 1992] P. Simard and Y. LeCun. Reverse TDNN: an architecture for trajectory generation. In J. M. Moody, S. J. Hanson, and R. P. Lippman, editors, *Advances in Neural Information Processing Systems 4 (NIPS*91)*, Denver, CO, 1992. Morgan Kaufman.

Improving Performance in Neural Networks Using a Boosting Algorithm

Harris Drucker
AT&T Bell Laboratories
Holmdel, NJ 07733

Robert Schapire
AT&T Bell Laboratories
Murray Hill, NJ 07974

Patrice Simard
AT&T Bell Laboratories
Holmdel, NJ 07733

Abstract

A boosting algorithm converts a learning machine with error rate less than 50% to one with an arbitrarily low error rate. However, the algorithm discussed here depends on having a large supply of independent training samples. We show how to circumvent this problem and generate an ensemble of learning machines whose performance in optical character recognition problems is dramatically improved over that of a single network. We report the effect of boosting on four databases (all handwritten) consisting of 12,000 digits from segmented ZIP codes from the United State Postal Service (USPS) and the following from the National Institute of Standards and Testing (NIST): 220,000 digits, 45,000 upper case alphas, and 45,000 lower case alphas. We use two performance measures: the raw error rate (no rejects) and the reject rate required to achieve a 1% error rate on the patterns not rejected. Boosting improved performance in some cases by a factor of three.

1 INTRODUCTION

In this article we summarize a study on the effects of a boosting algorithm on the performance of an ensemble of neural networks used in optical character recognition problems. Full details can be obtained elsewhere (Drucker, Schapire, and Simard, 1993). The "boosting by filtering" algorithm is based on Schapire's original work (1990) which showed that it is theoretically possible to convert a learning machine with error rate less than 50% into an ensemble of learning machines whose error rate is arbitrarily low. The work detailed here is the first practical implementation of this boosting algorithm.

As applied to an ensemble of neural networks using supervised learning, the algorithm proceeds as follows: Assume an oracle that generates a large number of independent training examples. First, generate a set of training examples and train a first network. After the first network is trained it may be used in combination with the oracle to produce a second training set in the following manner: Flip a fair coin. If the coin is heads, pass outputs from the oracle through the first learning machine until the first network misclassifies a pattern and add this pattern to a second training set. Otherwise, if the coin is tails pass outputs from the oracle through the first learning machine until the first network finds a pattern that it classifies correctly and add to the training set. This process is repeated until enough patterns have been collected. These patterns, half of which the first machine classifies correctly and half incorrectly, constitute the training set for the second network. The second network may then be trained.

The first two networks may then be used to produce a third training set in the following manner: Pass the outputs from the oracle through the first two networks. If the networks disagree on the classification, add this pattern to the training set. Otherwise, toss out the pattern. Continue this until enough patterns are generated to form the third training set. This third network is then trained.

In the final testing phase (of Schapire's original scheme), the test patterns (never previously used for training or validation) are passed through the three networks and labels assigned using the following voting scheme: If the first two networks agree, that is the label. Otherwise, assign the label as classified by the third network. However, we have found that if we add together the three sets of outputs from each of the three networks to obtain one set of ten outputs (for the digits) or one set of twenty-size outputs (for the alphas) we obtain better results. Typically, the error rate is reduced by .5% over straight voting.

The rationale for the better performance using addition is as follows: A voting criterion is a hard-decision rule. Each voter in the ensemble has an equal vote whether in fact the voter has high confidence (large difference between the two largest outputs in a particular network) or low confidence (small difference between the two largest outputs). By summing the outputs (a soft-decision rule) we incorporate the confidence of the networks into the total output. As will be seen later, this also allows us to build an ensemble with only two voters rather than three as called for in the original algorithm.

Conceptually, this process could be iterated in a recursive manner to produce an ensemble of nine networks, twenty-seven networks, etc. However, we have found significant improvement in going from one network to only three. The penalty paid is potentially an increase by a factor of three in evaluating the performance (we attribute no penalty to the increased training time). However it can show how to reduce this to a factor of 1.75 using sieving procedures.

2 A DEFORMATION MODEL

The proof that boosting works depends on the assumption of three independent training sets. Without a very large training set, this is not possible unless that error rates are large. After training the first network, unless the network has very poor performance, there are not enough remaining samples to generate the second training set. For example, suppose we had 9000 total examples and used the first 3000 to train the first network and that network achieves a 5% error rate. We would like the next training set to consist of 1500 patterns that the first network classifies incorrectly and 1500 that the first network classifies incorrectly. At a 5% error rate, we need approximately 30,000 new images to pass through the first network to find 1500 patterns that the first network classifies incorrectly. These many patterns are not available. Instead we will generate additional patterns by using small deformations around the finite training set based on the techniques of Simard (Simard, et. al., 1992).

The image consists of a square pixel array (we use both 16x16 and 20x20). Let the intensity of the image at coordinate location (i,j) be $F_{ij}(x,y)$ where the (x,y) denotes that F is a differentiable and hence continuous function of x and y. i and j take on the discrete values 0,1,...,15 for a 16x16 pixel array.

The change in F at location (i,j) due to small x-translation, y-translation, rotation, diagonal deformation, axis deformation, scaling and thickness deformation is given by the following respective matrix inner products:

$$\Delta F_{ij}(x,y) = \begin{bmatrix} \frac{\partial F_{ij}(x,y)}{\partial x} & \frac{\partial F_{ij}(x,y)}{\partial y} \end{bmatrix}$$

$$x \left\{ k_1 \begin{bmatrix} 1 \\ 0 \end{bmatrix} + k_2 \begin{bmatrix} 0 \\ 1 \end{bmatrix} + k_3 \begin{bmatrix} -y \\ x \end{bmatrix} + k_4 \begin{bmatrix} y \\ x \end{bmatrix} + k_5 \begin{bmatrix} -x \\ y \end{bmatrix} + k_6 \begin{bmatrix} x \\ y \end{bmatrix} + k_7 \begin{bmatrix} \frac{\partial F_{ij}(x,y)}{\partial x} \\ \frac{\partial F_{ij}(x,y)}{\partial y} \end{bmatrix} \right\}$$

where the k's are small values and x and y are referenced to the center of the image. This construction depends on obtaining the two partial derivatives.

For example, if all the k's except k_1 are zero, then $\Delta F_{ij}(x,y) = k_1 \frac{\partial F_{ij}(x,y)}{\partial x}$ is the amount by which $F_{ij}(x,y)$ at coordinate location (i,j) changes due to an x-translation of value k_1.

The diagonal deformation can be conceived of as pulling on two opposite corners of the image thereby stretching the image along the 45 degree axis (away from the center) while simultaneously shrinking the image towards the center along a - 45 degree axis. If k_4 changes sign, we push towards the center along the 45 degree axis and pull away along the - 45 degree axis. Axis deformation can be conceived as pulling (or pushing) away from the center along the x-axis while pushing (or pulling) towards the center along the y-axis.

If all the k's except k_7 are zero, then $\Delta F_{ij}(x,y) = k_7 \| \nabla F_{ij}(x,y) \|^2$ is the norm squared of the gradient of the intensity. It can be shown that this corresponds to varying the "thickness" of the image.

Typically the original image is very coarsely quantized and not differentiable. Smoothing of the original image is done by numerically convolving the original image with a 5x5 square kernel whose elements are values from the Gaussian: $\exp \frac{-(x^2+y^2)}{\sigma^2}$ to give us a 16x16 or 20x20 square matrix of smoothed values.

A matrix of partial derivatives (with respect to x) for each pixel location is obtained by convolving the original image with a kernel whose elements are the derivatives with respect to x of the Gaussian function. We can similarly form a matrix of partial derivatives with respect to y. A new image can then be constructed by adding together the smoothed image and a differential matrix whose elements are given by the above equation.

Using the above equation, we may simulate an oracle by cycling through a finite sized training set, picking random values (uniformly distributed in some small range) of the constants k for each new image. The choice of the range of k is somewhat critical: too small and the new image is too close to the old image for the neural network to consider it a "new" pattern. Too large and the image is distorted and nonrepresentative of "real" data. We will discuss the proper choice of k later.

3 NETWORK ARCHITECTURES

We use as the basic learning machine a neural network with extensive use of shared weights (LeCun, et. al., 1989, 1990). Typically the number of weights is much less than the number of connections. We believe this leads to a better ability to reject images (i.e., no decision made) and thereby minimizes the number of rejects needed to obtain a given error rate on images not rejected. However, there is conflicting evidence (Martin & Pitman, 1991) that given enough training patterns, fully connected networks give similar performance to networks using weight sharing. For the digits there is a 16 by 16 input surrounded by a six pixel border to give a 28 by 28 input layer. The network has 4645 neurons, 2578 different weights, and 98442 connections.

The networks used for the alpha characters use a 20 by 20 input surrounded by a six pixel border to give a 32 by 32 input layer. There are larger feature maps and more layers, but essentially the same construction as for the digits.

4 TRAINING ALGORITHM

The training algorithm is described in general terms: Ideally, the data set should be broken up into a training set, a validation set and a test set. The training set and validation set are smoothed (no deformations) and the first network trained using a quasi-Newton procedure. We alternately train on the training data and test on the validation data until the error rate on the validation data reaches a minimum. Typically, there is some overtraining in that the error rate on the training data continues to decrease after the error rate on the validation set reaches a minimum.

Once the first network is trained, the second set of training data is generated by cycling deformed training data through the first network. After the pseudo-random tossing of a fair coin, if the coin is heads, deformed images are passed though the first network until the network makes a mistake. If tails, deformed images are passed through the network until the network makes a correct labeling. Each deformed image is generated from the original image by randomly selecting values of the constants k. It may require multiple passes through the training data to generate enough deformed images to form the second training set.

Recall that the second training set will consist equally of images that the first network misclassifies and images that the the first network classifies correctly. The total size of the training set is that of the first training set. Correctly classified images are not hard to find if the error rate of the first network is low. However, we only accept these images with probability 50%. The choice of the range of the random variables k should be such that the deformed images do not look distorted. The choice of the range of the k's is good if the error rate using the first network on the deformed patterns is approximately the same as the error rate of the first network on the validation set (NOT the first training set).

A second network is now trained on this new training set in the alternate train/test procedure using the original validation set (not deformed) as the test set. Since this training data is much more difficult to learn than the first training data, typically the error rate on the second training set using the second trained network will be higher (sometimes much higher) than the error rates of the first network on either the first training set or the validation set. Also, the error rate on the validation set using the second network will be higher than that of the first network because the network is trying to generalize from difficult training data, 50% of which the first network could not recognize.

The third training set is formed by once again generating deformed images and presenting the images to both the first and second networks. If the networks disagree (whether both are wrong or just one is), then that image is added to the third training set. The network is trained using this new training data and tested on the original validation set. Typically, the error rate on the validation set using the third network will be much higher than either of the first two networks on the same validation set.

The three networks are then tested on the third set of data, which is the smoothed test data. According to the original algorithm we should observe the outputs of the first two networks. If the networks agree, accept that labeling, otherwise use the labeling assigned by the third network. However, we are interested in more than a low error rate. We have a second criterion, namely the percent of the patterns we have to reject (i.e. no classification decision) in order to achieve a 1% error rate. The rationale for this is that if an image recognizer is used to sort ZIP codes (or financial statements) it is much less expensive to hand sort some numbers than to accept all and send mail to the wrong address or credit the wrong account. From now on we shall call this latter criterion the reject rate (without appending each time the statement "for a 1% error rate on the patterns not rejected").

For a single neural network, a reject criterion is to compare the two (of the ten or twenty-six) largest outputs of the network. If the difference is great, there is high confidence that the maximum output is the correct classification. Therefore, a critical threshold is set such that if the difference is smaller then that threshold, the image is rejected. The threshold is set so that the error rate on the patterns not rejected is 1%.

5 RESULTS

The boosting algorithm was first used on a database consisting of segmented ZIP codes from the United States Postal Service (USPS) divided into 9709 training examples and 2007 validation samples.

The samples supplied to us from the USPS were machine segmented from zip codes and labeled but not size normalized. The validation set consists of approximately 2% badly segmented characters (incomplete segmentations, decapitated fives, etc.) The training set was cleaned thus the validation set is significantly more difficult than the training set.

The data was size normalized to fit inside a 16x16 array, centered, and deslanted. There is no third group of data called the "test set" in the sense described previously even though the validation error rate has been commonly called the test error rate in prior work (LeCun, et. al., 1989, 1990).

Within the 9709 training digits are some machine printed digits which have been found to improve performance on the validation set. This data set has an interesting history having been around for three years with an approximate 5% error rate and 10% reject rate using our best neural network. There has been a slight improvement using double backpropagation (Drucker & LeCun, 1991) bringing down the error rate to 4.7% and the reject rate to 8.9% but nothing dramatic. This network, which has a 4.7% error rate was retrained on smoothed data by starting from the best set of weights. The second and third networks were trained as described previously with the following key numbers:

The retrained first network has a training error rate of less than 1%, a test error rate of 4.9% and a test reject rate of 11.5%

We had to pass 153,000 deformed images (recycling the 9709 training set) through the trained first network to obtain another 9709 training images. Of these 9709 images, approximately one-half are patterns that the first network misclassifies. This means that the first network has a 3.2% error rate on the deformed images, far above the error rate on the original training images.

A second network is trained and gives a 5.8% test error rate.

To generate the last training set we passed 195,000 patterns (again recycling the 9709) to give another set of 9709 training patterns. Therefore, the first two nets disagreed on 5% of the deformed patterns.

The third network is trained and gives a test error rate of 16.9%

Using the original voting scheme for these three networks, we obtained a 4.0% error rate, a significant improvement over the 4.9% using one network. As suggested before, adding together the three outputs gives a method of rejecting images with low confidence scores (when the two highest outputs are too close). For curiosity, we also determined what would happen if we just added together the first two networks:

Original network: 4.9% test error rate and 11.5% reject rate.
Two networks added: 3.9% test error rate and 7.9% reject rate.
Three networks added: 3.6% test error rate and 6.6% reject rate.

The ensemble of three networks gives a significant improvement, especially in the reject rate.

In April of 1992, the National Institute of Standards and Technology (NIST) provided a labeled database of 220,000 digits, 45,000 lower case alphas and 45,000 upper case alphas. We divided these into training set, validation set, and test set. All data were resampled and size-normalized to fit into a 16x16 or 20x20 pixel array. For the digits, we deslanted and smoothed the data before retraining the first 16x16 input neural network used for the USPS data. After the second training set was generated and the second network trained the results from adding the two networks together were so good (Table 1) that we decided not to generate the third training set. For the NIST data, the error rates reported are those of the test data.

TABLE 1. Test error rate and reject rate in percent

DATABASE	USPS digits	NIST digits	NIST upper alphas	NIST lower alpha
ERROR RATE SINGLE NET	5.0	1.4	4.0	9.8
ERROR RATE USING BOOSTING	3.6	.8	2.4	8.1
REJECT RATE SINGLE NET	9.6	1.0	9.2	29.
REJECT RATE USING BOOSTING	6.6	*	3.1	21.

* Reject rate is not reported if the error rate is below 1%.

6 CONCLUSIONS

In all cases we have been able to boost performance above that of single net. Although others have used ensembles to improve performance (Srihari, 1990; Benediktsson and Swain, 1992; Xu, et. al., 1992) the technique used here is particularly straightforward since the usual multi-classifier system requires a laborious development of each classifier. There is also a difference in emphasis. In the usual multi-classifier design, each classifier is trained independently and the problem is how to best combine the classifiers. In boosting, each network (after the first) has parameters that depend on the prior networks and we know how to combine the networks (by voting or adding).

7 ACKNOWLEDGEMENTS

We hereby acknowledge the United State Postal Service and the National Institute of Standards and Technology in supplying the databases.

References

J.A. Benediktsson and P.H. Swain, "Consensus Theoretic Classification Methods", *IEEE trans. on Systems, Man, and Cybernetics*, Vol. 22, No. 4, July/August 1992, pp. 688-704.

H. Drucker, R. Schapire, and P. Simard "Boosting Performance in Neural Networks", *International Journal of Pattern Recognition and Artificial Intelligence*, (to be published, 1993)d

H. Drucker and Y. LeCun, "Improving Generalization Performance in Character Recognition", *Proceedings of the 1991 IEEE Workshop on Neural Networks for Signal Processing*, IEEE Press,pp. 198 - 207.

Y. LeCun, et. al., "Backpropagation Applied to Handwritten Zip Code Recognition", *Neural Computation 1*, 1989, pp. 541-551

Y. LeCun, et. al., Handwritten Digit Recognition with a Back-Propagation Network", In D.S. Touretsky (ed), *Advances in Neural Information Processing Systems 2*, (1990) pp. 396-404, San Mateo, CA: Morgan Kaufmann Publishers

G. L. Martin and J. A. Pitman, "Recognizing Handed-Printed Letters and Digits Using Backpropagation Learning", *Neural Computation*, Vol. 3, 1991, pp. 258-267.

R. Schapire, "The Strength of Weak Learnability", *Machine Learning*, Vol. 5, #2, 1990, pp. 197-227.

P. Simard, "Tangent Prop - A formalism for specifying selected invariances in an adaptive network", In J.E. Moody, S.J. Hanson, and R.P. Lippmann (eds.) *Advances in Neural Information Processing Systems 4*, (1992) p. 895-903, San Mateo, CA: Morgan Kaufmann Publishers

Sargur Srihari, "High-Performance Reading Machines", *Proceeding of the IEEE*, Vol 80, No. 7, July 1992, pp. 1120-1132.

C.Y. Suen, et. al., "Computer Recognition of Unconstrained Handwritten Numerals", *Proceeding of the IEEE*, Vol 80, No. 7, July 1992, pp. 1162-1180.

L. Xu, et. al., "Methods of Combining Multiple Classifiers", *IEEE Trans. on Systems Man, and Cybernetics*, Vol. 22, No. 3, May/June 1992, pp. 418-435.

Efficient Pattern Recognition Using a New Transformation Distance

Patrice Simard **Yann Le Cun** **John Denker**

AT&T Bell Laboratories, 101 Crawford Corner Road, Holmdel, NJ 07724

Abstract

Memory-based classification algorithms such as radial basis functions or K-nearest neighbors typically rely on simple distances (Euclidean, dot product...), which are not particularly meaningful on pattern vectors. More complex, better suited distance measures are often expensive and rather ad-hoc (elastic matching, deformable templates). We propose a new distance measure which (a) can be made locally invariant to any set of transformations of the input and (b) can be computed efficiently. We tested the method on large handwritten character databases provided by the Post Office and the NIST. Using invariances with respect to translation, rotation, scaling, shearing and line thickness, the method consistently outperformed all other systems tested on the same databases.

1 INTRODUCTION

Distance-based classification algorithms such as radial basis functions or K-nearest neighbors often rely on simple distances (such as Euclidean distance, Hamming distance, etc.). As a result, they suffer from a very high sensitivity to simple transformations of the input patterns that should leave the classification unchanged (e.g. translation or scaling for 2D images). This is illustrated in Fig. 1 where an unlabeled image of a "9" must be classified by finding the closest prototype image out of two images representing respectively a "9" and a "4". According to the Euclidean distance (sum of the squares of the pixel to pixel differences), the "4" is closer even though the "9" is much more similar once it has been rotated and thickened. The result is an incorrect classification. The key idea is to construct a distance measure which is invariant with respect to some chosen transformations such as translation, rotation and others. The special case of linear transformations has been well studied in statistics and is sometimes referred to as Procrustes analysis

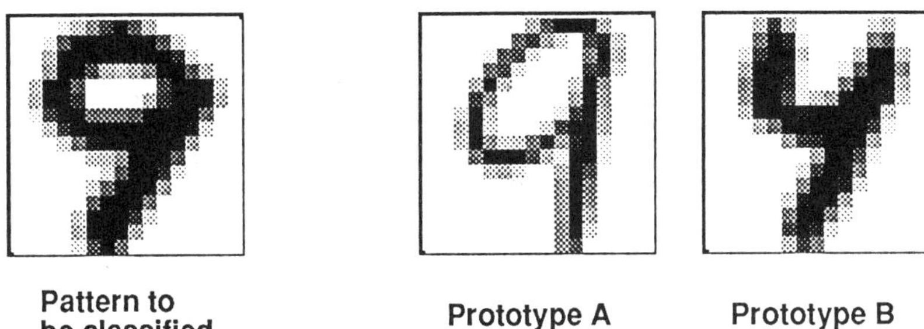

Figure 1: What is a good similarity measure? According to the Euclidean distance the pattern to be classified is more similar to prototype B. A better distance measure would find that prototype A is closer because it differs mainly by a rotation and a thickness transformation, two transformations which should leave the classification invariant.

(Sibson, 1978). It has been applied to on-line character recognition (Sinden and Wilfong, 1992).

This paper considers the more general case of non-linear transformations such as geometric transformations of gray-level images. Remember that even a simple image translation corresponds to a highly non-linear transformation in the high-dimensional pixel space[1]. In previous work (Simard et al., 1992b), we showed how a neural network could be trained to be invariant with respect to selected transformations of the input. We now apply similar ideas to distance-based classifiers.

When a pattern P is transformed (e.g. rotated) with a transformation s that depends on one parameter α (e.g. the angle of the rotation), the set of all the transformed patterns $S_P = \{x \mid \exists \vec{\alpha} \text{ such that } x = s(\vec{\alpha}, P)\}$ is a one-dimensional curve in the vector space of the inputs (see Fig. 2). In certain cases, such as rotations of digitized images, this curve must be made continuous using smoothing techniques (see (Simard et al., 1992b)). When the set of transformations is parameterized by n parameters α_i (rotation, translation, scaling, etc.), S_P is a manifold of at most n dimensions. The patterns in S_P that are obtained through *small* transformations of P, i.e. the part of S_P that is close to P, can be approximated by a plane tangent to the manifold S_P at the point P. Small transformations of P can be obtained by adding to P a linear combination of vectors that span the tangent plane (tangent vectors). The images at the bottom of Fig. 2 were obtained by that procedure. Tangent vectors for a transformation s can easily be computed by finite difference (evaluating $\partial s(\alpha, P)/\partial\alpha$); more details can be found in (Simard et al., 1992b; Simard et al., 1992a).

As we mentioned earlier, the Euclidean distance between two patterns P and E is in general not appropriate because it is sensitive to irrelevant transformations of P and of E. In contrast, the distance $\mathcal{D}(E, P)$ defined to be the minimal distance between the two manifolds S_P and S_E is truly invariant with respect to the transformation used to generate S_P and S_E. Unfortunately, these manifolds have no analytic expression in general, and finding the distance between them is a hard optimization problem with multiple local minima. Besides, true invariance is not

[1] If the image of a "3" is translated vertically upward, the middle top pixel will oscillate from black to white three times.

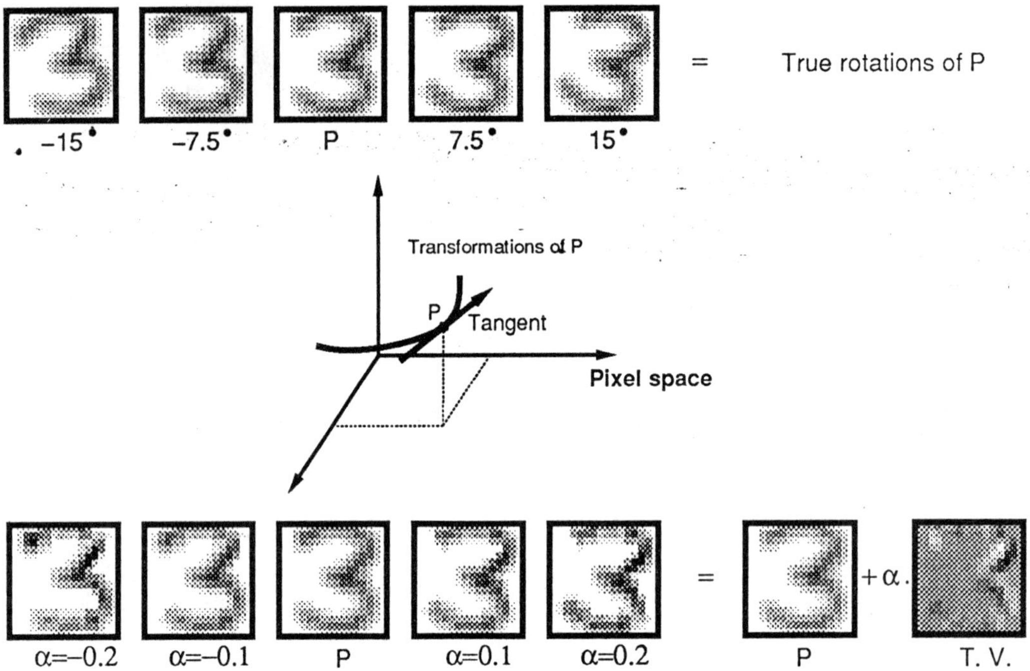

Figure 2: Top: Small rotations of an original digitized image of the digit "3". Middle: Representation of the effect of the rotation in pixel space (if there were only 3 pixels). Bottom: Images obtained by moving along the tangent to the transformation curve for the same original digitized image P by adding various amounts (α) of the tangent vector (T.V.).

necessarily desirable since a rotation of a "6" into a "9" does not preserve the correct classification.

Our approach consists of approximating the non-linear manifold S_P and S_E by linear surfaces and computing the distance $D(E, P)$ defined to be the minimum distance between them. This solves three problems at once: 1) linear manifolds have simple analytical expressions which can be easily computed and stored, 2) finding the minimum distance between linear manifolds is a simple least squares problem which can be solved efficiently and, 3) this distance is locally invariant but not globally invariant. Thus the distance between a "6" and a slightly rotated "6" is small but the distance between a "6" and a "9" is large. The different distances between P and E are represented schematically in Fig. 3.

The figure represents two patterns P and E in 3-dimensional space. The manifolds generated by s are represented by one-dimensional curves going through E and P respectively. The linear approximations to the manifolds are represented by lines tangent to the curves at E and P. These lines do not intersect in 3 dimensions and the shortest distance between them (uniquely defined) is $D(E, P)$. The distance between the two non-linear transformation curves $\mathcal{D}(E, P)$ is also shown on the figure.

An efficient implementation of the tangent distance $D(E, P)$ will be given in the

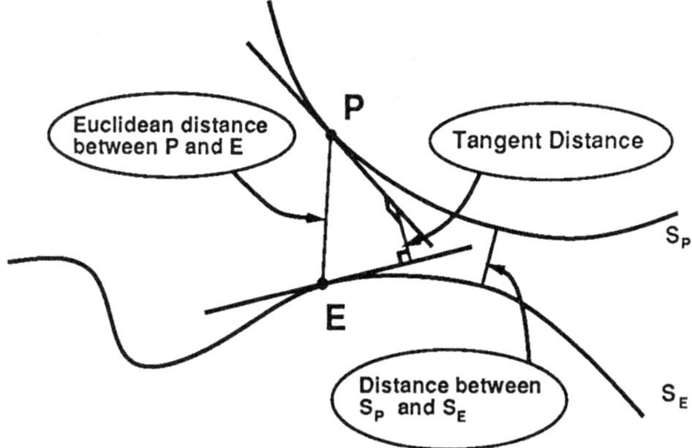

Figure 3: Illustration of the Euclidean distance and the tangent distance between P and E

next section. Although the tangent distance can be applied to any kind of patterns represented as vectors, we have concentrated our efforts on applications to image recognition. Comparison of tangent distance with the best known competing method will be described. Finally we will discuss possible variations on the tangent distance and how it can be generalized to problems other than pattern recognition.

2 IMPLEMENTATION

In this section we describe formally the computation of the tangent distance. Let the function s which map $u, \vec{\alpha}$ to $s(\vec{\alpha}, u)$ be a differentiable transformation of the input space, depending on a vector $\vec{\alpha}$ of parameter, verifying $s(\vec{0}, u) = u$.

If u is a 2 dimensional image for instance, $s(\vec{\alpha}, u)$ could be a rotation of u by the angle $\vec{\alpha}$. If we are interested in all transformations of images which conserve distances (isometry), $s(\vec{\alpha}, u)$ would be a rotation by α_r followed by a translation by α_x, α_y of the image u. In this case $\vec{\alpha} = (\alpha_r, \alpha_x, \alpha_y)$ is a vector of parameters of dimension 3. In general, $\vec{\alpha} = (\alpha_0, \dots, \alpha_{m-1})$ is of dimension m.

Since s is differentiable, the set $S_u = \{x \mid \exists \vec{\alpha} \text{ for which } x = s(\vec{\alpha}, u)\}$ is a differentiable manifold which can be approximated to the first order by a hyperplane T_u. This hyperplane is tangent to S_u at u and is generated by the columns of matrix

$$L_u = \left.\frac{\partial s(\vec{\alpha}, u)}{\partial \vec{\alpha}}\right|_{\vec{\alpha}=\vec{0}} = \left[\frac{\partial s(\vec{\alpha}, u)}{\partial \alpha_0}, \dots, \frac{\partial s(\vec{\alpha}, u)}{\partial \alpha_{m-1}}\right]_{\vec{\alpha}=\vec{0}} \tag{1}$$

which are vectors tangent to the manifold. If E and P are two patterns to be compared, the respective tangent planes T_E and T_P can be used to define a new distance D between these two patterns. The tangent distance $D(E, P)$ between E and P is defined by

$$D(E, P) = \min_{x \in T_E, y \in T_P} \|x - y\|^2 \tag{2}$$

The equation of the tangent planes T_E and T_P is given by:

$$E'(\vec{\alpha}_E) = E + L_E \vec{\alpha}_E \tag{3}$$

$$P'(\vec{\alpha}_P) = P + L_P \vec{\alpha}_P \tag{4}$$

where L_E and L_P are the matrices containing the tangent vectors (see Eq. 1) and the vectors $\vec{\alpha}_E$ and $\vec{\alpha}_P$ are the coordinates of E' and P' in the corresponding tangent planes. The quantities L_E and L_P are attributes of the patterns so in many cases they can be precomputed and stored.

Computing the tangent distance

$$D(E,P) = \min_{\vec{\alpha}_E, \vec{\alpha}_P} \|E'(\vec{\alpha}_E) - P'(\vec{\alpha}_P)\|^2 \tag{5}$$

amounts to solving a linear least squares problem. The optimality condition is that the partial derivatives of $D(E,P)$ with respect to $\vec{\alpha}_P$ and $\vec{\alpha}_E$ should be zero:

$$\frac{\partial D(E,P)}{\partial \vec{\alpha}_E} = 2(E'(\vec{\alpha}_E) - P'(\vec{\alpha}_P))^\top L_E = 0 \tag{6}$$

$$\frac{\partial D(E,P)}{\partial \vec{\alpha}_P} = 2(P'(\vec{\alpha}_P) - E'(\vec{\alpha}_E))^\top L_P = 0 \tag{7}$$

Substituting E' and P' by their expressions yields to the following linear system of equations, which we must solve for $\vec{\alpha}_P$ and $\vec{\alpha}_E$:

$$L_P^\top(E - P - L_P\vec{\alpha}_P + L_E\vec{\alpha}_E) = 0 \tag{8}$$

$$L_E^\top(E - P - L_P\vec{\alpha}_P + L_E\vec{\alpha}_E) = 0 \tag{9}$$

The solution of this system is

$$(L_{PE}L_{EE}^{-1}L_E^\top - L_P^\top)(E - P) = (L_{PE}L_{EE}^{-1}L_{EP} - L_{PP})\vec{\alpha}_P \tag{10}$$

$$(L_{EP}L_{PP}^{-1}L_P^\top - L_E^\top)(E - P) = (L_{EE} - L_{EP}L_{PP}^{-1}L_{PE})\vec{\alpha}_E \tag{11}$$

where $L_{EE} = L_E^\top L_E$, $L_{PE} = L_P^\top L_E$, $L_{EP} = L_E^\top L_P$ and $L_{PP} = L_P^\top L_P$. LU decompositions of L_{EE} and L_{PP} can be precomputed. The most expensive part in solving this system is evaluating L_{EP} (L_{PE} can be obtained by transposing L_{EP}). It requires $m_E \times m_P$ dot products, where m_E is the number of tangent vectors for E and m_P is the number of tangent vectors for P. Once L_{EP} has been computed, $\vec{\alpha}_P$ and $\vec{\alpha}_E$ can be computed by solving two (small) linear system of respectively m_E and m_P equations. The tangent distance is obtained by computing $\|E'(\vec{\alpha}_E) - P'(\vec{\alpha}_P)\|$ using the value of $\vec{\alpha}_P$ and $\vec{\alpha}_E$ in equations 3 and 4. If n is the length of vector E (or P), the algorithm described above requires roughly $n(m_E+1)(m_P+1)+3(m_E^3+m_P^3)$ multiply-adds. Approximations to the tangent distance can be computed more efficiently.

3 RESULTS

Before giving the results of handwritten digit recognition experiments, we would like to demonstrate the property of "local invariance" of tangent distance. A 16 by 16 pixel image similar to the "3" in Fig 2 was translated by various amounts. The tangent distance (using the tangent vector corresponding to horizontal translations) and the Euclidean Distance between the original image and its translated version were measured as a function of the size k (in pixels) of the translation. The result is plotted in Fig. 4. It is clear that the Euclidean Distance starts increasing linearly with k while the tangent distance remains very small for translations as large as two pixels. This indicates that, while Euclidean Distance is not invariant to translation, tangent distance is locally invariant. The extent of the invariance can be

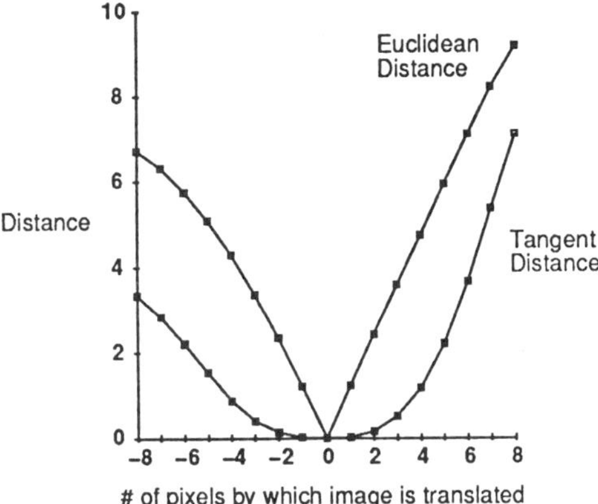

Figure 4: Euclidean and tangent distances between a 16x16 handwritten digit image and its translated version as a function of the amount of translation measured in pixels.

increased by smoothing the original image, but significant features may be blurred away, leading to confusion errors. The figure is not symmetric for large translations because the translated image is truncated to the 16 by 16 pixel field of the original image. In the following experiments, smoothing was done by convolution with a Gaussian of standard deviation $\sigma = 0.75$. This value, which was estimated visually, turned out to be nearly optimal (but not critical).

3.1 Handwritten Digit Recognition

Experiments were conducted to evaluate the performance of tangent distance for handwritten digit recognition. An interesting characteristic of digit images is that we can readily identify a set of local transformations which do not affect the identity of the character, while covering a large portion of the set of possible *instances* of the character. Seven such image transformations were identified: X and Y translations, rotation, scaling, two hyperbolic transformations (which can generate shearing and squeezing), and line thickening or thinning. The first six transformations were chosen to span the set of all possible linear coordinate transforms in the image plane (nevertheless, they correspond to highly non-linear transforms in pixel space). Additional transformations have been tried with less success.

The simplest possible use of tangent distance is in a Nearest Neighbor classifier. A set of prototypes is selected from a training set, and stored in memory. When a test pattern is to be classified, the K nearest prototypes (in terms of tangent distance) are found, and the pattern is given the class that has the majority among the neighbors. In our applications, the size of the prototype set is in the neighborhood of 10,000. In principle, classifying a pattern would require computing 10,000 tangent distances, leading to excessive classification times, despite the efficiency of the tangent distance computation. Fortunately, two patterns that are very far apart in terms of Euclidean Distance are likely to be far apart in terms of tangent distance. Therefore we can use Euclidean distance as a "prefilter", and eliminate prototypes that are unlikely to be among the nearest neighbors. We used the following 4-step classification procedure: 1) the Euclidean distance is computed between the test pattern and all the prototypes, 2) The closest 100 prototypes are selected, 3) the tangent distance between these 100 prototypes and the test pattern is computed

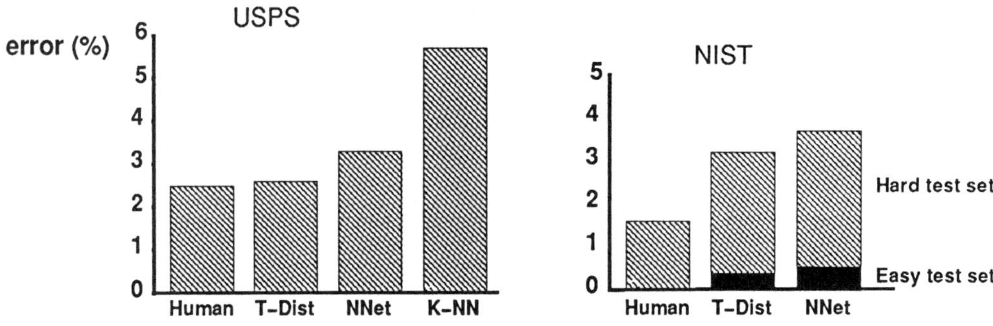

Figure 5: Comparison of the error rate of tangent nearest neighbors and other methods on two handwritten digit databases

and 4) the most represented label among the K closest prototype is outputed. This procedure is two orders of magnitude faster than computing all 10,000 tangent distances, and yields the same performance.

US Postal Service database: In the first experiment, the database consisted of 16 by 16 pixel size-normalized images of handwritten digits, coming from US mail envelopes. The entire training set of 9709 examples of was used as the prototype set. The test set contained 2007 patterns. The best performance was obtained with the "one nearest neighbor" rule. The results are plotted in Fig. 5. The error rate of the method is 2.6%. Two members of our group labeled the test set by hand with an error rate of 2.5% (using one of their labelings as the truth to test the other also yielded 2.5% error rate). This is a good indicator of the level of difficulty of this task[2]. The performance of our best neural network (Le Cun et al., 1990) was 3.3%. The performance of one nearest neighbor with the Euclidean distance was 5.9%. These results show that tangent distance performs substantially better than both standard K-nearest neighbor and neural networks.

NIST database: The second experiment was a competition organized by the National Institute of Standards and Technology. The object of the competition was to classify a test set of 59,000 handwritten digits, given a training set of 223,000 patterns. A total of 45 algorithms were submitted from 26 companies from 7 different countries. Since the training set was so big, a very simple procedure was used to select about 12,000 patterns as prototypes. The procedure consists of creating a new database (empty at the beginning), and classifying each pattern of the large database using the new database as a prototype set. Each time an error is made, the pattern is added to the new database. More than one pass may have to be made before the new database is stable. Since this filtering process would take too long with 223,000 prototypes, we split the large database into 22 smaller databases of 10,000 patterns each, filtered those (to about 550 patterns) and concatenated the result, yielding a database of roughly 12,000 patterns. This procedure has many drawbacks, and in particular, it is very good at picking up mislabeled characters in the training set. To counteract this unfortunate effect, a 3 nearest neighbors procedure was used with tangent distance. The organizers decided to collect the

[2]This is an extremely difficult test set. Procedures that achieve less than 0.5% error on other handwritten digit tasks barely achieve less than 4% on this one

training set and the test set among two very different populations (census bureau workers for the training set, high-school students for the test set), we therefore report results on the official NIST test set (named "hard test set"), and on a subset of the official training set, which we kept aside for test purposes (the "easy test set"). The results are shown in Fig. 5. The performance is much worse on the hard test set since the distribution was very different from that of the training set. Out of the 25 participants *who used the NIST training database*, tangent distance finished first. The overall winner did not use the training set provided by NIST (he used a much larger proprietary training set), and therefore was not affected by the different distributions in the training set and test set.

4 DISCUSSION

The tangent distance algorithm described in the implementation section can be improved/adjusted in at least four different ways: 1) approximating the tangent distance for better speed 2) modifying the tangent distance itself, 3) changing the set of transformations/tangent vectors and 4) using the tangent distance with classification algorithms other than K-nearest neighbors, perhaps in combination, to minimize the number of prototypes. We will discuss each of these aspects in turn.

Approximation: The distance between two hyperplanes T_E and T_P going through P and E can be approximated by computing the projection $\mathcal{P}_E(P)$ of P onto T_E and $\mathcal{P}_P(E)$ of E onto T_P. The distance $||\mathcal{P}_E(P) - \mathcal{P}_P(E)||$ can be computed in $O(n(m_E + m_P))$ multiply-adds and is a fairly good approximation of $D(E, P)$. This approximation can be improved at very low cost by computing the closest points between the lines defined by $(E, \mathcal{P}_E(P))$ and $(P, \mathcal{P}_P(E))$. This approximation was used with no loss of performance to reduce the number of computed tangent distance from 100 to 20 (this involves an additional "prefilter"). In the case of images, another time-saving idea is to compute tangent distance on progressively smaller sets of progressively higher resolution images.

Changing the distance: One may worry that the tangent planes of E and P may be parallel and be very close at a very distant region (a bad side effect of the linear approximation). This effect can be limited by imposing a constraint of the form $||\vec{\alpha_E}|| < K_E$ and $||\vec{\alpha_P}|| < K_P$. This constraint was implemented but did not yield better results. The reason is that tangent planes are mostly orthogonal in high dimensional space and the norms of $||\vec{\alpha_E}||$ and $||\vec{\alpha_P}||$ are already small.

The tangent distance can be normalized by dividing it by the norm of the vectors. This improves the results slightly because it offsets side effects introduced in some transformations such as scaling. Indeed, if scaling is a transformation of interest, there is a potential danger of finding the minimum distance between two images after they have been scaled down to a single point. The linear approximation of the scaling transformation does not reach this extreme, but still yields a slight degradation of the performance. The error rate reported on the USPS database can be improved to 2.4% using this normalization (which was not tried on NIST).

Tangent distance can be viewed as one iteration of a Newton-type algorithm which finds the points of minimum distance on the true transformation manifolds. The vectors $\vec{\alpha_E}$ and $\vec{\alpha_P}$ are the coordinates of the two closest points in the respective tangent spaces, but they can also be interpreted for real (non-linear) transformations. If $\alpha_{\vec{E},i}$ is the amount of the translation tangent vector that must be added to E to make it as close as possible to P, we can compute the true translation of image E by $\alpha_{\vec{E},i}$ pixels. In other words, $E'(\alpha_E)$ and $P'(\alpha_P)$ are projected onto close points of S_E and S_P. This involves a resampling but can be done efficiently. Once this new image has been computed, the corresponding tangent vectors can be computed for this new image and the process can be repeated. Eventually this will converge to a local minimum in the distance between the two transformation manifold of P and E. The tangent distance needs to be normalized for this iteration process to work.

A priori knowledge: The *a priori* knowledge used for tangent vectors depends greatly on the application. For character recognition, thickness was one of the most important transformations, reducing the error rate from 3.3% to 2.6%. Such a transformation would be meaningless in, say, speech or face recognition. Other transformations such as local rubber sheet deformations may be interesting for character recognition. Transformations can be known *a priori* or learned from the data.

Other algorithms, reducing the number of prototypes: Tangent distance is a general method that can be applied to problems other than image recognition, with classification methods other than K-nearest neighbors. Many distance-based classification schemes could be used in conjunction with tangent distance, among them LVQ (Kohonen, 1984), and radial basis functions. Since all the operators involved in the tangent distance are differentiable, it is possible to compute the partial derivative of the tangent distance (between an object and a prototype) with respect to the tangent vectors, or with respect to the prototype. Therefore the tangent distance operators can be inserted in gradient-descent based adaptive machines (of which LVQ and RBF are particular cases). The main advantage of learning the prototypes or the tangent vectors is that fewer prototypes may be needed to reach the same (or superior) level of performance as, say, regular K-nearest neighbors.

In conclusion, tangent distance can greatly improve many of the distance-based algorithms. We have used tangent distance in the simple K-nearest neighbor algorithm and outperformed all existing techniques on standard classification tasks. This surprising success is probably due the fact that *a priori* knowledge can be very effectively expressed in the form of tangent vectors. Fortunately, many algorithms are based on computing distances and can be adapted to express *a priori* knowledge in a similar fashion. Promising candidates include Parzen windows, learning vector quantization and radial basis functions.

References

Kohonen, T. (1984). Self-organization and Associative Memory. In *Springer Series in Information Sciences*, volume 8. Springer-Verlag.

Le Cun, Y., Boser, B., Denker, J. S., Henderson, D., Howard, R. E., Hubbard, W., and Jackel, L. D. (1990). Handwritten digit recognition with a back-propagation network. In Touretzky, D., editor, *Advances in Neural Information Processing Systems 2 (NIPS*89)*, Denver, CO. Morgan Kaufman.

Sibson, R. (1978). Studies in the Robustness of Multidimensional Scaling: Procrustes Statistices. *J. R. Statist. Soc.*, 40:234–238.

Simard, P. Y., LeCun, Y., Denker, J., and Victorri, B. (1992a). An Efficient Method for Learning Invariances in Adaptive classifiers. In *International Conference on Pattern Recognition*, volume 2, pages 651–655, The Hague, Netherlands.

Simard, P. Y., Victorri, B., LeCun, Y., and Denker, J. (1992b). Tangent Prop – A formalism for specifying selected invariances in an adaptive network. In *Neural Information Processing Systems*, volume 4, pages 895–903, San Mateo, CA.

Sinden, F. and Wilfong, G. (1992). On-line Recognition of Handwritten Symbols. Technical Report 11228-910930-02IM, AT&T Bell Laboratories.

Optimal Depth Neural Networks for Multiplication and Related Problems

Kai-Yeung Siu
Dept. of Electrical & Comp. Engineering
University of California, Irvine
Irvine, CA 92717

Vwani Roychowdhury
School of Electrical Engineering
Purdue University
West Lafayette, IN 47907

Abstract

An artificial neural network (ANN) is commonly modeled by a threshold circuit, a network of interconnected processing units called linear threshold gates. The depth of a network represents the number of unit delays or the time for parallel computation. The size of a circuit is the number of gates and measures the amount of hardware. It was known that traditional logic circuits consisting of only unbounded fan-in AND, OR, NOT gates would require at least $\Omega(\log n / \log\log n)$ depth to compute common arithmetic functions such as the product or the quotient of two n-bit numbers, unless we allow the size (and fan-in) to increase exponentially (in n). We show in this paper that ANNs can be much more powerful than traditional logic circuits. In particular, we prove that that iterated addition can be computed by depth-2 ANN, and multiplication and division can be computed by depth-3 ANNs with polynomial size and polynomially bounded integer weights, respectively. Moreover, it follows from known lower bound results that these ANNs are optimal in depth. We also indicate that these techniques can be applied to construct polynomial-size depth-3 ANN for powering, and depth-4 ANN for multiple product.

1 Introduction

Recent interest in the application of artificial neural networks [10, 11] has spurred research interest in the theoretical study of such networks. In most models of neural networks, the basic processing unit is a Boolean gate that computes a linear threshold function, or an analog element that computes a sigmoidal function. Artificial neural networks can be viewed as circuits of these processing units which are massively interconnected together.

While neural networks have found wide application in many areas, the behavior and the limitation of these networks are far from being understood. One common model of a neural network is a *threshold circuit.* Incidentally, the study of threshold circuits, motivated by some other complexity theoretic issues, has also gained much interest in the area of computer science. Threshold circuits are Boolean circuits in which each gate computes a linear threshold function, whereas in the classical model of *unbounded fan-in* Boolean circuits only AND, OR, NOT gates are allowed. A Boolean circuit is usually arranged in layers such that all gates in the same layer are computed concurrently and the circuit is computed layer by layer in some increasing *depth* order. We define the *depth* as the number of layers in the circuit. Thus each layer represents a unit delay and the depth represents the overall delay in the computation of the circuit.

2 Related Work

Theoretical computer scientists have used *unbounded fan-in* Boolean circuits as a model to understand fundamental issues of parallel computation. To be more specific, this computational model should be referred to as *unbounded fan-in* parallelism, since the number of inputs to each gate in the Boolean circuit is not bounded by a constant. The theoretical study of unbounded fan-in parallelism may give us insights into devising faster algorithms for various computational problems than would be possible with bounded fan-in parallelism. In fact, any nondegenerate Boolean function of n variables requires at least $\Omega(\log n)$ depth to compute in a bounded fan-in circuit. On the other hand, in some practical situations, (for example large fan-in circuits such as programmable logic arrays (PLAs) or multiple processors simultaneously accessing a shared bus), unbounded fan-in parallelism seems to be a natural model. For example, a PLA can be considered as a depth-2 AND/OR circuit.

In the Boolean circuit model, the amount of resources is usually measured by the number of gates, and is considered to be 'reasonable' as long as it is bounded by a polynomial (as opposed to exponential) in the number of the inputs. For example, a Boolean circuit for computing the sum of two n-bit numbers with $O(n^3)$ gates is 'reasonable', though circuit designers might consider the size of the circuit impractical for moderately large n. One of the most important theoretical issues in parallel computation is the following: *Given that the number of gates in the Boolean circuit is bounded by a polynomial in the size of inputs, what is the minimum depth (i.e. number of layers) that is needed to compute certain functions?*

A first step toward answering this important question was taken by Furst et al. [4] and independently by Ajtai [2]. It follows from their results that for many basic functions, such as the *parity* and the *majority* of n Boolean variables, or the multiplication of two n-bit numbers, any constant depth (*i.e.* independent of n) classical Boolean circuit of unbounded fan-in AND/OR gates computing these functions must have more than a polynomial (in n) number of gates. This lower bound on the size was subsequently improved by Yao [18] and Hastad [7]; it was proved that indeed an exponential number of AND/OR gates are needed. So functions such as *parity* and *majority* are computationally 'hard' with respect to constant depth and polynomial size classical Boolean circuits. Another way of interpreting these results is that circuits of AND/OR gates computing these 'hard' functions which use polynomial amount of chip area must have *unbounded delay* (*i.e.* delay that increases with n). In fact, the lower bound results imply that the minimum possible delay for multipliers (with polynomial number of AND/OR gates) is $\Omega(\log n/\log\log n)$. These results also give theoretical justification why it is impossible for circuit designers to implement fast parity circuit or multiplier in small chip area using AND, OR gates as the basic building blocks.

One of the 'hard' functions mentioned above is the *majority* function, a special case of a threshold function in which the *weights* or parameters are restricted. A natural extension is to study Boolean circuits that contain *majority gates*. This type of Boolean circuit is called a threshold circuit and is believed to capture some aspects of the computation in our brain [12]. In the rest of the paper, the term 'neural networks' refers to the threshold circuits model.

With the addition of majority gates, the resulting Boolean circuit model seems much more powerful than the classical one. Indeed, it was first shown by Muroga [13] three decades ago that any symmetric Boolean function (*e.g.* parity) can be computed by a two-layer neural network with $(n + 1)$ gates. Recently, Chandra et al. [3] showed that multiplication of two n-bit numbers and sorting of n n-bit numbers can be computed by neural networks with 'constant' depth and polynomial size. These 'constants' have been significantly reduced by Siu and Bruck [14, 15] to 4 in both cases, whereas a lower bound of depth-3 was proved by Hajnal et al. [6] in the case of multiplication. It is now known [8] that the size of the depth-4 neural networks for multiplication can be reduced to $O(n^2)$. However, the existence of depth-3 and polynomial-size neural networks for multiplication was left as an open problem [6, 5, 15] since the lower bound result in [6]. In [16], some depth-efficient neural networks were constructed for division and related arithmetic problems; the networks in [16] do not have optimal depth.

Our main contribution in this paper is to show that small constant depth neural networks for multiplication, division and related problems can be constructed. For the problems such as iterated addition, multiplication, and division, the neural networks constructed can be shown to have optimal depth. These results have the following implication on their practical significance: *Suppose we can use analog devices to build threshold gates with a cost (in terms of delay and chip area) that is comparable to that of AND, OR, logic gates, then we can compute many basic functions much faster than using traditional circuits.* Clearly, the particular weighting of depth, fan-in, and size that gives a realistic measure of a network's cost and speed depends on the technology used to build it. One case where circuit depth would seem to be the most important parameter is when the circuit is implemented using optical devices. We refer those who are interested in the optical implementation of neural networks to [1].

Due to space limitations, we shall only state some of the important results; further results and detailed proofs will appear in the journal version of this paper [17].

3 Main Results

Definition 1 Given n n-bit integers, $z_i = \sum_{j=0}^{n-1} z_{i,j} 2^j$, $i = 1, \ldots, n$, $z_{i,j} \in \{0, 1\}$, We define *iterated addition* to be the problem of computing the $(n + \log n)$-bit sum $\sum_{i=1}^{n} z_i$ of the n integers.

Definition 2 Given 2 n-bit integers, $x = \sum_{j=0}^{n-1} x_j 2^j$ and $y = \sum_{j=0}^{n-1} y_j 2^j$. We define *multiplication* to be the problem of computing the $(2n)$-bit product of x and y.

Using the notations of [15], let us denote the class of depth-d polynomial-size neural networks where the (integer) weights are polynomially bounded by $\widehat{LT}_d$ and the corresponding class where the weights are unrestricted by LT_d. It is easy to see that if iterated addition can be computed in $\widehat{LT}_2$, then multiplication can be computed in $\widehat{LT}_3$. We first prove the result on iterated addition. Our result hinges on a recent striking result of Goldmann, Håstad and Razborov [5]. The key observation is that iterated addition can be computed as a sum of polynomially many linear threshold (LT_1) functions (with exponential weights). Let us first state the result of Goldmann, Håstad and Razborov [5].

Lemma 1 [5] Let $\widetilde{LT}_d$ denote the class of depth-d polynomial-size neural networks where the weights at the output gate are polynomially bounded integers (with no restriction on the weights of the other gates). Then $\widetilde{LT}_d = \widehat{LT}_d$ for any fixed integer $d \geq 1$.

The following lemma is a generalization of the result in [13]. Informally, the result says that if a function is 1 when a weighted sum (possibly exponential) of its inputs lies in one of polynomially many intervals, and is 0 otherwise, then the function can be computed as a sum of polynomially many LT_1 functions.

Lemma 2 Let $S = \sum_{i=1}^{n} w_i x_i$ and $f(X)$ be a function such that $f = 1$ if $S \in [l_i, u_i]$ for $i = 1, \ldots, N$ and $f = 0$ otherwise, where N is polynomially bounded. Then f can be computed as a sum of polynomially many LT_1 functions and thus $f \in \widetilde{LT}_2$.

Combining the above two lemmas yields a depth-2 neural network for iterated addition.

Theorem 1 Iterated addition is in $\widehat{LT}_2$.

It is also easy to see that iterated addition cannot be computed in LT_1. Simply observe that the first bit of the sum is the parity function, which does not belong to LT_1. Thus the above neural network for iterated addition has minimum possible depth.

Theorem 2 Multiplication of 2 n-bit integers can be computed in $\widehat{LT}_3$.

It follows from the results in [6] that the depth-3 neural network for multiplication stated in the above theorem has optimal depth.

We can further apply the results in [5] to construct small depth neural networks for division, powering and multiple product. Let us give a formal definition of these problems.

Definition 3 Let X be an input n-bit integer ≥ 0. We define *powering* to be the n^2-bit representation of X^n.

Definition 4 Given n n-bit integers z_i, $i = 1, ..., n$, We define *multiple product* to be the n^2-bit representation of $\prod_{i=1}^{n} z_i$.

Suppose we want to compute the quotient of two integers. Some quotient in binary representation might require infinitely many bits, however, a circuit can only compute the most significant bits of the quotient. If a number has both finite and infinite binary representation (for example $0.1 = 0.0111...$), we shall always express the number in its finite binary representation. We are interested in computing the truncated quotient, defined below:

Definition 5 Let X and $Y \geq 1$ be two input n bit integers. Let $X/Y = \sum_{i=-\infty}^{n-1} z_i 2^i$ be the quotient of X divided by Y. We define $\text{DIV}_k(X/Y)$ to be X/Y *truncated* to the $(n + k)$-bit number, *i.e.*

$$\text{DIV}_k(X/Y) = \sum_{i=-k}^{n-1} z_i 2^i \qquad \square$$

In particular, $\text{DIV}_0(X/Y)$ is $\lfloor X/Y \rfloor$, the greatest integer $\leq X/Y$.

Theorem 3

1. Powering can be computed in $\widehat{LT}_3$.
2. $\text{DIV}_k(x/y)$ can be computed in $\widehat{LT}_3$.
3. Multiple Product can be computed in $\widehat{LT}_4$.

It can be shown from the lower-bound results in [9] that the neural networks for division are optimal in depth.

References

[1] Y. S. Abu-Mostafa and D. Psaltis. Optical Neural Computers. *Scientific American* , 256(3):88–95, 1987.

[2] M. Ajtai. $\sum_1^1$-formulae on finite structures . *Annals of Pure and Applied Logic*, 24:1–48, 1983.

[3] A. K. Chandra, L. Stockmeyer, and U. Vishkin. Constant depth reducibility. *Siam J. Comput.*, 13:423–439, 1984.

[4] M. Furst, J. B. Saxe, and M. Sipser. Parity, Circuits and the Polynomial-Time Hierarchy. *IEEE Symp. Found. Comp. Sci.*, 22:260–270, 1981.

[5] M. Goldmann, J. Håstad, and A. Razborov. Majority Gates vs. General Weighted Threshold Gates. preprint, 1991.

[6] A. Hajnal, W. Maass, P. Pudlak, M. Szegedy, and G. Turan. Threshold circuits of bounded depth. *IEEE Symp. Found. Comp. Sci.*, 28:99–110, 1987.

[7] J. Håstad and M. Goldmann. On the power of small-depth threshold circuits. In*Proceedings of the 31st IEEE FOCS*, pp. 610-618, 1990.

[8] T. Hofmeister, W. Hohberg and S. Köhling . Some notes on threshold circuits and multiplication in depth 4. *Information Processing Letters*, 39:219–225, 1991.

[9] T. Hofmeister and P. Pudlák, A proof that division is not in TC_2^0. Forschungsbericht Nr. 447, 1992, Uni Dortmund.

[10] J. J. Hopfield. Neural Networks and physical systems with emergent collective computational abilities. *Proceedings of the National Academy of Sciences*, 79:2554–2558, 1982.

[11] J. L. McClelland D. E. Rumelhart and the PDP Research Group. *Parallel Distributed Processing: Explorations in the Microstructure of Cognition, vol. 1.* MIT Press, 1986.

[12] W. S. McCulloch and W. Pitts. A Logical Calculus of Ideas Immanent in Nervous Activity. *Bulletin of Mathematical Biophysics*, 5:115–133, 1943.

[13] S. Muroga. The principle of majority decision logic elements and the complexity of their circuits. *Intl. Conf. on Information Processing, Paris, France*, June 1959.

[14] K. Y. Siu and J. Bruck. Neural Computation of Arithmetic Functions. *Proc. IEEE*, 78, No. 10:1669–1675, October 1990. Special Issue on Neural Networks.

[15] K.-Y. Siu and J. Bruck. On the Power of Threshold Circuits with Small Weights . *SIAM J. Discrete Math.*, 4(3):423–435, August 1991.

[16] K.-Y. Siu, J. Bruck, T. Kailath, and T. Hofmeister. Depth-Efficient Neural Networks for Division and Related Problems . to appear in *IEEE Trans. Information Theory*, 1993.

[17] K.-Y. Siu and V. Roychowdhury. On Optimal Depth Threshold Circuits for Mulitplication and Related Problems. to appear in *SIAM J. Discrete Math.*

[18] A. Yao. Separating the polynomial-time hierarchy by oracles. *IEEE Symp. Found. Comp. Sci.*, pages 1–10, 1985.

Using Prior Knowledge in a NNPDA to Learn Context-Free Languages

Sreerupa Das
Dept. of Comp. Sc. &
Inst. of Cognitive Sc.
University of Colorado
Boulder, CO 80309

C. Lee Giles*
NEC Research Inst.
4 Independence Way
Princeton, NJ 08540

Guo-Zheng Sun
*Inst. for Adv. Comp. Studies
University of Maryland
College Park, MD 20742

Abstract

Although considerable interest has been shown in language inference and automata induction using recurrent neural networks, success of these models has mostly been limited to regular languages. We have previously demonstrated that Neural Network Pushdown Automaton (NNPDA) model is capable of learning deterministic context-free languages (e.g., $a^n b^n$ and parenthesis languages) from examples. However, the learning task is computationally intensive. In this paper we discus some ways in which *a priori* knowledge about the task and data could be used for efficient learning. We also observe that such knowledge is often an experimental prerequisite for learning nontrivial languages (eg. $a^n b^n c b^m a^m$).

1 INTRODUCTION

Language inference and automata induction using recurrent neural networks has gained considerable interest in the recent years. Nevertheless, success of these models has been mostly limited to regular languages. Additional information in form of *a priori* knowledge has proved important and at times necessary for learning complex languages (Abu-Mostafa 1990; Al-Mashouq and Reed, 1991; Omlin and Giles, 1992; Towell, 1990). They have demonstrated that partial information incorporated in a connectionist model guides the learning process through constraints for efficient learning and better generalization.

We have previously shown that the NNPDA model can learn Deterministic Context

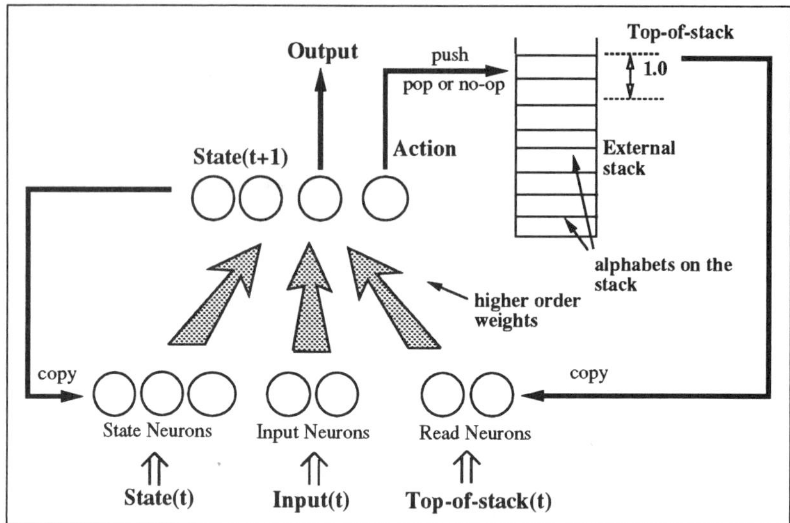

Figure 1: The figure shows the architecture of a third-order NNPDA. Each weight relates the product of Input(t), State(t) and Top-of-Stack information to the State(t+1). Depending on the activation of the Action Neuron, stack action (namely, push, pop or no operation) is taken and the Top-of-Stack (i.e. value of Read Neurons) is updated.

Free Languages (DCFLs) from a finite set of examples. However, the learning task requires considerable amount of time and computational resources. In this paper we discuss methods in which *a priori* knowledge, may be incorporated in a *Neural network Pushdown Automaton (NNPDA)* described in (Das, Giles and Sun, 1992; Giles et al, 1990; Sun et al, 1990).

2 THE NEURAL NETWORK PUSHDOWN AUTOMATA

2.1 ARCHITECTURE

The description of the network architecture is necessarily brief, for further details see the references above. The network consists of a set of recurrent units, called *state neurons* and an external stack memory. One state neuron is designated as the *output neuron*. The *state neurons* get input (at every time step) from three sources: from their own recurrent connections, from the *input neurons* and from the *read neurons*. The *input neurons* register external inputs which consist of strings of characters presented one at a time. The *read neurons* keep track of the symbol(s) on top of the stack. One non-recurrent state neuron, called the *action neuron*, indicates the stack action (push, pop or no-op) at any instance. The architecture is shown in Figure 1.

The stack used in this model is *continuous*. Unlike an usual discrete stack where an element is either present or absent, elements in a continuous stack may be present in varying degrees (values between [0, 1]). A continuous stack is essential in order to permit the use of a continuous optimization method during learning. The stack is manipulated by the continuous valued action neuron. A detailed discussion on the operations may be found in (Das, Giles and Sun, 1992).

2.2 LEARNABLE CLASS OF LANGUAGES

The class of language learnable by the NNPDA is a proper subset of deterministic context-free languages. A formal description of a Pushdown Automaton (PDA) requires two distinct sets of symbols – one is the input symbol set and the other is the stack symbol set[1]. We have reduced the complexity of this PDA model in the following ways: First, we use the same set of symbols for the input and the stack. Second, when a push operation is performed the symbol pushed on the stack is the one that is available as the current input. Third, no epsilon transitions are allowed in the NNPDA. Epsilon transition is one that performs state transition and stack action without reading in a new input symbol. Unlike a deterministic finite state automata, a deterministic PDA can make epsilon transitions under certain restrictions[1]. Although these simplifications reduce the language class learnable by NNPDA, nevertheless the languages in this class retain essential properties of CFLs and is therefore more complex than any regular language.

2.3 TRAINING

The activation of the state neurons **s** at time step $t+1$ may be formulated as follows (we will only consider third order NNPDA in this paper):

$$s_i(t+1) = g\left(\sum\sum\sum w_{ijkl} s_j(t) i_k(t) r_l(t)\right) \tag{1}$$

where $g(x) = frac1/1 + exp(-x)$, **i** is the activation of the input neurons and **r** is the activation of the read neuron and **W** is the weight matrix of the network. We use a localized representation for the input and the read symbols. During training, input sequences are presented one at a time and activations are allowed to propagate until the end of the string is reached. Once the end is reached the activation of the output neuron is matched with the *target* (which is 1.0 for positive string and 0.0 for a negative string) The learning rule used in the NNPDA is a significantly enhanced extension to *Real Time Recurrent Learning* (Williams and Zipser, 1989).

2.4 OBJECTIVE FUNCTION

The objective function used to train the network consists of two error terms: one for positive strings and the other for negative strings. For positive strings we require (a) the NNPDA must reach a final state and (b) the stack must be empty. This criterion can be reached by minimizing the error function:

$$Error = \frac{1}{2}[(1 - s_o(l))^2 + L(l)^2] \tag{2}$$

where $S_o(l)$ is the activation of an output neuron and $L(l)$ is the stack length, after a string of length l has been presented as input a character at a time. For negative

[1] For details refer to (Hopcroft, 1979).

avg of total presentations	parenthesis		postfix		$a^n b^n$	
	w IL	w/o IL	w IL	w/o IL	w IL	w/o IL
# of strings	2671	5644	8326	15912	108200	>200000
# of character	10628	29552	31171	82002	358750	>700000

Table 1: Effect of Incremental Learning (IL) is displayed in this table. The number of strings and characters required for learning the languages are provided here.

	parenthesis		$a^n b^n$	
	w SSP	w/o SSP	w SSP	w/o SSP
epochs	50–80	50–80	150–250	150–250
generalization	100%	100%	100%	98.97%
number of units	1+1	2	1+1	2
	$a^n b^n c b^m a^m$		$a^{n+m} b^n c^m$	
	w SSP	w/o SSP	w SSP	w/o SSP
epochs	150	***	150–250	***
generalization	96.02%	***	100%	***
number of units	1+1	***	1+1	***

Table 2: This table provides some statistics on epochs, generalization and number of hidden units required for learning with and without selective string presentation (SSP).

strings, the error function is modified as:

$$Error = \begin{cases} s_o(l) - L(l) & \text{if } (s_o(l) - L(l)) > 0.0 \\ 0 & \text{else} \end{cases} \tag{3}$$

Equation (2) reflects the criterion that, for a negative pattern we require either the final state $s_o(l) = 0.0$ or the stack length $L(l)$ to be greater than 1.0 (only when $s_o(l) = 1.0$ and the stack length $L(l)$ is close to zero, the error is high).

3 BUILDING IN PRIOR KNOWLEDGE

In practical inference tasks it may be possible to obtain prior knowledge about the problem domain. In such cases it often helps to build in knowledge into the system under study. There could be at least two different types of knowledge available to a model (a) knowledge that depends on the training data with absolutely no knowledge about the automaton, and (b) partial knowledge about the automaton being inferred. Some of ways in which knowledge can be provided to the model are discussed below.

3.1 KNOWLEDGE FROM THE DATA

3.1.1 Incremental Learning

Incremental Learning has been suggested by many (Elman, 1991; Giles et al, 1990, Sun et al, 1990), where the training examples are presented in order of increasing

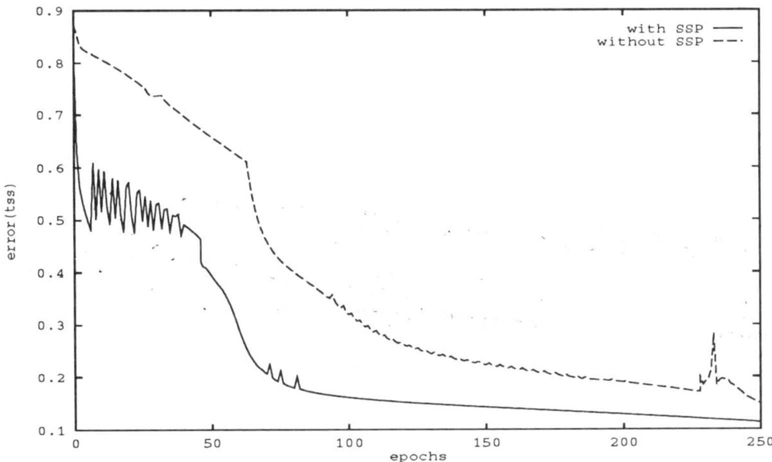

Figure 2: Faster convergence using selective string presentation (SSP) for parenthesis language task.

length. This model of learning starts with a training set containing short simple strings. Longer strings are added to the training set as learning proceeds.

We believe that incremental learning is very useful when (a) the data presented contains structure, and (b) the strings learned earlier embody simpler versions of the task being learned. Both these conditions are valid for context-free languages. Table 1 provides some results obtained when incremental learning was used. The figures are averages over several pairs of simulations, each of which were initialized with the same initial random weights.

3.1.2 Selective Input Presentation

Our training data contained both positive and negative examples. One problem with training on incorrect strings is that, once a symbol in the string is reached that makes it negative, no further information is gained by processing the rest of the string. For example, the fifth a in the string $aaaaba...$ makes the string a negative example of the language $a^n b^n$, irrespective of what follows it. In order to incorporate this idea we have introduced the concept of a *dead state.*

During training, we assume that there is a *teacher* or an *oracle* who has knowledge of the grammar and is able to identify the first (leftmost) occurrence of incorrect sequence of symbols in a negative string. When such a point is reached in the input string, further processing of the string is stopped and the network is trained so that one designated state neuron called the *dead state neuron* is active. To accommodate the idea of a *dead state* in the learning rule, the following change is made: if the network is being trained on negative strings that end in a *dead state* then the length $L(l)$ in the error function in equation (1) is ignored and it simply becomes

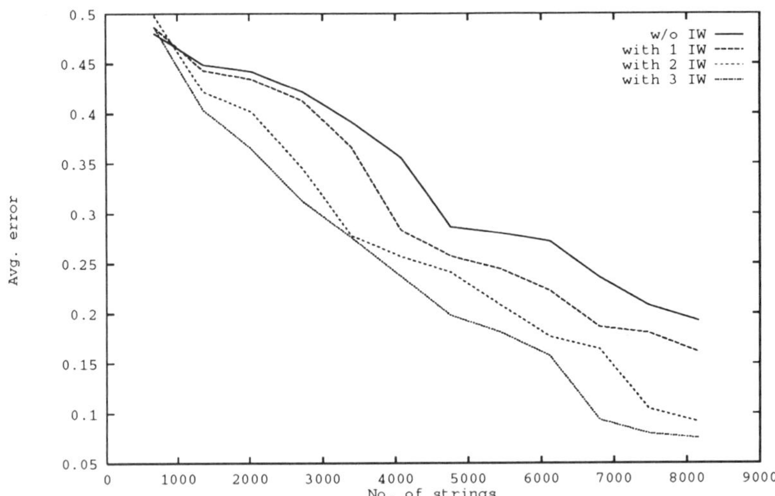

Figure 3: Learning curves when none, one or more initial weights (IW) were set for postfix language learning task

$Error = \frac{1}{2}(1 - S_{dead}(l))^2$. Since such strings have an negative subsequence, they cannot be a prefix to any positive string. Therefore at this point we do not care about the length of the stack. For strings that are either positive or negative but do not go to a dead state (an example would be a prefix of a positive string); the objective function remains the same as described earlier in Equations 1 and 2.

Such additional information provided during training resulted in efficient learning, helped in learning of exact pushdown automata and led to better generalization for the trained network. Information in this form was often a prerequisite for successfully learning certain languages. Figure 2 shows a typical plot of improvement in learning when such knowledge is used. Table 2 shows improvements in the statistics for generalization, number of units needed and number of epochs required for learning. The numbers in the tables were averages over several simulations; changing the initial conditions resulted in values of similar orders of magnitude.

3.2 KNOWLEDGE ABOUT THE TASK

3.2.1 Knowledge About The Target PDA's Dynamics

One way in which knowledge about the target PDA can be built into a system is by biasing the initial conditions of the network. This may be done by assigning predetermined initial values to a selected set of weights (or biases). For example a third order NNPDA has a dynamics that maps well onto the theoretical model of a PDA. Both allow a three to two mapping of a similar kind. This is because in the third order NNPDA, the product of the activations of the input neurons, the read neurons and the state neurons determine the next state and the next action to be

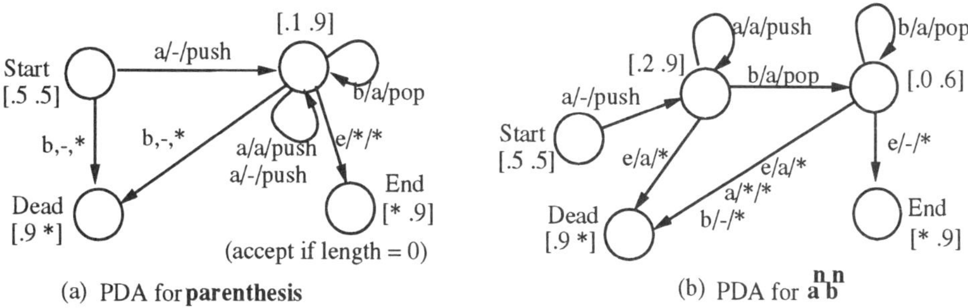

(a) PDA for **parenthesis** (b) PDA for $\mathbf{a^n b^n}$

Figure 4: The figure shows some of the PDAs inferred by the NNPDA. In the figure the nodes in the graph represent states inferred by the NNPDA and the numbers in "[ ]" indicates the state representations. Every transition is indicated by an arrow and is labeled as "x/y/z" where "x" corresponds to the current input symbol, "y" corresponds to the symbol on top of the stack and "z" corresponds to the action taken.

taken. It may be possible to determine some of the weights in a third order network if certain information about the automaton in known. Typical improvement in learning is shown in Figure 3 for a postfix language learning task.

3.2.2 Using Structured Examples

Structured examples from a grammar are a set of strings where the order of letter generation is indicated by brackets. An example would be the string ((ab)c) generated by the rules $S \rightarrow Xc; X \rightarrow ab$. Under the current dynamics and limitations of the model, this information could be interpreted as providing the stack actions (push and pop) to the NNPDA. Learning the palindrome language is a hard task because it necessitates remembering a precise history over a long period of time. The NNPDA was able to learn the palindrome language for two symbols when structured examples were presented.

4 AUTOMATON EXTRACTION FROM NNPDA

Once the network performs well on the training set, the transition rules in the inferred PDA can then be deduced. Since the languages learned by the NNPDA so far corresponded to PDAs with few states, the state representations in the induced PDA could be inferred by looking at the state neuron activations when presented with all possible character sequences. For larger PDAs clustering techniques could be used to infer the state representations. Various clustering techniques for similar tasks have been discussed in (Das and Das, 1992; Giles et al., 1992). Figure 4 shows some of the PDAs inferred by the NNPDA.

5 CONCLUSION

This paper has described some of the ways in which prior knowledge could be used to learn DCFGs in an NNPDA. Such knowledge is valuable to the learning process in two ways. It may reduce the solution space, and as a consequence may speed up the learning process. Having the right restrictions on a given representation can make learning simple: which reconfirms an old truism in Artificial Intelligence.

References

Y.S. Abu-Mostafa. (1990) Learning from hints in neural networks. *Journal of Complexity*, 6:192-198.

K.A. Al-Mashouq and I.S. Reed. (1991) Including hints in training neural networks. *Neural Computation*, 3(3):418-427.

S. Das and R. Das. (1992) Induction of discrete state-machine by stabilizing a continuous recurrent network using clustering. *To appear in CSI Journal of Computer Science and Informatics.* Special Issue on Neural Computing.

S. Das, C.L. Giles, and G.Z. Sun. (1992) Learning context free grammars: capabilities and limitations of neural network with an external stack memory. *Proc of the Fourteenth Annual Conf of the Cognitive Science Society*, pp. 791-795. Morgan Kaufmann, San Mateo, Ca.

J.L. Elman. (1991) Incremental learning, or the importance of starting small. CRL Tech Report 9101, Center for Research in Language, UCSD, La Jolla, CA.

C.L. Giles, G.Z. Sun, H.H. Chen, Y.C. Lee and D. Chen, (1990) Higher Order Recurrent Networks & Grammatical Inference, *Advances in Neural Information Processing Systems 2*, pp. 380-387, ed. D.S. Touretzky, Morgan Kaufmann, San Mateo, CA.

C.L. Giles, C.B. Miller, H.H. Chen, G.Z. Sun, and Y.C. Lee. (1992) Learning and extracting finite state automata with second-order recurrent neural networks. *Neural Computation*, 4(3):393-405.

J.E. Hopfcroft and J.D. Ullman. (1979) *Introduction to Automata Theory, Languages and Computation.* Addison-Wesley, Reading, MA.

C.W. Omlin and C.L. Giles. (1992) Training second-order recurrent neural networks using hints. *Proceedings of the Ninth Int Conf on Machine Learning*, pp. 363-368. D. Sleeman and P. Edwards (eds). Morgan Kaufmann, San Mateo, Ca.

G.Z. Sun, H.H. Chen, C.L. Giles, Y.C. Lee and D. Chen. (1991) Neural networks with external memory stack that learn context-free grammars from examples. *Proc of the Conf on Information Science and Systems*, Princeton U., Vol. II, pp. 649-653.

G.G. Towell, J.W. Shavlik and M.O Noordewier. (1990) Refinement of approximately correct domain theories by knowledge-based neural-networks. In *Proc of the Eighth National Conf on Artificial Intelligence*, Boston, MA. pp. 861.

R.J. Williams and D. Zipser. (1989) A learning algorithm for continually running fully recurrent neural networks. *Neural Computation* 1(2):270-280.

A Method for Learning from Hints

Yaser S. Abu-Mostafa
Departments of Electrical Engineering, Computer Science,
and Computation and Neural Systems
California Institute of Technology
Pasadena, CA 91125
e-mail: yaser@caltech.edu

Abstract

We address the problem of learning an unknown function by putting together several pieces of information (hints) that we know about the function. We introduce a method that generalizes learning from examples to learning from hints. A canonical representation of hints is defined and illustrated for new types of hints. All the hints are represented to the learning process by examples, and examples of the function are treated on equal footing with the rest of the hints. During learning, examples from different hints are selected for processing according to a given schedule. We present two types of schedules; fixed schedules that specify the relative emphasis of each hint, and adaptive schedules that are based on how well each hint has been learned so far. Our learning method is compatible with any descent technique that we may choose to use.

1 INTRODUCTION

The use of hints is coming to the surface in a number of research communities dealing with learning and adaptive systems. In the learning-from-examples paradigm, one often has access not only to examples of the function, but also to a number of hints (prior knowledge, or side information) about the function. The most common difficulty in taking advantage of these hints is that they are heterogeneous and cannot be easily integrated into the learning process. This paper is written with the specific goal of addressing this problem. The paper develops a systematic method for incorporating different hints in the usual learning-from-examples process.

Without such a systematic method, one can still take advantage of certain types of hints. For instance, one can implement an invariance hint by preprocessing the input to achieve the invariance through normalization. Alternatively, one can structure the learning model in a way that directly implements the invariance (Minsky and Papert, 1969). Whenever direct implementation is feasible, the full benefit of the hint is realized. This paper does not attempt to offer a superior alternative to direct implementation. *However, when direct implementation is not an option, we prescribe a systematic method for incorporating practically any hint in any descent technique for learning.* The goal is to automate the use of hints in learning to a degree where we can effectively utilize a large number of different hints that may be available in a practical situation. As the use of hints becomes routine, we are encouraged to exploit even the simplest observations that we may have about the function we are trying to learn.

The notion of hints is quite general and it is worthwhile to formalize what we mean by a hint as far as our method is concerned. Let f be the function that we are trying to learn. A hint is a property that f is known to have. Thus, all that is needed to qualify as a hint is to have a litmus test that f passes and that can be applied to different functions. Formally, a hint is a given subset of functions that includes f.

We start by introducing the basic nomenclature and notation. The *environment* X is the set on which the function f is defined. The points in the environment are distributed according to some probability distribution P. f takes on values from some set Y

$$f : X \to Y$$

Often, Y is just $\{0, 1\}$ or the interval $[0, 1]$. The *learning process* takes pieces of information about (the otherwise unknown) f as input and produces a *hypothesis* g

$$g : X \to Y$$

that attempts to approximate f. The degree to which a hypothesis g is considered an approximation of f is measured by a distance or 'error'

$$E(g, f)$$

The error E is based on the disagreement between g and f as seen through the eyes of the probability distribution P.

Two popular forms of the error measure are

$$E = \Pr[g(x) \neq f(x)]$$

and

$$E = \mathcal{E}[(g(x) - f(x))^2]$$

where $\Pr[.]$ denotes the probability of an event, and $\mathcal{E}[.]$ denotes the expected value of a random variable. The underlying probability distribution is P. E will always be a non-negative quantity, and we will take $E(g, f) = 0$ to mean that g and f are identical for all intents and purposes. We will also assume that when the set of hypotheses is parameterized by real-valued parameters (e.g., the weights in the case of a neural network), E will be well-behaved as a function of the parameters (in order to allow for derivative-based descent techniques). We make the same assumptions about the error measures that will be introduced in section 2 for the hints.

In this paper, the 'pieces of information' about f that are input to the learning process are more general than in the learning-from-examples paradigm. In that paradigm, a number of points $x_1, \cdots, x_N$ are picked from X (usually independently according to the probability distribution P) and the values of f on these points are provided. Thus, the input to the learning process is the set of examples

$$(x_1, f(x_1)), \cdots, (x_N, f(x_N))$$

and these examples are used to guide the search for a good hypothesis. We will consider the set of examples of f as only one of the available hints and denote it by H_0. The other hints $H_1, \cdots, H_M$ will be additional known facts about f, such as invariance properties for instance.

The paper is organized as follows. Section 2 develops a canonical way for representing different hints. This is the first step in dealing with any hint that we encounter in a practical situation. Section 3 develops the basis for learning from hints and describes our method, including specific learning schedules.

2 REPRESENTATION OF HINTS

As we discussed before, a hint H_m is defined by a litmus test that f satisfies and that can be applied to the set of hypotheses. This definition of H_m can be extended to a definition of 'approximation of H_m' in several ways. For instance, g can be considered to approximate H_m within ϵ if there is a function h that strictly satisfies H_m for which $E(g,h) \leq \epsilon$. In the context of learning, it is essential to have a notion of approximation since exact learning is seldom achievable. Our definitions for approximating different hints will be part of the scheme for representing those hints.

The first step in representing H_m is to choose a way of generating 'examples' of the hint. For illustration, suppose that H_m asserts that

$$f : [-1,+1] \rightarrow [-1,+1]$$

is an *odd* function. An example of H_m would have the form

$$f(-x) = -f(x)$$

for a particular $x \in [-1,+1]$. To generate N examples of this hint, we generate $x_1, \cdots, x_N$ and assert for each x_n that $f(-x_n) = -f(x_n)$. Suppose that we are in the middle of a learning process, and that the current hypothesis is g when the example $f(-x) = -f(x)$ is presented. We wish to measure how much g disagrees with this example. This leads to the second component of the representation, the error measure e_m. For the oddness hint, e_m can be defined as

$$e_m = (g(x) + g(-x))^2$$

so that $e_m = 0$ reflects total agreement with the example (i.e., $g(-x) = -g(x)$). Once the disagreement between g and an example of H_m has been quantified through e_m, the disagreement between g and H_m as a whole is automatically quantified through E_m, where

$$E_m = \mathcal{E}(e_m)$$

The expected value is taken w.r.t. the probability rule for picking the examples. Therefore, E_m can be estimated by averaging e_m over a number of examples that are independently picked.

The choice of representation of H_m is not unique, and E_m will depend on the form of examples, the probability rule for picking the examples, and the error measure e_m. A minimum requirement on E_m is that it should be zero when $E = 0$. This requirement guarantees that a hypothesis for which $E = 0$ (perfect hypothesis) will not be excluded by the condition $E_m = 0$.

Let us illustrate how to represent different types of hints. Perhaps the most common type of hint is **the invariance hint**. This hint asserts that $f(x) = f(x')$ for certain pairs x, x'. For instance, "f is shift-invariant" is formalized by the pairs x, x' that are shifted versions of each other. To represent the invariance hint, an invariant pair (x, x') is picked as an example. The error associated with this example is

$$e_m = (g(x) - g(x'))^2$$

Another related type of hint is **the monotonicity hint** (or inequality hint). The hint asserts for certain pairs x, x' that $f(x) \leq f(x')$. For instance, "f is monotonically nondecreasing in x" is formalized by all pairs x, x' such that $x < x'$. To represent the monotonicity hint, an example (x, x') is picked, and the error associated with this example is given by

$$e_m = \begin{cases} (g(x) - g(x'))^2 & \text{if } g(x) > g(x') \\ 0 & \text{if } g(x) \leq g(x') \end{cases}$$

The third type of hint we discuss here is **the approximation hint**. The hint asserts for certain points $x \in X$ that $f(x) \in [a_x, b_x]$. In other words, the value of f at x is known only approximately. The error associated with an example x of the approximation hint is

$$e_m = \begin{cases} (g(x) - a_x)^2 & \text{if } g(x) < a_x \\ (g(x) - b_x)^2 & \text{if } g(x) > b_x \\ 0 & \text{if } g(x) \in [a_x, b_x] \end{cases}$$

Another type of hints arises when the learning model allows non-binary values for g where f itself is known to be binary. This gives rise to **the binary hint**. Let $\hat{X} \subseteq X$ be the set where f is known to be binary (for Boolean functions, $\hat{X}$ is the set of binary input vectors). The binary hint is represented by examples of the form x, where $x \in \hat{X}$. The error function associated with an example x (assuming 0/1 binary convention, and assuming $g(x) \in [0,1]$) is

$$e_m = g(x)(1 - g(x))$$

This choice of e_m forces it to be zero when $g(x)$ is either 0 or 1, while it would be positive if $g(x)$ is between 0 and 1.

It is worth noting that the set of examples of f can be formally treated as a hint, too. Given $(x_1, f(x_1)), \cdots, (x_N, f(x_N))$, **the examples hint** asserts that these are the correct values of f at those particular points. Now, to generate an 'example' of this hint, we pick a number n from 1 to N and use the corresponding $(x_n, f(x_n))$. The error associated with this example is e_0 (we fix the convention that $m = 0$ for the examples hint)

$$e_0 = (g(x_n) - f(x_n))^2$$

Assuming that the probability rule for picking n is uniform over $\{1, \cdots, N\}$,

$$E_0 = \mathcal{E}(e_0) = \frac{1}{N}\sum_{n=1}^{N}(g(x_n) - f(x_n))^2$$

In this case, E_0 is also the best estimator of $E = \mathcal{E}[(g(x) - f(x))^2]$ given $x_1, \cdots, x_N$ that are independently picked according to the original probability distribution P. This way of looking at the examples of f justifies their treatment exactly as one of the hints, and underlines the distinction between E and E_0.

In a practical situation, we try to infer as many hints about f as the situation will allow. Next, we represent each hint according to the scheme discussed in this section. This leads to a list $H_0, H_1, \cdots, H_M$ of hints that are ready to produce examples upon the request of the learning algorithm. We now address how the algorithm should pick and choose between these examples as it moves along.

3 LEARNING SCHEDULES

If the learning algorithm had complete information about f, it would search for a hypothesis g for which $E(g, f) = 0$. However, f being unknown means that the point $E = 0$ cannot be directly identified. The most any learning algorithm can do given the hints $H_0, H_1, \cdots, H_M$ is to reach a hypothesis g for which all the error measures $E_0, E_1, \cdots, E_M$ are zeros. Indeed, we have required that $E = 0$ implies that $E_m = 0$ for all m.

If that point is reached, regardless of how it is reached, the job is done. However, it is seldom the case that we can reach the zero-error point because either (1) it does not exist (i.e., no hypothesis can satisfy all the hints simultaneously, which implies that no hypothesis can replicate f exactly), or (2) it is difficult to reach (i.e., the computing resources do not allow us to exhaustively search the space of hypotheses looking for that point). In either case, we will have to settle for a point where the E_m's are 'as small as possible'.

How small should each E_m be? A balance has to be struck, otherwise some E_m's may become very small at the expense of the others. This situation would mean that some hints are over-learned while the others are under-learned. We will discuss learning schedules that use different criteria for balancing between the hints. The schedules are used by the learning algorithm to simultaneously minimize the E_m's. Let us start by exploring how simultaneous minimization of a number of quantities is done in general.

Perhaps the most common approach is that of *penalty functions* (Wismer and Chattergy, 1978). In order to minimize $E_0, E_1, \cdots, E_M$, we minimize the penalty function

$$\sum_{m=0}^{M} \alpha_m \; E_m$$

where each α_m is a non-negative number that may be constant (exact penalty function) or variable (sequential penalty function). Any descent technique can be employed to minimize the penalty function once the α_m's are selected. The α_m's are weights that reflect the relative emphasis or 'importance' of the corresponding E_m's. The choice of the weights is usually crucial to the quality of the solution.

Even if the α_m's are determined, we still do not have the explicit values of the E_m's in our case (recall that E_m is the expected value of the error e_m on an example of the hint). Instead, we will estimate E_m by drawing several examples and averaging their error. Suppose that we draw N_m examples of H_m. The estimate for E_m would then be

$$\frac{1}{N_m} \sum_{n=1}^{N_m} e_m^{(n)}$$

where $e_m^{(n)}$ is the error on the nth example. Consider a batch of examples consisting of N_0 examples of H_0, N_1 examples of H_1, $\cdots$, and N_M examples of H_M. The total error of this batch is

$$\sum_{m=0}^{M} \sum_{n=1}^{N_m} e_m^{(n)}$$

If we take $N_m \propto \alpha_m$, this total error will be a proportional estimate of the penalty function

$$\sum_{m=0}^{M} \alpha_m \; E_m$$

In effect, we translated the weights into a **schedule**, where different hints are emphasized, not by magnifying their error, but by representing them with more examples.

A batch of examples can be either a *uniform batch* that consist of N examples of one hint at a time, or, more generally, a *mixed batch* where examples of different hints are allowed within the same batch. If the descent technique is linear and the learning rate is small, a schedule that uses mixed batches is equivalent to a schedule that alternates between uniform batches (with frequency equal to the frequency of examples in the mixed batch). If we are using a nonlinear descent technique, it is generally more difficult to ascertain a direct translation from mixed batches to uniform batches, but there may be compelling heuristic correspondences. All schedules discussed here are expressed in terms of uniform batches for simplicity.

The implementation of a given schedule goes as follows: (1) The algorithm decides which hint (which m for $m = 0, 1, \cdots, M$) to work on next, according to some criterion; (2) The algorithm then requests a batch of examples of this hint; (3) It performs its descent on this batch; and (4) When it is done, it goes back to step (1). We make a distinction between *fixed schedules*, where the criterion for selecting the hint can be 'evaluated' ahead of time (albeit time-invariant or time-varying, deterministic or stochastic), and *adaptive schedules*, where the criterion depends on what happens as the algorithm runs. Here are some fixed and adaptive schedules:

Simple Rotation: This is the simplest possible schedule that tries to balance between the hints. It is a fixed schedule that rotates between $H_0, H_1, \cdots, H_M$. Thus, at step k, a batch of N examples of H_m is processed, where $m = k \bmod (M+1)$. This simple-minded algorithm tends to do well in situations where the E_m's are somewhat similar.

Weighted Rotation: This is the next step in fixed schedules that tries to give different emphasis to different E_m's. The schedule rotates between the hints, visiting H_m with frequency ν_m. The choice of the ν_m's can achieve balance by emphasizing the hints that are more important or harder to learn.

Maximum Error: This is the simplest adaptive schedule that tries to achieve the same type of balance as simple rotation. At each step k, the algorithm processes the hint with the largest error E_m. The algorithm uses estimates of the E_m's to make its selection.

Maximum Weighted Error: This is the adaptive counterpart to weighted rotation. It selects the hint with the largest value of $\nu_m E_m$. The choice of the ν_m's can achieve balance by making up for disparities between the numerical ranges of the E_m's. Again, the algorithm uses estimates of the E_m's.

Adaptive schedules attempt to answer the question: Given a set of values for the E_m's, which hint is the most under-learned? The above schedules answer the question by comparing the individual E_m's. Although this works well in simple cases, it does not take into consideration the correlation between different hints. As we deal with more and more hints, the correlation between the E_m's becomes more significant. This leads us to the final schedule that achieves the balance between the E_m's through their relation to the actual error E.

Adaptive Minimization: Given the estimates of $E_0, E_1, \cdots, E_M$, make $M+1$ estimates of E, each based on all but one of the hints:

$$
\begin{gathered}
\hat{E}(\bullet, E_1, E_2, \cdots, E_M) \\
\hat{E}(E_0, \bullet, E_2, \cdots, E_M) \\
\hat{E}(E_0, E_1, \bullet, \cdots, E_M) \\
\cdots \\
\hat{E}(E_0, E_1, E_2, \cdots, \bullet)
\end{gathered}
$$

and choose the hint for which the corresponding estimate is the *smallest*.

In other words, E becomes the common thread between the E_m's. Knowing that we are really trying to minimize E, and that the E_m's are merely a vehicle to this end, *the criterion for balancing the E_m's should be based on what is happening to E as far as we can tell.*

CONCLUSION

This paper developed a systematic method for using different hints as input to the learning process, generalizing the case of invariance hints (Abu-Mostafa, 1990). The method treats all hints on equal footing, including the examples of the function. Hints are represented in a canonical way that is compatible with the common learning-from-examples paradigm. No restrictions are made on the learning model or the descent technique to be used.

The hints are captured by the error measures $E_0, E_1, \cdots, E_M$, and the learning algorithm attempts to simultaneously minimize these quantities. The simultaneous minimization of the E_m's gives rise to the idea of balancing between the different hints. A number of algorithms that minimize the E_m's while maintaining this balance were discussed in the paper. Adaptive schedules in particular are worth noting because they automatically compensate against many artifacts of the learning process.

It is worthwhile to distinguish between the quality of the hints and the quality of the learning algorithm that uses these hints. The quality of the hints is determined by how reliably one can predict that the actual error E will be close to zero for a given hypothesis based on the fact that $E_0, E_1, \cdots, E_M$ are close to zero for that hypothesis. The quality of the algorithm is determined by how likely it is that the E_m's will become nearly as small as they can be within a reasonable time.

Acknowledgements

The author would like to thank Ms. Zehra Kök for her valuable input. This work was supported by the AFOSR under grant number F49620-92-J-0398.

References

Abu-Mostafa, Y. S. (1990), Learning from hints in neural networks, *Journal of Complexity* **6**, 192-198.

Al-Mashouq, K. and Reed, I. (1991), Including hints in training neural networks, *Neural Computation* **3**, 418-427.

Minsky, M. L. and Papert, S. A. (1969), "Perceptrons," MIT Press.

Omlin, C. and Giles, C. L. (1992), Training second-order recurrent neural networks using hints, *Machine Learning: Proceedings of the Ninth International Conference (ML-92)*, D. Sleeman and P. Edwards (ed.), Morgan Kaufmann.

Suddarth, S. and Holden, A. (1991), Symbolic neural systems and the use of hints for developing complex systems, *International Journal of Machine Studies* **35**, p. 291.

Wismer, D. A. and Chattergy, R. (1978), "Introduction to Nonlinear Optimization," North Holland.

Q-Learning with Hidden-Unit Restarting

Charles W. Anderson
Department of Computer Science
Colorado State University
Fort Collins, CO 80523

Abstract

Platt's resource-allocation network (RAN) (Platt, 1991a, 1991b) is modified for a reinforcement-learning paradigm and to "restart" existing hidden units rather than adding new units. After restarting, units continue to learn via back-propagation. The resulting restart algorithm is tested in a Q-learning network that learns to solve an inverted pendulum problem. Solutions are found faster on average with the restart algorithm than without it.

1 Introduction

The goal of supervised learning is the discovery of a compact representation that generalizes well. Such representations are typically found by incremental, gradient-based search, such as error back-propagation. However, in the early stages of learning a control task, we are more concerned with fast learning than a compact representation. This implies a local representation with the extreme being the memorization of each experience. An initially local representation is also advantageous when the learning component is operating in parallel with a conventional, fixed controller. A learning experience should not generalize widely; the conventional controller should be preferred for inputs that have not yet been experienced.

Platt's resource-allocation network (RAN) (Platt, 1991a, 1991b) combines gradient search and memorization. RAN uses locally tuned (gaussian) units in the hidden layer. The weight vector of a gaussian unit is equal to the input vector for which the unit produces its maximal response. A new unit is added when the network's error magnitude is large and the new unit's radial domain would not significantly overlap domains of existing units. Platt demonstrated RAN on the supervised learning task of predicting values in the Mackey-Glass time series.

We have integrated Platt's ideas with the reinforcement-learning algorithm called Q-learning (Watkins, 1989). One major modification is that the network has a fixed number of hidden units, all in a single-layer, all of which are trained on every step. Rather than adding units, the least useful hidden unit is selected and its weights are set to new values, then continue the gradient-based search. Thus, the unit's search is *restarted.* The temporal-difference errors control restart events in a fashion similar to the way supervised errors control RAN's addition of new units.

The motivation for starting with all units present is that in a parallel implementation, the computation time for a layer of one unit is roughly the same as that for a layer with all of the units. All units are trained from the start. Any that fail to learn anything useful are *re*-allocated when needed.

Here the Q-learning algorithm with restarts is applied to the problem of learning to balance a simulated inverted pendulum. In the following sections, the inverted pendulum problem and Watkin's Q-Learning algorithm are described. Then the details of the restart algorithm are given and results of applying the algorithm to the inverted pendulum problem are summarized.

2 Inverted Pendulum

The inverted pendulum is a classic example of an inherently unstable system. The problem can be used to study the difficult credit assignment problem that arises when performance feedback is provided only by a failure signal. This problem has often used to test new approaches to learning control (from early work by Widrow and Smith, 1964, to recent studies such as Jordan and Jacobs, 1990, and Whitley, Dominic, Das, and Anderson, 1993). It involves a pendulum hinged to the top of a wheeled cart that travels along a track of limited length. The pendulum is constrained to move within the vertical plane. The state is specified by the position and velocity of the cart and the angle between the pendulum and vertical and the angular velocity of the pendulum.

The only information regarding the goal of the task is provided by the failure signal, or reinforcement, r_t, which signals either the pendulum falling past $\pm 12°$ or the cart hitting the bounds of the track at ± 1 m. The state at time t of the pendulum is presented to the network as a vector, x_t, of the four state variables scaled to be between 0 and 1.

For further details of this problem and other reinforcement learning approaches to this problem, see Barto, Sutton, and Anderson (1983) and Anderson (1987).

3 Q-Learning

The objective of many control problems is to optimize a performance measure over time. For the inverted pendulum problem, we define a *reinforcement signal* to be -1 when the pendulum angle or the cart position exceed their bounds, and 0 otherwise. The objective is to maximize the sum of this reinforcement signal over time.

If we had complete knowledge of state transition probabilities we could apply dynamic programming to find the sequence of pushes that maximize the sum of reinforcements. Reinforcement learning algorithms have been devised to learn control strategies when such knowledge is not available. In fact, Watkins has shown that one form of his Q-learning algorithm converges to the dynamic programming solution (Watkins, 1989; Watkins and Dayan, 1992).

The essence of Q-learning is the learning and use of a Q function, $Q(x, a)$, that is a prediction of a weighted sum of future reinforcement given that action a is taken when the controlled system is in a state represented by x. This is analogous to the value function in dynamic programming. Specifically, the objective of Q-learning is to form the following approximation:

$$Q(x_t, a_t) \approx \sum_{k=0}^{\infty} \gamma^k r_{t+k+1}$$

where $0 \leq \gamma < 1$ is a discount rate and r_t is the reinforcement received at time t.

Watkins (1989) presents a number of algorithms for adjusting the parameters of Q. Here we focus on using error back-propagation to train a neural network to learn the Q function. For Q-learning, the following *temporal-difference* error (Sutton, 1988)

$$e_t = r_{t+1} + \gamma \max_{a_{t+1}} [Q(x_{t+1}, a_{t+1})] - Q(x_t, a_t).$$

is derived by using $\max_{a_{t+1}} [Q(x_{t+1}, a_{t+1})]$ as an approximation to $\sum_{k=0}^{\infty} \gamma^k r_{t+k+2}$. See (Barto, Bradtke, and Singh, 1991) for further discussion of the relationships between reinforcement learning and dynamic programming.

4 Q-Learning Network

For the inverted pendulum experiments reported here, a neural network with a single hidden layer was used to learn the $Q(x, a)$ function. As shown in Figure 1, the network has four inputs for the four state variables of the inverted pendulum, and two outputs corresponding to the two possible actions for this problem, similar to Lin (1992). In addition to the weights shown, w and v, the two units in the output layer each have a single weight with a constant input of 0.5.

The activation function of the hidden units is the approximate gaussian function used by Platt. Let d_j be the squared distance between the current input vector, x, and the weights in hidden unit j.

$$d_j = \sum_{i=1}^{4} (x_i - w_{j,i})^2$$

Here x_i is the ith component of x at the current time. The output, y_j, of hidden unit j is

$$y_j = \begin{cases} \left(1 - \frac{d_j}{\rho}\right)^2, & \text{if } d_j < \rho; \\ 0, & \text{otherwise,} \end{cases}$$

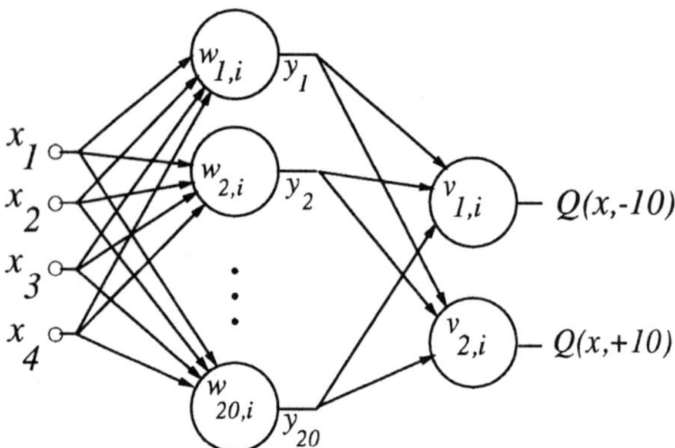

Figure 1: Q-Learning Network

where ρ controls the radius of the region in which the unit's output is nonzero. Unlike Platt, ρ is constant and equal for all units.

The output units calculate weighted sums of the hidden unit outputs and the constant input. The output values are the current estimates of $Q(x_t, -10)$ and $Q(x_t, 10)$, which are predictions of future reinforcement given the current observed state of the inverted pendulum and assuming a particular action will be applied in that state.

The action applied at each step is selected as the one corresponding to the larger of $Q(x_t, -10)$ and $Q(x_t, 10)$. To explore the effects of each action, the action with the lower Q value is applied with a probability that decreases with time:

$$p = \begin{cases} 1 - 0.5\lambda^t, & \text{if } Q(x_t, 10) > Q(x_t, -10); \\ 0.5\lambda^t, & \text{otherwise,} \end{cases}$$

$$a_t = \begin{cases} 10, & \text{with probability } p; \\ -10, & \text{with probability } 1-p. \end{cases}$$

To update all weights, error back-propagation is applied at each step using the following temporal-difference error

$$e_t = \begin{cases} \gamma \max\limits_{a_{t+1}} [Q(x_{t+1}, a_{t+1})] - Q(x_t, a_t), & \text{if failure does not occur on step } t+1, \\ r_{t+1} - Q(x_t, a_t), & \text{if failure occurs on step } t+1. \end{cases}$$

Note that $r_t = 0$ for all non-failure steps and drops out of the first expression.

Weights are updated by the following equations, assuming Unit j is the output unit corresponding to the action taken, and all variables are for the current time t.

$$\begin{aligned} \Delta w_{k,i} &= \frac{\beta_h}{\rho} \, e \, y_k \, v_{j,k} \, (x_i - w_{j,i}) \\ \Delta v_{j,i} &= \beta \, e \, y_i \end{aligned}$$

In all experiments, $\rho = 2$, $\lambda = 0.99999$, and $\gamma = 0.9$. Values of β and β_h are discussed in Section 6.

5 Restart Algorithm

After weights are modified by back-propagation, conditions for a restart are checked. If conditions are met, a unit is restarted, and processing continues with the next time step. Conditions and primary steps of the restart algorithm appear below as the numbered equations.

5.1 When to Restart

Several conditions must be met before a restart is performed. First, the magnitude of the error, e_t, must be larger than usual. To detect this, exponentially-weighted averages of the mean, μ, and variance, σ^2, of e_t are maintained and used to calculate a normalized error, e'_t

$$\begin{aligned} e'_t &= e_t - \frac{\mu_t}{(1-\kappa^t)}, \\ \mu_{t+1} &= \kappa\mu_t + (1-\kappa)e_t, \\ \sigma^2_{t+1} &= \kappa\sigma^2_t + (1-\kappa)e'^2_t, \end{aligned}$$

For our experiments, $\kappa = 0.99$.

Now we can state the first restart condition. A restart is considered on steps for which the magnitude of the error is greater than 0.01 and greater than a constant factor of the error's standard deviation, i.e., whenever

$$|e_t| > 0.01 \quad \text{and} \quad |e_t| > \alpha\sqrt{\frac{\sigma^2_t}{(1-\kappa^n)}}. \tag{1}$$

Of a small number of tested values, $\alpha = 0.2$ resulted in the best performance.

Before choosing a unit to restart for this step, we determine whether or not the current input vector is already "covered" by a unit. Assuming y_j is the output of Unit j for the current input vector, the restart procedure is continued only if

$$y_j < 0.5, \text{ for } j = 1, \ldots, 20 \tag{2}$$

5.2 Which Unit to Restart

As stated by Mozer and Smolensky (1989), ideally we would choose the least useful unit as the one that results in the largest error when removed from the network. For the Q-network, this requires the removal of one unit at a time, making multiple attempts to balance the pendulum, and determining which unit when removed results in the shortest balancing times. Rather than following this computationally expensive procedure, we simply took the sum of the magnitudes of a hidden unit's output weights as a measure of it's utility. This is one of several utility measures suggested by Mozer and Smolensky and others (e.g., Kloph and Gose, 1969).

After a unit is restarted, it may require further learning experience to acquire a useful function in the network. The amount of learning experience is defined as a sum of magnitudes of the error e_t. The sum of error magnitudes since Unit j was restarted is given by c_j. Once this sum surpasses a maximum, c_{max}, the unit is again eligible for restarting. Thus, Unit j is restarted when

$$u_j = \min_{j \in \{1,\ldots,20\}} (|v_{1,j}| + |v_{2,j}|) \tag{3}$$

and

$$c_j > c_{\max}. \tag{4}$$

Without a detailed search, a value of $c_{\max} = 10$ was found to result in good performance.

5.3 New Weights for Restarted Unit

Say Unit j is restarted. It's input weights are set equal to the current input vector, x, the one for which the output of the network was in error. One of the two output weights of Unit j is also modified. The output weight through which Unit j modifies the output of the unit corresponding to the action actually taken is set equal to the error, e_t. The other output weight is not modified.

$$w_{j,i} = x_i, \text{ for } i = 1, \ldots, 4, \tag{5}$$

$$v_{k,j} = e_t, \tag{6}$$

$$\text{where } k = \begin{cases} 1, & \text{if } a_t = -10; \\ 2, & \text{if } a_t = 10. \end{cases}$$

6 Results

The pendulum is said to be balanced when 90,000 steps (1/2 hour of simulated time) have elapsed without failure. After every failure, the pendulum is reset to the center of the track with a zero angle (straight up) and zero velocities. Performance is judged by the average number of failures before the pendulum is balanced. Averages were taken over 30 runs. Each run consists of choosing initial values for the hidden units' weights from a uniform distribution from 0 to 1, then training the net until the pendulum is balanced for 90,000 steps or a maximum number of 50,000 failures is reached.

To determine the effect of restarting, we compare the performance of the Q-learning algorithm with and without restarts. Back-propagation learning rates are given by β for the output units and β_h for the hidden units. β and β_h were optimized for the algorithm without restarts by testing a large number of values. The best values of those tried are $\beta = 0.05$ and $\beta_h = 1.0$. These values were used for both algorithms. A small number of values for the additional restart parameters were tested, so the restart algorithm is not optimized for this problem.

Figure 2 is a graph of the number of steps between failures versus the number of failures. Each algorithm was initialized with the same hidden unit weights. Without restarts the pendulum is balanced for this run after 6,879 failures. With restarts it is balanced after 3,415 failures.

The performances of the algorithms were averaged over 30 runs giving the following results. The restart algorithm balanced the pendulum in all 30 runs, within an

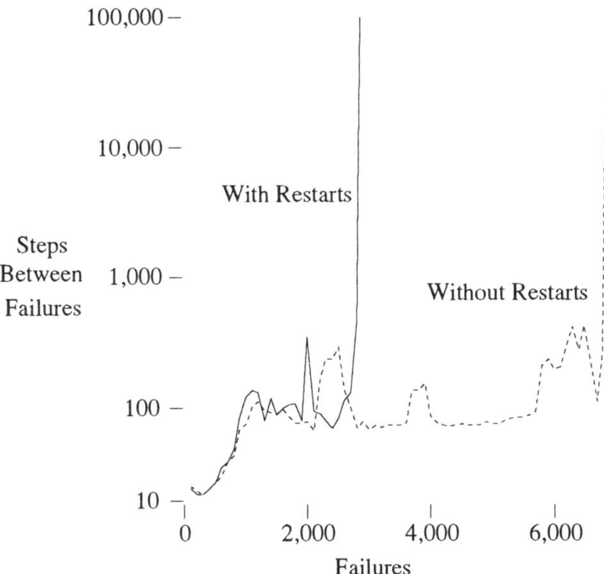

Figure 2: Learning Curves of Balancing Time Versus Failures (averaged over bins of 100 failures)

average of 3,303 failures. The algorithm without restarts was unsuccessful within 50,000 failures for two of the 30 runs. Not counting the unsuccessful runs, this algorithm balanced the pendulum within an average of 4,923 failures. Considering the unsuccessful runs, this average is 7,928 failures.

In studying the timing of restarts, we observe that initially the number of restarts is small, due to the high variance of e_t in the early stages of learning. During later stages, we see that a single unit might be restarted many times (15 to 20) before it becomes more useful (at least according to our measure) than some other unit.

7 Conclusion

This first test of an algorithm for restarting hidden units in a reinforcement-learning paradigm led to a decrease in learning time for this task. However, much work remains in studying the effects of each step of the restart procedure. Many alternatives exist, most significantly in the method for determining the utility of hidden units. A significant extension of this algorithm would be to consider units with variable-width domains, as in Platt's RAN algorithm.

Acknowledgements

The work was supported in part by the National Science Foundation through Grant IRI-9212191 and by Colorado State University through Faculty Research Grant 1-38592.

References

C. W. Anderson. (1987). Strategy learning with multilayer connectionist representations. Technical Report TR87-509.3, GTE Laboratories, Waltham, MA, 1987. Corrected version of article that was published in Proceedings of the Fourth International Workshop on Machine Learning, pp. 103–114, June, 1987.

A. G. Barto, S. J. Bradtke, and S. P. Singh. (1991). Real-time learning and control using asynchronous dynamic programming. Technical Report 91-57, Department of Computer Science, University of Massachusetts, Amherst, MA, Aug.

A. G. Barto, R. S. Sutton, and C. W. Anderson. (1983). Neuronlike elements that can solve difficult learning control problems. *IEEE Transactions on Systems, Man, and Cybernetics*, 13:835–846. Reprinted in J. A. Anderson and E. Rosenfeld, *Neurocomputing: Foundations of Research*, MIT Press, Cambridge, MA, 1988.

M. I. Jordan and R. A. Jacobs. (1990). Learning to control an unstable system with forward modeling. In D. S. Touretzky, editor, *Advances in Neural Information Processing Systems*, volume 2, pages 324–331. Morgan Kaufmann, San Mateo, CA.

A. H. Klopf and E. Gose. (1969). An evolutionary pattern recognition network. *IEEE Transactions on Systems, Science, and Cybernetics*, 15:247–250.

L.-J. Lin. (1992). Self-improving reactive agents based on reinforcement learning, planning, and teaching. *Machine Learning*, 8(3/4):293–321.

M. C. Mozer and P. Smolensky. (1989). Skeltonization: A technique for trimming the fat from a network via relevance assessment. In D. S. Touretzky, editor, *Advances in Neural Information Systems*, volume 1, pages 107–115. Morgan Kaufmann, San Mateo, CA, 1989.

J. C. Platt. (1991a). Learning by combining memorization and gradient descent. In R. P. Lippmann, J. E. Moody, and D. S. Touretzky, editors, *Advances in Neural Information Processing Systems 3*, pages 714–720. Morgan Kaufmann Publishers, San Mateo, CA.

J. C. Platt. (1991b) A resource-allocating network for function interpolation. *Neural Computation*, 3:213–225.

R. S. Sutton. (1988). Learning to predict by the method of temporal differences. *Machine Learning*, 3:9–44.

C. J. C. H. Watkins. (1989). *Learning with Delayed Rewards.* PhD thesis, Cambridge University Psychology Department.

C. J. C. H. Watkins and P. Dayan. (1992). Q-learning. *Machine Learning*, 8(3/4):279–292.

D. Whitley, S. Dominic, R. Das, and C. Anderson. (1993). Genetic reinforcement learning for neurocontrol problems. *Machine Learning*, to appear.

B. Widrow and F. W. Smith. (1964). Pattern-recognizing control systems. In *Proceedings of the 1963 Computer and Information Sciences (COINS) Symposium*, pages 288–317, Washington, DC. Spartan.

Nets with Unreliable Hidden Nodes Learn Error-Correcting Codes

Stephen Judd
Siemens Corporate Research
755 College Road East
Princeton NJ 08540
judd@learning.siemens.com

Paul W. Munro
Department of Information Science
University of Pittsburgh
Pittsburgh, PA 15260
munro@lis.pitt.edu

ABSTRACT

In a multi-layered neural network, any one of the hidden layers can be viewed as computing a distributed representation of the input. Several "encoder" experiments have shown that when the representation space is small it can be fully used. But computing with such a representation requires completely dependable nodes. In the case where the hidden nodes are noisy and unreliable, we find that error correcting schemes emerge simply by using noisy units during training; random errors injected during backpropagation result in spreading representations apart. Average and minimum distances increase with misfire probability, as predicted by coding-theoretic considerations. Furthermore, the effect of this noise is to protect the machine against permanent node failure, thereby potentially extending the useful lifetime of the machine.

1 INTRODUCTION

The encoder task described by Ackley, Hinton, and Sejnowski (1985) for the Boltzmann machine, and by Rumelhart, Hinton, and Williams (1986) for feed-forward networks, has been used as one of several standard benchmarks in the neural network literature. Cottrell, Munro, and Zipser (1987) demonstrated the potential of such autoencoding architectures to lossy compression of image data. In the encoder architecture, the weights connecting the input layer to the hidden layer play the role of an encoding mechanism, and the hidden-output weights are analogous to a decoding device. In the terminology of Shannon and Weaver (1949), the hidden layer corresponds to the communication channel. By analogy, channel noise corresponds to a fault (misfiring) in the hidden layer. Previous encoder studies have shown that the representations in the hidden layer correspond to optimally efficient (i.e., fully compressed) codes, which suggests that introducing noise in the form of random interference with hidden unit function may lead to the development of codes more robust to noise of the kind that prevailed during learning. Many of these ideas also appear in Chiueh and Goodman (1987) and Séquin and Clay (1990).

We have tested this conjecture empirically, and analyzed the resulting solutions, using a standard gradient-descent procedure (backpropagation). Although there are alternative techniques to encourage fault tolerance through construction of specialized error functions (eg., Chauvin, 1989) or direct attacks (eg., Neti, Schneider, and Young, 1990), we have used a minimalist approach that simply introduces intermittent node misfirings during training that mimic the errors anticipated during normal performance.

In traditional approaches to developing error-correcting codes (eg., Hamming, 1980), each symbol from a source alphabet is mapped to a *codeword* (a sequence of symbols from a *code alphabet*); the distance between codewords is directly related to the code's robustness.

2 METHODOLOGY

Computer simulations were performed using strictly layered feed forward networks. The nodes of one of the hidden layers randomly misfire during training; in most experiments, this "channel" layer was the sole hidden layer. Each input node corresponds to a transmitted symbol, output nodes to received symbols, channel representations to codewords; other layers are introduced as needed to enable nonlinear encoding and/or decoding. After training, the networks were analyzed under various conditions, in terms of performance and coding-theoretic measures, such as Hamming distance between codewords.

The response, r, of each unit in the channel layer is computed by passing the weighted sum, x, through the hyperbolic tangent (a sigmoid that ranges from -1 to +1). The responses of those units randomly designated to misfire are then multiplied by -1 as this is most comparable with concepts from coding theory for binary channels.[1] The misfire operation influences the course of learning in two ways, since the erroneous information is both passed on to units further "downstream" in the net, and used as the presynaptic factor in the synaptic modification rule. Note that the derivative factor in the backpropagation procedure is unaffected for units using the hyperbolic tangent, since $dr/dx = (1+r)(1-r)/2$.

These misfirings were randomly assigned according to various kinds of probability distributions: independent identically distributed (i.i.d), k-of-n, correlated across hidden units, and correlated over the input distribution. The hidden unit representations required to handle uncorrelated noise roughly correspond to Hamming spheres[2], and can be decoded by a

[1] Other possible misfire modes include setting the node's activity to zero (or some other constant) or randomizing it. The most appropriate mode depends on various factors, including the situation to be simulated and the type of analysis to be performed. For example, simulating neuronal death in a biological situation may warrant a different failure mode than simulating failure of an electronic component.

[2] Consider an n-bit block code, where each codeword lies on the vertex of an n-cube. The Hamming sphere of radius k is the neighborhood of vertices that differ from the codeword by a number of bits less than or equal to k.

single layer of weights; thus the entire network consists of just three sets of units: source-channel-sink. However, correlated noise generally necessitates additional layers.

All the experiments described below use the encoder task described by Ackley, Hinton, and Sejnowki (1986); that is, the input pattern consists of just one unit active and the others inactive. The task is to activate only the corresponding unit in the output layer. By comparison with coding theory, the input units are thus analogous to symbols to be encoded, and the hidden unit representations are analogous to the codewords.

3 RESULTS

3.1. PERFORMANCE

The first experiment supports the claim of Séquin and Clay (1990) that training with faults improves network robustness. Four 8-30-8 encoders were trained with fault probability p = 0, 0.05, 0.1, and 0.3 respectively. After training, each network was tested with fault probabilities varying from 0.05 to 1.0. The results show enhanced performance for networks trained with a higher rate of hidden unit misfiring. Figure 1 shows four performance curves (one for each *training* fault probability), each as a function of *test* fault probability.

Interesting convergence properties were also observed; as the training fault probabilty, p, was varied from 0 to 0.4, networks converge reliably faster for low nonzero values ($0.05<p<0.15$) than they do at $p=0$.

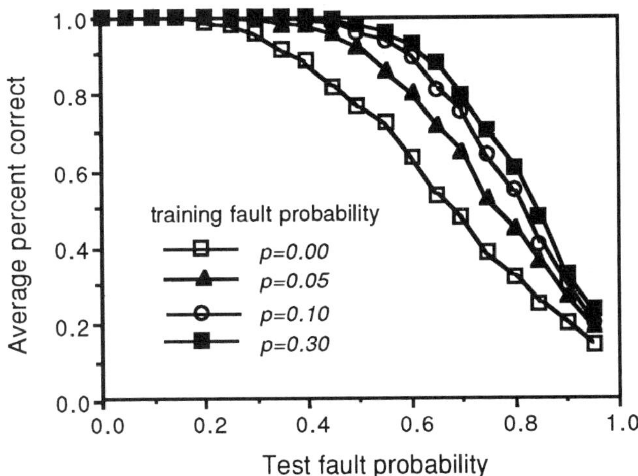

Figure 1. *Performance for various training conditions.* Four 8-30-8 encoders were trained with different probabilities for hidden unit misfiring. Each data point is an average over 1000 random stimuli with random hidden unit faults. Outputs are scored correct if the most active output node corresponds to the active input node.

3.2. DISTANCE

3.2.1 Distances increase with fault probability

Distances were measured between all pairs of hidden unit representations. Several networks trained with different fault probabilities and various numbers of hidden units were examined. As expected, both the minimum distances and average distances increase with the training fault probability until it approaches 0.5 per node (see Figure 2). For probabilities above 0.25, the minimum distances fall within the theoretical bounds for a 30 bit code of a 16 symbol alphabet given by Gilbert and Elias (see Blahut, 1987).

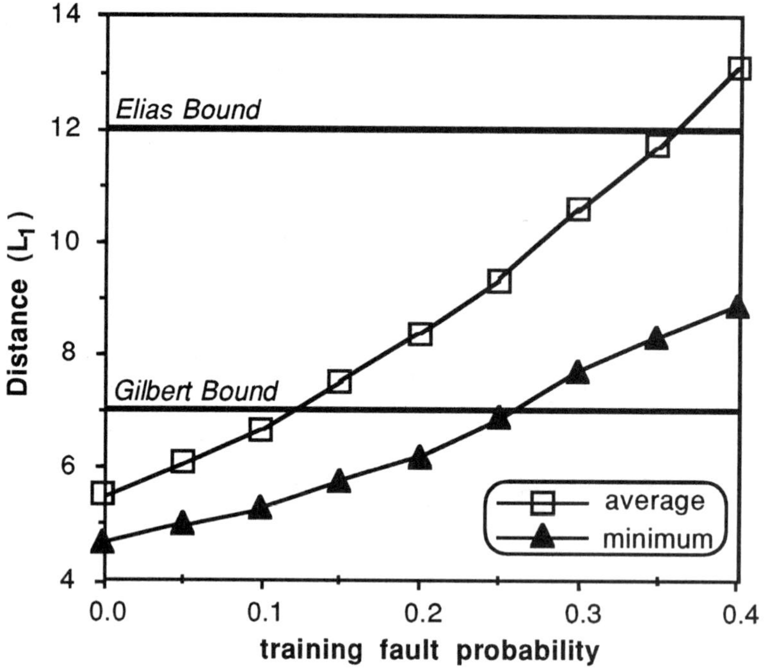

Figure 2. *Distance increases with fault probability.* Average and minimum L_1 distances are plotted for 16-30-16 networks trained with fault probabilities ranging from 0.0 to 0.4. Each data point represents an average over 100 networks trained using different weight initializations.

3.2.2. Input probabilities affect distance

The probability distribution over the inputs influences the relative distances of the representations at the hidden unit level. To illustrate this, a 4-10-4 encoder was trained using various probabilities for one of the four inputs (denoted P*), distributing the remaining probabilty uniformly among the other three. The average distance between the representation of P* and the others increases with its probability, while the average distance among the other three decreases as shown in the upper part of Figure 3. The more frequent patterns are generally expected to "claim" a larger region of representation space.

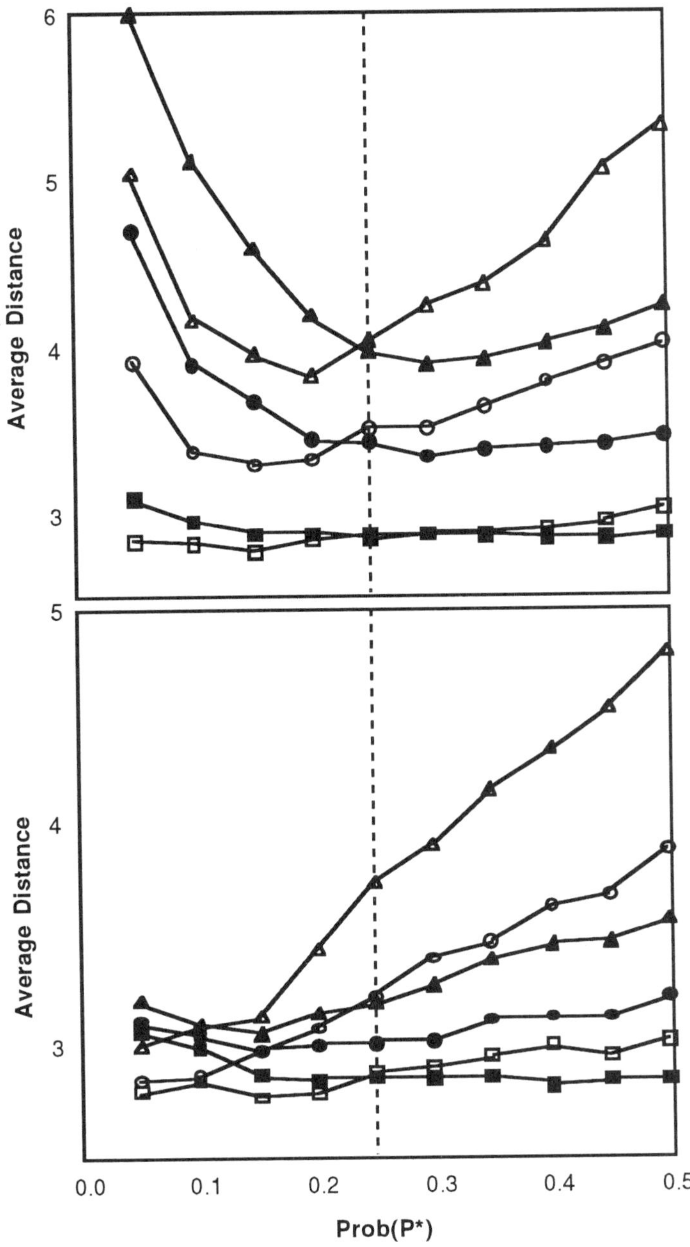

Figure 3. *Non-uniform input distribution.* 4-10-4 encoders were trained using failure probabilities of 0 (squares), 0.1 (circles), and 0.2 (triangles). The input distribution was skewed by varying the probability of one of the four items (denoted P*) in the training set from 0.05 to 0.5, keeping the other probabilities uniform. Average L_1 distances are shown from the manipulated pattern to the other three (open symbols) and among the equiprobables (filled symbols) as well. In the upper figure, failure is independent of the input, while in the lower figure, failure is induced only when P* is presented.

The dashed line in Figure 3 indicates a uniform input distribution, hence in the top figure, the average distance to P* is equal to the average distances among the other patterns. However this does not hold in the lower figure, indicating that the representations of stimuli that induce more frequent channel errors also claim more representation space.

3.3. CORRELATED MISFIRING

If the error probability for each bit in a message (or each hidden unit in a network layer) is uncorrelated with the other message bits (hidden units), then the principles of distance between codewords (representations) applies. On the other hand, if there is some structure to the noise (i.e. the misfirings are correlated across the hidden units), there may be different strategies to encoding and decoding, that require computations other than simple distance. While a Hamming distance criterion on a hypercube is a linearly separable classification function, and hence computable by a single layer of weights, the more general case is not linearly separable, as is demonstrated below.

Example: Misfiring in 2 of 6 channel units.
In this example, up to two of six channel units are randomly selected to misfire with each learning trial. In order to guarantee full recovery from two simultaneous faults, only two symbols can be represented, if the faults are independent; however, if one fault is always in one three-unit subset and the other is always in the complementary subset, it is possible to store four patterns. The following code can be considered with no loss of generality: Let the six hidden units (code bits) be partitioned into two sets of three, where there is at most one fault in each subset. The four code words, 000000, 000111, 111000, 111111 form an error correcting code under this condition; i.e. each subset is a triplicate code. Under the allowed fault combinations specified above, any given transmitted code string will be converted by noise to one of 9 strings of the 15 that lie at a Hamming distance of 2 (the 15 unconstrained two-bit errors of the string 000000 are shown in the table below with the 9 that satisfy the constraint in a box). Because of the symmetric distribution of these 9 allowed states, any category that includes all of them and is defined by a linear (hyperplane) boundary, must include all 15. Thus, this code cannot be decoded by a single layer of threshold (or sigmoidal) units; hence even if a 4-6-4 network discovers this code, it will not decode it accurately. However, our experiments show that *inserting a reliable (fault-free) hidden layer of just two units between the channel layer and the output layer (i.e., a 4-6-2-4 encoder)* enables the discovery of a code that is robust to errors of this kind. The representations of the four patterns in the channel layer show a triply redundant code in each half of the channel layer (Figure 4). The 2-unit layer provides a transformation that allows successful decoding of channel representations with faults.

Table. Possible two-bit error masks

000011				
000101	000110			
001001	001010	001100		
010001	010010	010100	011000	
100001	100010	100100	101000	110000

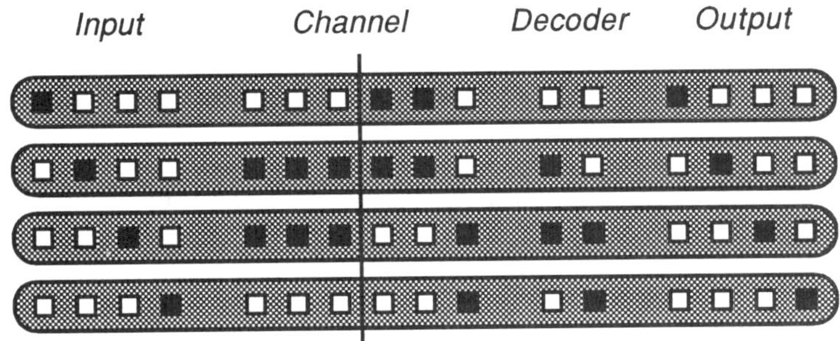

Figure 4. *Sample solution to 3-3 channel task.* Thresholded activation patterns are shown for a 4-6-2-4 network. Errors are introduced into the first hidden (channel) layer only. With each iteration, the outputs of one hidden unit from the left half of the hidden layer and one unit from the right half can be inverted. Note that the channel develops a triplicate code for each half-layer.

4 DISCUSSION

Results indicate that vanilla backpropagation on its own does not spread out the hidden unit representations (codewords) optimally, and that deliberate random misfiring during training induces wider separations, increasing resistance to node misfiring. Furthermore, non-uniform input distributions and non-uniform channel properties lead to asymmetries among the similarity relationships between hidden unit representations that are consistent with optimizing mutual information.

A mechanism of this kind may be useful for increasing fault tolerance in electronic systems, and may be used in neurobiological systems. The potential usefulness of inducing faults during training extends beyond fault tolerance. Clay and Séquin (1992) point out that training of this kind can enhance the capacity of a network to generalize. In effect, the probability of random faults can be used to vary the number of "effective parameters" (a term coined by Moody, 1992) available for adaptation, without dynamically altering network architecture. Thus, a naive system might begin with a relatively high probability of misfiring, and gradually reduce it as storage capacity needs increase with experience.

This technique may be particularly valuable for designing efficient, robust codes for channels with high order statistical properties, which defy traditional coding techniques. In such cases, a single layer of weights for encoding is not generally sufficient, as was shown above in the 4-6-2-4 example. Additional layers may enhance code efficiency for complex noiseless applications, such as image compression (Cottrell, Munro, and Zipser, 1987).

Acknowledgements

The second author participated in this research as a visiting research scientist during the summers of 1991 and 1992 at Siemens Corporate Research, which kindly provided financial support and a stimulating research environment.

References

Ackley, D. H., Hinton, G. E., and Sejnowski, T. J. (1985) A learning algorithm for Boltzmann machines. *Cognitive Science.* **9**: 147-169.

Blahut, R. E. (1987) *Principle and Practise of Information Theory*. Reading MA, Addison Wesley.

Chauvin, Y. (1989) A back-propagation algorithm with optimal use of hidden units. In: Touretsky, D.S. (ed.) *Advances in Neural Information Processing Systems 1*. San Mateo, CA: Morgan Kaufmann Publishers.

Chiueh, Tz-Dar and Rodney Goodman. (1987) A neural network classifier based on coding theory. In: Dana Z. Anderson, editor, *Neural Information Processing Systems*, pp 174--183, New York, A.I.P.

Clay, Reed D. and Séquin, Carlo H. (1992) Fault tolerance training improves generalization and robustness. *Proceedings of IJCNN92*, I-769, Baltimore.

Cottrell, G. W., P. Munro, and D. Zipser (1987) Image compression by back propagation: An example of extensional programming. *Ninth Ann Meeting of the Cognitive Science Society*, pp. 461-473.

Hamming, R. W. (1980) *Coding and Information Theory.* Prentice Hall: Englewood Cliffs, N.J.

Moody, J. (1992) The effective number of parameters. In: Moody, J. E., Hanson, S. J., Lippman, R., (eds.) *Advances in Neural Information Processing Systems 4*. San Mateo, CA: Morgan Kaufmann Publishers.

Neti, C., M. H. Schneider, and E. D. Young. (1990) Maximally fault-tolerant neural networks and nonlinear programming. *Proceedings of IJCNN*, II-483, San Diego.

Rumelhart D., Hinton G., and Williams R. (1986) Learning representations by back-propagating errors. *Nature* **323**:533-536.

Séquin, Carlo H. and Reed D. Clay (1990) Fault tolerance in artificial neural networks. *Proceedings of IJCNN*, I-703, San Diego.

Shannon, C. and Weaver, W. (1949) *The Mathematical Theory of Communication.* University of Illinois Press.

PART II

ARCHITECTURES AND ALGORITHMS

Interposing an ontogenic model between Genetic Algorithms and Neural Networks

Richard K. Belew
rik@cs.ucsd.edu

Cognitive Computer Science Research Group
Computer Science & Engr. Dept. (0014)
University of California - San Diego
La Jolla, CA 92093

Abstract

The relationships between learning, development and evolution in Nature is taken seriously, to suggest a model of the developmental process whereby the genotypes manipulated by the Genetic Algorithm (GA) might be expressed to form phenotypic neural networks (NNet) that then go on to learn. ONTOL is a grammar for generating polynomial NNets for time-series prediction. Genomes correspond to an ordered sequence of ONTOL productions and define a grammar that is expressed to generate a NNet. The NNet's weights are then modified by learning, and the individual's prediction error is used to determine GA fitness. A new gene doubling operator appears critical to the formation of new genetic alternatives in the preliminary but encouraging results presented.

1 Introduction

Two natural phenomena, the learning done by individuals' nervous systems and the evolution done by populations of individuals, have served as the basis of distinct classes of adaptive algorithms, neural networks (NNets) and Genetic Algorithms (GAs), resp. Interactions between learning and evolution in Nature suggests that combining NNet and GA algorithmic techniques might also yield interesting hybrid algorithms.

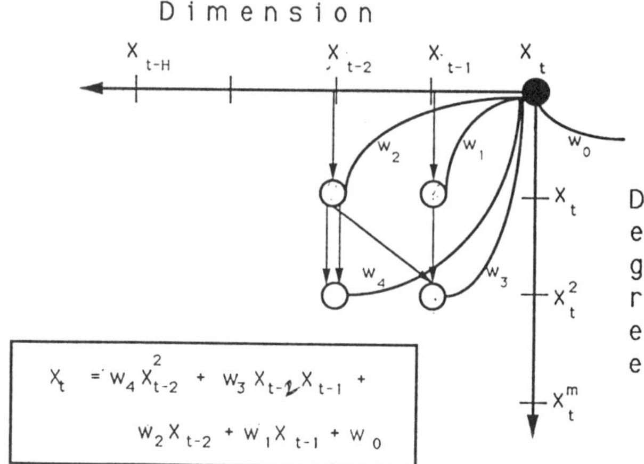

Figure 1: Polynomial networks

Taking the analogy to learning and evolution seriously, we propose that the missing feature is a the *developmental* process whereby the genotypes manipulated by the GA are *expressed* to form phenotypic NNets that then go on to learn. Previous attempts to use the GA to search for good NNet topologies have foundered exactly because they have assumed an overly direct genotype-to-phenotype correspondence. This research is therefore consistent with other NNet research the physiology of neural development [3] as well as those into "constructive" methods for changing network topologies adaptively during the training process [4]. Additional motivation derives from the growing body of neuroscience demonstrating the importance of developmental processes as the shapers of effective learning networks. Cognitively, the resolution of false dicotomies like "nature/nurture" and "nativist/empiricist" also depends on a richer language for describing the way genetically determined characteristics and within-lifetime changes by individuals can interact.

Because GAs and NNets are each complicated technologies in their own right, and because the focus of the current research is a model of development that can span between them, three major simplifications have been imposed for the preliminary research reported here. First, in order to stay close to the mathematical theory of functional approximation, we restrict the form of our NNets to what can be called "polynomials networks" (cf. [7]). That is, we will consider networks with a first layer of linear units (i.e., terms in the polynomial that are simply weighted input X_i), a second layer with units that form products of first-layer units, a third layer with units that form products of second-layer units, etc.; see Figure 1, and below for an example. As depicted in Figure 1 the space of polynomial networks can be viewed as two-dimensional, parameterized by *dimension* (i.e., how much history of the time series is used) and *degree*.

There remains the problem of finding the best parameter values for this particular polynomial form. Much of classicial optimization theory and more recent NNet research is concerned with various methods for performing this task. Previous research has demonstrated that the *global sampling* behavior of the GA works very effectively with any gradient, *local search* technique [2]. The second major simplification, then, is that for the time being we use only the most simple-minded gradient method: first-order, fixed-step gradient descent. Analytically, this is the most tractible, and the general algorithm design can readily replace this with any other local search technique.

The final simplification is that we focus on one of the most parsimonious of problems, time series prediction: The GA is used to evolve NNets that are good at predicting X_{t+1} given access to an unbounded history $X_t, X_{t-1}, X_{t-2}, \ldots$. Polynomial approximations of an arbitrary time series can vary in two dimensions: the extent to which they rely on this history, and (e.g., how far back in time), and in their degree. The Stone-Weierstrauss Aproximation Theorem guarantees that, within this two-dimensional space, there exists some polynomial that will match the desired temporal sequence to arbitrarily precision. The problem, of course, is that over a history H and allowing m degree terms there exists $O(H^m)$ terms, far too many to search effectively. From the perspective of function approximation, then, this work corresponds to a particular heuristic for searching for the correct polynomial form, the parameters of which will be tuned with a gradient technique.

2 Expression of the ONTOL grammar

Every multi-cellular organism has the problem of using a single genetic description contained in the first germ cell as specification for *all* of its various cell types. The genome therefore appears to contain a set of developmental instructions, subsets of which become "relevant" to the particular context in which each developing cell finds itself. If we imagine that each cell type is a unique symbol in some alphabet, and that the mature organism is a string of symbols, it becomes very natural to model the developmental process as a (context-sensitive) *grammar* generating this string [6, 5]. The initial germ cell becomes the start symbol. A series of production rules specify the expansion (mitosis) of this non-terminal (cell) into two other symbols that then develop according to the same set of genetically-determined rules, until all cells are in a mature, terminal state.

ONTOL is a grammar for generating cells in the two-dimensional space of polynomial networks. The left hand side (LHS) of productions in this grammar define conditions on the cells' internal *Clock* state and on the state of its eight Moore neighbors. The RHS of the production defines one of five cell-state update actions that are performed if the LHS condition is satisfied: A cell can mitosize either left or down ($MLeft, MDown$), meaning that this adjacent cell now becomes filled with an identical copy; *Die* (i.e., disappear entirely); *Tick* (simply decrement its internal *Clock* state); or *Terminate* (cease development). Only terminating cells form synaptic connections, and only to adjacent neighbors.

The developmental process is begun by placing a single "gamete" cell at the origin of the 2d polyspace, with its *Clock* state initialized to a maximal value $MaxClock = 4$; this state is decremented every time a gene is fired. If and when a gene causes this cell to undergo mitosis, a new cell, either to the left or below the originial cell, is created. Critically, the same set of genetic instructions contained in the original gametic cell are used to control transitions of *all* its progeny cells (much like a

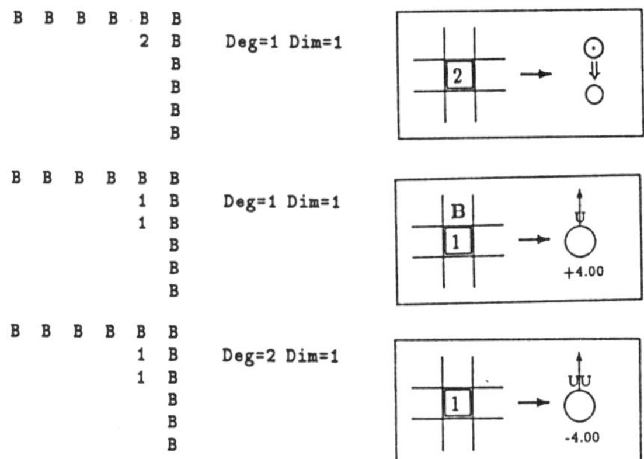

Figure 2: Logistic genome, engineered

cellular automaton's transition table), even though the differing contexts of each cell are likely to cause different genes to be applied in different cells. Figure 2 shows a trace of this developmental process: each snap-shot shows the *Clock* states of all active (non-terminated) cells, the coordinates of the cell being expressed, and the gene used to control its expression.

3 Experimental design

Each generation begins by developing and evaluating each genotype in the population. First, each genome in the population is expressed to form an executable Lisp lambda expression computing a polynomial and a corresponding set of initial weights for each of its terms. If this expression can be performed successfully and the individual is viable (i.e., their genomes can be interpretted to build well-formed networks), the individual is exposed to *NTrain* sequential instances of the time series. Fitness is then defined to be its cumulative error on the next *NTest* time steps.

After the entire population has been evaluated, the next generation is formed according to a relatively conventional genetic algorithm: more successful individuals are differentially reproduced and genetic operators are applied to these to experiment with novel, but similar, alternatives. Each genome is cloned zero, one or more times using a proportional selection algorithm that guarantees the expected number of offspring is proportional to an individual's relative fitness.

Variation is introduced into the population by *mutation* and *recombination* genetic operators that explore new genes and genomic combinations. Four types of mutation were applied, with the probability of a mutation proportional to genome length. First, some random portion of an extant gene might be randomly altered, e.g., changing an initial weight, adding or deleting a constraint on a condition, changing the gene's action. Because a gene's order in the genome can affect its probability of being expressed, a second form of mutation permutes the order of the genes on

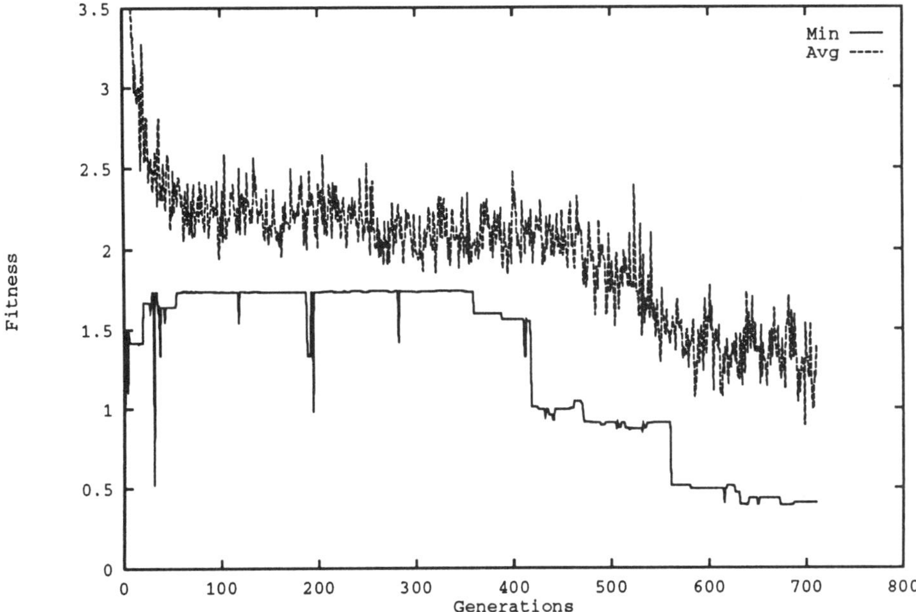

Figure 3: Poulation Minimum and Average Fitness

the genome. A third class of mutation removes genes from the genome, always "trimming" them from the end. Combined with the expression mechanism's bias towards the head of the genomic list, this trimming operation creates a pressure towards putting genes critical to early ontogeny near the head. The final and critical form of mutation randomly selects a gene to be *doubled*: a duplicate copy of the gene is constructed and inserted at a randomly selected position in the genome. After all mutations have been performed, cross-over is performed between pairs of individuals.

4 Experiments

To demonstrate, consider the problem of predicting a particularly difficult time series, the chaotic logistic map: $X_t = 4.0X_{t-1} - 4.0X_{t-1}^2$. The example of Figure 2 showed an ONTOL genome engineered to produce the desired logistic polynomial. This "genetically engineered" solution is merely evidence that a genetic solution exists that can be interpretted to form the desired phenotypic form; the real test is of course whether the GA can find it or something similar.

Early generations are not encouraging. Figure 3 shows the minimum (i.e., best) prediction error and population average error for the first 800 generations of a typical simulation. Initial progress is rapid because in the initial, randomly constructed population, fully half of the individuals are not even viable. These are strongly

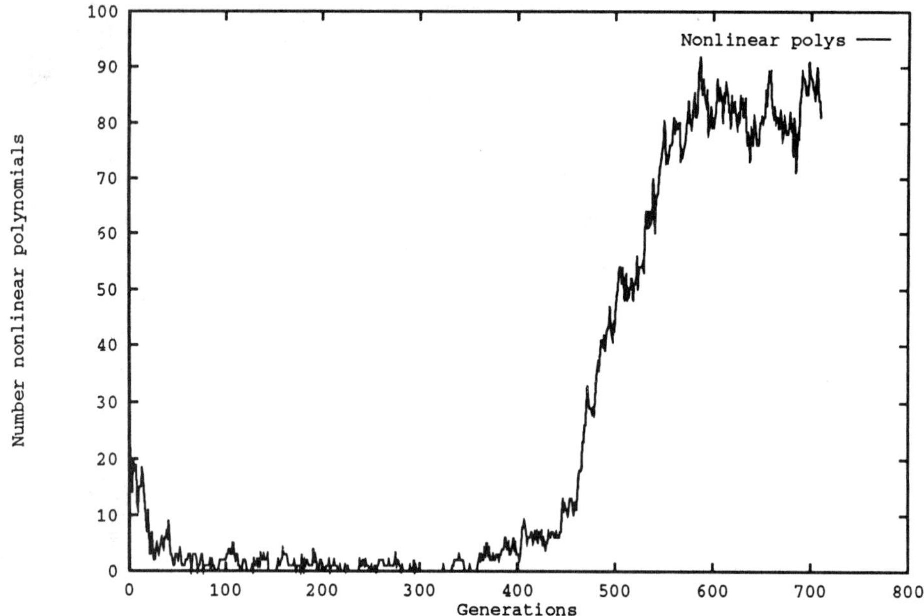

Figure 4: Complex polynomials

selected against, of course, and within the first two or three generations at least 95% of all generations remain viable.

For the next several hundred generations, however, all of ONTOL's developmental machinery appears for naught as the dominant phenotypic individuals are the most "simplistic" linear, first-degree approximators of the form $w_1X_1 + w_0$. Even here, however, the GA is able to work in conjunction with the gradient learning process is able to achieve Baldwin-like effects optimizing w_0 and w_1 [1]. The simulation reaches a "simplistic plateau," then, as it converges on a population composed of the best predictors the simplistic linear, first-degree network topology permits for this time series.

In the background, however, genetic operators are continuing to explore a wide variety of *genotypic* forms that all have the property of generating roughly the same simplistic *phenotypes*. Figure 4 shows that there are significant numbers of "complex" polynomials[1] in early generations, and some of these have much higher than average fitness[2] On average, however, genes leading to complex phenotypes provide lead to poorer approximations than the simplistic ones, and are quickly culled.

[1] I.e., either nonlinear terms or higher dimensional dependence on the past

[2] Note the good solutions in the first 50 generations, as well as subsequent dips during the simplistic plateau.

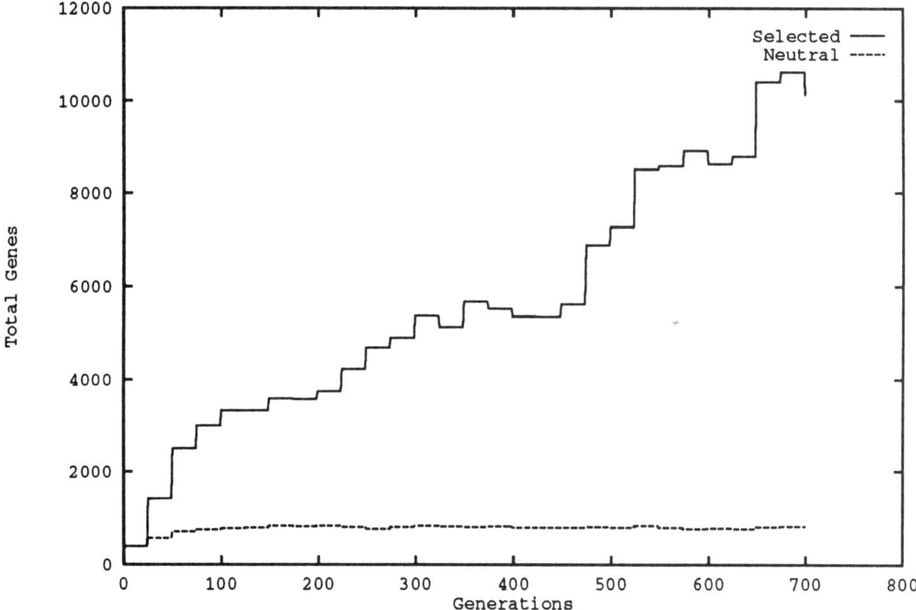

Figure 5: Genome length

A critical aspect of the redundancy introduced by gene doubling is that old genetic material is freed to mutate into new forms without threatening the phenotype's viability. When compared to a population of mediocre, simplistic networks any complex networks able to provide more accurate predictions have much higher fitness, and eventually are able to take over the population. Around generation 400, then, Figure 3 shows the fitness dropping from the simplistic plateau, and Figure 4 shows the number of complex polynomials increasing. Many of these individuals' genomes indeed encode grammars that form polynomials of the desired functional form.

A surprising feature of these simulations is that while the genes leading to complex phenotypes are present from the beginning and continue to be explored during the simplistic plateau, it takes many generations before these genes are successfully composed into robust, consistently viable genotypes. How do the complex genotypes discovered in later generations differ from those in the initial population?

One piece of the answer is revealed in Figure 5: later genomes are much longer. All 100 individuals in the initial population have exactly five genes, and so the initial "gene pool" size is 500. In the experiments just described, this number grows asymptotically to approximately 6000 total genes (i.e., 60 per individual, on average) during the simplistic plateau, and then explodes a second time to more than 10,000 as the population converts to complex polynomials. It appears that gene duplication creates a very constructive form of redundancy: mulitple copies of critical genes help the genotype maintain the more elaborate development programs required to form complex phenotypes. Micro-analysis of the most successful individuals in later generations supports this view. While many parts of their genomes appear inconsequential (for example, relative to the engineered genome of Figure 2), both the *MDown* gene and the two-element *Terminate* genes, critical to forming polynomials that are "morphologically isomorphic" with the correct solution, are consistently present.

This hypothesis is also supported by results from a second experiment, also plotted on Figure 5. Recall that the increase in genome size caused by gene doubling is offset by a trimming mutation that periodically shortens a genome. The curve labelled "Neutral" shows the results of these opposing operations when the next generation is formed randomly, rather than being selected for better prediction. Under neutral selection, genome size grows slightly from initial size, but gene doubling and genome trimming then quickly reach equilibrium. When we select for better predictors, however, longer genomes are clearly preferred, at least up to a point. The apparent asymptote accompanying the simplistic plateau suggests that if these simulations were extended, the length of complex genotypes would also stabalize.a

Acknowledgements

I gratefully acknowledge the warm and stimulating research environments provide by Domenico Parisi and colleagues at the Psychological Institute, CNR, Rome, Italy, and Jean-Arcady Meyer and colleagues in the Groupe de BioInformatique, Ecole Normale Superieure in Paris, France.

References

[1] R. K. Belew. Evolution, learning and culture: computational metaphors for adaptive search. *Complex Systems*, 4(1):11–49, 1990.

[2] R. K. Belew, J. McInerney, and N. N. Schraudolph. Evolving networks: Using the Genetic Algorithm with connectionist learning. In *Proc. Second Artificial Life Conference*, pages 511–547, New York, 1991. Addison-Wesley.

[3] J. D. Cowan and A. E. Friedman. Development and regeneration of eye-brain maps: A computational model. In *Advances in Neural Info. Proc. Systems 2*, pages 92–99. Morgan Kaufman, 1990.

[4] S. E. Fahlman and C. Lebiere. The Cascade-Correlation learning architecture. In D. S. Touretzky, editor, *Advances in Neural Info. Proc. Systems 4*, pages 524–532. Morgan Kaufmann, 1990.

[5] H. Kitano. Designing neural networks using genetic algorithms with graph generation system. *Complex Systems*, 4(4), 1990.

[6] A. Lindenmayer and G. Rozenberg. *Automata, languages, development.* North-Holland, Amsterdam, 1976.

[7] T. D. Sanger, R. S. Sutton, and C. J. Matheus. Iterative construction of sparse polynomials. In J. E. Moody, S. J. Hanson, and R. P. Lippman, editors, *Advances in Neural Info. Proc. Systems 4*, pages 1064–1071. Morgan Kaufmann, 1992.

Combining Neural and Symbolic Learning to Revise Probabilistic Rule Bases

J. Jeffrey Mahoney and Raymond J. Mooney
Dept. of Computer Sciences
University of Texas
Austin, TX 78712
mahoney@cs.utexas.edu, mooney@cs.utexas.edu

Abstract

This paper describes RAPTURE — a system for revising probabilistic knowledge bases that combines neural and symbolic learning methods. RAPTURE uses a modified version of backpropagation to refine the certainty factors of a MYCIN-style rule base and uses ID3's information gain heuristic to add new rules. Results on refining two actual expert knowledge bases demonstrate that this combined approach performs better than previous methods.

1 Introduction

In complex domains, learning needs to be biased with prior knowledge in order to produce satisfactory results from limited training data. Recently, both connectionist and symbolic methods have been developed for biasing learning with prior knowledge [Fu, 1989; Towell *et al.*, 1990; Ourston and Mooney, 1990]. Most of these methods revise an imperfect knowledge base (usually obtained from a domain expert) to fit a set of empirical data. Some of these methods have been successfully applied to real-world tasks, such as recognizing promoter sequences in DNA [Towell *et al.*, 1990; Ourston and Mooney, 1990]. The results demonstrate that revising an expert-given knowledge base produces more accurate results than learning from training data alone.

In this paper, we describe the RAPTURE system (**R**evising **A**pproximate

Probabilistic Theories Using Repositories of Examples), which combines connectionist and symbolic methods to revise both the parameters and structure of a certainty-factor rule base.

2 The Rapture Algorithm

The RAPTURE algorithm breaks down into three main phases. First, an initial rule-base (created by a human expert) is converted into a RAPTURE network. The result is then trained using certainty-factor backpropagation (CFBP). The theory is further revised through network architecture modification. Once the network is fully trained, the solution is at hand—there is no need for retranslation. Each of these steps is outlined in full below.

2.1 The Initial Rule-Base

RAPTURE uses propositional certainty factor rules to represent its theories. These rules have the form $A \stackrel{0.8}{\rightarrow} D$, which expresses the idea that belief in proposition A gives a 0.8 measure of belief in proposition D [Shafer and Pearl, 1990]. Certainty factors can range in value from -1 to $+1$, and indicate a degree of confidence in a particular proposition. Certainty factor rules allow updating of these beliefs based upon new observed evidence.

Rules combine evidence via probabilistic sum, which is defined as $a \oplus b \equiv a + b - ab$. In general, all positive evidence is combined to determine the *measure of belief* (MB) for a given proposition, and all negative evidence is combined to obtain a *measure of disbelief* (MD). The certainty factor is then calculated using $CF = MB + MD$.

RAPTURE uses this formalism to represent its rule base for a variety of reasons. First, it is perhaps the simplest method that retains the desired evidence-summing aspect of uncertain reasoning. As each rule fires, additional evidence is contributed towards belief in the rule's consequent. The use of probabilistic sum enables many small pieces of evidence to add up to significant evidence. This is lacking in formalisms that use only MIN or MAX for combining evidence [Valtorta, 1988]. Second, probabilistic sum is a simple, differentiable, non-linear function. This is crucial for implementing gradient descent using backpropagation. Finally, and perhaps most significantly, is the widespread use of certainty factors. Numerous knowledge-bases have been implemented using this formalism, which immediately gives our approach a large base of applicability.

2.2 Converting the Rule Base into a Network

Once the initial theory is obtained, it is converted into a RAPTURE -network. Building the network begins by mapping all identical propositions in the rule-base to the same node in the network. Input features (those only appearing as rule-antecedents) become input nodes, and output symbols (those only appearing as rule-consequents) become output nodes. The certainty factors of the rules become the weights on the links that connect nodes. Networks for classification problems contain one output for each category. When an example is presented, the certainty factor for each of the categories is computed and the example is assigned to the category with the

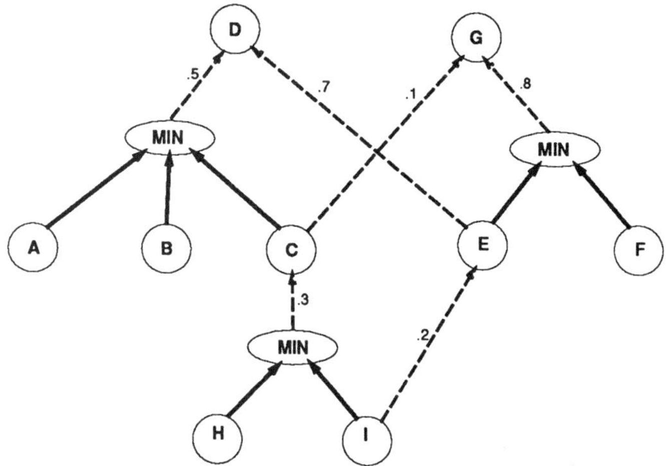

Figure 1: A RAPTURE NETWORK

highest value. Figure 1 illustrates the following set of rules.

$$ABC \xrightarrow{.5} D \quad E \xrightarrow{.7} D \quad C \xrightarrow{.1} G \quad EF \xrightarrow{.8} G \quad HI \xrightarrow{.3} C \quad I \xrightarrow{.2} E$$

As shown in the network, conjuncts must first pass through a MIN node before any activation reaches the consequent node. Note that each of the conjuncts is connected to the corresponding MIN mode with a solid line. This represents the fact that the link is non-adjustable, and simply passes its full activation value onto the MIN node. The standard (certainty-factor) links are drawn as dotted lines indicating that their values *are* adjustable.

This construction shows how easily a RAPTURE-network can model a MYCIN rule-base. Each representation can be converted into the other, without loss or corruption of information. They are two equivalent representations of the same set of rules.

2.3 Certainty Factor Backpropagation

Using the constructed RAPTURE-network, we desire to maximize its predictive accuracy over a set of training examples. Cycling through the examples one at a time, and slightly adjusting all relevant network weights in a direction that will minimize the output error, results in hill-climbing to a local minimum. This is the idea behind gradient descent [Rumelhart *et al.*, 1986], which RAPTURE accomplishes with Certainty Factor Backpropagation (CFBP), using the following equations.

$$\Delta_p w_{ji} = \eta \delta_{pj} (1 \pm \sum_{k \neq i} w_{jk} o_{pk}) \qquad (1)$$

If u_j is an output unit

$$\delta_{pj} = (t_{pj} - o_{pj}) \tag{2}$$

If u_j is not an output unit

$$\delta_{pj} = \sum_{k_{min}} \delta_{pk} w_{kj} (1 \pm \sum_{i \neq k} w_{jk} o_{pk}) \tag{3}$$

The "Sigma with circle" notation is meant to represent probabilistic sum over the index, and the $\pm$ notation is shorthand for two separate cases. If $w_{ji} o_{pi} \geq 0$, then $-$ is used, otherwise $+$ is used. The k_{min} subscript refers to the fact that we do not perform this summation for *every* unit k (as in standard backpropagation), but only those units that received some contribution from unit j. Since a unit j may be required to pass through a min or max-node before reaching the next layer (k), it is possible that its value may not reach k.

RAPTURE deems a classification correct when the output value for the correct category is greater than that of any other category. No error propagation takes place in this case ($\delta_{pj} = 0$). CFBP terminates when overall error reaches a minimal value.

2.4 Changing the Network Architecture

Whenever training accuracy fails to reach 100% through CFBP, it may be an indication that the network architecture is inappropriate for the current classification task. To date, RAPTURE has been given two ways of changing network architecture. First, whenever the weight of a link in the network approaches zero, it is removed from the network along with all of the nodes and links that become detached due to this removal. Further, whenever an intermediate node loses all of its input links due to link deletion, it too is removed from the network, along with its output link. This link/node deletion is performed immediately after CFBP, and before anything new is introduced into the network.

RAPTURE also has a method for adding new nodes into the network. Specific nodes are added in an attempt to maximize the number of training examples that are classified correctly. The simple solution employed by RAPTURE is to create new input nodes that connect directly, either positively or negatively, to one or more output nodes. These new nodes are created in a way that will best help the network distinguish among training examples that are being misclassified. Specifically, RAPTURE attempts to distinguish for each output category, those examples of that category that are being misclassified (i.e. being classified into a different output category), from those examples that *do* belong in these different output categories. Quinlan's ID3 information gain metric [Quinlan, 1986] has been adopted by RAPTURE to select this new node, which becomes positive evidence for the correct category, and negative evidence for mistaken categories.

With these new nodes in place, we can now return to CFBP, where hopefully more training examples will be successfully classified. This entire process (CFBP followed by deleting links and adding new nodes) repeats until all training examples are correctly classified. Once this has occurred, the network is considered trained, and testing may begin.

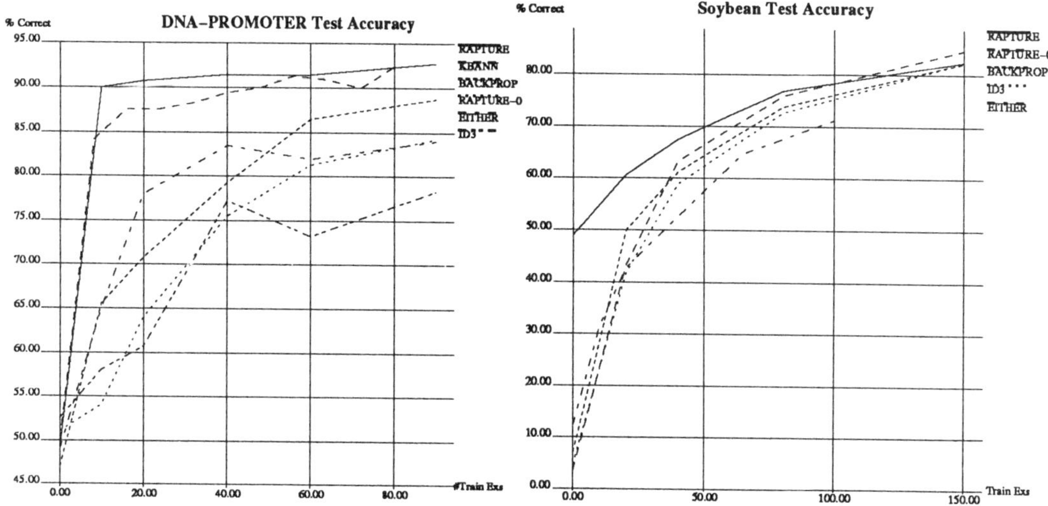

Figure 2: RAPTURE Testing Accuracy

3 Experimental Results

To date, RAPTURE has been tested on two real-world domains. The first of these is a domain for recognizing promoter sequences in strings of DNA-nucleotides. The second uses a theory for diagnosing soybean diseases. These datasets are discussed in detail in the following sections.

3.1 Promoter Recognition Results

A prokaryotic *promoter* is a short DNA sequence that precedes the beginnings of genes, and are locations where the protein RNA polymerase binds to the DNA structure [Towell *et al.*, 1990]. A set of propositional Horn-clause rules for recognizing promoters, along with 106 labelled examples (53 promoters, 53 non-promoters) was provided as the initial theory.

In order for this theory to used by RAPTURE it had to be modified into a certainty factor format. This was done by breaking up rules with multiple antecedents, into several rules. In this fashion, each antecedent is able to contribute some evidence towards belief in the consequent. Initial certainty factors were assigned in such a way that if *every* antecedent (from the original rule) were true, a certainty factor of 0.9 would result for the consequent.

To test RAPTURE using this dataset, standard training and test runs were performed, which resulted in the learning curve of Figure 2a. This graph is a plot of average performance in accuracy at classifying DNA strings over 25 independent trials. A single trial consists of providing each system with increasing numbers of examples to use for training, and then seeing how well it can classify unseen test examples. This graph clearly demonstrates the advantages of an evidence summing system like RAPTURE over a pure Horn-clause system such as EITHER, a pure inductive system such as ID3, or a pure connectionist system, like backprop. Also plotted in the graph, is KBANN [Towell *et al.*, 1990], a symbolic-connectionist system that uses standard backpropagation, and RAPTURE-0, which is simply RAPTURE given no initial theory, emphasizing the importance of the expert knowledge. For this dataset, CFBP alone was all that was required in order to train the network. The node addition module was never called.

3.2 Soybean Disease Diagnosis Results

The Soybean Data comes from [Michalski and Chilausky, 1980] and is a dataset of 562 examples of diseased soybean plants. Examples were described by a string of 35 features including the condition of the stem, the roots, the seeds, as well as information such as the time of year, temperature, and features of the soil. An expert classified each example into one of 15 soybean diseases. This dataset has been used as a benchmark for a number of learning systems. Figure 2b is a learning curve on this data comparing RAPTURE, RAPTURE-0, backpropagation, ID3, and EITHER.

The headstart given to RAPTURE does not last throughout testing in this domain. RAPTURE maintains a statistically significant lead over the other systems (except RAPTURE-0) through 80 examples, but by 150 examples, all systems are performing at statistically equivalent levels. A likely explanation for this is that the expert provided theory is more helpful on the easier to diagnose diseases than on those that are more difficult. But these easy ones are also easy to learn via pure induction, and good rules can be created after seeing only a few examples. Trials have actually been run out to 300 examples, though all systems are performing at equivalent levels of accuracy.

4 Related Work

The SEEK system [Ginsberg *et al.*, 1988] revises rule bases containing *M-of-N* rules, though can not modify real-valued weights and contains no means for adding new rules. Valtorta [Valtorta, 1988] has examined the computational complexity of various refinement tasks for probabilistic knowledge bases, and shows that refining the weights to fit a set of training data is an NP-Hard problem. Ma and Wilkins [Ma and Wilkins, 1991] have developed methods for improving the accuracy of a certainty-factor knowledge base by deleting rules, and they report modest improvements in the accuracy of a MYCIN rule base. Gallant [Gallant, 1988] designed and implemented a system that combines expert domain knowledge with connectionist learning, though is not suitable for multi-layer networks or for combination functions like probabilistic sum. KBANN [Towell *et al.*, 1990] uses standard backpropagation to refine a symbolic rule base, though the mapping between the symbolic rules and the network is only an approximation. Fu [Fu, 1989] and Lacher [Lacher, 1992] have also used backpropagation techniques to revise certainty factors on rules. However, the current publications on these two projects do not address the problem of altering the network architecture (i.e. adding new rules) and do not present results on revising actual expert knowledge bases.

5 Future Work

The current method for changing network architecture in RAPTURE is restricted to adding new input units that directly feed the outputs. We hope to incorporate newer techniques for creating and linking to hidden nodes, in order to improve the range of architectural changes that it can make.

Another area requiring further research concerns the differences between certainty-factor networks and traditional connectionist networks. Further comparison of the RAPTURE and KBANN approaches to knowledge-base refinement are also indicated.

Finally, in recent years, certainty-factors have been the subject of considerable criticism from researchers in uncertain reasoning [Shafer and Pearl, 1990]. However, the basic revision framework in RAPTURE should be applicable to other uncertain reasoning formalisms such as Bayesian networks, Dempster-Shafer theory, or fuzzy logic [Shafer and Pearl, 1990]. As long as the activation functions in the corresponding network implementations of these methods are differentiable, backpropagation techniques should be employable.

6 Conclusions

Automatic refinement of probabilistic rule bases is an under-studied problem with important applications to the development of intelligent systems. This paper has described and evaluated an approach to refining certainty-factor rule bases that integrates connectionist and symbolic learning. The approach is implemented in a system called RAPTURE, which uses a revised backpropagation algorithm to modify certainty factors and ID3's information gain criteria to determine new rules to add to the network. In other words, connectionist methods are used to adjust parameters and symbolic methods are used to make structural changes to the knowledge base.

In domains with limited training data or domains requiring meaningful explanations for conclusions, refining existing expert knowledge has clear advantages. Results on revising three real-world knowledge bases indicates that RAPTURE generally performs better than purely inductive systems (ID3 and backpropagation), a purely symbolic revision system (EITHER), and and purely connectionist revision system (KBANN).

The certainty-factor networks used in RAPTURE blur the distinction between connectionist and symbolic representations. They can be viewed either as connectionist networks or symbolic rule bases. RAPTURE demonstrates the utility of applying connectionist learning methods to "symbolic" knowledge bases and employing symbolic methods to modify "connectionist" networks. Hopefully these results will encourage others to explore similar opportunities for cross-fertilization of ideas between connectionist and symbolic learning.

Acknowledgements

This research was supported by the National Science Foundation under grant IRI-9102926, the NASA Ames Research Center under grant NCC 2-629, and the Texas Advanced Research Program under grant 003658114. We wish to thank R.S. Michalski for furnishing the soybean data, M. Noordewier, G.G. Towell, and J.W. Shavlik for supplying the DNA data, and the KBANN results.

References

[Fu, 1989] Li-Min Fu. Integration of neural heuristics into knowledge-based inference. *Connection Science*, 1(3):325–339, 1989.

[Gallant, 1988] S.I. Gallant. Connectionist expert systems. *Communications of the Association for Computing Machinery*, 31:152–169, 1988.

[Ginsberg *et al.*, 1988] A. Ginsberg, S. M. Weiss, and P. Politakis. Automatic knowledge based refinement for classification systems. *Artificial Intelligence*, 35:197–226, 1988.

[Lacher, 1992] R.C. Lacher. Expert networks: Paradigmatic conflict, technological rapprochement. Neuroprose FTP Archive, 1992.

[Ma and Wilkins, 1991] Y. Ma and D. C. Wilkins. Improving the performance of inconsistent knowledge bases via combined optimization method. In *Proceedings of the Eighth International Workshop on Machine Learning*, pages 23–27, Evanston, IL, June 1991.

[Michalski and Chilausky, 1980] R. S. Michalski and S. Chilausky. Learning by being told and learning from examples: An experimental comparison of the two methods of knowledge acquisition in the context of developing an expert system for soybean disease diagnosis. *Journal of Policy Analysis and Information Systems*, 4(2):126–161, 1980.

[Ourston and Mooney, 1990] D. Ourston and R. Mooney. Changing the rules: a comprehensive approach to theory refinement. In *Proceedings of the Eighth National Conference on Artificial Intelligence*, pages 815–820, Detroit, MI, July 1990.

[Quinlan, 1986] J. R. Quinlan. Induction of decision trees. *Machine Learning*, 1(1):81–106, 1986.

[Rumelhart *et al.*, 1986] D. E. Rumelhart, G. E. Hinton, and J. R. Williams. Learning internal representations by error propagation. In D. E. Rumelhart and J. L. McClelland, editors, *Parallel Distributed Processing, Vol. I*, pages 318–362. MIT Press, Cambridge, MA, 1986.

[Shafer and Pearl, 1990] G. Shafer and J. Pearl, editors. *Readings in Uncertain Reasoning*. Morgan Kaufmann, Inc., San Mateo,CA, 1990.

[Towell *et al.*, 1990] G. G. Towell, J. W. Shavlik, and Michiel O. Noordewier. Refinement of approximate domain theories by knowledge-based artificial neural networks. In *Proceedings of the Eighth National Conference on Artificial Intelligence*, pages 861–866, Boston, MA, July 1990.

[Valtorta, 1988] M. Valtorta. Some results on the complexity of knowledge-base refinement. In *Proceedings of the Sixth International Workshop on Machine Learning*, pages 326–331, Ithaca, NY, June 1988.

Learning Sequential Tasks by Incrementally Adding Higher Orders

Mark Ring
Department of Computer Sciences, Taylor 2.124
University of Texas at Austin
Austin, Texas 78712
(ring@cs.utexas.edu)

Abstract

An incremental, higher-order, non-recurrent network combines two properties found to be useful for learning sequential tasks: higher-order connections and incremental introduction of new units. The network adds higher orders when needed by adding new units that dynamically modify connection weights. Since the new units modify the weights at the next time-step with information from the previous step, temporal tasks can be learned without the use of feedback, thereby greatly simplifying training. Furthermore, a theoretically unlimited number of units can be added to reach into the arbitrarily distant past. Experiments with the Reber grammar have demonstrated speedups of two orders of magnitude over recurrent networks.

1 INTRODUCTION

Second-order recurrent networks have proven to be very powerful [8], especially when trained using complete back propagation through time [1, 6, 14]. It has also been demonstrated by Fahlman that a recurrent network that incrementally adds nodes during training—his Recurrent Cascade-Correlation algorithm [5]—can be superior to non-incremental, recurrent networks [2, 4, 11, 12, 15].

The incremental, higher-order network presented here combines advantages of both of these approaches in a non-recurrent network. This network (a simplified, continuous version of that introduced in [9]), adds higher orders when they are needed by the system to solve its task. This is done by adding new units that dynamically modify connection weights. The new units modify the weights at the next time-step with information from the last, which allows temporal tasks to be learned without the use of feedback.

2 GENERAL FORMULATION

Each unit (U) in the network is either an input (I), output (O), or high-level (L) unit.

$$\begin{aligned} U^i(t) &\stackrel{def}{=} \text{value of } i\text{th unit at time } t. \\ I^i(t) &\stackrel{def}{=} U^i(t) \text{ where } i \text{ is an input unit.} \\ O^i(t) &\stackrel{def}{=} U^i(t) \text{ where } i \text{ is an output unit.} \\ T^i(t) &\stackrel{def}{=} \text{Target value for } O^i(t) \text{ at time } t. \\ L^i_{xy}(t) &\stackrel{def}{=} U^i(t) \text{ where } i \text{ is the higher-order unit that} \\ & \quad\ \text{modifies weight } w_{xy} \text{ at time } t.^1 \end{aligned}$$

The output and high-level units are collectively referred to as non-input (N) units:

$$N^i(t) \stackrel{def}{=} \begin{cases} O^i(t) & \text{if } U^i \equiv O^i. \\ L^i_{xy}(t) & \text{if } U^i \equiv L^i_{xy}. \end{cases}$$

In a given time-step, the output and high-level units receive a summed input from the input units.

$$N^i(t) = \sum_j I^j(t) g(i, j, t). \tag{1}$$

g is a gating function representing the weight of a particular connection at a particular time-step. If there is a higher-order unit assigned to that connection, then the input value of that unit is added to the connection's weight at that time-step.[2]

$$g(i, j, t) = \begin{cases} w_{ij}(t) + L^n_{ij}(t-1) & \text{If } L^n_{ij} \text{ exists} \\ w_{ij}(t) & \text{Otherwise} \end{cases} \tag{2}$$

At each time-step, the values of the output units are calculated from the input units and the weights (possibly modified by the activations of the high-level units from the previous time-step). The values of the high-level units are calculated at the same time in the same way. The output units generate the output of the network. The high-level units simply alter the weights at the next time-step. All unit activations can be computed simultaneously since the activations of the L units are not required

---

[1]A connection may be modified by at most one L unit. Therefore L^i, L_{xy}, and L^i_{xy} are identical but used as appropriate for notational convenience.

[2]It can be seen that this is a higher-order connection in the usual sense if one substitutes the right-hand side of equation 1 for L^n_{ij} in equation 2 and then replaces g in equation 1 with the result. In fact, as the network increases in height, ever higher orders are introduced, while lower orders are preserved.

until the following time-step. The network is arranged hierarchically in that every higher-order units is always higher in the hierarchy than the units on either side of the weight it affects. Since higher-order units have no outgoing connections, the network is not recurrent. It is therefore impossible for a high-level unit to affect, directly or indirectly, its own input.

There are no hidden units in the traditional sense, and all units have a linear activation function. (This does not imply that non-linear functions cannot be represented, since non-linearities do result from the multiplication of higher-level and input units in equations 1 and 2.)

Learning is done through gradient descent to reduce the sum-squared error.

$$\begin{aligned} E(t) &= \frac{1}{2}\sum_i (T^i(t) - O^i(t))^2 \\ w_{ij}(t+1) &= w_{ij}(t) - \eta \Delta w_{ij}(t) \\ \Delta w_{ij}(t) &= \sum_{\tau=0}^{t} \frac{\partial E(t)}{\partial w_{ij}(\tau)}, \end{aligned} \tag{3}$$

where η is the learning rate. Since it may take several time-steps for the value of a weight to affect the network's output and therefore the error, equation 3 can be rewritten as:

$$\Delta w_{ij}(t) = \frac{\partial E(t)}{\partial w_{ij}(t - \tau^i)}, \tag{4}$$

where

$$\tau^i = \begin{cases} 0 & \text{if } U^i \equiv O^i \\ 1 + \tau^x & \text{if } U^i \equiv L^i_{xy} \end{cases}$$

The value τ^i is constant for any given unit i and specifies how "high" in the hierarchy unit i is. It therefore also specifies how many time-steps it takes for a change in unit i's activation to affect the network's output.

Due to space limitations, the derivation of the gradient is not shown, but is given elsewhere [10]. The resulting weight change rule, however, is:

$$\Delta w_{ij}(t) = I^j(t - \tau^i) \begin{cases} T^i(t) - O^i(t) & \text{If } U^i \equiv O^i \\ \Delta w_{xy}(t) & \text{If } U^i \equiv L^i_{xy} \end{cases} \tag{5}$$

The weights are changed after error values for the output units have been collected. Since each high-level unit is higher in the hierarchy than the units on either side of the weight it affects, weight changes are made bottom up, and the $\Delta w_{xy}(t)$ in equation 5 will already have been calculated at the time $\Delta w_{ij}(t)$ is computed.

The intuition behind the learning rule is that each high-level unit learns to utilize the context from the previous time-step for adjusting the connection it influences at the next time-step so that it can minimize the connection's error in that context. Therefore, if the information necessary to decide the correct value of a connection at one time-step is available at the previous time-step, then that information is used by the higher-order unit assigned to that connection. If the needed information is not available at the previous time-step, then new units may be built to look for the information at still earlier steps. This method concentrating on unexpected events is similar to the "hierarchy of decisions" of Dawkins [3], and the "history compression" of Schmidhuber [13].

3 WHEN TO ADD NEW UNITS

A unit is added whenever a weight is being pulled strongly in opposite directions (i.e. when learning is forcing the weight to increase and to decrease at the same time). The unit is created to determine the contexts in which the weight is pulled in each direction. This is done in the following way: Two long-term averages are kept for each connection. The first of these records the average change made to the weight,

$$\overline{\Delta w_{ij}(t)} = \sigma \Delta w_{ij}(t) + (1-\sigma)\overline{\Delta w_{ij}(t-1)}; \quad 0 \leq \sigma \leq 1.$$

The second is the long-term mean absolute deviation, given by:

$$\overline{|\Delta w_{ij}(t)|} = \sigma |\Delta w_{ij}(t)| + (1-\sigma)\overline{|\Delta w_{ij}(t-1)|}; \quad 0 \leq \sigma \leq 1.$$

The parameter, σ, specifies the duration of the long-term average. A lower value of σ means that the average is kept for a longer period of time. When $\overline{\Delta w_{ij}(t)}$ is small, but $\overline{|\Delta w_{ij}(t)|}$ is large, then the weight is being pulled strongly in conflicting directions, and a new unit is built.

$$\text{if} \qquad \frac{\overline{|\Delta w_{ij}(t)|}}{\epsilon + |\overline{\Delta w_{ij}(t)}|} > \Theta \qquad \text{then build unit } L_{ij}^{N+1},$$

where ϵ is a small constant that keeps the denominator from being zero, Θ is a threshold value, and N is the number of units in the network. A related method for adding new units in feed-forward networks was introduced by Wynne-Jones [16].

When a new unit is added, its incoming weights are initially zero. It has no output weights but simply learns to anticipate and reduce the error at each time-step of the weight it modifies. In order to keep the number of new units low, whenever a unit, L_{ij}^n is created, the statistics for all connections into the destination unit (U^i) are reset: $\overline{|\Delta w_{ij}(t)|} \leftarrow 0.0$ and $\overline{\Delta w_{ij}(t)} \leftarrow 1.0$.

4 RESULTS

The Reber grammar is a small finite-state grammar of the following form:

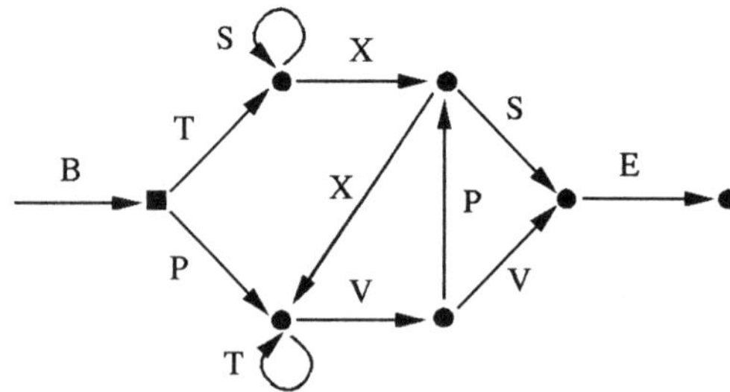

Transitions from one node to the next are made by way of the labeled arcs. The task of the network is: given as input the label of the arc just traversed, predict

		Elman Network	RTRL	Recurrent Cascade Correlation	Incremental Higher-Order Network
Sequences Seen:	Mean			25,000	206
	Best	20,000	19,000		176
"Hidden" Units		15	2	2-3	40

Table 1: The incremental higher-order network is compared against recurrent networks on the Reber grammar. The results for the recurrent networks are quoted from other sources [2, 5]. The mean and/or best performance is shown when available. RTRL is the real-time recurrent learning algorithm [15].

the arc that will be traversed next. A training sequence, or *string,* is generated by starting with a B transition and then randomly choosing an arc leading away from the current state until the final state is reached. Both inputs and outputs are encoded locally, so that there are seven output units (one each for B, T, S, X, V, P, and E) and eight input units (the same seven plus one bias unit). The network is considered correct if its highest activated outputs correspond to the arcs that can be traversed from the current state. Note that the current state cannot be determined from the current input alone.

An Elman-type recurrent network was able to learn this task after 20,000 string presentations using 15 hidden units [2]. (The correctness criteria for the Elman net was slightly more stringent than that described in the previous paragraph.) Recurrent Cascade-Correlation (RCC) was able to learn this task using only two or three hidden units in an average of 25,000 string presentations [5].

The incremental, higher-order network was trained on a continuous stream of input: the network was not reset before beginning a new string. Training was considered to be complete only after the network had correctly classified 100 strings in a row. Using this criterion, the network completed training after an average of 206.3 string presentations with a standard deviation of 16.7. It achieved perfect generalization on test sets of 128 randomly generated strings in all ten runs. Because the Reber grammar is stochastic, a ceiling of 40 higher-order units was imposed on the network to prevent it from continually creating new units in an attempt to outguess the random number generator.

Complete results for the network on the Reber grammar task are given in table 1. The parameter settings were: $\eta = 0.04, \sigma = 0.08, \Theta = 1.0, \epsilon = 0.1$ and Bias $= 0.0$. (The network seemed to perform better with no bias unit.)

The network has also been tested on the "variable gap" tasks introduced by Mozer [7], as shown in figure 1. These tasks were intended to test performance of networks over long time-delays. Two sequences are alternately presented to the network. Each sequence begins with an X or a Y and is followed by a fixed string of characters with an X or a Y inserted some number of time-steps from the beginning. In figure 1 the number of time-steps, or "gap", is 2. The only difference between the two sequences is that the first begins with an X and repeats the X after the gap, while the second begins with a Y and repeats the Y after the gap. The network must learn to predict the next item in the sequence given the current item as input

Time-step:	0	1	2	3	4	5	6	7	8	9	10	11	12
Sequence 1:	X	a	b	X	c	d	e	f	g	h	i	j	k
Sequence 2:	Y	a	b	Y	c	d	e	f	g	h	i	j	k

Figure 1: An example of a "variable gap" training sequence [7]. One item is presented to the network at each time-step. The target is the next item in the sequence. Here the "gap" is two, because there are two items in the sequence between the first X or Y and the second X or Y. In order to correctly predict the second X or Y, the network must remember how the sequence began.

(where all inputs are locally encoded). In order for the network to predict the second occurrence of the X or Y, it must remember how the sequence began. The length of the gap can be increased in order to create tasks of greater difficulty.

Results of the "gap" tasks are given in table 2. The values for the standard recurrent network and for Mozer's own variation are quoted from Mozer's paper [7]. The incremental higher-order net had no difficulty with gaps up to 24, which was the largest gap I tested. The same string was used for all tasks (except for the position of the second X or Y), and had no repeated characters (again with the exception of the X and Y). The network continued to scale linearly with every gap size both in terms of units and epochs required for training. Because these tasks are not stochastic, the network always stopped building units as soon as it had created those necessary to solve each task.

The parameter settings were: $\eta = 1.5, \sigma = 0.2, \Theta = 1.0, \epsilon = 0.1$ and Bias $= 0.0$. The network was considered to have correctly predicted an element in the sequence if the most strongly activated output unit was the unit representing the correct prediction. The sequence was considered correctly predicted if all elements (other than the initial X or Y) were correctly predicted.

Gap	Mean number of Training sets required by: Standard Recurrent Net	Mozer Network	Incremental Higher-Order Net	Units Created
2	468	328	4	10
4	7406	584	6	15
6	9830	992	8	19
8	> 10000	1312	10	23
10	> 10000	1630	12	27
24			26	49

Table 2: A comparison on the "gap" tasks of a standard recurrent-network and a network devised specifically for long time-delays (quoted from Mozer [7], who reported results for gaps up to ten) against an incremental higher-order network. The last column is the number of units created by the incremental higher-order net.

5 CONCLUSIONS

The incremental higher-order network performed much better than the networks that it was compared against on these tiny tests. A few caveats are in order, however. First, the parameters given for the tasks above were customized for those tasks. Second, the network may add a large number of new units if it contains many context-dependent events or if it is inherently stochastic. Third, though the network in principle can build an ever larger hierarchy that searches further and further back in time for a context that will predict what a connection's weight should be, many units may be needed to bridge a long time-gap. Finally, once a bridge across a time-delay is created, it does not generalize to other time-delays.

On the other hand, the network learns very fast due to its simple structure that adds high-level units only when needed. Since there is no feedback (i.e. no unit ever produces a signal that will ever feed back to itself), learning can be done without back propagation through time. Also, since the outputs and high-level units have a fan-in equal to the number of inputs only, the number of connections in the system is much smaller than the number of connections in a traditional network with the same number of hidden units.

Finally, the network can be thought of as a system of continuous-valued condition-action rules that are inserted or removed depending on another set of such rules that are in turn inserted or removed depending on another set, etc. When new rules (new units) are added, they are initially invisible to the system, (i.e., they have no effect), but only gradually learn to have an effect as the opportunity to decrease error presents itself.

Acknowledgements

This work was supported by NASA Johnson Space Center Graduate Student Researchers Program training grant, NGT 50594. I would like to thank Eric Hartman, Kadir Liano, and my advisor Robert Simmons for useful discussions and helpful comments on drafts of this paper. I would also like to thank Pavilion Technologies, Inc. for their generous contribution of computer time and office space required to complete much of this work.

References

[1] Jonathan Richard Bachrach. *Connectionist Modeling and Control of Finite State Environments.* PhD thesis, Department of Computer and Information Sciences, University of Massachusetts, February 1992.

[2] Axel Cleeremans, David Servan-Schreiber, and James L. McClelland. Finite state automata and simple recurrent networks. *Neural Computation*, 1(3):372–381, 1989.

[3] Richard Dawkins. Hierarchical organisation: a candidate principle for ethology. In P. P. G. Bateson and R. A. Hinde, editors, *Growing Points in Ethology*, pages 7–54, Cambridge, 1976. Cambridge University Press.

[4] Jeffrey L. Elman. Finding structure in time. CRL Technical Report 8801, University of California, San Diego, Center for Research in Language, April 1988.

[5] Scott E. Fahlman. The recurrent cascade-correlation architecture. In R. P. Lippmann, J. E. Moody, and D. S. Touretzky, editors, *Advances in Neural Information Processing Systems 3*, pages 190–196, San Mateo, California, 1991. Morgan Kaufmann Publishers.

[6] C. L. Giles, C. B. Miller, D. Chen, G. Z. Sun, H. H. Chen, and Y. C. Lee. Extracting and learning an unknown grammar with recurrent neural networks. In J. E. Moody, S. J. Hanson, and R. P. Lippman, editors, *Advances in Neural Information Processing Systems 4*, pages 317–324, San Mateo, California, 1992. Morgan Kaufmann Publishers.

[7] Michael C. Mozer. Induction of multiscale temporal structure. In John E. Moody, Steven J. Hanson, and Richard P. Lippmann, editors, *Advances in Neural Information Processing Systems 4*, pages 275–282, San Mateo, California, 1992. Morgan Kaufmann Publishers.

[8] Jordan B. Pollack. The induction of dynamical recognizers. *Machine Learning*, 7:227–252, 1991.

[9] Mark B. Ring. Incremental development of complex behaviors through automatic construction of sensory-motor hierarchies. In Lawrence A. Birnbaum and Gregg C. Collins, editors, *Machine Learning: Proceedings of the Eighth International Workshop (ML91)*, pages 343–347. Morgan Kaufmann Publishers, June 1991.

[10] Mark B. Ring. Sequence learning with incremental higher-order neural networks. Technical Report AI 93-193, Artificial Intelligence Laboratory, University of Texas at Austin, January 1993.

[11] A. J. Robinson and F. Fallside. The utility driven dynamic error propagation network. Technical Report CUED/F-INFENG/TR.1, Cambridge University Engineering Department, 1987.

[12] D. E. Rumelhart, G. E. Hinton, and R. J. Williams. Learning internal representations by error propagation. In D. E. Rumelhart and J. L. McClelland, editors, *Parallel Distributed Processing: Explorations in the Microstructure of Cognition. V1: Foundations.* MIT Press, 1986.

[13] Jürgen Schmidhuber. Learning unambiguous reduced sequence descriptions. In J. E. Moody, S. J. Hanson, and R. P. Lippman, editors, *Advances in Neural Information Processing Systems 4*, pages 291–298, San Mateo, California, 1992. Morgan Kaufmann Publishers.

[14] Raymond L. Watrous and Gary M. Kuhn. Induction of finite-state languages using second-order recurrent networks. In J. E. Moody, S. J. Hanson, and R. P. Lippman, editors, *Advances in Neural Information Processing Systems 4*, pages 309–316, San Mateo, California, 1992. Morgan Kaufmann Publishers.

[15] Ronald J. Williams and David Zipser. A learning algorithm for continually running fully recurrent neural networks. *Neural Computation*, 1(2):270–280, 1989.

[16] Mike Wynn-Jones. Node splitting: A constructive algorithm for feed-forward neural networks. *Neural Computing and Applications*, 1(1):17–22, 1993.

Kohonen Feature Maps and Growing Cell Structures – a Performance Comparison

Bernd Fritzke
International Computer Science Institute
1947 Center Street, Suite 600
Berkeley, CA 94704-1105, USA

Abstract

A performance comparison of two self-organizing networks, the Kohonen Feature Map and the recently proposed Growing Cell Structures is made. For this purpose several performance criteria for self-organizing networks are proposed and motivated. The models are tested with three example problems of increasing difficulty. The Kohonen Feature Map demonstrates slightly superior results only for the simplest problem. For the other more difficult and also more realistic problems the Growing Cell Structures exhibit significantly better performance by every criterion. Additional advantages of the new model are that all parameters are constant over time and that size as well as structure of the network are determined automatically.

1 INTRODUCTION

Self-organizing networks are able to generate interesting low-dimensional representations of high-dimensional input data. The most well-known of these models is the Kohonen Feature Map (Kohonen [1982]). So far it has been applied to a large variety of problems including vector quantization (Schweizer et al. [1991]), biological modelling (Obermayer, Ritter & Schulten [1990]), combinatorial optimization (Favata & Walker [1991]) and also processing of symbolic information(Ritter & Kohonen [1989]).

It has been reported by a number of researchers, that one disadvantage of Kohonen's model is the fact, that the network structure had to be specified in advance. This is generally not possible in an optimal way since a necessary piece of information, the probability distribution of the input signals, is usually not available. The choice of an unsuitable network structure, however, can badly degrade network performance.

Recently we have proposed a new self-organizing network model – the Growing Cell Structures – which can automatically determine a problem specific network structure (Fritzke [1992]). By now the model has been successfully applied to clustering (Fritzke [1991]) and combinatorial optimization (Fritzke & Wilke [1991]).

In this contribution we directly compare our model to that of Kohonen. We first review some general properties of self-organizing networks and several performance criteria for these networks are proposed and motivated. The new model is then briefly described. Simulation results are presented and allow a comparison of both models with respect to the proposed criteria.

2 SELF-ORGANIZING NETWORKS

2.1 CHARACTERISTICS

A self-organizing network consists of a set of neurons arranged in some topological structure which induces *neighborhood relations* among the neurons. An n-dimensional *reference vector* is attached to every neuron. This vector determines the specific n-dimensional input signal to which the neuron is maximally sensitive.

By assigning to every input signal the neuron with the nearest reference vector (according to a suitable norm), a mapping is defined from the space of all possible input signals onto the neural structure. A given set of reference vectors thus divides the input vector space into regions with a common nearest reference vector. These regions are commonly denoted as *Voronoi regions* and the corresponding partition of the input vector space is denoted *Voronoi partition*.

Self-organizing networks learn (change internal parameters) in an unsupervised manner from a stream of input signals. These input signals obey a generally unknown probability distribution. For each input signal the neuron with the nearest reference vector is determined, the so-called "best matching unit" (bmu). The reference vectors of the bmu *and* of a number of its topological neighbors are moved towards the input signal. The adaptation of topological neighbors distinguishes self-organization ("winner take most") from competitive learning where only the bmu is adapted ("winner take all").

2.2 PERFORMANCE CRITERIA

One can identify three main criteria for self-organizing networks. The importance of each criterion may vary from application to application.

Topology Preservation. This denotes two properties of the mapping defined by the network. We call the mapping *topology-preserving* if

a) similar input vectors are mapped onto identical or closely neighboring neurons and

b) neighboring neurons have similar reference vectors.

Property a) ensures, that small changes of the input vector cause correspondingly small changes in the position of the bmu. The mapping is *robust* against distortions of the input, a very important property for applications dealing with real, noisy data. Property b) ensures robustness of the inverse mapping. The topology preservation is especially interesting when the dimension of the input vectors is higher than the network dimension. Then the mapping reduces the data dimension but usually preserves important similarity relations among the input data.

Modelling of Probability Distribution. A set of reference vectors is said to *model the probability distribution*, if the local density of reference vectors in the input vector space approaches the probability density of the input vector distribution.

This property is desirable for two reasons. First, we get an implicit model of the unknown probability distribution underlying the input signals. Second, the network becomes *fault-tolerant* against damage, since every neuron is only "responsible" for a small fraction of all input vectors. If neurons are destroyed for some reason the mapping ability of the network degrades only proportionally to the number of the destroyed neurons (soft fail). This is a very desirable property for technical (as well as natural) systems.

Minimization of Quantization Error. The *quantization error* for a given input signal is the distance between this signal and the reference vector of the bmu. We call a set of reference vectors *error minimizing* for a given probability distribution if the mean quantization error is minimized.

This property is important, if the original signals have to be reconstructed from the reference vectors which is a very common situation in vector quantization. The quantization error in this case limits the accuracy of the reconstruction.

One should note that the optimal distribution of reference vectors for error minimization is generally different from the optimal distribution for distribution modelling.

3 THE GROWING CELL STRUCTURES

The Growing Cell Structures are a self-organizing network an important feature of which is the ability to automatically find a problem specific network structure through a growth process.

Basic building blocks are k-dimensional *hypertetrahedrons*: lines for $k = 1$, triangles for $k = 2$, tetrahedrons for $k = 3$ etc. The vertices of the hypertetrahedrons are the neurons and the edges denote neighborhood relations.

By insertion and deletion of neurons the structure is modified. This is done during a self-organization process which is similar to that in Kohonen's model. Input signals cause adaptation of the bmu and its topological neighbors. In contrast to Kohonen's model all parameters are constant including the width of the neighborhood around the bmu where adaptation takes place. Only *direct* neighbors and the bmu itself are being adapted.

3.1 INSERTION OF NEURONS

To determine the positions where new neurons should be inserted the concept of a *resource* is introduced. Every neuron has a local resource variable and new neurons are always inserted near the neuron with the highest resource value. New neurons get part of the resource of their neighbors so that in the long run the resource is distributed evenly among all neurons.

Every input signal causes an increase of the resource variable of the best matching unit. Choices for the resource examined so far are

- the summed quantization error caused by the neuron
- the number of input signals received by the neuron

Always after a constant number of adaptation steps (e.g. 100) a new neuron is inserted. For this purpose the neuron with the highest resource is determined and the edge connecting it to the neighbor with the most different reference vector is "split" by inserting the new neuron. Further edges are added to rebuild a structure consisting only of k-dimensional hypertetrahedrons.

The reference vector of the new neuron is interpolated from the reference vectors belonging to the ending points of the split edge. The resource variable of the new neuron is initialized by subtracting some resource from its neighbors, the amount of which is determined by the reduction of their Voronoi regions through the insertion.

3.2 DELETION OF NEURONS

By comparing the fraction of all input signals which a specific neuron has received and the volume of its Voronoi region one can derive a local *estimate of the probability density* of the input vectors.

Those neurons, whose reference vectors fall into regions of the input vector space with a very low probability density, are regarded as "superfluous" and are removed. The result are problem-specific network structures potentially consisting of several separate sub networks and accurately modelling a given probability distribution.

4 SIMULATION RESULTS

A number of tests have been performed to evaluate the performance of the new model. One series is described in the following.

Three methods have been compared.

a) Kohonen Feature Maps (KFM)

b) Growing Cell Structures with quantization error as resource (GCS-1)

c) Growing Cell Structures with number of input signals as resource (GCS-2)

Distribution A:
The probability density is uniform in the unit square

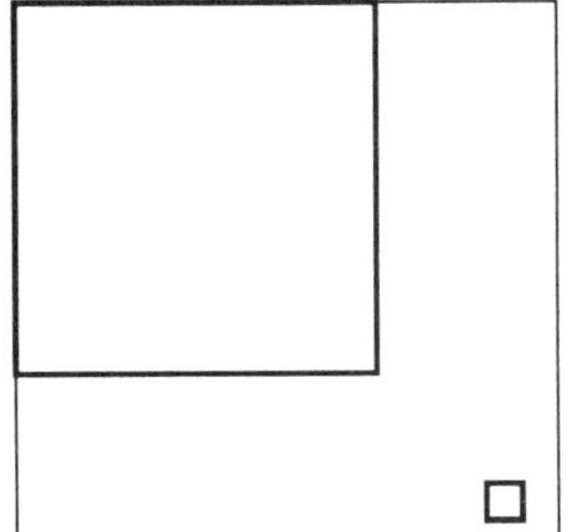

Distribution B:
The probability density is uniform in the 10 × 10-field, by a factor 100 higher in the 1 × 1-field and zero elsewhere

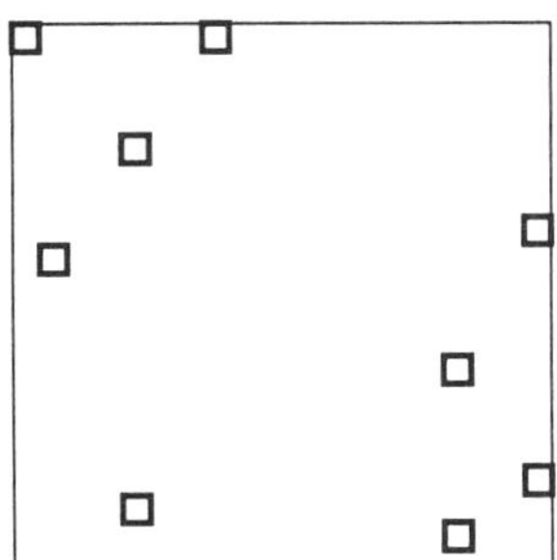

Distribution C:
The probability density is uniform inside the seven lower squares, by a factor 10 higher in the two upper squares and zero elsewhere.

Figure 1: Three different probability distributions used for a performance comparison. Distribution A is very simple and has a form ideally suited for the Kohonen Feature Map which uses a square grid of neurons. Distribution B was chosen to show the effects of a highly varying probability density. Distribution C is the most realistic with a number of separate regions some of which have also different probability densities.

These models were applied to the probability distributions shown in fig. 1. The Kohonen model was used with a 10×10-grid of neurons. The Growing Cell Structures were used to build up a two dimensional cell structure of the same size. This was achieved by stopping the growth process when the number of neurons had reached 100.

At the end of the simulation the proposed criteria were measured as follows:

- The topology preservation requires two properties. Property a) was measured by the *topographical product* recently proposed by Bauer e.a. for this purpose (Bauer & Pawelzik [1992]). Property b) was measured by computing the *mean edge length* in the input space, i.e. the mean difference between reference vectors of directly neighboring neurons.
- The distribution modelling was measured by generating 5000 test signals according to the specific probability distribution and counting for every neuron the number of test signals it has been bmu for. The standard deviation of all counter values was computed and divided by the mean value of the counters to get a normalized measure, the *distribution error*, for the modelling of the probability distribution.
- The error minimization was measured by computing the *mean square quantization error* of the test signals.

The numerical results of the simulations are shown in fig. 2. Typical examples of the final network structures can be seen in fig. 3. It can be seen from fig. 2 that the

model	A	B	C
KFM	0.0013	0.022	0.048
GCS-1	0.0085	0.014	0.044
GCS-2	0.0087	0.011	0.019

a) topographical product

model	A	B	C
KFM	0.09	0.092	0.110
GCS-1	0.11	0.056	0.015
GCS-2	0.11	0.071	0.013

b) mean edge length

model	A	B	C
KFM	0.20	0.84	0.90
GCS-1	0.26	0.31	0.59
GCS-2	0.26	1.57	0.73

c) distribution error

model	A	B	C
KFM	0.0020	0.00077	0.00086
GCS-1	0.0019	0.00089	0.00010
GCS-2	0.0019	0.00055	**0.00004**

d) quantization error

Figure 2: Simulation results of the performance comparison. The model of Kohonen(KFM) and two versions of the Growing Cell Structures have been compared with respect to different criteria. All criteria are such, that smaller values are better values. The best (smallest) value in each column is enclosed in a box. Simulations were performed with the probability distributions A, B and C from fig. 1.

model of Kohonen has superior values only for distribution A, which is very regular and formed exactly like the chosen network structure (a square). Since generally the probability distribution is unknown and irregular, the distributions B and C are by far more realistic. For these distributions the Growing Cell Structures have the best values.

The modelling of the distribution and the minimization of the quantization error are generally concurring objectives. One has to decide which objective is more important for the current application. Then the appropriate version of the Growing Cell Structures can optimize with respect to that objective. For the complicated distribution C, however, *either* version of the Growing Cell Structures performs for every criterion better than Kohonen's model.

Especially notable is the low quantization error for distribution C and the error minimizing version (GCS-2) of the Growing Cell Structures (see fig. 2d). This value indicates a good potential for vector quantization.

5 DISCUSSION

Our investigations indicate that – w.r.t the proposed criteria – the Growing Cell Structures are superior to Kohonen's model for all but very carefully chosen trivial examples. Although we used small examples for the sake of clarity, our experiments lead us to conjecture, that the difference will further increase with the difficulty and size of the problem.

There are some other important advantages of our approach. First, all parameters are constant. This eliminates the difficult choice of a "cooling schedule" which is necessary in Kohonen's model. Second, the network size does not have to be specified in advance. Instead the growth process can be continued until an arbitrary performance criterion is met. To meet a specific criterion with Kohonen's model, one generally has to try different network sizes. To start always with a very large

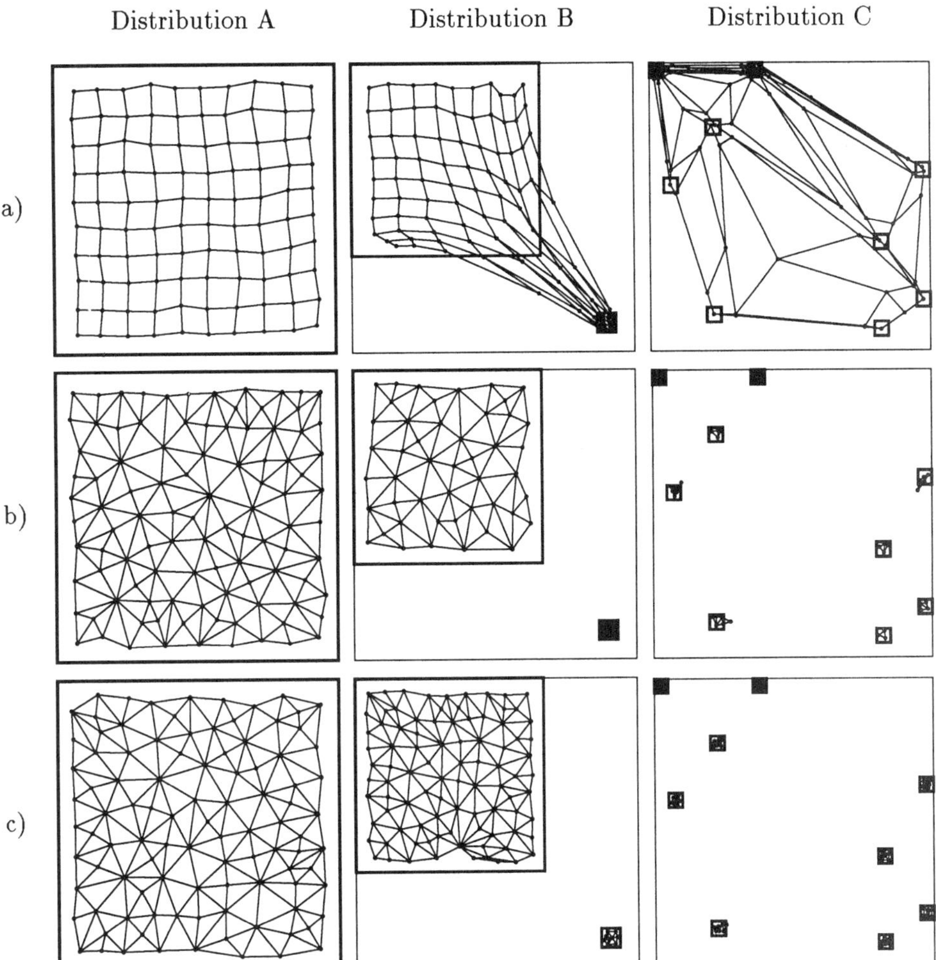

Figure 3: Typical simulation results for the model of Kohonen and the two versions of the Growing Cell Structures. The network size is 100 in every case. The probability distributions are described in fig. 1.

a) *Kohonen Feature Map* (KFM). For distributions B and C the fixed network structure leads to long connections and neurons in regions with zero probability density.

b) *Growing Cell Structures, distribution modelling variant* (GCS-1). The growth process combined with occasional removal of "superfluous" neurons has led to several sub networks for distributions B and C. For distribution B roughly half of the neurons are used to model either of the squares. This corresponds well to the underlying probability density.

c) *Growing Cell Structures, error minimizing variant* (GCS-2). The difference to the previous variant can be seen best for distribution B, where only a few neurons are used to cover the small square.

network is not a good solution to this problem, since the computational effort grows faster than quadratically with the network size.

Currently applications of variants of the new method to image compression and robot control are being investigated. Furthermore a new type of radial basis function network related to (Moody & Darken [1989]) is being explored, which is based on the Growing Cell Structures.

REFERENCES

Bauer, H.-U. & K. Pawelzik [1992], "Quantifying the neighborhood preservation of self-organizing feature maps," *IEEE Transactions on Neural Networks* 3, 570–579.

Favata, F. & R. Walker [1991], "A study of the application of Kohonen-type neural networks to the travelling Salesman Problem," *Biological Cybernetics* 64, 463–468.

Fritzke, B. [1991], "Unsupervised clustering with growing cell structures," *Proc. of IJCNN-91*, Seattle, 531–536 (Vol. II).

Fritzke, B. [1992], "Growing cell structures – a self-organizing network in k dimensions," in *Artificial Neural Networks II*, I. Aleksander & J. Taylor, eds., North-Holland, Amsterdam, 1051–1056.

Fritzke, B. & P. Wilke [1991], "FLEXMAP - A neural network with linear time and space complexity for the traveling salesman problem," *Proc. of IJCNN-91*, Singapore, 929–934.

Kohonen, T. [1982], "Self-organized formation of topologically correct feature maps," *Biological Cybernetics* 43, 59–69.

Moody, J. & C. Darken [1989], "Fast Learning in Networks of Locally-Tuned Processing Units," *Neural Computation* 1, 281–294.

Obermayer, K., H. Ritter & K. Schulten [1990], "Large-scale simulations of self-organizing neural networks on parallel computers: application to biological modeling," *Parallel Computing* 14, 381–404.

Ritter, H.J. & T. Kohonen [1989], "Self-Organizing Semantic Maps," *Biological Cybernetics* 61, 241–254.

Schweizer, L., G. Parladori, G.L. Sicuranza & S. Marsi [1991], "A fully neural approach to image compression," in *Artificial Neural Networks*, T. Kohonen, K. Mäkisara, O. Simula & J. Kangas, eds., North-Holland, Amsterdam, 815–820.

Metamorphosis Networks: An Alternative to Constructive Methods

Brian V. Bonnlander **Michael C. Mozer**
Department of Computer Science &
Institute of Cognitive Science
University of Colorado
Boulder, CO 80309–0430

Abstract

Given a set of training examples, determining the appropriate number of free parameters is a challenging problem. Constructive learning algorithms attempt to solve this problem automatically by adding hidden units, and therefore free parameters, during learning. We explore an alternative class of algorithms—called *metamorphosis algorithms*—in which the number of units is fixed, but the number of free parameters gradually increases during learning. The architecture we investigate is composed of RBF units on a lattice, which imposes flexible constraints on the parameters of the network. Virtues of this approach include variable subset selection, robust parameter selection, multiresolution processing, and interpolation of sparse training data.

1 INTRODUCTION

Generalization performance on a fixed-size training set is closely related to the number of free parameters in a network. Selecting either too many or too few parameters can lead to poor generalization. Geman et al. (1991) refer to this problem as the *bias/variance dilemma*: introducing too many free parameters incurs high variance in the set of possible solutions, and restricting the network to too few free parameters incurs high bias in the set of possible solutions.

Constructive learning algorithms (e.g., Fahlman & Lebiere, 1990; Platt, 1991) have

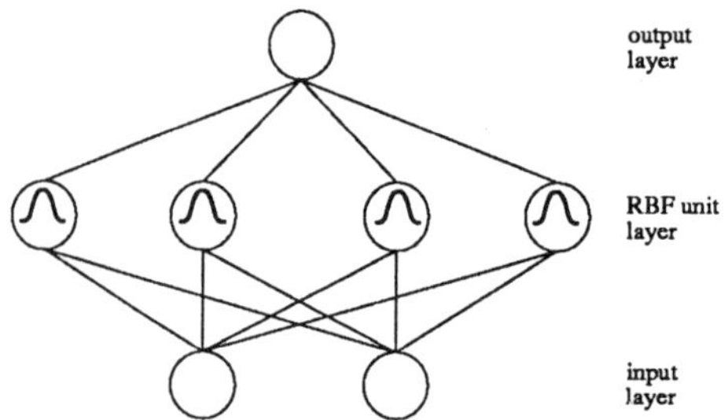

Figure 1: Architecture of an RBF network.

been proposed as a way of automatically selecting the number of free parameters in the network during learning. In these approaches, the learning algorithm gradually increases the number of free parameters by adding hidden units to the network. The algorithm stops adding hidden units when some validation criterion indicates that network performance is good enough.

We explore an alternative class of algorithms—called *metamorphosis algorithms*—for which the number of units is fixed, but heavy initial constraints are placed on the unit response properties. During learning, the constraints are gradually relaxed, increasing the flexibility of the network. Within this general framework, we develop a learning algorithm that builds the virtues of recursive partitioning strategies (Breiman et al., 1984; Friedman, 1991) into a Radial Basis Function (RBF) network architecture. We argue that this framework offers two primary advantages over constructive RBF networks: for problems with low input variable interaction, it can find solutions with far fewer free parameters, and it is less susceptible to noise in the training data. Other virtues include multiresolution processing and built-in interpolation of sparse training data.

Section 2 introduces notation for RBF networks and reviews the advantages of using these networks in constructive learning. Section 3 describes the idea behind metamorphosis algorithms and how they can be combined with RBF networks. Section 4 describes the advantages of this class of algorithm. The final section suggests directions for further research.

2 RBF NETWORKS

RBF networks have been used successfully for learning difficult input-output mappings such as phoneme recognition (Wettschereck & Dietterich, 1991), digit classification (Nowlan, 1990), and time series prediction (Moody & Darken, 1989; Platt, 1991). The basic architecture is shown in Figure 1. The response properties of each RBF unit are determined by a set of parameter values, which we'll call a *pset*. The pset for unit i, denoted $\mathbf{r}_i$, includes: the center location of the RBF unit in the input space, $\boldsymbol{\mu}_i^{\mathbf{r}}$; the width of the unit, $\sigma_i^{\mathbf{r}}$; and the strength of the connection(s) from the RBF unit to the output unit(s), $\mathbf{h}_i^{\mathbf{r}}$.

One reason why RBF networks work well with constructive algorithms is because the hidden units have the property of *noninterference*: the nature of their activation functions, typically Gaussian, allows new RBF units to be added without changing the global input-output mapping already learned by the network.

However, the advantages of constructive learning with RBF networks diminish for problems with high-dimensional input spaces (Hartman & Keeler, 1991). For these problems, a large number of RBF units are needed to cover the input space, even when the number of input dimensions relevant for the problem is small. The relevant input dimensions can be different for different parts of the input space, which limits the usefulness of a global estimation of input dimension relevance, as in Poggio and Girosi (1990). Metamorphosis algorithms, on the other hand, allow RBF networks to solve problems such as these without introducing a large number of free parameters.

3 METAMORPHOSIS ALGORITHMS

Metamorphosis networks contrast with constructive learning algorithms in that the number of units in the network remains fixed, but degrees of freedom are gradually added during learning. While metamorphosis networks have not been explored in the context of supervised learning, there is at least one instance of a metamorphosis network in unsupervised learning: a Kohonen net. Units in a Kohonen net are arranged on a lattice; updating the weights of a unit causes weight updates of the unit's neighbors. Units nearby on the lattice are thereby forced to have similar responses, reducing the effective number of free parameters in the network. In one variant of Kohonen net learning, the neighborhood of each unit gradually shrinks, increasing the degrees of freedom in the network.

3.1 MRBF NETWORKS

We have applied the concept of metamorphosis algorithms to ordinary RBF networks in supervised learning, yielding *MRBF networks*. Units are arranged on an n-dimensional lattice, where n is picked ahead of time and is unrelated to the dimensionality of the input space. The response of RBF unit i is constrained by deriving its pset, $\mathbf{r}_i$, from a collection of *underlying* psets, each denoted $\mathbf{u}_j$, that also reside on the lattice. The elements of $\mathbf{u}_j$ correspond to those of $\mathbf{r}_i$: $\mathbf{u}_j = (\boldsymbol{\mu}_j^{\mathbf{u}}, \sigma_j^{\mathbf{u}}, \mathbf{h}_j^{\mathbf{u}})$. Due to the orderly arrangement of the $\mathbf{u}_j$, the lattice is divided into nonoverlapping hyperrectangular regions that are bounded by 2^n $\mathbf{u}_j$. Consequently, each $\mathbf{r}_i$ is *enclosed* by 2^n $\mathbf{u}_j$. The pset $\mathbf{r}_i$ can then be derived by linear interpolation of the enclosing underlying psets $\mathbf{u}_j$, as shown in Figure 2 for a one-dimensional lattice.

Learning in MRBF networks proceeds by minimizing an error function E in the $\mathbf{u}_j$ components via gradient descent:

$$\Delta\mu_{jk}^{\mathbf{u}} = -\eta \sum_{i \in \mathrm{NEIGH}_j} \frac{\partial \mathrm{E}}{\partial \mu_{ik}^{\mathbf{r}}} \frac{\partial \mu_{ik}^{\mathbf{r}}}{\partial \mu_{jk}^{\mathbf{u}}}$$

where NEIGH_j is the set of RBF units whose values are affected by underlying pset j, and k indexes the input units of the network. The update expression is similar for $\sigma_j^{\mathbf{u}}$ and $\mathbf{h}_j^{\mathbf{u}}$. To better condition the search space, instead of optimizing the

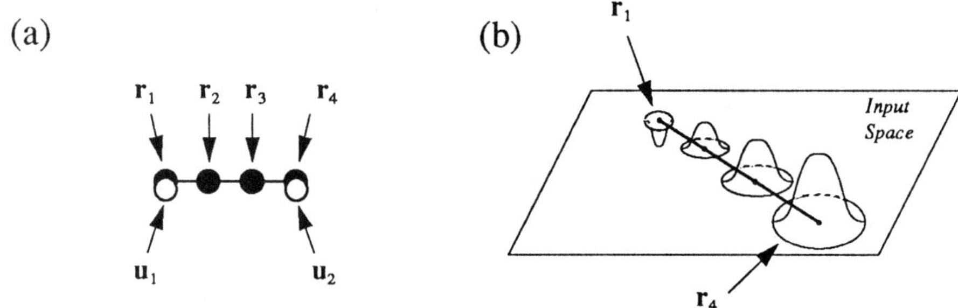

Figure 2: Constrained RBF units. (a) Four RBF units with psets $\mathbf{r}_1$–$\mathbf{r}_4$ are arranged on a one-dimensional lattice, enclosed by underlying psets $\mathbf{u}_1$ and $\mathbf{u}_2$. (b) An input space representation of the constrained RBF units. RBF center locations, widths, and heights are linearly interpolated.

$\sigma_i^{\mathbf{r}}$ directly, we follow Nowlan and Hinton's (1991) suggestion of computing each RBF unit width according to the transformation $\sigma_i^{\mathbf{r}} = exp(\gamma_i/2)$ and searching for the optimum value of γ_i. This forces RBF widths to remain positive and makes it difficult for a width to approach zero.

When a local optimum is reached, either learning is stopped or additional underlying psets are placed on the lattice in a process called *metamorphosis*.

3.2 METAMORPHOSIS

Metamorphosis is the process that gradually adds new degrees of freedom to the network during learning. For the MRBF network explored in this paper, introducing new free parameters corresponds to placing additional underlying psets on the lattice. The new psets split one hyperrectangular region—an n-dimensional sublattice bounded by 2^n underlying psets—into two nonoverlapping hyperrectangular regions. To achieve this, 2^{n-1} additional underlying psets, which we call the *split group*, are required (Figure 3). The splitting process implements a *recursive partitioning* strategy similar to the strategies employed in the CART (Breiman et al., 1984) and MARS (Friedman, 1991) statistical learning algorithms.

Many possible rules for region splitting exist. In the simulations presented later, we consider every possible region and every possible split of the region into two subregions. For each split group k, we compute the *tension* of the split, defined as

$$\sum_{j \in \text{split group } k} \left\| \frac{\partial E}{\partial \mathbf{u}_j} \right\|^2 .$$

We then select the split group that has the greatest tension. This heuristic is based on the assumption that the error gradient at the point in weight space where a split would take place reflects the long-term benefit of that split.

It may appear that this splitting process is computationally expensive, but it can be implemented quite efficiently; the cost of computing all possible splits and choosing

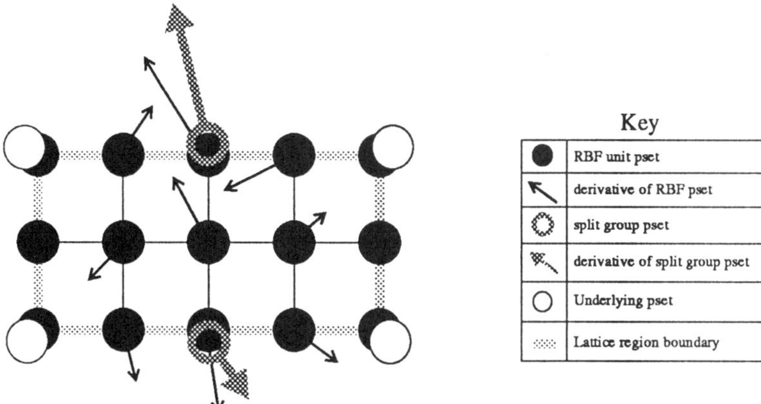

Figure 3: Computing the tension of a split group. Arrows are meant to represent derivatives of corresponding pset components.

the best one is linear in the number of RBF units on the lattice.

4 VIRTUES OF METAMORPHOSIS NETS

4.1 VARIABLE SUBSET SELECTION

One advantage of MRBF networks is that they can perform *variable subset selection*; that is, they can select a subset of input dimensions more relevant to the problem and ignore the other input dimensions. This is also a property of other recursive partitioning algorithms such as CART and MARS. In MRBF networks, however, region splitting occurs on a lattice structure, rather than in the input space. Consequently, the learning algorithm can orient a small number of regions to fit data that is not aligned with the lattice to begin with. CART and MARS have to create many regions to fit this kind of data (Friedman, 1991).

To see if this style of learning algorithm could learn to solve a difficult problem, we trained an MRBF network on the Mackey-Glass chaotic time series. Figure 4(a) compares normalized RMS error on the test set with Platt's (1991) RAN algorithm as the number of parameters increases during learning. Although RAN eventually finds a superior solution, the MRBF network requires a much smaller number of free parameters to find a reasonably accurate solution. This result agrees with the idea that ordinary RBF networks must use many free parameters to cover an input space with RBF units, whereas MRBF networks may use far fewer by concentrating resources on only the most relevant input dimensions.

4.2 ROBUST PARAMETER SELECTION

In RBF networks, the local response of a hidden unit makes it difficult for back propagation to move RBF centers far from where they are originally placed. Consequently, the choice of initial RBF center locations is critical for constructive al-

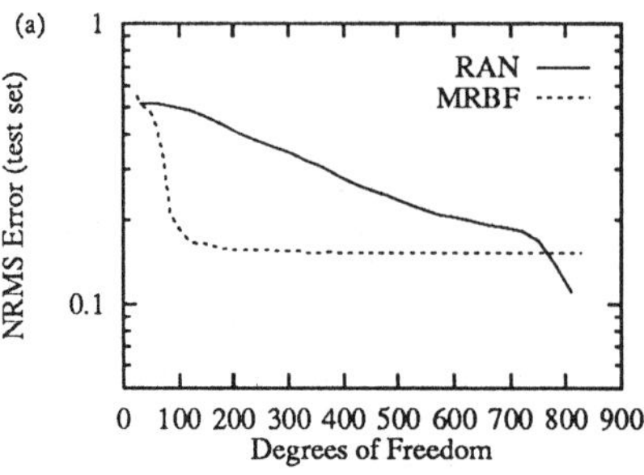

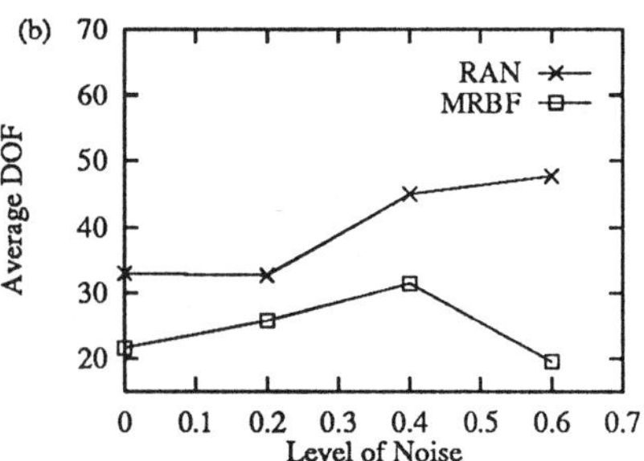

Figure 4: (a) Comparison on the Mackey-Glass chaotic time series. The curves for RAN and MRBF represent an average over ten and three simulation runs, respectively. The simulations used 300 training patterns and 500 test patterns as described in (Platt 1991). Simulation parameters for RAN match those reported in (Platt 1991) with $\epsilon = 0.02$. (b) Gaussian noise was added to the function $y = sin 8\pi x$, $0 < x < 1$, where the task was to predict y given x. The horizontal axis represents the standard deviation of the Gaussian distribution. For both algorithms, 20 simulations were run at each noise level. The number of degrees of freedom (DOF) needed to achieve a fixed error level was averaged.

gorithms. Poor choices could result in the allocation of more RBF units than are necessary. One apparent weakness of the RAN algorithm is that it chooses RBF center locations based on individual examples, which makes it susceptible to noise. Metamorphosis in MRBF networks, on the other hand, is based on the more global measure of tension.

Figure 4(b) shows the average number of degrees of freedom allocated by RAN and an MRBF network on a simple, one-dimensional function approximation task. Gaussian noise was added to the target output values in the training and test sets. As the amount of noise increases, the average number of free parameters allocated by RAN also increases, whereas for the MRBF network, the average remains low.

One interesting property of RAN is that allocating many extra RBF units does not necessarily hurt generalization performance. This is true when RAN starts with wide RBF units and decreases the widths of candidate RBF units slowly. The main disadvantage to this approach is wasted computational resources.

4.3 MULTIRESOLUTION PROCESSING

Our approach has the property of initially finding solutions sensitive to coarse problem features and using these solutions to find refinements more sensitive to finer features (Figure 5). This idea of *multiresolution processing* has been studied in the context of computer vision relaxation algorithms and is a property of algorithms proposed by other authors (e.g. Moody, 1989, Platt, 1991).

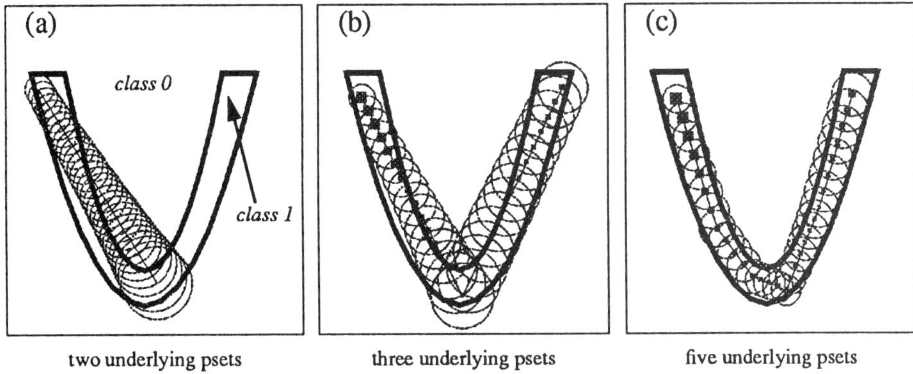

Figure 5: Example of multiresolution processing. The figure shows performance on a two-dimensional classification task, where the goal is to classify all inputs inside the U-shape as belonging to the same category. An MRBF network is constrained using a one-dimensional lattice. Circles represent RBF widths, and squares represent the height of each RBF.

4.4 INTERPOLATION OF SPARSE TRAINING DATA

For a problem with sparse training data, it is often necessary to make assumptions about the appropriate response at points in the input space far away from the training data. Like nearest-neighbor algorithms, MRBF networks have such an assumption built in. The constrained RBF units in the network serve to *interpolate* the values of underlying psets (Figure 6). Although ordinary RBF networks can, in principle, interpolate between sparse data points, the local response of an RBF unit makes it difficult to find this sort of solution by back propagation.

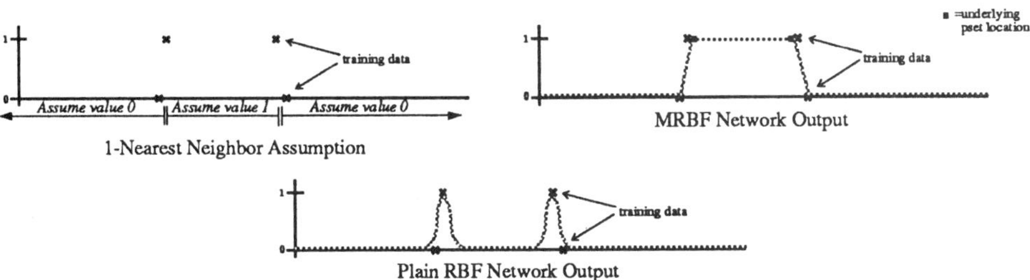

Figure 6: Assumptions made for sparse training data on a task with a one-dimensional input space and one-dimensional output space. Target output values are marked with an 'x'. Like nearest-neighbor algorithms, the assumption made by MRBF networks causes network response to interpolate between sparse data points. This assumption is not built into ordinary RBF networks.

5 DIRECTIONS FOR FURTHER RESEARCH

In our simulations to date, we have not observed astonishingly better generalization performance with metamorphosis nets than with alternative approaches, such as Platt's RAN algorithm. Nonetheless, we believe the approach worthy of further exploration. We've examined but one type of metamorphosis net and in only a few domains. The sorts of investigations we are considering next include: substituting finite-element basis functions for RBFs, implementing a "soft" version of the RBF pset constraint using regularization techniques, and using a supervised learning algorithm similar to Kohonen networks, where updating the weights of a unit causes weight updates of the unit's neighbors.

Acknowledgements

This research was supported by NSF PYI award IRI-9058450 and grant 90-21 from the James S. McDonnell Foundation. We thank John Platt for providing the Mackey-Glass time series data, and Chris Williams, Paul Smolensky, and the members of the Boulder Connectionist Research Group for helpful discussions.

References

L. Breiman, J. Friedman, R. A. Olsen & C. J. Stone. (1984) *Classification and Regression Trees.* Belmont, CA: Wadsworth.

S. E. Fahlman & C. Lebiere. (1990) The cascade-correlation learning architecture. In D. S. Touretzky (ed.), *Advances in Neural Information Processing Systems 2*, 524-532. San Mateo, CA: Morgan Kaufmann.

J. Friedman. (1991) Multivariate Adaptive Regression Splines. *Annals of Statistics* **19**:1-141.

S. Geman, E. Bienenstock & R. Doursat. (1992) Neural networks and the bias/variance dilemma. *Neural Computation* **4**(1):1-58.

E. Hartman & J. D. Keeler. (1991) Predicting the future: advantages of semilocal units. *Neural Computation* **3**(4):566-578.

T. Kohonen. (1982) Self-organized formation of topologically correct feature maps. *Biological Cybernetics* **43**:59-69.

J. Moody & C. Darken. (1989) Fast learning in networks of locally-tuned processing units. *Neural Computation* **1**(2):281-294.

J. Moody. (1989) Fast learning in multi-resolution hierarchies. In D. S. Touretzky (ed.), *Advances in Neural Information Processing 1*, 29-39. San Mateo, CA: Morgan Kaufmann.

S. J. Nowlan. (1990) Maximum likelihood competition in RBF networks. Tech. Rep. CRG-TR-90-2, Department of Computer Science, University of Toronto, Toronto, Canada.

S. J. Nowlan & G. Hinton. (1991) Adaptive soft weight-tying using Gaussian Mixtures. In Moody, Hanson, & Lippmann (eds.), *Advances in Neural Information Processing 4*, 993-1000. San Mateo, CA: Morgan-Kaufmann.

J. Platt. (1991) A resource-allocating network for function interpolation. *Neural Computation* **3**(2):213-225.

T. Poggio & F. Girosi. (1990) Regularization algorithms for learning that are equivalent to multilayer networks. *Science* **247**:978-982.

D. Wettschereck & T. Dietterich. (1991) Improving the performance of radial basis function networks by learning center locations. In Moody, Hanson, & Lippmann (eds.), *Advances in Neural Info. Processing 4*, 1133-1140. San Mateo, CA: Morgan Kaufmann.

A Boundary Hunting Radial Basis Function Classifier Which Allocates Centers Constructively

Eric I. Chang and Richard P. Lippmann
MIT Lincoln Laboratory
Lexington, MA 02173-0073, USA

Abstract

A new boundary hunting radial basis function (BH-RBF) classifier which allocates RBF centers constructively near class boundaries is described. This classifier creates complex decision boundaries only in regions where confusions occur and corresponding RBF outputs are similar. A predicted square error measure is used to determine how many centers to add and to determine when to stop adding centers. Two experiments are presented which demonstrate the advantages of the BH-RBF classifier. One uses artificial data with two classes and two input features where each class contains four clusters but only one cluster is near a decision region boundary. The other uses a large seismic database with seven classes and 14 input features. In both experiments the BH-RBF classifier provides a lower error rate with fewer centers than are required by more conventional RBF, Gaussian mixture, or MLP classifiers.

1 INTRODUCTION

Radial basis function (RBF) classifiers have been successfully applied to many pattern classification problems (Broomhead, 1988, Ng, 1991). These classifiers have the advantages of short training times and high classification accuracy. In addition, RBF outputs estimate minimum-error Bayesian *a posteriori* probabilities (Richard, 1991). Performing classification with RBF outputs requires selecting the output which is highest for each input. In regions where one class dominates, the Bayesian *a posteriori* probability for that class will be uniformly "high" and near 1.0. Detailed modeling of the variation of the Bayesian *a posteriori* probability in these regions is not necessary for classification. Only at the boundary between different classes is accurate estimation of the Bayesian *a posteriori* probability necessary for high classification accuracy. If the boundary between different classes can be located in the input space, RBF centers can be judiciously allocated in those regions without wasting RBF centers in regions where accurate estimation of the Bayesian *a posteriori* probability does not improve classification performance.

In general, having more RBF centers allows better approximation of the desired output. While training a RBF classifier, the number of RBF centers must be selected. The traditional approach has been to randomly choose patterns from the training set as centers, or to perform *K*-means clustering on the data and then to use these centers as the RBF centers. Frequently the correct number of centers to use is not known *a priori* and the number of centers has to be tuned. Also, with *K*-means clustering, the centers are distributed without considering their usefulness in classification. In contrast, a constructive approach to adding RBF centers based on modeling Bayesian *a posteriori* probabilities accurately only near class boundaries provides good performance with fewer centers than are required to separately model class PDF's.

Many algorithms have been proposed for constructively building up the structure of a RBF network (Mel, 1991). However, the algorithms proposed have all been designed for training a RBF network to perform function mapping. For mapping tasks, accuracy is important throughout the input region and the mean squared error is the criterion that is minimized. In classification tasks, only boundaries between different classes are important and the overall mean squared error is not as important as the error in class boundaries.

2 ALGORITHM DESCRIPTION

A block diagram of a new boundary hunting RBF (BH-RBF) classifier that adds centers constructively near class boundaries is presented in Figure 1. A simple unimodal Gaussian classifier is first formed by clustering the training patterns from a randomly selected class and assigning a center to that class. The confusion matrix generated by using this simple classifier is then examined to determine the pair of classes *A* and *B*, which have the most mutual confusion. Training patterns that are close to the boundary between these two classes are determined by looking at the outputs of the RBF classifier. Boundary patterns

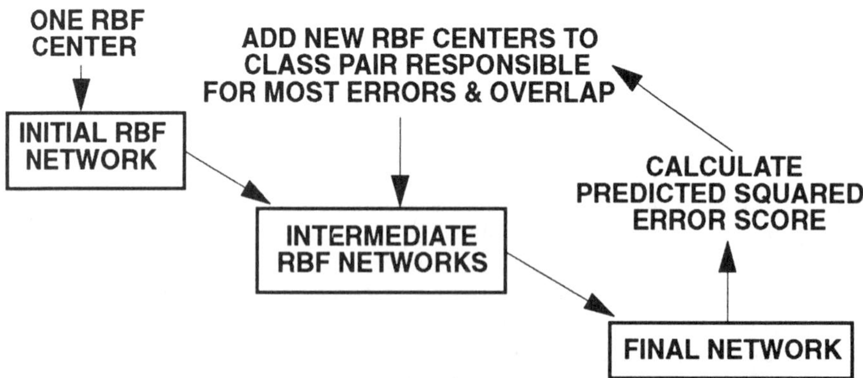

Figure 1: Block Diagram of Training of BH-RBF Network

which produce similar "high" outputs for both classes that are different by less than a "closecall" threshold are used to produce new cluster centers.

Figure 2 shows RBF outputs corresponding to class A and B as the input varies over a small range. This figure illustrates how network outputs are used to determine the "closecall" region between classes. Network outputs are high in regions dominated by a particular class and therefore these regions are outside the boundary between different classes. Network outputs are close in the region where the absolute difference of the two highest network outputs is less than the closecall threshold. Training patterns which fall into this closecall region plus all the points that are misclassified as the other class in the class pair are considered to be points in the boundary. For example, a pattern in class A which is misclassified as class B would be considered to be in the boundary between class A and B. On the other hand, a pattern in class A which is misclassified as class C would not be placed in the boundary between class A and B.

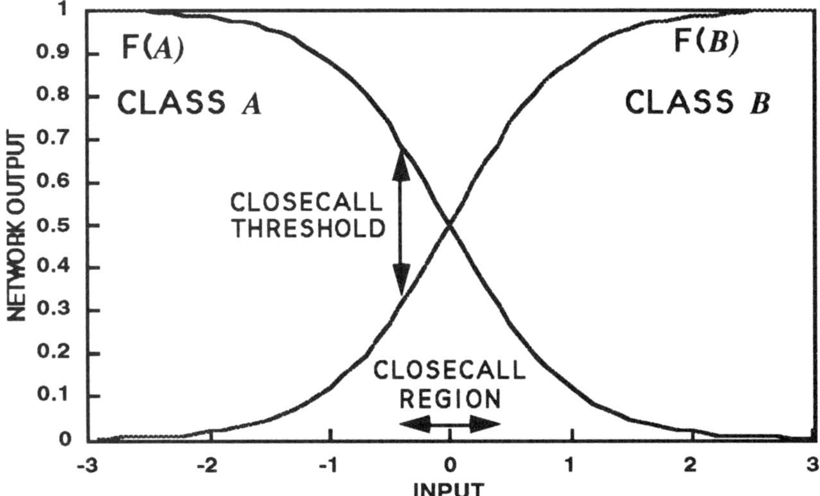

Figure 2: Using the Network Output to Determine Closecall Regions

After the patterns which belong in the boundary are determined, clustering is performed separately on boundary patterns from different classes using K-means clustering and a number of centers ranging from zero to a preset maximum number of centers. After the centers are found, new RBF classifiers are trained using the new sets of centers plus the original set of centers. The combined set of centers that provides the best performance is saved and the cycle repeats again by finding the next class pair which accounts for the most remaining confusions. Overfitting by adding too many centers at a time is avoided by using the predicted squared error (PSE) as the criterion for choosing new centers (Barron, 1984):

$$PSE = RMS + \frac{C \times \sigma^2}{N} \quad .$$

In this equation, *RMS* is the root mean squared error on the training set, σ^2 estimates the variance of the error, C is the total number of centers in the RBF classifier, and N is the total number of patterns in the training set. The error variance σ^2 is selected empirically using left-out evaluation data. Different values of σ^2 are tried and the value which provides the best performance on the evaluation data is chosen. On each cycle, different number of centers are tried for each class of the selected class pair and the PSE is used to select the best subset of centers. The best PSE on each cycle is used to determine when training should be stopped to prevent overfitting. Training stops after the PSE has not decreased for five consecutive cycles.

3 EXPERIMENTAL RESULTS

Two experiments were performed using the new BH-RBF classifier, a more conventional RBF classifier, a Gaussian mixture classifier (Ng, 1991), and a MLP classifier. Five regular RBF classifiers (RBF) were trained by assigning 1, 2, 3, 4, or 5 centers to each class. Similarly, five Gaussian mixture classifiers (GMIX) were trained with 1, 2, 3, 4, or 5 centers in each class. The means of each center were trained individually using K-means clustering to find the centers for patterns from each class. The diagonal covariance of each center was set using all the patterns that were assigned to a cluster during the last pass of K-means clustering. The structure of the regular RBF classifier and the Gaussian mixture classifier are identical when the number of centers are the same. The only difference between the classifiers is the method used to train parameters.

MLP classifiers were trained for 10 independent trials for each data set. The number of hidden nodes was varied from 2 to 30 in increments of 2. The goal of the experiment was to explore the relationship between the complexity of the classifier and the classification accuracy of the classifier. Training was stopped using cross validation to avoid overfitting.

3.1 FOUR-CLUSTER DATABASE

The first problem is an artificial data set designed to illustrate the difference between BH-RBF and other classifiers. There are two classes, each class consist of one large Gaussian cluster with 700 random points and three smaller clusters with 100 points each. Figure 3 shows the distribution of the data and the ideal decision boundary if the actual centers and variances are used to train a Bayesian minimum error classifier. There were 2000 training patterns, 2000 evaluation patterns, and 2000 test patterns. The BH-RBF classifier was trained with the closecall threshold set to 0.75, σ^2 set to 0.5, and a maximum of two extra centers per class at between each pair of classes. The theoretically optimal Bayesian classifier for this database provides the error rate of 1.95% on the test set. This optimal Bayesian classifier is obtained using the actual centers, variances, and *a priori* probability used to generate the data in a Gaussian mixture classifier. In a real classification task, these center parameters are not known and have to be estimated from training data.

Figure 4 shows the testing error rate of the three different classifiers. The BH-RBF classifier was able to achieve 2.35% error rate with only 5 centers and the error rate gradually decreased to 2.15% with 15 centers. The BH-RBF classifier performed well with few centers because it allocated these centers near the boundary between the two classes. On the other hand, the performance of the RBF classifier and the Gaussian mixture classifier was worse with few centers. These classifiers performed worse because they allocated centers

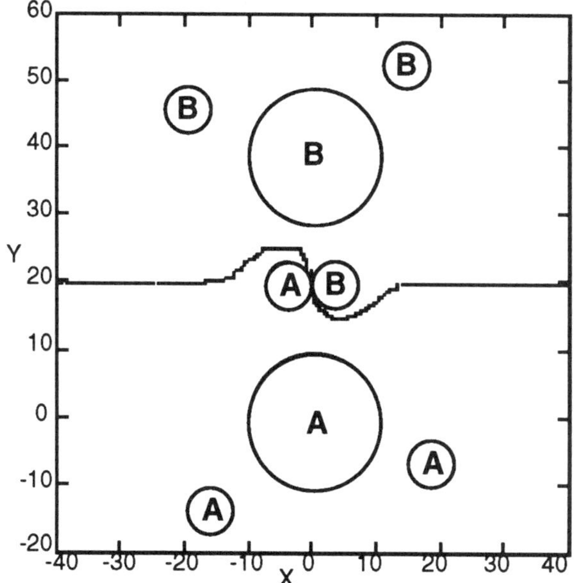

Figure 3: The Artificially Generated Four-Cluster Problem

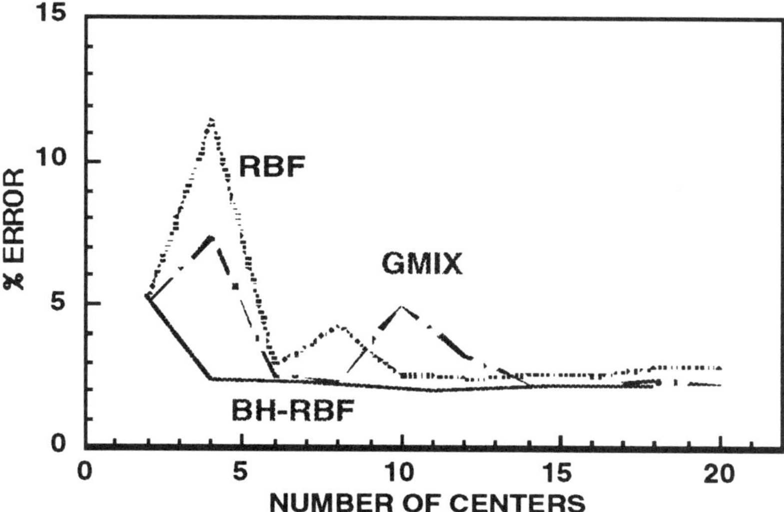

Figure 4: Testing Error Rate Of The BH-RBF Classifier, The Gaussian Mixture Classifier, And The Regular RBF Classifier On The Four-Cluster Problem.

in regions that had many patterns. The training algorithm did not distinguish between patterns that are easily confusable between classes (i.e. near the class boundary) and patterns that clearly belong in a given class. Furthermore, adding more centers did not monotonically decrease the error rate. For example, the RBF classifier had 5% error using two centers, but when the number of centers was increased to four, the error rate jumped to 11%. Only until the number of centers increased above 14 did the RBF classifier and the Gaussian mixture classifier's error rates converge. The RBF and the Gaussian mixture classifiers performed poorly with few centers because the centers were concentrated away from the decision boundary due to the high concentration of data far away from the boundary. Thus, there weren't enough centers to model the decision boundary accurately. The BH-RBF classifier added centers near the boundary and thus was able to define an accurate boundary with fewer centers.

Figure 5 presents the results from training MLP classifiers on the same data set using different numbers of hidden nodes. The learning rate was set to 0.001, the momentum term was set to 0.6, and each classifier was trained for 100 epochs. The error rate on a left out evaluation set was checked to assure that the net had not overfitted the training data. As the number of hidden nodes increased, the MLP classifier generally performed better. However, the testing error rate did not decrease monotonically as the number of hidden nodes increased. Furthermore, the random initial condition set by the different random seeds affected the classification error rate of each classifier. In comparison, the training algorithms used for BH-RBF, RBF, and GMIX classifiers do not exhibit such sensitivity to initial conditions.

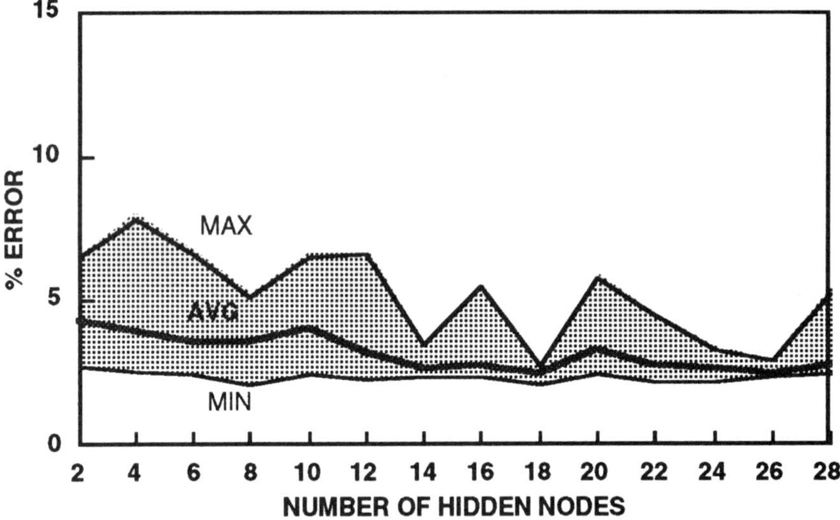

Figure 5: Testing Error Rate Of The MLP Classifiers On The Four-Cluster Problem

3.2 SEISMIC DATABASE

The second problem consists of data for classification of seismic events. The input consist of 14 continuous and binary measurements derived from seismic waveform signals. These features are used to classify a waveform as belonging to one of 7 classes which represent different seismic phases. There were 3038 training, 3033 evaluation, and 3034 testing pat-

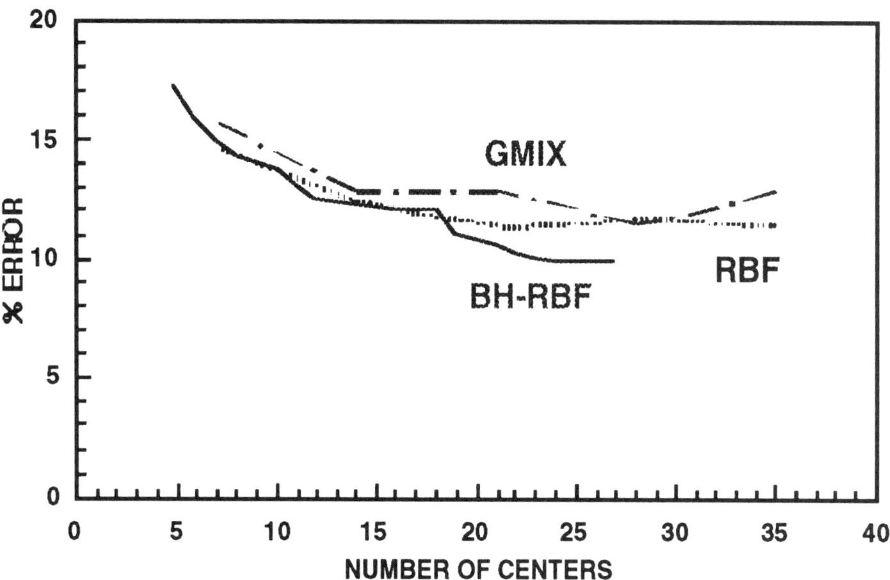

Figure 6: Error Rate Comparison Between The BH-RBF Classifier, The Regular RBF Classifier, And The Gaussian Mixture Classifier On The Seismic Problem

terns. Once again, the number of centers per class was varied from 1 to 5 for the regular RBF classifier and the Gaussian mixture classifier, while the BH-RBF classifier was started with 1 center in the first class and then more centers were automatically assigned. The BH-RBF classifier was trained with the closecall threshold set to 0.75, σ^2 set to 0.5, and a maximum of one extra center per class at each boundary. The parameters were chosen according to the performance of the classifier on the left-out evaluation data. For this problem, the closecall threshold and σ^2 turned out to be the same as the ones used in the four-cluster problem.

Figure 6 shows the error rate on the testing patterns for all three classifiers. The BH-RBF classifier clearly performed better than the regular RBF classifier and the Gaussian mixture classifier. The BH-RBF classifier added centers only at the boundary region where they improved discrimination. Also, the diagonal covariance of the added centers are more local in their influence and can improve discrimination of a particular boundary without affecting other decision region boundaries.

MLP classifiers were also trained on this data set with the number of hidden nodes varying from 2 to 32 in increments of 2. The learning rate was set to 0.001, the momentum term was set to 0.6, and each classifier was trained for 100 epochs. The classification error rate on the left-out evaluation set showed that the network had not overfitted on the training data. Once more, the MLP classifiers exhibited great sensitivity to initial conditions, especially when the number of hidden nodes were small. Also, for this high dimensionality classification task, even the best performance of the MLP classifier (15.5%) did not match the best performance of the BH-RBF classifier. This result suggests that for this high dimensionality data, the radially symmetric boundaries formed with local basis functions such as the RBF classifier are more appropriate than the ridge-like boundaries formed with the MLP classifier.

4 CONCLUSION

A new boundary-hunting RBF classifier was developed which adds RBF centers constructively near boundaries of classes which produce classification confusions. Experimental results from two problems differing in input dimension, number of classes, and difficulty show that the BH-RBF classifier performed better than traditional training algorithms used for RBF, Gaussian mixture, and MLP classifiers. Experiments have also been conducted on other problems such as Peterson and Barney's vowel database and the disjoint database used by Ng (Peterson, 1952, Ng, 1990). In all experiments, the BH-RBF constructive algorithm performed at least as well as the traditional RBF training algorithm. These results, and the experiments described above, confirm the hypothesis that better discrimination performance can be achieved by training a classifier to perform discrimination instead of probability density function estimation.

Acknowledgments

This work was supported by DARPA. The views expressed are those of the authors and do not reflect the official policy or position of the U.S. Government. Experiments were conducted using *LNKnet*, a general purpose classifier program developed at Lincoln Laboratory by Richard Lippmann, Dave Nation, and Linda Kukolich.

References

G. E. Peterson and H. L. Barney. (1952) Control Methods Used in a Study of Vowels. *The Journal of the Acoustical Society of America* **24:2**, 175-84.

A. Barron. (1984) Predicted squared error: a criterion for automatic model selection. In S. Farlow, Editor. *Self-Organizing Methods in Modeling*. New York, Marcel Dekker.

D. S. Broomhead and D. Lowe. (1988) *Radial Basis Functions, multi-variable functional interpolation and adaptive networks*. Technical Report RSRE Memorandum No. 4148, Royal Speech and Radar Establishment, Malvern, Worcester, Great Britain.

B. W. Mel and S. M. Omohundro. (1991) How Receptive Field Parameters Affect Neural Learning. In R. Lippmann, J. Moody and D. Touretzky (Eds.), *Advances in Neural Information Processing Systems 3*, 1991. San Mateo, CA: Morgan Kaufman.

K. Ng and R. Lippmann. (1991) A Comparative Study of the Practical Characteristics of Neural Networks and Conventional Pattern Classifiers. In R. Lippmann, J. Moody and D. Touretzky (Eds.), *Advances in Neural Information Processing Systems 3*, 1991. San Mateo, CA: Morgan Kaufman.

M.D. Richard and R. P. Lippmann. (1991) Neural Network Classifier Estimates Bayesian *a posteriori* Probabilities. *Neural Computation*, Volume 3, Number 4.

Automatic Capacity Tuning of Very Large VC-dimension Classifiers

I. Guyon
AT&T Bell Labs,
50 Fremont st., 6th floor,
San Francisco, CA 94105
isabelle@neural.att.com

B. Boser*
EECS Department,
University of California,
Berkeley, CA 94720
boser@eecs.berkeley.edu

V. Vapnik
AT&T Bell Labs,
Room 4G-314,
Holmdel, NJ 07733
vlad@neural.att.com

Abstract

Large VC-dimension classifiers can learn difficult tasks, but are usually impractical because they generalize well only if they are trained with huge quantities of data. In this paper we show that even high-order polynomial classifiers in high dimensional spaces can be trained with a small amount of training data and yet generalize better than classifiers with a smaller VC-dimension. This is achieved with a maximum margin algorithm (the Generalized Portrait). The technique is applicable to a wide variety of classifiers, including Perceptrons, polynomial classifiers (sigma-pi unit networks) and Radial Basis Functions. The effective number of parameters is adjusted automatically by the training algorithm to match the complexity of the problem. It is shown to equal the number of those training patterns which are closest patterns to the decision boundary (supporting patterns). Bounds on the generalization error and the speed of convergence of the algorithm are given. Experimental results on handwritten digit recognition demonstrate good generalization compared to other algorithms.

1 INTRODUCTION

Both experimental evidence and theoretical studies [1] link the generalization of a classifier to the error on the training examples and the capacity of the classifier.

*Part of this work was done while B. Boser was at AT&T Bell Laboratories. He is now at the University of California, Berkeley.

Classifiers with a large number of adjustable parameters, and therefore large capacity, likely learn the training set without error, but exhibit poor generalization. Conversely, a classifier with insufficient capacity might not be able to learn the task at all. The goal of capacity tuning methods is to find the optimal capacity which minimizes the expected generalization error for a given amount of training data.

Capacity tuning techniques include: starting with a low capacity system and allocating more parameters as needed or starting with an large capacity system and eliminating unnecessary adjustable parameters with regularization. The first method requires searching in the space of classifier structures which possibly contains many local minima. The second method is computationally inefficient since it does not avoid adjusting a large number of parameters although the effective number of parameters may be small.

With the method proposed in this paper, the capacity of some very large VC-dimension classifiers is adjusted automatically in the process of training. The problem is formulated as a quadratic programming problem which has a single global minimum. Only the effective parameters get adjusted during training which ensures computational efficiency.

1.1 MAXIMUM MARGIN AND SUPPORTING PATTERNS

Here is a familiar problem: Given is a limited number of training examples from two classes A and B; find the linear decision boundary which yields best generalization performance. When the training data is scarce, there exists usually many errorless separations (figure 1.1). This is especially true when the dimension of input space (i.e. the number of tunable parameters) is large compared to the number of training examples. The question arises which of these solutions to choose? The one solution that achieves the largest possible margin between the decision boundary and the training patterns (figure 1.2) is optimal in the "minimax" sense [2] (see section 2.2). This choice is intuitively justifiable: a new example from class A is likely to fall within or near the convex envelope of the examples of class A (and similarly for class B). By providing the largest possible "safety" margin, we minimize the chances that examples from class A and B cross the border to the wrong side.

An important property of the maximum margin solution is that it is only dependent upon a restricted number of training examples, called supporting patterns (or informative patterns). These are those examples which lie on the margin and therefore are closest to the decision boundary (figure 1.2). The number m of linearly independent supporting patterns satisfies the inequality:

$$m \leq \min(N+1, p). \tag{1}$$

In this inequality, $(N+1)$ is the number of adjustable parameters and equals the Vapnik-Chervonenkis dimension (VC-dimension) [2], and p is the number of training examples. In reference [3], we show that the generalization error is bounded by m/p and therefore m is a measure of complexity of the learning problem. Because m is bounded by p and is generally a lot smaller than p, the maximum margin solution obtains good generalization even when the problem is grossly underdetermined, i.e. the number of training patterns p is much smaller than the number of adjustable parameters, $N+1$. In section 2.3 we show that the existence of supporting patterns is advantageous for computational reasons as well.

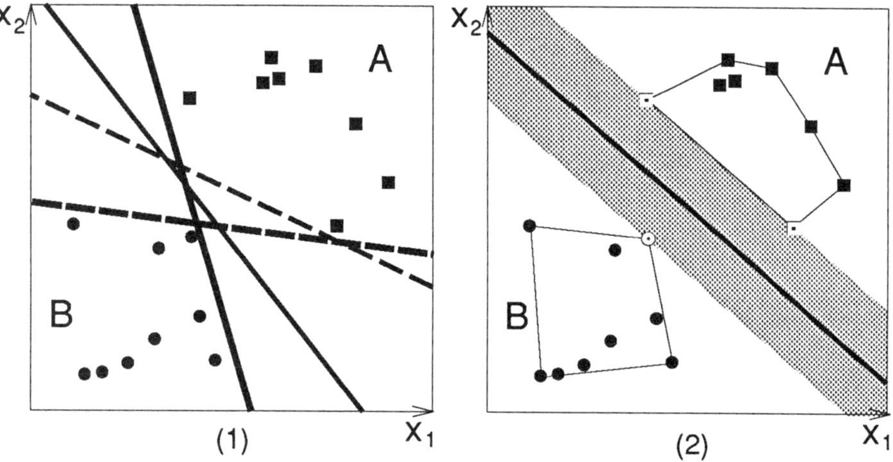

Figure 1: **Linear separations.**
(1) When many linear decision rules separate the training set, which one to choose?
(2) The maximum margin solution. The distance to the decision boundary of the closest training patterns is maximized. The grey shading indicates the margin area in which no pattern falls. The supporting patterns (in white) lie on the margin.

1.2 NON-LINEAR CLASSIFIERS

Although algorithms that maximize the margin between classes have been known for many years [4, 2], they have for computational reasons so far been limited to the special case of finding linear separations and consequently to relatively simple classification problems. In this paper, we present an extension to one of these maximum margin training algorithms called the "Generalized Portrait Method" (*GP*) [2] to various non-linear classifiers, including including Perceptrons, polynomial classifiers (sigma-pi unit networks) and kernel classifiers (Radial Basis Functions) (figure 2). The new algorithm trains efficiently very high VC-dimension classifiers with a huge number of tunable parameters. Despite the large number of free parameters, the solution exhibits good generalization due to the inherent regularization of the maximum margin cost function.

As an example, let us consider the case of a second order polynomial classifier. Its decision surface is described by the following equation:

$$\sum_i w_i x_i + \sum_{i,j} w_{ij} x_i x_j + b = 0. \qquad (2)$$

he w_i, w_{ij} and b are adjustable parameters, and x_i are the coordinates of a pattern $\mathbf{x}$. If n is the dimension of input pattern $\mathbf{x}$, the number of adjustable parameters of the second order polynomial classifier is $[n(n+1)/2]+1$. In general, the number of adjustable parameters of a qth order polynomial is of the order of $N \approx n^q$.

The GP algorithm has been tested on the problem of handwritten digit recognition. The input patterns consist of 16×16 pixel images ($n = 256$). The results achieved

q	N	$DB1$ (p=600) error	<m>	$DB2$ (p=7300) error	<m>
1 (linear)	256	3.2 %	36	10.5 %	97
2	$3 \cdot 10^4$	1.5 %	44	5.8 %	89
3	$8 \cdot 10^7$	1.7 %	50	5.2 %	79
4	$4 \cdot 10^9$			4.9 %	72
5	$1 \cdot 10^{12}$			5.2 %	69

Table 1: **Handwritten digit recognition experiments.** The first database ($DB1$) consists of 1200 clean images recorded from ten subjects. Half of this data is used for training, and the other half is used to evaluate the generalization performance. The other database ($DB2$) consists of 7300 images for training and 2000 for testing and has been recorded from actual mail pieces. We use ten polynomial classification functions of order q, separating one class against all others. We list the number N of adjustable parameters, the error rates on the test set and the average number <m>of supporting patterns per separating hypersurface. The results compare favorably to neural network classifiers which minimize the mean squared error with backpropagation. For the one layer network (linear classifier),the error on the test set is 12.7 % on $DB1$ and larger than 25 % on $DB2$. The lowest error rate for $DB2$, 4.9 %, obtained with a forth order polynomial, is comparable to the 5.1 % error obtained with a multi-layer neural network with sophisticated architecture being trained and tested on the same data [6].

with polynomial classifiers of order q are summarized in table 1. Also listed is the number of adjustable parameters, N. This quantity increases rapidly with q and quickly reaches a level that is computationally intractable for algorithms that explicitly compute each parameter [5]. Moreover, as N increases, the learning problem becomes grossly underdetermined: the number of training patterns ($p = 600$ for $DB1$ and $p = 7300$ for $DB2$) becomes very small compared to N. Nevertheless, good generalization is achieved as shown by the experimental results listed in the table. This is a consequence of the inherent regularization of the algorithm.

An important concern is the sensitivity of the maximum margin solution to the presence of outliers in the training data. It is indeed important to remove undesired outliers (such as meaningless or mislabeled patterns) to get best generalization performance. Conversely, "good" outliers (such as examples of rare styles) must be kept. Cleaning techniques have been developed based on the re-examination by a human supervisor of those supporting patterns which result in the largest increase of the margin when removed, and thus, are the most likely candidates for outliers [3]. In our experiments on $DB2$ with linear classifiers, the error rate on the test set dropped from 15.2% to 10.5% after cleaning the training data (not the test data).

2 ALGORITHM DESIGN

The properties of the GP algorithm arise from merging two separate ideas: Training in *dual space*, and minimizing the maximum loss. For large VC-dimension classifiers ($N \gg p$), the first idea reduces the number of *effective* parameters to be actually computed from N to p. The second idea reduces it from p to m.

2.1 DUALITY

We seek a decision function for pattern vectors $\mathbf{x}$ of dimension n belonging to either of two classes A and B. The input to the training algorithm is a set of p examples $\mathbf{x}_i$ with labels y_i:

$$(\mathbf{x}_1, y_1),\ (\mathbf{x}_2, y_2),\ (\mathbf{x}_3, y_3),\ \ldots,\ (\mathbf{x}_p, y_p) \tag{3}$$

$$\text{where } \begin{cases} y_k = 1 & \text{if } \mathbf{x}_k \in \text{class A} \\ y_k = -1 & \text{if } \mathbf{x}_k \in \text{class B.} \end{cases}$$

From these training examples the algorithm finds the parameters of the decision function $D(\mathbf{x})$ during a learning phase. After training, the classification of unknown patterns is predicted according to the following rule:

$$\begin{array}{ll} \mathbf{x} \in \text{A} & \text{if } D(\mathbf{x}) > 0 \\ \mathbf{x} \in \text{B} & \text{otherwise.} \end{array} \tag{4}$$

We limit ourselves to classifiers linear in their parameters, but not restricted to linear dependences in their input components, such as Perceptrons and kernel-based classifiers. Perceptrons [5] have a decision function defined as:

$$D(\mathbf{x}) = \mathbf{w} \cdot \varphi(\mathbf{x}) + b = \sum_{i=1}^{N} w_i \varphi_i(\mathbf{x}) + b, \tag{5}$$

where the φ_i are predefined functions of $\mathbf{x}$, and the w_i and b are the adjustable parameters of the decision function. This definition encompasses that of polynomial classifiers. In that particular case, the φ_i are products of components of vector $\mathbf{x}$(see equation 2). Kernel-based classifiers, have a decision function defined as:

$$D(\mathbf{x}) = \sum_{k=1}^{p} \alpha_k K(\mathbf{x}_k, \mathbf{x}) + b, \tag{6}$$

The coefficients α_k and the bias b are the parameters to be adjusted and the $\mathbf{x}_k$ are the training patterns. The function K is a predefined kernel, for example a potential function [7] or any Radial Basis Function (see for instance [8]).

Perceptrons and RBF's are often considered two very distinct approaches to classification. However, for a number of training algorithms, the resulting decision function can be cast either in the form of equation (5) or (6). This has been pointed out in the literature for the Perceptron and potential function algorithms [7], for the polynomial classifiers trained with pseudo-inverse [9] and more recently for regularization algorithms and RBF's [8]. In those cases, Perceptrons and RBF's constitute *dual* representations of the same decision function.

The duality principle can be understood simply in the case of Hebb's learning rule. The weight vector of a linear Perceptron ($\varphi_i(\mathbf{x}) = x_i$), trained with Hebb's rule, is simply the average of all training patterns $\mathbf{x}_k$, multiplied by their class membership polarity y_k:

$$\mathbf{w} = \frac{1}{p} \sum_{k=1}^{p} y_k \mathbf{x}_k \ .$$

Substituting this solution into equation (5), we obtain the dual representation

$$D(\mathbf{x}) = \mathbf{w} \cdot \mathbf{x} + b = \frac{1}{p} \sum_{k=1}^{p} y_k \; \mathbf{x}_k \cdot \mathbf{x} + b \; .$$

The corresponding kernel classifier has kernel $K(\mathbf{x}, \mathbf{x}') = \mathbf{x} \cdot \mathbf{x}'$ and the dual parameters α_k are equal to $(1/p) y_k$.

In general, a training algorithm for Perceptron classifiers admits a dual kernel representation if its solution is a linear combination of the training patterns in φ-space:

$$\mathbf{w} = \sum_{k=1}^{p} \alpha_k \varphi(\mathbf{x}_k) \; . \tag{7}$$

Reciprocally, a kernel classifier admits a dual Perceptron representation if the kernel function possesses a finite (or infinite) expansion of the form:

$$K(\mathbf{x}, \mathbf{x}') = \sum_{i} \varphi_i(\mathbf{x}) \, \varphi_i(\mathbf{x}') \; . \tag{8}$$

Such is the case for instance for some symmetric kernels [10]. Examples of kernels that we have been using include

$$\begin{array}{lcll}
K(\mathbf{x}, \mathbf{x}') & = & (\mathbf{x} \cdot \mathbf{x}' + 1)^q & \text{(polynomial of order q)}, \\
K(\mathbf{x}, \mathbf{x}') & = & \tanh(\gamma \, \mathbf{x} \cdot \mathbf{x}') & \text{(neural units)}, \\
K(\mathbf{x}, \mathbf{x}') & = & \exp(\gamma \, \mathbf{x} \cdot \mathbf{x}') \; - \; 1 & \text{(exponential)}, \\
K(\mathbf{x}, \mathbf{x}') & = & \exp\left(-||\mathbf{x} - \mathbf{x}'||^2 / \gamma\right) & \text{(gaussian RBF)}, \\
K(\mathbf{x}, \mathbf{x}') & = & \exp\left(-||\mathbf{x} - \mathbf{x}'|| / \gamma\right) & \text{(exponential RBF)}, \\
K(\mathbf{x}, \mathbf{x}') & = & (\mathbf{x} \cdot \mathbf{x}' + 1)^q \exp\left(-||\mathbf{x} - \mathbf{x}'|| / \gamma\right) & \text{(mixed polynomial \& RBF)}.
\end{array} \tag{9}$$

These kernels have positive parameters (the integer q or the real number γ) which can be determined with a Structural Risk Minimization or Cross-Validation procedure (see for instance [2]). More elaborate kernels incorporating known invariances of the data could be used also.

The *GP* algorithm computes the maximum margin solution in the kernel representation. This is crucial for making the computation tractable when training very large VC-dimension classifiers. Training a classifier in the kernel representation is computationally advantageous when the dimension N of vectors $\mathbf{w}$ (or the VC-dimension $N+1$) is large compared to the number of parameters α_k, which equals the number of training patterns p. This is always true if the kernel function possesses an infinite expansions (8). The experimental results listed in table 1 indicate that this argument holds in practice even for low order polynomial expansions when the dimension n of input space is sufficiently large.

2.2 MINIMIZING THE MAXIMUM LOSS

The margin, defined as the Euclidean distance between the decision boundary and the closest training patterns in φ-space can be computed as

$$M = \min_{k} \frac{y_k D(\mathbf{x}_k)}{||\mathbf{w}||} \; . \tag{10}$$

The goal of the maximum margin training algorithm is to find the decision function $D(\mathbf{x})$ which maximizes M, that is the solution of the optimization problem

$$\max_{\mathbf{w}} \min_{k} \frac{y_k D(\mathbf{x}_k)}{||\mathbf{w}||} . \tag{11}$$

The solution $\mathbf{w}$ of this problem depends only on those patterns which are on the margin, i.e. the ones that are closest to the decision boundary, called supporting patterns. It can be shown that $\mathbf{w}$ can indeed be represented as a linear combination of the supporting patterns in φ-space [4, 2, 3] (see section 2.3).

In the classical framework of loss minimization, problem 11 is equivalent to minimizing (over $\mathbf{w}$) the maximum loss. The loss function is defined as

$$l(\mathbf{x}_k) = -y_k D(\mathbf{x}_k)/||\mathbf{w}||.$$

This "minimax" approach contrasts with training algorithms which minimize the average loss. For example, backpropagation minimizes the mean squared error (MSE), which is the average of

$$l(\mathbf{x}_k) = (D(\mathbf{x}_k) - y_k)^2 .$$

The benefit of minimax algorithms is that the solution is a function only of a restricted number of training patterns, namely the supporting patterns. This results in high computational efficiency in those cases when the number m of supporting patterns is small compared to both the total number of training patterns p and the dimension N of φ-space.

2.3 THE GENERALIZED PORTRAIT

The *GP* algorithm consists in formulating the problem 11 in the dual α-space as the quadratic programming problem of maximizing the cost function

$$J(\alpha, b) = \sum_{k=1}^{p} \alpha_k (1 - b y_k) - \frac{1}{2}\alpha \cdot H \cdot \alpha,$$

under the constrains $\alpha_k > 0$ [4, 2]. The $p \times p$ square matrix H has elements:

$$H_{kl} = y_k y_l K(\mathbf{x}_k, \mathbf{x}_l).$$

where $K(\mathbf{x}, \mathbf{x}')$ is a kernel, such as the ones proposed in (9), which can be expanded as in (8). Examples are shown in figure 2. $K(\mathbf{x}, \mathbf{x}')$ is not restricted to the dot product $K(\mathbf{x}, \mathbf{x}') = \mathbf{x} \cdot \mathbf{x}'$ as in the original formulation of the *GP* algorithm [2].

In order for a unique solution to exist, H must be positive definite. The bias b can be either fixed or optimized together with the parameters α_k. This case introduces another set of constraints: $\sum_k y_k \alpha_k = 0$ [4].

The quadratic programming problem thus defined can be solved efficiently by standard numerical methods [11]. Numerical computation can be further reduced by processing iteratively small chunks of data [2]. The computational time is linear the dimension n of $\mathbf{x}$-space (not the dimension N of φ-space) and in the number p of training examples and polynomial in the number $m < \min(N+1, p)$ of supporting

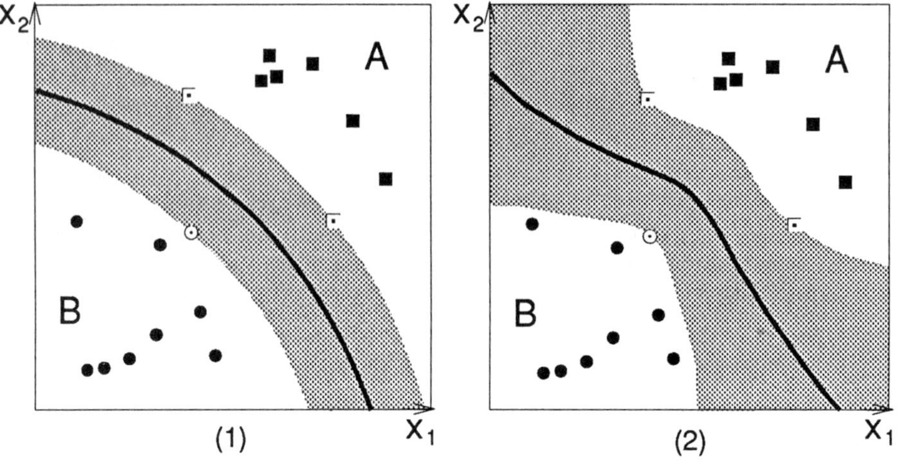

Figure 2: **Non-linear separations.**
Decision boundaries obtained by maximizing the margin in φ-space (see text). The grey shading indicates the margin area projected back to $\mathbf{x}$-space. The supporting patterns (white) lie on the margin. (1) Polynomial classifier of order two (sigma-pi unit network), with kernel $K(\mathbf{x},\mathbf{x}') = (\mathbf{x}\cdot\mathbf{x}'+1)^2$. (2) Kernel classifier (RBF) with kernel $K(\mathbf{x},\mathbf{x}) = (\exp - \|\mathbf{x}-\mathbf{x}'\|/10)$.

patterns. It can be theoretically proven that it is a polynomial in m of order lower than 10, but experimentally an order 2 was observed.

Only the supporting patterns appear in the solution with non-zero weight α_k:

$$D(\mathbf{x}) = \sum_k y_k \alpha_k K(\mathbf{x}_k, \mathbf{x}) + b, \qquad \alpha_k \geq 0 \ . \tag{12}$$

Substituting (8) in $D(\mathbf{x})$, we obtain:

$$\mathbf{w} = \sum_k y_k \alpha_k \varphi(x_k) \ . \tag{13}$$

Using the kernel representation, with a factorized kernel (such as 9), the classification time is linear in n (not N) and in m (not p).

3 CONCLUSIONS

We presented an algorithm to train in high dimensional spaces polynomial classifiers and Radial Basis functions which has remarquable computational and generalization performances. The algorithms seeks the solution with the largest possible margin on both side of the decision boundary. The properties of the algorithm arise from the fact that the solution is a function only of a small number of supporting patterns, namely those training examples that are closest to the decision boundary. The generalization error of the maximum margin classifier is bounded by the ratio of the number of linearly independent supporting patterns and the number of training examples. This bound is tighter than a bound based on the VC-dimension of the classifier family. For further improvement of the generalization error, outliers corresponding to supporting patterns with large α_k can be eliminated automatically or with the assistance of a supervisor. This feature suggests other interesting applications of the maximum margin algorithm for database cleaning.

Acknowledgements

We wish to thank our colleagues at UC Berkeley and AT&T Bell Laboratories for many suggestions and stimulating discussions. Comments by L. Bottou, C. Cortes, S. Sanders, S. Solla, A. Zakhor, are gratefully acknowledged. We are especially indebted to R. Baldick and D. Hochbaum for investigating the polynomial convergence property, S. Hein for providing the code for constrained nonlinear optimization, and D. Haussler and M. Warmuth for help and advice regarding performance bounds.

References

[1] I. Guyon, V. Vapnik, B. Boser, L. Bottou, and S.A. Solla. Structural risk minimization for character recognition. In J. Moody and et al., editors, *NIPS 4*, San Mateo CA, 1992. IEEE, Morgan Kaufmann.

[2] V.N. Vapnik. *Estimation of dependences based on empirical data.* Springer, New York, 1982.

[3] B. Boser, I. Guyon, and V. Vapnik. An training algorithm for optimal margin classifiers. In *Fifth Annual Workshop on Computational Learning Theory*, pages 144–152, Pittsburgh, July 1992. ACM.

[4] P. F. Lambert. Designing patterns recognizers with extremal paradigm information. In Watanabe S., editor, *Methodologies of Pattern Recognition*, pages 359–391. Academic Press, 1969.

[5] R.O. Duda and P.E. Hart. *Pattern Classification And Scene Analysis.* Wiley and Son, 1973.

[6] Y. Le Cun, B. Boser, J. S. Denker, D. Henderson, R. E. Howard, W. Hubbard, and L. D. Jackel. Back-propagation applied to handwritten zipcode recognition. *Neural Computation*, 1(4):541–551, 1989.

[7] M.A. Aizerman, E.M. Braverman, and L.I. Rozonoer. Theoretical foundations of the potential function method in pattern recognition learning. *Automation and Remote Control*, 25:821–837, 1964.

[8] T. Poggio and F. Girosi. Regularization algorithms for learning that are equivalent to multilayer networks. *Science*, 247:978 – 982, February 1990.

[9] T. Poggio. On optimal nonlinear associative recall. *Biol. Cybern.*, 19:201, 1975.

[10] G.F Roach. *Green's Functions.* Cambridge University Press, Cambridge, 1982 (second ed.).

[11] D. Luenberger. *Linear and Non-linear Programming.* Addidon Wesley, 1984.

Automatic Learning Rate Maximization by On-Line Estimation of the Hessian's Eigenvectors

Yann LeCun,[1] Patrice Y. Simard,[1] and Barak Pearlmutter[2]
[1]AT&T Bell Laboratories 101 Crawfords Corner Rd, Holmdel, NJ 07733
[2]CS&E Dept. Oregon Grad. Inst., 19600 NW vonNeumann Dr, Beaverton, OR 97006

Abstract

We propose a very simple, and well principled way of computing the optimal step size in gradient descent algorithms. The on-line version is very efficient computationally, and is applicable to large backpropagation networks trained on large data sets. The main ingredient is a technique for estimating the principal eigenvalue(s) and eigenvector(s) of the objective function's second derivative matrix (Hessian), which does not require to even calculate the Hessian. Several other applications of this technique are proposed for speeding up learning, or for eliminating useless parameters.

1 INTRODUCTION

Choosing the appropriate learning rate, or step size, in a gradient descent procedure such as backpropagation, is simultaneously one of the most crucial and expert-intensive part of neural-network learning. We propose a method for computing the best step size which is both well-principled, simple, very cheap computationally, and, most of all, applicable to on-line training with large networks and data sets. Learning algorithms that use Gradient Descent minimize an objective function E of the form

$$E(W) = \frac{1}{P}\sum_{p=0}^{P} E^p(W) \qquad E^p = E(W, X^p) \tag{1}$$

where W is the vector of parameters (weights), P is the number of training patterns, and X^p is the p-th training example (including the desired output if necessary). Two basic versions of gradient descent can be used to minimize E. In the first version, called the *batch* version, the exact gradient of E with respect to W is calculated, and the weights are updated by iterating the procedure

$$W \leftarrow W - \eta \nabla E(W) \tag{2}$$

where η is the *learning rate* or step size, and $\nabla E(W)$ is the gradient of E with respect to W. In the second version, called *on-line*, or *Stochastic* Gradient Descent, the weights are updated after each pattern presentation

$$W \leftarrow W - \eta \nabla E^p(W) \tag{3}$$

Before going any further, we should emphasize that our main interest is in training large networks on large data sets. As many authors have shown, Stochastic Gradient Descent (SGD) is much faster on large problems than the "batch" version. In fact, on large problems, a carefully tuned SGD algorithm outperforms most accelerated or second-order batch techniques, including Conjugate Gradient. Although there have been attempts to "stochasticize" second-order algorithms (Becker and Le Cun, 1988) (Moller, 1992), most of the resulting procedures also rely on a global scaling parameter similar to η. Therefore, there is considerable interest in finding ways of optimizing η.

2 COMPUTING THE OPTIMAL LEARNING RATE: THE RECIPE

In a somewhat unconventional way, we first give our simple "recipe" for computing the optimal learning rate η. In the subsequent sections, we sketch the theory behind the recipe.

Here is the proposed procedure for estimating the optimal learning rate in a back-propagation network trained with Stochastic Gradient Descent. Equivalent procedures for other adaptive machines are straightforward. In the following, the notation $\mathcal{N}(V)$ designates the normalized vector $V/||V||$. Let W be the N dimensional weight vector,

1. pick a normalized, N dimensional vector Ψ at random. Pick two small positive constants α and γ, say $\alpha = 0.01$ and $\gamma = 0.01$.
2. pick a training example (input and desired output) X^p. Perform a regular forward prop and a backward prop. Store the resulting gradient vector $G_1 = \nabla E^p(W)$.
3. add $\alpha\mathcal{N}(\Psi)$ to the current weight vector W,
4. perform a forward prop and a backward prop on the same pattern using the perturbed weight vector. Store the resulting gradient vector $G_2 = \nabla E^p(W + \alpha\mathcal{N}(\Psi))$
5. update vector Ψ with the running average formula $\Psi \leftarrow (1-\gamma)\Psi + \frac{\gamma}{\alpha}(G_2 - G_1)$.
6. restore the weight vector to its original value W.
7. loop to step 2 until $||\Psi||$ stabilizes.
8. set the learning rate η to $||\Psi||^{-1}$, and go on to a regular training session.

The constant α controls the size of the perturbation. A small α gives a better estimate, but is more likely to cause numerical errors. γ controls the tradeoff between the convergence speed of Ψ and the accuracy of the result. It is better to start with

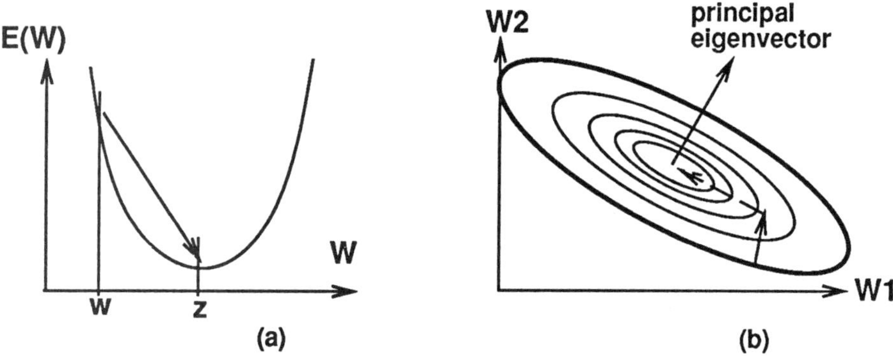

Figure 1: Gradient descent with optimal learning rate in (a) one dimension, and (b) two dimensions (contour plot).

a relatively large γ (say 0.1) and progressively decrease it until the fluctuations on $||\Psi||$ are less than say 10%. In our experience accurate estimates can be obtained with between one hundred and a few hundred pattern presentations: for a large problem, the cost is very small compared to a single learning epoch.

3 STEP SIZE, CURVATURE AND EIGENVALUES

The procedure described in the previous section makes $||\Psi||$ converge to the largest positive eigenvalue of the second derivative matrix of the average objective function. In this section we informally explain why the best learning rate is the inverse of this eigenvalue. More detailed analysis of gradient descent procedures can be found in Optimization, Statistical Estimation, or Adaptive Filtering textbooks (see for example (Widrow and Stearns, 1985)). For didactical purposes, consider an objective function of the form $E(w) = \frac{h}{2}(w - z)^2 + C$ where w is a scalar parameter (see fig 1(a)). Assuming w is the current value of the parameter, what is the optimal η that takes us to the minimum in one step? It is easy to visualize that, as it has been known since Newton, the optimal η is the inverse of the second derivative of E, i.e. $1/h$. Any smaller or slightly larger value will yield slower convergence. A value more then twice the optimal will cause divergence.

In multidimension, things are more complicated. If the objective function is quadratic, the surfaces of equal cost are ellipsoids (or ellipses in 2D as shown on figure 1(b)). Intuitively, if the learning rate is set for optimal convergence along the direction of largest second derivative, then it will be small enough to ensure (slow) convergence along all the other directions. This corresponds to setting the learning rate to the inverse of the second derivative *in the direction in which it is the largest.* The largest learning rate that ensures convergence is twice that value. The actual optimal η is somewhere in between. Setting it to the inverse of the largest second derivative is both safe, and close enough to the optimal. The second derivative information is contained in the *Hessian matrix* of $E(W)$: the symmetric matrix H whose (i,j) component is $\partial^2 E(W)/\partial w_i \partial w_j$. If the learning machine has N free parameters (weights), H is an N by N matrix. The Hessian can be decomposed (diagonalized) into a product of the form $H = R\Lambda R^T$, where Λ is a diagonal matrix whose diagonal terms (the *eigenvalues* of H) are the second derivatives of $E(W)$

along the principal axes of the ellipsoids of equal cost, and R is a rotation matrix which defines the directions of these principal axes. The direction of largest second derivative is the principal eigenvector of H, and the largest second derivative is the corresponding eigenvalue (the largest one). In short, it can be shown that the optimal learning rate is the inverse of the largest eigenvalue of H:

$$\eta_{\text{opt}} = \frac{1}{\lambda_{\text{max}}} \tag{4}$$

4 COMPUTING THE HESSIAN'S LARGEST EIGENVALUE WITHOUT COMPUTING THE HESSIAN

This section derives the recipe given in section 2. Large learning machines, such as backpropagation networks can have several thousand free parameters. Computing, or even storing, the full Hessian matrix is often prohibitively expensive. So at first glance, finding its largest eigenvalue in a reasonable time seems rather hopeless. We are about to propose a shortcut based on three simple ideas: 1- the Taylor expansion, 2- the power method, 3- the running average. The method described here is general, and can be applied to any differentiable objective function that can be written as an average over "examples" (e.g. RBFs, or other statistical estimation techniques).

Taylor expansion: Although it is often unrealistic to compute the Hessian H, there is a simple way to approximate the product of H by a vector of our choosing. Let Ψ be an N dimensional vector, and α a small real constant, the Taylor expansion of the *gradient* of $E(W)$ around W along the direction Ψ gives us

$$H\Psi = \frac{\nabla E(W + \alpha\Psi) - \nabla E(W)}{\alpha} + O(\alpha^2) \tag{5}$$

Assuming E is locally quadratic (i.e. ignoring the $O(\alpha^2)$ term), the product of H by any vector Ψ can be estimated by subtracting the gradient of E at point $(W + \alpha\Psi)$ from the gradient at W. This is an $O(N)$ process, compared to the $O(N^2)$ direct product. In the usual neural network context, this can be done with two forward propagations and two backward propagations. More accurate methods which do not use perturbations for computing $H\Psi$ exist, but they are more complicated to implement than this one. (Pearlmutter, 1993).

The power method: Let λ_{max} be the largest eigenvalue[1] of H, and V_{max} the corresponding normalized eigenvector (or a vector in the eigenspace if λ_{max} is degenerate). If we pick a vector Ψ (say, at random) which is non-orthogonal to V_{max}, then iterating the procedure

$$\Psi \leftarrow H\mathcal{N}(\Psi) \tag{6}$$

will make $\mathcal{N}(\Psi)$ converge to V_{max}, and $||\Psi||$ converge to $|\lambda_{\text{max}}|$. The procedure is slow if good accuracy is required, but a good estimate of the eigenvalue can be obtained with a very small number of iterations (typically about 10). The reason for introducing equation (5), is now clear: we can use it to compute the right hand side of (6), yielding

$$\Psi \leftarrow \frac{1}{\alpha}(\nabla E(W + \alpha\mathcal{N}(\Psi)) - \nabla E(W)) \tag{7}$$

[1]largest in absolute value, not largest algebraically

where Ψ is the current estimate of the principal eigenvector of H, and α is a small constant.

The "on-line" version: One iteration of the procedure (7) requires the computation of the gradient of E at two different points of the parameter space. This means that one iteration of (7) is roughly equivalent to two epochs of gradient descent learning (two passes through the entire training set). Since (7) needs to be iterated, say 10 times, the total cost of estimating $\lambda_{\max}$ would be approximately equivalent to 20 epochs.

This excessive cost can be drastically reduced with an "on-line" version of (7) which exploits the stationarity of the second-order information over large (and redundant) training sets. Essentially, the hidden "average over patterns" in ∇E can be replaced by a running average. The procedure becomes

$$\Psi \leftarrow (1-\gamma)\Psi + \gamma\frac{1}{\alpha}\left(\nabla E\left(W + \alpha\mathcal{N}(\Psi)\right) - \nabla E(W)\right) \tag{8}$$

where γ is a small constant which controls the tradeoff between the convergence speed and the accuracy [2]. The "recipe" given in section 2 is a direct implementation of (8). Empirically, this procedure yields sufficiently accurate values in a very short time. In fact, in all the cases we have tried, it converged with only a few dozen *pattern presentations*: a fraction of the time of an entire learning pass through the training set (see the results section). It looks like the essential features of the Hessian can be extracted from only a few examples of the training set. In other words, the largest eigenvalue of the Hessian seems to be mainly determined by the network architecture and initial weights, and by short-term, low-order statistics of the input data. It should be noted that the on-line procedure can only find positive eigenvalues.

5 A FEW RESULTS

Experiments will be described for two different network architectures trained on segmented handwritten digits taken from the NIST database. Inputs to the networks were 28x28 pixel images containing a centered and size-normalized image of the character. Network 1 was a 4-hidden layer, locally-connected network with shared weights similar to (Le Cun et al., 1990a) but with fewer feature maps. Each layer is only connected to the layer above. the input is 32x32 (there is a border around the 28x28 image), layer 1 is 2x28x28, with 5x5 convolutional (shared) connections. Layer 2 is 2x14x14 with 2x2 subsampled, averaging connections. Layer 3 is 4x10x10, with 2x5x5 convolutional connections. Layer 4 is 4x5x5 with 2x2 averaging connections, and the output layer is 10x1x1 with 4x5x5 convolutional connections. The network has a total of 64,638 connections but only 1278 free parameters because of the weight sharing. Network 2 was a regular 784x30x10 fully-connected network (23860 weights). The sigmoid function used for all units in both nets was $1.7159\tanh(2/3x)$. Target outputs were set to +1 for the correct unit, and -1 for the others.

To check the validity of our assumptions, we computed the full Hessian of Network 1 on 300 patterns (using finite differences on the gradient) and obtained the eigenvalues and eigenvectors using one of the EISPACK routines. We then computed

[2] the procedure (8) is not an unbiased estimator of (7). Large values of γ are likely to produce slightly underestimated eigenvalues, but this inaccuracy has no practical consequences.

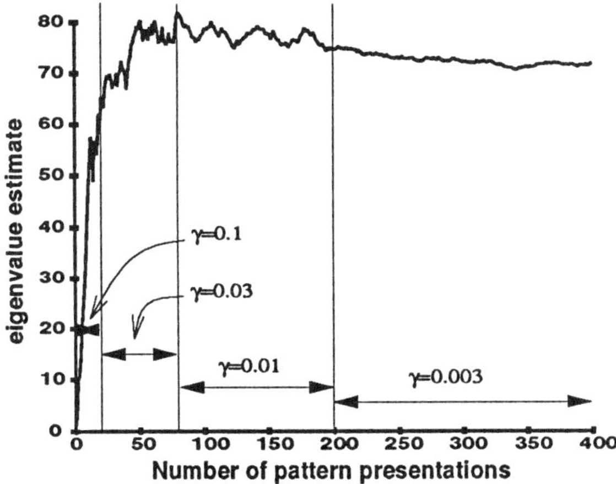

Figure 2: Convergence of the on-line eigenvalue estimation (Network 1)

the principal eigenvector and eigenvalue using procedures (7), and (8). All three methods agreed within less than a percent on the eigenvalue. An example run of (8) on a 1000 pattern set is shown on figure 2. A 10% accurate estimate of the largest eigenvalue is obtained in less than 200 pattern presentations (one fifth of the database). As can be seen, the value is fairly stable over small portions of the set, which means that increasing the set size would not require more iterations of the estimation procedure.

A second series of experiments were run to verify the accuracy of the learning rate prediction. Network 1 was trained on 1000 patterns, and network 2 on 300 patterns, both with SGD. Figure 3 shows the Mean Squared Error of the two networks after 1,2,3,4 and 5 passes through the training set as a function of the learning rate, for one particular initial weight vector. The constant γ was set to 0.1 for the first 20 patterns, 0.03 for the next 60, 0.01 for the next 120, and 0.003 for the next 200 (400 total pattern presentations), but it was found that adequate values were obtained after only 100 to 200 pattern presentations. The vertical bar represents the value predicted by the method for that particular run. It is clear that the predicted optimal value is very close to the correct optimal learning rate. Other experiments with different training sets and initial weights gave similar results. Depending on the initial weights, the largest eigenvalue for Network 1 varied between 80 and 250, and for Network 2 between 250 and 400. Experiments tend to suggest that the optimal learning rate varies only slightly during the early phase of training. The learning rate may need to be decreased for long learning sessions, as SGD converts from the "getting near the minimum" mode to the "wobbling around" mode.

There are many other method for adjusting the learning rate. Unfortunately, most of them are based on some measurement of the oscillations of the gradient (Jacobs, 1987). Therefore, they are difficult to apply to stochastic gradient descent.

6 MORE ON EIGENVALUES AND EIGENVECTORS

We believe that computing the optimal learning rate is only one of many applications of our eigenvector estimation technique. The procedure can be adapted to serve many applications.

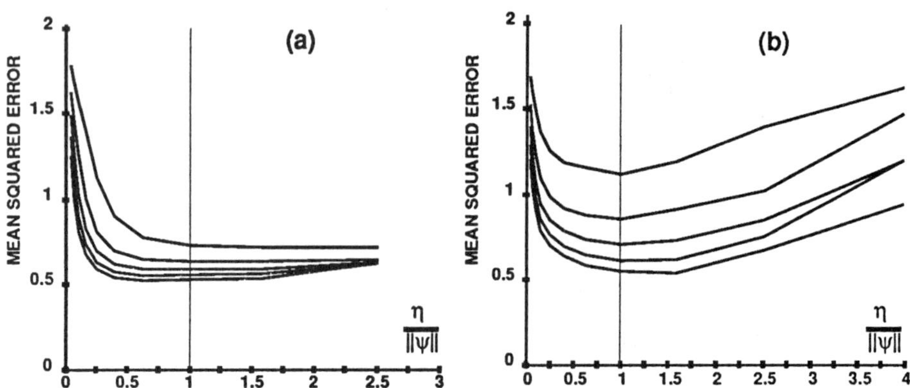

Figure 3: Mean Squared Error after 1,2,3,4, and 5 epochs (from top to bottom) as a function of the ratio between the learning rate η and the learning rate predicted by the proposed method $||\Psi||^{-1}$. (a) Network 1 trained on 1000 patterns, (b) Network 2 trained on 300 patterns.

An important variation of the learning rate estimation is when, instead of update rule 3, we use a "scaled SGD" rule of the form $W \leftarrow W - \eta\Phi\nabla E^p(W)$, where Φ is a diagonal matrix (each weight has its own learning rate $\eta\phi_i$). For example, each ϕ_i can be the inverse of the corresponding diagonal term of the average Hessian, which can be computed efficiently as suggested in (Le Cun, 1987; Becker and Le Cun, 1988). Then procedure 8 must be changed to

$$\Psi \leftarrow (1-\gamma)\Psi + \gamma\frac{1}{\alpha}\Phi^{\frac{1}{2}}\left(\nabla E\left(W + \alpha\Phi^{\frac{1}{2}}\mathcal{N}(\Psi)\right) - \nabla E(W)\right) \tag{9}$$

where the terms of $\Phi^{\frac{1}{2}}$ are the square root of the corresponding terms in Φ. More generally, the above formula applies to any transformation of the parameter space whose Jacobian is $\Phi^{\frac{1}{2}}$. The added cost is small since $\Phi^{\frac{1}{2}}$ is diagonal.

Another extension of the procedure can compute the first K principal eigenvectors and eigenvalues. The idea is to store K eigenvector estimates Ψ_k, $k = 1 \ldots K$, updated simultaneously with equation (8) (this costs a factor K over estimating only one). We must also ensure that the Ψ_k's remain orthogonal to each other. This can be performed by projecting each Ψ_k onto the space orthogonal to the space subtended by the Ψ_l, $l < k$. This is an NK process, which is relatively cheap if the network uses shared weights. A generalization of the acceleration method introduced in (Le Cun, Kanter and Solla, 1991) can be implemented with this technique. The idea is to use a "Newton-like" weight update formula of the type

$$W \leftarrow W - \sum_{k=1}^{K} ||\Psi_k||^{-1} P_k$$

where P_k, $k = 1 \ldots K-1$ is the projection of $\nabla E(W)$ onto Ψ_k, and P_K is the projection of $\nabla E(W)$ on the space orthogonal to the Ψ_k, $(k = 1 \ldots K-1)$. In theory, this procedure can accelerate the training by a factor $||\Psi_1||/||\Psi_K||$, which is between 3 and 10 for $K = 5$ in a typical backprop network. Results will be reported in a later publication.

Interestingly, the method can be slightly modified to yield the *smallest* eigenvalues/eigenvectors. First, the largest eigenvalue $\lambda_{\max}$ must be computed (or bounded above). Then, by iterating

$$\Psi \leftarrow (1-\gamma)\Psi + \lambda_{\max}\mathcal{N}(\Psi) - \gamma\frac{1}{\alpha}(\nabla E(W+\alpha\mathcal{N}(\Psi)) - \nabla E(W)) \quad (10)$$

one can compute the eigenvector corresponding to the smallest (probably negative) eigenvalue of $(H - \lambda_{\max} I)$, which is the same as H's. This can be used to determine the direction(s) of displacement in parameter space that will cause the least increase of the objective function. There are obvious applications of this to weight elimination methods: a better version of OBD (Le Cun et al., 1990b) or a more efficient version of OBS (Hassibi and Stork, 1993).

We have proposed efficient methods for (a) computing the product of the Hessian by any vector, and (b) estimating the few eigenvectors of largest or smallest eigenvalues. The methods were successfully applied the estimation of the optimal learning rate in Stochastic Gradient Descent learning We feel that we have only scratched the surface of the many applications of the proposed techniques.

Acknowledgements

Yann LeCun and Patrice Simard would like to thank the members of the Adaptive Systems Research dept for their support and comments. Barak Pearlmutter was partially supported by grants NSF ECS-9114333 and ONR N00014-92-J-4062 to John Moody.

References

Becker, S. and Le Cun, Y. (1988). Improving the Convergence of Back-Propagation Learning with Second-Order Methods. Technical Report CRG-TR-88-5, University of Toronto Connectionist Research Group.

Hassibi, B. and Stork, D. (1993). Optimal Brain Surgeon. In Giles, L., Hanson, S., and Cowan, J., editors, *Advances in Neural Information Processing Systems*, volume 5, (Denver, 1992). Morgan Kaufman.

Jacobs, R. A. (1987). Increased Rates of Convergence Through Learning Rate Adaptation. Department of Computer and Information Sciences COINS-TR-87-117, University of Massachusetts, Amherst, Ma.

Le Cun, Y. (1987). *Modeles connexionnistes de l'apprentissage (connectionist learning models)*. PhD thesis, Université P. et M. Curie (Paris 6).

Le Cun, Y., Boser, B., Denker, J. S., Henderson, D., Howard, R. E., Hubbard, W., and Jackel, L. D. (1990a). Handwritten digit recognition with a back-propagation network. In Touretzky, D., editor, *Advances in Neural Information Processing Systems 2 (NIPS*89)*, Denver, CO. Morgan Kaufman.

Le Cun, Y., Denker, J. S., Solla, S., Howard, R. E., and Jackel, L. D. (1990b). Optimal Brain Damage. In Touretzky, D., editor, *Advances in Neural Information Processing Systems 2 (NIPS*89)*, Denver, CO. Morgan Kaufman.

Le Cun, Y., Kanter, I., and Solla, S. (1991). Eigenvalues of covariance matrices: application to neural-network learning. *Physical Review Letters*, 66(18):2396–2399.

Moller, M. (1992). supervised learning on large redundant training sets. In *Neural Networks for Signal Processing 2*. IEEE press.

Pearlmutter, B. (1993). Phd thesis, Carnegie-Mellon University, Pittsburgh PA.

Widrow, B. and Stearns, S. D. (1985). *Adaptive Signal Processing*. Prentice-Hall.

Second order derivatives for network pruning: Optimal Brain Surgeon

Babak Hassibi* and **David G. Stork**
Ricoh California Research Center
2882 Sand Hill Road, Suite 115
Menlo Park, CA 94025-7022
stork@crc.ricoh.com

and

* Department of Electrical Engineering
Stanford University
Stanford, CA 94305

Abstract

We investigate the use of information from *all* second order derivatives of the error function to perform network pruning (i.e., removing unimportant weights from a trained network) in order to improve generalization, simplify networks, reduce hardware or storage requirements, increase the speed of further training, and in some cases enable rule extraction. Our method, Optimal Brain Surgeon (OBS), is significantly better than magnitude-based methods and Optimal Brain Damage [Le Cun, Denker and Solla, 1990], which often remove the wrong weights. OBS permits the pruning of more weights than other methods (for the same error on the training set), and thus yields better generalization on test data. Crucial to OBS is a recursion relation for calculating the inverse Hessian matrix $\mathbf{H}^{-1}$ from training data and structural information of the net. OBS permits a 90%, a 76%, and a 62% reduction in weights over backpropagation with weight decay on three benchmark MONK's problems [Thrun et al., 1991]. Of OBS, Optimal Brain Damage, and magnitude-based methods, only OBS deletes the correct weights from a trained XOR network in every case. Finally, whereas Sejnowski and Rosenberg [1987] used 18,000 weights in their NETtalk network, we used OBS to prune a network to just 1560 weights, yielding better generalization.

1 Introduction

A central problem in machine learning and pattern recognition is to minimize the system complexity (description length, VC-dimension, etc.) consistent with the training data. In neural networks this regularization problem is often cast as minimizing the number of connection weights. Without such weight elimination overfitting problems and thus poor generalization will result. Conversely, if there are too few weights, the network might not be able to learn the training data.

If we begin with a trained network having too many weights, the questions then become: Which weights should be eliminated? How should the remaining weights be adjusted for best performance? How can such network pruning be done in a computationally efficient way?

Magnitude based methods [Hertz, Krogh and Palmer, 1991] eliminate weights that have the smallest magnitude. This simple and naively plausible idea unfortunately often leads to the elimination of the wrong weights — small weights can be necessary for low error. Optimal Brain Damage [Le Cun, Denker and Solla, 1990] uses the criterion of minimal increase in training error for weight elimination. For computational simplicity, OBD assumes that the Hessian matrix is diagonal; in fact, however, Hessians for every problem we have considered are strongly *non*-diagonal, and this leads OBD to eliminate the wrong weights. The superiority of the method described here — Optimal Brain Surgeon — lies in great part to the fact that it makes no restrictive assumptions about the form of the network's Hessian, and thereby eliminates the correct weights. Moreover, unlike other methods, OBS does not demand (typically slow) retraining after the pruning of a weight.

2 Optimal Brain Surgeon

In deriving our method we begin, as do Le Cun, Denker and Solla [1990], by considering a network trained to a local minimum in error. The functional Taylor series of the error with respect to weights (or parameters, see below) is:

$$\delta E = \left(\frac{\partial E}{\partial \mathbf{w}}\right)^T \cdot \delta\mathbf{w} + \tfrac{1}{2}\delta\mathbf{w}^T \cdot \mathbf{H} \cdot \delta\mathbf{w} + O(\|\delta\mathbf{w}\|^3) \tag{1}$$

where $\mathbf{H} \equiv \partial^2 E/\partial \mathbf{w}^2$ is the Hessian matrix (containing all second order derivatives) and the superscript T denotes vector transpose. For a network trained to a local minimum in error, the first (linear) term vanishes; we also ignore the third and all higher order terms. Our goal is then to set one of the weights to zero (which we call w_q) to minimize the increase in error given by Eq. 1. Eliminating w_q is expressed as:

$$\delta w_q + w_q = 0 \qquad \text{or more generally} \quad \mathbf{e}_q^T \cdot \delta\mathbf{w} + w_q = 0 \tag{2}$$

where $\mathbf{e}_q$ is the unit vector in weight space corresponding to (scalar) weight w_q. Our goal is then to solve:

$$Min_q\{Min_{\delta\mathbf{w}}\{\tfrac{1}{2}\delta\mathbf{w}^{\mathrm{T}} \cdot \mathbf{H} \cdot \delta\mathbf{w}\} \quad \text{such that} \quad \mathbf{e}_q^T \cdot \delta\mathbf{w} + w_q = 0\} \tag{3}$$

To solve Eq. 3 we form a Lagrangian from Eqs. 1 and 2:

$$L = \tfrac{1}{2}\delta\mathbf{w}^{\mathrm{T}} \cdot \mathbf{H} \cdot \delta\mathbf{w} + \lambda(\mathbf{e}_q^T \cdot \delta\mathbf{w} + w_q) \tag{4}$$

where λ is a Lagrange undetermined multiplier. We take functional derivatives, employ the constraints of Eq. 2, and use matrix inversion to find that the optimal weight change and resulting change in error are:

$$\delta\mathbf{w} = -\frac{w_q}{[\mathbf{H}^{-1}]_{qq}}\mathbf{H}^{-1} \cdot \mathbf{e}_q \qquad \mathit{and} \qquad L_q = \frac{1}{2}\frac{w_q^2}{[\mathbf{H}^{-1}]_{qq}} \tag{5}$$

Note that neither $\mathbf{H}$ nor $\mathbf{H}^{-1}$ need be diagonal (as is assumed by Le Cun et al.); moreover, our method recalculates the magnitude of *all* the weights in the network, by the left side of Eq. 5. We call L_q the "saliency" of weight q — the increase in error that results when the weight is eliminated — a definition more general than Le Cun et al.'s, and which includes theirs in the special case of diagonal **H**.

Thus we have the following algorithm:

Optimal Brain Surgeon procedure

1. Train a "reasonably large" network to minimum error.
2. Compute $\mathbf{H}^{-1}$.
3. Find the q that gives the smallest saliency $L_q = w_q^2/(2[\mathrm{H}^{-1}]_{qq})$. If this candidate error increase is much smaller than E, then the qth weight should be deleted, and we proceed to step 4; otherwise go to step 5. (Other stopping criteria can be used too.)
4. Use the q from step 3 to update *all* weights (Eq. 5). Go to step 2.
5. No more weights can be deleted without large increase in E. (At this point it may be desirable to retrain the network.)

Figure 1 illustrates the basic idea. The relative magnitudes of the error after pruning (before retraining, if any) depend upon the particular problem, but to second order obey: E(mag) ≥ E(OBD) ≥ E(OBS), which is the key to the superiority of OBS. In this example OBS and OBD lead to the elimination of the same weight (weight 1). In many cases, however, OBS will eliminate *different* weights than those eliminated by OBD (cf. Sect. 6). We call our method Optimal Brain *Surgeon* because in addition to deleting weights, it calculates and *changes* the strengths of other weights without the need for gradient descent or other incremental retraining.

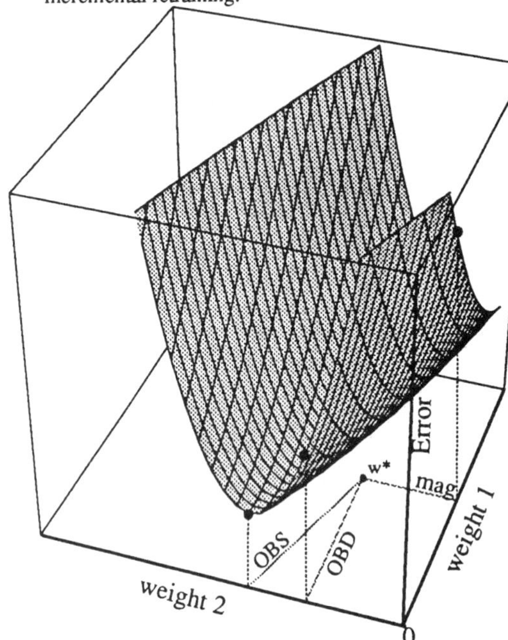

Figure 1: Error as a function of two weights in a network. The (local) minimum occurs at weight w*, found by gradient descent or other learning method. In this illustration, a magnitude based pruning technique (mag) then removes the smallest weight, weight 2; Optimal Brain Damage before retraining (OBD) removes weight 1. In contrast, our Optimal Brain Surgeon method (OBS) not only removes weight 1, but *also* automatically adjusts the value of weight 2 to minimize the error, without retraining. The error surface here is general in that it has different curvatures (second derivatives) along different directions, a minimum at a non-special weight value, and a non-diagonal Hessian (i.e., principal axes are *not* parallel to the weight axes). We have found (to our surprise) that every problem we have investigated has strongly *non*-diagonal Hessians — thereby explaining the improvment of our method over that of Le Cun et al.

3 Computing the inverse Hessian

The difficulty appears to be step 2 in the OBS procedure, since inverting a matrix of thousands or millions of terms seems computationally intractable. In what follows we shall give a general derivation of the inverse Hessian for a *fully trained* neural network. It makes no difference whether it was trained by backpropagation, competitive learning, the Boltzmann algorithm, or any other method, so long as derivatives can be taken (see below). We shall show that the Hessian can be reduced to the sample covariance matrix associated with certain gradient vectors. Furthermore, the gradient vectors necessary for OBS are normally available at small computational cost; the covariance form of the Hessian yields a recursive formula for computing the inverse.

Consider a general non-linear neural network that maps an input vector **in** of dimension n_i into an output vector o of dimension n_o, according to the following:

$$\mathbf{o} = \mathbf{F}(\mathbf{w}, \mathbf{in}) \tag{6}$$

where w is an n dimensional vector representing the neural network's weights or other parameters. We shall refer to w as a weight vector below for simplicity and definiteness, but it must be stressed that w could represent *any* continuous parameters, such as those describing neural transfer function, weight sharing, and so on. The mean square error corresponding to the training set is defined as:

$$E = \frac{1}{2P}\sum_{k=1}^{P}(\mathbf{t}^{[k]} - \mathbf{o}^{[k]})^T(\mathbf{t}^{[k]} - \mathbf{o}^{[k]}) \tag{7}$$

where P is the number of training patterns, and $\mathbf{t}^{[k]}$ and $\mathbf{o}^{[k]}$ are the desired response and network response for the kth training pattern. The first derivative with respect to **w** is:

$$\frac{\partial E}{\partial \mathbf{w}} = -\frac{1}{P}\sum_{k=1}^{P}\frac{\partial \mathbf{F}(\mathbf{w}, \mathbf{in}^{[k]})}{\partial \mathbf{w}}(\mathbf{t}^{[k]} - \mathbf{o}^{[k]}) \tag{8}$$

and the second derivative or Hessian is:

$$\mathbf{H} \equiv \frac{\partial^2 E}{\partial \mathbf{w}^2} = \frac{1}{P}\sum_{k=1}^{P}\left[\frac{\partial \mathbf{F}(\mathbf{w}, \mathbf{in}^{[k]})}{\partial \mathbf{w}} \cdot \frac{\partial \mathbf{F}(\mathbf{w}, \mathbf{in}^{[k]})}{\partial \mathbf{w}}^T - \frac{\partial^2 \mathbf{F}(\mathbf{w}, \mathbf{in}^{[k]})}{\partial \mathbf{w}^2} \cdot (\mathbf{t}^{[k]} - \mathbf{o}^{[k]})\right] \tag{9}$$

Next we consider a network fully trained to a local minimum in error at **w***. Under this condition the network response $\mathbf{o}^{[k]}$ will be close to the desired response $\mathbf{t}^{[k]}$, and hence we neglect the term involving $(\mathbf{t}^{[k]} - \mathbf{o}^{[k]})$. Even late in pruning, when this error is not small for a single pattern, this approximation can be justified (see next Section). This simplification yields:

$$\mathbf{H} = \frac{1}{P}\sum_{k=1}^{P} \frac{\partial \mathbf{F}(\mathbf{w},\mathbf{in}^{[k]})}{\partial \mathbf{w}} \cdot \frac{\partial \mathbf{F}(\mathbf{w},\mathbf{in}^{[k]})}{\partial \mathbf{w}}^{T} \tag{10}$$

If out network has just a single output, we may define the n-dimensional data vector $\mathbf{X}^{[k]}$ of derivatives as:

$$\mathbf{X}^{[k]} \equiv \frac{\partial \mathbf{F}(\mathbf{w},\mathbf{in}^{[k]})}{\partial \mathbf{w}} \tag{11}$$

Thus Eq. 10 can be written as:

$$\mathbf{H} = \frac{1}{P}\sum_{k=1}^{P} \mathbf{X}^{[k]} \cdot \mathbf{X}^{[k]T} \tag{12}$$

If instead our network has *multiple* output units, then **X** will be an n x n_o matrix of the form:

$$\mathbf{X}^{[k]} = \frac{\partial \mathbf{F}(\mathbf{w},\mathbf{in}^{[k]})}{\partial \mathbf{w}} = \left(\frac{\partial \mathbf{F}_1(\mathbf{w},\mathbf{in}^{[k]})}{\partial \mathbf{w}}, \ldots, \frac{\partial \mathbf{F}_{n_o}(\mathbf{w},\mathbf{in}^{[k]})}{\partial \mathbf{w}}\right) = (\mathbf{X}_1^{[k]}, \ldots, \mathbf{X}_{n_o}^{[k]}) \tag{13}$$

where $\mathbf{F}_i$ is the ith component of **F**. Hence in this multiple output unit case Eq. 10 generalizes to:

$$\mathbf{H} = \frac{1}{P}\sum_{k=1}^{P}\sum_{l=1}^{n_o} \mathbf{X}_l^{[k]} \cdot \mathbf{X}_l^{[k]T} \tag{14}$$

Equations 12 and 14 show that **H** is the sample covariance matrix associated with the gradient variable **X**. Equation 12 also shows that for the single output case we can calculate the full Hessian by sequentially adding in successive "component" Hessians as:

$$\mathbf{H}_{m+1} = \mathbf{H}_m + \frac{1}{P}\mathbf{X}^{[m+1]} \cdot \mathbf{X}^{[m+1]T} \quad \text{with} \quad \mathbf{H}_0 = \alpha\mathbf{I} \text{ and } \mathbf{H}_P = \mathbf{H} \tag{15}$$

But Optimal Brain Surgeon requires the *inverse* of **H** (Eq. 5). This inverse can be calculated using a standard matrix inversion formula [Kailath, 1980]:

$$(\mathbf{A} + \mathbf{B} \cdot \mathbf{C} \cdot \mathbf{D})^{-1} = \mathbf{A}^{-1} - \mathbf{A}^{-1} \cdot \mathbf{B} \cdot (\mathbf{C}^{-1} + \mathbf{D}.\mathbf{A}^{-1} \cdot \mathbf{B})^{-1} \cdot \mathbf{D} \cdot \mathbf{A}^{-1} \tag{16}$$

applied to each term in the analogous sequence in Eq. 16:

$$\mathbf{H}_{m+1}^{-1} = \mathbf{H}_m^{-1} - \frac{\mathbf{H}_m^{-1} \cdot \mathbf{X}^{[m+1]} \cdot \mathbf{X}^{[m+1]T} \cdot \mathbf{H}_m^{-1}}{P + \mathbf{X}^{[m+1]T} \cdot \mathbf{H}_m^{-1} \cdot \mathbf{X}^{[m+1]}} \quad \text{with} \quad \mathbf{H}_0^{-1} = \alpha^{-1}\mathbf{I} \text{ and } \mathbf{H}_P^{-1} = \mathbf{H}^{-1} \tag{17}$$

and α ($10^{-8} \le \alpha \le 10^{-4}$) a small constant needed to make $\mathbf{H}_0^{-1}$ meaningful, and to which our method is insensitive [Hassibi, Stork and Wolff, 1993b]. Actually, Eq. 17 leads to the calculation of the inverse of $(\mathbf{H} + \alpha\mathbf{I})$, and this corresponds to the introduction of a penalty term $\alpha||\delta\mathbf{w}||^2$ in Eq. 4. This has the benefit of penalizing large candidate jumps in weight space, and thus helping to insure that the neglecting of higher order terms in Eq. 1 is valid.

Equation 17 permits the calculation of $\mathbf{H}^{-1}$ using a *single* sequential pass through the training data $1 \le m \le P$. It is also straightforward to generalize Eq. 18 to the multiple output case of Eq. 15: in this case Eq. 15 will have recursions on both the indices m and *l* giving:

$$\begin{aligned} \mathbf{H}_{m\,l+1} &= \mathbf{H}_{m\,l} + \frac{1}{P}\mathbf{X}_{l+1}^{[m]} \cdot \mathbf{X}_{l+1}^{[m]T} \\ \mathbf{H}_{m+1\,1} &= \mathbf{H}_{m\,n_o} + \frac{1}{P}\mathbf{X}_{1}^{[m+1]} \cdot \mathbf{X}_{1}^{[m+1]T} \end{aligned} \tag{18}$$

To sequentially calculate $\mathbf{H}^{-1}$ for the multiple output case, we use Eq. 16, as before.

4 The (t - o) → 0 approximation

The approximation used for Eq. 10 can be justified on computational and functional grounds, even late in pruning when the training error is not negligible. From the computational view, we note first that normally **H** is degenerate — especially before significant pruning has been done — and its inverse not well defined.

The approximation guarantees that there are no singularities in the calculation of $\mathbf{H}^{-1}$. It also keeps the computational complexity of calculating $\mathbf{H}^{-1}$ the same as that for calculating $\mathbf{H}$ — $O(\mathrm{P}\,n^2)$. In Statistics the approximation is the basis of Fisher's method of scoring and its goal is to replace the true Hessian with its expected value and guarantee that $\mathbf{H}$ is positive definite (thereby avoiding stability problems that can plague Gauss-Newton methods) [Seber and Wild, 1989].

Equally important are the functional justifications of the approximation. Consider a high capactiy network trained to small training error. We can consider the network structure as involving both signal and noise. As we prune, we hope to eliminate those weights that lead to "overfitting," i.e., learning the noise. If our pruning method did *not* employ the $(\mathbf{t} - \mathbf{o}) \to 0$ approximation, every pruning step (Eqs. 9 and 5) would inject the noise back into the system, by penalizing for noise terms. A different way to think of the approximation is the following. After some pruning by OBS we have reached a new weight vector that is a local minimum of the error (cf. Fig. 1). Even if this error is not negligible, we want to stay as close to *that* value of the error as we can. Thus we imagine a new, effective teaching signal $\mathbf{t}^*$, that would keep the network near this new error minimum. It is then $(\mathbf{t}^* - \mathbf{o})$ that we in effect set to zero when using Eq. 10 instead of Eq. 9.

5 OBS and backpropagation

Using the standard terminology from backpropagation [Rumelhart, Hinton and Williams, 1986] and the single output network of Fig. 2, it is straightforward to show from Eq. 11 that the derivative vectors are:

$$\mathbf{X}^{[k]} = \begin{pmatrix} \mathbf{X}_{\mathrm{v}}^{[k]} \\ \mathbf{X}_{\mathrm{u}}^{[k]} \end{pmatrix} \tag{19}$$

where

$$[\mathbf{X}_{\mathrm{v}}^{[k]}]^{\mathrm{T}} = \left(\mathrm{f}'(\mathrm{net}^{[k]})\mathrm{o}_{j=1}^{[k]}, \ldots, \mathrm{f}'(\mathrm{net}^{[k]})\mathrm{o}_{n_j}^{[k]} \right) \tag{20}$$

refers to derivatives with respect to hidden-to-output weights v_j and

$$\begin{aligned}[\mathbf{X}_{\mathrm{u}}^{[k]}]^{\mathrm{T}} = \big(&\mathrm{f}'(\mathrm{net}^{[k]})\mathrm{f}'(\mathrm{net}_1^{[k]})\mathrm{v}_1^{[k]}\mathrm{o}_{i=1}^{[k]}, \ldots, \mathrm{f}'(\mathrm{net}^{[k]})\mathrm{f}'(\mathrm{net}_1^{[k]})\mathrm{v}_1^{[k]}\mathrm{o}_{n_i}^{[k]}, \ldots, \\ &\mathrm{f}'(\mathrm{net}^{[k]})\mathrm{f}'(\mathrm{net}_{n_j}^{[k]})\mathrm{v}_{n_j}^{[k]}\mathrm{o}_1^{[k]}, \ldots, \mathrm{f}'(\mathrm{net}^{[k]})\mathrm{f}'(\mathrm{net}_{n_j}^{[k]})\mathrm{v}_{n_j}^{[k]}\mathrm{o}_{n_i}^{[k]} \big)\end{aligned} \tag{21}$$

refers to derivatives with respect to input-to-hidden weights u_{ji}, and where lexicographical ordering has been used. The neuron nonlinearity is $\mathrm{f}(\cdot)$.

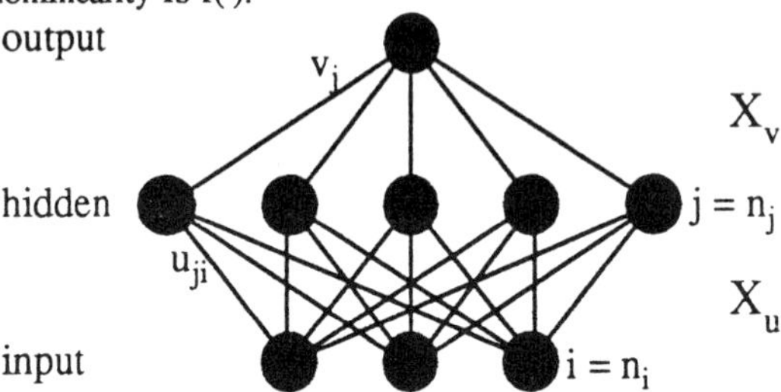

Figure 2: Backpropagation net with n_i inputs and n_j hidden units. The input-to-hidden weights are u_{ji} and hidden-to-output weights v_j. The derivative ("data") vectors are $\mathbf{X}_v$ and $\mathbf{X}_u$ (Eqs. 20 and 21).

6 Simulation results

We applied OBS, Optimal Brain Damage, and a magnitude based pruning method to the 2-2-1 network with bias unit of Fig. 3, trained on all patterns of the XOR problem. The network was first trained to a local minimum, which had zero error, and then the three methods were used to prune one weight. As shown, the methods deleted different weights. We then trained the original XOR network from different initial conditions, thereby leading to a different local minima. Whereas there were some cases in which OBD or magnitude methods deleted the correct weight, only OBS deleted the correct weight in *every* case. Moreover, OBS changed the values of the remaining weights (Eq. 5) to achieve perfect performance *without any retraining by the backpropagation algorithm.* Figure 4 shows the Hessian of the trained but unpruned XOR network.

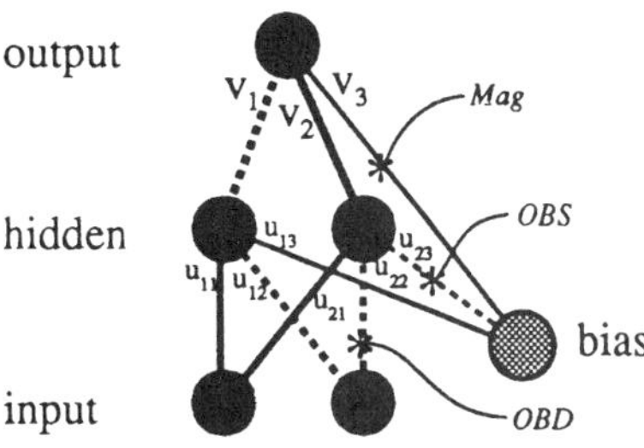

Figure 3: A nine weight XOR network trained to a local minimum. The thickness of the lines indicates the weight magnitudes, and inhibitory weights are shown dashed. Subsequent pruning using a magnitude based method (*Mag*) would delete weight v_3; using Optimal Brain Damage (*OBD*) would delete u_{22}. Even with retraining, the network pruned by those methods cannot learn the XOR problem. In contrast, Optimal Brain Surgeon (*OBS*) deletes u_{23} and furthermore changed all other weights (cf. Eq. 5) to achieve zero error on the XOR problem.

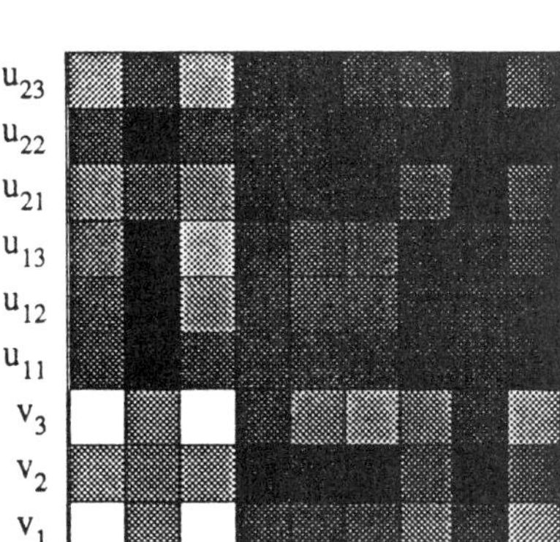

Figure 4: The Hessian of the trained but unpruned XOR network, calculated by means of Eq. 12. White represents large values and black small magnitudes. The rows and columns are labeled by the weights shown in Fig. 3. As is to be expected, the hidden-to-output weights have significant Hessian components. Note especially that the Hessian is far from being diagonal. The Hessians for all problems we have investigated, including the MONK's problems (below), are far from being diagonal.

Figure 5 shows two-dimensional "slices" of the nine-dimensional error surface in the neighborhood of a local minimum at **w*** for the XOR network. The cuts compare the weight elimination of Magnitude methods (left) and OBD (right) with the elimination and weight adjustment given by OBS.

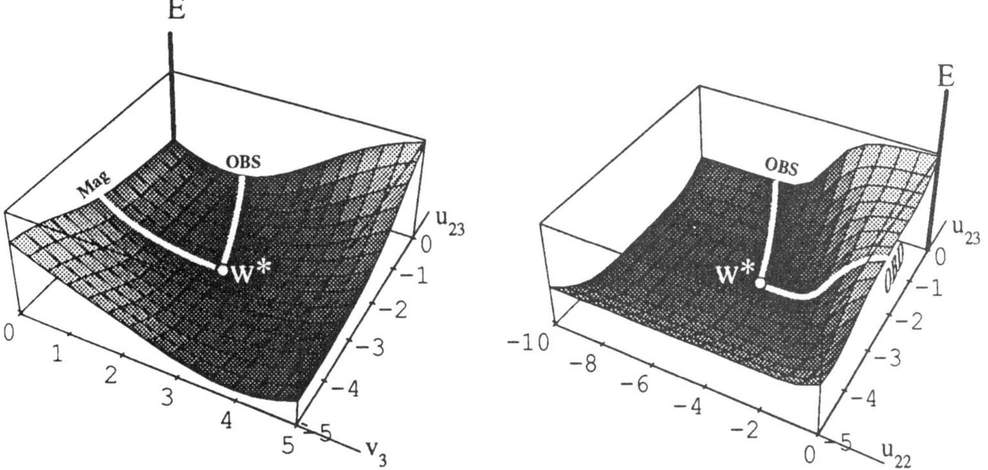

Figure 5: (Left) the XOR error surface as a function of weights v_3 and u_{23} (cf. Fig. 4). A magnitude based pruning method would delete weight v_3 whereas OBS deletes u_{23}. (Right) The XOR error surface as a function of weights u_{22} and u_{23}. Optimal Brain Damage would delete u_{22} whereas OBS deletes u_{23}. For this minimum, only deleting u_{23} will allow the pruned network to solve the XOR problem.

After all network weights are updated by Eq. 5 the system is at zero error (not shown). It is especially noteworthy that in neither case of pruning by magnitude methods nor Optimal Brain Damage will further retraining by gradient descent reduce the training error to zero. In short, magnitude methods and Optimal Brain Damage delete the wrong weights, and their mistake cannot be overcome by further network training. Only Optimal Brain Surgeon deletes the correct weight.

We also applied OBS to larger problems, three MONK's problems, and compared our results to those of Thrun et al. [1991], whose backpropagation network outperformed all other approaches (network and rule-based) on these benchmark problems in an extensive machine learning competition.

		Accuracy		# weights
		training	testing	
MONK 1	BPWD	100	100	58
	OBS	100	100	14
MONK 2	BPWD	100	100	39
	OBS	100	100	15
MONK 3	BPWD	93.4	97.2	39
	OBS	93.4	97.2	4

Table 1: The accuracy and number of weights found by backpropagation with weight decay (BPWD) found by Thrun et al. [1991], and by OBS on three MONK's problems.

Table 1 shows that for the same performance, OBS (without retraining) required only 24%, 38% and 10% of the weights of the backpropagation network, which was already regularized with weight decay (Fig. 6). The error increase L (Eq. 5) accompanying pruning by OBS negligibly affected accuracy.

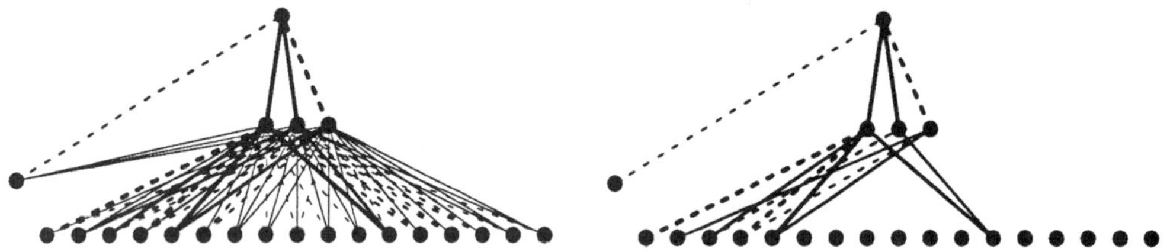

Figure 6: Optimal networks found by Thrun using backpropagation with weight decay (Left) and by OBS (Right) on MONK 1, which is based on logical rules. Solid (dashed) lines denote excitatory (inhibitory) connections; bias units are at left.

The dramatic reduction in weights achieved by OBS yields a network that is simple enough that the logical rules that generated the data can be recovered from the pruned network, for instance by the methods of Towell and Shavlik [1992]. Hence OBS may help to address a criticism often levied at neural networks: the fact that they may be unintelligible.

We applied OBS to a three-layer NETtalk network. While Sejnowski and Rosenberg [1987] used 18,000 weights, we began with just 5546 weights, which after backpropagation training had a test error of 5259. After pruning this net with OBS to 2438 weights, and then retraining and pruning again, we achieved a net with only 1560 weights and test error of only 4701 — a significant improvement over the original, more complex network [Hassibi, Stork and Wolff, 1993a]. Thus OBS can be applied to real-world pattern recognition problems such as speech recognition and optical character recognition, which typically have several thousand parameters.

7 Analysis and conclusions

Why is Optimal Brain Surgeon so successful at reducing excess degrees of freedom? Conversely, given this new standard in weight elimination, we can ask: Why are magnitude based methods so poor? Consider again Fig. 1. Starting from the local minimum at w^*, a magnitude based method deletes the wrong weight, weight 2, and through retraining, weight 1 will *increase*. The final "solution" is weight 1 $\rightarrow$ large, weight 2 = 0. This is precisely the *opposite* of the solution found by OBS: weight 1 = 0, weight 2 $\rightarrow$ large. Although the actual difference in error shown in Fig. 1 may be small, in large networks, differences from many incorrect weight elimination decisions can add up to a significant increase in error.

But most importantly, it is simply wishful thinking to believe that after the elimination of many incorrect weights by magnitude methods the net can "sort it all out" through further training and reach a global optimum, especially if the network has already been pruned significantly (cf. XOR discussion, above).

We have also seen how the approximation employed by Optimal Brain Damage — that the diagonals of the Hessian are dominant — does not hold for the problems we have investigated. There are typically many off-diagonal terms that are comparable to their diagonal counterparts. This explains why OBD often deletes the wrong weight, while OBS deletes the correct one.

We note too that our method is quite general, and subsumes previous methods for weight elimination. In our terminology, magnitude based methods assume isotropic Hessian ($\mathbf{H} \propto \mathbf{I}$); OBD assumes diagonal $\mathbf{H}$; FARM [Kung and Hu, 1991] assumes linear f(net) and only updates the hidden-to-output weights. We have shown that none of those assumptions are valid nor sufficient for optimal weight elimination.

We should also point out that our method is even more general than presented here [Hassibi, Stork and Wolff, 1993b]. For instance, rather than pruning a weight (parameter) by setting it to zero, one can instead reduce a degree of freedom by projecting onto an *arbitrary* plane, e.g., w_q = a constant, though such networks typically have a large description length [Rissanen, 1978]. The pruning constraint $w_q = 0$ discussed throughout this paper makes retraining (if desired) particularly simple. *Several* weights can be deleted simultaneously; bias weights can be exempt from pruning, and so forth. A slight generalization of OBS employs cross-entropy or the Kullback-Leibler error measure, leading to Fisher Information matrix rather than the Hessian (Hassibi, Stork and Wolff, 1993b). We note too that OBS does not by itself give a criterion for when to stop pruning, and thus OBS can be utilized with a wide variety of such criteria. Moreover, gradual methods such as weight decay during learning can be used in conjunction with OBS.

Acknowledgements

The first author was supported in part by grants AFOSR 91-0060 and DAAL03-91-C-0010 to T. Kailath, who in turn provided constant encouragement. Deep thanks go to Greg Wolff (Ricoh) for assistance with simulations and analysis, and Jerome Friedman (Stanford) for pointers to relevant statistics literature.

REFERENCES

Hassibi, B. Stork, D. G. and Wolff, G. (1993a). Optimal Brain Surgeon and general network pruning (submitted to ICNN, San Francisco)

Hassibi, B. Stork, D. G. and Wolff, G. (1993b). Optimal Brain Surgeon, Information Theory and network capacity control (in preparation)

Hertz, J., Krogh, A. and Palmer, R. G. (1991). ***Introduction to the Theory of Neural Computation*** Addison-Wesley.

Kailath, T. (1980). ***Linear Systems*** Prentice-Hall.

Kung, S. Y. and Hu, Y. H. (1991). A Frobenius approximation reduction method (FARM) for determining the optimal number of hidden units, ***Proceedings of the IJCNN-91*** Seattle, Washington.

Le Cun, Y., Denker, J. S. and Solla, S. A. (1990). Optimal Brain Damage, in ***Proceedings of the Neural Information Processing Systems-2***, D. S. Touretzky (ed.) 598-605, Morgan-Kaufmann.

Rissanen, J. (1978). Modelling by shortest data description, *Automatica* **14**, 465-471.

Rumelhart, D. E., Hinton, G. E., and Williams, R. J. (1986). Learning Internal representations by error propagation, Chapter 8 (318-362) in ***Parallel Distributed Processing I*** D. E. Rumelhart and J. L. McClelland (eds.) MIT Press.

Seber, G. A. F. and Wild, C. J. (1989). ***Nonlinear Regression*** 35-36 Wiley.

Sejnowski, T. J., and Rosenberg, C. R. (1987). Parallel networks that learn to pronounce English text, *Complex Systems* **1**, 145-168.

Thrun, S. B. and 23 co-authors (1991). The MONK's Problems — A performance comparison of different learning algorithms, CMU-CS-91-197 Carnegie-Mellon U. Department of Computer ScienceTech Report.

Towell, G. and Shavlik, J. W. (1992). Interpretation of artificial neural networks: Mapping knowledge-based neural networks into rules, in ***Proceedings of the Neural Information Processing Systems-4***, J. E. Moody, D. S. Touretzky and R. P. Lippmann (eds.) 977-984, Morgan-Kaufmann.

Directional-Unit Boltzmann Machines

Richard S. Zemel
Computer Science Dept.
University of Toronto
Toronto, ONT M5S 1A4

Christopher K. I. Williams
Computer Science Dept.
University of Toronto
Toronto, ONT M5S 1A4

Michael C. Mozer
Computer Science Dept.
University of Colorado
Boulder, CO 80309–0430

Abstract

We present a general formulation for a network of stochastic directional units. This formulation is an extension of the Boltzmann machine in which the units are not binary, but take on values in a cyclic range, between 0 and 2π radians. The state of each unit in a Directional-Unit Boltzmann Machine (DUBM) is described by a complex variable, where the phase component specifies a direction; the weights are also complex variables. We associate a quadratic energy function, and corresponding probability, with each DUBM configuration. The conditional distribution of a unit's stochastic state is a circular version of the Gaussian probability distribution, known as the von Mises distribution. In a mean-field approximation to a stochastic DUBM, the phase component of a unit's state represents its mean direction, and the magnitude component specifies the degree of certainty associated with this direction. This combination of a value and a certainty provides additional representational power in a unit. We describe a learning algorithm and simulations that demonstrate a mean-field DUBM's ability to learn interesting mappings.

Many kinds of information can naturally be represented in terms of angular, or directional, variables. A circular range forms a suitable representation for explicitly directional information, such as wind direction, as well as for information where the underlying range is periodic, such as days of the week or months of the year. In computer vision, tangent fields and optic flow fields are represented as fields of oriented line segments, each of which can be described by a magnitude and direction. Directions can also be used to represent a set of symbolic labels, e.g., object label A at 0, and object label B at $\pi/2$ radians. We discuss below some advantages of representing symbolic labels with directional units.

These and many other phenomena can be usefully encoded using a *directional* representation—a polar coordinate representation of complex values in which the phase parameter indicates a direction between 0 and 2π radians. We have devised a general formulation of networks of stochastic directional units. This paper describes a *directional-unit Boltzmann machine* (DUBM), which is a novel generalization of a Boltzmann machine (Ackley, Hinton and Sejnowski, 1985) in which the units are not binary, but instead take on directional values between 0 and 2π.

1 STOCHASTIC DUBM

A stochastic directional unit takes on values on the unit circle. We associate with unit j a random variable Z_j; a particular state of j is described by a complex number with magnitude one and direction, or phase τ_j: $z_j = e^{i\tau_j}$.

The weights of a DUBM also take on complex values. The weight from unit k to unit j is: $w_{jk} \equiv b_{jk}e^{i\theta_{jk}}$. We constrain the weight matrix W to be Hermitian: $W^T = W^*$, where the diagonal elements of the matrix are zero, and the asterisk indicates the complex conjugate operation. Note that if the components are real, then $\mathbf{W}^T = \mathbf{W}$, which is a real symmetric matrix. Thus, the Hermitian form is a natural generalization of weight symmetry to the complex domain.

This definition of $\mathbf{W}$ leads to a Hermitian quadratic form that generalizes the real quadratic form of the Hopfield energy function:

$$E(\mathbf{z}) = -1/2\ \mathbf{z}^{*T}\mathbf{W}\mathbf{z} = -1/2 \sum_{j,k} z_j z_k^* w_{jk} \tag{1}$$

where $\mathbf{z}$ is the vector of the units' complex states in a particular global configuration. Noest (1988) independently proposed this energy function. It is similar to that used in Fradkin, Huberman, and Shenker's (1978) generalization of the XY model of statistical mechanics to allow arbitary weight phases θ_{jk}, and coupled oscillator models, e.g., Baldi and Meir (1990).

We can define a probability distribution over the possible states of a stochastic network using the Boltzmann factor. In a DUBM, we can describe the energy as a function of the state of a particular unit j:

$$E(Z_j = z_j) = -1/2\ [\sum_k z_j z_k^* w_{jk} + \sum_k z_k z_j^* w_{kj}]$$

We define

$$x_j = \sum_k z_k w_{jk}^* = a_j e^{i\alpha_j}$$

to be the net input to unit j, where a_j and α_j denote the magnitude and phase of x_j, respectively.

Applying the Boltzmann factor, we find that the probability that unit j is in a particular state is proportional to:

$$p(Z_j = z_j) \propto e^{-\beta E(Z_j = z_j)} = e^{\beta a_j \cos(\tau_j - \alpha_j)} \tag{2}$$

where β is the reciprocal of the system temperature.

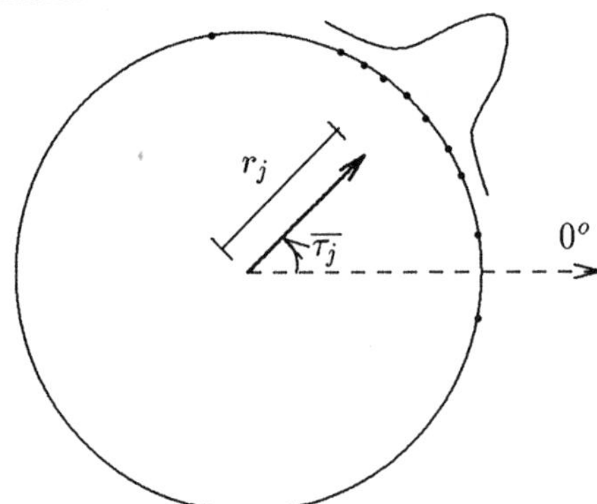

Figure 1: A circular normal density function laid over a unit circle. The dots along the circle represent samples of the circular normal random variable Z_j. The expected direction of Z_j, $\overline{\tau_j}$, is $\pi/4$; r_j is its resultant length.

This probability distribution for a unit's state corresponds to a distribution known as the *von Mises*, or *circular normal*, distribution (Mardia, 1972). Two parameters completely characterize this distribution: a mean direction $\overline{\tau} = (0, 2\pi]$ and a concentration parameter $m > 0$ that behaves like the reciprocal of the variance of a Gaussian distribution on a linear random variable. The probability density function of a circular normal random variable Z is[1]:

$$p(\tau;\ \overline{\tau}, m) \ = \ \frac{1}{2\pi I_0(m)} \ e^{m\ \cos(\tau - \overline{\tau})} \tag{3}$$

From Equations 2 and 3, we see that if a unit adopts states according to its contribution to the system energy, it will be a circular normal variable with mean direction α_j and concentration parameter $m_j \ = \ \beta a_j$. These parameters are directly determined by the net input to the unit.

Figure 1 shows a circular normal density function for Z_j, the state of unit j. This figure also shows the expected value of its stochastic state, which we define as:

$$y_j \ = < Z_j > = \ r_j e^{i\gamma_j} \tag{4}$$

where γ_j, the phase of y_j, is the mean direction and r_j, the magnitude of y_j, is the *resultant length*. For a circular normal random variable, $\gamma_j = \overline{\tau_j}$, and $r_j \ = \ \frac{I_1(m_j)}{I_0(m_j)}$.[2]

When samples of Z_j are concentrated on a small arc about the mean (see Figure 1), r_j will approach length one. This corresponds to a large concentration parameter ($m_j \ = \ \beta a_j$). Conversely, for small m_j, the distribution approaches the uniform distribution on the circle, and the resultant length falls toward zero. For a uniform distribution, $r_j \ = \ 0$. Note that the concentration parameter for a unit's circular

[1]The normalization factor $I_0(m)$ is the modified Bessel function of the first kind and order zero. An integral representation of this function is $I_0(m) = \frac{1}{\pi}\int_0^\pi e^{\pm m\cos\theta} d\theta$. It can be computed by numerical routines.

[2]An integral representation of the modified Bessel function of the first kind and order k is $I_k(m) = \frac{1}{\pi}\int_0^\pi e^{m\cos\theta}\cos(k\theta) d\theta$. Note that $I_1(m) = dI_0(m)/dm$.

normal density function is proportional to β, the reciprocal of the system temperature. Higher temperatures will thus have the effect of making this distribution more uniform, just as they do in a binary-unit Boltzmann machine.

2 EMERGENT PROPERTIES OF A DUBM

A network of directional units as defined above contains two important emergent properties. The first property is that the magnitude of the net input to unit j describes the extent to which its various inputs "agree". Intuitively, one can think of each component $z_k w^*_{jk}$ of the sum that comprises x_j as predicting a phase for unit j. When the phases of these components are equal, the magnitude of x_j, a_j, is maximized. If these phase predictions are far apart, then they will act to cancel each other out, and produce a small a_j. Given x_j, we can compute the expected value of the output of unit j. The expected direction of the unit roughly represents the weighted average of the phase predictions, while the resultant length is a monotonic function of a_j and hence describes the agreement between the various predictions.

The key idea here is that the resultant length directly describes the degree of certainty in the expected direction of unit j. Thus, a DUBM naturally incorporates a representation of the system's confidence in a value. This ability to combine several sources of evidence, and not only represent a value but also describe the certainty of that value is an important property that may be useful in a variety of domains.

The second emergent property is that the DUBM energy is globally *rotation-invariant*—E is unaffected when the same rotation is applied to all units' states in the network. For each DUBM configuration, there is an equivalence class of configurations which have the same energy. In a similar way, we find that the magnitude of x_j is *rotation-invariant*. That is, when we translate the phases of all units but one by some phase, the magnitude of that unit is unaffected. This property underlies one of the key advantages of the representation: both the magnitude of a unit's state as well as system energy depend on the *relative* rather than *absolute* phases of the units.

3 DETERMINISTIC DUBM

Just as in deterministic binary-unit Boltzmann machines (Peterson and Anderson, 1987; Hinton, 1989), we can greatly reduce the computational time required to run a large stochastic system if we invoke the *mean-field approximation*, which states that once the system has reached equilibrium, the stochastic variables can be approximated by their mean values. In this approximation, the variables are treated as independent, and the system probability distribution is simply the product of the probability distributions for the individual units.

Gislén, Peterson, and Söderberg (1992) originally proposed a mean-field theory for networks of directional (or "rotor") units, but only considered the case of real-valued weights. They derived the mean-field consistency equations by using the saddle-point method. Our approach provides an alternative, perhaps more intuitive derivation, due to the use of the circular normal distribution.

We can directly describe these mean values based on the circular normal interpretation. We still denote the net input to a unit j as x_j:

$$x_j = \sum_k y_k w_{jk}^* = a_j e^{i\alpha_j} \tag{5}$$

Once equilibrium has been reached, the state of unit j is y_j, the expected value of Z_j given the mean-field approximation:

$$y_j = r_j e^{i\gamma_j} = \frac{I_1(\beta a_j)}{I_0(\beta a_j)} e^{i\alpha_j} \tag{6}$$

In the stochastic as well as the deterministic system, units evolve to minimize the *free energy*, $F = < E > - TH$. The calculation of H, the entropy of the system, follows directly from the circular normal distribution and the mean-field approximation. We can derive mean-field consistency equations for x_j and y_j by minimizing the mean-field free energy, F_{MF}, with respect to each variable independently. The resulting equations match the mean-field equations (Equations 5 and 6) derived directly from the circular normal probability density function. They also match the special case derived by Gislén *et al.* for real-valued weights.

We have implemented a DUBM using the mean-field approximation. We solve for a consistent set of **x** and **y** values by performing synchronous updates of the discrete-time approximation of the set of differential equations based on the net input to each unit j. We update the x_j variables using the following differential equation:

$$\frac{dx_j}{dt} = -x_j + \sum_k y_k w_{jk}^* \tag{7}$$

which has Equation 5 as its steady-state solution. In the simulations, we use simulated annealing to help find good minima of F_{MF}.

Just as for the Hopfield binary-state network, it can be shown that the free energy always decreases during the dynamical evolution described in Equation 7 (Zemel, Williams and Mozer, 1992). The equilibrium solutions are free energy minima.

4 DUBM LEARNING

The units in a DUBM can be arranged in a variety of architectures. The appropriate method for determining weight values for the network depends on the particular class of network architecture. In an autoassociative network containing a single set of interconnected units, the weights can be set directly from the training patterns. If hidden units are required to perform a task, then an algorithm for learning the weights is required. We use an algorithm that generalizes the Boltzmann machine training algorithm (Ackley, Hinton and Sejnowski, 1985; Peterson and Anderson, 1987) to these networks.

As in the standard Boltzmann machine learning algorithm, the partial derivative of the objective function with respect to a weight depends on the difference between the partials of two mean-field free energies: one when both input and output units are clamped, and the other when only the input units are clamped. On a given training case, for each of these stages we let the network settle to equilibrium and then calculate the following derivatives:

$$\begin{aligned} \partial F_{MF}/\partial b_{jk} &= -r_j r_k \cos(\gamma_j - \gamma_k + \theta_{jk}) \\ \partial F_{MF}/\partial \theta_{jk} &= r_j r_k b_{jk} \sin(\gamma_j - \gamma_k + \theta_{jk}) \end{aligned}$$

The learning algorithm uses these gradients to find weight values that will minimize the objective over a training set.

5 EXPERIMENTAL RESULTS

We present below some illustrative examples to show that an adaptive network of directional units can be used in a range of paradigms, including associative memory, input/output mappings, and pattern completion.

5.1 SIMPLE AUTOASSOCIATIVE DUBM

The first set of experiments considers a simple autoassociative DUBM, which contains no hidden units, and the units are fully connected. As in a standard Hopfield network, the weights are set directly from the training patterns; they equal the superposition of the outer product of the patterns.

We have run several experiments with simple autoassociative DUBMs. The empirical results parallel those for binary-unit autoassociative networks. We find, for example, that a network containing 30 fully interconnected units is capable of reliably settling from a corrupted version of one of 4 stored patterns to a state near the pattern. These patterns thus form stable attractors, as the network can perform pattern completion and clean-up from noisy inputs. The rotation-invariance property of the energy function allows any rotated version of a training pattern to also act as an attractor. The network's performance rapidly degrades for more than 4 orthogonal patterns; the patterns themselves no longer act as fixed-points, and many random initial states end in states far from any stored pattern. In addition, more orthogonal patterns can be stored than random patterns. See Noest (1988) for an analysis of the capacity of an autoassociative DUBM with sparse and asymmetric connections.

5.2 LEARNING INPUT/OUTPUT MAPPINGS

We have also used the mean-field DUBM learning algorithm to learn the weights in networks containing hidden units. We have experimented with a task that is well-suited to a directional representation. There is a single-jointed robot arm, anchored at a point, as shown in Figure 2. The input consists of two angles: the angle between the first arm segment and the positive x-axis (λ), and the angle between the two arm segments (ρ). The two segments each have a fixed length, A and B; these are not explicitly given to the network. The output is the angle between the line connecting the two ends of the arm and the x-axis (μ). This target angle is related in a complex, non-linear way to the input angles—the network must learn to approximate the following trigonometric relationship:

$$\mu = \arctan\left(\frac{A\sin\lambda - B\sin(\lambda+\rho)}{A\cos\lambda - B\cos(\lambda+\rho)}\right)$$

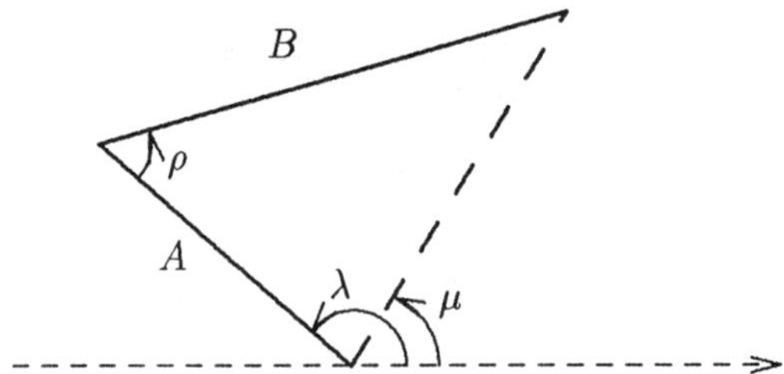

Figure 2: A sample training case for the robot arm problem. The arm consists of two fixed-length segments, A and B, and is anchored on the x-axis. The two angles, λ and ρ, are given as input for each case, and the target output is the angle μ.

With 500 training cases, a DUBM with 2 input units and 8 hidden units is able to learn the task so that it can accurately estimate μ for novel patterns. The learning requires 200 iterations of a conjugate gradient training algorithm. On each of 100 testing patterns, the resultant length of the output unit exceeds .85, and the mean error on the angle is less than .05 radians. The network can also learn the task with as few as 5 hidden units, with a concomitant decrease in learning speed. The compact nature of this network shows that the directional units form a natural, efficient representation for this problem.

5.3 COMPLEX PATTERN COMPLETION

Our earlier work described a large-scale DUBM that attacks a difficult problem in computer vision: image segmentation. In MAGIC (Mozer et al., 1992), directional values are used to represent alternative labels that can be assigned to image features. The goal of MAGIC is to learn to assign appropriate object labels to a set of image features (e.g., edge segments) based on a set of examples. The idea is that the features of a given object should have consistent phases, with each object taking on its own phase. The units in the network are arranged into two layers—feature and hidden—and the computation proceeds by randomly initializing the phases of the units in the feature layer, and settling on a labeling through a relaxation procedure. The units in the hidden layer learn to detect spatially local configurations of the image features that are labeled in a consistent manner across the training examples.

MAGIC successfully learns to segment novel scenes consisting of overlapping geometric objects. The emergent DUBM properties described above are essential to MAGIC's ability to perform this task. The complex weights are necessary in MAGIC, as the weights encode statistical regularities in the relationships between image features, e.g., that two features typically belong to the same object (i.e., have similar phase values) or to different objects (i.e., are out of phase). The fact that a unit's resultant length reflects the certainty in a phase label allows the system to decide which phase labels to use when updating labels of neighboring features: the initially random phases are ignored, while confident labels are propagated. Finally, the rotation-invariance property allows the system to assign labels to features in a manner consistent with the relationships described in the weights, where it is the *relative* rather than *absolute* phases of the units that are important.

6 CURRENT DIRECTIONS

We are currently extending this work in a number of directions. We are extending the definition of a DUBM to combine binary and directional units (Radford Neal, personal communication). This expanded representation may be useful in domains with directional data that is not present everywhere. For example, it can be directly applied to the object labeling problem explored in MAGIC. The binary aspect of the unit can describe whether a particular image feature is present or absent. This may enable the system to handle various complications, particularly labeling across gaps along the contour of an object. Finally, we are applying a DUBM network to the interesting and challenging problem of time-series prediction of wind directions.

Acknowledgements

The authors thank Geoffrey Hinton for his generous support and guidance. We thank Radford Neal, Peter Dayan, Conrad Galland, Sue Becker, Steve Nowlan, and other members of the Connectionist Research Group at the University of Toronto for helpful comments regarding this work. This research was supported by a grant from the Information Technology Research Centre of Ontario to Geoffrey Hinton, and NSF Presidential Young Investigator award IRI-9058450 and grant 90-21 from the James S. McDonnell Foundation to MM.

References

Ackley, D. H., Hinton, G. E., and Sejnowski, T. J. (1985). A learning algorithm for Boltzmann machines. *Cognitive Science*, 9:147–169.

Baldi, P. and Meir, R. (1990). Computing with arrays of coupled oscillators: An application to preattentive texture discrimination. *Neural Computation*, 2(4):458–471.

Fradkin, E., Huberman, B. A., and Shenker, S. H. (1978). Gauge symmetries in random magnetic systems. *Physical Review B*, 18(9):4789–4814.

Gislén, L., Peterson, C., and Söderberg, B. (1992). Rotor neurons: Basic formalism and dynamics. *Neural Computation*, 4(5):737–745.

Hinton, G. E. (1989). Deterministic Boltzmann learning performs steepest descent in weight-space. *Neural Computation*, 1(2):143–150.

Mardia, K. V. (1972). *Statistics of Directional Data*. Academic Press, London.

Mozer, M. C., Zemel, R. S., Behrmann, M., and Williams, C. K. I. (1992). Learning to segment images using dynamic feature binding. *Neural Computation*, 4(5):650–665.

Noest, A. J. (1988). Phasor neural networks. In *Neural Information Processing Systems*, pages 584–591, New York. AIP.

Peterson, C. and Anderson, J. R. (1987). A mean field theory learning algorithm for neural networks. *Complex Systems*, 1:995–1019.

Zemel, R. S., Williams, C. K. I., and Mozer, M. C. (1992). Adaptive networks of directional units. Technical Report CRG-TR-92-2, University of Toronto.

Time Warping Invariant Neural Networks

Guo-Zheng Sun, Hsing-Hen Chen and Yee-Chun Lee
Institute for Advanced Computer Studies
and
Laboratory for Plasma Research,
University of Maryland
College Park, MD 20742

Abstract

We proposed a model of Time Warping Invariant Neural Networks (TWINN) to handle the time warped continuous signals. Although TWINN is a simple modification of well known recurrent neural network, analysis has shown that TWINN completely removes time warping and is able to handle difficult classification problem. It is also shown that TWINN has certain advantages over the current available sequential processing schemes: Dynamic Programming(DP)[1], Hidden Markov Model(-HMM)[2], Time Delayed Neural Networks(TDNN) [3] and Neural Network Finite Automata(NNFA)[4].

We also analyzed the time continuity employed in TWINN and pointed out that this kind of structure can memorize longer input history compared with Neural Network Finite Automata (NNFA). This may help to understand the well accepted fact that for learning grammatical reference with NNFA one had to start with very short strings in training set.

The numerical example we used is a trajectory classification problem. This problem, making a feature of variable sampling rates, having internal states, continuous dynamics, heavily time-warped data and deformed phase space trajectories, is shown to be difficult to other schemes. With TWINN this problem has been learned in 100 iterations. For benchmark we also trained the exact same problem with TDNN and completely failed as expected.

I. INTRODUCTION

In dealing with the temporal pattern classification or recognition, time warping of input signals is one of the difficult problems we often encounter. Although there are a number of schemes available to handle time warping, e.g. Dynamic Programming (DP) and Hidden Markov Model(HMM), these schemes also have their own shortcomings in certain aspects. More depressing is that, as far as we know, there are no efficient neural network schemes to handle time warping. In this paper we proposed a model of Time Warping Invariant Neural Networks (TWINN) as a solution. Although TWINN is only a simple modification to the well known neural net structure, analysis shows that TWINN has the built-in ability to remove time warping completely.

The basic idea of TWINN is straightforward. If one plots the state trajectories of a continuous dynamical system in its phase space, these trajectory curves are independent of time warping because time warping can only change the time duration when traveling along these trajectories and does not affect their shapes and structures. Therefore, if we normalize the time dependence of the state variables with respect to any phase space variable, say the length of trajectory, the neural network dynamics becomes time warping invariant.

To illustrate the power of the TWINN we tested it with a numerical example of trajectory classification. This problem, chosen as a typical problem that the TWINN could handle, has the following properties: (1). The input signals obey a continuous time dynamics and are sampled with various sampling rates. (2). The dynamics of the de-warped signals has internal states. (3). The temporal patterns consist of severely time warped signals.

To our knowledge there have not been any neural network schemes which can deal with this case effectively. We tested it with TDNN and failed to learn.

In the next section we will introduce the TWINN and prove its time warping invariance. In Section III we analyze its features and identify the advantages over other schemes. The numerical example of the trajectory classification with TWINN is presented in Section IV.

II. TIME WARPING INVARIANT NEURAL NETWORKS (TWINN)

To process temporal signals, we consider a fully recurrent network, which consists of two groups of neurons: the state neurons (or recurrent units) represented by vector $\boldsymbol{S}(t)$ and the input neurons that are clamped to the external input signals $\{\boldsymbol{I}(t),\ t = 0,\ 1,\ 2,......,\ T\text{-}1)$. The Time Warping Invariant Neural Networks (TWINN) is simply defined as:

$$\boldsymbol{S}(t+1) = \boldsymbol{S}(t) + l(t)\boldsymbol{F}(\boldsymbol{S}(t), \boldsymbol{W}, \boldsymbol{I}(t)) \tag{1}$$

where $\boldsymbol{W}$ is the weight matrix, $l(t)$ is the distance between two consecutive input vectors defined by the norm

$$l(t) = \|\boldsymbol{I}(t+1) - \boldsymbol{I}(t)\| \tag{2}$$

and the mapping function $\boldsymbol{F}$ is a nonlinear function usually referred as neural activity function. For example of first order networks, it could take the form:

$$F_i(\boldsymbol{S}(t), \boldsymbol{W}, \boldsymbol{I}(t)) = Tanh\left(\sum_j W_{ij}(\boldsymbol{S}(t) \oplus \boldsymbol{I}(t))_j\right) \tag{3}$$

where $Tanh(x)$ is Hyperbolic Tangent function and symbol $\oplus$ stands for the vector concatenation.

For the purpose of classification (or recognition), we assign the target final state $\boldsymbol{S}_k$, (k=1,2,3,...K), for each category of patterns. After we feed into the TWINN the whole sequence $\{\boldsymbol{I}(0), \boldsymbol{I}(1), \boldsymbol{I}(2),......,\boldsymbol{I}(T\text{-}1)\}$, the state vector $\boldsymbol{S}(t)$ will reach the final state $\boldsymbol{S}(T)$. We then need to compare $\boldsymbol{S}(T)$ with the target final state $\boldsymbol{S}_k$ for each category k, (k=1,2,3,...K), and calculate the error:

$$e_k = \|\boldsymbol{S}(T) - \boldsymbol{S}_k\|^2 \tag{4}$$

The one with minimal error will be classified as such. The ideal error is zero.

For the purpose of training, we are given a set of training examples for each category. We then minimize the error functions given by Eq. (4) using either back-propagation[7] or forward propagation algorithm[8]. The training process can be terminated when the total error reach its minimum.

The formula of TWINN as shown in Eq. (1) does not look like new. The subtle difference from wildly used models is the introduction of normalization factor $l(t)$ as in Eq. (1). The main advantage by doing this lies in its built-in time warping ability. This can be directly seen from its continuous version.

As Eq. (1) is the discrete implementation of continuous dynamics, we can easily convert it into a continuous version by replacing "$t+1$" by "$t+\Delta t$" and let $\Delta t \to 0$. By doing so, we get

$$\lim_{\Delta t \to 0} \frac{S(t+\Delta t) - S(t)}{\| I(t+\Delta t) - I(t) \|} = \frac{dS}{dL} \tag{5}$$

where L is the input trajectory length, which can be expressed as an integral

$$L(t) = \int_0^t \left\| \frac{dI}{d\tau} \right\| d\tau \tag{6}$$

or summation (as in discrete version)

$$L(t) = \sum_{\tau=0}^{t} \| I(\tau+1) - I(\tau) \| \tag{7}$$

For deterministic dynamics, the distance $L(t)$ is a single-valued function. Therefore, we can make a unique mapping from t to L, $\prod: t \to L$, and any function of t can be transformed into a function of L in terms of this mapping. For instance, the input trajectory $I(t)$ and the state trajectory $S(t)$ can be transformed into $I(L)$ and $S(L)$. By doing so, discrete dynamics of Eq. (1) becomes, in the continuous limit,

$$\frac{dS}{dL} = F(S(L), W, I(L)) \tag{8}$$

It is obvious that there is no explicit time dependence in Eq. (8) and therefore the dynamics represented by Eq. (8) is time warping independent.

To be more specific, if we draw the trajectory curves of $I(t)$ and $S(t)$ in their phase spaces respectively, these two curves would not be deformed if we only change the time duration when traveling along the curves. Therefore, if we generate several input sequences $\{I(t)\}$ using different time warping functions and feed them into TWINN, represented by Eq. (8) or Eq. (1), the induced state dynamics of $S(L)$ would be the same. Meanwhile, the final state is the solo criterion for classification. Therefore, any time warped signals would be classified by the TWINN as the same. This is the so called "time warping invariant".

III. ANALYSIS OF TWINN VS. OTHER SCHEMES

We emphasize two points in this section. First, we would analyze the advantages of the TWINN over the other neural network structures, like TDNN, and other mature and well known algorithms for time warping, such as HMM and Dynamics Programming. Second, we would analyze the memory capacity of input history for both the continuous dynamical networks as illustrated in Eq. (1) and its discrete companion, Neural Network Finite Automata used in grammatical inference by Liu [3], Sun [4] and Giles [5]. And, we will show by mathematical estimation that the continuity employed in TWINN increases the power of memorizing history compared with NNFA

The Time Delayed Neural Networks (TDNN)[3] has been a useful neural network structure in processing temporal signals and achieves successes in several applications, e.g. speech recognition. The traditional neural network structures are either feedforward or recurrent. The TDNN is something in between. The power of TDNN is in its dynamic combination of the spatial processing (as in a feedforward net) and sequential processing (as in a recurrent net with short time memory). Therefore, the TDNN could detect the local features within each windowed frame and store their voting scores into the short time memory neurons, and then make a final decision at the end of input sequence. This technique is suitable for processing the temporal patterns where the classification is decided by the integration of local features. But, it could not handle the long time correlation across time frames like a state machine. It also does not tolerate time warping effectively. Each of time warped patterns will be treated as a new feature. Therefore, TDNN would not be able to handle the numerical example given in this paper which has both the severe time warping and the internal states (long time correlation). The benchmark test has been performed and it proved our prediction. Actually, it can be seen later that in our examples, no matter which category they belong to, all windowed frames would contain similar local features, the simple integration of local features do not contribute directly to the final classification, rather the whole sinal history will decide the classification.

As for the Dynamic Programming, it is to date the most efficient way to cope with time warping problem. The most impressing feature of dynamic programming is that it accomplishes a global search among all N^N possible paths using only ~O(N^2) operations, where N is the length of the input time series and, of course, one operation here represents all calculations involved in evaluating the 'score" of one path. But, on the other hand this is not ideal. If we can do the time warping using recurrent network, the number of operations will be reduced to ~O(N). This is a dramatic saving. Another undesirable feature of current dynamic warping scheme is that the recognition or classification result heavily depends on the pre-selected template and therefore one may need a large number of templates for a better classification rate. By adding one or two template we actually double or triple the number of operations. Therefore, search for a neural network time warping scheme is a pressing task.

Another available technique for time warping is Hidden Markov Model (HMM), which has been successfully applied in speech recognition. The way for HMM to deal with time warping is in terms of statistical behavior of its hidden state transition. Starting from one state q_i, HMM allows a certain probability a_{ij} to forward to another state q_j. Therefore, for any given HMM one could generate various state sequences, say, $q_1q_2q_2q_3q_4q_4q_5$, $q_1q_2q_2q_2q_3q_3q_4q_4q_5$, etc., each with a certain occurrence probability. But, these state sequences are "hidden", the observed part is a set of speech data or symbol represented by $\{s_k\}$ for example. HMM also includes a set of observation probability $B \equiv \{b_{jk}\}$, so that when it is in a certain state, say q_j, HMM allows each symbol from the set $\{s_k\}$ to occur with the probability b_{jk}. Therefore, for any state sequence one can generate various series of symbols. As an example, let us consider one simple way to generate symbols: in state q_j we generate symbol s_j (with probability b_{jj}). By doing so, the two state sequences mentioned above would correspond to two possible symbol sequences: $s_1s_2s_2s_3s_4s_4s_5$ and $s_1s_2s_2s_2s_3s_3s_4s_4s_5$. Examining the two strings closely, we find that the second one may be considered as the time warped version of the first one, or *vice versa*. If we present these two strings to the HMM for testing, it will accept them with similar probabilities. This is the way that HMM tolerates time warping. And, these state transition probabilities of HMM are learned from the statistics of training set by using re-estimation formula. In this sense, HMM does not deal with time warping directly, instead, it learns statistical distribution of training set which contains time warped patterns. Consequently, if one presents a test pattern with time warped signals which is far away from the statistical distribution of training set, it is very unlikely for a HMM to recognize this pattern.

On the contrary, the model of TWINN we proposed here has intrinsic built-in time warping nature. Although the TWINN itself has internal states, these internal states are not used for tolerating time warping. Instead, they are used to learn more complex behavior of the "de-warped" trajectories. In this sense, TWINN could be more powerful than HMM.

Another feature of TWINN needs be mention is its explicit expression of continuous mapping from $\boldsymbol{S}(t)$ to $\boldsymbol{S}(t+1)$ as shown in Eq. (1). In our early work of [4,5,6], to train a NNFA (Neural Network Finite Automaton), we used a discrete mapping

$$\boldsymbol{S}(t+1) = \boldsymbol{F}(\boldsymbol{S}(t), \boldsymbol{W}, \boldsymbol{I}(t)) \tag{9}$$

where $\boldsymbol{F}$ is a nonlinear function, say *Sigmoid* function $g(x) \equiv 1/(1+e^{-x})$. This model has been successfully applied into the grammatical inference. The reason we call Eq. (1) a continuous mapping but Eq. (9) a discrete one, even though both of them are implemented in discrete time steps, is because there is an explicit infinitesimal factor $l(t)$ used in Eq. (1). Due to this factor the continuous state dynamics is guaranteed, by which we mean that the state variation $\boldsymbol{S}(t+1)$ - $\boldsymbol{S}(t+1)$ approaches zero if the input variation $\boldsymbol{I}(t+1)$ - $\boldsymbol{I}(t+1)$ does so. But, In general, the state variation $S(t+1)$ - $S(t+1)$ generated by Eq. (9) is of order of one, regardless of what input variations are. If one starts from random initial weights, Eq. (9) provides a discrete jump between different, randomly distributed states, which is far away from any continuous dynamics.

We did numerical test using NNFA of Eq. (9) to learn the classification problem of continuous trajectories as shown in Section V. For simplicity we did not include time warping, but the NNFA still failed to learn. The reason is that when we tried to train a NNFA to learning the continuous dynamics, we were actually forcing the weights to generate an almost identical mapping F from $S(t)$ to $S(t+1)$. This is a very strong constrain on the weight parameters, such that it drives the diagonal terms to positive infinity and off-diagonal terms to negative infinity (*Sigmoid* function is used). When this happens, the learning is stuck due to the saturation effect.

The failure of NNFA may also comes from the short history memory capacity compared to the continuous mapping of Eq. (1). It has been shown by many numerical experiments on grammatical inference [3, 4, 5] that to train an NNFA as in Eq. (9) effectively, one has to start with short training patterns (usually, the sentence length ≤ 4). Otherwise, learning will fail or be very slow. This is exactly what happened to learning the trajectory classification using NNFA, where the lengths of our training patterns are in general considerably long (normally,~ 60). But, TWINN learned it easily. To understand the NNFA's failure and TWINN's success, in the following, we will analyze how the history information enters the learning process.

Consider the example of learning grammatical inference. Before training since we have no *a priori* knowledge about the target values of weights, we normally start with random initial values. On the other hand, during training the credit assignment (or the weight correction ΔW) can only be done at the end of each input sequence. Consequently, each ΔW should explicitly contain the information about all symbols contained in that string, otherwise the learning is meaningless. But, in numerical implementation, every variable, including both ΔW and W, has a finite precision and any information beyond the precision range will be lost. Therefore, to compare which model has the longer history memory we need to examine how the history information relates to the finite precisions of ΔW and W.

Let us illustrate this point with a simple second-order connected fully recurrent network and write both Eq. (1) and Eq. (9) in a unified form

$$S(t+1) = G^{t+1} \tag{10}$$

such that Eq. (1) is represented by

$$G^{t+1} = S(t) + l(t)\, g(K(t)) \tag{11}$$

and Eq. (9) is just

$$G^{t+1} = g(K(t)) \tag{12}$$

where $K(t)$ is the weighted sum of concatenation of vectors $S(t)$ and $I(t)$

$$K_i(t) = \sum_j W_{ij} (S(t) \oplus I(t))_j \tag{13}$$

For a grammatical inference problem the error is calculated from the final state $S(T)$ as

$$E = (S(T) - S_{target})^2 \tag{14}$$

Learning is to minimize this error function. According to the standard error back-propagation scheme, the recurrent net can be viewed as a multi-layered net with identical weights between neurons at adjacent time step: $w(t) = W$, where $w(t)$ is the "t_{th} layer" weights connecting *input* $S(t-1)$ to *output* $S(t)$. The total weight correction is the summation of all weight corrections at each layer. By using the gradient descent scheme one immediately has

$$\Delta W = \sum_{t=1}^{T} \delta w(t) = -\eta \sum_{t=1}^{T} \frac{\partial E}{\partial w(t)} = -\eta \sum_{t=1}^{T} \frac{\partial E}{\partial S(t)} \cdot \frac{\partial G^t}{\partial w(t)} \tag{15}$$

If we define new symbols: vector $u(t)$, second-order tensor $A(t)$ and third-order tensor $B(t)$ as

$$u_i(t) \equiv \frac{\partial E}{\partial S_i(t)} \qquad B_{ijk}(t) \equiv \frac{\partial G_i^t}{\partial W_{jk}} \qquad A_{ij}(t) \equiv \frac{\partial G_i^{t+1}}{\partial S_j(t)} \tag{16}$$

the weight correction can be simply written as

$$\Delta W = -\eta \sum_{t=1}^{T} u(t) \cdot B(t) \tag{17}$$

and the "error rate" $u(t)$ can be back-propagated using the Derivative Chain Rule

$$u(t) = u(t+1) \cdot A(t) \qquad t = 1, 2, \ldots, T-1; \tag{18}$$

so that it is easy to have

$$u(t) = u(T) \cdot A(T-1) \cdot A(T-2) \cdot \ldots \cdot A(t) \equiv u(T) \cdot \prod_{\tau = T-1}^{t} A(\tau) \qquad t = 1, 2, \ldots, T-1; \tag{19}$$

First, let us examine the model of NNFA in Eq. (9). Using Eqs. (12), (13) and (16), $A_{ij}(t)$ and $B_{ijk}(t)$ can be written as

$$A_{ij}(t) = g'(K_i(t))\, W_{ij} \qquad B_{ijk}(t) = \delta_{ij}(S(t-1) \oplus I(t-1))_k \tag{20}$$

where $g'(x) \equiv dg/dx = g(1-g)$ is the derivative of *Sigmoid* function and δ_{ij} is Kronecker delta function. If we substitute $B_{ijk}(t)$ into Eq. (17), ΔW becomes a weighted sum of all input symbols $\{I(0), I(1), I(2), \ldots\ldots, I(T-1)\}$, each with different weighting factor $u(t)$. Therefore, to guarantee that ΔW contain the information of all input symbols $\{I(0), I(1), I(2), \ldots\ldots, I(T-1)\}$, the ratio of $|u(t)|_{max}/|u(t)|_{min}$ should be within the range of precision of ΔW. This is the main point.

The exact mathematical analysis has not been done, but from a rough estimate we can gain some good understanding. From Eq. (19), $u(t)$ is a matrices product of $A_{ij}(t)$, and $u(1)$ the coefficient of $I(0)$ contains the highest order product of $A_{ij}(t)$. The key point is that the coefficient ratio between the adjacent symbols: $|u(t)|/|u(t+1)$ is of the order of $|A_{ij}(t)|$, which is a small value, therefore the earlier symbol information could be lost from ΔW due to its finite precision. It can be shown that $xg'(x) = x\, g(x)(1-g(x)) < 0.25$ for any real value of x. Then, we roughly have $|A_{ij}(t)| = |g' W_{ij}| = |g(1-g) W_{ij}| < 0.25$, if we assume the values of weights W_{ij} to be order 1. Thus, the ratio $R = |u(t)|_{max}/|u(t)|_{min}$ is estimated as

$$R \sim |u(1)| / |u(T)| \sim \prod_{t' = T-1}^{1} |A(t')| < 2^{-2.(T-1)} \tag{21}$$

From Eq. (21) we see that if the input pattern length is T=10 we need at least 2(T-1) ≅ 18 bits computer memory to store weight variables (including u, W and ΔW). If T= 60, as in the trajectory classification problem, it requires at least 128 bit weight variables. This is why the NNFA Eq. (9) could not work.

Similarly, for the dynamics of Eq. (1), we use Eqs. (11), (13) and (16), and obtain

$$A_{ij}(t) = 1 + l(t)\ (g'(K_i(t))\, W_{ij}) \qquad B_{ijk}(t) = l(t)\ (\delta_{ij}(S(t-1) \oplus I(t-1))_k) \tag{22}$$

From Eq. (22) we see that no matter how small the factor l(t) will be, $|A_{ij}(t)|$ remains a value of order of one, therefore the ratio $R = |u(t)|_{max}/|u(t)|_{min}$ which is estimated as a product of $|A_{ij}(t)|$ would be of order of one compared with result of discrete case as in Eq. (21). Therefore, the contributions from ***all*** $\{I(0), I(1), I(2), \ldots\ldots, I(T-1)\}$ to the weight correction ΔW are of the same order. This prevents the information loss during learning.

IV NUMERICAL SIMULATION

We demonstrate the power of TWINN with a trajectory classification problem. The three 2-

D trajectory equations are artificially given by

$$\begin{cases} x(t) = \sin(t+\beta)\,|\sin(t)| \\ y(t) = \cos(t+\beta)\,|\sin(t)| \end{cases} \begin{cases} x(t) = \sin(0.5t+\beta)\sin(1.5t) \\ y(t) = \cos(0.5t+\beta)\sin(1.5t) \end{cases} \begin{cases} x(t) = \sin(t+\beta)\sin(2t) \\ y(t) = \cos(t+\beta)\sin(2t) \end{cases} \quad (23)$$

where β is a uniformly distributed random parameter. When β is changed, these trajectories are distorted accordingly. Some examples (three for each class) are shown in Fig.1.

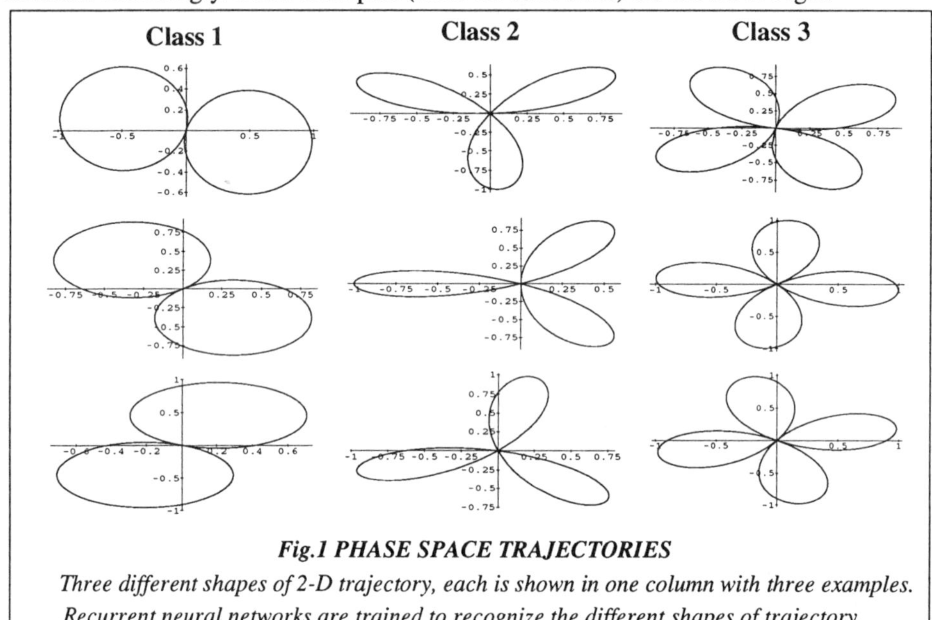

Fig.1 PHASE SPACE TRAJECTORIES

Three different shapes of 2-D trajectory, each is shown in one column with three examples. Recurrent neural networks are trained to recognize the different shapes of trajectory.

The trajectory data are the time series of two dimensional coordinate pairs $\{x(t), y(t)\}$ sampled along three different types of curves in the phase space. The neural net dynamics of TWINN is

$$S_i(t+1) = S_i(t) + l(t)\left(Tanh\left(\sum_{j=1}^{N+6} W_{ij}(S(t) \oplus \boldsymbol{I}(t))_j\right)\right) \quad and \quad l(t) = \sqrt{\sum_{i=1}^{6}(I_i(t) - I_i(t-1))^2} \quad (24)$$

where we used 6 input neurons $\boldsymbol{I} = \{1, x(t), y(t), x^2(t), y^2(t), x(t)y(t)\}$ (normalized to norm = 1.0) and 4 (N=4) state neurons $S = \{S_1, S_2, S_3, S_4\}$. The neural network structure is shown in Fig. 2.

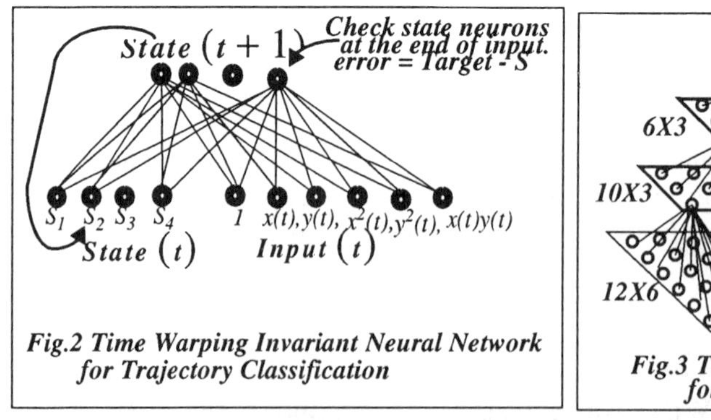

Fig.2 Time Warping Invariant Neural Network for Trajectory Classification

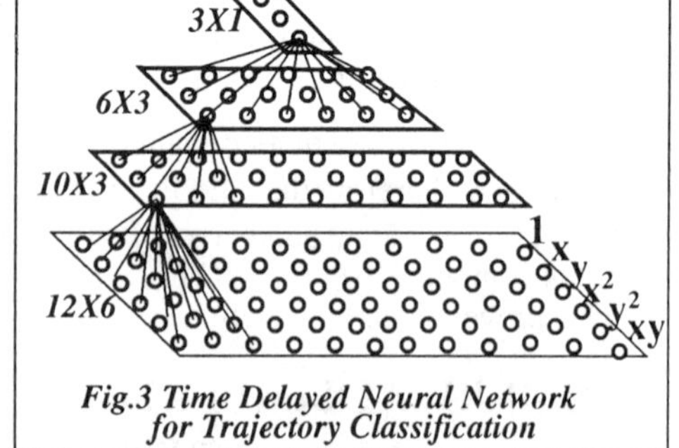

Fig.3 Time Delayed Neural Network for Trajectory Classification

For training, we assign the desired final output for the three trajectory classes to be (1,0,0),

(0,1,0) and (0,0,1) respectively. For recognition, each trajectory data sequence needs to be fed to the input neurons and the state neurons evolve according to the dynamics in Eq. (24). At the end of input series we check the last three state neurons and classify the input trajectory according to the "winner-take-all" rule.

In each iteration of training we randomly picked up 150 deformed trajectories, 50 for each of the three categories, by choosing different values of β within $0 \leq \beta \leq 2\pi$. To simulate time warping we randomly sampled the data by choosing the random time step $\Delta t = 2\pi r/T$ along each trajectory, where r is a random number between 0 and 2 and the sampling rate T=60 for training patterns, and T=20 to 200 for testing patterns. Therefore, each training pattern is a time warped trajectory data with averaged length = 60. Using RTRL algorithm[8] to minimize the error function, after 100 iterations of training it converged to Mean Square Error of $\cong 0.03$.

We tested the trained network with hundreds of randomly picked input sequences with different sampling rate (from $20/2\pi$ to $200/2\pi$) and different wrapping functions (non-uniform step length). All input trajectories are classified correctly. If the sampling rates are too large (>200) or too small(<20), some classification errors will occur.

We test the same example with TDNN. See Fig.3 for its parameters. The top layer contains three output neurons for the three classes of trajectories. The classification rules, error function and training patterns are the same as those of TWINN. After three days of training with DEC-3100 Workstation the training error (MSE) approaches 0.5 and in testing the error rate is 70%.

V. CONCLUSION

We have proposed a model of Time Warping Invariant Neural Network to handle temporal pattern classification where the severely time warped and deformed data may occur. This model is shown to have built-in time warping ability. We have analyzed the properties of TWINN and shown that for trajectory classification it has several advantages over other schemes: HMM, DP, TDNN and NNFA.

We also numerically implemented the TWINN and trained a trajectory classification easily. This problem is shown by analysis to be difficult to other schemes. It has been trained with TDNN but failed.

References

[1] H.Sakoe and S. Chiba, "Dynamic Programming Algorithm Optimization for Spoken Word Recognition", IEEE Transactions on Acoustics Speech and Signal Processing, Vol. ASSP-26, pp.43-49, Feb. 1978.

[2] L.R.Rabiner and B.H.Juang, "An Introduction to Hidden Markov Models", IEEE, ASSP Mag., Vol.3, No. 1, pp. 4-16, 1986.

[3]A. Weibel, T. Hanazawa, G. Hinton, K.shikano and K. Lang, "Phoneme Recognition Using Time-Delay Neural Networks", IEEE Transactions on Acoustics Speech and Signal Processing, March,1989.

[4]. Y.D. Liu, G.Z. Sun, H.H. Chen, C.L. Giles and Y.C. Lee, *"Grammatic Inference and Neural Network State Machine*", Proceedings of the International Joint Conference on Neural Networks, pp. I-285, Washington D.C. (1990).

[5]. G.Z. Sun, H.H. Chen, C.L. Giles, Y.C. Lee and D. Chen, "*Connectionist Pushdown Automata that Learn Context-Free Grammars*", Proceedings of the International Joint Conference on Neural networks, pp. I-577, Washington D.C. (1990).

[6]Giles, C.L., Sun, G.Z., Chen, H.H., Lee,Y.C., and Chen, D. (1990). "Higher Order Recurrent Networks & Grammatical Inference". *Advances in Neural Information Processing Systems 2*, D.S. Touretzky (editor), 380-386, Morgan Kaufmann, San Mateo, C.A. (7)

[7] D.Rumelhart, G. Hinton, and R. Williams. "Learning internal representations by error propagation", In PDP: Vol.I MIT press 1986. P. Werbos, "Beyond Regression: New tools for prediction and analysis in the behavior sciences", Ph.D. thesis, Harvard university, 1974.

[8] R. Williams and D. Zipser, "A learning algorithm for continually running fully recurrent neural networks", Neural Computation 1(1989), pp.270-280.

Generalization Abilities of Cascade Network Architectures

E. Littmann*
Department of Information Science
Bielefeld University
D-4800 Bielefeld, FRG
littmann@techfak.uni-bielefeld.de

H. Ritter
Department of Information Science
Bielefeld University
D-4800 Bielefeld, FRG
helge@techfak.uni-bielefeld.de

Abstract

In [5], a new incremental cascade network architecture has been presented. This paper discusses the properties of such cascade networks and investigates their generalization abilities under the particular constraint of small data sets. The evaluation is done for cascade networks consisting of local linear maps using the Mackey-Glass time series prediction task as a benchmark. Our results indicate that to bring the potential of large networks to bear on the problem of *extracting information from small data sets without running the risk of overfitting*, deeply cascaded network architectures are more favorable than shallow broad architectures that contain the same number of nodes.

1 Introduction

For many real-world applications, a major constraint for the successful learning from examples is the limited number of examples available. Thus, methods are required, that can learn from small data sets. This constraint makes the problem of generalization particularly hard. If the number of adjustable parameters in a

*to whom correspondence should be sent

network approaches the number of training examples, the problem of *overfitting* occurs and generalization becomes very poor. This severely limits the size of networks applicable to a learning task with a small data set. To achieve good generalization also in these cases, particular attention must be paid to *a proper architecture* chosen for the network. The better the architecture matches the structure of the problem at hand, the better is the chance to achieve good results even with small data sets and small numbers of units.

In the present paper, we address this issue for the class of so called *Cascade Network Architectures* [5, 6] on the basis of an empirical approach, where we use the Mackey-Glass time series prediction as a benchmark problem. In our experiments we want to exploit the potential of large networks to bear on the problem of *extracting information from small data sets without running the risk of overfitting*. Our results indicate that it is more favorable to use deeply cascaded network architectures than shallow broad architectures, provided the same number of nodes is used in both cases. The width of each individual layer is essentially determined by the size of the training data set. The cascade depth is then matched to the total number of nodes available.

2 Cascade Architecture

So far, mainly architectures with few layers containing many units have been considered, while there has been very little research on narrow, but deeply cascaded networks. One of the few exceptions is the work of Fahlman [1], who proposed networks trained by the cascade-correlation algorithm. In his original approach, training is strictly feed-forward and the nonlinearity is achieved by incrementally adding perceptron units trained to maximize the covariance with the residual error.

2.1 Construction Algorithm

In [5] we presented a new incremental cascade network architecture based on *error minimization* instead of *covariance maximization*. This leads to an architecture that differs significantly from Fahlman's proposal and allows an *inversion of the construction process* of the network. Thus, at each stage of the construction of the network *all* cascaded modules provide an approximation of the target function $t(\xi)$, albeit corresponding to different states of convergence (Fig. 1).

The algorithm starts with the training of a neural module with output $\mathbf{y}^{(0)}$ to approximate a target function $\mathbf{t}(\xi)$, yielding

$$\mathbf{y}^{(0)}(\xi) = f^{(0)}\left(\mathbf{w}^{(0)}, \mathbf{x}^{(0)}(\xi)\right), \tag{1}$$

the superscript $^{(0)}$ indicating the cascade level. After an arbitrary number of training epochs, the weight vector $\mathbf{w}^{(0)}$ becomes "frozen". Now we add the output $\mathbf{y}^{(0)}$ of this module as a *virtual* input unit and train another neural module *as new output*

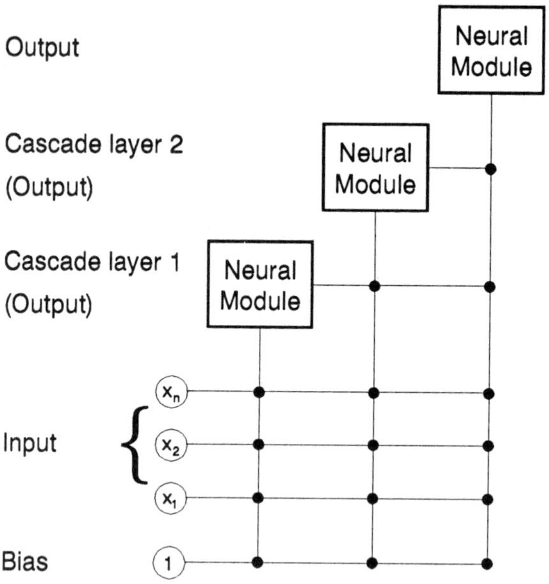

Figure 1: Cascade Network Architecture

unit $y^{(1)}$ with

$$\mathbf{y}^{(1)} = f^{(1)}\left(\mathbf{w}^{(1)}, \mathbf{x}^{(1)}(\xi)\right). \tag{2}$$

where $\mathbf{x}^{(1)}(\xi) = \{\mathbf{x}^{(0)}(\xi), \mathbf{y}^{(0)}(\xi)\}$ denotes the extended input. This procedure can be iterated arbitrarily and generates a network structure as shown in Fig. 1.

2.2 Cascade Modules

The details and advantages of this approach are discussed in [5, 6]. In particular, this architecture can be applied to *any arbitrary nonlinear* module. It *does not* rely on the availability of a procedure for error backpropagation. Therefore, it is also applicable to (and has been extensively tested with) pure feed-forward approaches like simple perceptrons [5] and vector quantization or "Local linear maps" ("LLM networks") [6, 7].

2.3 Local Linear Maps

LLM networks have been introduced earlier ((Fig. 2); for details, cf. [11, 12]) and are related to the GRBF–approach [10] and the self–organizing maps [2, 3, 11]. They consist of N units $r = 1, \ldots, N$, with an input weight vector $\mathbf{w}_r^{(in)} \in \mathbb{R}^L$, an output weight vector $\mathbf{w}_r^{(out)} \in \mathbb{R}^M$ and a MxL-matrix $\mathbf{A}_r$ for each unit r.

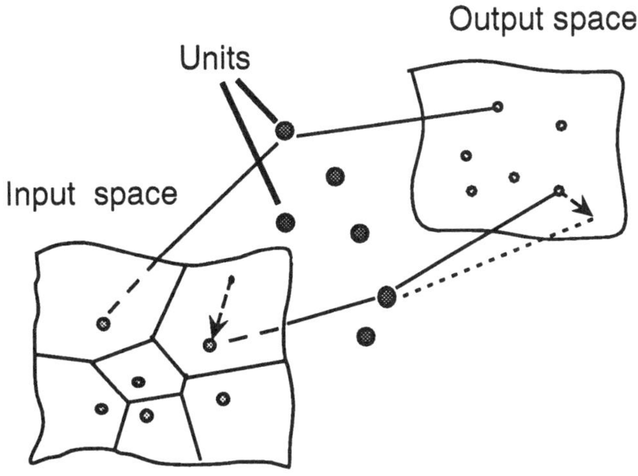

Figure 2: LLM Network Architecture

The output $\mathbf{y}^{(net)}$ of a single LLM-network for an input feature vector $\mathbf{x} \in \mathbb{R}^L$ is

$$\mathbf{y}^{(net)}(\mathbf{x}) = \mathbf{y}_s(\mathbf{x}) = \mathbf{w}_s^{(out)} + \mathbf{A}_s(\mathbf{x} - \mathbf{w}_s^{(in)}), \tag{3}$$

the "winner" node s determined by the minimality condition

$$\|\mathbf{x} - \mathbf{x}_s\| = min_r \|\mathbf{x} - \mathbf{w}_r^{(in)}\|. \tag{4}$$

This leads to the learning steps for a training sample $(\mathbf{x}^{(\alpha)}, \mathbf{y}^{(\alpha)})$:

$$\begin{aligned} \Delta\mathbf{w}_s^{(in)} &= \epsilon_1(\mathbf{x}^{(\alpha)} - \mathbf{w}_s^{(in)}), & (5)\\ \Delta\mathbf{w}_s^{(out)} &= \epsilon_2(\mathbf{y}^{(\alpha)} - \mathbf{w}_s^{(out)}) - \mathbf{A}_s\Delta\mathbf{w}_s^{(in)}, \text{ and} & (6)\\ \Delta\mathbf{A}_s &= \epsilon_3(d_s^2)^{-1}(\mathbf{y}^{(\alpha)} - \mathbf{y}^{(net)})(\mathbf{x}^{(\alpha)} - \mathbf{w}_s^{(in)})^T, & (7) \end{aligned}$$

applied for T samples $(\mathbf{x}^{(\alpha)}, \mathbf{y}^{(\alpha)}), \alpha = 1, 2, \ldots T$, and $0 < \epsilon_i << 1$, $i = 1, 2, 3$ denote learning step sizes. The additional term in (6), not given in [11, 12], leads to a better decoupling of the effects of (5) and (6,7).

3 Experiments

In order to evaluate the generalization performance of this architecture, we consider the problem of time series prediction based on the Mackey–Glass differential equation, for which results of other networks already have been reported in the literature.

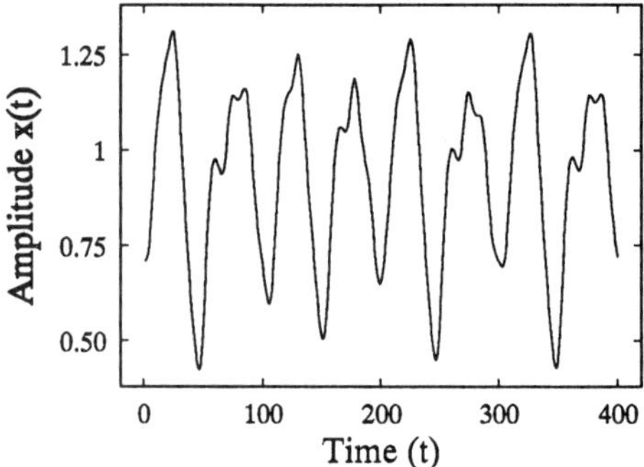

Figure 3: Mackey–Glass function

3.1 Time Series Prediction

Lapedes and Farber [4] introduced the prediction of chaotic time series as a benchmark problem. The data is based on the Mackey-Glass differential equation [8]:

$$\dot{x}(t) = -bx(t) + (ax(t-\tau))/(1 + x^{10}(t-\tau)). \tag{8}$$

With the parameters $a = 0.2$, $b = 0.1$, and $\tau = 17$, this equation produces a chaotic time series with a strange attractor of fractal dimension $d \approx 2.1$ (Fig. 3). The input data is a vector $\mathbf{x}(t) = \{x(t), x(t-\Delta), x(t-2\Delta), x(t-3\Delta)\}^T$. The learning task is defined to predict the value $x(t+P)$. To facilitate comparison, we adopt the standard choice $\Delta = 6$ and $P = 85$. Results with these parameters have been reported in [4, 9, 13].

The data was generated by integration with 30 steps per time unit. We performed different numbers of training epochs with samples randomly chosen from training sets consisting of 500 (5000 resp.) samples. The performance was measured on an independent test set of 5000 samples. All results are averages over ten runs. The error measure is the *normalized root mean square error* (**NRMSE**), i.e. predicting the average value yields an error value of 1.

4 Results and Discussion

The training of the single LLM networks was performed without extensive parameter tuning. If fine tuning for each cascade unit would be necessary, the training would be unattractively expensive.

The first results were achieved with cascade networks consisting of LLM units after 30 training epochs per layer on a learning set of 500 samples. Figs. 4 and 5 represent the performance of such LLM cascade networks *on the independent test set* for different numbers of cascaded layers as a function of the number of nodes per layer

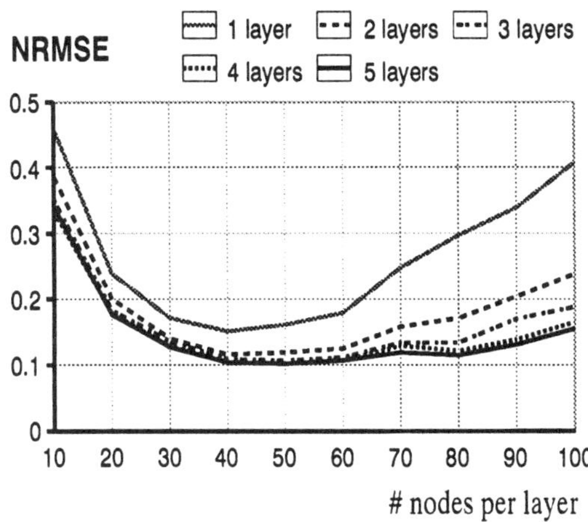

Figure 4: Iso-Layer-Dependence

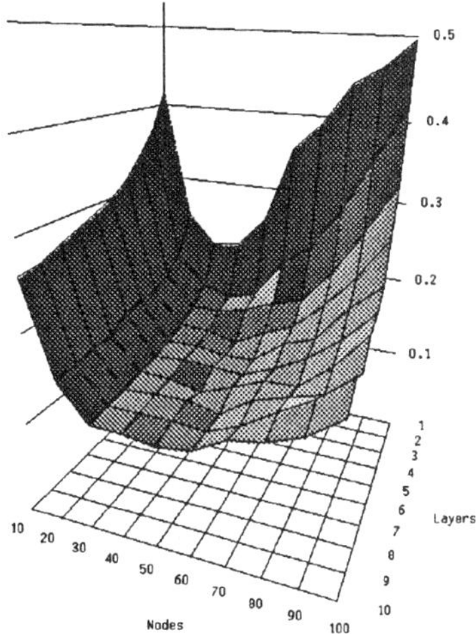

Figure 5: Error Landscape

("iso-layer-curves"). The graphs indicate that there is an optimal number $N_{opt}^{(1)}$ of nodes for which the performance of the single layer network has a best value $P_{opt}^{(1)}$. Within the single layer architecture, additional nodes lead to a decrease of performance due to overfitting. This can only be avoided if the training set is enlarged, since $N_{opt}^{(1)}$ grows with the number of available training examples.

However, Figs. 4 and 5 show that adding more units in the form of an additional, cascaded layer allows to increase performance *significantly beyond* $P_{opt}^{(1)}$. Similarly, the optimal performance of the resulting two-layer network cannot be improved beyond an optimal value $P_{opt}^{(2)}$ by arbitrarily increasing the number of nodes in the two-layer system. However, adding a third cascaded layer again allows to make use of more nodes to improve performance further, although this time the relative gain is smaller than for the first cascade step. The same situation repeats for larger numbers of cascaded layers. This suggests that the cascade architecture is very suitable to exploit the computational capabilities of large numbers of nodes for the task of building networks that *generalize well from small data sets without running into the problem of overfitting when many nodes are used.*

A second way of comparing the benefits of shallow and broad versus narrow and deep architectures is to compare the performance achieveable by distributing a fixed number N of nodes over different numbers L of cascaded layers. Fig. 6 shows the result for the same benchmark problem as in Fig. 4, each graph belonging to one of the values $N = 40, 60, 120, 240$ nodes and representing the NRMSE for distributing the N nodes among L layers of N/L nodes each[1], L ranging from 1 to 10 layers ("iso-nodes-curves").

[1]rounding to the nearest integral, whenever N/L is nonintegral.

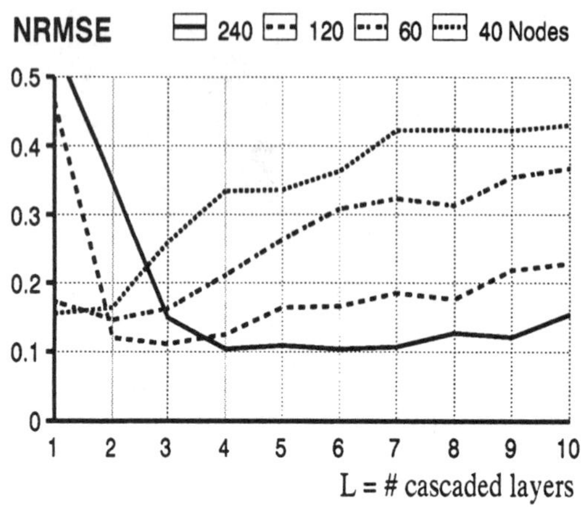

Figure 6: Iso-Nodes-Dependence

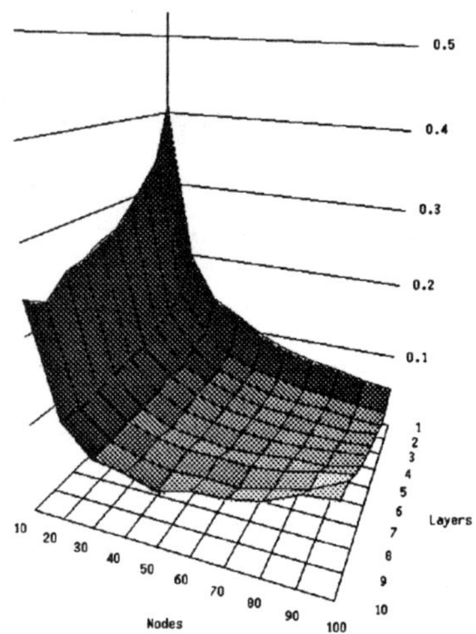

Figure 7: Nodes-Layer-Dependence

The results show that

(i) the optimal number of layers increases monotonously with — and is roughly proportional to — the number of nodes to be used.

(ii) if for each number of nodes the optimal number of layers is used, performance increases monotonously with the number of available nodes, and thus, as a consequence of (i), with the number of cascaded layers.

These results are not restricted to small data sets only. The application of the cascade algorithm is also useful if larger training sets are available. Fig. 7 represents the performance of LLM cascade networks on the test set after 300 training epochs overall on a learning set consisting of *5000 samples*. As could be expected, there is still no sign of overfitting, even using LLM networks with 100 nodes per layer. But regardless of the size of the single LLM unit, network performance is improved by the cascade process at least in a zone involving a total of some 300 nodes in the whole cascade.

5 Conclusions

Summarizing, we find that Cascade Network Architectures allow to use the benefits of large numbers of nodes even for small training data sets, and still bypass the problem of overfitting. To achieve this, the "width" of each layer must be matched to the size of the training set. The "depth" of the cascade then is determined by the total number of nodes available.

Acknowledgements

This work was supported by the German Ministry of Research and Technology (BMFT), Grant No. ITN9104AO. Any responsibility for the contents of this publication is with the authors.

References

[1] Fahlman, S.E., and Lebiere, C. (1989), "The Cascade-Correlation Learning Architecture", in *Advances in Neural Information Processing Systems II*, ed. D.S. Touretzky, pp. 524–532.

[2] Kohonen, T. (1984), *Self-Organization and Associative Memory*, Springer Series in Information Sciences 8, Springer, Heidelberg.

[3] Kohonen, T. (1990), "The Self-Organizing Map", in *Proc. IEEE* **78**, pp. 1464–1480.

[4] Lapedes, A., and Farber, R. (1987), "Nonlinear signal processing using neural networks; Prediction and system modeling", TR LA–UR–87–2662

[5] Littmann, E., Ritter, H. (1992), "Cascade Network Architectures", in *Proc. Intern. Joint Conference On Neural Networks*, pp. II/398-404, Baltimore.

[6] Littmann, E., Ritter, H. (1992), "Cascade LLM Networks", in *Artificial Neural Networks II*, eds. I. Aleksander, J. Taylor, pp. 253-257, Elsevier Science Publishers (North Holland).

[7] Littmann, E., Meyering, A., Ritter, H. (1992), "Cascaded and Parallel Neural Network Architectures for Machine Vision — A Case Study", in *Proc. 14. DAGM-Symposium 1992, Dresden*, ed. S. Fuchs, pp. 81-87, Springer, Heidelberg.

[8] Mackey, M., and Glass, L. (1977), "Oscillations and chaos in physiological control systems", in *Science*, pp. 287–289.

[9] Moody, J., Darken, C. (1988). "Learning with Localized Receptive Fields", in *Proc. of the 1988 Connectionist Models Summer School*, Pittsburg, pp. 133–143, Morgan Kaufman Publishers, San Mateo, CA.

[10] Poggio, T., Edelman, S. (1990), "A network that learns to recognize three-dimensional objects", in *Nature* **343**, pp. 263–266.

[11] Ritter, H. (1991), "Learning with the Self-organizing Map", in *Artificial Neural Networks 1*, eds. T. Kohonen, K. Mäkisara, O. Simula, J. Kangas, pp. 357-364, Elsevier Science Publishers (North-Holland).

[12] Ritter, H., Martinetz, T., Schulten, K. (1992). *Neural Computation and Self-organizing Maps*, Addison-Wesley, Reading, MA.

[13] Walter, J., Ritter, H., Schulten, K. (1990). "Non-linear prediction with self-organizing maps", in *Proc. Intern. Joint Conference On Neural Networks*, San Diego, Vol.1, pp. 587–592.

Assessing and Improving Neural Network Predictions by the Bootstrap Algorithm

Gerhard Paass
German National Research Center for Computer Science (GMD)
D-5205 Sankt Augustin, Germany
e-mail: paass@gmd.de

Abstract

The bootstrap algorithm is a computational intensive procedure to derive nonparametric confidence intervals of statistical estimators in situations where an analytic solution is intractable. It is applied to neural networks to estimate the predictive distribution for unseen inputs. The consistency of different bootstrap procedures and their convergence speed is discussed. A small scale simulation experiment shows the applicability of the bootstrap to practical problems and its potential use.

1 INTRODUCTION

Bootstrapping is a strategy for estimating standard errors and confidence intervals for parameters when the form of the underlying distribution is unknown. It is particularly valuable when the parameter of interest is a complicated functional of the true distribution. The key idea first promoted by Efron (1979) is that the relationship between the true cumulative distribution function (cdf) F and the sample of size n is similar to the relationship between the empirical cdf $\hat{F}_n$ and a secondary sample drawn from it. So one uses the primary sample to form an estimate $\hat{F}_n$ and calculates the sampling distribution of the parameter estimate under $\hat{F}_n$. This calculation is done by drawing many secondary samples and finding the estimate, or function of the estimate, for each. If $\mathcal{F}_n$ is a good approximation of F, then H_n, the sampling distribution of the estimate under $\hat{F}_n$, is a generally good approximation to the sampling distribution for the estimate under F. H_n is called the *bootstrap distribution* of the parameter. Introductory articles are Efron and Gong (1983) and Efron and Tibshirani (1986). For a survey of bootstrap results see Hinkley (1988) and DiCiccio and Romano (1988).

A neural networks often may be considered as a nonlinear or nonparametric regression model

$$z = g_\beta(y) + \epsilon \tag{1}$$

which defines the relation between the vectors y and z of input and output variables. The term ϵ can be interpreted as a random 'error' and the function g_β depends on some unkown parameter β which may have infinite dimension. Usually the network is used to determine a prediction $z_0 = g_\beta(y_0)$ for some new input vector y_0. If the data is a random sample, an estimate $\hat{\beta}$ differs from the true value of β because of the sampling error and consequently the prediction $g_{\hat{\beta}}(y_0)$ is different from the true prediction. In this paper the bootstrap approach is used to approximate a sampling distribution of the prediction (or a function thereof) and to estimate parameters of that distribution like its mean value, variance, percentiles, etc. Bootstrapping procedures are closely related to other resampling methods like cross validation and jackknife (Efron 1982). The jackknife can be considered as a linear approximation to the bootstrap (Efron, Tibshirani 1986).

In the next section different versions of the bootstrap procedure for feedforward neural networks are defined and their theoretical properties are reviewed. Main points are the convergence of the bootstrap distribution to true theoretical distribution and the speed of that convergence. In the following section the results of a simulation experiment for a simple backprop model are reported and the application of the bootstrap to model selection is discussed. The final section gives a short summary.

2 CONSISTENCY OF THE BOOTSTRAP FOR FEEDFORWARD NEURAL NETWORKS

Assume $X(n) := (x_1, \ldots, x_n)$ is the available independent, identically distributed (iid) sample from an underlying cdf F where $x_i = (z_i, y_i)$ and $\hat{F}_n$ is the corresponding empirical cdf. For a given y_0 let $\eta = \eta(g_\beta(y_0))$ be a parameter of interest of the prediction, e.g. the mean value of the prediction of a component of z for y_0.

The *pairwise bootstrap* algorithm is an intuitive way to apply the bootstrap notion to regression. It was proposed by Efron (1982) and involves the independent repetition of following steps for $b = 1, \ldots, B$.

1. A sample $X_b^*(n)$ of size n is generated from $\hat{F}_n$. Notice that this amounts to the random selection of n elements from $X(n)$ *with replacement.*
2. An estimate $\hat{\eta}_b$ is determined from $X_b^*(n)$.

The resulting empirical cdf of the $\hat{\eta}_b$, $b = 1, \ldots, n$ is denoted by $\hat{H}_B$ and approximates the sampling distribution for the estimate $\hat{\eta}$ under $\hat{F}_n$. The standard deviation of H_B is an estimate of the standard error of $\eta(\hat{F}_n)$, and $[\hat{H}_B^{-1}(\alpha), \hat{H}_B^{-1}(1-\alpha)]$ is an approximate $(1 - 2\alpha)$ central confidence interval.

In general two conditions are necessary for the bootstrap to be consistent:

- The estimator, e.g. $\hat{\eta}_b$ has to be consistent.
- The functional which maps F to $\hat{H}_B$ has to be smooth.

This requirement can be formalized by a uniform weak convergence condition (DiCiccio, Romano 1988). Using these concepts Freedman (1981) proved that for the parameters of a linear regression model the pairwise bootstrap procedure is consistent, i.e. yields the desired limit distribution for $n, B \to \infty$. Mammen (1991) showed that this also holds for the preaictive distribution of a linear model (i.e. linear contrasts). These results hold even if the errors are heteroscedastic, i.e. if the distribution of ϵ_i depends on the value of y_i.

The performance of the bootstrap for *linear* regression is extensively discussed by Wu (1986). It turns out that the small sample properties can be different from the asymptotic relations and the bootstrap may exhibit a sizeable bias. Various procedures of bias correction have been proposed (DiCiccio, Romano 1988). Beran (1990) discusses a calibrated bootstrap prediction region containing the prediction $g_\beta(y_0)+\epsilon$ with prescribed probability α. It requires a sequence of nested bootstraps. Its coverage probability tends to α at a rate up to n^{-2}. Note that this procedure can be applied to *nonlinear* regression models (1) with homoscedastic errors (Example 3 in Beran (1990, p.718) can be extended to this case).

Biases especially arise if the errors are heteroscedastic. Hinkley (1988) discusses the parametric modelling of dependency of the error distribution (or its variance) from y and the application of the bootstrap algorithm using this model. The problem is here to determine this parametric dependency from the data. As an alternative Wu (1986) and Liu (1988) take into account heteroscedasticity in a nonparametric way. They propose the following *wild bootstrap* algorithm which starts with a consistent estimate $\hat{\beta}$ based on the sample $X(n)$. Then the set of residuals $(\hat{\epsilon}_1, \ldots, \hat{\epsilon}_n)$ with $\hat{\epsilon}_i := z_i - g_{\hat{\beta}}(y_i)$ is determined. The approach attempts to mimic the conditional distribution of z given y_i in a very crude way by defining a distribution $\hat{G}_i$ whose first three moments coincide with the observed residual $\hat{\epsilon}_i$:

$$\int u d\hat{G}_i(u) = 0 \qquad \int u^2 d\hat{G}_i(u) = \hat{\epsilon}_i^2 \qquad \int u^3 d\hat{G}_i(u) = \hat{\epsilon}_i^3 \tag{2}$$

Two point distributions are used which are uniquely defined by this requirement (Mammen 1991, p.121). Then the following steps are repeated for $b = 1, \ldots, B$:

1. Independently generate residuals $\tilde{\epsilon}_i$ according to $\hat{G}_i$ and generate observations $z_i^* := g_{\hat{\beta}}(y_i) + \tilde{\epsilon}_i$ for $i = (1, \ldots, n)$. This yields a new sample $X_b^*(n)$ of size n.
2. An estimate $\hat{\eta}_b^*$ is determined from $X_b^*(n)$.

The resulting empirical cdf of the $\hat{\eta}_b^*$ is then taken as the bootstrap distribution $\hat{H}_B$ which approximates the sampling distribution for the estimate $\hat{\eta}$ under $\hat{F}_n$. Mammen (1991, p.123) shows that this algorithm is consistent for the prediction of linear regression models if the least square estimator or M-estimators are used and discusses the convergence speed of the procedure.

The bootstrap may also be applied to nonparameric regression models like kernel-type estimators of the form

$$\hat{g}(y) = \frac{\left[\sum_{i=1}^{n} z_i K\left(\frac{y-y_i}{h}\right)\right]}{\left[\sum_{i=1}^{n} K\left(\frac{y-y_i}{h}\right)\right]} \tag{3}$$

with kernel K and bandwidth h. These models are related to radial basis functions discussed in the neural network literature. For those models the pairwise bootstrap does not work (Härdle, Mammen 1990) as the algorithm is not forced to perform local a.eraging. To account for heteroscedasticity in the errors of (1) Härdle (1990, p.103) advocates the use of the wild bootstrap algorithm described above. Under some regularity conditions he shows the convergence of the bootstrap distribution of the kernel estimator to the correct limit distribution.

To summarize the bootstrap often is used simply because an analytic derivation of the desired sampling distribution is too complicated. The asymptotic investigations offer two additional reasons:

- There exist versions of the bootstrap algorithm that have a better rate of convergence than the usual asymptotic normal approximation. This effect has been extensively discussed in literature e.g. by Hall (1988), Beran (1988), DiCiccio and Romano (1988, p.349), Mammen (1991, p.74).
- There are cases where the bootstrap works, even if the normal approximation breaks down. Bickel and Freedman (1983) for instance show, that the bootstrap is valid for linear regression models in the presence of outliers and if the number of parameters changes with n. Their results are discussed and extended by Mammen (1991, p.88ff).

3 SIMULATION EXPERIMENTS

To demonstrate the performance of the bootstrap for real real problems we investigated a small neural network. To get a nonlinear situation we chose a "noisy" version of the xor model with eight input units $y_1, \ldots, y_8$ and a single output unit z. The input variables may take the values 0 and 1. The output unit of the true model is stochastic. It takes the values 0.1 and 0.9 with the following probabilities:

$$\begin{array}{llll}
p(y=0.9)=0.9 & \text{if} & x_1+x_2+x_3+x_4<3 & \text{and} \quad x_5+x_6+x_7+x_8<3 \\
p(y=0.9)=0.1 & \text{if} & x_1+x_2+x_3+x_4<3 & \text{and} \quad x_5+x_6+x_7+x_8\geq 3 \\
p(y=0.9)=0.1 & \text{if} & x_1+x_2+x_3+x_4\geq 3 & \text{and} \quad x_5+x_6+x_7+x_8<3 \\
p(y=0.9)=0.9 & \text{if} & x_1+x_2+x_3+x_4\geq 3 & \text{and} \quad x_5+x_6+x_7+x_8\geq 3
\end{array}$$

In contrast to the simple xor model generalization is possible in this setup. We generated a training set $X(n)$ of $n = 100$ inputs using the true model.

We used the pairwise bootstrap procedure described above and generated $B = 30$ different bootstrap samples $X_b^*(n)$ by random selection from $X(n)$ with replacement. This number of bootstrap samples is rather low and only will yield reliable information on the central tendency of the prediction. More sensitive parameters of

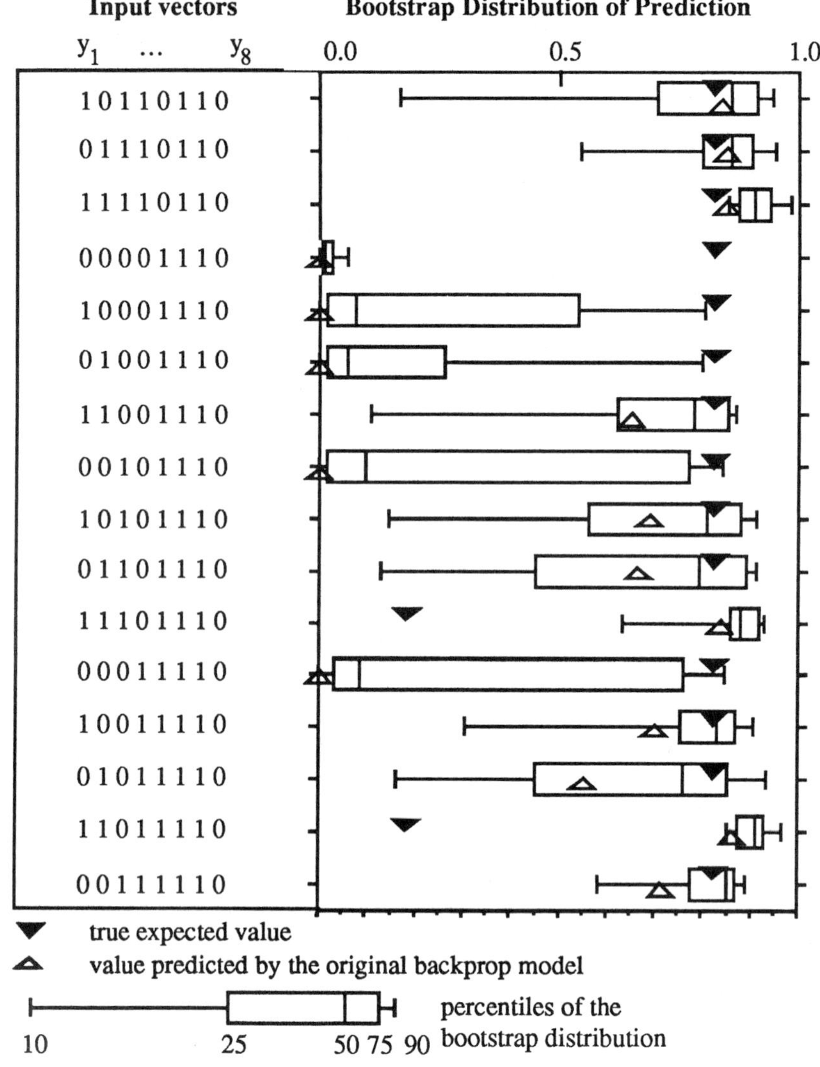

Figure 1: **Box-Plots of the Bootstrap Predictive Distribution for a Series of Different Input Vectors**

the distribution like low percentiles and the standard deviation can be expected to exhibit larger fluctuations. We estimated 30 weight vectors $\hat{\beta}_b$ from those samples by the backpropagation method with random initial weights. Subsequently for each of the 256 possible input vectors y_i we determined the prediction $g_{\hat{\beta}_b}(y_i)$ yielding a predictive distribution. For comparison purposes we also estimated the weights of the original backprop model with the full data set $X(n)$ and the corresponding

Table 1: Mean Square Deviation from the True Prediction

INPUT TYPE	HIDDEN UNITS	MEAN SQUARE DIFFERENCE BOOTSTRAP D_B	FULL DATA D_F
training inputs	2	0.18	0.19
	3	0.17	0.19
	4	0.17	0.19
non-training inputs	2	0.30	0.34
	3	0.35	0.38
	4	0.37	0.42

Table 2: Coverage Probabilities of the Bootstrap Confidence Interval for Prediction

HIDDEN UNITS	FRACTION OF CASES WITH TRUE PREDICTION IN $[q_{25}, q_{75}]$	$[q_{10}, q_{90}]$
2	0.47	0.77
3	0.44	0.70
4	0.43	0.70

predictions.

For some of those input vectors the results are shown in figure 1. The distributions differ greatly in size and form for the different input vectors. Usually the spread of the predictive distribution is large if the median prediction differs substantially from the true value. This reflects the situation that the observed data does not have much information on the specific input vector. Simply by inspecting the predictive distribution the reliability of a predictions may be assessed in a heuristic way. This may be a great help in practical applications.

In table 1 the mean square difference $D_B := \left(\frac{1}{n}\sum_{i=1}^{n}(z_i - q_{50})^2\right)^{1/2}$ between the true prediction z_i and the median q_{50} of the bootstrap predictive distribution is compared to the mean square difference $D_S := \left(\frac{1}{n}\sum_{i=1}^{n}(z_i - \hat{z}_{i,F})^2\right)^{1/2}$ between the true prediction and the value $\hat{z}_{i,F}$ estimated with full data backprop model. For the non-training inputs the bootstrap median has a lower mean deviation from the true value. This effect is a real practical advantage and occurs even for this simple bootstrap procedure. It may be caused in part by the variation of the initial weight values (cf. Pearlmutter, Rosenfeld 1991). The utilization of bootstrap procedures with higher order convergence has the potential to improve this effect.

Table 2 list the fraction of cases in the full set of all 256 possible inputs where the true value is contained in the central 50% and 80% prediction interval. Note that the intervals are based on only 30 cases. For the correct model with 2 hidden units the difference is 0.03 which corresponds to just one case. Models with more hidden units exhibit larger fluctuations. To arrive at more reliable intervals the number of

Table 3: Spread of the Predictive Distribution

HIDDEN UNITS	MEAN INTERQUARTILE RANGE FOR TRAINING INPUTS	NON-TRAINING INPUTS
2	0.13	0.29
3	0.11	0.35
4	0.11	0.37

bootstrap samples has to be increased by an order of magnitude.

If we use a model with more than two hidden units the fit to the training sample cannot be improved but remains constant. For nontraining inputs, however, the predictions of the model deteriorate. In table 1 we see that the mean square deviation from the true prediction increases. This is just a manifestation of 'Occam's razor' which states that unnecessary complex models should not be prefered to simpler ones (MacKay 1992). Table 3 shows that the spread of the predictive distribution is increased for non-training inputs in the case of models with more than two hidden units. Therefore Occam's razor is supported by the bootstrap predictive distribution *without* knowing the correct prediction.

This effect shows that bootstrap procedures may be utilized for *model selection.* Analoguous to Liu (1993) we may use a crossvalidation strategy to determine the prediction error for the bootstrap estimate $\hat{\beta}_b$ for sample elements of $X(n)$ which are not contained in the bootstrap sample $X_b^*(n)$. In a similar way Efron (1982, p.52f) determines the error for the predictions $g_{\hat{\beta}_b}(y)$ within the full sample $X(n)$ and uses this as an indicator of the model performance.

4 SUMMARY

The bootstrap method offers an computation intensive alternative to estimate the predictive distribution for a neural network even if the analytic derivation is intractable. The available asymptotic results show that it is valid for a large number of linear, nonlinear and even nonparametric regression problems. It has the potential to model the distribution of estimators to a higher precision than the usual normal asymptotics. It even may be valid if the normal asymptotics fail. However, the theoretical properties of bootstrap procedures for neural networks – especially nonlinear models – have to be investigated more comprehensively. In contrast to the Bayesian approach no distributional assumptions (e.g. normal errors) are have to be specified. The simulation experiments show that bootstrap methods offer practical advantages as the performance of the model with respect to a new input may be readily assessed.

Acknowledgements

This research was supported in part by the German Federal Department of Reserach and Technology, grant ITW8900A7.

References

Beran, R. (1988): Prepivoting Test Statistics: A Bootstrap View of Asymptotic Refinements. *Journal of the American Statistical Association.* vol. 83, pp.687-697.

Beran, R. (1990): Calibrating Prediction Regions. *Journal of the American Statistical Association.*, vol. 85, pp.715-723.

Bickel, P.J., Freedman, D.H. (1981): Some Asymptotic Theory for the Bootstrap. *The Annals of Statistics,* vol. 9, pp.1196-1217.

Bickel, P.J., Freedman, D.H. (1983): Bootstrapping Regression Models with many Parameters. In P. Bickel, K. Doksum, J.C. Hodges (eds.) *A Festschrift for Erich Lehmann.* Wadsworth, Belmont, CA, pp.28-48.

DiCiccio, T.J., Romano, J.P. (1988): A Review of Bootstrap Confidence Intervals. *J. Royal Statistical Soc.,* Ser. B, vol. 50, pp.338-354.

Efron, B. (1979): Bootstrap Methods: Another Look at the Jackknife. *The Annals of Statistics,* vol 7, pp.1-26.

Efron, B. (1982): *The Jackknife, the Bootstrap and Other Resampling Plans.* SIAM, Philadelphia.

Efron, B., Gong, G. (1983): A leisure look at the bootstrap, the jackknife and crossvalidation. *American Statistician,* vol. 37, pp.36-48.

Efron, B., Tibshirani (1986): Bootstrap methods for Standard Errors, Confidence Intervals, and other Measures of Statistical Accuracy . *Statistical Science,* vol 1, pp.54-77.

Freedman, D.H. (1981): Bootstrapping Regression Models. *The Annals of Statistics,* vol 9, p.1218-1228.

Härdle, W.(1990): *Applied Nonparametric Regression.* Cambridge University Press, Cambridge.

Härdle, W., Mammen, E. (1990): Bootstrap Methods in Nonparametric Regression. *Preprint Nr. 593.* Sonderforschungsbereich 123, University of Heidelberg.

Hall, P. (1988): Theoretical Comparison of Bootstrap Confidence Intervals. *The Annals of Statistics,* vol 16, pp.927-985.

Hinkley, D. . (1988): Bootstrap Methods. *Journal of the Royal Statistical Society,* Ser. B, vol.50, pp.321-337.

Liu, R. (1988): Bootstrap Procedures under some non i.i.d. Models. *The Annals of Statistics,* vol.16, pp. 1696-1708.

Liu, Y. (1993): Neural Network Model Selection Using Asymptotic Jackknife Estimator and Cross-Validation Method. This volume.

MacKay, D. J. C. (1992): Bayesian Model Comparison and Backprop Nets. In Moody, J.E., Hanson, S.J., Lippman, R.P. (eds.) *Advances in Neural Information Processing Systems 4.* Morgan Kaufmann, San Mateo, pp.839-846.

Mammen, E. (1991): When does Bootstrap Work: Asymptotic Results and Simulations. *Preprint Nr. 623.* Sonderforschungsbereich 123, University of Heidelberg.

Pearlmutter, B.A., Rosenfeld, R. (1991): Chaitin-Kolmogorov Complexity and Generalization in Neural Networks. in Lippmann et al. (eds.): *Advances in Neural Information Processing Systems 3,* Morgan Kaufmann, pp.925-931.

C.F.J. Wu (1986): Jackknife, Bootstrap and other Resampling Methods in Regression Analysis. *The Annals of Statistics,* vol. 14, p.1261-1295.

Discriminability-Based Transfer between Neural Networks

L. Y. Pratt
Department of Mathematical and Computer Sciences
Colorado School of Mines
Golden, CO 80401
lpratt@mines.colorado.edu

Abstract

Previously, we have introduced the idea of neural network *transfer*, where learning on a *target* problem is sped up by using the weights obtained from a network trained for a related *source* task. Here, we present a new algorithm, called *Discriminability-Based Transfer* (DBT), which uses an information measure to estimate the utility of hyperplanes defined by source weights in the target network, and rescales transferred weight magnitudes accordingly. Several experiments demonstrate that target networks initialized via DBT learn significantly faster than networks initialized randomly.

1 INTRODUCTION

Neural networks are usually trained from scratch, relying only on the training data for guidance. However, as more and more networks are trained for various tasks, it becomes reasonable to seek out methods that avoid "reinventing the wheel", and instead are able to build on previously trained networks' results. For example, consider a speech recognition network that was only trained on American English speakers. However, for a new application, speakers might have a British accent. Since these tasks are sub-distributions of the same larger distribution (English speakers), they may be related in a way that can be exploited to speed up learning on the British network, compared to when weights are randomly initialized.

We have previously introduced the question of how trained neural networks can be "recycled' in this way [Pratt *et al.*, 1991]; we've called this the ***transfer*** problem. The idea of transfer has strong roots in psychology (as discussed in [Sharkey and Sharkey, 1992]), and is a standard paradigm in neurobiology, where synapses almost always come "pre-wired".

There are many ways to formulate the transfer problem. Retaining performance on the source task may or may not be important. When it is, the problem has been called *sequential learning*, and has been explored by several authors (cf. [McCloskey and Cohen, 1989]). Our paradigm assumes that source task performance is not important, though when the source task training data is a subset of the target training data, our method may be viewed as addressing sequential learning as well. Transfer knowledge can also be inserted into several different *entry points* in a back-propagation network (see [Pratt, 1993a]). We focus on changing a network's initial weights; other studies change other aspects, such as the objective function (cf. [Thrun and Mitchell, 1993, Naik *et al.*, 1992]).

Transfer methods may or may not use back-propagation for target task training. Our formulation does, because this allows it to degrade, in the worst case of no source task relevance, to back-propagation training on the target task with randomly initialized weights. An alternative approach is described by [Agarwal *et al.*, 1992].

Several studies have explored *literal* transfer in back-propagation networks, where the final weights from training on a source task are used as the initial conditions for target training (cf. [Martin, 1988]). However, these studies have shown that often networks will demonstrate worse performance after literal transfer than if they had been randomly initialized.

This paper describes the Discriminability-Based Transfer (DBT) algorithm, which overcomes problems with literal transfer. DBT achieves the same asymptotic accuracy as randomly initialized networks, and requires substantially fewer training updates. It is also superior to literal transfer, and to just using the source network on the target task.

2 ANALYSIS OF LITERAL TRANSFER

As mentioned above, several studies have shown that networks initialized via literal transfer give worse asymptotic performance than randomly initialized networks. To understand why, consider the situation when only a subset of the source network input-to-hidden (IH) layer hyperplanes are relevant to the target problem, as illustrated in Figure 1. We've observed that some hyperplanes initialized by source network training don't shift out of their initial positions, despite the fact that they don't help to separate the target training data. The weights defining such hyperplanes often have high magnitudes [Dewan and Sontag, 1990]. Figure 2 (a) shows a simulation of such a situation, where a hyperplane that has a high magnitude, as if it came from a source network, causes learning to be slowed down.[1]

Analysis of the back-propagation weight update equations reveals that high source weight magnitudes retard back-propagation learning on the target task because this

[1]Neural network visualization will be explored more thoroughly in an upcoming paper. An X-based animator is available from the author via anonymous ftp. Type "archie ha".

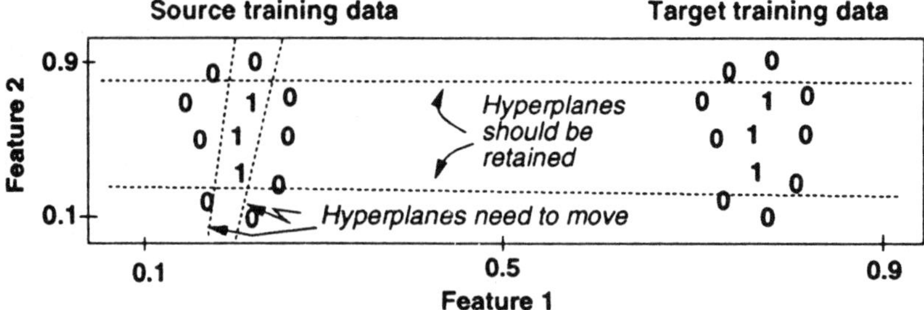

Figure 1: Problem Illustrating the need for DBT. The source and target tasks are identical, except that the target task has been shifted along one axis, as represented by the training data shown. Because of this shift, two of the source hyperplanes are helpful in separating class-0 from class-1 data in the target task, and two are not.

equation is not scaled relative to weight magnitudes. Also, the weight update equation contains the factor $y(1-y)$ (where y is a unit's activation), which is small for large weights. Considering this analysis, it might at first appear that a simple solution to the problem with literal transfer is to uniformly lower all weight magnitudes. However, we have also observed that hyperplanes in separating positions will move unless they are given high weight magnitudes. To address both of these problems, we must rescale hyperplanes so that useful ones are defined by high-magnitude weights and less useful hyperplanes receive low magnitudes. To implement such a method, we need a metric for evaluating hyperplane utility.

3 EVALUATING CLASSIFIER COMPONENTS

We borrow the *IM* metric for evaluating hyperplanes from decision tree induction [Quinlan, 1983]. Given a set of training data and a hyperplane that crosses through it, the IM function returns a value between 0 and 1, indicating the amount that the hyperplane helps to separate the data into different classes.

The formula for IM, for a decision surface in a multi-class problem, is: $\mathrm{IM} = \frac{1}{N}(\sum\sum x_{ij}\log x_{ij} - \sum x_{i.}\log x_{i.} - \sum x_{.j}\log x_{.j} + N\log N)$ [Mingers, 1989]. Here, N is the number of patterns, i is either 0 or 1, depending on the side of a hyperplane on which a pattern falls, j indexes over all classes, x_{ij} is the count of class j patterns on side i of the hyperplane, $x_{i.}$ is the count of all patterns on side i, and $x_{.j}$ is the total number of patterns in class j.

4 THE DBT ALGORITHM

The DBT algorithm is shown in Figure 3. It inputs the target training data and weights from the source network, along with two parameters C and S (see below). DBT outputs a modified set of weights, for initializing training on the target task. Figure 2 (b) shows how the problem of Figure 2 (a) was repaired via DBT.

DBT modifies the weights defining each source hyperplane to be proportional to the

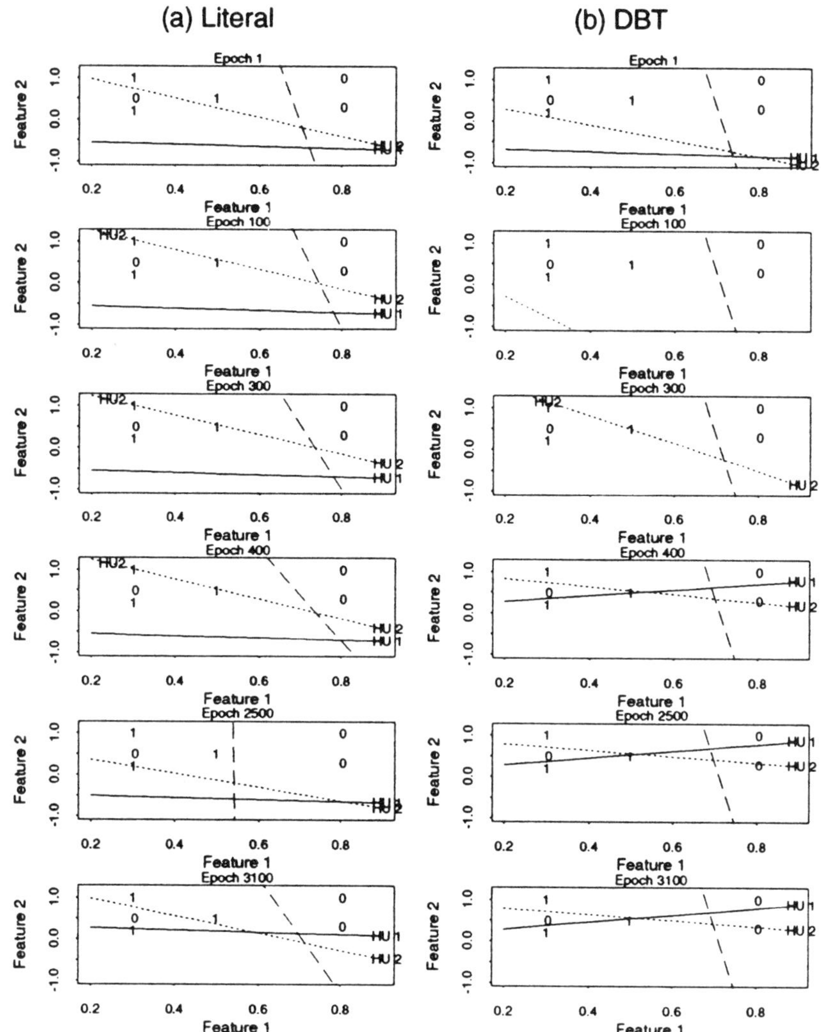

Figure 2: Hyperplane Movement speed in Literal Transfer, Compared to DBT. Each image in this figure shows the hyperplanes implemented by IH weights at a different epoch of training. Hidden unit 1's hyperplane is a solid line; HU2's is a dotted line, and HU3's hyperplane is shown as a dashed line. In (a) note how HU1 seems fixed in place. Its high magnitude causes learning to be slow (taking about 3100 epochs to converge). In (b) note how DBT has given HU1 a small magnitude, allowing it to be flexible, so that the training data is separated by epoch 390. A randomly initialized network on this problem takes about 600 epochs.

Input:
Source network weights
Target training data
Parameters: C (cutoff factor), S (scaleup factor)
Output:
Initial weights for target network, assuming same topology as source network
Method:
For each source network hidden unit i
Compare the hyperplane defined by incoming weights to i to the target training data, calculating IM_{ti} ($\in [0,1]$)
Rescale IM_{ti} values so that largest has value S. Put result in s_i.
For IM_{ti}'s that are less than C
If highest magnitude ratio between weights defining hyperplane i is > 100.0, reset weights for that hyperplane randomly
Else uniformly scale down hyperplane to have low-valued weights (maximum magnitude of 0.5), but to be in the same position.
For each remaining IH hidden unit i
For each weight w^t_{ji} defining hyperplane i in target network
Let w^t_{ji} = source weight $w^s_{ji} \times s_i$
Set hidden-to-output target network weights randomly in $[-0.5, 0.5]$

Figure 3: The Discriminability-Based Transfer (DBT) Algorithm.

IM value, according to an input parameter, S. DBT is based on the idea that the best initial magnitude M_t for a target hyperplane is $M_t = S \times M_s \times IM_t$, where S ("scaleup") is a constant of proportionality, M_s is the magnitude of a source network hyperplane, and IM_t is the discriminability of the source hyperplane on the target training data. We assume that this simple relationship holds over some range of IM_t values. A second parameter, C, determines a cut-off in this relationship - source hyperplanes with $IM_t < C$ receive very low magnitudes, so that the hyperplanes are effectively equivalent to those in a randomly initialized network. The use of the C parameter was motivated by empirical experiments that indicated that the multiplicative scaling via S was not adequate.

To determine S and C for a particular source and target task, we ran DBT several times for a small number of epochs with different S and C values. We chose the S and C values that yielded the best average TSS (total sum of squared errors) after a few epochs. We used local hill climbing in average TSS space to decide how to move in S, C space.

DBT randomizes the weights in the network's hidden-to-output (HO) layer. See [Sharkey and Sharkey, 1992] for an extension to this work showing that literal transfer of HO weights might also be effective.

5 EMPIRICAL RESULTS

DBT was evaluated on seven tasks: female-to-male speaker transfer on a 10-vowel recognition task (PB), a 3-class subset of the PB task (PB123), transfer from all females to a single male in the PB task (Onemale), transfer for a heart disease diagnosis problem from Hungarian to Swiss patients (Heart-HS), transfer for the same task from patients in California to Swiss patients (Heart-VAS), transfer from a subset of DNA pattern recognition examples to a superset (DNA), and transfer from a subset of chess endgame problems to a superset (Chess). Note that the DNA and chess tasks effectively address the sequential learning problem; as long as the source data is a subset of the target data, the target network can build on the previous results.

DBT was compared to randomly initialized networks on the target task. We measured generalization performance in both conditions by using 10-way cross-validation on 10 different initial conditions for each target task, resulting in 100 different runs for each of the two conditions, and for each of the seven tasks. Our empirical methodology controlled carefully for initial conditions, hidden unit count, back-propagation parameters η (learning rate) and α (momentum), and DBT parameters S and C.

5.1 SCENARIOS FOR EVALUATION

There are at least two different practical situations in which we may want to speed up learning. First, we may have a limited amount of computer time, all of which will be used because we have no way of detecting when a network's performance has reached some criterion. In this case, if our speed-up method (i.e. DBT) is significantly superior to a baseline for a large proportion of epochs during training, then the probability that we'll have to stop during that period of significant superiority is high If we do stop at an epoch when our method is significantly better, then this justifies it over the baseline, because the resulting network has better performance.

A second situation is when we have some way of detecting when performance is "good enough" for an application. In contrast to the above situation, here a DBT network may be run for a shorter time than a baseline network, because it reaches this criterion faster. In this case, the number of epochs of DBT significant superiority is less important than the speed with which it achieves the criterion.

5.2 RESULTS

To evaluate networks according to the first scenario, we tested for statistical significance at the 99.0% level between the 100 DBT and the 100 randomly initialized networks at each training epoch. We found (1) that asymptotic DBT performance scores were the same as for random networks and (2), that DBT was superior for much of the training period. Figure 4 (a) shows the number of weight updates for which a significant difference was found for the seven tasks.

For the second scenario, we also found (3) that DBT networks required many fewer epochs to reach a criterion performance score. For this test, we found the last significantly different epoch between the two methods. Then we measured the number of epochs required to reach 98%, 95%, and 66% of that level. The number of weight updates required for DBT and randomly initialized networks to reach the 98% criterion are shown in Figure 4 (b). Note that the y axis is logarithmic, so, for example, over 30 million weight updates were saved by using DBT instead of random initialization in the PB123 problem. Results for the 95% and 66% criteria also showed DBT to be at least as fast as random initialization for every task.

Using the same tests described for DBT above, we also tested literal networks on the seven transfer tasks. We found that, unlike DBT, literal networks reached sig-

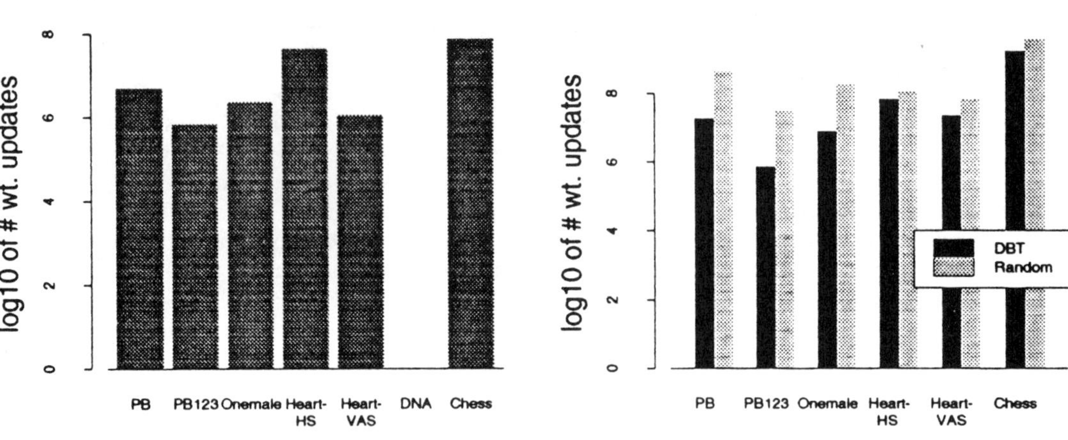

Figure 4: Summary of DBT Empirical Results.

nificantly worse asymptotic performance scores than randomly initialized networks. Literal networks also learned slower for some tasks. These results justify the use of the more complicated DBT method over literal transfer.

We also evaluated the source networks directly on the target tasks, without any back-propagation training on the target training data. Scores were significantly and substantially worse than random networks. This result indicates that the transfer scenarios we chose for evaluation were nontrivial.

6 CONCLUSION

We have described the DBT algorithm for transfer between neural networks.[2] DBT demonstrated substantial and significant learning speed improvement over randomly initialized networks in 6 out of 7 tasks studied (and the same learning speed in the other task). DBT never displayed worse asymptotic performance than a randomly initialized network. We have also shown that DBT is superior to literal transfer, and to simply using the source network on the target task.

Acknowledgements

The author is indebted to John Smith. Gale Martin, and Anshu Agarwal for their valuable comments on this paper, and to Jack Mostow and Haym Hirsh for their contribution to this research program.

[2]See [Pratt, 1993b] for more details.

References

[Agarwal *et al.*, 1992] A. Agarwal, R. J. Mammone, and D. K. Naik. An on-line training algorithm to overcome catastrophic forgetting. In *Intelligence Engineering Systems through Artificial Neural Networks*, volume 2, pages 239–244. The American Society of Mechanical Engineers, ASME Press, 1992.

[Dewan and Sontag, 1990] Hasanat M. Dewan and Eduardo Sontag. Using extrapolation to speed up the backpropagation algorithm. In *Proceedings of the International Joint Conference on Neural Networks, Washington, DC*, volume 1, pages 613–616. IEEE Publications, Inc., January 1990.

[Martin, 1988] Gale Martin. The effects of old learning on new in Hopfield and Backpropagation nets. Technical Report ACA-HI-019, Microelectronics and Computer Technology Corporation (MCC), 1988.

[McCloskey and Cohen, 1989] Michael McCloskey and Neal J. Cohen. Catastrophic interference in connectionist networks: the sequential learning problem. *The psychology of learning and motivation*, 24, 1989.

[Mingers, 1989] John Mingers. An empirical comparison of selection measures for decision- tree induction. *Machine Learning*, 3(4):319–342, 1989.

[Naik *et al.*, 1992] D. K. Naik, R. J. Mammone, and A. Agarwal. Meta-neural network approach to learning by learning. In *Intelligence Engineering Systems through Artificial Neural Networks*, volume 2, pages 245–252. The American Society of Mechanical Engineers, ASME Press, 1992.

[Pratt *et al.*, 1991] Lorien Y. Pratt, Jack Mostow, and Candace A. Kamm. Direct transfer of learned information among neural networks. In *Proceedings of the Ninth National Conference on Artificial Intelligence (AAAI-91)*, pages 584–589, Anaheim, CA, 1991.

[Pratt, 1993a] Lorien Y. Pratt. Experiments in the transfer of knowledge between neural networks. In S. Hanson, G. Drastal, and R. Rivest, editors, *Computational Learning Theory and Natural Learning Systems, Constraints and Prospects*, chapter 4.1. MIT Press, 1993. To appear.

[Pratt, 1993b] Lorien Y. Pratt. Non-literal transfer of information among inductive learners. In R.J.Mammone and Y. Y. Zeevi, editors, *Neural Networks: Theory and Applications II*. Academic Press, 1993. To appear.

[Quinlan, 1983] J. R. Quinlan. Learning efficient classification procedures and their application to chess end games. In *Machine Learning*, pages 463–482. Palo Alto, CA: Tioga Publishing Company, 1983.

[Sharkey and Sharkey, 1992] Noel E. Sharkey and Amanda J. C. Sharkey. Adaptive generalisation and the transfer of knowledge, 1992. Working paper, Center for Connection Science, University of Exeter, 1992.

[Thrun and Mitchell, 1993] Sebastian B. Thrun and Tom M. Mitchell. Integrating inductive neural network learning and explanation-based learning. In C.L. Giles, S. J. Hanson, and J. D. Cowan, editors, *Advances in Neural Information Processing Systems 5*. Morgan Kaufmann Publishers, San Mateo, CA, 1993.

Summed Weight Neuron Perturbation: An O(N) Improvement over Weight Perturbation.

Barry Flower and Marwan Jabri
SEDAL
Department of Electrical Engineering
University of Sydney
NSW 2006 Australia

Abstract

The algorithm presented performs gradient descent on the weight space of an Artificial Neural Network (ANN), using a finite difference to approximate the gradient. The method is novel in that it achieves a computational complexity similar to that of Node Perturbation, $O(N^3)$, but does not require access to the activity of hidden or internal neurons. This is possible due to a stochastic relation between perturbations at the weights and the neurons of an ANN. The algorithm is also similar to Weight Perturbation in that it is optimal in terms of hardware requirements when used for the training of VLSI implementations of ANN's.

1 INTRODUCTION

Optimization of the weights of an ANN may be performed by, the application of a gradient descent technique. The gradient may be calculated directly as in Backpropagation, or it may be approximated by a Finite Difference Method which is what we concern ourselves with in this paper. These methods lend themselves to the task of training hardware implementations of ANNs where real estate is at a premium and synaptic density is of great importance. Neuron Perturbation (NP), as described by the Madaline Rule III (MRIII) (Widrow and Lehr, 1990), is a technique that approximates the gradient of the Mean Square Error (MSE) *with respect to* the change at a given neuron by applying a small perturbation to the input of the neuron and measuring the change in the MSE. The weight

$$\Delta w_{ij} = -\eta . \frac{\partial E}{\partial net_i} . x_j , \qquad (1)$$

update is then calculated from the product of this gradient measure and the activation of the neuron from which the weight is fed, as described by (1).

Weight Perturbation (WP), as described by Jabri and Flower (Jabri and Flower, 1992) is a neural network training techniques based on gradient descent using a Finite Difference method to approximate the gradient. The gradient of the MSE *with respect to* a weight is approximated by applying a small pertubation to the weight and measuring the change in the MSE. This gradient is then used to calculated the weight update such that:

$$\Delta w_{ij} = -\eta \cdot \frac{\partial E}{\partial w_{ij}} \tag{2}$$

The advantages of WP over NP are that it performs better when limited precision weights are used, as shown by Xie and Jabri (Xie and Jabri, 1992), and is optimal with respect to hardware requirements when used to train VLSI implementations of ANNs. However, WP has $O(N^4)$ computational complexity whilst NP has $O(N^3)$ computational complexity.

Summed Weight Neuron Perturbation (SWNP) is similar to NP in that it has a computational complexity of $O(N^3)$ but it has the added advantage that the activation of internal neurons does not need to be known. The cost of this reduced computational complexity is that SWNP needs to save the perturbation vector used.

In the following sections a description of the SWNP algorithm is provided and, finally, some experimental results are presented.

2 THE SUMMED WEIGHT NEURON PERTURBATION ALGORITHM

A subsection of a feedforward ANN containing N neurons is shown in Figure 1. on which nomenclature the following derivation is based.

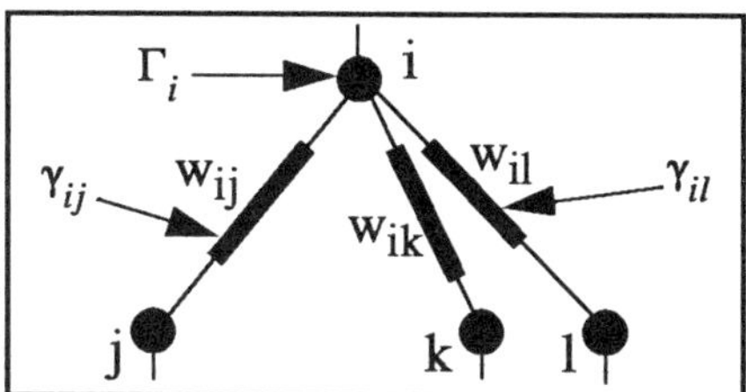

FIGURE 1: Description Of Indices Used To Describe The Neurons Weights And Perturbations In An ANN.

In a feedforward network of size N neurons the activation of a given neuron is determined by:

$$x_i(p) = f_i(net_i(p)), \quad \text{and} \quad net_i(p) = \sum_l w_{il} x_l(p), \tag{3}$$

and $f_i(y)$ is the ith neuron transfer function, $x_i(p)$ is the activation of the ith neuron for the pth pattern, and w_{il} is the weight connecting the lth neuron's output to the ith neuron's input. The error function, (MSE), is defined as in (4), where T is the set of output neurons and $d_k(p)$ is the expected value of the output on the kth neuron. The change in $E(p)$

with respect to a given weight may then be expressed as (5).

$$E(p) = \frac{1}{2}\sum_{k \in T}(d_k(p) - x_k(p))^2. \tag{4}$$

$$\frac{\partial E(p)}{\partial w_{ij}} = \frac{\partial E(p)}{\partial net_i(p)} . x_j(p) . \tag{5}$$

The first term of on the right-hand side of (5) can be determined using a Finite Difference, which in this case is a Forward Difference, so that:

$$\frac{\partial E(p)}{\partial net_i(p)} = \frac{\Delta E_{\Gamma_i}(p)}{\Gamma_i} + O(\Gamma_i), \tag{6}$$

where,

$$\Delta E_{\Gamma_i}(p) = E_{\Gamma_i}(p) - E(p), \tag{7}$$

and Γ_i is the perturbation applied to the ith neuron, $E_{\Gamma_i}(p)$ is the error for the pth pattern with a perturbation applied to the ith neuron and $E(p)$ is the error for the pth pattern without a perturbation applied to any neurons. The error introduced by the approximation is represented by the last term on the right-hand side in (6).

The perturbation of one or more of the weights that are inputs to the qth neuron can be thought of as being equal to some perturbation applied directly to that neuron. Hence:

$$\Gamma_q = \sum_l \gamma_{ql} x_l(p), \tag{8}$$

where γ_{ql} is the perturbation applied to weight w_{ql}. As will be shown, perturbing the qth neuron by perturbing all the weights feeding into it, enables the sign of the gradient $\frac{\partial E(p)}{\partial w_{ij}}$ to be determined without performing the product on the right-hand side of (5). Further more, the activation of hidden neurons, (i.e. $x_j(p)$ in (5)) need not be known. The contribution of the perturbation of weight w_{ij} to the perturbation of the ith neuron is

$$\gamma_{ij} x_j(p). \tag{9}$$

Let us take the degenerate case where there is only one weight for the ith neuron. Then the gradient of the MSE *with respect to* weight w_{ij} is:

$$\frac{\partial E(p)}{\partial w_{ij}} = \frac{\Delta E_{\Gamma_i}(p) x_j(p)}{\Gamma_i} + O(\Gamma_i) = \frac{\Delta E_{\Gamma_i}(p) x_j(p)}{\gamma_{ij} x_j(p)} + O(\Gamma_i)$$

$$= \frac{\Delta E_{\Gamma_i}(p)}{\gamma_{ij}} + O(\Gamma_i), \tag{10}$$

noting that $x_j(p)$ has been eliminated. In the general case where the ith neuron has more than one weight the gradient *with respect to* weight w_{ij} is shown in (11).

$$\frac{\partial E(p)}{\partial w_{ij}} = \frac{\Delta E_{\Gamma_i}(p)\,x_j(p)}{\Gamma_i} + O(\Gamma_i)$$

$$= \frac{\Delta E_{\Gamma_i}(p)}{\Psi_{ij}} + O(\Gamma_i) \tag{11}$$

where,

$$\Psi_{ij} = \frac{\Gamma_i}{x_j(p)}. \tag{12}$$

The form of (10) and (11) are the same and it will be shown that γ_{ij} can be substituted for Ψ_{ij} in (11) due to a stochastic relationship between them.

Let us represent the sign of γ_{ij} and Ψ_{ij} as either +1 or -1 such that:

$$\mu_{ij} = \frac{|\gamma_{ij}|}{\gamma_{ij}} \quad \text{and} \quad \nu_{ij} = \frac{|\Psi_{ij}|}{\Psi_{ij}}. \tag{13}$$

The set of all possible states for the system represented by the vector (μ_{ij}, ν_{ij}), assuming γ_{ij} and Ψ_{ij} are never zero, is:

$$\{(-1,-1), (-1,1), (1,-1), (1,1)\}. \tag{14}$$

and it can be seen that when $\mu_{ij} = \nu_{ij}$ then the sign of the gradient of the MSE *with respect to* weight w_{ij} given by (10) is the same as that given by (11). If the sign of γ_{ij} is chosen randomly then the probability of $\mu_{ij} = \nu_{ij}$ being true is 0.5, from (14), and so (10) will generate a gradient that is in the correct direction 50% of the time. This in itself is not sufficient to allow the network to be trained as it will take as many steps in the incorrect direction as the correct direction if the steps themselves are of the same size, (i.e. the magnitude of Γ_i is the same for a step in the correct direction as a step in the incorrect direction).

Fortunately it can be shown that the size of the steps in the correct direction are greater than those in the incorrect direction. Let us take the case where a particular γ_{ij} is chosen such that

$$\mu_{ij} = \nu_{ij}. \tag{15}$$

Now by substituting (8), (12) and (13) into (15) we get:

$$\frac{|\gamma_{ij}|}{\gamma_{ij}} = \frac{\left|\frac{\sum_k \gamma_{ik} x_k(p)}{x_j}\right|}{\frac{\sum_k \gamma_{ik} x_k(p)}{x_j}} \tag{16}$$

rearranging to give,

$$\frac{|\gamma_{ij} x_j|}{\gamma_{ij} x_j} = \frac{\left|\sum_k \gamma_{ik} x_k(p)\right|}{\sum_k \gamma_{ik} x_k(p)}, \tag{17}$$

which implies that the contribution to Γ_i made by the perturbation γ_{ij} is of the same sign as Γ_i. Let us designate this neuron perturbation as $\Gamma_i(A)$. Now we take the other possible case where,

$$\mu_{ij} \neq \nu_{ij}, \tag{18}$$

assuming every other parameter is the same, and only the sign of γ_{ij} is changed. The equality in (17) is now untrue and the contribution to Γ_i made by the perturbation γ_{ij} is of the opposite sign as Γ_i. Let us designate this neuron perturbation as $\Gamma_i(B)$. From (8) we can determine that,

$$|\Gamma_i(A)| = |\Gamma_i(B)| + 2|\gamma_{ij} x_j|. \tag{19}$$

Equation (19) shows the relationship between the two possible states of the system where $\Gamma_i(A)$ represents the summed neuron perturbation for a selected weight perturbation γ_{ij} that generates a step in the corrected direction and $\Gamma_i(B)$ is similar but for a step in the incorrect direction. Clearly the correct step is always calculated from an approximated gradient that is larger than that for an incorrect step as the neuron perturbation is larger. The weight update rule then becomes:

$$\Delta w_{ij} = -\eta . \frac{\Delta E_{\Gamma_i}(p)}{\gamma_{ij}}. \tag{20}$$

The algorithm for SWNP is shown as pseudo code in Figure 2.

2.1 HARDWARE COMPATIBILITY OF SWNP

This optimisation technique is ideally suited to the training of hardware implementations of ANN's whether they consist of discrete components or are VLSI technology. The speed up over WP of $O(N)$ achieved is at the cost of an $O(N)$ storage requirement but this storage can be achieved with a single bit per neuron. SWNP is the same order of complexity as NP but does not require access to the activation of internal neurons and therefore can treat a network as a "black box" into which an input vector and weight matrix is fed and an output vector is received.

```
While (total error > error threshold) {
  For (all patterns in training set) {
      Select next pattern and training vector;
      Forward Prop.;Measure, (calculate) and save error;
      Accumulate total error;
      For (all non-input neurons) {
          For (all weights of current neuron) {
              Apply & Save perturbation of random polarity;
          }
          Forward Prop.;Measure, (calculate) and save Δerror;
          For (all weights of current neuron) {
              Restore value of weight;
              Calculate weight delta using saved perturbation value;
              If (Online Mode) Update current weight;
          }
          If (Online Mode)
              Forward Prop.; Measure, (calculate) and save new error;
      }
      If (Batch Mode) {
          For (all weights)
              Update current weight;
      }
  }
}
```

FIGURE 2: Algorithm in Pseudo Code for Summed Weight Neuron Perturbation.

3 TEST RESULTS USING SWNP

The results for a series of tests are shown in the next three tables and are summarised in Figure 4. The headings are, **N** the number of neurons in the network, **P** the number of patterns in the training set, **FF-SWNP** the number of feedforward passes for the SWNP Algorithm, **FF-WP** the number of feedforward passes for the WP Algorithm, and **RATIO** the ratio between the number of feedforward passes for WP against SWNP. The feedforward passes are recorded to 1 significant figure.

The results for a series of simulations comparing the performance of SWNP against WP are shown in Table 1. The simulations utilised floating point synaptic and neuron precisions.

The results for a series of simulations comparing the performance of SWNP against WP are shown in Table 2. The simulations utilised limited synaptic precision, (i.e. 6 bits) and floating point neuron precisions

The results for a series of experiments comparing the performance of SWNP against WP are shown in Table 2. Note: the training algorithm are the variations of WP and SWNP that are combined with the Random Search Algorithm (RSA). The results reported are averaged over 10 trials.

An example of the training error trajectories of WP and SWNP for the Monk 2 problem are shown in Figure 3.

Table 1: Performance Of SWMP Versus WP, Comparing Feedforward Operations To Convergence. (Simulations With Floating Point Precision)

PROBLEM	N	P	FF-SWNP	FF-WP	ERROR	RATIO
XOR	3	4	1.6×10^3	1.9×10^3	0.0125	1. 22
4 Encoder	5	4	0.9×10^3	1.8×10^3	0.0125	1.84
8 Encoder	11	8	1.5×10^5	4.5×10^5	0.0125	2.88
ICEG	15	119	3.7×10^5	7.9×10^6	0.0125	21.34

Table 2: Performance Of SWNP Versus WP, Comparing Feedforward Operations To Convergence. (Simulations With Limited Precision)

PROBLEM	N	P	SWNP	WP	ERROR	RATIO
Monk1	4	129	1.0×10^5	1.9×10^6	0.001	19.38
Monk2	17	169	3.6×10^5	6.8×10^6	0.0005	18.71
Monk3	17	122	1.2×10^6	7.1×10^6	0.022	5.87
IECG 55	5	8	1.6×10^4	7.2×10^4	0.0001	4.2

Table 3: Performance Of SWNP Versus WP, Comparing Feedforward Operations To Convergence. (Hardware Implementation)

PROBLEM	N	P	SWNP	WP	ERROR	RATIO
ECG 55	5	8	3.1×10^3	3.6×10^3	0.00001	1.13
ECG 045	5	8	1.1×10^4	2.0×10^4	0.001	1.78

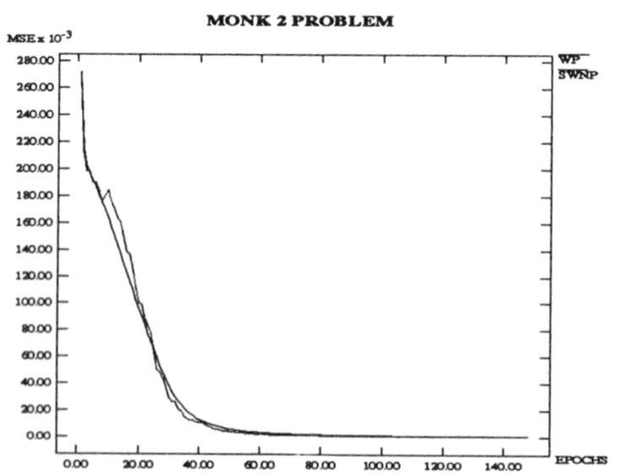

FIGURE 3: Comparison of WP and SWNP For Monk 2 Problem

FIGURE 4: Comparison of the number of Feedforward passes performed to achieve convergence on a range of problems using SWNP and WP.

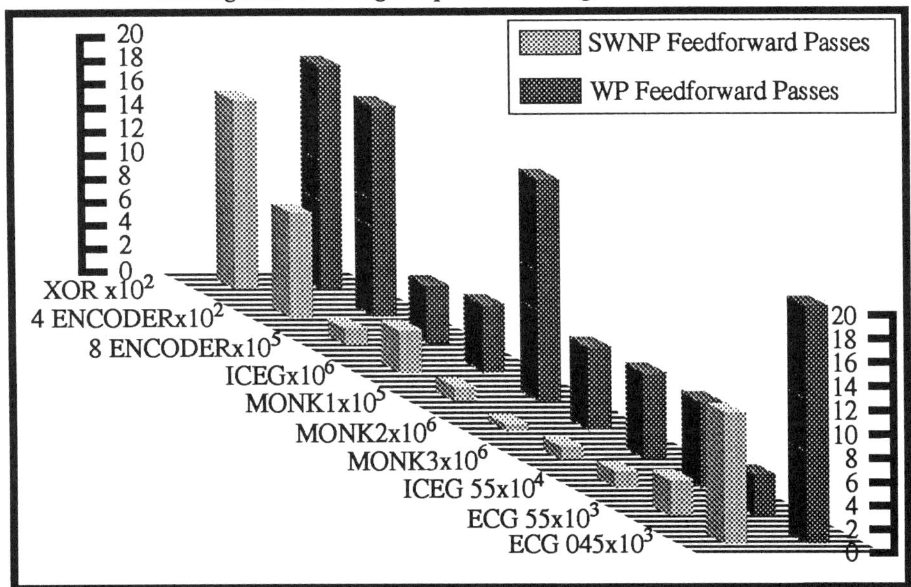

4 CONCLUSION

The algorithm presented, SWNP, performs gradient descent on the weight space of an ANN, using a finite difference to approximate the gradient. The method is novel in that it achieves $O(N^3)$ computational complexity similar to that of Node Perturbation but does not require access to the activity of hidden or internal neurons. The algorithm is also similar to Weight Perturbation in that it is optimal in terms of hardware requirements when used for the training of VLSI implementations of ANN's. Results are presented that show the algorithm in operation on floating point simulations, limited precision simulations and an actual hardware implementation of an ANN.

References

Jabri, M. and Flower, B. (1992). Weight perturbation: An optimal architecture and learning technique for analog vlsi feedforward and recurrent multilayer networks. *IEEE Transactions on Neural Networks*, 3(1):154–157.

Widrow, B. and Lehr, M. A. (1990). 30 years of adaptive neural networks: Perceptron, madaline, and backpropagation. *Proceedings of the IEEE*, 78(9):1415–1442.

Xie, Y. and Jabri, M. (1992). Analysis of the effects of quantization in multilayer neural networks using a statistical model. *IEEE Transactions on Neural Networks*, 3(2):334–338.

A Note on Learning Vector Quantization

Virginia R. de Sa
Department of Computer Science
University of Rochester
Rochester, NY 14627

Dana H. Ballard
Department of Computer Science
University of Rochester
Rochester, NY 14627

Abstract

Vector Quantization is useful for data compression. Competitive Learning which minimizes reconstruction error is an appropriate algorithm for vector quantization of unlabelled data. Vector quantization of labelled data for classification has a different objective, to minimize the number of misclassifications, and a different algorithm is appropriate. We show that a variant of Kohonen's LVQ2.1 algorithm can be seen as a multi-class extension of an algorithm which in a restricted 2 class case can be proven to converge to the Bayes optimal classification boundary. We compare the performance of the LVQ2.1 algorithm to that of a modified version having a decreasing window and normalized step size, on a ten class vowel classification problem.

1 Introduction

Vector quantization is a form of data compression that represents data vectors by a smaller set of codebook vectors. Each data vector is then represented by its nearest codebook vector. The goal of vector quantization is to represent the data with the fewest codebook vectors while losing as little information as possible.

Vector quantization of unlabelled data seeks to minimize the reconstruction error. This can be accomplished with Competitive learning[Grossberg, 1976; Kohonen, 1982], an iterative learning algorithm for vector quantization that has been shown to perform gradient descent on the following energy function [Kohonen, 1991]

$$\int ||x - w_{s^*(x)}||^2 p(x)dx.$$

where $p(x)$ is the probability distribution of the input patterns and w_s are the reference or codebook vectors and $s^*(x)$ is defined by $||x - w_{s^*(x)}|| \leq ||x - w_i||$ (for all i). This minimizes the square reconstruction error of unlabelled data and may work reasonably well for classification tasks if the patterns in the different classes are segregated.

In many classification tasks, however, the different member patterns may not be segregated into separate clusters for each class. In these cases it is more important that members of the same class be represented by the same codebook vector than that the reconstruction error is minimized. To do this, the quantizer can make use of the labelled data to encourage appropriate quantization.

2 Previous approaches to Supervised Vector Quantization

The first use of labelled data (or a teaching signal) with Competitive Learning by Rumelhart and Zipser [Rumelhart and Zipser, 1986] can be thought of as assigning a class to each codebook vector and only allowing patterns from the appropriate class to influence each reference vector.

This simple approach is far from optimal though as it fails to take into account interactions between the classes. Kohonen addressed this in his LVQ(1) algorithm[Kohonen, 1986]. He argues that the reference vectors resulting from LVQ(1) tend to approximate for a particular class r,

$$P(x|C_r)P(C_r) - \Sigma_{s \neq r} P(x|C_s)P(C_s).$$

where $P(C_i)$ is the a priori probability of Class i and $P(x|C_i)$ is the conditional density of Class i.

This approach is also not optimal for classification, as it addresses optimal places to put the codebook vectors instead of optimal placement of the *borders* of the vector quantizer which arise from the Voronoi tessellation induced by the codebook vectors. [1]

3 Minimizing Misclassifications

In classification tasks the goal is to minimize the numbers of misclassifications of the resultant quantizer. That is we want to minimize:

$$E = \sum_j \int_{D\_R_j} \sum_{i, i \neq j} P(Class_i) P(x|Class_i) dx \tag{1}$$

where , $P(Class_i)$ is the a priori probability of $Class_i$ and $P(x|Class_i)$ is the conditional density of $Class_i$ and D_R_j is the decision region for class j (which in this case is all x such that $||x - w_k|| < ||x - w_i||$ (for all i) and w_k is a codebook vector for class j).

Consider a One-Dimensional problem of two classes and two codebook vectors $w1$ and $w2$ defining a class boundary $b = (w1 + w2)/2$ as shown in Figure 1. In this case Equation 1 reduces to:

[1] Kohonen [1986] showed this by showing that the use of a "weighted" Voronoi tessellation (where the relative distances of the borders from the reference vectors was changed) worked better. However no principled way to calculate the relative weights was given and the application to real data used the unweighted tessellation.

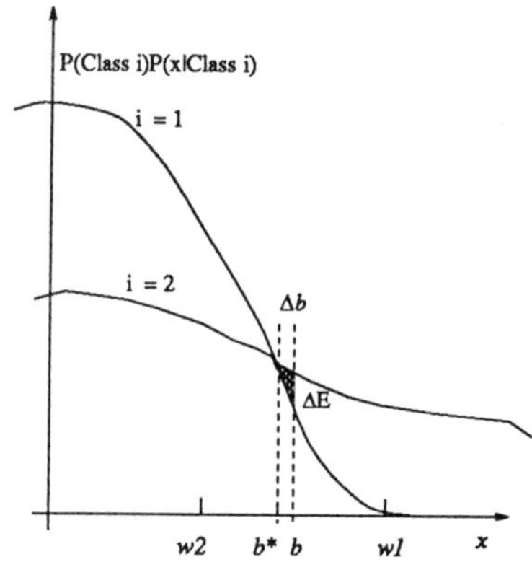

Figure 1: Codebook vectors w_1 and w_2 define a border b. The optimal place for the border is at b^* where $P(C_1)P(x|C_1) = P(C_2)P(x|C_2)$. The extra misclassification errors incurred by placing the border at b is shown by the shaded region.

$$E(b) = \int_{-\infty}^{b} P(C_2)P(x|C_2)dx + \int_{b}^{\infty} P(C_1)P(x|C_1)dx. \quad (2)$$

The derivative of Equation 2 with respect to b is

$$dE/db = P(Class_1)P(b|Class_1) - P(Class_2)P(b|Class_2)$$

That is, the minimum number of misclassifications occurs at b^* where

$$P(Class_1)P(b^*|Class_1) = P(Class_2)P(b^*|Class_2).$$

If $f(x) = (Class_1)P(x|Class_1) - P(Class_2)P(x|Class_2)$ was a regression function then we could use stochastic approximation [Robbins and Monro, 1951] to estimate b* iteratively as

$$b(n+1) = b(n) + \alpha(n)Z_n$$

where Z_n is a sample of the random variable Z whose expected value is $P(Class_1)P(b(n)|Class_1) - P(Class_2)P(b(n)|Class_2))$ and

$$\lim_{n\to\infty} \alpha(n) = 0$$

$$\Sigma_1^\infty \alpha(n) = \infty$$

$$\Sigma_1^\infty \alpha^2(n) < \infty$$

However, we do not have immediate access to an appropriate random variable Z but can express $P(Class_1)P(x|Class_1) - P(Class_2)P(x|Class_2)$ as the limit of a sequence of regression functions using the Parzen Window technique. In the Parzen window technique, probability density functions are estimated as the sum of appropriately normalized pulses centered at the observed values. More formally, we can estimate $P(x|Class_i)$ as [Sklansky and Wassel, 1981]

$$\hat{P}_i^n(x) = \frac{1}{n}\sum_{j=1}^{n} \Psi_n(x - X_j, c_n)$$

where X_j is the sample data point at time j, and $\Psi_n(x-z, c(n))$ is a Parzen window function centred at z with width parameter $c(n)$ that satisfies the following conditions

$$\Psi_n(x-z, c(n)) \geq 0, \forall x, z$$

$$\int_{-\infty}^{\infty} \Psi_n(x-z, c(n))dx = 1$$

$$\lim_{n\to\infty} \frac{1}{n} \int_{-\infty}^{\infty} \Psi_n^2(x-z, c(n))dx = 0$$

$$\lim_{n\to\infty} \Psi_n(x-z, c(n)) = \delta(x-z)$$

We can estimate $f(x) = P(Class_1)P(x|Class_1) - P(Class_2)P(x|Class_2)$ as

$$\hat{f}^n(x) = \frac{1}{n}\sum_{j=1}^{n} S(X_j)\Psi_n(x - X_j, c(n))$$

where $S(X_j)$ is +1 if X_j is from $Class_1$ and −1 if X_j is from $Class_2$.

Then

$$\lim_{n\to\infty} \hat{f}^n(x) = P(Class_1)P(x|Class_1) - P(Class_2)P(x|Class_2)$$

and

$$\lim_{n\to\infty} E[S(X)\Psi_n(x-X, c(n)] = P(Class_1)P(x|Class_1) - P(Class_2)P(x|Class_2)$$

Wassel and Sklansky [1972] have extended the stochastic approximation method of Robbins and Monro [1951] to find the zero of a function that is the limit of a sequence of regression functions and show rigourously that for the above case (where the distribution of $Class_1$ is to the left of that of $Class_2$ and there is only one crossing point) the stochastic approximation procedure

$$b(n+1) = b(n) + \alpha(n)Z_n(x_n, Class(n), b(n), c(n)) \tag{3}$$

using

$$Z_n = \begin{cases} 2c(n)\Psi(X_n - b(n), c(n)) & \text{for } X_n \in Class1 \\ -2c(n)\Psi(X_n - b(n), c(n)) & \text{for } X_n \in Class2 \end{cases}$$

converges to the Bayes optimal border with probability one where $\Psi(x-b, c)$ is a Parzen window function. The following standard conditions for stochastic approximation convergence are needed in their proof

$$\alpha(n), c(n) > 0, \qquad \lim_{n\to\infty} c(n) = 0 \qquad \lim_{n\to\infty} \alpha(n) = 0,$$

$$\Sigma_1^{\infty} \alpha(n)c(n) = \infty, \qquad \Sigma_1^{\infty} \alpha(n)^2 c(n)^2 < \infty$$

as well as a condition that for rectangular Parzen functions reduces to a requirement that $P(Class_1)P(x|Class_1) - P(Class_2)P(x|Class_2)$ be strictly positive to the left of b^* and strictly negative to the right of b^* (for full details of the proof and conditions see [Wassel and Sklansky, 1972]).

The above argument has only addressed the motion of the border. But b is defined as $b = (w1 + w2)/2$, thus we can move the codebook vectors according to

$$dE/dw1 = dE/dw2 = .5dE/db.$$

We could now write Equation 3 as

$$w_i(n+1) = w_i(n) + \alpha_2(n)\frac{(X_n - w_i(n-1))}{|X_n - w_i(n-1)|}$$

$$w_j(n+1) = w_j(n) - \alpha_2(n)\frac{(X_n - w_j(n-1))}{|X_n - w_j(n-1)|}$$

if X_n lies in window of width $2c(n)$ centred at $b(n)$, otherwise

$$w_i(n+1) = w_i(n), \qquad w_j(n+1) = w_j(n)$$

where we have used rectangular Parzen window functions and X_n is from $Class_i$. This holds if $Class_1$ is to the right or left of $Class_2$ as long as w_1 and w_2 are relatively ordered appropriately.

Expanding the problem to more dimensions, and more classes with more codebook vectors per class, complicates the analysis as a change in two codebook vectors to better adjust their border affects more than just the border between the two codebook vectors. However ignoring these effects for a first order approximation suggests the following update procedure:

$$w_i^*(n) = w_i^*(n-1) + \alpha(n)\frac{(X_n - w_i^*(n-1))}{\|X_n - w_i^*(n-1)\|}$$

$$w_j^*(n) = w_j^*(n-1) - \alpha(n)\frac{(X_n - w_j^*(n-1))}{\|X_n - w_j^*(n-1)\|}$$

where $\alpha(n)$ obeys the constraints above, X_n is from $Class_i$, and w_i^*, w_j^* are the two nearest codebook vectors, one each from class i and j ($j \neq i$) and x_n lies within c(n) of the border between them. (No changes are made if all the above conditions are not true). As above this algorithm assumes that the initial positions of the codebook vectors are such that they will not have to cross during the algorithm.

The above algorithm is similar to Kohonen's LVQ2.1 algorithm (which is performed after appropriate initialization of the codebook vectors) except for the normalization of the step size, the decreasing size of the window width c(n) and constraints on the learning rate α.

4 Simulations

Motivated by the theory above, we decided to modify Kohonen's LVQ2.1 algorithm to add normalization of the step size and a decreasing window. In order to allow closer comparison with LVQ2.1, all other parts of the algorithm were kept the same. Thus α decreased linearly. We used a linear decrease on the window size and defined it as in LVQ2.1 for easier parameter matching. For a window size of w all input vectors satisfying $d_i/d_j > \frac{(1-w)}{(1+w)}$ where d_i is the distance to the closest codebook vector and d_j is the distance to the next closest codebook vector, fall into the window between those two vectors (Note however, that updates only occur if the two closest codebook vectors belong to different classes).

The data used is a version of the Peterson and Barney vowel formant data [2]. The dataset consists of the first and second formants for ten vowels in a /hVd/ context from 75 speakers (32 males, 28 females, 15 children) who repeated each vowel twice [3]. As we were not testing generalization , the training set was used as the test set.

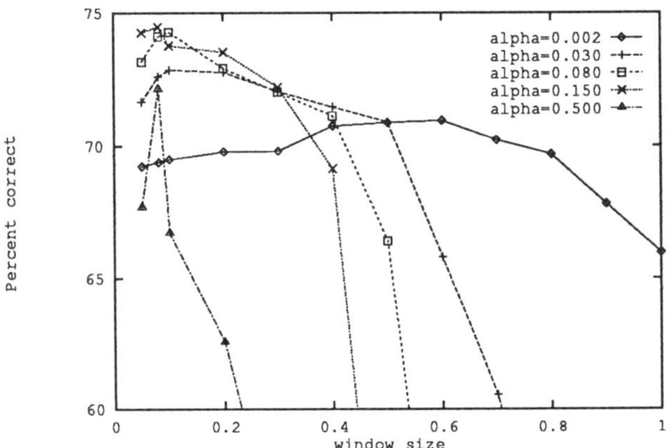

Figure 2: The effect of different window sizes on the accuracy for different values of initial α.

We ran three sets of experiments varying the number of codebook vectors and the number of pattern presentations. For the first set of experiments there were 20 codebook vectors and the algorithms ran for 40000 steps. Figure 2 shows the effect of varying the window size for different initial learning rates $\alpha(1)$ in the LVQ2.1 algorithm. The values plotted are averaged over three runs (The order of presentation of patterns is different for the different runs). The sensitivity of the algorithm to the window size as mentioned in [Kohonen, 1990] is evident. In general we found that as the learning rate is increased the peak accuracy is improved at the expense of the accuracy for other window widths. After a certain value

[2]obtained from Steven Nowlan

[3]3 speakers were missing one vowel and the raw data was linearly transformed to have zero mean and fall within the range $[-3, 3]$ in both components

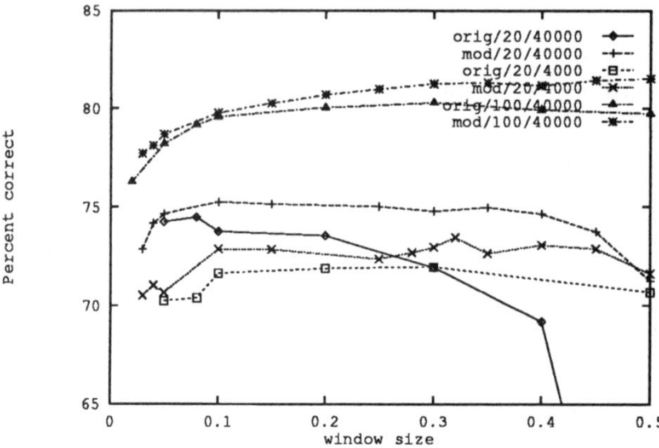

Figure 3: The performance of LVQ2.1 with and without the modifications (normalized step size and decreasing window) for 3 different conditions. The legend gives in order [the alg type/ the number of codebook vectors/ the number of pattern presentations]

the accuracy declines for further increases in learning rate.

Figure 3 shows the improvement achieved with normalization and a linearly decreasing window size for three sets of experiments : (20 code book vectors/40000 pattern presentations), (20 code book vectors/ 4000 pattern presentations) and (100 code book vectors/40000 pattern presentations). For the *decreasing window* algorithm, the x-axis represents the window size in the middle of the run. As above, the values plotted were averaged over three runs. The values of $\alpha(1)$ were the same within each algorithm over all three conditions. A graph using the best α found for each condition separately is almost identical. The graph shows that the modifications provide a modest but consistent improvement in accuracy across the conditions.

In summary the preliminary experiments indicate that a decreasing window and normalized step size can be worthwhile additions to the LVQ2.1 algorithm and further experiments on the generalization properties of the algorithm and with other data sets may be warranted. For these tests we used a linear decrease of the window size and learning rate to allow for easier comparison with the LVQ2.1 algorithm. Further modifications on the algorithm that experiment with different functions (that obey the theoretical constraints) for the learning rate and window size decrease may result in even better performance.

5 Summary

We have shown that Kohonen's LVQ2.1 algorithm can be considered as a variant on a generalization of an algorithm which is optimal for a 1Dimensional/2 codebook vector problem. We added a decreasing window and normalized step size, suggested from the one dimensional algorithm, to the LVQ2.1 algorithm and found a small but consistent improvement in accuracy.

Acknowledgements

We would like to thank Steven Nowlan for his many helpful suggestions on an earlier draft and for making the vowel formant data available to us. We are also grateful to Leonidas Kontothanassis for his help in coding and discussion. This work was supported by a grant from the Human Frontier Science Program and a Canadian NSERC 1967 Science and Engineering Scholarship to the first author who also received A NIPS travel grant to attend the conference.

References

[Grossberg, 1976] Stephen Grossberg, "Adaptive Pattern Classification and Universal Recoding: I. Parallel Development and Coding of Neural Feature Detectors," *Biological Cybernetics*, 23:121–134, 1976.

[Kohonen, 1982] Teuvo Kohonen, "Self-Organized Formation of Topologically Correct Feature Maps," *Biological Cybernetics*, 43:59–69, 1982.

[Kohonen, 1986] Teuvo Kohonen, "Learning Vector Quantization for Pattern Recognition," Technical Report TKK-F-A601, Helsinki University of Technology, Department of Technical Physics, Laboratory of Computer and Information Science, November 1986.

[Kohonen, 1990] Teuvo Kohonen, "Statistical Pattern Recognition Revisited," In R. Eckmiller, editor, *Advanced Neural Computers*, pages 137–144. Elsevier Science Publishers, 1990.

[Kohonen, 1991] Teuvo Kohonen, "Self-Organizing Maps: Optimization Approaches," In T. Kohonen, K. Makisära, O. Simula, and J. Kangas, editors, *Artificial Neural Networks*, pages 981–990. Elsevier Science Publishers, 1991.

[Robbins and Monro, 1951] Herbert Robbins and Sutton Monro, "A Stochastic Approximation Method," *Annals of Math. Stat.*, 22:400—407, 1951.

[Rumelhart and Zipser, 1986] D. E. Rumelhart and D. Zipser, "Feature Discovery by Competitive Learning," In David E. Rumelhart, James L. McClelland, and the PDP Research Group, editors, *Parallel Distributed Processing: Explorations in the Microstructure of Cognition*, volume 2, pages 151–193. MIT Press, 1986.

[Sklansky and Wassel, 1981] Jack Sklansky and Gustav N. Wassel, *Pattern Classifiers and Trainable Machines*, Springer-Verlag, 1981.

[Wassel and Sklansky, 1972] Gustav N. Wassel and Jack Sklansky, "Training a One-Dimensional Classifier to Minimize the Probability of Error," *IEEE Transactions on Systems, Man, and Cybernetics*, SMC-2(4):533—541, 1972.

Extended Regularization Methods for Nonconvergent Model Selection

W. Finnoff, F. Hergert and H.G. Zimmermann
Siemens AG, Corporate Research and Development
Otto-Hahn-Ring 6
8000 Munich 83, Fed. Rep. Germany

Abstract

Many techniques for model selection in the field of neural networks correspond to well established statistical methods. The method of 'stopped training', on the other hand, in which an oversized network is trained until the error on a further validation set of examples deteriorates, then training is stopped, is a true innovation, since model selection doesn't require convergence of the training process.

In this paper we show that this performance can be significantly enhanced by extending the 'nonconvergent model selection method' of stopped training to include dynamic topology modifications (dynamic weight pruning) and modified complexity penalty term methods in which the weighting of the penalty term is adjusted during the training process.

1 INTRODUCTION

One of the central topics in the field of neural networks is that of model selection. Both the theoretical and practical side of this have been intensively investigated and a vast array of methods have been suggested to perform this task. A widely used class of techniques starts by choosing an 'oversized' network architecture then either removing redundant elements based on some measure of saliency (pruning), adding a further term to the cost function penalizing complexity (penalty terms), and finally, observing the error on a further validation set of examples, then stopping training as soon as this performance begins to deteriorate (stopped training). The first two methods can be viewed as variations of long established statistical techniques corresponding in the case of pruning to specification searches, and with respect to penalty terms as regularization or biased regression.

The method of stopped training, on the other hand, seems to be one of the true innovations to come out of neural network research. Here, the model chosen doesn't require the training process to converge, rather, the training process is used to perform a directed search of weight space to find a model with superior generalization performance. Recent theoretical ([B,C,91], [F,91], [F,Z,91]) and empirical results ([H,F,Z,92], [W,R,H,90]) have provided strong evidence for the efficiency of stopped training. In this paper we will show that generalization performance can be further enhanced by expanding the 'nonconvergent method' of stopped training to include dynamic topology modifications (dynamic pruning) and modified complexity penalty term methods in which the weighting of the penalty term is adjusted during the training process. Here, the empirical results are based on an extensive sequence of simulation examples designed to reduce the effects of domain dependence on the performance comparisons.

2 CLASSICAL MODEL SELECTION

Classical model selection methods are generally divided into a number of steps that are performed independently. The first step consists of choosing a network architecture, then either an objective function (possibly including a penalty term) is chosen directly, or in a Bayesian setting, prior distributions on the elements of the data generating process (noise, weights in the model, regularizers, etc.) are specified from which an objective function is derived. Next, using the specified objective function, the training process is started and continued until a convergence criterion is fulfilled. The resulting parametrization of the given architecture is then placed in a 'pool' from which a final model will be selected.

The next step can consist of a modification of the network architecture (for example by pruning weights/hidden-neurons/input-neurons), or of the penalty term (for example by changing its weighting in the objective function) or of the Bayesian prior distributions. The last two modifications then result in a modification of the objective function. This establishes a new framework for the training process which is then restarted and continued until convergence, producing another model for the pool. This process is iterated until the model builder is satisfied that the pool contains a reasonable diversity of candidate models, which are then compared with one another using some estimator of generalization ability, (for example, the performance on a validation set).

Stopped training, on the other hand, has a fundamentally different character. Although the choice of framework remains the same, the essential innovation consists of considering every parametrization of a given architecture as a potential model. This contrasts with classical methods in which only those parametrizations corresponding to minima of the objective function are taken into consideration for the model pool.

Under the weight of accumulated empirical evidence (see [W,R,H,90], [H,F,Z,92]) theorists have begun to investigate the properties of this technique and have been able to show that stopped training has the same sort of regularization effect (i.e. reduction of model variance at the cost of bias) that penalty terms provide (see

[B,C,91], [F,91]). Since the basic effect of pruning procedures is also to reduce network complexity (and consequent model variance) one sees that there is a close relationship in the instrumental effects of stopped training, pruning and regularization. The question remains whether (or under what circumstances) any one or combination of these methods produces superior results.

3 THE METHODS TESTED

In our expirements a single hidden layer feedforward network with tanh activation functions and ten hidden units was used to fit data sets generated in such a manner that network complexity had to be reduced or constrained to prevent overfitting. A variety of both classical and nonconvergent methods were tested for this purpose. The first we will discuss used weight pruning. To characterize the relevance of a weight in a given network, three different test variables were used. The first simply measures weight size under the assumption that the training process naturally forces nonrelevant weights into a region around zero. The second test variable is that used in the Optimal Brain Damage (OBD) pruning procedure of Le Cun et al. (see [L,D,S,90]). The final test variables considered are those proposed by Finnoff and Zimmermann in [F,Z,91], based on significance tests for deviations from zero in the weight update process.

Two pruning algorithms were used in the experiments, both of which attempt to emulate successful interactive methods. In the first algorithm, one removes a certain fixed percentage of weights in the network after a stopping criterion is reached. The reduced network is then trained further until the stopping criterion is once again fulfilled. This process is then repeated until performance breaks down completely. This method will be referred to in the following as *auto-pruning* and was implemented using all three types of test variables to determine the weights to be removed. The only difference lay in the stopping criterion used. In the case of the OBD test variables, training was stopped after the training process converged. In the case of the statistical and small weight test variables, training was stopped whenever overtraining (defined by a repeated increase in the error on a validation set) was observed. A final (restart) variant of auto-pruning using the statistical test variables was also tested. This version of auto-pruning only differs in that the weights are reinitialized (on the reduced topology) after every pruning step. In the tables of results presented in the appendix, the results for auto-pruning using the statistical (resp. small weight, resp. OBD) test variables will be denoted by P^* (resp. G^*, resp. O^*). The version of auto-pruning using restarts will be denoted by p^*.

The second method uses the statistical test variables to both remove and reactivate weights. As in auto-pruning the network is trained until overfitting is observed after a fixed number of epochs, then test values are calculated for all active and inactive weights. Here a fixed number $\varepsilon > 0$ is given, corresponding to some quantile value of a probability distribution. If the test variable for an active weight falls below ε the weight is pruned (deactivated). For weights that have already been set to zero, the value of the test variables are compared with ε, and if larger, the weight is reactivated with a small random value. Furthermore, the value of ε is increased by some $\Delta\varepsilon > 0$ after each pruning step until some value ε_{max} is reached. This method is referred to as *epsi-pruning*. Epsi-pruning was tested in versions both with (e^*)

and without restarts (E*).

Two complexity penalty terms were considered. These consist of a further term $C_\lambda(w)$ added to the error function which forces the network to achieve a compromise between fit and network complexity during the training process; here, the parameter $\lambda \in [0, \infty)$ controls the strength of the complexity penalty. The first is the quadratic term, the first derivative of which leads to the so-called weight decay term in the weight updates (see [H,P,89]). The second is the Weigend/Rumelhart penalty term (see [W,R,H,91]). The weight decay penalty term was tested using two techniques. In the first of these, (D*), λ was held constant throughout the training process. In the second, (d*), λ was set to zero until overtraining was observed, then turned on and held constant for the remainder of the training process. The Weigend/Rumelhart penalty term was also tested using these two methods (denoted in the following tables by W*, resp. w*). Further, the algorithm suggested by A. Weigend in [W,R,H,91] in which the value of λ is varied during training was considered (wF).

In addition to the pruning and penalty term methods investigated, two (simple) versions of stopped training were tested, in one case (nN) with a constant learning step throughout, and in the other (nF) with the step size reduced after overtraining was observed. Finally three benchmarks were included. All these involved training a network until convergence to emulate the situation when no precautions are taken to prevent overfitting other than varying the number of hidden units. The number of hidden units in these benchmark tests was set at three, six and ten, (#3, #6, ##) this last network having then the same topology as that used in the remaining tests.

4 THE DATA GENERATION PROCESSES

To test the methods under consideration, a number of processes were used to generate data sets. By testing on a sufficiently wide range of controlled examples one hopes to reduce the domain dependence that might arise in the performance comparisons. The data used in our experiments was based on pairs $(\widetilde{y}_i, x_i)$, $i = 1, ..., T$, $T \in \mathbf{N}$ with targets $\widetilde{y}_i \in \mathbf{R}$ and inputs $x_i = (x_i^1, ..., x_i^K) \in [-1, 1]^K$, where $\widetilde{y}_i = g(x_i^1, ..., x_i^j) + u_i$, for $j, K \in \mathbf{N}$. Here, g represents the *structure* in the data, $x^1, ..., x^j$ the *relevant* inputs, $x^{j+1}, ..., x^K$, the irrelevant or *decoy* inputs and u_i a stochastic disturbance term.

The first group of experiments was based on an additive structure g having the following form with $j = 5$ and $K = 10$, $g(x_i^1, ..., x_i^5) = \sum_{k=1}^{5} f(\alpha^k x_i^k)$, $\alpha^k \in \mathbf{R}$ and f either the identity on $\mathbf{R}$ or sin. The second class of models investigated had a highly nonlinear product structure g with $j = 3$, $K = 10$ and $g(x_i^1, ..., x_i^3) = \prod_{k=1}^{3} f(\alpha^k x_i^k)$, $\alpha^k \in \mathbf{R}$ and f once again either the identity on $\mathbf{R}$ or sin. The next structure considered was constructed using sums of Radial Basis Functions (RBF's) as follows, $g(x_i^1, ..., x_i^5) = \sum_{l=1}^{8} (-1)^l \exp\left(\sum_{k=1}^{5} \frac{(\alpha^{k,l} - x_i^k)^2}{2\sigma^2}\right)$, with $\alpha^{k,l} \in \mathbf{R}$ for $k = 1, ..., 5$, $l = 1, ..., 8$. Here, for every $l = 1, ..., 8$ the vector parameter $(\alpha^{1,l}, ..., \alpha^{5,l})$ corresponds to the center of the RBF. The final group of experiments were conducted using data generated by feedforward network activation functions. The network used for this task had fifty input units, two hundred hidden units and one output. In every experiment, the data was divided into three disjoint subsets $\mathcal{D}_t, \mathcal{D}_v, \mathcal{D}_g$: The first set $\mathcal{D}_t$ was used for training, the second $\mathcal{D}_v$ (validation) set to test for overfitting and to steer the pruning algorithms and the third $\mathcal{D}_g$ (generalization) set to test the quality of the model selection process.

5 DISCUSSION

The results of the experiments are given below. Here we give a short review of the most interesting phanomena observed.

Notable in a general sense is a striking domain dependence in the performance, which illustrates the danger of basing a comparison of methods on tests using a single (particularly small) data set. Another valuable observation is that by testing at higher levels of significance, apparent performance differences can dwindle or even disappear. Finally, one sees that even in the examples without noise that overfitting occurs, which contradicts the frequently stated conviction that overfitting is noise fitting.

With regard to specific methods, one sees that all the methods tested significantly improved generalization performance when compared to the benchmarks. Further, the results show that the extended nonconvergent methods are on average superior (sometimes dramatically so) than their classical counterparts. In particular, the performance of penalty terms is greatly enhanced if they are first introduced in the training process *after* overtraining is observed. Further, dynamic pruning using the statistical or even the small weight test variables produces significantly better results than stopped training alone or using the Optimal Brain Damage (OBD) weight elimination method which requires training to minima of the objective function. A final notable observation is that the pruning methods (especially those using resarts) generally work better in the examples with a great deal of noise, while the penalty term methods are superior when the structure is highly nonlinear.

6 TABLES OF RESULTS

The experiments were performed as follows: First, each data generating process was used to produce six independent sets of data and initial weights to increase the statistical significance of observed effects and to help reduce the effects of any data set specific anomalies. In a second step, the parameters of the training processes were optimized for each example by extensive testing, then a fixed value for each parameter was chosen for use across the entire range of experiments. With these parameters, each method was tested on all of the six data sets produced by one data generating process. Both the penalty terms and the pruning methods were tested with different settings of the relevant parameters in each model. The parameter values used in the simulations and an overview of the methods tested are collected in the following two tables.

6.1 Parameter Settings of the Experiments

Symbol	Structure	Noise Var.	Size $\mathcal{D}_t/\mathcal{D}_v/\mathcal{D}_g$	Learn Step before/after overfitting
exp_0_n	Sum of RBF's	0.0	400/200/1000	0.05/0.005
exp_3_n	Sum of RBF's	0.3	400/200/1000	0.05/0.005
exp_6_n	Sum of RBF's	0.6	400/200/1000	0.05/0.005
id_7_n	$\sum_{k=0}^{5} \alpha_k x_k$	0.7	200/100/1000	0.05/0.005
id_8_n	$\sum_{k=0}^{5} \alpha_k x_k$	0.8	200/100/1000	0.05/0.005
id_9_n	$\sum_{k=0}^{5} \alpha_k x_k$	0.9	200/100/1000	0.05/0.005
n_0_id	$\prod_{k=0}^{3} x_k$	0.0	1400/600/1000	0.05/0.01
n_1_id	$\prod_{k=0}^{3} x_k$	0.1	1400/600/1000	0.05/0.01
n_2_id	$\prod_{k=0}^{3} x_k$	0.2	1400/600/1000	0.05/0.01
n_0_sin	$\sum_{k=0}^{5} \sin(\alpha_k x_k)$	0.0	1400/600/1000	0.05/0.01
n_1_sin	$\sum_{k=0}^{5} \sin(\alpha_k x_k)$	0.1	1400/600/1000	0.05/0.01
n_2_sin	$\sum_{k=0}^{5} \sin(\alpha_k x_k)$	0.2	1400/600/1000	0.05/0.01
net_0_n	50/200/1 Network	0.0	400/200/1000	0.05/0.005
net_3_n	50/200/1 Network	0.3	400/200/1000	0.05/0.005
net_6_n	50/200/1 Network	0.6	400/200/1000	0.05/0.005
sin_0_n	$\sum_{k=0}^{5} \sin(\alpha_k x_k)$	0.0	400/200/1000	0.05/0.005
sin_3_n	$\sum_{k=0}^{5} \sin(\alpha_k x_k)$	0.3	400/200/1000	0.05/0.005
sin_6_n	$\sum_{k=0}^{5} \sin(\alpha_k x_k)$	0.6	400/200/1000	0.05/0.005

6.2 Overview of Methods Tested

Method Type	Method	Explanation
Classical	D*	Weight Decay, constant λ
Penalty Term	W*	Weigend/Rumelhart, constant λ
Nonconvergent	d*	Weight Decay, 1-Step λ adaptation
Penalty Term	w*	Weigend/Rumelhart, 1-Step λ adaptation
	wF	Weigend/Rumelhart, λ-adapt by Weigend algorithm
Auto-Pruning	G*	Small weight pruning
	o*	Optimal Brain Damage
	P*	Pruning with statistical test var., no restarts
	p*	Pruning with statistical test var., using restarts
Epsi-Pruning	E*	Pruning with statistical test var., no restarts
	e*	Pruning with statistical test var., using restarts
Stopped	nF	Stopped training with reduced η
Training	nN	Stopped training with constant η
Benchmarks	3#	Training to convergence, 3 Neurons im hidden Layer
	6#	Training to convergence, 6 neurons im hidden layer
	##	Training to convergence, 10 neurons im hidden layer

The following tables give categorical rankings of the results. The rankings were calculated as follows: The method with the best performance was given ranking 1, then the performance of each following method was compared with that of the method on the first position using a modified t-test statistic. The first method in the list whose test results deviated from that on the first position to at least the quantile value of the statistic given at the head of the table was then used to start the second category. All those whose test results did not deviate by at least this amount were given the same ranking as the leading method of the category, (in this case 1). Following categories were then formed in an analogous fashion using test results measured against the performance of the leading method at the head of the category.

The results are presented in two tables. The first contains the results for the data generating processes without noise and the second for the models with noise. The categorical rankings given were determined using the procedure described above at a 0.9 level of significance. The ordering of the methods given, listed in the first column, is based on the average ranking over all the simulations listed in the table. This average is given in the second column.

6.2.1 Data Generating Processes without Noise

Classification by objective function, $t_\alpha = 0.9$

method	av	exp_0_n	n_0_id	n_0_sin	net_0_n	sin_0_n
d*	1.6	1	3	1	2	1
P*	1.8	2	2	2	1	2
w*	2.0	1	2	3	3	1
wF	2.0	2	1	3	2	2
G*	2.2	2	3	3	1	2
E*	2.6	2	5	3	1	2
o*	2.6	3	4	2	2	2
p*	2.6	4	5	2	1	1
nF	3.0	3	5	3	2	2
e*	3.8	4	6	4	3	2
nN	3.8	4	7	4	1	3
##	5.2	5	8	4	3	6
W*	5.6	8	10	7	1	2
D*	5.8	8	11	7	2	1
6#	6.2	6	9	6	5	5
3#	6.4	7	12	5	4	4

6.2.2 Data Generating Processes with Noise

Classification by objective function, $t_\alpha = 0.9$

method	av	exp _3_n	exp _6_n	id _9_n	n_1 _id	n_1 _sin	n_2 _id	n_2 _sin	net _3_n	net _6_n	sin _3_n	sin _6_n
P*	2.1	3	1	4	2	2	1	3	3	1	2	2
d*	2.2	5	5	3	1	1	2	1	1	1	2	2
p*	2.2	2	1	1	3	5	3	2	1	2	1	1
wF	2.2	4	5	3	1	4	1	2	2	1	2	1
e*	2.2	1	2	1	4	5	3	4	2	2	1	1
E*	2.6	3	3	2	4	4	3	3	2	1	2	2
G*	2.7	4	4	3	3	3	3	3	2	1	2	2
o*	2.8	5	5	3	3	5	4	1	1	1	2	1
w*	2.8	5	5	3	3	5	3	3	1	1	2	2
nF	2.9	5	5	3	3	5	3	3	1	1	2	2
nN	3.5	5	5	4	4	5	3	3	3	1	3	3
D*	3.7	5	4	5	1	5	7	5	2	2	1	1
W*	4.1	5	4	5	5	6	7	5	2	2	1	1
##	5.2	6	6	6	6	5	5	5	5	4	5	5
3#	5.3	7	7	7	7	5	7	6	4	3	4	4
6#	5.4	8	8	8	5	4	6	3	4	4	5	5

7 REFERENCES

[B,C,91] Baldi, P. and Chauvin, Y., Temporal evolution of generalization during learning in linear networks, *Neural Computation* 3, 1991, pp. 589-603.

[F,91] Finnoff, W., Complexity measures for classes of neural networks with variable weight bounds, in *Proc. Int. Joint Conf. on Neural Networks*, Singapore, 1991.

[F,Z,91] Finnoff, W., Zimmermann, H.G., Detecting structure in small datasets by network fitting under complexity constraints, to appear in *Proc. of 2nd Ann. Workshop Computational Learning Theory and Natural Learning Systems*, Berkeley, 1991.

[H,P,89], Hanson, S. J., and Pratt, L. Y., Comparing biases for minimal network construction with back-propagation, in *Advances in Neural Information Processing I*, D. S. Touretzky, Ed., Morgan Kaufman, 1989.

[H,F,Z,92] Hergert, F., Finnoff, W. and H.G. Zimmermann, A comparison of weight elimination methods for reducing complexity in neural networks. To be presented at *Int. Joint Conf. on Neural Networks*, Baltimore, 1992.

[L,D,S,90] Le Cun, Y., Denker J. and Solla, S., Optimal Brain Damage, in *Proceedings of Neural Information Processing Systems II*, Denver, 1990.

[W,R,H,91] Weigend, A., Rumelhart, D., and Huberman, B., Generalization by weight elimination with application to forecasting, *Advances in Neural Information Processing III*, Ed. R. P. Lippman and J. Moody, Morgan Kaufman, 1991.

Synchronization and Grammatical Inference in an Oscillating Elman Net

Bill Baird
Dept Mathematics,
U.C.Berkeley,
Berkeley, Ca. 94720,
baird@math.berkeley.edu

Todd Troyer
Dept Mathematics,
U.C.Berkeley,
Berkeley, Ca. 94720

Frank Eeckman
Lawrence Livermore
National Laboratory,
P.O. Box 808 (L-426),
Livermore, Ca. 94551

Abstract

We have designed an architecture to span the gap between biophysics and cognitive science to address and explore issues of how a discrete symbol processing system can arise from the continuum, and how complex dynamics like oscillation and synchronization can then be employed in its operation and affect its learning. We show how a discrete-time recurrent "Elman" network architecture can be constructed from recurrently connected oscillatory associative memory modules described by continuous nonlinear ordinary differential equations. The modules can learn connection weights between themselves which will cause the system to evolve under a clocked "machine cycle" by a sequence of transitions of attractors within the modules, much as a digital computer evolves by transitions of its binary flip-flop attractors. The architecture thus employs the principle of "computing with attractors" used by macroscopic systems for reliable computation in the presence of noise. We have specifically constructed a system which functions as a finite state automaton that recognizes or generates the infinite set of six symbol strings that are defined by a Reber grammar. It is a symbol processing system, but with analog input and oscillatory subsymbolic representations. The time steps (machine cycles) of the system are implemented by rhythmic variation (clocking) of a bifurcation parameter. This holds input and "context" modules clamped at their attractors while 'hidden and output modules change state, then clamps hidden and output states while context modules are released to load those states as the new context for the next cycle of input. Superior noise immunity has been demonstrated for systems with dynamic attractors over systems with static attractors, and synchronization ("binding") between coupled oscillatory attractors in different modules has been shown to be important for effecting reliable transitions.

1 Introduction

Patterns of 40 to 80 Hz oscillation have been observed in the large scale activity (local field potentials) of olfactory cortex [Freeman and Baird, 1987] and visual neocortex [Gray and Singer, 1987], and shown to predict the olfactory [Freeman and Baird, 1987] and visual pattern recognition responses of a trained animal. Similar observations of 40 Hz oscillation in auditory and motor cortex (in primates), and in the retina and EMG have been reported. It thus appears that cortical computation in general may occur by dynamical interaction of resonant modes, as has been thought to be the case in the olfactory system.

The oscillation can serve a macroscopic clocking function and entrain or "bind" the relevant microscopic activity of disparate cortical regions into a well defined phase coherent collective state or "gestalt". This can overide irrelevant microscopic activity and produce coordinated motor output. There is further evidence that although the oscillatory activity appears to be roughly periodic, it is actually chaotic when examined in detail.

If this view is correct, then oscillatory/chaotic network modules form the actual cortical substrate of the diverse sensory, motor, and cognitive operations now studied in static networks. It must then be shown how those functions can be accomplished with oscillatory and chaotic dynamics, and what advantages are gained thereby. It is our expectation that nature makes good use of this dynamical complexity, and our intent is to search here for novel design principles that may underly the superior computational performance of biological systems over man made devices in many task domains. These principles may then be applied in artificial systems to engineering problems to advance the art of computation. We have therefore constructed a parallel distributed processing architecture that is inspired by the structure and dynamics of cerebral cortex, and applied it to the problem of grammatical inference.

The construction assumes that cortex is a set of coupled oscillatory associative memories, and is also guided by the principle that attractors must be used by macroscopic systems for reliable computation in the presence of noise. Present day digital computers are built of flip-flops which, at the level of their transistors, are continuous dissipative dynamical systems with different attractors underlying the symbols we call "0" and "1".

2 Oscillatory Network Modules

The network modules of this architecture were developed previously as models of olfactory cortex, or caricatures of "patches"of neocortex [Baird, 1990a]. A particular subnetwork is formed by a set of neural populations whose interconnections also contain higher order synapses. These synapses determine attractors for that subnetwork independent of other subnetworks. Each subnetwork module assumes only minimal coupling justified by known olfactory anatomy. An N node module can be shown to function as an associative memory for up to $N/2$ oscillatory and $N/3$ chaotic memory attractors [Baird, 1990b, Baird and Eeckman, 1992b]. Single modules with static, oscillatory, and three types of chaotic attractors – Lorenz, Roessler, Ruelle-Takens – have been sucessfully used for recognition of handwritten characters [Baird and Eeckman, 1992b].

We have shown in these modules a superior stability of oscillatory attractors over static attractors in the presence of additive Gaussian noise perturbations with the 1/f spectral character of the noise found experimentally by Freeman in the brain[Baird and Eeckman, 1992a]. This may be one reason why the brain uses dynamic attractors. An oscillatory attractor acts like a a bandpass filter and is effectively immune to the many slower macroscopic bias perturbations in the theta-alpha-beta range (3 - 25 Hz) below its 40 -80 Hz passband, and the more microscopic perturbations of single neuron spikes in the 100 - 1000 Hz range.

The mathematical foundation for the construction of network modules is contained in the **normal form projection algorithm**[Baird, 1990b]. This is a learning algorithm for recurrent analog neural networks which allows associative memory storage of analog patterns, continuous periodic sequences, and chaotic attractors in the same network. A key feature of a net constructed by this algorithm is that the underlying dynamics is explicitly isomorphic to any of a class of standard, well understood nonlinear dynamical systems - a "normal form" [Guckenheimer and Holmes, 1983]. This system is chosen in advance, independent of both the patterns to be stored and the learning algorithm to be used. This control over the dynamics permits the design of important aspects of the network dynamics independent of the particular patterns to be stored. Stability, basin geometry, and rates of convergence to attractors can be programmed in the standard dynamical system.

By analyzing the network in the polar form of these "normal form coordinates", the amplitude and phase dynamics have a particularly simple interaction. When the input to a module is synchronized with its intrinsic oscillation, the amplitudes of the periodic activity may be considered separately from the phase rotation, and the network of the module may be viewed as a static network with these amplitudes as its activity. We can further show analytically that the network modules we have constructed have a strong tendency to synchronize as required.

3 Oscillatory Elman Architecture

Because we work with this class of mathematically well-understood associative memory networks, we can take a constructive approach to building a cortical computer architecture, using these networks as modules in the same way that digital computers are designed from well behaved continuous analog flip-flop circuits. The architecture is such that the larger system is itself a special case of the type of network of the submodules, and can be analysed with the same tools used to design the subnetwork modules.

Each module is described in normal form or "mode" coordinates as a k-winner-take-all network where the winning set of units may have static, periodic or chaotic dynamics. By choosing modules to have only two attractors, networks can be built which are similar to networks using binary units. There can be fully recurrent connections between modules. The entire super-network of connected modules, however, is itself a polynomial network that can be projected into standard network coordinates. The attractors within the modules may then be distributed patterns like those described for the biological model [Baird, 1990a], and observed experimentally in the olfactory system [Freeman and Baird, 1987]. The system is still equivalent to the architecture of modules in normal form, however, and may easily be designed, simulated, and theoretically evaluated in these coordinates. *In this paper all networks are discussed in normal form coordinates.*

As a benchmark for the capabilities of the system, and to create a point of contact to standard network architectures, we have constructed a discrete-time recurrent "Elman" network [Elman, 1991] from oscillatory modules defined by ordinary differential equations. We have at present a system which functions as a finite state automaton that perfectly recognizes or generates the infinite set of strings defined by the Reber grammar described in Cleeremans et. al. [Cleeremans et al., 1989]. The connections for this network were found by psuedo-inverting to find the connection matrices between a set of pre-chosen automata states for the hidden layer modules and the proper possible output symbols of the Reber grammar, and between the proper next hidden state and each legal combination of a new input symbol and the present state contained in the context modules.

We use two types of modules in implementing the Elman network architecture. The input and output layer each consist of a single associative memory module with six oscillatory attractors (six competing oscillatory modes), one for each of the six possible symbols in the grammar. An attractor in these winner-take-all normal form cordinates is one oscillator at its maximum amplitude, with the others near zero amplitude. The hidden and context layers consist of binary "units" composed of a two competing oscillator module. We think of one mode within the unit as representing "1" and the other as representing"0" (see fig.1).

A "weight" for this unit is simply defined to be the weight of a driving unit to the input of the 1 attractor. The weights for the 0 side of the unit are then given as the compliment of these, $w^0 = A - w^1$. This forces the input to the 0 side of the unit be the complement of the input to the 1 side, $I_i^0 = A - I_i^0$, where A is a bias constant chosen to divide input equally between the oscillators at the midpoint of activation.

Figure 1.

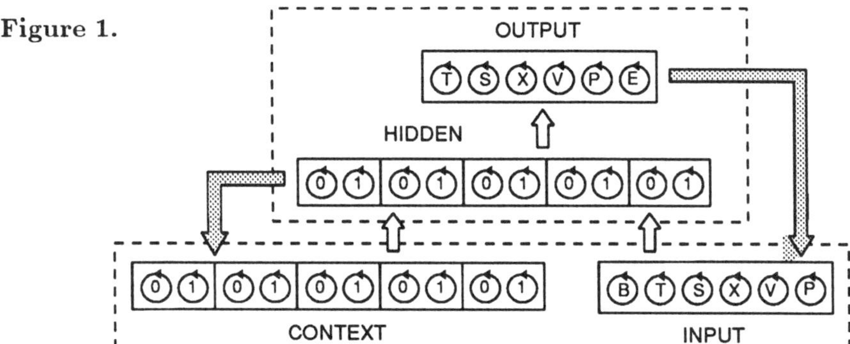

Information flow in the network is controlled by a "machine cycle" implemented by the sinusoidal clocking of a bifurcation parameter which controls the level of inhibitory inter-mode coupling or "competition" between the individual oscillatory modes within each winner-take-all module.

For illustration, we use a binary module represnting either a single hidden or context unit; the behavior of the larger input and output modules is similar. Such a unit is defined in polar normal form coordinates by the following equations:

$$\begin{aligned}
\dot{r}_{1i} &= u_i r_{1i} - c r_{1i}(r_{1i}^2 + (d - b\sin(\omega_{clock} t))r_{0i}^2) + \sum_j w_{ij} I_j \cos(\theta_j - \theta_{1i}) \\
\dot{r}_{0i} &= u_i r_{0i} - c r_{0i}(r_{0i}^2 + (d - b\sin(\omega_{clock} t))r_{1i}^2) + \sum_j (A - w_{ij}) I_j \cos(\theta_j - \theta_{0i}) \\
\dot{\theta}_{1i} &= \omega_i + \sum_j w_{ij}(I_j / r_{1i}) \sin(\theta_j - \theta_{1i}) \\
\dot{\theta}_{0i} &= \omega_i + \sum_j (A - w_{ij})(I_j / r_{0i}) \sin(\theta_j - \theta_{0i})
\end{aligned}$$

The clocked parameter $bsin(\omega_{clock}t)$ has lower (1/10) frequency than the intrinsic frequency of the unit ω_i. Asuming that all inputs to the unit are phase-locked, examination of the phase equations shows that the unit will synchronize with this input. When the oscillators are phase-locked to the input, $\theta_j - \theta_{1i} = 0$, and the phase terms $\cos(\theta_j - \theta_{1i}) = \cos(0) = 1$ dissappear. This leaves the amplitude equations $\dot{r}_{1i}$ and $\dot{r}_{0i}$ with static inputs $\sum_j w_{ij} I_j$ and $\sum_j (A - w_{ij}) I_j$. The phase equations show a strong tendency to phase-lock, since there is an attractor at zero phase difference $\phi = \theta_0 - \theta_I = \theta_0 - \omega_I t = 0$, and a repellor at 180 degrees in the phase difference equations $\dot{\phi}$ for either side of a unit driven by an input of the same frequency, $\omega_I - \omega_0 = 0$.

$$\dot{\phi} = \omega_0 - \omega_I + (r_I/r_0)\sin(-\phi) \quad , \quad so \quad , \quad \hat{\phi} = -sin^{-1}[(r_0/r_I)(\omega_I - \omega_0)]$$

Thus we have a network module which approximates a static network unit in its amplitude activity when fully phase-locked. Amplitude information is transmitted between modules, with an oscillatory carrier. If the frequencies of attractors in the architecture are randomly dispersed by a significant amount, phase-lags appear, then synchronization is lost and improper transitions begin to occur.

For the remainder of the paper we assume the entire system is operating in the synchronized regime and examine the flow of information characterized by the pattern of amplitudes of the oscillatory modes within the network.

4 Machine Cycle by Clocked Bifurcation

Given this assumption of a phase-locked system, the amplitude dynamics behave as a gradient dynamical system for an energy function given by

$$E_i = -\frac{1}{2}u_i(r_{1i}^2 + r_{0i}^2) + \frac{1}{4}c((r_{1i}^4 + r_{0i}^4) + \frac{1}{2}(d \pm bsin(\omega_{clock}t))(r_{1i}^2 r_{0i}^2) - (Ir_{1i} + (B - I)r_{0i})$$

where the total input $I = \sum_j w_{ij} I_j$ and $B = \sum_j I_j$. Figures 2a and 2b show the energy landscape with no external input for minimal and maximal levels of competition respectively. External input simply adds a linear "tilt" to the landscape, with large I giving a larger tilt toward the r_{1i} axis and small I a larger tilt toward the r_{0i} axis.

Note that for low levels of competition, there is a broad circular valley. When tilted by external input, there is a unique equilibrium that is determined by the bias in tilt along one axis over the other. Thinking of r_{1i} as the "acitivity" of the unit, this acitivity becomes an increasing function of I. *The module behaves as analog connectionist unit whose transfer function can be approximated by a sigmoid.*

With high levels of competition, the unit will behave as a binary (bistable) "digital" flip-flop element. There are two deep valleys, one on each axis. Hence the final steady state of the unit is determined by which basin contains the initial state of the system reached during the analog mode of operation before competition is increased by the clock. This state changes little under the influence of external input: a tilt will move the location of the valleys only slightly. Hence *the unit performs a winner-take-all choice on the coordinates of its initial state and maintains that choice independent of external input.*

Figure 2a.

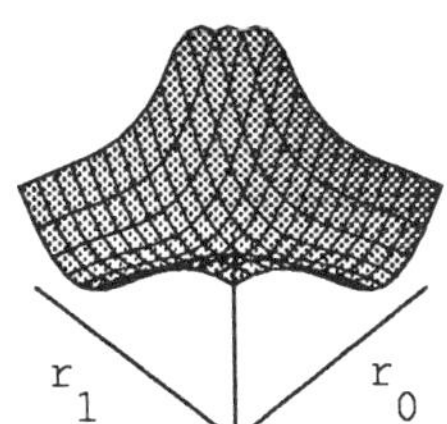

Low Competition

Figure 2b.

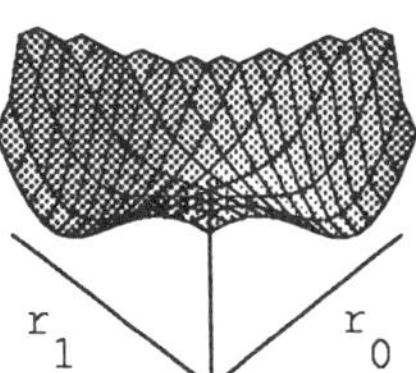

High Competition

We use this bifurcation in the behavior of the modules to control information flow within the network. We think of the input and context modules as "sensory", and the hidden and output modules as "motor" modules. The action of the clock is applied reciprocally to these two sets (grouped by dotted lines in fig.1) so that they alternatively open to receive input from each other and make transitions of attractors. *This enables a network completely defined as a set of ordinary differential equations to implement the discrete-time recurrent Elman network.*

At the beginning of a machine cycle, the input and context layers are at high competition and hence their activity is "clamped" at the bottom of deep attractors. The hidden and output modules are at low competition and therefore behave as traditional feedforward network free to take on analog values. Then the situation reverses. As the competition comes up in the output module, it makes a winner-take-all choice as to the next symbol. Meanwhile high competition has quantized and clamped the activity in the hidden layer to a fixed binary vector. Then competition is lowered in the input and context layers, freeing these modules from their attractors.

Identity mappings from hidden to context and from output to input (gray arrows in fig.1) "load" the binarized activity of the hidden layer to the context layer for the next cycle, and "place" the generated output symbol into the input layer. For a Reber grammar there are always two equally possible next symbols being generated in the output layer, and we apply noise to break this symmetry and let the winner-take-all dynamics of the output module chose one. For the recognition mode of operation, these symbols are thought of as "predicted" by the output, and one of them must always match the next actual input of a string to be recognized or the string is instantly rejected.

Note that even though the clocking is sinusiodal and these transitions are not sharp, the system is robust and reliable. It is only necessary to set the rates of convergence within modules to be faster than the rate of change of the clocked bifurcation parameter, so that the modules are operating "adiabatically" – i.e. always internally relaxed to an equilibrium that is moved slowly by the clocked parameter.

It is the bifurcation in the phase portrait of a module from one to two attractors that contributes the essential "digitization" of the system in time and state. A bifurcation is a discontinuous (topologically sharp) change in the phase portrait of possibilities for the continuous dynamical behavior of a system that occurs as a bifurcation parameter reaches a "critical" value. We can think of the analog mode for a module as allowing input to prepare its initial state for the binary "decision" between attractor basins that occurs as competition rises and the double potential well appears.

The feedback between sensory and motor modules is effectively cut when one set is clamped at high competition. The system can thus be viewed as operating in discrete time by alternating transitions between a finite set of attracting states. This kind of clocking and "buffering" (clamping) of some states while other states relax is essential to the reliable operation of digital architectures. The clock input on a flip-flop clamps it's state until its signal inputs have settled and the choice of transition can be made with the proper information available. In our simulations, if we clock all modules to transition at once, the programmed sequences lose stability, and we get transitions to unprogrammed fixed points and simple limit cycles for the whole system.

5 Training

When the input and context modules are clamped at their attractors, and the hidden and output modules are in the analog operating mode and synchronized to their inputs, the network approximates the behavior of a standard feedforward network in terms of its amplitude activities. Thus a real valued error can be defined for the hidden and output units and standard learning algorithms like backpropagation can be used to train the connections.

We can use techniques of Giles et. al. [Giles et al., 1992] who have trained simple recurrent networks to become finite state automata that can recognize the regular Tomita languages and others. If the context units are clamped with high competition, they are essentially "quantized" to take on only their 0 or 1 attractor values, and the feedback connections from the hidden units cannot affect them. While Giles, et. al. often do not quantize their units until the end of training to extract a finite state automaton, they find that quantizing of the context units during training like this increases learning speed in many cases[Giles et al., 1992]. In preparation for learning in the dynamic architecture, we have sucessfully trained the backpropogation network of Cleermans et. al. with digititized context units and a shifted sigmoid activation function that approximates the one calculated for our oscillatory units.

In the dynamic architecture, we have also the option of leaving the competition within the context units at intermediate levels to allow them to take on analog values in a variable sized neighborhood of the 0 or 1 attractors. Since our system is recurrently connected by an identity map from hidden to context units, it will relax to some equilibrium determined by the impact of the context units and the clamped input on the hidden unit states, and the effect of the feedback from those hidden states on the context states. We can thus further explore the impact on learning of this range of operation between discrete time and space automaton and continuous analog recurrent network.

6 Discusion

The ability to operate as an finite automaton with oscillatory/chaotic "states" is an important benchmark for this architecture, but only a subset of its capabilities. At low to zero competition, the supra-system reverts to one large continuous dynamical system. We expect that this kind of variation of the operational regime, especially with chaotic attractors inside the modules, though unreliable for habitual behaviors, may nontheless be very useful in other areas such as the search process of reinforcement learning.

An important element of intra-cortical communication in the brain, and between modules in this architecture, is the ability of a module to detect and respond to the proper input signal from a particular module, when inputs from other modules which is irrelevant to the present computation are contributing cross-talk and noise. This is smilar to the problem of coding messages in a computer architecture like the connection machine so that they can be picked up from the common communication buss line by the proper receiving module. We believe that sychronization is one important aspect of how the brain solves this coding problem. Attractors in modules of the architecture may be frequency coded during learning so that they will sychronize only with the appropriate active attractors in other modules that have a similar resonant frequency. The same hardware (or "wetware") and connection matrix can thus subserve many different networks of interaction between modules at the same time without cross-talk problems.

This type of computing architecture and its learning algorithms for computation with oscillatory spatial modes may be ideal for implementation in optical systems, where electromagnetic oscillations, very high dimensional modes, and high processing speeds are available. The mathematical expressions for optical mode competition are nearly identical to our normal forms.

Acknowledgements

Supported by AFOSR-91-0325, and a grant from LLNL. It is a pleasure to acknowledge the invaluable assistance of Morris Hirsch and Walter Freeman.

References

[Baird, 1990a] Baird, B. (1990a). Bifurcation and learning in network models of oscillating cortex. In Forest, S., editor, *Emergent Computation*, pages 365–384. North Holland. also in Physica D, 42.

[Baird, 1990b] Baird, B. (1990b). A learning rule for cam storage of continuous periodic sequences. In *Proc. Int. Joint Conf. on Neural Networks, San Diego*, pages 3: 493–498.

[Baird and Eeckman, 1992a] Baird, B. and Eeckman, F. H. (1992a). A hierarchical sensory-motor architecture of oscillating cortical area subnetworks. In Eeckman, F. H., editor, *Analysis and Modeling of Neural Systems II*, pages 96–204, Norwell, Ma. Kluwer.

[Baird and Eeckman, 1992b] Baird, B. and Eeckman, F. H. (1992b). A normal form projection algorithm for associative memory. In Hassoun, M. H., editor, *Associative Neural Memories: Theory and Implementation*, New York, NY. Oxford University Press. in press.

[Cleeremans et al., 1989] Cleeremans, A., Servan-Schreiber, D., and McClelland, J. (1989). Finite state automata and simple recurrent networks. *Neural Computation*, 1(3):372–381.

[Elman, 1991] Elman, J. (1991). Distributed representations, simple recurrent networks and grammatical structure. *Machine Learning*, 7(2/3):91.

[Freeman and Baird, 1987] Freeman, W. and Baird, B. (1987). Relation of olfactory eeg to behavior: Spatial analysis. *Behavioral Neuroscience*, 101:393–408.

[Giles et al., 1992] Giles, C., Miller, C.B.and Chen, D., Chen, H., Sun, G., and Lee, Y. (1992). Learning and extracting finite state automata with second order recurrent neural networks. *Neural Computation*, pages 393–405.

[Gray and Singer, 1987] Gray, C. M. and Singer, W. (1987). Stimulus dependent neuronal oscillations in the cat visual cortex area 17. *Neuroscience [Suppl]*, 22:1301P.

[Guckenheimer and Holmes, 1983] Guckenheimer, J. and Holmes, D. (1983). *Nonlinear Oscillations, Dynamical Systems, and Bifurcations of Vector Fields.* Springer, New York.

A Fast Stochastic Error-Descent Algorithm for Supervised Learning and Optimization

Gert Cauwenberghs
California Institute of Technology
Mail-Code 128-95
Pasadena, CA 91125
E-mail: gert@cco.caltech.edu

Abstract

A parallel stochastic algorithm is investigated for error-descent learning and optimization in deterministic networks of arbitrary topology. No *explicit* information about internal network structure is needed. The method is based on the model-free distributed learning mechanism of Dembo and Kailath. A modified parameter update rule is proposed by which each individual parameter vector perturbation contributes a decrease in error. A substantially faster learning speed is hence allowed. Furthermore, the modified algorithm supports learning time-varying features in dynamical networks. We analyze the convergence and scaling properties of the algorithm, and present simulation results for dynamic trajectory learning in recurrent networks.

1 Background and Motivation

We address general optimization tasks that require finding a set of constant parameter values p_i that minimize a given error functional $\mathcal{E}(\mathbf{p})$. For supervised learning, the error functional consists of some quantitative measure of the deviation between a desired state $\mathbf{x}^T$ and the actual state of a network $\mathbf{x}$, resulting from an input $\mathbf{y}$ and the parameters $\mathbf{p}$. In such context the components of $\mathbf{p}$ consist of the connection strengths, thresholds and other adjustable parameters in the network. A typical specification for the error in learning a discrete set of pattern associations $(\mathbf{y}^{(\alpha)}, \mathbf{x}^{T(\alpha)})$ for a steady-state network is the Mean Square Error (MSE)

$$\mathcal{E}(\mathbf{p}) = \frac{1}{2} \sum_{\alpha} \sum_{k} (x_k^{T(\alpha)} - x_k^{(\alpha)})^2 \tag{1}$$

and similarly, for learning a desired response $(\mathbf{y}(t), \mathbf{x}^T(t))$ in a dynamic network

$$\mathcal{E}(\mathbf{p}) = \frac{1}{2} \int_{t_0}^{t_f} \sum_{k} (x_k^T(t) - x_k(t))^2 \mathrm{d}t \ . \tag{2}$$

For $\mathcal{E}(\mathbf{p})$ to be uniquely defined in the latter dynamic case, initial conditions $\mathbf{x}(t_{\text{init}})$ need to be specified.

A popular method for minimizing the error functional is steepest error descent (gradient descent) [1]-[6]

$$\Delta \mathbf{p} = -\eta \frac{\partial \mathcal{E}}{\partial \mathbf{p}} \ . \tag{3}$$

Iteration of (3) leads asymptotically to a local minimum of $\mathcal{E}(\mathbf{p})$, provided η is strictly positive and small. The computation of the gradient is often cumbersome, especially for time-dependent problems [2]-[5], and is even ill-posed for analog hardware learning systems that unavoidably contain unknown process impurities. This calls for error descent methods avoiding *calculation* of the gradients but rather probing the dependence of the error on the parameters *directly*. Methods that use some degree of explicit internal information other than the adjustable parameters, such as Madaline III [6] which assumes a specific feedforward multi-perceptron network structure and requires access to internal nodes, are therefore excluded. Two typical methods which satisfy the above condition are illustrated below:

- **Weight Perturbation** [7], a simple sequential parameter perturbation technique. The method updates the individual parameters in sequence, by measuring the change in error resulting from a perturbation of a single parameter and adjusting that parameter accordingly. This technique effectively measures the components of the gradient sequentially, which for a complete knowledge of the gradient requires as many computation cycles as there are parameters in the system.
- **Model-Free Distributed Learning** [8], which is based on the "M.I.T." rule in adaptive control [9]. Inspired by analog hardware, the distributed algorithm makes use of time-varying perturbation signals $\pi_i(t)$ supplied in parallel to the parameters p_i, and correlates these $\pi_i(t)$ with the instantaneous network response $\mathcal{E}(\mathbf{p} + \pi)$ to form an incremental update Δp_i. Unfortunately, the distributed model-free algorithm does not support learning of dynamic features (2) in networks with delays, and the learning speed degrades sensibly with increasing number of parameters [8].

2 Stochastic Error-Descent: Formulation and Properties

The algorithm we investigate here combines both above methods, yielding a significant improvement in performance over both. Effectively, at *every* epoch the constructed algorithm decreases the error along a single randomly selected direction in the parameter space. Each such decrement is performed using a *single* synchronous parallel parameter perturbation per epoch. Let $\hat{\mathbf{p}} = \mathbf{p} + \boldsymbol{\pi}$ with parallel perturbations π_i selected from a random distribution. The perturbations π_i are assumed reasonably small, but not necessarily mutually orthogonal. For a given *single* random instance of the perturbation $\boldsymbol{\pi}$, we update the parameters with the rule

$$\Delta \mathbf{p} = -\mu \, \hat{\mathcal{E}} \, \boldsymbol{\pi} \quad , \tag{4}$$

where the scalar

$$\hat{\mathcal{E}} = \mathcal{E}(\hat{\mathbf{p}}) - \mathcal{E}(\mathbf{p}) \tag{5}$$

is the error contribution due to the perturbation $\boldsymbol{\pi}$, and μ is a small strictly positive constant. Obviously, for a sequential activation of the π_i, the algorithm reduces to the weight perturbation method [7]. On the other hand, by omitting $\mathcal{E}(\mathbf{p})$ in (5) the original distributed model-free method [8] is obtained. The subtraction of the unperturbed reference term $\mathcal{E}(\mathbf{p})$ in (5) contributes a significant increase in speed over the original method. Intuitively, the incremental error $\hat{\mathcal{E}}$ specified in (5) isolates the *specific* contribution due to the perturbation, which is obviously more relevant than the total error which includes a bias $\mathcal{E}(\mathbf{p})$ unrelated to the perturbation $\boldsymbol{\pi}$. This bias necessitates stringent zero-mean and orthogonality conditions on the π_i and requires many perturbation cycles in order to effect a consistent decrease in the error [8].[1] An additional difference concerns the assumption on the dynamics of the perturbations π_i. By fixing the perturbation $\boldsymbol{\pi}$ during every epoch in the present method, the dynamics of the π_i no longer interfere with the time delays of the network, and dynamic optimization tasks as (2) come within reach.

The rather simple and intuitive structure (4) and (5) of the algorithm is somewhat reminiscent of related models for reinforcement learning, and likely finds parallels in other fields as well. Random direction and line-search error-descent algorithms for trajectory learning have been suggested and analyzed by P. Baldi [12]. As a matter of coincidence, independent derivations of basically the same algorithm but from different approaches are presented in this volume as well [13],[14]. Rather than focussing on issues of originality, we proceed by analyzing the virtues and scaling properties of this method. We directly present the results below, and defer the formal derivations to the appendix.

2.1 The algorithm performs **gradient descent on average**, provided that the perturbations π_i are mutually uncorrelated with uniform auto-variance, that is $\mathrm{E}(\pi_i \pi_j) = \sigma^2 \delta_{ij}$ with σ the perturbation strength. The effective gradient descent learning rate corresponding to (3) equals $\eta_{\text{eff}} = \mu\sigma^2$.

Hence on average the learning trajectory follows the steepest path of error descent. The stochasticity of the parameter perturbations gives rise to fluctuations around the mean path of descent, injecting diffusion in the learning process. However, the individual fluctuations satisfy the following desirable regularity:

[1] An interesting noise-injection variant on the model-free distributed learning paradigm of [8], presented in [10], avoids the bias due to the offset level $\mathcal{E}(\mathbf{p})$ as well, by differentiating the perturbation and error signals prior to correlating them to construct the parameter increments. A complete demonstration of an analog VLSI system based on this approach is presented in this volume [11]. As a matter of fact, the modified noise-injection algorithm corresponds to a continuous-time version of the algorithm presented here, for networks and error functionals free of time-varying features.

2.2 The error $\mathcal{E}(\mathbf{p})$ **always decreases** under an update (4) for *any* $\boldsymbol{\pi}$, provided that $|\boldsymbol{\pi}|^2$ is "small", and μ is strictly positive and "small".

Therefore, the algorithm is guaranteed to converge towards local error minima just like gradient descent, as long as the perturbation vector π statistically explores all directions of the parameter space, provided the perturbation strength and learning rate are sufficiently small. This property holds only for methods which bypass the bias due to the offset error term $\mathcal{E}(\mathbf{p})$ for the calculation of the updates, as is performed here by subtraction of the offset in (5).

The guaranteed decrease in error of the update (4) under any small, single instance of the perturbation π removes the need of averaging multiple trials obtained by different instances of π in order to reduce turbulence in the learning dynamics. We intentionally omit any smoothing operation on the constructed increments (4) prior to effecting the updates Δp_i, unlike the estimation of the true gradient in [8],[10],[13] by essentially accumulating and averaging contributions (4) over a large set of random perturbations. Such averaging is unnecessary here (and in [13]) since each individual increment (4) contributes a decrease in error, and since the smoothing of the ragged downward trajectory on the error surface is effectively performed by the integration of the incremental updates (4) anyway. Furthermore, from a simple analysis it follows that such averaging is actually detrimental to the effective speed of convergence.[2] For a correct measure of the convergence speed of the algorithm relative to that of other methods, we studied the boundaries of learning stability regions specifying maximum learning rates for the different methods. The analysis reveals the following scaling properties with respect to the size of the trained network, characterized by the number of adjustable parameters P:

2.3 The **maximum attainable average speed** of the algorithm is a factor $P^{1/2}$ slower than that of pure gradient descent, as opposed to the maximum average speed of sequential weight perturbation which is a factor P slower than gradient descent.

The reduction in speed of the algorithm vs. gradient descent by the square root of the number of parameters can be understood as well from an information-theoretical point of view using physical arguments. At each epoch, the stochastic algorithm applies perturbations in all P dimensions, injecting information in P different "channels". However, only *scalar* information about the global response of the network to the perturbations is available at the outside, through a single "channel". On average, such an algorithm can extract knowledge about the response of the network in at most $P^{1/2}$ effective dimensions, where the upper limit is reached only if the perturbations are truly statistically independent, exploiting the full channel capacity. In the worst case the algorithm only retains scalar information through a single, low-bandwidth channel, which is e.g. the case for the sequential weight perturbation algorithm. Hence, the stochastic algorithm achieves a speed-up of a factor $P^{1/2}$ over the technique of sequential weight perturbation, by using parallel statistically independent perturbations as opposed to serial single perturbations. The original model-free algorithm by Dembo and Kailath [8] does not achieve this $P^{1/2}$

[2]Sure enough, averaging say M instances of (4) for different random perturbations will improve the estimate of the gradient by decreasing its variance. However, the variance of the update $\Delta\mathbf{p}$ decreases by a factor of M, allowing an increase in learning rate by only a factor of $M^{1/2}$, while to that purpose M network evaluations are required. In terms of total computation efforts, the averaged method is hence a factor $M^{1/2}$ slower.

speed-up over the sequential perturbation method (and may even do worse), partly because the information about the specific error contribution by the perturbations is contaminated due to the constant error bias signal $\mathcal{E}(\mathbf{p})$.

Note that up to here the term "speed" was defined in terms of the number of epochs, which does not necessarily directly relate to the physical speed, in terms of the total number of operations. An equally important factor in speed is the amount of computation involved per epoch to obtain values for the updates (3) and (4). For the stochastic algorithm, the most intensive part of the computation involved at every epoch is the evaluation of $\mathcal{E}(\mathbf{p})$ for two instances of $\mathbf{p}$ in (5), which typically scales as $\mathcal{O}(P)$ for neural networks. The remaining operations relate to the generation of random perturbations π_i and the calculation of the correlations in (4), scaling as $\mathcal{O}(P)$ as well. Hence, for an accurate comparison of the learning speed, the scaling of the computations involved in a single gradient descent step needs to be balanced against the computation effort by the stochastic method corresponding to an equivalent error descent rate, which combining both factors scales as $\mathcal{O}(P^{3/2})$. An example where the scaling for this computation balances in favor of the stochastic error-descent method, due to the expensive calculation of the full gradient, will be demonstrated below for dynamic trajectory learning.

More importantly, the intrinsic parallelism, fault tolerance and computational simplicity of the stochastic algorithm are especially attractive with hardware implementations in mind. The complexity of the computations can be furthermore reduced by picking a *binary* random distribution for the parallel perturbations, $\pi_i = \pm\sigma$ with equal probability for both polarities, simplifying the multiply operations in the parameter updates. In addition, powerful techniques exist to generate large-scale streams of pseudo-random bits in VLSI [15].

3 Numerical Simulations

For a test of the learning algorithm on time-dependent problems, we selected dynamic trajectory learning (a "Figure 8") as a representative example [2]. Several exact gradient methods based on an error functional of the form (2) exist [2]-[5], with a computational complexity scaling as either $\mathcal{O}(P)$ per epoch for an *off-line*[3] method [2] (requiring history storage over the complete time interval of the error functional), or as $\mathcal{O}(P^2)$ [3] and recently as $\mathcal{O}(P^{3/2})$ [4]-[5] per epoch for an *on-line* method (with only most current history storage). The stochastic error-descent algorithm provides an *on-line* alternative with an $\mathcal{O}(P)$ per epoch complexity. As a consequence, including the extra $P^{1/2}$ factor for the convergence speed relative to gradient descent, the overall computation complexity of the stochastic error-descent still scales like the best on-line exact gradient method currently available.

For the simulations, we compared several runs of the stochastic method with a single run of an exact gradient-descent method, all runs starting from the same initial conditions. For a meaningful comparison, the equivalent learning rate for

[3]The distinction between on-line and off-line methods here refers to issues of time reversal in the computation. On-line methods process incoming data strictly in the order it is received, while off-line methods require extensive access to previously processed data. On-line methods are therefore more desirable for real-time learning applications.

stochastic descent $\eta_{\text{eff}} = \mu\sigma^2$ was set to η, resulting in equal average speeds. We implemented binary random perturbations $\pi_i = \pm\sigma$ with $\sigma = 1 \times 10^{-3}$. We used the network topology, the teacher forcing mechanism, the values for the learning parameters and the values for the initial conditions from [4], case 4, except for η (and η_{eff}) which we reduced from 0.1 to 0.05 to avoid strong instabilities in the stochastic sessions. Each epoch represents one complete period of the figure eight. We found no local minima for the learning problem, and all sessions converged successfully within 4000 epochs as shown in Fig. 1 (a). The occasional upward transitions in the stochastic error are caused by temporary instabilities due to the elevated value of the learning rate. At lower values of the learning rate, we observed significantly less frequent and articulate upward transitions. The measured distribution for the decrements in error at $\eta_{\text{eff}} = 0.01$ is given in Fig. 1 (b). The values of the stochastic error decrements in the histogram are normalized to the mean of the distribution, *i.e.* the error decrements by gradient descent (8). As expected, the error decreases at practically all times with an average rate equal to that of gradient descent, but the largest fraction of the updates cause little change in error.

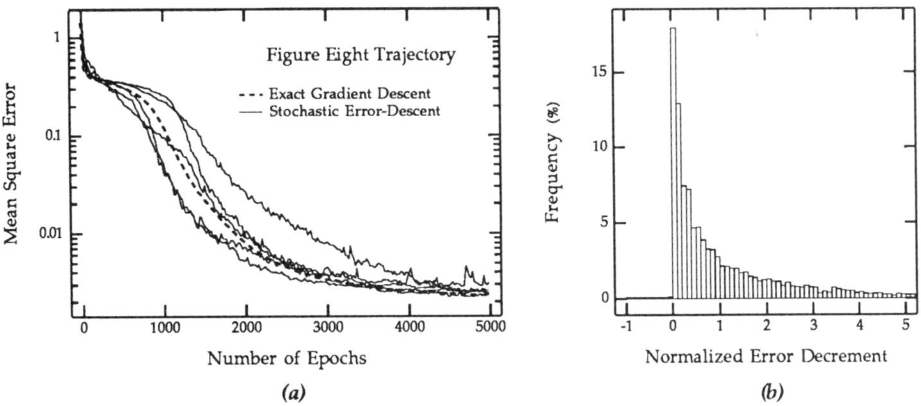

Figure 1 Exact Gradient and Stochastic Error-Descent Methods for the Figure "8" Trajectory. *(a)* Convergence Dynamics ($\eta = 0.05$). *(b)* Distribution of the Error Decrements.($\eta = 0.01$).

4 Conclusion

The above analysis and examples serve to demonstrate the solid performance of the error-descent algorithm, in spite of its simplicity and the minimal requirements on explicit knowledge of internal structure. While the functional simplicity and fault-tolerance of the algorithm is particularly suited for hardware implementations, on conventional digital computers its efficiency compares favorably with pure gradient descent methods for certain classes of networks and optimization problems, owing to the involved effort to obtain full gradient information. The latter is particularly true for complex optimization problems, such as for trajectory learning and adaptive control, with expensive scaling properties for the calculation of the gradient. In particular, the discrete formulation of the learning dynamics, decoupled from the dynamics of the network, enables the stochastic error-descent algorithm to handle dynamic networks and time-dependent optimization functionals gracefully.

Appendix: Formal Analysis

We analyze the algorithm for small perturbations π_i, by expanding (5) into a Taylor series around $\mathbf{p}$:

$$\hat{\mathcal{E}} = \sum_j \frac{\partial \mathcal{E}}{\partial p_j} \pi_j + \mathcal{O}(|\pi|^2) \ , \tag{6}$$

where the $\partial \mathcal{E}/\partial p_j$ represent the components of the true error gradient, reflecting the physical structure of the network. Substituting (6) in (4) yields:

$$\Delta p_i = -\mu \sum_j \frac{\partial \mathcal{E}}{\partial p_j} \pi_i \pi_j + \mathcal{O}(|\pi|^2)\pi_i \ . \tag{7}$$

For mutually uncorrelated perturbations π_i with uniform variance σ^2, $\mathrm{E}(\pi_i \pi_j) = \sigma^2 \delta_{ij}$, the parameter vector on average changes as

$$\mathrm{E}(\Delta \mathbf{p}) = -\mu \sigma^2 \frac{\partial \mathcal{E}}{\partial \mathbf{p}} + \mathcal{O}(\sigma^3) \ . \tag{8}$$

Hence, on average the algorithm performs pure gradient descent as in (3), with an effective learning rate $\eta = \mu\sigma^2$. The fluctuations of the parameter updates (7) with respect to their average (8) give rise to diffusion in the error-descent process. Nevertheless, regardless of these fluctuations the error will *always* decrease under the updates (4), provided that the increments Δp_i are sufficiently small (μ small):

$$\Delta \mathcal{E} = \sum_i \frac{\partial \mathcal{E}}{\partial p_i} \Delta p_i + \mathcal{O}(|\Delta \mathbf{p}|^2) \approx -\mu \sum_i \sum_j \frac{\partial \mathcal{E}}{\partial p_i} \pi_i \frac{\partial \mathcal{E}}{\partial p_j} \pi_j \approx -\mu \ \hat{\mathcal{E}}^2 \leq 0 \ . \tag{9}$$

Note that this is a direct consequence of the offset bias subtraction in (5), and (9) is no longer valid when the compensating reference term $\mathcal{E}(\mathbf{p})$ in (5) is omitted. The algorithm will converge towards local error minima just like gradient descent, as long as the perturbation vector π statistically explores all directions of the parameter space. In principle, statistical independence of the π_i is not required to ensure convergence, though in the case of cross-correlated perturbations the learning trajectory (7) does not on average follow the steepest path (8) towards the optima, resulting in slower learning.

The constant μ cannot be increased arbitrarily to boost the speed of learning. The value of μ is constrained by the allowable range for $|\Delta \mathbf{p}|$ in (9). The maximum level for $|\Delta \mathbf{p}|$ depends on the steepness and nonlinearity of the error functional $\mathcal{E}$, but is largely independent of which algorithm is being used. A value of $|\Delta \mathbf{p}|$ exceeding the limit will likely cause instability in the learning process, just as it would for an exact gradient descent method. The constraint on $|\Delta \mathbf{p}|$ allows us to formulate the maximum attainable speed of the stochastic algorithm, relative to that of other methods. From (4),

$$|\Delta \mathbf{p}|^2 = \mu^2 |\pi|^2 \hat{\mathcal{E}}^2 \approx P \mu^2 \sigma^2 \hat{\mathcal{E}}^2 \tag{10}$$

where P is the number of parameters. The approximate equality at the end of (10) holds for large P, and results from the central limit theorem for $|\pi|^2$ with $\mathrm{E}(\pi_i \pi_j) = \sigma^2 \delta_{ij}$. From (6), the expected value of (10) is

$$\mathrm{E}(|\Delta \mathbf{p}|^2) = P \ (\mu\sigma^2)^2 \left| \frac{\partial \mathcal{E}}{\partial \mathbf{p}} \right|^2 \ . \tag{11}$$

The maximum attainable value for μ can be expressed in terms of the maximum value of η for gradient descent learning. Indeed, from a worst-case analysis of (3)

$$|\Delta \mathbf{p}|^2_{\mathrm{max}} = \eta^2_{\mathrm{max}} \left| \frac{\partial \mathcal{E}}{\partial \mathbf{p}} \right|^2_{\mathrm{max}} \tag{12}$$

and from a similar worst-case analysis of (11), we obtain $P\mu_{max}\sigma^2 \sim \eta_{max}$ to a first order approximation. With the derived value for μ_{max}, the maximum effective learning rate η_{eff} associated with the mean field equation (8) becomes $\eta_{eff} = P^{-1/2}\ \eta_{max}$ for the stochastic method, as opposed to η_{max} for the exact gradient method. This implies that on average and under optimal conditions the learning process for the stochastic error descent method is a factor $P^{1/2}$ slower than optimal gradient descent. From similar arguments, it can be shown that for *sequential* perturbations π_i the effective learning rate for the mean field gradient descent satisfies $\eta_{eff} = P^{-1}\ \eta_{max}$. Hence under optimal conditions the sequential weight perturbation technique is a factor P slower than optimal gradient descent.

Acknowledgements

We thank J. Alspector, P. Baldi, B. Flower, D. Kirk, M. van Putten, A. Yariv, and many other individuals for valuable suggestions and comments on the work presented here.

References

[1] D.E. Rumelhart, G.E. Hinton, and R.J. Williams, "Learning Internal Representations by Error Propagation," in *Parallel Distributed Processing, Explorations in the Microstructure of Cognition,* vol. **1**, D.E. Rumelhart and J.L. McClelland, eds., Cambridge, MA: MIT Press, 1986.

[2] B.A. Pearlmutter, "Learning State Space Trajectories in Recurrent Neural Networks," *Neural Computation,* vol. **1** (2), pp 263-269, 1989.

[3] R.J. Williams and D. Zipser, "A Learning Algorithm for Continually Running Fully Recurrent Neural Networks," *Neural Computation,* vol. **1** (2), pp 270-280, 1989.

[4] N.B. Toomarian, and J. Barhen, "Learning a Trajectory using Adjoint Functions and Teacher Forcing," *Neural Networks,* vol. **5** (3), pp 473-484, 1992.

[5] J. Schmidhuber, "A Fixed Size Storage $\mathcal{O}(n^3)$ Time Complexity Learning Algorithm for Fully Recurrent Continually Running Networks," *Neural Computation,* vol. **4** (2), pp 243-248, 1992.

[6] B. Widrow and M.A. Lehr, "30 years of Adaptive Neural Networks. Perceptron, Madaline, and Backpropagation," *Proc. IEEE,* vol. **78** (9), pp 1415-1442, 1990.

[7] M. Jabri and B. Flower, "Weight Perturbation: An Optimal Architecture and Learning Technique for Analog VLSI Feedforward and Recurrent Multilayered Networks," *IEEE Trans. Neural Networks,* vol. **3** (1), pp 154-157, 1992.

[8] A. Dembo and T. Kailath, "Model-Free Distributed Learning," *IEEE Trans. Neural Networks,* vol. **1** (1), pp 58-70, 1990.

[9] H.P. Whitaker, "An Adaptive System for the Control of Aircraft and Spacecraft," in *Institute for Aeronautical Sciences,* pap. 59-100, 1959.

[10] B.P. Anderson and D.A. Kerns, "Using Noise Injection and Correlation in Analog Hardware to Estimate Gradients," *submitted,* 1992.

[11] D. Kirk, D. Kerns, K. Fleischer, and A. Barr, "Analog VLSI Implementation of Gradient Descent," in *Advances in Neural Information Processing Systems,* San Mateo, CA: Morgan Kaufman Publishers, vol. **5**, 1993.

[12] P. Baldi, "Learning in Dynamical Systems: Gradient Descent, Random Descent and Modular Approaches," JPL Technical Report, California Institute of Technology, 1992.

[13] J. Alspector, R. Meir, B. Yuhas, and A. Jayakumar, "A Parallel Gradient Descent Method for Learning in Analog VLSI Neural Networks," in *Advances in Neural Information Processing Systems,* San Mateo, CA: Morgan Kaufman Publishers, vol. **5**, 1993.

[14] B. Flower and M. Jabri, "Summed Weight Neuron Perturbation: An $\mathcal{O}(n)$ Improvement over Weight Perturbation," in *Advances in Neural Information Processing Systems,* San Mateo, CA: Morgan Kaufman Publishers, vol. **5**, 1993.

[15] J. Alspector, J.W. Gannett, S. Haber, M.B. Parker, and R. Chu, "A VLSI-Efficient Technique for Generating Multiple Uncorrelated Noise Sources and Its Application to Stochastic Neural Networks," *IEEE T. Circuits and Systems,* **38** (1), pp 109-123, 1991.

PART III

CONTROL, NAVIGATION, AND PLANNING

Global Regularization of Inverse Kinematics for Redundant Manipulators

David DeMers
Dept. of Computer Science & Engr.
Institute for Neural Computation
University of California, San Diego
La Jolla, CA 92093-0114

Kenneth Kreutz-Delgado
Dept. of Electrical & Computer Engr.
Institute for Neural Computation
University of California, San Diego
La Jolla, CA 92093-0407

Abstract

The inverse kinematics problem for redundant manipulators is ill–posed and nonlinear. There are two fundamentally different issues which result in the need for some form of regularization; the existence of multiple solution branches (global ill–posedness) and the existence of excess degrees of freedom (local ill–posedness). For certain classes of manipulators, learning methods applied to input–output data generated from the forward function can be used to globally regularize the problem by partitioning the domain of the forward mapping into a finite set of regions over which the inverse problem is well–posed. Local regularization can be accomplished by an appropriate parameterization of the redundancy consistently over each region. As a result, the ill–posed problem can be transformed into a finite set of well–posed problems. Each can then be solved separately to construct approximate direct inverse functions.

1 INTRODUCTION

The robot forward kinematics function maps a vector of joint variables to the end–effector configuration space, or *workspace*, here assumed to be Euclidean. We denote this mapping by $f(\cdot) : \Theta^n \to \mathcal{W}^m \subseteq \mathcal{X}^m$, $f(\theta) \mapsto \mathbf{x}$, for $\theta \in \Theta^n$ (the *input space* or *joint space*) and $\mathbf{x} \in \mathcal{W}^m$ (the *workspace*). When $m < n$, we say that the manipulator has redundant degrees–of–freedom (dof).

The inverse kinematics problem is the following: given a desired workspace location $\mathbf{x}$, find joint variables θ such that $f(\theta) = \mathbf{x}$. Even when the forward kinematics is known, the inverse kinematics for a manipulator is not generically solvable in closed form (Craig, 1986). This problem is ill-posed[1] due to two separate phenomena. First, multiple solution branches can exist (for both non–redundant as well as redundant manipulators). The second source of ill–posedness arises because of the redundant dofs. Each of the inverse solution branches consists of a submanifold of dimensionality equal to the number of redundant dofs. Thus the inverse solution requires two regularizations; *global* regularization to select a solution branch, and *local* regularization, to resolve the redundancy. In this paper the existence of at least one solution is assumed; that is, inverses will be sought only for points in the reachable workspace, i.e. desired $\mathbf{x}$ in the image of $f(\cdot)$.

Given input–output data generated from the kinematics mapping (pairs consisting of joint variable values & corresponding end–effector location), can the inverse mapping be learned without making any *a priori* regularizing assumptions or restrictions? We show that the answer can be "yes". The approach taken towards the solution is based on the use of learning methods to partition the data into groups such that the inverse kinematics problem, when restricted to each group, is well–posed, after which a direct inverse function can be approximated on each group.

A direct inverse function is desireable. For instance, a direct inverse is computable quickly; if implemented by a feedforward network were used, one function evaluation is equivalent to a single forward propagation. More importantly, theoretical results show that an algorithm for tracking a cyclic path in the workspace will produce a cyclic trajectory of joint angles if and only if it is equivalent to a direct inverse function (Baker, 1990). That is, inverse functions are necessary to ensure that when following a closed loop the arm configurations which result in the same end–effector location will be the same.

Unfortunately, topological results show that a single *global* inverse function does not exist for generic robot manipulators. However, a global topological analysis of the kinematics function and the nature of the manifolds induced in the input space and workspace show that for certain robot geometries the mapping may be expressed as the union of a finite set of well–behaved local regions (Burdick, 1991). In this case, the redundancy takes the form of a submanifold which can be parameterized (locally) consistently by, for example, the use of topology preserving neural networks.

2 TOPOLOGY AND ROBOT KINEMATICS

It is known that for certain robot geometries the input space can be partitioned into disjoint regions which have the property that no more than one inverse solution branch lies within any one of the regions (Burdick, 1988). We assume in the following that the manipulator in question has such a geometry, and has all revolute joints. Thus $\Theta^n = T^n$, the n–torus. The redundancy manifolds in this case have the topology of T^{n-m}, $n - m$–dimensional torii.

For Θ^n a compact manifold of dimensionality n, $\mathcal{W}^m$ a compact manifold of dimensionality m, and f a smooth map from Θ^n to $\mathcal{W}^m$, let the differential $d_\Theta f$ be the map from the tangent space of Θ^n at $\theta \in \Theta^n$ to the tangent space of $\mathcal{W}^m$ at $f(\theta)$. The set of points in Θ^n which

[1]Ill–posedness can arise from having either too many or too few constraints to result in a unique and valid solution. That is, an overconstrained system may be ill–posed and have no solutions; such systems are typically solved by finding a least–squares or some such minimum cost solution. An underconstrained system may have multiple (possibly infinite) solutions. The inverse kinematics problem for redundant manipulators is underconstrained.

map to $\mathbf{x} \in \mathcal{W}^m$ is the *pre–image* of $\mathbf{x}$, denoted by $f^{-1}(\mathbf{x})$. The differential $d_{\Theta}f$ has a natural representation given by an m by n *Jacobian* matrix whose elements consist of the first partial derivatives of f w.r.t. a basis of Θ^n. Define $\mathcal{S}$ as the set of *critical points* of f, which are the set of all $\theta \in \Theta^n$ such that $d_{\Theta}f(\theta)$ has rank less than the dimensionality of $\mathcal{W}^m$. Elements of the image of $\mathcal{S}$, $f(\mathcal{S})$ are called the *critical values*. The set $\mathcal{R} \triangleq \mathcal{W}^m \backslash \mathcal{S}$ are the *regular values* of f. For $\theta \in \Theta^n$, if $\exists \theta^* \in f^{-1}(f(\theta))$, $\theta^* \in \mathcal{S}$, we call θ a *co–regular point* of f.

The kinematic mapping of certain classes of manipulators (with the geometry herein assumed) can be decomposed based on the co–regular surfaces which divide Θ^n into a finite number of disjoint, connected regions, $\mathcal{C}_i$. The image of each $\mathcal{C}_i$ under f is a connected region in the workspace, $\mathcal{W}_i$. We denote the kinematics mapping restricted to $\mathcal{C}_i$ to be f_i; $f_i : \mathcal{C}_i \rightarrow \mathcal{W}_i$.

Locally, one inverse solution branch for a region in the workspace has the structure of a product space. We conjecture that $(\mathcal{W}_i, \mathcal{T}^{n-m}, \mathcal{C}_i, f|_{\mathcal{C}_i})$ forms a locally trivial fiber bundle[2] and that the $\mathcal{C}_i$, therefore, form regions where the inverse is unique modulo the redundancy.

Given a point in the workspace, $\mathbf{x}$, for which a configuration is sought, global regularization requires choosing from among the multiple pre–image torii. Local regularization (redundancy resolution) requires finding a location on the chosen torus. We would like to effectively "mod out" the redundancy manifolds by constructing an indexed one–to–one, invertible mapping from each pre–image manifold to a point in $\mathcal{X}^m$, and to obtain a consistent representation of the manifold by constructing an invertible mapping from itself to a set of $n - m$ "location" parameters.

3 GLOBAL REGULARIZATION

The existence of multiple solutions for even non–redundant manipulators poses difficult problems. Usually (and often for plausible reasons) the manipulator's allowable configurations or task space is effectively constrained so that there exists only a single inverse solution (Martinetz et al., 1990; Kuperstein, 1991). This approach regularizes the problem by allowing the existence of only one–to–one data. We seek to generalize to the multi–solution case and to learn all of the possible solutions.

For an all revolute manipulator there typically will be multiple pre–image torii for a particular point in the workspace. The topology of the pre–image solution branches will generally be known from the type of geometry, although their number may not be obvious by inspection, and will usually be different for different regions of the workspace. An upper bound on the number of inverse solutions is known (Burdick, 1988); consequently, the determination of the number could be made by search for the best fit among the possibilities.

The sampling and clustering approach described in (DeMers & Kreutz–Delgado, 1992) can be used to partition input–output data into disjoint pre–image sets. This approach uses samples of the forward behavior to identify the sets in the input space which map to

[2]A fiber bundle is a four-tuple consisting of a **base space**, a **fiber** (here, $\mathcal{T}^{m-n}$), a **total space** and a projection p mapping the total space to the base space with certain properties (here, the projection is equivalent to f_i restricted to the total space). A locally trivial fiber bundle is one for which a consistent parameterization of the fibers is possible.

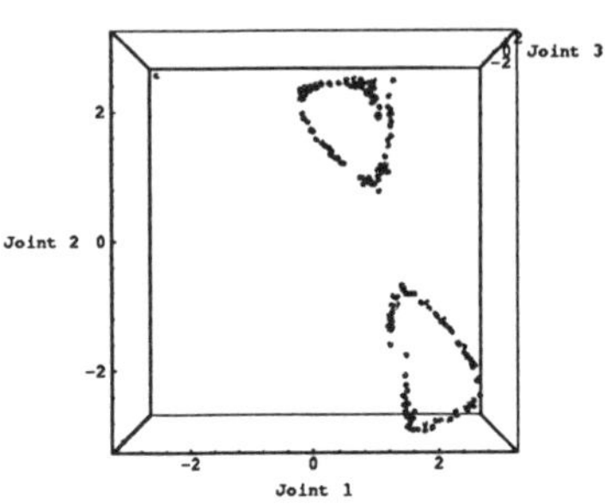

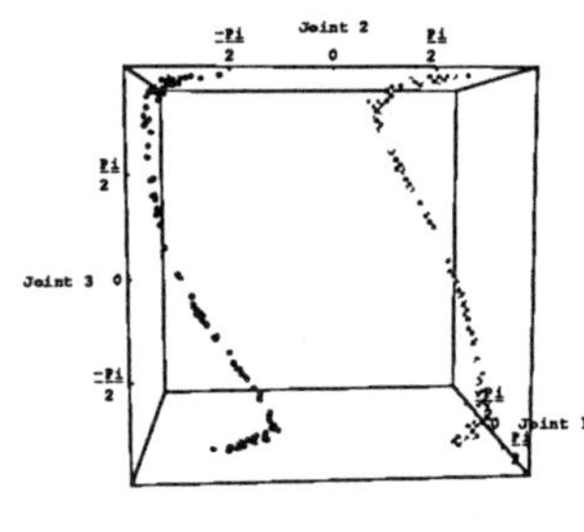

Figure 1: *The two pre–image manifolds for positioning the end–effector of the 3–R planar manipulator at a specific (x, y) location.*

within a small distance of a specific location in the workspace. The pre–image points will lie on the disjoint pre–image manifolds. These manifolds will typically be separable by clustering[3]. Figures 1 shows two views of the two redundancy, or "self–motion" manifolds for a particular end–effector location of the 3–R planar arm. All of the input space points shown position the arm's end–effector near the same (x,y) location. Note that the input space is the 3–torus, T^3. In order to visualize the space, the torus is "sliced" along each dimension. Thus opposite faces of the "cube" shown are identified with each other.

4 LOCAL REGULARIZATION

The inverse kinematics problem for manipulators with redundant dofs is usually solved either by using differential methods, which attempt to exploit the redundancy by optimizing a task–dependent objective function, or by using learning methods which regularize at training time by adding constraints equal to the number of redundant dof. The former may be computationally inefficient in that iterative solution of derivatives or matrix inversions are required, and may be unsatisfactory for real–time control. The latter is unsatisfying as it eliminates the run–time dexterity available from the redundancy; that is, it imposes prior constraints on the use of any extra dofs.

Although in practice numerical, differential methods are used for redundancy resolution, it has recently been shown that simple recurrent neural networks can resolve the redundancy by optimization of certain side–constraints at run–time, (Jordan & Rumelhart, 1992), (Kindermann & Linden, 1990). The differential methods have a number of desireable properties. In general it is possible to iterate in order to achieve a solution of arbitrary accuracy. They also tend to be capable of handling very flexible constraints. Global regularization as discussed above can be used to augment such methods. For example, once a choice of a solution branch has been made, an initial starting location away from singularities can be selected, and differential methods used to achieve an accurate solution on that branch.

Our work shows that construction of redundancy–parameterized approximations to di-

[3]For end–effector locations near the co–regular values, the pre–image manifolds tend to merge. This phenomenon can be identified by our methods.

rect inverses are achievable. That is, the mapping from the workspace (augmented by a parameterization of the redundancy) to the input space can be approximated. This local regularization is accomplished by parameterizing the pre–image solution branch torii. Given (enough) samples of θ points paired with their $\mathbf{x}$ image, a parameterization can be discovered for each branch. The method used exploits the fact that neighborhoods within each $\mathcal{C}_i$ map to neighborhoods, and that neighborhoods within each $\mathcal{W}_i$ have as pre-images a finite number of solution branches.

First, all points in our sample which have their image near some initial point $\mathbf{x}_0$ are found. Pulling back to the input space by accessing the θ component of each of these $(\theta, \mathbf{x})$ data pairs finds the points in the pre–image set of the neighborhood of $\mathbf{x}_0$. Now, because the topology of the pre–image set is known (here, the torus), a self–organizing map of appropriate topology can be fit to the pre–image points in order to parameterize this manifold. Neighboring torii have similar parameterizations; thus by repeating this process for a point $\mathbf{x}_1$ near $\mathbf{x}_0$ and using the parameterization of the pre–image of $\mathbf{x}_0$ as initial conditions, a parameterization of the pre–image of $\mathbf{x}_1$ qualitatively similar to that for $\mathbf{x}_0$ can be constructed efficiently. By stepping between such "query points", $\mathbf{x}_i$ a set of parameterizations can be obtained.

5 THE 3–R REDUNDANT PLANAR ARM

This approach can be used to provide a global and local regularization for a three–link manipulator performing the task of positioning in the plane. For this manipulator, $f : T^3 \to \mathbb{R}^2$. The map f restricted to each connected region in the input space bounded by the co–regular separating surfaces defines $f_i : T \times \mathbb{R} \times S^1 \to \mathbb{R} \times S^1$.

The pre–image of a point in the workspace thus consists of either one or two 1–torii (the actual number can be no more than the number of inverse solutions for a non–redundant manipulator of the same type, (Burdick, 1988)). Each torus is the pre–image of one of the restricted mappings f_i. The goal is to identify these torii and parameterize them. Figure 2 shows the input space and workspace of this arm, and their separating surfaces. These partition the workspace into disjoint annular regions, and the input space into disjoint tubular regions. The circles indicate workspace locations which can be reached in a kinematically singular configuration. The inverse image of these circles form the co–regular separating surfaces in the input space. For the link lengths used here ($l_1 = 5$, $l_2 = 4$, $l_3 = 3$), there is a single self–motion manifold for workspace locations in regions A and C, and two self–motion manifolds for workspace locations in B and D. Figure 3 shows two views of the data points near the pre–image manifolds for an end effector location in region A, and its parameterization by a self–organizing map (using the elastic net algorithm). Such a parameterization can be made for various locations in the workspace. Inverse kinematics can thus be computed by first locating the nearest parameterization network for a given workspace position and then choosing a configuration on the manifold, which can be done at run–time. Because the kinematics map is locally smooth, interpolation between networks and nodes on the networks can be done for greater accuracy. For convenience, a node on each torus was chosen as a canonical zero-point, and the remaining nodes assigned values based on their normalized distance from this point. Therefore all parameter values are scaled to be in the interval [0,1].

For some end–effector locations, there are two pre–image manifolds. These first need to be identified by a global partitioning, then the individual manifolds parameterized. The

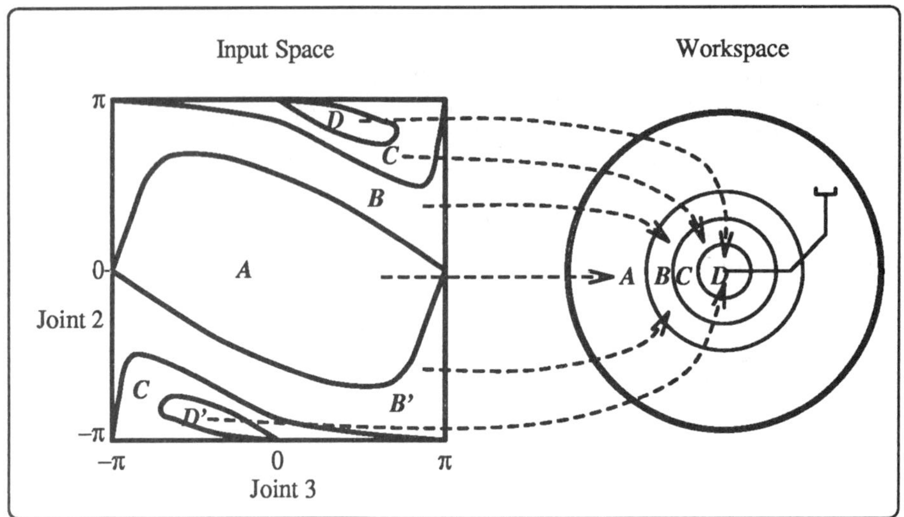

Figure 2: *The forward kinematics for a generic three–link planar manipulator. The separating surfaces in the input space do not depend on the value of joint angle 1, therefore the input space is shown projected to the joint 2 - joint 3 space. All end–effector locations inside regions A and C of the workspace have a single pre–image manifold in A and C, respectively, of the input space. End–effector locations inside regions B and D of the workspace have two pre–image manifolds, one in each of B and B' (resp. D and D') of the input space.*

manifolds may belong to one of a finite set of homotopy classes; that is, because they "live" in an ambient space which is a torus, they may or may not wrap around one or more of the dimensions of the torus. Unlike in Euclidean space, where there are only two possible one–dimensional manifolds, there are multiple topologically distinct types (homotopy classes) of closed loops which can serve as self–motion manifolds. Fortunately, because physical robots rarely have joints with unlimited range of motion, in practice the manifolds will usually not have wraparound. However, we should like to be able to parameterize any possibility. Appropriate choice of topology for a topology–preserving net results in an effective parameterization. Figure 4 shows two views of a parameterization for one of the self–motion manifolds shown above in Figure 1, which is the pre–image for an end–effector location in region B of Figure 2.

6 DISCUSSION

The global regularization accomplished by the method described above partitions the original input/output data into sets for each of the distinct C_i regions. The redundancy parameters, t, obtained by local regularization can be used to augment this data, resulting in a transformation of the $(\theta, \mathbf{x})$ data into $(\theta_i, (\mathbf{x}_i, t))$. Let $\mathcal{T} : \theta \mapsto t$ be a function that computes a parameter value for each θ in the input space. Let $\hat{f}_i(\theta) = (f_i(\theta), \mathcal{T}(\theta))$. By construction, the regularized mapping $\hat{f}_i : \theta \mapsto (\mathbf{x}, t)$ is one–to–one and onto. Now, given examples from a one–to–one mapping, the inverse map $\hat{f}_i^{-1}(\mathbf{x}, t) \mapsto \theta$ can be directly approximated by, e.g., a feedforward neural network.

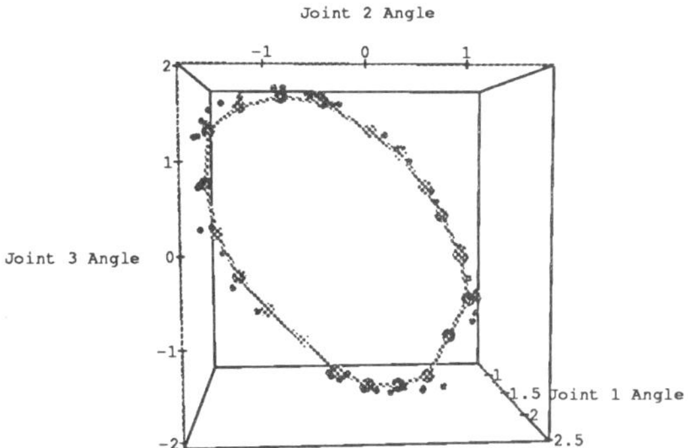

Figure 3: *The data points in the "self–motion" pre–image manifold of a point in the workspace of the 3–R planar arm, and a closed, 1–D elastic network after adaptation to them. This manifold is smoothly contractible to a point since it does not "wrap around" any of the dimensions of* T^3.

This method requires data sample sizes exponential in the number of degrees of freedom of the manipulator and thus will not be adequate for large dof "snake" manipulators. However, practical industrial robots of 7–dof may be amenable to our technique, especially if, as is common, it is designed with a separable wrist and is thus composable into a 4–dof redundant positioner plus a 3–dof non–redundant orienter.

This work can also be used to augment the differential methods of redundancy resolution. An approximate solution can be found extremely rapidly, and used to initialize gradient-based methods, which can then iterate to achieve a highly accurate solution. Global decisions such as choosing between multiple manifolds and identifying criteria for choosing locations on the manifold can now be made at run–time. Computation of an approximate direct inverse can then be made in constant time.

Acknowledgements

This work was supported in part by NSF Presidential Young Investigator award IRI–9057631 and Fellowships from the California Space Institute and the McDonnell-Pew Center for Cognitive Neuroscience. The first author would like to thank the NIPS Foundation for providing student travel grants.

References

Daniel Baker (1990), "Some Topological Problems in Robotics", *The Mathematical Intelligencer*, Vol. 12, No. 1, pp. 66–76.

Joel Burdick (1988), "Kinematics and Design of Redundant Robot Manipulators", Stanford Ph.D. Thesis, Dept. of Mechanical Engineering.

Joel Burdick (1991), "A Classification of 3R Regional Manipulator Singularities and Geometries", *Proc. 1991 IEEE Intl. Conf. Robotics & Automation*, Sacramento.

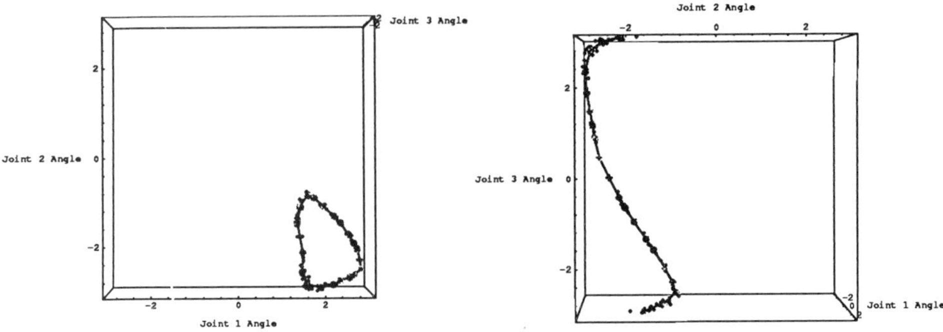

Figure 4: *Two views of the same data points in one of the two "self–motion" pre–image manifolds of a point in region B, and an elastic net after adaptation. It belongs to a different homotopy class than that of Fig 3 – it is not contractible to a point.*

John Craig (1986), *Introduction to Robotics.*

David DeMers & Kenneth Kreutz-Delgado (1992), "Learning Global Direct Inverse Kinematics", in Moody, J. E., Hanson, S.J. and Lippmann, R.P., eds, *Advances in Neural Information Processing Systems 4*, 589–594.

Michael I. Jordan & David Rumelhart (1992), "Forward Models: Supervised Learning with a Distal Teacher", *Cognitive Science 16*, 307–354.

J. Kindermann & Alexander Linden (1990), "Inversion of Neural Networks by Gradient Descent", *J. Parallel Computing 14*, 277–286.

Michael Kuperstein (1991), "INFANT Neural Controller for Adaptive Sensory–Motor Control", *Neural Networks*, Vol. 4, pp. 131–145.

Thomas Martinetz, Helge Ritter, & Klaus Schulten (1990), "Three–Dimensional Neural Networks for Learning Visuomotor Coordination of a Robot Arm", *IEEE Trans. Neural Networks*, Vol. 1, No. 1.

Charles Nash & Siddhartha Sen (1983), *Topology and Geometry for Physicists.*

Philippe Wenger (1992), "On the Kinematics of Manipulators with General Geometry: Application to the Feasibility Analysis of Continuous Trajectories", in M. Jamshidi, et al., eds, *Robotics and Manufacturing: Recent Trends in Research, Education and Applications 4*, 15–20 (ISRAM–92, Santa Fe).

Memory-based Reinforcement Learning: Efficient Computation with Prioritized Sweeping

Andrew W. Moore
awm@ai.mit.edu
NE43-759 MIT AI Lab.
545 Technology Square
Cambridge MA 02139

Christopher G. Atkeson
cga@ai.mit.edu
NE43-771 MIT AI Lab.
545 Technology Square
Cambridge MA 02139

Abstract

We present a new algorithm, Prioritized Sweeping, for efficient prediction and control of stochastic Markov systems. Incremental learning methods such as Temporal Differencing and Q-learning have fast real time performance. Classical methods are slower, but more accurate, because they make full use of the observations. Prioritized Sweeping aims for the best of both worlds. It uses all previous experiences both to prioritize important dynamic programming sweeps and to guide the exploration of state-space. We compare Prioritized Sweeping with other reinforcement learning schemes for a number of different stochastic optimal control problems. It successfully solves large state-space real time problems with which other methods have difficulty.

1 STOCHASTIC PREDICTION

The paper introduces a memory-based technique, *prioritized sweeping*, which is used both for stochastic prediction and reinforcement learning. A fuller version of this paper is in preparation [Moore and Atkeson, 1992]. Consider the 500 state Markov system depicted in Figure 1. The system has sixteen absorbing states, depicted by white and black circles. The prediction problem is to estimate, for every state, the long-term probability that it will terminate in a white, rather than black, circle. The data available to the learner is a sequence of observed state transitions. Let us consider two existing methods along with prioritized sweeping.

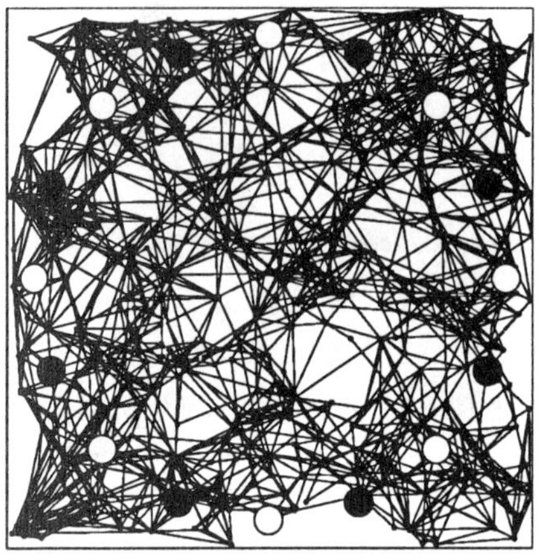

Figure 1: A 500-state Markov system. Each state has a random number (mean 5) of random successors chosen within the local neighborhood.

Temporal Differencing (TD) is an elegant incremental algorithm [Sutton, 1988] which has recently had success with a very large problem [Tesauro, 1991].

The **classical method** proceeds by building a maximum likelihood model of the state transitions. q_{ij} (the transition probability from i to j) is estimated by

$$\hat{q}_{ij} = \frac{\text{Number of observations } i \rightarrow j}{\text{Number of occasions in state } i} \tag{1}$$

After $t+1$ observations the new absorption probability estimates are computed to satisfy, for each terminal state k, the linear system

$$\hat{\pi}_{ik}[t+1] = \hat{q}_{ik} + \sum_{j \in \mathbf{succs}(i) \cap \mathsf{NONTERMS}} \hat{q}_{ij} \hat{\pi}_{jk}[t+1] \tag{2}$$

where the $\hat{\pi}_{ik}[t]$'s are the absorption probabilities we are trying to learn, where $\mathbf{succs}(i)$ is the set of all states which have been observed as immediate successors of i and NONTERMS is the set of non-terminal states.

This set of equations is solved after each transition is observed. It is solved using Gauss-Seidel—an iterative method. What initial estimates should be used to start the iteration? An excellent answer is to use the previous absorption probability estimates $\hat{\pi}_{ik}[t]$.

Prioritized sweeping is designed to combine the advantages of the classical method with the advantages of TD. It is described in the next section, but let us first examine performance on the original 500-state example of Figure 1. Figure 2 shows the result. TD certainly learns: by 100,000 observations it is estimating the terminal-white probability to an RMS accuracy of 0.1. However, the performance of the classical method appears considerably better than TD: the same error of 0.1 is obtained after only 3000 observations.

Figure 3 indicates why temporal differencing may nevertheless often be more useful. TD requires far less computation per observation, and so can obtain more data in real time. Thus, after 300 seconds, TD has had 250,000 observations and is down

Mean ± Standard Dev'n	TD	Classical	Pri. Sweep
After 100,000 observations	0.40 ± 0.077	0.024 ± 0.0063	0.024 ± 0.0061
After 300 seconds	0.079 ± 0.067	0.23 ± 0.038	0.021 ± 0.0080

Table 1: RMS prediction error: mean and standard deviation for ten experiments.

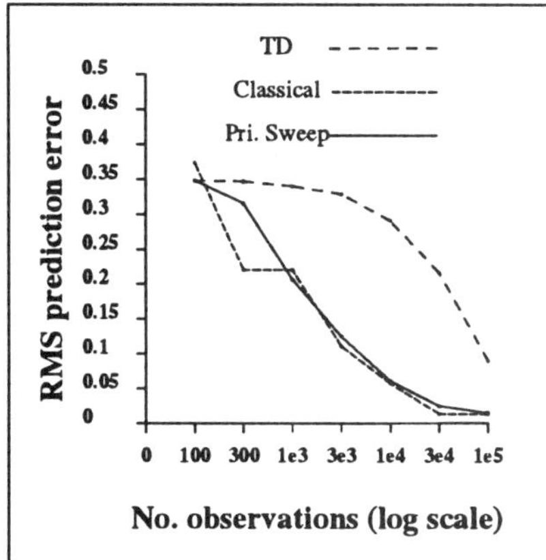

Figure 2: RMS prediction against observation during three learning algorithms.

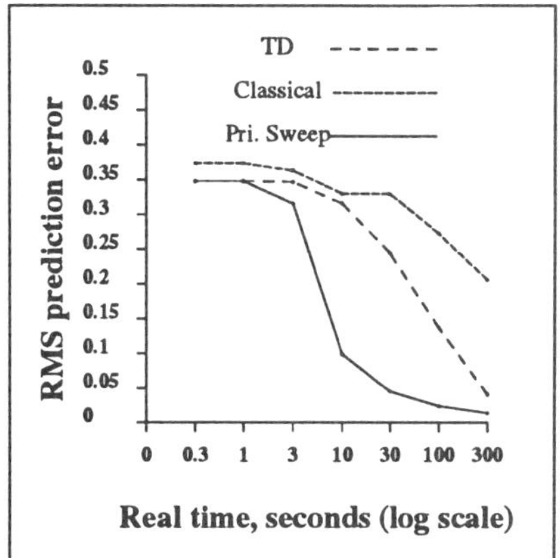

Figure 3: RMS prediction against real time

to an error of 0.05, whereas even after 300 seconds the classical method has only 1000 observations and a much cruder estimate.

In the same figures we see the motivation behind prioritized sweeping. Its performance relative to observations is almost as good as the classical method, while its performance relative to real time is even better than TD.

The graphs in Figures 2 and 3 were based on only one learning experiment each. Ten further experiments, each with a different random 500 state problem, were run. The results are given in Table 1.

2 PRIORITIZED SWEEPING

A longer paper [Moore and Atkeson, 1992] will describe the algorithm in detail. Here we summarize the essential insights, and then simply present the algorithm in Figure 4. The closest relation to prioritized sweeping is the search scheduling technique of the A^* algorithm [Nilsson, 1971]. Closely related research is being performed by [Peng and Williams, 1992] into a similar algorithm to prioritized sweeping, which they call Dyna-Q-queue.

- The memory requirements of learning a $N_s \times N_s$ matrix, where N_s is the number of states, may initially appear prohibitive, especially since we intend to operate with more than 10,000 states. However, we need only allocate memory for the

1. Promote state i_{recent} (the source of the most recent transition) to top of priority queue.
2. While we are allowed further processing and priority queue not empty
   2.1 Remove the top state from the priority queue. Call it i
   2.2 $\Delta_{\max} = 0$
   2.3 for each $k \in$ TERMS

$$\rho_{\text{new}} = \hat{q}_{ik} + \sum_{j \in \text{succs}(i) \cap \text{NONTERMS}} \hat{q}_{ij} \hat{\pi}_{jk}$$

$$\Delta := | \rho_{\text{new}} - \hat{\pi}_{ik} |$$

$$\hat{\pi}_{ik} := \rho_{\text{new}}$$

$$\Delta_{\max} := \max(\Delta_{\max}, \Delta)$$

   2.4 for each $i' \in$ **preds**(i)

$$P := \hat{q}_{i'i} \Delta_{\max}$$

   if i' not on queue, or P exceeds the current priority of i', then promote i' to new priority P.

Figure 4: The prioritized sweeping algorithm. This sequence of operations is executed each time a transition is observed.

experiences the system actually has, and for a wide class of physical systems there is not enough time in the lifetime of the physical system to run out of memory.

- We keep a record of all predecessors of each state. When the eventual absorption probabilities of a state are updated, its predecessors are alerted that they may need to change. A priority value is assigned to each predecessor according to how large this change could be possibly be, and it is placed in a priority queue.

- After each real-world observation $i \rightarrow j$, the transition probability estimate $\hat{q}_{ij}$ is updated along with the probabilities of transition to all other previously observed successors of i. Then state i is promoted to the top of the priority queue so that its absorption probabilities are updated immediately. Next, we continue to process further states from the top of the queue. Each state that is processed may result in the addition or promotion of its predecessors within the queue. This loop continues for a preset number of processing steps or until the queue empties.

If a real world observation is interesting, all its predecessors and their earlier ancestors quickly find themselves near the top of the priority queue. On the other hand, if the real world observation is unsurprising, then the processing immediately proceeds to other, more important areas of state-space which had been under consideration on the previous time step. These other areas may be different from those in which the system currently finds itself.

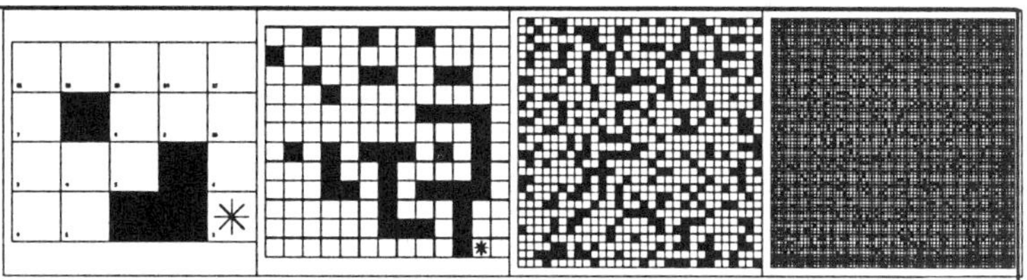

	15 States	117 States	605 States	4528 States
Q	800	> 25000	> 500000	> 500000
Dyna-PI+	400	500	36000	> 500000
Dyna-OPT	300	900	21000	245000
PriSweep	150	1200	6000	59000

Table 2: Number of observations before 98% of decisions were subsequently optimal. Dyna and Prioritized Sweeping were each allowed to process ten states per real-world observation.

3 LEARNING CONTROL FROM REINFORCEMENT

Prioritized sweeping is also directly applicable to stochastic control problems. Remembering all previous transitions allows an additional advantage for control—exploration can be guided towards areas of state space in which we predict we are ignorant. This is achieved using the exploration philosophy of [Kaelbling, 1990] and [Sutton, 1990]: optimism in the face of uncertainty.

4 RESULTS

Results of some maze problems of significant size are shown in Table 2. Each state has four actions: one for each direction. Blocked actions do not move. One goal state (the star in subsequent figures) gives 100 units of reward, all others give no reward, and there is a discount factor of 0.99. Trials start in the bottom left corner. The system is reset to the start state whenever the goal state has been visited ten times since the last reset. The reset is outside the learning task: it is not observed as a state transition. Prioritized sweeping is tested against a highly tuned Q-learner [Watkins, 1989] and a highly tuned Dyna [Sutton, 1990]. The optimistic experimentation method (described in the full paper) can be applied to other algorithms, and so the results of optimistic Dyna-learning is also included.

The same mazes were also run as a stochastic problem in which requested actions were randomly corrupted 50% of the time. The gap between Dyna-OPT and Prioritized Sweeping was reduced in these cases. For example, on a stochastic 4528-state maze Dyna-OPT took 310,000 steps and Prioritized sweeping took 200,000.

We also have results for a five state bench-mark problem described in [Sato *et al.*, 1988, Barto and Singh, 1990]. Convergence time is reduced by a factor of twenty over the incremental methods.

	Experiences to converge	Real time to converge
Q	never	
Dyna-PI+	never	
Optimistic Dyna	55,000	1500 secs
Prioritized Sweeping	14,000	330 secs

Table 3: Performance on the deterministic rod-in-maze task. Both Dynas and prioritized sweeping were allowed 100 backups per experience.

Finally we consider a task with a 3-d state space quantized into 15,000 potential discrete states (not all reachable). The task is shown in Figure 5 and involves finding the shortest path for a rod which can be rotated and translated.

Q, Dyna-PI+, Optimistic Dyna and prioritized sweeping were all tested. The results are in Table 3. Q and Dyna-PI+ did not even travel a quarter of the way to the goal, let alone discover an optimal path, within 200,000 experiences. Optimistic Dyna and prioritized sweeping both eventually converged, with the latter requiring a third the experiences and a fifth the real time.

When 2000 backups per experience were permitted, instead of 100, then both optimistic Dyna and prioritized sweeping required fewer experiences to converge. Optimistic Dyna took 21,000 experiences instead of 55,000 but took 2,900 seconds—almost twice the real time. Prioritized sweeping took 13,500 instead of 14,000 experiences—very little improvement, but it used no extra time. This indicates that for prioritized sweeping, 100 backups per observation is sufficient to make almost complete use of its observations, so that all the long term reward (J_i) estimates are very close to the estimates which would be globally consistent with the transition probability estimates ($\hat{q}^a_{ij}$). Thus, we conjecture that even full dynamic programming after each experience (which would take days of real time) would do little better.

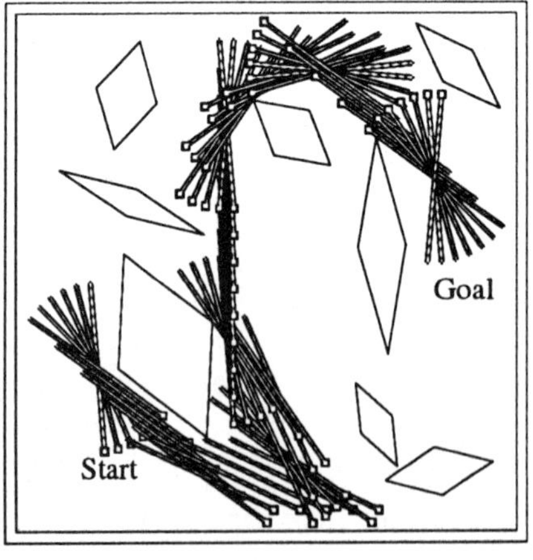

Figure 5: A three-DOF problem, and the optimal solution path.

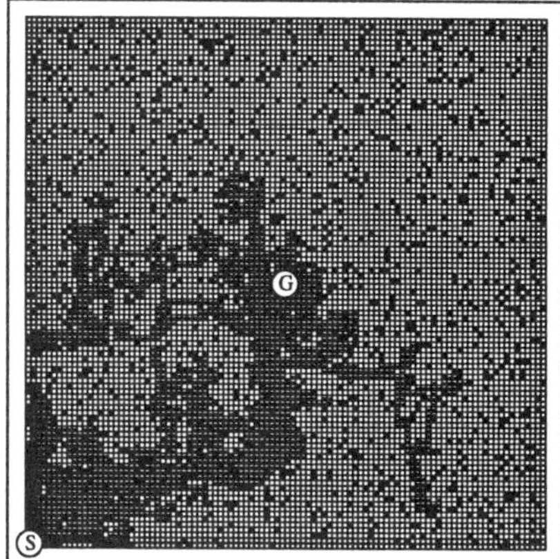

Figure 6: Dotted states are all those visited when the Manhattan heuristic was used

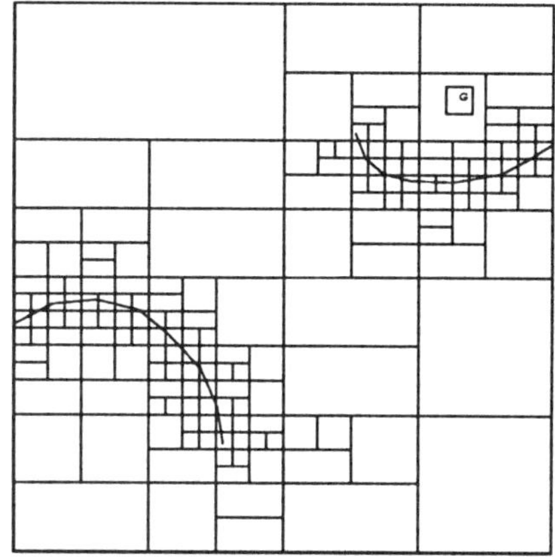

Figure 7: A *kd*-tree tessellation of state space of a sparse maze

5 DISCUSSION

Our investigation shows that Prioritized Sweeping can solve large state-space real-time problems with which other methods have difficulty. An important extension allows heuristics to constrain exploration decisions. For example, in finding an optimal path through a maze, many states need not be considered at all. Figure 6 shows the areas explored using a Manhattan heuristic when finding the optimal path from the lower left to the center. For some tasks we may be even satisfied to cease exploration when we have obtained a solution known to be, say, within 50% of the optimal solution. This can be achieved by using a heuristic which lies: it tells us that the best possible reward-to-go is that of a path which is twice the length of the true shortest possible path.

Furthermore, another promising avenue is prioritized sweeping in conjunction with *kd*-tree tessellations of state space to concentrate prioritizing sweeping on the important regions [Moore, 1991]. Other benefits of the memory-based approach, described in [Moore, 1992], allow us to control forgetting in changing environments and automatic scaling of state variables.

Acknowledgements

Thanks to Mary Soon Lee, Satinder Singh and Rich Sutton for useful comments on an early draft. Andrew W. Moore is supported by a Postdoctoral Fellowship from SERC/NATO. Support was also provided under Air Force Office of Scientific Research grant AFOSR-89-0500, an Alfred P. Sloan Fellowship, the W. M. Keck Foundation Associate Professorship in Biomedical Engineering, Siemens Corporation, and a National Science Foundation Presidential Young Investigator Award to Christopher G. Atkeson.

References

[Barto and Singh, 1990] A. G. Barto and S. P. Singh. On the Computational Economics of Reinforcement Learning. In D. S. Touretzky, editor, *Connectionist Models: Proceedings of the 1990 Summer School.* Morgan Kaufmann, 1990.

[Kaelbling, 1990] L. P. Kaelbling. Learning in Embedded Systems. PhD. Thesis; Technical Report No. TR-90-04, Stanford University, Department of Computer Science, June 1990.

[Moore and Atkeson, 1992] A. W. Moore and C. G. Atkeson. Memory-based Reinforcement Learning: Converging with Less Data and Less Real Time. In preparation, 1992.

[Moore, 1991] A. W. Moore. Variable Resolution Dynamic Programming: Efficiently Learning Action Maps in Multivariate Real-valued State-spaces. In L. Birnbaum and G. Collins, editors, *Machine Learning: Proceedings of the Eighth International Workshop.* Morgan Kaufman, June 1991.

[Moore, 1992] A. W. Moore. Fast, Robust Adaptive Control by Learning only Forward Models. In J. E. Moody, S. J. Hanson, and R. P. Lippman, editors, *Advances in Neural Information Processing Systems 4.* Morgan Kaufmann, April 1992.

[Nilsson, 1971] N. J. Nilsson. *Problem-solving Methods in Artificial Intelligence.* McGraw Hill, 1971.

[Peng and Williams, 1992] J. Peng and R. J. Williams. Efficient Search Control in Dyna. College of Computer Science, Northeastern University, March 1992.

[Sato *et al.*, 1988] M. Sato, K. Abe, and H. Takeda. Learning Control of Finite Markov Chains with an Explicit Trade-off Between Estimation and Control. *IEEE Trans. on Systems, Man, and Cybernetics*, 18(5):667–684, 1988.

[Sutton, 1988] R. S. Sutton. Learning to Predict by the Methods of Temporal Differences. *Machine Learning*, 3:9–44, 1988.

[Sutton, 1990] R. S. Sutton. Integrated Architecture for Learning, Planning, and Reacting Based on Approximating Dynamic Programming. In *Proceedings of the 7th International Conference on Machine Learning.* Morgan Kaufman, June 1990.

[Tesauro, 1991] G. J. Tesauro. Practical Issues in Temporal Difference Learning. RC 17223 (76307), IBM T. J. Watson Research Center, NY, 1991.

[Watkins, 1989] C. J. C. H. Watkins. Learning from Delayed Rewards. PhD. Thesis, King's College, University of Cambridge, May 1989.

Feudal Reinforcement Learning

Peter Dayan
CNL
The Salk Institute
PO Box 85800
San Diego CA 92186-5800, USA
dayan@helmholtz.sdsc.edu

Geoffrey E Hinton
Department of Computer Science
University of Toronto
6 Kings College Road, Toronto,
Canada M5S 1A4
hinton@ai.toronto.edu

Abstract

One way to speed up reinforcement learning is to enable learning to happen simultaneously at multiple resolutions in space and time. This paper shows how to create a Q-learning managerial hierarchy in which high level managers learn how to set tasks to their sub-managers who, in turn, learn how to satisfy them. Sub-managers need not initially understand their managers' commands. They simply learn to maximise their reinforcement in the context of the current command.

We illustrate the system using a simple maze task.. As the system learns how to get around, satisfying commands at the multiple levels, it explores more efficiently than standard, flat, Q-learning and builds a more comprehensive map.

1 INTRODUCTION

Straightforward reinforcement learning has been quite successful at some relatively complex tasks like playing backgammon (Tesauro, 1992). However, the learning time does not scale well with the number of parameters. For agents solving rewarded Markovian decision tasks by learning dynamic programming value functions, some of the main bottlenecks (Singh, 1992b) are *temporal resolution* – expanding the unit of learning from the smallest possible step in the task, *division-and-conquest* – finding smaller subtasks that are easier to solve, *exploration*, and *structural generalisation* – generalisation of the value function between different locations. These are obviously related – for instance, altering the temporal resolution can have a dramatic effect on exploration.

Consider a control hierarchy in which managers have sub-managers, who work for them, and super-managers, for whom they work. If the hierarchy is *strict* in the sense that managers control exactly the sub-managers at the level below them and only the very lowest level managers can actually act in the world, then intermediate level managers have essentially two instruments of control over their sub-managers at any time – they can choose amongst them and they can set them sub-tasks. These sub-tasks can be incorporated into the *state* of the sub-managers so that they in turn can choose their own sub-sub-tasks and sub-sub-managers to execute them based on the task selection at the higher level.

An appropriate hierarchy can address the first three bottlenecks. Higher level managers should sustain a larger grain of temporal resolution, since they leave the sub-sub-managers to do the actual work. Exploration for actions leading to rewards can be more efficient since it can be done non-uniformly – high level managers can decide that reward is best found in some other region of the state space and send the agent there directly, without forcing it to explore in detail on the way.

Singh (1992a) has studied the case in which a manager picks one of its sub-managers rather than setting tasks. He used the degree of accuracy of the Q-values of sub-managerial Q-learners (Watkins, 1989) to train a gating system (Jacobs, Jordan, Nowlan & Hinton, 1991) to choose the one that matches best in each state. Here we study the converse case, in which there is only one possible sub-manager active at any level, and so the only choice a manager has is over the tasks it sets. Such systems have been previously considered (Hinton, 1987; Watkins, 1989).

The next section considers how such a strict hierarchical scheme can learn to choose appropriate tasks at each level, section 3 describes a maze learning example for which the hierarchy emerges naturally as a multi-grid division of the space in which the agent moves, and section 4 draws some conclusions.

2 FEUDAL CONTROL

We sought to build a system that mirrored the hierarchical aspects of a feudal fiefdom, since this is one extreme for models of control. Managers are given absolute power over their sub-managers – they can set them tasks and reward and punish them entirely as they see fit. However managers ultimately have to satisfy their own super-managers, or face punishment themselves – and so there is recursive reinforcement and selection until the whole system satisfies the goal of the highest level manager. This can all be made to happen without the sub-managers initially "understanding" the sub-tasks they are set. Every component just acts to maximise its expected reinforcement, so after learning, the meaning it attaches to a specification of a sub-task consists of the way in which that specification influences its choice of sub-sub-managers and sub-sub-tasks. Two principles are key:

Reward Hiding Managers must reward sub-managers for doing their bidding *whether or not* this satisfies the commands of the super-managers. Sub-managers should just learn to obey their managers and leave it up to them to determine what it is best to do at the next level up. So if a sub-manager fails to achieve the sub-goal set by its manager it is not rewarded, even if its actions result in the satisfaction of of the manager's own goal. Conversely, if a sub-manager achieves the sub-goal it is given it is rewarded, even if this does not lead to satisfaction of the manager's own goal. This allows the sub-manager to learn to achieve sub-goals even when the manager was mistaken in setting these sub-goals. So in the early stages of learning, low-level managers can become quite competent at achieving low-level goals even if the highest level goal has never been satisfied.

Information Hiding Managers only need to know the state of the system at the granularity of their own choices of tasks. Indeed, allowing some decision making to take place at a coarser grain is one of the main goals of the hierarchical decomposition. Information is hidden both downwards – sub-managers do not know the task the super-manager has set the manager – and upwards – a super-manager does not know what choices its manager has made to satisfy its command. However managers do need to know the satisfaction conditions for the tasks they set and some measure of the actual cost to the system for achieving them using the sub-managers and tasks it picked on any particular occasion.

For the special case to be considered here, in which managers are given no choice of which sub-manager to use in a given state, their choice of a task is very similar to that of an action for a standard Q-learning system. If the task is completed successfully, the cost is determined by the super-manager according to how well (*eg* how quickly, or indeed whether) the manager satisfied its super-tasks. Depending on how its own task is accomplished, the manager rewards or punishes the sub-manager responsible. When a manager chooses an action, control is passed to the sub-manager and is only returned when the state changes *at the managerial level.*

3 THE MAZE TASK

To illustrate this feudal system, consider a standard maze task (Barto, Sutton & Watkins, 1989) in which the agent has to learn to find an initially unknown goal. The grid is split up at successively finer grains (see figure 1) and managers are assigned to separable parts of the maze at each level. So, for instance, the level 1 manager of area 1-(1,1) sets the tasks for and reinforcement given to the level 2 managers for areas 2-(1,1), 2-(1,2), 2-(2,1) and 2-(2,2). The successive separation into quarters is fairly arbitrary – however if the regions at high levels did not cover contiguous areas at lower levels, then the system would not perform very well.

At all times, the agent is effectively performing an action at every level. There are five actions, NSEW and *, available to the managers at all levels other than the first and last. NSEW represent the standard geographical moves and * is a special action that non-hierarchical systems do not require. It specifies that lower level managers should search for the goal within the confines of the current larger state instead of trying to move to another region of the space at the same level. At the top level, the only possible action is *; at the lowest level, only the geographical moves are allowed, since the agent cannot search at a finer granularity than it can move.

Each manager maintains Q values (Watkins, 1989; Barto, Bradtke & Singh, 1992) over the actions it instructs its sub-managers to perform, based on the location of

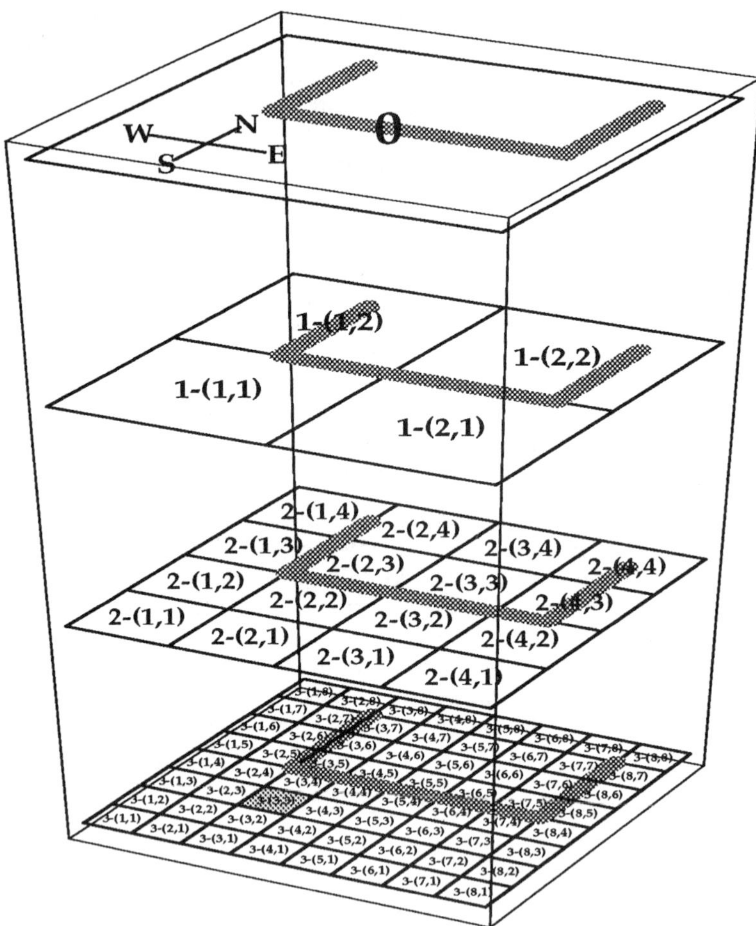

Figure 1: Figure 1: The Grid Task. This shows how the maze is divided up at different levels in the hierarchy. The 'U' shape is the barrier, and the shaded square is the goal. Each high level state is divided into four low level ones at every step.

---

the agent at the subordinate level of detail and the command it has received from above. So, for instance, if the agent currently occupies 3-(6,6), and the instruction from the level 0 manager is to move South, then the 1-(2,2) manager decides upon an action based on the Q values for NSEW giving the total length of the path to either 2-(3,2) or 2-(4,2). The action the 1-(2,2) manager chooses is communicated one level down the hierarchy and becomes part of the state determining the level 2 Q values.

When the agent starts, actions at successively lower levels are selected using the standard Q-learning softmax method and the agent moves according to the finest grain action (at level 3 here). The Q values at every level at which this causes

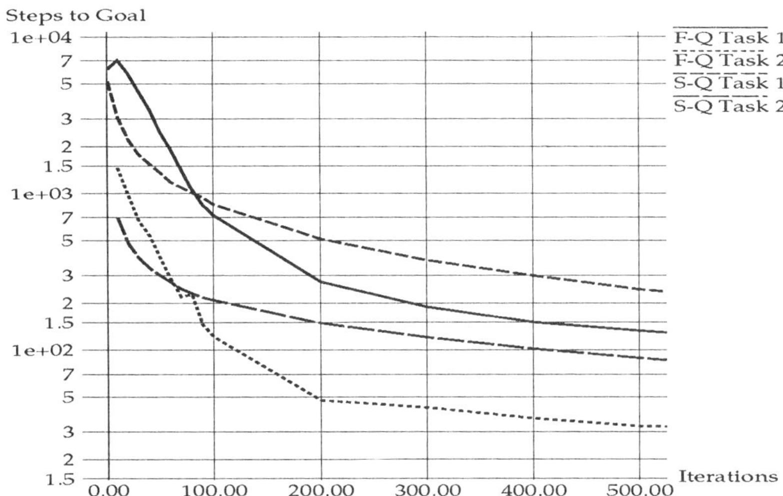

Figure 2: Learning Performance. F-Q shows the performance of the feudal architecture and S-Q of the standard Q-learning architecture.

---

a state transition are updated according to the length of path *at that level*, if the state transition is what was ordered at all lower levels. This restriction comes from the constraint that super-managers should only learn from the fruits of the honest labour of sub-managers, *ie* only if they obey their managers.

Figure 2 shows how the system performs compared with standard, one-step, Q-learning, first in finding a goal in a maze similar to that in figure 1, only having 32x32 squares, and second in finding the goal after it is subsequently moved. Points on the graph are averages of the number of steps it takes the agent to reach the goal across all possible testing locations, after the given number of learning iterations. Little effort was made to optimise the learning parameters, so care is necessary in interpreting the results.

For the first task the feudal system is initially slower, but after a while, it learns much more quickly how to navigate to the goal. The early sloth is due to the fact that many low level actions are wasted, since they do not implement desired higher level behaviour and the system has to learn not to try impossible actions or * in inappropriate places. The late speed comes from the feudal system's superior exploratory behaviour. If it decides at a high level that the goal is in one part of the maze, then it has the capacity to specify large scale actions at that level to take it there. This is the same advantage that Singh's (1992b) variable temporal resolution system garners, although this is over a single task rather than explicitly composite sub-tasks. Tests on mazes of different sizes suggested that the number of iterations after which the advantage of exploration outweighs the disadvantage of wasted actions gets less as the complexity of the task increases.

A similar pattern emerges for the second task. Low level Q values embody an implicit knowledge of how to get around the maze, and so the feudal system can explore efficiently once it (slowly) learns not to search in the original place.

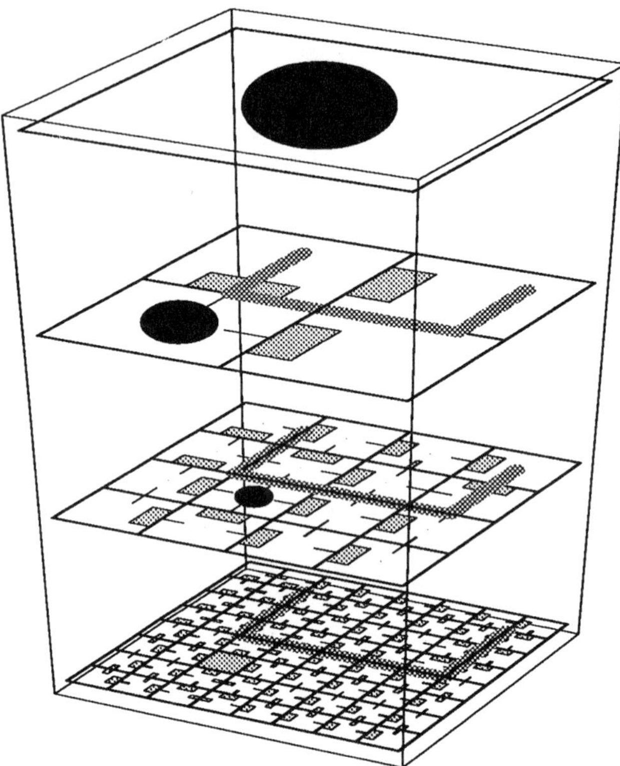

Figure 3: The Learned Actions. The area of the boxes and the radius of the central circle give the probabilities of taking action NSEW and * respectively.

Figure 3 shows the probabilities of each move at each location once the agent has learnt to find the goal at 3-(3,3). The length of the NSEW bars and the radius of the central circle are proportional to the probability of selecting actions NSEW or * respectively, and action choice flows from top to bottom. For instance, the probability of choosing action S at state 2-(1,3) is the sum of the products of the probabilities of choosing actions NSEW and * at state 1-(1,2) and the probabilities, conditional on this higher level selection, of choosing action S at state 2-(1,3). Apart from the right hand side of the barrier, the actions are generally correct – however there are examples of sub-optimal behaviour caused by the decomposition of the space, *eg* the system decides to move North at 3-(8,5) despite it being more felicitous to move South.

Closer investigation of the course of learning reveals that, as might be expected from the restrictions in updating the Q values, the system initially learns in a completely bottom-up manner. However after a while, it learns appropriate actions at the highest levels, and so top-down learning happens too. This generally beneficial effect arises because there are far fewer states at coarse resolutions, and so it is easier for the agent to calculate what to do.

4 DISCUSSION

The feudal architecture partially addresses one of the major concerns in reinforcement learning about how to divide a single task up into sub-tasks at multiple levels. A demonstration was given of how this can be done separately from choosing between different possible sub-managers at a given level.

It depends on there being a plausible managerial system, preferably based on a natural hierarchical division of the available state space. For some tasks it can be very inefficient, since it forces each sub-manager to learn how to satisfy all the sub-tasks set by its manager, whether or not those sub-tasks are appropriate. It is therefore more likely to be useful in environments in which the set tasks can change. Managers need not necessarily know in advance the consequences of their actions. They could learn, in a self-supervised manner, information about the state transitions that they have experienced. These observed next states can be used as goals for their sub-managers – consistency in providing rewards for appropriate transitions is the only requirement.

Although the system gains power through hiding information, which reduces the size of the state spaces that must be searched, such a step also introduces inefficiencies. In some cases, if a sub-manager only knew the super-task of its super-manager then it could bypass its manager with advantage. However the *reductio* of this would lead to each sub-manager having as large a state space as the whole problem, negating the intent of the feudal architecture. A more serious concern is that the non-Markovian nature of the task at the higher levels (the future course of the agent is determined by more detailed information than just the high level states) can render the problem insoluble. Moore and Atkeson's (1993) system for detecting such cases and choosing finer resolutions accordingly should integrate well with the feudal system.

For the maze task, the feudal system learns much more about how to navigate than the standard Q-learning system. Whereas the latter is completely concentrated on a particular target, the former knows how to execute arbitrary high level moves efficiently, even ones that are not used to find the current goal such as going East from one quarter of the space 1-(2,2) to another 1-(1,2). This is why exploration can be more efficient. It doesn't require a map of the space, or even a model of `state x action` → `next state` to be learned explicitly.

Jameson (1992) independently studied a system with some similarities to the feudal architecture. In one case, a high level agent learned on the basis of external reinforcement to provide on a slow timescale direct commands (like reference trajectories) to a low level agent – which learned to obey it based on reinforcement proportional to the square trajectory error. In another, low and high level agents received the same reinforcement from the world, but the former was additionally tasked on making its prediction of future reinforcement significantly dependent on the output of the latter. Both systems learned very effectively to balance an upended pole for long periods. They share the notion of hierarchical structure with the feudal architecture, but the notion of control is somewhat different.

Multi-resolution methods have long been studied as ways of speeding up dynamic programming (see Morin, 1978, for numerous examples and references). Standard methods focus effectively on having a single task at every level and just having coarser and finer representations of the value function. However, here we have studied a slightly different problem in which managers have the flexibility to specify different tasks which the sub-managers have to learn how to satisfy. This is more complicated, but also more powerful.

From a psychological perspective, we have replaced a system in which there is a single external reinforcement schedule with a system in which the rat's mind is composed of a hierarchy of little Skinners.

Acknowledgements

We are most grateful to Andrew Moore, Mark Ring, Jürgen Schmidhuber, Satinder Singh, Sebastian Thrun and Ron Williams for helpful discussions. This work was supported by SERC, the Howard Hughes Medical Institute and the Canadian Institute for Advanced Research (CIAR). GEH is the Noranda fellow of the CIAR.

References

[1] Barto, AG, Bradtke, SJ & Singh, SP (1991). *Real-Time Learning and Control using Asynchronous Dynamic Programming*. COINS technical report 91-57. Amherst: University of Massachusetts.

[2] Barto, AG, Sutton, RS & Watkins, CJCH (1989). Learning and sequential decision making. In M Gabriel & J Moore, editors, *Learning and Computational Neuroscience: Foundations of Adaptive Networks*. Cambridge, MA: MIT Press, Bradford Books.

[3] Hinton, GE (1987). *Connectionist Learning Procedures*. Technical Report CMU-CS-87-115, Department of Computer Science, Carnegie-Mellon University.

[4] Jacobs, RA, Jordan, MI, Nowlan, SJ & Hinton, GE. Adaptive mixtures of local experts. *Neural Computation*, **3**, pp 79-87.

[5] Jameson, JW (1992). Reinforcement control with hierarchical backpropagated adaptive critics. Submitted to *Neural Networks*.

[6] Moore, AW & Atkeson, CG (1993). Memory-based reinforcement learning: efficient computation with prioritized sweeping. In SJ Hanson, CL Giles & JD Cowan, editors *Advances in Neural Information Processing Systems 5*. San Mateo, CA: Morgan Kaufmann.

[7] Morin, TL (1978). Computational advances in dynamic programming. In ML Puterman, editor, *Dynamic Programming and its Applications*. New York: Academic Press.

[8] Moore, AW (1991). Variable resolution dynamic programming: Efficiently learning action maps in multivariate real-valued state spaces. *Proceedings of the Eighth Machine Learning Workshop*. San Mateo, CA: Morgan Kaufmann.

[9] Singh, SP (1992a). Transfer of learning by composing solutions for elemental sequential tasks. *Machine Learning*, **8**, pp 323-340.

[10] Singh, SP (1992b). Scaling reinforcement learning algorithms by learning variable temporal resolution models. Submitted to *Machine Learning*.

[11] Tesauro, G (1992). Practical issues in temporal difference learning. *Machine Learning*, **8**, pp 257-278.

[12] Watkins, CJCH (1989). *Learning from Delayed Rewards*. PhD Thesis. University of Cambridge, England.

Input Reconstruction Reliability Estimation

Dean A. Pomerleau
School of Computer Science
Carnegie Mellon University
Pittsburgh, PA 15213

Abstract

This paper describes a technique called *Input Reconstruction Reliability Estimation* (IRRE) for determining the response reliability of a restricted class of multi-layer perceptrons (MLPs). The technique uses a network's ability to accurately encode the input pattern in its internal representation as a measure of its reliability. The more accurately a network is able to reconstruct the input pattern from its internal representation, the more reliable the network is considered to be. IRRE is provides a good estimate of the reliability of MLPs trained for autonomous driving. Results are presented in which the reliability estimates provided by IRRE are used to select between networks trained for different driving situations.

1 Introduction

In many real world domains it is important to know the reliability of a network's response since a single network cannot be expected to accurately handle all the possible inputs. Ideally, a network should not only provide a response to a given input pattern, but also an indication of the likelihood that its response is "correct". This reliability measure could be used to weight the outputs from multiple networks and to determine when a new network needs to be trained.

This paper describes a technique for estimating a network's reliability called *Input Reconstruction Reliability Estimation* (IRRE). IRRE relies on the fact that the hidden representation developed by an artificial neural network can be considered to be a compressed representation of important input features. For example, when the network shown in Figure 1 is trained to produce the correct steering direction from images of the road ahead, the hidden units learn to encode the position and orientation of important features like the road edges and lane markers (See [Pomerleau, 1991] for more details). Because there are many fewer hidden units than input units in the network, the hidden units cannot accurately represent all the details of an

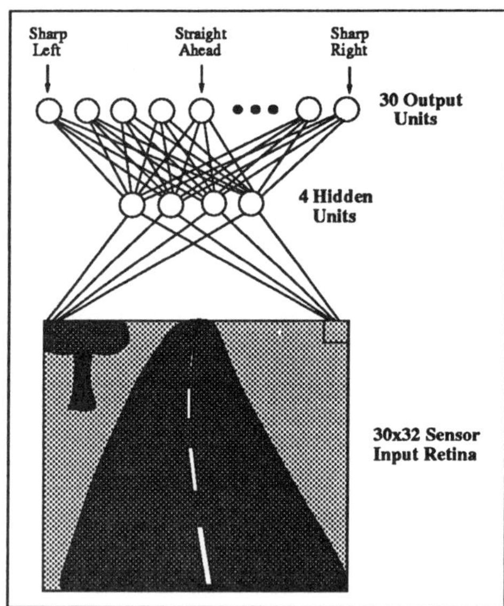

Figure 1: Original driving network architecture.

arbitrary input pattern. Instead, the hidden units learn to devote their limited representational capabilities to encoding the position and orientation of consistent, frequently-occurring features from the training set. When presented with an atypical input, such as a road with a different number of lanes, the feature detectors developed by the hidden units will not be capable of accurately encode all the actual input features.

Input Reconstruction Reliability Estimation exploits this limitation in representational capacity to estimate a network's reliability. In IRRE, the network's internal representation is used to reconstruct in the input pattern being presented. The more closely the reconstructed input matches the actual input, the more familiar the input and hence the more reliable the network's response.

2 Reconstructing the Input

IRRE utilized an additional set of output units to perform input reconstruction called the encoder output array, as depicted in Figure 2. This second set of output units has the same dimensionality as the input retina. In the experiments described in this paper, the input layer and encoder output array have 30 rows and 32 columns. The desired activation for each of these additional output units is identical to the activation of the corresponding input unit. In essence, these additional output units turn the network into an autoencoder.

The network is trained using backpropagation both to produce the correct steering response on the steering output units, and to reconstruct the input image as accurately as possible on the encoder output array. During the training process, the network is presented with several hundred images taken with a camera onboard our test vehicle as a person drives (See [Pomerleau, 1991] for more details). Training typically requires approximately 3 minutes during which the person drives over a 1/4 to 1/2 mile stretch of road.

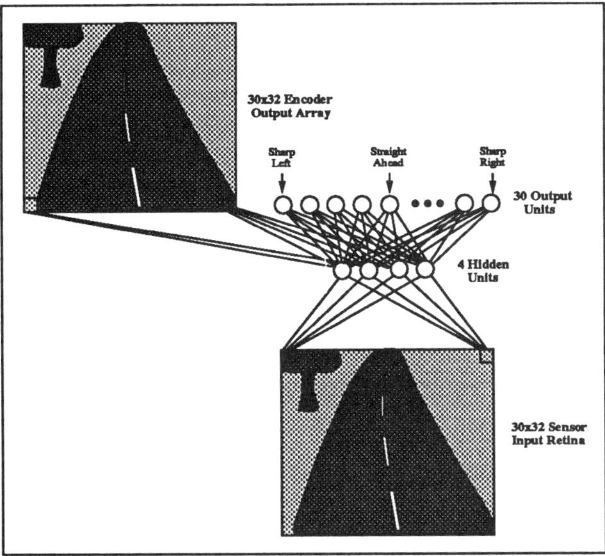

Figure 2: Network architecture augmented to include an encoder output array.

During testing on a new stretch of road, images are presented to the network and activation is propagated forward through the network to produce a steering response and a reconstructed input image. The reliability of the steering response is estimated by computing the correlation coefficient $\rho(\mathbf{I}, \mathbf{R})$ between the activation levels of units in the actual input image **I** and the reconstructed input image **R** using the following formula:

$$\rho(\mathbf{I}, \mathbf{R}) = \frac{\overline{\mathbf{IR}} - \overline{\mathbf{I}} \cdot \overline{\mathbf{R}}}{\sigma_I \, \sigma_R}$$

where $\overline{\mathbf{I}}$ and $\overline{\mathbf{R}}$ are the mean activation value of the actual and the reconstructed images, $\overline{\mathbf{IR}}$ is the mean of the set formed by the unit-wise product of the two images, and σ_I and σ_R represent the standard deviations of the activation values of each image. The higher the correlation between the two images, the more reliable the network's response is estimated to be. The reason correlation is used to measure the degrees of match between the two images is that, unlike Euclidean distance, the correlation measure is invariant to differences in the mean and variance between the two images. This is important since the mean and variance of the input and the reconstructed images can sometimes vary, even when the input image depicts a familiar situation.

3 Results and Applications

The degree of correlation between the actual and the reconstructed input images is an extremely good indicator of network response accuracy in the domain of autonomous driving, as shown in Figure 3. It shows a trained network's steering error and reconstruction error as the vehicle drives down a quarter mile stretch of road that starts out as a single lane path and eventually becomes a two-lane street. The solid line indicates the network's steering error, as measured by the difference in turn curvature between the network's steering response and a person's

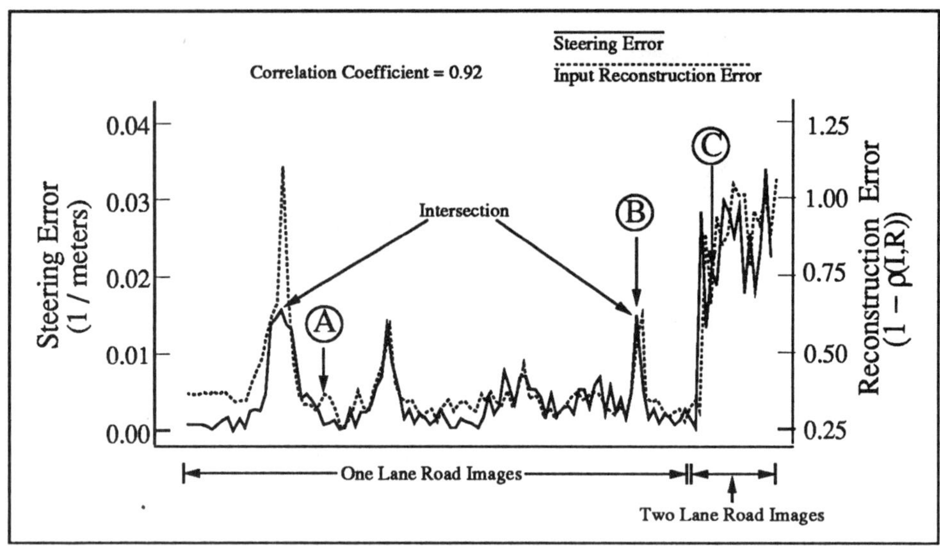

Figure 3: Reconstruction error obtained using autoencoder reconstruction versus network steering error over a stretch of one-lane and two-lane road.

steering response at that point along the road. The dashed line represents the network's "reconstruction error", which is defined to be the degree of statical independence between the actual and reconstructed images, or $1 - \rho(\mathbf{I}, \mathbf{R})$.

The two curves are nearly identical, having a correlation coefficient of 0.92. This close match between the curves demonstrates that when the network is unable to accurately reconstruct the input image, it is also probably suggesting an incorrect steering direction. Visual inspection of the actual and reconstructed input images demonstrates that the degree of resemblance between them is a good indication of the actual input's familiarity, as shown in Figure 4. It depicts the input image, network response, and reconstructed input at the three points along the road, labeled A, B and C in Figure 3. When presented with the image at point A, which closely resembles patterns from training set, the network's reconstructed image closely resembles the actual input, as shown by the close correspondence between the images labeled "Input Acts" and "Reconstructed Input" in the left column of Figure 4. This close correspondence between the input and reconstructed images suggests that the network can reliably steer in this situation. It in fact it can steer accurately on this image, as demonstrated by the close match between the network's steering response labeled "Output Acts" and the desired steering response labeled "Target Acts" in the upper left corner of Figure 4.

When presented with a situation the network did not encounter during training, such as the fork image and the two-lane road image shown in the other two columns of Figure 4, the reconstructed image bears much less resemblance to the original input. This suggests that the network is confused. This confusion results in an incorrect steering response, illustrated in the discrepancy between the network's steering response and the target steering response for the two atypical images.

The reliability prediction provided by IRRE has been used to improve the performance of the neural network based autonomous driving system in a number of ways. The simplest is

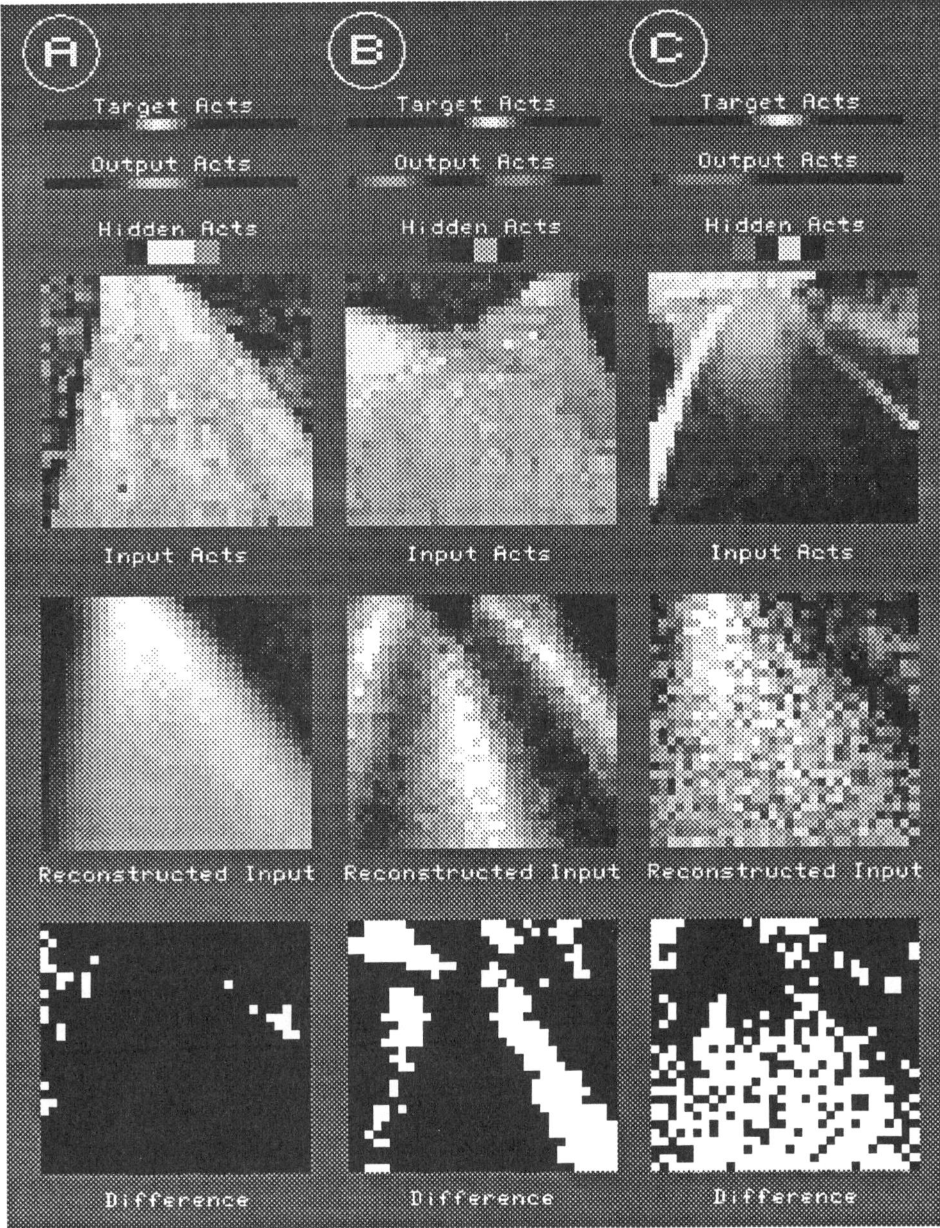

Figure 4: The actual input, the reconstructed input and the point-wise absolute difference between them on a road image similar to those in the training set (labeled A), and on two atypical images (labeled B and C).

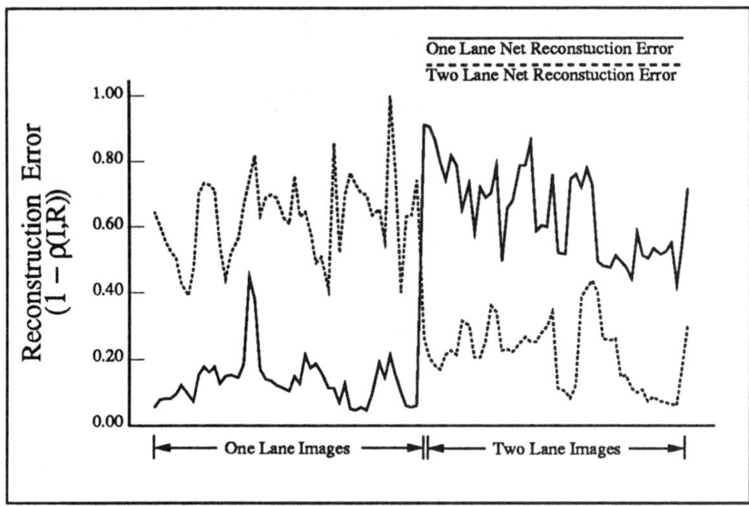

Figure 5: Reconstruction error of networks trained for one-lane road driving (solid line) and two-lane road driving (dashed line).

to use IRRE to control vehicle speed. The more accurate the input reconstruction, the more confident the network, and hence the faster the system drives the vehicle. A second use the system makes of the reliability estimate provided by IRRE is to update the vehicle's position on a rough map of the area being driven over. When the map indicates there should be an intersection or other confusing situation up ahead, a subsequent sharp rise in reconstruction error is a good indication that the vehicle has actually reached that location, allowing the system to pinpoint the vehicle's position. Knowing the vehicle's location on a map is useful for integrating symbolic processing, such as planning, into the neural network driving system (for more details, see [Pomerleau et al., 1991]).

Figure 5 illustrates how IRRE can be used to integrate the outputs from multiple expert networks. The two lines in this graph illustrate the reconstruction error of two networks, one trained to steer on one-lane roads (solid line), and the other trained to steer on two-lane roads (dashed line). The reconstruction error for the one-lane network is low on the one-lane road images, and high on the two-lane road images. The opposite is true for the network trained for two-lane road driving. The reliability estimate provided by IRRE allows the system to determine which network is most reliable for driving in the current situation. By simulating multiple networks in parallel, and then selecting the one with the highest reliability, the system have been able to drive the Navlab test vehicle on one, two and four lane roads automatically at speeds of up to 30 miles per hour.

4 Discussion

The effectiveness of input reconstruction reliable estimation stems from the fact that the network has a small number of hidden units and is only trained in a narrow range of situations. These constraints prevent the network from faithfully encoding arbitrary input patterns. Instead, the hidden units learn to encode features in the training images that are most important for the task. Baldi and Hornik [Baldi & Hornik, 1989] have shown that if an autoencoder network with a single layer of N linear hidden units is trained with back-propagation, the activation levels of the hidden units will represent the first N principal components of the training set. Since the units in the driving network are non-linear, this assertion does not strictly hold in this case. However, Cottrell and Munro [Cottrell & Munro, 1988] have found empirically that autoencoder networks with a sigmoidal activation function develop hidden units that span the principal subspace of the training images, with some noise on the first principal component due to network non-linearity. Because the principal components represent the dimensions along which the training examples varies most, it can be shown that using linear combinations of the principal components to represent the individual training patterns optimally preserves the information contained in the training set [Linsker, 1989].

However the compressed representation developed by a linear autoencoder network is only optimal for encoding images from the same distribution as the training set. When presented with images very different from those in the training set, the image reconstructed from the internal representation is not as accurate. The results presented in this paper demonstrate that this reconstruction error can be employed to estimate the likelihood and magnitude of error in MLPs trained for autonomous driving.

However the input reconstruction technique presented here has a serious potential shortcoming, namely that it forces the network's hidden units to encode all input features, including potentially irrelevant ones. While this increased representation load on the hidden units has the potential to degrade network performance, this effect has not been observed in the tests conducted so far. In support of this finding, Gluck [Gluck, personal communications] has found that forcing a network to autoencode its input frequently *improves* its generalization. In [Gluck & Myers, 1992], Gluck and Myers use the representation developed by an autoencoder network as a model for simple types of learning in biological systems. The model suggests that the hippocampus acts as an autoencoder, developing internal representations that are then used to perform other tasks.

But if interference from the autoencoder task proves to be a problem, one way to eliminate it would be to have separate groups of hidden units connected exclusively to one group of outputs or the other. Having a separate set of hidden units for the autoencoder task would ensure that the representation developed for the input reconstruction does not interfere with representation developed for the "normal" task. It remains to be seen if this decoupling of internal representations will adversely affect IRRE's ability to predict network errors.

As a technique for multi-network integration, IRRE has several advantages over existing connectionist arbitration methods, such as Hampshire and Waibel's Meta-Pi architecture [Hampshire & Waibel, 1992] and the Adaptive Mixture of Experts Model of Jacobs et al. [Jacobs et al., 1991]. It is a more modular approach, since each expert can be trained entirely in isolation and then later combined with other experts without any additional training by simply selecting the most reliable network for the current input. Since IRRE provides an absolute measure of a single network's reliability, and not just a measure of how appropriate a network is relative to others, IRRE can be also used to determine when none of the experts is capable of coping with the current situation.

A potentially interesting extension to IRRE is the development of techniques for reasoning about the difference between the actual input and the reconstructed input. For instance, it should be possible to recognize when the vehicle has reached a fork in the road by the characteristic mistakes the network makes in reconstructing the input image. Another important component of future work in is to test the ability of IRRE to estimate network reliability in domains other than autonomous driving.

Acknowledgements

I thank Dave Touretzky, Chuck Thorpe and the entire Unmanned Ground Vehicle Group at CMU for their support and suggestions. Principle support for this research has come from DARPA, under contracts "Perception for Outdoor Navigation" (contract number DACA76-89-C-0014, monitored by the US Army Topographic Engineering Center) and "Unmanned Ground Vehicle System" (contract number DAAE07-90-C-R059, monitored by TACOM).

References

[Baldi & Hornik, 1989] Baldi, P. and Hornik, K. (1989) Neural networks and principal component analysis: Learning from examples without local minima. *Neural Networks, Vol. 2* pp. 53-58.

[Cottrell & Munro, 1988] Cottrell, G.W. and Munro, P. (1988) Principal components analysis of images via back-propagation. *Proc. Soc. of Photo-Optical Instr. Eng.*, Cambridge MA.

[Gluck, personal communications] Gluck, M.A. (1992) Personal Communications. Rutgers Univ., Newark NJ.

[Gluck & Myers, 1992] Gluck, M.A. and Myers, C.E. (1992) Hippocampal function in representation and generalization: a computational theory. *Proc. 1992 Cogn. Sci. Soc. Conf.* Hillsdale, NJ: Erlbaum Assoc.

[Hampshire & Waibel, 1992] Hampshire J.B. and Waibel, A.H. (1989) The Meta-Pi network: building distributed knowledge representations for robust pattern recognition. *IEEE Trans. on Pattern Analysis and Machine Intelligence.*

[Jacobs et al., 1991] Jacobs, R.A., Jordan, M.I. Nowlan, S.J. and Hinton, G.E. (1991) Adaptive mixtures of local experts. *Neural Computation, 3:1*, Terrence Sejnowski (ed).

[Linsker, 1989] Linsker, R. (1989) Designing a sensory processing system: What can be learned from principal component analysis? IBM Technical Report RC14983 (#66896).

[Pomerleau, 1991] Pomerleau, D.A. (1991) Efficient Training of Artificial Neural Networks for Autonomous Navigation. *Neural Computation 3:1*, Terrence Sejnowski (ed).

[Pomerleau et al., 1991] Pomerleau, D.A., Gowdy, J., Thorpe, C.E. (1991) Combining artificial neural networks and symbolic processing for autonomous robot guidance. *Engineering Applications of Artificial Intelligence, 4:4* pp. 279-285.

Explanation-Based Neural Network Learning for Robot Control

Tom M. Mitchell
School of Computer Science
Carnegie Mellon University
Pittsburgh, PA 15213
E-mail: mitchell@cs.cmu.edu

Sebastian B. Thrun
University of Bonn
Institut für Informatik III
Römerstr. 164, D-5300 Bonn, Germany
thrun@uran.informatik.uni-bonn.de

Abstract

How can artificial neural nets generalize better from fewer examples? In order to generalize successfully, neural network learning methods typically require large training data sets. We introduce a neural network learning method that generalizes rationally from many fewer data points, relying instead on prior knowledge encoded in previously learned neural networks. For example, in robot control learning tasks reported here, previously learned networks that model the effects of robot actions are used to guide subsequent learning of robot control functions. For each observed training example of the target function (e.g. the robot control policy), the learner *explains* the observed example in terms of its prior knowledge, then *analyzes* this explanation to infer additional information about the shape, or slope, of the target function. This shape knowledge is used to bias generalization when learning the target function. Results are presented applying this approach to a simulated robot task based on reinforcement learning.

1 Introduction

Neural network learning methods generalize from observed training data to new cases based on an inductive bias that is similar to smoothly interpolating between observed training points. Theoretical results [Valiant, 1984], [Baum and Haussler, 1989] on learnability, as well as practical experience, show that such purely inductive methods require significantly larger training data sets to learn functions of increasing complexity. This paper introduces explanation-based neural network learning (EBNN), a method that generalizes successfully from fewer training examples, relying instead on prior knowledge encoded in previously learned neural networks.

EBNN is a neural network analogue to symbolic explanation-based learning methods (EBL) [DeJong and Mooney, 1986], [Mitchell *et al.*, 1986]. Symbolic EBL methods generalize based upon pre-specified domain knowledge represented by collections of symbolic rules.

For example, in the task of learning general rules for robot control EBL can use prior knowledge about the effects of robot actions to analytically generalize from specific training examples of successful control actions. This is achieved by a. *observing* a sequence of states and actions leading to some goal, b. *explaining* (i.e., post-facto predicting) the outcome of this sequence using the domain theory, then c. *analyzing* this explanation in order to determine which features of the initial state are relevant to achieving the goal of the sequence, and which are not. In previous approaches to EBL, the initial domain knowledge has been represented symbolically, typically by propositional rules or horn clauses, and has typically been assumed to be complete and correct.

2 EBNN: Integrating inductive and analytical learning

EBNN extends explanation-based learning to cover situations in which prior knowledge (also called the domain theory) is approximate and is itself learned from scratch. In EBNN, this domain theory is represented by real-valued neural networks. By using neural network representations, it becomes possible to learn the domain theory using training algorithms such as the Backpropagation algorithm [Rumelhart *et al.*, 1986]. In the robot domains addressed in this paper, such domain theory networks correspond to *action models*, i.e., networks that model the effect of actions on the state of the world $M: s \times a \longrightarrow s'$ (here a denotes an action, s a state, and s' the successor state). This domain theory is used by EBNN to bias the learning of the robot control function. Because the action models may be only approximately correct, we require that EBNN be *robust* with respect to severe errors in the domain theory.

The remainder of this section describes the EBNN learning algorithm. Assume that the robot agent's action space is discrete, and that its domain knowledge is represented by a collection of pre-trained action models $M_i: s \longrightarrow s'$, one for each discrete action i. The learning task of the robot is to learn a policy for action selection that maximizes the *reward*, denoted by R, which defines the task. More specifically, the agent has to learn an *evaluation function* $Q(s, a)$, which measures the *cumulative future expected reward* when action a is executed at state s. Once learned, the function $Q(s, a)$ allows the agent to select actions that maximize the reward R (greedy policy). Hence learning control reduces to learning the evaluation function Q.[1]

How can the agent use its previously learned action models to focus its learning of Q? To illustrate, consider the episode shown in Figure 1. The EBNN learning algorithm for learning the target function Q consists of two components, an *inductive learning component* and an *analytical learning component.*

2.1 The inductive component of EBNN

The observed episode is used by the agent to construct training examples, denoted by $\hat{Q}$, for the evaluation function Q:

$$\hat{Q}(s_1, a_1) := R \qquad \hat{Q}(s_2, a_2) := R \qquad \hat{Q}(s_3, a_3) := R$$

Q could for example be realized by a monolithic neural network, or by a collection of networks trained with the Backpropagation training procedure. As observed training episodes are accumulated, Q will become increasingly accurate. Such pure inductive learning typ-

[1]This approach to learning a policy is adopted from recent research on *reinforcement learning* [Barto *et al.*, 1991].

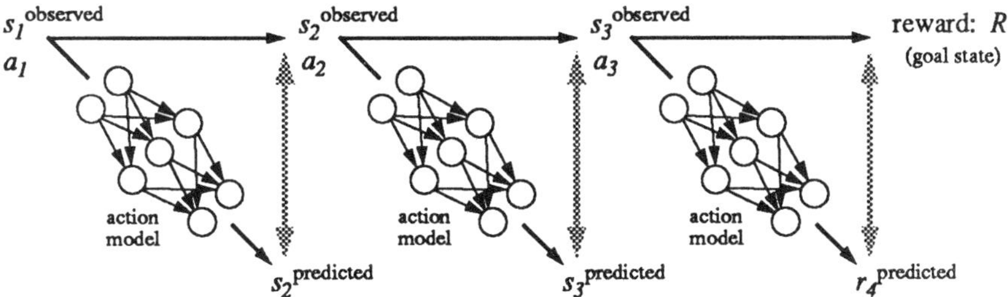

Figure 1: Episode: Starting with the initial state s_1, the action sequence a_1, a_2, a_3 was observed to produce the final reward R. The domain knowledge represented by neural network action models is used to post-facto predict and analyze each step of the observed episode.

ically requires large amounts of training data (which will be costly in the case of robot learning).

2.2 The analytical component of EBNN

In EBNN, the agent exploits its domain knowledge to extract additional shape knowledge about the target function Q, to speed convergence and reduce the number of training examples required. This shape knowledge, represented by the estimated *slope* of the target function Q, is then used to guide the generalization process. More specifically, EBNN combines the above inductive learning component with an analytical learning component that performs the following three steps for each observed training episode:

1. **Explain:** Post-facto predict the observed episode (states and final reward), using the action models M_i (c.f. Fig. 1). Note that there may be a deviation between predicted and observed states, since the domain knowledge is only approximately correct.
2. **Analyze:** Analyze the explanation to estimate the *slope* of the target function for each observed state-action pair $\langle s_k, a_k \rangle$ ($k = 1..3$), i.e., extract the *derivative* of the final reward R with respect to the features of the states s_k, according to the action models M_i. For instance, consider the explanation of the episode shown in Fig. 1. The domain theory networks M_i represent differentiable functions. Therefore it is possible to extract the derivative of the final reward R with respect to the preceding state s_3, denoted by $\nabla_{s_3} R$. Using the chain rule of differentiation, the derivatives of the final reward R with respect to all states s_k can be extracted. These derivatives $\nabla_{s_k} R$ describe the dependence of the final reward upon features of the previous states. They provide the *target slopes*, denoted by $\widehat{\nabla_{s_k} Q}$, for the target function Q:

$$\widehat{\nabla_{s_3} Q}(s_3, a_3) = \nabla_{s_3} R = \frac{\partial M_{a_3}(s_3)}{\partial s_3}$$

$$\widehat{\nabla_{s_2} Q}(s_2, a_2) = \nabla_{s_2} R = \frac{\partial M_{a_3}(s_3)}{\partial s_3} \cdot \frac{\partial M_{a_2}(s_2)}{\partial s_2}$$

$$\widehat{\nabla_{s_1} Q}(s_1, a_1) = \nabla_{s_1} R = \frac{\partial M_{a_3}(s_3)}{\partial s_3} \cdot \frac{\partial M_{a_2}(s_2)}{\partial s_2} \cdot \frac{\partial M_{a_1}(s_1)}{\partial s_1}$$

3. **Learn:** Update the learned target function to better fit both the target values and target slopes. Fig. 2 illustrates training information extracted by both the inductive (values) and the analytical (slopes) components of EBNN. Assume that the "true" Q-function

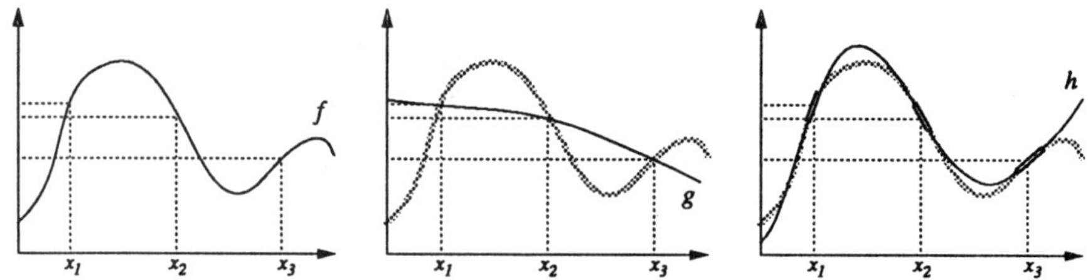

Figure 2: Fitting slopes: Let f be a target function for which three examples $\langle x_1, f(x_1)\rangle$, $\langle x_2, f(x_2)\rangle$, and $\langle x_3, f(x_3)\rangle$ are known. Based on these points the learner might generate the hypothesis g. If the slopes are also known, the learner can do much better: h.

---

is shown in Fig. 2a, and that three training instances at x_1, x_2 and x_3 are given. When only values are used for learning, i.e., as in standard inductive learning, the learner might conclude the hypothesis g depicted in Fig. 2b. If the slopes are known as well, the learner can better estimate the target function (Fig. 2c). From this example it is clear that the analysis in EBNN may reduce the need for training data, provided that the estimated slopes extracted from the explanations are sufficiently accurate.

In EBNN, the function Q is learned by a real-valued function approximator that fits both the target values and target slopes. If this approximator is a neural network, an extended version of the Backpropagation algorithm can be employed to fit these slope constraints as well, as originally shown by [Simard *et al.*, 1992]. Their algorithm *"Tangent Prop"* extends the Backpropagation error function by a second term measuring the mean square error of the slopes. Gradient descent in slope space is then combined with Backpropagation to minimize both error functions. In the experiments reported here, however, we used an instance-based function approximation technique described in Sect. 3.

2.3 Accommodating imperfect domain theories

Notice that the slopes extracted from explanations will be only approximately correct, since they are derived from the approximate action models M_i. If this domain knowledge is weak, the slopes can be arbitrarily poor, which may mislead generalization.

EBNN reduces this undesired effect by estimating the *accuracy* of the extracted slopes and weighting the analytical component of learning by these estimated slope accuracies. Generally speaking, *the accuracy of slopes is estimated by the prediction accuracy of the explanation* (this heuristic has been named LOB*). More specifically, each time the domain theory is used to post-facto predict a state s_{k+1}, its prediction $s_{k+1}^{\text{predicted}}$ may deviate from the observed state $s_{k+1}^{\text{observed}}$. Hence the 1-step prediction accuracy at state s_k, denoted by $c_1(i)$, is defined as 1 minus the normalized prediction error:

$$c_1(i) \quad := \quad 1 - \frac{||s_{k+1}^{\text{predicted}} - s_{k+1}^{\text{observed}}||}{\text{max\_prediction\_error}}$$

For a given episode we define the n-step accuracy $c_n(i)$ as the product of the 1-step accuracies in the next n steps. The n-step accuracy, which measures the accuracy of the derived slopes n steps away from the end of the episode, posseses three desireable properties: a. It is 1 if the learned domain theory is perfectly correct, b. it decreases monotonically as the length of the chain of inferences increases, and c. it is bounded below by 0. The n-step accuracy is used to determine the ratio with which the analytical and inductive components are weighted when learning the target concept. If an observation is n steps away from the end of the episode, the analytically derived training information (slopes) is weighted by the n-step accuracy times the weight of the inductive component (values). Although the experimental results reported in section 3 are promising, the generality of this approach is an open question, due to the heuristic nature of the assumption LOB*.

2.4 EBNN and Reinforcement Learning

To make EBNN applicable to robot learning, we extend it here to a more sophisticated scheme for learning the evaluation function Q, namely Watkins' Q-Learning [Watkins, 1989] combined with Sutton's temporal difference methods [Sutton, 1988]. The reason for doing so is the *problem of suboptimal action choices* in robot learning: Robots must explore their environment, i.e., they must select non-optimal actions. Such non-optimal actions can have a negative impact on the final reward of an episode which results in both underestimating target values and misleading slope estimates.

Watkins' Q-Learning [Watkins, 1989] permits non-optimal actions during the course of learning Q. In his algorithm targets for Q are constructed *recursively*, based on the maximum possible Q-value at the next state:[2]

$$\hat{Q}(s_k, a_k) = \begin{cases} R & \text{if } k \text{ is the final step and } R \text{ final reward} \\ \gamma \max\limits_{a \text{ action}} Q(s_{k+1}, a) & \text{otherwise} \end{cases}$$

Here γ $(0 \leq \gamma \leq 1)$ is a *discount factor* that discounts reward over time, which is commonly used for minimizing the number of actions. Sutton's TD(λ) [Sutton, 1988] can be used to combine both Watkins' Q-Learning and the non-recursive Q-estimation scheme underlying the previous section. Here the parameter λ $(0 \leq \lambda \leq 1)$ determines the ratio between recursive and non-recursive components:

$$\hat{Q}(s_k, a_k) = \begin{cases} R & \text{if } k \text{ final step} \\ (1-\lambda)\,\gamma\, \max_a Q(s_{k+1}, a) \;+\; \lambda\,\gamma\, \hat{Q}(s_{k+1}, a_{k+1}) & \text{otherwise} \end{cases} \quad (1)$$

Eq. (1) describes the extended inductive component of the EBNN learning algorithm. The extension of the analytical component in EBNN is straightforward. Slopes are extracted via the *derivative* of Eq. (1), which is computed via the derivative of both the models M_i and the derivative of Q.

$$\widehat{\nabla_{s_k} Q}(s_k, a_k) = \begin{cases} \dfrac{\partial M_{a_k}(s_k)}{\partial s_k} & \text{if } k \text{ last step} \\ (1\text{-}\lambda)\,\gamma\, \dfrac{\partial Q(s_{k+1}, a)}{\partial s_{k+1}} \dfrac{\partial M_{a_k}(s_k)}{\partial s_k} \;+\; \lambda\,\gamma\, \widehat{\nabla_{s_{k+1}} Q}(s_{k+1}, a_{k+1}) & \text{otherwise} \end{cases}$$

3 Experimental results

EBNN has been evaluated in a simulated robot navigation domain. The world and the action space are depicted in Fig. 3a&b. The learning task is to find a Q function, for which the greedy policy navigates the agent to its goal location (circle) from arbitrary starting locations, while avoiding collisions with the walls or the obstacle (square). States are

[2] In order to simplify the notation, we assume that reward is only received at the end of the episode, and is also modeled by the action models. The extension to more general cases is straightforward.

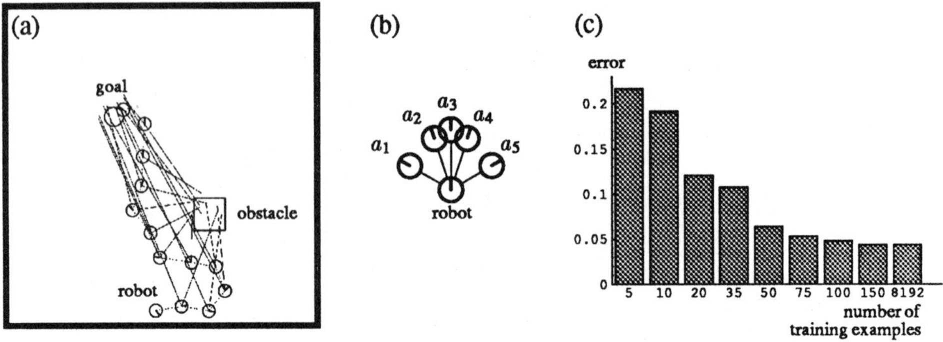

Figure 3: a. The simulated robot world. b. Actions. c. The squared generalization error of the domain theory networks decreases monotonically as the amount of training data increases. These nine alternative domain theories were used in the experiments.

described by the local view of the agent, in terms of distances and angles to the center of the goal and to the center of the obstacle. Note that the world is deterministic in these experiments, and that there is no sensor noise.

We applied Watkins' Q-Learning and TD(λ) as described in the previous section with λ=0.7 and a discount factor γ=0.8. Each of the five actions was modeled by a separate neural network (12 hidden units) and each had a separate Q evaluation function. The latter functions were represented by a instance-based local approximation technique. In a nutshell, this technique memorizes all training instances and their slopes explicitly, and fits a local quadratic model over the l=3 nearest neighbors to the query point, fitting both target values and target slopes. We found empirically that this technique outperformed Tangent Prop in the domain at hand.[3] We also applied an *experience replay* technique proposed by Lin [Lin, 1991] in order to optimally exploit the information given by the observed training episodes.

Fig. 4 shows average performance curves for EBNN using nine different domain theories (action models) trained to different accuracies, with (Fig. 4a) and without (Fig. 4b) taking the n-step accuracy of the slopes into account. Fig. 4a shows the main result. It shows clearly that (1) EBNN outperforms purely inductive learning, (2) more accurate domain theories yield better performance than less accurate theories, and (3) EBNN learning degrades gracefully as the accuracy of the domain theory decreases, eventually matching the performance of purely inductive learning. In the limit, as the size of the training data set grows, we expect all methods to converge to the same asymptotic performance.

4 Conclusion

Explanation-based neural network learning, compared to purely inductive learning, generalizes more accurately from less training data. It replaces the need for large training data sets by relying instead on a previously learned domain theory, represented by neural networks. In this paper, EBNN has been described and evaluated in terms of robot learning tasks. Because the learned action models M_i are independent of the particular control task (reward function), this knowledge acquired during one task transfers directly to other tasks.

[3] Note that in a second experiment not reported here, we applied EBNN using neural network representation for Q and Tangent Prop successfully in a real robot domain.

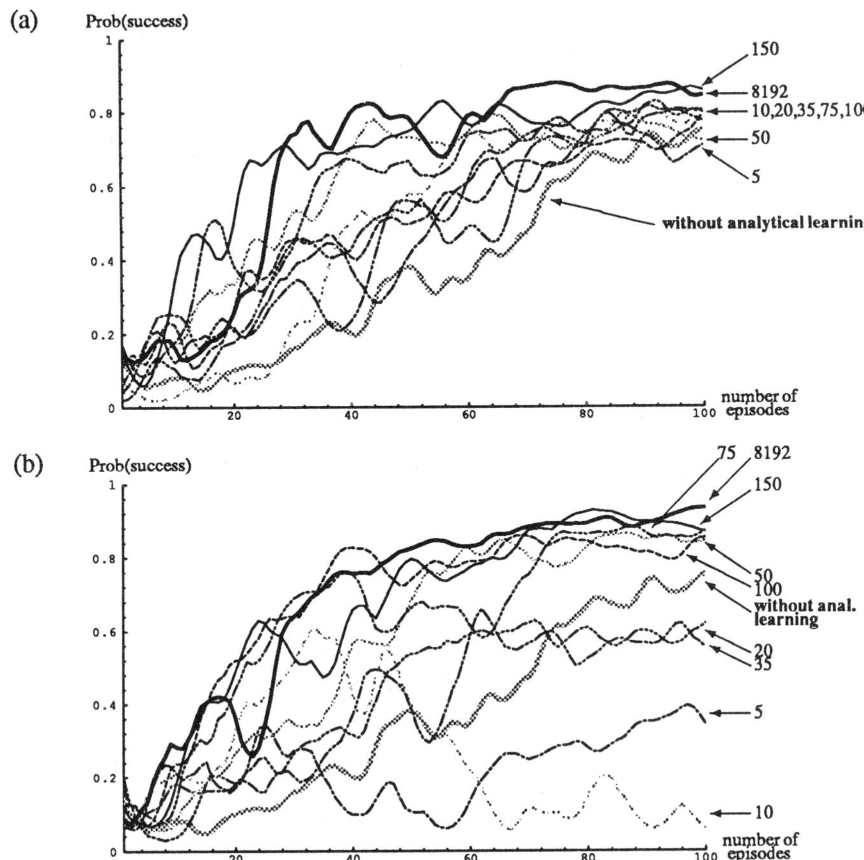

Figure 4: How does domain knowledge improve generalization? a. Averaged results for EBNN domain theories of differing accuracies, pre-trained with from 5 to 8 192 training examples for each action model network. In contrast, the bold grey line reflects the learning curve for pure inductive learning, i.e., Q-Learning and TD(λ). b. Same experiments, but without weighting the analytical component of EBNN by its accuracy, illustrating the importance of the LOB* heuristic. All curves are averaged over 3 runs and are also locally window-averaged. The performance (vertical axis) is measured on an independent test set of starting positions.

EBNN differs from other approaches to knowledge-based neural network learning, such as Shavlik/Towell's KBANNs [Shavlik and Towell, 1989], in that the domain knowledge and the target function are strictly separated, and that both are learned from scratch. A major difference from other model-based approaches to robot learning, such as Sutton's DYNA architecture [Sutton, 1990] or Jordan/Rumelhart's distal teacher method [Jordan and Rumelhart, 1990], is the ability of EBNN to operate across the spectrum of strong to weak domain theories (using LOB*). EBNN has been found to degrade gracefully as the accuracy of the domain theory decreases.

We have demonstrated the ability of EBNN to transfer knowledge among robot learning tasks. However, there are several open questions which will drive future research, the most significant of which are: a. Can EBNN be extended to real-valued, parameterized action spaces? So far we assume discrete actions. b. Can EBNN be extended to handle first-order predicate logic, which is common in symbolic approaches to EBL? c. How will EBNN perform in highly stochastic domains? d. Can knowledge other than slopes (such as higher order derivatives) be extracted via explanations? e. Is it feasible to automatically partition/modularize the domain theory as well as the target function, as this is the case with symbolic EBL methods? More research on these issues is warranted.

Acknowledgments

We thank Ryusuke Masuoka, Long-Ji Lin, the CMU Robot Learning Group, Jude Shavlik, and Mike Jordan for invaluable discussions and suggestions. This research was sponsored in part by the Avionics Lab, Wright Research and Development Center, Aeronautical Systems Division (AFSC), U. S. Air Force, Wright-Patterson AFB, OH 45433-6543 under Contract F33615-90-C-1465, Arpa Order No. 7597 and by a grant from Siemens Corporation.

References

[Barto *et al.*, 1991] Andy G. Barto, Steven J. Bradtke, and Satinder P. Singh. Real-time learning and control using asynchronous dynamic programming. Technical Report COINS 91-57, Department of Computer Science, University of Massachusetts, MA, August 1991.

[Baum and Haussler, 1989] Eric Baum and David Haussler. What size net gives valid generalization? *Neural Computation*, 1(1):151–160, 1989.

[DeJong and Mooney, 1986] Gerald DeJong and Raymond Mooney. Explanation-based learning: An alternative view. *Machine Learning*, 1(2):145–176, 1986.

[Jordan and Rumelhart, 1990] Michael I. Jordan and David E. Rumelhart. Forward models: Supervised learning with a distal teacher. submitted to Cognitive Science, 1990.

[Lin, 1991] Long-Ji Lin. Programming robots using reinforcement learning and teaching. In *Proceedings of AAAI-91*, Menlo Park, CA, July 1991. AAAI Press / The MIT Press.

[Mitchell *et al.*, 1986] Tom M. Mitchell, Rich Keller, and Smadar Kedar-Cabelli. Explanation-based generalization: A unifying view. *Machine Learning*, 1(1):47–80, 1986.

[Pratt, 1993] Lori Y. Pratt. Discriminability-based transfer between neural networks. Same volume.

[Rumelhart *et al.*, 1986] David E. Rumelhart, Geoffrey E. Hinton, and Ronald J. Williams. Learning internal representations by error propagation. In D. E. Rumelhart and J. L. McClelland, editors, *Parallel Distributed Processing. Vol. I + II.* MIT Press, 1986.

[Shavlik and Towell, 1989] Jude W. Shavlik and G.G. Towell. An approach to combining explanation-based and neural learning algorithms. *Connection Science*, 1(3):231–253, 1989.

[Simard *et al.*, 1992] Patrice Simard, Bernard Victorri, Yann LeCun, and John Denker. Tangent prop – a formalism for specifying selected invariances in an adaptive network. In J. E. Moody, S. J. Hanson, and R. P. Lippmann, editors, *Advances in Neural Information Processing Systems 4*, pages 895–903, San Mateo, CA, 1992. Morgan Kaufmann.

[Sutton, 1988] Richard S. Sutton. Learning to predict by the methods of temporal differences. *Machine Learning*, 3, 1988.

[Sutton, 1990] Richard S. Sutton. Integrated architectures for learning, planning, and reacting based on approximating dynamic programming. In *Proceedings of the Seventh International Conference on Machine Learning, June 1990*, pages 216–224, 1990.

[Valiant, 1984] Leslie G. Valiant. A theory of the learnable. *Communications of the ACM*, 27:1134–1142, 1984.

[Watkins, 1989] Chris J. C. H. Watkins. *Learning from Delayed Rewards*. PhD thesis, King's College, Cambridge, England, 1989.

Reinforcement Learning Applied to Linear Quadratic Regulation

Steven J. Bradtke
Computer Science Department
University of Massachusetts
Amherst, MA 01003
bradtke@cs.umass.edu

Abstract

Recent research on reinforcement learning has focused on algorithms based on the principles of Dynamic Programming (DP). One of the most promising areas of application for these algorithms is the control of dynamical systems, and some impressive results have been achieved. However, there are significant gaps between practice and theory. In particular, there are no convergence proofs for problems with continuous state and action spaces, or for systems involving non-linear function approximators (such as multilayer perceptrons). This paper presents research applying DP-based reinforcement learning theory to Linear Quadratic Regulation (LQR), an important class of control problems involving continuous state and action spaces and requiring a simple type of non-linear function approximator. We describe an algorithm based on Q-learning that is proven to converge to the optimal controller for a large class of LQR problems. We also describe a slightly different algorithm that is only *locally* convergent to the optimal Q-function, demonstrating one of the possible pitfalls of using a non-linear function approximator with DP-based learning.

1 INTRODUCTION

Recent research on reinforcement learning has focused on algorithms based on the principles of Dynamic Programming. Some of the DP-based reinforcement learning algorithms that have been described are Sutton's Temporal Differences methods (Sutton, 1988), Watkins' Q-learning (Watkins, 1989), and Werbos' Heuristic Dynamic Programming (Werbos, 1987). However, there are few convergence results for DP-based reinforcement learning algorithms, and these are limited to discrete time, finite-state systems, with either lookup-tables or linear function approximators. Watkins and Dayan (1992) show that the Q-learning algorithm converges, under appropriate conditions, to the optimal Q-function for finite-state Markovian decision tasks, where the Q-function is represented by a lookup-table. Sutton (1988) and Dayan (1992) show that the linear TD(λ) learning rule, when applied to Markovian decision tasks where the states are representated by a linearly independent set of feature vectors, converges in the mean to V_U, the value function for a given control policy U. Dayan (1992) also shows that linear TD(λ) with linearly *dependent* state representations converges, but not to V_U, the function that the algorithm is supposed to learn.

Despite the paucity of theoretical results, applications have shown promise. For example, Tesauro (1992) describes a system using TD(λ) that learns to play championship level backgammon entirely through self-play[1]. It uses a multilayer perceptron (MLP) trained using backpropagation as a function approximator. Sofge and White (1990) describe a system that learns to improve process control with continuous state and action spaces. Neither of these applications, nor many similar applications that have been described, meet the convergence requirements of the existing theory. Yet they produce good results experimentally. We need to extend the theory of DP-based reinforcement learning to domains with continuous state and action spaces, and to algorithms that use non-linear function approximators.

Linear Quadratic Regulation (e.g., Bertsekas, 1987) is a good candidate as a first attempt in extending the theory of DP-based reinforcement learning in this manner. LQR is an important class of control problems and has a well-developed theory. LQR problems involve continuous state and action spaces, and value functions can be exactly represented by quadratic functions. The following sections review the basics of LQR theory that will be needed in this paper, describe Q-functions for LQR, describe the Q-learning algorithm used in this paper, and describe an algorithm based on Q-learning that is proven to converge to the optimal controller for a large class of LQR problems. We also describe a slightly different algorithm that is only *locally* convergent to the optimal Q-function, demonstrating one of the possible pitfalls of using a non-linear function approximator with DP-based learning.

2 LINEAR QUADRATIC REGULATION

Consider the deterministic, linear, time-invariant, discrete time dynamical system given by

$$\begin{aligned} x_{t+1} &= f(x_t, u_t) \\ &= Ax_t + Bu_t \\ u_t &= Ux_t, \end{aligned}$$

where A, B, and U are matrices of dimensions $n \times n$, $n \times m$, and $m \times n$ respectively. x_t is the state of the system at time t, and u_t is the control input to the system at

[1]Backgammon can be viewed as a Markovian decision task.

time t. U is a linear feedback controller. The cost at every time step is a quadratic function of the state and the control signal:

$$\begin{aligned} r_t &= r(x_t, u_t) \\ &= x_t' E x_t + u_t' F u_t, \end{aligned}$$

where E and F are symmetric, positive definite matrices of dimensions $n \times n$ and $m \times m$ respectively, and x' denotes x transpose.

The value $V_{\mathrm{U}}(x_t)$ of a state x_t under a given control policy U is defined as the discounted sum of all costs that will be incurred by using U for all times from t onward, *i.e.*, $V_{\mathrm{U}}(x_t) = \sum_{i=0}^{\infty} \gamma^i r_{t+i}$, where $0 \leq \gamma \leq 1$ is the discount factor. Linear-quadratic control theory (e.g., Bertsekas, 1987) tells us that V_{U} is a quadratic function of the states and can be expressed as $V_{\mathrm{U}}(x_t) = x_t' K_{\mathrm{U}} x_t$, where K_{U} is the $n \times n$ *cost matrix* for policy U. The optimal control policy, U^*, is that policy for which the value of every state is minimized. We denote the cost matrix for the optimal policy by K^*.

3 Q-FUNCTIONS FOR LQR

Watkins (1989) defined the Q-function for a given control policy U as $Q_{\mathrm{U}}(x, u) = r(x, u) + \gamma V_{\mathrm{U}}(f(x, u))$. This can be expressed for an LQR problem as

$$\begin{aligned} Q_{\mathrm{U}}(x, u) &= r(x, u) + \gamma V_{\mathrm{U}}(f(x, u)) \\ &= x' E x + u' F u + \gamma (Ax + Bu)' K_{\mathrm{U}} (Ax + Bu) \\ &= [x, u]' \begin{bmatrix} E + \gamma A' K_{\mathrm{U}} A & \gamma A' K_{\mathrm{U}} B \\ \gamma B' K_{\mathrm{U}} A & F + \gamma B' K_{\mathrm{U}} B \end{bmatrix} [x, u], \end{aligned} \tag{1}$$

where $[x, u]$ is the column vector concatenation of the column vectors x and u.

Define the parameter matrix H_{U} as

$$H_{\mathrm{U}} = \begin{bmatrix} E + \gamma A' K_{\mathrm{U}} A & \gamma A' K_{\mathrm{U}} B \\ \gamma B' K_{\mathrm{U}} A & F + \gamma B' K_{\mathrm{U}} B \end{bmatrix} = \begin{bmatrix} H_{11} & H_{12} \\ H_{21} & H_{22} \end{bmatrix}. \tag{2}$$

H_{U} is a symmetric positive definite matrix of dimensions $(n+m) \times (n+m)$.

4 Q-LEARNING FOR LQR

The convergence results for Q-learning (Watkins & Dayan, 1992) assume a discrete time, finite-state system, and require the use of lookup-tables to represent the Q-function. This is not suitable for the LQR domain, where the states and actions are vectors of real numbers. Following the work of others, we will use a parameterized representation of the Q-function and adjust the parameters through a learning process. For example, Jordan and Jacobs (1990) and Lin (1992) use MLPs trained using backpropagation to approximate the Q-function. Notice that the function Q_{U} is a quadratic function of its arguments, the state and control action, but it is a *linear* function of the quadratic combinations from the vector $[x, u]$. For example, if $x = [x_1, x_2]$, and $u = [u_1]$, then $Q_{\mathrm{U}}(x, u)$ is a linear function of the vector $[x_1^2, x_2^2, u_1^2, x_1x_2, x_1u_1, x_2u_1]$. This fact allows us to use linear Recursive Least Squares (RLS) to implement Q-learning in the LQR domain.

There are two forms of Q-learning. The first is the rule Watkins described in his thesis (Watkins, 1989) . Watkins called this rule *Q-learning*, but we will refer to it as *optimizing Q-learning* because it attempts to learn the Q-function of the optimal policy directly. The optimizing Q-learning rule may be written as

$$Q_{t+1}(x_t, u_t) = Q_t(x_t, u_t) + \alpha \left[r(x_t, u_t) + \gamma \min_a Q_t(x_{t+1}, a) - Q_t(x_t, u_t) \right], \quad (3)$$

where Q_t is the tth approximation to Q^*. The second form of Q-learning attempts to learn Q_U, the Q-function for some designated policy, U. U may or may not be the policy that is actually followed during training. This *policy-based Q-learning* rule may be written as

$$Q_{t+1}(x_t, u_t) = Q_t(x_t, u_t) + \alpha \left[r(x_t, u_t) + \gamma Q_t(x_{t+1}, Ux_{t+1}) - Q_t(x_t, u_t) \right], \quad (4)$$

where Q_t is the tth approximation to Q_U. Bradtke, Ydstie, and Barto (paper in preparation) show that a linear RLS implementation of the policy-based Q-learning rule will converge to Q_U for LQR problems.

5 POLICY IMPROVEMENT FOR LQR

Given a policy U_k, how can we find an improved policy, U_{k+1}? Following Howard (1960) , define U_{k+1} as

$$U_{k+1}x = \operatorname*{argmin}_u \left[r(x, u) + \gamma V_{U_k}(f(x, u)) \right].$$

But equation (1) tells us that this can be rewritten as

$$U_{k+1}x = \operatorname*{argmin}_u Q_{U_k}(x, u).$$

We can find the minimizing u by taking the partial derivative of $Q_{U_k}(x, u)$ with respect to u, setting that to zero, and solving for u. This yields

$$u = \underbrace{-\gamma \left(F + \gamma B' K_{U_k} B\right)^{-1} B' K_{U_k} A}_{U_{k+1}} x.$$

Using (2), U_{k+1} can be written as

$$U_{k+1} = -H_{22}^{-1} H_{21}.$$

Therefore we can use the definition of the Q-function to compute an improved policy.

6 POLICY ITERATION FOR LQR

The RLS implementation of policy-based Q-learning (Section 4) and the policy improvement process based on Q-functions (Section 5) are the key elements of the policy iteration algorithm described in Figure 1. Theorem 1, proven in (Bradtke,

Ydstie, & Barto, in preparation), shows that the sequence of policies generated by this algorithm converges to the optimal policy. Standard policy iteration algorithms, such as those described by Howard (1960) for discrete time, finite state Markovian decision tasks, or by Bertsekas (1987) and Kleinman (1968) for LQR problems, require exact knowledge of the system model. *Our algorithm requires no system model. It only requires a suitably accurate estimate of* H_{U_k}.

Theorem 1: If (1) $\{A, B\}$ is controllable, (2) U_0 is stabilizing, and (3) the control signal, which at time step t and policy iteration step k is $U_k x_t$ plus some "exploration factor", is strongly persistently exciting, then there exists a number N such that the sequence of policies generated by the policy iteration algorithm described in Figure 1 will converge to U^* when policy updates are performed at most every N time steps.

```
Initialize the Q-function parameters, Ĥ_0.
t = 0, k = 0.
do forever {
        Initialize the Recursive Least Squares estimator.
        for i = 1 to N {
                • u_t = U_k x_t + e_t, where e_t is the "exploration" com-
                  ponent of the control signal.
                • Apply u_t to the system, resulting in state x_{t+1}.
                • Define a_{t+1} = U_k x_{t+1}.
                • Update the Q-function parameters, Ĥ_k using the
                  Recursive Least Squares implementation of the
                  policy-based Q-learning rule, equation (4).
                • t = t + 1.
        }
        Policy improvement based on Ĥ_k: U_{k+1} = -Ĥ_22^{-1} Ĥ_21
        Initialize parameters Ĥ_{k+1} = Ĥ_k.
        k = k + 1
}
```

Figure 1: The Q-function based policy iteration algorithm. It starts with the system in some initial state x_0 and with some stabilizing controller U_0. k keeps track of the number of policy iteration steps. t keeps track of the total number of time steps. i counts the number of time steps since the last change of policy. When $i = N$, one policy improvement step is executed.

Figure 2 demonstrates the performance of the Q-function based policy iteration algorithm. We do not know how to characterize a persistently exciting exploratory signal for this algorithm. Experimentally, however, a random exploration signal generated from a normal distribution has worked very well, even though it does not meet condition (3) of the theorem. The system is a 20-dimensional discrete time approximation of a flexible beam supported at both ends. There is one control point. The control signal is a scalar representing acceleration to be applied at that point. U_0 is an arbitrarily selected stabilizing controller for the system. x_0 is a random point in a neighborhood around $0 \in \mathcal{R}^{20}$. We used a normal random variable with mean 0 and variance 1 as the exploratory signal. There are 231 parameters to be estimated for this system, so we set $N = 500$, approximately twice that. Panel A of Figure 2 shows the norm of the difference between the current controller and the optimal controller. Panel B of Figure 2 shows the norm of the difference between the estimate of the Q-function for the current controller and the Q-function for the optimal controller. After only eight policy iteration steps the Q-function based policy iteration algorithm has converged close enough to U^* and Q^* that further improvements are limited by the machine precision.

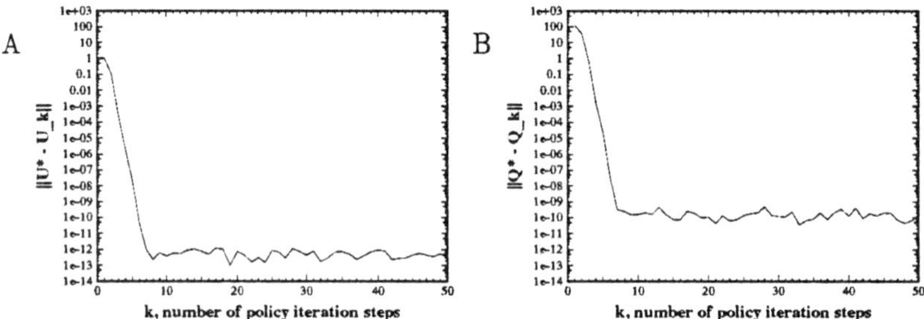

Figure 2: Performance of the Q-function based policy iteration algorithm on a discretized beam system.

7 THE OPTIMIZING Q-LEARNING RULE FOR LQR

Policy iteration would seem to be a slow method. It has to evaluate each policy before it can specify a new one. Why not do as Watkins' optimizing Q-learning rule does (equation 3), and try to learn Q^* directly? Figure 3 defines this algorithm precisely. This algorithm does not update the policy actually used during training. It only updates the estimate of Q^*. The system is started in some initial state x_0 and some stabilizing controller U_0 is specified as the controller to be used during training.

To what will this algorithm converge, if it does converge? A fixed point of this algorithm must satisfy

$$[x,u]' \begin{bmatrix} H_{11} & H_{12} \\ H_{21} & H_{22} \end{bmatrix} [x,u] =$$

$$x'Ex + u'Eu + \gamma[Ax+Bu,a]' \begin{bmatrix} H_{11} & H_{12} \\ H_{21} & H_{22} \end{bmatrix} [Ax+Bu,a], \qquad (5)$$

where $a = -H_{22}^{-1}H_{21}(Ax+Bu)$. Equation (5) actually specifies $(n+m)(n+m+1)/2$ polynomial equations in $(n+m)(n+m+1)/2$ unknowns (remember that H_U is symmetric). We know that there is at least one solution, that corresponding to the optimal policy, but there may be other solutions as well.

As an example of the possibility of multiple solutions, consider the 1-dimensional system with $A = B = E = F = [1]$ and $\gamma = 0.9$. Substituting these values into

Initialize the Q-function parameters, $\hat{H}_0$.
Initialize Recursive Least Squares estimator.
$t = 0$.
do forever {

- $u_t = U_0 x_t + e_t$, where e_t is the "exploration" component of the control signal.
- Apply u_t to the system, resulting in state x_{t+1}.
- Define $a_{t+1} = -\hat{H}_{22}^{-1}\hat{H}_{21}x_{t+1}$.
- Update the Q-function parameters, $\hat{H}_t$, using the Recursive Least Squares implementation of the optimizing Q-learning rule, equation (3).
- $t = t + 1$.

}

Figure 3: The optimizing Q-learning rule in the LQR domain. U_0 is the policy followed during training. t keeps track of the total number of time steps.

equation (5) and solving for the unknown parameters yields two solutions. They are

$$\begin{bmatrix} 2.4296 & 1.4296 \\ 1.4296 & 2.4296 \end{bmatrix} \text{ and } \begin{bmatrix} 0.3704 & -0.6296 \\ -0.6296 & 0.3704 \end{bmatrix}.$$

The first solution is Q^*. The second solution, if used to define an "improved" policy as describe in Section 5, results in a destablizing controller. This is certainly not a desirable result. Experiments show that the algorithm in Figure 3 will converge to either of these solutions if the initial parameter estimates are close enough to that solution. Therefore, this method of using Watkins' Q-learning rule directly on an LQR problem will not necessarily converge to the optimal Q-function.

8 CONCLUSIONS

In this paper we take a first step toward extending the theory of DP-based reinforcement learning to domains with continuous state and action spaces, and to algorithms that use non-linear function approximators. We concentrate on the problem of Linear Quadratic Regulation. We describe a policy iteration algorithm for LQR problems that is proven to converge to the optimal policy. In contrast to standard methods of policy iteration, it does not require a system model. It only requires a suitably accurate estimate of H_{U_k}. This is the first result of which we are aware showing convergence of a DP-based reinforcement learning algorithm in a domain with continuous states and actions. We also describe a straightforward implementation of the optimizing Q-learning rule in the LQR domain. This algorithm is only locally convergent to Q^*. This result demonstrates that we cannot expect the theory developed for finite-state systems using lookup-tables to extend to continuous state systems using parameterized function representations.

The convergence proof for the policy iteration algorithm described in this paper requires exact matching between the form of the Q-function for LQR problems and the form of the function approximator used to learn that function. Future work will explore convergence of DP-based reinforcement learning algorithms when applied to non-linear systems for which the form of the Q-functions is unknown.

Acknowledgements

The author thanks Andrew Barto, B. Erik Ydstie, and the ANW group for their contributions to these ideas. This work was supported by the Air Force Office of Scientific Research, Bolling AFB, under Grant AFOSR-89-0526 and by the National Science Foundation under Grant ECS-8912623.

References

[1] D. P. Bertsekas. *Dynamic Programming: Deterministic and Stochastic Models.* Prentice Hall, Englewood Cliffs, NJ, 1987.

[2] S. J. Bradtke, B. E. Ydstie, and A. G. Barto. Convergence to optimal cost of adaptive policy iteration. In preparation.

[3] P. Dayan. The convergence of TD(λ) for general λ. *Machine Learning*, 1992.

[4] R. A. Howard. *Dynamic Programming and Markov Processes.* John Wiley & Sons, Inc., New York, 1960.

[5] M. I. Jordan and R. A. Jacobs. Learning to control an unstable system with forward modeling. In *Advances in Neural Information Processing Systems 2.* Morgan Kaufmann Publishers, San Mateo, CA, 1990.

[6] D. L. Kleinman. On an iterative technique for Riccati equation computations. *IEEE Transactions on Automatic Control*, pages 114–115, February 1968.

[7] L.-J. Lin. Self-improving reactive agents based on reinforcement learning, planning and teaching. *Machine Learning*, 1992.

[8] D. A. Sofge and D. A. White. Neural network based process optimization and control. In *Proceedings of the 29th IEEE Conference on Decision and Control*, Honolulu, Hawaii, December 1990.

[9] R. S. Sutton. Learning to predict by the method of temporal differences. *Machine Learning*, 3:9–44, 1988.

[10] G. J. Tesauro. Practical issues in temporal difference learning. *Machine Learning*, 8(3/4):257–277, May 1992.

[11] C. J. C. H. Watkins. *Learning from Delayed Rewards.* PhD thesis, Cambridge University, Cambridge, England, 1989.

[12] C. J. C. H. Watkins and P. Dayan. Q-learning. *Machine Learning*, 1992.

[13] P. J. Werbos. Building and understanding adaptive systems: A statistical/numerical approach to factory automation and brain research. *IEEE Transactions on Systems, Man, and Cybernetics*, 17(1):7–20, 1987.

Neural Network On-Line Learning Control of Spacecraft Smart Structures

Dr. Christopher Bowman
Ball Aerospace Systems Group
P.O. Box 1062
Boulder, CO 80306

Abstract

The overall goal is to reduce spacecraft weight, volume, and cost by on-line adaptive non-linear control of flexible structural components. The objective of this effort is to develop an adaptive Neural Network (NN) controller for the Ball C-Side 1m x 3m antenna with embedded actuators and the RAMS sensor system. A traditional optimal controller for the major modes is provided perturbations by the NN to compensate for unknown residual modes. On-line training of recurrent and feed-forward NN architectures have achieved adaptive vibration control with unknown modal variations and noisy measurements. On-line training feedback to each actuator NN output is computed via Newton's method to reduce the difference between desired and achieved antenna positions.

1 ADAPTIVE CONTROL BACKGROUND

The two traditional approaches to adaptive control are 1) direct control (such as performed in direct model reference adaptive controllers) and 2) indirect control (such as performed by explicit self-tuning regulators). Direct control techniques (e.g. model-reference adaptive control) provide good stability however are susceptible to noise. Whereas indirect control techniques (e.g. explicit self-tuning regulators) have low noise susceptibility and good convergence rate. However they require more control effort and have worse stability and are less robust to mismodeling. NNs synergistically augment traditional adaptive control techniques by providing improved mismodeling robustness both adaptively on-line for time-varying dynamics as well as in a learned control mode at a slower rate.

The NN control approaches which correspond to direct and indirect adaptive control are commonly known as inverse and forward modeling, respectively. More specifically, a NN which maps the plant state and its desired performance to the control command is called an inverse model, a NN mapping both the current plant state and control to the next state and its performance is called the forward model.

When given a desired performance and the current state, the inverse model generates the control, see Figure 1. The actual performance is observed and is used to train/update the inverse model. A significant problem occurs when the desired and achieved performance differ greatly since the model near the desired state is not changed. This condition is corrected by adding random noise to the control outputs so as to extend the state space being explored. However, this correction has the effect of slowing the learning and reducing broadband stability.

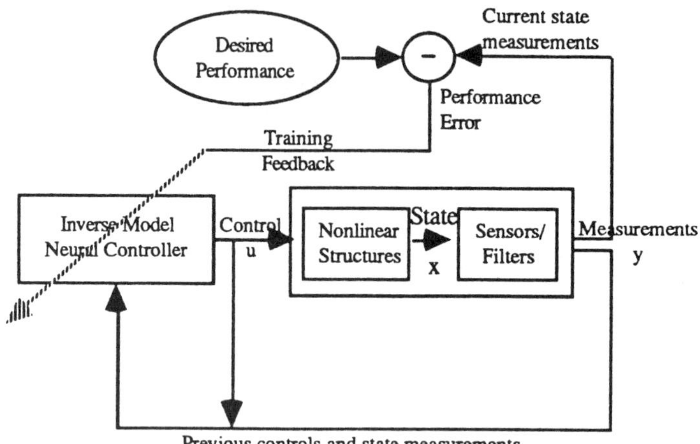

Figure 1: Direct Adaptive Control Using Inverse Modeling Neural Network Controller

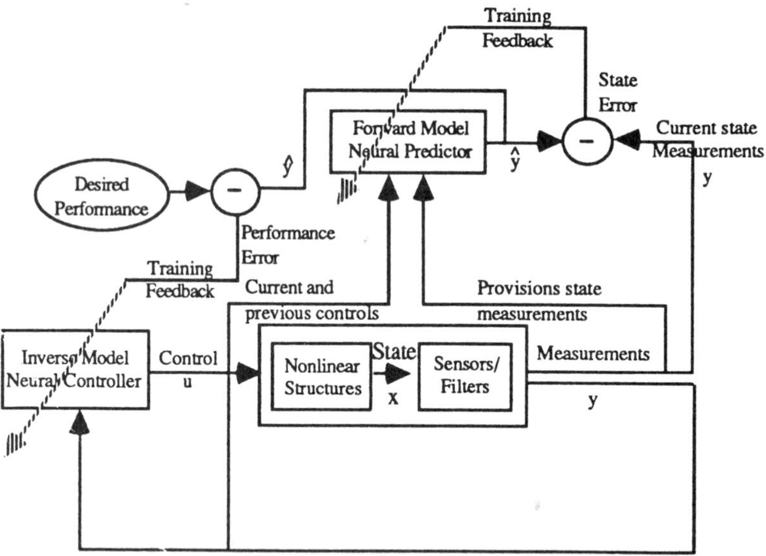

Figure 2: Dual (Indirect and Direct) Adaptive Control Using Forward Modeling Neural Network State Predictor To Aid Inverse Model Convergence

For forward modeling the map from the current control and state to the resulting state and performance is learned, see Figure 2. For cases where the performance is evaluated at a future time (i.e. distal in time), a predictive critic [Barto and Sutton, 1989] NN model is learned. In both cases the Jacobian of this performance can be computed to iteratively generate the next control action. However, this differentiating of the critic NN for back-propagation training of the controller network is very slow and in some cases steers the searching the wrong direction due to initial erroneous forward model estimates. As the NN adapts itself the performance flattens which results in the slow halting of learning at an unacceptable solution. Adding noise to the controller's output [Jordan and Jacobs, 1990] breaks the redundancy but forces the critic to predict the effects of future noise. This problem has been solved by using a separately trained intermediate plant model to predict the next state from the prior state and control while having an independent predictor model generate the performance evaluation from the plant model predicted state [Werbos, 1990] and [Brody, 1991]. The result is a 50-100 fold learning speed improvement over reinforcement training of the forward model controller NN.

However, this method still relies on a "good" forward model to incrementally train the inverse model. These incremental changes can still lead to undesirable solutions. For control systems which follow the stage 1, 2 or 3 models given in [Narendra, 1991) the control can be analytically computed from a forward-only model. For the most general, non-linear (stage 4) systems, an alternative is the memory-based forward model [Moore, 1992]. Using only a forward NN model, a direct hill-climbing or Newton's method search of candidate actions can be applied until a control decision is reached. The resulting state and its performance are used for on-line training of the forward model. Judicial random control actions are applied to improve behavior only where the forward model error is predicted to be large (e.g. via cross-validation). Also using robust regression, experiences can be deweighted according to their quality and their age. The high computational burden of these cross-validation techniques can be reduced by parallel on-line processing providing the "policy" parameters for fast on-line NN control.

For control problems which are distal in time and space, a hybrid of these two forward-modeling approaches can be used. Namely, a NN plant model is added which is trained off-line in real-time and updated as necessary at a slower rate than the on-line forward model which predicts performance based upon the current plant model. This slower rate trained forward-model NN supports learned control (e.g. via numerical inversion) whereas the on-line forward model provides the faster response adaptive control. Other NN control techniques such as using a Hopfield net to solve the optimal-control quadratic-programming problem or the supervised training of ART II off-line with adaptive vigilance for on-line pole placement have been proposed. However, their on-line robustness appears limited due to their sensitivity to a priori parameter assumptions.

A forward model NN which augments a traditional controller for unmodeled modes and unforeseen situations is presented in the following section. Performance results for both feed-forward and current learning versions are compared in Section 3.

2 RESIDUAL FORWARD MODEL NEURAL NETWORK (RFM-NN) CONTROLLER

A type of forward model NN which acts as a residual mode filter to support a reduced-order model (ROM) traditional optimal state controller has been evaluated, see Figure 3. The ROM determines the control based upon its model coordinate approximate representation of the structure. Model coordinates are obtained by a transformation using known primary vibration modes, [Young, 1990]. The transformation operator is a set of eigenvectors (mode shapes) generated by finite element modeling. The ROM controller is traditionally augmented by a residual-mode filter (RMF). Ball's RFM-NN Ball's RFM-NN replaces the RMF in order to better capture the mismodeled, unmodeled and changing modes.

The objective of the RFM-NN is to provide ROM controller with ROM derivative state perturbations, so that the ROM controls the structure as desired by the user. The RFM-NN is trained on-line using scored supervised feedback to generate these desired ROM state perturbations. The scored supervised training provides a score for each perturbation output based upon the measured position of the structure. The measured deviations, Y*(t), from the desired structure position are converted to errors in the estimated ROM state using the ROM transformation. Specifically, the training score, S(t), for each ROM derivative state $\dot{x}_N(t)$ is expressed in the following discrete equation:

$$S(t) = B_N Y*(t) - \hat{\dot{x}}_N(t)$$

$$\text{where } \hat{\dot{x}}_N(t) = [A_N + B_N G_N - K_N C_N]\hat{x}_N(t-1) + K_N Y(t-1)$$

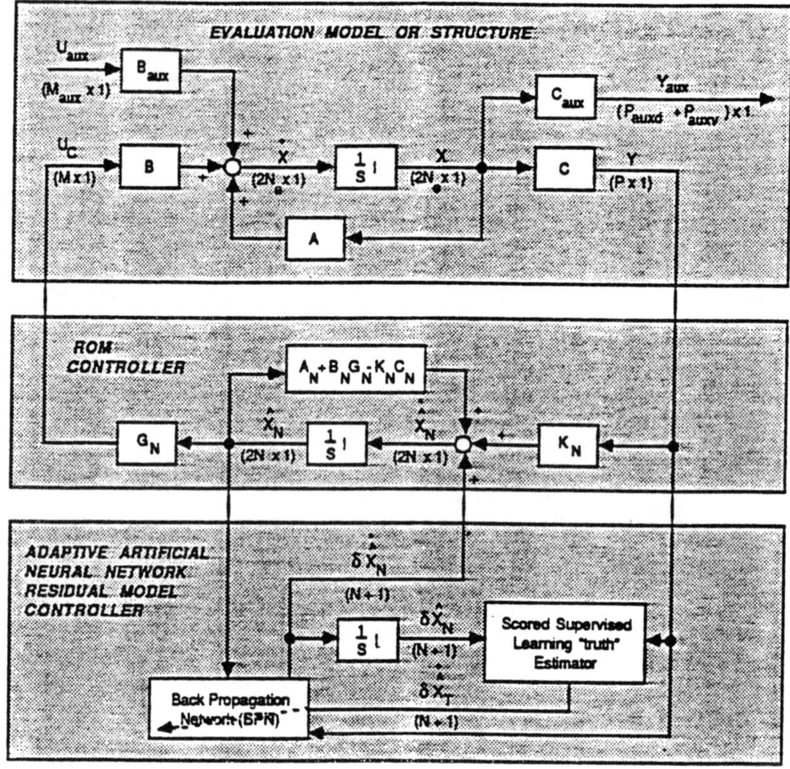

Figure 3: Residual Forward Model Neural Network Adaptive Controller Replaces Traditional Residual Mode Filter

Newton's method is then applied to find the $\delta\hat{\dot{x}}_N(t)$ ROM state perterbations which zero the score. First, the score is smoothed, $\bar{S}(t) = \delta\bar{S}(t-1) + (1-\delta)S(t)$ and the neural network output is smoothed similarly. Second, Newton's method computes the adjustments needed to zero the scores,

$$\Delta(\delta\hat{\dot{x}}_N(t)) = -\bar{S}(t)(\delta\hat{\dot{x}}_N(t) - \delta\hat{\dot{x}}_N(t-1)) / [\bar{S}(t) - \bar{S}(t-1)]$$
$$= -\varepsilon x_N(t) \text{ (if either difference} = 0)$$

Third, the NN is trained, $\delta\hat{\dot{x}}_T(t+1) = \alpha\Delta(\delta\hat{\dot{x}}_N(t)) + \delta\hat{\dot{x}}_N(t)$ with the appropriate learning rate, α (e.g. approximation to inverse of largest eigenvalue of the Hessian weight matrix).

3 RFM-NN ON-LINE LEARNING RESULTS

Both feed-forward and recurrent RFM-NNs have been incorporated into an interactive simulation of Ball's Control-Structure Interaction Demonstration Experiment (C-SIDE) see Figure 4. This 1m x 3m lightweight antenna facesheet has 8 embedded actuators plus three auxiliary input actuators and uses 8 remote angular measurement sensors (RAMS) plus 4 displacement and 3 velocity auxiliary sensors. In order to evaluate the on-line performance of the RFM-NNs the ROM controller was given insufficient and partially incorrect modes. The ROM without the RFM-NN grew unstable (i.e. greater than 10 millimeter C-SIDE displacements) in 13 seconds. The initial feed-forward RFM-NN used 8 sensor and 6 ROM state feedback estimate inputs as well as 5 hidden units and 3 ROM velocity state perturbation outputs. This RFM-NN had random initial weights, logistic activation functions, and back-propagation training using one sixth the learning rate for the output layers (e.g. .06 and .01). Newton RFM-NN training search used a step size of one with smoothing factor of one tenth.

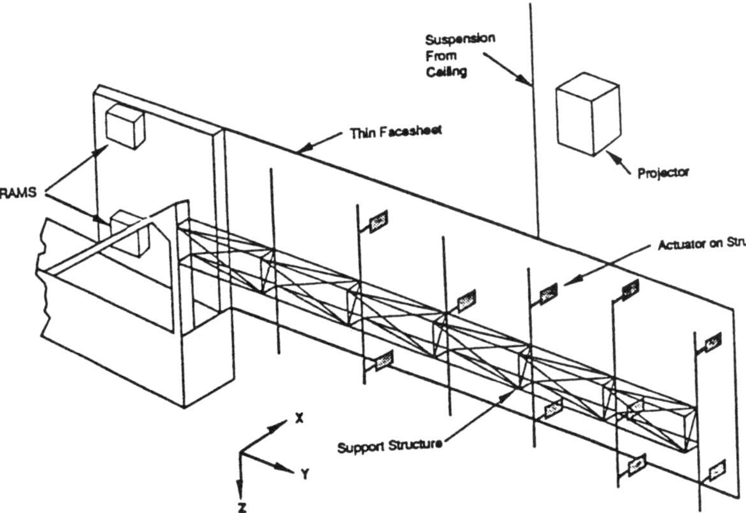

Figure 4: 1m x 3m C-SIDE Antenna Facesheet With Embedded Actuators.

This RFM-NN learned on-line to stabilized and reduce vibration to less than ±1mm within 20 seconds, see Figure 5. A five Newton force applied a few seconds later is compensated for within nine seconds, see Figure 6. This is accomplished with learning off as well as when on. To test the necessity of the RFM-NN the ROM was given the scored supervised training (i.e. Newton's search estimates) directly instead of the RFM-NN outputs. This caused immediate unstable behavior. To test the RFM-NN sensitivity to measurement accuracy a uniform error of ±5% was added. Starting from the same random weight start the RFM-NN required 25 seconds to learn to stabilize the antenna, see Figure 7. The best stability was achieved when the product of the Newton and BPN steps was approximately .01. This feed-forward NN was compared to an Elman-type recurrent NN (i.e. hidden layer feedback to itself with one-step BP training). The recurrent RFM-NN on-line learning stability was much less sensitive to initial weights. The recurrent RFM-NN stabilized C-SIDE with up to 10% - 20% measurement noise versus 5% - 10% limit for feed-forward RFM-NN.

4 SUMMARY AND RECOMMENDATIONS

Adaptive smart structures promise to reduce spacecraft weight and dependence on extensive ground monitoring. A recurrent forward model NN is used as a residual mode filter to augment a traditional reduced-order model (ROM) controller. It was more robust than the feed-forward NN and the traditional-only controller in the presence of unmodeled modes and noisy measurements. Further analyses and hardware implementations will be performed to better quantify this robustness including the sensitivity to the ROM controller mode fidelity, number of output modes, learning rates, measurement-to-state errors, and time quantization effects.

To improve robustness to ROM mode changes a comparison to the dual forward/inverse NN control approach is recommended. The forward model will adjust the search used to train an inverse model which provides control augmentations to the ROM controller. This will enable control searches to occur both off-line faster than real-time using the forward model (i.e. imagination) and on-line using direct search trials with varying noise levels. The forward model will adapt using quality experiences (e.g. via cross validation) which improves inverse models searches. The inverse model reliance on forward model will reduce until forward model prediction errors increase. Future challenges, include solving

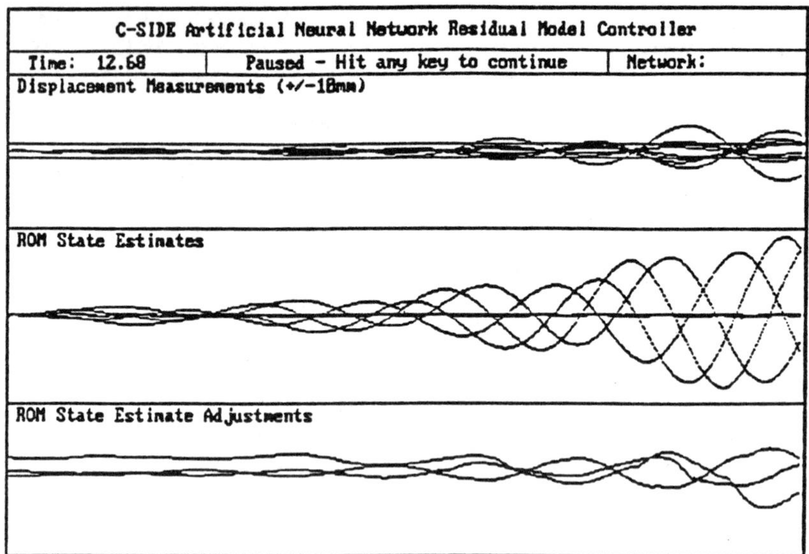

Figure 5: RFM-NN On-Line Learning To Achieve Stable Control

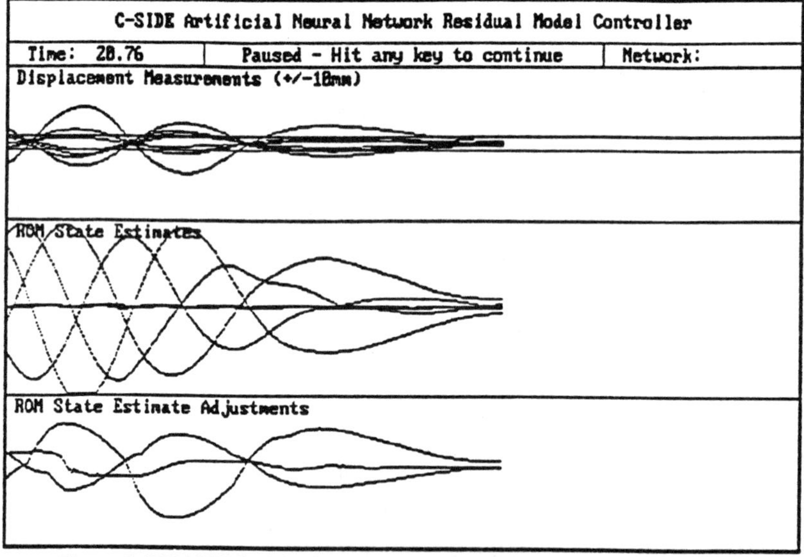

Figure 5: RFM-NN On-Line Learning To Achieve Stable Control (concluded)

the temporal credit assignment problem, partitioning to restricted chip sizes, combining with incomplete a priori knowledge, and balancing adaptivity of response with long-term learning. The goal is to extend stability-dominated, fixed-goal traditional control with adaptive robotic-type neural control to enable better autonomous control where fully-justified fixed models and complete system knowledge are not required. The resultant robust autonomous control will capitalize on the speed of massively parallel analog neural-like computations (e.g. with NN pulse stream chips).

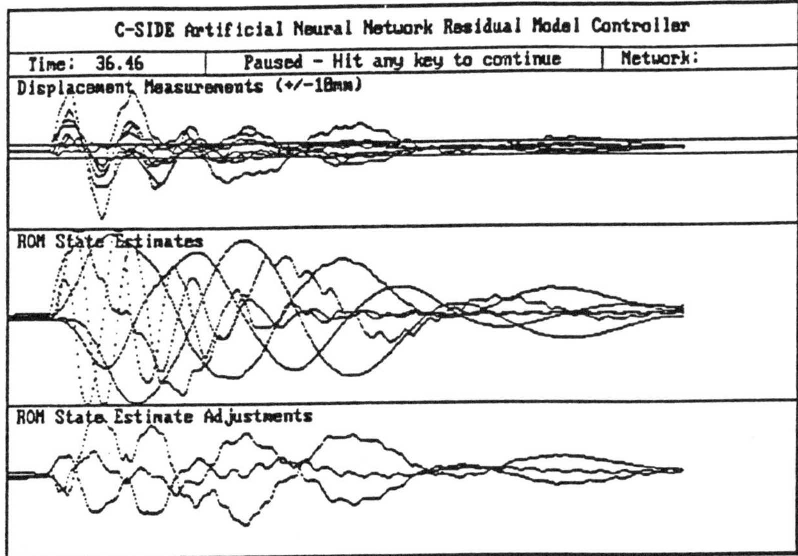

Figure 6: 5 Newton Force Vibration Removed Using RFM-NN Learned Forward Model

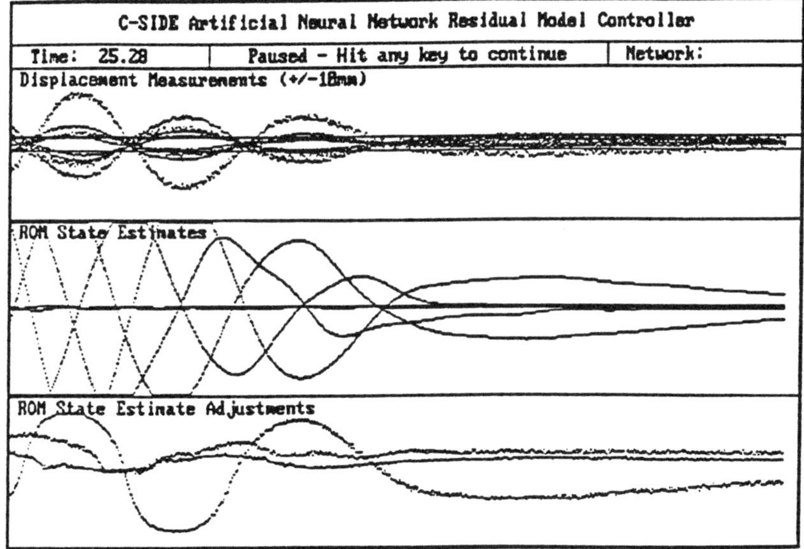

Figure 7: RFM-NN Learning to Remove Vibrations in C-SIDE With ±15% Noisy Displacement Measurements

5 REFERENCES

Barto, A.G., Sutton, R.S., and Watkins, C.J.C.H., *Learning and Sequential Decision Making*, Univ. of Mass. at Amherst COINS Technical Report 89-95, September 1989

Bowman, C.L., *Adaptive Neural Networks Applied to Signal Recognition*, 3rd Tri-Service Data fusion Symposium, May 1989

Brody, Carlos, *Fast Learning With Predictive Forward Models*, Neural Information Processing Systems 4 (NIPS4), 1992

Jorden, M.I., and Jacobs, R.A., *Learning to Control and Unstable System with Forward Modeling*, in D.S. Touretzky, ed., Advances in NIPS 2, Morgan Kaufmann 1990.

Moore, A.W., *Fast, Robust Adaptive Control by Learning Only Forward Models*, NIPS 4, 1992

Mukhopadhyay S. and Narendra, D.S., *Disturbance Rejection in Nonlinear Systems Using Neural Networks* Yale University Report No. 9114 December 1991

Werbos, P., *Architectures For Reinforcement Learning*, in Miller, Sutton and Werbos, ed., Neural Networks for Control, MIT Press 1990

Young, D.D., *Distributed Finite-Element Modeling and Control Approach for Large Flexible Structures*, J. of Guidance, Control and Dynamics, Vol. 13 (4), 703-713, 1990

Integration of Visual and Somatosensory Information for Preshaping Hand in Grasping Movements

Yoji Uno
ATR Human Information Processing
Research Laboratories
2-2 Hikaridai, Seika-cho, Soraku-gun,
Kyoto 619-02, Japan

Naohiro Fukumura*
Faculty of Engineering
University of Tokyo
7-3-1 Hongo, Bunkyo-ku,
Tokyo 113, Japan

Ryoji Suzuki
Faculty of Engineering
University of Tokyo
7-3-1 Hongo, Bunkyo-ku,
Tokyo 113, Japan

Mitsuo Kawato
ATR Human Information Processing
Research Laboratories
2-2 Hikaridai, Seika-cho, Soraku-gun,
Kyoto 619-02, Japan

Abstract

The primate brain must solve two important problems in grasping movements. The first problem concerns the recognition of grasped objects: specifically, how does the brain integrate visual and motor information on a grasped object? The second problem concerns hand shape planning: specifically, how does the brain design the hand configuration suited to the shape of the object and the manipulation task? A neural network model that solves these problems has been developed. The operations of the network are divided into a *learning phase* and an *optimization phase*. In the learning phase, internal representations, which depend on the grasped objects and the task, are acquired by integrating visual and somatosensory information. In the optimization phase, the most suitable hand shape for grasping an object is determined by using a relaxation computation of the network.

*Present Address: Parallel Distributed Processing Research Dept., Sony Corporation, 6-7-35 Kitashinagawa, Shinagawa-ku, Tokyo 141, Japan

1 INTRODUCTION

It has previously been established that, while reaching out to grasp an object, the human hand preshapes according to the shape of the object and the planned manipulation (Jeannerod, 1984; Arbib et al., 1985). The preshaping of the human hand suggests that prior to grasping an object the 3-dimensional form of the object is recognized and the most suitable hand configuration is preset depending on the manipulation task.

It is supposed that the human recognizes objects using not only visual information but also somatosensory information when the hand grasps them. Visual information is made from the 2-dimensional image in the visual system of the brain. Somatosensory information is closely related to motor information, because it depends on the prehensile hand shape (i.e., finger configuration). We hypothesize that an internal representation of a grasped object is formed in the brain by integrating visual and somatosensory information. Some physiological studies support our hypothesis. For example, Taira et al. (1990) found that the activity of *hand-movement-related neurons* in the posterior parietal association cortex were highly selective to the shape and/or the orientation of manipulated switches.

How can the neural network integrate different kinds of information? Merely uniting visual image with somatosensory information does not lead to any interesting representation. Our basic idea is that information compression is applied to integrating different kinds of information. It is useful to extract the essential information by compressing the visual and somatosensory information.

Irie & Kawato (1991) pointed out that multi-layered perceptrons have the ability to extract features from the input signals by compressing the information from input signals. Katayama & Kawato (1990) proposed a learning schema in which an internal representation of the grasped object was acquired using information compression. Developing the schema of Katayama et al., we have devised a neural network model for recognizing objects and planning hand shapes (e.g., Fukumura et al. 1991). This neural network consists of five layers of neurons with only forward connections as shown in Figure 1. The input layer (1st layer) and the output layer (5th layer) of the network have the same structure. There are fewer neurons in the 3rd layer than in the 1st and 5th layers. The operations of the network are divided into the *learning phase*, which is discussed in section 2 and the *optimization phase*, which is discussed in section 3.

2 INTEGRATION OF VISUAL AND SOMATOSENSORY INFORMATION USING NETWORK LEARNING

In the learning phase, the neural network learns the relation between the visual information (i.e.,visual image) and the somatosensory information which, in this paper, is regarded as information on the prehensile hand configuration (i.e., finger configuration).

Both vector $\mathbf{x}$ representing the visual image of an object and vector $\mathbf{y}$ representing the prehensile hand configuration to grasp it are fed into the 1st layer (the input layer). The synaptic weights of the network are repeatedly adjusted so that the 5th layer outputs the same vectors $\mathbf{x}$ and $\mathbf{y}$ as are fed into the 1st layer. In other words, the network comes to realize the **identity map** between the 1st layer and the 5th layer through a learning process. The most important point of the neural network model is that the number of neurons in the 3rd layer is smaller than the number of neurons in the 1st layer (which is equal to the number of neurons in the 5th layer). Therefore, the information from $\mathbf{x}$ and $\mathbf{y}$ is compressed between

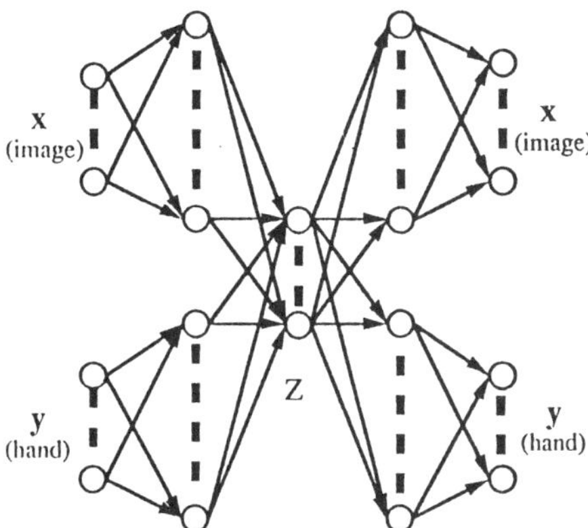

Figure 1: A neural network model for integrating visual image **x** and prehensile hand configuration **y**. The internal representation **z** of a grasped object is acquired in the third layer.

the 1st layer and the 3rd layer, and restored between the 3rd layer and the 5th layer. Once the network learning process is complete, visual image **x** and prehensile hand configuration **y** are integrated in the network. Consequently, the internal representation **z** of the grasped object, which should include enough information to reproduce **x** and **y**, is formed in the 3rd layer.

Prehensile hand configuration in grasping movements were measured and the learning of the network was simulated by a computer. In behavioral experiments, three kinds of wooden objects were prepared: five circular cylinders whose diameters were 3 cm, 4 cm, 5 cm, 6 cm and 7 cm; four quadrangular prisms whose side lengths were 3 cm, 4 cm, 5 cm and 6 cm; and three spheres whose diameters were 3 cm, 4 cm and 5 cm. Data input to the network was comprised of visual image **x** and prehensile hand configuration **y**.

Visual images of objects are formed through complicated processes in the visual system of the brain. For simplicity, however, projections of objects onto a side plane and/or a bottom plane were used instead of real visual images. The area of each pixel of the projected image was fed into the network as an element of visual image **x**. A $DataGlove^{TM}(VPL)$ was used to measure finger configurations in grasping movements. We attached sixteen optical fibers, whose outputs were roughly inversely proportional to finger joint-angles, to the DataGlove. The subject was instructed to grasp the objects on the table tightly with the palm and all the fingers. The subject grasped twelve objects thirty times each, which produced 360 prehensile patterns for use as training data for network learning.

In the computer simulation, six neurons were set in the 3rd layer. The back-propagation learning method was applied in order to modify the synaptic weights in the network. Figure 2 shows the activity of neurons in the 3rd layer after the learning had sufficiently been performed. Some interesting features of the internal representations were found in Figure 2. The first is that the level of neuron activity in the 3rd layer increased monotonically as the size of the object increased. The second is that, except for the magnitude, the neuron activation patterns for the same kinds of objects were almost the same. Furthermore, the activation patterns were similar for circular cylinders and quadrangular prisms, but were quite different for spheres. In other words, similar representations were acquired for similarly shaped objects. We concluded that the internal representations were formed in the 3rd

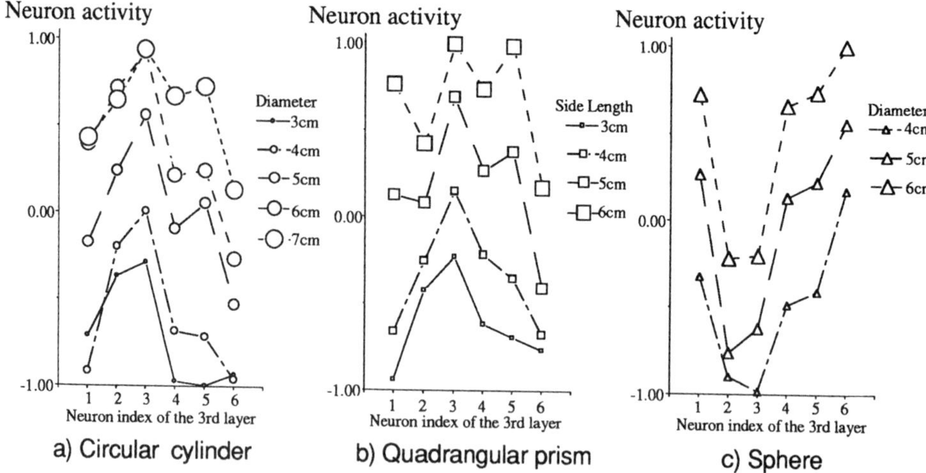

Figure 2: Internal representations of grasped objects. Graph **a)** shows the neuron activation patterns for five circular cylinders whose diameters were 3 cm, 4 cm, 5 cm, 6 cm and 7 cm. Graph **b)** shows the neuron activation patterns for four quadrangular prisms whose side lengths were 3 cm, 4 cm, 5 cm and 6 cm. Finally, Graph **c)** shows the neuron activation patterns for three spheres whose diameters were 3 cm, 4 cm and 5 cm. The abscissa represents the index of the six neurons in the 3rd layer, while the ordinate represents their activity. These values were normalized from -1 to +1.

layer and changed topologically according to the shapes and sizes of the grasped objects.

3 DESIGN OF PREHENSILE HAND SHAPES

The neural network that has completed the learning can design hand shapes to grasp any objects in the optimization phase. Determining prehensile hand shape (i.e., finger configuration) is an ill-posed problem, because there are many ways to grasp any given object. In other words, prehensile hand configuration cannot be determined uniquely for any one object. In order to solve this indeterminacy, a criterion, a measure of performance for any possible prehensile configuration is introduced.

The criterion should normally be defined based on the dynamics of the human hand and the manipulation task. However, for simplicity, the criterion is defined based only on the static configuration of the fingers, which is represented by vector **y**. We assumed that the central nervous system adopts a stable hand configuration to grasp an object, which corresponds to flexing the fingers as much as possible. The output of the DataGlove sensor decreases as finger flexion increases. Therefore, the criterion $C_1(\mathbf{y})$ is defined as follows:

$$C_1(\mathbf{y}) = \frac{1}{2}\sum_i y_i^2, \tag{1}$$

where y_i represents the ith output of the sixteen DataGlove sensors. Minimizing the criterion $C_1(\mathbf{y})$ requires as much finger flexing as possible.

Finding values of y_i ($i = 1, 2, \ldots, 16$) so as to minimize $C_1(\mathbf{y})$ is an optimization problem with constraints. In the optimization phase, the neural network can solve this optimization problem using a relaxation computation as follows. When an object is specified, the visual image $\mathbf{x}^*$ of the object is input to the 1st layer as an input signal and given to the 5th layer as a reference signal. We call neurons in the 1st and the 5th layers which represent visual image $\mathbf{x}$ *image neurons*, and call neurons in the 1st and the 5th layers which represent finger configuration $\mathbf{y}$ *hand neurons*. Let us define the following energy function of the network.

$$E(\mathbf{y}) = \frac{1}{2}\sum_i (x_i^* - x_i')^2 + \frac{1}{2}\sum_j (y_j - y_j')^2 + \lambda \cdot \frac{1}{2}\sum_j y_j^2. \tag{2}$$

Here, x_i^* is the ith element of the image $\mathbf{x}^*$ which is fed into the ith image neuron in the 1st layer, and x_i' is the output of the ith image neuron in the 5th layer. y_j is the activity of the jth hand neuron in the 1st layer, and y_j' is the output of the jth hand neuron in the 5th layer. λ is a positive regularization parameter which decreases gradually during the relaxation computation. The first term and the second term of equation (2) require that the network realizes the identity map between the input layer and the output layer as well as in the learning phase. This requirement guarantees that a hand whose configuration is specified by vector $\mathbf{y}$ can grasp an object whose visual image is $\mathbf{x}^*$. The third term of equation (2) represents the criterion $C_1(\mathbf{y})$. In the optimization phase, the values of the synaptic weights are fixed. Instead, the hand neuron changes its state autonomously while obeying the following differential equation:

$$c\frac{dy_k}{ds} = -\frac{\partial E}{\partial y_k}, \quad k = 1, 2, \ldots, 16. \tag{3}$$

Here, s is the relaxation time required for the state change of the hand neuron, and c is a positive time constant. The right-hand side of equation (3) can be transformed as follows:

$$-\frac{\partial E}{\partial y_k} = \sum_i (x_i^* - x_i')\frac{\partial x_i'}{\partial y_k} + \sum_j (y_j - y_j')\frac{\partial y_j'}{\partial y_k} + (y_k - y_k')\left(\frac{\partial y_k'}{\partial y_k} - 1\right) - \lambda y_k. \tag{4}$$

It is straightforward to show that the first three terms of equation (4) are the error signals at the kth hand neuron, which can be calculated backward from the output layer to the input layer. The fourth term of equation (4) is a suppressive signal which is given to the hand neuron by itself. When the state of the hand neuron obeys the differential equation (3), the time change E can be expressed as :

$$\frac{dE}{ds} = \sum_k \frac{dy_k}{ds}\frac{\partial E}{\partial y_k} = -c\sum_k \left(\frac{dy_k}{ds}\right)^2 \leq 0. \tag{5}$$

Therefore, the energy function E always decreases and the network comes to the equilibrium state that is the (local) minimum energy state. The outputs of the hand neurons in the equilibrium state represent the solution of the optimization problem which corresponds to the most suitable finger configuration.

The relaxation computation of the neural network was simulated. For example, when given the image of a circular cylinder whose diameter was 5 cm, the prehensile finger configuration was computed. After a hundred-thousand iterations for the relaxation computation, we had the results shown in Figure 3. The left sied shows the hand shape that had the minimum value of the criterion of all the training data recorded when the subject grasped a circular cylinder whose diameter was 5 cm. The right side shows the hand shape produced by relaxation computation. These two hand shapes were very similar, which indicated that the network reproduced hand shape by using relaxation computation.

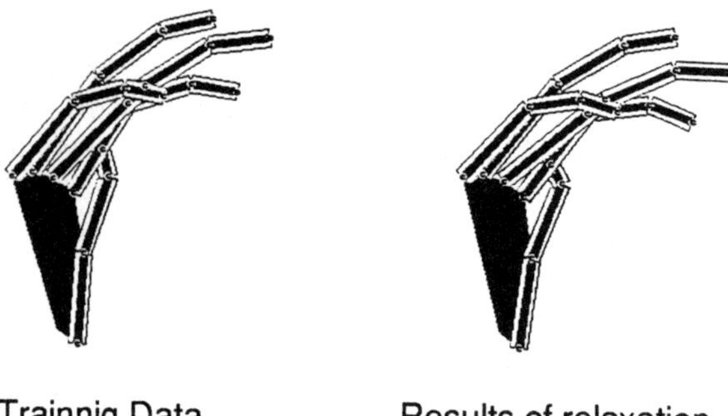

Figure 3: Prehesile hand shapes for grasping a circular cylinder whose diameter was 5cm.

4 VARIOUS TYPES OF PREHENSIONS

In the sections above, the subject was instructed to grasp objects using only one type of prehension. It is, however, thought that a human chooses different types of prehensions depending on the manipulation tasks. In order to investigate the dependence of the internal representation on the type of prehension, the second behavioral experiment was conducted. In this experiment, five circular cylinders and three spheres which were the same size as those in the first experiment were prepared. The subject was first instructed to grasp the objects tightly with his palm and all of his fingers, and then to grasp the same objects with only his fingertips. Iberall et al.(1988) referred to the first prehension and the second prehension as *palm opposition* and *pad opposition*, respectively. The subject grasped eight objects in two different types of prehensions twenty times each, which produced 320 prehensile patterns. Four neurons were set in the 3rd layer of the network and the network learning was simulated using these prehensile patterns as training data. Figure 4 shows the neuronal activation patterns formed in the 3rd layer after the network learning. Even if the grasped objects were the same, the neuron activation pattern for palm opposition was quite different from that for palm opposition.

The neural network can reproduce different prehension, by introducing different criteria. $C_1(\mathbf{y})$ is definded corresponding to palm opposition. Furthermore, we defind another criterion $C_2(\mathbf{y})$, corresponding to pad opposition.

$$C_2(\mathbf{y}) = \sum^{i \epsilon MP,CM} y_i^2 + \sum^{i \epsilon IP} (1.0 - y_j)^2. \tag{6}$$

Minimizing the criterion $C_2(\mathbf{y})$ demands that the MP joints (metacarpophalangeal joints) of the four fingers and the CM joint (carpometacarpal joint) of the thumb be flexed as much as possible and that the IP joints (interphalangeal joints) of all five fingers be stretched as much as possible. The relaxation computation of the neural network was simulated, when given the image of a sphere whose diameter was 5 cm. The results of the relaxation computation are shown in Figure 5. Adopting the different criteria, the neural network reproduced different prehensile hand configurations which corresponded to **a**) palm opposition and **b**) pad opposition.

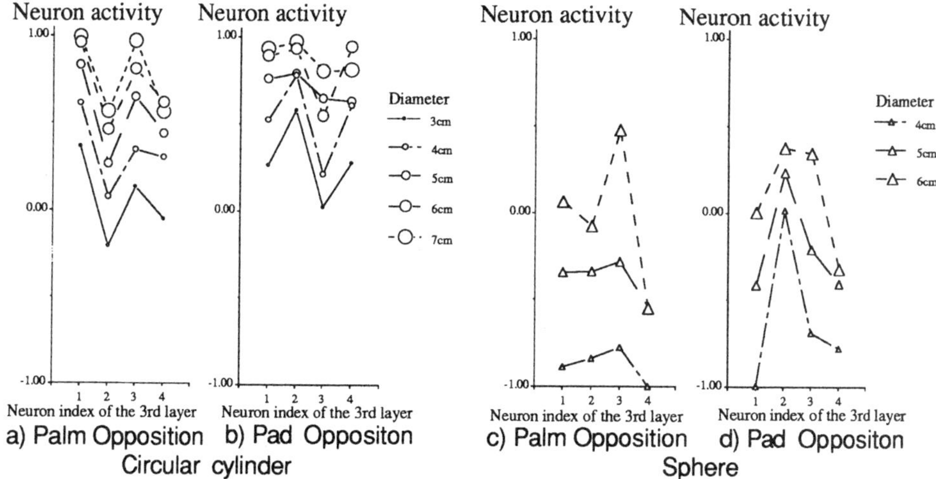

Figure 4: Internal representations of grasped objects formed in the 3rd layer of the network. Graphs **a**), **b**), **c**) and **d**) show the activation patterns of neurons for palm oppositions when grasping 5 circular cylinders, for pad oppositions when grasping 5 circular cylinders, for palm oppositions when grasping 3 spheres and for pad oppositions when grasping 3 spheres, respectively. See Figure 2 legend for description.

5 DISCUSSION

In view of the function of neurons in the posterior parietal association cortex, we have devised a neural network model for integrating visual and motor information. The proposed neural network model is an active sensing model, as it learns only when an object is successfully grasped. In this paper, tactile information is not treated, as the materials of the grasped objects are not considered for simplicity. We know that tactile information plays an important role in the recognition of grasped objects. The neural network model shown in Figure 1 can easily be developed so as to integrate visual, motor and tactile information. However, it is not clear how the internal representations of grasped objects is changed by adding tactile information.

The critical problem in our neural network model is how many neurons should be set in the 3rd layer to represent the shapes of grasped objects. If there are too few neurons in the 3rd layer, the 3rd layer cannot represent enough information to restor $\mathbf{x}$ and $\mathbf{y}$ between the 3rd layer and the 5th layer; that is, the network cannot learn to realize the identity map between the input layer and the output layer. If there are too many neurons in the 3rd layer, the network cannot obtain useful representations of the grasped objects in the 3rd layer and the relaxation computation sometimes fails. In the present stage, we have no method to decide an adequate number of neurons for the 3rd layer. This is an important task for the future.

Acknowledgements

The main part of this study was done while the first author (Y.U.) was working at University of Tokyo. Y. Uno, N. Fukumura and R. Suzuki was supported by Japanese Ministry of

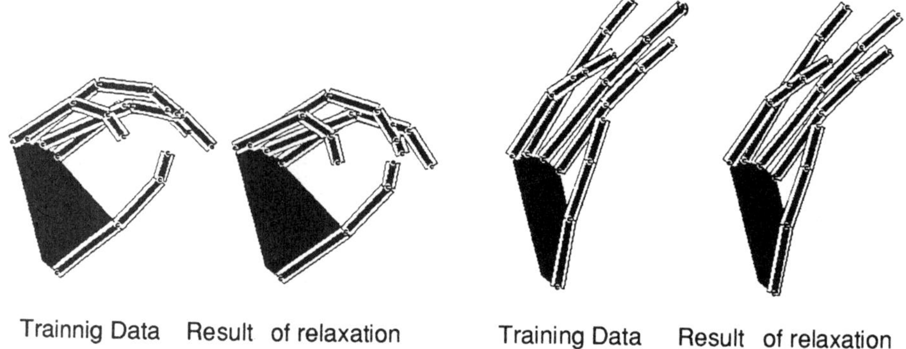

Figure 5: Prehensile hand configuration **a**) for palm opposition and prehensile hand configuration **b**) for pad opposition when grasping a sphere whose diameter was 5 cm. The left sides show the hand shapes with the minimum values of the criterions for all training data recorded when the subject grasped a sphere whose diameter was 5 cm. The right sides show the hand shapes made by the relaxation computation.

Education, Science and Culture Grants, No.03251102 and No.03650338. M. Kawato was supported by Human Frontier Science Project Grant.

References

M. Jeannerod. (1984) The timing of natural prehension movements, *J. Motor Behavior,* **16**: 235-254.

M.A. Arbib, T. Iberall and D. Lyons. (1985) Coordinated control programs for movements of the hand. *Hand Function and the Neocortex. Experimental Brain Research*, suppl.**10**, 111-129.

N. Fukumura, Y. Uno, R. Suzuki and K. Kawato (1991) A neural network model which recognizes shape of a grasped object and decides hand configuration. *Japan IEICE Technical Report,* NC90-104: 213-218 (in Japanese).

Katayama and M. Kawato (1990) Neural network model integrating visual and somatic information. *J. Robotics Society of Japan,* **8**: 117-125 (in Japanese).

T. Iberall (1998) A neural network for planning hand shapes in human prehension. *proc. Automation and controls Conf.*: 2288-2293.

B. Irie and Kawato (1991) "Acquisition of Internal Representation by Multilayered Perceptrons." *Electronics and Communications in Japan,* Part 3, **74**: 112-118.

M. Taira, S. Mine, A.P. Georgopoulos, A. Murata and S. Sakata. (1990) Parietal cortex neurons of the monkey related to the visual guidance of hand movement. *Exp. Brain Res.*, **83**: 29-36.

On-Line Estimation of the Optimal Value Function: HJB-Estimators

James K. Peterson
Department of Mathematical Sciences
Martin Hall Box 341907
Clemson University
Clemson, SC 29634-1907
email: peterson@math.clemson.edu

Abstract

In this paper, we discuss on-line estimation strategies that model the optimal value function of a typical optimal control problem. We present a general strategy that uses local corridor solutions obtained via dynamic programming to provide *local* optimal control sequence training data for a neural architecture model of the optimal value function.

1 ON-LINE ESTIMATORS

In this paper, the problems of adaptive control using neural architectures are explored in the setting of general on-line estimators. We will try to pay close attention to the underlying mathematical structure that arises in the on-line estimation process.

The complete effect of a control action u_k at a given time step t_k is clouded by the fact that the state history depends on the control actions taken after time step t_k. So the effect of a control action over *all future time* must be monitored. Hence, choice of control must inevitably involve knowledge of the future history of the state trajectory. In other words, the optimal control sequence can not be determined until after the fact. Of course, standard optimal control theory supplies an optimal control sequence to this problem for a variety of performance criteria. Roughly, there are two approaches of interest: solving the two-point boundary value problem arising from the solution of Pontryagin's maximum or minimum principle or solving the Hamilton-Jacobi-Bellman (HJB) partial differential equation. However, the computational burdens associated with these schemes may be too high for real-time use. Is it possible to essentially use on-line estimation to build a solution to either of these two classical techniques at a lower cost? In other words, if η samples are taken of the system from some initial point under some initial sequence of control actions, can this time series be use to obtain information about the true optimal sequence of controls that should be used in the next η time steps?

We will focus here on algorithm designs for on-line estimation of the optimal control law that are implementable in a control step time of 20 milliseconds or less. We will use local learning methods such as CMAC (Cerebellar Model Articulated Controllers) architectures (Albus, 1 and W. Miller, 7), and estimators for characterizations of the optimal value function via solutions of the Hamilton-Jacobi-Bellman equation, (adaptive critic type methods), (Barto, 2; Werbos, 12).

2 CLASSICAL CONTROL STRATEGIES

In order to discuss on-line estimation schemes based on the Hamilton- Jacobi-Bellman equation, we now introduce a common sample problem:

$$\min_{u \in \mathcal{U}} \quad \hat{J}(x,u,t) \tag{1}$$

where

$$\hat{J}(x,u,t) = dist(y(t_f),\Gamma) + \int_t^{t_f} L(y(s),u(s),s)\,ds \tag{2}$$

Subject to:

$$y'(s) = f(y(s),u(s),s), \; t \leq s \leq t_f \tag{3}$$

$$y(t) = x \tag{4}$$

$$y(s) \in \mathcal{Y}(s) \subseteq R^N, \; t \leq s \leq t_f \tag{5}$$

$$u(s) \in U(s) \subseteq R^M, \; t \leq s \leq t_f \tag{6}$$

Here y and u are the *state vector* and *control vector* of the system, respectively; $\mathcal{U}$ is the space of functions that the control must be chosen from during the minimization process and (4) - (6) give the initialization and constraint conditions that the state and control must satisfy. The set Γ represents a target constraint set and $dist(y(t_f),\Gamma)$ indicates the distance from the final state $y(t_f)$ to the constraint set Γ. The optimal value of this problem for the initial state x and time t will be denoted by $J(x,t)$ where

$$J(x,t) = \min_u \hat{J}(x,u,t).$$

It is well known that the optimal value function $J(x,t)$ satisfies a generalized partial differential equation known as the Hamilton-Jacobi-Bellman (HJB) equation.

$$
\begin{aligned}
-\frac{\partial J(x,t)}{\partial t} &= \min_u \left\{ L(x,u,t) + \frac{\partial J(x,t)}{\partial x} f(x,u,t) \right\} \\
J(x,t_f) &= dist(x,\Gamma)
\end{aligned}
$$

In the case that J is indeed differentiable with respect to both the state and time arguments, this equation is interpreted in the usual way. However, there are many problems where the optimal value function is not differentiable, even though it is bounded and continuous. In these cases, the optimal value function J can be interpreted as a *viscosity solution* of the HJB equation and the partial derivatives of J are replaced by the *sub* and *superdifferentials* of J (Crandall, 5). In general, once the HJB equation is solved, the optimal control from state x and time t is then given by the minimum condition

$$
u \in arg \min_u \left\{ L(x,u,t) + \frac{\partial J(x,t)}{\partial x} f(x,u,t) \right\}
$$

If the underlying state and time space are discretized using a state mesh of resolution r and a time mesh of resolution s, the HJB equation can be rewritten into the form of the standard Bellman Principle of Optimality (BPO):

$$
J_{rs}(x_i,t_j) = \min_u \{ L(x_i,u,t_j)(t_{j+1}-t_j) + J_{rs}(x(x_i,u),t_{j+1}) \}
$$

where $x(x_i,u)$ indicates the new state achieved by using control u over time interval $[t_j,t_{j+1}]$ from initial state x_i. In practice, this equation is solved by successive iterations of the form:

$$
J_{rs}^{\tau+1}(x_i,t_j) = \min_u \{ L(x_i,u,t_j)(t_{j+1}-t_j) + J_{rs}^{\tau}(x(x_i,u),t_{j+1}) \}
$$

where τ denotes the iteration cycle and the process is started by initializing $J_{rs}^0(x_i,t_j)$ in a suitable manner. Generally, the iterations continue until the values $J_{rs}^{\tau+1}(x_i,t_j)$ and $J_{rs}^{\tau+1}(x_i,t_j)$ differ by negligible amounts. This iterative process is usually referred to as *dynamic programming* (DP). Once this iterative process converges, let $J_{rs}(x_i,t_j) = \lim_{\tau\to\infty} J_{rs}^{\tau}$, and consider $\lim_{(r,s)\to(0,0)} J_{rs}(x_i^r,t_j^s)$, where (x_i^r,t_j^s) indicates that the discrete grid points depend on the resolution (r,s). In many situations, this limit gives the viscosity solution $J(x,t)$ to the HJB equation.

Now consider the problem of finding $J(x,0)$. The Pontryagin minimum principle gives first order necessary conditions that the optimal state x and costate p variables must satisfy. Letting $\hat{H}(x,u,p,t) = L(x,u,t) + p^T f(x,u,t)$ and defining

$$H(x,p,t) = \min_u \hat{H}(x,u,p,t), \tag{7}$$

the optimal state and costate then must satisfy the following two-point boundary value problem (TPBVP):

$$\begin{array}{ll} x'(t) = \frac{\partial H(x,p,t)}{\partial p}, & p'(t) = -\frac{\partial H(x,p,t)}{\partial x} \\ x(0) = x, & p(t_f) = 0 \end{array} \tag{8}$$

and the optimal control is obtained from (7) once the optimal state and costate are determined. Note that (7) can not necessarily be solved for the control u in terms of x and p, i.e. a feedback law may not be possible. If the TPBVP can not be solved, then we set $J(x,0) = \infty$. In conclusion, in this problem, we are led inevitably to an optimal value function that can be poorly behaved; hence, we can easily imagine that at many (x,t), $\frac{\partial J}{\partial x}$ is not available and hence J will not satisfy the HJB equation in the usual sense. So if we estimate J directly using some form of on-line estimation, how can we hope to back out the control law if $\frac{\partial J}{\partial x}$ is not available?

3 HJB ESTIMATORS

A potential on-line estimation technique can be based on approximations of the optimal value function. Since the optimal value function should satisfy the HJB equation, these methods will be grouped under the broad classification **HJB estimators**.

Assume that there is a given initial state x_0 with start time 0. Consider a local patch, or *local corridor*, of the state space around the initial state x_0, denoted by $\Omega(x_0)$. The exact size of $\Omega(x_0)$ will depend on the nature of the state dynamics and the starting state. If $\Omega(x_0)$ is then discretized using a coarse grid of resolution r and the time domain is discretized using resolution s, an approximate dynamic programming problem can be formulated and solved using the BPO equations. Since the new states obtained via integration of the plant dynamics will in general not land on coarse grid lines, some sort of interpolation must be used to assign the integrated new state value an appropriate coarse grid value. This can be done using the coarse encoding implied by the grid resolution r of $\Omega(x_0)$. In addition, multiple grid resolutions may be used with coarse and fine grid approximations interacting with one another as in multigrid schemes (Briggs, 3). The optimal value function so obtained will be denoted by $J_{rs}(z_i, t_j)$ for any discrete grid point $z_i \in \Omega(x_0)$ and time point t_j. This approximate solution also supplies an estimate of the optimal control sequence $(u^*)_{ij}^{\eta-1} \equiv (u^*)_j^{\eta-1}(z_i, t_j)$. Some papers on approximate dynamic programming are (Peterson, 8; (Sutton, 10; Luus, 6). It is also possible to obtain estimates of the optimal control sequences, states and costates using an η step look-ahead and the Pontryagin minimum principle. The associated two point boundary value problem is solved and the controls computed via $u_i \in arg\min_u \hat{H}(x_i^*, u, p_i^*, t_i)$ where $(x^*)_0^\eta$ and $(p^*)_0^\eta$ are the calculated optimal state and costate sequences respectively. This approach is developed in (Peterson, 9) and implementated for vibration suppression in a large space structure, by (Carlson, Rothermel and Lee, 4)

For any $z_i \in \Omega(x_0)$, let $(u)_{ij}^{\eta-1} \equiv (u)_j^{\eta-1}(z_i, t_j)$ be a control sequence used from initial state z_i and time point t_j. Thus u_{ij} is the control used on time interval $[t_j, t_{j+1}]$ from start point z_i. Define $z_{ij}^{j+1} \equiv z(z_i, u_{ij}, t_j)$, the state obtained by integrating the plant dynamics one time step using control u_{ij} and initial state z_i. Then $u_{i,j+1}$ is the control used on time interval $[t_{j+1}, t_{j+2}]$ from start point z_{ij}^{j+1} and the new state is $z_{ij}^{j+2} \equiv z(z_{ij}^{j+1}, u_{i,j+1}, t_{j+1})$; in general, $u_{i,j+k}$ is the control used on time interval $[t_{j+k}, t_{j+k+1}]$ from start point z_{ij}^{j+k} and the new state is $z_{ij}^{j+k+1} \equiv z(z_{ij}^{j+k}, u_{i,j+k}, t_{j+k})$, where $z_{ij}^{j} \equiv z_i$.

Let's now assume that optimal control information u_{ij} (we will dispense with the superscript $*$ labeling for expositional cleanness) is available at each of the discrete grid points $(z_i, t_j) \in \Omega(x_0)$. Let $\phi_{rs}(z_i, t_j)$ denote the value of a neural architecture (CMAC, feedforward, associative etc.) which is trained as follows using this optimal information for $0 \leq k < \eta - j - 1$ (the equation below holds for the converged value of the network's parameters and the actual dependence of the network on those parameters is notationally suppressed):

$$\phi_{rs}(z_{ij}^{j+k}, t_{j+k}) = \xi \phi_{rs}(z_{ij}^{j+k+1}, t_{j+k+1}) + \zeta \Re(z_{ij}^{j+k}, u_{i,j+k}) \tag{9}$$

where $0 < \xi, \zeta \leq 1$ and we define a typical reinforcement function $\Re$ by

$$\Re(z_{ij}^{j+k}, u_{i,j+k}, t_{j+k}, t_{j+k+1}) = \tag{10}$$

$$\begin{cases} L(z_{ij}^{j+k}, u_{i,j+k}, t_{j+k})(t_{j+k+1} - t_{j+k}) & \text{if } j \leq k < \eta - j - 1 \\ L(z_{ij}^{\eta-1}, u_{i,\eta-1}, t_{\eta-1})(t_\eta - t_{\eta-1}) & \text{if } k = \eta - 1 \\ \quad + dist(z_{ij}^{\eta}, \Gamma) & \end{cases} \tag{11}$$

For notational convenience, we will now drop the notational dependence on the time grid points and simply refer to the reinforcement by $\Re(z_{ij}^{j+k}, u_{i,j+k})$

Then applying (9) repeatedly, for any $0 \leq p \leq \eta - i$,

$$\phi_{rs}(z_i, t_j) = \xi^p \phi_{rs}(z_{ij}^{j+p}, t_{j+p}) + \zeta \sum_{k=0}^{p-1} \xi^k \Re(z_{ij}^{j+k}, u_{i,j+k}) \tag{12}$$

Thus, the function Ψ_{rs} can be defined by

$$\begin{aligned} \Psi_{rs}(z_i, t_j, \xi, \zeta) &= (\zeta)^{-1} \phi_{rs}(z_i, t_j) - \xi^p \phi_{rs}(z_{ij}^{\eta}, t_\eta) \\ &= \sum_{k=0}^{\eta-j-1} \xi^k \Re(z_{ij}^{j+k}, u_{i,j+k}), \end{aligned}$$

where the term $u_{j\eta}$ will be interpreted as $u_{j,\eta-1}$.

It follows then that since u_{ij} is optimal,

$$\Psi_{rs}(z_i, t_j, 1, 1) \quad = \quad J_{rs}(z_i, t_j)$$

Clearly, the function $\Phi_{rs}(z_i, t_j) = \Psi_{rs}(z_i, t_j, 1, 1)$ estimates the optimal value $J_{rs}(z_i, t_j)$ itself. (See, Q-Learning (Watkins, 11)).

An alternate approach that does not model J indirectly, as is done above, is to train a neural model $\Phi_{rs}(z_i, t_j)$ directly on the data $J(z_i, t_j)$ that is computed in each local corridor calculation. In either case, the above observations lead to the following algorithm:

Initialization:

Here, the iteration count is $\tau = 0$. For given starting state x_0 and local look ahead of η time steps, form the local corridor $\Omega(x_0)$ and solve the associated approximate BPO equation for $J_{rs}(z_i, t_j)$. Compute the associated optimal control sequences for each (z_i, t_j) pair, $(u^*)_{ij}^{\eta-1} \equiv (u^*)_j^{\eta-1}(z_i, t_j)$. Initialize the neural architecture for the optimal value estimate using $\Phi_{rs}^0(z_i, t_j) = J_{rs}(z_i, t_j)$.

Estimate of New Optimal Control Sequence:

For the next η time steps, an estimate must be made of the next optimal control action in time interval $[t_{\eta+k}, t_{\eta+k+1}]$. The initial state is any z_i in $\Omega(x_\eta)$ (x_η is one such choice) and the initial time is t_η. For the time interval $[t_\eta, t_{\eta+1}]$, if the model $\Phi_{rs}^0(z_i, t_j)$ is differentiable, the new control can be estimated by

$$\hat{u}_{\eta+1} \quad \in \quad arg \min_u \left\{ \begin{array}{l} L(z_\eta, u, t_\eta)(t_{\eta+1} - t_\eta) \\ +\frac{\partial \Phi_{rs}^0}{\partial x}(z_\eta, t_\eta) \\ f(z_\eta, u, t_\eta)(t_{\eta+1} - t_\eta) \end{array} \right\}$$

For ease of notation, let $z_{\eta+1}$ denote the new state obtained using the control $u_{\eta+1}$ on the interval $[t_\eta, t_{\eta+1}]$. Then choose the next control via

$$\hat{u}_{\eta+2} \quad \in \quad arg \min_u \left\{ \begin{array}{l} L(z_{\eta+1}, u, t_{\eta+1})(t_{\eta+2} - t_{\eta+1}) \\ +\frac{\partial \Phi_{rs}^0}{\partial x}(z_{\eta+1}, t_{\eta+1}) \\ f(z_{\eta+1}, u, t_{\eta+1})(t_{\eta+2} - t_{\eta+1}) \end{array} \right\}$$

Clearly, if $z_{\eta+k}$ denote the new state obtained using the control $u_{\eta+k-1}$ on the interval $[t_{\eta+k}, t_{\eta+k+1}]$, the next control is chosen to satisfy

$$\hat{u}_{\eta+k} \quad \in \quad arg \min_u \left\{ \begin{array}{l} L(z_{\eta+k}, u, t_{\eta+k})(t_{\eta+k+1} - t_{\eta+k}) \\ +\frac{\partial \Phi_{rs}^0}{\partial x}(z_{\eta+k}, t_{\eta+k}) \\ f(z_{\eta+k}, u, t_{\eta+k})(t_{\eta+k+1} - t_{\eta+k}) \end{array} \right\}$$

Alternately, if the neural architecture is not differentiable (that is $\frac{\partial \Phi^0_{rs}}{\partial x}$ is not available), the new control action can be computed via

$$\hat{u}_{\eta+k} \in arg \min_u \left\{ \begin{array}{l} L(z_{\eta+k}, u, t_{\eta+k})(t_{\eta+k+1} - t_{\eta+k}) \\ +\Phi^0_{rs}(z_{\eta+k}(u), t_{\eta+k+1}) \end{array} \right\}.$$

Update of the Neural Estimator:

The new starting point for the dynamics is now x_η and there is a new associated local corridor $\Omega(x_\eta)$. The neural estimator is then updated using either the HJB or the BPO equations over the local corridor $\Omega(x_\eta)$. Using the BPO equations, for all $z_i \in \Omega(x_\eta)$ the updates are:

$$\Phi^1_{rs}(z_i, t_{\eta+j}) = \min_u \{L(z_i, u, t_{\eta+j})(t_{\eta+j+1} - t_{\eta+j}) + \Phi^0_{rs}(z_i, t_{\eta+j})\}$$

where $(\hat{u})^{\eta-1}_j$ indicates the optimal control estimates obtained in the previous algorithm step. Finally, using the HJB equation, for all $z_i \in \Omega(x_\eta)$ the updates are:

$$\Phi^1_{rs}(z_i, t_{\eta+j}) = \Phi^0_{rs}(z_i, t_{\eta+j+1}) + \min_u \left\{ \begin{array}{l} L(z_i, u, t_{\eta+j})(t_{\eta+j+1} - t_{\eta+j}) \\ +\frac{\partial \Phi^0_{rs}}{\partial x}(z_i, t_{\eta+j}) \\ f(z_i, u, t_{\eta+j})(t_{\eta+j+1} - t_{\eta+j}) \end{array} \right\}$$

Comparison to BPO optimal control sequence:

Now solve the associated approximate BPO equation for each z_i in the local corridor $\Omega(x_\eta)$ for $J_{rs}(z_i, t_{\eta+j})$. Compute the new approximate optimal control sequences for each $(z_i, t_{\eta+j})$ pair, $(u^*)^{2\eta-1}_{\eta+j} \equiv (u^*)^{2\eta-1}_{\eta+j}(z_i, t_{\eta+j})$ and compare them to the estimated sequences $(\hat{u})^{2\eta-1}_{\eta+j}$. If the discrepancy is out of tolerance (this is a design decision) initialize the neural architecture for the optimal value estimate using $\Phi^1_{rs}(z_i, t_{\eta+i}) = J_{rs}(z_i, t_{\eta+j})$. If the discrepancy is acceptable, terminate the BPO approximation calculations for M future iterations and use the neural architectures alone for on-line estimation.

The determination of the stability and convergence properties of any on-line approximation procedure of this sort is intimately connected with the the optimal value function which solves the generalized HJB equation. We conjecture the following limit converges to a viscosity solution of the HJB equation for the given optimal control problem:

$$lim_{(r,s)\to(0,0)} lim_{\tau\to\infty} \Phi^\tau_{rs}(x^r_i, t^s_j) = J(x,t)$$

Further, there are stability questions and there are interesting issues relating to the use of multiple state resolutions r_1 and r_2 and the corresponding different approximations to J, leading to the use of multigrid like methods on the HJB equation (see, for example, Briggs, 3). Also note that there is an advantage to using CMAC architectures for the approximation of the optimal value function J; since J need not be smooth, the CMAC's lack of differentiability with respect to its inputs is not a problem and in fact is a virtue.

Acknowledgements

We acknowledge the partial support of NASA grant NAG 3-1311 from the Lewis Research Center.

References

1. Albus, J. 1975. "A New Approach to Manipulator Control: The Cerebellar Model Articulation Controller (CMAC)." *J. Dynamic Systems, Measurement and Control*, 220 - 227.
2. Barto, A., R. Sutton, C. Anderson. 1983 "Neuronlike Adaptive Elements That Can Solve Difficult Learning Control Problems." *IEEE Trans. Systems, Man Cybernetics*, Vol. SMC-13, No. 5, September/October, 834 - 846.
3. Briggs, W. 1987. **A Multigrid Tutorial**, SIAM, Philadelphia, PA.
4. Carlson, R., C. Lee and K. Rothermel. 1992. "Real Time Neural Control of an Active Structure", **Artificial Neural Networks in Engineering 2**, 623 - 628.
5. Crandall, M. and P. Lions. 1983. "Viscosity solutions of Hamilton-Jacobi Equations." *Trans. American Math. Soc.*, Vol. 277, No. 1, 1 - 42.
6. Luus, R. 1990. "Optimal Control by Dynamic Programming Using Systematic Reduction of Grid Size", *Int. J. Control*, Vol. 51, No. 5, 995 - 1013.
7. Miller, W. 1987. "Sensor-Based Control of Robotic Manipulators Using as General Learning Algorithm." *IEEE J. Robot. Automat.*, Vol RA-3, No. 2, 157 - 165
8. Peterson, J. 1992. "Neural Network Approaches to Estimating Directional Cost Information and Path Planning in Analog Valued Obstacle Fields", *HEURISTICS: The Journal of Knowledge Engineering*, Special Issue on Artificial Neural Networks, Vol. 5, No. 2, Summer, 50 - 61.
9. Peterson, J. 1992. "On-Line Estimation of Optimal Control Sequences: Pontryagin Estimators", **Artificial Neural Networks in Engineering 2**, ed. Dagli et. al., 579 - 584.
10. Sutton, R. 1991. "Planning by Incremental Dynamic Programming", *Proceedings of the Ninth International Workshop on Machine Learning*, 353 - 357.
11. Watkins, C. 1989. **Learning From Delayed Rewards**, Ph. D. Dissertation, King's College.
12. Werbos, P. 1990. "A Menu of Designs for Reinforcement Learning Over Time". In **Neural Networks for Control**, Ed. Miller, W. R. Sutton and P. Werbos, 67 - 96.

Learning Control Under Extreme Uncertainty

Vijaykumar Gullapalli
Computer Science Department
University of Massachusetts
Amherst, MA 01003

Abstract

A peg-in-hole insertion task is used as an example to illustrate the utility of direct associative reinforcement learning methods for learning control under real-world conditions of uncertainty and noise. Task complexity due to the use of an unchamfered hole and a clearance of less than $0.2mm$ is compounded by the presence of positional uncertainty of magnitude exceeding 10 to 50 times the clearance. Despite this extreme degree of uncertainty, our results indicate that direct reinforcement learning can be used to learn a robust reactive control strategy that results in skillful peg-in-hole insertions.

1 INTRODUCTION

Many control tasks of interest today involve controlling complex nonlinear systems under uncertainty and noise.[1] Because traditional control design techniques are not very effective under such circumstances, methods for learning control are becoming increasingly popular. Unfortunately, in many of these control tasks, it is difficult to obtain training information in the form of prespecified instructions on how to perform the task. Therefore supervised learning methods are not directly applicable. At the same time, evaluating the performance of a controller on the task is usually fairly straightforward, and hence these tasks are ideally suited for the application of *associative reinforcement learning* (Barto & Anandan, 1985).

[1] For our purposes, noise can be regarded simply as one of the sources of uncertainty.

In associative reinforcement learning, the learning system's interactions with its environment are evaluated by a critic, and the goal of the learning system is to learn to respond to each input with the action that has the best expected evaluation. In learning control tasks, the learning system is the controller, its actions are control signals, and the critic's evaluations are based on the performance criterion associated with the control task. Two kinds of associative reinforcement learning methods, direct and indirect, can be distinguished (e.g., Gullapalli, 1992). Indirect reinforcement learning methods construct and use a model of the environment and the critic (modeled either separately or together), while direct reinforcement learning methods do not.

We have previously argued (Gullapalli, 1992; Barto & Gullapalli, 1992) that in the presence of uncertainty, hand-crafting or learning an adequate model—imperative if one is to use indirect methods for training the controller—can be very difficult. Therefore, it can be expeditious to use direct reinforcement learning methods in such situations. In this paper, a peg-in-hole insertion task is used as an example to illustrate the utility of direct associative reinforcement learning methods for learning control under real-world conditions of uncertainty.

2 PEG-IN-HOLE INSERTION

Peg-in-hole insertion has been widely used by roboticists for testing various approaches to robot control and has also been studied as a canonical robot assembly operation (Whitney, 1982; Gustavson, 1984; Gordon, 1986). Although the abstract peg-in-hole task can be solved quite easily, real-world conditions of uncertainty due to (1) errors and noise in sensory feedback, (2) errors in execution of motion commands, and (3) uncertainty due to movement of the part grasped by the robot can substantially degrade the performance of traditional control methods. Approaches proposed for peg-in-hole insertion under uncertainty can be grouped into two major classes: methods based on off-line planning, and methods based on reactive control.

Off-line planning methods combine geometric analysis of the peg-hole configuration with analysis of the task statics to determine motion strategies that will result in successful insertion (Whitney, 1982; Gustavson, 1984; Gordon, 1986). In the presence of uncertainty in sensing and control, researchers have suggested incorporating the uncertainty into the geometric model of the task in configuration space (e.g., Lozano-Perez et al., 1984; Erdmann, 1986; Caine et al., 1989; Donald, 1986). Off-line planning is based on the assumption that a realistic characterization of the margins of uncertainty is available, which is a strong assumption when dealing with real-world systems.

Methods based on reactive control, in comparison, try to counter the effects of uncertainty with on-line modification of the motion control based on sensory feedback. Often, *compliant* motion control is used, in which the trajectory is modified by contact forces or tactile stimuli occurring during the motion. The compliant behavior either is actively generated or occurs passively due to the physical characteristics of the robot (Whitney, 1982; Asada, 1990). However, as Asada (1990) points out, many tasks including the peg insertion task require complex nonlinear compliance or admittance behavior that is beyond the capability of a passive mechanism. Unfortunately, humans find it quite difficult to prespecify appropriate compliant behavior (Lozano-Perez et al., 1984), especially in the presence of uncertainty. Hence techniques for learning compliant behavior can be very useful.

We demonstrate our approach to learning a reactive control strategy for peg-in-hole insertion by training a controller to perform peg-in-hole insertions using a Zebra Zero robot. The Zebra Zero is equipped with joint position encoders and a six-axis force sensor at its wrist, whose outputs are all subject to uncertainty. Before describing the controller and presenting its performance in peg insertion, we present some experimental data quantifying the uncertainty in position and force sensors.

3 QUANTIFYING THE SENSOR UNCERTAINTY

In order to quantify the position uncertainty under varying load conditions similar to those that occur when the peg is interacting with the hole, we compared the sensed peg position with its actual position in cartesian space under different load conditions. In one such experiment, the robot was commanded to maintain a fixed position under five different loads conditions applied sequentially: no load, and a fixed load of 0.12Kgf applied in the $\pm x$ and $\pm y$ directions. Under each condition, the position and force feedback from the robot sensors, as well as the actual x-y position of the peg were recorded.

The sensed and actual x-y positions of the peg are shown in Table 1. The sensed x-y positions were computed from the joint positions sensed by the Zero's joint position encoders. As can be seen from the table, there is a large discrepancy between the sensed and actual positions of the peg: while the actual change in the peg's position under the external load was of the order of 2 to $3mm$, the largest sensed change in position was less than $0.025mm$. In comparison, the clearance between the peg and the hole (in the 3D task) was $0.175mm$. From observations of the robot, we could determine that the uncertainty in position was primarily due to gear backlash. Other factors affecting the uncertainty include the posture of the robot arm, which affects the way the backlash is loaded, and interactions between the peg and the environment.

Table 1: Sensed And Actual Positions Under 5 Different Load Conditions

Load Condition	Sensed x-y Position (mm)	Actual x-y Position (mm)
No load position	(0.0, 0.000000)	(0.0, 0.0)
With $-y$ load	$(0.0, -0.014673)$	$(0.0, -2.5)$
With $+x$ load	$(0.0, 0.000000)$	$(1.9, -0.3)$
With $+y$ load	$(0.0, 0.024646)$	$(-2.9, -0.2)$
With $-x$ load	$(0.0, 0.010026)$	$(0.3, 2.2)$
Final (no load) position	$(0.0, 0.000000)$	$(0.0, -0.6)$

Figure 1 shows 30 time-step samples of the force sensor output for each of the load conditions described above. As can be seen from the figure, there is considerable sensor noise, especially in recording moments. Although designing a controller that can robustly perform peg insertions despite the large uncertainty in sensory input is difficult, our results indicate that a controller can learn a robust peg insertion strategy.

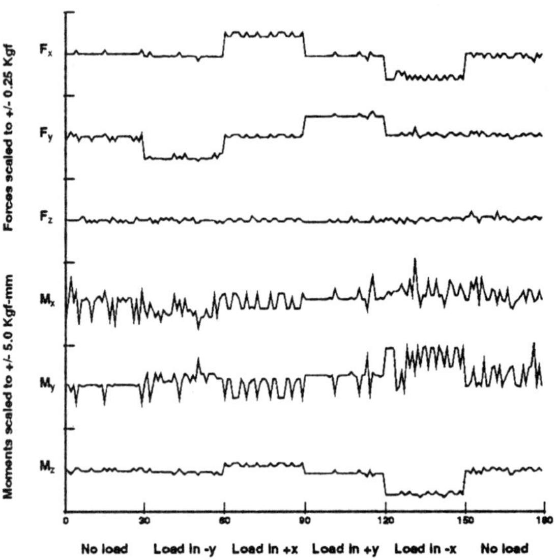

Figure 1: 30 Time-step Samples Of The Sensed Forces and Moments Under 5 Different Load Conditions. With An Ideal Sensor, The Readings Would Be Constant In Each 30 Time-step Interval.

4 LEARNING PEG-IN-HOLE INSERTION

Our approach to learning a reactive control strategy for peg insertion under uncertainty is based on active generation of compliant behavior using a nonlinear mapping from sensed positions and forces to position commands.[2] The controller learns this mapping through repeated attempts at peg insertion.

The Peg Insertion Tasks As depicted in Figure 2, both 2D and 3D versions of the peg insertion task were attempted. In the 2D version of the task, the peg used was $50mm$ long and $22.225mm$ $(7/8in)$ wide, while the hole was $23.8125mm$ $(15/16in)$ wide. Thus the clearance between the peg and the hole was $0.79375mm$ $(1/32in)$. In the 3D version, the peg used was $30mm$ long and $6mm$ in diameter, while the hole was $6.35mm$ in diameter. Thus the clearance in the 3D case was $0.175mm$.

The Controller The controller was implemented as a connectionist network that operated in closed loop with the robot so that it could learn a reactive control strategy for performing peg insertions. The network used in the 2D task had 6 inputs, viz., the sensed positions and forces, (X, Y, Θ) and (F_x, F_y, M_z), three

[2]See also (Gullapalli et al., 1992).

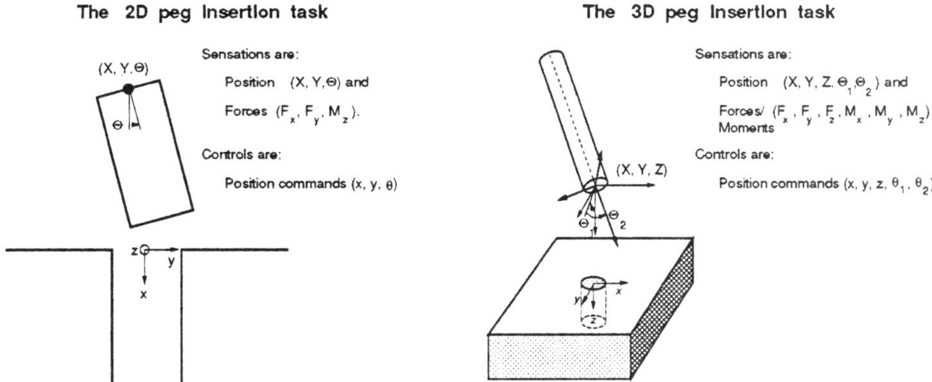

Figure 2: The 2D And 3D Peg-in-hole Insertion Tasks.

outputs forming the position command (x, y, θ), and two hidden layers of 15 units each. For the 3D task, the network had 11 inputs, the sensed positions and forces, $(X, Y, Z, \Theta_1, \Theta_2)$ and $(F_x, F_y, F_z, M_x, M_y, M_z)$, five outputs forming the position command $(x, y, z, \theta_1, \theta_2)$, and two hidden layers of 30 units each.

In both networks, the hidden units used were back-propagation units, while the output units used were stochastic real-valued (SRV) reinforcement learning units (Gullapalli, 1990). SRV units use a direct reinforcement learning algorithm to find the best real-valued output for each input (see Gullapalli (1990) for details). The position inputs to the network were computed from the sensed joint positions using the forward kinematics equations for the Zero. The force and moment inputs were those sensed by the six-axis force sensor. A PD servo loop was used to servo the robot to the position output by the network at each time step.

Training Methodology The controller network was trained in a sequence of trials, each of which started with the peg at a random position and orientation with respect to the hole and ended either when the peg was successfully inserted in the hole, or when 100 time steps had elapsed. An insertion was termed successful when the peg was inserted to a depth of $25mm$ into the hole. At each time step during training, the sensed peg position and forces were input to the network, and the computed control output was executed by the robot, resulting in some motion of the peg. An evaluation of the controller's performance, r, ranging from 0 to 1 with 1 denoting the best possible evaluation, was computed based on the new peg position and the forces acting on the peg as

$$r = \begin{cases} \max(0.0, 1.0 - 0.01\|\text{position error}\|) & \text{if all forces} \leq 0.5\text{Kgf}, \\ \max(0.0, 1.0 - 0.01\|\text{position error}\| - 0.1F_{\max}) & \text{otherwise}, \end{cases}$$

where $F_{\max}$ denotes the largest magnitude force component. Thus, the closer the sensed peg position was to the desired position with the peg inserted in the hole, the higher the evaluation. Large sensed forces, however, reduced the evaluation. Using this evaluation, the network adjusted its weights appropriately and the cycle was repeated.

5 PERFORMANCE RESULTS

A learning curve showing the final evaluation over 500 consecutive trials on the 2D task is shown in Figure 3 (a). The final evaluation levels off close to 1 after about

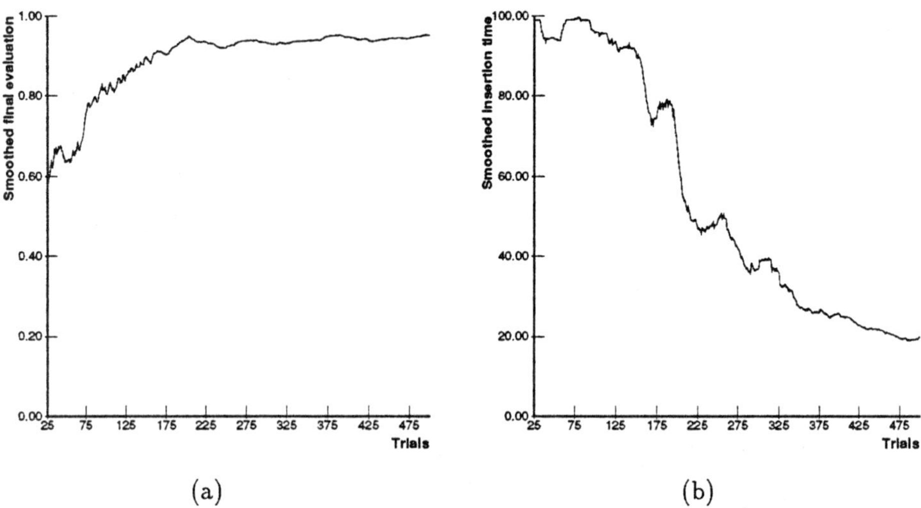

Figure 3: Smoothed Final Evaluation Received And Smoothed Insertion Time (In Simulation Time Steps) Taken On Each Of 500 Consecutive Trials On The 2D Peg Insertion Task. The Smoothed Curve Was Obtained By Filtering The Raw Data Using A Moving-Average Window Of 25 Consecutive Values.

150 trials because after that amount of training, the controller is consistently able to perform successful insertions within 100 time steps. However, performance as measured by insertion time continues to improve, as is indicated by the learning curve in Figure 3 (b), which shows the time to insertion decreasing continuously over the 500 trials. These curves indicate that the controller becomes progressively more *skillful* at peg insertion with training. Similar results were obtained for the 3D task, although learning was slower in this case. The performance curves for the 3D task are shown in Figure 4.

6 DISCUSSION AND CONCLUSIONS

The high degree of uncertainty in the sensory feedback from the Zebra Zero, coupled with the fine motion control requirements of peg-in-hole insertion make the task under consideration an example of learning control under extreme uncertainty. The positional uncertainty, in particular, is of the order of 10 to 50 times the clearance between the peg and the hole and is primarily due to gear backlash. There is also significant uncertainty in the sensed forces and moments due to sensor noise. Our results indicate that direct reinforcement learning can be used to learn a reactive control strategy that works robustly even in the presence of a high degree of uncertainty.

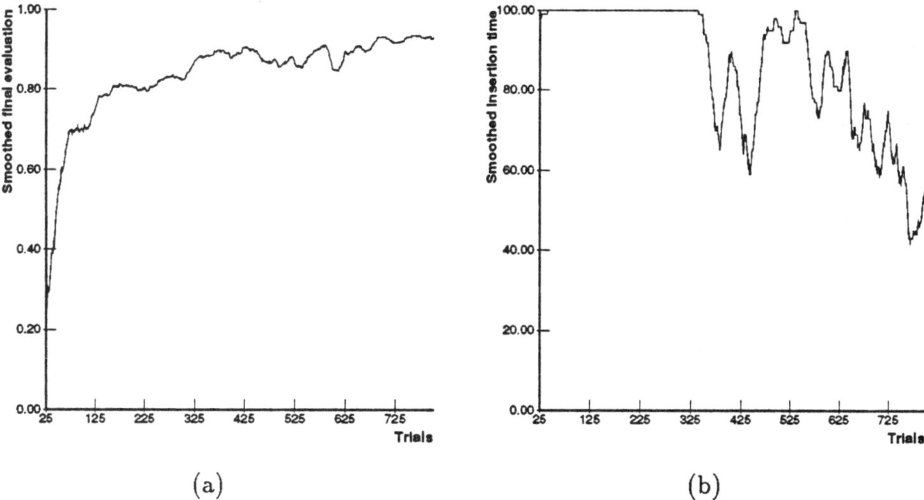

(a) (b)

Figure 4: Smoothed Final Evaluation Received And Smoothed Insertion Time (In Simulation Time Steps) Taken On Each Of 800 Consecutive Trials On The 3D Peg Insertion Task. The Smoothed Curve Was Obtained By Filtering The Raw Data Using A Moving-Average Window Of 25 Consecutive Values.

Although others have studied similar tasks, in most other work on learning peg-in-hole insertion (e.g., Lee & Kim, 1988) it is assumed that the positional uncertainty is about an order of magnitude *less* than the clearance. Moreover, results are often presented using simulated peg-hole systems. Our results indicate that our approach works well with a physical system, despite the much higher magnitudes of noise and consequently greater degree of uncertainty inherent in dealing with physical systems. Furthermore, the success of the direct reinforcement learning approach to training the controller indicates that this approach can be useful for automatically synthesizing robot control strategies that satisfy constraints encoded in the performance evaluations.

Acknowledgements

This paper has benefited from many useful discussions with Andrew Barto and Roderic Grupen. I would also like to thank Kamal Souccar for assisting with running the Zebra Zero. This material is based upon work supported by the Air Force Office of Scientific Research, Bolling AFB, under Grant AFOSR-89-0526 and by the National Science Foundation under Grant ECS-8912623.

References

[1] H. Asada. Teaching and learning of compliance using neural nets: Representation and generation of nonlinear compliance. In *Proceedings of the 1990 IEEE International Conference on Robotics and Automation*, pages 1237–1244, 1990.

[2] A. G. Barto and P. Anandan. Pattern recognizing stochastic learning automata. *IEEE Transactions on Systems, Man, and Cybernetics*, 15:360–375, 1985.

[3] A. G. Barto and V. Gullapalli. Neural Networks and Adaptive Control. In P. Rudomin, M. A. Arbib, and F. Cervantes-Perez, editors, *Natural and Artificial Intelligence. Research Notes in Neural Computation*, Springer-Verlag: Washington. (in press).

[4] M. E. Caine, T. Lozano-Pérez, and W. P. Seering. Assembly strategies for chamferless parts. In *Proceedings of the IEEE International Conference on Robotics and Automation*, pages 472–477, May 1989.

[5] B. R. Donald. Robot motion planning with uncertainty in the geometric models of the robot and environment: A formal framework for error detection and recovery. In *Proceedings of the IEEE International Conference on Robotics and Automation*, pages 1588–1593, 1986.

[6] M. Erdmann. Using backprojections for fine motion planning with uncertainty. *International Journal of Robotics Research*, 5(1):19–45, 1986.

[7] S. J. Gordon. *Automated assembly using feature localization.* PhD thesis, Massachusetts Institute of Technology, MIT AI Laboratory, Cambridge, MA, 1986. Technical Report 932.

[8] V. Gullapalli. A stochastic reinforcement learning algorithm for learning real-valued functions. *Neural Networks*, 3:671–692, 1990.

[9] V. Gullapalli. *Reinforcement Learning and its application to control.* PhD thesis, University of Massachusetts, Amherst, MA 01003, 1992.

[10] V. Gullapalli, R. A. Grupen, and A. G. Barto. Learning reactive admittance control. In *Proceedings of the 1992 IEEE International Conference on Robotics and Automation*, pages 1475–1480, Nice, France, 1992.

[11] R. E. Gustavson. A theory for the three-dimensional mating of chamfered cylindrical parts. *Journal of Mechanisms, Transmissions, and Automated Design*, December 1984.

[12] S. Lee and M. H. Kim. Learning expert systems for robot fine motion control. In H. E. Stephanou, A. Meystal, and J. Y. S. Luh, editors, *Proceedings of the 1988 IEEE International Symposium on Intelligent Control*, pages 534–544, Arlington, Virginia, USA, 1989. IEEE Computer Society Press: Washington.

[13] T. Lozano-Pérez, M. T. Mason, and R. H. Taylor. Automatic synthesis of fine-motion strategies for robots. *The International Journal of Robotics Research*, 3(1):3–24, Spring 1984.

[14] D. E. Whitney. Quasi-static assembly of compliantly supported rigid parts. *Journal of Dynamic Systems, Measurement, and Control*, 104, March 1982. Also in *Robot Motion: Planning and Control*, (Brady, M., et al. eds.), MIT Press, Cambridge, MA, 1982.

A Practice Strategy for Robot Learning Control

Terence D. Sanger
Department of Electrical Engineering and Computer Science
Massachusetts Institute of Technology, room E25-534
Cambridge, MA 02139
tds@ai.mit.edu

Abstract

"Trajectory Extension Learning" is a new technique for Learning Control in Robots which assumes that there exists some parameter of the desired trajectory that can be smoothly varied from a region of easy solvability of the dynamics to a region of desired behavior which may have more difficult dynamics. By gradually varying the parameter, practice movements remain near the desired path while a Neural Network learns to approximate the inverse dynamics. For example, the average speed of motion might be varied, and the inverse dynamics can be "bootstrapped" from slow movements with simpler dynamics to fast movements. This provides an example of the more general concept of a "Practice Strategy" in which a sequence of intermediate tasks is used to simplify learning a complex task. I show an example of the application of this idea to a real 2-joint direct drive robot arm.

1 INTRODUCTION

The most general definition of Adaptive Control is one which includes any controller whose behavior changes in response to the controlled system's behavior. In practice, this definition is usually restricted to modifying a small number of controller parameters in order to maintain system stability or global asymptotic stability of the errors during execution of a single trajectory (Sastry and Bodson 1989, for review). Learning Control represents a second level of operation, since it uses Adaptive Control to modify parameters during repeated performance trials of a desired trajectory so that future trials result in greater accuracy (Arimoto *et al.* 1984). In this paper I present a third level called a "Practice Strategy", in which Learning Control is applied to a sequence of intermediate trajectories leading ultimately to the true desired trajectory. I claim that this can significantly increase learning speed and make learning possible for systems which would otherwise become unstable.

1.1 LEARNING CONTROL

During repeated practice of a single desired trajectory, the actual trajectory followed by the robot may be significantly different. Many Learning Control algorithms modify the commands stored in a sequence memory to minimize this difference (Atkeson 1989, for review). However, the performance errors are usually measured in a sensory coordinate system, while command corrections must be made in the motor coordinate system. If the relationship between these two coordinate systems is not known, then command corrections might be in the wrong direction and inadvertently worsen performance. However, if the practice trajectory is close to the desired trajectory, then the errors will be small and the relationship between command and sensory errors can be approximated by the system Jacobian.

An alternative to a stored command sequence is to use a Neural Network to learn an approximation to the inverse dynamics in the region of interest (Sanner and Slotine 1992, Yabuta and Yamada 1991, Atkeson 1989). In this case, the commands and results from the actual movement are used as training data for the network, and smoothness properties are assumed such that the error on the desired trajectory will decrease. However, a significant problem with this method is that if the actual practice trajectory is far from the desired trajectory, then its inverse dynamics information will be of little use in training the inverse dynamics for the desired trajectory. In fact, the network may achieve perfect approximation on the actual trajectory while still making significant errors on the desired trajectory. In this case, learning will stop (since the training error is zero) leading to the phenomenon of "learning lock-up" (An *et al.* 1988). So whether Learning Control uses a sequence memory or a Neural Network, learning may proceed poorly if large errors are made during the initial practice movements.

1.2 PRACTICE STRATEGIES

I define a "practice strategy" as a sequence of trajectories such that the first element in the sequence is any previously learned trajectory, and the last element in the sequence is the ultimate desired trajectory. A well designed practice strategy will result in a seqence for which learning control of the trajectory for any particular step is simplified if prior steps have already been learned. This will occur if learning of prior trajectories reduces the initial performance error for subsequent trajectories, so that a network will be less likely to experience learning lock-up.

One example of a practice strategy is a three-step sequence in which the intermediate step is a set of independently executable subtasks which partition the desired trajectory into discrete pieces. Another example is a multi-step sequence in which intermediate steps are a set of trajectories which are somehow related to the desired trajectory. In this paper I present a multi-step sequence which gradually

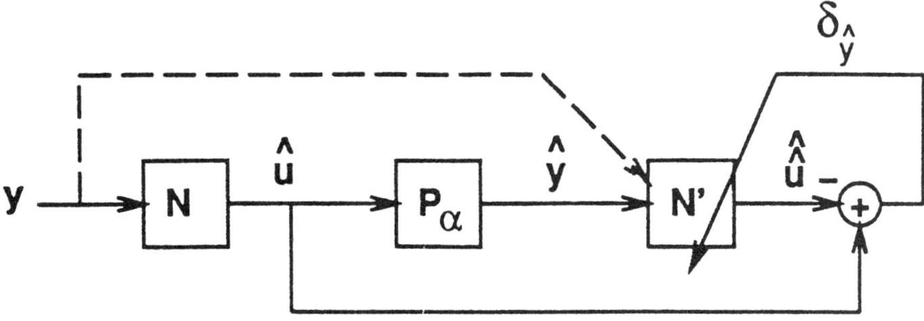

Figure 1: Training signals for network learning.

transforms some known trajectory into the desired trajectory by varying a single parameter. This method has the advantage of not requiring detailed knowledge of the task structure in order to break it up into meaningful subtasks, and conditions for convergence can be stated explicitly. It has a close relationship to Continuation Methods for solving differential equations, and can be considered to be a particular application of the Banach Extension Theorem.

2 METHODS

As in (Sanger 1992), we need to specify 4 aspects of the use of a neural network within a control system:

1. the networks' function in the control system,
2. the network learning algorithm which modifies the connection weights,
3. the training signals used for network learning, and
4. the practice strategy used to generate sample movements.

The network's function is to learn the inverse dynamics of an equilibrium-point controlled plant (Shadmehr 1990). The LMS-tree learning algorithm trains the network (Sanger 1991b, Sanger 1991a). The training signals are determined from the actual practice data using either "Actual Trajectory Training" or "Desired Trajectory Training", as defined below. And the practice strategy is "Trajectory Extension Learning", in which a parameter of the movement is gradually modified during training.

2.1 TRAINING SIGNALS

Figure 1 shows the general structure of the network and training signals. A desired trajectory y is fed into the network N to yield an estimated command $\hat{u}$. This command is then applied to the plant P_α where the subscript indicates that the plant is parameterized by the variable α. Although the true command u which achieves y is unknown, we do know that the estimated command $\hat{u}$ produces $\hat{y}$, so these signals are used for training by comparing the network response to $\hat{y}$ given by $\hat{\hat{u}} = N\hat{y}$ to the known value $\hat{u}$ and subtracting these to yield the training error $\delta_{\hat{y}}$.

Normally, network training would use this error signal to modify the network output for inputs near $\hat{y}$, and I refer to this as "Actual Trajectory Training". However, if $\hat{y}$ is far from y then no change in response may occur at y and this may lead even more quickly to learning lock-up. Therefore an alternative is to use the error $\delta_{\hat{y}}$ to train the network output for inputs near y. I refer to this as "Desired Trajectory Training", and in the figure it is represented by the dotted arrow.

The following discussion will summarize the convergence conditions and theorems presented in (Sanger 1992).

Define

$$Ru \doteq (I - NP(x))u = u - \hat{u}$$

to be an operator which maps commands into command errors for states x on the desired trajectory. Similarly, let

$$\hat{R}\hat{u} = (I - NP(\hat{x}))\hat{u} = \hat{u} - \hat{\hat{u}}$$

map commands into command errors for states $\hat{x}$ on the actual trajectory.

Convergence depends upon the following assumptions:

A1: The plant P is smooth and invertible with respect to both the state x and the input u with Lipschitz constants k_x and k_u, and it has stable zero-dynamics.

A2: The network N is smooth with Lipschitz constant k_N.

A3: Network learning reduces the error in response to a pair (y, δ_y).

A4: The change in network output in response to training is smooth with Lipschitz constant k_L.

A5: There exists a smoothly controllable parameter α such that an inverse dynamics solution is available at $\alpha = \alpha_0$, and the desired performance occurs when $\alpha = \alpha_d$.

A6: The change in command required to produce a desired output after any change in α is bounded by the change in α multiplied by a constant k_α.

A7: The change in plant response for any fixed input is bounded by the change in α multiplied by a constant k_p.

Under assumptions A1-A3 we can prove convergence of Desired Trajectory Training:

Theorem 1:
If there exists a k_{R_n} such that

$$\|R_n u - \hat{R}_n \hat{u}\| < k_{R_n} \|u - \hat{u}\|$$

then if the learning rate $0 < \gamma \leq 1$,

$$\|R_{n+1}u\| < (1 - \gamma + \gamma k_{R_n}))\|R_n u\|.$$

If $k_{R_n} < 1$ and $\gamma \leq 1$, then the network output $\hat{u}$ approaches the correct command u.

Under assumptions A1-A4, we can prove convergence of Actual Trajectory Training:

Theorem 2:
If there exists a k_{R_n} *such that*

$$\|R_n u - \hat{R}_n \hat{u}\| < k_{R_n} \|u - \hat{u}\|$$

then if the learning rate $0 < \gamma \leq 1$,

$$\|R_{n+1}u\| < (1 - \gamma + \gamma k_L k_u + \gamma k_{R_n})\|R_n u\| + \gamma k_L k_x \|x - \hat{x}\|$$

2.2 TRAJECTORY EXTENSION LEARNING

Let α be some modifiable parameter of the plant such that for $\alpha = \alpha_0$ there exists a simple inverse dynamics solution, and we seek a solution when $\alpha = \alpha_d$. For example, if the plant uses Equilibrium Point Control (Shadmehr 1990), then at low speeds the inverse dynamics behave like a perfect servo controller yielding desired trajectories without the need to solve the dynamics. We can continue to train a learning controller as the average speed of movement (α) is gradually increased. The inverse dynamics learned at one speed provide an approximation to the inverse dynamics for a slightly faster speed, and thus the performance errors remain small during practice. This leads to significantly faster learning rates and greater likelihood that the conditions for convergence at any given speed will be satisfied. Note that unlike traditional learning schemes, the error does not decrease monotonically with practice, but instead maintains a steady magnitude as the speed increases, until the network is no longer able to approximate the inverse dynamics.

The following is a summary of a result from (Sanger 1992). Let α change from α_1 to α_2, and let $P = P_{\alpha_1}$ and $P' = P_{\alpha_2}$. Then under assumptions A1-A7 we can prove convergence of Trajectory Extension Learning:

Theorem 3:
If there exists a k_R *such that for* $\alpha = \alpha_1$

$$\|Ru - \hat{R}\hat{u}\| < k_R \|u - \hat{u}\|$$

then for $\alpha = \alpha_2$

$$\|R'u' - \hat{R}'\hat{u}\| < k_R \|u' - \hat{u}\| + (2k_\alpha + k_N k_p)|\alpha_2 - \alpha_1|$$

This shows that given the smoothness assumptions and a small enough change in α, the error will continue to decrease.

3 EXAMPLE

Figure 2 shows the result of 15 learning trials performed by a real direct-drive two-joint robot arm on a sampled desired trajectory. The initial trial required 11.5 seconds to execute, and the speed was gradually increased until the final trial required only 4.5 seconds. Simulated equilibrium point control was used (Bizzi *et al.* 1984) with stiffness and damping coefficients of 15 nm/rad and 1.5 nm/rad/sec, respectively. The grey line in figure 2 shows the equilibrium point control signal which generated the actual movement represented by the solid line. The difference between these two indicates the nontrivial nature of the dynamics calculations required to derive the control signal from the desired trajectory. Note that without Trajectory Extension Learning, the network does not converge and the arm becomes unstable. The neural network was an LMS tree (Sanger 1991b, Sanger 1991a) with 10 Gaussian basis functions for each of the 6 input dimensions, and a total of 15 subtrees were grown per joint (see (Sanger 1992) for further explanation).

4 CONCLUSION

Trajectory Extension Learning is one example of the way in which a practice strategy can be used to improve convergence for Learning Control. This or other types of practice strategies might be able to increase the performance of many different types of learning algorithms both within and outside the Control domain. Such strategies may also provide a theoretical model for the practice strategies used by humans to learn complex tasks, and the theoretical analysis and convergence conditions could potentially lead to a deeper understanding of human motor learning and successful techniques for optimizing performance.

Acknowledgements

Thanks are due to Simon Giszter, Reza Shadmehr, Sandro Mussa-Ivaldi, Emilio Bizzi, and many people at the NIPS conference for their comments and criticisms. This report describes research done within the laboratory of Dr. Emilio Bizzi in the department of Brain and Cognitive Sciences at MIT. The author was supported during this work by a National Defense Science and Engineering Graduate Fellowship, and by NIH grants 5R37AR26710 and 5R01NS09343 to Dr. Bizzi.

References

An C. H., Atkeson C. G., Hollerbach J. M., 1988, *Model-Based Control of a Robot Manipulator*, MIT Press, Cambridge, MA.

Arimoto S., Kawamura S., Miyazaki F., 1984, Bettering operation of robots by learning, *Journal of Robotic Systems*, 1(2):123–140.

Atkeson C. G., 1989, Learning arm kinematics and dynamics, *Ann. Rev. Neurosci.*, 12:157–183.

Bizzi E., Accornero N., Chapple W., Hogan N., 1984, Posture control and trajectory formation during arm movement, *J. Neurosci*, 4:2738–2744.

Sanger T. D., 1991a, A tree-structured adaptive network for function approximation in high dimensional spaces, *IEEE Trans. Neural Networks*, 2(2):285–293.

Sanger T. D., 1991b, A tree-structured algorithm for reducing computation in networks with separable basis functions, *Neural Computation*, 3(1):67–78.

Sanger T. D., 1992, Neural network learning control of robot manipulators using gradually increasing task difficulty, submitted to *IEEE Trans. Robotics and Automation.*

Sanner R. M., Slotine J.-J. E., 1992, Gaussian networks for direct adaptive control, IEEE Trans. Neural Networks, in press. Also MIT NSL Report 910303, 910503, March 1991 and Proc. American Control Conference, Boston pages 2153–2159, June 1991.

Sastry S., Bodson M., 1989, *Adaptive Control: Stability, Convergence, and Robustness*, Prentice Hall, New Jersey.

Shadmehr R., 1990, Learning virtual equilibrium trajectories for control of a robot arm, *Neural Computation*, 2:436–446.

Yabuta T., Yamada T., 1991, Learning control using neural networks, *Proc. IEEE Int'l Conf. on Robotics and Automation, Sacramento*, pages 740–745.

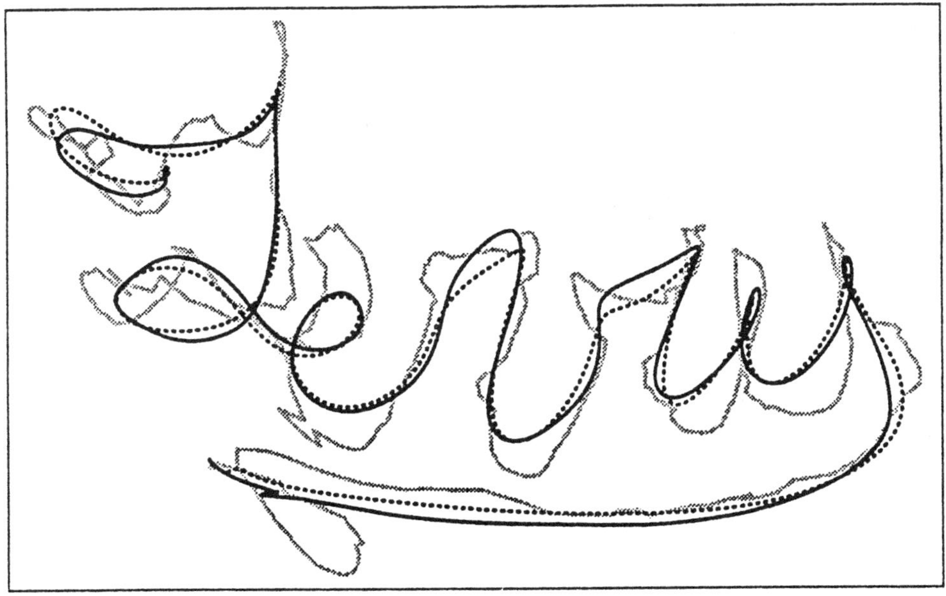

Figure 2: Dotted line is the desired trajectory, solid line is the actual trajectory, and the grey line is the equilibrium point control trajectory.

Learning Spatio-Temporal Planning from a Dynamic Programming Teacher: Feed-Forward Neurocontrol for Moving Obstacle Avoidance

Gerald Fahner *
Department of Neuroinformatics
University of Bonn
Römerstr. 164
W-5300 Bonn 1, Germany

Rolf Eckmiller
Department of Neuroinformatics
University of Bonn
Römerstr. 164
W-5300 Bonn 1, Germany

Abstract

Within a simple test-bed, application of feed-forward neurocontrol for short-term planning of robot trajectories in a dynamic environment is studied. The action network is embedded in a sensory-motoric system architecture that contains a separate world model. It is continuously fed with short-term predicted spatio-temporal obstacle trajectories, and receives robot state feedback. The action net allows for external switching between alternative planning tasks. It generates goal-directed motor actions – subject to the robot's kinematic and dynamic constraints – such that collisions with moving obstacles are avoided. Using supervised learning, we distribute examples of the optimal planner mapping over a structure-level adapted parsimonious higher order network. The training database is generated by a Dynamic Programming algorithm. Extensive simulations reveal, that the local planner mapping is highly nonlinear, but can be effectively and sparsely represented by the chosen powerful net model. Excellent generalization occurs for unseen obstacle configurations. We also discuss the limitations of feed-forward neurocontrol for growing planning horizons.

*Tel.: (228)–550–364 FAX: (228)–550–425 e–mail: gerald@nero.uni-bonn.de

1 INTRODUCTION

Global planning of goal directed trajectories subject to cluttered spatio-temporal, state-dependent constraints – as in the kinodynamic path planning problem (Donald, 1989) considered here – is a difficult task, probably best suited for systems with embedded sequential behavior; theoretical insights indicate that the related problem of connectedness is of unbounded order (Minsky, 1969). However, considering practical situations, there is a lack of globally disposable constraints at planning time, due to partially unmodelled environments. The question then arises, to what extent feed-forward neurocontrol may be effective for *local* planning horizons.
In this paper, we put aside problems of credit assignment, and world model identification. We focus on the complexity of representing a local version of the generic kinodynamic path planning problem by a feed-forward net. We investigate the capacity of sparse distributed planner representations to *generalize from example plans.*

2 ENVIRONMENT AND ROBOT MODELS

2.1 ENVIRONMENT

The world around the robot is a two-dimensional scene, occupied by obstacles moving all in parallel to the y-axis, with randomly choosen discretized x-positions, and with a continuous velocity spectrum. The environment's state is given by a list reporting position $(x_i, y_i) \in (\mathcal{X}, \mathcal{Y})$, $\mathcal{X} \in \{0, ..., 8\}$, $\mathcal{Y} = [y^-, y^+]$, and velocity $(0, v_i)$; $v_i \in [v^-, v^+]$ of each obstacle i. The environment dynamics is given by

$$y_i(t+1) = y_i(t) + v_i \; . \tag{1}$$

Obstacles are inserted at random positions, and with random velocities, into some region distant from the robot's workspace. At each time step, the obstacle's positions are updated according to eqn.(1), so that they will cross the robot's workspace some time.

2.2 ROBOT

We consider a point-like robot of unit mass, which is confined to move within some interval along the x-axis. Its state is denoted by $(x_r, \dot{x}_r) \in (\mathcal{X}, \dot{\mathcal{X}})$; $\dot{\mathcal{X}} = \{-1, 0, 1\}$. At each time step, a motor command $u \in \ddot{\mathcal{X}} = \{-1, 0, 1\}$ is applied to the robot. The robot dynamics is given by

$$\begin{aligned} \dot{x}_r(t+1) &= \dot{x}_r(t) + u(t) \\ x_r(t+1) &= x_r(t) + \dot{x}_r(t+1) \; . \end{aligned} \tag{2}$$

Notice that the set of admissible motor commands depends on the present robot state. With these settings, the robot faces a fluctuating number of obstacles crossing its baseline, similar to the situation of a pedestrian who wants to cross a busy street (Figure 1).

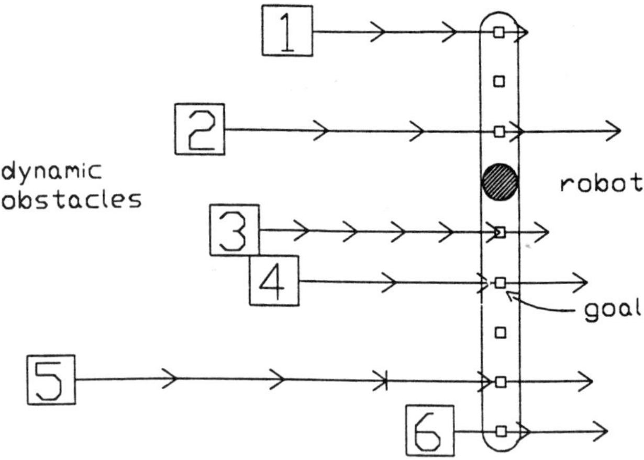

Figure 1: Obstacles Crossing the Robot's Workspace

3 SYSTEM ARCHITECTURE AND FUNCTIONALITY

Adequate modeling of the perception-action cycle is of decisive importance for the design of intelligent reactive systems. We partition the overall system into two modules: an active Perception Module (PM) with built-in capabilities for short-term environment forecasts, and a subsequent Action Module (AM) for motor command generation (Figure 2). Either module may be represented by a 'classical' algorithm, or by a neural net. PM is fed with a sensory data stream reporting the observed

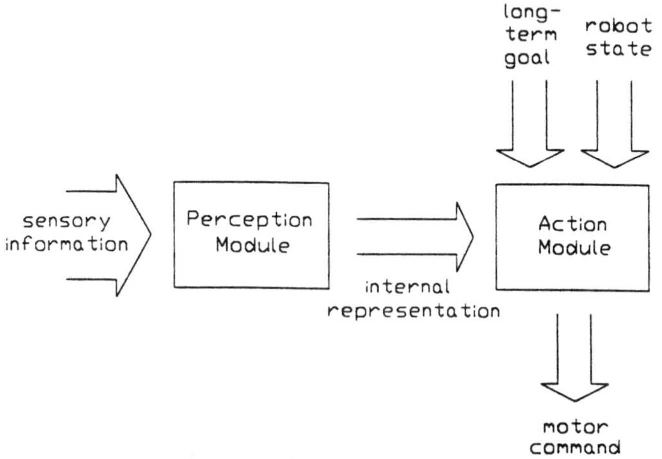

Figure 2: Sensory-Motoric System Architecture

dynamic scene of time-varying obstacle positions. From this, it assembles a spatio-temporal internal representation of near-future obstacle trajectories. At each time step t, it actualizes the incidence function

$$occupancy(x,k) = \begin{cases} 1 & : \ (x = x_i \ and \ -s < y_i(t+k) < s) \ for \ any \ obstacle \ i \\ -1 & : \ otherwise \ , \end{cases}$$

where s is some safety margin accounting for the y-extension of obstacles. The incidence function is defined on a spatio-temporal cone-shaped cell array, based at the actual robot position:

$$|x - x_r(t)| \leq k \ ; \ k = 1, ..., HORIZON \tag{3}$$

The opening angle of this cone-shaped region is given by the robot's speed limit (here: one cell per time step). Only those cells that can potentially be reached by the robot within the local prediction-/planning horizon are thus represented by PM (see Figure 3). The functionality of AM is to map the current PM representation to

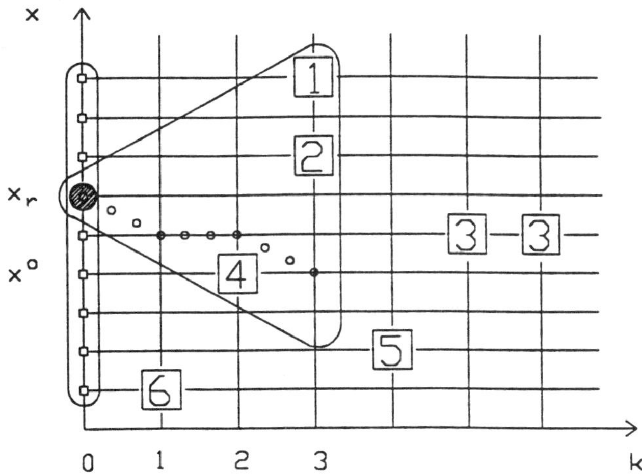

Figure 3: Space-Time Representation with Solution Path Indicated

an appropriate robot motor command, taking into account the present robot state, and paying regard to the currently specified long-term goal. Firstly, we realize the optimal AM by the Dynamic Programming (DP) algorithm (Bellman, 1957). Secondly, we use supervised learning to distribute optimal planning examples over a neural network.

4 DYNAMIC PROGRAMMING SOLUTION

Given PM's internal representation at time t, the present robot state, and some specification of the desired long-term goal, DP determines a sequence of motor commands minimizing some cost functional. Here we use

$$cost_{\{u(t),...,u(t+HORIZON)\}} = \sum_{k=0}^{HORIZON} (x_r(t+k) - x^o)^2 + c\, u(t+k)^2 \ , \tag{4}$$

with $x_r(t+k)$ given by the dynamics eqns.(2) (see solution path in Figure 3). By x^o, we denote the desired robot position or long-term goal. Deviations from this position are punished by higher costs, just as are costly accelerations. Obstacle collisions are excluded by restricting search to admissible cells $(x, \dot{x}, t+k)_{admissible}$ in phase-space-time (obeying $occupancy(x, t+k) = -1$). Training targets for time t are constituted by the optimal present motor actions $u^{opt}(t)$, for which the minimum is attained in eqn.(4). For cases with degenerated optimal solutions, we consistently break symmetry, in order to obtain a deterministic target mapping.

5 NEURAL ACTION MODEL

For neural motor command generation, we use a single layer of structure-adapted *parsi*monious Higher Order Neurons (*parsi*HONs) (Fahner, 1992a, b), computing outputs $y_i \in [0,1]$; $i = 1,2,3$. Target values for each single neuron are given by $y_i^{des} = 1$, if motor-action i is the optimal one, otherwise, $y_i^{des} = 0$. As input, each neuron receives a bit-vector $\mathbf{x} = x_1, ..., x_N \in \{-1,1\}^N$, whose components specify the values of PM's incidence function, the binary encoded robot state, and some task bits encoding the long-term goal. Using batch training, we maximize the log-likelihood criterion for each neuron independently. For recall, the motor command is obtained by a winner-takes-all decision: the index of the most active neuron yields the motor action applied.

Generally, atoms for nonlinear interactions within a bipolar-input HON are modelled by input monomials of the form

$$\eta_\alpha \equiv \prod_{j=1}^{N} x_j^{\alpha_j} \quad ; \quad \alpha = \alpha_1 ... \alpha_N \in \mathcal{R} \equiv \{0,1\}^N . \tag{5}$$

Here, the jth bit of α is understood as exponent of x_j. It is well known that the complete set of monomials forms a basis for Boolean functions expansions (Karpovski, 1976). Combinatorial growth of the number of terms with increasing input dimension renders allocation of the complete basis impractical in our case. Moreover, an action model employing excessive numbers of basis functions would overfit trainig data, thus preventing generalization.

We therefore use a structural adaptation algorithm, as discussed in detail in (Fahner, 1992a, b), for automatic identification and inclusion of a sparse set of *relevant* nonlinearities present in the problem. In effect, this algorithm performs a guided stochastic search exploring the space of nonlinear interactions by means of an intertwined process of weight adaptation, and competition between nonlinear terms. The *parsi*HON model restricts the *number* of terms used, not their *orders*: instead of the exponential size set $\{\eta_\alpha : \alpha \in \mathcal{R}\}$, just a small subset $\{\eta_\beta : \beta \in \mathcal{S} \subset \mathcal{R}\}$ of terms is used within a parsimonious higher order function expansion

$$y^{est}(\mathbf{x}) = f\left[\sum_{\beta \in \mathcal{S}} w^\beta \eta_\beta(\mathbf{x})\right] \quad ; \quad w^\beta \in I\!R . \tag{6}$$

Here, f denotes the usual sigmoid transfer function.

*parsi*HONs with high degrees of sparsity were effectively trained and emerged robust generalization for difficult nonlinear classification benchmarks (Fahner, 1992a, b).

6 SIMULATION RESULTS

We performed extensive simulations to evaluate the neural action network's capabilities to generalize from learned optimal planning examples. The planner was trained with respect to two alternative long-term goals: $x^o = 0$, or $x^o = 8$. Firstly, optimal DP planner actions were assembled over about 6,000 time steps of the simulated environment (fairly crowded with moving obstacles), for both long-term goals. At each time step, optimal motor commands were computed for all $9 \times 3 = 27$ available robot states. From this bunch of situations we excluded those, where no collision-free path existed within the planning horizon considered: $(HORIZON = 3)$. A total of 115,000 admissible training situations were left, out of the $6,000 \times 27 = 162,000$ one's generated . Thus, out of the full spectrum of robot states which were checked every time step, just about 19 states were not doomed to collide, at an average. These findings corroborate the difficulty of the choosen task.
Many repetitions are present in these accumulated patterns, reflecting the statistics of the simulated environment. We collapsed the original training set by removing repeated patterns, providing the learner with more information per pattern: a working data base containing about 20.000 different patterns was left.
Input to the neural action net consisted of a bit-vector of length $N = 21$, where $3 + 5 + 7$ bits encode PM's internal representation (cone size in Figure 3), 6 bits encode the robot's state, and a single task bit reports the desired goal. For training, we delimited single neuron learning to a maximum of 1000 epochs. In most cases, this was sufficient for successful training set classification for any of the three neurons ($y_i < .8$ for $y_i^{des} = 0$, and $y_i > .8$ for $y_i^{des} = 1$; $i = 1, 2, 3$). But even if some training patterns were misclassified by individual motor neurons, additional robustness stemming from the winner-takes-all decision rescued fault-free recall of the voting community. To test generalization of the neural action model, we par-

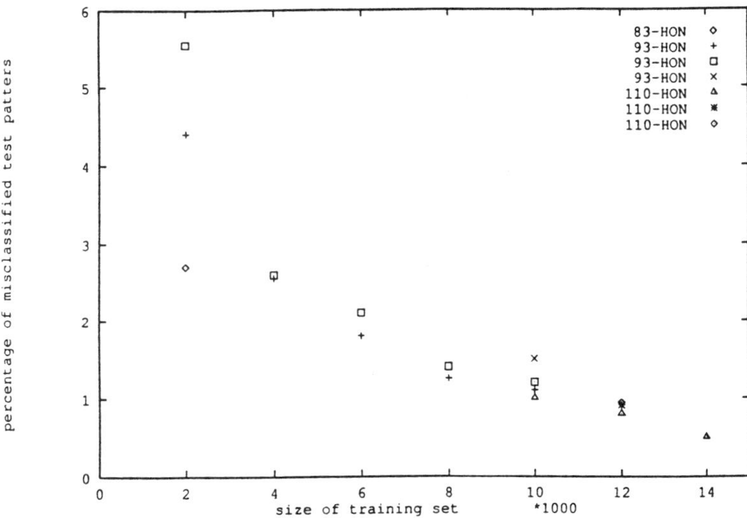

Figure 4: Generalization Behavior

titioned the data base into two parts, one containing training patterns, the other

containing new test patterns, not present in the training set. Several runs were performed with *parsi*HONs of sizes between 83 and 110 terms. Results for varying training set sizes are depicted in Figure 4. Test error decreases with increasing training set size, and falls as low as about one percent for about 12,000 training patterns. It continues to decrease for larger training sets. These findings corroborate that the trained architectures emerge sensible robust generalization.
To get some insight into the complexity of the mapping, we counted the number of terms which carry a given order. The resulting distribution has its maximum at order 3, exhibits many terms of orders 4 and higher, and finally decreases to zero for orders exceeding 10 (Figure 5). This indicates that the planner mapping considered is highly nonlinear.

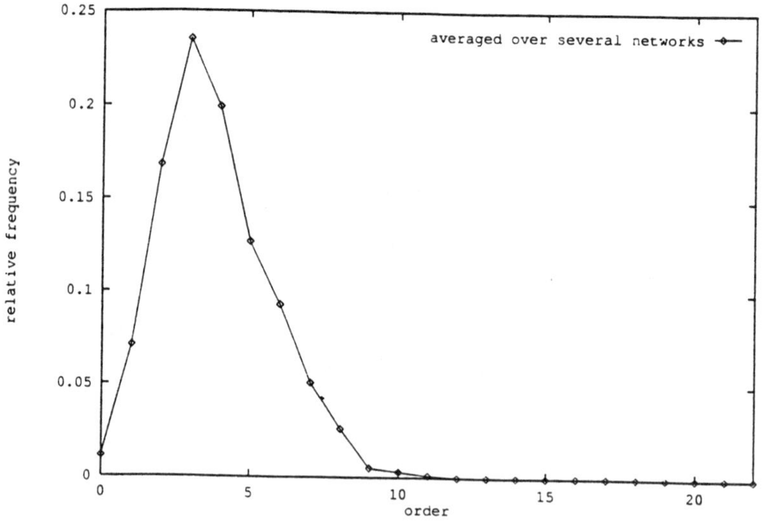

Figure 5: Distribution of Orders

7 DISCUSSION AND CONCLUSIONS

Sparse representation of planner mappings is desirable when representation of complete policy look-up tables becomes impracticable (Bellman's "curse of dimensionality"), or when computation of plans becomes expensive or conflicting with real-time requirements. For these reasons, it is urgent to investigate the capacity of neurocontrol for effective distributed representation and for robust generalization of planner mappings.
Here, we focused on a new type of shallow feed-forward action network for the local kinodynamic trajectory planning problem. An advantage with feed- forward nets is their low-latency recall, which is an important requirement for systems acting in rapidly changing environments. However, from theoretical considerations concerning the related problem of connectedness with its inherent serial character (Minsky, 1969), the planning problem under focus is expected to be hard for feed-forward nets. Even for rather local planning horizons, complex and nonlinear planner map-

pings must be expected. Using a powerful new neuron model that identifies the relevant nonlinearities inherent in the problem, we determined extremely parsimonious architectures for representation of the planner mapping. This indicates that some compact set of important features determines the optimal plan. The adapted networks emerged excellent generalization.
We encourage use of feed-forward nets for difficult local planning tasks, if care is taken that the models support effective representation of high-order nonlinearities. For growing planning horizons, it is expected that feed-forward neurocontrol will run into limitations (Werbos, 1992). The simple test-bed presented here would allow for insertion and testing also of other net models and system designs, including recurrent networks.

Acknowledgements

This work was supported by Federal Ministry of Research and Technology (BMFT-project SENROB), grant 01 IN 105 A/0)

References

E. B. Baum, F. Wilczek (1987). Supervised Learning of Probability Distributions by Neural Networks. In D. Anderson (Ed.), *Neural Information Processing Systems*, 52-61. Denver, CO: American Institute of Physics.

R. E. Bellman (1957). *Dynamic Programming.* Princeton University Press.

B. Donald (1989). *Near-Optimal Kinodynamic Planning for Robots With Coupled Dynamic Bounds*, Proc. IEEE Int. Conf. on Robotics and Automation.

G. Fahner, N. Goerke, R. Eckmiller (1992). *Structural Adaptation of Boolean Higher Order Neurons: Superior Classification with Parsimonious Topologies*, Proc. ICANN, Brighton, UK.

G. Fahner, R. Eckmiller. *Structural Adaptation of Parsimonious Higher Order Classifiers*, subm. to Neural Networks.

M. G. Karpovski (1976). *Finite Orthogonal Series in the Design of Digital Devices.* New York: John Wiley & Sons.

M. Minsky, S. A. Papert (1969). *Perceptrons.* Cambridge: The MIT Press.

P. Werbos (1992). Approximate Dynamic Programming for Real-Time Control and Neural Modeling. In D. White, D. Sofge (eds.) *Handbook of Intelligent Control*, 493-525. New York: Van Nostrand.

Learning Fuzzy Rule-Based Neural Networks for Control

Charles M. Higgins and Rodney M. Goodman
Department of Electrical Engineering, 116-81
California Institute of Technology
Pasadena, CA 91125

Abstract

A three-step method for function approximation with a fuzzy system is proposed. First, the membership functions and an initial rule representation are learned; second, the rules are compressed as much as possible using information theory; and finally, a computational network is constructed to compute the function value. This system is applied to two control examples: learning the truck and trailer backer-upper control system, and learning a cruise control system for a radio-controlled model car.

1 Introduction

Function approximation is the problem of estimating a function from a set of examples of its independent variables and function value. If there is prior knowledge of the type of function being learned, a mathematical model of the function can be constructed and the parameters perturbed until the best match is achieved. However, if there is no prior knowledge of the function, a model-free system such as a neural network or a fuzzy system may be employed to approximate an arbitrary nonlinear function. A neural network's inherent parallel computation is efficient for speed; however, the information learned is expressed only in the weights of the network. The advantage of fuzzy systems over neural networks is that the information learned is expressed in terms of linguistic rules. In this paper, we propose a method for learning a complete fuzzy system to approximate example data. The membership functions and a minimal set of rules are constructed automatically from the example data, and in addition the final system is expressed as a computational

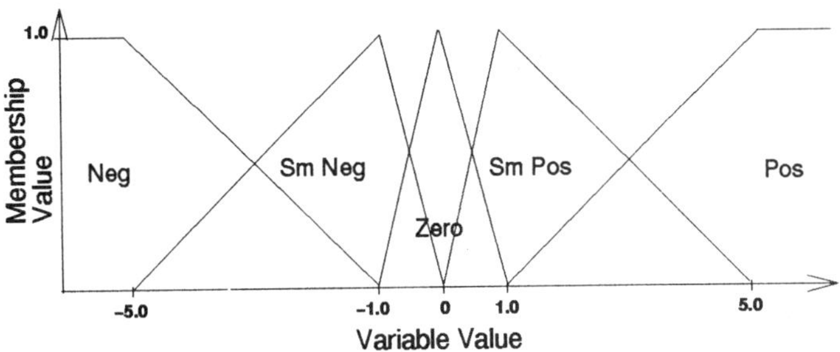

Figure 1: Membership function example

(neural) network for efficient parallel computation of the function value, combining the advantages of neural networks and fuzzy systems. The proposed learning algorithm can be used to construct a fuzzy control system from examples of an existing control system's actions.

Hereafter, we will refer to the function value as the output variable, and the independent variables of the function as the input variables.

2 Fuzzy Systems

In a fuzzy system, a function is expressed in terms of membership functions and rules. Each variable has membership functions which partition its range into overlapping classes (see figure 1). Given these membership functions for each variable, a function may be expressed by making rules from the input space to the output space and smoothly varying between them.

In order to simplify the learning of membership functions, we will specify a number of their properties beforehand. First, we will use piecewise linear membership functions. We will also specify that membership functions are *fully overlapping*; that is, at any given value of the variable the total membership sums to one. Given these two properties of the membership functions, we need only specify the positions of the peaks of the membership functions to completely describe them.

We define a fuzzy rule as *if* y *then* X, where y (the condition side) is a conjunction in which each clause specifies an input variable and one of the membership functions associated with it, and X (the conclusion side) specifies an output variable membership function.

3 Learning a Fuzzy System from Example Data

There are three steps in our method for constructing a fuzzy system: first, learn the membership functions and an initial rule representation; second, simplify (compress) the rules as much as possible using information theory; and finally, construct a computational network with the rules and membership functions to calculate the function value given the independent variables.

3.1 Learning the Membership Functions

Before learning, two parameters must be specified. First, the maximum allowable RMS error of the approximation from the example data; second, the maximum number of membership functions for each variable. The system will not exceed this number of membership functions, but may use fewer if the error is reduced sufficiently before the maximum number is reached.

3.1.1 Learning by Successive Approximation to the Target Function

The following procedure is performed to construct membership functions and a set of rules to approximate the given data set. All of the rules in this step are *cell-based*, that is, they have a condition for every input variable; there is a rule for every combination of input variables (*cell*).

We begin with input membership functions at input extrema. The closest example point to each "corner" of the input space is found and a membership function for the output is added at its value at the corner point. The initial rule set contains a rule for each corner, specifying the closest output membership function to the actual value at that corner.

We now find the example point with the greatest RMS error from the current model and add membership functions *in each variable* at that point. Next, we construct a new set of rules to approximate the function. Constructing rules simply means determining the output membership function to associate with each cell. While constructing this rule set, we also add any output membership functions which are needed. The best rule for a given cell is found by finding the closest example point to the rule (recall each rule specifies a point in the input space). If the output value at this point is "too far" from the closest output membership function value, this output value is added as a new output membership. After this addition has been made, if necessary, the closest output membership function to the value at the closest point is used as the conclusion of the rule. At this point, if the error threshold has been reached or all membership functions are full, we exit. Otherwise, we go back to find the point with the greatest error from the model and iterate again.

3.2 Simplifying the Rules

In order to have as simple a fuzzy system as possible, we would like to use the minimum possible number of rules. The initial cell-based rule set can be "compressed" into a minimal set of rules; we propose the use of an information-theoretic algorithm for induction of rules from a discrete data set [1] for this purpose. The key to the use of this method is the interpretation of each of the original rules as a discrete example. The rule set becomes a discrete data set which is input to a rule-learning algorithm. This algorithm learns the best rules to describe the data set.

There are two components of the rule-learning scheme. First, we need a way to tell which of two candidate rules is the best. Second, we need a way to search the space of all possible rules in order to find the best rules without simply checking every rule in the search space.

3.2.1 Ranking Rules

Smyth and Goodman[2] have developed an information-theoretic measure of rule value with respect to a given discrete data set. This measure is known as the j-measure; defining a rule as *if y then X*, the j-measure can be expressed as follows:

$$j(X|y) = p(X|y)\log_2(\frac{p(X|y)}{p(X)}) + p(\bar{X}|y)\log_2(\frac{p(\bar{X}|y)}{p(\bar{X})})$$

[2] also suggests a modified rule measure, the J-measure:

$$J(X|y) = p(y)j(X|y)$$

This measure discounts rules which are not as useful in the data set in order to remove the effects of "noise" or randomness. The probabilities in both measures are computed from relative frequencies counted in the given discrete data set.

Using the j-measure, examples will be combined only when no error is caused in the prediction of the data set. The J-measure, on the other hand, will combine examples even if some prediction ability of the data is lost. If we simply use the j-measure to compress our original rule set, we don't get significant compression. However, we can only tolerate a certain margin of error in prediction of our original rule set and maintain the same control performance. In order to obtain compression, we wish to allow some error, but not so much as the J-measure will create. We thus propose the following measure, which allows a gradual variation of the amount of noise tolerance:

$$L(X|y) = f\left(p(y), \alpha\right) j(X|y) \quad \text{where} \quad f(x, \alpha) = \frac{1 - e^{-\alpha x}}{1 - e^{-\alpha}}$$

The parameter α may be set at 0^+ to obtain the J-measure since $f(x, 0^+) = x$ or at ∞ to obtain the j-measure, since $f(x, \infty) = 1 \quad (x > 0)$. Any value of α between 0 and ∞ will result in an amount of compression between that of the J-measure and the j-measure; thus if we are able to tolerate some error in the prediction of the original rule set, we can obtain more compression than the j-measure could give us, but not as much as the J-measure would require. We show an example of the variation of α for the truck backer-upper control system in section 4.1.

3.2.2 Searching for the Best Rules

In [1], we presented an efficient method for searching the space of all possible rules to find the most representative ones for discrete data sets. The basic idea is that each example is a very specific (and quite perfect) rule. However, this rule is applicable to only one example. We wish to generalize this very specific rule to cover as many examples as possible, while at the same time keeping it as correct as possible. The goodness-measures shown above are just the tool for doing this. If we calculate the "goodness" of all the rules generated by *removing a single input variable* from the very specific rule, then we will be able to tell if any of the slightly more general rules generated from this rule are better. If so, we take the best and continue in this manner until no more general rule with a higher "goodness" exists. When we have performed this procedure on the very specific rule generated from each example (and removed duplicates), we will have a set of rules which represents the data set.

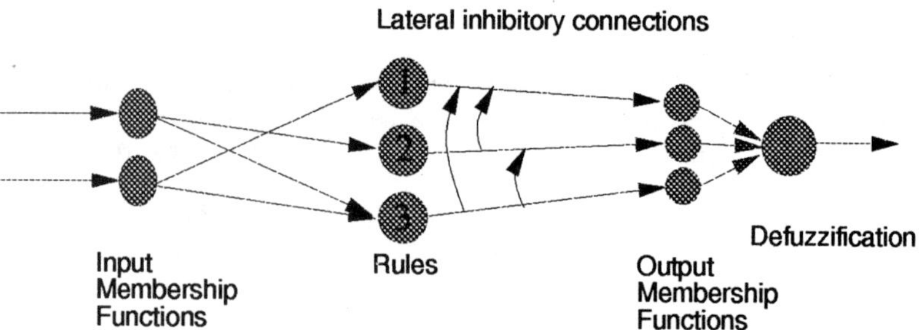

Figure 2: Computational network constructed from fuzzy system

3.3 Constructing a Network

Constructing a computational network to represent a given fuzzy system can be accomplished as shown in figure 2. From input to output, layers represent input membership functions, rules, output membership functions, and finally defuzzification. A novel feature of our network is the lateral links shown in figure 2 between the outputs of various rules. These links allow inference with dependent rules.

3.3.1 The Layers of the Network

The first layer contains a node for every input membership function used in the rule set. Each of these nodes responds with a value between zero and one to a certain region of the input variable range, implementing a single membership function. The second layer contains a node for each rule – each of these nodes represents a fuzzy AND, implemented as a product. The third layer contains a node for every output membership function. Each of these nodes sums the outputs from each rule that concludes that output fuzzy set. The final node simply takes the output memberships collected in the previous layer and performs a defuzzification to produce the final crisp output by normalizing the weights from each output node and performing a convex combination with the peaks of the output membership functions.

3.3.2 The Problem with Dependent Rules and a Solution

There is a problem with the standard fuzzy inference techniques when used with dependent rules. Consider a rule whose conditions are all contained in a more specific rule (i.e. one with more conditions) which contradicts its conclusion. Using standard fuzzy techniques, the more general rule will drive the output to an intermediate value between the two conclusions. What we really want is that a more general rule dependent on a more specific rule should only be allowed to fire *to the degree that the more specific rule is not firing.* Thus the degree of firing of the more specific rule should gate the maximum firing allowed for the more general rule. This is expressed in network form in the links between the rule layer and the output membership functions layer. The lateral arrows are inhibitory connections which take the value at their input, invert it (subtract it from one), and multiply it by the value at their output.

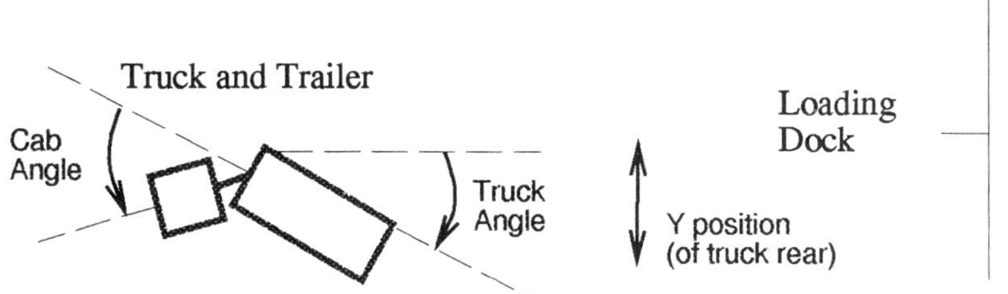

Figure 3: The truck and trailer backer-upper problem

4 Experimental Results

In this section, we show the results of two experiments: first, a truck backer-upper in simulation; and second, a simple cruise controller for a radio-controlled model car constructed in our laboratory.

4.1 Truck and Trailer Backer-Upper

Jenkins and Yuhas [3] have developed by hand a very efficient neural network for solving the problem of backing up a truck and trailer to a loading dock. The truck and trailer backer-upper problem is parameterized in figure 3.

The function approximator system was trained on 225 example runs of the Yuhas controller, with initial positions distributed symmetrically about the field in which the truck operates. In order to show the effect of varying the number of membership functions, we have fixed the maximum number of membership functions for the y position and cab angle at 5 and set the maximum allowable error to zero, thus guaranteeing that the system will fill out all of the allowed membership functions. We varied the maximum number of truck angle membership functions from 3 to 9. The effects of this are shown in figure 4. Note that the error decreases sharply and then holds constant, reaching its minimum at 5 membership functions. The Yuhas network performance is shown as a horizontal line. At its best, the fuzzy system performs slightly better than the system it is approximating.

For this experiment, we set a goal of 33% rule compression. We varied the parameter α in the L-measure for each rule set to get the desired compression. Note in figure 4 the performance of the system with compressed rules. The performance is in every case almost identical to that of the original rule sets. The number of rules and the amount of rule compression obtained can be seen in table 1.

4.2 Cruise Controller

In this section, we describe the learning of a cruise controller to keep a radio controlled model car driving at a constant speed in a circle. We designed a simple PD controller to perform this task, and then learned a fuzzy system to perform the same task. This example is not intended to suggest that a fuzzy system should replace a simple PD controller, since the fuzzy system may represent far more complex

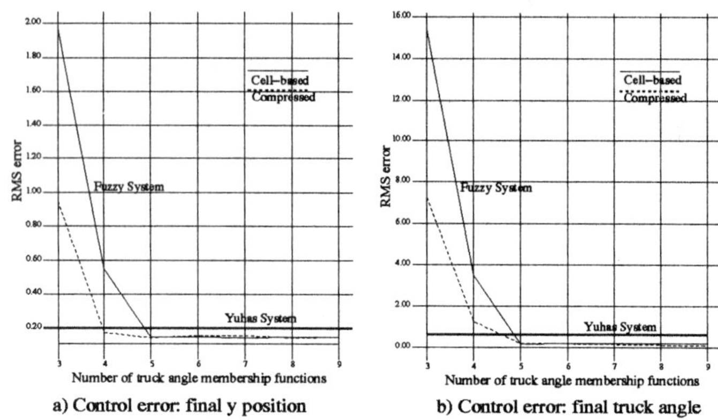

Figure 4: Results of experiments with the truck backer-upper

		Number of truck angle membership functions						
		3	4	5	6	7	8	9
Number of Rules	Cell-Based	75	100	125	150	175	200	225
	Compressed	48	67	86	100	114	138	154
Compression		36%	33%	31%	33%	35%	31%	32%

Table 1: Number of rules and compression figures for learned TBU systems

functions, but rather to show that the fuzzy system can learn from real control data and operate in real-time.

The fuzzy system was trained on 6 runs of the PD controller which included runs going forward and backward, and conditions in which the car's speed was perturbed momentarily by blocking the car or pushing it. Figure 5 shows the error trajectory of both the hand-crafted PD and learned fuzzy control systems from rest. The car builds speed until it reaches the desired set point with a well-damped response, then holds speed for a while. At a later time, an obstacle was placed in the path of the car to stop it and then removed; figure 5 shows the similar recovery responses of both systems. It can be seen from the numerical results in table 2 that the fuzzy system performs as well as the original PD controller.

No compression was attempted because the rule sets are already very small.

	PD Controller	Learned Fuzzy System
Time from 90% error to 10% error (s)	0.9	0.7
RMS error at steady state (uncal)	59	45
Time to correct after obstacle (s)	6.2	6.2

Table 2: Analysis of cruise control performance

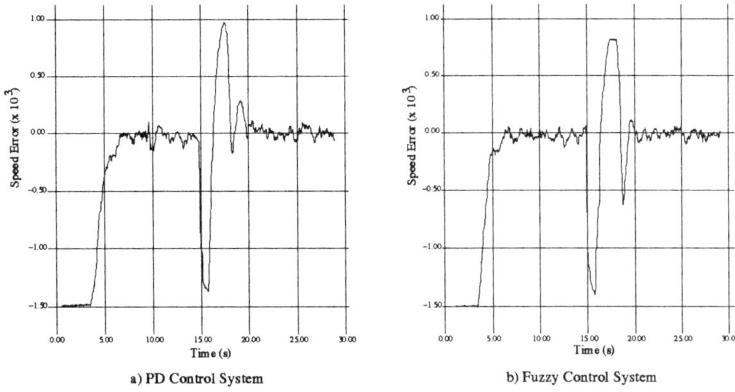

a) PD Control System b) Fuzzy Control System

Figure 5: Performance of PD controller vs. learned fuzzy system

5 Summary and Conclusions

We have presented a method which, given examples of a function and its independent variables, can construct a computational network based on fuzzy logic to predict the function given the independent variables. The user must only specify the maximum number of membership functions for each variable and the maximum RMS error from the example data.

The final fuzzy system's actions can be explicitly explained in terms of rule firings. If a system designer does not like some aspect of the learned system's performance, he can simply change the rule set and the membership functions to his liking. This is in direct contrast to a neural network system, in which he would have no recourse but another round of training.

Acknowledgements

This work was supported in part by Pacific Bell, and in part by DARPA and ONR under grant no. N00014-92-J-1860.

References

[1] C. Higgins and R. Goodman, "Incremental Learning using Rule-Based Neural Networks," *Proceedings of the International Joint Conference on Neural Networks*, vol. 1, 875-880, July 1991.

[2] R. Goodman, C. Higgins, J. Miller, P. Smyth, "Rule-Based Networks for Classification and Probability Estimation," *Neural Computation* 4(6), 781-804, November 1992.

[3] R. Jenkins and B. Yuhas, "A Simplified Neural-Network Solution through Problem Decomposition: The Case of the Truck Backer-Upper," *Neural Computation* 4(5), 647-9, September 1992.

PART IV

VISUAL PROCESSING

Learning to categorize objects using temporal coherence

Suzanna Becker*
The Rotman Research Institute
Baycrest Center
3560 Bathurst St.
Toronto, Ontario, M6A 2E1

Abstract

The invariance of an objects' identity as it transformed over time provides a powerful cue for perceptual learning. We present an unsupervised learning procedure which maximizes the mutual information between the representations adopted by a feed-forward network at consecutive time steps. We demonstrate that the network can learn, entirely unsupervised, to classify an ensemble of several patterns by observing pattern trajectories, even though there are abrupt transitions from one object to another between trajectories. The same learning procedure should be widely applicable to a variety of perceptual learning tasks.

1 INTRODUCTION

A promising approach to understanding human perception is to try to model its developmental stages. There is ample evidence that much of perception is learned. Even some very low level perceptual abilities such as stereopsis (Held, Birch and Gwiazda, 1980; Birch, Gwiazda and Held, 1982) are not present at birth, and appear to be learned. Once rudimentary feature detection abilities have been established, the infant can learn to segment the sensory input, and eventually classify it into familiar patterns. These earliest stages of learning seem to be inherently unsuper-

*Address as of July 1993: Department of Psychology, McMaster University, 1280 Main Street West, Hamilton Ontario, Canada, L8S 4K1

vised (or "self-supervised"). Gradually, the infant learns to detect regularities in the world. One kind of structure that is ubiquitous in sensory information is spatio-temporal coherence. For example, in speech signals, speaker characteristics such as the fundamental frequency are relatively constant over time. At shorter time scales, individual words are typically composed of long intervals having relatively constant spectral characteristics, corresponding to vowels, with short intervening bursts and rapid transitions corresponding to consonants. The consonants also change across time in very regular ways. This temporal coherence at various scales makes speech predictable, to a certain degree. As one moves about in the world, the visual field flows by in characteristic patterns of expansion, dilation and translation. Since most objects in the visual world move slowly, if at all, the visual scene changes slowly over time, exhibiting the same temporal coherence as other sensory sources. Independently moving rigid objects are invariant with respect to shape, texture and many other features, up to very high level properties such as the object's identity. Even under nonlinear shape distortions, images like clouds drifting across the sky are perceived to have coherent features, in spite of undergoing highly non-rigid transformations. Thus, temporal coherence of the sensory input may provide important cues for segmenting signals in space and time, and for object localization and identification.

2 PREVIOUS WORK

A common approach to training neural networks to perform transformation-invariant object recognition is to build in hard constraints which enforce invariance with respect to the transformations of interest. For example, equality constraints among feature-detecting kernels have been used to enforce translation-invariance (Fukushima, 1988; Le Cun et al., 1990). Various other higher-order constraints have been used to enforce viewpoint-invariance (Hinton and Lang, 1985; Zemel, Hinton and Mozer, 1990) and invariance with respect to arbitrary group transformations (Giles and Maxwell, 1987). While in the case of translation-invariance it is straightforward to hard-wire the appropriate constraints, more general linear transformation-invariance requires rather cumbersome machinery, and for arbitrary non-linear transformations the approach is difficult if not impossible.

In contrast to the above approaches, Földiák's model of complex cell development results in translation-invariant orientation detectors without the imposition of any hard constraints (Földiák, 1991). Further, his method is unsupervised. He proposed a modified Hebbian learning rule, in which each weight change depends on the unit's output history:

$$\Delta w_{ij}(t) = \alpha\, \overline{y}_i(t)\ (x_j(t) - w_{ij}(t))$$

where $x_j(t)$ is the activity of the jth presynaptic unit at the tth time step, and $\overline{y}_i(t)$ is a temporally low-pass filtered trace of the postsynaptic activity of the ith unit. Whereas a standard Hebb-rule encourages a unit to detect correlations between its inputs, this rule encourages a unit to produce outputs which are correlated over time. A single unit can therefore learn to group patterns which have zero overlap. Földiák demonstrated this by presenting trajectories of moving lines, with line orientation held constant within each trajectory, to a network whose input features were local orientation detectors. Units became tuned to particular orientations, independent of location.

While Földiák's work is of interest as a model of cell development in early visual cortex, there are several reasons why it cannot be applied directly to the more general problem of transformation-invariant object recognition. One reason that Földiák's learning rule worked well on the line trajectory problem is that the input representation (oriented line features) made the problem linearly separable: there was no overlap between input features present in successive trajectories, hence it was easy to categorize lines of the same orientation. Generally, in more difficult pattern classification problems (such as digit or speech recognition) the optimal input features cannot be preselected but must be learned, and there is considerable overlap between the component features of different pattern classes. Hence, a multi-layer network is required, and it must be able to optimally select features so as to improve its classification performance. The question of interest here is whether it is possible to train such a network entirely unsupervised? As mentioned above, the temporal coherence of the sensory input may be an important cue for solving this problem in biological systems.

3 TEMPORAL-COHERENCE BASED LEARNING

One way to capture the constraint of temporal coherence in a learning procedure is to build it into the objective function. For example, we could try to build representations that are relatively predictable, at least over short time scales. We also need a constraint which captures the notion of high information content; for example, we could require that the network be *unpredictable* over long time scales. A measure which satisfies both criteria is the mutual information between the classifications produced by the network at successive time steps. If the network produces classification $C(t)$ at time t and classification $C(t+1)$ at time $t+1$, the mutual information between the two successive classifications, averaged over the entire sequence of patterns, is given by

$$\begin{aligned} I_{C_t;C_{t+1}} &= H(C_t) + H(C_{t+1}) - H(C_t, C_{t+1}) \\ &= -\sum_i \langle p_i{}^t \rangle_t \log \langle p_i{}^t \rangle_t - \sum_j \langle p_j{}^{t+1} \rangle_t \log \langle p_j{}^{t+1} \rangle_t \\ &\quad + \sum_{ij} \langle p_i{}^t p_j{}^{t+1} \rangle_t \log \langle p_i{}^t p_j{}^{t+1} \rangle_t \end{aligned}$$

where the angle brackets denote time-averaged quantities.

A set of n output units can be forced to represent a probability distribution over n classes, $C \in \{c_1 \cdots c_n\}$, by adopting states whose probabilities sum to one. This can be done, for example, by using the "softmax" activation function suggested by Bridle (1990):

$$p_i{}^t = \frac{e^{x_i(t)}}{\sum_{j=1}^n e^{x_j(t)}} \quad = \quad P(C(t) = c_i)$$

where x_i is the total weighted summed input to the ith unit, and $p_i{}^t$, the output of the ith unit, stands for the probability of the ith class, $P(C(t) = c_i)$.

Once we know the probability of the network assigning each pattern to each class, we can compute the mutual information between the classifications produced by the network at neighboring time steps, $C(t)$ and $C(t+1)$. This requires sampling, over the entire training set, the average probability of each class, as well as the joint probabilities of each possible pair of classifications being produced as successive time steps. The learning involves adjusting the weights in the network so as to maximize the mutual information between the representations produced by the network at adjacent time steps. In the experiments reported here, a gradient ascent procedure was used with the method of conjugate gradients.

One problem with maximizing the information measure described above is that for a fixed amount of entropy in the classifications, $H(C_t)$, the network can always improve the mutual information by decreasing the joint entropy, $H(C_t, C_{t_1})$. In order to achieve low joint entropy, the network must try to assign class probabilities with high certainty, i.e., produce output values near zero or one. Thus the network can always improve its current solution by simply make the weights very large. Unfortunately, this often occurs during learning. To discourage the network from getting stuck in such locally optimal (but very poor) solutions, we introduce a constant λ to weight the importance of the joint entropy term in the objective function, so as to maximize the following:

$$I_{C_t;C_{t+1}} = H(C_t) + H(C_{t+1}) - \lambda H(C_t, C_{t+1})$$

In the simulations reported here, we used a value of 0.5 for λ. This effectively prevents the network from concentrating all its effort on reducing the joint entropy, and forces it to learn more gradually, resulting in more globally optimal solutions.

We have tested this learning procedure on a simple signal classification problem. The pattern set consisted of trajectories of random intensity patterns, drawn from six classes, shown in figure 1. Members of the same class consisted of translated versions of the same pattern, shifted one to five pixels with wrap-around. A trajectory consisted of a block of ten randomly selected patterns from the same class. Between trajectories, the pattern class changed randomly. The network had six input units, twenty hidden units, and six output units. The hidden units used the logistic nonlinearity, $\frac{1}{1+e^{-x}}$, and the output units used the softmax activation function. The hidden units had biases but the outputs did not.[1] After training the network on 1200 patterns (20 trajectories of 10 examples of each of the six patterns) for 300 conjugate gradient iterations, the output units always became reasonably specific to particular pattern classes, as shown for a typical run in Figure 2a). The general pattern is that each output unit responds maximally to one or two pattern classes, although some of the units have mixed responses.

This classification problem is extremely difficult for an unsupervised learning procedure, as there is considerable overlap between patterns in different classes, and essentially no overlap between patterns in the same class. It is therefore easy to see why a single unit might end up capturing a few patterns from one class and a few from another. We can create an easier subproblem by only training the network on half the patterns in each class. In this case, the network always learns to separate the six pattern classes either perfectly, or nearly so, as shown in figure 2b).

[1]Removing biases from the outputs helps prevent the network from getting trapped in local maxima during learning.

Figure 1: *The set of 6 random patterns used to create pattern trajectories. Each pattern was created by randomly setting the intensities of the 6 pixels, and normalizing the intensity profile to have zero mean.*

4 DISCUSSION

Becker and Hinton (1992) showed that a network could learn to extract a continuous parameter of visual scenes which is coherent across space, by maximizing the mutual information between the outputs of two network modules that receive input from spatially adjacent parts of the input. Here, we have shown how the same idea can be applied to the temporal domain, to perform a discrete classification of the input assuming temporal coherence. We could also apply the same algorithm to the problem of unsupervised multi-sensory integration, by forming classifications which are coherent across different sensory modalities, as well as across time.

One advantage of the approach presented here over unsupervised learning procedures such as competitive learning is that units must co-operate to try to find a globally optimal solution. There is therefore incentive for each unit to try to improve the temporal predictability of *all* of the output units' classifications over time, including its own; this discourages any one unit from trying to model all of

a)

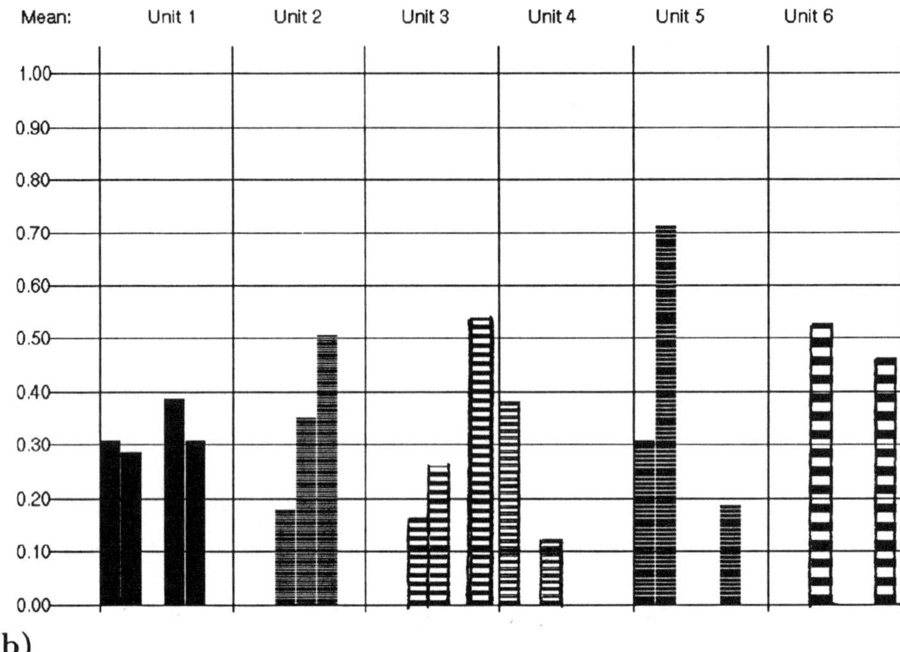

b)

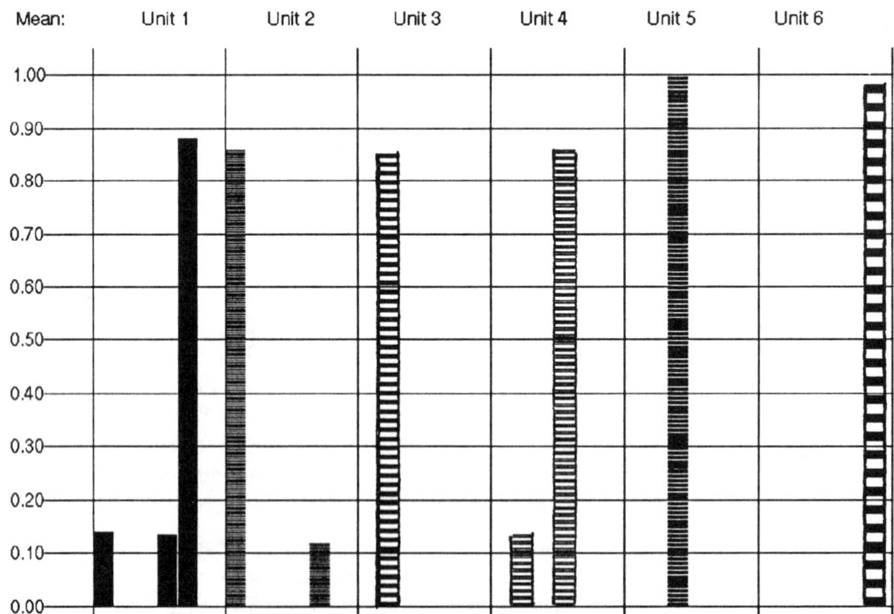

Figure 2: *The probability of each output unit responding for each of the six classes of patterns, averaged over 1200 cases. In a) the pattern trajectories contained six shifted examples of each class, while in b) there were three examples of each class.*

the patterns. Additionally, because we have a well-defined objective function for the learning, the procedure can be applied to multi-layer networks which discover features specifically tuned to the classification problem.

However, there are a few drawbacks to using this learning procedure. One is that if any lower-order temporally coherent structure exists, the network will invariably discover it. So, for example, if the pattern classes differ in their average intensity, the network can easily learn to separate them simply by detecting the average intensity of the inputs and ignoring all other information. Similarly, if the spatial location of pattern features varies slowly and predictably over time, the network tends to learn a spatial map rather than solving the higher-order problem of pattern classification. On the other hand, this suggests that a sequential approach to modelling temporally coherent structure may be possible: an initial processing stage could try to model low-order temporal structure such as local spatial correlations, a second processing stage could model the remaining structure in the output of the first over a larger spatio-temporal extent, and so on.

A second drawback is the space complexity of the algorithm: for a network with n output units, each must store n^2 joint probability statistics and n individual probabilities.[2] The storage complexity can be reduced from $n^2 + n$ to just two statistics per output unit by optimizing a more constrained objective function in which each output unit assumes a maximum entropy distribution for the other $n-1$ units. It then need only consider the average probability of its own output, and the joint probability of its output at successive time steps. In this case, the mutual information can be approximated by a sum of n terms:

$$\begin{aligned} I_{C_t;C_{t+1}} &\simeq \sum_i I_{c_{i,t};c_{i,t+1}} \\ &= \sum_i H(c_{i,t}) + H(c_{i,t+1}) - H(c_{i,t}, c_{i,t+1}) \end{aligned}$$

where $H(c_{i,t}) = -\langle p_i{}^t \rangle_t \log \langle p_i{}^t \rangle_t - \frac{n-1}{n} \langle 1 - p_i{}^t \rangle_t \log \frac{n-1}{n} \langle 1 - p_i{}^t \rangle_t$ is the entropy of the ith output unit under the maximum entropy assumption for the other output units, and the other constrained entropies are computed similarly.

A final drawback of the learning procedure presented here, as discussed earlier, is its tendency to become trapped in local optima with very large weights. We dealt with this by introducing a constant parameter, λ, to dampen the importance of the joint entropy term. A more principled way to deal with the problem of local optima is to use stochastic rather than deterministic output units, resulting in a stochastic gradient descent learning procedure (although this would increase the simulation time considerably). Another way of obtaining more globally optimal solutions might be to consider the predictability of classifications over longer time scales rather than just at pairwise time steps, as was done in Földiák's model (1991). The network could thus maximize the mutual information between its current response and a weighted average of its responses over the last few time steps.

[2] Note, however, that the complexity (both in time and space) of the computation of these statistics is negligible relative to that of the gradient calculations, assuming there are many more weights than the squared number of output units in the network.

5 CONCLUSIONS

The invariance of an objects' identity over time, with respect to transformations it may undergo as it and/or the observer move, provides a powerful cue for perceptual learning. We have demonstrated that a network can learn, entirely unsupervised, to build translation-invariant object detectors based on the assumption of temporal coherence about the input. This procedure should be widely applicable to a variety of perceptual learning tasks, such as identifying phonemes in speech, segmenting objects in images of trajectories, and classifying textures in tactile input.

Acknowledgments

I thank Geoff Hinton for many fruitful discussions that led to the ideas presented in this paper.

References

Becker, S. and Hinton, G. E. (1992). A self-organizing neural network that discovers surfaces in random-dot stereograms. *Nature*, 355:161–163.

Birch, E. E., Gwiazda, J., and Held, R. (1982). Stereoacuity development for crossed and uncrossed disparities in human infants. *Vison research*, 22:507–513.

Bridle, J. S. (1990). Training stochastic model recognition algorithms as networks can lead to maximum mutual information estimation of parameters. In Touretzky, D. S., editor, *Neural Information Processing Systems, Vol. 2*, pages 111–217, San Mateo, CA. Morgan Kaufmann.

Földiák, P. (1991). Learning invariance from transformation sequences. *Neural Computation*, 3(2):194–200.

Fukushima, K. (1988). Neocognition: A hierarchical neural network capable of visual pattern pattern recognition. *Neural networks*, 1:119–130.

Giles, C. L. and Maxwell, T. (1987). Learning, invariance, and generalization in high-order neural networks. *Applied Optics*, 26(23):4972–4978.

Held, R., Birch, E. E., and Gwiazda, J. (1980). Stereoacuity of human infants. *Proceedings of the national academy of sciences USA*, 77(9):5572–5574.

Hinton, G. E. and Lang, K. (1985). Shape recognition and illusory conjunctions. In *IJCAI 9*, Los Angeles.

Le Cun, Y., Boser, B., Denker, J., Henderson, D., Howard, R., Hubbard, W., and Jackel, L. (1990). Handwritten digit recognition with a back-propagation network. In Touretzky, D., editor, *Advances in Neural Information Processing Systems*, pages 396–404, Denver 1989. Morgan Kaufmann, San Mateo.

Zemel, R. S., Hinton, G. E., and Mozer, M. C. (1990). TRAFFIC: object recognition using hierarchical reference frame transformations. In *Advances in Neural Information Processing Systems 2*, pages 266–273. Morgan Kaufmann Publishers.

Filter Selection Model for Generating Visual Motion Signals

Steven J. Nowlan*
CNL, The Salk Institute
P.O. Box 85800, San Diego, CA
92186-5800

Terrence J. Sejnowski
CNL, The Salk Institute
P.O. Box 85800, San Diego, CA
92186-5800

Abstract

Neurons in area MT of primate visual cortex encode the velocity of moving objects. We present a model of how MT cells aggregate responses from V1 to form such a velocity representation. Two different sets of units, with local receptive fields, receive inputs from motion energy filters. One set of units forms estimates of local motion, while the second set computes the utility of these estimates. Outputs from this second set of units "gate" the outputs from the first set through a gain control mechanism. This active process for selecting only a subset of local motion responses to integrate into more global responses distinguishes our model from previous models of velocity estimation. The model yields accurate velocity estimates in synthetic images containing multiple moving targets of varying size, luminance, and spatial frequency profile and deals well with a number of transparency phenomena.

1 INTRODUCTION

Humans, and primates in general, are very good at complex motion processing tasks such as tracking a moving target against a moving background under varying luminance. In order to accomplish such tasks, the visual system must integrate many local motion estimates from cells with limited spatial receptive fields and marked orientation selectivity. These local motion estimates are sensitive not just

*Current address, Synaptics Inc., 2698 Orchard Parkway, San Jose, CA 95134.

to the velocity of a visual target, but also to many other features of the target such as its spatial frequency profile or local edge orientation. As a result, the integration of these motion signals cannot be performed in a fixed manner, but must be a dynamic process dependent on the visual stimulus.

Although cells with motion-sensitive responses are found in primary visual cortex (V1 in primates), mounting physiological evidence suggests that the integration of these responses to produce responses which are tuned primarily to the velocity of a visual target first occurs in primate visual area MT (Albright 1992, Maunsell and Newsome 1987). We propose a computational model for integrating local motion responses to estimate the velocity of objects in the visual scene. These velocity estimates may be used for eye tracking or other visuo-motor skills. Previous computational approaches to this problem (Grzywacz and Yuille 1990, Heeger 1987, Heeger 1992, Horn and Schunk 1981, Nagel 1987) have primarily focused on *how* to combine local motion responses into local velocity estimates at all points in an image (the velocity flow field). We propose that the integration of local motion measurements may be much simpler, if one does not try to integrate across all of the local motion measurements but only a subset. Our model learns to estimate the velocity of visual targets by solving the problems of *what* to integrate and *how* to integrate in parallel. The trained model yields accurate velocity estimates from synthetic images containing multiple moving targets of varying size, luminance, and spatial frequency profile.

2 THE MODEL

The model is implemented as a cascade of networks of locally connected units which has two parallel processing pathways (figure 1). All stages of the model are represented as "layers" of units with a roughly retinotopic organization. The figure schematically represents the activity in the model at one instant of time. Conceptually, it is easier to think of the model as computing evidence for particular velocities in an image rather than computing velocity directly. Processing in the model may be divided into 3 stages, to be described in more detail below. In the first stage, the input intensity image is converted into 36 local motion "images" (9 of which are shown in the figure) which represent the outputs of 36 motion energy filters from each region of the input image. In the second stage, the operations of *integration* and *selection* are performed in parallel. The integration pathway combines information from motion energy filters tuned to different directions and spatial and temporal frequencies to compute the local evidence in favor of a particular velocity. The selection pathway weights each region of the image according to the amount of evidence for a particular velocity that region contains. In the third stage, the global evidence for a visual target moving at a particular velocity $v_k(t)$ is computed as a sum over the product of the outputs of the integration and selection pathways:

$$v_k(t) = \sum_{x,y} I_k(x,y,t) S_k(x,y,t) \tag{1}$$

where $I_k(x,y,t)$ is the local evidence for velocity k computed by the integration pathway from region (x,y) at time t, and $S_k(x,y,t)$ is the weight assigned by the selection pathway to that region.

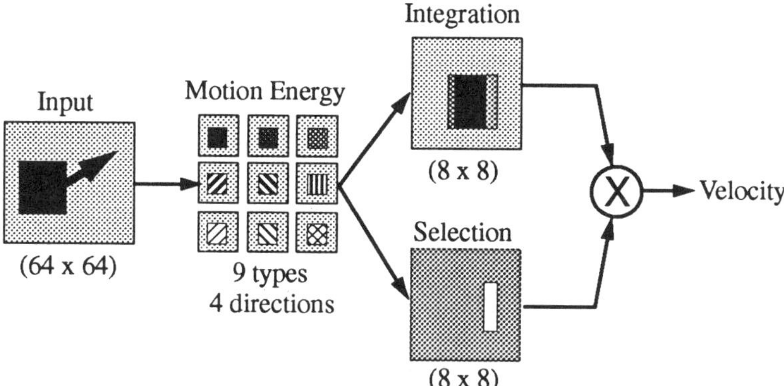

Figure 1: Diagram of motion processing model. Processing proceeds from left to right in the model, but the integration and selection stages operate in parallel. Shading within the boxes indicates different levels of activity at each stage. The responses shown in the diagram are intended to be *indicative* of the responses at different stages of the model but do not represent actual responses from the model.

2.1 LOCAL MOTION ESTIMATES

The first stage of processing is based on the motion energy model (Adelson and Bergen 1985, Watson 1985). This model relies on the observation that an intensity edge moving at a constant velocity produces a line at a particular orientation in space-time. This means that an oriented space-time filter will respond most strongly to objects moving at a particular velocity.[1] A motion energy filter uses the squared outputs of a quadrature pair (90° out of phase) of oriented filters to produce a phase independent local velocity estimate. The motion energy model was selected as a biologically plausible model of motion processing in mammalian V1, based primarily on the similarity of responses of simple and complex cells in cat area V1 to the output of different stages of the motion energy model (Heeger 1992, Grywacz and Yuille 1990, Emerson 1987).

The particular filters used in our model had spatial responses similar to a two-dimensional Gabor filter, with the physiologically more plausible temporal responses suggested by Adelson and Bergen (1985). The motion energy layer was divided into a grid of 49 by 49 receptive field locations and at each grid location there were filters tuned to four different directions of motion (up, down, left, and right). For each direction of motion there were nine different filters representing combinations of three spatial and three temporal frequencies. The filter center frequency spacings were 1 octave spatially and 1.5 octaves temporally. The filter parameters and spacings were chosen to be physiologically realistic, and were *fixed* during training of the model. In addition, there was a correspondence between the size of the filter

[1]These filters actually respond most strongly to a narrow band of spatial frequencies (SF) and temporal frequencies (TF), which represent a range of velocities, $v = TF/SF$.

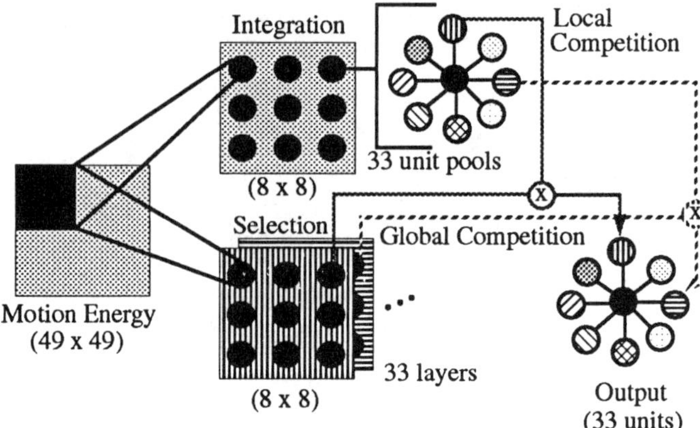

Figure 2: Diagram of integration and selection processing stages. Different shadings for units in the integration and output pools correspond to different directions of motion. Only two of the selection layers are shown and the backgrounds of these layers are shaded to match their corresponding integration and output units. See text for description of architecture.

receptive fields and the spatial frequency tuning of the filters with lower frequency filters having larger spatial extent to their receptive fields. This is also similar to what has been found in visual cortex (Maunsell and Newsome, 1987).

The input intensity image is first filtered with a difference of gaussians filter which is a simplification of retinal processing and provides smoothing and contrast enhancement. Each motion energy filter is then convolved with the smoothed input image producing 36 motion energy responses at each location in the receptive field grid which serve as the input to the next stage of processing.

2.2 INTEGRATION AND SELECTION

The integration and selection pathways are both implemented as locally connected networks with a single layer of weights. The integration pathway can be thought of as a layer of units organized into a grid of 8 by 8 receptive field locations (figure 2). Units at each receptive field location look at all 36 motion energy measurements from each location within a 9 by 9 region of the motion energy receptive field grid. Adjacent receptive field locations receive input from overlapping regions of the motion energy layer.

At each receptive field location in the integration layer there is a pool of 33 integration units (9 units in one of these pools are shown in figure 2). These units represent motion in 8 different directions with units representing four different speeds for each direction plus a central unit indicating no motion. These units form a log polar representation of the local velocity at that receptive field location, since as one moves out along any "arm" of the pool of units each unit represents a speed twice as large as the preceding unit in that arm. All of the integration pools share a common set of weights, so in the final trained model all compute the same function.

The activity of an integration unit (which lies between 0 and 1) represents the amount of local support for the corresponding velocity. *Local competition* between the units in each integration pool enforces the important constraint that *each integration pool can only provide strong support for one velocity.* The competition is enforced using a *softmax* non-linearity: If $I'_k(x,y,t)$ represents the net input to unit k in one of the integration pools, the state of that unit is computed as

$$I_k(x,y,t) = e^{I'_k(x,y,t)} / \sum_j e^{I'_j(x,y,t)}.$$

Note that the summation is performed over all units within a single pool, all of which share the same (x,y) receptive field location.

The output of the model is also represented by a pool of 33 units, organized in the same way as each pool of integration units. The state of each unit in the output pool represents the global evidence within the entire image supporting a particular velocity. The state of each of these output units $v_k(t)$ is computed as the weighted sum of the state of the corresponding integration unit in all 64 integration receptive field locations (equation (1)). The weights assigned to each receptive field location are computed by the state of the corresponding selection unit (figure 2). Although the activity of output units can be treated as evidence for a particular velocity, the activity across the entire pool of units forms a distributed representation of a continuous range of velocities (*i.e.* activity split between two adjacent units represents a velocity between the optimal velocities of those two units).

The selection units are also organized into a grid of 8 by 8 receptive field locations which are in one to one correspondence with the integration receptive field locations (figure 2). However, it is convenient to think of the selection units as being organized not as a single layer of units but rather as 33 layers of units, one for each output unit. In each layer of selection units, there is one unit for each receptive field location. Two of the selection layers are shown in figure 2. The layer with the vertically shaded background corresponds to the output unit for upward motion (also shaded with vertical stripes) and states of units in this selection layer weight the states of upward motion units in each integration pool (again shaded vertically).

There is *global competition* among all of the units in each selection layer. Again this is implemented using a softmax non-linearity: If $S'_k(x,y,t)$ is the net input to a selection unit in layer k, the state of that unit is computed as

$$S_k(x,y,t) = e^{S'_k(x,y,t)} / \sum_{x',y'} e^{S'_k(x',y',t)}.$$

Note that unlike the integration case, the summation in this case is performed over all receptive field locations. This global competition enforces the second important constraint in the model, that *the total amount of support for each velocity across the entire image cannot exceed one.* This constraint, combined with the fact that the integration unit outputs can never exceed 1 ensures that the states of the output units are constrained to be between 0 and 1 and can be interpreted as the global support within the image for each velocity, as stated earlier.

The combination of global competition in the selection layers and local competition within the integration pools means that the only way to produce strong support for a particular output velocity is for the corresponding selection network to focus all its support on regions that strongly support that velocity. This allows the selection network to learn to estimate how useful information in different regions of an image is for predicting velocities within the visual scene. The weights of both the selection and integration networks are adapted in parallel as is discussed next.

2.3 OBJECTIVE FUNCTION AND TRAINING

The outputs of the integration and selection networks in the final trained model are combined as in equation (1), so that the final outputs represent the global support for each velocity within the image. During training of the system however, the outputs of each pool of integration units are treated as if each were an independent estimate of support for a particular velocity. If a training image sequence contains an object moving at velocity v_k then the target for the corresponding output unit is set to 1, otherwise it is set to 0. The system is then trained to maximize the likelihood of generating the targets:

$$\log L = \sum_t \sum_k \log \left(\sum_{x,y} S_k(x,y,t) \exp\left[-(v_k - I_k(x,y,t))^2\right] \right) \quad (2)$$

To optimize this objective, each integration output $I_k(x,y,t)$ is compared to the target v_k directly, and the outputs closest to the target value are assigned the most *responsibility* for that target, and hence receive the largest error signal. At the same time, the selection network states are trained to try and estimate from the input alone (*i.e.* the local motion measurements), which integration outputs are most accurate. This interpretation of the system during training is identical to the interpretation given to the *mixture of experts* (Nowlan, 1990) and the same training procedure was used. Each pool of integration units functions like an expert network, and each layer of selection units functions like a gating network.

There are, however, two important differences between the current system and the mixture of experts. First, this system uses multiple gating networks rather than a single one, allowing the system to represent more than a single velocity within an image. Second, in the mixture of experts, each expert network has an independent set of weights and essentially learns to compute a different function (usually different functions of the same input). In the current model, each pool of integration units shares the same set of weights and is constrained to compute the same function. The effect of the training procedure in this system is to bias the computations of the integration pools to favor certain types of local image features (for example, the integration stage may only make reliable velocity estimates in regions of shear or discontinuities in velocity). The selection networks learn to identify which features the integration stage is looking for, and to weight image regions most heavily which contain these kinds of features.

3 RESULTS AND DISCUSSION

The system was trained using 500 image sequences containing 64 frames each. These training image sequences were generated by randomly selecting one or two visual targets for each sequence and moving these targets through randomly selected trajectories. The targets were rectangular patches that varied in size, texture, and intensity. The motion trajectories all began with the objects stationary and then one or both objects rapidly accelerated to constant velocities maintained for the remainder of the trajectory. Targets moved in one of 8 possible directions, at speeds ranging between 0 and 2.5 pixels per unit of time. In training sequences containing multiple targets, the targets were permitted to overlap (targets were assigned to different depth planes at random) and the upper target was treated as opaque in some cases and partially transparent in other cases. The system was trained using a conjugate gradient descent procedure until the response of the system on the training sequences deviated by less than 1% on average from the desired response.

The performance of the trained system was tested using a separate set of 50 test image sequences. These sequences contained 10 novel visual targets with random trajectories generated in the same manner as the training sequences. The responses on this test set remained within 2.5% of the desired response, with the largest errors occurring at the highest velocities. Several of these test sequences were designed so that targets contained edges oriented obliquely to the direction of motion, demonstrating the ability of the model to deal with aspects of the aperture problem. In addition, only small, transient increases in error were observed when two moving objects intersected, whether these objects were opaque or partially transparent.

A more challenging test of the system was provided by presenting the system with "plaid patterns" consisting of two square wave gratings drifting in different directions (Adelson and Movshon, 1982). Human observers will sometimes see a single coherent motion corresponding to the intersection of constraints (IOC) direction of the two grating motions, and sometimes see the two grating motions separately, as one grating sliding through the other. The percept reported can be altered by changing the contrast of the regions where the two gratings intersect relative to the contrast of the grating itself (Stoner *et al*, 1990). We found that for most grating patterns the model reliably reported a single motion in the IOC direction, but by manipulating the intensity of the intersection regions it was possible to find regions where the model would report the motion of the two gratings separately. Coherent grating motion was reported when the model tended to select most strongly image regions corresponding to the intersections of the gratings, while two motions were reported when the regions between the grating intersections were strongly selected.

We also explored the response properties of selection and integration units in the trained model using drifting sinusoidal gratings. These stimuli were chosen because they have been used extensively in exploring the physiological response properties of visual motion neurons in cortical visual areas (Albright 1992, Maunsell and Newsome 1987). Integration units tended to be tuned to a fairly narrow band of velocities over a broad range of spatial frequencies, like many MT cells (Maunsell and Newsome, 1987). The selection units had quite different response properties. They responded primarily to velocity shear (neighboring regions of differing velocity) and to flicker (temporal frequency) rather than true velocity. Cells with many of these properties are also common in MT (Maunsell and Newsome, 1987). A final important difference between the integration and selection units is their response to whole field motion. Integration units tend to have responses which are somewhat enhanced by whole field motion in their preferred direction, while selection unit responses are generally suppressed by whole field motion. This difference is similar to the recent observation that area MT contains two classes of cell, one whose responses are suppressed by whole field motion, while responses of the second class are not suppressed (Born and Tootell, 1992).

Finally, the model that we have proposed is built on the premise of an active mechanism for selecting subsets of unit responses to integrate over. While this is a common aspect of many accounts of attentional phenomena, we suggest that active selection may represent a fundamental aspect of cortical processing that occurs with many pre-attentive phenomena, such as motion processing.

References

Adelson, E. H. and Bergen, J. R. (1985) Spatiotemporal energy models for the perception of motion. *J. Opt. Soc. Am.* A, **2**, 284-299.

Adelson, M. and Movshon, J. A. (1982) Phenomenal coherence of moving visual patterns. *Nature*, **300**, 523-525.

Albright, T. D. (1992) Form-cue invariant motion processing in primate visual cortex. *Science.* **255**, 1141-1143.

Born, R. T. and Tootell, R. B. H. (1992) Segregation of global and local motion processing in primate middle temporal visual area. *Nature*, **357**, 497-500.

Emerson, R.C., Citron, M.C., Vaughn W.J., Klein, S.A. (1987) Nonlinear directionally selective subunits in complex cells of cat striate cortex. *J. Neurophys.* **58**, 33-65.

Grzywacz, N.M. and Yuille, A.L. (1990) A model for the estimate of local image velocity by cells in the visual cortex. *Proc. R. Soc. Lond.* B **239**, 129-161.

Heeger, D.J. (1987) Model for the extraction of image flow. *J. Opt. Soc. Am.* A **4**, 1455-1471.

Heeger, D.J. (1992) Normalization of cell responses in cat striate cortex. *Visual Neuroscience*, in press.

Horn, B.K.P. and Schunk, B.G. (1981) Determining optical flow. *Artificial Intelligence* **17**, 185-203.

Maunsell J.H.R. and Newsome, W.T. (1987) Visual processing in monkey extrastriate cortex. *Ann. Rev. Neurosci.* **10**, 363-401.

Nowlan, S.J. (1990) Competing experts: An experimental investigation of associative mixture models. Technical Report CRG-TR-90-5, Department of Computer Science, University of Toronto.

Nagel, H.H. (1987) On the estimation of optical flow: relations between different approaches and some new results. *Artificial Intelligence* **33**, 299-324.

Stoner G.R., Albright T.D., Ramachandran V.S. (1990) Transparency and coherence in human motion perception. *Nature* **344**, 153-155.

Watson, A.B. and Ahumada, A.J. (1985) Model of human visual-motion sensing. *J. Opt. Soc. Am.* A, **2**, 322-342.

STIMULUS ENCODING BY MULTIDIMENSIONAL RECEPTIVE FIELDS IN SINGLE CELLS AND CELL POPULATIONS IN V1 OF AWAKE MONKEY

Edward Stern
Center for Neural Computation
and Department of Neurobiology
Life Sciences Institute
Hebrew University
Jerusalem, Israel

Ad Aertsen
Institut fur Neuroinformatik
Ruhr-Universitat-Bochum
Bochum, Germany

Eilon Vaadia
Center for Neural Computation
and Physiology Department
Hadassah Medical School
Hebrew University
Jerusalem, Israel

Shaul Hochstein
Center for Neural Computation
and Department of Neurobiology,
Life Sciences Institute
Hebrew University
Jerusalem, Israel

ABSTRACT

Multiple single neuron responses were recorded from a single electrode in V1 of alert, behaving monkeys. Drifting sinusoidal gratings were presented in the cells' overlapping receptive fields, and the stimulus was varied along several visual dimensions. The degree of dimensional separability was calculated for a large population of neurons, and found to be a continuum. Several cells showed different temporal response dependencies to variation of different stimulus dimensions, i.e. the tuning of the modulated firing was not necessarily the same as that of the mean firing rate. We describe a multidimensional receptive field, and use simultaneously recorded responses to compute a multi-neuron receptive field, describing the information processing capabilities of a group of cells. Using dynamic correlation analysis, we propose several computational schemes for multidimensional spatiotemporal tuning for groups of cells. The implications for neuronal coding of stimuli are discussed.

INTRODUCTION

The receptive field is perhaps the most useful concept for understanding neuronal information processing. The ideal definition of the receptive field is that set of stimuli which cause a change in the neuron's firing properties. However, as with many such concepts, the use of the receptive field in describing the behavior of sensory neurons falls short of the ideal. The classical method for describing the receptive field has been to measure the "tuning curve" i.e. the response of the neuron as a function of the value of one dimension of the stimulus. This presents a problem because the sensory world is multidimensional: For example, even a simple visual stimulus, such as a patch of a sinusoidal grating, may vary in location, orientation, spatial frequency, temporal frequency, movement direction and speed, phase, contrast, color, etc. Does the tuning to one dimension remain constant when other dimensions are varied? i.e. are the dimensions linearly separable? It is not unreasonable to expect inseparability: Consider an oriented, spatially discrete receptive field. The excitation generated by passing a bar through the receptive field will of course change with orientation. However, the shape of this tuning curve will depend upon the bar width, related to the spatial frequency. This effect has not been studied quantitatively, however. If interactions among dimensions exist, do they account for a large portion of the cell's response variance? Are there discrete populations of cells, with some cells showing interactions among dimensions and others not? These question have clear implications for the problem of neural coding.

Related to the question of dimensional separability is that of stimulus encoding: Given that the receptive field is multidimensional in nature, how can the cell maximize the amount of stimulus information it encodes? Does the neuron use a single code to represent all the stimulus dimensions? It is possible that interactions lead to greater uncertainty in stimulus identification. Does the small number of visual cortical cells encode all the possible combinations of stimuli using only spike rate as the dependent variable? We present data indicating that more information is indeed present in the neuronal response, and propose a new approach for its utilization.

The final problem that we address is the following: Clearly, many cells participate in the stimulus encoding process. Arriving at a valid concept of a multidimensional receptive field, can we generalize this concept to more than one cell introducing the notion of a multi-cellular receptive field?

METHODS

Drifting sinusoidal gratings were presented for 500 msec to the central 10 degrees of the visual field of monkeys performing a fixation task. The gratings were varied in orientation, spatial frequency, temporal frequency, and movement direction. We recorded from up to 3 cells simultaneously with a single electrode in the monkey's primary visual cortex (V1). The cells described in this study were well separated, using a template-matching procedure. The responses of the neurons were plotted as Peri-Stimulus Time Histograms (PSTHs) and their parameters quantified (Abeles, 1982), and offline Fourier analysis and time-dependent crosscorrelation analysis (Aertsen et al, 1989) were performed.

RESULTS

Recording the responses of visual cortical neurons to stimuli varied over a number of dimensions, we found that in some cases, the tuning curve to one dimension depended on the value of another dimension. Figure 1A shows the spatial-frequency tuning curve of a single cell measured at 2 different stimulus orientations. When the orientation of the stimulus is 72 degrees, the peak response is at a spatial frequency of 4.5 cycles/degree (cpd), while at an orientation of 216 degrees, the spatial frequency of peak response is 2.3 cpd. If the responses to different visual dimensions were truly linearly separable, the tuning curve to any single dimension would have the same shape and, in particular, position of peak, despite any variations in other dimensions. If the tuning curves are not parallel, then interactions must exist between dimensions. Clearly, this is an example of a cell whose responses are not linearly separable. In order to quantify the inseparability phenomenon, analyses of variance were performed, using spike rate as the dependent variable, and the visual dimensions of the stimuli as the independent variables. We then measured the amount of interaction as a percentage of the total between-conditions

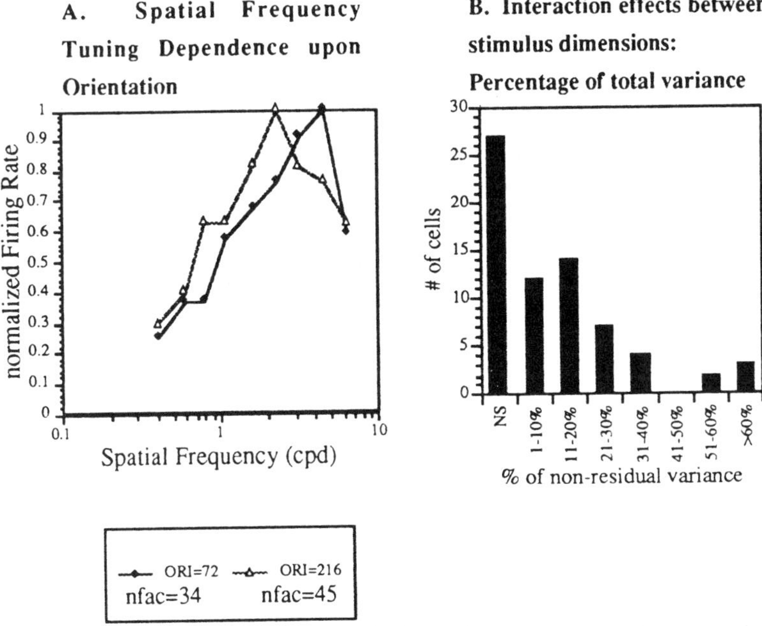

Figure 1: Dimensional Inseparability of Visual Cortical Neurons. A: An example of dimensionsional inseparability in the response of a single cell; B: Histogram of dimensional inseparability as a percentage of total response variance.

variance divided by the residuals. The resulting histogram for 69 cells is shown in Figure 1B. Although there are several cells with non-significant interactions, i.e. linearly separable dimensions, this is not the majority of cells. The amount of dimensional inseparability seems to be a continuum. We suggest that separability is a significant variable in the coding capability of the neurons, which must be taken into account when modeling the representation of sensory information by cortical neural networks.

We found that the time course of the response was not always constant, but varied with stimulus parameters. Cortical cell responses may have components which are sustained (constant over time), transient (with a peak near stimulus onset and/or offset), or modulated (varying with the stimulus period). For example, Figure 2 shows the responses of a single neuron in V1 to 50 stimuli, varying in orientation and spatial frequency. Each response is plotted as a PSTH, and the stippled bar under the PSTH indicates the time of

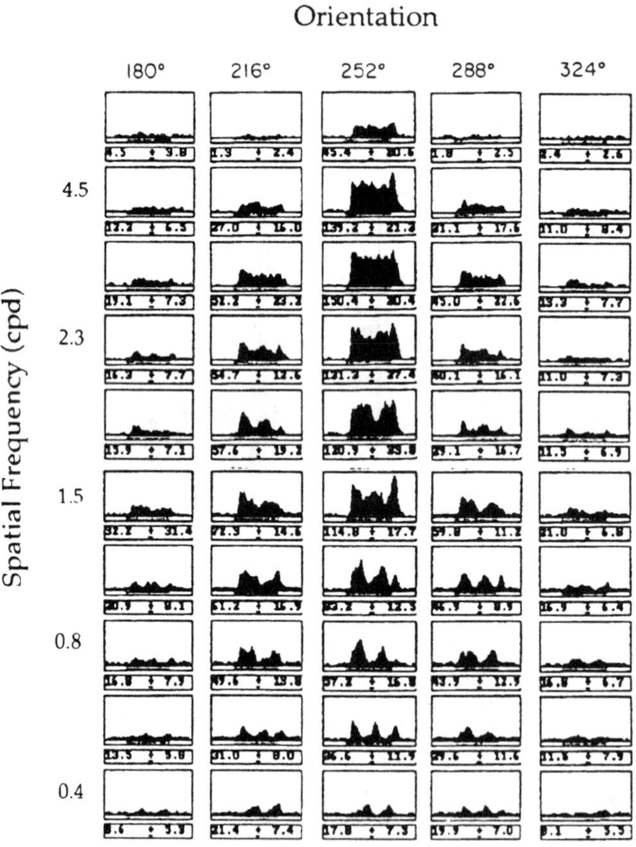

Figure 2: Spatial Frequency/Orientation Tuning of Responses of V1 Cell

the stimulus presentation (500 msec). The numbers beneath each PSTH are the firing rate averaged over the response time, and the standard deviations of the response over repetitions of the stimulus (in this case 40). Clearly, the cell is orientation selective, and the neuronal response is also tuned to spatial frequency. The stimulus eliciting the highest firing rate is ORI=252 degrees; SF=3.2 cycles/degree (cpd). However, when looking at the responses to lower spatial frequencies, we see a modulation in the PSTH. The modulation, when present, has 2 peaks, corresponding to the temporal frequency of the stimulus grating (4 cycles/second). Therefore, although the response rate of the cell is lower at low spatial frequencies than for other stimuli, the spike train carries additional information about another stimulus dimension.

If the visual neuron is considered as a linear system, the predicted response to a drifting sinusoidal grating would be a (rectified) sinusoid of the same (temporal) frequency as that of the stimulus, i.e. a modulated response (Enroth-Cugell & Robson, 1966; Hochstein & Shapley, 1976; Spitzer & Hochstein, 1988). However, as seen in Figure 2, in some stimulus regimes the cell's response deviates from linearity. We conclude that the linearity or nonlinearity of the response is dependent upon the stimulus conditions (Spitzer & Hochstein, 1985). A modulated response is one that would be expected from simple cells, while the sustained response seen at higher spatial frequencies is that expected from complex cells. Our data therefore suggest that the simple/complex cell categorization is not complete.

A further example of response time-course dependence on stimulus parameters is seen in Figure 3A. In this case, the stimulus was varied in spatial frequency and temporal frequency, while other dimensions were held constant. Again, as spatial frequency is raised, the modulation of the PSTH gives way to a more sustained response. Furthermore, as temporal frequency is raised, both the sustained and the modulated responses are replaced by a single transient response. When present, the frequency of the modulation follows that of the temporal frequency of the stimulus. Fourier analysis of the response histograms (Figure 3B) reveals that the DC and fundamental component (FC) are not tuned to the same stimulus values (arrows indicating peaks). We propose that this information may be available to the cell readout, enabling the single cell to encode multiple stimulus dimensions simultaneously.

Thus, a complete description of the receptive field must be multidimensional in nature. Furthermore, in light of the evidence that the spike train is not constant, one of the dimensions which must be used to display the receptive field must be time.

Figure 4 shows one method of displaying a multidimensional response map, with time along the abscissa (in 10 msec bins) and orientation along the ordinate. In the top two figures, the z axis, represented in gray-scale, is the number of counts (spikes) per bin. Therefore, each line is a PSTH, with counts (bin height) coded by shading. In this example, cell 2 (upper picture) is tuned to orientation, with peaks at 90 and 270 degrees. The cell is only slightly direction selective, as represented by the fact that the 2 areas of high activity are similarly shaded. However, there is a transient peak at 270 degrees which

A.

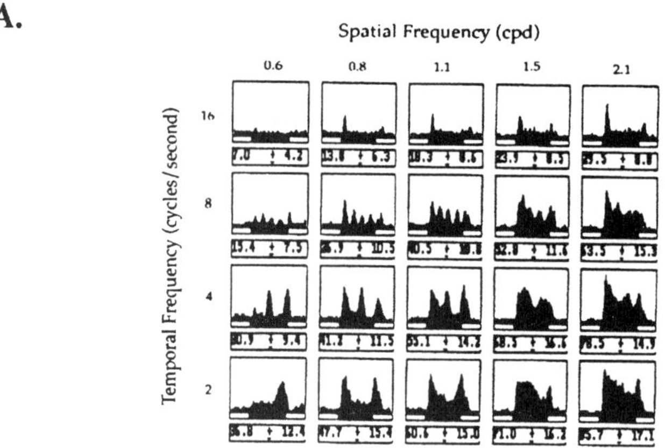

B.

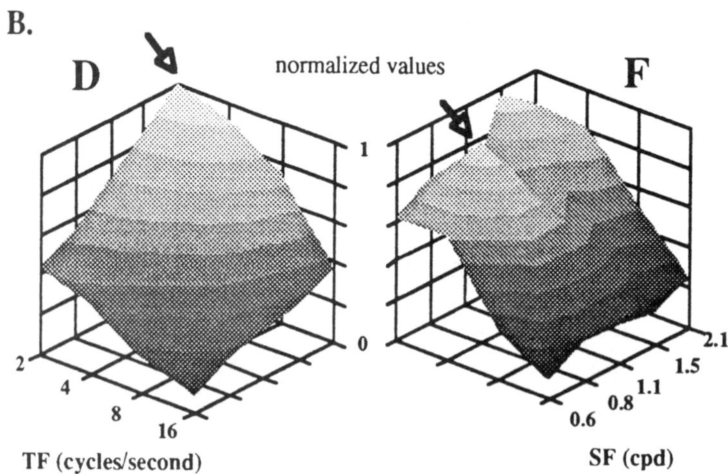

**Figure 3: A. TF/SF Tuning of response of V1 cell.
B. Tuning of DC and FC of response to stimulus parameters.**

is absent at 90 degrees. The middle picture, representing a simultaneously recorded cell shows a different pattern of activity. The orientation tuning of this cell is similar to that of cell 2, but it has stronger directional selectivity, (towards 90 degrees). In this case, the transient is also at 90 degrees. The bottom picture shows the joint activity of these 2 cells. Rather than each line being a PSTH, each line is a Joint PSTH (JPSTH; Aertsen et al, 1989). This histogram represents the time-dependent correlated activity of a pair of cells. It is equivalent to sliding a window across a spike train of one neuron and

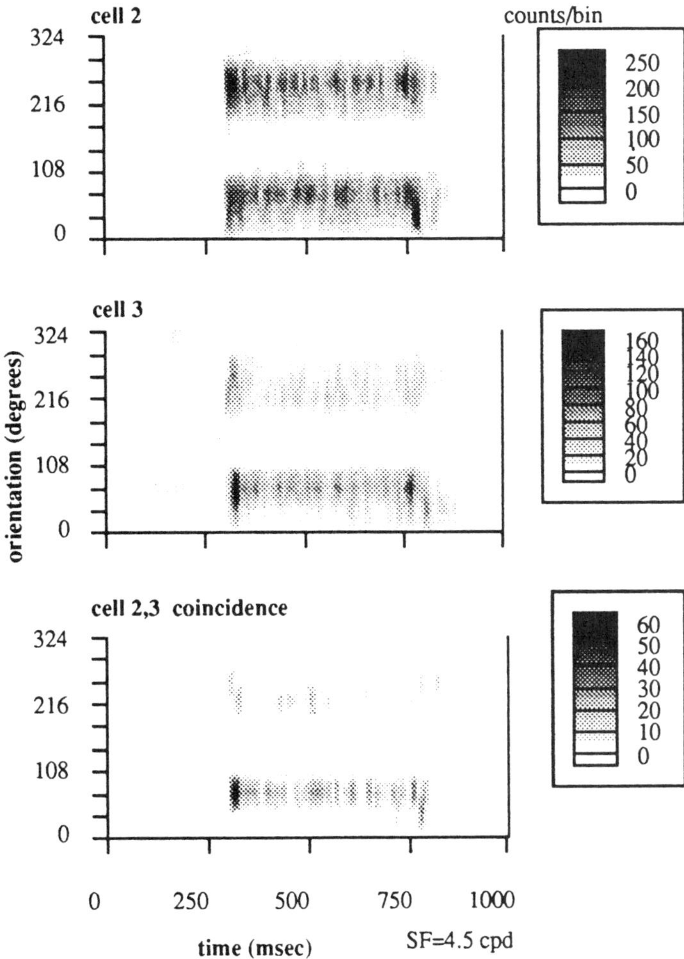

Figure 4: Response Maps.

Top, Middle: Single-cell Multidimensional Receptive Fields;

Bottom: Multi-Cell Multidimensional Receptive Field

asking when a spike from another neuron falls within the window. The size of the window can be varied; here we used 2 msec. Therefore, we are asking when these cells fire within 2 msec of each other, and how this is connected to the stimulus. The z axis is now coincidences per bin. We may consider this the logical AND activity of these cells; if there is a cell receiving information from both of these neurons, this is the receptive field which would describe its input. Clearly, it is different from the each of the 2 individual cells. In our results, it is more narrowly tuned, and the tuning can not be predicted from the individual components. We emphasize that this is the "raw" JPSTH, which is not corrected for stimulus effects, common input, or normalized. This is because we want a measure comparable to the PSTHs themselves, to compare a multi-unit receptive field to its single unit components. In this case, however, a significant ($p<0.01$; Palm et al, 1988) "mono-directional" interaction is present. For a more complete description of the receptive field, this type of figure, shown here for one spatial frequency only, can be shown for all spatial frequencies as "slices" along a fourth axis. However, space limitations prevent us from presenting this multidimensional aspect of the multicellular receptive field.

CONCLUSIONS

We have shown that interactions among stimulus dimensions account for a significant proportion of the response variance of V1 cells. The variance of the interactions itself may be a useful parameter when considering a population response, as the amount and location of the dimensional inseparability varies among cells. We have also shown that different temporal characteristics of the spike trains can be tuned to different dimensions, and add to the encoding capabilities of the cell in a neurobiologically realistic manner. Finally, we use these results to generate multidimensional receptive fields, for single cells and small groups of cells. We emphasize that this can be generalized to larger populations of cells, and to compute the population responses of cells that may be meaningful for the cortex as a biological neuronal network.

Acknowledgements

We thank Israel Nelken, Hagai Bergman, Volodya Yakovlev, Moshe Abeles, Peter Hillman, Robert Shapley and Valentino Braitenberg for helpful discussions. This study was supported by grants from the U.S.-Israel Bi-National Science Foundation (BSF) and the Israel Academy of Sciences.

References

1. Abeles, M. Quantification, Smoothing, and Confidence Limits for Single Units' Histograms *J. Neurosci. Methods 5* , 317-325, 1982.

2. Aertsen, A.M.H.J., Gerstein, G. L., Habib, M.K., and Palm, G. Dynamics of Neuronal Firing Correlation: Modulation of "Effective Connectivity" *J. Neurophysiol 51* (5), 900-917, 1989.

3. Enroth-Cugell, C. and Robson, J.G. The Contrast Sensitivity of Retinal Ganglion Cells of the Cat *J Physiol. Lond 187*, 517-552, 1966.

4. Hochstein, S. and Shapley, R. M. Linear and Nonlinear Spatial Subunits in Y Cat Retinal Ganglion Cells *J Physiol. Lond 262*, 265-284, 1976.

5. Palm, G., Aertsen, A.M.H.J. and Gerstein, G.L. On the Significance of Correlations Among Neuronal Spike Trains *Biol. Cybern. 59* , 1-11, 1988.

6. Spitzer, H. and Hochstein, S. Simple and Complex-Cell Response Dependencies on Stimulation Parameters *J.Neurophysiol 53*, 1244-1265, 1985.

7. Spitzer, H. and Hochstein, S. Complex Cell Receptive Field Models *Prog. in Neurobiology, 31* , 285-309, 1988.

The Computation of Stereo Disparity for Transparent and for Opaque Surfaces

Suthep Madarasmi
Computer Science Department
University of Minnesota
Minneapolis, MN 55455

Daniel Kersten
Department of Psychology
University of Minnesota

Ting-Chuen Pong
Computer Science Department
University of Minnesota

Abstract

The classical computational model for stereo vision incorporates a uniqueness inhibition constraint to enforce a one-to-one feature match, thereby sacrificing the ability to handle transparency. Critics of the model disregard the uniqueness constraint and argue that the smoothness constraint can provide the excitation support required for transparency computation. However, this modification fails in neighborhoods with sparse features. We propose a Bayesian approach to stereo vision with priors favoring cohesive over transparent surfaces. The disparity and its segmentation into a multi-layer "depth planes" representation are simultaneously computed. The smoothness constraint propagates support within each layer, providing mutual excitation for non-neighboring transparent or partially occluded regions. Test results for various random-dot and other stereograms are presented.

1 INTRODUCTION

The horizontal disparity in the projection of a 3-D point in a parallel stereo imaging system can be used to compute depth through triangulation. As the number of points in the scene increases, the correspondence problem increases in complexity due to the matching ambiguity. Prior constraints on surfaces are needed to arrive at a correct solution. Marr and Poggio [1976] use the smoothness constraint to resolve matching ambiguity and the uniqueness constraint to enforce a 1-to-1 match. Their smoothness constraint tends to oversmooth at occluding boundaries and their uniqueness assumption discourages the computation of stereo transparency for two overlaid surfaces. Prazdny [1985] disregards the uniqueness inhibition term to enable transparency perception. However, their smoothness constraint is locally enforced and fails at providing excitation for spatially disjoint regions and for sparse transparency.

More recently, Bayesian approaches have been used to incorporate prior constraints (see [Clark and Yuille, 1990] for a review) for stereopsis while overcoming the problem of oversmoothing. Line processes are activated for disparity discontinuities to mark the smoothness boundaries while the disparity is simultaneously computed. A drawback of such methods is the lack of an explicit grouping of image sites into piece-wise smooth regions. In addition, when presented with a stereogram of overlaid (transparent) surfaces such as in the random-dot stereogram in figure 5, multiple edges in the image are obtained while we clearly perceive two distinct, overlaid surfaces. With edges as output, further grouping of overlapping surfaces is impossible using the edges as boundaries. This suggests that surface grouping should be performed simultaneously with disparity computation.

2 THE MULTI-LAYER REPRESENTATION

We propose a Bayesian approach to computing disparity and its segmentation that uses a different output representation from the previous, edge-based methods. Our representation was inspired by the observations of Nakayama *et al.* [1989] that mid-level processing such as the grouping of objects behind occluders is performed for objects within the same "depth plane".

As an example consider the stereogram of a floating square shown in figure 1a. The edge-based segmentation method computes the disparity and marks the disparity edges as shown in figure 1b. Our approach produces two types of output at each pixel: a layer (depth plane) number and a disparity value for that layer. The goal of the system is to place points that could have arisen from a single smooth surface in the scene into one distinct layer. The output for our multi-surface representation is shown in figure 1c. Note that the floating square has a unique layer label, namely layer 4, and the background has another label of 2. Layers 1 and 3 have no data support and are, therefore, inactive.

The rest of the pixels in each layer that have no data support obtain values by a membrane fitting process using the computed disparity as anchors. The occluded parts of surfaces are, thus, represented in each layer. In addition, disjoint regions of a single surface due to occlusion are represented in a single layer. This representation of occluded parts is an important difference between our representation and a similar representation for segmentation by Darrell and Pentland [1991].

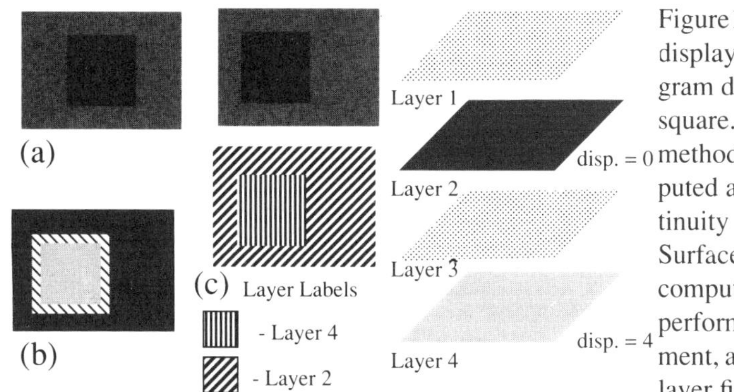

Figure 1: a) A gray scale display of a noisy stereogram depicting a floating square. b. Edge based method: disparity computed and disparity discontinuity computed. c. Multi-Surface method: disparity computed, surface grouping performed by layer assignment, and disparity for each layer filled in.

3 ALGORITHM AND SIMULATION METHOD

We use Bayes' [1783] rule to compute the scene attribute, namely disparity u and its layer assignment l for each layer:

$$p(u,l|d^L,d^R) = \frac{p(d^L,d^R|u,l)p(u,l)}{p(d^L,d^R)}$$

where d^L and d^R are the left and right intensity image data. Each constraint is expressed as a local cost function using the Markov Random Field (MRF) assumption [Geman and Geman, 1984], that pixels values are conditional only on their nearest neighbors. Using the Gibbs-MRF equivalence, the energy function can be written as a probability function:

$$p(x) = \frac{1}{Z}e^{-\frac{E(x)}{T}}$$

where Z is the normalizing constant, T is the temperature, E is the energy cost function, and x is a random variable

Our energy constraints can be expressed as

$$E = \lambda_D V_D + \lambda_S V_S + \lambda_G V_G + \lambda_E V_E + \lambda_R V_R$$

where the λ's are the weighting factors and the V_D,V_S, V_G, V_E, V_R functions are the data matching cost, the smoothness term, the gap term, the edge shape term, and the disparity versus intensity edge coupling term, respectively.

The data matching constraint prefers matches with similar intensity and contrast:

$$V_D = \sum_i^M \left[|d_i^R - d_k^L| + \gamma \sum_{j \in N_i} |(d_j^R - d_i^R) - (d_m^L - d_k^L)| \right]$$

with the image indices k and m given by the ordered pairs $k = (row(i), col(i) + u_{C_i i})$, $m = (row(j), col(j) + u_{C_i i})$, M is the number of pixels in the image, C_i is the layer classification for site i, and u_{li} is the disparity at layer l. The γ weighs absolute intensity versus contrast matching.

The λ_D is higher for points that belong to unambiguous features such as straight vertical contours, so that ambiguous pixels rely more on their prior constraints.

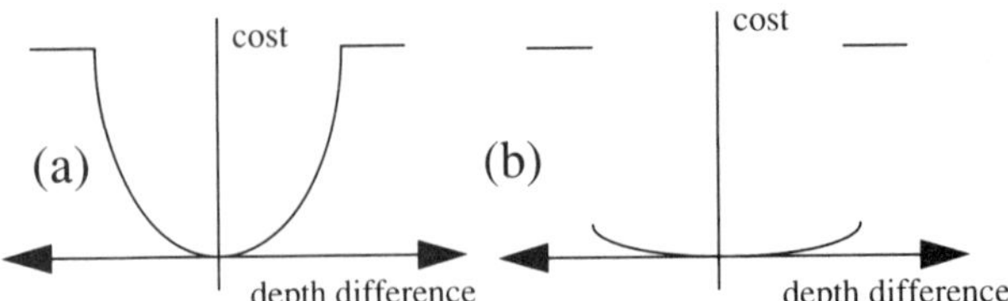

Figure 2: Cost function V_S. a) The smoothness cost is quadratic until the disparity difference is high and an edge process is activated. b) In our simulations we use a threshold below which the smoothness cost is scaled down and above which a different layer assignment is accepted at a constant high cost.

Also, if neighboring pixels have a higher disparity than the current pixel and are in a different layer, its λ_D is lowered since its corresponding point in the left image is likely to be occluded.

The equation for the smoothness term is given by:

$$V_S = \sum_i^M \sum_l^L \sum_{j \in N_i} V_s(u_{li}, u_{lj}) a_l$$

where, N_i are the neighbors of i, V_s is the local smoothness potential, a_l is the activity level for layer l defined by the percent of pixels belonging to layer l, and L is the number layers in the system. The local smoothness potential is given by:

$$V_s = \sigma_1(u_{li}, u_{lj}) + \mu \sum_k \sigma_2(\Delta_k u_{li}, \Delta_k u_{lj}); \quad \sigma_n(a, b) = \begin{cases} \frac{(a-b)^2}{\beta_n} & \text{if } (a-b)^2 < T_n \\ 1 & \text{otherwise} \end{cases}$$

where μ is the weighting term between depth smoothness and directional derivative smoothness. The Δ_k is the difference operation in various directions k, and T is the threshold. Instead of the commonly used quadratic smoothness function graphed in figure 2a, we use the σ function graphed in figure 2b which resembles the Ising potential. This allows for some flexibility since λ_S is set rather high in our simulations.

The V_G term ensures a gap in the values of corresponding pixels between layers:

$$V_G = \sum_i^M \sum_{l \neq C_i}^L \sum_{j \in N_i} V_g(u_{C_i i}, u_{lj}) a_l a_{C_i}; \quad V_g(u_{C_i i}, u_{lj}) = \begin{cases} 0 & \text{if } |u_{C_i i} - u_{lj}| \geq T \\ 1 & \text{otherwise} \end{cases}$$

This ensures that if a site i belongs to layer C_i, then all points j neighboring i for each layer l must have different disparity values u_{lj} than $u_{C_i i}$.

The edge or boundary shape constraint V_E incorporates two types of constraints: a cohesive measure and a saliency measure. The costs for various neighborhood configurations are given in figure 3.

The constraint V_R ensures that if there is no edge in intensity then there should be no edge in the disparity. This is particularly important to avoid local minima for gray scale images since there is so much ambiguity in the matching.

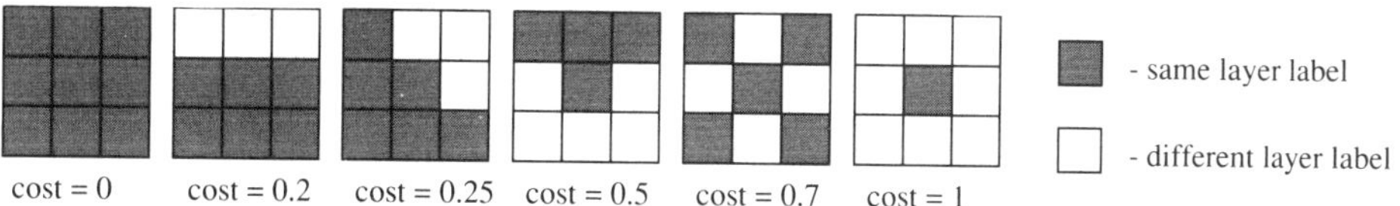

Figure 3: Cost function V_E. The costs associated nearest neighborhood layer label configurations. a) Fully cohesive region (lowest cost) b) Two opaque regions with straight line boundary. c) Two opaque regions with diagonal line boundary. d) Opaque regions with no figural continuity. e) Transparent region with dense samplings. f) Transparent region with no other neighbors (highest cost).

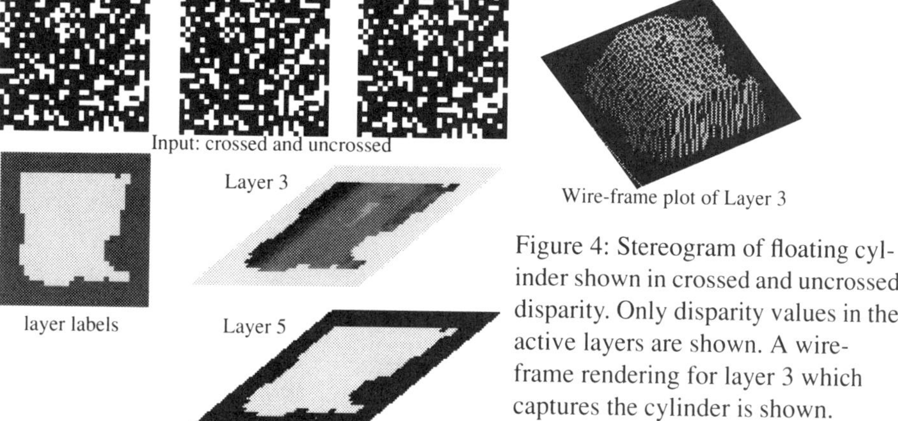

Figure 4: Stereogram of floating cylinder shown in crossed and uncrossed disparity. Only disparity values in the active layers are shown. A wire-frame rendering for layer 3 which captures the cylinder is shown.

The Gibbs Sampler [Geman and Geman, 1984] with simulated annealing is used to compute the disparity and layer assignments. After each iteration of the Gibbs Sampler, the missing values within each layer are filled-in using the disparity at the available sites. A quadratic energy functional enforces smoothness of disparity and of disparity difference in various directions. A gradient descent approach minimizes this energy and the missing values are filled-in.

4 SIMULATION RESULTS

After normalizing each of the local costs to lie between 0 and 1, the values for the weighting parameters used in decreasing order are: $\lambda_S, \lambda_R, \lambda_D, \lambda_E, \lambda_G$ with the λ_D value moved to follow λ_G if a pixel is partially occluded. The results for a random-dot stereogram with a floating half-cylinder are shown in figure 4. Note that for clarity only the visible pixels within each layer are displayed, though the remaining pixels are filled-in. A wire-frame rendering for layer 3 is also provided.

Figure 5 is a random-dot stereogram with features from two transparent fronto-parallel surfaces. The output consists primarily of two labels corresponding to the foreground and the background. Note that when the stereogram is fused, the percept is of two overlaid surfaces with various small, noisy regions of incorrect matches.

Figure 6 is a random-dot stereogram depicting many planar-parallel surfaces. Note

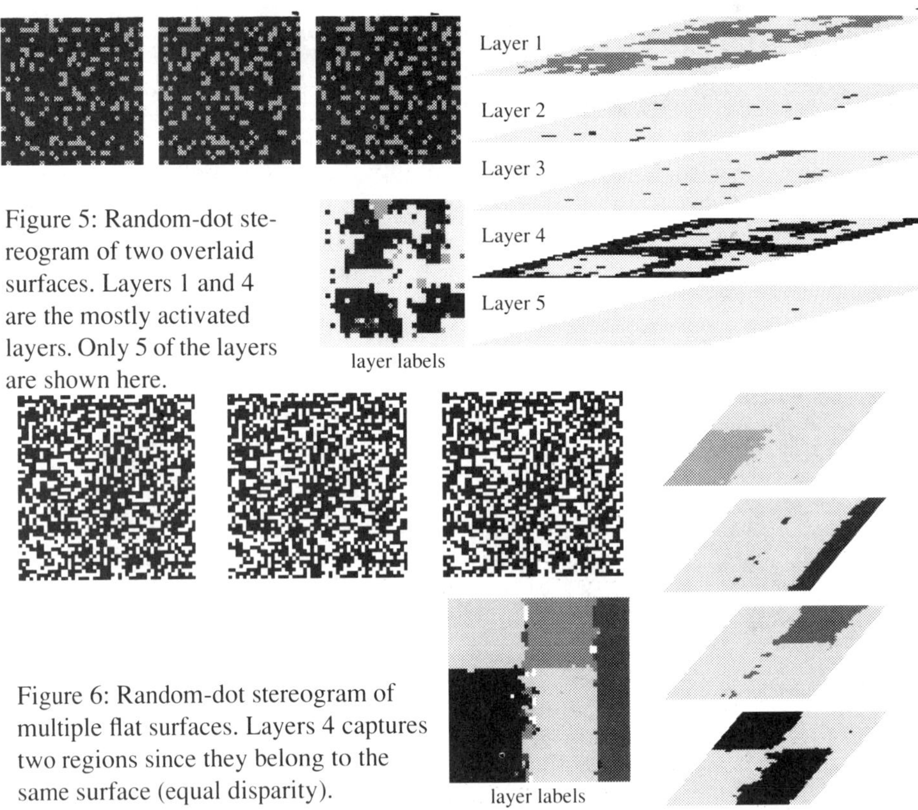

Figure 5: Random-dot stereogram of two overlaid surfaces. Layers 1 and 4 are the mostly activated layers. Only 5 of the layers are shown here.

Figure 6: Random-dot stereogram of multiple flat surfaces. Layers 4 captures two regions since they belong to the same surface (equal disparity).

that there are two disjoint regions which are classified into the same layer since they form a single surface.

A gray-scale stereogram depicting a floating square occluding the letter 'C' also floating above the background is shown in figure 7. A feature-based matching scheme is bound to fail here since locally one cannot correctly attribute the computed disparity at a matched corner of the rectangle, for example, to either the rectangle, the background, or to both regions. Our V_R constraint forces the system to attempt various matches until points with no intensity discontinuity have no disparity discontinuity. Another important feature is that the two ends of the letter 'C' are in the same "depth plane" [Nakayama *et al.*, 1989] and may later be merged to complete the letter.

Figure 8 is a gray scale stereogram depicting 4 distant surfaces with planar disparity. At occluding boundaries, the region corresponding to the further surface in the right image has no corresponding region in the left image. A high λ_D would only force these points to find an incorrect match and add to the systems errors. The λ_D reduction factor for partially occluded points reduces the data matching requirement for such points. This is crucial for obtaining correct matches especially since the images are sparsely textured and the dependence on accurate information from the textured regions is high.

A transparency example of a fence in front a bill-board is given in figure 9. Note

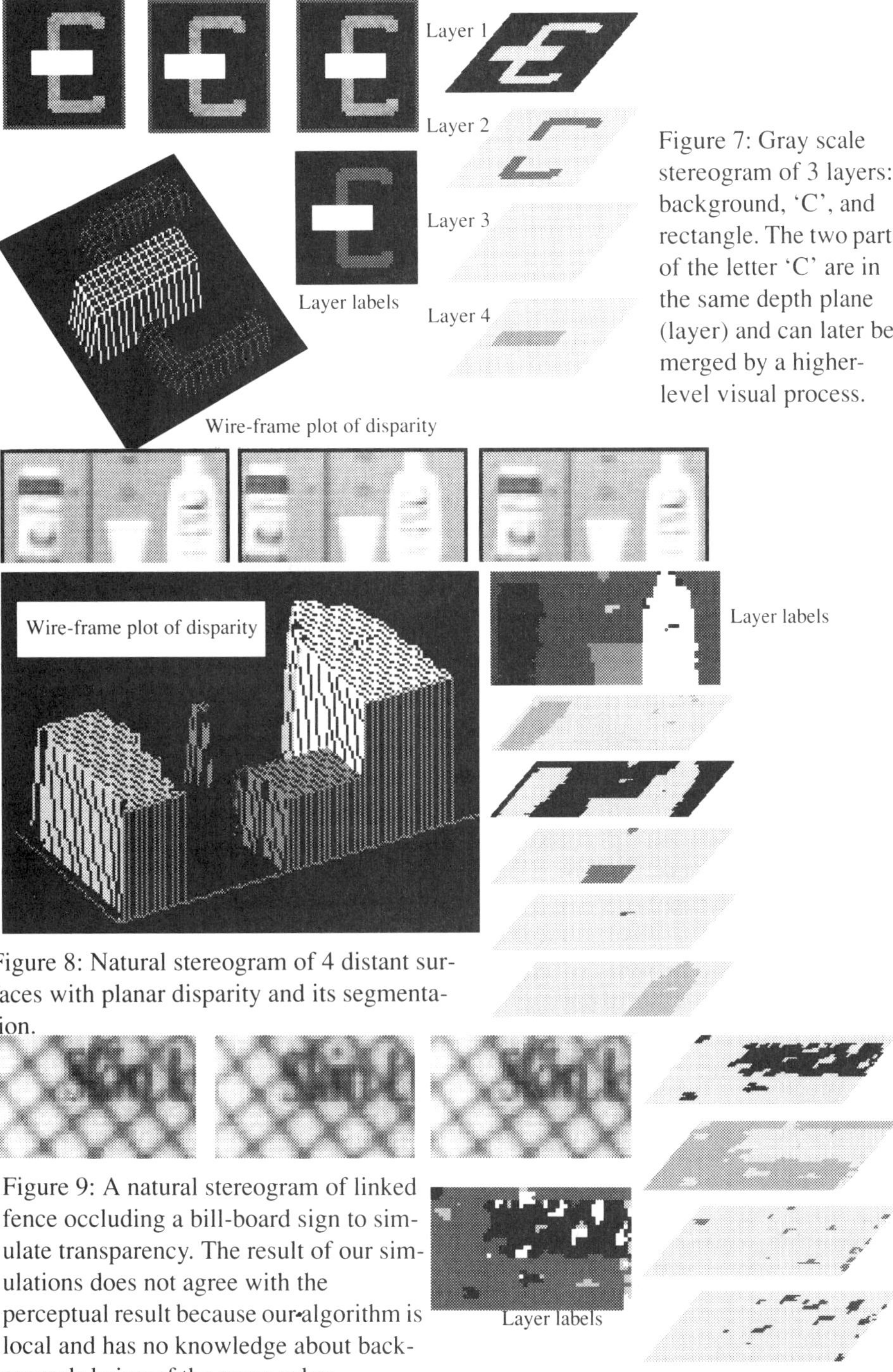

Figure 7: Gray scale stereogram of 3 layers: background, 'C', and rectangle. The two parts of the letter 'C' are in the same depth plane (layer) and can later be merged by a higher-level visual process.

Figure 8: Natural stereogram of 4 distant surfaces with planar disparity and its segmentation.

Figure 9: A natural stereogram of linked fence occluding a bill-board sign to simulate transparency. The result of our simulations does not agree with the perceptual result because our algorithm is local and has no knowledge about backgrounds being of the same color.

that our results do not match human perception in that the entire background and the entire fence do not belong to two separate layers. Note, however, that when fusing only the lower half of the stereogram by covering the upper half of both images, the background will be captured with the fence and a constant disparity region will be observed. Our algorithm is local, and, therefore, does not associate the white background in the bottom half of the images with the upper half to perform the correct segmentation. It appears that some knowledge about surface intensity segmentation and backgrounds is required to solve this problem correctly. The algorithm does, however, produce two disparity surfaces.

5 CONCLUSION

To conclude, the advantages of our Bayesian approach to stereopsis include:

- An explicit segmentation and grouping via local computations.
- The computation of transparency defined by overlaid random-dot surfaces.
- The filling-in of occluded regions.
- The removal of outliers by placing them in a separate layer.
- The model is consistent with the idea of "depth planes" as inferred from psychophysical studies.

Acknowledgements

This work was supported in part by the University of Minnesota/Army High Performance Computing Research Center and in part by AFOSR 90-0274.

References

[Bayes, 1783] T. Bayes. An essay towards solving a problem in the doctrine of chances. *Phil. Trans. Roy. Soc.*, 53, 1783.

[Clark and Yuille, 1990] J. Clark and A. Yuille. *Data Fusion for Sensory Information Processing Systems.* Kluwer Academic Publishers, 1990.

[Darrell and Pentland, 1991] T. Darrell and A. Pentland. Discontinuity models and multi-layer description networks. M.I.T. Media Lab Technical Report no. 162, 1991.

[Geman and Geman, 1984] S. Geman and D. Geman. Stochastic relaxation, gibbs distribution, and the bayesian restoration of images. *IEEE Transactions on Pattern Analysis and Machine Intelligence*, 6(6):721–741, 1984.

[Marr and Poggio, 1976] D. Marr and T. Poggio. Cooperative computation of stereo disparity. *Science*, 194:283–287, 1976.

[Nakayama *et al.*, 1989] K. Nakayama, S. Shimojo, and G. H. Silverman. Stereoscopic depth: Its relation to image segmentation, grouping, and the recognition of occluded objects. *Perception*, 18:55–68, 1989.

[Prazdny, 1985] K. Prazdny. Detection of binocular disparities. *Biological Cybernetics*, 52:93–99, 1985.

Some Solutions to the Missing Feature Problem in Vision

Subutai Ahmad
Siemens AG,
Central Research and Development
ZFE ST SN61, Otto-Hahn Ring 6
8000 München 83, Germany.
ahmad@icsi.berkeley.edu

Volker Tresp
Siemens AG,
Central Research and Development
ZFE ST SN41, Otto-Hahn Ring 6
8000 München 83, Germany.
tresp@inf21.zfe.siemens.de

Abstract

In visual processing the ability to deal with missing and noisy information is crucial. Occlusions and unreliable feature detectors often lead to situations where little or no direct information about features is available. However the available information is usually sufficient to highly constrain the outputs. We discuss Bayesian techniques for extracting class probabilities given partial data. The optimal solution involves integrating over the missing dimensions weighted by the local probability densities. We show how to obtain closed-form approximations to the Bayesian solution using Gaussian basis function networks. The framework extends naturally to the case of noisy features. Simulations on a complex task (3D hand gesture recognition) validate the theory. When both integration and weighting by input densities are used, performance decreases gracefully with the number of missing or noisy features. Performance is substantially degraded if either step is omitted.

1 INTRODUCTION

The ability to deal with missing or noisy features is vital in vision. One is often faced with situations in which the full set of image features is not computable. In fact, in 3D object recognition, it is highly unlikely that all features will be available. This can be due to self-occlusion, occlusion from other objects, shadows, etc. To date the issue of missing features has not been dealt with in neural networks in a systematic way. Instead the usual practice is to substitute a single value for the missing feature (e.g. *0*, the mean value of the feature, or a pre-computed value) and use the network's output on that feature vector.

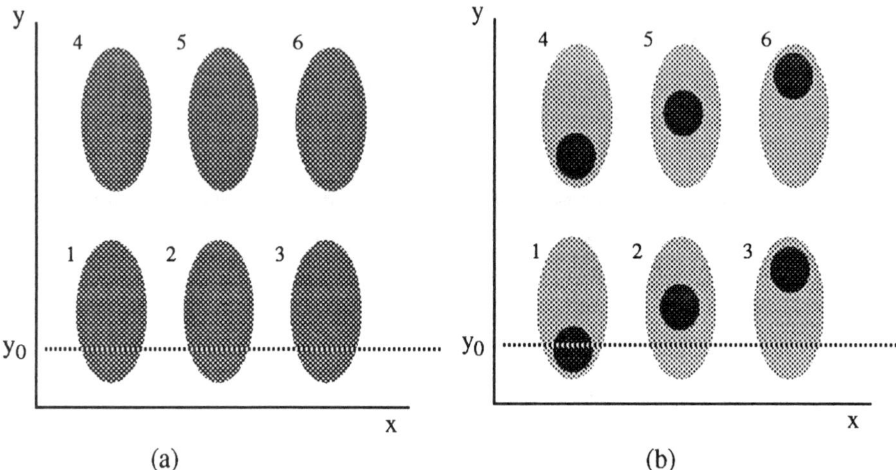

Figure 1. The images show two possible situations for a 6-class classification problem. (Dark shading denotes high-probability regions.) If the value of feature x is unknown, the correct solution depends both on the classification boundaries along the missing dimension and on the distribution of exemplars.

When the features are known to be noisy, the usual practice is to just use the measured noisy features directly. The point of this paper is to show that these approaches are not optimal and that it is possible to do much better.

A simple example serves to illustrate why one needs to be careful in dealing with missing features. Consider the situation depicted in Figure 1(a). It shows a *2-d* feature space with *6* possible classes. Assume a network has already been trained to correctly classify these regions. During classification of a novel exemplar, only feature *y* has been measured, as y_0; the value of feature *x* is unknown. For each class C_i, we would like to compute $p(C_i|y)$. Since nothing is known about x, the classifier should assign equal probability to classes 1, 2, and 3, and zero probability to classes 4, 5, and 6. Note that substituting any *single* value will always produce the wrong result. For example, if the mean value of x is substituted, the classifier would assign a probability near 1 for class 2. To obtain the correct posterior probability, it is necessary to integrate the network output over all values of x. But there is one other fact to consider: the probability distribution over x may be highly constrained by the known value of feature y. With a distribution as in Figure 1(b) the classifier should assign class 1 the highest probability. Thus it is necessary to *integrate over x along the line* $y=y_0$ *weighted by the joint distribution p(x,y).*

2 MISSING FEATURES

We first show how the intituitive arguments outlined above for missing inputs can be formalized using Bayes rule. Let $\vec{x}$ represent a complete feature vector. We assume the classifier outputs good estimates of $p(C_i|\vec{x})$ (most reasonable classifiers do - see (Richard & Lippmann, 1991)). In a given instance, $\vec{x}$ can be split up into $\vec{x}_c$, the vector of known (certain) features, and $\vec{x}_u$, the unknown features. When features are missing the task is to estimate $p(C_i|\vec{x}_c)$. Computing marginal probabilities we get:

$$p(C_i|\vec{x}_c) = \frac{p(C_i, \vec{x}_c)}{p(\vec{x}_c)} = \frac{\int p(C_i, \vec{x}_c, \vec{x}_u)\, d\vec{x}_u}{p(\vec{x}_c)} = \frac{\int p(C_i|\vec{x}_c, \vec{x}_u)\, p(\vec{x}_c, \vec{x}_u)\, d\vec{x}_u}{p(\vec{x}_c)} \tag{1}$$

Note that $p(C_i|\vec{x}_c, \vec{x}_u)$ is approximated by the network output and that in order to use (1) effectively we need estimates of the joint probabilities of the inputs.

3 NOISY FEATURES

The missing feature scenario can be extended to deal with noisy inputs. (Missing features are simply noisy features in the limiting case of complete noise.) Let $\vec{x}_c$ be the vector of features measured with complete certainty, $\vec{x}_u$ the vector of measured, uncertain features, and $\vec{x}_{tu}$ the true values of the features in $\vec{x}_u$. $p(\vec{x}_u|\vec{x}_{tu})$ denotes our knowledge of the noise (i.e. the probability of measuring the (uncertain) value $\vec{x}_u$ given that the true value is $\vec{x}_{tu}$). We assume that this is independent of $\vec{x}_c$ and C_i, i.e. that $p(\vec{x}_u|\vec{x}_{tu}, \vec{x}_c, C_i) = p(\vec{x}_u|\vec{x}_{tu})$. (Of course the value of $\vec{x}_{tu}$ is dependent on $\vec{x}_c$ and C_i.) We want to compute $p(C_i|\vec{x}_c, \vec{x}_u)$. This can be expressed as:

$$p(C_i|\vec{x}_c, \vec{x}_u) = \frac{\int p(\vec{x}_c, \vec{x}_u, \vec{x}_{tu}, C_i)\, d\vec{x}_{tu}}{p(\vec{x}_c, \vec{x}_u)} \tag{2}$$

Given the independence assumption, this becomes:

$$p(C_i|\vec{x}_c, \vec{x}_u) = \frac{\int p(C_i|\vec{x}_c, \vec{x}_{tu})\, p(\vec{x}_c, \vec{x}_{tu})\, p(\vec{x}_u|\vec{x}_{tu})\, d\vec{x}_{tu}}{\int p(\vec{x}_c, \vec{x}_{tu})\, p(\vec{x}_u|\vec{x}_{tu})\, d\vec{x}_{tu}} \tag{3}$$

As before, $p(C_i|\vec{x}_c, \vec{x}_{tu})$ is given by the classifier. (3) is almost the same as (1) except that the integral is also weighted by the noise model. Note that in the case of complete uncertainty about the features (i.e. the noise is uniform over the entire range of the features), the equations reduce to the missing feature case.

4 GAUSSIAN BASIS FUNCTION NETWORKS

The above discussion shows how to optimally deal with missing and noisy inputs in a Bayesian sense. We now show how these equations can be approximated using networks of Gaussian basis functions (GBF nets). Let us consider GBF networks where the Gaussians have diagonal covariance matrices (Nowlan, 1990). Such networks have proven to be useful in a number of real-world applications (e.g. Röscheisen *et al*, 1992). Each hidden unit is characterized by a mean vector $\vec{\mu}_j$ and by $\vec{\sigma}_j$, a vector representing the diagonal of the covariance matrix. The network output is:

$$y_i(\vec{x}) = \frac{\sum_j w_{ij} b_j(\vec{x})}{\sum_j b_j(\vec{x})}$$

$$\text{with } b_j(\vec{x}) = \pi_j n(\vec{x};\vec{\mu}_j,\vec{\sigma}_j^2) = \frac{\pi_j}{(2\pi)^{\frac{d}{2}} \prod_k^d \vec{\sigma}_{kj}} exp\left[-\sum_i \frac{(x_i-\mu_{ji})^2}{2\vec{\sigma}_{ji}^2}\right] \tag{4}$$

w_{ji} is the weight from the j'th basis unit to the i'th output unit, π_j is the probability of choosing unit j, and d is the dimensionality of $\vec{x}$.

4.1 GBF NETWORKS AND MISSING FEATURES

Under certain training regimes such as Gaussian mixture modeling, EM or "soft clustering" (Duda & Hart, 1973; Dempster *et al*, 1977; Nowlan, 1990) or an approximation as in (Moody & Darken, 1988) the hidden units adapt to represent local probability densities. In particular $y_i(\vec{x}) \approx p(C_i|\vec{x})$ and $p(\vec{x}) \approx \sum_j b_j(\vec{x})$. This is a major advantage of this architectur and can be exploited to obtain closed form solutions to (1) and (3). Substituting into (3) we get:

$$p(C_i|\vec{x}_c,\vec{x}_u) \approx \frac{\int (\sum_j w_{ij} b_j(\vec{x}_c,\vec{x}_{tu}))\, p(\vec{x}_u|\vec{x}_{tu})\, d\vec{x}_{tu}}{\int (\sum_j b_j(\vec{x}_c,\vec{x}_{tu}))\, p(\vec{x}_u|\vec{x}_{tu})\, d\vec{x}_{tu}} \tag{5}$$

For the case of missing features equation (5) can be computed directly. As noted before, equation (1) is simply (3) with $p(\vec{x}_u|\vec{x}_{tu})$ uniform. Since the infinite integral along each dimension of a multivariate normal density is equal to one we get:

$$p(C_i|\vec{x}_c) \approx \frac{\sum_j w_{ji} b_j(\vec{x}_c)}{\sum_j b_j(\vec{x}_c)} \tag{6}$$

(Here $b_j(\vec{x}_c)$ denotes the same function as in except that it is only evaluated over the known dimensions given by $\vec{x}_c$.) Equation (6) is appealing since it gives us a simple closed form solution. Intuitively, the solution is nothing more than projecting the Gaussians onto the dimensions which are available and evaluating the resulting network. As the number of training patterns increases, (6) will approach the optimal Bayes solution.

4.2 GBF NETWORKS AND NOISY FEATURES

With noisy features the situation is a little more complicated and the solution depends on the form of the noise. If the noise is known to be uniform in some region $[\vec{a},\vec{b}]$ then equation (5) becomes:

$$p(C_i|\vec{x}_c,\vec{x}_u) \approx \frac{\sum_j w_{ij} b_j(\vec{x}_c) \prod_{i\in U} [N(b_i;\mu_{ij},\sigma_{ij}^2) - N(a_i;\mu_{ij},\sigma_{ij}^2)]}{\sum_j b_j(\vec{x}_c) \prod_{i\in U} [N(b_i;\mu_{ij},\sigma_{ij}^2) - N(a_i;\mu_{ij},\sigma_{ij}^2)]} \tag{7}$$

Here $\vec{\mu}_{ij}$ and $\vec{\sigma}_{ij}^2$ select the i'th component of the j'th mean and variance vectors. U ranges over the noisy feature indices. Good closed form approximations to the normal distribution function $N(x;\mu,\sigma^2)$ are available (Press et al, 1986) so (7) is efficiently computable.

With zero-mean Gaussian noise with variance σ_u^2, we can also write down a closed form solution. In this case we have to integrate a product of two Gaussians and end up with:

$$p(C_i|\vec{x}_c, \vec{x}_u) = \frac{\sum_j w_{ij} b'_j(\vec{x}_c, \vec{x}_u)}{\sum_j b'_j(\vec{x}_c, \vec{x}_u)} \quad \text{with } b'_j(\vec{x}_c, \vec{x}_u) = n(\vec{x}_u; \vec{\mu}_{ju}, \vec{\sigma}_u^2 + \vec{\sigma}_{ju}^2)\, b_j(\vec{x}_c).$$

5 BACKPROPAGATION NETWORKS

With a large training set, the outputs of a sufficiently large network trained with backpropagation converges to the optimal Bayes *a posteriori* estimates (Richard & Lippmann, 1992). If $B_i(\vec{x})$ is the output of the i'th output unit when presented with input $\vec{x}$, $B_i(\vec{x}) \approx p(C_i|\vec{x})$. Unfortunately, access to the input distribution is not available with backpropagation. Without prior knowledge it is reasonable to assume a uniform input distribution, in which case the right hand side of (3) simplifies to:

$$p(C_i|\vec{x}_c) \approx \frac{\int p(C_i|\vec{x}_c, \vec{x}_{tu})\, p(\vec{x}_u|\vec{x}_{tu})\, d\vec{x}_{tu}}{\int p(\vec{x}_u|\vec{x}_{tu})\, d\vec{x}_{tu}} \qquad (8)$$

The integral can be approximated using standard Monte Carlo techniques. With uniform noise in the interval $[\vec{a}, \vec{b}]$, this becomes (ignoring normalizing constants):

$$p(C_i|\vec{x}_c) \approx \int_{\vec{a}}^{\vec{b}} B_i(\vec{x}_c, \vec{x}_{tu})\, d\vec{x}_{tu} \qquad (9)$$

With missing features the integral in (9) is computed over the entire range of each feature.

6 AN EXAMPLE TASK: 3D HAND GESTURE RECOGNITION

A simple realistic example serves to illustrate the utility of the above techniques. We consider the task of recognizing a set of hand gestures from single 2D images independent of 3D orientation (Figure 2). As input, each classifier is given the 2D polar coordinates of the five fingertip positions relative to the 2D center of mass of the hand (so the input space is 10-dimensional). Each classifier is trained on a training set of 4368 examples (624 poses for each gesture) and tested on a similar independent test set.

The task forms a good benchmark for testing performance with missing and uncertain inputs. The classification task itself is non-trivial. The classifier must learn to deal with hands (which are complex non-rigid objects) and with perspective projection (which is non-linear and non-invertible). In fact it is impossible to obtain a perfect score since in certain poses some of the gestures are indistinguishable (e.g. when the hand is pointing directly at the screen). Moreover, the task is characteristic of real vision problems. The

Figure 2. Examples of the 7 gestures used to train the classifier. A 3D computer model of the hand is used to generate images of the hand in various poses. For each training example, we choose a 3D orientation, compute the 3D positions of the fingertips and project them onto 2D. For this task we assume that the correspondence between image and model features are known, and that during training all feature values are always available.

position of each finger is highly (but not completely) constrained by the others resulting in a very non-uniform input distribution. Finally it is often easy to see what the classifier should output if features are uncertain. For example suppose the real gesture is "five" but for some reason the features from the thumb are not reliably computed. In this case the gestures "four" and "five" should both get a positive probability whereas the rest should get zero. In many such cases only a single class should get the highest score, e.g. if the features for the little finger are uncertain the correct class is still "five".

We tried three classifiers on this task: standard sigmoidal networks trained with backpropagation (BP), and two types of gaussian networks as described in . In the first (Gauss-RBF), the gaussians were radial and the centers were determined using k-means clustering as in (Moody & Darken, 1988). σ^2 was set to twice the average distance of each point to its nearest gaussian (all gaussians had the same width). After clustering, π_j was set to $\sum_k \left[\frac{n(\vec{x}_k;\vec{\mu}_j;\vec{\sigma}_j^2)}{\sum_i n(\vec{x}_k;\vec{\mu}_i;\vec{\sigma}_i^2)}\right]$. The output weights were then determined using LMS gradient descent. In the second (Gauss-G), each gaussian had a unique diagonal covariance matrix. The centers and variances were determined using gradient descent on all the parameters (Röscheisen *et al*, 1992). Note that with this type of training, even though gaussian hidden units are used, there is no guarantee that the distribution information will be preserved.

All classifiers were able to achieve a reasonable performance level. BP with 60 hidden units managed to score 95.3% and 93.3% on the training and test sets, respectively. Gauss-G with 28 hidden units scored 94% and 92%. Gauss-RBF scored 97.7% and 91.4% and required 2000 units to achieve it. (Larger numbers of hidden units led to overfitting.) For comparison, nearest neighbor achieves a score of 82.4% on the test set.

6.1 PERFORMANCE WITH MISSING FEATURES

We tested the performance of each network in the presence of missing features. For backpropagation we used a numerical approximation to equation (9). For both gaussian basis function networks we used equation (6). To test the networks we randomly picked samples from the test set and deleted random features. We calculated a performance score as the percentage of samples where the correct class was ranked as one of the top two classes. Figure 3 displays the results. For comparison we also tested each classifier by substituting the mean value of each missing feature and using the normal update equation.

As predicted by the theory the performance of Gauss-RBF using (6) was consistently better than the others. The fact that BP and Gauss-G performed poorly indicates that the distribution of the features must be taken into account. The fact that using the mean value is

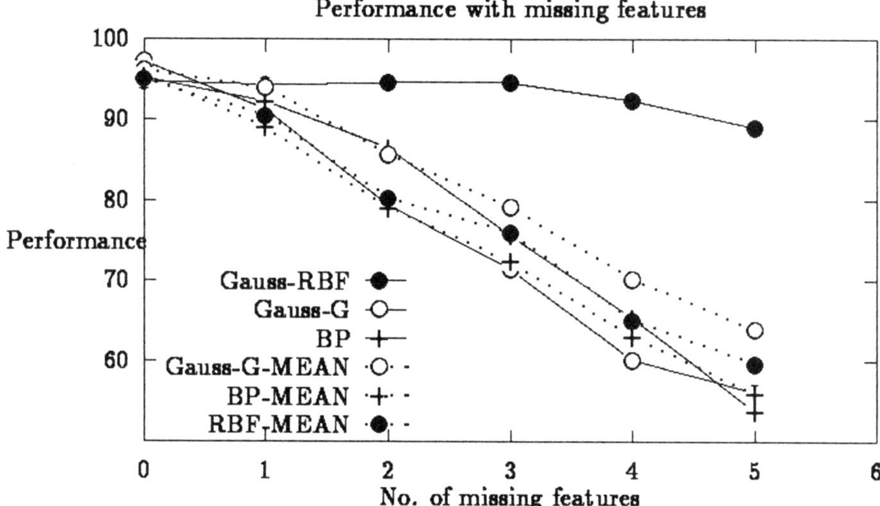

Figure 3. The performance of various classifiers when dealing with missing features. Each data point denotes an average over 1000 random samples from an independent test set. For each sample, random features were considered missing. Each graph plots the percentage of samples where the correct class was one of the top two classes.

insufficient indicates that the integration step must also be carried out. Perhaps most encouraging is the result that even with 50% of the features missing, Gauss-RBF ranks the correct class among the top two 90% of the time. This clearly shows that a significant amount of information can be extracted even with a large number of missing features.

6.2 PERFORMANCE WITH NOISY FEATURES

We also tested the performance of each network in the presence of noisy features. We randomly picked samples from the test set and added uniform noise to random features. The noise interval was calculated as $[x_i - 2\sigma_i, x_i + 2\sigma_i]$ where x_i is the feature value and σ_i is the standard deviation of that feature over the training set. For BP we used equation (9) and for the GBF networks we used equation (7). Figure 3 displays the results. For comparison we also tested each classifier by substituting the noisy value of each noisy feature and using the normal update equation (RBF-N, BP-N, and Gauss-GN). As with missing features, the performance of Gauss-RBF was significantly better than the others when a large number of features were noisy.

7 DISCUSSION

The results demonstrate the advantages of estimating the input distribution and integrating over the missing dimensions, at least on this task. They also show that good classification performance alone does not guarantee good missing feature performance. (Both BP and Gauss-G performed better than Gauss-RBF on the test set.) To get the best of both worlds one could use a hybrid technique utilizing separate density estimators and classifiers although this would probably require equations (1) and (3) to be numerically integrated.

One way to improve the performance of BP and Gauss-G might be to use a training set that contained missing features. Given the unusual distributions that arise in vision, in order to guarantee accuracy such a training set should include every possible combination

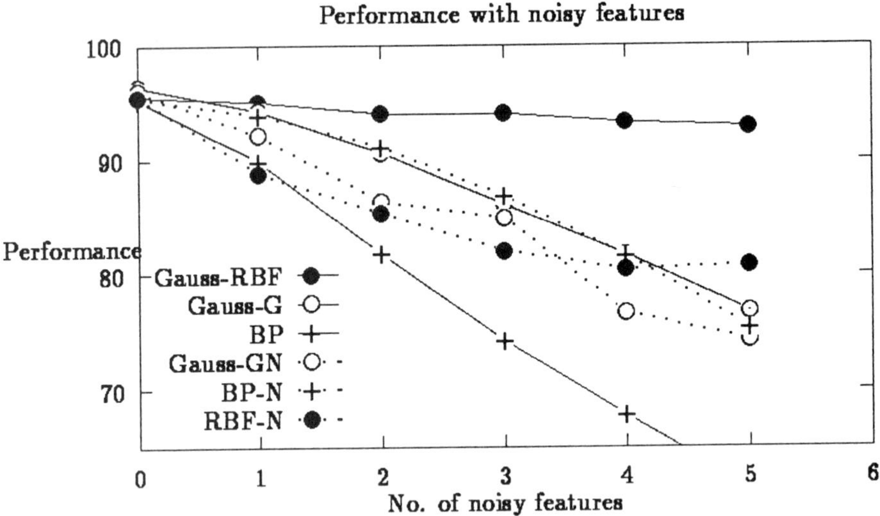

Figure 4. As in Figure 3 except that the performance with noisy features is plotted.

of missing features. In addition, for each such combination, enough patterns must be included to accurately estimate the posterior density. In general this type of training is intractable since the number of combinations is exponential in the number of features. Note that if the input distribution is available (as in Gauss-RBF), then such a training scenario is unnecessary.

Acknowledgements

We thank D. Goryn, C. Maggioni, S. Omohundro, A. Stolcke, and R. Schuster for helpful discussions, and especially B. Wirtz for providing the computer hand model. V.T. is supported in part by a grant from the Bundesministerium für Forschung und Technologie.

References

A.P. Dempster, N.M. Laird, and D.B. Rubin. (1977) Maximum-likelihood from incomplete data via the EM algorithm. *J. Royal Statistical Soc. Ser. B*, **39**:1-38.

R.O. Duda and P.E. Hart. (1973) *Pattern Classification and Scene Analysis.* John Wiley & Sons, New York.

J. Moody and C. Darken. (1988) Learning with localized receptive fields. In: D. Touretzky, G. Hinton, T. Sejnowski, editors, *Proceedings of the 1988 Connectionist Models Summer School*, Morgan Kaufmann, CA.

S. Nowlan. (1990) Maximum Likelihood Competitive Learning. In: *Advances in Neural Information Processing Systems 4*, pages 574-582.

W.H. Press, B.P. Flannery, S.A. Teukolsky, and W.T. Vetterling. (1986) *Numerical Recipes: The Art of Scientific Computing*, Cambridge University Press, Cambridge, UK.

M. D. Richard and R.P. Lippmann. (1991) Neural Network Classifiers Estimate Bayesian *a posteriori* Probabilities, *Neural Computation*, **3**:461-483.

M. Röscheisen, R. Hofman, and V. Tresp. (1992) Neural Control for Rolling Mills: Incorporating Domain Theories to Overcome Data Deficiency. In: *Advances in Neural Information Processing Systems 4*, pages 659-666.

Improving Convergence in Hierarchical Matching Networks for Object Recognition

Joachim Utans* **Gene Gindi**†
Department of Electrical Engineering
Yale University
P. O. Box 2157 Yale Station
New Haven, CT 06520

Abstract

We are interested in the use of analog neural networks for recognizing visual objects. Objects are described by the set of parts they are composed of and their structural relationship. Structural models are stored in a database and the recognition problem reduces to matching data to models in a structurally consistent way. The object recognition problem is in general very difficult in that it involves coupled problems of grouping, segmentation and matching. We limit the problem here to the simultaneous labelling of the parts of a single object and the determination of analog parameters. This coupled problem reduces to a weighted match problem in which an optimizing neural network must minimize $E(\mathbf{M}, \mathbf{p}) = \sum_{\alpha i} M_{\alpha i} W_{\alpha i}(\mathbf{p})$, where the $\{M_{\alpha i}\}$ are binary match variables for data parts i to model parts α and $\{W_{\alpha i}(\mathbf{p})\}$ are weights dependent on parameters $\mathbf{p}$. In this work we show that by first solving for estimates $\hat{\mathbf{p}}$ without solving for $M_{\alpha i}$, we may obtain good initial parameter estimates that yield better solutions for $\mathbf{M}$ and $\mathbf{p}$.

*Current address: International Computer Science Institute, 1947 Center Street, Suite 600, Berkeley, CA 94704, utans@icsi.berkeley.edu

†Current address: SUNY Stony Brook, Department of Electrical Engineering, Stony Brook, NY 11784

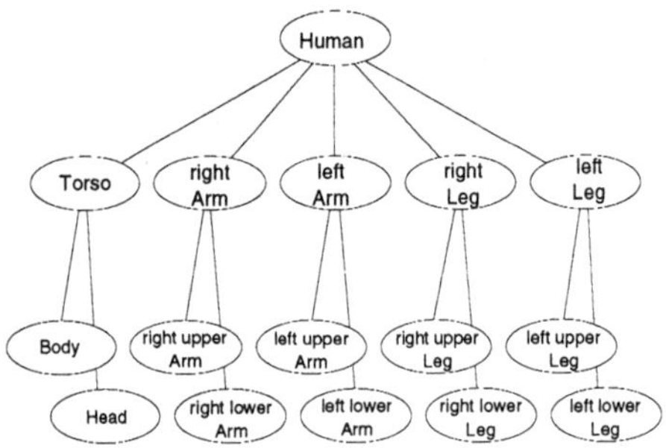

Figure 1: Stored Model for a 3-Level Compositional Hierarchy (compare Figure 3).

1 Recognition via Stochastic Forward Models

The Frameville object recognition system introduced by Mjolsness *et al* [5, 6, 1] makes use of a compositional hierarchy to represent stored models. The recognition problem is formulated as the minimization of an objective function. Mjolsness [3, 4] has proposed to derive the objective function describing the recognition problem in a principled way from a stochastic model that describes the objects the system is designed to recognize (*stochastic visual grammar*). The description mirrors the data representation as a compositional hierarchy, at each stage the description of the object becomes more detailed as parts are added.

The stochastic model assigns a probability distribution at each stage of that process. Thus at each level of the hierarchy a more detailed description of parts in terms of their subparts is given by specifying a probability distribution for the coordinates of the subparts. Explicitly specifying these distributions allows for finer control over individual part descriptions than the rather general parameter error terms used before [1, 8]. The goal is to derive a joint probability distribution for an instance of an object and its parts as it appears in the scene. This gives the probability of observing such an object prior to the arrival of the data. Given an observed image, the recognition problem can be stated as a Bayesian inference problem that the neural network solves.

1.1 3–Level Stochastic Model

For example, consider the model shown in Figure 1 and 3. The object and its parts are represented as line segments (sticks), the parameters were $\mathbf{p} = (x, y, l, \theta)^T$ with x, y denoting position, l the length of a stick and θ its orientation. The model considers only a rigid translation of an object in the image.

Only one model is stored. From a central position $\mathbf{p} = (x, y, l, \theta)$, itself chosen from a uniform density, the N_β parts at the first level are placed. Their structural relationships is stored as coordinates $\mathbf{u}_\beta$ in an object-centered coordinate frame, i.e. relative to $\mathbf{p}$. While placing the parts, Gaussian distributed noise with mean 0 and is added to the position coordinates to capture the notion of natural variation of the object's shape. The variance is coordinate specific, but we assume the same distribution for the x and y coordinates, σ^2_{1x}; σ^2_{1l} is the variance for the length component and $\sigma_{1\theta}^2$ for the relative angle. In addition, here we assume for simplicity that all parts are independently distributed. Each of the parts β is composed of subparts. For simplicity of notation, we assume that each part β is composed from the same number of subparts N_m (note that the index γ in Figure 2 here corresponds to the double index βm to keep track of which part β subpart βm belongs to on the model side, i.e. the index βm denotes the mth sub-part of part β). The next step models the *unordering* of parts in the image via a permutation matrix $\mathbf{M}$, chosen with probability $P(\mathbf{M})$, by which their identity is lost. If this step were omitted, the recognition problem would reduce to the problem of estimating part parameters because the parts would already be labeled.

From the grammar we compute the final joint probability distribution (all constant terms are collected in a constant C):

$$\begin{aligned}
&P(M, \{\mathbf{p}_{\beta m}\}, \{\mathbf{p}_\beta\}, \mathbf{p}) = \\
&\quad C \exp\Bigg(\sum_\beta \Bigg(-\frac{1}{2\sigma_{\beta x}^2}(x_\beta - (x + u_{\beta x}))^2 - \frac{1}{2\sigma_{\beta x}^2}(y_\beta - (y + u_{\beta y}))^2 \\
&\qquad -\frac{1}{2\sigma_{\beta l}^2}(l_\beta - (l + u_{\beta l}))^2 - \frac{1}{2\sigma_{\beta \theta}^2}(\theta_\beta - (\theta + u_{\beta\theta}))^2 \Bigg)\Bigg) \\
&\quad \exp\Bigg(\sum_{\beta m\, k} M_{\beta m k} \Bigg(-\frac{1}{2\sigma_{\beta m x}^2}(x_k - (x_\beta + u_{\beta m x}))^2 - \frac{1}{2\sigma_{\beta m x}^2}(y_k - (y_\beta + u_{\beta m y}))^2 \\
&\qquad -\frac{1}{2\sigma_{\beta m l}^2}(l_k - (l_\beta + u_{\beta m l}))^2 - \frac{1}{2\sigma_{\beta m \theta}^2}(\theta_k - (\theta_\beta + u_{\beta m \theta}))^2 \Bigg)\Bigg) \qquad (1)
\end{aligned}$$

1.2 Frameville Architecture for Part Labelling within a single Object

The stochastic forward model for the part labelling problem with only a single object present in the scene translates into a reduced Frameville architecture as depicted in Figure 2. The compositional hierarchy parallels the steps in the stochastic model as parts are added at each level. Match variables appear only at the lowest level, corresponding to the permutation step of the grammar. Parts in the image must be matched to model parts and parts found to belong to the stored object must be grouped together.

The single match neuron $M_{\alpha i}$ at the highest level can be set to unity since we assume we know the object's identity and only a single object is present. Similarly, all terms ina_{ij} from the first to the second level can be set to unity for the correct grouping since the grouping is known at this point from the forward model description. In addition, at the intermediate (second) level, we may set all $M_{\beta j} = 1$ for $\beta = j$ and $M_{\beta j} = 0$ otherwise with no loss of generality. These mid–level frames may be matched ahead of time, but their parameters must be computed from data. Introducing a part permutation at the intermediate levels thus is redundant. Given this, an additional simplification **ina** grouping variables at the lowest (third) level is possible. Since parts are pre-matched at all but the lowest level, ina_{jk} can be expressed in terms of the part match $M_{\gamma k}$ as $ina_{jk} = M_{\gamma k} INA_{\gamma\beta} M_{\beta j}$ and explicitly representing ina_{jk} as variables is not necessary.

The input to the system are the $\{\mathbf{p}_k\}$, recognition involves finding the parameters

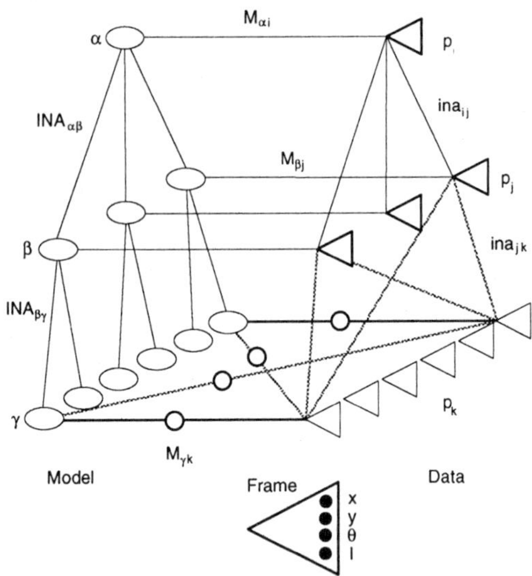

Figure 2: Frameville Architecture for the Stochastic Model. The 3–level grammar leads to a reduced "Frameville" style network architecture: a single model is stored on the model side and only one instance of the model is present in the input data. The ovals on the model side represent the object, its parts and subparts (compare Figure 1); the arcs *INA* represent their structural relationship. On the data side, the triangles represent parameter vectors (or *frames*) describing an instance of the object in the scene. At the lowest level the p_k represent the input data, parameters at higher levels in the hierarchy must be computed by the network (represented as bold triangles). *ina* represents the grouping of parts on the data side (see text). The horizontal lines represent assignments from frames on the data side to nodes on the model side. At the intermediate level, frames are prematched to the corresponding parts on the model side; match variables are necessary only at the lowest level (represented as bold lines with circles).

$\mathbf{p}$ and $\{\mathbf{p}_j\}$ as well as the labelling of parts $\mathbf{M}$. Thus, from Bayes Theorem

$$P(\mathbf{M},\mathbf{p},\{\mathbf{p}_j\}|\{\mathbf{p}_k\}) = \frac{P(\{\mathbf{p}_k\}|\mathbf{M},\mathbf{p},\{\mathbf{p}_j\})P(\mathbf{M},\mathbf{p},\{\mathbf{p}_j\})}{P(\{\mathbf{p}_k\})}$$
$$\propto P(\mathbf{M},\mathbf{p},\{\mathbf{p}_j\},\{\mathbf{p}_k\}) \quad (2)$$

and recognition reduces to finding the most probable values for $\mathbf{p}$, $\{\mathbf{p}_j\}$ and $\mathbf{M}$ given the data:

$$\arg\max_{\mathbf{M},\mathbf{p},\{\mathbf{p}_j\}} P(\mathbf{M},\mathbf{p},\{\mathbf{p}_j\},\{\mathbf{p}_k\}) \quad (3)$$

Solving the inference problem involves finding the MAP estimate and is is equivalent to minimizing the exponent in equation (1) with respect to $\mathbf{M}$, $\mathbf{p}$ and $\{\mathbf{p}_j\}$.

2 Bootstrap: Coarse Scale Hints to Initialize the Network

2.1 Compositional Hierarchy and Scale Space

In some labelling approaches found in the vision literature, an object is first labelled at the coarse, low resolution, level and approximate parameters are found. In this top–down approach the information at the higher, more abstract, levels is used

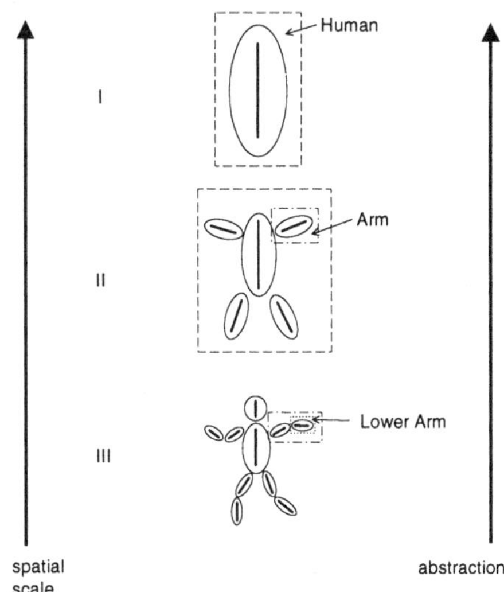

Figure 3: Compositional Hierarchy vs. Scale Space Hierarchy. A compositional hierarchy can represent a scale space hierarchy. At successive levels in the hierarchy, more and more detail is added to the object.

to select initial values for the parts at the next lower level of abstraction. The segmentation and labelling at this next lowest level is thus not done blindly; rather it is strongly influenced contextually by the results at the level above.

In fact, in very general terms such a scheme was described by Marr and Nishihara [2]. They advocate in essence a hierarchical model base in which a shape is first matched to the highest levels, and defaults in terms of relative object–based parameters of parts at the next level are recalled from memory. These defaults then serve as initial values in an unspecified segmentation algorithm that derives part parameters; this step is repeated recursively until the lowest level is reached.

Note that the highest level of abstractions correspond to the coarsest levels of spatial scale. There is nothing in the design of the model base that demands this, but invariably, elements at the top of a compositional hierarchy are of coarser scale since they must both include the many subparts below, and summarize this inclusion with relatively few parameters. Figure 3 illustrates the correspondence between these representations. In this sense, the compositional hierarchy as applied to shapes includes a notion of scale, but there is no "scale–space" operation of intentionally blurring data. The notion of Scale Space as utilized here thus differs from the application of the method to low-level computations in the visual domain where auxiliary coarse scale representations are computed explicitly. The object representations in the Frameville system as described earlier combines both, bottom–up and top–down elements. If the top–down aspects of the scheme described by Marr and Nishihara [2] could be incorporated into the Frameville architecture, then our previous simulation results [8] suggest that much better performance can be expected from the neural network. Two problems must be addressed: (1) How do we obtain, from the observed raw data alone, a coarse estimate of the slot parameters at the highest level and (2) given these crude estimates how do we utilize them to recall default settings for the segmentation one level below?

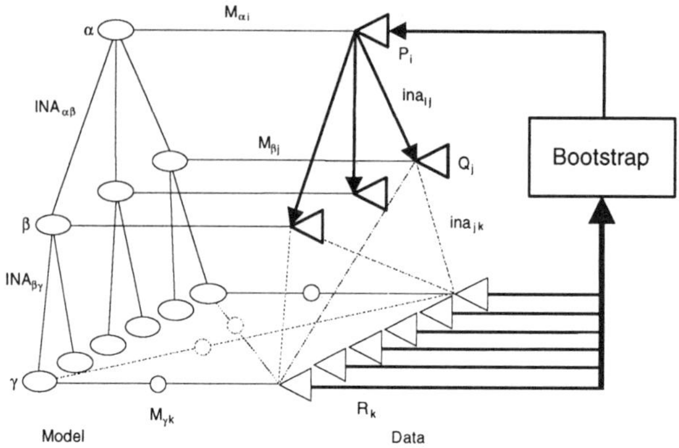

Figure 4: Bootstrap computation for a network from a 3–level grammar. Analog frame variables at the top and intermediate level are initialized from data by a bootstrap computation (bold lines indicate the flow of information)

2.2 Initialization of Coarse Scale Parameters

We propose to aid convergence by supplying initial values for the analog variables $\mathbf{p}$ and $\{\mathbf{p}_j\}$; these must be computed from data without making use of the labelling. In general, it is not possible to solve for the analog parameters without knowledge of the correct permutation matrix $\mathbf{M}$. However, for the purpose of obtaining an approximation $\hat{\mathbf{p}}$ one can derive a new objective function that does not depend on $\mathbf{M}$ and the parameters $\{\mathbf{p}_j\}$ by integrating over the $\{\mathbf{p}_j\}$ and summing over all possible permutation matrices $\mathbf{M}$:

$$P(\mathbf{p}, \{\mathbf{p}_k\}) = \sum_{\substack{\{\mathbf{M}\} \mid \mathbf{M} \text{ is a} \\ \text{permutation}}} \int d\{\mathbf{p}_j\} P(\mathbf{p}, \{\mathbf{p}_j\}, \{\mathbf{p}_k\}, \mathbf{M}) \tag{4}$$

This formulation leads to an Elastic Net type network [9, 7]. However, this implementation of a separate network for the bootstrap computations is expensive.

Here we use simpler computation where the coarse scale parameters are estimated by computing sample averages, corresponding to finding the solution for the Elastic Net in the high temperature limit [7]. For the position $\mathbf{x}$ we find, after integrating over the $\{\mathbf{x}_j\}$,

$$\begin{aligned} x \;=\; & \frac{1}{\sum_{\beta m} 1/(\sigma^2_{\beta x}\sigma^2_{\beta m x})} \sum_{\beta m\, k} \frac{M_{\beta m k}\, x_k}{\sigma^2_{\beta x}\sigma^2_{\beta m x}} - \frac{1}{\sum_{\beta m} 1/(\sigma^2_{\beta x}\sigma^2_{\beta m x})} \sum_{\beta m} \frac{u_{\beta m x}}{\sigma^2_{\beta x}\sigma^2_{\beta m x}} \\ & - \frac{1}{\sum_{\beta} 1/\sigma^2_{\beta x}} \sum_{\beta} \frac{u_{\beta x}}{\sigma^2_{\beta x}} \end{aligned} \tag{5}$$

and similarly for y. Since the assignment $M_{\beta m\, k}$ of subparts k on the data side to subparts βm on the model side is not known at this point, the first term in equations (5) cannot be evaluated. After approximating the actual variance with an average variance, these equations reduce to

$$\hat{x} = \frac{1}{N_\beta N_m}\sum_k x_k - \frac{1}{N_\beta N_m}\sum_{\beta m} u_{\beta m x} - \frac{1}{N_\beta}\sum_\beta u_{\beta x} \qquad (6)$$

In terms of the objective function this translates into assuming that here the error terms for all parts are weighted equally. Since these weights would depend on the actual part match, this just corresponds to our ignorance regarding identity of the parts. This approximation assumes that the variances do not differ by a large amount, otherwise the approximation $\hat{\mathbf{p}}$ will not be close to the true values. Since the model can be designed such that the part primitives used at the lowest level of the grammar are not highly specialized as would be the case for abstractions at higher levels of the model, the approximation proved sufficient for the problems studied here.

The neural network can be used to perform the calculation. The Elastic Net formulation assigns approximately equal weights to all possible assignments at high temperatures. Thus, this behavior can be expressed in the original network with match variables by choosing $M_{\beta mk} = 1/(N_\beta N_m)\ \forall\, i, j$. This leads to the following two-pass bootstrap computation. Using this specific choice for $\mathbf{M}$ only the analog variables need to be updated to compute the coarse scale estimates. The network with constant $\mathbf{M}$ is just the neural network implementation for computing $\hat{\mathbf{x}}$ from equation (6). After these have converged, $\hat{\mathbf{x}}$ can be used to compute $\hat{\mathbf{x}}_j = \hat{\mathbf{x}} + \mathbf{u}_\beta$. Thus, the parameters for intermediate levels can by hypothesized from the coarse scale estimate $\hat{\mathbf{x}}$ by adding the known transformation (recall that for intermediate levels, the part identity is preserved and no permutation steps takes place (see Figure 2)). Then the network is restarted with random values for the match variables to compute the correct labelling and the correct parameters.

2.3 Simulation Results

The bootstrap procedure has been implemented for a 3-level hierarchical model. The model describes a "gingerbread man" as shown in Figure 3. The incorrect solutions observed did not, in the vast majority of cases, violate the permutation matrix constraint, i.e. the assignment was unique. However, even though the assignment is unique, parts where not always assigned correctly. Most commonly, the identity of neighboring parts was interchanged, in particular for cases with large variance.

The advantage of using the bootstrap initialization is clear from Figure 5. For the simulation, $\sigma_2^2 = 2\sigma_1^2$; the noise variance was identical for all parts. The network computed the solution reliably for large noise variances. In such cases the performance of the network without initialization deteriorates rapidly. Only one set of 10 experiments was used for the graph but in all simulations performed, the network with initialization consistently outperformed the network without initialization. Figure 5(right) shows the time measured in the number of iterations necessary for the network to converge; it is almost unaffected by the increase in the noise variance. This is because the initial values derived from data are still close to the final solution. While in some cases, the random starting point happens to be close to the correct solution and the network without initialization converges rapidly, Figure 5 reflect the typical behavior and demonstrate the advantage of computing approximate initial values.

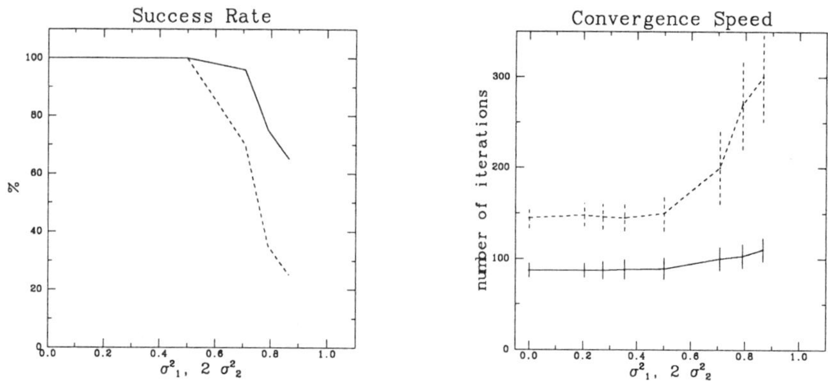

Figure 5: Results Comparing the Network without and with Initialization (solid line).
Left: The success rate indicates the rate at which the network converged to the correct solutions. σ_1^2 denotes the noise variance at the intermediate level of the model and σ_2^2 the noise variance at the lowest level. Only one set of 10 experiments was used for the graph but in all simulations performed, the network with initialization consistently outperformed the network without initialization.
Right: The graph shows the average time it takes for the network to converge (as measured by the number of iterations) averaged over 10 experiments. Only simulations where the network converged to the correct solution are used to compute the average time for convergence. The stopping criterion used required all the match neurons to assume values $M_{ij} > 0.95$ or $M_{ij} < 0.05$. The error bars denote the standard deviation.

Acknowledgements

This work was supported in part by AFOSR grant AFOSR 90-0224. We thank E. Mjolsness and A. Rangarajan for many helpful discussions.

References

[1] G. Gindi, E. Mjolsness, and P. Anandan. Neural networks for model based recognition. In *Neural Networks: Concepts, Applications and Implementations*, pages 144–173. Prentice–Hall, 1991.

[2] David Marr. *Vision*. W. H. Freeman and Co., New York, 1982.

[3] E. Mjolsness. Bayesian inference on visual grammars by neural nets that optimize. Technical Report YALEU–DCS–TR–854, Yale University, Dept. of Computer Science, 1991.

[4] E. Mjolsness. Visual grammars and their neural nets. In R.P. Lippmann J.E. Moody, S.J. Hanson, editor, *Advances in Neural Information Processing Systems 4*. Morgan Kaufmann Publishers, San Mateo, CA, 1992.

[5] Eric Mjolsness, Gene Gindi, and P. Anandan. Optimization in model matching and perceptual organization: A first look. Research report yaleu/dcs/rr-634, Yale University, Department of Computer Science, 1988.

[6] Eric Mjolsness, Gene R. Gindi, and P. Anandan. Optimization in model matching and perceptual organization. *Neural Computation*, vol. 1, no. 2, 1989.

[7] Joachim Utans. *Neural Networks for Object Recognition within Compositional Hierarchies*. PhD thesis, Department of Electrical Engineering, Yale University, New Haven, CT 06520, 1992.

[8] Joachim Utans, Gene R. Gindi, Eric Mjolsness, and P. Anandan. Neural networks for object recognition within compositional hierarchies: Initial experiments. Technical report 8903, Yale University, Center for Systems Science, Department Electrical Engineering, 1989.

[9] A. L. Yuille. Generalized deformable models, statistical physics, and matching problems. *Neural Computation*, 2(2):1–24, 1990.

A Model of Feedback to the Lateral Geniculate Nucleus

Carlos D. Brody
Computation and Neural Systems Program
California Institute of Technology
Pasadena, CA 91125

Abstract

Simplified models of the lateral geniculate nucles (LGN) and striate cortex illustrate the possibility that feedback to the LGN may be used for robust, low-level pattern analysis. The information fed back to the LGN is rebroadcast to cortex using the LGN's full fan-out, so the cortex→LGN→cortex pathway mediates extensive cortico-cortical communication while keeping the number of necessary connections small.

1 INTRODUCTION

The lateral geniculate nucleus (LGN) in the thalamus is often considered as just a relay station on the way from the retina to visual cortex, since receptive field properties of neurons in the LGN are very similar to retinal ganglion cell receptive field properties. However, there is a massive projection from cortex back to the LGN: it is estimated that 3-4 times more synapses in the LGN are due to corticogeniculate connections than those due to retinogeniculate connections [12]. This suggests some important processing role for the LGN, but the nature of the computation performed has remained far from clear.

I will first briefly summarize some anatomical facts and physiological results concerning the corticogeniculate loop, and then present a simplified model in which its function is to (usefully) mediate communication between cortical cells.

1.1 SOME ANATOMY AND PHYSIOLOGY

The LGN contains both principal cells, which project to cortex, and inhibitory interneurons. The projection to cortex sends collaterals into a sheet of inhibitory cells called the perigeniculate nucleus (PGN). PGN cells, in turn, project back to the LGN. The geniculocortical projection then proceeds into cortex, terminating principally in layers 4 and 6 in the cat [11, 12]. Areas 17, 18, and to a lesser extent, 19 are all innervated. Layer 6 cells in area 17 of the cat have particularly long, non-end-stopped receptive fields [2]. It is from layer 6 that the corticogeniculate projection back originates.[1] It, too, passes through the PGN, sending collaterals into it, and then contacts both principal cells and interneurons in the LGN, mostly in the more distal parts of their dendrites [10, 13]. Both the forward and the backward projection are retinotopically ordered.

Thus there is the possibility of both excitatory and inhibitory effects in the corticogeniculate projection, which is principally what shall be used in the model.

The first attempts to study the physiology of the corticogeniculate projection involved inactivating cortex in some way (often cooling cortex) while observing geniculate responses to simple visual stimuli. The results were somewhat inconclusive: some investigators reported that the projection was excitatory, some that it was inhibitory, and still others that it had no observable effect at all. [1, 5, 9] Later studies have emphasized the need for using stimuli which optimally excite the cortical cells which project to the LGN; inactivating cortex should then make a significant difference in the inputs to geniculate cells. This has helped to reveal some effects: for example, LGN cells *with* corticogeniculate feedback are end-stopped (that is, respond much less to long bars than to short bars), while the end-stopping is quite clearly reduced when the cortical input is removed [8].

One study [13] has used cross-correlation analysis between cortical and geniculate cells to suggest that there is spatial structure in the corticogeniculate projection: an excitatory corticogeniculate interaction was found if cells had receptive field centers that were close to each other, while an inhibitory interaction was found if the centers were farther apart. However, the precise spatial structure of the projection remains unknown.

2 A FEEDBACK MODEL

I will now describe a simplified model of the LGN and the corticogeniculate loop. The very simple connection scheme shown in fig 1 originated in a suggestion by Christof Koch [3] that the long receptive fields in layer 6 might be used to facilitate contour completion at the LGN level. In the model, then, striate cortex simple cells feed back positively to the LGN, enhancing the conditions which gave rise to their firing. This reinforces, or completes, the oriented bar or edge patterns to which they are tuned. Assuming that the visual features of interest are for the most part oriented, while much of the noise in images may be isotropic and unoriented, enhancing the oriented features improves the signal-to-noise ratio.

[1] In all areas innervated by the LGN.

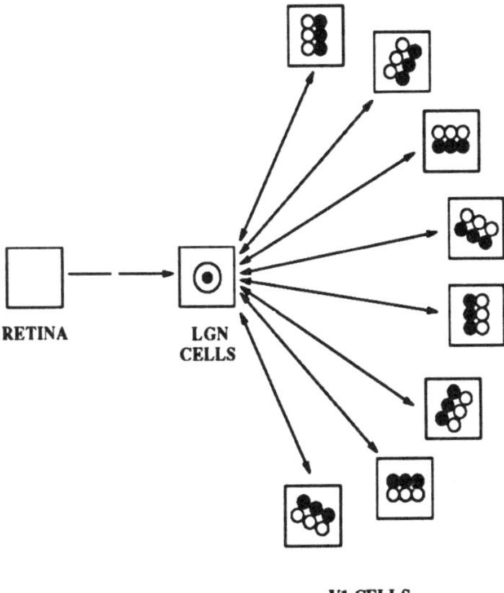

Figure 1: **Basic model connectivity**: A schematic diagram showing the connections between different pools of units in the single spatial frequency channel model. LGN cells first filter the image linearly through a center-surround filter ($\nabla^2 G$), the result of which is then passed through a sigmoid nonlinearity (tanh). (In the simulations presented here G was a Gaussian with standard deviation 1.4 pixels.) V1 cells then provide oriented filtering, which is also passed through a nonlinearity (logistic; but see details in text) and fed back positively to the LGN to reinforce detected oriented edges. V1 cells excite LGN cells which have excitatory connections to them, and inhibit those that have inhibitory connections to them. Inhibition is implicitly assumed to be mediated by interneurons. (Note that there are no intracortical or intrageniculate connections: communication takes place entirely through the feedback loop.) See text for further details.

For simplicity, only striate cortex simple "edge-detecting" cells were modeled. Two models are presented. In the first one, all cortical cells have the same spatial frequency characteristics. In the second one, two channels, a high frequency channel and a low frequency channel, interact simultaneously.

2.1 SINGLE SPATIAL FREQUENCY CHANNEL MODEL

A schematic diagram of the model is shown in figure 1. The retina is used simply as an input layer. To each input position (pixel) in the retina there corresponds one LGN unit. Linear weights from the retina to the LGN implement a $\nabla^2 G$ filter, where $G(x, y)$ is a two-dimensional Gaussian. The LGN units then project to eight different pools of "orientation-tuned" cells in V1. Each of these pools has as many units as there are pixels in the input "retina". The weights in the projection forward to V1 represent eight rotations of the template shown in figure 2a, covering 360 degrees. This simulates basic orientation tuning in V1. Cortical cells then feed back positively to the geniculus, using rotations of the template shown in fig 2(b).

The precise dynamics of the model are as follows: R_i are real-valued retinal inputs, L_i are geniculate unit outputs, and V_i are cortical cell outputs. G_{ji} represent weights from retina → LGN, F_{ji} forward weights from LGN → V1, and B_{ji} backward weights from V1 → LGN. $\alpha, \beta, \gamma, T_{C1}$ and T_{C2} are all constants. For geniculate units:

$$\frac{\mathrm{d}l_j}{\mathrm{dt}} = -\gamma l_j + \sum_i G_{ji} R_i + \sum_k B_{jk} V_k \qquad L_j = \tanh(l_j)$$

While for cortical cell units:

$$\frac{\mathrm{d}v_j}{\mathrm{dt}} = -\alpha v_j + \sum_i F_{ji} L_i - \beta\Big(\sum_i |F_{ji}| L_i\Big)^2 \qquad V_j = \begin{cases} g(v_j - T_{C1}) & \text{if } v_j > T_{C2} \\ 0 & \text{otherwise} \end{cases}$$

Here $g()$ is the logistic function.

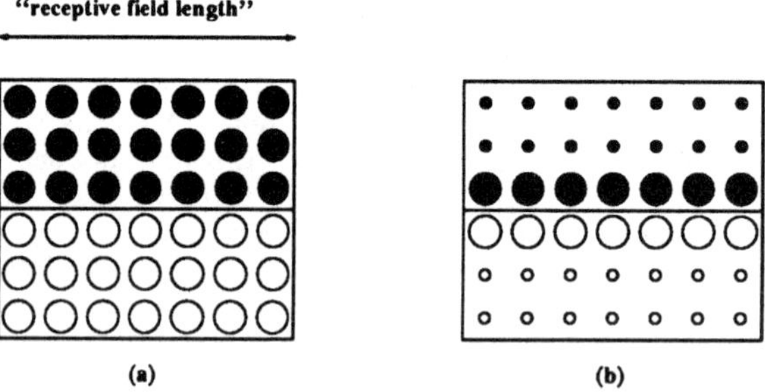

Figure 2: **Weights between the LGN and V1.** Figure **2(a)**: Forward weights, from the LGN to V1. Each circle represents the weight from a cell in the LGN; dark circles represent positive weights, light circles negative weights (assumed mediated by interneurons). The radius of each circle represents the strength of the corresponding weight. These weights create "edge-detecting" neurons in V1. Figure **2(b)**: Backwards weights, from V1 back to the LGN. Only cells close to the contrast edge receive strong feedback.

In the scheme described above many cortical cells have overlapping receptive fields, both in the forward projection from the geniculus and in the backwards projection from cortex. A cell which is reinforcing an edge within its receptive field will also partially reinforce the edge for retinotopically nearby cortical cells. For nearby cells with similar orientation tuning, the reinforcement will enhance their own firing; they will then enhance the firing of other, similar, cells farther along; and so on. That is, the overlapping feedback fields allow the edge detection process to *follow contours* (note that the process is tempered at the geniculate level by actual input from the retina). This is illustrated in figure 3.

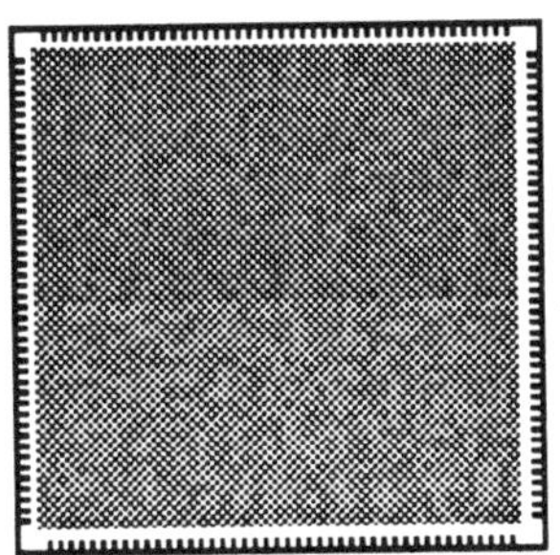
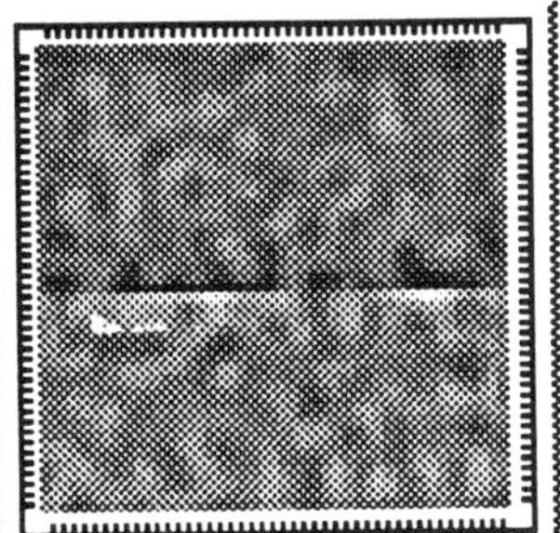
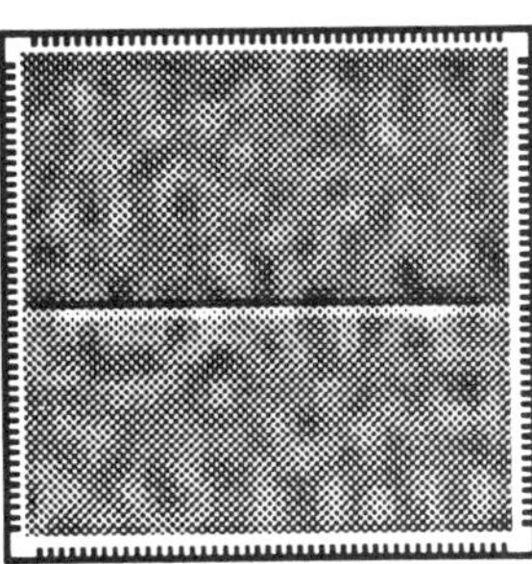

Figure 3: **Following contours**: This figure shows the effect on the LGN of the feedback enhancement. The image on the left is the retinal input: a very weak, noisy horizontal edge. The center image is the LGN after two iterations of the simulation. Note that initially only certain sectors of the edge are detected (and hence enhanced). The rightmost image is the LGN after 8 iterations: the enhanced region has spread to cover the entire edge through the effect of horizontally oriented, overlapping receptive fields. This is the final stable point of the dynamics.

2.2 MULTIPLE SPATIAL FREQUENCY CHANNELS MODEL

In the model described above the LGN is integrating and summarizing the information provided by each of the orientation-tuned pools of cortical cells.[2] It does so in a way which would easily extend to cover other types of cortical cells (bar or grating "detectors", or varying spatial frequency channels). To experiment simply with this possibility, an extra set of eight pools of orientation-tuned "edge-detecting" cortical cells was added. The new set's weights were similar to the original weights described above, except they had a "receptive field length" (see figure 2) of 3 pixels: the original set had a "receptive field length" of 9 pixels.

Thus one set was tuned for detecting short edges, while the other was tuned for detecting long edges. The effect of using both of these sets is illustrated in figure 4. Both sets interact nonlinearly to produce edge detection rather more robust than either set used alone: the image produced using both simultaneously is not a linear addition of those produced using each set separately. Note how little noise is accepted as an edge. The same model, running with the same parameters but more pixels, was also tested on a real image. This is shown in figure 5.

3 DISCUSSION ON CONNECTIVITY

A major function fulfilled by the LGN in this model is that of providing a communications pathway between cortical cells, both between cells of similar orientation but different location or spatial frequency tuning, and between cells of different orienta-

[2]A function not unlike that suggested by Mumford [7], except that here the "experts" are extremely low-level orientation-tuned channels.

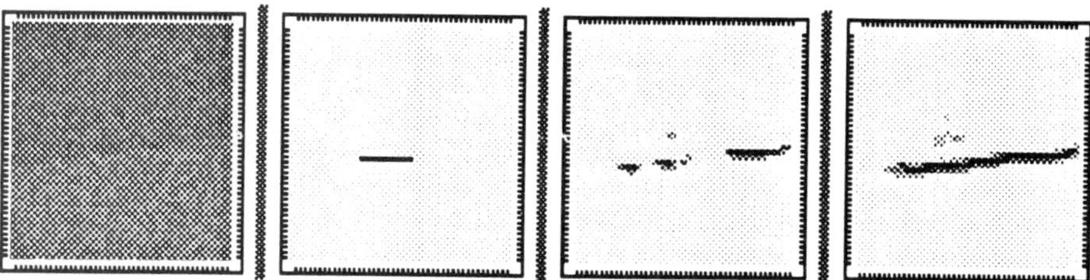

Figure 4: **Combined spatial frequency channels**: The leftmost image is the retinal input, a weak noisy edge. (The other three images are "summary outputs", obtained as follows: the model produces activations in many pools of cortical cell units; the activations from all V1 units corresponding to a particular retinotopic position are added together to form a real-valued number corresponding to that position; and this is then displayed as a grey-scale pixel. Since only "edge-detecting" units were used, this provides a rough estimate of the certainty of there being an edge at that point.) Second from left we see the summary output of the model after 20 iterations (by which time it has stabilized), using only the low spatial frequency channel. Only a single segment of the edge is detected. Third from left is the output after 20 iterations using only the high frequency channel. Only isolated, short, segments of the edge are detected. The rightmost image is the output using both channels simultaneously. Now the segments detected by the high frequency channel can combine with the original image to provide edges long enough for the low frequency channel to detect and complete into a single, long continuous edge.

tion tuning: for example, these last compete to reinforce their particular orientation preference on the geniculus. The model qualitatively shows that such a pathway, while mediated by a low-level representation like that of the LGN, can nevertheless be used effectively, producing contour-following and robust edge-detection. We must now ask whether such a function could not be performed without feedback. Clearly, it **could** be done without feedback to the LGN, purely through intracortical connections, since *any* feedback network can in principle be "unfolded in time" into a feedforward network which performs the same computation– provided we have enough units and connections available.

In other words, any suggested functional role for corticogeniculate feedback must not only include an account of the proposed computation performed, but also an account of why it is preferable to perform that computation through a feedback process, in terms of some efficiency measure (like the number of cells or synapses necessary, for example). There can be no other rationale, apart from fortuitous coincidence, for constructing an elaborate feedback mechanism to perform a computation that could just as well be done without it.

With this view in mind, it is worth re-stating that in this model any two cortical cells whose receptive fields overlap are connected (disynaptically) through the LGN. How many connections would we require in order to achieve similar communication if we only used direct connections between cortical orientation-tuned cells instead? In monkey, each cell's receptive field overlaps with approximately 10^6 others [4]– thus,

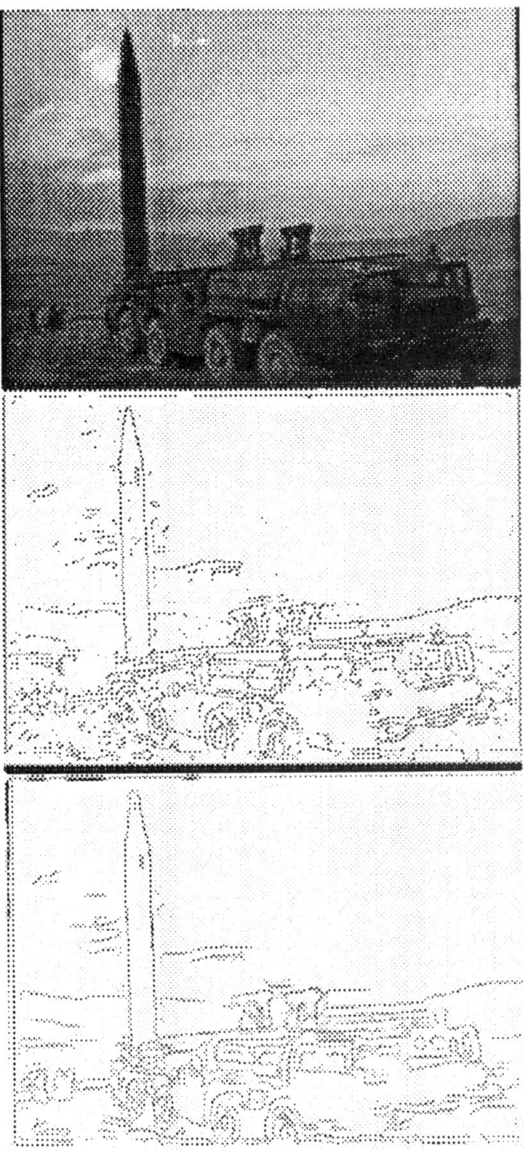

Figure 5: **A real image**: The top image is the retinal input. Stippling is due to printing only. The center image is that obtained through detecting the zero-crossings of $\nabla^2 G$. To reduce spurious edges, a minimum slope threshold was placed on the point of the zero-crossing below which edges were not accepted. The image shown here was the best that could be obtained through varying both the width of the Gaussian G and the slope threshold value. The last image shows the summary output from the model, using two simultaneous spatial frequency channels. Note how noise is reduced compared to the center image, straight lines are smoother, and resolution is not impaired, but is better in places (group of people at lower left, or "smoke stacks" atop launcher).

any cortical cell would need to synapse onto at least 10^6 cells. If the information can be sent via the LGN, geniculate cell fan-out can reduce the number of necessary synapses by a significant factor. It is estimated that geniculate cells (in the cat) synapse onto at least 200 cortical cells (probably more) [6], reducing the number of necessary connections considerably.

4 BIOLOGY AND CONCLUSIONS

In section 1.1 I noted one important study [8] which established that corticogeniculate input reduces firing of geniculate cells for long bars; this is in direct contradiction to the prediction which would be made by this model, where the feedback enhances firing for long features (here, edges). Thus, the model does not agree with known physiology.

However, the model's value lies simply in clearly illustrating the possibility that feedback in a hierarchical processing scheme like the corticogeniculate loop can be utilized for robust, low-level pattern analysis, through the use of the cortex→LGN→cortex communications pathway. The possibility that a great deal of different types of information could be flowing through this pathway for this purpose should not be left unconsidered.

Acknowledgements

The author is supported by fellowships from the Parsons Foundation and from CONACYT (Mexico). Thanks are due to Michael Lyons for careful reading of the manuscript.

References

[1] Baker, F. H. and Malpeli, J. G. 1977 *Exp. Brain Res.* **29** pp. 433-444

[2] Gilbert, C.D. 1977, *J. Physiol.*, **268**, pp. 391-421

[3] Koch, C. 1992, personal communication.

[4] Hubel, D.H. and Wiesel, T. N. 1977, *Proc. R. Soc. Lond. (B)* **198** pp. 1-59

[5] Kalil, R. E. and Chase, R. 1970, *J. Neurophysiol.* **33** pp. 459-474

[6] Martin, K.A.C. 1988, *Q. J. Exp. Phy.* **73** pp. 637-702

[7] Mumford, D. 1991 *Biol. Cybern.* **65** pp. 135-145

[8] Murphy, P.C. and Sillito, A.M. 1987, *Nature* **329** pp. 727-729

[9] Richard, D. et. al. 1975, *Exp. Brain Res.* **22** pp. 235-242

[10] Robson, J. A. 1983, *J. Comp. Neurol.* **216** pp. 89-103

[11] Sherman, S. M. 1985, *Prog. in Psychobiol. and Phys. Psych.* **11** pp. 233-314

[12] Sherman, S.M. and Koch, C. 1986, *Exp. Brain Res.* **63** pp. 1-20

[13] Tsumoto, T. et. al. 1978, *Exp. Brain Res.* **32** pp. 345-364

Unsmearing Visual Motion: Development of Long-Range Horizontal Intrinsic Connections

Kevin E. Martin **Jonathan A. Marshall**
Department of Computer Science, CB 3175, Sitterson Hall
University of North Carolina, Chapel Hill, NC 27599-3175, U.S.A.

Abstract

Human vision systems integrate information nonlocally, across long spatial ranges. For example, a moving stimulus appears smeared when viewed briefly (30 ms), yet sharp when viewed for a longer exposure (100 ms) (Burr, 1980). This suggests that visual systems combine information along a trajectory that matches the motion of the stimulus. Our self-organizing neural network model shows how developmental exposure to moving stimuli can direct the formation of horizontal trajectory-specific motion integration pathways that unsmear representations of moving stimuli. These results account for Burr's data and can potentially also model other phenomena, such as visual inertia.

1 INTRODUCTION

Nonlocal interactions strongly influence the processing of visual motion information and the response characteristics of visual neurons. Examples include: attentional modulation of receptive field shape; modulation of neural response by stimuli beyond the classical receptive field; and neural response to large-field background motion.

In this paper we present a model of the development of nonlocal neural mechanisms for visual motion processing. Our model (Marshall, 1990a, 1991) is based on the long-range excitatory horizontal intrinsic connections (LEHICs) that have been identified in the visual cortex of a variety of animal species (Blasdel, Lund, & Fitzpatrick, 1985; Callaway & Katz, 1990; Gabbott, Martin, & Whitteridge, 1987; Gilbert & Wiesel, 1989; Luhmann, Martínez Millán, & Singer, 1986; Lund, 1987; Michalski, Gerstein, Czarkowska, & Tarnecki, 1983; Mitchison & Crick, 1982; Nelson & Frost, 1985; Rockland & Lund, 1982, 1983; Rockland, Lund, & Humphrey, 1982; Ts'o, Gilbert, & Wiesel, 1986).

2 VISUAL UNSMEARING

Human visual systems summate signals over a period of approximately 120 ms in daylight (Burr 1980; Ross & Hogben, 1974). This slow summation reinforces stationary stimuli but would tend to smear any moving object. Nevertheless, human observers report perceiving both stationary and moving stimuli as sharp (Anderson, Van Essen, & Gallant, 1990; Burr, 1980; Burr, Ross, & Morrone, 1986; Morgan & Benton, 1989; Welch & McKee, 1985). Why do moving objects not appear smeared? Burr (1980) measured perceived smear of moving spots as a function of exposure time. He found that a moving visual spot appears smeared (with a comet-like tail) when it is viewed for a brief exposure (30 ms) yet perfectly sharp when viewed for a longer exposure (100 ms) (Figure 1). The ability to counteract smear at longer exposures suggests that human visual systems combine (or integrate) and sharpen motion information from multiple locations along a specific spatiotemporal *trajectory* that matches the motion of the stimulus (Barlow, 1979, 1981; Burr, 1980; Burr & Ross, 1986) in the domains of direction, velocity, position, and time.

This unsmearing phenomenon also suggests the existence of a memory-like effect, or persistence, which would cause the behavior of processing mechanisms to differ in the early, smeared stages of a spot's motion and in the later, unsmeared stages.

3 NETWORK ARCHITECTURE

We built a biologically-modeled self-organizing neural network (SONN) containing long-range excitatory horizontal intrinsic connections (LEHICs) that learns to integrate visual motion information nonlocally. The network laterally propagates predictive moving stimulus information in a trajectory-specific manner to successive image locations where a stimulus is likely to appear. The network uses this propagated information sharpen its representation of visual motion.

3.1 LONG-RANGE EXCITATORY HORIZONTAL INTRINSIC CONNECTIONS

The network's LEHICs modeled several characteristics consistent with neurophysiological data:

- They are *highly specific* and anisotropic (Callaway & Katz, 1990).

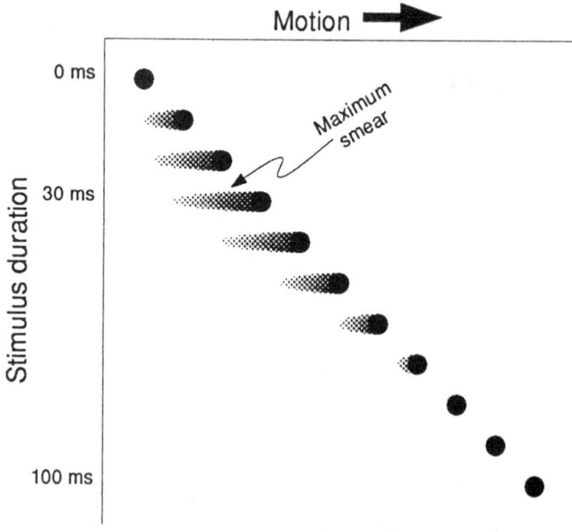

Figure 1: Motion unsmearing. A spot presented for 30 ms appears to have a comet-like tail, but a spot presented for 100 ms appears sharp and unsmeared (Burr, 1980).

- They typically run between neurons with *similar stimulus preferences* (Callaway & Katz, 1990).
- They can run for very *long distances* across the network space (e.g., 10 mm horizontally across cortex) (Luhmann, Martínez Millán, & Singer, 1986).
- They can be *shaped adaptively* through visual experience (Callaway & Katz, 1990; Luhmann, Martínez Millán, & Singer, 1986).
- They may serve to *predictively prime* motion-sensitive neurons (Gabbott, Martin, & Whitteridge, 1987).

Some characteristics of our modeled LEHICs are also consistent with those of the horizontal connections described by Hirsch & Gilbert (1991). For instance, we predicted (Marshall, 1990a) that horizontal excitatory input alone should not cause suprathreshold activation, but horizontal excitatory input should amplify activation when local bottom-up excitation is present. Hirsch & Gilbert (1991) directly observed these characteristics in area 17 pyramidal neurons in the cat.

Since LEHICs are found in early vision processing areas like V1, we hypothesize that similar connections are likely to be found within "higher" cortical areas as well, like areas MT and STS. Our simulated networks may correspond to structures in such higher areas. Although our long-range lateral signals are modeled as being excitatory (Orban, Gulyás, & Vogels, 1987), they are also functionally homologous to long-range trajectory-specific lateral inhibition of neurons tuned to *null*-direction motion (Ganz & Felder, 1984; Marlin, Douglas, & Cynader, 1991; Motter, Steinmetz, Duffy, & Mountcastle, 1987).

LEHICs constitute one possible means by which nonlocal communication can take place in visual cortex. Other means, such as large bottom-up receptive fields, can also cause information to be transmitted nonlocally. However, the main difference between LEHICs and bottom-up receptive fields is that LEHICs provide lateral *feedback* information about the *outcome* of other processing within a given stage. This generates a form of memory, or persistence. Purely bottom-up networks (without LEHICs or other feedback) would perform processing afresh at each step, so that the outcome of processing would be influenced only by the direct, feedforward *inputs* at each step.

3.2 RESULTS OF NETWORK DEVELOPMENT

In our model, developmental exposure to moving stimuli guides the formation of motion-integration pathways that unsmear representations of moving stimuli. Our model network is repeatedly exposed to training input sequences of smeared motion patterns through bottom-up excitatory connections. Smear is modeled as an exponential decay and represents the responses of temporally integrating neurons to moving visual stimuli. The network contains a set of initially nonspecific LEHICs with fixed signal transmission latencies. The moving stimuli cause the pattern of weights across the LEHICs to become refined, eventually forming "chains" that correspond to trajectories in the visual environment.

To model unsmearing fully, we would need a 2-D retinotopically organized layer of neurons tuned to different directions of motion and different velocities. Each trajectory in visual space would be represented by a set of like velocity and direction sensitive neurons whose receptive fields are located along the trajectory. These neurons would be connected through a trajectory-specific chain of time-delayed LEHICs. Lateral inhibition between chains would be organized selectively to allow representations of multiple stimuli to be simultaneously active (Marshall, 1990a), thereby letting most trajectory representations operate independently.

Our simulation consists of a 1-D subnetwork of the full 2-D network, with 32 neurons sensitive to a single velocity and direction of motion (Figure 2a). The lateral inhibitory connections are fixed in a Gaussian distribution, but the LEHIC weights can change according to a modified Hebbian rule (Grossberg, 1982):

$$\frac{d}{dt} z_{ji}^{+} = \epsilon \, f(x_i)\left(-z_{ji}^{+} + h(x_j)\right),$$

where z_{ji}^{+} represents the weight of the LEHIC from the jth neuron to the ith neuron, x_i represents the value of the activation level of the ith neuron, ϵ is a slow learning rate, $h(x_j) = \max(0, x_j)^2$ is a faster-than-linear signal function, and $f(x_i) = \max(0, x_i)^2$ is a faster-than-linear sampling function. To model multiple-step trajectories, we used LEHICs with three different signal transmission delays. Initially the LEHICs were all represented, but their weights were zero.

As stimuli move across the receptive fields of the neurons in the network, many neurons are coactive because the network is unable to resolve the smear. By the learning rule, the weights of the LEHICs between these coactive neurons increase. This leads to a profusion of connection weights (Figure 2b), analogous to the "crude clusters" proposed by Callaway and Katz (1990) to describe the early (postnatal days 14-35) structure of horizontal connections in cat area V1.

After sufficient exposure to moving stimuli, the "crude clusters" in our simulation become sharper (Figure 2c) because of the faster-than-linear signal functions. This refinement of the pattern of connection weights into chains might correspond to the later (postnatal day 42+) development of "refined clusters" described by Callaway and Katz (1990).

3.3 RESULTS OF NETWORK OPERATION

Before learning begins the network is incapable of unsmearing a stimulus moving across the receptive fields of the neurons (Figure 3a). As the stimulus moves from one position to the next, the pattern of neuron activations is no less smeared than

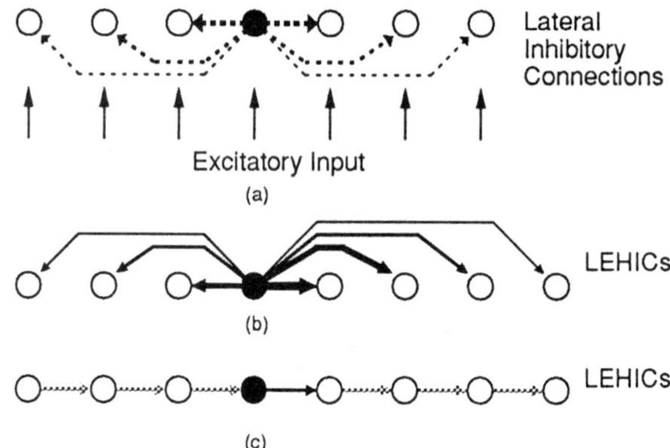

Figure 2: Three phases of modeled development. (a) Initial. Lateral excitatory connections were modifiable and had zero weight. Lateral inhibition was fixed in a Gaussian distribution (thickness of dotted arrows). The neurons received sequences of smeared rightward-moving excitatory input patterns. (b) Profusion. During early development lateral excitatory connections went through a phase of weight profusion. The output LEHIC weights (thickness of arrows) from one neuron (filled circle) are shown; weights were biased toward rightward motion. (c) Refinement. During later development, the pattern of weights settled into sets of regular anisotropic chains; most of the early profuse connections were eliminated. No external parameters were manipulated during the simulation to induce the initial→profusion→refinement phase transitions. The simulation contained three different signal transmission latencies, but only one is shown here.

the moving input pattern. No information is built up along the trajectory since the LEHIC weights are still zero.

After training, the network is able to resolve the smear (Figure 3b) in a manner reminiscent of Burr's results (Figure 1). As a stimulus moves, it excites a sequence of neurons whose receptive fields lie along its trajectory. As each neuron receives excitatory input in turn from the moving stimulus, it becomes activated and emits excitatory signals along its trajectory-specific LEHICs. Subsequent neurons along the trajectory then receive both direct stimulus-generated excitation *and* lateral time-delayed excitation. The combination causes these neurons to become even more active; thus activation accumulates along the chain toward an asymptote. The accumulating activation lets neurons farther along the trajectory more effectively suppress (via lateral inhibition) the activation of the neurons carrying the trailing smear. The comet-like tail contracts progressively, and the representation of the

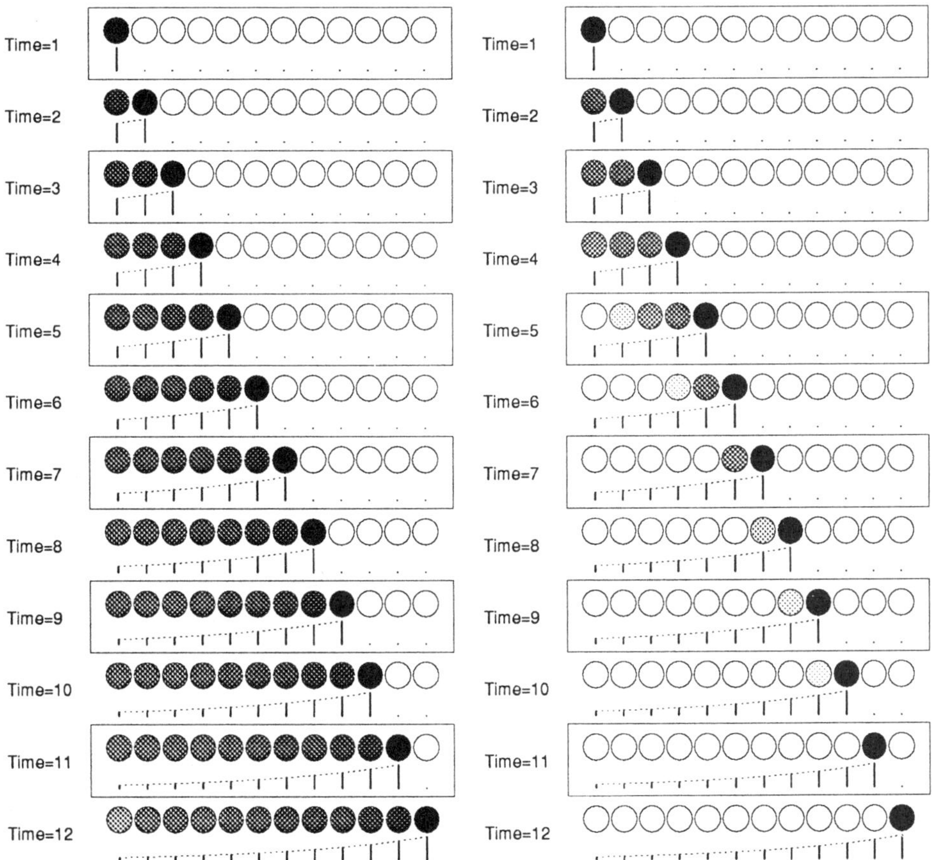

Figure 3: Results of unsmearing simulation. A simulated spot moves rightward for 12 time steps along a 1-D model retina. Smeared input patterns are plotted as vertical lines, and relative output neuron activation patterns are plotted as shading intensity of circles (neurons). (a) Before learning (left) the network is unable to resolve the smear in the input, but (b) after learning (right), the smear is resolved by time step 11. The same test input patterns are used both before and after learning.

moving stimulus becomes increasingly sharp.

Each neuron's activation value x_i changes according to a shunting differential equation (Grossberg, 1982):

$$\frac{d}{dt}x_i = -Ax_i + (B - x_i)E_i - (C + x_i)I_i,$$

where the neuron's total excitatory input $E_i = K_i(1 + L_i)$ combines bottom-up input K_i (the smeared motion) with summed lateral excitation input $L_i = L\sum_j h(x_j)z_{ji}^+$, the neuron's inhibitory input is $I_i = \gamma\sum_j g(x_j)z_{ji}^-$, $h(x_j) = \max(0, x_j)^2$ and $g(x_j) = \max(0, x_j)^3$ are faster-than-linear signal functions, and A, B, C, L, β, and γ are constants.

4 CONCLUSIONS AND FUTURE RESEARCH

One might wonder why visual systems allow smear to be represented during the first 30 ms of a stimulus' motion, since simple winner-take-all lateral inhibition could easily eliminate the smear in the representation. Our research leads us to suggest that representing smear lets human visual systems tolerate and even exploit initial uncertainty in local motion measurements. A system with winner-take-all sharpening could not generate a reliable trajectory prediction from an initial inaccurate local motion measurement because the motion can be determined accurately only after multiple measurements along the trajectory are combined (Figure 4a). The inaccurate trajectory predictions of such a network would impair its ability to develop or maintain circuits for combining motion measurements (Marshall, 1990ab). We conclude that motion perception systems need to represent explicitly both initial smear and subsequent unsmearing.

Figure 4a illustrates that when a moving object first appears, the direction in which it will move is uncertain. As the object continues to move, its successor positions become increasingly predictable, in general. The initial smear in the representation is necessary for communicating prior trajectory information to the representations of many possible future trajectory positions.

Faster-than-linear signal functions (Figure 4b) were used so that a neuron would generate little lateral excitation and inhibition when it is uncertain about the presence of the moving stimulus in its receptive field (when a new stimulus appears) and so that a highly active neuron (more certain about the presence of the stimulus in its receptive field) would generate strong lateral excitation and inhibition.

Our results illustrate how visual systems may become able both to propagate motion

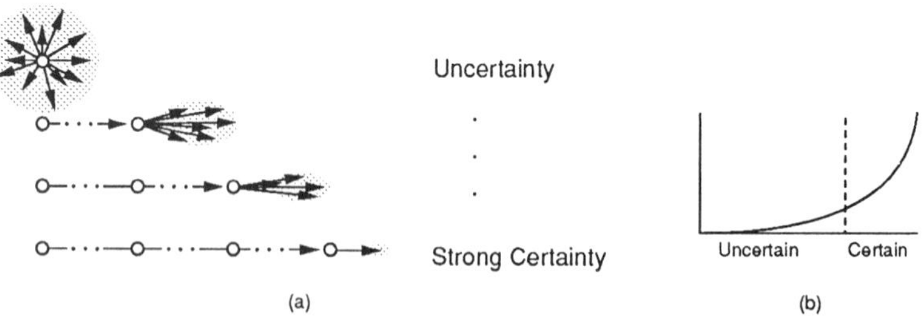

Figure 4: Visual motion system uncertainty. (a) When a moving object first appears, the direction in which it will move is uncertain (top row, circular shaded region). As motion proceeds (second, third, and fourth rows), the set of possible stimulus locations becomes increasingly predictable (smaller shaded regions). (b) Faster-than-linear signal functions maintain smear of uncertain data but sharpen more certain data.

information in a trajectory-specific manner and to use the propagated information to unsmear representations of moving objects: (1) Regular anisotropic "chain" patterns of time-delayed horizontal excitatory connections become established through a learning procedure, in response to exposure to ordinary moving visual scenes. (2) Accumulation of propagated motion information along these chains causes a sharpening that unsmears representations of moving visual stimuli.

These results let us model the integration-along-trajectory revealed by Burr's (1980) experiment, within a developmental framework that corresponds to known neurophysiological data; they can potentially also let other nonlocal motion phenomena, such as visual inertia (Anstis & Ramachandran, 1987), be modeled.

ACKNOWLEDGEMENTS

This work was supported in part by the National Eye Institute (EY09669), by the Office of Naval Research (Cognitive and Neural Sciences, N00014-93-1-0130), and by an Oak Ridge Associated Universities Junior Faculty Enhancement Award.

REFERENCES

Anderson, C.H., Van Essen, D.C., & Gallant, J.L. (1990). "Blur into Focus." *Nature*, 343, 419–420.

Anstis, S.M. & Ramachandran, V.S. (1987). "Visual Inertia in Apparent Motion." *Vision Research*, 27(5), 755–764.

Barlow, H.B. (1979). "Reconstructing the Visual Image in Space and Time." *Nature*, 279, 189–190.

Barlow, H.B. (1981). "Critical Limiting Factors in the Design of the Eye and Visual Cortex." *Proceedings of the Royal Society of London, Ser. B*, 212, 1–34.

Blasdel, G.G., Lund, J.S., & Fitzpatrick, D. (1985). "Intrinsic Connections of Macaque Striate Cortex: Axonal Projections of Cells Outside Lamina 4C." *Journal of Neuroscience*, 5(12), 3350–3369.

Burr, D. (1980). "Motion Smear." *Nature*, 284, 164–165.

Burr, D. & Ross, J. (1986). "Visual Processing of Motion." *Trends in Neuroscience*, 9(7), 304–307.

Burr, D.C., Ross, J., & Morrone, M.C. (1986). "Seeing Objects in Motion." *Proceedings of the Royal Society of London, Ser. B*, 227, 249–265.

Callaway, E.M. & Katz, L.C. (1990). "Emergence and Refinement of Clustered Horizontal Connections in Cat Striate Cortex." *J. Neurophysiol.*, 10, 1134–1153.

Gabbott, P.L.A., Martin, K.A.C., & Whitteridge, D. (1987). "Connections Between Pyramidal Neurons in Layer 5 of Cat Visual Cortex (Area 17)." *Journal of Comparative Neurology*, 259, 364–381.

Ganz, L. & Felder, R. (1984). "Mechanism of Directional Selectivity is Simple Neurons of the Cat's Visual Cortex Analyzed with Stationary Flash Sequences." *Journal of Neurophysiology*, 51, 294-324.

Gilbert, C.D. & Wiesel, T.N. (1989). "Columnar Specificity of Intrinsic Horizontal and Corticocortical Connections in Cat Visual Cortex." *Journal of Neuroscience*, 9, 2432–2442.

Hirsch, J. & Gilbert, C.D. (1991). "Synaptic Physiology of Horizontal Connections in the Cat's Visual Cortex." *Journal of Neuroscience*, 11, 1800–1809.

Luhmann, H.J., Martínez Millán, L., & Singer, W. (1986). "Development of

Horizontal Intrinsic Connections in Cat Striate Cortex." *Experimental Brain Research*, 63, 443–448.

Lund, J.S. (1987). "Local Circuit Neurons of Macaque Monkey Striate Cortex: I. Neurons of Laminae 4C and 5A." *Journal of Comparative Neurology*, 257, 60–92.

Marlin, S.G., Douglas, R.M., & Cynader, M.S. (1991). "Position-Specific Adaptation in Simple Cell Receptive Fields of the Cat Striate Cortex." *Journal of Neurophysiology*, 66(5), 1769–1784.

Marshall, J.A. (1990a). "Self-Organizing Neural Networks for Perception of Visual Motion." *Neural Networks*, 3, 45–74.

Marshall, J.A. (1990b). "Representation of Uncertainty in Self-Organizing Neural Networks." *Proceedings of the International Neural Network Conference*, Paris, France, July 1990, 809–812.

Marshall, J.A. (1991). "Challenges of Vision Theory: Self-Organization of Neural Mechanisms for Stable Steering of Object-Grouping Data in Visual Motion Perception." Invited Paper, in *Stochastic and Neural Methods in Signal Processing, Image Processing, and Computer Vision*, Su-Shing Chen, Ed., Proceedings of the SPIE 1569, San Diego, CA, July 1991, pp. 200–215.

Michalski, A., Gerstein, G.L., Czarkowska, J., & Tarnecki, R. (1983). "Interactions Between Cat Striate Cortex Neurons." *Experimental Brain Research*, 51, 97–107.

Mitchison, G. & Crick, F. (1982). "Long Axons Within the Striate Cortex: Their Distribution, Orientation, and Patterns of Connection." *Proceedings of the National Academy of Sciences of the U.S.A.*, 79, 3661–3665.

Morgan, M.J. & Benton, S. (1989). "Motion-Deblurring in Human Vision." *Nature*, 340, 385–386.

Motter, B.C., Steinmetz, M.A., Duffy, C.J., & Mountcastle, V.B. (1987). "Functional Properties of Parietal Visual Neurons: Mechanisms of Directionality Along a Single Axis." *Journal of Neuroscience*, 7(1), 154–176.

Nelson, J.I. & Frost, B.J. (1985). "Intracortical Facilitation Among Co-Oriented, Co-Axially Aligned Simple Cells in Cat Striate Cortex." *Experimental Brain Research*, 61, 54–61.

Orban, G.A., Gulyás, B., & Vogels, R. (1987). "Influence of a Moving Textured Background on Direction Selectivity of Cat Striate Neurons." *Journal of Neurophysiology*, 57(6), 1792–1812.

Rockland, K.S. & Lund, J.S. (1982). "Widespread Periodic Intrinsic Connections in the Tree Shrew Visual Cortex." *Science*, 215, 1532–1534.

Rockland, K.S. & Lund, J.S. (1983). "Intrinsic Laminar Lattice Connections in Primate Visual Cortex." *Journal of Comparative Neurology*, 216, 303–318.

Rockland, K.S., Lund, J.S., & Humphrey, A.L. (1982). "Anatomical Banding of Intrinsic Connections in Striate Cortex of Tree Shrews (*Tupaia glis*)." *Journal of Comparative Neurology*, 209, 41–58.

Ross, J. & Hogben, J.H. (1974). *Vision Research*, 14, 1195–1201.

Ts'o, D.Y., Gilbert, C.D., & Wiesel, T.N. (1986). "Relationships Between Horizontal Interactions and Functional Architecture in Cat Striate Cortex as Revealed by Cross-Correlation Analysis." *Journal of Neuroscience*, 6(4), 1160–1170.

Welch, L. & McKee, S.P. (1985). "Colliding Targets: Evidence for Spatial Localization Within the Motion System." *Vision Research*, 25(12), 1901–1910.

Remote Sensing Image Analysis via a Texture Classification Neural Network

Hayit K. Greenspan and Rodney Goodman
Department of Electrical Engineering
California Institute of Technology, 116-81
Pasadena, CA 91125
hayit@electra.micro.caltech.edu

Abstract

In this work we apply a texture classification network to remote sensing image analysis. The goal is to extract the characteristics of the area depicted in the input image, thus achieving a segmented map of the region. We have recently proposed a combined neural network and rule-based framework for texture recognition. The framework uses unsupervised and supervised learning, and provides probability estimates for the output classes. We describe the texture classification network and extend it to demonstrate its application to the Landsat and Aerial image analysis domain.

1 INTRODUCTION

In this work we apply a texture classification network to remote sensing image analysis. The goal is to segment the input image into homogeneous textured regions and identify each region as one of a prelearned library of textures, e.g. tree area and urban area distinction. Classification o f remote sensing imagery is of importance in many applications, such as navigation, surveillance and exploration. It has become a very complex task spanning a growing number of sensors and application domains. The applications include: landcover identification (with systems such as the AVIRIS and SPOT), atmospheric analysis via cloud-coverage mapping (using the AVHRR sensor), oceanographic exploration for sea/ice type classification (SAR input) and more.

Much attention has been given to the use of the spectral signature for the identification of region types (Wharton, 1987; Lee and Philpot, 1991). Only recently has the idea of adding on spatial information been presented (Ton et al, 1991). In this work we investigate the possibility of gaining information from textural analysis. We have recently developed a texture recognition system (Greenspan et al, 1992) which achieves state-of-the-art results on natural textures. In this paper we apply the system to remote sensing imagery and check the system's robustness in this noisy environment. Texture can play a major role in segmenting the images into homogeneous areas and enhancing other sensors capabilities, such as multispectra analysis, by indicating areas of interest in which further analysis can be pursued. Fusion of the spatial information with the spectral signature will enhance the classification and the overall automated analysis capabilities.

Most of the work in the literature focuses on human expert-based rules with specific sensor data calibration. Some of the existing problems with this classic approach are the following (Ton et al, 1991):
- Experienced photointerpreters are required to spend a considerable amount of time generating rules.
- The rules need to be updated for different geographical regions.
- No spatial rules exist for the complex Landsat imagery.

An interesting question is if one can automate the rule generation. In this paper we present a learning framework in which spatial rules are learned by the system from a given database of examples.

The learning framework and its contribution in a texture-recognition system is the topic of section 2. Experimental results of the system's application to remote sensing imagery are presented in section 3.

2 The texture-classification network

We have previously presented a texture classification network which combines a neural network and rule-based framework (Greenspan et al, 1992) and enables both unsupervised and supervised learning. The system consists of three major stages, as shown in Fig. 1. The first stage performs feature extraction and transforms the image space into an array of 15-dimensional feature vectors, each vector corresponding to a local window in the original image. There is much evidence in animal visual systems supporting the use of multi-channel orientation selective band-pass filters in the feature-extraction phase. An open issue is the decision regarding the appropriate number of frequencies and orientations required for the representation of the input domain. We define an initial set of 15 filters and achieve a computationally efficient filtering scheme via the multi-resolution pyramidal approach.

The learning mechanism shown next derives a minimal subset of the above filters which conveys sufficient information about the visual input for its differentiation and labeling. In an unsupervised stage a machine-learning clustering algorithm is used to quantize the continuous input features. A supervised learning stage follows in which labeling of the input domain is achieved using a rule-based network. Here an information theoretic measure is utilized to find the most informative correlations between the attributes and the pattern class specification, while providing probability estimates for the output classes. Ultimately, a minimal representation for a library of patterns is learned in a training mode, following which the classification

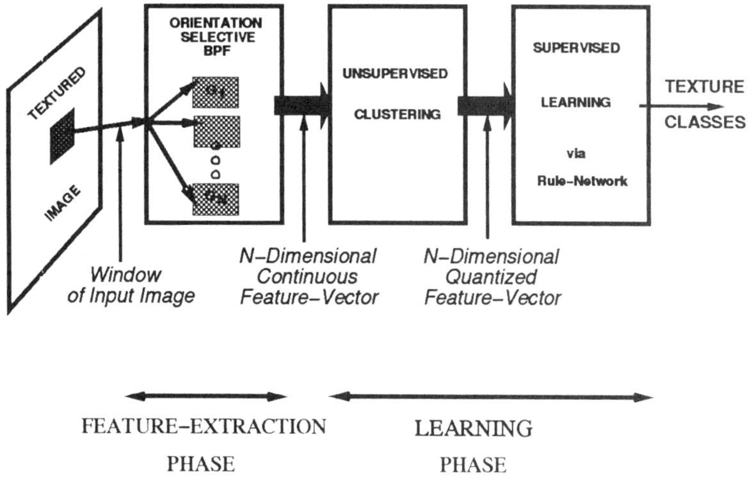

Figure 1: System block diagram

of new patterns is achieved.

2.1 The system in more detail

The initial stage for a classification system is the feature extraction phase. In the texture-analysis task there is both biological and computational evidence supporting the use of Gabor-like filters for the feature-extraction. In this work, we use the Log Gabor pyramid, or the Gabor wavelet decomposition to define an initial finite set of filters. A computational efficient scheme involves using a pyramidal representation of the image which is convolved with fixed spatial support oriented Gabor filters (Greenspan at al, 1993). Three scales are used with 4 orientations per scale (0,90,45,135 degrées), together with a non-oriented component, to produce a 15-dimensional feature vector as the output of the feature extraction stage. Using the pyramid representation is computationally efficient as the image is subsampled in the filtering process. Two such size reduction stages take place in the three scale pyramid. The feature values thus generated correspond to the average power of the response, to specific orientation and frequency ranges, in an $8 * 8$ window of the input image. Each such window gets mapped to a 15-dimensional attribute vector as the output of the feature extraction stage.

The goal of the learning system is to use the feature representation described above to discriminate between the input patterns, or textures. Both unsupervised and supervised learning stages are utilized. A minimal set of features are extracted from the 15-dimensional attribute vector, which convey sufficient information about the visual input for its differentiation and labeling.

The unsupervised learning stage can be viewed as a preprocessing stage for achieving a more compact representation of the filtered input. The goal is to quantize the continuous valued features which are the result of the initial filtering, thus shifting to a more symbolic representation of the input domain. This clustering stage was found experimentally to be of importance as an initial learning phase in a classification system. The need for discretization becomes evident when trying to learn associations between attributes in a symbolic representation, such as rules.

The output of the filtering stage consists of N (=15), continuous valued feature maps; each representing a filtered version of the original input. Thus, each local area of the input image is represented via an N-dimensional feature vector. An array of such N-dimensional vectors, viewed across the input image, is the input to the learning stage. We wish to detect characteristic behavior across the N-dimensional feature space, for the family of textures to be learned. In this work, each dimension, out of the 15-dimensional attribute vector, is individually clustered. All training samples are thus projected onto each axis of the space and one-dimensional clusters are found using the K-means clustering algorithm (Duda and Hart, 1973). This statistical clustering technique consists of an iterative procedure of finding K means in the training sample space, following which each new input sample is associated with the closest mean in Euclidean distance. The means, labeled 0 thru K minus 1 arbitrarily, correspond to discrete codewords. Each continuous-valued input sample gets mapped to the discrete codeword representing its associated mean. The output of this preprocessing stage is a 15-dimensional quantized vector of attributes which is the result of concatenating the discrete-valued codewords of the individual dimensions.

In the final, supervised stage, we utilize the existing information in the feature maps for higher level analysis, such as input labeling and classification. A rule - based information theoretic approach is used which is an extension of a first order Bayesian classifier, because of its ability to output probability estimates for the output classes (Goodman et al, 1992). The classifier defines correlations between input features and output classes as probabilistic rules. A data driven supervised learning approach utilizes an information theoretic measure to learn the most informative links or rules between features and class labels. The classifier then uses these links to provide an estimate of the probability of a given output class being true. When presented with a new input evidence vector, a set of rules R can be considered to "fire". The classifier estimates the posterior probability of each class given the rules that fire in the form $log(p(x)|R)$, and the largest estimate is chosen as the initial class label decision. The probability estimates for the output classes can now be used for feedback purposes and further higher level processing.

The rule-based classification system can be mapped into a 3 layer feed forward architecture as shown in Fig. 2 (Greenspan et al, 1993). The input layer contains a node for each attribute. The hidden layer contains a node for each rule and the output layer contains a node for each class. Each rule (second layer node j) is connected to a class via a multiplicative weight of evidence W_j.

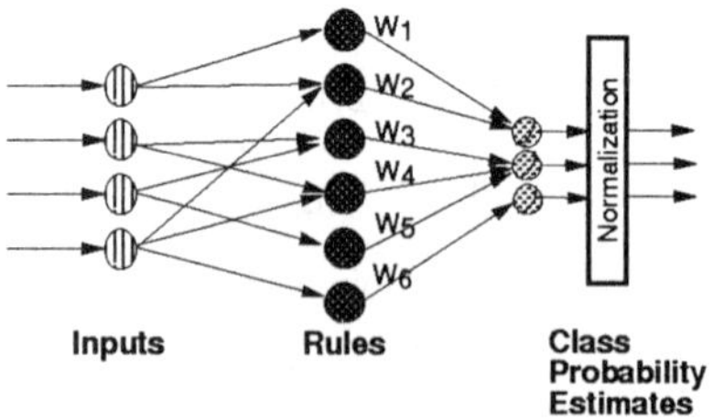

Figure 2: Rule-Based Network

3 Results

The above-described system has achieved state-of-the-art results on both structured and unstructured natural texture classification [5]. In this work we present initial results of applying the network to the noisy environment of satellite and air-borne imagery.

Fig. 3 presents two such examples. The first example (top) is an image of Pasadena, California, taken via the AVIRIS system (Airborne Visible/Infrared Imaging Spectrometer). The AVIRIS system covers 224 contiguous spectral bands simultaneously, at 20 meters per pixel resolution. The presented example is taken as an average of several bands in the visual range. In this input image we can see that a major distinguishing characteristic is urban area vs. hilly surround. These are the two categories we set forth to learn. The training consists of a 128*128 image sample for each category. The test input is a 512*512 image which is very noisy and because of its low resolution, very difficult to segment into the two categories, even to our own visual perception. In the presented output (top right), the urban area is labeled in white, the hillside in gray and unknown, undetermined areas are in darker gray. We see that a rough segmentation into the desired regions has been achieved. The probabilistic network's output allows for the identification of unknown or unspecified regions, in which more elaborate analysis can be pursued (Greenspan et al, 1992). The dark gray areas correspond to such regions; one example is the hill and urban contact (bottom right) in which some urban suburbs on the hill slopes form a mixture of the classes. Note that in the initial results presented the blockiness perceived is the result of the analysis resolution chosen. Fusing into the system additional spectral bands as our input, would enable pixel resolution as well as enable detecting additional classes (not visually detectable), such as concrete material, a variety of vegetation etc.

A higher resolution Airborne image is presented at the bottom of Fig. 3. The classes learned are bush (output label dark gray), ground (output label gray) and a structured area, such as a field present or the man-made structures (white). Here, the training was done on 128*128 image examples (1 example per class). The input image is 800*800. In the result presented (right) we see that the three classes have been found and a rough segmentation into the three regions is achieved. Note in particular the detection of the bush areas and the three main structured areas in the image, including the man-made field, indicated in white.

Our final example relates to an autonomous navigation scenario. Autonomous vehicles require an automated scene analysis system to avoid obstacles and navigate through rough terrain. Fusion of several visual modalities, such as intensity-based segmentation, texture, stereo, and color, together with other domain inputs, such as soil spectral decomposition analysis, will be required for this challenging task. In Fig. 4. we present preliminary results on outdoor photographed scenes taken by an autonomous vehicle at JPL (Jet Propulsion Laboratory, Pasadena). The presented scenes (left) are segmented into bush and gravel regions (right). The training set consists of 4 $64 * 64$ image samples from each category. In the top example (a 256*256 pixel image), light gray indicates gravel while black represents bushy regions. We can see that intensity alone can not suffice in this task (for example, top right corner). The system has learned some textural characteristics which guided

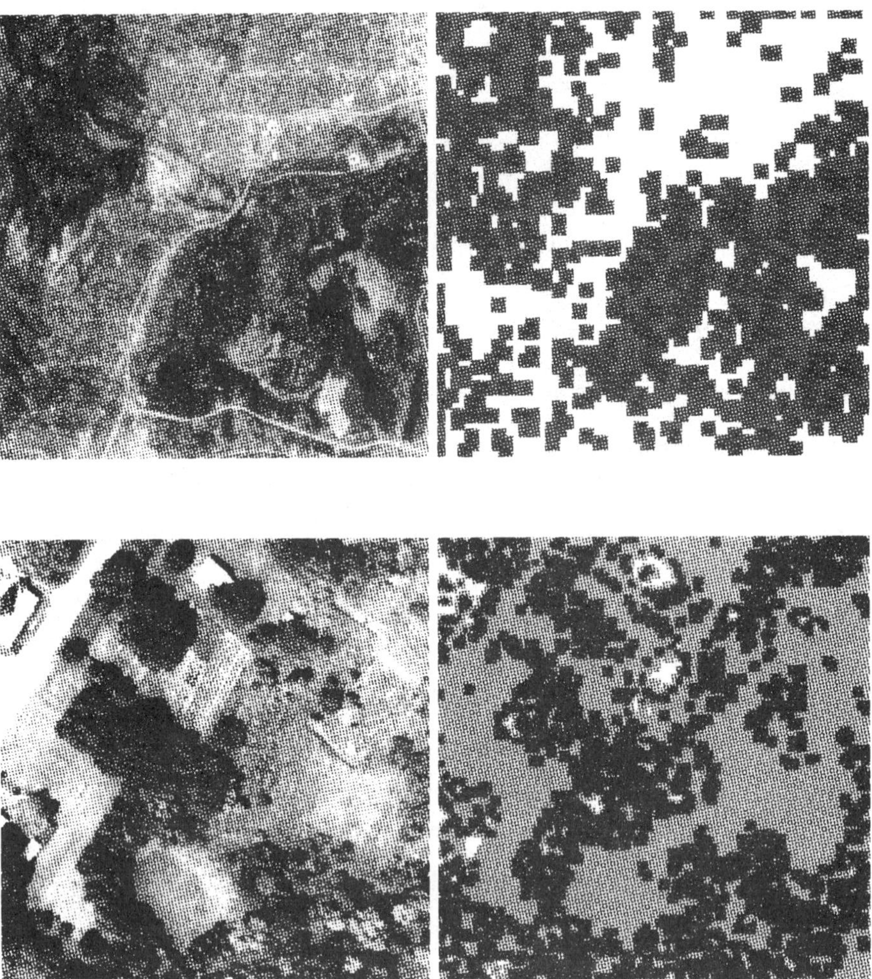

Figure 3: Remote sensing image analysis results. The input test image is shown (left) followed by the system output classification map (right). In the AVIRIS (top) input, white indicates urban regions, gray is a hilly area and dark gray reflects undetermined or different region types. In the Airborne output (bottom), dark gray indicates a bush area, light gray is a ground cover region and white indicates man-made structures. Both robustness to noise and generalization are demonstrated in these two challenging real-world problems.

the segmentation in otherwise similar-intensity regions. Note that this is also probably the cause for identifying the track-like region (e.g., center bottom) as bush regions. We could learn track-like regions as a third category, or specifically include such examples as gravel in our training set.

In the second example (a 400*400 input image, bottom) light gray indicates gravel, dark gray represents a bush-like region, and black represents the unknown category. Here, the top right region of the sky, is labeled correctly as an unknown, or new category. Note that intensity alone would have confused that region as being gravel. Overall, the texture classification neural-network succeeds in achieving a correct, yet rough, segmentation of the scene based on textural characteristics alone. These are encouraging results indicating that the learning system has learned informative characteristics of the domain.

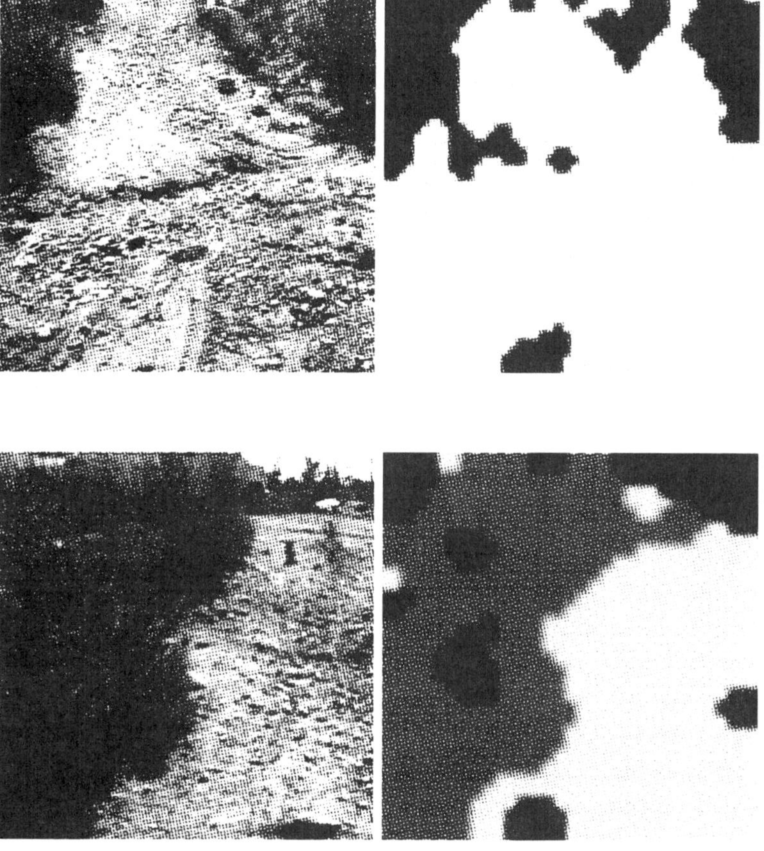

Fig 4: Image Analysis for Autonomous Navigation

4 Summary and Discussion

The presented results demonstrate the network's capability for generalization and robustness to noise in very challenging real-world problems. In the presented framework a learning mechanism automates the rule generation. This framework can answer some of the current difficulties in using the human expert's knowledge. Further more, the automation of the rule generation can enhance the expert's knowledge regarding the task at hand. We have demonstrated that the use of textural spatial information can segment complex scenery into homogeneous regions. Some of the system's strengths include generalization to new scenes, invariance to intensity, and the ability to enlarge the feature vector representation to include additional inputs (such as additional spectral bands) and learn rules characterizing the integrated modalities. Future work includes fusing several modalities within the learning framework for enhanced performance and testing the performance on a large database.

Acknowledgements

This work is supported in part by Pacific Bell, and in part by DARPA and ONR under grant no. N00014-92-J-1860. H. Greenspan is supported in part by an Intel fellowship. The research described in this paper was carried out in part by the Jet Propulsion Laboratories, California Institute of Technology. We would like to thank Dr. C. Anderson for his pyramid software support and Dr. L. Matthies for the autonomous vehicle images.

References

S. Wharton. (1987) A Spectral-Knowledge-Based Approach for Urban Land-Cover Discrimination. *IEEE Transactions on Geoscience and Remote Sensing*, Vol. GE-25[3]:272-282.

J. Lee and W. Philpot. (1991) Spectral Texture Pattern Matching: A Classifier For Digital Imagery. *IEEE Transactions on Geoscience and Remote Sensing*, Vol. 29[4]:545-554.

J. Ton, J. Sticklen and A. Jain. (1991) Knowledge-Based Segmentation of Landsat Images. *IEEE Transactions on Geoscience and Remote Sensing*, Vol. 29[2]:222-232.

H. Greenspan, R. Goodman and R. Chellappa. (1992) Combined Neural Network and Rule-Based Framework for Probabilistic Pattern Recognition and Discovery. In J. E. Moody, S. J. Hanson, and R. P. Lippman (eds.), *Advances in Neural Information Processing Systems 4.*, 444-452, San Mateo, CA: Morgan Kaufmann Publishers.

H. Greenspan, R. Goodman, R. Chellappa and C. Anderson. (1993) Learning Texture Discrimination Rules in a Multiresolution System. Submitted to *IEEE Transactions on Pattern Analysis and Machine Intelligence.*

R. O. Duda and P. E. Hart. (1973) *Pattern Classification and Scene Analysis.* John Wiley and Sons, Inc.

R. Goodman, C. Higgins, J. Miller and P. Smyth. (1992) Rule-Based Networks for Classification and Probability Estimation. *Neural Computation*, [4]:781-804.

Computation of Heading Direction From Optic Flow in Visual Cortex

Markus Lappe* **Josef P. Rauschecker**

Laboratory of Neurophysiology, NIMH, Poolesville, MD, U.S.A. and
Max–Planck–Institut für Biologische Kybernetik, Tübingen, Germany

Abstract

We have designed a neural network which detects the direction of ego–motion from optic flow in the presence of eye movements (Lappe and Rauschecker, 1993). The performance of the network is consistent with human psychophysical data, and its output neurons show great similarity to "triple component" cells in area MSTd of monkey visual cortex. We now show that by using assumptions about the kind of eye movements that the observer is likely to perform, our model can generate various other cell types found in MSTd as well.

1 INTRODUCTION

Following the ideas of Gibson in the 1950's a number of studies in human psychophysics have demonstrated that optic flow can be used effectively for navigation in space (Rieger and Toet, 1985; Stone and Perrone, 1991; Warren *et al.*, 1988). In search for the neural basis of optic flow processing, an area in the cat's extrastriate visual cortex (PMLS) was described as having a centrifugal organization of neuronal direction preferences, which suggested an involvement of area PMLS in the processing of expanding flow fields (Rauschecker *et al.*, 1987; Brenner and Rauschecker, 1990). Recently, neurons in the dorsal part of the medial superior temporal area (MSTd) in monkeys have been described that respond to various combinations of large expanding/contracting, rotating, or shifting dot patterns (Duffy and Wurtz, 1991; Tanaka and Saito, 1989). Cells in MSTd show a continuum of response properties ranging from selectivity for only one movement pattern ("single

*Present address: Neurobiologie, ND7, Ruhr–Universität Bochum, 4630 Bochum, Germany.

component cells") to selectivity for one mode of each of the three movement types ("triple component cells"). An interesting property of many MSTd cells is their position invariance (Andersen *et al.*, 1990). A sizable proportion of cells, however, do change their selectivity when the stimulus is displaced by several tens of degrees of visual angle, and their position dependence seems to be correlated with the type of movement selectivity (Duffy and Wurtz, 1991; Orban *et al.*, 1992): It is most common for triple component cells and occurs least often in single component cells. Taken together, the wide range of directional tuning and the apparent lack of specificity for the spatial position of a stimulus seem to suggest, that MSTd cells do not possess the selectivity needed to explain the high accuracy of human observers in psychophysical experiments. Our simulation results, however, demonstrate that a population encoding can be used, in which individual neurons are rather broadly tuned while the whole network gives very accurate results.

2 THE NETWORK MODEL

The major projections to area MST originate from the middle temporal area (MT). Area MT is a well known area of monkey cortex specialized for the processing of visual motion. It contains a retinotopic representation of local movement directions (Allman and Kaas, 1971; Maunsell and Van Essen, 1983). In our model we assume that area MT comprises a population encoding of the optic flow and that area MST uses this input from MT to extract the heading direction. Therefore, the network consists of two layers. In the first layer, 300 optic flow vectors at random locations within 50 degrees of eccentricity are represented. Each flow vector is encoded by a population of directionally selective neurons. It has been shown previously that a biologically plausible population encoding like this can also be modelled by a neural network (Wang *et al.*, 1989). For simplicity we use only four neurons to represent an optic flow vector $\boldsymbol{\theta}_i$ as

$$\boldsymbol{\theta}_i = \sum_{k=1}^{4} s_{ik}\mathbf{e}_{ik}, \tag{1}$$

with equally spaced preferred directions $\mathbf{e}_{ik} = (\cos(\pi k/2), \sin(\pi k/2))^t$. A neuron's response to a flow vector of direction ϕ_i and speed θ_i is given by the tuning curve

$$s_{ik} = \begin{cases} \theta_i \cos(\phi_i - \pi k/2) & \text{if } \cos(\phi_i - \pi k/2) > 0 \\ 0 & \text{otherwise.} \end{cases}$$

The second layer contains a retinotopic grid of possible translational heading directions $\mathbf{T}_j$. Each direction is represented by a population of neurons, whose summed activities give the likelihood that $\mathbf{T}_j$ is the correct heading. The perceived direction is finally chosen to be the one that has the highest population activity.

The calculation of this likelihood is based on the subspace algorithm by Heeger and Jepson (1992). It employs the minimization of a residual function over all possible heading directions. The neuronal populations in the second layer evaluate a related function that is maximal for the correct heading. The subspace algorithm works as follows: When an observer moves through a static environment all points in space share the same six motion parameters, the translation $\mathbf{T} = (T_x, T_y, T_z)^t$ and the rotation $\boldsymbol{\Omega} = (\Omega_x, \Omega_y, \Omega_z)^t$. The optic flow $\boldsymbol{\theta}(x, y)$ is the projection of the movement of a 3D–point $(X, Y, Z)^t$ onto the retina, which, for simplicity, is modelled as an image plane. In a viewer centered coordinate system the optic flow can be written as:

$$\boldsymbol{\theta}(x,y) = \frac{1}{Z(x,y)}\mathbf{A}(x,y)\mathbf{T} + \mathbf{B}(x,y)\boldsymbol{\Omega} \tag{2}$$

with the matrices

$$\mathbf{A}(x,y) = \begin{pmatrix} -f & 0 & x \\ 0 & -f & y \end{pmatrix} \text{ and } \mathbf{B}(x,y) = \begin{pmatrix} xy/f & -f - x^2/f & y \\ f + y^2/f & -xy/f & -x \end{pmatrix}$$

depending only on coordinates (x, y) in the image plane and on the "focal length" f (Heeger and Jepson, 1992). In trying to estimate $\mathbf{T}$, given the optic flow $\boldsymbol{\theta}$, we first have to note that the unknowns $Z(x, y)$ and $\mathbf{T}$ are multiplied together. They can thus not be determined independently so that the translation is considered a unit vector pointing in the direction of heading. Eq. (2) now contains six unknowns, $Z(x, y)$, $\mathbf{T}$ and $\boldsymbol{\Omega}$, but only two measurements θ_x and θ_y. Therefore, flow vectors from m distinct image points are combined into the matrix equation

$$\boldsymbol{\Theta} = \mathbf{C}(\mathbf{T})\mathbf{q}, \tag{3}$$

where $\boldsymbol{\Theta} = (\boldsymbol{\theta}_1, \ldots, \boldsymbol{\theta}_m)^t$ is a $2m$–dimensional vector consisting of the components of the m image velocities, $\mathbf{q} = (1/Z(x_1, y_1), \ldots, 1/Z(x_m, y_m), \Omega_x, \Omega_y, \Omega_z)^t$ an $(m + 3)$–dimensional vector, and

$$\mathbf{C}(\mathbf{T}) = \begin{pmatrix} \mathbf{A}(x_1,y_1)\mathbf{T} & \cdots & 0 & \mathbf{B}(x_1,y_1) \\ \vdots & \ddots & \vdots & \vdots \\ 0 & \cdots & \mathbf{A}(x_m,y_m)\mathbf{T} & \mathbf{B}(x_m,y_m) \end{pmatrix} \tag{4}$$

a $2m \times (m + 3)$ matrix. Heeger and Jepson (1992) show that the heading direction can be recovered by minimizing the residual function

$$\mathrm{R}(\mathbf{T}) = ||\boldsymbol{\Theta}^t\mathbf{C}^{\perp}(\mathbf{T})||^2.$$

In this equation $\mathbf{C}^{\perp}(\mathbf{T})$ is defined as follows: Provided that the columns of $\mathbf{C}(\mathbf{T})$ are linearly independent, they form a basis of an $(m + 3)$–dimensional subspace of the $\mathcal{R}^{2m}$, which is called the range of $\mathbf{C}(\mathbf{T})$. The matrix $\mathbf{C}^{\perp}(\mathbf{T})$ spans the remaining $(2m-(m+3))$–dimensional subspace which is called the orthogonal complement of $\mathbf{C}(\mathbf{T})$. Every vector in the orthogonal complement of $\mathbf{C}(\mathbf{T})$ is orthogonal to every vector in the range of $\mathbf{C}(\mathbf{T})$.

In the network, the population of neurons representing a certain $\mathbf{T}_j$ shall be maximally excited when $\mathrm{R}(\mathbf{T}_j) = 0$. Two steps are necessary to accomplish this. First an individual neuron evaluates part of the argument of $\mathrm{R}(\mathbf{T}_j)$ by picking out one of the column vectors of $\mathbf{C}^{\perp}(\mathbf{T}_j)$, denoted by $\mathbf{C}_l^{\perp}(\mathbf{T}_j)$, and computing $\boldsymbol{\Theta}^t\mathbf{C}_l^{\perp}(\mathbf{T}_j)$. This is done in the following way: m first layer populations are chosen to form the neuron's input receptive field. The neuron's output is given by the sigmoid function

$$u_{jl} = \mathrm{g}(\sum_{i=1}^{m}\sum_{k=1}^{4} J_{ijkl}s_{ik} - \mu), \tag{5}$$

in which J_{ijkl} denotes the strength of the synaptic connection between the l–th output neuron in the second layer population representing heading direction $\mathbf{T}_j$ and the k–th input neuron in the first layer population representing the optic flow vector $\boldsymbol{\theta}_i$, μ denotes the threshold. For the synaptic strengths we require that:

$$\sum_{i=1}^{m}\sum_{k=1}^{4} J_{ijkl}s_{ik} = \boldsymbol{\Theta}^t\mathbf{C}_l^{\perp}(\mathbf{T}_j). \tag{6}$$

At a single image location i this is:

$$\sum_{k=1}^{4} J_{ijkl} s_{ik} = \boldsymbol{\theta}_i^t \begin{pmatrix} C_{l,2i-1}^{\perp}(\mathbf{T}_j) \\ C_{l,2i}^{\perp}(\mathbf{T}_j) \end{pmatrix}.$$

Substituting eq. (1) we find:

$$\sum_{k=1}^{4} J_{ijkl} s_{ik} = \sum_{k=1}^{4} s_{ik} \mathbf{e}_{ik}^t \begin{pmatrix} C_{l,2i-1}^{\perp}(\mathbf{T}_j) \\ C_{l,2i}^{\perp}(\mathbf{T}_j) \end{pmatrix}.$$

Therefore we set the synaptic strengths to:

$$J_{ijkl} = \mathbf{e}_{ik}^t \begin{pmatrix} C_{l,2i-1}^{\perp}(\mathbf{T}_j) \\ C_{l,2i}^{\perp}(\mathbf{T}_j) \end{pmatrix}.$$

Then, whenever $\mathbf{T}_j$ is compatible with the measured optic flow, i.e. when $\boldsymbol{\Theta}$ is in the range of $\mathbf{C}(\mathbf{T}_j)$, the neuron receives a net input of zero. In the second step, another neuron $u_{jl'}$ is constructed so that the sum of the activities of the two neurons is maximal in this situation. Both neurons are connected to the same set of image locations but their connection strengths satisfy $J_{ijkl'} = -J_{ijkl}$. In addition, the threshold μ is given a slightly negative value. Then both their sigmoid transfer functions overlap at zero input, and the sum has a single peak. Finally, the neurons in every second layer population are organized in such matched pairs so that each population j generates its maximal activity when $\mathrm{R}(\mathbf{T}_j) = 0$.

In simulations, our network is able to compute the direction of heading with a mean error of less than one degree in agreement with human psychophysical data (see Lappe and Rauschecker, 1993). Like heading detection in human observers it functions over a wide range of speeds, it works with sparse flow fields and it needs depth in the visual environment when eye movements are performed.

3 DIFFERENT RESPONSE SELECTIVITIES

For the remainder of this paper we will focus on the second layer neuron's response properties by carrying out simulations analogous to neurophysiological experiments (Andersen *et al.*, 1990; Duffy and Wurtz, 1991; Orban *et al.*, 1992). A single neuron is constructed that receives input from 30 random image locations forming a 60×60 degree receptive field. The receptive field occupies the lower left quadrant of the visual field and also includes the fovea (Fig. 1A). The neuron is then presented with shifting, expanding/contracting and rotating optic flow patterns. The center (x_c, y_c) of the expanding/contracting and rotating patterns is varied over the 100×100 degree visual field in order to test the position dependence of the neuron's responses. Directional tuning is assessed via the direction Φ of the shifting patterns. All patterns are obtained by choosing suitable translations and rotations in eq. (2). For instance, rotating patterns centered at (x_c, y_c) are generated by

$$\mathbf{T} = 0 \quad \text{and} \quad \boldsymbol{\Omega} = \frac{\pm\Omega}{\sqrt{x_c^2 + y_c^2 + f^2}} \begin{pmatrix} x_c \\ y_c \\ f \end{pmatrix}. \tag{7}$$

In keeping with the most common experimental condition, all depth values $Z(x_i, y_i)$ are taken to be equal.

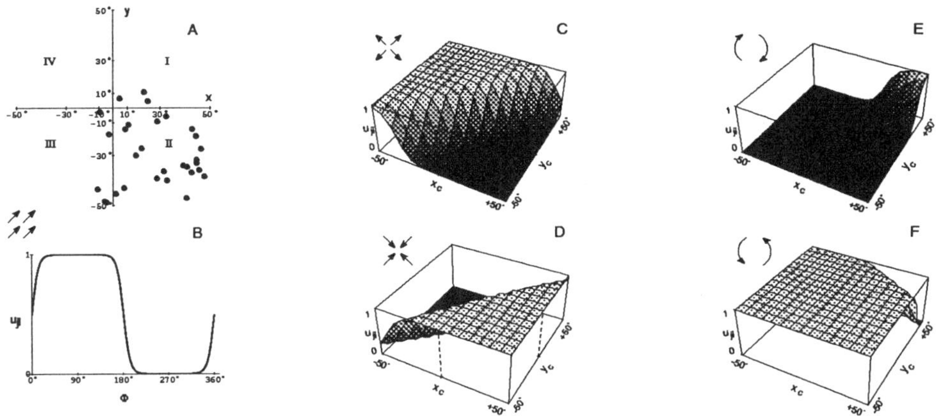

Figure 1: Single Neuron Responding To All Three Types Of Optic Flow Stimuli ("Triple Component Cell")

In the following we consider different assumptions about the observer's eye movements. These assumptions change the equations of the subspace algorithm. The rotational matrix $\mathbf{B}(x, y)$ takes on different forms. We will show that these changes result in different cell types. First let us restrict the model to the biologically most important case: During locomotion in a static environment the eye movements of humans or higher animals are usually the product of intentional behavior. A very common situation is the fixation of a visible object during locomotion. A specific eye rotation is necessary to compensate for the translational body–movement and to keep the object fixed in the center $(0, 0)$ of the visual field, so that its image velocity eq. (2) vanishes:

$$\boldsymbol{\theta}(0,0) = \frac{1}{Z_F}\begin{pmatrix} -fT_X \\ -fT_Y \end{pmatrix} + \begin{pmatrix} -f\Omega_Y \\ +f\Omega_X \end{pmatrix} = \begin{pmatrix} 0 \\ 0 \end{pmatrix}. \tag{8}$$

Z_F denotes the distance of the fixation point. We can easily calculate Ω_X and Ω_Y from eq. (8) and chose $\Omega_Z = 0$. The optic flow eq. (2) in the case of the fixation of a stationary object then is

$$\tilde{\boldsymbol{\theta}}(x,y) = \frac{1}{Z(x,y)}\mathbf{A}(x,y)\mathbf{T} + \frac{1}{Z_F}\tilde{\mathbf{B}}(x,y)\mathbf{T},$$

with

$$\tilde{\mathbf{B}}(x,y) = \begin{pmatrix} f + x^2/f & (xy)/f & 0 \\ (xy)/f & f + y^2/f & 0 \end{pmatrix}.$$

We would like to emphasize that another common situation, namely no eye movements at all, can be approximated by $Z_F \to \infty$. We can now construct a new matrix

$$\tilde{\mathbf{C}}(\mathbf{T}) = \begin{pmatrix} \mathbf{A}(x_1,y_1)\mathbf{T} & \cdots & 0 & \tilde{\mathbf{B}}(x_1,y_1)\mathbf{T} \\ \vdots & \ddots & \vdots & \vdots \\ 0 & \cdots & \mathbf{A}(x_m,y_m)\mathbf{T} & \tilde{\mathbf{B}}(x_m,y_m)\mathbf{T} \end{pmatrix}$$

and form synaptic connections in the same way as described above. The resulting network is able to deal with the most common types of eye movements. The response properties of a

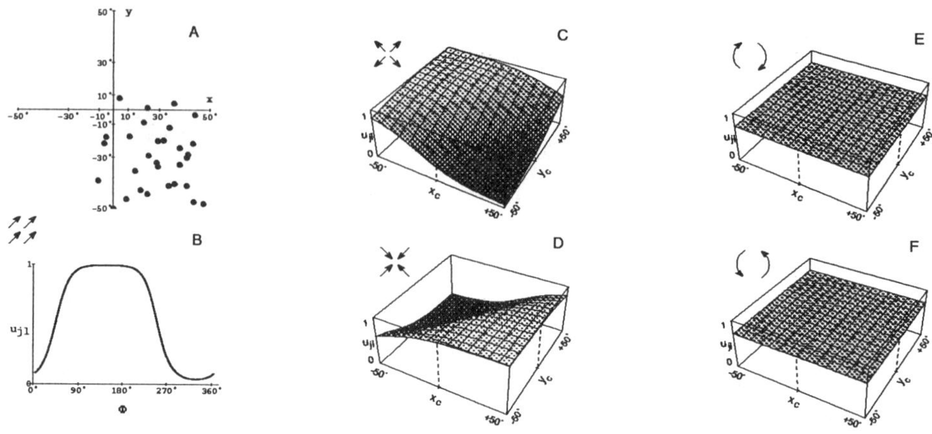

Figure 2: Neuron Selective For Two Components ("Double Component Cell")

single neuron from such a network are shown in Fig. 1. The neuron is selective for all three types of flow patterns. It exhibits broad directional tuning (Fig. 1B) for upward shifting patterns ($\Phi = 90$ deg.). The responses to expanding (Fig. 1C), contracting (Fig. 1D) and rotating (Fig. 1E–F) patterns show large areas of position invariant selectivity. Inside the receptive field, which covers the second quadrant (see destribution of input locations in Fig. 1A), the neuron favors upward shifts, contractions and counterclockwise rotations. It is thus compatible with a triple component cell in MSTd. Also, lines are visible along which the selectivities reverse. This happens because the neuron's input is a linear function of the stimulus position (x_c, y_c). For example, for rotational patterns we can calculate the input using eqs. (2), (6), and (7):

$$\sum_{i=1}^{m}\sum_{k=1}^{4} J_{ijkl}s_{ik} = \frac{\pm\Omega}{\sqrt{x_c^2+y_c^2+f^2}} \sum_{i=1}^{m} \frac{1}{Z_F}(x_c, y_c, f)\tilde{\mathbf{B}}^t(x_i, y_i)\begin{pmatrix} C^{\perp}_{l,2i-1}(\mathbf{T}_j) \\ C^{\perp}_{l,2i}(\mathbf{T}_j) \end{pmatrix}.$$

As long as the threshold μ is small, the neuron's output is halfway between its maximal and minimal values whenever its input is zero, i.e. when

$$(x_c, y_c, f) \sum_{i=1}^{m} \left[\tilde{\mathbf{B}}^t(x_i, y_i) \begin{pmatrix} C^{\perp}_{l,2i-1}(\mathbf{T}_j) \\ C^{\perp}_{l,2i}(\mathbf{T}_j) \end{pmatrix} \right] = 0.$$

This is the equation of a line in the (x_c, y_c) plane. The neuron's selectivity for rotations reverses along this line. A similar equation holds expansion/contraction selectivity.

Now, what would the neuron's selectivity look like, if we had not restricted the eye movements to the case of the fixation of an object. The responses of a neuron that is constructed following the unconstrained version of the algorithm, as described in section 2, is shown in Fig. 2. There is no selectivity for clockwise versus counterclockwise rotations at all, since both patterns elicit the same response everywhere in the visual field. Inside the receptive field the neuron favors contractions and shifts towards the upper left ($\Phi = 150$ deg.). It can thus be regarded as a double component cell. To understand the absence of rotational selectivity we have to calculate the whole rotational optic flow pattern Θ_{rot} by inserting **T**

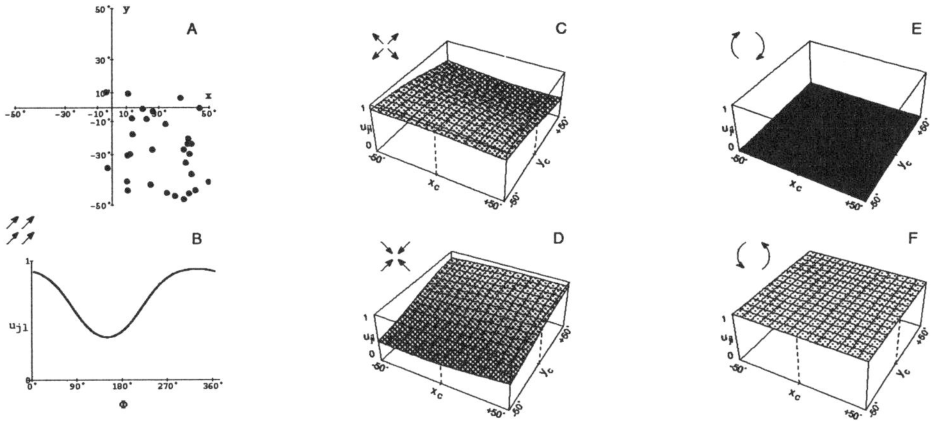

Figure 3: Predominantly Rotation Selective Neuron ("Single Component Cell")

and Ω from eq. (7) into eq. (3). $\mathbf{C}(\mathbf{T})$ becomes

$$\mathbf{C}(0) = \begin{pmatrix} 0 & \cdots & 0 & \mathbf{B}(x_1, y_1) \\ \vdots & \ddots & \vdots & \vdots \\ 0 & \cdots & 0 & \mathbf{B}(x_m, y_m) \end{pmatrix}.$$

Denoting the three rightmost column vectors of $\mathbf{C}(\mathbf{T})$ by $\mathbf{B}_1$, $\mathbf{B}_2$, and $\mathbf{B}_3$ we find

$$\Theta_{\text{rot}} = \frac{\pm\Omega}{\sqrt{x_c^2 + y_c^2 + f^2}}(x_c\mathbf{B}_1 + y_c\mathbf{B}_2 + f\mathbf{B}_3).$$

Comparison to $\mathbf{C}(\mathbf{T})$, eq. (4), shows that Θ_{rot} can be written as a linear combination of column vectors of $\mathbf{C}(\mathbf{T})$. Thus Θ_{rot} lies in the range of $\mathbf{C}(\mathbf{T})$ and is orthogonal to $\mathbf{C}^{\perp}(\mathbf{T})$, so that $\Theta_{\text{rot}}\ \mathbf{C}_l^{\perp}(\mathbf{T}_j) = 0$ for all j and l. From eqs. (5) and (6) it follows, that the neuron's response to any rotational pattern is always $u_{jl} = \mathrm{g}(-\mu)$.

The last type of eye movements we want to consider is that of a general frontoparallel rotation, which is defined by $\Omega_Z = 0$. In addition to the fixation of a stationary object, frontoparallel rotations also include smooth pursuit eye movements necessary for the fixation of a moving object. Inserting $\Omega_Z = 0$ into eq. (2) gives

$$\hat{\theta}(x,y) = \frac{1}{Z(x,y)}\mathbf{A}(x,y)\mathbf{T} + \hat{\mathbf{B}}(x,y)\begin{pmatrix}\Omega_X \\ \Omega_Y\end{pmatrix}$$

with

$$\hat{\mathbf{B}}(x,y) = \begin{pmatrix} xy/f & -(f + x^2/f) \\ f + y^2/f & -xy/f \end{pmatrix}$$

now being a 2×2 matrix, so that $\mathbf{C}(\mathbf{T})$, eq. (4), becomes a $2m \times (m+2)$ matrix $\hat{\mathbf{C}}(\mathbf{T})$. A neuron that is constructed using $\hat{\mathbf{C}}(\mathbf{T})$ can be seen in Fig. 3. It best responds to counterclockwise rotational patterns showing complete position invariance over the visual field. The neuron is much less selective to expansions and unidirectional shifts, since the responses never reach saturation. It therefore resembles a single component rotation selective cell. The position invariant behavior can again be explained by looking at the rotational optic flow pattern. Using the same argument as above, one can show that the neuron's input is zero whenever Ω_Z vanishes, i.e. when the rotational axis lies in the (X, Y)–plane. Then the flow pattern becomes

$$\Theta_{\mathrm{rot}} = \frac{\pm\Omega}{\sqrt{x_c^2 + y_c^2 + f^2}}(x_c\hat{\mathbf{B}}_1 + y_c\hat{\mathbf{B}}_2),$$

and is an element of the range of $\hat{\mathbf{C}}(\mathbf{T}_j)$. The (X, Y)–plane thus splits the space of all rotational axes into two half spaces, one in which the neuron's input is always positive and one in which it is always negative. Clockwise rotations are characterized by $\Omega_Z > 0$ and hence all lie in the same half space, while counterclockwise rotations lie in the other. As a result the neuron is exclusively excited by one mode of rotation in all of the visual field.

4 Conclusion

Our neural network model for the detection of ego–motion proposes a computational map of heading directions. A similar map could be contained in area MSTd of monkey visual cortex. Cells in MSTd exhibit a varying degree of selectivity for basic optic flow patterns, but often show a substantial indifference towards the spatial position of a stimulus. By using a population encoding of the heading directions, individual neurons in the model exhibit similar position invariant responses within large parts of the visual field. Different neuronal selectivities found in MSTd can be modelled by assuming specializations pertaining to different types of eye movements. Consistent with experimental findings the position invariance of the model neurons is largest in the single component cells and less developed in the double and triple component cells.

References

Allman, J. M. and Kaas, J. H. 1971. *Brain Res.* **31**, 85–105.

Andersen, R., Graziano, M., and Snowden, R. 1990. *Soc. Neurosci. Abstr.* **16**, 7.

Brenner, E. and Rauschecker, J. P. 1990. *J. Physiol.* **423**, 641–660.

Duffy, C. J. and Wurtz, R. H. 1991. *J. Neurophysiol.* **65(6)**, 1329–1359.

Gibson, J. J. 1950. *The Perception of the Visual World.* Houghton Mifflin, Boston.

Heeger, D. J. and Jepson, A. 1992. *Int. J. Comp. Vis.* **7(2)**, 95–117.

Lappe, M. and Rauschecker, J. P. 1993. *Neural Computation (in press).*

Maunsell, J. H. R. and Van Essen, D. C. 1983. *J. Neurophysiol.* **49(5)**, 1127–1147.

Orban, G. A., Lagae, L., Verri, A., Raiguel, S., Xiao, D., Maes, H., and Torre, V. 1992. *Proc. Nat. Acad. Sci.* **89**, 2595–2599.

Rauschecker, J. P., von Grünau, M. W., and Poulin, C. 1987. *J. Neurosci.* **7(4)**, 943–958.

Rieger, J. H. and Toet, L. 1985. *Biol. Cyb.* **52**, 377–381.

Stone, L. S. and Perrone, J. A. 1991. In *Soc. Neurosci. Abstr.* **17**, 857.

Tanaka, K. and Saito, H.-A. 1989. *J. Neurophysiol.* **62(3)**, 626–641.

Wang, H. T., Mathur, B. P. and Koch, C. 1989. *Neural Computation* **1**, 92–103.

Warren, W. H. Jr., and Hannon, D. J. 1988. *Nature* **336**, 162–163.

Learning to See Where and What: Training a Net to Make Saccades and Recognize Handwritten Characters

Gale Martin, Mosfeq Rashid, David Chapman, and James Pittman
MCC, 3500 Balcones Center Drive, Austin, Texas 78759

ABSTRACT

This paper describes an approach to integrated segmentation and recognition of hand–printed characters. The approach, called *Saccade*, integrates ballistic and corrective saccades (eye movements) with character recognition. A single backpropagation net is trained to make a classification decision on a character centered in its input window, as well as to estimate the distance of the current and next character from the center of the input window. The net learns to accurately estimate these distances regardless of variations in character width, spacing between characters, writing style and other factors. During testing, the system uses the net–extracted classification and distance information, along with a set of jumping rules, to jump from character to character.

The ability to read rests on multiple foundation skills. In learning how to read, people learn how to recognize individual characters centered in the visual field. They also learn how to move their eyes along a line of text, sequentially centering the visual field on successive characters. We believe that the key to developing optical character recognition (OCR) systems that can mimic human reading capabilities, is to develop systems that can learn these and other skills in an integrated fashion. In this paper, we demonstrate that a backpropagation net can learn to navigate along a line of handwritten characters, as well as to recognize the characters centered in its visual field. The system, called *Saccade*, extends the current state of the art in OCR technology by using a single classifier to accurately and efficiently locate and recognize characters, regardless of whether they touch each other or are separate. The *Saccade* system was described briefly at the last NIPS conference (Martin & Rashid, 1992). In this paper, we describe it more fully and report on results demonstrating its accuracy and efficiency in recognizing handwritten digits.

The *Saccade* system takes a cue from the ballistic and corrective saccades (eye movements) of natural vision systems. Natural saccades make it possible to efficiently move from one informative area to another by jumping. The eye typically initiates a ballistic saccade to move the center of focus to the general area of interest, followed, if necessary, by one or more corrective saccades for fine-grained position corrections. Recognition processes are applied only at these multiple fixation points.

We have copied some of these aspects in the artificial *Saccade* system by training a neural network to know about the locations of characters in its input window, as well as to know about the identity of the character centered in its input window. During run-time, the *Saccade* system accesses this information computed by the net for successive input windows, along with a set of simple jumping rules, to yield an OCR system that jumps from character to character, classifying each character in a sequence.

1 TRAINING DETAILS

As shown in Figure 1, the Saccade system has a wide input window, large enough to contain

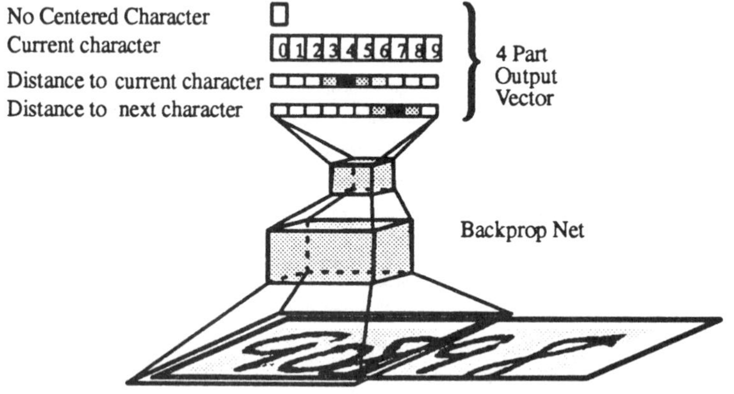

Figure 1. The *Saccade* system uses an enlarged input window and a 4–part output vector.

several characters. Prior to training, each field image of a line of characters is labeled with the horizontal center position of each character in the field, as well as with the category of each character. During training, the input window slides horizontally across a field of characters, and at each position, the contents of the input window are paired with a four–part target output vector, the values of which are computed from the labeled information. The target values answer the following four questions about the contents of the input window:

1. Is a character centered in the input window?
2. What character is closest to the center of the window?
3. How far off–center (horizontally) is the centermost character?
4. How far is the next character to the right from the center of the window?

The first node in the output vector represents the *no–centered–character* state. It's target value is set high (e.g., 1.0) when the center of the input window falls between characters, and set low (e.g., 0.0) when the center of the input window falls on the center of a character. When the net is trained, the value of the *no–centered–character* node indicates whether the input window is centered over a character, or whether a corrective saccade is needed to better center the character.

The second part of the output vector contains a node for each character category. When the center of the input window falls on a character, the target value for its corresponding node is set high; otherwise it is set low. When the net is trained, the values in these nodes are used to classify the centered character. The target values for both the *no–centered–character* and the *character–category* nodes are defined continuously across the horizontal dimension as trapezoidal functions, such that there are plateaus surrounding the off and on positions, with linearly increasing and decreasing values connecting the plateaus.

The third and fourth components of the output vector represent distance values, each encoded in a distributed fashion across multiple nodes, using localized receptive fields (Moody & Darken, 1988). The first of these two parts represents the distance by which the character closest to the center of the window is off–center. The target value can be positive, indicating that the center of the window is to the left of the center of character, or it can be negative, indicating that the center of the window has passed over the character, to the right of it's center. When trained, the value of the *current–character–distance* set of nodes is accessed to determine the magnitude of a corrective saccade, to make a fine–grained position adjustment.

The fourth component represents the distance from the center of the window to the center of the next character to the right. The target value can only be positive. When trained, the value of this set of nodes is accessed to determine the magnitude of a ballistic saccade, to jump to the next character to the right.

It is important to note that for both distance components, the maximum target value can not exceed half the window width. The net is never trained to make a distance judgment that extends beyond its field of view, since it is not given any information about what exists outside of it's input window. For example, when the center of the next character to the right is positioned outside of the current input window, the distance value is set to the maximum value of half the window width. Since the distance values vary with different characters, different writers, and of course, at different positions with respect to a character, the net is forced to learn to use the visual characteristics particular to each window to estimate the distance values. In other words, the net does NOT simply learn average values for each of the two distance metrics. Moreover, as the results will show, the trained net does not seem to use simple density histogram cues to estimate the distance values. It is able to reliably estimate the distance values even when characters overlap, and hence would appear as a single clump in a density histogram.

2 RUN–TIME SACCADE RULES

During run–time, the labeled values are, of course, not available. The system uses the computed values in the character classification and distance components of the output vector, and some heuristics, to navigate horizontally along a character field, jumping from one character to the next, and occasionally making a corrective saccade to improve its ability to classify a character. When the net recognizes a character, it executes a ballistic saccade to the next character, obtaining the distance to jump by reading the *next–character–distance* component of the output vector. When this action fails to center a character, as indicated by a low value in the *no–centered–character* output node, the system executes a corrective saccade to better center the character. It obtains the distance and direction to jump by reading the *current–character–distance* component of the output vector. Multiple corrective saccades can be executed.

3 TESTING ON NIST HANDWRITTEN DIGIT FIELDS

We tested the performance of the system on a set of hand–printed digits collected and distributed by the National Institute of Standards and Technology (NIST). This is a database containing 273,000 samples of handwritten numerals. Each of 2100 Census workers filled in a form with 33 fields, 28 fields of which only contain handwritten digits. The scanning resolution of the samples was 300 pixels/inch. The neural net was trained on about 80,000 characters from 20,000 fields, written by 800 different individuals. The fields varied in length from 2 characters per field to 6 characters per field. The horizontal positions of each of the characters in these training–data fields were extracted by a person. The test data contained about 20,000 digits from 5,000 fields, written by a different group of 200 individuals. The test set was chosen to be this large because use of smaller test sets (e.g., 5,000 digits, 1250 fields) yielded significant between–set variations in reported accuracy. Each field image was preprocessed to remove the box around the field of characters, and any surrounding white space. Each field image was size normalized, with respect to the vertical axis, to a height of 20 pixels. Aspect ratio was maintained. An input pattern generator was then passed over the field to create input windows for training the net. The input window size was 36 pixels wide and 20 pixels high. The input window scanned the field at 2–pixel increments during training. Subsequent experiments have shown that training can be speeded up considerably by training on the character centers and at random points between the character centers, without causing decreased accuracy.

The backpropagation network architecture is described more fully in Martin & Rashid (1992). It has 2 hidden layers with local, shared connections in the first hidden layer, and local connections in the second hidden layer. **Shared weights are not used in the second hidden layer** because early experiments showed that this retards learning, presumably because extending the position invariance to second–hidden–layer nodes inhibits the net in learning the position specific information regarding what is centered in its input window. The learning rate of the net was initially set at .05, and then successively lowered as training reached an asymptote. The momentum term was set at .9 throughout training. All nodes in the net used logistic activation functions.

Table 1 reports on the test results in terms of field–based reject rates, for 1% and .5% percent of the fields rejected. The error rates are field–based in the sense that if the net mis–classifies one character in the field, the entire field is considered as mis–classified. Error rates pertain to the fields remaining after rejection. Rejections are based on placing a threshold for the acceptable distance between the highest and next highest running activation total. In this way, by varying the threshold, the error rate can be traded off against the percentage of rejections. In addition, recognized fields were also rejected if the number of recognized digits differed from the expected number of digits.

Table 1: Field–Based Error Rates For Saccade System

Field Size	Field Error Rate	Field Reject Rate
2–digits	1.0%	6.4%
	0.5%	9.3%
3–digits	1.0%	12.7%
	0.5%	19.6%
4–digits	1.1%	19.5%
	0.5%	35.0%
5–digits	1.1%	23.2%
	0.5%	28.3%
6–digits	1.1%	26.8%
	0.5%	35.0 %

Figure 2 presents some of the fields of connected characters that the system correctly recognized. Conventional OCR systems typically fail on connected characters because they employ an independent character segmentation stage, in which the character is isolated from its surround using features, such as intervening white spaces. This character segmentation stage typically fails when characters are connected. The *Saccade* system goes beyond conventional OCR systems by integrating segmentation and recognition, and thereby is able to recognize touching characters.

The *Saccade* system is also efficient in the sense that it typically jumps from one character to the next without making a corrective saccades. Corrective saccades tend to be more likely when characters are touching. In addition, there is almost always a corrective saccade for the first character in the field, since the system starts at the beginning of the field, with

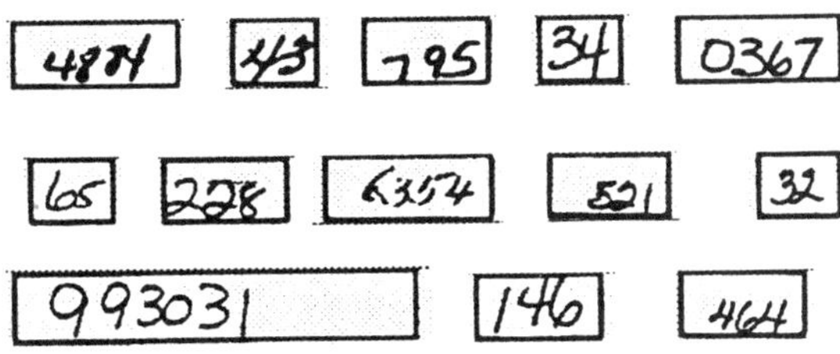

Figure 2. Examples of connected and broken characters that the *Saccade* system correctly recognizes.

no knowledge of the location of the character. For fields containing two digits, the average number of passes of the net on a small test set was about 2 saccades per character. For field containing five digits, the average number of saccades per character was 1.3.

4 COMPARISONS WITH OTHER SYSTEMS

The *Saccade* system is an extension of a related integrated segmentation and recognition system we reported on at last years NIPS conference (Martin & Rashid, 1992). That system employed an exhaustive scan technique, rather than saccades, to navigate along a line of text. Essentially, the net was convolved horizontally across a field image at a scan increment of 2 pixels. The net architecture was very similar to that of the *Saccade* system, except that it did not have the two distance components in the output vector. The accuracy rates of the two systems are essentially equivalent. However, the exhaustive scan version was considerably less efficient, requiring a forward pass of the network at every 2–pixel incremental scan position. On average it required about 5.5 forward passes per character, rather than the 1.3 forward passes per character required by the *Saccade* system.

Over the past two years, an approach similar to the exhaustive scan method has been advanced by a number of researchers (**Keeler & Rumelhart, 1992; Matan, Burges, Le Cun, & Denker, 1992). This approach also involves convolving a network across a field image, but uses a time–delay–neural–net (TDNN), or completely local, shared weight, architecture, a smaller input window, and no explicit position labeling of characters. The TDNN approach has algorithmic advantages over the exhaustive scan version described in the previous paragraph, because the completely shared–weight architecture enables the number of forward passes of the net to be reduced considerably.**

5 CONCLUSIONS AND FUTURE WORK

As stated at the beginning of this paper, we believe that the key to developing optical character recognition (OCR) systems that can mimic human reading capabilities is to develop systems that can learn the multiple foundation skills underlying human reading. This paper has reported some progress in this regard. We have demonstrated that a relatively simple backpropagation network can integrate its learning of position and category information, thereby enabling efficient navigation along a field of text through ballistic and corrective saccades, and accurate recognition of touching or broken characters.

There is however, a long way to go before we can claim a system with capabilities similar to human reading. The present *Saccade* system only moves horizontally, in one dimension. Human reading operates in two–dimensions, and in a sense, it operates in three–dimensions because it automatically operates across different scales. Human vision also employs automatic contrast adjustment; the *Saccade* system does not. Human vision has a wider field of view and employs a foveal transform, such that objects centered in the field of vision are represented at a higher resolution than objects in the periphery. This effectively expands the field of vision beyond what would be estimated simply by the size of the receptive area on the retina. As a result, saccades enable very effective means of scanning a large visual area. The present artificial *Saccade* system has only a small field of vision, and no foveal transform, so it's saccades must necessarily be limited in size. The present system is also only oriented toward recognizing a single character centered in its input window at a time. Human reading typically only makes one or two saccades per word. Finally, human reading capabilities clearly integrate recognition processes with higher–level processes, to enable the redundancies of natural language to constrain the recognition decisions.

References

Keeler, J, & Rumelhart, D. E. (1992) A self–organizing integrated segmentation and recognition neural network. In Moody, J.E., Hanson, S.J., and Lippmann, R.P., (eds.) *Advances in Neural Information Processing Systems 4*. San Mateo, CA: Morgan Kaufmann Publishers.

Matan, O., Burges, J. C., Le Cun, Y., and Denker, J. S. (1992) Multi–Digit Recognition Using a Space Displacement Neural Network. In Moody, J.E., Hanson, S.J., and Lippmann, R.P., (eds.) *Advances in Neural Information Processing Systems 4*. San Mateo, CA: Morgan Kaufmann Publishers, 488–495.

Martin, G. L. & Rashid, M. (1992) Recognizing overlapping hand–printed characters by centered–object integrated segmentation and recognition. In Moody, J.E., Hanson, S.J., and Lippmann, R.P., (eds.) *Advances in Neural Information Processing Systems 4*. San Mateo, CA: Morgan Kaufmann Publishers.

Moody, J. & Darken, C. (1988) Learning with localized receptive fields. Technical Report Yaleu/DCS/RR–649.

PART V

STOCHASTIC LEARNING AND ANALYSIS

Weight Space Probability Densities in Stochastic Learning: I. Dynamics and Equilibria

Todd K. Leen and John E. Moody
Department of Computer Science and Engineering
Oregon Graduate Institute of Science & Technology
19600 N.W. von Neumann Dr.
Beaverton, OR 97006-1999

Abstract

The ensemble dynamics of stochastic learning algorithms can be studied using theoretical techniques from statistical physics. We develop the equations of motion for the weight space probability densities for stochastic learning algorithms. We discuss equilibria in the diffusion approximation and provide expressions for special cases of the LMS algorithm. The equilibrium densities are not in general thermal (Gibbs) distributions in the objective function being minimized, but rather depend upon an effective potential that includes diffusion effects. Finally we present an exact analytical expression for the time evolution of the density for a learning algorithm with weight updates proportional to the *sign* of the gradient.

1 Introduction: Theoretical Framework

Stochastic learning algorithms involve weight updates of the form

$$\omega(n+1) \;=\; \omega(n) \;+\; \mu(n)\, H[\,\omega(n), x(n)\,] \tag{1}$$

where $\omega \in \mathbb{R}^m$ is the vector of m weights, μ is the learning rate, $H[\cdot] \in \mathbb{R}^m$ is the update function, and $x(n)$ is the exemplar (input or input/target pair) presented to the network at the nth iteration of the learning rule. Often the update function is based on the gradient of a cost function $H(\omega, x) = -\partial\mathcal{E}(\omega, x)/\partial\omega$. We assume that the exemplars are i.i.d. with underlying probability density $\rho(x)$.

We are interested in studying the time evolution and steady state behavior of the weight space probability density $P(\omega, n)$ for ensembles of networks trained by stochastic learning. Stochastic process theory and classical statistical mechanics provide tools for doing this. As we shall see, the ensemble behavior of stochastic learning algorithms is similar to that of diffusion processes in physical systems, although significant differences do exist.

1.1 Dynamics of the Weight Space Probability Density

Equation (1) defines a Markov process on the weight space. Given the *particular input* x, the single time-step transition probability density for this process is a Dirac delta function whose arguments satisfy the weight update (1):

$$W(\omega' \to \omega \mid x) = \delta(\omega - \omega' - \mu H[\omega', x]) \quad . \tag{2}$$

From this conditional transition probability, we calculate the *total* single time-step transition probability (Leen and Orr 1992, Ritter and Schulten 1988)

$$W(\omega' \to \omega) = \langle\ \delta(\omega - \omega' - \mu H[\omega', x])\ \rangle_x \tag{3}$$

where $\langle \ldots \rangle_x$ denotes integration over the measure on the random variable x.

The time evolution of the density is given by the Kolmogorov equation

$$P(\omega, n+1) = \int d\omega'\ P(\omega', n)\ W(\omega' \to \omega)\ , \tag{4}$$

which forms the basis for our dynamical description of the weight space probability density [1].

Stationary, or equilibrium, probability distributions are eigenfunctions of the transition probability

$$P_s(\omega) = \int d\omega'\ P_s(\omega')\ W(\omega' \to \omega). \tag{5}$$

It is particularly interesting to note that for problems in which there exists an optimal weight ω_* such that

$$H(\omega_*, x) = 0, \quad \forall x\ ,$$

one stationary solution is a delta function at $\omega = \omega_*$. An important class of such examples are noise-free mapping problems for which weight values exist that realize the desired mapping over all possible input/target pairs. For such problems, the ensemble can settle into a sharp distribution at the optimal weights (for examples see Leen and Orr 1992, Orr and Leen 1993).

Although the Kolmogorov equation can be integrated numerically, we would like to make further analytic progress. Towards this end we convert the Kolmogorov

[1] An alternative is to base the time evolution on a suitable master equation. Both approaches give the same results.

equation into a differential-difference equation by expanding (3) as a power series in μ. Since the transition probability is defined in the sense of generalized functions (i.e. distributions), the proper way to proceed is to smear (4) with a smooth test function of compact support $f(\omega)$ to obtain

$$\int d\omega\, f(\omega)\, P(\omega, n+1) \;=\; \int d\omega\, d\omega'\, f(\omega)\, P(\omega', n)\, W(\omega' \to \omega) \quad . \tag{6}$$

Next we use the transition probability (3) to perform the integration over ω and expand the resulting expression as a power series in μ. Finally, we integrate by parts to take derivatives off f, dropping the surface terms. This results in a discrete time version of the classic Kramers-Moyal expansion (Risken 1989)

$$P(\omega, n+1) \;-\; P(\omega, n) \;=$$

$$\sum_{i=1}^{\infty} \frac{(-1)^i}{i!} \sum_{j_1,\ldots j_i=1}^{m} \frac{\partial^i}{\partial\omega_{j_1}\,\partial\omega_{j_2}\ldots\partial\omega_{j_i}} \left\{ \langle \mu H_{j_1}\, \mu H_{j_2} \ldots \mu H_{j_i} \rangle_x \; P(\omega, n) \right\} , \tag{7}$$

where H_{j_a} denotes the $j_a{}^{th}$ component of the m-component vector H.

In section 3, we present an algorithm for which the Kramers-Moyal expansion can be explicitly summed. In general the full expansion is not analytically tractable, and to make further analytic progress we will truncate it at second order to obtain the Fokker-Planck equation.

1.2 The Fokker-Planck (Diffusion) Approximation

For small enough $|\mu H|$, the Kramers-Moyal expansion (7) can be truncated to second order to obtain a Fokker-Planck equation:[2]

$$P(\omega, n+1) \;-\; P(\omega, n) \;=$$

$$-\mu \frac{\partial}{\partial\omega_i} [\, A_i(\omega)\, P(\omega, n)\,] \;+\; \frac{\mu^2}{2} \frac{\partial^2}{\partial\omega_i \partial\omega_j} [\, B_{ij}(\omega)\, P(\omega, n)\,] \; . \tag{8}$$

In (8), and throughout the remainder of the paper, repeated indices are summed over. In the Fokker-Planck approximation, only two coefficients appear: $A_i(\omega) \equiv \langle H_i \rangle_x$, called the *drift vector*, and $B_{ij}(\omega) \equiv \langle H_i\, H_j \rangle_x$, called the *diffusion matrix*. The drift vector is simply the average update applied at ω. Since the diffusion coefficients can be strongly dependent on the position in weight space, the equilibrium densities will, in general, *not be thermal* (Gibbs) distributions in the potential corresponding to $\langle H(\omega, x) \rangle_x$. This is exemplified in our discussion of equilibrium densities for the LMS algorithm in section 2.1 below[3].

[2]Radons *et al.* (1990) independently derived a Fokker-Planck equation for backpropagation. Earlier, Ritter and Schulten (1988) derived a Fokker-Planck equation (for Kohonen's self-ordering feature map) that is valid in the neighborhood of a local optimum.

[3]See (Leen and Orr 1992, Orr and Leen 1993) for further examples.

2 Equilibrium Densities in the Fokker-Planck Approximation

In equilibrium the probability density is stationary, $P(\omega, n+1) = P(\omega, n) \equiv P_s(\omega)$, so the Fokker-Planck equation (8) becomes

$$0 = -\frac{\partial}{\partial \omega_i} J_i(\omega) \equiv -\frac{\partial}{\partial \omega_i} \left(\mu A_i(\omega) P_s(\omega) - \frac{\mu^2}{2} \frac{\partial}{\partial \omega_j} [\, B_{ij}(\omega) P_s(\omega) \,] \right) . \tag{9}$$

Here, we have implicitly defined the probability density current $J(\omega)$. In equilibrium, its divergence is zero.

If the drift and diffusion coefficients satisfy *potential conditions*, then the equilibrium current itself is zero and *detailed balance* is obtained. The potential conditions are (Gardiner, 1990)

$$\frac{\partial Z_k}{\partial \omega_l} - \frac{\partial Z_l}{\partial \omega_k} \equiv 0, \quad \text{where} \quad Z_k(\omega) \equiv B_{ki}^{-1}(\omega) \left[\frac{\mu}{2} \frac{\partial}{\partial \omega_j} B_{ij}(\omega) - A_i(\omega) \right] . \tag{10}$$

Under these conditions the solution to (9) for the equilibrium density is:

$$P_s(\omega) = \frac{1}{K} e^{-2\mathcal{F}(\omega)/\mu}, \quad \mathcal{F}(\omega) \equiv \int_{\omega} d\omega_k \, Z_k(\omega) \tag{11}$$

where K is a normalization constant and $\mathcal{F}(\omega)$ is called the *effective potential.*

In general, the potential conditions are not satisfied for stochastic learning algorithms in multiple dimensions.[4] In this respect, stochastic learning differs from most physical diffusion processes. However for LMS with inputs whose correlation matrix is isotropic, the conditions *are* satisfied and the equilibrium density can be reduced to the quadrature in (11).

2.1 Equilibrium Density for the LMS Algorithm

The best known on-line learning system is the LMS adaptive filter. For the LMS algorithm, the training examples consist of input/target pairs $x(n) = \{s(n), t(n)\}$, the model output is $u(n) = \omega \cdot s(n)$, and the cost function is the squared error:

$$\mathcal{E}(\,\omega, x(n)\,) = \frac{1}{2} [t(n) - u(n)]^2 = \frac{1}{2} [t(n) - \omega \cdot s(n)]^2 . \tag{12}$$

The resulting update equations (for constant learning rate μ) are

$$\omega(n+1) = \omega(n) + \mu \, [t(n) - \omega \cdot s(n)] \, s(n) . \tag{13}$$

We assume that the training data are generated according to a "signal plus noise" model:

$$t(n) = \omega_* \cdot s(n) + \epsilon(n) , \tag{14}$$

where ω_* is the "true" weight vector and $\epsilon(n)$ is i.i.d. noise with mean zero and variance σ^2. We denote the correlation matrix of the inputs $s(n)$ by R and the

[4] For one-dimensional algorithms, the potential conditions are *trivially* satisfied.

fourth order correlation tensor of the inputs by S. It is convenient to shift the origin of coordinates in weight space and define the *weight error* vector

$$v \equiv \omega - \omega_*.$$

In terms of v, the weight update is

$$v(n+1) = v(n) - \mu\,[\,s(n)\cdot v(n)\,]\,s(n) + \mu\,\epsilon(n)\,s(n).$$

The drift vector and diffusion matrix are given by

$$A_i = -\langle\, s_i s_j \,\rangle_s\, v_j = -R_{ij}\, v_j \tag{15}$$

and

$$B_{ij} = \left\langle\, s_i\, s_j\, s_k\, s_l\, v_k\, v_l + \epsilon^2\, s_i\, s_j \,\right\rangle_{s,\epsilon} = S_{ijkl}\, v_k\, v_l + \sigma^2\, R_{ij} \tag{16}$$

respectively. Notice that the diffusion matrix is quadratic in v. Thus as we move away from the global minimum at $v = 0$, diffusive spreading of the probability density is enhanced. Notice also that, in general, both terms of the diffusion matrix contribute an *anisotropy*.

We further assume that the inputs are drawn from a zero-mean Gaussian process. This assumption allows us to appeal to the Gaussian moment factoring theorem (Haykin, 1991, p318) to express the fourth-order correlation S in terms of R

$$S_{ijkl} = R_{ij}\, R_{kl} + R_{ik}\, R_{jl} + R_{il}\, R_{jk}\ .$$

The diffusion matrix reduces to

$$B = (\, v^T R\, v + \sigma^2\,)\, R + 2\,(\, Rv\,)(\, Rv\,)^T\ . \tag{17}$$

To compute the effective potential (10 and 11) the diffusion matrix is inverted using the Sherman-Morrison formula (Press, 1987, p67). As a final simplification, we assume that the input distribution is spherically symmetric. Thus

$$R = r\, I\ ,$$

where I denotes the identity matrix.

Together these assumptions insure detailed balance, and we can integrate (11) in closed form. In figure 1, we compare the effective potential $\mathcal{F}(v)$ (for 1-D LMS) with the potential corresponding to the quadratic cost function.

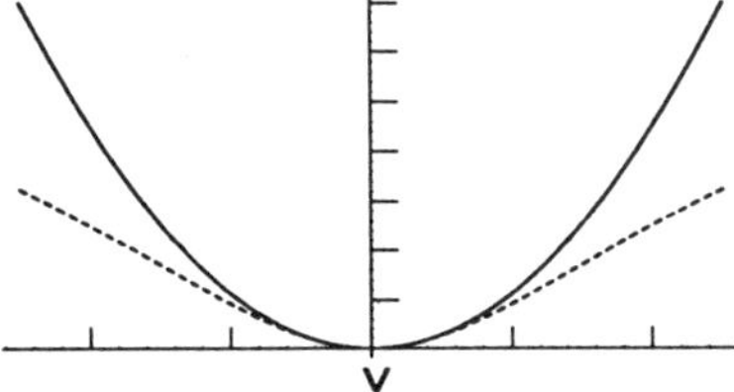

Fig.1: Effective potential (dashed curve) and cost function (solid curve) for 1-D LMS.

The spatial dependence of the the diffusion coefficient forces the effective potential to soften relative to the cost function for large $|v|$. This accentuates the tails of the distribution relative to a gaussian.

The equilibrium density is

$$P_s(v) = \frac{1}{K}\left[1+\frac{3r}{\sigma^2}|v|^2\right]^{-\left(\frac{2+m}{3}+\frac{1}{3r\mu}\right)}, \tag{18}$$

where, as before, m and K denote the dimension of the weight vector and the normalization constant for the density respectively. For a *1-D filter*, the equilibrium density can be found in closed form without assuming Gaussian input data. We find

$$P_s(v) = \frac{1}{K}\left[1+\frac{S}{r\,\sigma^2}v^2\right]^{-\left(1+\frac{r}{\mu S}\right)}. \tag{19}$$

With gaussian inputs (for which $S = 3r^2$) (19) properly reduces to (18) with $m = 1$.

The equilibrium densities (18) and (19) are clearly *not* gaussian, however in the limit of very small μr they reduce to gaussian distributions with variance $\mu\sigma^2/2$. Figure 2 shows a comparison between the theoretical result and a histogram of 200,000 values of v generated by simulation with $\mu = 0.005$, and $\sigma^2 = 1.0$. The input data were drawn from a zero-mean Gaussian distribution with $r = 4.0$.

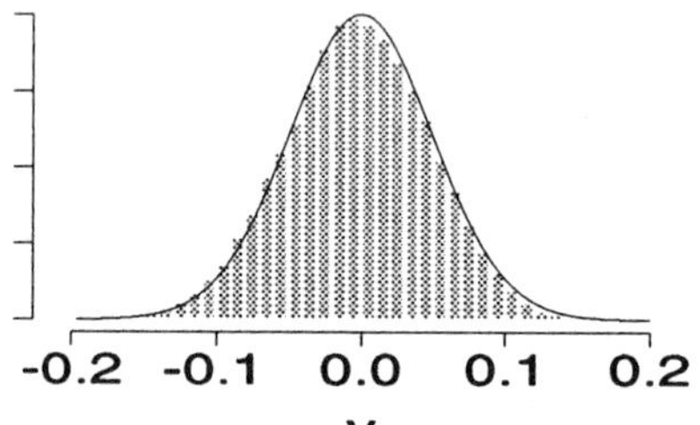

Fig.2: Equilibrium density for 1-D LMS

3 An Exactly Summable Model

As in the case of LMS learning above, stochastic gradient descent algorithms update weights based on an instantaneous estimate of the gradient of some average cost function $\mathcal{E}(\omega) = \langle\, \mathcal{E}(\omega, x)\,\rangle_x$. That is, the update is given by

$$H_i(\omega, x) = -\frac{\partial}{\partial\omega_i}\,\mathcal{E}(\omega, x).$$

An alternative is to increment or decrement each weight by a fixed amount depending only on the *sign* of $\partial\mathcal{E}/\partial\omega_i$. We formulated this alternative update rule because it avoids a common problem for sigmoidal networks, getting stuck on "flat spots" or "plateaus". The standard gradient descent update rule yields very slow movement on plateaus, while second order methods such as gauss-newton can be unstable. The sign-of-gradient update rule suffers from neither of these problems.[5]

[5]The use of the sign of the gradient has been suggested previously in the stochastic approximation literature by Fabian (1960) and in the neural network literature by Derthick (1984).

If at each iteration one chooses a weight at random for updating, then the Kramers-Moyal expansion can be exactly summed. Thus at each iteration we 1) choose a weight ω_i and an exemplar x at random, and 2) update ω_i with

$$H_i(\omega, x) \;=\; -\operatorname{sign}\left(\frac{\partial \mathcal{E}(\,\omega, x(n)\,)}{\partial \omega_i} \right) \quad . \tag{20}$$

With this update rule, $H_j = \pm 1$ or 0 and $H_i\, H_j = \delta_{ij}$ (or 0). All of the coefficients $\langle\, H_i H_j H_k \ldots \rangle_x$ in the Kramers-Moyal expansion (7) vanish *unless* $i = j = k = \ldots$. The remaining series can be summed by breaking it into odd and even parts. This leaves

$$\begin{aligned} P(\omega, n+1) \;&-\; P(\omega, n) \;= \\ &-\; \frac{1}{2m} \sum_{j=1}^{m} \{\; P(\omega + \mu_j, n)\, A_j(\omega + \mu_j) - P(\omega - \mu_j, n)\, A_j(\omega - \mu_j)\; \} \\ &+\; \frac{1}{2m} \sum_{j=1}^{m} \{\; P(\omega + \mu_j, n)\, B_{jj}(\omega + \mu_j) - 2\, P(\omega, n)\, B_{jj}(\omega) \\ &\qquad\qquad + P(\omega - \mu_j, n)\, B_{jj}(\omega - \mu_j)\; \} \end{aligned} \tag{21}$$

where μ_j denotes a displacement along ω_j a distance μ, $A_j(\omega) \equiv \langle\, H_j(\omega, x)\,\rangle_x$, and $B_{jj}(\omega) \equiv \langle H_j^2(\omega, x)\rangle_x$. Note that $B_{jj}(\omega) = 1$ unless $H(\omega, x) = 0$, for all x, in which case $B_{jj}(\omega) \equiv 0$. Although exact, (21) curiously has the form of a second order finite difference approximation to the Fokker-Planck equation with diagonal diffusion matrix. This form is understandable, since the dynamics (20) restrict the weight values ω to a hypercubic lattice with cell length μ and generate only nearest neighbor interactions.

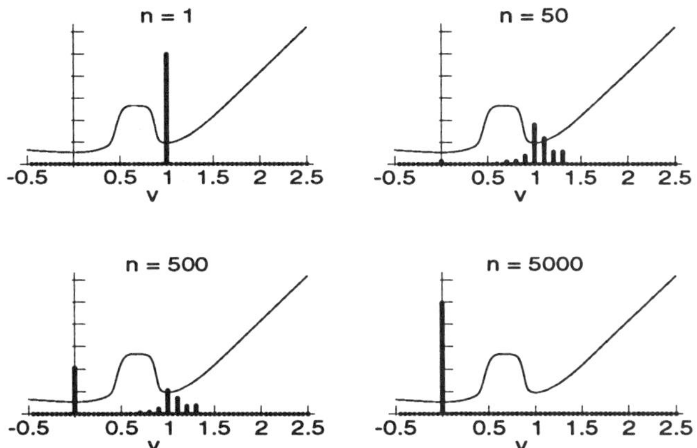

Fig.3: Sequence of densities for the XOR problem

As an example, figure 3 shows the cost function evaluated along a 1-D slice through the weight space for the XOR problem. Along this line are local and global minima at $v = 1$ and $v = 0$ respectively. Also shown is the probability density (vertical lines). The sequence shows the spreading of the density from its initialization at the local minimum, and its eventual collection at the global minimum.

4 Discussion

A theoretical approach that focuses on the dynamics of the weight space probability density, as we do here, provides powerful tools to extend understanding of stochastic search. Both transient and equilibrium behavior can be studied using these tools. We expect that knowledge of equilibrium weight space distributions can be used in conjunction with theories of generalization (e.g. Moody, 1992) to assess the influence of stochastic search on prediction error. Characterization of transient phenomena should facilitate the design and evaluation of search strategies such as data batching and adaptive learning rate schedules. Transient phenomena are treated in greater depth in the companion paper in this volume (Orr and Leen, 1993).

Acknowledgements

T. Leen was supported under grants N00014-91-J-1482 and N00014-90-J-1349 from ONR. J. Moody was supported under grants 89-0478 from AFOSR, ECS-9114333 from NSF, and N00014-89-J-1228 and N00014-92-J-4062 from ONR.

References

Todd K. Leen and Genevieve B. Orr (1992), Weight-space probability densities and convergence times for stochastic learning. In *International Joint Conference on Neural Networks*, pages IV 158–164. IEEE, June.

H. Ritter and K. Schulten (1988), Convergence properties of Kohonen's topology conserving maps: Fluctuations, stability and dimension selection, *Biol. Cybern.*, 60, 59-71.

Genevieve B. Orr and Todd K. Leen (1993), Probability densities in stochastic learning: II. Transients and Basin Hopping Times. In Giles, C.L., Hanson, S.J., and Cowan, J.D. (eds.), *Advances in Neural Information Processing Systems 5.* San Mateo, CA: Morgan Kaufmann Publishers.

H. Risken (1989), *The Fokker-Planck Equation* Springer-Verlag, Berlin.

G. Radons, H.G. Schuster and D. Werner (1990), Fokker-Planck description of learning in backpropagation networks, *International Neural Network Conference - INNC 90*, Paris, II 993-996, Kluwer Academic Publishers.

C.W. Gardiner (1990), *Handbook of Stochastic Methods, 2nd Ed.* Springer-Verlag, Berlin.

Simon Haykin (1991), *Adaptive Filter Theory, 2nd edition.* Prentice Hall, Englewood Cliffs, N.J.

W.H. Press, B.P. Flannery, S.A. Teukolsky, and W.T. Vetterling (1987) *Numerical Recipes - the Art of Scientific Computing.* Cambridge University Press, Cambridge / New York.

V. Fabian (1960), Stochastic approximation methods. *Czechoslovak Math J.*, 10, 123–159.

Mark Derthick (1984), Variations on the Boltzmann machine learning algorithm. Technical Report CMU-CS-84-120, Department of Computer Science, Carnegie-Mellon University, Pittsburgh, PA, August.

John E. Moody (1992), The effective number of parameters: An analysis of generalization and regularization in nonlinear learning systems. In J.E. Moody, S.J. Hanson, and R.P. Lipmann, editors, *Advances in Neural Information Processing Systems 4.* Morgan Kaufmann Publishers, San Mateo, CA.

Diffusion Approximations for the Constant Learning Rate Backpropagation Algorithm and Resistence to Local Minima

William Finnoff
Siemens AG, Corporate Research and Development
Otto-Hahn-Ring 6
8000 Munich 83, Fed. Rep. Germany

Abstract

In this paper we discuss the asymptotic properties of the most commonly used variant of the backpropagation algorithm in which network weights are trained by means of a local gradient descent on examples drawn randomly from a fixed training set, and the learning rate η of the gradient updates is held constant (simple backpropagation). Using stochastic approximation results, we show that for $\eta \to 0$ this training process approaches a batch training and provide results on the rate of convergence. Further, we show that for small η one can approximate simple back propagation by the sum of a batch training process and a Gaussian diffusion which is the unique solution to a linear stochastic differential equation. Using this approximation we indicate the reasons why simple backpropagation is less likely to get stuck in local minima than the batch training process and demonstrate this empirically on a number of examples.

1 INTRODUCTION

The original (simple) backpropagation algorithm, incorporating pattern for pattern learning and a constant learning rate $\eta \in (0, \infty)$, remains in spite of many real (and imagined) deficiencies the most widely used network training algorithm, and a vast body of literature documents its general applicability and robustness. In this paper we will draw on the highly developed literature of stochastic approximation theory to demonstrate several asymptotic properties of simple backpropagation. The close relationship between backpropagation and stochastic approximation methods has been long recognized, and various properties of the algorithm for the case of decreasing learning rate $\eta_{n+1} < \eta_n$, $n \in \mathbf{N}$ were shown for example by White [W,89a], [W,89b] and Darken and Moody [D,M,91]. Hornik and Kuan [H,K,91] used comparable results for the algorithm with constant learning rate to derive weak convergence results.

In the first part of this paper we will show that simple backpropagation has the same asymptotic dynamics as batch training in the small learning rate limit. As such, anything that can be expected of batch training can also be expected in simple backpropagation as long as the learning rate of the algorithm is very small. In the special situation considered here (in contrast to that in [H,K,91]) we will also be able to provide a result on the speed of convergence. As such, anything that can be expected of batch training can also be expected in simple backpropagation as long as the learning rate of the algorithm is very small. In the next part of the paper, Gaussian approximations for the difference between the actual training process and the limit are derived. It is shown that this difference, (properly renormalized), converges to the solution of a linear stochastic differential equation. In the final section of the paper, we combine these results to provide an approximation for the simple backpropagation training process and use this to show why simple backpropagation will be less inclined to get stuck in local minima than batch training. This ability to avoid local minima is then demonstrated empirically on several examples.

2 NOTATION

Define the parametric version of a single hidden layer network activation function with h inputs, m outputs and q hidden units

$$f : \mathbf{R}^d \times \mathbf{R}^h \rightarrow \mathbf{R}^m, (\theta, x) \rightarrow (f^1(\theta, x), ..., f^m(\theta, x)),$$

by setting for $x \in \mathbf{R}^h$, $\overline{x} = (x_1, ..., x_h, 1)$, $\theta = (\gamma_{\cdot}^{\cdot}, \beta_{\cdot}^{\cdot})$ and $u = 1, ..., m$,

$$f^u(\theta, x) = f^u((\gamma_{\cdot}^{\cdot}, \beta_{\cdot}^{\cdot}), x) = \phi\left(\sum_{j=1}^{q} \gamma_j^u \phi(\beta_j^{\cdot} \overline{x}^T) + \gamma_{q+1}^u\right),$$

where $\overline{x}^T$ denotes the transpose of $\overline{x}$ and $d = m(q+1) + q(h+1)$ denotes the number of weights in the network. Let $((Y_k, X_k))_{k=1,...,T}$ be a set of training examples, consisting of targets $(Y_k)_{k=1,...,T}$ and inputs $(X_k)_{k=1,...,T}$. We then define the parametric error function

$$U(y, x, \theta) = \|y - f(\theta, x)\|^2, .$$

and for every θ, the cummulative gradient

$$h(\theta) = -\frac{1}{T}\sum_{k=1}^{T}\frac{\partial U}{\partial \theta}(Y_k, X_k, \theta).$$

3 APPROXIMATION WITH THE ODE

We will be considering the asymptotic properties of network training processes induced by the starting value θ_0, the gradient (or direction) function $-\frac{\partial U}{\partial \theta}$ the learning rate η and an infinite training sequence $(y_n, x_n)_{n\in\mathbf{N}}$, where each (y_n, x_n) example is drawn at random from the set $\{(Y_1, X_1), ..., (Y_T, X_T)\}$. One defines the discrete parameter process $\theta = \theta^\eta = (\theta_n^\eta)_{n\in\mathbf{Z}_+}$ of weight updates by setting

$$\theta_n^\eta = \begin{cases} \theta_0 & \text{for } n = 0 \\ \theta_{n-1}^\eta - \eta\frac{\partial U}{\partial \theta}(y_n, x_n, \theta_{n-1}^\eta) & \text{for } n \in \mathbf{N} \end{cases}$$

and the corresponding continuous parameter process $(\theta^\eta(t))_{t\in[0,\infty)}$, by setting

$$\theta_n^\eta(t) = \theta_{n-1}^\eta - (t-(n-1)\eta)\frac{\partial U}{\partial \theta}(y_n, x_n, \theta_{n-1}^\eta)$$

for $t \in [(n-1)\eta, n\eta)$, $n \in \mathbf{N}$. The first question that we will investigate is that of the 'small learning rate limit' of the continuous parameter process θ^η, i.e. the limiting properties of the family θ^η for $\eta \to 0$. We show that the family of (stochastic) processes $(\theta^\eta)_{\eta>0}$ converges with probability one to a limit process $\overline{\theta}$, where $\overline{\theta}$ denotes the solution to the cummulative gradient equation,

$$\overline{\theta}(t) = \theta_0 + \int_0^t h(\overline{\theta}(s))ds.$$

Here, for $\theta_0 = a = constant$, this solution is deterministic. This result corresponds to a 'law of large numbers' for the weight update process, in which the small learning rate (in the limit) averages out the stochastic fluctuations.

Central to any application of the stochastic approximation results is the derivation of local Lipschitz and linear growth bounds for $\frac{\partial U}{\partial \theta}$ and h. That is the subject of the following,

Lemma(3.1) i) There exists a constant $K > 0$ so that

$$\sup_{(y,x)}\left\|\frac{\partial U}{\partial \theta}(y, x, \theta)\right\| \leq K(1 + ||\theta||)$$

and

$$||h(\theta)|| \leq K(1 + ||\theta||).$$

ii) For every $G > 0$ there exists a constant L_G so that for any $\theta, \widetilde{\theta} \in [-G, G]^d$,

$$\sup_{(y,x)} \left\| \frac{\partial U}{\partial \theta}(y,x,\theta) - \frac{\partial U}{\partial \theta}(y,x,\widetilde{\theta}) \right\| \leq L_G \|\theta - \widetilde{\theta}\|$$

and

$$\|h(\theta) - h(\widetilde{\theta})\| \leq L_G \|\theta - \widetilde{\theta}\|.$$

Proof: The calculations on which this result are based are tedious but straightforward, making repeated use of the fact that products and sums of locally Lipschitz continuous functions are themselves locally Lipschitz continuous. It is even possible to provide explicit values for the constants given above.

•

Denoting with **P** (resp. **E**) the probability (resp. mathematical expectation) of the processes defined above, we can present the results on the probability of deviations of the process θ from the limit $\overline{\theta}$.

Theorem(3.2) Let $r, \delta \in (0, \infty)$. Then there exists a constant B_r (which doesn't depend on η) so that

i) $\mathbf{E}\left(\sup_{s \leq r} \|\theta^\eta(s) - \overline{\theta}(s)\|^2\right) \leq B_r \eta.$

ii) $\mathbf{P}\left(\sup_{s \leq r} \|\theta(s) - \overline{\theta}(s)\| > \delta\right) \leq \frac{1}{\delta^2} B_r \eta.$

Proof: The first part of the proof requires that one finds bounds for $\theta^\eta(t)$ and $\overline{\theta}(t)$ for $t \in [0, r]$. This is accomplished using the results of Lemma(3.1) and Gronwall's Lemma. This places η independent bounds on B_r. The remainder of the proof uses Theorem(9), §1.5, Part II of [Ben,Met,Pri,87]. The required conditions (A1), (A2) follow directly from our hypotheses, and (A3), (A4) from Lemma(3.1). Due to the boundedness of the variables $(y_n, x_n)_{n \in \mathbf{N}}$ and θ_0, condition (A5) is trivially fulfilled.

•

It should be noted that the constant B_r is usually dependent on r and may indeed increase exponentially (in r) unless it is possible to show that the training process remains in some bounded region for $t \to \infty$. This is not necessarily due exclusively to the difference between the stochastic approximation and the discrete parameter cummulative gradient process, but also to the the error between the discrete (Euler approximation) and continuous parameter versions of (3.3).

4 GAUSSIAN APPROXIMATIONS

In this section we will give a Gaussian approximation for the difference between the training process θ^η and the limit $\overline{\theta}$. Although in the limit these coincide, for $\eta > 0$ the training process fluctuates away from the limit in a stochastic fashion. The following Gaussian approximation provides an estimate for the size and nature of these fluctuations depending on the second order statistics (variance/covariance matrix) of the weight update process. Define for any $t \in [0, \infty)$,

$$\Theta^\eta(t) = \frac{\theta^\eta(t) - \overline{\theta}(t)}{\sqrt{\eta}}.$$

Further, for $i = 1, ..., d$ we denote with $\frac{\partial U}{\partial \theta}^i(y, x, \theta)$, (resp. $h^i(\theta)$) the i-th coordinate vector of $\frac{\partial U}{\partial \theta}(y, x, \theta)$ (resp. $h(\theta)$). Then define for $i, j = 1, ..., d$, $\theta \in \mathbf{R}^d$

$$R^{ij}(\theta) = \frac{1}{T}\sum_{k=1}^{T}\left(\frac{\partial U}{\partial \theta}^i(Y_k, X_k, \theta) - h^i(\theta)\right)\left(\frac{\partial U}{\partial \theta}^j(Y_k, X_k, \theta) - h^j(\theta)\right).$$

Thus, for any $n \in \mathbf{N}$, $\theta \in \mathbf{R}^d$, $R(\theta)$ represents the covariance matrix of the random elements $\frac{\partial U}{\partial \theta}(y_n, x_n, \theta)$. We can then define for the symmetric matrix $R(\theta)$ a further $\mathbf{R}^{d \times d}$ valued matrix $R^{\frac{1}{2}}(\theta)$ with the property that $R(\theta) = R^{\frac{1}{2}}(\theta)(R^{\frac{1}{2}}(\theta))^T$.

The following result represents a central limit theorem for the training process. This permits a type of second order approximation of the fluctuations of the stochastic training process around its deterministic limit.

Theorem(4.1): Under the assumptions given above, the distributions of the processes Θ^η, $\eta > 0$, converge weakly (in the sense of weak convergence of measures) for $\eta \to 0$ to a uniquely defined measure $\mathcal{L}\{\widetilde{\theta}\}$, where $\widetilde{\theta}$ denotes the solution to the following stochastic differential equation

$$\widetilde{\theta}(t) = \int_0^t \frac{\partial h}{\partial \theta}(\overline{\theta}(s))\widetilde{\theta}(s)ds + \int_0^t R^{\frac{1}{2}}(\overline{\theta}(s))dW(s),$$

where W denotes a standard d−dimensional Brownian motion (i.e. with covariance matrix equal to the identity matrix).

Proof: The proof here uses Theorem(7), §4.4, Part II of [Ben,Met,Pri,87]. As noted in the proof of Theorem(3.2), under our hypotheses, the conditions (A1)-(A5) are fulfilled. Define for $i, j = 1, ..., d$, $(y, x) \in I^{m+h}$, $\theta \in \mathbf{R}^d$, $w^{ij}(y, x, \theta) = \rho^i(y, x, \theta)\rho^j(y, x, \theta) - h^i(\theta)h^j(\theta)$, and $\nu = \rho$. Under our hypotheses, h has continuous first and second order derivatives for all $\theta \in \mathbf{R}^d$ and the function $R = (R^{ij})_{i,j=1,...,d}$ as well as $W = (w^{ij})_{i,j=1,...,d}$ fulfill the remaining requirements of (A8) as follows: (A8)i) and (A8)ii) are trivial consequence of the definition of R and W. Finally, setting $p_3 = p_4 = 0$ and $\mu = 1$, (A8)iii) then can be derived directly from the definitions of W and R and Lemma(5.1)ii).

•

5 RESISTENCE TO LOCAL MINIMA

In this section we combine the results of the two preceding sections to provide a Gaussian approximation of simple backpropagation. Recalling the results and notation of Theorem(3.2) and Theorem(4.1) we have for any $t \in [0,\infty)$,

$$\theta^{\eta}(t) = \overline{\theta}(t) + \eta^{\frac{1}{2}}\widetilde{\theta}(t) + o(\eta^{\frac{1}{2}}).$$

Using this approximation we have:

-For 'very small' learning rate η, simple backpropagation and batch learning will produce essentially the same results since the stochastic portion of the process (controlled by $\eta^{\frac{1}{2}}$) will be negligible.

-Otherwise, there is a nonnegligible stochastic element in the training process which can be approximated by the Gaussian diffusion $\widetilde{\theta}$.

-This diffusion term gives simple backpropagation a 'quasi-annealing' character, in which the cummulative gradient is continuously perturbed by the Gaussian term $\widetilde{\theta}$, allowing it to escape local minima with small shallow basins of attraction.

It should be noted that the rest term will actually have a better convergence rate than the indicated $o(\eta^{\frac{1}{2}})$. The calculation of exact rates, though, would require a generalized version of the Berry-Esséen theorem. To our knowledge, no such results are available which would be applicable to the situation described above.

6 EMPIRICAL RESULTS

The imperviousness of simple backpropagation to local minima, which is part of neural network 'folklore' is documented here in four examples. A single hidden layer feedforward network with $\phi = tanh$, ten hidden units n and one output was trained with both simple backpropagation and batch training using data generated by four different models. The data consisted of pairs (y_i, x_i), $i = 1, \ldots, T$, $T \in \mathbf{N}$ with targets $y_i \in \mathbf{R}$ and inputs $x_i = (x_i^1, \ldots, x_i^K) \in [-1,1]^K$, where $y_i = g((x_i^1, \ldots, x_i^j)) + u_i$, for $j, K \in \mathbf{N}$. The first experiment was based on an additive structure g having the following form with $j = 5$ and $K = 10$, $g((x_i^1, \ldots, x_i^5)) = \sum_{k=1}^{5} \sin(\alpha^k x_i^k)$, $\alpha^k \in \mathbf{R}$. The second model had a product structure g with $j = 3$, $K = 10$ and $g((x_i^1, \ldots, x_i^3)) = \prod_{k=1}^{3} x_i^k$, $\alpha^k \in \mathbf{R}$. The third structure considered was constructed with $j = 5$ and $K = 10$, using sums of Radial Basis Functions (RBF's) as follows: $g((x_i^1, \ldots, x_i^5)) = \sum_{l=1}^{8} (-1)^l \exp\left(\sum_{k=1}^{5} \frac{(\alpha^{k,l} - x_i^k)^2}{2\sigma^2}\right)$. These points were chosen by independent drawings from a uniform distribution on $[-1,1]^5$. The final experiment was conducted using data generated by a feedforward network activation function. For more details concerning the construction of the examples used here consult [F,H,Z,92].

For each model three training runs were made using the same vector of starting weights for both simple backpropagation and batch training. As can be seen, in all but one example the batch training process got stuck in a local minimum producing much worse results than those found using simple backpropagation. Due to the wide array of structures used to generate data and the number of data sets used, it would be hard to dismiss the observed phenomena as being example dependent.

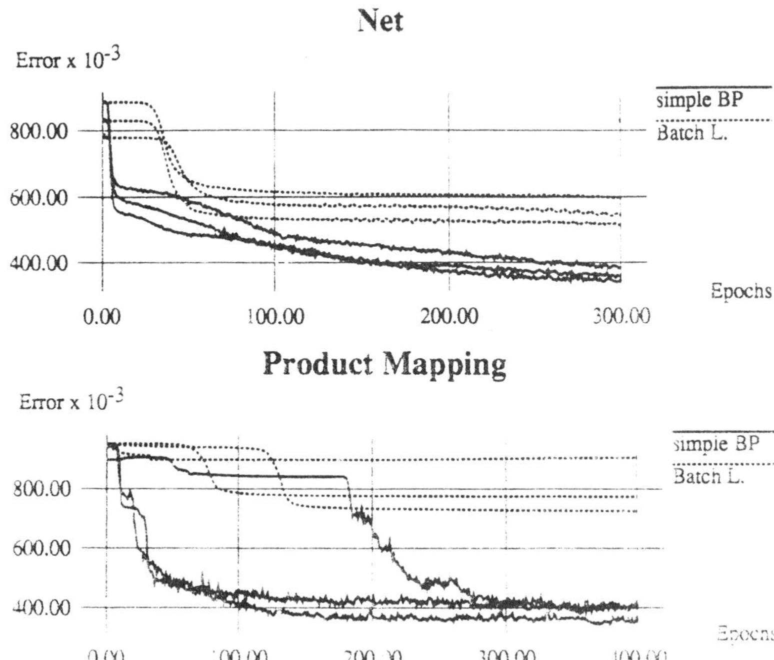
Net
Error x 10^{-3}
800.00
600.00
400.00
0.00
100.00
200.00
300.00
simple BP
Batch L.
Epochs
Product Mapping
Error x 10^{-3}
800.00
600.00
400.00
0.00
100.00
200.00
300.00
400.00
simple BP
Batch L.
Epochs

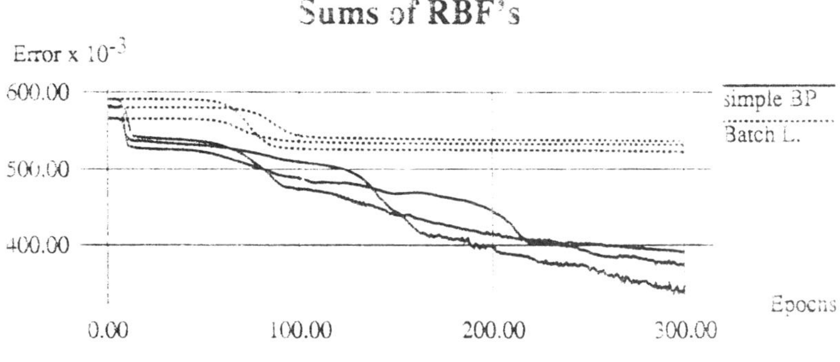
Sums of RBF's
Error x 10^{-3}
600.00
500.00
400.00
0.00
100.00
200.00
300.00
simple BP
Batch L.
Epochs

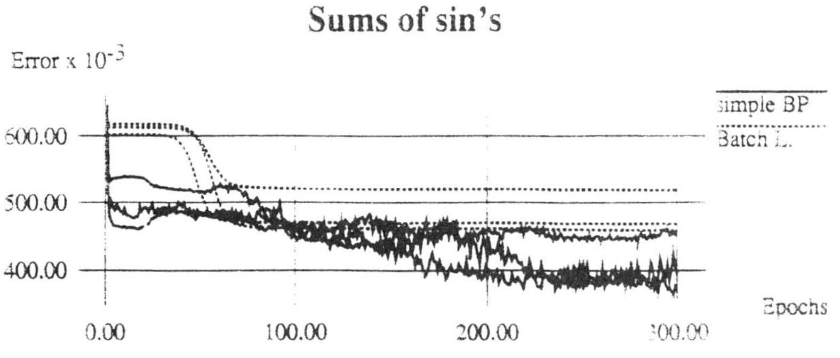
Sums of sin's
Error x 10^{-3}
600.00
500.00
400.00
0.00
100.00
200.00
300.00
simple BP
Batch L.
Epochs

7 REFERENCES

[Ben,Met,Pri,87] Benveniste, A., Métivier, M., Priouret, P., *Adaptive Algorithms and Stochastic Approximations*, Springer Verlag, 1987.

[Bou,85] Bouton C., Approximation Gaussienne d'algorithmes stochastiques a dynamique Markovienne. Thesis, Paris VI, (in French), 1985.

[Da,M,91] Darken C. and Moody J., Note on learning rate schedules for stochastic optimization, in*Advances in Neural Information Processing Systems 3*, Lippmann, R. Moody, J., and Touretzky, D., ed., Morgan Kaufmann, San Mateo, 1991.

[F,H,Z,92] Improving model selection by nonconvergent methods. To appear in *Neural Networks.*

[H,K,91], Hornik, K. and Kuan, C.M., Convergence of Learning Algorithms with constant learning rates, *IEEE Trans. on Neural Networks* 2, pp. 484-489, (1991).

[Wh,89a] White, H., Some asymptotic results for learning in single hidden-layer feedforward network models, *Jour. Amer. Stat. Ass.* 84, no. 408, p. 1003-1013, 1989.

[W,89b] White, H., Learning in artificial neural networks: A statistical perspective, *Neural Computation* 1, p.425-464, 1989.

Self-Organizing Rules for Robust Principal Component Analysis

Lei Xu[1,2]* **and Alan Yuille**[1]
1. Division of Applied Sciences, Harvard University, Cambridge, MA 02138
2. Dept. of Mathematics, Peking University, Beijing, P.R.China

Abstract

In the presence of outliers, the existing self-organizing rules for *Principal Component Analysis (PCA)* perform poorly. Using statistical physics techniques including the Gibbs distribution, binary decision fields and effective energies, we propose self-organizing PCA rules which are capable of resisting outliers while fulfilling various PCA-related tasks such as obtaining the first principal component vector, the first k principal component vectors, and directly finding the subspace spanned by the first k vector principal component vectors without solving for each vector individually. Comparative experiments have shown that the proposed robust rules improve the performances of the existing PCA algorithms significantly when outliers are present.

1 INTRODUCTION

Principal Component Analysis (PCA) is an essential technique for data compression and feature extraction, and has been widely used in statistical data analysis, communication theory, pattern recognition and image processing. In the neural network literature, a lot of studies have been made on learning rules for implementing PCA or on networks closely related to PCA (see Xu & Yuille, 1993 for a detailed reference list which contains more than 30 papers related to these issues). The existing rules can fulfil various PCA-type tasks for a number of application purposes.

*Present address: Dept. of Brain and Cognitive Sciences, E10–243, Massachusetts Institute of Technology, Cambridge, MA 02139.

However, almost all the previously mentioned PCA algorithms are based on the assumption that the data has not been spoiled by outliers (except Xu, Oja&Suen 1992, where outliers can be resisted to some extent.). In practice, real data often contains some outliers and usually they are not easy to separate from the data set. As shown by the experiments described in this paper, these outliers will significantly worsen the performances of the existing PCA learning algorithms. Currently, little attention has been paid to this problem in the neural network literature, although the problem is very important for real applications.

Recently, there have been some success in applying the statistical physics approach to a variety of computer vision problems (Yuille, 1990; Yuille, Yang&Geiger 1990; Yuille, Geiger&Bulthoff, 1991). In particular, it has also been shown that some techniques developed in robust statistics (e.g., redescending M-estimators, least-trimmed squares estimators) appear naturally within the Bayesian formulation by the use of the statistical physics approach. In this paper we adapt this approach to tackle the problem of robust PCA. Robust rules are proposed for various PCA-related tasks such as obtaining the first principal component vector, the first k principal component vectors, and principal subspaces. Comparative experiments have been made and the results show that our robust rules improve the performances of the existing PCA algorithms significantly when outliers are present.

2 PCA LEARNING AND ENERGY MINIMIZATION

There exist a number of self-organizing rules for finding the first principal component. Three of them are listed as follows (Oja 1982, 85; Xu, 1991, 93):

$$\vec{m}(t+1) = \vec{m}(t) + \alpha_a(t)(\vec{x}y - \vec{m}(t)y^2), \tag{1}$$

$$\vec{m}(t+1) = \vec{m}(t) + \alpha_a(t)(\vec{x}y - \frac{\vec{m}(t)}{\vec{m}(t)^T\vec{m}(t)}y^2), \tag{2}$$

$$\vec{m}(t+1) = \vec{m}(t) + \alpha_a(t)[y(\vec{x} - \vec{u}) + (y - y')\vec{x}]. \tag{3}$$

where $y = \vec{m}(t)^T\vec{x}$, $\vec{u} = y\vec{m}(t)$, $y' = \vec{m}(t)^T\vec{u}$ and $\alpha_a(t) \geq 0$ is the learning rate which decreases to zero as $t \to \infty$ while satisfying certain conditions, e.g., $\sum_t \alpha_a(t) = \infty$, $\sum_t \alpha_a(t)^q < \infty$ *for some* $q > 1$.

Each of the three rules will converge to the principal component vector $\vec{\phi}$ almost surely under some mild conditions which are studied in detail in by Oja (1982&85) and Xu (1991&93). Regarding $\vec{m}$ as the weight vector of a linear neuron with output $y = \vec{m}^T\vec{x}$, all the three rules can be considered as modifications of the well known Hebbian rule $\vec{m}(t+1) = \vec{m}(t) + \alpha_a(t)\vec{x}y$ through introducing additional terms for preventing $||\vec{m}(t)||$ from going to ∞ as $t \to \infty$.

The performances of these rules deteriorate considerably when data contains outliers. Although some outlier-resisting versions of eq.(1) and eq.(2) have also been recently proposed (Xu, Oja & Suen, 1992), they work well only for data which is not severely spoiled by outliers. In this paper, we adopt a totally different approach—we generalize eq.(1),eq.(2) and eq.(3) into more robust versions by using the statistical physics approach.

To do so, first we need to connect these rules to energy functions. It follows from Xu (1991&93) and Xu & Yuille(1993) that the rules eq.(2) and eq.(3) are respectively *on-line* gradient descent rules for minimizing $J_1(\vec{m})$, $J_2(\vec{m})$ respectively[1]:

$$J_1(\vec{m}) = \frac{1}{N}\sum_{i=1}^{N}(\vec{x}_i^T\vec{x}_i - \frac{\vec{m}^T\vec{x}_i\vec{x}_i^T\vec{m}}{\vec{m}^T\vec{m}}) \tag{4}$$

$$J_2(\vec{m}) = \frac{1}{N}\sum_{i=1}^{N}||\vec{x}_i - \vec{u}_i||^2. \tag{5}$$

It has also been proved that the rule given by eq.(1) satisfies (Xu, 1991, 93): (a) $\vec{h}_1^T\vec{h}_2 \geq 0, E(\vec{h}_1)^T E(\vec{h}_1) \geq 0$, with $\vec{h}_1 = \vec{x}y - \vec{m}y^2$, $\vec{h}_2 = \vec{x}y - \frac{\vec{m}}{\vec{m}^T\vec{m}}y^2$; (b) $E(\vec{h}_1)^T E(\vec{h}_3) \geq 0$, with $\vec{h}_3 = y(\vec{x}-\vec{u}) + (y-y')\vec{x}$; (c) Both J_1 and J_2 have only one local (also global) minimum $tr(\Sigma) - \vec{\phi}^T\Sigma\vec{\phi}$, and all the other critical points (i.e., the points satisfy $\frac{\partial J_i(\vec{m})}{\partial \vec{m}} = 0, i = 1,2$) are saddle points. Here $\Sigma = E\{\vec{x}\vec{x}^{\,t}\}$, and $\vec{\phi}$ is the eigenvector of Σ corresponding to the largest eigenvalue.

That is, the rule eq.(1) is a downhill algorithm for minimizing J_1 in both the *on line* sense and the *average* sense, and for minimizing J_2 in the *average* sense.

3 GENERALIZED ENERGY AND ROBUST PCA

We further regard $J_1(\vec{m})$, $J_2(\vec{m})$ as special cases of the following general energy:

$$J(\vec{m}) = \frac{1}{N}\sum_{i=1}^{N} z(\vec{x}_i, \vec{m}), \quad z(\vec{x}_i, \vec{m}) \geq 0. \tag{6}$$

where $z(\vec{x}_i, \vec{m})$ is the portion of energy contributed by the sample $\vec{x}_i$, and

$$\begin{aligned} z(\vec{x}_i, \vec{m}) = & \quad (\vec{x}_i^T\vec{x}_i - \tfrac{\vec{m}^T\vec{x}_i\vec{x}_i^T\vec{m}}{\vec{m}^T\vec{m}})\ for\ J_1, \\ = & \quad ||\vec{x}_i - \vec{u}_i||^2\ for\ J_2 \end{aligned} \tag{7}$$

Following (Yuille, 1990 a& b), we now generalize energy eq.(6) into

$$E(\vec{V}, \vec{m}) = \sum_{i=1}^{N} V_i\ z(\vec{x}_i, \vec{m}) + E_{prior}(\vec{V}) \tag{8}$$

where $\vec{V} = \{V_i, i = 1, \cdots, N\}$ is a binary field $\{V_i\}$ with each V_i being a random variable taking value either 0 or 1. V_i acts as a decision indicator for deciding whether $\vec{x}_i$ is an outlier or a sample. When $V_i = 1$, the portion of energy contributed by the sample $\vec{x}_i$ is taken into consideration; otherwise, it is equivalent to discarding $\vec{x}_i$ as an outlier. $E_{prior}(\vec{V})$ is the *a priori* portion of energy contributed by the *a priori* distribution of $\{V_i\}$. A natural choice is

$$E_{prior}(\vec{V}) = \eta\sum_{i=1}^{N}(1 - V_i) \tag{9}$$

This choice of priori has a natural interpretation: for fixed $\vec{m}$ it is energetically favourable to set $V_i = 1$ (i.e., not regarding $\vec{x}_i$ as an outlier) if $z(\vec{x}_i, \vec{m}) < \sqrt{\eta}$ (i.e.,

[1]We have $J_1(\vec{m}) \geq 0$, since $\vec{x}^T\vec{x} - \frac{y^2}{\vec{m}^T\vec{m}} = ||\vec{x}||^2 \sin^2\theta_{\vec{x}\vec{m}} \geq 0$.

the portion of energy contributed by $\vec{x}_i$ is smaller than a prespecified threshold) and to set it to 0 otherwise.

Based on $E(\vec{V}, \vec{m})$, we define a Gibbs distribution (Parisi 1988):

$$P[\vec{V}, \vec{m}] = \frac{1}{Z} e^{-\beta E[\vec{V}, \vec{m}]}, \tag{10}$$

where Z is the partition function which ensures $\sum_{\vec{V}} \sum_{\vec{m}} P[\vec{V}, \vec{m}] = 1$. Then we compute

$$\begin{aligned} P_{margin}(\vec{m}) &= \frac{1}{Z} \sum_{\vec{V}} e^{-\beta \sum_i \{V_i z(\vec{x}_i, \vec{m}) + \eta(1-V_i)\}} \\ &= \frac{1}{Z} \prod_i \sum_{V_i = \{0,1\}} e^{-\beta \{V_i z(\vec{x}_i, \vec{m}) + \eta(1-V_i)\}} = \frac{1}{Z_m} e^{-\beta E_{eff}(\vec{m})}. \end{aligned} \tag{11}$$

$$Z_m = Z e^{N\beta\eta}, \qquad E_{eff}(\vec{m}) = \frac{-1}{\beta} \sum_i \log\{1 + e^{-\beta\{z(\vec{x}_i, \vec{m}) - \eta\}}\}. \tag{12}$$

E_{eff} is called the effective energy. Each term in the sum for E_{eff} is approximately $z(\vec{x}_i, \vec{m})$ for small values of z but becomes constant as $z(\vec{x}_i, \vec{m}) \to \infty$. In this way outliers, which are more likely to yield large values of $z(\vec{x}_i, \vec{m})$, are treated differently from samples, and thus the estimation $\vec{m}$ obtained by minimizing $E_{eff}(\vec{m})$ will be robust and able to resist outliers.

$E_{eff}(\vec{m})$ is usually not a convex function and may have many local minima. The statistical physics framework suggests using deterministic annealing to minimize $E_{eff}(\vec{m})$. That is, by the following gradient descent rule eq.(13), to minimize $E_{eff}(\vec{m})$ for small β and then track the minimum as β increases to infinity (the zero temperature limit):

$$\vec{m}(t+1) = \vec{m}(t) - \alpha_b(t) \sum_i \frac{1}{1 + e^{\beta(z(\vec{x}_i, \vec{m}(t)) - \eta)}} \frac{\partial z(\vec{x}_i, \vec{m}(t))}{\partial \vec{m}(t)}. \tag{13}$$

More specifically, with z's chosen to correspond to the energies J_1 and J_2 respectively, we have the following *batch-way* learning rules for robust PCA:

$$\vec{m}(t+1) = \vec{m}(t) + \alpha_b(t) \sum_i \frac{1}{1 + e^{\beta(z(\vec{x}_i, \vec{m}(t)) - \eta)}} (\vec{x}_i y_i - \frac{\vec{m}(t)}{\vec{m}(t)^T \vec{m}(t)} y_i^2), \tag{14}$$

$$\vec{m}(t+1) = \vec{m}(t) + \alpha_b(t) \sum_i \frac{1}{1 + e^{\beta(z(\vec{x}_i, \vec{m}(t)) - \eta)}} [y_i(\vec{x}_i - \vec{u}_i) + (y_i - y_i')\vec{x}_i]. \tag{15}$$

For data that comes incrementally or in the *on-line* way, we correspondingly have the following *adaptive or stochastic approximation* versions

$$\vec{m}(t+1) = \vec{m}(t) + \alpha_a(t) \frac{1}{1 + e^{\beta(z(\vec{x}_i, \vec{m}(t)) - \eta)}} (\vec{x}_i y_i - \frac{\vec{m}(t)}{\vec{m}(t)^T \vec{m}(t)} y_i^2), \tag{16}$$

$$\vec{m}(t+1) = \vec{m}(t) + \alpha_a(t) \frac{1}{1 + e^{\beta(z(\vec{x}_i, \vec{m}(t)) - \eta)}} [y_i(\vec{x}_i - \vec{u}_i) + (y_i - y_i')\vec{x}_i]. \tag{17}$$

It can be observed that the difference between eq.(2) and eq.(16) or eq.(3) and eq.(17) is that the learning rate $\alpha_a(t)$ has been modified by a multiplicative factor

$$\alpha_m(t) = \frac{1}{1+e^{\beta(z(\vec{x}_i,\vec{m}(t))-\eta)}}. \tag{18}$$

which adaptively modifies the learning rate to suit the current input $\vec{x}_i$. This modifying factor has a similar function as that used in Xu, Oja&Suen(1992) for robust line fitting. But the modifying factor eq.(18) is more sophisticated and performs better.

Based on the connection between the rule eq.(1) and J_1 or J_2, given in sec.2, we can also formally use the modifying factor $\alpha_m(t)$ to turn the rule eq.(1) into the following robust version:

$$\vec{m}(t+1) = \vec{m}(t) + \alpha_a(t)\frac{1}{1+e^{\beta(z(\vec{x}_i,\vec{m}(t))-\eta)}}(\vec{x}_i y_i - \vec{m}(t)y_i^2), \tag{19}$$

4 ROBUST RULES FOR k PRINCIPAL COMPONENTS

In a similar way to SGA (Oja, 1992) and GHA (Sanger, 1989) we can generalize the robust rules eq.(19), eq.(16) and eq.(17) into the following general form of robust rules for finding the first k principal components:

$$\vec{m}_j(t+1) = \vec{m}_j(t) + \alpha_a(t)\frac{1}{1+e^{\beta(z(\vec{x}_i(j),\vec{m}_j(t))-\eta)}}\Delta\vec{m}_j(\vec{x}_i(j),\vec{m}_j(t)), \tag{20}$$

$$\vec{x}_i(0) = \vec{x}_i, \quad \vec{x}_i(j+1) = \vec{x}_i(j) - \sum_{r=1}^{j-1} y_i(r)\vec{m}_r(t), \quad y_i(j) = \vec{m}_j^T(t)\vec{x}_i(j), \tag{21}$$

where $\Delta\vec{m}_j(\vec{x}_i(j),\vec{m}_j(t))$, $z(\vec{x}_i(j),\vec{m}_j(t))$ have four possibilities (Xu & Yuille, 1993). As an example, one of them is given here

$$\Delta\vec{m}_j(\vec{x}_i(j),\vec{m}_j(t)) = (\vec{x}_i(j)y_i(j) - \vec{m}_j(t)y_i(j)^2),$$

$$z(\vec{x}_i(j),\vec{m}_j(t)) = \vec{x}_i(j)^T\vec{x}_i(j) - \frac{y_i(j)^2}{\vec{m}_j(t)^T\vec{m}_j(t)}.$$

In this case, eq.(20) can be regarded as the generalization of GHA (Sanger, 1989).

We can also develop an alternative set of rules for a type of nets with asymmetric lateral weights as used in (Rubner&Schulten, 1990). The rules can also get the first k principal components robustly in the presence of outliers (Xu & Yuille, 1993).

5 ROBUST RULES FOR PRINCIPAL SUBSPACE

Let $M = [\vec{m}_1, \cdots, \vec{m}_k]$, $\Phi = [\vec{\phi}_1, \cdots, \vec{\phi}_k]$, $\vec{y} = [y_1, \cdots, y_k]^T$ and $\vec{y} = M^T\vec{x}$, it follows from Oja(1989) and Xu(1991) the rules eq.(1), eq.(3) can be generalized into eq.(22) and eq.(23) respectively:

$$\vec{M}(t+1) = \vec{M}(t) + \alpha_A(t)(\vec{y}\vec{x}^T - \vec{y}\vec{y}^T M(t)) \tag{22}$$

$$\vec{M}(t+1) = \vec{M}(t) + \alpha_A(t)(\vec{y}(\vec{x}-\vec{u})^T - (\vec{y}-\vec{y}')\vec{x}^T), \quad \vec{u} = M\vec{y}, \quad \vec{y}' = M^T\vec{u} \quad (23)$$

In the case without outliers, by both the rules, the weight matrix $M(t)$ will converge to a matrix M^{∞} whose column vectors $m_j^{\infty}, j = 1, \cdots, k$ span the k-dimensional principal subspace (Oja, 1989; Xu, 1991&93), although the vectors are, in general, not equal to the k principal component vectors $\vec{\phi}_j, j = 1, \cdots, k$.

Similar to the previously used procedure, we have the following results:

(1). We can show that eq.(23) is an *on-line* or *stochastic approximation* rule which minimizes the energy J_3 in the gradient descent way (Xu, 1991& 93):

$$J_3(\vec{m}) = \frac{1}{N}\sum_{i=1}^{N} ||\vec{x}_i - \vec{u}_i||^2, \quad \vec{u} = M\vec{y}, \quad \vec{y}' = M^T\vec{u}. \quad (24)$$

and that in the *average sense* the subspace rule eq.(22) is also an *on-line* "down-hill" rule for minimizing the energy function J_3.

(2). We can also generalize the non-robust rules eq.(22) and eq.(23) into robust versions by using the statistical physics approach again:

$$\vec{M}(t+1) = \vec{M}(t) + \alpha_A(t)\frac{1}{1+e^{\beta(||\vec{x}_i - \vec{u}_i||^2 - \eta)}}[\vec{y}_i(\vec{x}_i - \vec{u}_i)^T - (\vec{y}_i - \vec{y}_i')\vec{x}_i^T], \quad (25)$$

$$\vec{M}(t+1) = \vec{M}(t) + \alpha_A(t)\frac{1}{1+e^{\beta(||\vec{x}_i - \vec{u}_i||^2 - \eta)}}[\vec{y}_i\vec{x}_i^T - \vec{y}_i\vec{y}_i^T M(t)] \quad (26)$$

6 EXAMPLES OF EXPERIMENTAL RESULTS

Let $\vec{x}$ from a population of 400 samples with zero mean. These samples are located on an elliptic ring centered at the origin of R^3, with its largest elliptic axis being along the direction $(-1, 1, 0)$, the plane of its other two axes intersecting the $x-y$ plane with an acute angle (30°). Among the 400 samples, 10 points (only 2.5%) are randomly chosen and replaced by outliers. The obtained data set is shown in Fig.1.

Before the outliers were introduced, either the conventional simple-variance-matrix based approach (i.e., solving $S\vec{\phi} = \lambda\vec{\phi}$, $S = \frac{1}{N}\sum_{i=1}^{N}\vec{x}_i\vec{x}_i^T$) or the unrobust rules eqs.(1)(2)(3) can find the correct 1st principal component vector of this data set.

On the data set contaminated by outliers , shown in Fig.1, the result of the simple-variance-matrix based approach has an angular error of $\vec{\phi}_p$ by 71.04^o—a result definitely unacceptable. The results of using the proposed robust rules eq.(19), eq.(16) and eq.(17) are shown in Fig.2(a) in comparison with those of their unrobust counterparts— the rules eq.(1), eq.(2) and eq.(3). We observe that all the unrobust rules get the solutions with errors of more than 21° from the correct direction of $\vec{\phi}_p$. By contrast, the robust rules can still maintain a very good accuracy—the error is about 0.36^o. Fig.2(b) gives the results of solving for the first two principal component vectors. Again, the unrobust rule produce large errors of around 23°, while the robust rules have an error of about 1.7^o. Fig.3 shows the results of solving for the 2-dimensional principal subspace, it is easy to see the significant improvements obtained by using the robust rules.

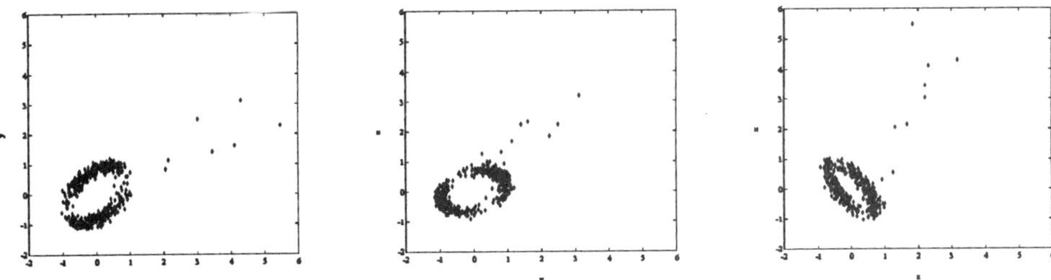

Figure 1: The projections of the data on the $x-y$, $y-z$ and $z-x$ planes, with 10 outliers.

Acknowledgements

We would like to thank DARPA and the Air Force for support with contracts AFOSR-89-0506 and F4969092-J-0466.

We like to menta ion that some further issues about the proposed robust rules are studied in Xu & Yuille (1993), including the selection of parameters α, β and η, the extension of the rules for robust *Minor Component Analysis (MCA)*, the relations between the rules to the two main types of existing robust PCA algorithms in the literature of statistics, as well as to Maximal Likelihood (ML) estimation of finite mixture distributions.

References

E. Oja, *J. Math. Bio. 16*, 1982, 267-273.

E. Oja & J. Karhunen, *J. Math. Anal. Appl. 106*, 1985, 69-84.

E. Oja, *Int. J. Neural Systems 1*, 1989, 61-68.

E. Oja, *Neural Networks 5*, 1992, 927-935.

G. Parisi, *Statistical Field Theory*, Addison-Wesley, Reading, Mass., 1988.

J. Rubner & K. Schulten, *Biological Cybernetics, 62*, 1990, 193-199.

T.D. Sanger, *Neural Networks, 2*, 1989, 459-473.

L. Xu, *Proc. of IJCNN'91-Singapore*, Nov., 1991, 2368-2373.

L. Xu, Least mean square error reconstruction for self-organizing neural-nets, *Neural Networks 6*, 1993, in press.

L. Xu, E. Oja & C.Y. Suen, *Neural Networks 5*, 1992, 441-457.

L. Xu & A.L. Yuille, Robust principal component analysis by self-organizing rules based on statistical physics approach, *IEEE Trans. Neural Networks*, 1993, in press.

A.L. Yuille, *Neural computation 2*, 1990, 1-24.

A.L. Yuille, D. Geiger and H.H. Bulthoff, *Networks* **2**, 1991. 423-442.

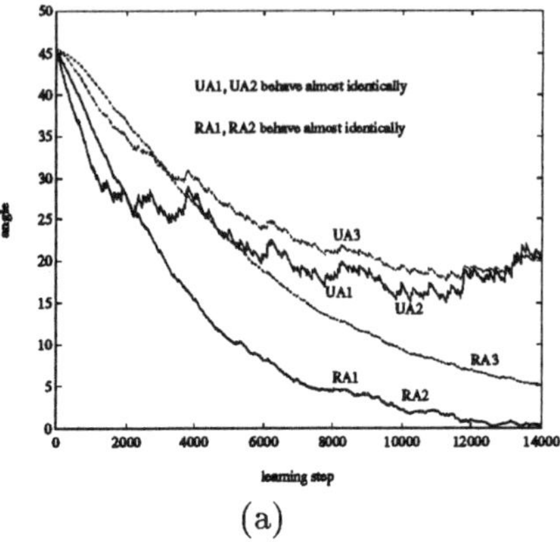

(a)

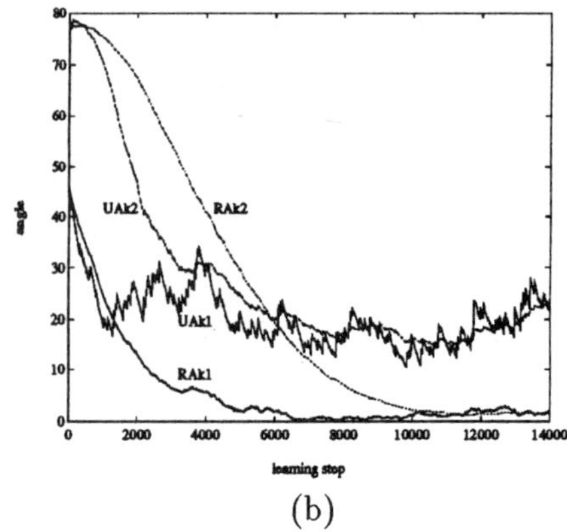

(b)

Figure 2: The learning curves obtained in the comparative experiments for principal component vectors. (a) for the first principal component vector, $RA1, RA2, RA3$ denote the robust rules eq.(19), eq.(16) and eq.(17) respectively, and $UA1, UA2, UA3$ denote the rules eq.(1), eq.(2) and eq.(3) respectively. The horizontal axis denotes the learning steps, and the vertical axis is $\theta_{\vec{m}(t)\vec{\phi}_{p1}}$ with $\theta_{\vec{x},\vec{y}}$ denoting the acute angle between $\vec{x}$ and $\vec{y}$. (b) for the first two principal component vectors, by the robust rule eq.(20) and its unrobust counterpart GHA. $UAk1$, $UAk2$ denote the learning curves of angles $\theta_{\vec{m}_1(t)\vec{\phi}_{p1}}$ and $\theta_{\vec{m}_2(t)\vec{\phi}_{p2}}$ respectively, obtained by GHA . $RAk1$, $RAk2$ denote the learning curves of the angles obtained by using the robust rule eq.(20). In both (a) & (b), $\vec{\phi}_{pj}, j = 1, 2$ is the correct 1st and 2nd principal component vector respectively.

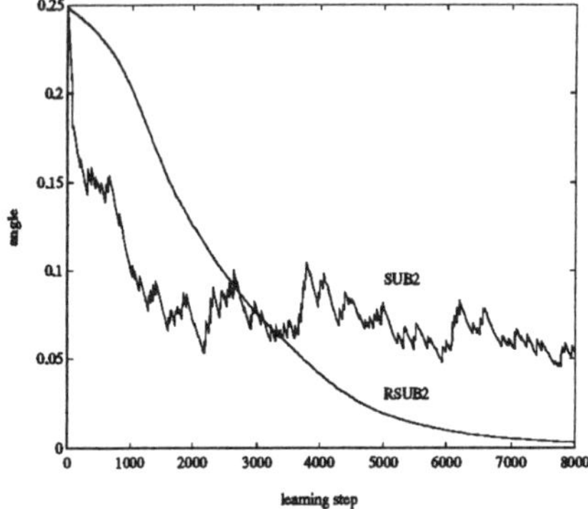

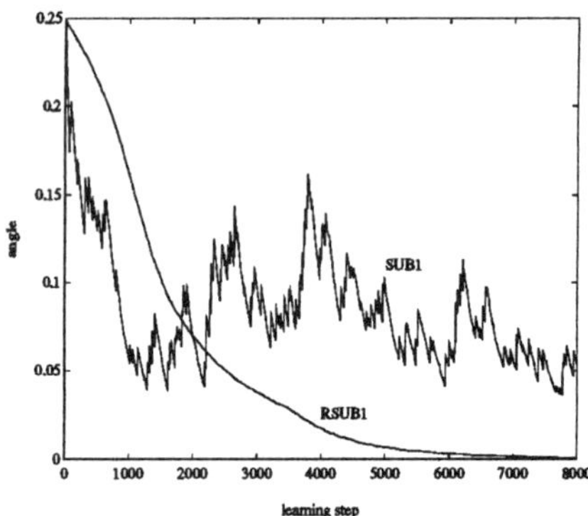

Figure 3: The learning curves obtained in the comparative experiments for for solving the 2-dimensional principal subspace. Each learning curve expresses the change of the residual $e_r(t) = \sum_{j=1}^{2} \|\vec{m}_j(t) - \sum_{r=1}^{2} (\vec{m}_j(t)^T \vec{\phi}_{pr})\vec{\phi}_{pr}\|^2$ with learning steps. The smaller the residual, the closer the estimated principal subspace to the correct one. $SUB1$, $SUB2$ denote the unrobust rules eq.(22) and eq.(23) respectively, and $RSUB1$, $RSUB2$ denote the robust rules eq.(26) and eq.(25) respectively.

Bayesian Learning via Stochastic Dynamics

Radford M. Neal
Department of Computer Science
University of Toronto
Toronto, Ontario, Canada M5S 1A4

Abstract

The attempt to find a single "optimal" weight vector in conventional network training can lead to overfitting and poor generalization. Bayesian methods avoid this, without the need for a validation set, by averaging the outputs of many networks with weights sampled from the posterior distribution given the training data. This sample can be obtained by simulating a stochastic dynamical system that has the posterior as its stationary distribution.

1 CONVENTIONAL AND BAYESIAN LEARNING

I view neural networks as probabilistic models, and learning as statistical inference. Conventional network learning finds a single "optimal" set of network parameter values, corresponding to maximum likelihood or maximum penalized likelihood inference. Bayesian inference instead integrates the predictions of the network over all possible values of the network parameters, weighting each parameter set by its posterior probability in light of the training data.

1.1 NEURAL NETWORKS AS PROBABILISTIC MODELS

Consider a network taking a vector of real-valued inputs, $\mathbf{x}$, and producing a vector of real-valued outputs, $\overline{\mathbf{y}}$, perhaps computed using hidden units. Such a network architecture corresponds to a function, f, with $\overline{\mathbf{y}} = f(\mathbf{x}, \mathbf{w})$, where $\mathbf{w}$ is a vector of connection weights. If we assume the observed outputs, $\mathbf{y}$, are equal to $\overline{\mathbf{y}}$ plus Gaussian noise of standard deviation σ, the network defines the conditional probability for an observed output vector given an input vector as follows:

$$P(\mathbf{y} \mid \mathbf{x}, \sigma) \;\propto\; \exp(-|\mathbf{y} - f(\mathbf{x}, \mathbf{w})|^2 / 2\sigma^2) \tag{1}$$

The probability of the outputs in a training set $(\mathbf{x}_1, \mathbf{y}_1), \ldots, (\mathbf{x}_n, \mathbf{y}_n)$ given this fixed noise level is therefore

$$P(\mathbf{y}_1, \ldots, \mathbf{y}_n \mid \mathbf{x}_1, \ldots, \mathbf{x}_n, \sigma) \;\propto\; \exp(-\sum_c |\mathbf{y}_c - f(\mathbf{x}_c, \mathbf{w})|^2 / 2\sigma^2) \tag{2}$$

Often σ is unknown. A Bayesian approach to handling this is to assign σ a vague prior distribution and then integrating it away, giving the following probability for the training set (see (Buntine and Weigend, 1991) or (Neal, 1992) for details):

$$P(\mathbf{y}_1, \ldots, \mathbf{y}_n \mid \mathbf{x}_1, \ldots, \mathbf{x}_n) \;\propto\; \left(s_0 + \sum_c |\mathbf{y}_c - f(\mathbf{x}_c, \mathbf{w})|^2\right)^{-\frac{m_0 + nD}{2}} \tag{3}$$

where s_0 and m_0 are parameters of the prior for σ.

1.2 CONVENTIONAL LEARNING

Conventional backpropagation learning tries to find the weight vector that assigns the highest probability to the training data, or equivalently, that minimizes minus the log probability of the training data. When σ is assumed known, we can use (2) to obtain the following objective function to minimize:

$$M(\mathbf{w}) \;=\; \sum_c |\mathbf{y}_c - f(\mathbf{x}_c, \mathbf{w})|^2 \,/\, 2\sigma^2 \tag{4}$$

When σ is unknown, we can instead minimize the following, derived from (3):

$$M(\mathbf{w}) \;=\; \frac{m_0 + nD}{2} \log\left(s_0 + \sum_c |\mathbf{y}_c - f(\mathbf{x}_c, \mathbf{w})|^2\right) \tag{5}$$

Conventional learning often leads to the network *overfitting* the training data — modeling the noise, rather than the true regularities. This can be alleviated by stopping learning when the the performance of the network on a separate *validation* set begins to worsen, rather than improve. Another way to avoid overfitting is to include a *weight decay* term in the objective function, as follows:

$$M'(\mathbf{w}) \;=\; \lambda |\mathbf{w}|^2 \;+\; M(\mathbf{w}) \tag{6}$$

Here, the data fit term, $M(\mathbf{w})$, may come from either (4) or (5). We must somehow find an appropriate value for λ, perhaps, again, using a separate validation set.

1.3 BAYESIAN LEARNING AND PREDICTION

Unlike conventional training, Bayesian learning does not look for a single "optimal" set of network weights. Instead, the training data is used to find the *posterior* probability distribution over weight vectors. Predictions for future cases are made by averaging the outputs obtained with all possible weight vectors, with each contributing in proportion to its posterior probability.

To obtain the posterior, we must first define a *prior* distribution for weight vectors. We might, for example, give each weight a Gaussian prior of standard deviation ω:

$$P(\mathbf{w}) \;\propto\; \exp(-|\mathbf{w}|^2 / 2\omega^2) \tag{7}$$

We can then obtain the posterior distribution over weight vectors given the training cases $(\mathbf{x}_1, \mathbf{y}_1), \ldots, (\mathbf{x}_n, \mathbf{y}_n)$ using Bayes' Theorem:

$$P(\mathbf{w} \mid (\mathbf{x}_1, \mathbf{y}_1), \ldots, (\mathbf{x}_n, \mathbf{y}_n)) \;\propto\; P(\mathbf{w})\, P(\mathbf{y}_1, \ldots, \mathbf{y}_n \mid \mathbf{x}_1, \ldots, \mathbf{x}_n,\, \mathbf{w}) \qquad (8)$$

Based on the training data, the best prediction for the output vector in a test case with input vector $\mathbf{x}_*$, assuming squared-error loss, is

$$\widehat{\mathbf{y}}_* \;=\; \int f(\mathbf{x}_*, \mathbf{w})\, P(\mathbf{w} \mid (\mathbf{x}_1, \mathbf{y}_1), \ldots, (\mathbf{x}_n, \mathbf{y}_n))\, d\mathbf{w} \qquad (9)$$

A full predictive distribution for the outputs in the test case can also be obtained, quantifying the uncertainty in the above prediction.

2 INTEGRATION BY MONTE CARLO METHODS

Integrals such as that of (9) are difficult to evaluate. Buntine and Weigend (1991) and MacKay (1992) approach this problem by approximating the posterior distribution by a Gaussian. Instead, I evaluate such integrals using Monte Carlo methods.

If we randomly select weight vectors, $\mathbf{w}_0, \ldots, \mathbf{w}_{N-1}$, each distributed according to the posterior, the prediction for a test case can be found by approximating the integral of (9) by the average output of networks with these weights:

$$\widehat{\mathbf{y}}_* \;\approx\; \frac{1}{N} \sum_t f(\mathbf{x}_*, \mathbf{w}_t) \qquad (10)$$

This formula is valid even if the $\mathbf{w}_t$ are dependent, though a larger sample may then be needed to achieve a given error bound. Such a sample can be obtained by simulating an ergodic Markov chain that has the posterior as its stationary distribution. The early part of the chain, before the stationary distribution has been reached, is discarded. Subsequent vectors are used to estimate the integral.

2.1 FORMULATING THE PROBLEM IN TERMS OF ENERGY

Consider the general problem of obtaining a sample of (dependent) vectors, $\mathbf{q}_t$, with probabilities given by $P(\mathbf{q})$. For Bayesian network learning, $\mathbf{q}$ will be the weight vector, or other parameters from which the weights can be obtained, and the distribution of interest will be the posterior.

It will be convenient to express this probability distribution in terms of a *potential energy* function, $E(\mathbf{q})$, chosen so that

$$P(\mathbf{q}) \;\propto\; \exp(-E(\mathbf{q})) \qquad (11)$$

A *momentum* vector, $\mathbf{p}$, of the same dimensions as $\mathbf{q}$, is also introduced, and defined to have a *kinetic energy* of $\frac{1}{2}|\mathbf{p}|^2$. The sum of the potential and kinetic energies is the *Hamiltonian*:

$$H(\mathbf{q}, \mathbf{p}) \;=\; E(\mathbf{q}) \;+\; \tfrac{1}{2}|\mathbf{p}|^2 \qquad (12)$$

From the Hamiltonian, we define a joint probability distribution over $\mathbf{q}$ and $\mathbf{p}$ (*phase space*) as follows:

$$P(\mathbf{q}, \mathbf{p}) \;\propto\; \exp(-H(\mathbf{q}, \mathbf{p})) \qquad (13)$$

The marginal distribution for $\mathbf{q}$ in (13) is that of (11), from which we wish to sample.

We can therefore proceed by sampling from this joint distribution for $\mathbf{q}$ and $\mathbf{p}$, and then just ignoring the values obtained for $\mathbf{p}$.

2.2 HAMILTONIAN DYNAMICS

Sampling from the distribution (13) can be split into two subproblems — first, to sample *uniformly* from a surface where H, and hence the probability, is constant, and second, to visit points of differing H with the correct probabilities. The solutions to these subproblems can then be interleaved to give an overall solution.

The first subproblem can be solved by simulating the *Hamiltonian dynamics* of the system, in which $\mathbf{q}$ and $\mathbf{p}$ evolve through a fictitious time, τ, according to the following equations:

$$\frac{d\mathbf{q}}{d\tau} = \frac{\partial H}{\partial \mathbf{p}} = \mathbf{p}, \qquad \frac{d\mathbf{p}}{d\tau} = -\frac{\partial H}{\partial \mathbf{q}} = -\nabla E(\mathbf{q}) \tag{14}$$

This dynamics leaves H constant, and preserves the volumes of regions of phase space. It therefore visits points on a surface of constant H with uniform probability.

When simulating this dynamics, some discrete approximation must be used. The *leapfrog* method exactly maintains the preservation of phase space volume. Given a size for the time step, ϵ, an iteration of the leapfrog method goes as follows:

$$\begin{aligned} \mathbf{p}(\tau+\epsilon/2) &= \mathbf{p}(\tau) - (\epsilon/2)\nabla E(\mathbf{q}(\tau)) \\ \mathbf{q}(\tau+\epsilon) &= \mathbf{q}(\tau) + \epsilon\,\mathbf{p} \\ \mathbf{p}(\tau+\epsilon) &= \mathbf{p}(\tau+\epsilon) - (\epsilon/2)\nabla E(\mathbf{q}(\tau+\epsilon)) \end{aligned} \tag{15}$$

2.3 THE STOCHASTIC DYNAMICS METHOD

To create a Markov chain that converges to the distribution of (13), we must interleave leapfrog iterations, which keep H (approximately) constant, with steps that can change H. It is convenient for the latter to affect only $\mathbf{p}$, since it enters into H in a simple way. This general approach is due to Anderson (1980).

I use stochastic steps of the following form to change H:

$$\mathbf{p}' = \alpha\mathbf{p} + (1-\alpha^2)^{1/2}\mathbf{n} \tag{16}$$

where $0 \leq \alpha < 1$, and $\mathbf{n}$ is a random vector with components picked independently from Gaussian distributions of mean zero and standard deviation one. One can show that these steps leave the distribution of (13) invariant. Alternating these stochastic steps with dynamical leapfrog steps will therefore sample values for $\mathbf{q}$ and $\mathbf{p}$ with close to the desired probabilities. In so far as the discretized dynamics does not keep H exactly constant, however, there will be some degree of bias, which will be eliminated only in the limit as ϵ goes to zero.

It is best to use a value of α close to one, as this reduces the random walk aspect of the dynamics. If the random term in (16) is omitted, the procedure is equivalent to ordinary batch mode backpropagation learning with momentum.

2.4 THE HYBRID MONTE CARLO METHOD

The bias introduced into the stochastic dynamics method by using an approximation to the dynamics is eliminated in the Hybrid Monte Carlo method of Duane, Kennedy, Pendleton, and Roweth (1987).

This method is a variation on the algorithm of Metropolis, *et al* (1953), which generates a Markov chain by considering randomly-selected changes to the state. A change is always accepted if it lowers the energy (H), or leaves it unchanged. If it increases the energy, it is accepted with probability $\exp(-\Delta H)$, and is rejected otherwise, with the old state then being repeated.

In the Hybrid Monte Carlo method, candidate changes are produced by picking a random value for $\mathbf{p}$ from its distribution given by (13) and then performing some predetermined number of leapfrog steps. If the leapfrog method were exact, H would be unchanged, and these changes would always be accepted. Since the method is actually only approximate, H sometimes increases, and changes are sometimes rejected, exactly cancelling the bias introduced by the approximation.

Of course, if the errors are very large, the acceptance probability will be very low, and it will take a long time to reach and explore the stationary distribution. To avoid this, we need to choose a step size (ϵ) that is small enough.

3 RESULTS ON A TEST PROBLEM

I use the "robot arm" problem of MacKay (1992) for testing. The task is to learn the mapping from two real-valued inputs, x_1 and x_2, to two real-valued outputs, y_1 and y_2, given by

$$\bar{y}_1 = 2.0\cos(x_1) + 1.3\cos(x_1 + x_2) \tag{17}$$

$$\bar{y}_2 = 2.0\sin(x_1) + 1.3\sin(x_1 + x_2) \tag{18}$$

Gaussian noise of mean zero and standard deviation 0.05 is added to $(\bar{y}_1, \bar{y}_2)$ to give the observed position, (y_1, y_2). The training and test sets each consist of 200 cases, with x_1 picked randomly from the ranges $[-1.932, -0.453]$ and $[+0.453, +1.932]$, and x_2 from the range $[0.534, 3.142]$.

A network with 16 sigmoidal hidden units was used. The output units were linear. Like MacKay, I group weights into three categories — input to hidden, bias to hidden, and hidden/bias to output. MacKay gives separate priors to weights in each category, finding an appropriate value of ω for each. I fix ω to one, but multiply each weight by a scale factor associated with its category before using it, giving an equivalent effect. For conventional training with weight decay, I use an analogous scheme with three weight decay constants (λ in (6)).

In all cases, I assume that the true value of σ is not known. I therefore use (3) for the training set probability, and (5) for the data fit term in conventional training. I set $s_0 = m_0 = 0.1$, which corresponds to a very vague prior for σ.

3.1 PERFORMANCE OF CONVENTIONAL LEARNING

Conventional backpropagation learning was tested on the robot arm problem to gauge how difficult it is to obtain good generalization with standard methods.

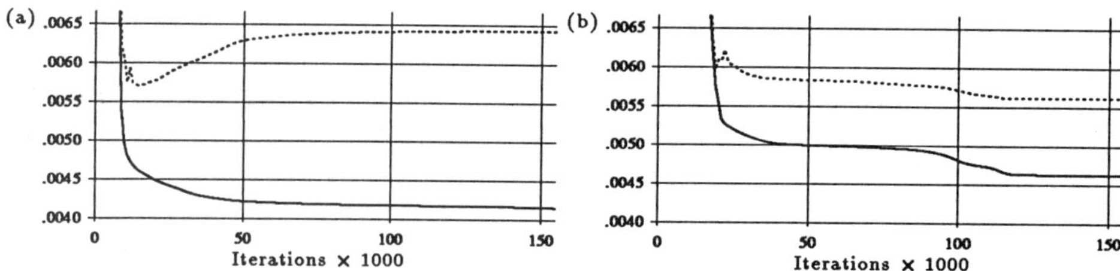

Figure 1: Conventional backpropagation learning — (a) with no weight decay, (b) with carefully-chosen weight decay constants. The solid lines give the squared error on the training data, the dotted lines the squared error on the test data.

Fig. 1(a) shows results obtained without using weight decay. Error on the test set declined initially, but then increased with further training. To achieve good results, the point where the test error reaches its minimum would have to be identified using a separate validation set.

Fig. 1(b) shows results using good weight decay constants, one for each category of weights, taken from the Bayesian runs described below. In this case there is no need to stop learning early, but finding the proper weight decay constants by non-Bayesian methods would be a problem. Again, a validation set seems necessary, as well as considerable computation.

Use of a validation set is wasteful, since data that could otherwise be included in the training set must be excluded. Standard techniques for avoiding this, such as "N-fold" cross-validation, are difficult to apply to neural networks.

3.2 PERFORMANCE OF BAYESIAN LEARNING

Bayesian learning was first tested using the unbiased Hybrid Monte Carlo method. The parameter vector in the simulations ($\mathbf{q}$) consisted of the unscaled network weights together with the scale factors for the three weight categories. The actual weight vector ($\mathbf{w}$) was obtained by multiplying each unscaled weight by the scale factor for its category.

Each Hybrid Monte Carlo run consisted of 500 Metropolis steps. For each step, a trajectory consisting of 1000 leapfrog iterations with $\epsilon = 0.00012$ was computed, and accepted or rejected based on the change in H at its end-point. Each run therefore required 500,000 batch gradient evaluations, and took approximately four hours on a machine rated at about 25 MIPS.

Fig. 2(a) shows the training and test error for the early portion of one Hybrid Monte Carlo run. After initially declining, these values fluctuate about an average. Though not apparent in the figure, some quantities (notably the scale factors) require a hundred or more steps to reach their final distribution. The first 250 steps of each run were therefore discarded as not being from the stationary distribution.

Fig. 2(b) shows the training and test set errors produced by networks with weight vectors taken from the last 250 steps of the same run. Also shown is the error on the test set using the *average* of the outputs of all these networks — that is, the estimate given by (10) for the Bayesian prediction of (9). For the run shown, this

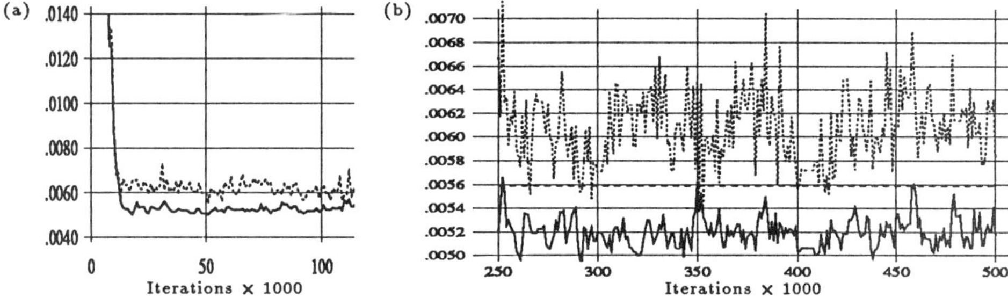

Figure 2: Bayesian learning using Hybrid Monte Carlo — (a) early portion of run, (b) last 250 iterations. The solid lines give the squared error on the training set, the dotted lines the squared error on the test set, for individual networks. The dashed line in (b) is the test error when using the average of the outputs of all 250 networks.

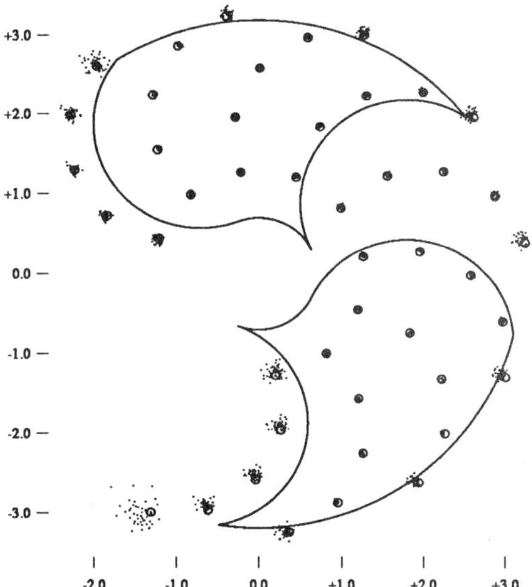

Figure 3: Predictive distribution for outputs. The two regions from which training data was drawn are outlined. Circles indicate the true, noise-free outputs for a grid of cases in the input space. The dots in the vicinity of each circle (often piled on top of it) are the outputs of every fifth network from the last 250 iterations of a Hybrid Monte Carlo run.

test set error using averaged outputs is 0.00559, which is (slightly) better than any results obtained using conventional training. Note that with Bayesian training no validation set is necessary. The analogues of the weight decay constants — the weight scale factors — are found during the course of the simulation.

Another advantage of the Bayesian approach is that it can provide an indication of how uncertain the predictions for test cases are. Fig. 3 demonstrates this. As one would expect, the uncertainty is greater for test cases with inputs outside the region where training data was supplied.

3.3 STOCHASTIC DYNAMICS VS. HYBRID MONTE CARLO

The uncorrected stochastic dynamics method will have some degree of systematic bias, due to inexact simulation of the dynamics. Is the amount of bias introduced of any practical importance, however?

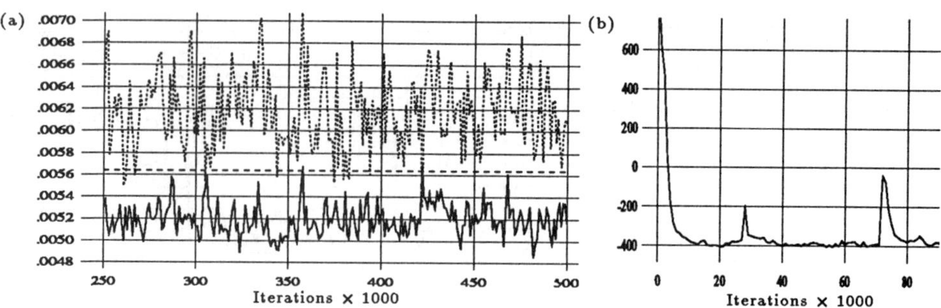

Figure 4: Bayesian learning using uncorrected stochastic dynamics — (a) Training and test error for the last 250 iterations of a run with $\epsilon = 0.00012$, (b) potential energy (E) for a run with $\epsilon = 0.00030$. Note the two peaks where the dynamics became unstable.

To help answer this question, the stochastic dynamics method was run with parameters analogous to those used in the Hybrid Monte Carlo runs. The step size of $\epsilon = 0.00012$ used in those runs was chosen to be as large as possible while keeping the number of trajectories rejected low (about 10%). A smaller step size would not give competitive results, so this value was used for the stochastic dynamics runs as well. A value of 0.999 for α in (16) was chosen as being (loosely) equivalent to the use of trajectories 1000 iterations long in the Hybrid Monte Carlo runs.

The results shown in Fig. 4(a) are comparable to those obtained using Hybrid Monte Carlo in Fig. 2(b). Fig. 4(b) shows that with a larger step size the uncorrected stochastic dynamics method becomes unstable. Large step sizes also cause problems for the Hybrid Monte Carlo method, however, as they lead to high rejection rates.

The Hybrid Monte Carlo method may be the more robust choice in some circumstances, but uncorrected stochastic dynamics can also give good results. As it is simpler, the stochastic dynamics method may be better for hardware implementation, and is a more plausible starting point for any attempt to relate Bayesian methods to biology. Numerous other variations on these methods are possible as well, some of which are discussed in (Neal, 1992).

References

Andersen, H. C. (1980) "Molecular dynamics simulations at constant pressure and/or temperature", *Journal of Chemical Physics*, vol. 72, pp. 2384-2393.

Buntine, W. L. and Weigend, A. S. (1991) "Bayesian back-propagation", *Complex Systems*, vol. 5, pp. 603-643.

Duane, S., Kennedy, A. D., Pendleton, B. J., and Roweth, D. (1987) "Hybrid Monte Carlo", *Physics Letters B*, vol. 195, pp. 216-222.

MacKay, D. J. C. (1992) "A practical Bayesian framework for backpropagation networks", *Neural Computation*, vol. 4, pp. 448-472.

Metropolis, N., Rosenbluth, A. W., Rosenbluth, M. N., Teller, A. H., and Teller, E. (1953) "Equation of state calculations by fast computing machines", *Journal of Chemical Physics*, vol. 21, pp. 1087-1092.

Neal, R. M. (1992) "Bayesian training of backpropagation networks by the hybrid Monte Carlo method", CRG-TR-92-1, Dept. of Computer Science, University of Toronto.

Information, prediction, and query by committee

Yoav Freund
Computer and Information Sciences
University of California, Santa Cruz
yoav@cse.ucsc.edu

H. Sebastian Seung
AT&T Bell Laboratories
Murray Hill, New Jersey
seung@physics.att.com

Eli Shamir
Institute of Computer Science
Hebrew University, Jerusalem
shamir@cs.huji.ac.il

Naftali Tishby
Institute of Computer Science and
Center for Neural Computation
Hebrew University, Jerusalem
tishby@cs.huji.ac.il

Abstract

We analyze the "query by committee" algorithm, a method for filtering informative queries from a random stream of inputs. We show that if the two-member committee algorithm achieves information gain with positive lower bound, then the prediction error decreases exponentially with the number of queries. We show that, in particular, this exponential decrease holds for query learning of thresholded smooth functions.

1 Introduction

For the most part, research on supervised learning has utilized a *random input* paradigm, in which the learner is both trained and tested on examples drawn at random from the same distribution. In contrast, in the *query* paradigm, the learner is given the power to ask questions, rather than just passively accept examples. What does the learner gain from this additional power? Can it attain the same prediction performance with fewer examples?

Most work on query learning has been in the *constructive* paradigm, in which the learner *constructs* inputs on which to query the teacher. For some classes of boolean functions and finite automata that are not PAC learnable from random inputs, there are algorithms that can successfully PAC learn using "membership queries"[Val84, Ang88]. Query algorithms are also known for neural network learning[Bau91]. The general relevance of these positive results is unclear, since each is specific to the learning of a particular concept class. Moreover, as shown by Eisenberg and Rivest in [ER90], constructed membership queries cannot be used to reduce the number of examples required for PAC learning. That is because *random* examples provide the learner with information not only about the correct mapping, but also about the distribution of future test inputs. This information is lacking if the learner must construct inputs.

In the statistical literature, some attempt has been made towards a more fundamental understanding of query learning, there called "sequential design of experiments."[1]. It has been suggested that the optimal experiment (query) is the one with maximal Shannon information[Lin56, Fed72, Mac92]. Similar suggestions have been made in the perceptron learning literature[KR90]. Although the use of an entropic measure seems sensible, its relationship with prediction error has remained unclear.

Understanding this relationship is a main goal of the present work, and enables us to prove a positive result about the power of queries. Our work is derived within the *query filtering* paradigm, rather than the constructive paradigm. In this paradigm, proposed by [CAL90], the learner is given access to a stream of inputs drawn at random from a distribution. The learner sees every input, but chooses whether or not to query the teacher for the label. This paradigm is realistic in contexts where it is cheap to get unlabeled examples, but expensive to label them. It avoids the problems with the constructive paradigm described in [ER90] because it gives the learner free access to the input distribution.

In [CAL90] there are several suggestions for query filters together with some empirical tests of their performance on simple problems. Seung et al.[SOS92] have suggested a filter called "query by committee," and analytically calculated its performance for some perceptron-type learning problems. For these problems, they found that the prediction error decreases exponentially fast in the number of queries. In this work we present a more complete and general analysis of query by committee, and show that such an exponential decrease is guaranteed for a general class of learning problems.

We work in a Bayesian model of concept learning[HKS91] in which the target concept f is chosen from a concept class C according to some prior distribution $\mathcal{P}$. The concept class consists of boolean-valued functions defined on some input space X. An example is an input $x \in X$ along with its label $l = f(x)$. For any set of examples, we define the *version space* to be the set of all hypotheses in C that are consistent with the examples. As each example arrives, it eliminates inconsistent hypotheses, and the probability of the version space (with respect to $\mathcal{P}$) is reduced. The *instantaneous information gain* (i.i.g.) is defined as the logarithm of the ratio

[1]The paradigm of (non-sequential) experimental design is analogous to what might be called "batch query learning," in which all of the inputs are chosen by the learner before a single label is received from the teacher

of version space probabilities before and after receiving the example. In this work, we study a particular kind of learner, the Gibbs learner, which chooses a hypothesis at random from the version space. In Bayesian terms, it chooses from the posterior distribution on the concept class, which is the restriction of the prior distribution to the version space.

If an *unlabeled* input x is provided, the expected i.i.g. of its label can be defined by taking the expectation with respect to the probabilities of the unknown label. The input x divides the version space into two parts, those hypotheses that label it as a positive example, and those that label it negative. Let the *probability ratios* of these two parts to the whole be χ and $1-\chi$. Then the expected i.i.g. is

$$\mathcal{H}(\chi) = -\chi \log \chi - (1-\chi)\log(1-\chi) \ . \tag{1}$$

The goal of the learner is to minimize its *prediction error*, its probability of error on an input drawn from the *input distribution* $\mathcal{D}$. In the case of random input learning, every input x is drawn independently from $\mathcal{D}$. Since the expected i.i.g. tends to zero (see [HKS91]), it seems that random input learning is inefficient. We will analyze query construction and filtering algorithms that are designed to achieve high information gain.

The rest of the paper is organized as follows. In section 2 we exhibit query construction algorithms for the high-low game. The bisection algorithm for high-low illustrates that constructing queries with high information gain can improve prediction performance. But the failure of bisection for multi-dimensional high-low exposes a deficiency of the query construction paradigm. In section 3 we define the query filtering paradigm, and discuss the relation between information gain and prediction error for queries filtered by a committee of Gibbs learners. In section 4 lower bounds for information gain are proved for the learning of some nontrivial concept classes. Section 5 is a summary and discussion of open problems.

2 Query construction and the high-low game

In this section, we give examples of query construction algorithms for the high-low game and its generalizations. In the high-low game, the concept class C consists of functions of the form

$$f_w(x) = \begin{cases} 1, & w < x \\ 0, & w > x \end{cases} , \tag{2}$$

where $0 \le w, x \le 1$. Thus both X and C are naturally mapped to the interval $[0,1]$. Both $\mathcal{P}$, the prior distribution for the parameter w, and $\mathcal{D}$, the input distribution for x, are assumed to be uniform on $[0,1]$. Given any sequence of examples, the version space is $[x_L, x_R]$ where x_L is the largest negative example and x_R is the smallest positive example. The posterior distribution is uniform in the interval $[x_L, x_R]$ and vanishes outside.

The prediction error of a Gibbs learner is $\Pr(f_v(x) \neq f_w(x))$ where x is chosen from $\mathcal{D}$, and v and w from the posterior distribution. It is easy to show that $\Pr(f_v(x) \neq f_w(x)) = (x_R - x_L)/3$. Since the prediction error is proportional to the version space volume, always querying on the midpoint $(x_R + x_L)/2$ causes the prediction error after m queries to decrease like 2^{-m}. This is in contrast to the case of random input learning, for which the prediction error decreases like $1/m$.

The strategy of bisection is clearly maximally informative, since it achieves $\mathcal{H}(1/2) = 1$ bit per query, and can be applied to the learning of any concept class. Naive intuition suggests that it should lead to rapidly decreasing prediction error, but this is not necessarily so. Generalizing the high-low game to d dimensions provides a simple counterexample. The target concepts are functions of the form

$$f_{\vec{w}}(i, x) = \begin{cases} 1, & w_i < x \\ 0, & w_i > x \end{cases} . \tag{3}$$

The prior distribution of $\vec{w}$ is uniform on the concept class $C = [0,1]^d$. The inputs are pairs (i, x), where i takes on the values $1, \ldots, d$ with equal probability, and x is uniformly distributed on $[0,1]$. Since this is basically d concurrent high-low games (one for each component of $\vec{w}$), the version space is a product of subintervals of $[0,1]$. For $d = 2$, the concept class is the unit square, and the version space is a rectangle. The prediction error is proportional to the perimeter of the rectangle. A sequence of queries with $i = 1$ can bisect the rectangle along one dimension, yielding 1 bit per query, while the perimeter tends to a finite constant. Hence the prediction error tends to a finite constant, in spite of the maximal information gain.

3 The committee filter: information and prediction

The dilemma of the previous section was that constructing queries with high information gain does not necessarily lead to rapidly decreasing prediction error. This is because the constructed query distribution may have nothing to do with the input distribution $\mathcal{D}$. This deficiency can be avoided in a different paradigm in which the query distribution is created by filtering $\mathcal{D}$. Suppose that the learner receives a stream of unlabeled inputs $x_1, x_2, \ldots$ drawn independently from the distribution $\mathcal{D}$. After seeing each input x_i, the learner has the choice of whether or not to query the teacher for the correct label $l_i = f(x_i)$.

In [SOS92] it was suggested to filter queries that cause disagreement in a committee of Gibbs learners. In this paper we concentrate on committees with two members. The algorithm is:

Query by a committee of two

Repeat the following until n queries have been accepted

1. Draw an unlabeled input $x \in X$ at random from $\mathcal{D}$.
2. Select two hypotheses h_1, h_2 from the posterior distribution. In other words, pick two hypotheses that are consistent with the labeled examples seen so far.
3. If $h_1(x) \neq h_2(x)$ then query the teacher for the label of x, and add it to the training set.

The committee filter tends to select examples that split the version space into two parts of comparable size, because if one of the parts contains most of the version space, then the probability that the two hypotheses will disagree is very small. More precisely, if x cuts the version space into parts of size χ and $1 - \chi$, then the probability of accepting x is $2\chi(1 - \chi)$. One can show that the i.i.g. of the queries is lower bounded by that obtained from random inputs.

In this section, we assume something stronger: that the expected i.i.g. of the committee has positive lower bound. Conditions under which this assumption holds will be discussed in the next section. The bound implies that the cumulative information gain increases linearly with the number of queries n. But the version space resulting from *the queries alone* must be larger than the version space that would result if the learner knew *all of the labels*. Hence the cumulative information gain from the queries is upper bounded by the cumulative information gain which would be obtained from the labels of all m inputs, which behaves like $O(d \log \frac{m}{d})$ for a concept class C with finite VC dimension d ([HKS91]). These $O(n)$ and $O(\log m)$ behaviors are consistent only if the gap between consecutive queries increases exponentially fast. This argument is depicted in Figure 1.

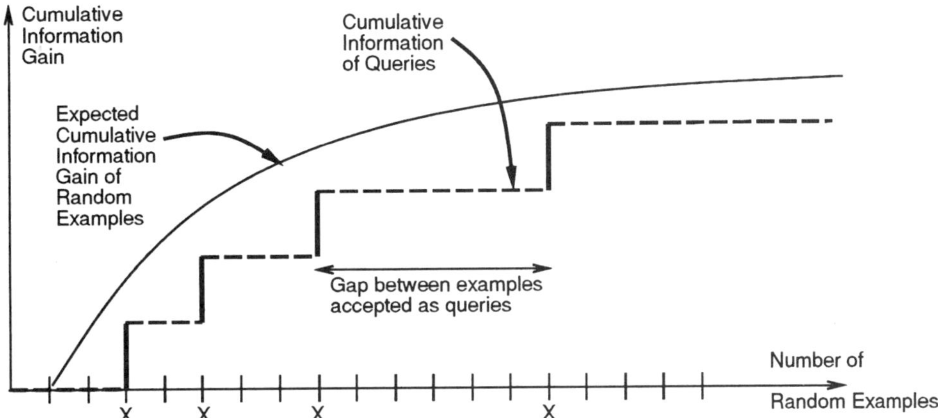

Figure 1: Each tag on the x axis denotes a random example in a specific typical sequence. The symbol X under a tag denotes the fact that the example was chosen as a query.

Recall that an input is accepted if it provokes disagreement between the two Gibbs learners that constitute the committee. Thus a large gap between consecutive queries is equivalent to a small *probability* of disagreement. But in our Bayesian framework the probability of disagreement between two Gibbs learners is equal to the probability of disagreement between a Gibbs learner and the teacher, which is the expected prediction error. Thus the prediction error is exponentially small as a function of the number of queries. The exact statement of the result is given below, a detailed proof of which will be published elsewhere.

Theorem 1 *Suppose that a concept class C has VC-dimension $d < \infty$ and the expected information gained by the two member committee algorithm is bounded by $c > 0$, independent of the query number and of the previous queries. Then the probability that one of the two committee members makes a mistake on a randomly chosen example with respect to a randomly chosen $f \in C$ is bounded by*

$$(3 + O(e^{-c_1 n}))\frac{n}{d}\exp\left(-\frac{c}{2(d+1)}n\right) \tag{4}$$

for some constant $c_1 > 0$, where n is the number of queries asked so far.

4 Lower bounds on the information gain

Theorem 1 is applicable to learning problems for which the committee achieves i.i.g. with positive lower bound. A simple case of this is the d-dimensional high-low game of section 2, for which the i.i.g. is $7/(12 \ln 2) \approx 0.84$, independent of dimension. This exact result is simple to derive because the high-low game is geometrically trivial: all version spaces are similar to each other. In general, the shape of the version space is more complex, and depends on the randomness of the examples. Nevertheless, the expected i.i.g. can be lower bounded even for some learning problems with nontrivial version space geometry.

4.1 The information gain for convex version spaces

Define a class of functions $f_{\vec{w}}$ by

$$f_{\vec{w}}(\vec{x}, t) = \begin{cases} 1, & \vec{w} \cdot \vec{x} > t \ , \\ 0, & \vec{w} \cdot \vec{x} < t \ . \end{cases} \tag{5}$$

The vector $\vec{w} \in \mathbf{R}^d$ is drawn at random from a prior distribution $\mathcal{P}$, which is uniform over some convex body contained in the unit ball. The distribution of inputs $(\vec{x}, t) \in B^d \times [-1, 1]$, is a product of any distribution over B^d (the unit ball centered at the origin) and the uniform distribution over $[-1, +1]$. Since each example defines a plane in the concept space, all version spaces for this problem are convex. We show that there is a uniform lower bound on the expected i.i.g. for any convex version space when a two member committee filters inputs drawn from $\mathcal{D}$. In the next paragraphs we sketch our proof, the full details of which shall appear elsewhere.

In fact, we prove a stronger statement, a bound on the expected i.i.g. for any fixed $\vec{x}$. Fix $\vec{x}$ and define $\chi(t)$ as the fraction of the version space volume for which $\vec{x} \cdot \vec{w} < t$. Since the probability of filtering a query at t is proportional to $2\chi(t)[1 - \chi(t)]$, the expected i.i.g. is given by

$$\mathcal{I}[\chi(t)] = \frac{\int_{-1}^{1} 2\chi(t)[1 - \chi(t)]\mathcal{H}(\chi(t))dt}{\int_{-1}^{1} 2\chi(t)[1 - \chi(t)]dt} \ . \tag{6}$$

In the following, it is more convenient to define the expected i.i.g. as a functional of $r(t) = \sqrt[d-1]{d\chi/dt}$, which is the radius function of the body of revolution with equivalent cross sectional area $d\chi/dt$. Using the Brunn-Minkowski inequality, it can be shown that any convex body has a concave radius function $r(t)$.

We have found a set of four transformations of $r(t)$ which decrease $\mathcal{I}[r]$. The only concave function that is a fixed point of these transformations is (up to volume preserving rescaling transformations):

$$r^*(t) = \sqrt[d-1]{d/2}\,(1 - |t|) \ .$$

This corresponds to the body constructed by placing two cones base to base with their axes pointing along $\vec{x}$. We can calculate $\mathcal{I}[r^*]$ explicitly for each dimension d. As the dimension of the space increases to infinity this value converges from above to a strictly positive value which is $1/9 + 7/(18 \ln 2) \approx 0.672$ bits, which is surprisingly close to the upper bound of 1 bit.

4.2 The information gain for thresholded continuous functions

Consider a concept class consisting of functions of the form

$$f_{\vec{w}}(x) = \begin{cases} 1, & F(\vec{w}, \vec{x}) \geq 0 \ , \\ 0, & F(\vec{w}, \vec{x}) < 0 \ , \end{cases} \tag{7}$$

where $\vec{x} \in \mathbf{R}^l$, $\vec{w} \in \mathbf{R}^d$ and F is a smooth function of both $\vec{x}$ and $\vec{w}$. Random input learning of this type of concept class has been studied within the annealed approximation by [AFS92]. We assume that both $\mathcal{D}$ and $\mathcal{P}$ are described by density functions that are smooth and nonvanishing almost everywhere. Let the target concept be denoted by $f_{\vec{w}_0}(\vec{x})$. We now argue that in the small version space limit (reached in the limit of a large number of examples), the expected i.i.g. for query learning of this concept class has the same lower bound that was derived in section 4.1.

This is because a linear expansion of F becomes a good approximation in the version space,

$$F(\vec{w}, \vec{x}) = F(\vec{w}_0, \vec{x}) + (\vec{w} - \vec{w}_0) \cdot \nabla_{\vec{w}} F(\vec{w}_0, \vec{x}) \ . \tag{8}$$

Consequently, the version space is a convex body containing $\vec{w}_0$, each boundary of which is a hyperplane perpendicular to $\nabla_w F(\vec{w}_0, \vec{x})$ for some $\vec{x}$ in the training set. Because the prior density $\mathcal{P}$ is smooth and nonvanishing, the posterior becomes uniform on the version space.

From Eq. (8) it follows that a small version space is only cut by hyperplanes corresponding to inputs $\vec{x}$ for which $F(\vec{w}_0, \vec{x})$ is small. Such inputs can be parametrized by using coordinates on the decision boundary (the manifold in $\vec{x}$ space determined by $F(\vec{w}_0, \vec{x}) = 0$), plus an additional coordinate for the direction normal to the decision boundary. Varying the normal coordinate of $\vec{x}$ changes the distance of the corresponding hyperplane from $\vec{w}_0$, but does not change its direction (to lowest order). Hence each normal average is governed by the lower bound of 0.672 bits that was derived in section 4.1 for planar cuts along a fixed axis of a convex version space. The expected i.i.g. is obtained by integrating the normal average over the rest of the coordinates, and therefore is governed by the same lower bound.

5 Summary and open questions

In this work we have shown that the number of examples required for query learning behaves like the logarithm of the number required for random input learning. This result on the power of query filtering applies generally to concept classes for which the committee filter achieves information gain with positive lower bound, and in particular to concept classes consisting of thresholded smooth functions. A wide variety of learning architectures in common use fall in this group, including radial basis function networks and layered feedforward neural networks with smooth transfer functions. Our main unrealistic assumption is that the learned rule is assumed to be realizable and noiseless. Understanding how to filter queries for learning unrealizable or noisy concepts remains an important open problem.

Acknowledgments

Part of this research was done at the Hebrew University of Jerusalem. Freund, Shamir and Tishby would like to thank the US-Israel Binational Science Foundation (BSF) Grant no. 90-00189/2 for support of their work. We would also like to thank Yossi Azar and Manfred Opper for helpful discussions regarding this work.

References

[AFS92] S. Amari, N. Fujita, and S. Shinomoto. Four types of learning curves. *Neural Comput.*, 4:605–618, 1992.

[Ang88] D. Angluin. Queries and concept learning. *Machine Learning*, 2:319–342, 1988.

[Bau91] E. Baum. Neural net algorithms that learn in polynomial time from examples and queries. *IEEE Trans. Neural Networks*, 2:5–19, 1991.

[CAL90] D. Cohn, L. Atlas, and R. Ladner. Training connectionist networks with queries and selective sampling. *Advances in Neural Information Processing Systems*, 2:566–573, 1990.

[ER90] B. Eisenberg and R. Rivest. On the sample complexity of PAC-learning using random and chosen examples. In M. Fulk and J. Case, editors, *Proceedings of the Third Annual ACM Workshop on Computational Learning Theory*, pages 154–162, San Mateo, Ca, 1990. Kaufmann.

[Fed72] V. V. Fedorov. *Theory of Optimal Experiments.* Academic Press, New York, 1972.

[HKS91] D. Haussler, M. Kearns, and R. Schapire. Bounds on the sample complexity of Bayesian learning using information theory and the VC dimension. In M. K. Warmuth and L. G. Valiant, editors, *Proceedings of the Fourth Annual Workshop on Computational Learning Theory*, pages 61–74, San Mateo, CA, 1991. Kaufmann.

[KR90] W. Kinzel and P. Ruján. Improving a network generalization ability by selecting examples. *Europhys. Lett.*, 13:473–477, 1990.

[Lin56] D. V. Lindley. On a measure of the information provided by an experiment. *Ann. Math. Statist.*, 27:986–1005, 1956.

[Mac92] D. J. C. MacKay. *Bayesian methods for adaptive models.* PhD thesis, California Institute of Technology, Pasadena, 1992.

[SOS92] H. S. Seung, M. Opper, and H. Sompolinsky. Query by committee. In *Proceedings of the fifth annual ACM workshop on computational learning theory*, pages 287–294, New York, 1992. ACM.

[Val84] L. G. Valiant. A theory of the learnable. *Comm. ACM*, 27:1134–1142, 1984.

Synaptic Weight Noise During MLP Learning Enhances Fault-Tolerance, Generalisation and Learning Trajectory

Alan F. Murray
Dept. of Electrical Engineering
Edinburgh University
Scotland

Peter J. Edwards
Dept. of Electrical Engineering
Edinburgh University
Scotland

Abstract

We analyse the effects of analog noise on the synaptic arithmetic during MultiLayer Perceptron training, by expanding the cost function to include noise-mediated penalty terms. Predictions are made in the light of these calculations which suggest that fault tolerance, generalisation ability and learning trajectory should be improved by such noise-injection. Extensive simulation experiments on two distinct classification problems substantiate the claims. The results appear to be perfectly general for all training schemes where weights are adjusted incrementally, and have wide-ranging implications for all applications, particularly those involving "inaccurate" analog neural VLSI.

1 Introduction

This paper demonstrates both by consideration of the cost function and the learning equations, and by simulation experiments, that injection of random noise on to MLP weights during learning enhances fault-tolerance without additional supervision. We also show that the nature of the hidden node states and the learning trajectory is altered fundamentally, in a manner that improves training times and learning quality. The enhancement uses the mediating influence of noise to distribute information optimally across the existing weights.

Taylor[Taylor, 72] has studied noisy synapses, largely in a biological context, and infers that the noise might assist learning. We have already demonstrated that noise injection both reduces the learning time and improves the network's generalisation ability[Murray, 91],[Murray, 92]. It is established[Matsuoka, 92],[Bishop, 90] that adding noise to the *training data* in neural (MLP) learning improves the "quality" of learning, as measured by the trained network's ability to generalise. Here we infer (synaptic) noise-mediated terms that sculpt the error function to favour faster learning, and that generate more robust internal representations, giving rise to better generalisation and immunity to small variations in the characteristics of the test data. Much closer to the spirit of this paper is the work of Hanson[Hanson, 90]. His stochastic version of the delta rule effectively adapts weight means and standard deviations. Also Sequin and Clay[Sequin, 91] use stuck-at faults during training which imbues the trained network with an ability to withstand such faults. They also note, but do not pursue, an increased generalisation ability.

This paper presents an outline of the mathematical predictions and verification simulations. A full description of the work is given in [Murray, 93].

2 Mathematics

Let us analyse an MLP with I input, J hidden and K output nodes, with a set of P training input vectors $\underline{o}_p = \{o_{ip}\}$, looking at the effect of noise injection into the error function itself. We are thus able to infer, from the additional terms introduced by noise, the characteristics of solutions that tend to **reduce** the error, and those which tend to **increase** it. The former will clearly be favoured, or at least stabilised, by the additional terms, while the latter will be de-stabilised.

Let each weight T_{ab} be augmented by a random noise source, such that $T_{ab} \rightarrow T_{ab} + \Delta_{ab} T_{ab}$, for all weights $\{T_{ab}\}$. Neuron thresholds are treated in precisely the same way. Note in passing, but importantly, that this **synaptic** noise is **not** the same as noise on the input data. Input noise is correlated across the synapses leaving an input node, while the synaptic noise that forms the basis of this study is not. The effect is thus quite distinct.

Considering, therefore, an error function of the form :-

$$\epsilon_{tot,p} = \frac{1}{2}\sum_{k=0}^{K-1} {\epsilon_{kp}}^2 = \frac{1}{2}\sum_{k=0}^{K-1} (o_{kp}(\{T_{ab}\}) - \tilde{o}_{kp})^2 \tag{1}$$

Where $\tilde{o}_{kp}$ is the target output. We can now perform a Taylor expansion of the output o_{kp} to second order, around the noise-free weight set, $\{T_N\}$, and thus augment the error function :-

$$o_{kp} \rightarrow o_{kp} + \sum_{ab} T_{ab}\Delta_{ab}\left(\frac{\partial o_{kp}}{\partial T_{ab}}\right) + \frac{1}{2}\sum_{ab,cd} T_{ab}\Delta_{ab}T_{cd}\Delta_{cd}\left(\frac{\partial^2 o_{kp}}{\partial T_{ab}\partial T_{cd}}\right) + O(>3) \tag{2}$$

If we ignore terms of order Δ^3 and above, and taking the time average over the learning phase, we can infer that two terms are added to the error function :-

$$<\epsilon_{tot}> = <\epsilon_{tot}(\{T_N\})> + \frac{1}{2P}\sum_{p=1}^{P}\sum_{k=0}^{K-1}\Delta^2\sum_{ab}{T_{ab}}^2\left[\left(\frac{\partial o_{kp}}{\partial T_{ab}}\right)^2 + \epsilon_{kp}\left(\frac{\partial^2 o_{kp}}{\partial {T_{ab}}^2}\right)\right] \tag{3}$$

Consider also the perceptron rule update on the hidden-output layer along with the expanded error function :-

$$< \delta T_{kj} >= -\tau \sum_{p} < \epsilon_{kp} o_{jp} o'_{kp} > -\tau \frac{\Delta^2}{2} \sum_{P} < o_{jp} o'_{kp} > \times \sum_{ab} {T_{ab}}^2 \frac{\partial^2 o_{kp}}{\partial {T_{ab}}^2} \quad (4)$$

averaged over several training epochs (which is acceptable for small values of τ the *adaption rate* parameter).

3 Simulations

The simulations detailed below are based on the *virtual targets* algorithm [Murray, 92], a variant on backpropagation, with broadly similar performance. The "targets" algorithm was chosen for its faster convergence properties. Two contrasting classification tasks were selected to verify the predictions made in the following section by simulation. The first, a feature location task, uses *real world* normalised greyscale image data. The task was to locate eyes in facial images - to classify sections of these as either "eye" or "not-eye". The network was trained on 16 × 16 preclassified sections of the images, classified as eyes and not-eyes. The not-eyes were random sections of facial images, avoiding the eyes (see Fig. 1). The second,

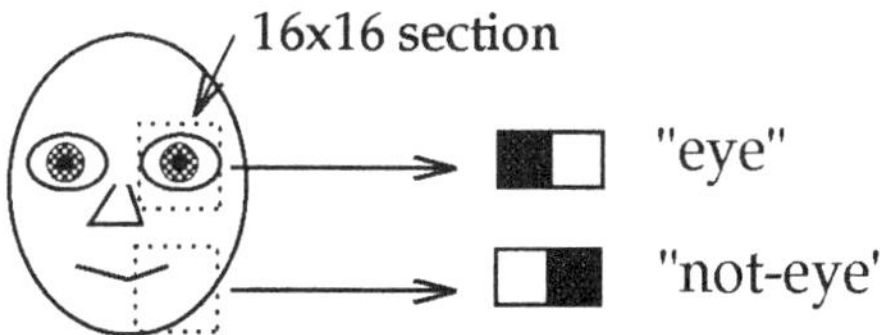

Figure 1: The eye/not-eye classifier.

a more artificial task, was the ubiquitous character encoder (Fig. 2) where a 25-

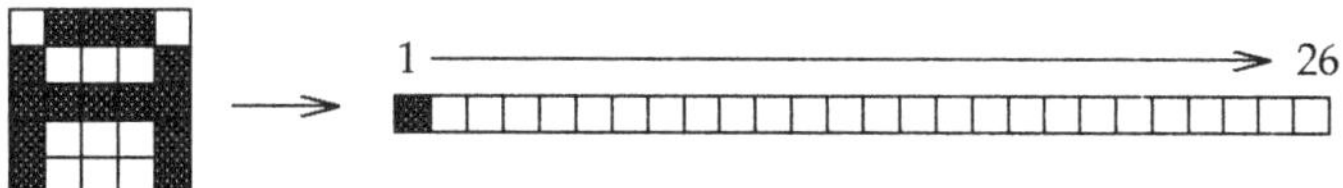

Figure 2: The character encoder task.

dimensional binary input vector describing the 26 alphabetic characters (each 5 × 5 pixels) was used to train the network with a one-out-of-26 output code.

During the simulations noise was added to the weights at a level proportional to the weight size and at a probability distribution of uniform density (i.e. $-\Delta_{max} < \Delta < \Delta_{max}$). Levels of up to 40% were probed in detail - although it is clear that the expansion above is not quantitatively valid at this level. Above these percentages further improvements were seen in the network performance, although the dynamics of the training algorithm became chaotic. The injected noise level was reduced smoothly to a minimum value of 1% as the network approached convergence (as evidenced by the highest output bit error). As in all neural network simulations, the results depended upon the training parameters, network sizes and the random start position of the network. To overcome these factors and to achieve a meaningful result 35 weight sets were produced for each noise level. All other characteristics of the training process were held constant. The results are therefore not simply pathological freaks.

4 Prediction/Verification

4.1 Fault Tolerance

Consider the first derivative penalty term in the expanded cost function (3), averaged over all patterns, output nodes and weights :-

$$K \times \Delta^2 \left[{T_{ab}}^2 \left(\frac{\partial o_{kp}}{\partial T_{ab}} \right)^2 \right] \tag{5}$$

The implications of this term are straightforward. For large values of the (weighted) average magnitude of the derivative, the overall error is increased. This term therefore causes solutions to be favoured where the dependence of outputs on individual weights is evenly distributed across the entire weight set. Furthermore, weight saliency should not only have a lower average value, but a smaller scatter across the weight set as the training process attempts to reconcile the competing pressures to reduce both (1) and (5). This more distributed representation should be manifest in an improved tolerance to faulty weights.

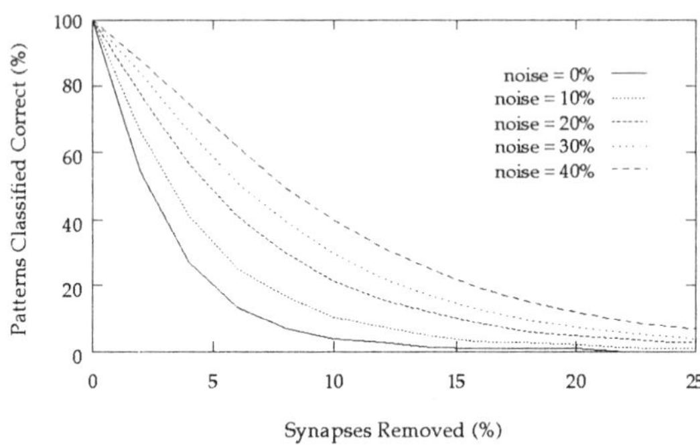

Figure 3: Fault tolerance in the character encoder problem.

Simulations were carried out on 35 weight sets produced for each of the two problems at each of 5 levels of noise injected during training. Weights were then randomly removed and the networks tested on the training data. The resulting graphs (Fig. 3, 4) show graceful degradation with an increased tolerance to faults with injected noise during training. The networks were highly constrained for these simulations to remove some of the natural redundancy of the MLP structure. Although the eye/not-eye problem contains a high proportion of redundant information, the

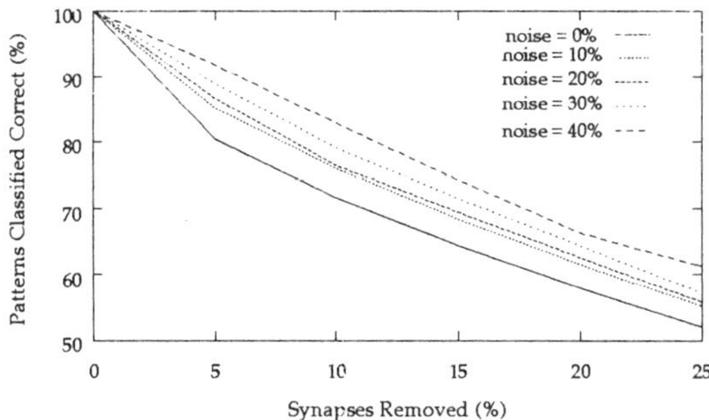

Figure 4: Fault tolerance enhancement in the eye/not-eye classifier.

improvement in the networks ability to withstand damage, with injected noise, is clear.

4.2 Generalisation Ability

Considering the derivative in equation 5, and looking at the input-hidden weights. The term that is added to the error function, again averaged over all patterns, output nodes and weights is :-

$$K \times \Delta^2 \left[{T_{ji}}^2 \, {o'_{kp}}^2 \, {T_{kj}}^2 \, {o'_{jp}}^2 \, {o_{ip}}^2 \right] \tag{6}$$

If an output neuron has a non-zero connection from a particular hidden node ($T_{kj} \neq 0$), and provided the input o_{ip} is non-zero and is connected to the hidden node ($T_{ji} \neq 0$), there is also a term o'_{jp} that will **tend to favour solutions with the hidden nodes also turned firmly ON or OFF** (i.e. $o_{jp} = 0 \; or \; 1$). Remembering, of course, that all these terms are noise-mediated, and that during the early stages of training, the "actual" error ϵ_{kp}, in (1), will dominate, this term will de-stabilise final solutions that balance the hidden nodes on the slope of the sigmoid. Naturally, hidden nodes o_j that are firmly ON or OFF are less likely to change state as a result of small variations in the input data $\{o_i\}$. This should become evident in an increased tolerance to input perturbations and therefore an increased generalisation ability.

Simulations were again carried out on the two problems using 35 weight sets for each level of injected synaptic noise during training. For the character encoder problem generalisation is not really an issue, but it is possible to verify the above prediction by introducing random gaussian noise into the input data and noting the degradation in performance. The results of these simulations are shown in Fig. 5, and clearly show an increased ability to withstand input perturbation, with injected noise into the synapses during training.

Generalisation ability for the eye/not-eye problem is a real issue. This problem therefore gives a valid test of whether the synaptic noise technique actually improves generalisation performance. The networks were therefore tested on previously unseen facial images and the results are shown in Table 1. These results show

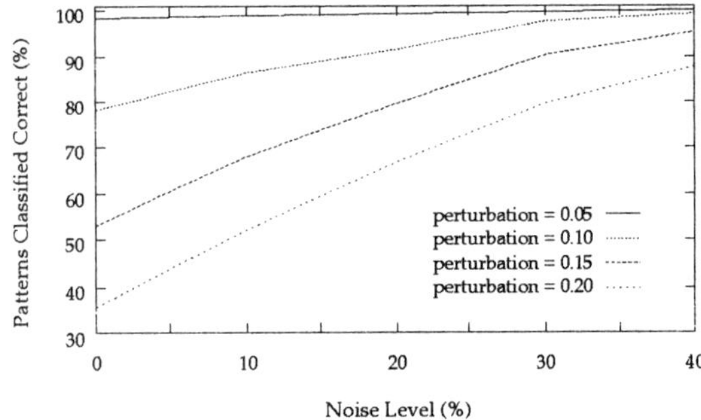

Figure 5: Generalisation enhancement shown through increased tolerance to input perturbation, in the character encoder problem.

	Correctly Classified (%)				
Noise Levels	0%	10%	20%	30%	40%
Test Patterns	67.875	70.406	70.416	72.454	75.446

Table 1: Generalisation enhancement shown through increased ability to classifier previously unseen data, in the eye/not-eye task.

dramatically improved generalisation ability with increased levels of injected synaptic noise during training. An improvement of approximately 8% is seen - consistent with earlier results on a different "real" problem [Murray, 91].

4.3 Learning Trajectory

Considering now the second derivative penalty term in the expanded cost function (2). This term is complex as it involves second order derivatives, and also depends upon the sign and magnitude of the errors themselves $\{\epsilon_{kp}\}$. The simplest way of looking at its effect is to look at a single exemplar term :-

$$K\Delta^2 \; \epsilon_{kp} {T_{ab}}^2 \left(\frac{\partial^2 o_{kp}}{\partial {T_{ab}}^2} \right) \tag{7}$$

This term implies that when the combination of $\epsilon_{kp} \frac{\partial^2 o_{kp}}{\partial {T_{ab}}^2}$ is negative then the overall cost function error is reduced and *vice versa*. The term (7) is therefore constructive as it can actually lower the error locally via noise injection, whereas (6) always increases it. (7) can therefore be viewed as a sculpting of the error surface during the early phases of training (i.e. when ϵ_{kp} is substantial). In particular, a weight set with a higher "raw" error value, calculated from (1), may be favoured over one with a lower value if noise-injected terms indicate that the "poorer" solution is located in a promising area of weight space. This "look-ahead" property should lead to an enhanced learning trajectory, perhaps finding a solution more rapidly.

In the augmented weight update equation (4), the noise is acting as a medium projecting statistical information about the character of the entire weight set on to the update equation for each particular weight. So, the effect of the noise term is to account not only for the weight currently being updated, but to add in a term that estimates what the other weight changes are likely to do to the output, and adjust the size of the weight increment/decrement as appropriate.

To verify this by simulation is not as straightforward as the other predictions. It is however possible to show the mean training time for each level of injected noise. For each noise level, 1000 random start points were used to allow the underlying properties of the training process to emerge. The results are shown in Fig. 6 and

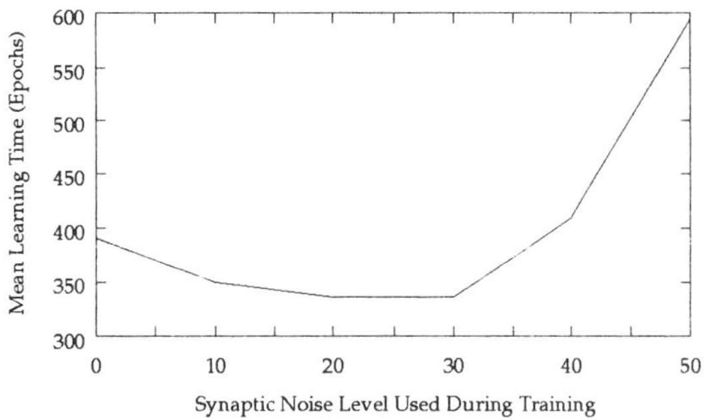

Figure 6: Training time as a function of injected synaptic noise during training.

clearly show that at low noise levels ($\leq 30\%$ for the case of the character encoder) a definite reduction in training times are seen. At higher levels the chaotic nature of the "noisy learning" takes over.

It is also possible to plot the combination of $\epsilon_{kp}\frac{\partial^2 o_{kp}}{\partial T_{ab}{}^2}$. This is shown in Fig. 7, again for the character encoder problem. The term (7) is reduced more quickly

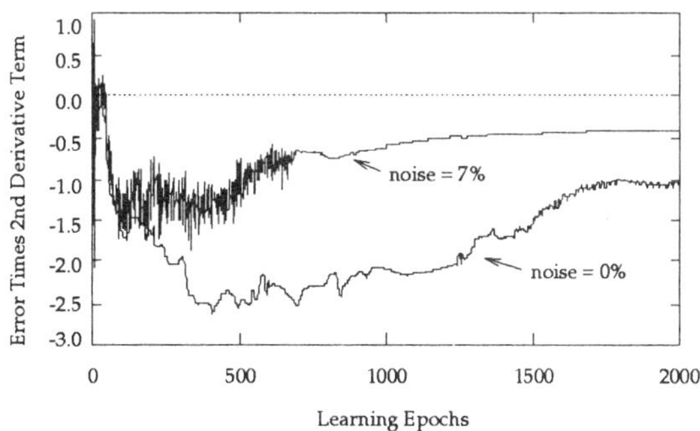

Figure 7: The second derivative $\times$ error term trajectory for injected synaptic noise levels 0% and 7%.

with injected noise, thus effecting better weight changes via (4). At levels of noise $> 7\%$ the effect is exaggerated, and the noise mediated improvements take place during the first 100-200 epochs of training. The level of 7% is displayed simply because it is visually clear what is happening, and is also typical.

5 Conclusion

We have shown both by mathematical expansion and by simulation that injecting random noise on to the synaptic weights of a MultiLayer Perceptron during the training phase enhances fault-tolerance, generalisation ability and learning trajectory. It has long been held that any inaccuracy during training is detrimental to MLP learning. This paper proves that **analog** inaccuracy is not. The mathematical predictions are perfectly general and the simulations relate to a non-trivial classification task and a "real" world problem. The results are therefore important for the designers of analog hardware and also as a non-invasive technique for producing learning enhancements in the software domain.

Acknowledgements

We are grateful to the Science and Engineering Research Council for financial support, and to Lionel Tarassenko and Chris Bishop for encouragement and advice.

References

[Taylor, 72] J. G. Taylor, "Spontaneous Behaviour in Neural Networks", *J. Theor. Biol.*, vol. 36, pp. 513-528, 1972.

[Murray, 91] A. F. Murray, "Analog Noise-Enhanced Learning in Neural Network Circuits," *Electronics Letters,* vol. 2, no. 17, pp. 1546-1548, 1991.

[Murray, 92] A. F. Murray, "Multi-Layer Perceptron Learning Optimised for On-Chip Implementation - a Noise Robust System," *Neural Computation,* vol. 4, no. 3, pp. 366-381, 1992.

[Matsuoka, 92] K. Matsuoka, "Noise Injection into Inputs in Back-Propagation Learning", *IEEE Trans. Systems, Man and Cybernetics*, vol. 22, no. 3, pp. 436-440, 1992.

[Bishop, 90] C. Bishop, "Curvature-Driven Smoothing in Backpropagation Neural Networks," *IJCNN*, vol. 2, pp. 749-752, 1990.

[Hanson, 90] S. J. Hanson, "A Stochastic Version of the Delta Rule", *Physica D*, vol. 42, pp. 265-272, 1990.

[Sequin, 91] C. H. Sequin, R. D. Clay, "Fault Tolerance in Feed-Forward Artificial Neural Networks", Neural Networks : Concepts, Applications and Implementations, vol. 4, pp. 111-141, 1991.

[Murray, 93] A. F. Murray, P. J. Edwards, "Enhanced MLP Performance and Fault Tolerance Resulting from Synaptic Weight Noise During Training", *IEEE Trans. Neural Networks*, 1993, In Press.

Unsupervised Discrimination of Clustered Data via Optimization of Binary Information Gain

Nicol N. Schraudolph
Computer Science & Engr. Dept.
University of California, San Diego
La Jolla, CA 92093–0114
nici@cs.ucsd.edu

Terrence J. Sejnowski
Computational Neurobiology Laboratory
The Salk Institute for Biological Studies
San Diego, CA 92186-5800
tsejnowski@ucsd.edu

Abstract

We present the information-theoretic derivation of a learning algorithm that clusters unlabelled data with linear discriminants. In contrast to methods that try to preserve information about the input patterns, we maximize the information gained from observing the output of robust binary discriminators implemented with sigmoid nodes. We derive a local weight adaptation rule via gradient ascent in this objective, demonstrate its dynamics on some simple data sets, relate our approach to previous work and suggest directions in which it may be extended.

1 INTRODUCTION

Unsupervised learning algorithms may perform useful preprocessing functions by preserving some aspects of their input while discarding others. This can be quantified as maximization of the information the network's output carries about those aspects of the input that are deemed important.

(Linsker, 1988) suggests maximal preservation of information about all aspects of the input. This *Infomax* principle provides for optimal reconstruction of the input in the face of noise and resource limitations. The *I-max* algorithm (Becker and Hinton, 1992), by contrast, focusses on coherent aspects of the input, which are extracted by maximizing the mutual information between networks looking at different patches of input.

Our work aims at recoding *clustered* data with adaptive discriminants that selectively emphasize gaps between clusters while collapsing patterns within a cluster onto near-identical output representations. We achieve this by maximizing *information gain* — the information gained through observation of the network's outputs under a probabilistic interpretation.

2 STRATEGY

Consider a node that performs a weighted summation on its inputs $\vec{x}$ and squashes the resulting net input y through a sigmoid function f:

$$z = f(y), \text{ where } f(y) = \frac{1}{1 + e^{-y}} \text{ and } y = \vec{w} \cdot \vec{x}\,. \tag{1}$$

Such a sigmoid node can be regarded as a "soft" discriminant: with a large enough weight vector, the output will essentially be binary, but smaller weights allow for the expression of varying degrees of confidence in the discrimination.

To make this notion more precise, consider y a random variable with bimodal distribution, namely an even mixture of two Gaussian distributions. Then if their means equal $\pm$ half their variance, z is the posterior probability for discriminating between the two source distributions (Anderson, 1972).

This probabilitstic interpretation of z can be used to design a learning algorithm that seeks such bimodal projections of the input data. In particular, we search for highly informative discriminants by maximizing the information gained about the binary discrimination through observation of z. This *binary information gain* is given by

$$\Delta H(z) = H(\hat{z}) - H(z), \tag{2}$$

where $H(z)$ is the entropy of z under the above interpretation, and $\hat{z}$ is an estimate of z based on prior knowledge.

3 RESULTS

3.1 THE ALGORITHM

In the Appendix, we present the derivation of a learning algorithm that maximizes binary information gain by gradient ascent. The resulting weight update rule is

$$\Delta\vec{w} \propto f'(y)\,\vec{x}\,(y - \hat{y}), \tag{3}$$

where $\hat{y}$, the estimated net input, must meet certain conditions[1] (see Appendix). The weight change dictated by (3) is thus proportional to the product of three factors:

- the derivative of the sigmoid squashing function,
- the presynaptic input $\vec{x}$, and
- the difference between actual and anticipated net input.

[1] In what follows, we have successfully used estimators that merely approximate these conditions.

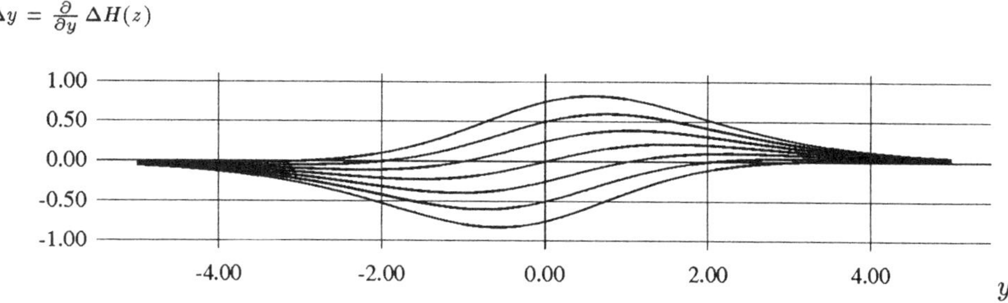

Figure 1: Phase plot of Δy against net input y for $\hat{y} = \{-3, -2, \ldots 3\}$. See text for details.

3.2 SINGLE NODE DYNAMICS

For a single, isolated node, we use $\langle y \rangle$, the average net input over a batch of input patterns, as estimator for y. The behavior of our algorithm in this setting is best understood from a *phase plot* as shown in Figure 1, where the change in net input resulting from a weight change according to (3) is graphed against the net input that causes this weight change.

Curves are plotted for seven different values of $\hat{y}$. The central curve ($\hat{y} = 0$) is identical to that of the straightforward Hebb rule for sigmoid nodes: both positive and negative net inputs are equally amplified until they reach saturation. For non-zero values of $\hat{y}$, however, the curves become asymmetric: positive $\hat{y}$ favor negative changes Δy and vice versa. For $\hat{y} = \langle y \rangle$, it is easy to see that this will have the effect of centering net inputs around zero.

The node will therefore converge to a state where its output is one for half of the input patterns, and zero for the other half. Note that this can be achieved by *any* sufficiently large weight vector, regardless of its direction! However, since simple gradient ascent is both greedy and local in weight space, starting it from small random initial weights is equivalent to a bias towards discriminations that can be made confidently with smaller weight vectors.

To illustrate this effect, we have tested a single node running our algorithm on a set of vowel formant frequency data due to (Peterson and Barney, 1952). The most prominent feature of this data is a central gap that separates front from back vowels; however, this feature is near-orthogonal to the principal component of the data and thus escapes detection by standard Hebbian learning rules.

Figure 2 shows the initial, intermediate and final phase of this experiment, using a visualization technique suggested by (Munro, 1992). Each plot shows the pre-image of zero net input superimposed on a scatter plot of the data set in input space. The two flanking lines delineate the "active region" where the sigmoid is not saturated, and thus provide an indication of weight vector size.

As demonstrated in this figure, our algorithm is capable of proceeding smoothly from a small initial weight vector that responds in principal component direction to a solution which uses a large weight vector in near-orthogonal direction to successfully discriminate between the two data clusters.

Figure 2: Single node discovers distinction between front and back vowels in unlabelled data set of 1514 multi-speaker vowel utterances (Peterson and Barney, 1952). Superimposed on a scatter plot of the data are the pre-images of $y = 0$ (solid center line) and $y = \pm 1.31696$ (flanking lines) in input space. Discovered feature is far from principal component direction.

3.3 EXTENSION TO A LAYER OF NODES

A learning algorithm for a single sigmoid node has of course only limited utility. When extending it to a layer of such nodes, some form of lateral interaction is needed to ensure that each node makes a different binary discrimination. The common technique of introducing lateral competition for activity or weight changes would achieve this only at the cost of severely distorting the behavior of our algorithm.

Fortunately our framework is flexible enough to accommodate lateral differentiation in a less intrusive manner: by picking an estimator that uses the activity of every other node in the layer to make its prediction, we force each node to maximize its information gain with respect to the entire layer. To demonstrate this technique we use the linear second-order estimator

$$\hat{y}_i = \langle y_i \rangle + \sum_{j \neq i} (y_j - \langle y_j \rangle)\, \varrho_{ij} \tag{4}$$

to predict the net input y_i of the ith node in the layer, where the $\langle \cdot \rangle$ operator denotes averaging over a batch of input patterns, and ϱ_{ij} is the empirical correlation coefficient

$$\varrho_{ij} = \frac{\langle (y_i - \langle y_i \rangle)(y_j - \langle y_j \rangle) \rangle}{\sqrt{\langle (y_i - \langle y_i \rangle)^2 \rangle \, \langle (y_j - \langle y_j \rangle)^2 \rangle}} . \tag{5}$$

Figure 3 shows a layer of three such nodes adapting to a mixture of three Gaussian distributions, with each node initially picking a different Gaussian to separate from the other two. After some time, all three discriminants rotate in concert so as to further maximize information gain by splitting the input data evenly. Note that throughout this process, the nodes always remain well-differentiated from each other.

For most initial conditions, however, the course of this experiment is that depicted in Figure 4: two nodes discover a more efficient way to discriminate between the three input clusters, to the detriment of the third. The latecomer repeatedly tries to settle into one of the gaps in the data, but this would result in a high degree of predictability. Thus the node with the shortest weight vector and hence most volatile discriminant is weakened further, its weight vector all but eliminated in an effective demonstration of Occam's razor.

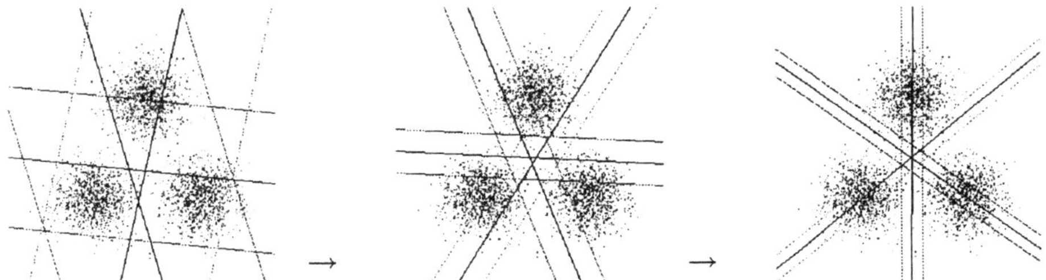

Figure 3: Layer of three nodes adapts to a mixture of three Gaussian distributions. In the final state, each node splits the input data evenly.

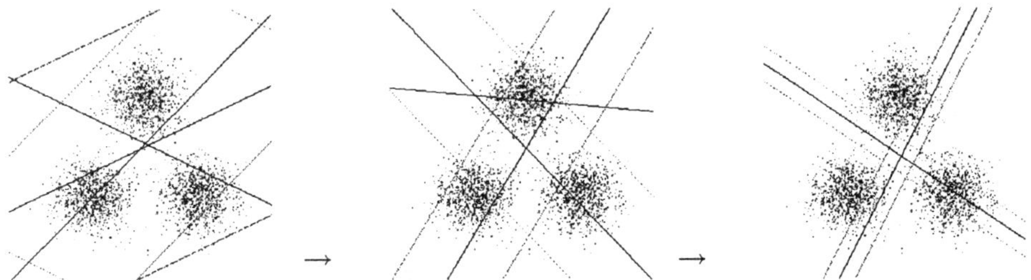

Figure 4: Most initial conditions, however, lead to a minimal solution involving only two nodes. The weakest node is "crowded out" by Occam's razor, its weight vector reduced to near-zero length.

4 DISCUSSION

4.1 RELATED WORK

By maximizing the difference of actual from anticipated response, our algorithm makes binary discriminations that are highly informative with respect to clusters in the input. The weight change in proportion to a *difference* in activity is reminiscent of the *covariance rule* (Sejnowski, 1977) but generalizes it in two important respects:

- it explicitly incorporates a sigmoid nonlinearity, and
- $\hat{y}$ need not necessarily be the average net input.

Both of these are critical improvements: the first allows the node to respond only to inputs in its non-saturated region, and hence to learn local features in projections other than along the principal component direction. The second provides a convenient mechanism for extending the algorithm by incorporating additional information in the estimator.

We share the goal of seeking highly informative, bimodal projections of the input with the *Bienenstock-Cooper-Munro* (BCM) algorithm (Bienenstock et al., 1982; Intrator, 1992). A critical difference, however, is that BCM uses a complex, asymmetric nonlinearity that increases the *selectivity* of nodes and hence produces a localized, 1-of-n recoding of the input, whereas our algorithm makes symmetric, robust and independent binary discriminations.

4.2 FUTURE DIRECTIONS

Since the learning algorithm described here has demonstrated flexibility and efficiency in our initial experiments, we plan to scale it up to address high-dimensional, real-world problems. The algorithm itself is likely to be further extended and improved as its applications grow more demanding.

For instance, although the size of the weight vector represents commitment to a discriminant in our framework, it is not explicitly controlled. The dynamics of weight adaptation happen to implement a reasonable bias in this case, but further refinements may be possible. Other priors implicit in our approach — such as the preference for splitting the data evenly — could be similarly relaxed or modified.

Another attractive generalization of this learning rule would be to implement nonlinear discriminants by backpropagating weight derivatives through hidden units. The dynamic stability of our algorithm is a significant asset for its expansion into an efficient unsupervised multi-layer network.

In such a network, linear estimators are no longer sufficient to fully remove redundancy between nodes. In his closely related *predictability minimization* architecture, (Schmidhuber, 1992) uses backpropagation networks as nonlinear estimators for this purpose with some success.

Since the notion of estimator in our framework is completely general, it may combine evidence from multiple, disparate sources. Thus a network running our algorithm can be trained to complement a heterogeneous mix of pattern recognition methods by maximizing information gain relative to an estimator that utilizes all such available sources of information. This flexibility should greatly aid the integration of binary information gain optimization into existing techniques.

APPENDIX: MATHEMATICAL DERIVATION

We derive a straightforward batch learning algorithm that performs gradient ascent in the binary information gain objective. On-line approximations may be obtained by using exponential traces in place of the batch averages denoted by the $\langle\cdot\rangle$ operator.

CONDITIONS ON THE ESTIMATOR

To eliminate the derivative term from (11d) below we require that the estimator $\hat{z}$ be

- unbiased: $\langle\hat{z}\rangle = \langle z\rangle$, and
- *honest*: $\frac{\partial}{\partial z}\,\hat{z} = \frac{\partial}{\partial z}\,\langle\hat{z}\rangle$.

The *honesty* condition ensures that the estimator has access to the estimated variable only on the slow timescale of batch averaging, thus eliminating trivial "solutions" such as $\hat{z} = z$.

For an unbiased and *honest* estimator,

$$\frac{\partial\hat{z}}{\partial z} = \frac{\partial}{\partial z}\,\langle\hat{z}\rangle = \frac{\partial}{\partial z}\,\langle z\rangle = \left\langle\frac{\partial z}{\partial z}\right\rangle = 1\,. \tag{6}$$

BINARY ENTROPY AND ITS DERIVATIVE

The entropy of a binary random variable X as a function of $z = Pr(X = 1)$ is given by

$$H(z) = -z \log z - (1 - z) \log(1 - z)\,; \tag{7}$$

its derivative with respect to z is

$$\frac{\partial}{\partial z} H(z) = \log(1 - z) - \log z\,. \tag{8}$$

Since z in our case is produced by the sigmoid function f given in (1), this conveniently simplifies to

$$\frac{\partial}{\partial z} H(z) = -y\,. \tag{9}$$

GRADIENT ASCENT IN INFORMATION GAIN

The information ΔH gained from observing the output z of the discriminator is

$$\Delta H(z) = H(\hat{z}) - H(z), \tag{10}$$

where $\hat{z}$ is an estimate of z based on prior knowledge. We maximize $\Delta H(z)$ by batched gradient ascent in weight space:

$$\begin{aligned}
\Delta\vec{w} &\propto \left\langle \frac{\partial}{\partial \vec{w}} \Delta H(z) \right\rangle & \text{(11a)}\\
&= \left\langle \frac{\partial z}{\partial \vec{w}} \cdot \frac{\partial}{\partial z} \left[H(\hat{z}) - H(z) \right] \right\rangle & \text{(11b)}\\
&= \left\langle z\,(1 - z)\,\frac{\partial y}{\partial \vec{w}} \left[\frac{\partial \hat{z}}{\partial z} \cdot \frac{\partial}{\partial \hat{z}} H(\hat{z}) - \frac{\partial}{\partial z} H(z) \right] \right\rangle & \text{(11c)}\\
&= \left\langle z\,(1 - z)\,\vec{x} \left(y - \frac{\partial \hat{z}}{\partial z} \cdot \hat{y} \right) \right\rangle, & \text{(11d)}
\end{aligned}$$

where estimation of the node's output z has been replaced by that of its net input y. Substitution of (6) into (11d) yields the binary information gain optimization rule

$$\Delta\vec{w} \propto \langle z\,(1 - z)\,\vec{x}\,(y - \hat{y}) \rangle\,. \tag{12}$$

■

Acknowledgements

We would like to thank Steve Nowlan, Peter Dayan and Rich Zemel for stimulating and helpful discussions. This work was supported by the Office of Naval Research and the McDonnell-Pew Center for Cognitive Neuroscience at San Diego.

References

Anderson, J. (1972). Logistic discrimination. *Biometrika*, 59:19–35.

Anderson, J. and Rosenfeld, E., editors (1988). *Neurocomputing: Foundations of Research*. MIT Press, Cambridge.

Becker, S. and Hinton, G. E. (1992). A self-organizing neural network that discovers surfaces in random-dot stereograms. *Nature*, 355:161–163.

Bienenstock, E., Cooper, L., and Munro, P. (1982). Theory for the development of neuron selectivity: Orientation specificity and binocular interaction in visual cortex. *Journal of Neuroscience*, 2. Reprinted in (Anderson and Rosenfeld, 1988).

Intrator, N. (1992). Feature extraction using an unsupervised neural network. *Neural Computation*, 4:98–107.

Linsker, R. (1988). Self-organization in a perceptual network. *Computer*, pages 105–117.

Munro, P. W. (1992). Visualizations of 2-d hidden unit space. In *International Joint Conference on Neural Networks*, volume 3, pages 468–473, Baltimore 1992. IEEE.

Peterson, G. E. and Barney, H. L. (1952). Control methods used in a study of the vowels. *Journal of the Acoustical Society of America*, 24:175–184.

Schmidhuber, J. (1992). Learning factorial codes by predictability minimization. *Neural Computation*, 4:863–879.

Sejnowski, T. J. (1977). Storing covariance with nonlinearly interacting neurons. *Journal of Mathematical Biology*, 4:303–321.

Weight Space Probability Densities in Stochastic Learning: II. Transients and Basin Hopping Times

Genevieve B. Orr and Todd K. Leen
Department of Computer Science and Engineering
Oregon Graduate Institute of Science & Technology
19600 N.W. von Neumann Drive
Beaverton, OR 97006-1999

Abstract

In stochastic learning, weights are random variables whose time evolution is governed by a Markov process. At each time-step, n, the weights can be described by a probability density function $P(\omega, n)$. We summarize the theory of the time evolution of P, and give graphical examples of the time evolution that contrast the behavior of stochastic learning with true gradient descent (batch learning). Finally, we use the formalism to obtain predictions of the time required for noise-induced hopping between basins of different optima. We compare the theoretical predictions with simulations of large ensembles of networks for simple problems in supervised and unsupervised learning.

1 Weight-Space Probability Densities

Despite the recent application of convergence theorems from stochastic approximation theory to neural network learning (Oja 1982, White 1989) there remain outstanding questions about the search dynamics in stochastic learning. For example, the convergence theorems do not tell us to which of several optima the algorithm is likely to converge[1]. Also, while it is widely recognized that the intrinsic noise in the weight update can move the system out of sub-optimal local minima (for a graphical example, see Darken and Moody 1991), there have been no theoretical predictions of the time required to escape from local optima, or of its dependence on learning rates.

In order to more fully understand the dynamics of stochastic search, we study the weight-space probability density and its time evolution. In this paper we summarize a theoretical framework that describes this time evolution. We graphically portray the motion of the density for examples that contrast stochastic and batch learning. Finally we use the theory to predict the statistical distribution of times required for escape from local optima. We compare the theoretical results with simulations for simple examples in supervised and unsupervised learning.

2 Stochastic Learning and Noisy Maps

2.1 Motion of the Probability Density

We consider stochastic learning algorithms of the form

$$\omega(n+1) \;=\; \omega(n) \;+\; \mu\, H[\,\omega(n), x(n)\,] \tag{1}$$

where $\omega(n) \in \mathbb{R}^m$ is the weight, $x(n)$ is the data exemplar input to the algorithm at time-step n, μ is the learning rate, and $H[\cdots] \in \mathbb{R}^m$ is the weight update function. The exemplars $x(n)$ can be either inputs or, in the case of supervised learning, input/target pairs. We assume that the $x(n)$ are i.i.d. with density $\rho(x)$. Angled brackets $\langle \ldots \rangle_x$ denote averaging over this density. In what follows, the learning rate will be held constant.

The learning algorithm (1) is a noisy map on ω. The weights are thus random variables described by the probability density function $P(\omega, n)$. The time evolution of this density is given by the Kolmogorov equation

$$P(\omega, n+1) \;=\; \int d\omega'\, P(\omega', n)\, W(\omega' \to \omega) \tag{2}$$

where the single time-step transition probability is given by (Leen and Orr 1992, Leen and Moody 1993)

$$W(\omega' \to \omega) \;=\; \langle\; \delta(\,\omega - \omega' - \mu H[\,\omega', x\,]\,)\;\rangle_x \tag{3}$$

and $\delta(\cdots)$ is the Dirac delta function.

The Kolmogorov equation can be recast as a differential-difference equation by expanding the transition probability (3) as a power series in μ. This gives a Kramers-Moyal expansion (Leen and Orr 1992, Leen and Moody 1993)

[1]However Kushner (1987) has proved convergence to global optima for stochastic approximation algorithms with added Gaussian noise subject to logarithmic annealing schedules.

$$P(\omega, n+1) - P(\omega, n) = \sum_{i=1}^{\infty} \frac{(-\mu)^i}{i!} \sum_{j_1,\ldots j_i=1}^{m} \frac{\partial^i}{\partial\omega_{j_1}\,\partial\omega_{j_2}\ldots\partial\omega_{j_i}} \left(\langle H_{j_1} H_{j_2} \ldots H_{j_i} \rangle_x \, P(\omega, n) \right), \tag{4}$$

where ω_{j_α} and H_{j_α} are the j_α^{th} component of weight, and weight update, respectively.

Truncating (4) to second order in μ leaves a Fokker-Planck equation[2] that is valid for small $|\,\mu H\,|$. The drift coefficient $\langle H \rangle_x$ is simply the average update. It is important to note that the diffusion coefficients, $\langle H_{j_\alpha} H_{j_\beta} \rangle_x$, can be *strongly* dependent on location in the weight-space. This spatial dependence influences both equilibria and transient phenomena. In section 3.1 we will use both the Kolmogorov equation (2), and the Fokker-Planck equation to track the time evolution of network ensemble densities.

2.2 First Passage Times

Our discussion of basin hopping will use the notion of the first passage time (Gardiner, 1990); the time required for a network initialized at ω_0 to first pass into an ϵ-neighborhood D of a global or local optimum ω_* (see Figure 1). The first passage time is a random variable. Its distribution function $\mathcal{P}(n;\omega_0)$ is the probability that a network initialized at ω_0 makes its first passage into D at the nth iteration of the learning rule.

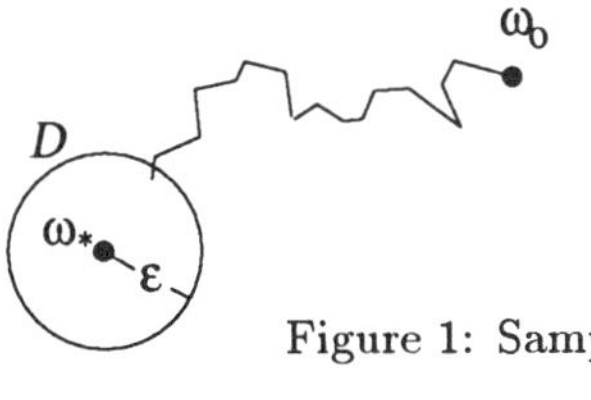

Figure 1: Sample search path.

To arrive at an expression for $\mathcal{P}(n;\omega_0)$, we first examine the probability of passing from the initial weight ω_0 to the weight ω after n iterations. This probability can be expressed as

$$P(\omega, n \mid \omega_0, 0) = \int d\omega' \, P(\omega, n \mid \omega', 1) \, W(\,\omega_0 \to \omega'\,). \tag{5}$$

Substituting the single time-step transition probability (3) into the above expression, integrating over ω', and making use of the time-shift invariance of the system[3] we find

$$P(\omega, n \mid \omega_0, 0) = \langle\, P(\omega, n-1 \mid \omega_0 + \mu H(\omega_0, x), 0)\, \rangle_x \ . \tag{6}$$

Next, let $G(n;\omega_0)$ denote the probability that a network initialized at ω_0 has *not* passed into the region D by the nth iteration. We obtain $G(n;\omega_0)$ by integrating $P(\omega, n \mid \omega_0, 0)$ over weights ω *not in D*;

$$G(n;\omega_0) = \int_{D^c} d\omega \, P(\omega, n \mid \omega_0, 0) \tag{7}$$

[2] See (Ritter and Schulten 1988) and (Radons *et al.* 1990) for independent derivations.

[3] With our assumptions of a constant learning rate μ and stationary sample density $\rho(x)$, the system is time-shift invariant. Mathematically stated, $P(\omega, n \mid \omega', m) = P(\omega, n-1 \mid \omega', m-1)$

where D^c is the complement of D. Substituting equation (6) into (7) and integrating over ω we obtain the recursion

$$G(n;\omega_0) \;=\; \langle\, G(n-1;\omega_0+\mu H[\,\omega_0,x\,])\,\rangle_x \;. \tag{8}$$

Before any learning takes place, none of the networks in the ensemble have entered D. Thus the initial condition for G is

$$G(0;\omega_0) \;=\; 1\,, \quad \omega_0\in D^c \;. \tag{9}$$

Networks that have entered D are removed from the ensemble (i.e. ∂D is an absorbing boundary). Thus G satisfies the boundary condition

$$G(n;\omega_0) \;=\; 0\,, \quad \omega_0\in D \;. \tag{10}$$

Finally, the probability that the network has *not* passed into the region D on or before iteration $n-1$ minus the probability the network has *not* passed into D on or before iteration n is simply the probability that the network *has* passed into D *exactly at iteration* n. This is just the probability for first passage into D at time-step n. Thus

$$\mathcal{P}(n;\omega_0) \;=\; G(n-1;\omega_0) \;-\; G(n;\omega_0) \;. \tag{11}$$

Finally the recursion (8) for G can be expanded in a power series in μ to obtain the *backward* Kramers-Moyal equation

$$G(n;\omega) \;-\; G(n-1;\omega) \;=$$

$$\sum_{i=1}^{\infty}\frac{\mu^i}{i!}\sum_{j_1,\ldots j_i=1}^{m}\langle\, H_{j_1}H_{j_2}\ldots H_{j_i}\rangle_x\,\frac{\partial^i}{\partial\omega_{j_1}\,\partial\omega_{j_2}\ldots\partial\omega_{j_i}}\,G(n-1;\omega)\;. \tag{12}$$

Truncation to second order in μ results in the *backward* Fokker-Planck equation. In section 3.2 we will use both the full recursion (8) and the Fokker-Planck approximation to (12) to predict basin hopping times in stochastic learning.

3 Backpropagation and Competitive Nets

We apply the above formalism to study the time evolution of the probability density for simple backpropagation and competitive learning problems. We give graphical examples of the time evolution of the weight space density, and calculate times for passage from local to global optima.

3.1 Densities for the XOR Problem

Feed-forward networks trained to solve the XOR problem provide an example of supervised learning with well-characterized local optima (Lisboa and Perantonis, 1991). We use a 2-input, 2-hidden, 1-output network (9 weights) trained by stochastic gradient descent on the cross-entropy error function in Lisboa and Perantonis (1991). For computational tractability, we reduce the state space dimension by constraining the search to one- or two-dimensional subspaces of the weight space. To provide global optima at *finite* weight values, the output targets are set to δ and $1-\delta$, with $\delta << 1$.

Figure 2a shows the cost function evaluated along a line in the weight space. This line, parameterized by v, is chosen to pass through a global optimum at $v = 0$, and a local optimum at $v = 1.0$. In this one-dimensional slice, another local optimum occurs at $v = 1.24$. Figure 2b shows the evolution of $P(v,n)$ obtained by numerical integration of the Fokker-Planck equation. Figure 2c shows the evolution of $P(v,n)$ estimated by simulation of 10,000 networks, each receiving a different random sequence of the four input/target patterns. Initially the density is peaked up about the local optimum at $v = 1.24$. At intermediate times, there is a spike of density at the local optimum at $v = 1.0$. This spike is narrow since the diffusion coefficient is small there. At late times the density collects at the global optimum. We note that for the learning rate used here, the local optimum at $v = 1.24$ is asymptotically stable under true gradient descent, and no escape would occur.

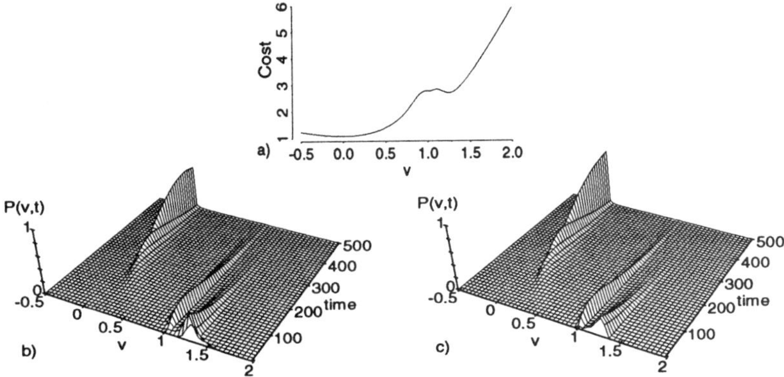

Figure 2: a) XOR cost function. b) Predicted density. c) Simulated density.

Figure 3 shows a series of snapshots of the density superimposed on the cost function for a 2-D slice through the XOR weight space. The first frame shows the weight evolution under true gradient descent. The weights are initialized at the upper right-hand corner of the frame, travel down the gradient and settle into a *local* optimum. The remaining frames show the evolution of the density calculated by direct integration of the Kolmogorov equation (2). Here one sees an early spreading of the initial density and the ultimate concentration at the global optimum.

3.2 Basin Hopping Times

The above examples graphically illustrate the intuitive notion that the noise inherent in stochastic learning can move the system out of local optima[4] In this section we calculate the statistical distribution of times required to pass between basins.

---

[4]The reader should not infer from these examples that stochastic update necessarily converges to global optima. It is straightforward to construct examples for which stochastic learning convergences to local optima with probability one.

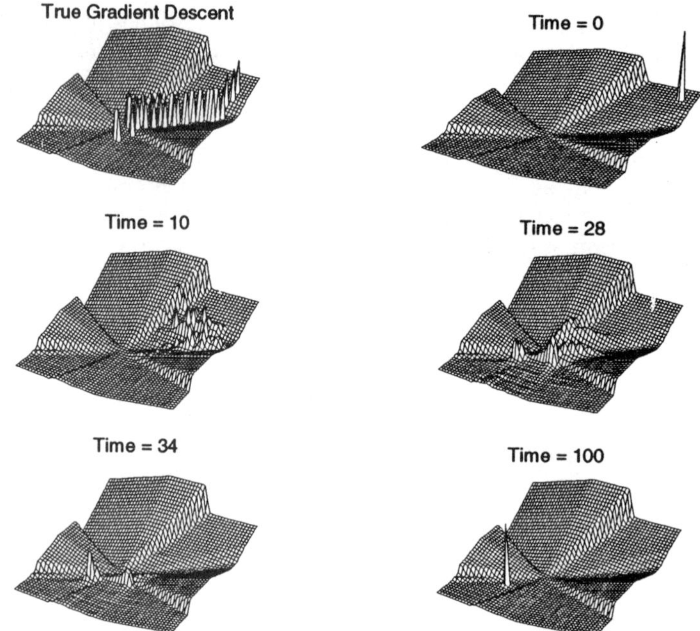

Figure 3: Weight evolution for 2-D XOR. The density is superimposed on top of the cost function. The first frame shows density using true gradient descent for all 100 timesteps. The remaining frames show the density for selected timesteps using stochastic descent.

3.2.1 Basin Hopping in Back-propagation

For the search direction used in the example of Figure 2, we calculated the distribution of times required for networks initialized at $v = 1.2$ to first pass within $\epsilon = 0.1$ of the global optimum at $v = 0.0$. For this example we numerically integrated the backward Fokker-Planck equation. We verified the theoretical predictions by obtaining first passage times from an ensemble of 10,000 networks initialized at $v = 1.2$. See Figure 4. For this example the agreement is good at the small learning rate ($\mu = 0.025$) used, but degrades for larger μ as higher order terms in the expansion (12) become significant.

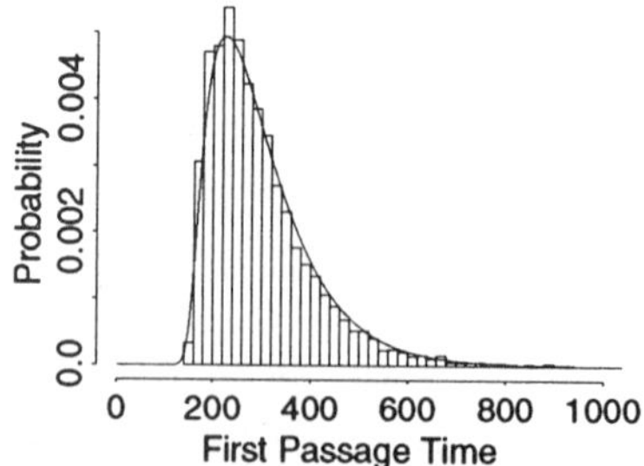

Figure 4: XOR problem. Simulated (histogram) and theoretical (solid line) distributions of first passage times for the cost function of Figure 1a.

When the Fokker-Planck approximation fails, results obtained from the exact expression (8) are in excellent agreement with experimental results. One such example is shown in Figure 5. Similar to Figure 2a, we have chosen a one-dimensional subspace of the XOR weight space (but in a different direction). Here, the Fokker-Planck solution is quite poor because the steepness of the cost function results in large contributions from higher order terms in (12). As one would expect, the exact solution obtained using (8) agrees well with the simulations.

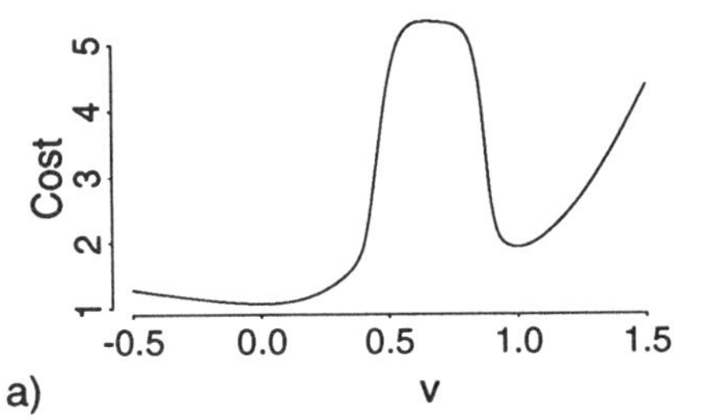

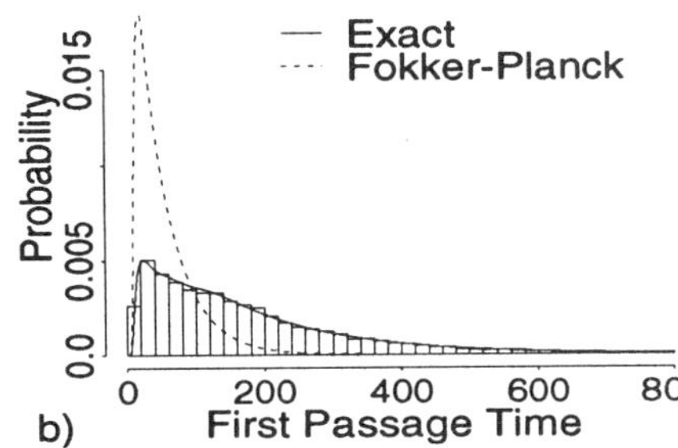

Figure 5: Second 1-D XOR example. a) Cost function. b) Simulated (histogram) and theoretical (lines) distributions of first passage times.

3.2.2 Basin Hopping in Competitive Learning

As a final example, we consider competitive learning with two 2-D weight vectors symmetrically placed about the center of a rectangle. Inputs are uniformly distributed in a rectangle of width 1.1 and height 1. This configuration has both global and local optima.

Figure 6a shows a sample path with weights started near the local optimum (crosses) and switching to hover around the global optimum. The measured and predicted (from numerical integration of (8)) distribution of times required to first pass within a distance $\epsilon = 0.1$ of the global optimum are shown in Figure 6b.

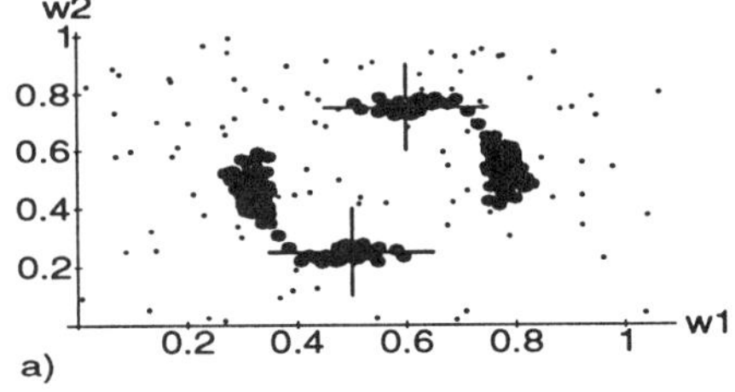

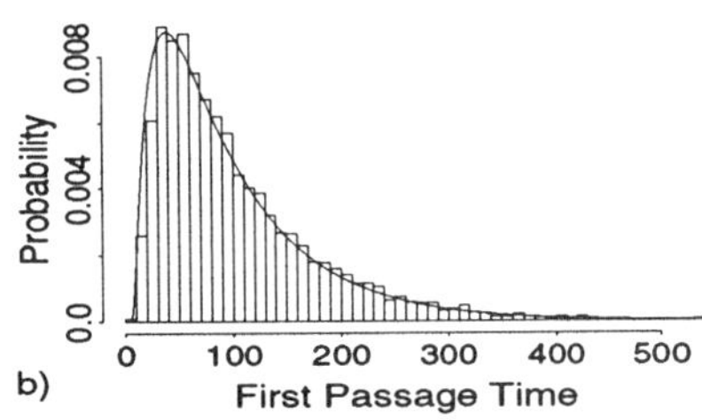

Figure 6: Competitive Learning a) Data (small dots) and sample weight path (large dots). b) First passage times.

4 Discussion

The dynamics of the time evolution of the weight space probability density provides a direct handle on the performance of learning algorithms. This paper has focused on transient phenomena in stochastic learning with constant learning rate. The same theoretical framework can be used to analyze the asymptotic properties of stochastic search with decreasing learning rates, and to analyze equilibrium densities. For a discussion of the latter, see the companion paper in this volume (Leen and Moody 1993).

Acknowledgements

This work was supported under grants N00014-90-J-1349 and N000-91-J-1482 from the Office of Naval Research.

References

E. Oja (1982), A simplified neuron model as a principal component analyzer. *J. Math. Biology*, 15:267–273.

Halbert White (1989), Learning in artificial neural networks: A statistical perspective. *Neural Computation*, 1:425–464.

J.J. Kushner (1987), Asymptotic global behavior for stochastic approximation and diffusions with slowly decreasing noise effects: Global minimization via monte carlo. *SIAM J. Appl. Math.*, 47:169–185.

Christian Darken and John Moody (1991), Note on learning rate schedules for stochastic optimization. In *Advances in Neural Information Processing Systems 3*, San Mateo, CA, Morgan Kaufmann.

Todd K. Leen and Genevieve B. Orr. (1992), Weight-space probability densities and convergence times for stochastic learning. In *International Joint Conference on Neural Networks*, pages IV 158–164. IEEE.

Todd K. Leen and John Moody (1993), Probability Densities in Stochastic Learning: Dynamics and Equilibria. In Giles, C.L., Hanson, S.J., and Cowan, J.D. (eds.), *Advances in Neural Information Processing Systems 5*. San Mateo, CA: Morgan Kaufmann Publishers.

H. Ritter and K. Schulten (1988), Convergence properties of Kohonen's topology conserving maps: Fluctuations, stability and dimension selection, *Biol. Cybern.*, 60, 59-71.

G. Radons, H.G. Schuster and D. Werner (1990), Fokker-Planck description of learning in backpropagation networks, *International Neural Network Conference*, Paris, II 993-996, Kluwer Academic Publishers.

C.W. Gardiner (1990), *Handbook of Stochastic Methods, 2nd Ed.* Springer-Verlag, Berlin.

P. Lisboa and S. Perantonis (1991), Complete solution of the local minima in the XOR problem. *Network: Computation in Neural Systems*, 2:119.

Information Theoretic Analysis of Connection Structure from Spike Trains

Satoru Shiono*
Central Research Laboratory
Mitsubishi Electric Corporation
Amagasaki, Hyogo 661, Japan

Satoshi Yamada
Central Research Laboratory
Mitsubishi Electric Corporation
Amagasaki, Hyogo 661, Japan

Michio Nakashima
Central Research Laboratory
Mitsubishi Electric Corporation
Amagasaki, Hyogo 661, Japan

Kenji Matsumoto
Faculty of Pharmaceutical Science
Hokkaidou University
Sapporo, Hokkaidou 060, Japan

Abstract

We have attempted to use information theoretic quantities for analyzing neuronal connection structure from spike trains. Two point mutual information and its maximum value, channel capacity, between a pair of neurons were found to be useful for sensitive detection of crosscorrelation and for estimation of synaptic strength, respectively. Three point mutual information among three neurons could give their interconnection structure. Therefore, our information theoretic analysis was shown to be a very powerful technique for deducing neuronal connection structure. Some concrete examples of its application to simulated spike trains are presented.

1 INTRODUCTION

The deduction of neuronal connection structure from spike trains, including synaptic strength estimation, has long been one of the central issues for understanding the structure and function of the neuronal circuit and thus the information processing

*corresponding author

mechanism at the neuronal circuitry level. A variety of crosscorrelational techniques for two or more neurons have been proposed and utilized (*e.g.*, Melssen and Epping, 1987; Aertsen *et. al.*, 1989). There are, however, some difficulties with those techniques, as discussed by, *e.g.*, Yang and Shamma (1990). It is sometimes difficult for the method to distinguish a significant crosscorrelation from noise, especially when the amount of experimental data is limited. The quantitative estimation of synaptic connectivity is another difficulty. And it is impossible to determine whether two neurons are directly connected or not, only by finding a significant crosscorrelation between them.

The information theory has been shown to afford a powerful tool for the description of neuronal input-output relations, such as in the investigation on the neuronal coding of the visual cortex (Eckhorn *et. al.*, 1976; Optican and Richmond, 1987). But there has been no extensive study to apply it to the correlational analysis of action potential trains. Because a correlational method using information theoretic quantities is considered to give a better correlational measure, the information theory is expected to offer a unique correlational method to overcome the above difficulties.

In this paper, we describe information theory-based correlational analysis for action potential trains, using two and three point mutual information (MI) and channel capacity. Because the information theoretic analysis by two point MI and channel capacity will be published in near future (Yamada *et. al.*, 1993a), more detailed description is given here on the analysis by three point MI for infering the relationship among three neurons.

2 CORRELATIONAL ANALYSIS BASED ON INFORMATION THEORY

2.1 INFORMATION THEORETIC QUANTITIES

According to the information theory, the n point mutual information expresses the amount of information shared among n processes (McGill, 1955). Let X, Y and Z be processes, and t and s be the time delays of X and Y from Z, respectively. Using Shannon entropies H, two point MI between X and Y and three point MI, are defined (Shannon, 1948; Ikeda *et. al.*, 1989):

$$I(X_t : Y_s) = H(X_t) + H(Y_s) - H(X_t, Y_s), \tag{1}$$

$$I(X_t : Y_s : Z) = H(X_t) + H(Y_s) + H(Z) - H(X_t, Y_s) - H(Y_s, Z) - H(Z, X_t) + H(X_t, Y_s, Z). \tag{2}$$

$I(X_t : Y_s : Z)$ is related to $I(X_t : Y_s)$ as follows:

$$I(X_t : Y_s : Z) = I(X_t : Y_s) - I(X_t : Y_s|Z), \tag{3}$$

where $I(X_t : Y_s|Z)$ means the two point conditional MI between X and Y if the state of Z is given. On the other hand, channel capacity is given by $(\tau = s - t)$,

$$CC(X : Y_\tau) = \max_{p(x_i)} I(X : Y_\tau). \tag{4}$$

We consider now X, Y and Z to be neurons whose spike activity has been measured.

Two point MI and two point conditional MI are obtained by $(i, j, k = 0, 1)$,

$$I(X : Y_\tau) = \sum_{i,j} p(y_{j,\tau}|x_i)p(x_i) \log \frac{p(y_{j,\tau}|x_i)}{p(y_{j,\tau})}, \tag{5}$$

$$I(X_t : Y_s|Z) = \sum_{i,j,k} p(x_{i,t}, y_{j,s}|z_k)p(z_k) \log \frac{p(x_{i,t}, y_{j,s}|z_k)}{p(x_{i,t}|z_k)p(y_{j,s}|z_k)}. \tag{6}$$

where x, y and z mean the states of neurons, *e.g.*, x_1 for the firing state and x_0 for the non-firing state of X, and $p(\ )$ denotes probability. And three point MI is obtained by using Equation (3). Those information theoretic quantities are calculated by using the probabilities estimated from the spike trains of X, Y and Z after the spike trains are converted into time sequences consisting of 0 and 1 with discrete time steps, as described elswhere (Yamada *et. al.*, 1993a).

2.2 PROCEDURE FOR THREE POINT MUTUAL INFORMATION ANALYSIS

Suppose that a three point MI peak is found at (t_0, s_0) in the t, s-plane (see Figure 1). The three time delays, t_0, s_0 and $\tau = s_0 - t_0$, are obtained. They are supposed to be time delays in three possible interconnections between any pair of neurons. Because the peak is not significant if only one pair of the three neurons is interconnected, two or three of the possible interconnections with corresponding time delays should truly work to produce the peak. We will utilize $I(n : m)$ and $I(n : m|l)$ $(n, m, l = X, Y$ or $Z)$ at the peak to find working interconnections out of them. These quantities are obtained by recalculating each probability in Equations (5) and (6) over the whole peak region.

If two neurons, *e.g.*, X and Y, are not interconnected either $I(X : Y)$ or $I(X : Y|Z)$ is equal to zero. The reverse proposition, however, is not true. The necessary and sufficient condition for having no interconnection is obtained by calculating $I(n : m)$ and $I(n : m|l)$ for all possible interconnection structures. The neurons are rearranged and renamed A, B and C in the order of the time delays. There are only four interconnection structures, as shown in Table 1.

I: No interconnection between A and B. A and B are statistically independent, *i.e.*, $p(a_i, b_j) = p(a_i)p(b_j)$, $I(A : B) = 0$. The three point MI peak is negative.

II: No interconnection between A and C. The states of A and C are statistically independent when the state of B is given, *i.e.*, $p(a_i, c_k|b_j) = p(a_i|b_j)p(c_k|b_j)$, $I(A : C|B) = 0$. The peak is positive.

III: No interconnection between B and C. Similar to case II, because $p(b_j, c_k|a_i) = p(b_j|a_i)p(c_k|a_i)$, $I(B : C|A) = 0$. The peak is positive.

IV: Three interconnections. The above three cases are considered to occur concomitantly in this case. The peak is positive or negative, depending on their relative contributions. Because A and B should have an apparent effect on the firing-probability of the postsynaptic neurons, $I(A : B)$, $I(A : C|B)$ and $I(B : C|A)$ are all non-zero except for the case where the activity of B completely coincides with that of A with the specified time delay (in this case, both $I(A : C|B)$ and $I(B : C|A)$ are zero (see Yamada *et. al.*, 1993b)).

Table 1. Interconnection Structure and Information Theoretic Quantities

Interconnection Structure	I 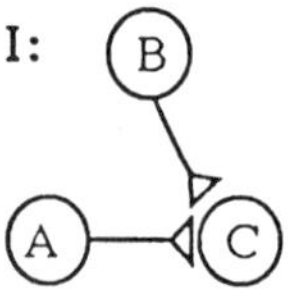	II 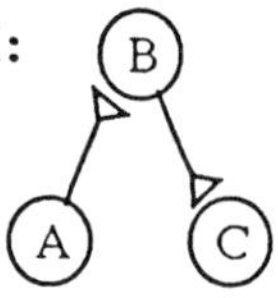	III 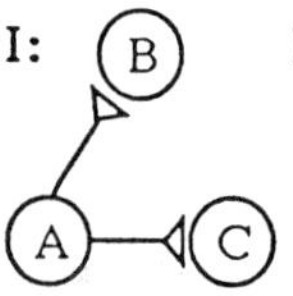	IV 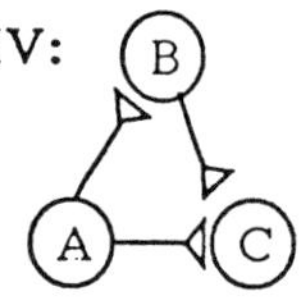
2 point MI				
I(A:B)	$=0$	>0	>0	>0
I(A:C)	$\geqq 0$	>0	>0	$\geqq 0$
I(B:C)	$\geqq 0$	>0	>0	$\geqq 0$
2 point condition MI				
I(A:B | C)	>0	$\geqq 0$	$\geqq 0$	$\geqq 0$
I(A:C | B)	>0	$=0$	$\geqq 0$	>0
I(B:C | A)	>0	$\geqq 0$	$=0$	>0
3 point MI				
I(A:B:C)	$-$	$+$	$+$	$+$ or $-$

From what we have described above, the interconnection structure for a three point MI peak is deduced utilizing the following procedure;

(a) A negative 3pMI peak: it corresponds to case I or IV. The problem is to determine whether A and B are interconnected or not.

(1) If $I(A:B) = 0$, case I.

(2) If $I(A:B) > 0$, case IV.

(b) A positive 3pMI peak: it corresponds to case II, III or IV. The existence of the $A-C$ and $B-C$ interconnections has to be checked.

(1) If $I(A:C|B) > 0$ and $I(B:C|A) > 0$, case IV.

(2) If $I(A:C|B) = 0$ and $I(B:C|A) > 0$, case II.

(3) If $I(A:C|B) > 0$ and $I(B:C|A) = 0$, case III.

(4) If $I(A:C|B) = 0$ and $I(B:C|A) = 0$, the interconnection structure cannot be deduced except for the $A-B$ interconnection.

This procedure is applicable, if all the time delays are non-zero. If otherwise, some of the interconnections cannot be determined (Yamada *et. al.*, 1993b).

3 SIMULATED SPIKE TRAINS

In order to characterize our information theoretic analysis, simulations of neuronal network models were carried out. We used a model neuron described by the Hodgkin-Huxley equations (Yamada *et. al.*, 1989). The used equations and parameters were described (Yamada *et. al.*, 1993a). The Hodgkin-Huxley equations were mathematically integrated by the Runge-Kutta-Gill technique.

4 RESULTS AND DISCUSSION

4.1 ANALYSIS BY TWO POINT MUTUAL INFORMATION AND CHANNEL CAPACITY

The performance was previously reported of the information theoretic analysis by two point MI and channel capacity (Yamada *et. al.*, 1993a).

Briefly, this anlytical method was compared with some conventional ones for both excitatory and inhibitory connections using action potential trains obtained by the simulation of a model neuronal network. It was shown to have the following advantages. First, it reduced correlational measures within the bounds of noise and simultaneously amplified beyond the bounds by its nonlinear function. It should be easier in its crosscorrelation graph to find a neuron pair having a weak but significant interaction, especially when the synaptic strength is small or the amount of experimental data is limited. Second, channel capacity was shown to allow fairly effective estimation of synaptic strength, being independent of the firing probability of a presynaptic neuron, as long as this firing probability was not large enough to have the overlap of two successive postsynaptic potentials.

4.2 ANALYSIS BY THREE POINT MUTUAL INFORMATION

The practical application of the analysis by three point MI is shown below in detail, using spike trains obtained by simulation of the three-neuron network models shown in Figures 1 and 2 (Yamada *et. al.*, 1993b).

The network model in Figure 1(1) has three interconnections. In Figure 1(2), three point MI has two positive peaks at (17ms, 12ms) (unit "ms" is omitted hereafter) and $(17, 30)$, and one negative peak at $(0, 12)$. For the peak at $(17, 12)$, the neurons are renamed A, B and C from the time delays (Z as A, Y as B and X as C), as in Table 1. Because only $I(B : C|A) \doteq 0$ (see Figure 1 legend), the peak indicates case III with $A \rightarrow B$ ($Z \rightarrow Y$) ($s = 12$) and $A \rightarrow C$ ($Z \rightarrow X$) ($t = 17$) interconnections. Similarly, the peak at $(17, 30)$ indicates $Z \rightarrow X$ and $X \rightarrow Y$ ($s - t = 13$) interconnections, and the peak at $(0, 12)$ indicates $Z \rightarrow Y$ and $X \rightarrow Y$ interconnections. The interconnection structure deduced from each three point MI peak is consistent with each other, and in agreement with the network model.

Alternatively, the three point MI graphical presentation such as shown in Figure 1(2) itself gives indication of some truly existing interconnections. If more than two three point MI peaks are found on one of the three lines, $t = t_0$, $s = s_0$ and $s - t = \tau_0$, the interconnection with the time delay represented by this line is considered to be real. For example, because the peaks at $(17, 12)$ and $(17, 30)$ are on the line of $t = 17$ (Figure 1(2)), the interconnection represented by $t = 17$ ($Z \rightarrow X$) are considered to be real. In a similar manner, the interconnections of $s = 12$ ($Z \rightarrow Y$) and $s - t = 12$ ($X \rightarrow Y$) are obtained. But this graphical indication is not complete, and thus the calculation of two point MI's and two point conditional MI's should be always

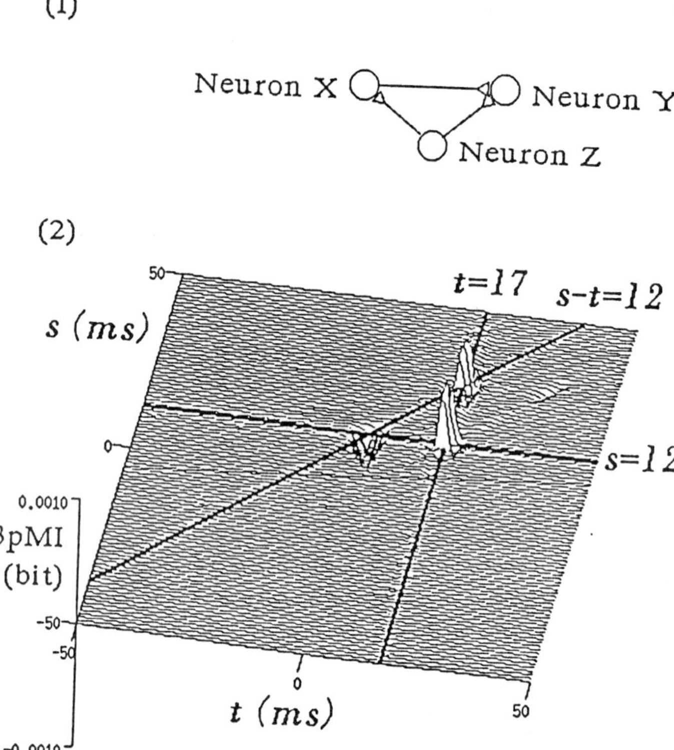

Figure 1. Three point MI analysis of simulated spike trains. (1) A three-neuron network model with $Z \rightarrow X$ $Z \rightarrow Y$ and $X \rightarrow Y$ interconnections. The total number of spikes; X:4000, Y:5400, Z:3150. (2) Three point MI analysis of spike trains. Three point MI has two positive peaks at $(17, 12)$ and $(17, 30)$, and one negative peak at $(0, 12)$. For the peak at $(17, 12)$ the neurons are renamed (Z as A, Y as B and X as C). Two point MI and two point conditional MI for the peak at $(17, 12)$ are: $I(A:B) = 0.03596$, $I(A:C) = 0.06855$, $I(B:C) = 0.01375$, $I(A:B|C) = 0.02126$, $I(A:C|B) = 0.05376$, $I(B:C|A) = 0.00011$. So, $I(B:C|A) \doteq 0$, indicating case III (see Table 1) with $A \rightarrow B$ ($Z \rightarrow Y$) and $A \rightarrow C$ ($Z \rightarrow X$) interconnections. Similarly, for the peaks at $(17, 30)$ and at $(0, 12)$, $Z \rightarrow X$ and $X \rightarrow Y$ interconnections, and $Z \rightarrow Y$ and $X \rightarrow Y$ interconnections are obtained, respectively.

performed for confirmation.

The network model in Figure 2(1) has four interconnections. Three point MI has five major peaks: four positive peaks at $(17, -12)$, $(17, 30)$, $(-24, -12)$ and $(17, 12)$ and one negative peak at $(0, 10)$. The peaks at $(17, -12)$, $(17, 12)$ and $(17, 30)$ are on the line of $t = 17$ ($Z \rightarrow X$), the peaks at $(17, -12)$ and $(-24, -12)$ are on the line of $s = -12$ ($Z \leftarrow Y$), the peaks at $(17, 12)$ and $(0, 10)$ are on the line of $s = 12$ ($Z \rightarrow Y$), and the peaks at $(-24, -12)$, $(0, 10)$ and $(17, 30)$ are on the line of

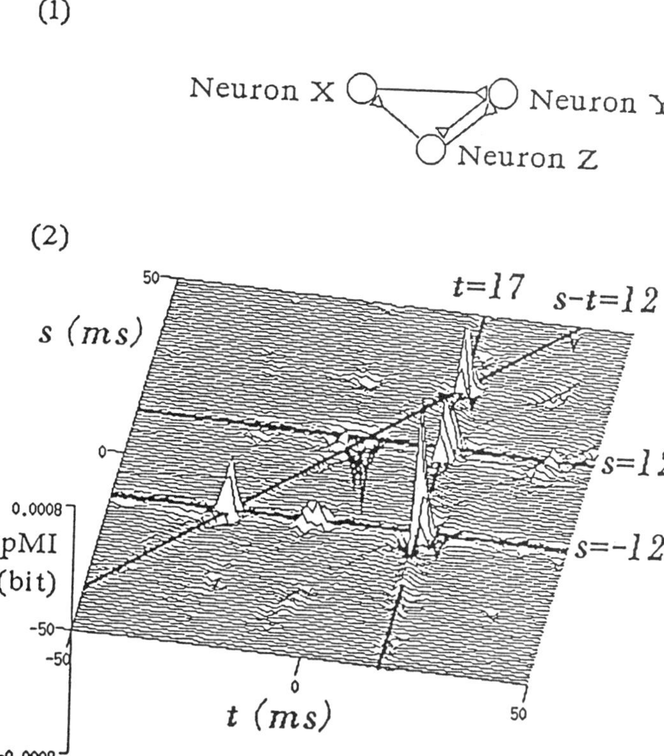

Figure 2. Three point MI analysis of simulated spike trains. (1) A three-neuron network model with $Z \rightarrow X$ $Z \rightarrow Y$, $Z \leftarrow Y$ and $X \rightarrow Y$ interconnections. The total number of spikes; X:4300, Y:5150, Z:4850. (2) Three point MI analysis of spike trains. Three point MI has five major peaks, four positive peaks at $(17, -12)$, $(17, 12)$, $(17, 30)$ and $(-24, -12)$, and one negative peak at $(0, 10)$.

$s - t = 12$ ($X \rightarrow Y$). The calculation of two point MI and two point conditional MI for each peak gives the confirmation that each three point MI peak was produced by two interconnections. Namely, their calculation indicates $Z \rightarrow X$ ($t = 17$), $Z \leftarrow Y$ ($s = -12$), $Z \rightarrow Y$ ($s = 12$) and $X \rightarrow Y$ ($s - t = 12$) interconnections. There are also some small peaks. They are considered to be ghost peaks due to two or three interconnections, at least one of which is a combination of two interconnections found by analyzing the major peaks. For example, the positive peak at $(-7, -12)$ indicates $Z \leftarrow Y$ and $X \rightarrow Y$ interconnections, but the latter ($s - t = -5$) is the combination of the $Z \rightarrow X$ interconnection ($t = 17$) and the $Z \rightarrow Y$ interconnection ($s = 12$).

The interconnection structure of a network containing an inhibitory interconnection or consisting of more than four neurons can also be deduced, although it becomes more difficult to perform the three point MI analysis.

References

A. M. H. J. Aertsen, G. L. Gerstein, M. K. Habib & G. Palm. (1989) Dynamics of neuronal firing correlation: modulation of "effective connectivity". *J. Neurophysiol.* **61**: 900-917.

R. Eckhorn, O. J. Grüsser, J. Kröller, K. Pellnitz & B. Pöpel. (1976) Efficiency of different neuronal codes: information transfer calculations for three different neuronal systems. *Biol. Cybern.* **22**: 49-60.

K. Ikeda, K. Otsuka & K. Matsumoto. (1989) Maxwell-Bloch turbulence. *Prog. Theor. Phys., Suppl.* **99**: 295-324.

W. J. McGill. (1955) Multivariate information transmission. *IRE Trans. Inf. Theory* **1**: 93-111.

W. J. Melssen & W. J. M. Epping. (1987) Detection and estimation of neural connectivity based on crosscorrelation analysis. *Biol. Cybern.* **57**: 403-414.

L. M. Optican & B. J. Richmond. (1987) Temporal encoding of two-dimensional patterns by single units primate inferior temporal cortex. III. Information theoretic analysis. *J. Neurophysiol.* **57**: 162-178.

C. E. Shannon. (1948) A mathematical theory of communication. *Bell. Syst. Techn. J.* **27**: 379-423.

S. Yamada, M. Nakashima, K. Matsumoto & S. Shiono. (1993a) Information theoretic analysis of action potential trains: I. Analysis of correlation between two neurons. *Biol. Cybern.*, in press.

S. Yamada, M. Nakashima, K. Matsumoto & S. Shiono. (1993b) Information theoretic analysis of action potential trains: II. Analysis of correlation among three neurons. submitted to *Biol. Cybern.*

W. M. Yamada, C. Koch & P. R. Adams. (1989) Multiple channels and calcium dynamics. In C. Koch & I. Segev (ed), *Methods in Neuronal Modeling: From Synapses to Neurons*, 97-133, Cambridge, MA, USA: MIT Press.

X. Yang & S. A. Shamma. (1990) Identification of connectivity in neural networks. *Biophys. J.* **57**: 987-999.

Statistical Mechanics of Learning in a Large Committee Machine

Holm Schwarze
CONNECT, The Niels Bohr Institute
Blegdamsvej 17, DK-2100 Copenhagen Ø, Denmark

John Hertz*
Nordita
Blegdamsvej 17, DK-2100 Copenhagen Ø, Denmark

Abstract

We use statistical mechanics to study generalization in large committee machines. For an architecture with nonoverlapping receptive fields a replica calculation yields the generalization error in the limit of a large number of hidden units. For continuous weights the generalization error falls off asymptotically inversely proportional to α, the number of training examples per weight. For binary weights we find a discontinuous transition from poor to perfect generalization followed by a wide region of metastability. Broken replica symmetry is found within this region at low temperatures. For a fully connected architecture the generalization error is calculated within the annealed approximation. For both binary and continuous weights we find transitions from a symmetric state to one with specialized hidden units, accompanied by discontinuous drops in the generalization error.

1 Introduction

There has been a good deal of theoretical work on calculating the *generalization ability* of neural networks within the framework of statistical mechanics (for a review

*Address in 1993: Laboratory of Neuropsychology, NIMH, Bethesda, MD 20892, USA

see e.g. Watkin et.al., 1992; Seung et.al., 1992). This approach has mostly been applied to single-layer nets (e.g. Györgyi and Tishby, 1990; Seung et.al., 1992). Extensions to networks with a hidden layer include a model with small hidden receptive fields (Sompolinsky and Tishby, 1990), some general results on networks whose outputs are continuous functions of their inputs (Seung et.al., 1992; Krogh and Hertz, 1992), and calculations for a so-called *committee machine* (Nilsson, 1965), a two-layer Boolean network, which implements a majority decision of the hidden units (Schwarze et.al., 1992; Schwarze and Hertz, 1992; Mato and Parga, 1992; Barkai et.al., 1992; Engel et.al., 1992). This model has previously been studied when learning a function which could be implemented by a simple perceptron (i.e. one with no hidden units) in the high-temperature (i.e. high-noise) limit (Schwarze et.al., 1992). In most practical applications, however, the function to be learnt is not linearly separable. Therefore, we consider here a committee machine trained on a rule which itself is defined by another committee machine (the 'teacher' network) and hence not linearly separable.

We calculate the generalization error, the probability of misclassifying an arbitrary new input, as a function of α, the ratio of the number of training examples P to the number of adjustable weights in the network. First we present results for the 'tree' committee machine, a restricted version of the model in which the receptive fields of the hidden units do not overlap. In section 3 we study a fully connected architecture allowing for correlations between different hidden units in the student network. In both cases we study a large-net limit in which the total number of inputs (N) and the number of hidden units (K) both go to infinity, but with $K \ll N$.

2 Committee machine with nonoverlapping receptive fields

In this model each hidden unit receives its input from N/K input units, subject to the restriction that different hidden units do not share common inputs. Therefore there is only one path from each input unit to the output. The hidden-output weights are all fixed to $+1$ as to implement a majority decision of the hidden units. The overall network output for inputs $\underline{S}_l \in \mathbb{R}^{N/K}$, $l = 1, \ldots, K$, to the K branches is given by

$$\sigma(\{\underline{S}_l\}) = \text{sign}\left(\frac{1}{\sqrt{K}}\sum_{l=1}^{K}\sigma_l\left(\underline{S}_l\right)\right), \tag{1}$$

where σ_l is the output of the lth hidden unit, given by

$$\sigma_l(\underline{S}_l) = \text{sign}\left(\sqrt{\frac{K}{N}}\,\underline{W}_l \cdot \underline{S}_l\right). \tag{2}$$

Here $\underline{W}_l$ is the N/K-dimensional weight vector connecting the input with the lth hidden unit. The training examples $(\{\underline{\xi^\mu}_l\}, \tau(\{\underline{\xi^\mu}_l\}), \mu = 1, \ldots, P$, are generated by another committee machine with weight vectors $\underline{V}_l$ and an overall output $\tau(\{\underline{\xi^\mu}_l\})$, defined analogously to (1). There are N adjustable weights in the network, and therefore we have $\alpha = P/N$.

As in the corresponding calculations for simple perceptrons (Gardner and Derrida, 1988; Györgyi and Tishby, 1990; Seung et.al., 1992), we consider a stochastic learning algorithm which for long training times yields a Gibbs distribution of networks. The statistical mechanics approach starts out from the partition function $Z = \int d\rho_0(\{\underline{W}_l\})\, e^{-\beta E(\{\underline{W}_l\})}$, an integral over weight space with a priori measure $\rho_0(\{\underline{W}_l\})$, weighted with a thermal factor $e^{-\beta E(\{\underline{W}_l\})}$, where E is the total error on the training examples

$$E(\{\underline{W}_l\}) = \sum_{\mu=1}^{P} \Theta\Big[-\sigma\Big(\{\underline{\xi}^{\mu}_{l}\}\Big) \cdot \tau\Big(\{\underline{\xi}^{\mu}_{l}\}\Big)\Big]. \tag{3}$$

The formal temperature $T = 1/\beta$ defines the level of noise during the training process. For $T = 0$ this procedure corresponds to simply minimizing the training error E.

From this the average free energy $F = -T\,\langle\langle \ln Z \rangle\rangle$, averaged over all possible sets of training examples can be calculated using the replica method (for details see Schwarze and Hertz, 1992). Like the calculations for simple perceptrons, our theory has two sets of order parameters:

$$q_l^{\alpha\beta} = \frac{K}{N}\, \underline{W}_l^{\alpha} \cdot \underline{W}_l^{\beta} \qquad R_l^{\alpha} = \frac{K}{N}\, \underline{W}_l^{\alpha} \cdot \underline{V}_l.$$

Note that these are the only order parameters in this model. Due to the tree structure no correlations between different hidden units exist. Assuming both replica symmetry and 'translational symmetry' we are left with two parameters: q, the pattern average of the square of the average input–hidden weight vector, and R, the average overlap between this weight vector and a corresponding one for the teacher.

We then obtain expressions for the replica–symmetric free energy of the form $G(q, R, \hat{q}, \hat{R}) = \alpha\, G_1(q, R) + G_2(q, R, \hat{q}, \hat{R})$, where the 'entropy' terms G_2 for the continuous– and binary–weight cases are exactly the same as in the simple perceptron (Györgyi and Tishby, 1990, Seung et.al., 1992). In the large–K limit another simplification similar to the zero–temperature capacity calculation (Barkai et.al., 1992) is found in the tree model. The 'energy' term G_1 is the same as the corresponding term in the calculation for the simple perceptron, except that the order parameters have to be replaced by $f(q) = (2/\pi)\sin^{-1} q$ and $f(R) = (2/\pi)\sin^{-1} R$. The generalization error

$$\epsilon_g = \frac{1}{\pi} \arccos\left[f(R)\right] \tag{4}$$

can then be obtained from the value of R at the saddle point of the free energy.

For a network with continuous weights, the solution of the saddle point equations yields an algebraically decreasing generalization error. There is no phase transition at any value of α or T. For $T = 0$ the asymptotic form of the generalization error in powers of $1/\alpha$ can be easily obtained as $1.25/\alpha + \mathcal{O}(1/\alpha^2)$, twice the ϵ_g found for the simple perceptron in this limit.

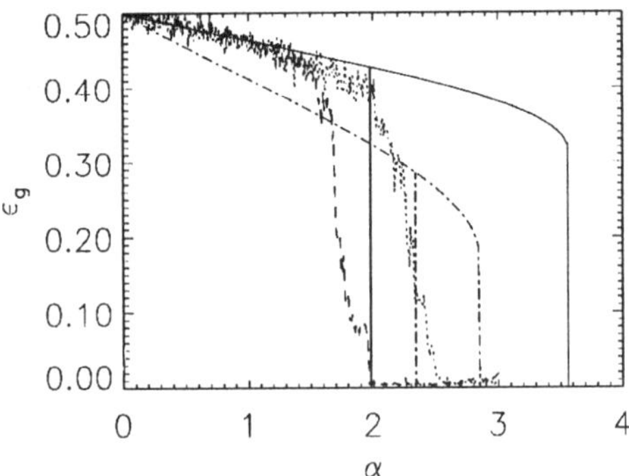

Figure 1: Learning curve for the large–K tree committee (solid line) with binary weights at $T = 1$. The phase transition occurs at $\alpha_c = 1.98$, and the spinodal point is at $\alpha_s = 3.56$. The analytic results are compared with Monte Carlo simulations with $K = 9$, $N = 75$ and $T = 1$, averaged over 10 runs. In each simulation the number of training examples is gradually increased (dotted line) and decreased (dashed line), respectively. The broken line shows the generalization error for the simple perceptron.

In contrast, the model with binary weights exhibits a phase transition at all temperatures from poor to perfect generalization. The corresponding generalization error as a function of α is shown in figure 1. At small values of α the free energy has two saddle points, one at $R < 1$ and the other at $R = 1$. Initially the solution with $R < 1$ and poor generalization ability has the lower free energy and therefore corresponds to the equilibrium state. When the load parameter is increased to a critical value α_c, the situation changes and the solution at $R = 1$ becomes the global minimum of the free energy. The system exhibits a first order phase transition to the state of perfect generalization. In the region $\alpha_c < \alpha < \alpha_s$ the $R < 1$ solution remains metastable and disappears at the spinodal point α_s. We find the same qualitative picture at all temperatures, and the complete replica symmetric phase diagram is shown in figure 2. The solid line corresponds to the phase transition to perfect generalization, and in the region between the solid and the dashed lines the $R < 1$ state of poor generalization is metastable. Below the dotted line, the replica–symmetric solution yields a negative entropy for the metastable state. This is unphysical in a binary system and replica symmetry has to be broken in this region, indicating the existence of many different metastable states.

The simple perceptron without hidden units corresponds to the case $K = 1$ in our model. A comparison of the generalization properties with the large–K limit shows that both limits exhibit qualitatively similar behavior. The locations of the thermodynamic transitions and the spinodal line, however, are different and the generalization error of the $R < 1$ state in the large–K committee machine is higher than in the simple perceptron.

The case of general finite K is rather more involved, but the annealed approximation

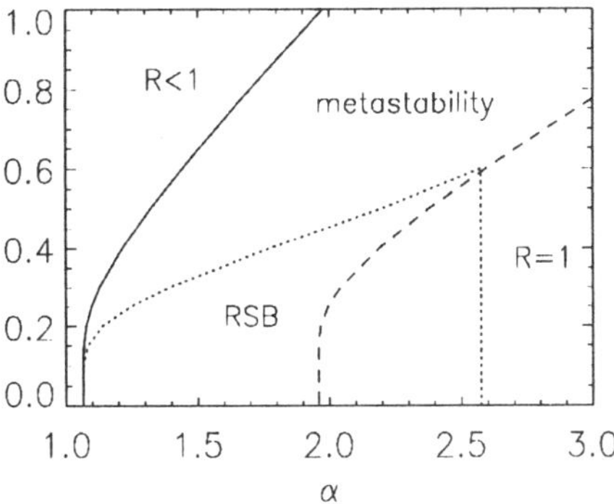

Figure 2: Replica–symmetric phase diagram of the large–K tree committee machine with binary weights. The solid line shows the locations of the phase transition, and the spinodal line is shown dashed. Below the the dotted line the replica–symmetric solution is incorrect.

for finite K indicates a rather smooth K–dependence for $1 < K < \infty$ (Mato and Parga, 1992).

We performed Monte–Carlo simulations to check the validity of the assumptions made in our calculation and found good agreements with our analytic results. Figure 1 compares the analytic predictions for large K with Monte Carlo simulations for $K = 9$. The simulations were performed for a slowly increasing and decreasing training set size, respectively, yielding a hysteresis loop around the location of the phase transition.

3 Fully connected committee machine

In contrast to the previous model the hidden units in the fully connected committee machine receive inputs from the entire input layer. Their output for a given N–dimensional input vector $\underline{S}$ is given by

$$\sigma_l(\underline{S}) = \text{sign}\left(\frac{1}{\sqrt{N}}\,\underline{W}_l \cdot \underline{S}\right), \tag{5}$$

while the overall output is again of the form (1). Note that the weight vectors $\underline{W}_l$ are now N–dimensional, and the load parameter is given by $\alpha = P/(KN)$.

For this model we solved the annealed approximation, which replaces $\langle\langle \ln Z \rangle\rangle$ by $\ln \langle\langle Z \rangle\rangle$. This approximation becomes exact at high temperatures (high noise level during training). For learnable target rules, as in the present problem, previous work indicates that the annealed approximation yields qualitatively correct results and correctly predicts the shape of the learning curves even at low temperatures (Seung et.al., 1992). Performing the average over all possible training sets again leads to two sets of order parameters: the overlaps between the student and teacher weight vectors, $R_{lk} = N^{-1}\underline{W}_l \cdot \underline{V}_k$, and the mutual overlaps in the student network $C_{lk} = N^{-1}\underline{W}_l \cdot \underline{W}_k$. The weight vectors of the target rule are assumed to be uncorrelated and normalized, $N^{-1}\underline{V}_l \cdot \underline{V}_k = \delta_{lk}$. As in the previous model we make symmetry assumptions for the order parameters. In the fully connected architecture we have to allow for correlations between different hidden units ($R_{lk}, C_{lk} \neq 0$ for $l \neq k$) but also include the possibility of a specialization of individual units ($R_{ll} \neq R_{lk}$). This is necessary because the ground state of the system with vanishing generalization error is achieved for the choice $R_{lk} = C_{lk} = \delta_{lk}$. Therefore we make the ansatz

$$R_{lk} = R + \Delta\delta_{lk}, \qquad C_{lk} = C + (1-C)\delta_{lk} \tag{6}$$

and evaluate the annealed free energy of the system using the saddle point method (details will be reported elsewhere). The values of the order parameters at the minimum of the free energy finally yield the average generalization error ϵ_g as a function of α.

For a network with continuous weights and small α the global minimum of the free energy occurs at $\Delta = 0$ and $R \sim \mathcal{O}(K^{-3/4})$. Hence, for small training sets each hidden unit in the student network has a small symmetric overlap to all the hidden units in the teacher network. The information obtained from the training examples is not sufficient for a specialization of hidden units, and the generalization error approaches a plateau. To order $1/\sqrt{K}$, this approach is given by

$$\epsilon_g = \epsilon_0 + \sqrt{\frac{\gamma(\beta)}{\alpha K}} + \mathcal{O}(1/K), \quad \epsilon_0 = \frac{1}{\pi}\arccos\left(\sqrt{2/\pi}\right) \approx 0.206, \tag{7}$$

with $\gamma(\beta) = \sqrt{\pi/2 - 1}\,[(1-e^{-\beta})^{-1} - \epsilon_0]/(4\pi)$. Figure 3 shows the generalization error as a function of α, including $1/\sqrt{K}$–corrections for different values of K.

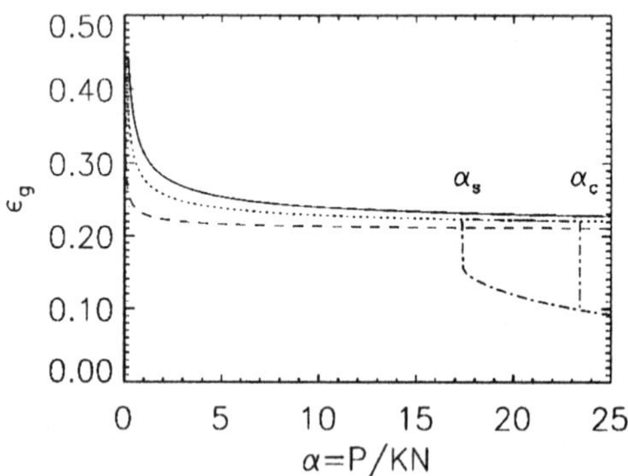

Figure 3: Generalization error for continuous weights and $T = 0.5$. The approach to the residual error is shown including $1/\sqrt{K}$–corrections for K=5 (solid line), K=11 (dotted line), and K=100 (dashed line). The broken line corresponds to the solution with nonvanishing Δ.

When the training set size is increased to a critical value α_s of the load parameter, a second minimum of the free energy appears at a finite value of Δ close to 1. For a larger value $\alpha_c > \alpha_s$ this becomes the global minimum of the free energy and the system exhibits a first order phase transition. The generalization error of the specialized solution decays smoothly with an asymptotic behavior inversely proportional to α. However, the poorly–generalizing symmetric state remains metastable for all $\alpha > \alpha_c$. Therefore, a stochastic learning procedure starting with $\Delta = 0$ will first settle into the metastable state. For large N it will take an exponentially long time to cross the free energy barrier to the global minimum of the free energy.

In a network with binary weights and for large K we find the same initial approach to a finite generalization error as in (7) for continuous weights. In the large–K limit the discreteness of the weights does not influence the behavior for small training sets. However, while a perfect match of the student to the teacher network ($R_{lk} = C_{lk} = \delta_{lk}$) cannot happen for $\alpha < \infty$ in the continuous model, such a 'freezing' is possible in a discrete system. The free energy of the binary model always has a local minimum at $R_{lk} = C_{lk} = \delta_{lk}$. When the load parameter is increased to a critical value, this minimum becomes the global minimum of the free energy, and a discontinuous transition into this perfectly generalizing state occurs, just as in the binary–weight simple perceptron and the tree described in section 2. As in the case of continuous weights, the symmetric solution remains metastable here even for large values of α. Figure 4 shows the generalization error for binary weights, including $1/\sqrt{K}$–corrections for $K = 5$. The predictions of the large–K theory are compared with Monte Carlo simulations. Although we cannot expect a good quantitative agreement for such a small committee, the simulations support our qualitative results. Note that the leading order correction to ϵ_0 in eqn. (7) is only small for $\alpha \gg 1/K$. However, we have obtained a different solution, which is valid for $\alpha \sim \mathcal{O}(1/K)$. The corresponding generalization error is shown as a dotted line in figure 4.

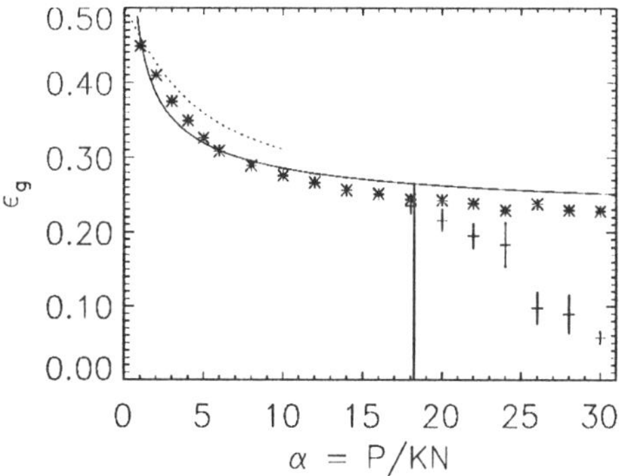

Figure 4: Generalization error for binary weights at $T = 5$. The large–K theory for different regions of α is compared with simulations for $K = 5$ and $N = 45$ averaged over all simulations (+) and simulations, in which no freezing occurred (*), respectively. The solid line shows the finite–α results including $1/\sqrt{K}$–corrections. The dotted line shows the small–α solution.

Compared to the tree model the fully connected committee machine shows a qualitatively different behavior. This difference is particularly pronounced in the continuous model. While the generalization error of the tree architecture decays smoothly for all values of α, the fully connected model exhibits a discontinuous phase transition. Compared to the tree model, the fully connected architecture has an additional symmetry, because each permutation of hidden units in the student network yields the same output for a given input (Barkai et.al., 1992). This additional degree of freedom causes the poor generalization ability for small training sets. Only if the training set size is sufficiently large can the hidden units specialize on one of the hidden units in the teacher network and achieve good generalization. However, the poorly generalizing states remain metastable even for arbitrarily large α. A similar phenomenon has also been found in a different architecture with only 2 hidden units performing a parity operation (Hansel et.al., 1992).

Acknowledgements

H. Schwarze acknowledges support from the EC under the SCIENCE programme and by the Danish Natural Science Council and the Danish Technical Research Council through CONNECT.

References

E. Barkai, D. Hansel, and H. Sompolinsky (1992), Phys.Rev. A **45**, 4146.

A. Engel, H.M. Köhler, F. Tschepke, H. Vollmayr, and A. Zippelius (1992), Phys.Rev. A **45**, 7590.

E. Gardner, B. Derrida (1989), J.Phys. A **21**, 271.

G. Györgyi and N. Tishby (1990) in *Neural Networks and Spin Glasses*, edited K. Thuemann and R. Köberle (World Scientific, Singapore).

D. Hansel, G. Mato, and C. Meunier (1992), Europhys.Lett. **20**, 471.

A. Krogh, J. Hertz (1992), *Advances in Neural Information Processing Systems IV*, edited by J.E. Moody, S.J. Hanson, and R.P. Lippmann, (Morgan Kaufmann, San Mateo).

G. Mato, N. Parga (1992), J.Phys. A **25**, 5047.

N.J. Nilsson (1965) *Learning Machines,* (McGraw–Hill, New York).

H. Schwarze, M. Opper, and W. Kinzel (1992), Phys.Rev. A **45**, R6185.

H. Schwarze, J. Hertz (1992), Europhys.Lett. **20**, 375.

H.S. Seung, H. Sompolinsky, and N. Tishby (1992), Phys.Rev. A **45**, 6056.

H. Sompolinsky, N. Tishby (1990), Europhys.Lett. **13**, 567.

T. Watkin, A. Rau, and M. Biehl (1992), to be published in Review of Modern Physics.

Probability Estimation from a Database Using a Gibbs Energy Model

John W. Miller
Microsoft Research (9/1051)
One Microsoft Way
Redmond, WA 98052

Rodney M. Goodman
Dept. of Electrical Engineering (116-81)
California Institute of Technology
Pasadena, CA 91125

Abstract

We present an algorithm for creating a neural network which produces accurate probability estimates as outputs. The network implements a Gibbs probability distribution model of the training database. This model is created by a new transformation relating the joint probabilities of attributes in the database to the weights (Gibbs potentials) of the distributed network model. The theory of this transformation is presented together with experimental results. One advantage of this approach is the network weights are prescribed without iterative gradient descent. Used as a classifier the network tied or outperformed published results on a variety of databases.

1 INTRODUCTION

This paper addresses the problem of modeling a discrete database. The database is viewed as a collection of independent samples from a probability distribution. This distribution is called the *underlying* distribution. In contrast, the empirical distribution is the distribution obtained if you take independent random samples from the database (with replacement). The task of creating a probability model can be separated into two parts. The first part is the problem of choosing statistics of the samples which are expected to accurately represent the underlying distribution. The second part is the problem of choosing a model which is consistent with these statistics. Under reasonable assumptions, the optimal solution to the second problem is the method of *Maximum Entropy*. For a broad class of statistics, the

Maximum Entropy solution is a *Gibbs* probability distribution (Slepian, 1972). In this paper, the background and theoretical result of a transformation from joint statistics to a Gibbs energy (or network weight) representation is presented. We then outline the experimental test results of an efficient algorithm implementing this transform without using gradient descent iteration.

2 BACKGROUND

Define a set T to be the set of attributes (or fields) in a database. For a particular entry (or record) of the database, define the associated set of attribute values to be the configuration ω of the attributes. The set of attribute values associated with a subset $b \subset T$ is called a subconfiguration ω_b. Using this set notation the Gibbs probability distribution may be defined:

$$p(\omega) = Z^{-1} \cdot e^{V_T(\omega)} \tag{1}$$

where

$$V_T(\omega) = \sum_{b \subseteq T} J_b(\omega) \tag{2}$$

The function V is called the *energy*. The function J_b, called the *potential function*, defines a real value for every subconfiguration of the set b. Z is the normalizing constant that makes the sum of probabilities of all configurations equal to unity.

Prior work in the neural network literature using the Gibbs distribution (such as the Boltzmann Machine) has primarily used second order models ($J_b = 0$ if $|b| > 2$) (Hinton, 1986). By adding new attributes not in the original database, second order potentials have been used to model complex distributions. The work presented in this paper, in contrast, uses higher order potentials to model complex probability distributions. We begin by considering the case where every potential of every order is used to model the distribution.

The Principle of Inclusion-Exclusion from set theory states that the following two equations are equivalent:

$$g(A) = \sum_{b \subseteq A} f(b) \tag{3}$$

$$f(A) = \sum_{b \subseteq A} (-1)^{|A-b|} \, g(b). \tag{4}$$

The method of inverting an equation from the form of (3) into one in the form of (4) is a special case of *Möbius Inversion.* Clifford-Hammersley (Kindermann, 1980) used this relation to invert formula (2):

$$J_A(\omega) = \sum_{b \subseteq A} (-1)^{|A-b|} \, V_b(\omega) \tag{5}$$

Define the probability of a subconfiguration $p(\omega_b)$ to be the probability that the attributes in set b take on the values defined in the configuration ω. Using (1) to describe the probability distribution of subconfigurations, equation (5) can be written:

$$J_A(\omega) = \sum_{b \subseteq A} (-1)^{|A-b|} \ln(\, p(\omega_b)\,) \tag{6}$$

3 A TRANSFORMATION TO GIBBS POTENTIALS

Equation (6) provides a technique for modeling distributions by potential functions rather than directly through the observable joint statistics of sets of attributes. If the model is truncated by setting high order potentials to zero, then the energy model becomes an estimate of the model obtained by collecting the joint statistics, rather than an exact equivalent. If equation (6) is used directly, the error in the energy due to setting all potentials of order d to zero grows quickly with d. For this reason (6) must be normalized if it is going to be used in a truncated modeling scheme. A normalization version of equation (2) that corrects for the unequal number of potentials of different orders is:

$$V_A(\omega) = \sum_{b \subseteq A} \binom{|A|-1}{|b|-1}^{-1} J_b(\omega) \tag{7}$$

This equation can be inverted to show the surprising result, a weight associated with ω_A:

$$J_A(\omega) = \ln(p_A(\omega)) - (|A|-1)^{-1} \sum_{\substack{t \in A \\ b = A - t}} \ln(p_b(\omega)) \tag{8}$$

For example, with three attribute values $\{x, y, z\}$, the following potentials are defined:

$$\begin{aligned}
J_{\{x\}} &= \ln(p(x)) \\
J_{\{y\}} &= \ln(p(y)) \\
J_{\{z\}} &= \ln(p(z)) \\
J_{\{xy\}} &= \ln\left(\frac{p(xy)}{p(x)p(y)}\right) \\
J_{\{yz\}} &= \ln\left(\frac{p(yz)}{p(y)p(z)}\right) \\
J_{\{xz\}} &= \ln\left(\frac{p(xz)}{p(x)p(z)}\right) \\
J_{\{xyz\}} &= \ln\left(\frac{p(xyz)}{\sqrt{p(xy)p(yz)p(xz)}}\right)
\end{aligned}$$

For a given database sample, a potential is *activated* if all of its defined attribute values are true for the sample. The weighted sum of all activated potentials recovers an approximation of the probability of the database sample. If all potentials of every order have been used to create the model, then this approximation is exactly the probability of the sample in the empirical distribution. The correct weighting is given by equation (7). For example it is easily verified that:

$$\begin{aligned}
\ln(p(xyz)) &= \binom{2}{2}^{-1} J_{\{xyz\}} + \binom{2}{1}^{-1} (J_{\{xy\}} + J_{\{xz\}} + J_{\{yz\}}) \\
&\quad + \binom{2}{0}^{-1} (J_{\{x\}} + J_{\{y\}} + J_{\{z\}}).
\end{aligned}$$

The Gibbs model truncated to second order potentials would estimate the probability in this example by:

$$\begin{aligned}\ln(p(xyz)) &\approx \binom{2}{1}^{-1}(J_{\{xy\}}+J_{\{xz\}}+J_{\{yz\}})+\binom{2}{0}^{-1}(J_{\{x\}}+J_{\{y\}}+J_{\{z\}}).\\ &\approx \ln\sqrt{p(xy)p(yz)p(xz)}\end{aligned}$$

4 PROOF OF THE INVERSION FORMULA

Theorem:
Let T be a finite set. Each element of T will be called an attribute. Each attribute can take on one of a finite set of states called attribute values. A collection of attribute values for every element of T is called a configuration ω. For all $A \subseteq T$ (including both the empty set $A = \emptyset$ and the full set $A = T$), let $V_A(\omega)$ and $J_A(\omega)$ be functions mapping the states of the elements of A to the real numbers. Define $\binom{m}{n} = m!/((m-n)! \cdot n!)$ to be "m choose n."
Let $V_\emptyset(\omega) = 0$, $J_\emptyset(\omega) = 0$, and let $V_A(\omega) = J_A(\omega)$ if $|A| = 1$.
Then for $|A| > 1$:

$$V_A(\omega) = \sum_{b \subseteq A} \binom{|A|-1}{|b|-1}^{-1} J_b(\omega), \tag{9}$$

and

$$J_A(\omega) = V_A(\omega) \quad - \sum_{\substack{b \subset A \\ |b|=|A|-1}} (|A|-1)^{-1} \cdot V_b(\omega) \tag{10}$$

are equivalent in that any assignment of V_A and J_A values for all $A \subseteq T$ will satisfy (9) if and only if they also satisfy (10).

Proof:
Let $\mathcal{J}$ be any assignment of the values $J_A(\omega)$ for all $A \subseteq T$. Let $\mathcal{V}$ be any assignment of all the values $V_A(\omega)$ for all $A \subseteq T$. Then clearly (9) maps any assignment $\mathcal{J}$ to a unique $\mathcal{V}$. We will represent this mapping by the function f, so (9) is abbreviated $\mathcal{V} = f(\mathcal{J})$. Similarly (10) maps any assignment $\mathcal{V}$ to a unique $\mathcal{J}$. Equation (10) will be abbreviated $\mathcal{J} = g(\mathcal{V})$. The result of Lemma C1 below, applied with the value $\mathcal{D}$ set to n, shows that $f(g(\mathcal{V})) = \mathcal{V}$. In Lemma C2 below, it is shown $g(f(\mathcal{J})) = \mathcal{J}$. Therefore the equations (9) and (10) are inverse one-to-one mappings and the association of assignments between $\mathcal{J}$ and $\mathcal{V}$ are identical for the two equations. *Q.E.D.*

Lemma C1:
Rather than simply showing $f(g(\mathcal{V})) = \mathcal{V}$, a more general result will be shown. Since the number of potentials of a given order increases exponentially with the order, it is useful to approximate the energy of a configuration by defining a maximum order $\mathcal{D}$ such that all potentials of greater order are assumed to be zero

$$J_b(\omega) = 0 \quad \forall \;\; b \text{ such that } \; |b| > \mathcal{D}.$$

Let $\hat{V}_A(\omega)$ be the resulting approximation to the energy $V_A(\omega)$. Let $|A| = n$.

Given

$$J_A(\omega) = V_A(\omega) \; - \sum_{\substack{b \subset A \\ |b|=n-1}} (n-1)^{-1} \cdot V_b(\omega) \tag{11}$$

and the order $\mathcal{D}$ approximation to equation (7):

$$\hat{V}_A(\omega) = \sum_{i=1}^{\mathcal{D}} \binom{n-1}{i-1}^{-1} \sum_{\substack{b \subseteq A \\ |b|=i}} J_b(\omega), \tag{12}$$

then

$$\hat{V}_A(\omega) = \sum_{\substack{b \subseteq A \\ |b|=\mathcal{D}}} \binom{n-1}{\mathcal{D}-1}^{-1} V_b(\omega).$$

Note:
For the case $\mathcal{D} = n$, the approximation is exact

$$\hat{V}_A(\omega) = V_A(\omega).$$

and so $f(g(\mathcal{V})) = \mathcal{V}$ is shown.

The lemma's result has a simple interpretation. The energy of a configuration is approximated by a scaled average of the energies of the configurations of order $\mathcal{D}$. Using equation (1) to relate energies to probabilities, shows that the estimated probability is a scaled geometric mean of the order $\mathcal{D}$ marginal probabilities.

Proof:
We start with the given equation for $\hat{V}_A(\omega)$

$$\hat{V}_A(\omega) \;=\; \sum_{i=1}^{\mathcal{D}} \binom{n-1}{i-1}^{-1} \sum_{\substack{b \subseteq A \\ |b|=i}} J_b(\omega).$$

Use equation (11) to substitute $J_b(\omega)$ out of the equation:

$$\hat{V}_A(\omega) \;=\; \sum_{i=1}^{\mathcal{D}} \binom{n-1}{i-1}^{-1} \sum_{\substack{b \subseteq A \\ |b|=i}} \left(V_b(\omega) - \sum_{\substack{c \subset b, |b| \neq 1 \\ |c|=|b|-1}} (i-1)^{-1} \cdot V_c(\omega) \right)$$

Separate the term in the first sum where $i = \mathcal{D}$

$$\hat{V}_A(\omega) \;=\; \sum_{\substack{b \subseteq A \\ |b|=\mathcal{D}}} \binom{n-1}{\mathcal{D}-1}^{-1} V_b(\omega) + \left(\sum_{i=1}^{n-1} \binom{n-1}{i-1}^{-1} \sum_{\substack{b \subset A \\ |b|=i}} V_b(\omega) \right)$$
$$- \sum_{i=1}^{n} \binom{n-1}{i-1}^{-1} \sum_{\substack{b \subseteq A \\ |b|=i}} \sum_{\substack{c \subset b, |b| \neq 1 \\ |c|=|b|-1}} (i-1)^{-1} \cdot V_c(\omega).$$

By subtracting $\hat{V}_A(\omega)$ from both sides using equation (12) and noting the second summation over i has no terms when $i = 1$ we see that it is sufficient to show

$$\sum_{i=1}^{\mathcal{D}-1} \binom{n-1}{i-1}^{-1} \sum_{\substack{b \subset A \\ |b|=i}} V_b(\omega) \;=\; \sum_{i=2}^{\mathcal{D}} \binom{n-1}{i-1}^{-1} \sum_{\substack{b \subseteq A \\ |b|=i}} \sum_{\substack{c \subset b \\ |c|=|b|-1}} (i-1)^{-1} \cdot V_c(\omega).$$

The right hand side inner double summation counts a given $V_c(\omega)$ once for every b such that $c \subset b \subseteq A$ with $i = |b| = |c| + 1$. This occurs exactly $|A| - |c| = n - i + 1$ times. Thus

$$\sum_{i=1}^{\mathcal{D}-1} \binom{n-1}{i-1}^{-1} \sum_{\substack{b \subset A \\ |b|=i}} V_b(\omega) = \sum_{i=2}^{\mathcal{D}} \binom{n-1}{i-1}^{-1} \sum_{\substack{c \subset A \\ |c|=i-1}} \frac{n-i+1}{i-1} \cdot V_c(\omega).$$

Now perform a change of variables. Let $j = i - 1$ on the right hand side

$$\sum_{i=1}^{\mathcal{D}-1} \binom{n-1}{i-1}^{-1} \sum_{\substack{b \subset A \\ |b|=i}} V_b(\omega) = \sum_{j=1}^{\mathcal{D}-1} \binom{n-1}{j}^{-1} \sum_{\substack{c \subset A \\ |c|=j}} \frac{n-j}{j} \cdot V_c(\omega).$$

Clearly both sides are identical since

$$\binom{n-1}{i-1}^{-1} = \binom{n-1}{i}^{-1} \frac{n-i}{i}.$$

Q.E.D.

Lemma C2: $g(f(\mathcal{J})) = \mathcal{J}$

Let $|A| = n$. It is sufficient to show that substituting V_b out of (10) using (9) yields an identity:

$$\begin{aligned} J_A(\omega) &= V_A(\omega) - \sum_{\substack{b \subset A, n \neq 1 \\ |b|=n-1}} (n-1)^{-1} \cdot V_b(\omega) \\ &= \sum_{b \subseteq A} \binom{n-1}{|b|-1}^{-1} J_b(\omega) - \sum_{\substack{b \subset A, n \neq 1 \\ |b|=n-1}} (n-1)^{-1} \sum_{c \subseteq b} \binom{|b|-1}{|c|-1}^{-1} J_c(\omega). \end{aligned}$$

Separate the term in the first sum for which $b = A$

$$\begin{aligned} J_A(\omega) &= J_A(\omega) \\ &+ \sum_{\substack{b \subset A \\ b \neq A}} \binom{n-1}{|b|-1}^{-1} J_b(\omega) - \sum_{\substack{b \subset A, n \neq 1 \\ |b|=n-1}} (n-1)^{-1} \sum_{c \subseteq b} \binom{|b|-1}{|c|-1}^{-1} J_c(\omega). \end{aligned}$$

Subtract $J_A(\omega)$ from both sides. The right hand side double sum counts a given $J_c(\omega)$ once for every b such that $c \subseteq b \subset A$ with $|b| = |A| - 1 = n - 1$. This occurs $|A| - |c| = n - |c|$ times. It is sufficient to show

$$\sum_{b \subset A, b \neq A} \binom{n-1}{|b|-1}^{-1} J_b(\omega) = \sum_{c \subset A, c \neq A} \frac{n-|c|}{n-1} \binom{n-2}{|c|-1}^{-1} J_c(\omega).$$

Both sides are identical since:

$$\binom{n-1}{i-1}^{-1} = \frac{n-i}{n-1} \binom{n-2}{i-1}^{-1}.$$

Q.E.D.

5 USING THE INVERSION FORMULA TO SET NETWORK WEIGHTS

Our method of probability estimation is to first collect empirical frequencies of patterns (subconfigurations) from the database. (An efficient hash table implementation of the algorithm is described in (Miller, 1993). The basic idea is to remove from the database a pattern with low potential whenever there is a hash collision which prevents a new pattern count from being stored.) Second, interpreting these frequencies as probabilities, we convert each pattern frequency to a potential using equation (8). We assume patterns with unknown or uncalculated frequencies have zero potential. Low order patterns which never occur are assigned a large negative potential (this approximation is needed to model events with zero probability in the empirical distribution). Finally, we calculate the probability of any new pattern not in the training set using the neural network implementation of equations (7) and (1).

6 RESULTS

One way to validate the performance of a probability model is to test its performance as a classifier. The probability model is used as a classifier by calculating the probabilities of each unknown class value together with the known attribute values. The most probable combination is then chosen as the predicted class. Used as a classifier the Gibbs model tied or outperformed published results on a variety of databases. Table 1 outlines results on three datasets taken from the UC Irvine archive (Murphy, 1992). The Gibbs model results were collected from the very first experiment using the algorithm with the datasets. No difficult parameter adjustment is necessary to get the algorithm to classify at these rates. The iris database has 4 real value attributes. Each attribute was quantized into a decile ranking for use by the algorithm.

7 CONCLUSION

A new method of extracting a Gibbs probability model from a database has been presented. The approach uses the Principle of Inclusion-Exclusion to invert a set of collected statistics into a set of potentials for a Gibbs energy model. A hash table implementation is used to efficiently process database records in order to collect the most important potentials, or weights, which can be stored in the available memory. Although the model is designed to give accurate probability estimates rather than simply class labels, the model in practice works well as a classifier on a variety of databases.

Acknowledgements

This work is funded in part by DARPA and ONR under grant N00014-92-J-1860.

Table 1: Summary of Classification Results

Database	A	C	R	Train	Test	Trials	Gibbs Rate	Compare
House Voting	16	2	435	335	100	50	95.3%	95%
Iris	4	3	150	120	30	100	96.3%	n.a.
Iris	4	3	150	149	1	1000	97.1%	98.0%
Breast Cancer	9	2	699	599	100	100	97.3%	n.a.
Breast Cancer	9	2	369	200	169	100	95.7%	93.7%

A = Attribute count in the database, excluding the class attribute
C = Class count
R = Record count
Train = Number of records used to create the energy for one trial
Test = Number of records tested in a single trial
Trials = Number of independent train-test trials used to calculate the rate
Gibbs Rate = Gibbs energy model classification rate
Compare = Baseline classification result of other methods (Schlimmer, 1987), (Weiss, 1992),(Zhang, 1992) respectively

References

D. Slepian, "On Maxentropic Discrete Stationary Processes," *Bell System Technical Journal*, **51**, pp.629–653, 1972.

G.E. Hinton and T.J. Sejnowski, "Learning and Relearning in Boltzmann Machines," in *Parallel Distributed Processing*, Vol. I., pp.282–317, Cambridge MA: MIT Press, 1986.

R. Kindermann, J.L. Snell, *Markov Random Fields and their Applications*, Providence, RI: American Mathematical Society, 1980.

J. W. Miller,"Building Probabilistic Models from Databases" California Institute of Technology, Ph.D. Thesis 1993.

P. Murphy, and D. Aha, *UCI Repository of Machine Learning Databases* [Machine-readable data repository at ics.uci.edu in directory /pub/machine-learning-databases]. Irvine, CA: University of California, Department of Information and Computer Science, 1992.

Schlimmer, J. C., "Concept Acquisition Through Representational Adjustment" University of California at Irvine, Ph.D. Thesis 1987.

S. Weiss, and I. Kapouleas, "An Empirical Comparison of Pattern Recognition, Neural Nets, and Machine Learning Classification Methods," in *Proceedings of the 11th International Joint Conference on Artificial Intelligence* Vol. 1, pp.781–787, Los Gatos, CA: Morgan Kaufmann, 1992.

J. Zhang, "Selecting Typical Instances in Instance-Based Learning," in *Proceedings of the Ninth International Machine Learning Conference* Aberdeen, Scotland, pp.470–479, San Mateo CA: Morgan Kaufmann, 1992.

On the Use of Evidence in Neural Networks

David H. Wolpert
The Santa Fe Institute
1660 Old Pecos Trail
Santa Fe, NM 87501

Abstract

The Bayesian "evidence" approximation has recently been employed to determine the noise and weight-penalty terms used in back-propagation. This paper shows that for neural nets it is far easier to use the exact result than it is to use the evidence approximation. Moreover, unlike the evidence approximation, the exact result neither has to be re-calculated for every new data set, nor requires the running of computer code (the exact result is closed form). In addition, it turns out that the evidence procedure's MAP estimate for neural nets is, *in toto*, approximation error. Another advantage of the exact analysis is that it does not lead one to incorrect intuition, like the claim that using evidence one can "evaluate different priors in light of the data". This paper also discusses sufficiency conditions for the evidence approximation to hold, why it can sometimes give "reasonable" results, etc.

1 THE EVIDENCE APPROXIMATION

It has recently become popular to consider the problem of training neural nets from a Bayesian viewpoint (Buntine and Weigend 1991, MacKay 1992). The usual way of doing this starts by assuming that there is some underlying target function f from $\mathbf{R}^n$ to $\mathbf{R}$, parameterized by an N-dimensional weight vector **w**. We are provided with a training set L of noise-corrupted samples of f. Our goal is to make a guess for **w**, basing that guess only on L. Now assume we have i.i.d. additive gaussian noise resulting in $P(L \mid \mathbf{w}, \beta) \propto \exp(-\beta\, \chi^2))$, where $\chi^2(\mathbf{w}, L)$ is the usual sum-squared training set error, and β reflects the noise level. Assume further that $P(\mathbf{w} \mid \alpha) \propto \exp(-\alpha W(\mathbf{w}))$, where $W(\mathbf{w})$ is the sum of the squares of the weights. If the values of α and β are known and fixed, to the values α_t and β_t respectively, then $P(\mathbf{w})$

$= P(\mathbf{w} \mid \alpha_t)$ and $P(L \mid \mathbf{w}) = P(L \mid \mathbf{w}, \beta_t)$. Bayes' theorem then tells us that the *posterior* is proportional to the product of the *likelihood* and the *prior*, i.e., $P(\mathbf{w} \mid L) \propto P(L \mid \mathbf{w})\, P(\mathbf{w})$. Consequently, finding the *maximum a posteriori* (MAP) **w** - the **w** which maximizes $P(\mathbf{w} \mid L)$ - is equivalent to finding the **w** minimizing $\chi^2(\mathbf{w}, L) + (\alpha_t / \beta_t)W(\mathbf{w})$. This can be viewed as a justification for performing gradient descent with weight-decay.

One of the difficulties with the foregoing is that we almost never know α_t and β_t in real-world problems. One way to deal with this is to estimate α_t and β_t, for example via a technique like cross-validation. In contrast, a Bayesian approach to this problem would be to set priors over α and β, and then examine the consequences for the posterior of **w**.

This Bayesian approach is the starting point for the "evidence" approximation created by Gull (Gull 1989). One makes three assumptions, for $P(\mathbf{w} \mid \gamma)$, $P(L \mid \mathbf{w}, \gamma)$, and $P(\gamma)$. (For simplicity of the exposition, from now on the two hyperparameters α and β will be expressed as the two components of the single vector γ.) The quantity of interest is the posterior:

$$\begin{aligned} P(\mathbf{w} \mid L) &= \int d\gamma\, P(\mathbf{w}, \gamma \mid L) \\ &= \int d\gamma\, [\{P(\mathbf{w}, \gamma \mid L) / P(\gamma \mid L)\} \times P(\gamma \mid L)] \end{aligned} \tag{1}$$

The evidence approximation suggests that if $P(\gamma \mid L)$ is sharply peaked about $\gamma = \gamma'$, while the term in curly brackets is smooth about $\gamma = \gamma'$, then one can approximate the **w**-dependence of $P(\mathbf{w} \mid L)$ as $P(\mathbf{w}, \gamma' \mid L) / P(\gamma' \mid L) \propto P(L \mid \mathbf{w}, \gamma')\, P(\mathbf{w} \mid \gamma')$. In other words, with the evidence approximation, one sets the posterior by taking $P(\mathbf{w}) = P(\mathbf{w} \mid \gamma')$ and $P(L \mid \mathbf{w}) = P(L \mid \mathbf{w}, \gamma')$, where γ' is the MAP γ. $P(L \mid \gamma) = \int d\mathbf{w}\, [P(L \mid \mathbf{w}, \gamma)\, P(\mathbf{w} \mid \gamma)]$ is known as the "evidence" for L given γ. For relatively smooth $P(\gamma)$, the peak of $P(\gamma \mid L)$ is the same as the peak of the evidence (hence the name "evidence approximation"). Although the current discussion will only explicitly consider using evidence to set hyperparameters like α and β, most of what will be said also applies to the use of evidence to set other characteristics of the learner, like its architecture.

MacKay has applied the evidence approximation to finding the posterior for the neural net $P(\mathbf{w} \mid \alpha)$ and $P(L \mid \mathbf{w}, \beta)$ recounted above combined with a $P(\gamma) = P(\alpha, \beta)$ which is uniform over all α and β from 0 to $+\infty$ (MacKay 1992). In addition to the error introduced by the evidence approximation, additional error is introduced by his need to approximate γ'. MacKay states that although he expects his approximation for γ' to be valid, "it is a matter of further research to establish [conditions for] this approximation to be reliable".

2 THE EXACT CALCULATION

It is always true that the *exact* posterior is given by

$$\begin{aligned} P(\mathbf{w}) &= \int d\gamma\, P(\mathbf{w} \mid \gamma)\, P(\gamma), \\ P(L \mid \mathbf{w}) &= \int d\gamma\, \{P(L \mid \mathbf{w}, \gamma) \times P(\mathbf{w} \mid \gamma) \times P(\gamma)\} / P(\mathbf{w}); \\ P(\mathbf{w} \mid L) &\propto \int d\gamma\, \{P(L \mid \mathbf{w}, \gamma) \times P(\mathbf{w} \mid \gamma) \times P(\gamma)\} \end{aligned} \tag{2}$$

where the proportionality constant, being independent of **w**, is irrelevant.

Using the neural net $P(\mathbf{w} \mid \alpha)$ and $P(L \mid \mathbf{w}, \beta)$ recounted above, and MacKay's $P(\gamma)$, it is trivial to use equation 2 to calculate that $P(\mathbf{w}) \propto [W(\mathbf{w})]^{-(N/2 + 1)}$, where N is the number of weights. Similarly, with m the number of pairs in L, $P(L \mid \mathbf{w}) \propto [\chi^2(\mathbf{w}, L)]^{-(m/2 + 1)}$. (See (Wolpert 1992) and (Buntine and Weigend 1991), and allow the output values in L to range from $-\infty$ to $+\infty$.) These two results give us the exact expression for the posterior $P(\mathbf{w} \mid L)$. In contrast, the evidence-approximated posterior $\propto \exp[-\alpha'(L)\, W(\mathbf{w}) - \beta'(L)\, \chi 2(\mathbf{w}, L)]$.

It is illuminating to compare this exact calculation to the calculation based on the evidence approximation. A good deal of relatively complicated mathematics followed by some computer-based numerical estimation is necessary to arrive at the answer given by the evidence approximation. (This is due to the need to approximate γ'.) In contrast, to perform the exact calculation one only need evaluate a simple gaussian integral, which can be done in closed form, and in particular one doesn't need to perform any computer-based numerical estimation. In addition, with the evidence procedure γ' must be re-evaluated for each new data set, which means that the formula giving the posterior must be re-derived every time one uses a new data set. In contrast, the exact calculation's formula for the posterior holds for any data set; no re-calculations are required. So as a practical tool, the exact calculation is both far simpler and quicker to use than the calculation based on the evidence approximation.

Another advantage of the exact calculation, of course, is that it is *exact*. Indeed, consider the simple case where the noise is fixed, i.e., $P(\gamma) = P(\gamma_1)\, \delta(\gamma_2 - \beta_t)$, so that the only term we must "deal with" is $\gamma_1 = \alpha$. Set all other distributions as in (MacKay 1992). For this case, the $\mathbf{w}$-dependence of the exact posterior can be quite different from that of the evidence-approximated posterior. In particular, note that the MAP estimate based on the exact calculation is $\mathbf{w} = \mathbf{0}$. This is, of course, a silly answer, and reflects the poor choice of distributions made in (MacKay 1992). In particular, it directly reflects the un-normalizability of MacKay's $P(\alpha)$. However the important point is that this is the *exactly correct* answer for those distributions. On the other hand, the evidence procedure will result in an MAP estimate of $\text{argmin}_{\mathbf{w}}\, [\chi^2(\mathbf{w}, L) + (\alpha' / \beta')W(\mathbf{w})]$, where α' and β' are derived from L. This answer will often be far from the correct answer of $\mathbf{w} = \mathbf{0}$. Note also that the evidence approximations's answer will vary, perhaps greatly, with L, whereas the correct answer is L-independent. Finally, since the correct answer is $\mathbf{w} = \mathbf{0}$, the difference between the evidence procedure's answer and the correct answer is equal to the evidence procedure's answer. In other words, although there exist scenarios for which the evidence approximation is valid, neural nets with flat $P(\gamma_1)$ is not one of them; for this scenario, the evidence procedure's answer is *in toto* approximation error. (A possible reason for this is presented in section 4.)

If one were to use a more reasonable $P(\alpha)$, uniform only from 0 to an upper cut-off α_{max}, the results would be essentially the same, for large enough α_{max}. The effect on the exact posterior, to first order, is to introduce a small region around $\mathbf{w} = \mathbf{0}$ in which $P(\mathbf{w})$ behaves like a decaying exponential in $W(\mathbf{w})$ (the exponent being set by α_{max}) rather than like $[W(\mathbf{w})]^{-(N/2+1)}$ (T. Wallstrom, private communication). For large enough α_{max}, the region is small enough so that the exact posterior still has a peak very close to $\mathbf{0}$. On the other hand, for large enough α_{max}, there is no change in the evidence procedure's answer. (Generically, the major effect on the evidence procedure of modifying $P(\gamma)$ is not to change its guess for $P(\mathbf{w} \mid L)$, but rather to change the associated error, i.e., change whether sufficiency conditions for the validity of the approximation are met. See below.) Even with a normalizable prior, the evidence procedure's answer is still essentially all approximation error.

Consider again the case where the prior over both α and β is uniform. With the evidence approximation, the log of the posterior is $-\{\, \chi^2(\mathbf{w}, L) + (\alpha' / \beta')W(\mathbf{w})\, \}$, where α' and β' are set by the data. On the other hand, the exact calculation shows that the log of the posterior is really given by $-\{\ \ln[\chi^2(\mathbf{w}, L)] + (N+2 / m+2) \ln[W(\mathbf{w})]\ \}$. What's interesting about this is not simply the logarithms, absent from the evidence approximation's answer, but also the factor multiplying the term involving the "weight penalty" quantity $W(\mathbf{w})$. In the evidence approximation, this factor is data-dependent, whereas in the exact calculation it only depends on the number of data. Moreover, the value of this factor in the exact calculation tells us that if the number of weights increases, or alternatively the number of training examples decreases, the "weight penalty" term becomes more important, and fitting the training examples becomes less important. (It is not at all clear that this trade-off between N and m is reflected in (α' / β'), the corresponding factor from the evidence approximation.) As before, if we have upper cut-offs on $P(\gamma)$, so that the MAP estimate may be reasonable, things don't change much. For such a scenario, the N vs. m trade-off governing the relative importance of $W(\mathbf{w})$ and $\chi^2(\mathbf{w}, L)$ still holds, but only to lowest order, and only in the region sufficiently far from the ex-singularities (like $\mathbf{w} = \mathbf{0}$) so that $P(\mathbf{w} \mid L)$ behaves like $[W(\mathbf{w})]^{-(N/2 + 1)} \times [\chi^2(\mathbf{w}, L)]^{-(m/2 + 1)}$.

All of this notwithstanding, the evidence approximation has been reported to give good results in practice. This should not be all that surprising. There are many procedures which are formally illegal but which still give reasonable advice. (Some might classify all of non-Bayesian statistics that way.) The evidence procedure fixes γ to a single value, essentially by maximum likelihood. That's not unreasonable, just usually illegal (as well as far more laborious than the correct Bayesian procedure).

In addition, the tests of the evidence approximation reported in (MacKay 1992) are not all that convincing. For paper 1, the evidence approximation gives $\alpha' = 2.5$. For any other α in an interval extending *three orders of magnitude* about this α', test set error is essentially unchanged (see figure 5 of (MacKay 1992)). Since such error is what we're ultimately interested in, this is hardly a difficult test of the evidence approximation. In paper 2 of (MacKay 1992) the initial use of the evidence approximation is "a failure of Bayesian prediction"; $P(\gamma \mid L)$ doesn't correlate with test set error (see figure 7). MacKay addresses this by arguing that poor Bayesian results are never wrong, but only "an opportunity to learn" (in contrast to poor non-Bayesian results?). Accordingly, he modifies the system *while looking at the test set*, to get his desired correlation on the test set. To do this legally, he should have instead modified his system while looking at a validation set, separate from the test set. However if he had done that, it would have raised the question of why one should use evidence at all; since one is already assuming that behavior on a validation set corresponds to behavior on a test set, why not just set α and β via cross-validation?

3 EVIDENCE AND THE PRIOR

Consider again equation 1. Since γ' depends on the data L, it would appear that when the evidence approximation is valid, the data determines the prior, or as MacKay puts it, "the modern Bayesian ... does not assign the priors - many different priors can be ... compared in the light of the data by evaluating the evidence" (MacKay 1992). If this were true, it would remove perhaps the most major objection which has been raised concerning Bayesian analysis - the need to choose priors in a subjective manner, independent of the data. However the exact $P(\mathbf{w})$ given by equation 2 is data-independent. So one *has* chosen the prior, in a subjective way. The evidence procedure is simply providing a data-dependent approximation to a data-independent quantity. In no sense does the evidence procedure allow one to side-step the need to make subjective assumptions which fix $P(\mathbf{w})$.

Since the true P(**w**) doesn't vary with L whereas the evidence approximation's P(**w**) does, one might suspect that that approximation to P(**w**) can be quite poor, even when the evidence approximation to the posterior is good. Indeed, if $P(\mathbf{w} \mid \gamma_1)$ is exponential, there is no non-pathological scenario for which the evidence approximation to P(**w**) is correct:

Theorem 1: *Assume that* $P(\mathbf{w} \mid \gamma_1) \propto e^{-\gamma_1 U(\mathbf{w})}$. *Then the only way that one can have* $P(\mathbf{w}) \propto e^{-\alpha U(\mathbf{w})}$ *for some constant* α *is if* $P(\gamma_1) = 0$ *for all* $\gamma_1 \neq \alpha$.

Proof: Our proposed equality is $\exp(-\alpha \times U) = \int d\gamma_1 \{P(\gamma_1) \times \exp(-\gamma_1 \times U)\}$ (the normalization factors having all been absorbed into $P(\gamma_1)$). We must find an α and a normalizable $P(\gamma_1)$ such that this equality holds for all allowed U. Let u be such an allowed value of U. Take the derivative with respect to U of both sides of the proposed equality t times, and evaluate for U = u. The result is $\alpha^t = \int d\gamma_1((\gamma_1)^t \times R(\gamma_1))$ for any integer $t \geq 0$, where $R(\gamma_1) \equiv P(\gamma_1) \exp(u(\alpha - \gamma_1))$. Using this, we see that $\int d\gamma_1((\gamma_1 - \alpha)^2 \times R(\gamma_1)) = 0$. Since both $R(\gamma_1)$ and $(\gamma_1 - \alpha)^2$ are nowhere negative, this means that for all γ_1 for which $(\gamma_1 - \alpha)^2 \neq 0$, $R(\gamma_1)$ must equal zero. Therefore $R(\gamma_1)$ must equal zero for all $\gamma_1 \neq \alpha$. QED.

Since the evidence approximation for the prior is always wrong, how can its approximation for the posterior ever be good? To answer this, write $P(\mathbf{w} \mid L) = P(L \mid \mathbf{w}) \times [P'(\mathbf{w}) + E(\mathbf{w})] / P(L)$, where P'(**w**) is the evidence approximation to P(**w**). (It is assumed that we know the likelihood exactly.) This means that $P(\mathbf{w} \mid L) - \{P(L \mid \mathbf{w}) \times P'(\mathbf{w}) / P(L)\}$, the error in the evidence procedure's estimate for the posterior, equals $P(L \mid \mathbf{w}) \times E(\mathbf{w}) / P(L)$. So we *can* have arbitrarily large E(**w**) and not introduce sizable error into the posterior of **w**, but only for those **w** for which $P(L \mid \mathbf{w})$ is small. As L varies, the **w** with non-negligible likelihood vary, and the γ such that *for those* **w** $P(\mathbf{w} \mid \gamma)$ is a good approximation to P(**w**) varies. When it works, the γ' given by the evidence approximation reflects this changing of γ with L.

4 SUFFICIENCY CONDITIONS FOR EVIDENCE TO WORK

Note that regardless of how peaked the evidence is, $-\{ \chi^2(\mathbf{w}, L) + (\alpha' / \beta')W(\mathbf{w}) \} \neq -\{ \ln[\chi^2(\mathbf{w}, L)] + (N+2 / m+2) \ln[W(\mathbf{w})] \}$; the evidence approximation always has non-negligible error for neural nets used with flat $P(\gamma)$. To understand this, one must carefully elucidate a set of sufficiency conditions necessary for the evidence approximation to be valid. (Unfortunately, this has never been done before. A direct consequence is that no one has ever checked, formally, that a particular use of the evidence approximation is justified.)

One such set of sufficiency conditions, the one implicit in all attempts to date to justify the evidence approximation (i.e., the one implicit in the logic of equation 1), is the following:

$P(\gamma \mid L)$ is sharply peaked about a particular γ, γ'. (i)

$P(\mathbf{w}, \gamma \mid L) / P(\gamma \mid L)$ varies slowly around $\gamma = \gamma'$. (ii)

$P(\mathbf{w}, \gamma \mid L)$ is infinitesimal for all γ sufficiently far from γ'. (iii)

Formally, condition (iii) can be taken to mean that there exists a not too large positive constant k, and a small positive constant δ, such that $\left| P(\mathbf{w} \mid L) - k \int_{\gamma-\delta}^{\gamma+\delta} d\gamma\, P(\mathbf{w}, \gamma \mid L) \right|$ is bounded by a small constant ε for all **w**. (As stated, (iii) has k = 1. This will almost always be the case in practice and will usually be assumed, but it is not needed to prove theorem 2.) Condition (ii) can be taken to mean that across $[\gamma' - \delta, \gamma' + \delta]$, $|P(\mathbf{w} \mid \gamma, L) - P(\mathbf{w} \mid \gamma' L)| < \tau$, for some small positive constant τ, for all $\mathbf{w}$. (Here and throughout this paper, when γ is multi-dimensional, "δ" is taken to be a small positive vector.)

Theorem 2: *When conditions (i), (ii), and (iii) hold,* $P(\mathbf{w} \mid L) \cong P(L \mid \mathbf{w}, \gamma') \times P(\mathbf{w} \mid \gamma')$, *up to an (irrelevant) overall proportionality constant.*

Proof: Condition (iii) gives $| P(\mathbf{w} \mid L) - k \int_{\gamma-\delta}^{\gamma+\delta} d\gamma [P(\mathbf{w} \mid \gamma L) \times P(\gamma \mid L)] | < \varepsilon$ for all $\mathbf{w}$. However $| k \int_{\gamma-\delta}^{\gamma+\delta} d\gamma [P(\mathbf{w} \mid \gamma, L) \times P(\gamma \mid L)] - k P(\mathbf{w} \mid \gamma' L) \int_{\gamma-\delta}^{\gamma+\delta} d\gamma P(\gamma \mid L) | < \tau k \times \int_{\gamma-\delta}^{\gamma+\delta} d\gamma P(\gamma \mid L)$, by condition (ii). If we now combine these two results, we see that $| P(\mathbf{w} \mid L) - k P(\mathbf{w} \mid \gamma' L) \int_{\gamma-\delta}^{\gamma+\delta} d\gamma P(\gamma \mid L) | < \varepsilon + \tau k \times \int_{\gamma-\delta}^{\gamma+\delta} d\gamma P(\gamma \mid L)$. Since the integral is bounded by 1, $| P(\mathbf{w} \mid L) - k P(\mathbf{w} \mid \gamma' L) \int_{\gamma-\delta}^{\gamma+\delta} d\gamma P(\gamma \mid L) | < \varepsilon + \tau k$. Since the integral is independent of $\mathbf{w}$, up to an overall proportionality constant (that integral times k) the w-dependence of $P(\mathbf{w} \mid L)$ can be approximated by that of $P(\mathbf{w} \mid \gamma', L) \propto P(L \mid \mathbf{w}, \gamma') \times P(\mathbf{w} \mid \gamma')$, incurring error less than $\varepsilon + \tau k$. Take k not too large and both ε and τ small. QED.

Note that the proof would go through even if $P(\gamma \mid L)$ were not peaked about γ', or if $P(\gamma \mid L)$ were peaked about some point far from the γ' for which (ii) and (iii) hold; nowhere in the proof is the definition of γ' from condition (i) used. However in practice, when condition (iii) is met, $k = 1$, $P(\gamma \mid L)$ falls to 0 outside of $[\gamma' - \delta, \gamma' + \delta]$, and $P(\mathbf{w} \mid \gamma, L)$ stays reasonably bounded for all such γ. (If this weren't the case, then $P(\mathbf{w} \mid \gamma, L)$ would have to fall to 0 outside of $[\gamma' - \delta, \gamma' + \delta]$, something which is rarely true.) So we see that we could either just give conditions (ii) and (iii), or we could give (i), (ii), and the extra condition that $P(\mathbf{w} \mid \gamma, L)$ is bounded small enough so that condition (iii) is met. (In addition, one can prove that if the evidence approximation is valid, then conditions (i) and (ii) give condition (iii).)

In any case, it should be noted that conditions (i) and (ii) by themselves are *not* sufficient for the evidence approximation to be valid. To see this, have $\mathbf{w}$ be one-dimensional, and let $P(\mathbf{w}, \gamma \mid L) = 0$ both for $\{|\gamma - \gamma'| < \delta, |\mathbf{w} - \mathbf{w}^*| < \nu\}$ and for $\{|\gamma - \gamma'| > \delta, |\mathbf{w} - \mathbf{w}^*| > \nu\}$. Let it be constant everywhere else (within certain bounds of allowed γ and $\mathbf{w}$). Then for both δ and ν small, conditions (i) and (ii) hold: the evidence is peaked about γ', and $\tau = 0$. Yet for the true MAP $\mathbf{w}$, $\mathbf{w}^*$, the evidence approximation fails badly. (Generically, this scenario will also result in a big error if rather than using the evidence-approximated posterior to guess the MAP $\mathbf{w}$, one instead uses it to evaluate the posterior-averaged f, $\int df\, f\, P(f \mid L)$.)

Gull mentions only condition (i). MacKay also mentions condition (ii), but not condition (iii). Neither author plugs in for ε and τ, or in any other way uses their distributions to infer bounds on the error accompanying their use of the evidence approximation.

Since by (i) $P(\gamma \mid L)$ is sharply peaked about γ', one would expect that for (ii) to hold $P(\mathbf{w}, \gamma \mid L)$ must also be sharply peaked about γ'. Although this line of reasoning can be formalized, it turns out to be easier to prove the result using sufficiency condition (iii):

Theorem 3: *If condition (iii) holds, then for all* $\mathbf{w}$ *such that* $P(\mathbf{w} \mid L) > c > \varepsilon$, *for each component i of* γ, $P(\mathbf{w}, \gamma_i \mid L)$ *must have a* γ_i*-peak somewhere within* $\delta_i[1 + 2\varepsilon / (c - \varepsilon)]$ *of* $(\gamma')_i$.

Proof: Condition (iii) with $k = 1$ tells us that $P(\mathbf{w} \mid L) - \int_{\gamma-\delta}^{\gamma+\delta} \delta\gamma P(\mathbf{w}, \gamma \mid L) < \varepsilon$. Extending the integrals over $\gamma_{j\neq i}$ gives $P(\mathbf{w} \mid L) - \int_{(\gamma'-\delta)_i}^{(\gamma'+\delta)_i} d\gamma_i\, P(\mathbf{w}, \gamma_i \mid L) < \varepsilon$. From now on the i subscript on γ and δ will be implicit. We have $\varepsilon > \int_{\gamma'+\delta}^{\gamma'+\delta+r} d\gamma\, P(\mathbf{w}, \gamma \mid L)$ for any scalar r > 0. Assume that $P(\mathbf{w}, \gamma \mid L)$ doesn't have a peak anywhere in $[\gamma' - \delta, \gamma' + \delta + r]$. Without loss of generality, assume also that $P(\mathbf{w}, \gamma' + \delta \mid L) \geq P(\mathbf{w}, \gamma' - \delta \mid L)$. These two assumptions mean that for any $\gamma \in [\gamma' + \delta, \gamma' + \delta + r]$, the value of $P(\mathbf{w}, \gamma \mid L)$ exceeds the maximal value it takes on in the interval $[\gamma' - \delta, \gamma' + \delta]$. Therefore $\int_{\gamma'+\delta}^{\gamma'+\delta+r} d\gamma\, P(\mathbf{w}, \gamma \mid L) \geq (r / 2\delta) \times \int_{\gamma'-\delta}^{\gamma'+\delta} d\gamma\, P(\mathbf{w}, \gamma \mid L)$. This means that $\int_{\gamma'-\delta}^{\gamma'+\delta} d\gamma\, P(\mathbf{w}, \gamma \mid L) < 2\delta\varepsilon / r$. But since $P(\mathbf{w} \mid L) < \varepsilon + \int_{\gamma'-\delta}^{\gamma'+\delta} d\gamma\, P(\mathbf{w}, \gamma \mid L)$, this means that $P(\mathbf{w} \mid L) < \varepsilon(1 + 2\delta / r)$. So if $P(\mathbf{w} \mid L) > c > \varepsilon$, $r < 2\varepsilon / (c - \varepsilon)$, and there must be a peak of $P(\mathbf{w}, \gamma \mid L)$ within $\delta(1 + 2\varepsilon/(c - \varepsilon))$ of γ'. QED.

So for those $\mathbf{w}$ with non-negligible posterior, for ε small, the γ-peak of $P(\mathbf{w}, \gamma \mid L) \propto P(L \mid \mathbf{w}, \gamma) \times P(\mathbf{w} \mid \gamma) \times P(\gamma)$ must lie essentially within the peak of $P(\gamma \mid L)$. Therefore:

Theorem 4: *Assume that* $P(\mathbf{w} \mid \gamma_1) = \exp(-\gamma_1\, U(\mathbf{w})) / Z_1(\gamma_1)$ *for some function U(.),* $P(L \mid \mathbf{w}, \gamma_2) = \exp(-\gamma_2\, V(\mathbf{w}, L)) / Z_2(\gamma_2, \mathbf{w})$ *for some function V(., .), and* $P(\gamma) = P(\gamma_1)P(\gamma_2)$. *(The* Z_i *act as normalization constants.) Then if condition (iii) holds, for all* **w** *with non-negligible posterior the* γ*-solution to the equations*

$$-U(\mathbf{w}) + \partial_{\gamma_1} [\ln(P(\gamma_1) - \ln(Z_1(\gamma_1))] = 0$$

$$-V(\mathbf{w}, L) + \partial_{\gamma_2} [\ln(P(\gamma_2) - \ln(Z_2(\gamma_2, \mathbf{w}))] = 0$$

must like within the γ*-peak of* $P(\gamma \mid L)$.

Proof: $P(\mathbf{w}, \gamma \mid L) \propto \{P(\gamma_1) \times P(\gamma_2) \times \exp[-\gamma_1 U(\mathbf{w}) - \gamma_2\, V(\mathbf{w}, L)]\} / \{Z_1(\gamma_1) \times Z_2(\gamma_2, \mathbf{w})\}$. For both i = 1 and i = 2, evaluate $\partial_{\gamma_i} \{\int d\gamma_{j\neq i}\, P(\mathbf{w}, \gamma \mid L)\}$, and set it equal to zero. This gives the two equations. Now define "the γ-peak of $P(\gamma \mid L)$" to mean a cube with i-component width $\delta_i[1 + 2\varepsilon / (c - \varepsilon)]$, centered on γ', where having a "non-negligible posterior" means $P(\mathbf{w} \mid L) > c$. Applying theorem 3, we get the result claimed. QED.

In particular, in MacKay's scenario, $P(\gamma)$ is uniform, $W(\mathbf{w}) = \Sigma^m_{i=1} (w_i)^2$, and $V(\mathbf{w}, L) = \chi^2(\mathbf{w}, L)$. Therefore Z_1 and Z_2 are proportional to $(\gamma_1)^{-N/2}$ and $(\gamma_2)^{-m/2}$ respectively. This means that if the vector $\{\gamma_1, \gamma_2\} = \{N / [2W(\mathbf{w})],\ m / [2\chi^2(\mathbf{w}, L)]\}$ does not lie within the peak of the evidence for the MAP **w**, condition (iii) does not hold. That γ'_1 / γ'_2 must approximately equal $[N\, \chi^2(\mathbf{w}, L)] / [m\, W(\mathbf{w})]$ should not be too surprising. If we set the **w**-gradient of both the evidence-approximated and exact $P(\mathbf{w} \mid L)$ to zero, and demand that the same **w**,**w'**, solves both equations, we get $\gamma'_1 / \gamma'_2 = -[(N + 2)\, \chi^2(\mathbf{w}', L)] / [(m + 2)W(\mathbf{w}')]$. (Unfortunately, if one continues and evaluates $\partial_{w_i}\partial_{w_j} P(\mathbf{w} \mid L)$ at **w'**, often one finds that it has opposite signs for the two posteriors - a graphic failure of the evidence approximation.)

It is not clear from the provided neural net data whether this condition is met in (MacKay 1992). However it appears that the corresponding condition is <u>not</u> met, for γ_1 at least, for the scenario in (Gull 1992) in which the evidence approximation is used with U(.) being the entropy. (See (Strauss et al. 1993, Wolpert et al. 1993).) Since conditions (i) through (iii) are sufficient conditions, not necessary ones, this does not prove that Gull's use of evidence is invalid. (It is still an open problem to delineate the full iff for when the evidence approximation is valid, though it appears that matching of peaks as in theorem 3 is necessary. See (Wolpert et al. 1993).) However this does mean that the *justification* offered by Gull for his use of evidence is apparently invalid. It might also help explain why Gull's results were "visually disappointing and ... clearly ... 'over-fitted'", to use his terms.

The first equation in theorem 4 can be used to set restrictions on the set of **w** which both have non-negligible posterior and for which condition (iii) holds. Consider for example MacKay's scenario, where that equation says that $N / 2W(\mathbf{w})$ must lie within the width of the evidence peak. If the evidence peak is sharp, this means that unless all **w** with non-negligible posterior have essentially the same $W(\mathbf{w})$, condition (iii) can not hold for all of them.

Finally, if for some reason one wishes to know γ', theorem 4 can sometimes be used to circumvent the common difficulty of evaluating $P(\gamma \mid L)$. To do this, one assumes that conditions (i) through (iii) hold. Then one finds *any* **w** with a non-negligible posterior (say by use of the evidence approximation coupled with approximations to $P(\gamma \mid L)$) and uses it in theorem 4 to find a γ which must lie within the peak of $P(\gamma \mid L)$, and therefore must lie close to the correct value of γ'.

To summarize, there might be scenarios in which the exact calculation of the quantity of interest is intractable, so that some approximation like evidence is necessary. Alternatively, if one's choice of $P(\mathbf{w} \mid \gamma)$, $P(\gamma)$, and $P(L \mid \mathbf{w}, \gamma)$ is poor, the evidence approximation would be useful if the error in that approximation somehow "cancels" error in the choice of distributions. However if one believes one's choice of distributions, and if the quantity of interest is $P(\mathbf{w} \mid L)$, then at a minimum one should check conditions (i) through (iii) before using the evidence approximation. When one is dealing with neural nets, one needn't even do that; the exact calculation is quicker and simpler than using the evidence approximation.

Acknowledgments

This work was done at the SFI and was supported in part by NLM grant F37 LM00011. I would like to thank Charlie Strauss and Tim Wallstrom for stimulating discussion.

References

Buntine, W., Weigend, A. (1991). Bayesian back-propagation. *Complex Systems*, **5**, 603.

Gull, S.F. (1989). Developments in maximum entropy data analysis. In "Maximum-entropy and Bayesian methods", J. Skilling (Ed.). Kluwer Academics publishers.

MacKay, D.J.C. (1992). Bayesian Interpolation. A Practical Framework for Backpropagation Networks. *Neural Computation*, **4**, 415 and 448.

Strauss, C.E.M, Wolpert, D.H., Wolf, D.R. (1993). Alpha, Evidence, and the Entropic Prior. In "Maximum-entropy and Bayesian methods", A. Mohammed-Djafari (Ed.). Kluwer Academics publishers. In press

Wolpert, D.H. (1992). A Rigorous Investigation of "Evidence" and "Occam Factors" in Bayesian Reasoning. SFI TR 92-03-13. Submitted.

Wolpert, D.H., Strauss, C.E.M., Wolf, D.R. (1993). On evidence and the marginalization of alpha in the entropic prior. In preparation.

PART VI

Network Dynamics and Chaos

Destabilization and Route to Chaos in Neural Networks with Random Connectivity

Bernard Doyon
Unité INSERM 230
Service de Neurologie
CHU Purpan
F-31059 Toulouse Cedex, France

Bruno Cessac
Centre d'Etudes et de Recherches
de Toulouse
2, avenue Edouard Belin, BP 4025
F-31055 Toulouse Cedex, France

Mathias Quoy
Centre d'Etudes et de Recherches
de Toulouse
2, avenue Edouard Belin, BP 4025
F-31055 Toulouse Cedex, France

Manuel Samuelides
Ecole Nationale Supérieure
de l'Aéronautique et de l'Espace
10, avenue Edouard Belin, BP 4032
F-31055 Toulouse Cedex, France

Abstract

The occurence of chaos in recurrent neural networks is supposed to depend on the architecture and on the synaptic coupling strength. It is studied here for a randomly diluted architecture. By normalizing the variance of synaptic weights, we produce a bifurcation parameter, dependent on this variance and on the slope of the transfer function but independent of the connectivity, that allows a sustained activity and the occurence of chaos when reaching a critical value. Even for weak connectivity and small size, we find numerical results in accordance with the theoretical ones previously established for fully connected infinite sized networks. Moreover the route towards chaos is numerically checked to be a quasi-periodic one, whatever the type of the first bifurcation is (Hopf bifurcation, pitchfork or flip).

1 INTRODUCTION

Most part of studies on recurrent neural networks assume sufficient conditions of convergence. Models with symmetric synaptic connections have dynamical properties strongly connected with those of spin-glasses. In particular, they have relaxationnal dynamics caracterised by the decreasing of a function which is analogous to the energy in spin-glasses (or free energy for models submitted to thermal noise). Networks with asymmetric synaptic connections lose this convergence property and can have more complex dynamics, but searchers try to obtain such a convergence because the relaxation to a stable network state is simply interpreted as a stored pattern.

However, as pointed out by Hirsch (1989), it might be very interesting, from an engineering point of view, to investigate non convergent networks because their dynamical possibilities are much richer for a given number of units. Moreover, the real brain is a highly dynamic system. Recent neurophysiological findings have focused attention on the rich temporal structures (oscillations) of neuronal processes (Gray *et al.*, 1989), which might play an important role in information processing. Chaotic behavior has been found out in the nervous system (Gallez & Babloyantz, 1991) and might be implicated in cognitive processes (Skarda & Freeman, 1987).

We have studied the emergent dynamics of a general class of non convergent networks. Some results are already available in this field. Sompolinsky *et al.* (1988) established strong theoretical results concerning the occurrence of chaos for *fully connected networks* in the thermodynamic limit ($N \to \infty$) by using the Dynamic Mean Field Theory. Their model is a continuous time, continuous state dynamical system with N fully connected neurons. Each connection J_{ij} is a gaussian random variable with zero mean and a *normalized* variance J^2/N. As the J_{ij}'s are independent, the constant term J^2 can be seen as the variance of the sum of the weights connected to a given unit. Thus, the global strength of coupling remains constant for each neuron as N increases. The output function of each neuron is sigmoidal with a slope g. Sompolinsky *et al.* established that, in the limit $N \to \infty$, there is a sharp transition from a stationary state to a chaotic flow. The onset of chaos is given by the critical value $gJ=1$. For $gJ<1$ the system admits the only fixed point zero, while for $gJ>1$ it is chaotic. The same authors performed simulations on finite and large values of N and showed the existence of an intermediate regime (nonzero stationary states or limit cycles) separating the stationary and the chaotic phase, but the routes to chaos were not systematically explored. The range of gJ where this intermediate behavior is observed shrinks as N increases.

2 THE MODEL

The hypothesis of a fully connected network being not biologically plausible, it could be interesting to inspect how far these results could be extended as the dilution increases for a general class of networks. The model we study is defined as follows: the number of units is N, and K is the fixed number of connections received by one unit ($K>1$). There is no connection from one unit to itself. The K connections are randomly selected (with an uniform law) among the N-1's. The state of each neuron i at time t is characterized by its output $x_i\ (t)$ which is a real variable varying between -1 and 1. The discrete and parallel dynamics is given by :

$$x_i(t+1) = tanh\left(g\sum_j J_{ij}\, x_j\ (t)\right)$$

J_{ij} is the synaptic weight which couples the output of unit j to the input of unit i. These weights are random independent variables chosen with a uniform law, with zero mean and a *normalized* variance J^2/K. Notice that, with such a normalization, the standard deviation of the sum of the weights afferent to a given neuron is the constant J.

One has to distinguish two effects of coupling on the behavior of such a class of models. The first effect is due to the strength of coupling, independent of the number of connections. The second one is due to the architecture of coupling, which can be studied by keeping constant the global synaptic effect of coupling. The genericity of our model cancels the peculiar dynamic features which may occur due to geometrical effects. Moreover it allows to study a model at different scales of dilution.

3 FIRST BIFURCATION

For such a system, zero is always a fixed point and for low bifurcation parameter value it is the only fixed point and it is stable. Let us call λ_{max} the eigenvalue of the matrix of synaptic weights with the greatest modulus and $\rho = |\lambda_{max}|$ the spectral radius of this matrix. The loss of stability arises when the product $g\rho$ is larger than 1. Our numerical simulations allow us to state that *ρ is approximately equal to J* for sufficiently large-sized networks. This statement can be derived rigorously for an approximate regularized model in the thermodynamic limit (Doyon *et al.*, 1993).

Table 1: Mean Value of the Bifurcation Parameter gJ over 30 Networks.
Destabilization of the zero fixed point / Onset of Chaos

Connectivity K	Number of neurons		
	128	256	512
4	.954 / 1.337	.965 / 1.298	.970 / 1.258
8	.950 / 1.449	.966 / 1.301	.978 / 1.233
16	.951 / 1.434	.965 / 1.315	.969 / 1.239
32	.961 / 1.360	.958 / 1.333	.972 / 1.246

We have studied by intensive simulations on a Cray I-XMP computer the statistical spectral distribution for N ranging from 4 to 512 and for K ranging from 2 to 32. Figure 1 shows two examples of spectra (for convenience, J is set to 1). The apparent drawing of a real axis is due to the real eigenvalue density but the distribution converges to a uniform one over the J radius disk, as N increases. A similar result has been theoretically achieved for full gaussian matrices (Girko, 1985 ; Sommers *et al.*, 1988). Thus ρ quickly decreases to J, so the loss of stability arises for a mean gJ value that increases to 1 for increasing size (Tab. 1). For a given N value, ρ is nearly independent of K.

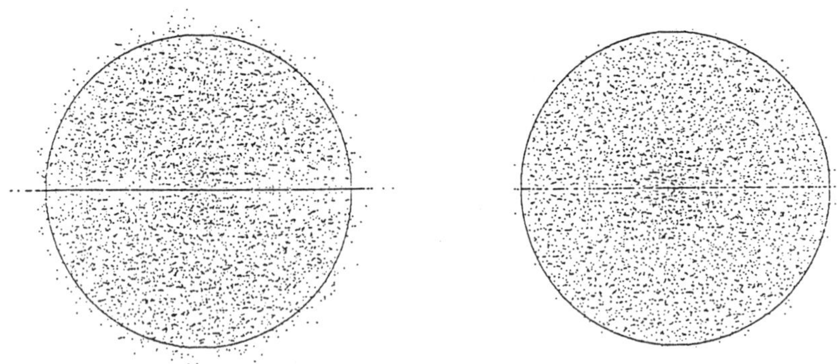

Figure 1: Plot of the Unit Disk and of the Eigenvalues in the Complex Plane.
Left: 100 Spectra for N=64, K=4. Right: 10 Spectra for N=512, K=4.

Three types of first bifurcation can occur, depending on the eigenvalue λ_{max} :

a) *Hopf Bifurcation*: this corresponds to the appearance of oscillations. There are two complex conjugate eigenvalues with maximal modulus ρ.

b) *Pitchfork bifurcation*: if λ_{max} is real positive, the bifurcation arises when $g\lambda_{max} = 1$. Zero loses its stability and two branches of stable equilibria emerge.

c) *Flip Bifurcation*: for λ_{max} real and negative a flip bifurcation occurs when $g\lambda_{max} = -1$. This corresponds to the appearance of a period two oscillation.

As the network size increases, the proportion of Hopf bifurcations increases because the proportion of real λ_{max} decreases, nearly independent of K.

4 ROUTE TO CHAOS

To study the following bifurcations, we chose the global observable:

$$m(t) = \frac{1}{N}\sum_{i=1}^{N} x_i(t)$$

The value $m(t)$ correctly characterizes all types of first bifurcation that can occur. Indeed the route to chaos is *qualitatively* well described by this observable, as we checked it by studying simultaneously $x_i(t)$. The onset of chaos was computed by testing the sensitivity on initial conditions for $m(t)$. We observed the onset of chaos occurs for quite low parameter values. The transient zone from fixed point to chaos shrinks slowly to zero as the network size increases (Tab. 1).

The qualitative study of the routes to chaos was made on a span of networks with various connectivity and quite important size. The route towards chaos that was observed was a quasi-periodic one in all cases with some variations due to the particular symmetry $x \rightarrow -x$. The following figures are obtained by plotting $m(t+1)$ versus $m(t)$ after discarding the transient (Fig. 2). They are not qualitatively different with a reconstruction in a higher dimensional space. The dominant features are the following ones.

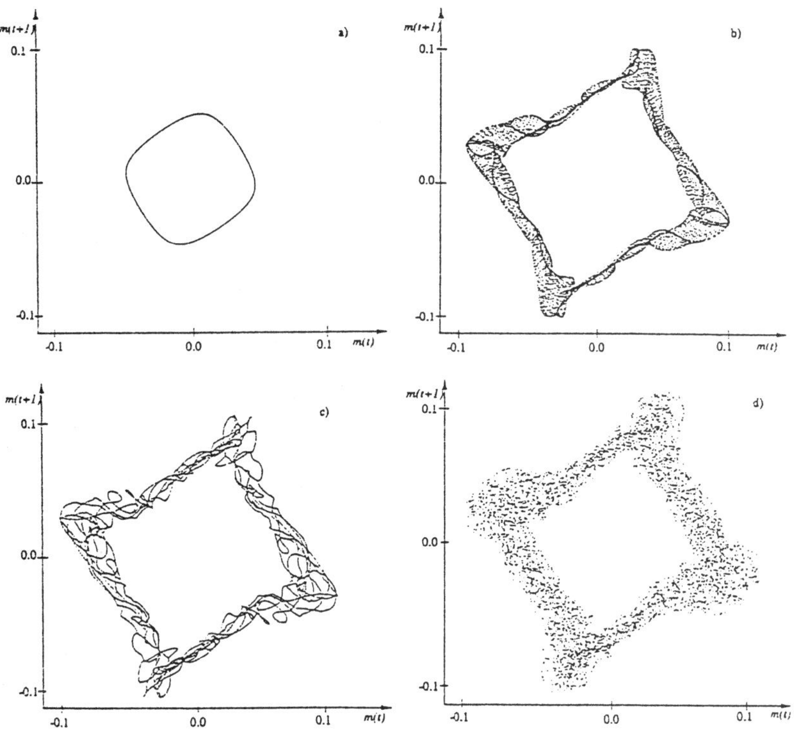

Figure 2: Example of route to chaos when the first bifurcation is a Hopf one. (N=128, K=16).

a) After the first bifurcation, the zero fixed point has lost its stability. The series of points $(m(t), m(t+1))$ densely covers a cycle (gJ=1.0).

b) After the second Hopf bifurcation: projection of a T^2 torus (gJ=1.23).

c) Frequency locking on the T^2 torus (gJ=1.247).

d) Chaos (gJ=1.26).

When the first bifurcation is a Hopf one (Fig. 2a), it is followed by a second Hopf bifurcation (Fig. 2b). Then there is a frequency locking occuring on the T^2 torus born from the second Hopf bifurcation (Fig. 2c), followed by chaos (Fig. 2d). This route is then a quasi-periodic one (Ruelle & Takens, 1971 ; Newhouse *et al.*, 1978). A slightly different feature emerges when the first bifurcation is followed by a stable resonance due to discrete time occuring before the second Hopf bifurcation. Then the limit cycle reduces to periodic points. When the second bifurcation occurs, the resonance persists until chaos is reached.

When the first bifurcation is a pitchfork, it is followed by a Hopf bifurcation for *each* stable point of the pitchfork (due to the symmetry $x \rightarrow -x$). Then a second Hopf bifurcation occurs followed, via a frequency locking, by chaos. It follows then, despite the pitchfork bifurcation, a quasi-periodicity route. Notice that in this case, we get two symmetric strange attractors. When gJ increases, the two attractors fuse.

For a first bifurcation of flip type, the route followed is like the one described by Bauer & Martienssen (1989). The flip bifurcation leads to an oscillatory system with two states. A first Hopf bifurcation arises followed by a second one leading to a quasi-periodic state, followed by a frequency locking preceeding chaos.

5 CONCLUSION

We have presented a type of neural network exhibiting a chaotic behavior when increasing a bifurcation parameter. As in Sompolinsky's model, gJ is *the* control parameter of the network dynamics. The variance of the synaptic weights being normalized, the bifurcation values are nearly independent of the connectivity K. The magnitude of dilution is not important for the behavior. The route to chaos by quasi-periodicity seems to be generic. It suggests that such high-dimensional networks behave like low-dimensional dynamical systems. It could be much simpler to control such networks than *a priori* expected.

From a biological point of view, we built our model to provide a tool that could be used to investigate the influence of chaotic dynamics in the cognitive processes in the brain. We clearly chose to simplify the biological complexity in order to understand a complex dynamic. We think that, if chaos plays a role in cognitive processes, it does neither depend on a specific architecture, nor on the exact internal modelling of the biological neuron. However, it could be interesting to introduce some biological caracteristics in the model. The next step will be to study the influence of non-zero entries on the behavior of the system, leading to the modelling of learning in a chaotic network.

Acknowledgements

This research has been partly supported by the COGNISCIENCE research program of the C.N.R.S. through PRESCOT, the Toulouse network of searchers in Cognitive Sciences.

References

M. Bauer & W. Martienssen. (1989) Quasi-Periodicity Route to Chaos in Neural Networks. *Europhys. Lett.* **10**: 427-431.

B. Doyon, B. Cessac, M. Quoy & M. Samuelides. (1993) Control of the Transition to Chaos in Neural Networks with Random Connectivity. *Int. J. Bifurcation and Chaos (in press)*.

D. Gallez & A. Babloyantz. (1991) Predictability of human EEG: a dynamical approach. *Biol. Cybern.* **64**: 381-392.

V.L. Girko. (1985) Circular Law. *Theory Prob. Its Appl. (USSR)* **29**: 694-706.

C.M. Gray, P. Koenig, A.K. Engel & W. Singer. (1989) Oscillatory responses in cat visual cortex exhibit intercolumnar synchronisation which reflects global stimulus properties. *Nature* **338**: 334-337.

M. W. Hirsch. (1989) Convergent Activation Dynamics in Continuous Time Networks. *Neural Networks* **2**: 331-349.

S. Newhouse, D. Ruelle & F. Takens. (1978) Occurrence of Strange Axiom *A* Attractors Near Quasi Periodic Flows on T^m, $m \geq 3$. *Commun. math. Phys.* **64**: 35-40.

D. Ruelle & F. Takens. (1971) On the nature of turbulence. *Comm. math. Phys.* **20**: 167-192.

C.A. Skarda & W.J. Freeman. (1987) How brains makes chaos in order to make sense of the world. *Behav. Brain Sci.* **10**: 161-195.

H.J. Sommers, A. Crisanti, H. Sompolinsky & Y. Stein. (1988) Spectrum of large random asymmetric matrices. *Phys. Rev. Lett.* **60**: 1895-1898.

H. Sompolinsky, A. Crisanti & H.J. Sommers. (1988) Chaos in random neural networks. *Phys. Rev. Lett.* **61**: 259-262.

Predicting Complex Behavior in Sparse Asymmetric Networks

Ali A. Minai and William B. Levy
Department of Neurosurgery
Box 420, Health Sciences Center
University of Virginia
Charlottesville, VA 22908

Abstract

Recurrent networks of threshold elements have been studied intensively as associative memories and pattern-recognition devices. While most research has concentrated on fully-connected symmetric networks, which relax to stable fixed points, asymmetric networks show richer dynamical behavior, and can be used as sequence generators or flexible pattern-recognition devices. In this paper, we approach the problem of predicting the complex global behavior of a class of random asymmetric networks in terms of network parameters. These networks can show fixed-point, cyclical or effectively aperiodic behavior, depending on parameter values, and our approach can be used to set parameters, as necessary, to obtain a desired complexity of dynamics. The approach also provides qualitative insight into why the system behaves as it does and suggests possible applications.

1 INTRODUCTION

Recurrent neural networks of threshold elements have been intensively investigated in recent years, in part because of their interesting dynamics. Most of the interest has focused on networks with *symmetric connections*, which always relax to stable fixed points (Hopfield, 1982) and can be used as associative memories or pattern-recognition devices. Networks with *asymmetric connections*, however, have the potential for much richer dynamic behavior and may be used for learning sequences (see, e.g., Amari, 1972; Sompolinsky and Kanter, 1986).

In this paper, we introduce an approach for predicting the complex global behavior of an interesting class of random sparse asymmetric networks in terms of network parameters. This approach can be used to set parameter values, as necessary, to obtain a desired activity level and qualitatively different varieties of dynamic behavior.

2 NETWORK PARAMETERS AND EQUATIONS

A network consists of n identical 0/1 neurons with threshold θ. The fixed pattern of excitatory connectivity between neurons is generated prior to simulation by a Bernoulli process with a probability p of connection from neuron j to neuron i. All excitatory connections have the fixed value w, and there is a global inhibition that is linear in the number of active neurons. If $m(t)$ is the number of active neurons at time t, K the inhibitory weight, $y_i(t)$ the net excitation and $z_i(t)$ the firing status of neuron i at t, and c_{ij} a 0/1 variable indicating the presence or absence of a connection from j to i, then the equations for i are:

$$y_i(t) = \frac{w \sum_{j=1}^{n} c_{ij} z_j(t-1)}{w \sum_{j=1}^{n} c_{ij} z_j(t-1) + Km(t-1)}, \qquad 1 \le m(t-1) \le n \tag{1}$$

$$z_i(t) = \begin{cases} 1 & \text{if } y_i(t) \ge \theta \\ 0 & \textit{otherwise} \end{cases}, \qquad 0 < \theta < 1 \tag{2}$$

If $m(t-1) = 0$, $y_i(t) = 0\ \forall i$. Equation (1) is a simple variant of the *shunting inhibition* neuron model studied by several researchers, and the network is similar to the one proposed by Marr (Marr, 1971). Note that (1) and (2) can be combined to write the neuron equations in a more familiar *subtractive inhibition* format. Defining $\alpha \equiv \theta K/(1-\theta)w$,

$$z_i(t) = \begin{cases} 1 & \text{if } \sum_{j=1}^{n} c_{ij} z_j(t-1) - \alpha \sum_{j=1}^{n} z_j(t-1) \ge 0 \\ 0 & \textit{otherwise} \end{cases} \tag{3}$$

3 NETWORK BEHAVIOR

In this paper, we study the evolution of total activity, $m(t)$, as the system relaxes. From Equation (3), the firing condition for neuron i at time t, given the activity $m(t-1)=M$ at time $t-1$, is: $e_i(t) \equiv \sum_{j=1}^{n} c_{ij} z_j(t-1) \ge \alpha M$. Thus, in order to fire at time t, neuron i must have at least $\lceil \alpha M \rceil$ active inputs. This allows us to calculate the average firing probability of a neuron given the prior activity M as:

$$P\{\#\ \textit{of active inputs} \ge \lceil \alpha M \rceil\} = \sum_{k=\lceil \alpha M \rceil}^{M} \binom{M}{k} p^k (1-p)^{M-k} \equiv \rho(M; n, p, \alpha) \tag{4}$$

If M is large enough, we can use a Gaussian approximation to the binomial distribution and a hyperbolic tangent approximation to the error function to get

$$\rho(M;n,p,\alpha) \approx \frac{1}{2}\left[1 - erf\left[\frac{X}{\sqrt{2}}\right]\right] \approx \frac{1}{2}\left[1 - \tanh\left[\sqrt{\frac{2}{\pi}}X\right]\right] \tag{5}$$

where

$$X \equiv \frac{\lceil \alpha M \rceil - Mp}{\sqrt{Mp(1-p)}}$$

Finally, when M is large enough to assume $\lceil \alpha M \rceil \approx \alpha M$, we get an even simpler form:

$$\rho(M;n,p,\alpha) \approx \frac{1}{2}\left[1 - \tanh\frac{\sqrt{M}}{T}\right] \tag{6}$$

where

$$T \equiv \frac{1}{\alpha - p}\sqrt{\frac{\pi p(1-p)}{2}}, \qquad \alpha \neq p$$

Assuming that neurons fire independently, as they will tend to do in such large, sparse networks (Minai and Levy, 1992a,b), the network's activity at time t is distributed as

$$P\{m(t)=N \mid m(t-1)=M\} \approx \binom{n}{N} \rho(M)^N (1-\rho(M))^{n-N} \tag{7}$$

which leads to a stochastic return map for the activity:

$$m(t) = n\,\rho(m(t-1)) + O(\sqrt{n}) \tag{8}$$

In Figure 1, we plot $m(t)$ against $m(t-1)$ for a 120 neuron network and two different values of α. The vertical bars show two standard deviations on either side of $n\rho(m(t-1))$. It is clear that the network's activity falls within the range predicted by (8).

After an initial transient period, the system either switches off permanently (corresponding to the zero activity fixed point) or gets trapped in an $O(\sqrt{n})$ region around the point $\bar{m}$ defined by $m(t) = m(t-1)$. We call this the *attracting region* of the map. The size and location of the attracting region are determined by α and largely dictate the qualitative dynamic behavior of the network.

As α ranges from 0 to 1, networks show three kinds of behavior: fixed points, short cycles, and effectively aperiodic dynamics. Before describing these behaviors, however, we introduce the notion of *available neurons*. Let k_i be the number of input connections to neuron i (the *fan-in* of i). Given $m(t-1) = M$, if $k_i < \lceil \alpha M \rceil$, neuron i cannot possibly meet the firing criterion at time t. Such a neuron is said to be disabled by activity M. The group of neurons not disabled are considered available neurons. At any specific activity M, there is a unique set, $N_a(M)$, of available neurons in a given network, and only neurons from this set can be active at the next time step. Clearly, $N_a(M_1) \subseteq N_a(M_2)$ if $M_1 \geq M_2$. The average size of the available set at a given activity M is

$$n_a(M;n,p,\alpha) \equiv n\left[1 - P\{k_i < \lceil \alpha M \rceil\}\right] = n \sum_{k=\lceil \alpha M \rceil}^{n} \binom{n}{k} p^k (1-p)^{n-k} \tag{9}$$

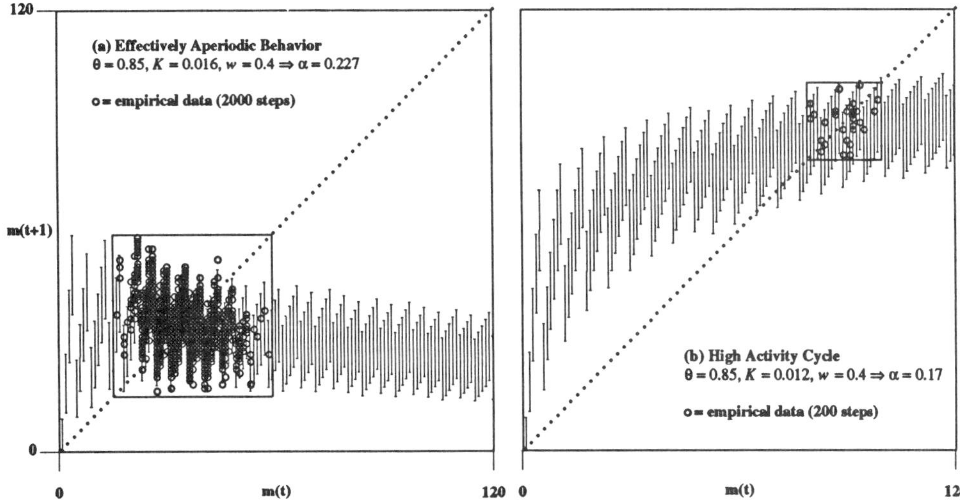

Figure 1: Predicted Distribution of $m(t+1)$ given $m(t)$, and Empirical Data (o) for Two Networks A and B. The vertical bars represent 4 standard deviations of the predicted distribution for each $m(t)$. Note that the empirical values fall in the predicted range.

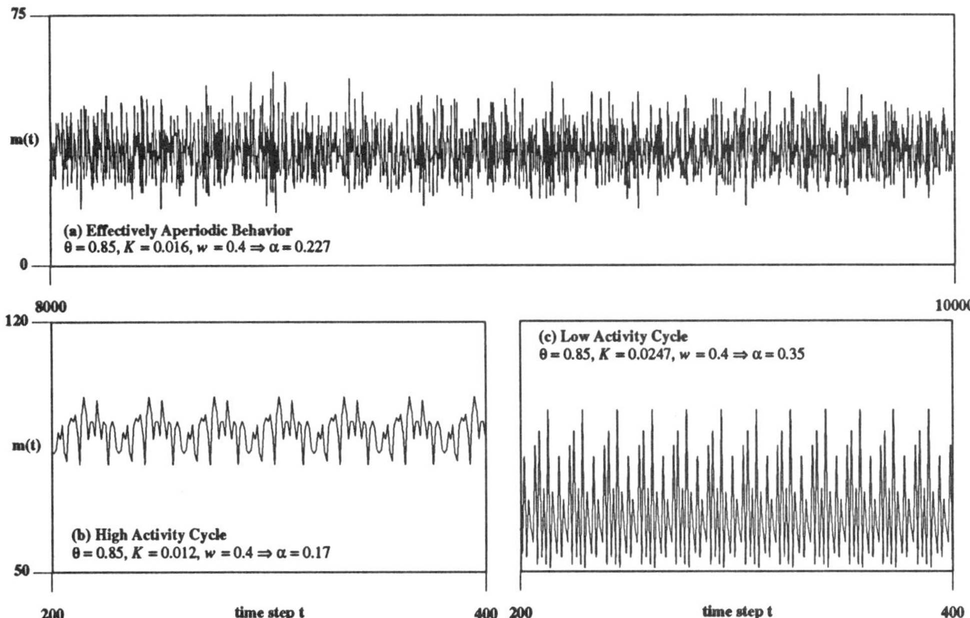

Figure 2: Activity time-series for three kinds of behavior shown by a 120 neuron network. Graphs (a) and (b) correspond to the data shown in Figure 1.

It can be shown that $n_a(M) \geq n\,\rho(M)$, so there are usually enough neurons available to achieve the average activity as per (8).

We now describe the three kinds of dynamic behavior exhibited by our networks.

(1) **Fixed Point Behavior:** If α is very small, $\bar{m}$ is close to n, inhibition is not strong enough to control activity and almost all neurons switch on permanently. If α is too large, $\bar{m}$ is close to 0 and the stochastic dynamics eventually finds, and remains at, the zero activity fixed point.

(2) **Effectively Aperiodic Behavior:** While deterministic, finite state systems such as our networks cannot show truly aperiodic or chaotic behavior, the time to repetition can be so long as to make the dynamics effectively aperiodic. This occurs when the attracting region is at a moderate activity level, well below the ceiling defined by the number of available neurons. In such a situation, the network, starting from an initial condition, successively visits a very large number of different states, and the activity, $m(t)$, yields an effvectively aperiodic time-series of amplitude $O(\sqrt{n})$, as shown in Figure 2(a).

(3) **Cyclical Behavior:** If the attracting region is at a high activity level, most of the available neurons must fire at every time step in order to maintain the activity predicted by (8). This forces network states to be very similar to each other, which, in turn, leads to even more similar successor states and the network settles into a relatively short limit cycle of high activity (Figure 2(b)). When the attracting region is at an activity level just above switch-off, the network can get into a low-activity limit cycle mediated by a very small group of high fan-in neurons (Figure 2(c)). This effect, however, is unstable with regard to initial conditions and the value of α; it is expected to become less significant with increasing network size.

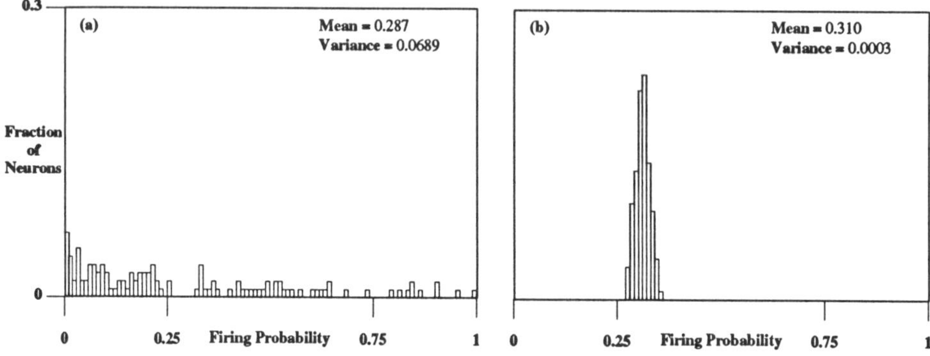

Figure 3: Neuron firing probability histograms for two 120-neuron networks in the effectively aperiodic phase ($\alpha \doteq 0.227$). Graph (a) is for a network with random connectivity generated through a Bernoulli process with $p = 0.2$, while Graph (b) is for a network with a fixed fan-in of exactly 24, which corresponds to the mean fan-in for $p = 0.2$.

One interesting issue that arises in the context of effectively aperiodic behavior is that of state-space sampling within the $O(\sqrt{n})$ constraint on activity. We assess this by looking at the histogram of individual neuron firing rates. Figure 3(a) shows the histogram for a 120 neuron network in the effectively aperiodic phase. Clearly, some subspaces are being sampled much more than others and the histogram is very broad. This is mainly due to differences in the fan-in of individual neurons, and will diminish in larger networks. Figure 3(b) shows the neuron firing histogram for a 120 neuron network where each neuron has a fan-in of 24. The sampling is clearly much more "ergodic" and the dynamics less biased towards certain subspaces.

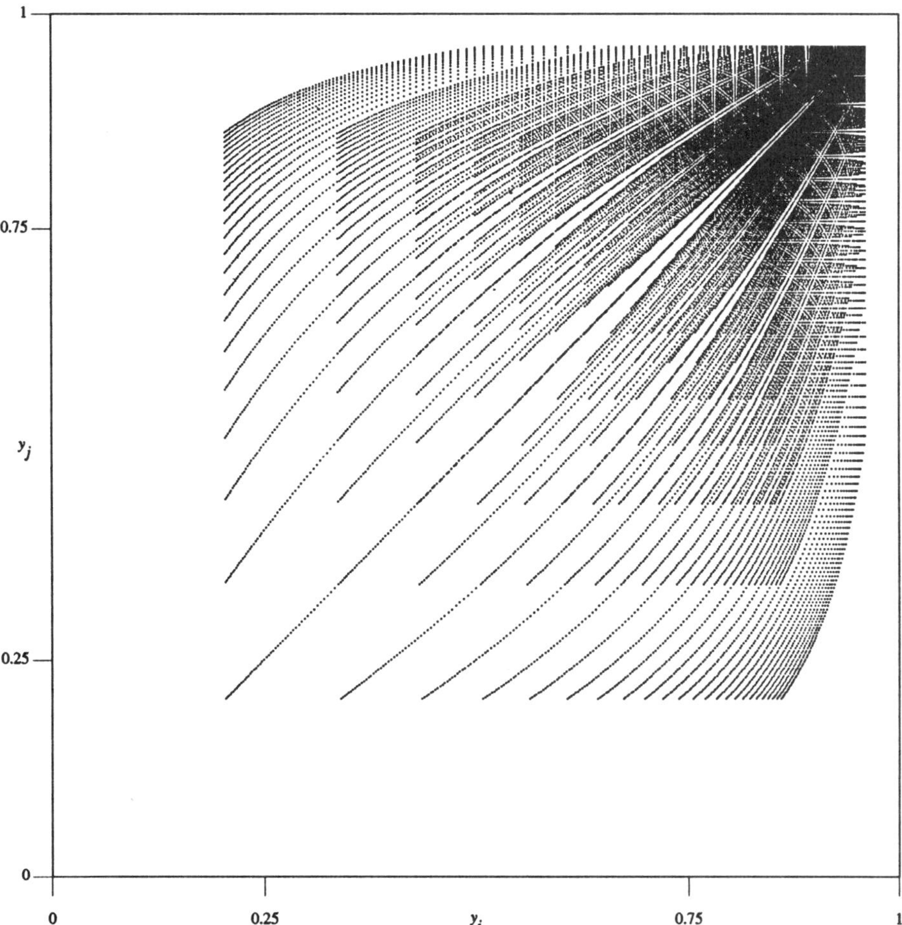

Figure 4: The complete set of non-zero activation values available to two identical neurons i and j with fan-in 24 in a 120-neuron network.

4 ACTIVATION DYNAMICS

While our modeling so far has focused on neural firing, it is instructive to look at the underlying neuron activation values, y_i. If $m(t-1) = M$, the possible $y_i(t)$ values for a neuron i with fan-in k_i are given by the set

$$Y(M, k_i) \equiv \left\{ \frac{wq}{wq + KM} \mid MAX(0, k_i - n + M) \leq q \leq MIN(M, k_i) \right\} \quad M > 0 \qquad (10)$$

with $Y(0, k_i) \equiv \{0\}$. Here q represents the number of active inputs to i, and the set $\mathbf{Y}_i \equiv \bigcup_{M=0}^{n} Y(M, k_i)$ represents the set of all possible activation values for the neuron. The network's n-dimensional activation state, $\mathbf{y}(t) \equiv [y_1, y_2, ..., y_n]$, evolves upon the *activation space* $\mathbf{Y}_1 \times \mathbf{Y}_2 \times \cdots \times \mathbf{Y}_n$, which is an extremely complex but regular object. In Figure 4, we plot a 2-dimensional subspace projection — called a y–y plot – of the activation space for a 120-neuron network excluding the zero states. Both neurons shown have a fan-in of 24. In actuality, only a small subset of the activation space is sampled due to the constraining effects of the dynamics and the improbability of most q values.

5 RELATING THE ACTIVITY LEVEL TO α

From a practical standpoint, it would be useful to know how the average activity in a network is related to its α parameter. This can be done using the hyperbolic tangent approximation of Equation (6). First, we define the *activity level* at time t as $r(t) \equiv n^{-1} m(t)$, i.e., the proportion of active neurons. This is a *macrostate* variable in the sense of (Amari, 1974). In the long term, the activity level becomes confined to a $O(1/\sqrt{n})$ region around the value corresponding to the activity fixed point. Thus, it is reasonable to use $\bar{r}$ as an estimate for the time-averaged activity level $\langle r \rangle$. To relate $\bar{m}$ (and thus $\bar{r}$) to α, we must solve the fixed point equation $\bar{m} = n\,\rho(\bar{m})$. Substituting this and the definition of $\bar{r}$ into

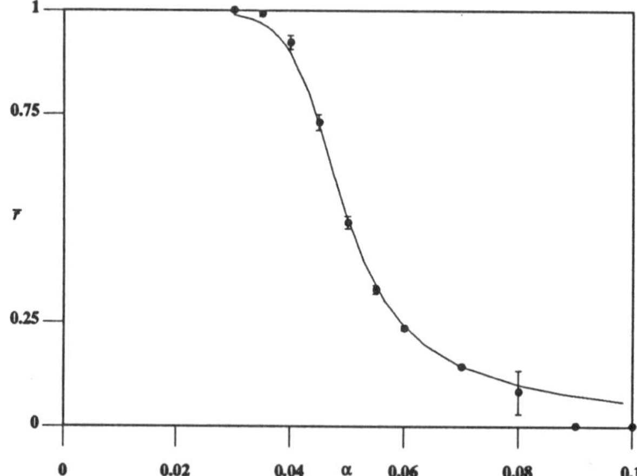

Figure 5: Predicted and empirical activities for 1000 neuron networks with $p = 0.05$. Each data point is averaged over 7 networks.

(6) gives:

$$\alpha(\bar{r}) \approx p + \sqrt{\frac{\pi p(1-p)}{2n\bar{r}}}\tanh^{-1}(1-2\bar{r}) \quad (11)$$

While α can range from 0 to 1, the approximation of (11) breaks down at very high or very small values of $\bar{r}$. However, the range of its applicability gets wider as n increases. Figure 5 shows the performance of (11) in predicting the average activity level in a 1000-neuron network. Note that $\alpha = p$ always leads to $\bar{r} = 0.5$ by Equation (11).

6 CONCLUSION

We have studied a general class of asymmetric networks and have developed a statistical model to relate its dynamical behavior to its parameters. This behavior, which is largely characterized by a composite parameter α, is richly varied. Understanding such behavior provides insight into the complex possibilities offered by sparse asymmetric networks, especially with regard to modeling such brain regions as the hippocampal CA3 area in mammals. The complex behavior of random asymmetric networks has been discussed before by Parisi (Parisi, 1986), Nützel (Nützel, 1991), and others. We show how to *control* this complexity in our networks by setting parameters appropriately.

Acknowledgements: This research was supported by NIMH MH00622 and NIMH MH48161 to WBL, and by the Department of Neurosurgery, University of Virginia, Dr. John A. Jane, Chairman.

References

S. Amari (1972). Learning Patterns and Pattern Sequences by Self-Organizing Nets of Threshold Elements. *IEEE Trans. on Computers* **C-21**, 1197-1206

S. Amari (1974). A Method of Statistical Neurodynamics. *Kybernetik* **14**, 201-215

J.J. Hopfield (1982). Neural Networks and Physical Systems with Emergent Collective Computational Abilities. *Proc. Nat. Acad. Sci. USA* **79**, 2554-2558.

D. Marr (1971). Simple Memory: A Theory for Archicortex. *Phil. Trans. R. Soc. Lond. B* **262**, 23-81.

A.A. Minai and W.B. Levy (1992a). The Dynamics of Sparse Random Networks. *In Review.*

A.A. Minai and W.B. Levy (1992b). Setting the Activity Level in Sparse Random Networks. *In Review.*

K. Nützel (1991). The Length of Attractors in Asymmetric Random Neural Networks with Deterministic Dynamics. *J. Phys. A: Math. Gen* **24**, L151-157.

G. Parisi (1982). Asymmetric Neural Networks and the Process of Learning. *J. Phys. A: Math. Gen.* **19**, L675-L680.

H. Sompolinsky and I. Kanter (1986), Temporal Association in Asymmetric Neural Networks. *Phys. Rev. Lett.* **57**, 2861-2864.

Single-iteration Threshold Hamming Networks

Isaac Meilijson **Eytan Ruppin**

Moshe Sipper
School of Mathematical Sciences
Raymond and Beverly Sackler Faculty of Exact Sciences
Tel Aviv University, 69978 Tel Aviv, Israel

Abstract

We analyze in detail the performance of a Hamming network classifying inputs that are distorted versions of one of its m stored memory patterns. The activation function of the memory neurons in the original Hamming network is replaced by a simple threshold function. The resulting Threshold Hamming Network (THN) correctly classifies the input pattern, with probability approaching 1, using only $O(m \ln m)$ connections, in a single iteration. The THN drastically reduces the time and space complexity of Hamming Network classifiers.

1 Introduction

Originally presented in (Steinbuch 1961, Taylor 1964) the Hamming network (HN) has received renewed attention in recent years (Lippmann et. al. 1987, Baum et. al. 1988). The HN calculates the Hamming distance between the input pattern and each memory pattern, and selects the memory with the smallest distance. It is composed of two subnets: The *similarity* subnet, consisting of an n-neuron input layer connected with an m-neuron memory layer, calculates the number of equal bits between the input and each memory pattern. The *winner-take-all* (WTA) subnet, consisting of a fully connected m-neuron topology, selects the memory neuron that best matches the input pattern.

The similarity subnet uses mn connections and performs a single iteration. The WTA subnet has m^2 connections. With randomly generated input and memory patterns, it converges in $\Theta(m\ln(mn))$ iterations (Floreen 1991). Since m is exponential in n, the space and time complexity of the network is primarily due to the WTA subnet (Domany & Orland 1987). We analyze the performance of the HN in the practical scenario where the input pattern is a distorted version of some stored memory vector. We show that it is possible to replace the original activation function of the neurons in the memory layer by a simple threshold function, and completely discard the WTA subnet. If the threshold is properly tuned, only the neuron standing for the 'correct' memory is likely to be activated. The resulting Threshold Hamming Network (THN) will perform correctly (with probability approaching 1) in a single iteration, using only $O(m\ln m)$ connections instead of the $O(m^2)$ connections in the original HN. We identify the optimal threshold, and measure its performance relative to the original HN.

2 The Threshold Hamming Network

We examine a HN storing $m+1$ memory patterns ξ^μ, $1 \le \mu \le m+1$, each being an n-dimensional vector of ± 1. The input pattern x is generated by selecting some memory pattern ξ^μ (w.l.g., ξ^{m+1}), and letting each bit x_i be either ξ_i^μ or $-\xi_i^\mu$ with probabilities α and $(1-\alpha)$ respectively, where $\alpha > 0.5$. To analyze this HN, we use some tight approximations to the binomial distribution. Due to space considerations, their proofs are omitted.

Lemma 1.
Let $X \sim Bin(n,p)$. If x_n are integers such that $lim_{n\to\infty}\frac{x_n}{n} = \beta \in (p,1)$, then

$$P(X \ge x_n) \approx \frac{1-p}{(1-\frac{p}{\beta})\sqrt{2\pi n\beta(1-\beta)}} \exp\{-n[\beta\ln\frac{\beta}{p} + (1-\beta)\ln\frac{1-\beta}{1-p}]\} \tag{1}$$

in the sense that the ratio between LHS and RHS converges to 1 as $n \to \infty$. For the special case $p=\frac{1}{2}$, let $G(\beta) = \ln 2 + \beta\ln\beta + (1-\beta)\ln(1-\beta)$, then

$$P(X \ge x_n) \approx \frac{\exp\{-nG(\beta)\}}{(2-\frac{1}{\beta})\sqrt{2\pi n\beta(1-\beta)}}\ . \tag{2}$$

Lemma 2.
Let $X_i \sim Bin(n,\frac{1}{2})$ be independent, $\gamma \in (0,1)$, and let x_n be as in Lemma 1. If

$$m = (2-\frac{1}{\beta})\sqrt{2\pi n\beta(1-\beta)}\left(\ln\frac{1}{\gamma}\right)e^{nG(\beta)}, \tag{3}$$

then

$$P(max(X_1, X_2, \cdots, X_m) < x_n) \approx \gamma \tag{4}$$

Lemma 3.
Let $Y \sim Bin(n,\alpha)$ with $\alpha > \frac{1}{2}$, let (X_i) and γ be as in Lemma 2, and let $\eta \in (0,1)$. Let x_n be the integer closest to $n\beta$, where

$$\beta = \alpha - \sqrt{\frac{\alpha(1-\alpha)}{n}}z_\eta - \frac{1}{2n} \tag{5}$$

and z_η is the η - quantile of the standard normal distribution, i.e.,

$$\eta = \frac{1}{\sqrt{2\pi}} \int_{-\infty}^{z_\eta} e^{-x^2/2} dx \tag{6}$$

Then, if Y and (X_i) are independent

$$P(max(X_1, X_2, \cdots, X_m) < Y) \geq P(max(X_1, X_2, \cdots, X_m) < x_n \leq Y) \Rightarrow \gamma\eta \tag{7}$$

as $n \to \infty$, for m as in (3).

Based on the above binomial probability approximations, we can now propose and analyze a n-neuron Threshold Hamming Network (THN) that classifies the input patterns with probability of error not exceeding ϵ, when the input vector is generated with an initial bit-similarity α: Let X_j be the similarity between the input vector and the $j'th$ memory pattern ($1 \leq j \leq m$), and let Y be the similarity with the 'correct' memory pattern ξ^{m+1}. Choose γ and η so that $\gamma\eta \geq 1 - \epsilon$, e.g., $\gamma = \eta = \sqrt{1-\epsilon}$; determine β by (5) and m by (3). Discard the WTA subnet, and simply replace the neurons of the memory layer by m neurons having a threshold x_n , the integer closest to $n\beta$. If any memory neuron with similarity at least x_n is declared 'the winner', then, by Lemma 3, the probability of error is at most ϵ, where 'error' may be due to the existence of no winner, wrong winner, or multiple winners.

3 The Hamming Network and an Optimal Threshold Hamming Network

We now calculate the choice of the threshold x_n that maximizes the storage capacity $m = m(n, \epsilon, \alpha)$. Let ϕ (Φ) denote the standard normal density (cumulative distribution function), and let $r = \phi/(1-\Phi)$ denote the corresponding failure rate function. Then,

Lemma 4.
The optimal proportion between the two error probabilities is

$$\frac{1-\gamma}{1-\eta} \approx \frac{r(z_\eta)}{\sqrt{n\alpha(1-\alpha)} \ln \frac{\beta}{1-\beta}}, \tag{8}$$

which we will denote by δ.

Proof:
Let $M = max(X_1, X_2, \cdots, X_m)$, and let Y denote the similarity with the 'correct' memory pattern, as before. We have seen that $P(M < x) \approx \exp\{-m\frac{\exp\{-nG(\beta)\}}{\sqrt{2\pi n\beta(1-\beta)(2-\frac{1}{\beta})}}\}$. Since $G'(\beta) = \ln\frac{\beta}{(1-\beta)}$, then by Taylor expansion

$$P(M < x) = P(M < x_0 + x - x_0) \approx \exp\{-m\frac{\exp\{-n[G(\beta + \frac{x-x_0}{n})]\}}{\sqrt{2\pi n\beta(1-\beta)(2-\frac{1}{\beta})}}\} \approx$$

$$\exp\{-m\frac{\exp\{-nG(\beta) - (x - x_0)\ln\frac{\beta}{(1-\beta)}\}}{\sqrt{2\pi n\beta(1-\beta)(2-\frac{1}{\beta})}}\} = \gamma^{(\frac{\beta}{1-\beta})^{x_0 - x}} \tag{9}$$

(in accordance with Gnedenko extreme-value distribution of type 1 (Leadbetter et. al. 1983)). Similarly,

$$P(Y < x) = \exp\{\ln P(Y < x_0 + x - x_0)\} \approx$$
$$P(Y < x_0)\exp\{\frac{\phi(z)}{\Phi^*(z)}\frac{x - x_0}{\sqrt{n\alpha(1-\alpha)}}\} = (1-\eta)\exp\{r(z)\frac{x - x_0}{\sqrt{n\alpha(1-\alpha)}}\} \quad (10)$$

where ϕ is the standard normal density function, Φ is the standard normal cumulative distribution function, $\Phi^* = 1 - \Phi$ and $r = \frac{\phi}{\Phi^*}$ is the corresponding failure rate function. The probability of correct recognition using a threshold x can now be expressed as

$$P(M < x)P(Y \geq x) = \gamma^{(\frac{\beta}{1-\beta})^{x_0 - x}}(1 - (1-\eta)\exp\{r(z)\frac{x - x_0}{\sqrt{n\alpha(1-\alpha)}}\}) \quad (11)$$

We differentiate expression (11) with respect to $x_0 - x$, and equate the derivative at $x_0 = x$ to zero, to obtain the relation between γ and η that yields the optimal threshold, i.e., that which maximizes the probability of correct recognition. This yields

$$\gamma = \exp\{-\frac{r(z)}{\sqrt{n\alpha(1-\alpha)}\ln\frac{\beta}{1-\beta}}\frac{1-\eta}{\eta}\} \quad (12)$$

We now approximate

$$1 - \gamma \approx -\ln\gamma \approx \frac{r(z)}{\sqrt{n\alpha(1-\alpha)}\ln\frac{\beta}{1-\beta}}(1-\eta) \quad (13)$$

and thus the optimal proportion between the two error probabilities is

$$\frac{1-\gamma}{1-\eta} \approx \frac{r(z)}{\sqrt{n\alpha(1-\alpha)}\ln\frac{\beta}{1-\beta}} = \delta. \quad (14)$$

□

Based on Lemma 4, if the desired probability of error is ϵ, we choose

$$\gamma = 1 - \frac{\delta\epsilon}{1+\delta}, \qquad \eta = 1 - \frac{\epsilon}{(1+\delta)}\ . \quad (15)$$

We start with $\gamma = \eta = \sqrt{1-\epsilon}$, obtain β from (5) and δ from (8), and recompute η and γ from (15). The limiting values of β and γ in this iterative process give the maximal capacity m and threshold x_n.

We now compute the error probability $\epsilon(m, n, \alpha)$ of the original HN (with the WTA subnet) for arbitrary m, n and α, and compare it with ϵ.

Lemma 5.
For arbitrary n, α and ϵ, let m, β, γ, η and δ be as calculated above. Then, the probability of error $\epsilon(m, n, \alpha)$ of the HN satisfies

$$\epsilon(m, n, \alpha) \approx \Gamma(1-\delta)\frac{1 - e^{-\delta\ln\frac{\beta}{1-\beta}}}{\delta\ln\frac{\beta}{1-\beta}}\frac{\delta^{\delta}}{(1+\delta)^{1+\delta}}\epsilon^{1+\delta} \quad (16)$$

where

$$\Gamma(t) = \int_0^\infty x^{t-1} e^{-x} dx \tag{17}$$

is the Gamma function.

Proof:

$$P(Y \leq M) = \sum_x P(Y \leq x) P(M = x) =$$

$$\sum_x P(Y \leq x)[P(M < x+1) - P(M < x)] \approx$$

$$\sum_x P(Y \leq x_0) e^{-\delta(x_0 - x) \ln \frac{\beta}{1-\beta}}$$

$$\left[(P(M < x_0))^{(\frac{\beta}{1-\beta})^{x_0 - x - 1}} - (P(M < x_0))^{(\frac{\beta}{1-\beta})^{x_0 - x}} \right] \tag{18}$$

We now approximate this sum by the integral of the summand: let $b = \frac{\beta}{1-\beta}$ and $c = \delta \ln \frac{\beta}{1-\beta}$. We have seen that the probability of incorrect performance of the WTA subnet is equal to

$$P(Y \leq M) \approx$$

$$\sum_x P(Y \leq x_0) e^{-c(x_0 - x)} [(P(M < x_0))^{b^{(x_0 - x - 1)}} - (P(M < x_0))^{b^{(x_0 - x)}}] \approx$$

$$(1 - \eta) \int_{-\infty}^{\infty} (\gamma^{b^{y-1}} - \gamma^{b^y}) e^{-cy} dy \tag{19}$$

Now we transform variables $t = b^y \ln \frac{1}{\gamma}$ to get the integral in the form

$$e^{-c}(1 - \eta) \int_0^\infty (e^{-t} - e^{-bt}) \left(\frac{t}{\ln \frac{1}{\gamma}}\right)^{\frac{-c}{\ln b}} \frac{dt}{t \ln b} = K_1 \int_0^\infty (e^{-t} - e^{-bt}) t^{-(1+K_2)} dt \tag{20}$$

This is the convergent difference between two divergent Gamma function integrals. We perform integration by parts to obtain a representation as an integral with t^{-K_2} instead of $t^{-(1+K_2)}$ in the integrand. For $0 \leq K_2 < 1$, the corresponding integral converges. The final result is then

$$(1 - \eta) \frac{1 - e^{-c}}{c} \Gamma\left(1 - \frac{c}{\ln b}\right) \left(\ln \frac{1}{\gamma}\right)^{\frac{c}{\ln b}} \tag{21}$$

Hence, we have

$$P(Y \leq M) \approx (1 - \eta) \frac{1 - e^{-\delta \ln \frac{\beta}{1-\beta}}}{\delta \ln \frac{\beta}{1-\beta}} \Gamma(1 - \delta) \left(\ln \frac{1}{\gamma}\right)^\delta \approx$$

$$\Gamma(1 - \delta) \frac{1 - e^{-\delta \ln \frac{\beta}{1-\beta}}}{\delta \ln \frac{\beta}{1-\beta}} \frac{(\epsilon \delta)^\delta}{(1 + \delta)^{1+\delta}} \epsilon \tag{22}$$

% error → threshold , m ↓	predicted THN	predicted HN	experimental THN	experimental HN
133 , 145	2.46 ($1-\gamma = 1.03$ $1-\eta = 1.46$)	0.144	2.552 ($1-\gamma = 1.0$ $1-\eta = 1.552$)	0.103
134 , 346	3.4 ($1-\gamma = 1.37$ $1-\eta = 2.11$)	0.272	3.468 ($1-\gamma = 1.373$ $1-\eta = 2.168$)	0.253
135 , 825	4.714 ($1-\gamma = 1.776$ $1-\eta = 2.991$)	0.494	4.152 ($1-\gamma = 1.606$ $1-\eta = 2.576$)	0.485
136 , 1970	6.346 ($1-\gamma = 2.274$ $1-\eta = 4.167$)	0.857	6.447 ($1-\gamma = 2.335$ $1-\eta = 4.162$)	0.863

Table 1: The performance of a HN and optimal THN: A comparison between calculated and experimental results ($\alpha = 0.7, n = 210$).

as claimed. Expression (22) is presented as $K(\epsilon, \delta, \beta)\epsilon$, where $K(\epsilon, \delta, \beta)$ is the factor (≤ 1) by which the probability of error ϵ of the THN should be multiplied in order to get the probability of error of the original HN with the WTA subnet. For small δ, K is close to 1, however, as will be seen in the next section, K is typically larger.

4 Numerical results

The experimental results presented in table 1 testify to the accuracy of the HN and THN calculations. Figure 1 presents the calculated error probabilities for various values of input similarity α and memory capacity m, as a function of the input size n. As is evident, the performance of the THN is worse than that of the HN, but due to the exponential growth of m, it requires only a minor increment in n to obtain a THN that performs as well as the original HN.

To examine the sensitivity of the THN network to threshold variation, we have fixed $\alpha = 0.7$, $n = 210$, $m = 825$, and let the threshold vary between 132 and 138. As we can see in figure 2, the threshold 135 is indeed optimal, but the performance with threshold values of 134 and 136 is practically identical. The magnitude of the two error types varies considerably with the threshold value, but this variation has no effect on the overall performance near the optimum. These two error probabilities might as well be taken equal to each other.

Conclusion In this paper we analyzed in detail the performance of a Hamming Network and a Threshold Hamming Network. Given a desired storage capacity and performance, we described how to compute the corresponding minimal network size required. The THN drastically reduces the time and connectivity requirements of Hamming Network classifiers.

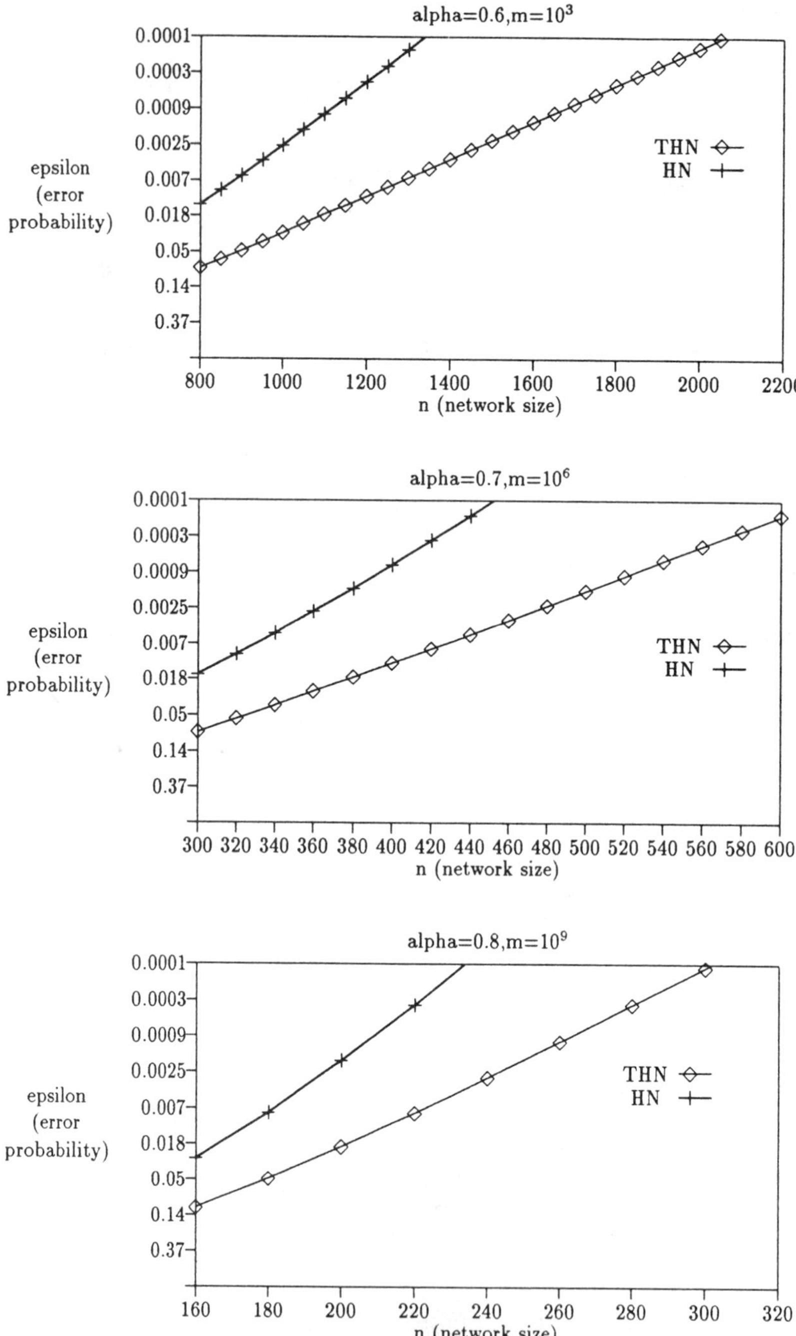

Figure 1: Probability of error as a function of network size: three networks are depicted, displaying the performance at various values of α and m. For graphical convenience, we have plotted $\log \frac{1}{\epsilon}$ versus n.

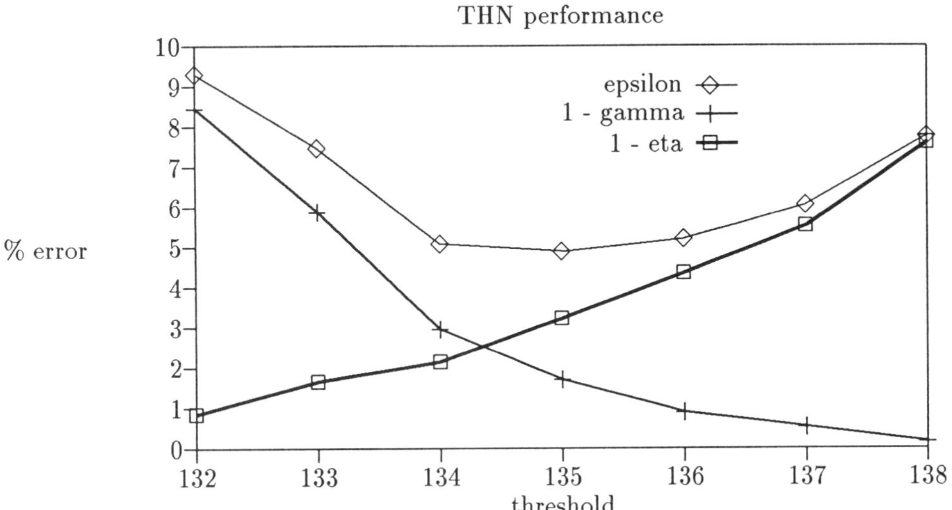

Figure 2: Threshold sensitivity of the THN ($\alpha = 0.7$, $n = 210$, $m = 825$).

References

[1] K. Steinbuch. Dei lernmatrix. *Kybernetic*, 1:36–45, 1961.

[2] W.K. Taylor. Cortico-thalamic organization and memory. *Proc. of the Royal Society of London B*, 159:466–478, 1964.

[3] R.P. Lippmann, B. Gold, and M.L. Malpass. A comparison of Hamming and Hopfield neural nets for pattern classification. Technical Report TR-769, MIT Lincoln Laboratory, 1987.

[4] E.E. Baum, J. Moody, and F. Wilczek. Internal representations for associative memory. *Biological Cybernetics*, 59:217–228, 1987.

[5] P. Floreen. The convergence of hamming memory networks. *IEEE Trans. on Neural Networks*, 2(4):449–457, 1991.

[6] E. Domany and H. Orland. A maximum overlap neural network for pattern recognition. *Physics Letters A*, 125:32–34, 1987.

[7] M.R. Leadbetter, G. Lindgren, and H. Rootzen. *Extremes and related properties of random sequences and processes.* Springer-Verlag, Berlin-Heidelberg-NewYork, 1983.

History-dependent Attractor Neural Networks

Isaac Meilijson **Eytan Ruppin**
School of Mathematical Sciences
Raymond and Beverly Sackler Faculty of Exact Sciences
Tel-Aviv University, 69978 Tel-Aviv, Israel.

Abstract

We present a methodological framework enabling a detailed description of the performance of Hopfield-like attractor neural networks (ANN) in the first two iterations. Using the Bayesian approach, we find that performance is improved when a history-based term is included in the neuron's dynamics. A further enhancement of the network's performance is achieved by judiciously choosing the *censored* neurons (those which become active in a given iteration) on the basis of the magnitude of their post-synaptic potentials. The contribution of biologically plausible, censored, history-dependent dynamics is especially marked in conditions of low firing activity and sparse connectivity, two important characteristics of the mammalian cortex. In such networks, the performance attained is higher than the performance of two 'independent' iterations, which represents an upper bound on the performance of history-independent networks.

1 Introduction

Associative Attractor Neural Network (ANN) models provide a theoretical background for the understanding of human memory processes. Considerable effort has been devoted recently to narrow the gap between the original ANN Hopfield model (Hopfield 1982) and the realm of the structure and dynamics of the brain (e.g., Amit & Tsodyks 1991). In this paper, we contribute to the examination of the performance of ANNs under cortical-like architectures, where neurons are typically connected to only a fraction of their neighboring neurons, and have a low firing activity (Abeles et. al. 1990). We develop a general framework for examining various *signalling* mechanisms (firing functions) and *activation* rules (the mechanism for deciding which neurons are active in some interval of time).

The Hopfield model is based on *memoryless dynamics*, which identify the notion of 'post-synaptic potential' with the input field received by a neuron from the neurons active in the current iteration. We follow a Bayesian approach under which the neuron's signalling and activation decisions are based on the current a-posteriori probabilities assigned to its two possible true memory states, ± 1. As we shall see, the a-posteriori belief in $+1$ is the sigmoidal function evaluated at a neuron's *generalized field*, a linear combination of present and past input fields. From a biological perspective, this *history-dependent* approach is strongly motivated by the observation that the time span of the different channel conductances in a given neuron is very broad (see Lytton 1991 for a review). While some channels are active for only microseconds, some slow-acting channels may remain open for seconds. Hence, a synaptic input currently impending on the neuron may influence both its current post-synaptic membrane potential, and its post-synaptic potential at some future time.

2 The Model

The neural network model presented is characterized as follows. There are m 'random memories' ξ^{μ}, $1 \leq \mu \leq m$, and one 'true' memory $\xi^{m+1} = \xi$. The $(m+1)N$ entries of these memories are independent and identically distributed, with equally likely values of $+1$ or -1. The initial state X has *similarity* $P(X_i = \xi_i) = (1+\epsilon)/2$, $P(X_i = -\xi_i) = (1-\epsilon)/2$, independently of everything else. The weight of the synaptic connection between neurons i and j ($i \neq j$) is given by the simple Hebbian law

$$W_{ij}{}^{*} = \sum_{\mu=1}^{m+1} \xi^{\mu}{}_{i} \xi^{\mu}{}_{j} \tag{1}$$

Each neuron receives incoming synaptic connections from a random choice of K of the N neurons in the network in such a way that if a synapse exists, the synapse in the opposite direction exists with probability r, the *reflexivity* parameter. In the first iteration, a random sample of L_1 neurons become *active* (i.e., 'fire'), thus on the average $n_1 = L_1 K/N$ neurons update the state of each neuron. The field $f_i{}^{(1)}$ of neuron i in the first iteration is

$$f_i{}^{(1)} = \frac{1}{n_1} \sum_{j=1}^{N} W_{ij}{}^{*} I_{ij} I_j{}^{(1)} X_j \ , \tag{2}$$

where I_{ij} denotes the indicator function of the event 'neuron i receives a synaptic connection from neuron j', and $I_j{}^{(t)}$ denotes the indicator function of the event 'neuron j is active in the t'th iteration'. Under the Bayesian approach we adopt, neuron i assigns an a-priori probability $\lambda_i{}^{(0)} = P(\xi_i = +1 | X_i) = (1 + \epsilon X_i)/2$ to having $+1$ as the correct memory state and evaluates the corresponding a-posteriori probability $\lambda_i{}^{(1)} = P(\xi_i = +1 | X_i, f_i{}^{(1)})$, which turns out to be expressible as the sigmoidal function $1/(1+exp(-2x))$ evaluated at some linear combination of X_i and ${f_i}^{(1)}$.

In the second iteration the belief ${\lambda_i}^{(1)}$ of a neuron determines the probability that the neuron is active. We illustrate two extreme modes for determining the active updating neurons, or *activation*: the *random* case where L_2 active neurons are randomly chosen, independently of the strength of their fields, and the *censored* case, which consists of selecting the L_2 neurons whose belief belongs to some set. The most appealing censoring rule from the biological point of view is *tail-censoring*, where the active neurons are those with the strongest beliefs. Performance, however, is improved under *interval-censoring*, where the active neurons are those with mid-range beliefs, and even further by combining tail and interval censoring into a *hybrid* rule.

Let $n_2 = L_2K/N$. The activation rule is given by a function $C : [\frac{1}{2}, 1] \rightarrow [0, 1]$. Neuron j, with belief ${\lambda_j}^{(1)}$ in $+1$, becomes active with probability $C(max({\lambda_j}^{(1)}, 1 - {\lambda_j}^{(1)}))$, independently of everything else. For example, the random case corresponds to $C \equiv \frac{L_2}{N}$ and the tail-censored case corresponds to $C(\lambda) = 1$ or 0 depending on whether $max(\lambda, 1-\lambda)$ exceeds some threshold. The output of an active neuron j is a *signal function* $S({\lambda_j}^{(1)})$ of its current belief. The field ${f_i}^{(2)}$ of neuron i in the second iteration is

$$ {f_i}^{(2)} = \frac{1}{n_2} \sum_{j=1}^{N} {W_{ij}}^* I_{ij} {I_j}^{(2)} S({\lambda_j}^{(1)}) \ . \tag{3} $$

Neuron i now evaluates its a-posteriori belief ${\lambda_i}^{(2)} = P(\xi_i = +1 | X_i, {I_i}^{(1)}, {f_i}^{(1)}, {f_i}^{(2)})$. As we shall see, ${\lambda_i}^{(2)}$ is, again, the sigmoidal function evaluated at some linear combination of the neuron's history $X_i, X_i{I_i}^{(1)}, {f_i}^{(1)}$ and ${f_i}^{(2)}$. In contrast to the common history-independent Hopfield dynamics where the signal emitted by neuron j in the $t'th$ iteration is a function of ${f_j}^{(t-1)}$ only, Bayesian history-dependent dynamics involve signals and activation rules which depend on the neuron's generalized field, obtained by adaptively incorporating ${f_j}^{(t-1)}$ to its previous generalized field. The final state ${X_i}^{(2)}$ of neuron i is taken as -1 or $+1$, depending on which of $1 - {\lambda_i}^{(2)}$ and ${\lambda_i}^{(2)}$ exceeds $1/2$.

For n_1/N, n_2/N, m/N, K/N constant, and N large, we develop explicit expressions for the performance of the network, for any signal function (e.g., $S_1(\lambda) = Sgn(\lambda - 1/2)$ or $S_2(\lambda) = 2\lambda - 1$) and activation rule. Performance is measured by the final *overlap* $\epsilon'' = \frac{1}{N}\sum \xi_i {X_i}^{(2)}$ (or equivalently by the final similarity $(1+\epsilon'')/2$). Various possible combinations of activation modes and signal functions described above are then examined under varying degrees of connectivity and neuronal activity.

3 Single-iteration optimization: the Bayesian approach

Consider the following well known basic fact in Bayesian Hypothesis Testing,
Lemma 1
Express the prior probability as

$$ P(\xi = 1) = \frac{1}{1 + e^{-2x}} \tag{4} $$

and assume an observable Y which, given ξ, is distributed according to

$$Y|\xi \sim N(\mu\xi, \sigma^2) \tag{5}$$

for some constants $\mu \in (-\infty, \infty)$ and $\sigma^2 \in (0, \infty)$. Then the posterior probability is

$$P(\xi = 1|Y = y) = \frac{1}{1 + e^{-2(x+(\mu/\sigma^2)y)}}. \tag{6}$$

Applying this Lemma to $Y = f_i^{(1)}$, with $\mu = \epsilon$ and $\sigma^2 = \frac{m}{n_1} \equiv \alpha_1$, we see that

$$\lambda_i^{(1)} = P(\xi_i = 1|X_i, f_i^{(1)}) = \frac{1}{1 + e^{-2\epsilon\left(\gamma(\epsilon)X_i + f_i^{(1)}/\alpha_1\right)}}\ , \tag{7}$$

where $\gamma(\epsilon) = \frac{1}{2\epsilon}\log\frac{1+\epsilon}{1-\epsilon}$. Hence, $P(\xi = 1|X_i, f_i^{(1)}) > 1/2$ if and only if $f_i^{(1)} + \alpha_1\gamma(\epsilon)X_i > 0$. The single-iteration performance is then given by the similarity

$$\frac{1+\epsilon'}{2} = P\left((f_i^{(1)} + \alpha_1\gamma(\epsilon)X_i)\xi_i > 0|\xi_i\right) = \tag{8}$$

$$\frac{1+\epsilon}{2}\Phi\left(\frac{\epsilon}{\sqrt{\alpha_1}} + \gamma(\epsilon)\sqrt{\alpha_1}\right) + \frac{1-\epsilon}{2}\Phi\left(\frac{\epsilon}{\sqrt{\alpha_1}} - \gamma(\epsilon)\sqrt{\alpha_1}\right)$$

$$\equiv Q(\epsilon, \alpha_1)$$

where Φ is the standard normal distribution function. The Hopfield dynamics, modified by redefining W_{ii} as $m\gamma(\epsilon)$ (in the Neural Network terminology) is equivalent (in the Bayesian jargon) to the obvious optimal policy, under which a neuron sets for itself the sign with posterior probability above 1/2 of being correct.

4 Two-iterations optimization

For mathematical convenience, we will relate signals and activation rules to normalized generalized fields rather than to beliefs. We let

$$h(x) = S\left(\frac{1}{1 + e^{-2cx}}\right)\ ,\ p(x) = C\left(max\left(\frac{1}{1 + e^{-2cx}}, 1 - \frac{1}{1 + e^{-2cx}}\right)\right) \tag{9}$$

for $c = \epsilon/\sqrt{\alpha_1}$. The signal function h is assumed to be odd, and the activation function p, even.

In order to evaluate the belief $\lambda_i^{(2)}$, we need the conditional distribution of $f_i^{(2)}$ given $X_i, I_i^{(1)}$ and $f_i^{(1)}$, for $\xi_i = -1$ or $\xi_i = +1$. We adopt the working assumption that the pair of random variables $(f_i^{(1)}, f_i^{(2)})$ has a bivariate normal distribution given ξ_i, $I_i^{(1)}$ and X_i, with ξ_i, $I_i^{(1)}$ and X_i affecting means but not variances or correlations. Under this working assumption, $f_i^{(2)}$ is conditionally normal given $(\xi_i, I_i^{(1)}, X_i, f_i^{(1)})$, with constant variance and a mean which we will identify. This working assumption allows us to model performance via the following well known regression model.

Lemma 2

If two random variables U and V with finite variances are such that $E(V|U)$ is a linear function of U and $Var(V|U)$ is constant, then

$$E(V|U) = E(V) + \frac{Cov(U,V)}{Var(U)}(U - E(U)) \tag{10}$$

and

$$Var(V|U) = Var(V) - \frac{(Cov(U,V))^2}{Var(U)}. \tag{11}$$

Letting $U = f_i^{(1)}$ and $V = f_i^{(2)}$, we obtain

$$\lambda_i^{(2)} = P(\xi_i = 1|X_i, I_i^{(1)}, f_i^{(1)}, f_i^{(2)}) = \tag{12}$$

$$\frac{1}{1+\exp\{-2\left[\epsilon\left(f_i^{(1)}/\alpha_1 + \gamma(\epsilon)X_i\right) + \frac{\epsilon^*-a\epsilon}{\tau^2}\left(f_i^{(2)} - bX_iI_i^{(1)} - af_i^{(1)}\right)\right]\}} =$$

$$\frac{1}{1+\exp\{-2\left[\left(\epsilon\gamma(\epsilon) - \frac{b(\epsilon^*-a\epsilon)}{\tau^2}I_i^{(1)}\right)X_i + \left(\frac{\epsilon}{\alpha_1} - \frac{a(\epsilon^*-a\epsilon)}{\tau^2}\right)f_i^{(1)} + \frac{\epsilon^*-a\epsilon}{\tau^2}f_i^{(2)}\right]\}}$$

which is the sigmoidal function evaluated at some generalized field. Expression (12) shows that the correct definition of a final state $X_i^{(2)}$, as the most likely value among $+1$ or -1, is

$$X_i^{(2)} = Sgn\left[\left(\epsilon\gamma(\epsilon) - \frac{b(\epsilon^*-a\epsilon)}{\tau^2}I_i^{(1)}\right)X_i + \left(\frac{\epsilon}{\alpha_1} - \frac{a(\epsilon^*-a\epsilon)}{\tau^2}\right)f_i^{(1)} + \frac{\epsilon^*-a\epsilon}{\tau^2}f_i^{(2)}\right] \tag{13}$$

and the performance is given by

$$P(X_i^{(2)} = \xi_i|\xi_i) = \frac{1+\epsilon}{2}\Phi\left(\frac{\epsilon}{\sqrt{\alpha^*}} + \gamma(\epsilon)\sqrt{\alpha^*}\right) + \frac{1-\epsilon}{2}\Phi\left(\frac{\epsilon}{\sqrt{\alpha^*}} - \gamma(\epsilon)\sqrt{\alpha^*}\right) = \tag{14}$$

$$Q(\epsilon, \alpha^*)$$

where the one-iteration performance function Q is defined by (8), and

$$\alpha^* = \frac{m}{n^*} = \frac{m}{n_1 + m\left(\frac{\epsilon^*/\epsilon - a}{\tau}\right)^2}. \tag{15}$$

We see that the performance is conveniently expressed as the single-iteration optimal performance, had this iteration involved n^* rather than n_1 sampled neurons. This formula yields a numerical and analytical tool to assess the network's performance with different signal functions, activation rules and architectures. Due to space restrictions, the identification of the various parameters used in the above formulas is not presented. However, it can be shown that in the sparse limit arrived at by fixing α_1 and α_2 and letting both K/m and N/K go to infinity, it is always better to replace an iteration by two smaller ones. This suggests that Bayesian updating dynamics should be essentially asynchronous. We also show that the two-iterations performance $Q\left(\epsilon, \frac{1}{\frac{1}{\alpha_1}+\frac{1}{\alpha_2}\left(\frac{Q(\epsilon,\alpha_1)}{\epsilon}\right)^2}\right)$ is superior to the performance $Q\left(2Q(\epsilon,\alpha_1)-1,\alpha_2\right)$ of two *independent* optimal single iterations.

5 Heuristics on activation and signalling

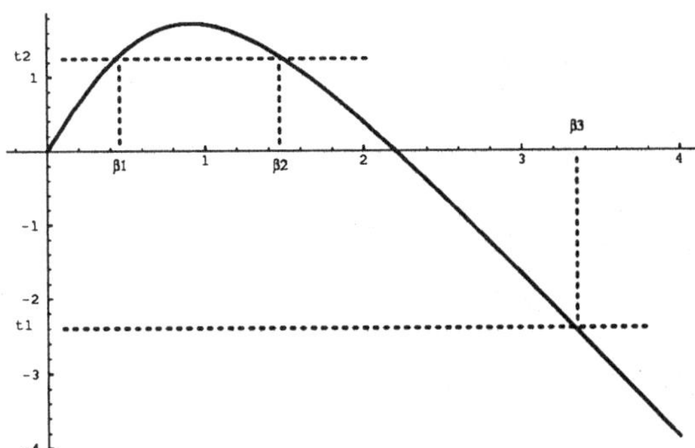

Figure 1: A typical plot of $R(x) = \phi_1(x)/\phi_0(x)$. Network parameters are $N = 500$, $K = 500$, $n_1 = n_2 = 50$ and $m = 10$.

By (14) and (15), performance is mostly determined by the magnitude of $(\epsilon^* - a\epsilon)^2$. It can be shown that

$$(\epsilon^* - a\epsilon)\bar{\Psi}_a = \int_0^\infty p(x)h(x)\phi_1(x)dx \tag{16}$$

and

$$\bar{\Psi}_a = \int_0^\infty p(x)\phi_0(x)dx \tag{17}$$

where ϕ_1 and ϕ_0 are some specific linear combinations of Gaussian densities and their derivatives, and $\bar{\Psi}_a = n_2/K$ is the activity level. High performance is achieved by maximizing over p and possibly over h the absolute value of expression (16) keeping (17) fixed. In complete analogy to Hypothesis Testing in Statistics, where $\bar{\Psi}_a$ takes the role of *level of significance* and $(\epsilon^* - a\epsilon)\bar{\Psi}_a$ the role of *power*, $p(x)$ should be 1 or 0 (activate the neuron or don't) depending on whether the field value x is such that the *likelihood ratio* $h(x)\phi_1(x)/\phi_0(x)$ is above or below a given threshold, determined by (17). Omitting details, the ratio $R(x) = \phi_1(x)/\phi_0(x)$ looks as in figure 1, and converges to $-\infty$ as $x \to \infty$.

We see that there are three reasonable ways to make the ratio $h(x)\phi_1(x)/\phi_0(x)$ large: we can take a negative threshold such as t_1 in figure 1, activate all neurons with generalized field exceeding β_3 (tail-censoring) and signal $h(x) = -Sgn(x)$, or take a positive threshold such as t_2 and activate all neurons with field value between β_1 and β_2 (interval-censoring) and signal $h(x) = Sgn(x)$. Better still, we can consider the ***hybrid signalling-censoring rule***: Activate all neurons with absolute field value between β_1 and β_2, or beyond β_3. The first group should signal their preferred sign, while those in the second group should signal the sign opposite to the one they so strongly believe in !

6 Numerical results

Performance	predicted	experimental
Random activation	0.955	0.951
Tail censoring	0.972	0.973
Interval/Hybrid censoring	0.975	0.972
Hopfield - zero diagonal	–	0.902,0.973
Independent $\gamma(\epsilon)$ diagonal	0.96	–
Independent zero diagonal	0.913	–

Table 1: Sparsely connected, low activity network: $N = 1500, K = 50, n_1 = n_2 = 20, m = 5$.

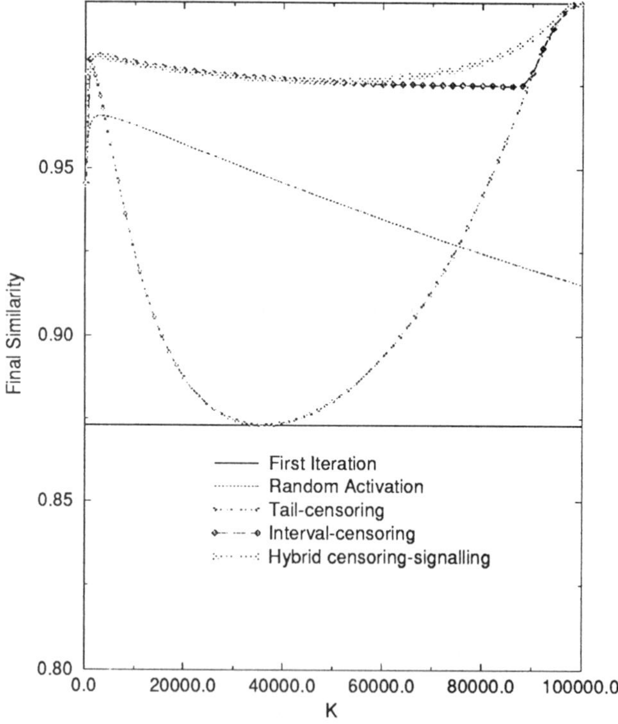

Figure 2: Performance of a large-scale cortical-like 'columnar' ANN, at different values of connectivity K, for initial similarity 0.75. $N = 10^5$, $n_1 = n_2 = 200$, $m = 50$. The horizontal line denotes the performance of a single iteration.

Our theoretical performance predictions show good correspondence with simulation results, already at fairly small-scale networks. The superiority of history-dependent dynamics is apparent. Table 1 shows the performance achieved in a sparsely-connected network. The predicted similarity after two iterations is reported, starting from initial similarity 0.75, and compared with experimental results averaged over 100 trials.

Figure 2 illustrates the theoretical two-iterations performance of large, low-activity 'cortical-like' networks, as a function of connectivity. We see that interval-censoring can maintain high performance throughout the connectivity range. The performance of tail-censoring is very sensitive to connectivity, almost achieving the performance of interval censoring at a narrow low-connectivity range, and becoming optimal only at very high connectivity. The superior hybrid rule improves on the others only under high connectivity. As a cortical neuron should receive the concomitant firing of about $200 - 300$ neurons in order to be activated (Treves & Rolls 1991), we have set $n = 200$. We find that the optimal connectivity per neuron, for biologically plausible tail-censoring activation, is of the same order of magnitude as actual cortical connectivity. The actual number nN/K of neurons firing in every iteration is about 5000, which is in close correspondence with the evidence suggesting that about 4% of the neurons in a module fire at any given moment (Abeles et. al. 1990).

References

[1] J.J. Hopfield. Neural networks and physical systems with emergent collective abilities. *Proc. Nat. Acad. Sci. USA*, 79:2554, 1982.

[2] D. J. Amit and M. V. Tsodyks. Quantitative study of attractor neural network retrieving at low spike rates: I. substrate–spikes, rates and neuronal gain. *Network*, 2:259–273, 1991.

[3] M. Abeles, E. Vaadia, and H. Bergman. Firing patterns of single units in the prefrontal cortex and neural network models. *Network*, 1:13–25, 1990.

[4] W. Lytton. Simulations of cortical pyramidal neurons synchronized by inhibitory interneurons. *J. Neurophysiol.*, 66(3):1059–1079, 1991.

[5] A. Treves and E. T. Rolls. What determines the capacity of autoassociative memories in the brain? *Network*, 2:371–397, 1991.

Non–Linear Dimensionality Reduction

David DeMers* **& Garrison Cottrell**†
Dept. of Computer Science & Engr., 0114
Institute for Neural Computation
University of California, San Diego
9500 Gilman Dr.
La Jolla, CA, 92093-0114

Abstract

A method for creating a non–linear encoder–decoder for multidimensional data with compact representations is presented. The commonly used technique of autoassociation is extended to allow non–linear representations, and an objective function which penalizes activations of individual hidden units is shown to result in minimum dimensional encodings with respect to allowable error in reconstruction.

1 INTRODUCTION

Reducing dimensionality of data with minimal information loss is important for feature extraction, compact coding and computational efficiency. The data can be tranformed into "good" representations for further processing, constraints among feature variables may be identified, and redundancy eliminated. Many algorithms are exponential in the dimensionality of the input, thus even reduction by a single dimension may provide valuable computational savings.

Autoassociating feedforward networks with one hidden layer have been shown to extract the principal components of the data (Baldi & Hornik, 1988). Such networks have been used to extract features and develop compact encodings of the data (Cottrell, Munro & Zipser, 1989). Principal Components Analysis projects the data into a linear subspace

*email: demers@cs.ucsd.edu
†email: gary@cs.ucsd.edu

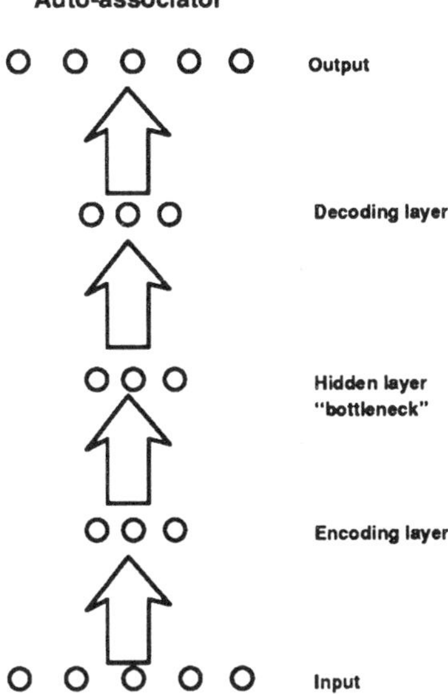

Figure 1: *A network capable of non–linear lower dimensional representations of data.*

with minimum information loss, by multiplying the data by the eigenvectors of the sample covariance matrix. By examining the magnitude of the corresponding eigenvalues one can estimate the minimum dimensionality of the space into which the data may be projected and estimate the loss. However, if the data lie on a non–linear submanifold of the feature space, then Principal Components will overestimate the dimensionality. For example, the covariance matrix of data sampled from a helix in $\mathbb{R}^3$ will have full–rank and thus three principal components. However, the helix is a one–dimensional manifold and can be (smoothly) parameterized with a single number.

The addition of hidden layers between the inputs and the representation layer, and between the representation layer and the outputs provides a network which is capable of learning non–linear representations (Kramer, 1991; Oja, 1991; Usui, Nakauchi & Nakano, 1991). Such networks can perform the non–linear analogue to Principal Components Analysis, and extract "principal manifolds". Figure 1 shows the basic structure of such a network. However, the dimensionality of the representation layer is problematic. Ideally, the dimensionality of the encoding (and hence the number of representation units needed) would be determined from the data.

We propose a pruning method for determining the dimensionality of the representation. A greedy algorithm which successively eliminates representation units by penalizing variances results in encodings of minimal dimensionality with respect to the allowable reconstruction error. The algorithm therefore performs non–linear dimensionality reduction (NLDR).

2 DIMENSIONALITY ESTIMATION BY REGULARIZATION

The *a priori* assignment of the number of units for the representation layer is problematic. In order to achieve maximum data compression, this number should be as small as possible; however, one also wants to preserve the information in the data and thus encode the data with minimum error. If the intrinsic dimensionality is not known ahead of time (as is typical), some method to estimate the dimensionality is desired. Minimization of the variance of a representation unit will essentially squeeze the variance of the data into the other hidden units. Repeated minimization results in increasingly lower–dimensional representation.

More formally, let the dimensionality of the raw data be n. We wish to find F and its approximate inverse such that $\mathbf{R}^n \xrightarrow{F} \mathbf{R}^p \xrightarrow{F^{-1}} \mathbf{R}^n$ where $p < n$. Let y denote the p–dimensional vector whose elements are the p univalued functions f_i which make up F. If one of the component functions f_i is always constant, it is not contributing to the autoassociation and can be eliminated, yielding a function F with $p-1$ components. A constant value for f_i means that the variance of f_i over the data is zero. We add a regularization term to the objective function penalizing the variance of one of the representation units. If the variance can be driven to near zero while simultaneously achieving a target error in the primary task of autoassociation, then the unit being penalized can be pruned.

Let $H_p = \lambda_p(\Sigma_{j=1}^{N}(h_p(\mathrm{net}^j) - E(h_p(\mathrm{net}^j)))^2)$ where net^j is the net input to the unit given the jth training pattern, $h_p(\mathrm{net}^j)$ is the activation of the pth hidden unit in the representation layer (the one being penalized) and E is the expectation operator. For notational clarity, the superscripts will be suppressed hereafter. $E(h_i(x_j))$ can be estimated as $\bar{h}_p$, the mean activation of h_p over all patterns in the training data.

$$\frac{\partial H_p}{\partial w_{pl}} = \frac{\partial H_p}{\partial \mathrm{net}_p}\frac{\partial net_p}{\partial w_{pl}} = 2\lambda_p(h_p - \bar{h}_p)h'_p o_l$$

where h'_p is the derivative of the activation function of unit h_p with respect to its input, and o_l is the output of the lth unit in the preceding layer. Let $\delta_p = 2\lambda_p h'_p(h_p - \bar{h}_p)$. We simply add δ_p to the delta of h_p due to backpropagation from the output layer.

We first train a multi–layer[1] network to learn the identity map. When error is below a user–specified threshold, λ_i is increased for the unit with lowest variance. If network weights can be found[2] such that the variance can be reduced below a small threshold while the remaining units are able to encode the data, the hidden unit in question is no longer contributing to the autoencoding, and its connections are excised from the network. The process is repeated until the variance of the unit in question cannot be reduced while maintaining low error.

[1]There is no reason to suppose that the encoding and decoding layers must be of the same size. In fact, it may be that two encoding or decoding layers will provide superior performance. For the helix example, the decoder had two hidden layers and linear connections from the representation to the output, while the encoder had a single layer. Kramer (1991) uses information theoretic measures for choosing the size of the encoding and decoding layers; however, only a fixed representation layer and equal encoding and decoding layers are used.

[2]Unbounded weights will allow the same amount of information to pass through the layer with arbitrarily small variance and using arbitrarily large weights. Therefore the weights in the network must be bounded. Weight vectors with magnitudes larger than 10 are renormalized after each epoch.

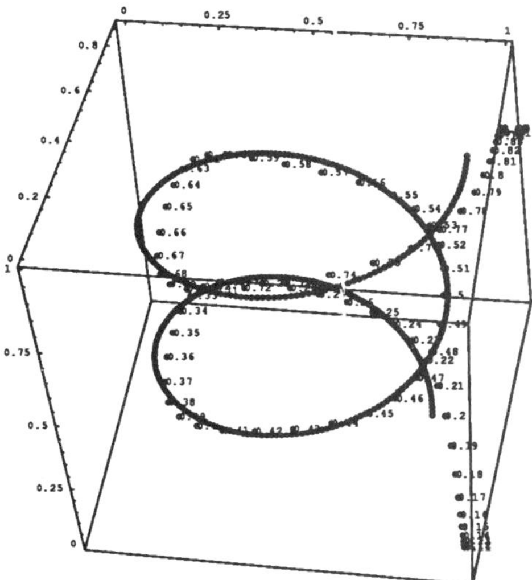

Figure 2: *The original 3–D helix data plus reconstruction from a single parameter encoding.*

3 RESULTS

We applied this method to several problems:

1. a closed 1–D manifold in $\mathbb{R}^3$.
2. a 1–D helix in $\mathbb{R}^3$.
3. Time series data generated from the Mackey–Glass delay–differential equation.
4. 160 64 by 64 pixel, 8-bit grayscale face images.

A number of parameter values must be chosen; error threshold, maximum magnitude of weights, value of λ_i when increased, and when to "give up" training. For these experiments, they were chosen by hand; however, reasonable values can be selected such that the method can be automated.

3.1 Static Mappings: Circle and Helix

The first problem is interesting because it is known that there is no diffeomorphism from the circle to the unit interval. Thus (smooth) single parameter encodings cannot cover the entire circle, though the region of the circle left unparameterized can be made arbitrarily small. Depending on initial conditions, our technique found one of three different solutions. Some simulations resulted in a two–dimensional representation with the encodings lying on a circle in $\mathbb{R}^2$. This is a failure to reduce the dimensionality. The other solutions were both 1–D representations; one "wrapping" the unit interval around the circle, the other "splitting" the interval into two pieces. The initial architecture consisted of a single 8-unit encoding layer and two 8-unit decoding layers. η was set to 0.01, $\Delta\lambda$ to 0.1, and the error threshold, ϵ, to 0.001.

The helix problem is interesting because the data appears to be three–dimensional to PCA. NLDR consistently finds an invertible one–dimensional representation of the data. Figure 2

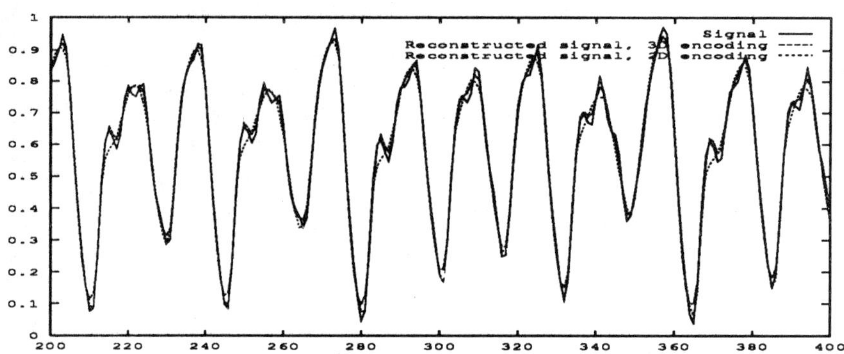

Figure 3: *Data from the Mackey–Glass delay–differential equation with $\tau = 17$, correlation dimension 2.1, and the reconstructed signal encoded in two and three dimensions.*

shows the original data, along with the network's output when the representation layer was stimulated with activation ranging from 0.1 to 0.9. The training data were mapped into the interval 0.213 – 0.778 using a single (sigmoidal) representation unit. The initial architecture consisted of a single 10-unit encoding layer and two 10-unit decoding layers. η was set to 0.01, $\Delta\lambda$ to 0.1, and the error threshold, ϵ, to 0.001.

3.2 NLDR Applied to Time Series

The Mackey–Glass problem consists of estimation of the intrinsic dimensionality of a scalar signal. Classically, such time series data is embedded in a space of "high enough" dimension such that one expects the geometric invariants to be preserved. However, this may significantly overestimate the number of variables needed to describe the data. Two different series were examined; parameter settings for the Mackey–Glass equation were chosen such that the intrinsic dimensionality is 2.1 and 3.5. The data was embedded in a high dimensional space by the standard technique of recoding as vectors of lagged data. A 3 dimensional representation was found for the 2.1 dimensional data and a 4 dimensional representation was found for the 3.5 dimensional data. Figure 3 shows the original data and its reconstruction for the 2.1 dimensional data. Allowing higher reconstruction error resulted in a 3 dimensional representation for the 3.5 dimensional data, effectively smoothing the original signal (DeMers, 1992). Figure 4 shows the original data and its reconstruction for the 3.5 dimensional data. The initial architecture consisted of a two 10-unit encoding layers and two 10-unit decoding layers, and a 7-unit representation layer. The representation layer was connected directly to the output layer. η was set to 0.01, $\Delta\lambda$ to 0.1, and the error threshold, ϵ, to 0.001.

3.3 Faces

The face image data is much more challenging. The face data are 64 × 64 pixel, 8–bit grayscale images taken from (Cottrell & Metcalfe, 1991), each of which can be considered to be a point in a 4,096 dimensional "pixel space". The question addressed is whether NLDR can find low–dimensional representations of the data which are more useful than principal components. The data was preprocessed by reduction to the first 50 principal

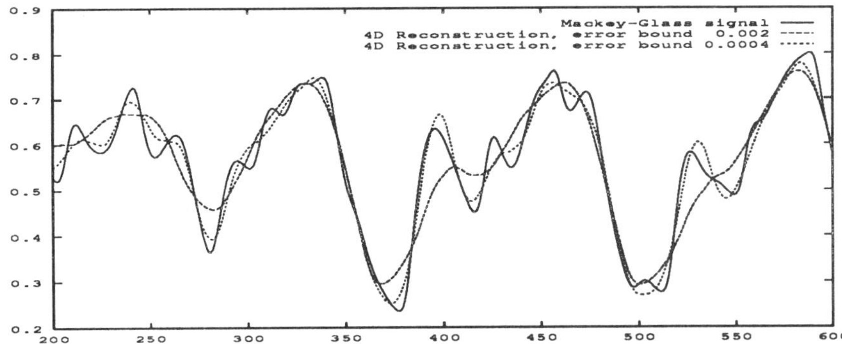

Figure 4: *Data from the Mackey–Glass delay–differential equation with* $\tau = 35$*, correlation dimension 3.5, and the reconstructed signal encoded in four dimensions with two different error thresholds.*

components[3] of the images. These reduced representations were then processed further by NLDR. The architecture consisted of a 30-unit encoding layer and a 30-unit decoding layer, and an initial representation layer of 20 units. There were direct connections from the representation layer to the output layer. η was 0.05, $\Delta\lambda$ was 0.1 and ϵ was 0.001. NLDR found a five–dimensional representation. Figure 5 shows four of the 160 images after reduction to the first 50 principal components (used as training) and the same images after reconstruction from a five dimensional encoding. We are unable to determine whether the dimensions are meaningful; however, experiments with the decoder show that points inside the convex hull of the representations project to images which look like faces. Figure 6 shows the reconstructed images from a linear interpolation in "face space" between the two encodings which are furthest apart.

How useful are the representations obtained from a training set for identification and classification of other images of the same subjects? The 5–D representations were used to train a feedforward network to recognize the identity and gender of the subjects, as in (Cottrell & Metcalfe, 1991). 120 images were used in training and the remaining 40 used as a test set. The network correctly identified 98% of the training data subjects, and 95% on the test set. The network achieved 95% correct gender recognition on both the training and test sets. The misclassified subject is shown in Figure 7. An informal poll of visitors to the poster in Denver showed that about 2/3 of humans classify the subject as male and 1/3 as female.

Although NLDR resulted in five dimensional encodings of the face data, and thus superficially compresses the data to approximately 55 bits per image or 0.013 bits per pixel, there is no data compression. Both the decoder portion of the network and the eigenvectors used in the initial processing must also be stored. These amortize to about 6 bits per pixel, whereas the original images require only 1.1 bits per pixel under run–length encoding. In order to achieve data compression, a much larger data set must be obtained in order to find the underlying human face manifold.

[3]50 was chosen by eyeballing a graph of the eigenvalues for the point at which they began to "flatten"; any value between about 40 and 80 would be reasonable.

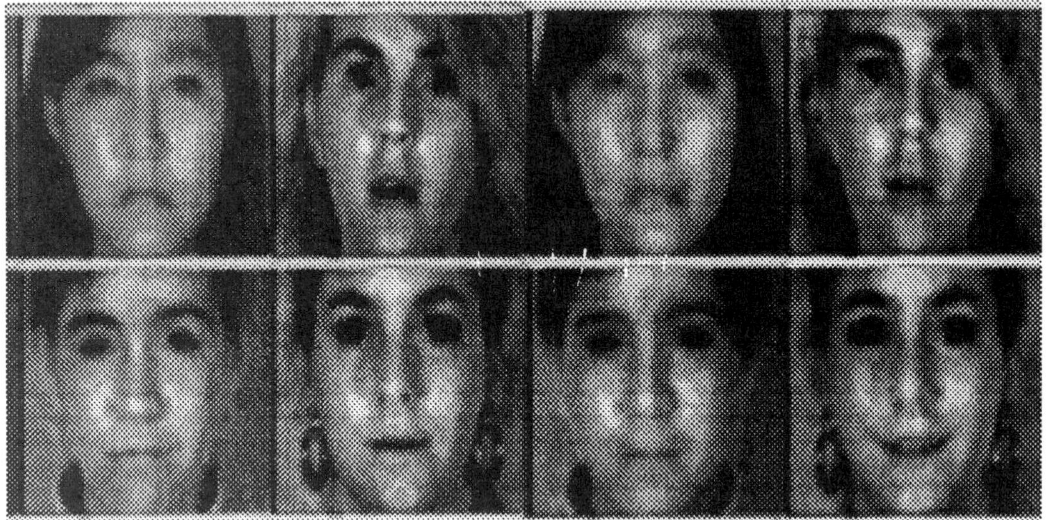

Figure 5: *Four of the original face images and their reconstruction after encoding as five dimensional data.*

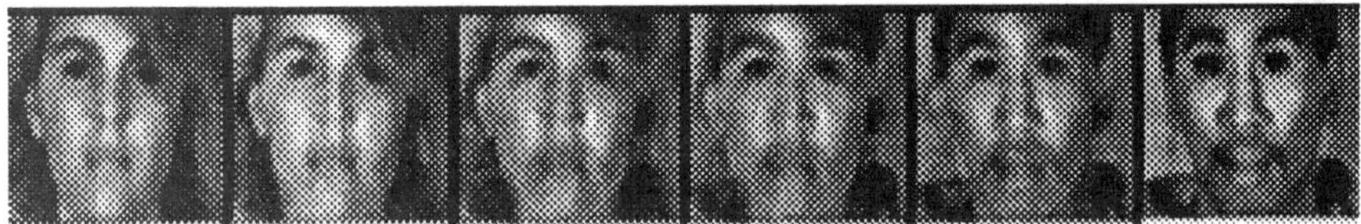

Figure 6: *The two images with 5–D encodings which are the furthest apart, and the reconstructions of four 5–D points equally spaced along the line joining them.*

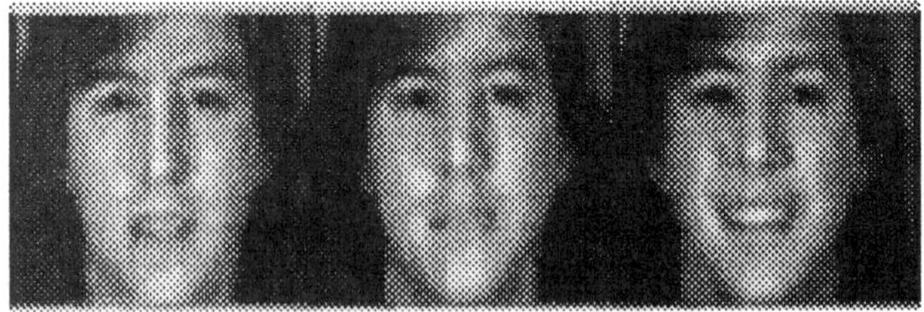

Figure 7: *"Pat"; the subject whose gender a feedforward network classified incorrectly.*

4 CONCLUSIONS

A method for automatically generating a non–linear encoder/decoder for high dimensional data has been presented. The number of representation units in the final network is an estimate of the intrinsic dimensionality of the data. The results are sensitive to the choice of error bound, though the precise relationship is as yet unknown. The size of the encoding and decoding hidden layers must be controlled to avoid over–fitting; any data set can be encoded into scalar values given enough resolution. Since we are using gradient search to solve a global non–linear optimization problem, there is no guarantee that this method will find the global optimum and avoid convergence to local minima. However, NLDR consistently constructed low dimensional encodings which were decodeable with low loss.

Acknowledgements

We would like to thank Matthew Turk & Alex Pentland for making their *facerec* software available, which was used to extract the eigenvectors of the original face data. The first author was partially supported by Fellowships from the California Space Institute and the McDonnell–Pew Foundation.

References

Pierre Baldi and Kurt Hornik (1988) "Neural Networks and Principal Component Analysis: Learning from Examples without Local Minima", *Neural Networks* 2, 53–58.

Garrison Cottrell and Paul Munro (1988) "Principal Components Analysis of Images via Backpropagation", in *Proc. SPIE* (Cambridge, MA).

Garrison Cottrell, Paul Munro, and David Zipser (1989) "Image Compression by Backpropagation: A Demonstration of Extensional Programming", In Sharkey, Noel (Ed.), *Models of Cognition: A review of Cognitive Science*, vol. 1.

Garrison Cottrell and Janet Metcalfe (1991) "EMPATH — Face, Emotion and Gender Recognition using Holons" in Lippmann, R., Moody, J. & Touretzky, D., (eds), *Advances in Neural Information Processing Systems* **3**.

David DeMers (1992) "Dimensionality Reduction for Non–Linear Time Series", *Neural and Stochastic Methods in Image and Signal Processing* (SPIE 1766).

Mark Kramer (1991) "Nonlinear Principal Component Analysis Using Autoassociative Neural Networks", *AIChE Journal* **37**:233-243.

Erkki Oja (1991) "Data Compression, Feature Extraction, and Autoassociation in Feedforward Neural Networks" in Kohonen, T., Simula, O. and Kangas, J., eds, *Artificial Neural Networks*, 737-745.

Shiro Usui, Shigeki Nakauchi, and Masae Nakano (1991) "Internal Color Representation Acquired by a Five–Layer Neural Network", in Kohonen, T., Simula, O. and Kangas, J., eds, *Artificial Neural Networks*, 867-872.

PART VII

Theory and Analysis

On Learning μ-Perceptron Networks with Binary Weights

Mostefa Golea
Ottawa-Carleton Institute for Physics
University of Ottawa
Ottawa, Ont., Canada K1N 6N5
050287@acadvm1.uottawa.ca

Mario Marchand
Ottawa-Carleton Institute for Physics
University of Ottawa
Ottawa, Ont., Canada K1N 6N5
mmmsj@acadvm1.uottawa.ca

Thomas R. Hancock
Siemens Corporate Research
755 College Road East
Princeton, NJ 08540
hancock@learning.siemens.com

Abstract

Neural networks with binary weights are very important from both the theoretical and practical points of view. In this paper, we investigate the learnability of single binary perceptrons and unions of μ-binary-perceptron networks, *i.e.* an "OR" of binary perceptrons where each input unit is connected to one and only one perceptron. We give a polynomial time algorithm that PAC learns these networks under the uniform distribution. The algorithm is able to identify both the network connectivity and the weight values necessary to represent the target function. These results suggest that, under reasonable distributions, μ-perceptron networks may be easier to learn than fully connected networks.

1 Introduction

The study of neural networks with binary weights is well motivated from both the theoretical and practical points of view. Although the number of possible states in the weight space of a binary network are finite, the capacity of the network is not much inferior to that of its continuous counterpart (Barkai and Kanter 1991). Likewise, the hardware realization of binary networks may prove simpler.

A major obstacle impeding the development of binary networks is that, under an arbitrary distribution of examples, the problem of learning binary weights is NP-complete(Pitt and Valiant 1988). However, the question of the learnability of this class of networks under some *reasonable* distributions is still open. A first step in this direction was reported by Venkatesh (1991) for single majority functions.

In this paper we investigate, within the PAC model (Valiant 1984; Blumer *et al.* 1989), the learnability of two interesting concepts under the uniform distribution: 1) Single binary perceptrons with arbitrary thresholds and 2) Unions of μ-binary perceptrons, *i.e.* an "OR" of binary perceptrons where each input unit is connected to one and only one perceptron (fig. 1) [1]. These functions are related to so-called μ or read-once formulas (Kearns *et al.* 1987). Learning these functions on special distributions is presently a very active research area (Pagallo and Haussler 1989; Valiant and Warmuth 1991). The μ restriction may seem to be a severe one but it is not. First, under an arbitrary distribution, μ-formulas are not easier to learn than their unrestricted counterpart (Kearns *et al.* 1987). Second, the μ assumption brings up a problem of its own: determining the network *connectivity*, which is a challenging task in itself.

Our main results are polynomial time algorithms that PAC learn single binary perceptrons and unions of μ-binary perceptrons under the uniform distribution of examples. These results suggest that μ-perceptron networks may be somewhat easier to learn than fully connected networks if one restricts his attention to reasonable distributions of examples. Because of the limited space, only a sketch of the proofs is given in this abstract.

2 Definitions

Let I denote the set $\{0,1\}$. A perceptron g on I^n is specified by a vector of n real valued weights w_i and a single real valued threshold θ. For $\mathbf{x} = (x_1, x_2, ..., x_n) \in I^n$, we have:

$$g(\mathbf{x}) = \begin{cases} 1 & \text{if } \sum_{i=1}^{i=n} w_i x_i \geq \theta \\ 0 & \text{if } \sum_{i=1}^{i=n} w_i x_i < \theta \end{cases} \tag{1}$$

A perceptron is said to be positive if $w_i \geq 0$ for $i = 1, ..., n$. We are interested in the case where the weights are binary valued (± 1). We assume, without loss of generality (w.l.o.g.), that θ is integer.

A function f is said to be a union of perceptrons if it can be written as a disjunction of perceptrons. If these perceptrons do not share any variables, f is said to be a union of μ-perceptrons (fig. 1), and we write

$$f = g^{(1)} \vee g^{(2)} \vee ... \vee g^{(s)} \quad 1 \leq s \leq n \tag{2}$$

We shall assume, w.l.o.g., that f is expressed with the maximum possible number of $g^{(i)}$'s, and has the minimum possible number of non-zero weights.

[1]The intersection is simply the complement of the union and can be treated similarly.

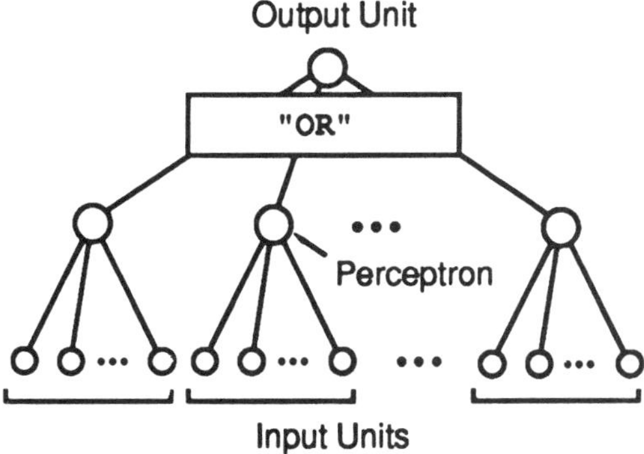

Figure 1: A two layer network representing a union of μ-perceptrons. Note that each input unit is connected to one and only one perceptron (hidden unit). The output unit computes an OR function.

We denote by $P(A)$ the probability of an event A and by $\hat{P}(A)$ its empirical estimate based on a given finite sample. All probabilities are taken with respect to the uniform distribution D on I^n. If $a \in \{0,1\}$, we denote by $P(f=1|x_i=a)$ the conditional probability that $f=1$ given the fact that $x_i=a$.
The algorithm will make use of the following probabilistic quantities:
The *influence* of a variable x_i, denoted $Inf(x_i)$, is defined as

$$Inf(x_i) = P(f=1|x_i=1) - P(f=1|x_i=0).$$

Intuitively, the influence of a variable is positive (negative) if its weight is positive (negative).
The *correlation* of a variable x_j with x_i, denoted $C(x_i,x_j)$, is defined as

$$C(x_i,x_j) = \frac{P(f=1|x_ix_j=1) - P(f=1|x_i=1)}{P(f=1|x_j=1) - P(f=1)}$$

where $x_ix_j=1$ stands for $x_i=x_j=1$. This quantity depends largely on whether or not the two variables are in same perceptron.

In what follows, we adopt the PAC learning model (Valiant 1984; Blumer *et al.* 1989). Here the methodology is to draw a sample of a certain size labeled according to the unknown target function f and then to find a "good" approximation h of f. The error of the hypothesis function h, with respect to the target f, is defined to be $P(h \neq f) = P(h(\mathbf{x}) \neq f(\mathbf{x}))$, where $\mathbf{x}$ is distributed according to D. An algorithm learns from examples a target class F using an hypothesis class H under the distribution D on I^n, if for every $f \in F$, and any $0 < \epsilon, \delta < 1$, the algorithm runs in time polynomial in (n, ϵ, δ) and outputs an hypothesis $h \in H$ such that

$$P[\ P(h \neq f) > \epsilon\ ] < \delta$$

3 Learning Networks with Binary Weights

3.1 Learning Single Binary Perceptrons

Let us assume that the target function f is a single binary perceptron g given by eq. (1). Let us assume also that the distribution generating the examples is uniform on $\{0,1\}^n$. The learning algorithm proceeds in two steps:

1. Estimating the weight values (signs). This is done by estimating the ***influence*** of each variable. Then the target perceptron is reduced to a ***positive*** perceptron by simply changing x_i to $1-x_i$ whenever $w_i=-1$.
2. Estimating the threshold of the positive target perceptron and hence the threshold of the original perceptron.

To simplify the analysis, we introduce the following notation. Let N be the number of negative weights in g and let $\mathbf{y}$ be defined as

$$y_i = \begin{cases} x_i & \text{if } w_i = 1 \\ 1-x_i & \text{if } w_i = -1 \end{cases} \tag{3}$$

Then eq. (1) can be written as

$$g(\mathbf{y}) = \begin{cases} 1 & \text{if } \sum_{i=1}^{i=n} y_i \geq \Omega \\ 0 & \text{if } \sum_{i=1}^{i=n} y_i < \Omega \end{cases} \tag{4}$$

where the renormalized threshold Ω is related to the original threshold θ by: $\Omega = \theta + N$. We assume, w.l.o.g., that $1 \leq \Omega \leq n$. Note that $D(\mathbf{x}) = D(\mathbf{y})$.

The following lemma, which follows directly from Bahadur's expansion (Bahadur 1960), will be used throughout this paper to approximate binomial distributions.

Lemma 1 *Let d and n be two integers. Then, if $\frac{n}{2} \leq d \leq n$,*

$$\sum_{i=d}^{n} \binom{n}{i} \leq \frac{1}{2}\binom{n}{d}\frac{1}{1-z}$$

where $z = \frac{1}{2}\frac{n+1}{d+1}$. And if $0 \leq d \leq \frac{n}{2}$,

$$\sum_{i=0}^{d} \binom{n}{i} \leq \frac{1}{2}\binom{n}{d}\frac{1}{1-z'}$$

where $z' = \frac{1}{2}\frac{n+1}{n-d+1}$.

As we said earlier, intuition suggests that the influence of a variable is positive (negative) if its weight is positive (negative). The following lemma strengthens this intuition by showing that there is a measurable *gap* between the two cases. This gap will be used to estimate the weight values (signs).

Lemma 2 *Let g be a perceptron such that $P(g=1)$, $P(g=0) > \rho$, where $0 < \rho < 1$. Then,*

$$Inf(x_i) \begin{cases} > \frac{\rho}{n+2} & \text{if } w_i = 1 \\ < -\frac{\rho}{n+2} & \text{if } w_i = -1 \end{cases}$$

Proof sketch for $w_i = 1$: We exploit the equivalence between eq. (1) and eq. (4), and the fact that the distribution is uniform:

$$\begin{aligned} Inf(x_i) &= P(g(\mathbf{x}) = 1|x_i = 1) - P(g(\mathbf{x}) = 1|x_i = 0) \\ &= P(g(\mathbf{y}) = 1|y_i = 1) - P(g(\mathbf{y}) = 1|y_i = 0) \\ &= 2\frac{\binom{n-1}{\Omega-1}}{\sum_{i=\Omega}^{n}\binom{n}{i}}P(g=1) \qquad (5) \\ &= 2\frac{\binom{n-1}{\Omega-1}}{\sum_{i=0}^{\Omega-1}\binom{n}{i}}P(g=0) \qquad (6) \end{aligned}$$

Applying lemma 1 to either eq. (5) (case: $\Omega \geq \frac{n}{2}$) or eq.(6) (case: $\Omega \leq \frac{n}{2}$) yields the desired result.□

Once we determine the weight values, we reduce g to its positive form by changing x_i to $1 - x_i$ whenever $w_i = -1$. The next step is to estimate the renormalized threshold Ω and hence, the original threshold θ.

Lemma 3 *Let g be the positive perceptron with a renormalized threshold Ω. Let g' the positive perceptron obtained from g by substituting r for Ω. Then, if $r \leq \Omega$,*

$$P(g \neq g') \leq 1 - P(g = 1|g' = 1)$$

So, if we estimate $P(g = 1|g' = 1)$ for $r = 1, 2, \ldots$ and then choose as the renormalized threshold the *least* r for which $P(g = 1|g' = 1) \geq (1 - \epsilon)$, we are guaranteed to have $P(g \neq g') \leq \epsilon$. Obviously, such r exists and is always $\leq \Omega$ because $P(g = 1|g' = 1) = 1$ for $r = \Omega$.

A sketch of the algorithm for learning single binary perceptrons is given in fig. 2.

Theorem 1 *The class of binary perceptrons is PAC learnable under the uniform distribution.*

Proof sketch: A sample of size $O(\frac{n^2}{\epsilon^4} \ln \frac{n}{\delta})$ is sufficient to ensure that the different probabilities are estimated to within a sufficient precision (Hagerup and Rub 1989). Steps 2 and 3 of the algorithm are obvious. If we reach step 5, $P(g = 1) > \frac{\epsilon}{2}$ and $P(g = 0) > \frac{\epsilon}{2}$. Then one has only to set $\rho = \frac{\epsilon}{2}$ and apply lemma 2 and 3 to step 5 and 6 respectively. Finally, the algorithm runs in time polynomial in n, ϵ and δ.□

3.2 Learning Unions of μ-binary Perceptrons

Let us assume now that the target function f is a union of μ-binary perceptrons as in eq. (2). Note that we do not assume that the architecture (connectivity) is known in advance. Rather, it is the task of the learning algorithm to determine which variables are in a given perceptron. The learning algorithm proceeds in three steps:

Algorithm *LEARN-BINARY-PERCEPTRON*(n,ϵ,δ)
Parameters: n is the number of input variables, ϵ is the accuracy parameter and δ is the confidence parameter.
Output: a binary perceptron h.
Description:

1. Call $M = \frac{[80(n+2)]^2}{\epsilon^4} \ln \frac{8n}{\delta}$ examples. This sample is be used to estimate the different probabilities. Initialize h to the constant perceptron 0. Initialize N to 0.
2. (Are most examples positive?) If $\hat{P}(g=1) \geq (1-\frac{\epsilon}{4})$ then set $h=1$. Return h.
3. (Are most examples negative?) If $\hat{P}(g=1) \leq \frac{\epsilon}{4}$ then return h.
4. Set $\rho = \frac{\epsilon}{2}$.
5. (Reduce g to a positive perceptron) For each input variable x_i:
   (a) If $\hat{Inf}(x_i) > \frac{1}{2}\frac{\rho}{n+2}$, set $w_i = 1$.
   (b) Else if $\hat{Inf}(x_i) < -\frac{1}{2}\frac{\rho}{n+2}$, set $N = N+1$, $w_i = -1$, and change x_i to $1-x_i$
   (c) Else delete x_i (update n accordingly).
6. (Estimating the bias) Let g' be as defined in lemma 3. Initialize r to 1.
   (a) Estimate $P(g=1|g'=1)$.
   (b) If $\hat{P}(g=1|g'=1) > 1-\frac{1}{2}\epsilon$, set $\Omega = r$ and go to step 7.
   (c) $r = r+1$. Go to step 6a.
7. Set $\theta = \Omega - N$. Return h (that is $(w_1, ..., w_n; \theta)$).

Figure 2: An algorithm for learning single binary perceptrons.

1. Estimating the weight values (signs). This is again done by estimating the *influence* of each variable. Then the target function is reduced to a union of *positive* perceptrons by simply changing x_i to $1-x_i$ whenever $w_i = -1$.
2. Estimating which variables belong to the *same* perceptron. This is done by estimating correlations between different variables.
3. Estimating the renormalized threshold of the each positive target perceptron and hence, the threshold of the original perceptron.

The following lemma is a straightforward generalization of lemma 2.

Lemma 4 *Let f be a union of μ-perceptrons as in (2). Let $g^{(a)}$ be a perceptron in f and let $x_i \in g^{(a)}$. Assume that $P(f=1) < 1-\gamma$ and $P(g=1), P(g=0) > \rho$ where $0 < \gamma,\ \rho < 1$. Then*

$$Inf(x_i)\begin{cases} > \frac{\gamma\rho}{n+2} & \text{if } w_i = 1 \\ < -\frac{\gamma\rho}{n+2} & \text{if } w_i = -1 \end{cases}$$

Proof sketch for $w_i = 1$: Let m be the disjunction of all perceptrons in f except g. Then, using the inclusion-exclusion property and the fact that perceptrons in f do not share any variables,

$$Inf(x_i) = (1-P(m=1))(P(g=1|x_i=1) - (P(g=1|x_i=0))$$

$$> \gamma(P(g=1|x_i=1) - (P(g=1|x_i=0)) > \frac{\gamma\rho}{n+2} \quad (7)$$

Inequality (7) follows from the fact that $1 - P(m=1) > 1 - P(f=1) > \gamma$ and from lemma 2.□

Lemma 4 enables us to determine the weight values and reduce f to its positive form. Note that we can assume, w.l.o.g., that $\gamma \geq \epsilon/2$ and $\rho \geq \epsilon/2n$. The next step is to determine which variables belong to the same perceptron. Starting with a variable, say x_i, the procedure uses the correlation measure to decide whether or not another variable, say x_j, belongs to x_i's perceptron. We appeal to the following lemma where we assume that f is already reduced to its positive form.

Lemma 5 *Let f be a union of μ-perceptrons (positive form). Let $g^{(a)}$ be a perceptron in f. Let $x_i \in g^{(a)}$ and let x_j and x_k be two other influential variables in f. Then*

$$C(x_i,x_j) - C(x_i,x_k) = \begin{cases} 0 & \text{if } x_j \in g^{(a)} \text{ and } x_k \in g^{(a)} \\ 0 & \text{if } x_j \notin g^{(a)} \text{ and } x_k \notin g^{(a)} \\ \geq \frac{1}{n^2} & \text{if } x_j \in g^{(a)} \text{ and } x_k \notin g^{(a)} \end{cases}$$

The lengthy proof of this important lemma will appear in the full paper.

If we estimate the correlations to within a sufficient precision, the *correlation gap*, established in lemma 5, enables us to decide which variables are in the same perceptron.

The last step is to estimate the bias of each perceptron. Let g be a perceptron in f and let g' be the perceptron obtained from g by setting its renormalized bias to r. Estimating g's bias may be done by simply estimating $P(f=1|g'=1)$ for different values of the renormalized threshold, $r = 2, 3, ...$, and choosing the least r such that $P(f=1|g'=1) \geq (1-\epsilon/n)$ (see lemma 3 and step 6 in figure 2).

Theorem 2 *The class of μ-binary perceptron unions are PAC learnable under the uniform distribution.*

4 Conclusion and Open Problems

We presented a simple algorithm for PAC learning single binary perceptrons and μ-binary-perceptron unions, under the uniform distribution of examples. The hardness results reported in the literature (see (Lin and Vitter 1991)) suggest that one can not avoid the training difficulties simply by considering only very simple neural networks. Our results (see also (Marchand and Golea 1992)) suggest that the combination of simple networks and reasonable distributions may be needed to achieve any degree of success.

The results reported here are part of an ongoing research aimed at understanding *nonoverlapping* perceptron networks (Hancock *et al.* 1991). The extension of these results to more complicated networks will appear in the full paper.

Acknowledgements

M. Golea and M. Marchand are supported by NSERC grant OGP0122405. This research was conducted while T. Hancock was a graduate student at Harvard University, supported by ONR grant N00014-85-K-0445 and NSF grant NSF-CCR-89-02500.

References

[1] Bahadur R. (1960) "Some Approximations to the Binomial Distribution Function", *Annals Math. Stat.*, Vol.31, 43–54.

[2] Barkai E. & Kanter I. (1991) "Storage Capacity of a Multilayer Neural Network with Binary weights", *Europhys. Lett.*, Vol. 14, 107–112.

[3] Blumer A., Ehrenfeucht A., Haussler D., and Warmuth K. (1989) "Learnability and the Vapnik-Chervonenkis Dimension", *J. ACM*, Vol. 36, 929–965.

[4] Hagerup T. & Rub C. (1989) "A Guided Tour to Chernoff Bounds", *Info. Proc. Lett.*, Vol. 33, 305–308.

[5] Hancock T., Golea M., and Marchand M. (1991) "Learning Nonoverlapping Perceptron Networks From Examples and Membership Queries", TR-26-91, Center for Research in Computing Technology, Harvard University. *Submitted* to Machine Learning.

[6] Kearns M., Li M., Pitt L., and Valiant L. (1987) "On the Learnability of Boolean Formulas", in *Proc. of the 19th Annual ACM Symposium on Theory of Computing*, 285-295, New York, NY.

[7] Lin J.H. & Vitter J.S. (1991) "Complexity Results on Learning by Neural Nets", *Machine Learning*, Vol. 6, 211-230.

[8] Marchand M. & Golea M. (1992) "On Learning Simple Neural Concepts", to appear in *Network*.

[9] Pagallo G. & Haussler D. (1989) "A Greedy Method for learning μDNF functions under the Uniform Distribution". Technical Report UCSC-CRL-89-12, Santa Cruz: Dept. of Computer and Information Science, University of California at Santa Cruz.

[10] Pitt L. & Valiant L.G. (1988) "Computational Limitations on Learning from Examples", *J. ACM*, Vol. 35, 965–984.

[11] Valiant L.G. (1984) "A Theory of the Learnable", *Comm. ACM*, Vol. 27, 1134–1142.

[12] Valiant L.G. & Warmuth K. (Editors) (1991) *Proc. of the 4st Workshop on Computational Learning Theory*, Morgan Kaufman.

[13] Venkatesh S. (1991) "On Learning Binary Weights for Majority Functions", in *Proc. of the 4th Workshop on Computational Learning Theory*, 257–266, Morgan Kaufman.

Neural Network Model Selection Using Asymptotic Jackknife Estimator and Cross-Validation Method

Yong Liu
Department of Physics and
Institute for Brain and Neural Systems
Box 1843, Brown University
Providence, RI, 02912

Abstract

Two theorems and a lemma are presented about the use of jackknife estimator and the cross-validation method for model selection. Theorem 1 gives the asymptotic form for the jackknife estimator. Combined with the model selection criterion, this asymptotic form can be used to obtain the fit of a model. The model selection criterion we used is the negative of the average predictive likehood, the choice of which is based on the idea of the cross-validation method. Lemma 1 provides a formula for further exploration of the asymptotics of the model selection criterion. Theorem 2 gives an asymptotic form of the model selection criterion for the regression case, when the parameters optimization criterion has a penalty term. Theorem 2 also proves the asymptotic equivalence of Moody's model selection criterion (Moody, 1992) and the cross-validation method, when the distance measure between response y and regression function takes the form of a squared difference.

1 INTRODUCTION

Selecting a model for a specified problem is the key to generalization based on the training data set. In the context of neural network, this corresponds to selecting an architecture. There has been a substantial amount of work in model selection (Lindley, 1968; Mallows, 1973; Akaike, 1973; Stone, 1977; Atkinson, 1978; Schwartz,

1978; Zellner, 1984; MacKay, 1991; Moody, 1992; etc.). In Moody's paper (Moody, 1992), the author generalized Akaike Information Criterion (AIC) (Akaike, 1973) in the regression case and introduced the term *effective number of parameters.* It is thus of great interest to see what the link between this criterion and the cross-validation method (Stone, 1974) is and what we can gain from it, given the fact that AIC is asymptotically equivalent to the cross-validation method (Stone, 1977).

In the method of cross-validation (Stone, 1974), a data set, which has a data point deleted from the original training data set, is used to estimate the parameters of a model by optimizing a parameters optimization criterion. The optimal parameters thus obtained are called the jackknife estimator (Miller, 1974). Then the predictive likelihood of the deleted data point is calculated, based on the estimated parameters. This is repeated for each data point in the original training data set. The fit of the model, or the model selection criterion, is chosen as the negative of the average of these predictive likelihoods. However, the computational cost of estimating parameters for different data point deletion is expensive. In section 2, we obtained an asymptotic formula (theorem 1) for the jackknife estimator based on optimizing a parameters optimization criterion with one data point deleted from the training data set. This somewhat relieves the computational cost mentioned above. This asymptotic formula can be used to obtain the model selection criterion by plugging it into the criterion. Furthermore, in section 3, we obtained the asymptotic form of the model selection criterion for the general case (Lemma 1) and for the special case when the parameters optimization criterion has a penalty term (theorem 2). We also proved the equivalence of Moody's model selection criterion (Moody, 1992) and the cross-validation method (theorem 2). Only sketchy proofs are given when these theorems and lemma are introduced. The detail of the proofs are given in section 4.

2 APPROXIMATE JACKKNIFE ESTIMATOR

Let the parameters optimization criterion, with data set $\omega = \{(x_i, y_i),\ i = 1,\ \ldots,\ n\}$ and parameters θ, be $C_\omega(\theta)$, and let ω_{-i} denote the data set with ith data point deleted from ω. If we denote $\hat{\theta}$ and $\hat{\theta}_{-i}$ as the optimal parameters for criterion $C_\omega(\theta)$ and $C_{\omega_{-i}}(\theta)$, respectively, ∇_θ as the derivative with respect to θ and superscript t as transpose, we have the following theorem about the relationship between $\hat{\theta}$ and $\hat{\theta}_{-i}$.

Theorem 1 *If the criterion function $C_\omega(\theta)$ is an infinite-order differentiable function and its derivatives are bounded around $\hat{\theta}$. The estimator $\hat{\theta}_{-i}$ (also called jackknife estimator (Miller, 1974)) can be approximated as*

$$\hat{\theta}_{-i} - \hat{\theta} \approx -(\nabla_\theta \nabla_\theta^t C_\omega(\hat{\theta}) - \nabla_\theta \nabla_\theta^t C_i(\hat{\theta}))^{-1} \nabla_\theta C_i(\hat{\theta}) \tag{1}$$

in which $C_i(\theta) = C_\omega(\theta) - C_{\omega_{-i}}(\theta)$.

Proof. Use the Taylor expansion of equation $\nabla_\theta C_{\omega_{-i}}(\hat{\theta}_{-i}) = 0$ around $\hat{\theta}$. Ignore terms higher than the second order.

Example 1: Using the *generalized maximum likelihood* method from Bayesian analysis[1] (Berger, 1985), if $\pi(\theta)$ is the prior on the parameters and the observations are mutually independent, for which the distribution is modeled as $y|x \sim f(y|x,\theta)$, the parameters optimization criterion is

$$C_\omega(\theta) = \log[\prod_{(x_i,y_i)\in\omega} f(y_i|x_i,\theta)\pi(\theta)] = \sum_{(x_i,y_i)\in\omega} \log f(y_i|x_i,\theta) + \log\pi(\theta). \quad (2)$$

Thus $C_i(\theta) = \log f(y_i|x_i,\theta)$. If we ignore the influence of the deleted data point in the denominator of equation 1, we have

$$\hat{\theta}_{-i} - \hat{\theta} \approx -(\nabla_\theta \nabla_\theta^t C_\omega(\hat{\theta}))^{-1} \nabla_\theta \log f(y_i|x_i,\hat{\theta}). \quad (3)$$

Example 2: In the special case of example 1, with noninformative prior $\pi(\theta) = 1$, the criterion is the ordinary log-likelihood function, thus

$$\hat{\theta}_{-i} - \hat{\theta} \approx -[\sum_{(x_i,y_i)\in\omega} \nabla_\theta \nabla_\theta^t \log f(y_j|x_j,\hat{\theta})]^{-1} \nabla_\theta \log f(y_i|x_i,\hat{\theta}). \quad (4)$$

3 CROSS-VALIDATION METHOD AND MODEL SELECTION CRITERION

Hereafter we use the negative of the average predictive likelihood, or,

$$\mathcal{T}_m(\omega) = -\frac{1}{n} \sum_{(x_i,y_i)\in\omega} \log f(y_i|x_i,\hat{\theta}_{-i}) \quad (5)$$

as the model selection criterion, in which n is the size of the training data set ω, $m \in \mathcal{M}$ denotes parametric probability models $f(y|x,\theta)$ and $\mathcal{M}$ is the set of all the models in consideration. It is well known that $\mathcal{T}_m(\omega)$ is an unbiased estimator of $r(\theta_0, \hat{\theta}(\cdot))$, the risk of using the model m and estimator $\hat{\theta}$, when the true parameters are θ_0 and the training data set is ω (Stone, 1974; Efron and Gong, 1983; etc.), i.e.,

$$\begin{aligned} r(\theta_0, \hat{\theta}(\cdot)) &= E\{\mathcal{T}_m(\omega)\} \\ &= E\{-\log f(y|x, \hat{\theta}(\omega))\} \\ &= \mathrm{E}\{ -\frac{1}{k} \sum_{(x_j,y_j)\in\omega_n} \log f(y_j|x_j,\hat{\theta}(\omega)) \} \end{aligned} \quad (6)$$

in which $\omega_n = \{(x_j, y_j),\ j = 1,\ \dots\ k\}$ is the test data set, $\hat{\theta}(\cdot)$ is an implicit function of the training data set ω and it is the estimator we decide to use after we have observed the training data set ω. The expectation above is taken over the randomness of ω, x, y and ω_n. The optimal model will be the one that minimizes this criterion. This procedure of using $\hat{\theta}_{-i}$ and $\mathcal{T}_m(\omega)$ to obtain an estimation of risk is often called the cross-validation method (Stone, 1974; Efron and Gong, 1983).

Remark: After we have obtained $\hat{\theta}$ for a model, we can use equation 1 to calculate $\hat{\theta}_{-i}$ for each i, and put the resulting $\hat{\theta}_{-i}$ into equation 5 to get the fit of the model, thus we will be able to compare different models $m \in \mathcal{M}$.

[1]Strictly speaking, it is a method to find the posterior mode.

Lemma 1 *If the probability model $f(y|x,\theta)$, as a function of θ, is differentiable up to infinite order and its derivatives are bounded around $\hat{\theta}$. The approximation to the model selection criterion, equation 5, can be written as*

$$\mathcal{T}_m(\omega) \approx -\frac{1}{n}\sum_{(x_i,y_i)\in\omega} \log f(y_i|x_i,\hat{\theta}) - \frac{1}{n}\sum_{(x_i,y_i)\in\omega} \nabla_\theta^t \log f(y_i|x_i,\hat{\theta})(\hat{\theta}_{-i}-\hat{\theta}) \tag{7}$$

Proof. Igoring the terms higher than the second order of the Taylor expansion of $\log f(y_j|x_j,\hat{\theta}_{-i})$ around $\hat{\theta}$ will yield the result.

Example 2 (continued): Using equation 4, we have, for the model selection criterion,

$$\begin{aligned}\mathcal{T}_m(\omega) &= -\frac{1}{n}\sum_{(x_i,y_i)\in\omega} \log f(y_i|x_i,\hat{\theta}) - \\ &\quad \frac{1}{n}\sum_{(x_i,y_i)\in\omega} \nabla_\theta^t \log f(y_i|x_i,\hat{\theta}) A^{-1}\nabla_\theta \log f(y_i|x_i,\hat{\theta}).\end{aligned} \tag{8}$$

in which $A = \sum_{(x_j,y_j)\in\omega} \nabla_\theta\nabla_\theta^t \log f(y_j|x_j,\hat{\theta})$. If the model $f(y|x,\theta)$ is the true one, the second term is asymptotically equal to p, the number of parameters in the model. So the model selection criterion is

$-$ log-likelihood $+$ number of parameters of the model.

This is the well known Akaike's Information Criterion (AIC) (Akaike, 1973).

Example 1(continued): Consider the probability model

$$f(y|x,\theta) = \beta\exp(-\frac{1}{2\sigma^2}\mathcal{E}(y,\eta_\theta(x))) \tag{9}$$

in which β is a normalization factor, $\mathcal{E}(y,\eta_\theta(x))$ is a distance measure between y and regression function $\eta_\theta(x)$. $\mathcal{E}(\cdot)$ as function of θ is assumed differentiable. Denoting[2] $\mathcal{U}(\theta,\lambda,\omega) = \sum_{(x_i,y_i)\in\omega}\mathcal{E}(y_i,\eta_\theta(x_i)) - 2\sigma^2\log\pi(\theta|\lambda)$, we have the following theorem,

Theorem 2 *For the model specified in equation 9 and the parameters optimization criterion specified in equation 2 (example 1), under regular condition, the unbiased estimator of*

$$E\{\frac{1}{k}\sum_{(x_i,y_i)\in\omega_n}\mathcal{E}(y_i,\eta_{\hat{\theta}}(x_i))\} \tag{10}$$

asymptotically equals to

$$\begin{aligned}&\frac{1}{n}\sum_{(x_i,y_i)\in\omega}\mathcal{E}(y_i,\eta_{\hat{\theta}}(x_i)) + \\ &\frac{1}{n}\sum_{(x_i,y_i)\in\omega}\nabla_\theta^t\mathcal{E}(y_i,\eta_{\hat{\theta}}(x_i))\{\nabla_\theta\nabla_\theta^t\mathcal{U}(\hat{\theta},\lambda,\omega)\}^{-1}\nabla_\theta\mathcal{E}(y_i,\eta_{\hat{\theta}}(x_i)).\end{aligned} \tag{11}$$

[2]For example, $\pi(\theta|\lambda) = \mathcal{N}_p(0,\sigma^2/\lambda)$, this corresponds to

$$\mathcal{U}(\theta,\lambda,\omega) = \sum_{(x_i,y_i)\in\omega}\mathcal{E}(y_i,\eta_\theta(x_i)) + \lambda\theta^2 + \text{const}(\lambda,\sigma^2).$$

For the case when $\mathcal{E}(y,\eta_\theta(x)) = (y-\eta_\theta(x))^2$, we get, for the asymptotic equivalency of the equation 11,

$$\mathcal{E}(\hat{\theta},\omega) + \frac{2\sigma^2}{n}\frac{1}{2}\times$$
$$\sum_{(x_i,y_i)\in\omega} \frac{\partial}{\partial y_i}\nabla_\theta^t n\mathcal{E}(\hat{\theta},\omega)\{\nabla_\theta\nabla_\theta^t \mathcal{U}(\hat{\theta},\lambda,\omega)\}^{-1}\frac{\partial}{\partial y_i}\nabla_\theta n\mathcal{E}(\hat{\theta},\omega) \quad (12)$$

in which $\omega = \{(x_i,y_i),\ i=1,\ \ldots,\ n\}$ is the training data set, $\omega_n = \{(x_i,y_i),\ i = 1,\ \ldots,\ k\}$ is the test data set, and $\mathcal{E}(\theta,\omega) = \frac{1}{n}\sum_{(x_i,y_i)\in\omega}\mathcal{E}(y_i,\eta_\theta(x_i))$.

Proof. This result comes directly from theorem 1 and lemma 1. Some asymptotic technique has to be used.

Remark: The result in equation 12 was first proposed by Moody (Moody, 1992). The *effective number of parameters* formulated in his paper corresponds to the summation in equation 12. Since the result in this theorem comes directly from the asymptotics of the cross-validation method and the jackknife estimator, it gives the equivalency proof between Moody's model selection criterion and the cross-validation method. The detailed proof of this theorem, presented in section 4, is in spirit the same as the one presented in Stone's paper about the proof of the asymptotic equivalence of AIC and the cross-validation method (Stone, 1977).

4 DETAILED PROOF OF LEMMAS AND THEOREMS

In order to prove theorem 1, lemma 1 and theorem 2, we will present three auxiliary lemmas first.

Lemma 2 *For random variable sequence x_n and y_n, if $\lim_{n\to\infty} x_n = x$ and $\lim_{n\to\infty} y_n = x$, then x_n and y_n are asymptotically equivalent.*

Proof. This comes from the definition of asymptotic equivalence. Because asymptotically the two random variable will behave the same as random variable x.

Lemma 3 *Consider the summation $\sum_i h(x_i,y_i)g(x_i,z)$. If $E(h(x,y)|x,z)$ is a constant c independent of x, y, z, then the summation is asymptotically equivalent to $c\sum_i g(x_i,z)$.*

Proof. According to the theorem of large number,

$$\begin{aligned}\lim_{n\to\infty}\frac{1}{n}\sum_i h(x_i,y_i)g(x_i,z) &= E(h(x,y)g(x,z)) \\ &= E(E(h(x,y)|x,z)g(x,z)) = cE(g(x,z))\end{aligned}$$

which is the same as the limit of $\frac{c}{n}\sum_i g(x_i,z)$. Using lemma 2, we get the result of this lemma.

Lemma 4 *If $\eta_\theta(\cdot)$ and $g(\theta,\cdot)$ are differentiable up to the second order, and the model $y = \eta_\theta(x) + \epsilon$ with $\epsilon \sim \mathcal{N}(0,\sigma^2)$ is the true model, the second derivative with* *respect to θ of*

$$\mathcal{U}(\theta, \lambda, \omega) = \sum_{i=1}^{n}(y_i - \eta_\theta(x_i))^2 + g(\theta, \lambda)$$

evaluated at the minimum of $\mathcal{U}$, i.e., $\hat{\theta}$, is asymptotically independent of random variable $\{y_i, i = 1, ..., n\}$.

Proof. Explicit calculation of the second derivative of $\mathcal{U}$ with respect to θ, evaluated at $\hat{\theta}$, gives

$$\nabla_\theta \nabla_\theta^t \mathcal{U}(\hat{\theta}, \lambda, \omega) = 2\sum_{i=1}^{n} \nabla_\theta \eta_{\hat{\theta}}(x_i) \nabla_\theta^t \eta_{\hat{\theta}}(x_i) \quad - \quad 2\sum_{i=1}^{n}(y_i - \eta_{\hat{\theta}}(x_i))\nabla_\theta \eta_{\hat{\theta}}(x_i) \\ + \quad \nabla_\theta \nabla_\theta^t g(\hat{\theta}, \lambda)$$

As n approaches infinite, the effect of the second term in $\mathcal{U}$ vanishes, $\hat{\theta}$ approach the mean squared error estimator with infinite amount of data points, or the true parameters θ_0 of the model (consistency of MSE estimator (Jennrich, 1969)), $E(y - \eta_{\hat{\theta}}(x))$ approaches $E(y - \eta_{\theta_0}(x))$ which is 0. According to lemma 2 and lemma 3, the second term of this second derivative vanishes asymptotically. So as n approaches infinite, the second derivative of $\mathcal{U}$ with respect to θ, evaluated at $\hat{\theta}$, approaches

$$\nabla_\theta \nabla_\theta^t \mathcal{U}(\theta_0), \lambda, \omega) = 2\sum_{i=1}^{n} \nabla_\theta \eta_{\theta_0}(x_i) \nabla_\theta^t \eta_{\theta_0}(x_i) + \nabla_\theta \nabla_\theta^t g(\theta_0, \lambda)$$

which is independent of $\{y_i,\ i = 1,\ ...,\ n\}$. According to lemma 2, the result of this lemma is readily obtained.

Now we give the detailed proof of theorem 1, lemma 1 and theorem 2.

Proof of Theorem 1. The jackknife estimator $\hat{\theta}_{-i}$ satisfies, $\nabla_\theta \mathcal{C}_{\omega_{-i}}(\hat{\theta}_{-i}) = 0$. The Taylor expansion of the left side of this equation around $\hat{\theta}$ gives

$$\nabla_\theta \mathcal{C}_{\omega_{-i}}(\hat{\theta}) + \nabla_\theta \nabla_\theta^t \mathcal{C}_{\omega_{-i}}(\hat{\theta})(\hat{\theta}_{-i} - \hat{\theta}) + O(|\hat{\theta}_{-i} - \hat{\theta}|^2) = 0$$

According to the definition of $\hat{\theta}$ and $\hat{\theta}_{-i}$, their difference is thus a small quantity. Also because of the boundness of the derivatives, we can ignore higher order terms in the Taylor expansion and get the approximation

$$\hat{\theta}_{-i} - \hat{\theta} \approx -(\nabla_\theta \nabla_\theta^t \mathcal{C}_{\omega_{-i}}(\hat{\theta}))^{-1} \nabla_\theta \mathcal{C}_{\omega_{-i}}(\hat{\theta})$$

Since $\hat{\theta}$ satisfies $\nabla_\theta \mathcal{C}_\omega(\hat{\theta}) = 0$, we can rewrite this equation and obtain equation 1.

Proof of Lemma 1. The Taylor expansion of $\log f(y_i|x_i, \hat{\theta}_{-i})$ around $\hat{\theta}$ is

$$\log f(y_i|x_i, \hat{\theta}_{-i}) = \log f(y_i|x_i, \hat{\theta}) + \nabla_\theta^t \log f(y_i|x_i, \hat{\theta})(\hat{\theta}_{-i} - \hat{\theta}) + O(|\hat{\theta}_{-i} - \hat{\theta}|^2)$$

Putting this into equation 5 and ignoring higher order terms for the same argument as that presented in the proof of theorem 1, we readily get equation 7.

Proof of Theorem 2. Up to an additive constant dependent only on λ and σ^2, the optimization criterion, or equation 2, can be rewritten as

$$\mathcal{C}_\omega(\theta) = -\frac{1}{2\sigma^2}\mathcal{U}(\theta, \lambda, \omega) \tag{13}$$

Now putting equation 9 and 13 into equation 3, we get,

$$\hat{\theta}_{-i} - \hat{\theta} \approx -\{\nabla_\theta \nabla_\theta^t \mathcal{U}(\hat{\theta}, \lambda, \omega)\}^{-1} \nabla_\theta \mathcal{E}(y_i, \eta_{\hat{\theta}}(x_i)) \tag{14}$$

Putting equation 14 into equation 7, we get, for the model selection criterion,

$$\mathcal{T}_m(\omega) = \frac{1}{n} \sum_{(x_i,y_i)\in\omega} \frac{1}{2\sigma^2} \mathcal{E}(y_i, \eta_{\hat{\theta}}(x_i)) +$$

$$\frac{1}{n} \sum_{(x_i,y_i)\in\omega} \frac{1}{2\sigma^2} \nabla_\theta^t \mathcal{E}(y_i, \eta_{\hat{\theta}}(x_i)) \{\nabla_\theta \nabla_\theta^t \mathcal{U}(\hat{\theta}, \lambda, \omega)\}^{-1} \nabla_\theta \mathcal{E}(y_i, \eta_{\hat{\theta}}(x_i)) \tag{15}$$

Recall the discussion associated with equation 6 and now

$$\mathrm{E}\{ -\frac{1}{k} \sum_{(x_j,y_j)\in\omega_n} \log f(y_j | x_j, \hat{\theta}) \} = \mathrm{E}\{\frac{1}{k} \sum_{(x_j,y_j)\in\omega_n} \frac{1}{2\sigma^2} \mathcal{E}(y_j, \eta_{\hat{\theta}}(x_j)) \} \tag{16}$$

after some simple algebra, we can obtain the unbiased estimator of equation 10. The result is equation 15 multiplied by $2\sigma^2$, or equation 11. Thus we prove the first part of the theorem.
Now consider the case when

$$\mathcal{E}(y, \eta_\theta(x)) = (y - \eta_\theta(x))^2 \tag{17}$$

The second term of equation 11 now becomes

$$\frac{1}{n} \sum_{(x_i,y_i)\in\omega} 4(y_i - \eta_{\hat{\theta}}(x_i))^2 \nabla_\theta^t \eta_{\hat{\theta}}(x_i) \{\nabla_\theta \nabla_\theta^t \mathcal{U}(\hat{\theta}, \lambda, \omega)\}^{-1} \nabla_\theta \eta_{\hat{\theta}}(x_i) \tag{18}$$

As n approaches infinite, $\hat{\theta}$ approach the true parameters θ_0, $\nabla_\theta \eta_{\hat{\theta}}(x.)$ approaches $\nabla_\theta \eta_{\theta_0}(x.)$ and $E((y - \eta_{\hat{\theta}}(x)))^2$ asymptotically equals to σ^2. Using lemma 4 and lemma 3, we get, for the asymptotic equivalency of equation 18,

$$\frac{1}{n}\sigma^2 \sum_{(x_i,y_i)\in\omega} 2\nabla_\theta^t \eta_{\hat{\theta}}(x_i) \{\nabla_\theta \nabla_\theta^t \mathcal{U}(\hat{\theta}, \lambda, \omega)\}^{-1} 2\nabla_\theta \eta_{\hat{\theta}}(x_i) \tag{19}$$

If we use notation $\mathcal{E}(\theta, \omega) = \frac{1}{n} \sum_{(x_i,y_i)\in\omega} \mathcal{E}(y_i, \eta_\theta(x_i))$, with $\mathcal{E}(y, \eta_\theta(x))$ of the form specified in equation 17, we can get,

$$\frac{\partial}{\partial y_i} \nabla_\theta n \mathcal{E}(\theta, \omega) = -2\nabla_\theta \eta_\theta(x_i) \tag{20}$$

Combining this with equation 19 and equation 11, we can readily obtain equation 12.

5 SUMMARY

In this paper, we used asymptotics to obtain the jackknife estimator, which can be used to get the fit of a model by plugging it into the model selection criterion. Based on the idea of the cross-validation method, we used the negative of the average predicative likelihood as the model selection criterion. We also obtained the asymptotic form of the model selection criterion and proved that when the parameters optimization criterion is the mean squared error plus a penalty term, this asymptotic form is the same as the form presented by (Moody, 1992). This also served to prove the asymptotic equivalence of this criterion to the method of cross-validation.

Acknowledgements

The author thanks all the members of the Institute for Brain and Neural Systems, in particular, Professor Leon N Cooper for reading the draft of this paper, and Dr. Nathan Intrator, Michael P. Perrone and Harel Shouval for helpful comments. This research was supported by grants from NSF, ONR and ARO.

References

Akaike, H. (1973). Information theory and an extension of the maximum likelihood principle. In Petrov and Czaki, editors, *Proceedings of the 2nd International Symposium on Information Theory*, pages 267–281.

Atkinson, A. C. (1978). Posterior probabilities for choosing a regression model. *Biometrika*, 65:39–48.

Berger, J. O. (1985). *Statistical Decision Theory and Bayesian Analysis*. Springer-Verlag.

Efron, B. and Gong, G. (1983). A leisurely look at the bootstrap, the jackknife and cross-validation. *Amer. Stat.*, 37:36–48.

Jennrich, R. (1969). Asymptotic properties of nonlinear least squares estimators. *Ann. Math. Stat.*, 40:633–643.

Lindley, D. V. (1968). The choice of variables in multiple regression (with discussion). *J. Roy. Stat. Soc.*, Ser. B, 30:31–66.

MacKay, D. (1991). *Bayesian methods for adaptive models*. PhD thesis, California Institute of Technology.

Mallows, C. L. (1973). Some comments on Cp. *Technometrics*, 15:661–675.

Miller, R. G. (1974). The jackknife - a review. *Biometrika*, 61:1–15.

Moody, J. E. (1992). The effective number of parameters, an analysis of generalization and regularization in nonlinear learning system. In Moody, J. E., Hanson, S. J., and Lippmann, R. P., editors, *Advances in Neural Information Processing System 4*. Morgan Kaufmann Publication.

Schwartz, G. (1978). Estimating the dimension of a model. *Ann. Stat*, 6:461–464.

Stone, M. (1974). Cross-validatory choice and assessment of statistical predictions (with discussion). *J. Roy. Stat. Soc.*, Ser. B.

Stone, M. (1977). An asymptotic equivalence of choice of model by cross-validation and Akaike's criterion. *J. Roy. Stat. Soc.*, Ser. B, 39(1):44–47.

Zellner, A. (1984). Posterior odds ratios for regression hypotheses: General consideration and some specific results. In Zellner, A., editor, *Basic Issues in Econometrics*, pages 275–305. University of Chicago Press.

Learning Curves, Model Selection and Complexity of Neural Networks

Noboru Murata
Department of Mathematical Engineering and Information Physics
University of Tokyo, Tokyo 113, JAPAN
E-mail: mura@sat.t.u-tokyo.ac.jp

Shuji Yoshizawa
Dept. Mech. Info.
University of Tokyo

Shun-ichi Amari
Dept. Math. Eng. and Info. Phys.
University of Tokyo

Abstract

Learning curves show how a neural network is improved as the number of training examples increases and how it is related to the network complexity. The present paper clarifies asymptotic properties and their relation of two learning curves, one concerning the predictive loss or generalization loss and the other the training loss. The result gives a natural definition of the complexity of a neural network. Moreover, it provides a new criterion of model selection.

1 INTRODUCTION

The learning curve shows how well the behavior of a neural network is improved as the number of training examples increases and how it is related with the complexity of neural networks. This provides us with a criterion for choosing an adequate network in relation to the number of training examples. Some researchers have attacked this problem by using statistical mechanical methods (see Levin et al. [1990], Seung et al. [1991], etc.) and some by information theory and algorithmic methods (see Baum and Haussler

[1989], etc.). The present paper elucidates asymptotic properties of the learning curve from the statistical point of view, giving a new criterion for model selection.

2 STATEMENT OF THE PROBLEM

Let us consider a stochastic neural network, which is parameterized by a set of m weights $\theta = (\theta^1, \cdots, \theta^m)$ and whose input-output relation is specified by a conditional probability $p(y|x, \theta)$. In other words, for an input signal is $x \in \boldsymbol{R}^{n_{in}}$, the probability distribution of output $y \in \boldsymbol{R}^{n_{out}}$ is given by $p(y|x, \theta)$.

A typical form of the stochastic neural network is as follows: let us consider a multi-layered network $f(x, \theta)$ where θ is a set of m parameters $\theta = (\theta^1, \cdots, \theta^m)$ and its components correspond to weights and thresholds of the network. When some input x is given, the network produce an output

$$y = f(x, \theta) + \eta(x), \tag{1}$$

where $\eta(x)$ is noise whose conditional distribution is given by $a(\eta|x)$. Then the conditional distribution of the network, which specifies the input-output relation, is given by

$$p(y|x, \theta) = a(y - f(x, \theta)|x). \tag{2}$$

We define a training sample $\xi^t = \{(x_1, y_1), \cdots, (x_t, y_t)\}$ as a set of t examples generated from the true conditional distribution $q(y|x)$, where x_i is generated from a probability distribution $r(x)$ independently. We should note that both $r(x)$ and $q(y|x)$ are unknown and we need not assume the faithfulness of the model, that is, we do not assume that there exists a parameter θ^* which realize the true distribution $q(y|x)$ such that $p(y|x, \theta^*) = q(y|x)$.

Our purpose is to find an appropriate parameter θ which realizes a good approximation $p(y|x, \theta)$ to $q(y|x)$. For this purpose, we use a loss function

$$L(\theta) = D(r; q|p(\theta)) + S(\theta) \tag{3}$$

as a criterion to be minimized, where $D(r; q|p(\theta))$ represents a general divergence measure between two conditional probabilities $q(y|x)$ and $p(y|x, \theta)$ in the expectation form under the true input-output probability

$$D(r; q|p(\theta)) = \int r(x) q(y|x) k(x, y, \theta) dx dy \tag{4}$$

and $S(\theta)$ is a regularization term to fit the smoothness condition of outputs (Moody [1992]). So the loss function is rewritten as a expectation form

$$L(\theta) = \int r(x) q(y|x) d(x, y, \theta) dx dy, \quad d(x, y, \theta) = k(x, y, \theta) + S(\theta), \tag{5}$$

and $d(x, y, \theta)$ is called the pointwise loss function.

A typical case of the divergence D of the multi-layered network $f(x, \theta)$ with noise is the squared error

$$D(r; q|p(\theta)) = \int r(x) q(y|x) ||y - f(x, \theta)||^2 dx dy, \tag{6}$$

The error function of an ordinary multi-layered network is in this form, and the conventional Back-Propagation method is derived from this type of loss function.

Another typical case is the Kullback-Leibler divergence

$$D(r;q|p(\theta)) = \int r(x)q(y|x)\log\frac{q(y|x)}{p(y|x,\theta)}dxdy. \tag{7}$$

The integration $\int r(x)q(y|x)\log q(y|x)dxdy$ is a constant called a conditional entropy, and we usually use the following abbreviated form instead of the previous divergence:

$$D(r;q|p(\theta)) = -\int r(x)q(y|x)\log p(y|x,\theta)dxdy. \tag{8}$$

Next, we define an optimum of the parameter in the sense of the loss function that we introduced. We denote by θ^* the optimal parameter that minimizes the loss function $L(\theta)$, that is,

$$L(\theta^*) = \min_\theta L(\theta), \tag{9}$$

and we regard $p(y|x,\theta^*)$ as the best realization of the model.

When a training sample ξ^t is given, we can also define an empirical loss function:

$$\hat{L}(\theta) = D(\hat{r};\hat{q}|p(\theta)) + S(\theta), \tag{10}$$

where $\hat{r}$, $\hat{q}$ are the empirical distributions given by the sample ξ^t, that is,

$$D(\hat{r};\hat{q}|p(\theta)) = \frac{1}{t}\sum_{i=1}^{t} k(x_i,y_i,\theta), \quad (x_i,y_i)\in\xi^t. \tag{11}$$

In practical case, we consider the empirical loss function and search for the quasi-optimal parameter $\hat{\theta}$ defined by

$$\hat{L}(\hat{\theta}) = \min_\theta \hat{L}(\theta), \tag{12}$$

because the true distributions $r(x)$ and $q(y|x)$ are unknown and we can only use examples (x_i,y_i) observed from the true distribution $r(x)q(y|x)$. We should note that the quasi-optimal parameter $\hat{\theta}$ is a random variable depending on the sample ξ^t, each element of which is chosen randomly.

The following lemma guarantees that we can use the empirical loss function instead of the actual loss function when the number of examples t is large.

Lemma 1 *If the number of examples t is large enough, it is shown that the quasi-optimal parameter $\hat{\theta}$ is normally distributed around the optimal parameter θ^*, that is,*

$$\hat{\theta} \sim N\left(\theta^*, \frac{1}{t}Q^{-1}GQ^{-1}\right), \tag{13}$$

where

$$G = \int r(x)q(y|x)\nabla d(x,y,\theta^*)\nabla d(x,y,\theta^*)^{\mathrm{T}}dxdy, \tag{14}$$

$$Q = \int r(x)q(y|x)\nabla\nabla d(x,y,\theta^*)dxdy, \tag{15}$$

and ∇ denotes the differential operator with respect to θ.

This lemma is proved by using the usual statistical methods.

3 LEARNING PROCEDURE

In many cases, however, it is difficult to obtain the quasi-optimal parameter $\hat{\theta}$ by minimizing the equation (10) directly. We therefore often use a stochastic descent method to get an approximation to the quasi-optimal parameter $\hat{\theta}$.

Definition 1 (Stochastic Descent Method) *In each learning step, an example is re-sampled from the given sample ξ^t randomly, and the following modification is applied to the parameter θ_n at step n,*

$$\theta_{n+1} = \theta_n - \varepsilon \nabla d(x_{i(n)}, y_{i(n)}, \theta_n), \tag{16}$$

where ε is a positive value called a learning coefficient and $(x_{i(n)}, y_{i(n)})$ is the re-sampled example at step n.

This is a sequential learning method and the operations of random sampling from ξ^t in each learning step is called *the re-sampling plan.* The parameter θ_n at step n is a random variable as a function of the re-sampled sequence $\omega = \{(x_{i(1)}, y_{i(1)}), \cdots, (x_{i(n)}, y_{i(n)})\}$. However, if the initial value of θ is appropriate (this assumption prevents being stuck in local minima) and if the learning step n is large enough, it is shown that the learned parameter θ_n is normally distributed around the quasi-optimal parameter.

Lemma 2 *If the learning step n is large enough and the learning coefficient ε is small enough, the parameter θ_n is normally distributed asymptotically, that is,*

$$\theta_n \sim N(\hat{\theta}, \varepsilon V), \tag{17}$$

where V satisfies the following relation

$$G = \hat{Q}V + V\hat{Q}, \tag{18}$$

$$G = \frac{1}{t}\sum_{i=1}^{t} \nabla d(x_i, y_i, \hat{\theta}) \nabla d(x_i, y_i, \hat{\theta})^{\mathrm{T}}, \quad \hat{Q} = \frac{1}{t}\sum_{i=1}^{t} \nabla\nabla d(x_i, y_i, \hat{\theta}).$$

In the following discussion, we assume that n is large enough and ε is small enough, and we denote the learned parameter by

$$\tilde{\theta}(= \theta_n). \tag{19}$$

The distribution of the random variable $\tilde{\theta}$, therefore, can be regarded as the normal distribution $N(\hat{\theta}, \varepsilon V)$.

4 LEARNING CURVES

It is important to evaluate the difference between two quantities $L(\tilde{\theta})$ and $\hat{L}(\tilde{\theta})$. The quantity $L(\tilde{\theta})$ is called the predictive loss or the generalization error, which shows the average loss of the trained network when a novel example is given. On the other hand, the quantity $\hat{L}(\tilde{\theta})$ is called the training loss or the training error, which shows the average loss evaluated by the examples used in training. Since these quantities depend on the sample ξ^t and the re-sampled sequence ω, we take the expectation E and the variance Var with respect to the sample ξ^t and the re-sampling sequence ω.

First, let us consider the predictive loss which is the average loss of the trained network when a new example (which does not belong to the sample ξ^t) is given. This averaging operation is replaced by averaging all over the input-output pairs, because the measure of the sample ξ^t is zero. Then the predictive loss is written as

$$L(\tilde{\theta}) = \int r(x)q(y|x)d(x, y, \tilde{\theta})dxdy. \tag{20}$$

From the properties of $\tilde{\theta}$ and $\hat{\theta}$, we can prove the following important relations.

Theorem 1 *The predictive loss asymptotically satisfies*

$$\mathrm{E}[L(\tilde{\theta})] = L(\theta^*) + \frac{1}{2t}\mathrm{tr}GQ^{-1} + \frac{\varepsilon}{2}\mathrm{tr}QV, \tag{21}$$

$$\mathrm{Var}[L(\tilde{\theta})] = \frac{1}{2t^2}\mathrm{tr}GQ^{-1}GQ^{-1} + \frac{\varepsilon^2}{2}\mathrm{tr}QVQV + \frac{\varepsilon}{t}\mathrm{tr}GV. \tag{22}$$

Roughly speaking, there exist two random values Y_1 and Y_2, and the predictive loss can be written as the following form:

$$\begin{aligned} L(\tilde{\theta}) &= L(\theta^*) + \frac{1}{2t}\mathrm{tr}GQ^{-1} + \frac{\varepsilon}{2}\mathrm{tr}QV \\ &\quad + \frac{1}{t}Y_1 + \varepsilon Y_2 + o_p(\frac{1}{t}) + o_p(\varepsilon), \end{aligned} \tag{23}$$

where Y_1 and Y_2 satisfy

$$\mathrm{E}[Y_1] = 0, \qquad \mathrm{Var}[Y_1] = \frac{1}{2}\mathrm{tr}GQ^{-1}GQ^{-1},$$

$$\mathrm{E}[Y_2] = 0, \qquad \mathrm{Var}[Y_2] = \frac{1}{2}\mathrm{tr}QVQV,$$

$$\mathrm{Cov}[Y_1Y_2] = \mathrm{tr}GV,$$

E, Var and Cov denote the expectation, the variance and the covariance respectively.

Next, we consider the training loss, i.e., the average loss evaluated by the examples used in training. Just as we did in the previous theorem, we can get the following relations.

Theorem 2 *The training loss asymptotically satisfy*

$$\mathrm{E}[\hat{L}(\tilde{\theta})] = L(\theta^*) - \frac{1}{2t}\mathrm{tr}GQ^{-1} + \frac{\varepsilon}{2}\mathrm{tr}QV, \tag{24}$$

$$\begin{aligned} \mathrm{Var}[\hat{L}(\tilde{\theta})] &= \frac{1}{t}\Big(\int r(x)q(y|x)d(x, y, \theta^*)^2dxdy \\ &\quad - \Big(\int r(x)q(y|x)d(x, y, \theta^*)dxdy\Big)^2\Big). \end{aligned} \tag{25}$$

Intuitively speaking like the predictive loss, the training loss can be expanded as

$$\hat{L}(\tilde{\theta}) = L(\theta^*) - \frac{1}{2t}\mathrm{tr}GQ^{-1} + \frac{\varepsilon}{2}\mathrm{tr}QV + \frac{1}{\sqrt{t}}Y_3 + o_p(\frac{1}{\sqrt{t}}) + O_p(\varepsilon), \tag{26}$$

where Y_3 satisfies

$$\mathrm{E}[Y_3] = 0,$$

$$\mathrm{Var}[Y_3] = \int r(x)q(y|x)d(x,y,\theta^*)^2 dxdy - \left(\int r(x)q(y|x)d(x,y,\theta^*)dxdy\right)^2.$$

When we look at two curves $\mathrm{E}[L(\tilde{\theta})]$ and $\mathrm{E}[\hat{L}(\tilde{\theta})]$ as functions of t, they are called learning curves which represent the characteristics of learning. The expectations of the predictive loss and the training loss look quite similar. They are different in the sign of the term $1/t$. As the learning coefficient ε increases, the expectations $\mathrm{E}[L(\tilde{\theta})]$ and $\mathrm{E}[\hat{L}(\tilde{\theta})]$ increase, but as the number of examples t increases, the average predictive loss $\mathrm{E}[L(\tilde{\theta})]$ decreases and the average training loss $\mathrm{E}[\hat{L}(\tilde{\theta})]$ conversely increases. Moreover, their variances are different in the order of t. The coefficients $\mathrm{tr}GQ^{-1}$, $\mathrm{tr}QV$, etc. are calculated from the matrices G, Q and V, which reflect the architecture of the network and the loss criterion to be minimized. We can consider these matrices as representing the complexity of the network. In earlier work, Amari and Murata [1991] introduced an effective complexity of the network, $\mathrm{tr}GQ^{-1}$, by analogy to Akaike's Information Criterion (AIC) (see Akaike [1974]).

5 AN APPLICATION FOR MODEL SELECTION

These results naturally leads us to a model selection criterion, which is like the AIC criterion of statistical model selection and which is related those proposed by some researchers (see Murata et al. [1991], Moody [1992]). From the previous relations, we can easily show the following relation

$$L(\tilde{\theta}) = \hat{L}(\tilde{\theta}) + \frac{1}{t}\mathrm{tr}GQ^{-1} + c, \tag{27}$$

where c is a quantity of order $1/\sqrt{t}$ and common to all the networks of the same architecture. We compare the abilities of two different networks, which have the same architecture and are trained by the same sample, but differ in the number of weights or neurons (see Fig.1). We can use a quantity, NIC (Network Information Criterion),

$$\mathrm{NIC}(\tilde{\theta}) = \hat{L}(\tilde{\theta}) + \frac{1}{t}\mathrm{tr}\tilde{G}\tilde{Q}^{-1}, \tag{28}$$

where

$$\tilde{G} = \frac{1}{t}\sum_{i=1}^{t}\nabla d(x_i,y_i,\tilde{\theta})\nabla d(x_i,y_i,\tilde{\theta})^{\mathrm{T}}, \quad \tilde{Q} = \frac{1}{t}\sum_{i=1}^{t}\nabla\nabla d(x_i,y_i,\tilde{\theta}), \tag{29}$$

for selecting an optimal network model. Note that this quantity NIC is directly calculable, since all elements of it, $\hat{L}(\tilde{\theta})$, $\tilde{G}$, $\tilde{Q}$, are given by summing over the sample ξ^t. When we have two models M_1 and M_2, and the NIC of M_1 is smaller than that of M_2, the predictive loss of M_1 is expected smaller than that of M_2, so M_1 can be regarded as a better model in the sense of the loss function.

This criterion cannot be used when we compare two networks of different architectures, for example a multi-layered network and a radial basis expansion network. This is because the value c of the order $1/\sqrt{t}$ term is common only to two networks in which one is included in the other as a submodel. The criterion is in general valid only for such a family of networks (see Fig.2).

6 CONCLUSIONS

In this paper, we show that there is nice relation between the expectation of the predictive loss and that of the training loss. This result naturally leads us to a new model selection criterion.

We will consider the application of this result as an algorithm for automatically changing the number of hidden units in the learning as future work.

References

H. Akaike. (1974) A new look at the statistical model identification. *IEEE Trans. AC*, **19**(6):716–723.

S. Amari. (1967) Theory of adaptive pattern classifiers. *IEEE Trans. EC*, **16**(3):299–307.

S. Amari and N. Murata. (1991) Statistical theory of learning curves under entropic loss criterion. Technical Report METR 91-12, University of Tokyo, Tokyo, Japan.

E. B. Baum and D. Haussler. (1989) What size net gives valid generalization? *Neural Computation*, 1:151–160.

E. Levin, N. Tishby, and S. A. Solla. (1990) A statistical approach to learning and generalization in layered neural networks. *Proc. of IEEE*, **78**(10):1568–1574.

J. E. Moody. (1992) The effective number of parameters: An analysis of generalization and regularization in nonlinear learning systems. In J. E. Moody, S. J. Hanson, and R. P. Lippmann, (eds.), *Advances in Neural Information Processing Systems 4*. San Mateo, CA: Morgan Kaufmann.

N. Murata. (1992) *Statistical asymptotic study on learning* (In Japanese). PhD thesis, University of Tokyo, Tokyo, Japan.

N. Murata, S. Yoshizawa, and S. Amari. (1991) A criterion for determining the number of parameters in an artificial neural network model. In T. Kohonen et al., (eds.), *Artificial Neural Networks*, 9–14. Holland: Elsevier Science Publishers.

H. S. Seung, H. Sompolinsky, and N. Tishby. (1991) Statistical mechanics of learning from examples II. quenched theory and unrealizable rules. Submitted to Physical Review A.

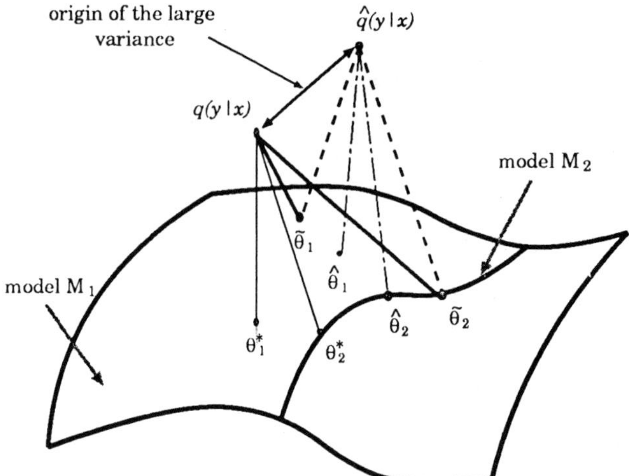

Figure 1: Geometrical representation of hierarchical models: the solid lines between $q(y|x)$ and $\tilde{\theta}_i$ show predictive losses, and the dashed lines between $\hat{q}(y|x)$ and $\tilde{\theta}_i$ show training losses. The large variance of the training loss originated in the discrepancy of $q(y|x)$ and $\hat{q}(y|x)$. When we estimate the prediction loss from the training loss, the large variance still remains. But in the case that the model M_1 includes the model M_2, this variance is common to two models, so we do not have to take care of it.

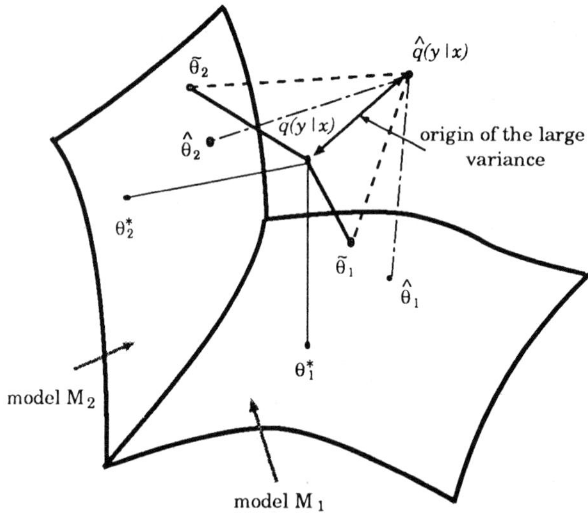

Figure 2: Geometrical representation of non-hierarchical models: the solid lines between $q(y|x)$ and $\tilde{\theta}_i$ show predictive losses, and the dashed lines between $\hat{q}(y|x)$ and $\tilde{\theta}_i$ show training losses. The discrepancy of $q(y|x)$ and $\hat{q}(y|x)$ works differently on two models M_1 and M_2 in estimating predictive losses.

The Power of Approximating: a Comparison of Activation Functions

Bhaskar DasGupta
Department of Computer Science
University of Minnesota
Minneapolis, MN 55455-0159
email: dasgupta@cs.umn.edu

Georg Schnitger
Department of Computer Science
The Pennsylvania State University
University Park, PA 16802
email: georg@cs.psu.edu

Abstract

We compare activation functions in terms of the approximation power of their feedforward nets. We consider the case of analog as well as boolean input.

1 Introduction

We consider efficient approximations of a given multivariate function $f : [-1,1]^m \rightarrow \mathcal{R}$ by feedforward neural networks. We first introduce the notion of a feedforward net.

Let Γ be a class of real-valued functions, where each function is defined on some subset of $\mathcal{R}$. A Γ-net C is an unbounded fan-in circuit whose edges and vertices are labeled by real numbers. The real number assigned to an edge (resp. vertex) is called its *weight* (resp. its *threshold*). Moreover, to each vertex v an activation function $\gamma_v \in \Gamma$ is assigned. Finally, we assume that C has a single sink w.

The net C computes a function $f_C : [-1,1]^m \rightarrow \mathcal{R}$ as follows. The components of the input vector $x = (x_1, \ldots, x_m) \in [-1,1]^m$ are assigned to the sources of C. Let $v_1, \ldots, v_n$ be the immediate predecessors of a vertex v. The input for v is then $s_v(x) = \sum_{i=1}^{n} w_i y_i - t_v$, where w_i is the weight of the edge (v_i, v), t_v is the threshold of v and y_i is the value assigned to v_i. If v is not the sink, then we assign the value $\gamma_v(s_v(x))$ to v. Otherwise we assign $s_v(x)$ to v.

Then $f_C = s_w$ is the function computed by C where w is the unique sink of C.

A great deal of work has been done showing that nets of two layers can approximate (in various norms) large function classes (including continuous functions) arbitrarily well (Arai, 1989; Carrol and Dickinson, 1989; Cybenko, 1989; Funahashi, 1989; Gallant and White, 1988; Hornik *et al.* 1989; Irie and Miyake,1988; Lapades and Farber, 1987; Nielson, 1989; Poggio and Girosi, 1989; Wei *et al.*, 1991). Various activation functions have been used, among others, *the cosine squasher, the standard sigmoid, radial basis functions, generalized radial basis functions, polynomials, trigonometric polynomials and binary thresholds.* Still, as we will see, these functions differ greatly in terms of their approximation power when we only consider efficient nets; i.e. nets with *few layers* and *few vertices.*

Our goal is to compare activation functions in terms of *efficiency* and *quality of approximation*. We measure efficiency by the *size* of the net (i.e. the number of vertices, not counting input units) and by its *number of layers*. Another resource of interest is *the Lipschitz-bound* of the net, which is a measure of the numerical stability of the net. We say that net C has Lipschitz-bound L if all weights and thresholds of C are bounded in absolute value by L and for each vertex v of C and for all inputs $x, y \in [-1,1]^m$,

$$|\gamma_v(s_v(x)) - \gamma_v(s_v(y))| \leq L \cdot |s_v(x) - s_v(y)|.$$

(Thus we do not demand that activation function γ_v has Lipschitz-bound L, but only that γ_v has Lipschitz-bound L for the inputs it receives.) We measure the quality of an approximation of function f by function f_C by the Chebychev norm; i.e. by the maximum distance between f and f_C over the input domain $[-1,1]^m$.

Let Γ be a class of activation functions. We are particularly interested in the following two questions.

• Given a function $f : [-1,1]^m \to \mathcal{R}$, how well can we approximate f by a Γ-net with d layers, size s, and Lipschitz-bound L? Thus, we are particularly interested in the behavior of the approximation error $e(s,d)$ as a *function of size and number of layers*. This set-up allows us to investigate how much the approximation error decreases with increased size and/or number of layers.

• Given two classes of activation functions Γ_1 and Γ_2, when do Γ_1-nets and Γ_2-nets have *essentially* the same "approximation power" with respect to some error function $e(s,d)$?

We first formalize the notion of "essentially the same approximation power".

Definition 1.1 *Let $e : \mathcal{N}^2 \to \mathcal{R}_+$ be a function. Γ_1 and Γ_2 are classes of activation functions.*

(a). *We say that Γ_1 simulates Γ_2 with respect to e if and only if there is a constant k such that for all functions $f : [-1,1]^m \to \mathcal{R}$ with Lipschitz-bound $1/e(s,d)$,*

> *if f can be approximated by a Γ_2-net with d layers, size s, Lipschitz-bound 2^s and approximation error $e(s,d)$, then f can also be approximated with error $e(s,d)$ by a Γ_1-net with $k(d+1)$ layers, size $(s+1)^k$ and Lipschitz-bound 2^{s^k}.*

(b). *We say that Γ_1 and Γ_2 are equivalent with respect to e if and only if Γ_2 simulates Γ_1 with respect to e and Γ_1 simulates Γ_2 with respect to e.*

In other words, when comparing the approximation power of activation functions, we allow size to increase polynomially and the number of layers to increase by a constant factor, but we insist on at least the same approximation error. Observe that we have linked the approximation error $e(s,d)$ and the Lipschitz-bound of the function to be approximated. The reason is that approximations of functions with high Lipschitz-bound "tend" to have an inversely proportional approximation error. Moreover observe that the Lipschitz-bounds of the involved nets are allowed to be exponential in the size of the net. We will see in section 3, that for some activation functions far smaller Lipschitz-bounds suffice.

Below we discuss our results. In section 2 we consider the case of tight approximations, i.e. $e(s,d) = 2^{-s}$. Then in section 3 the more relaxed error model $e(s,d) = s^{-d}$ is discussed. In section 4 we consider the computation of boolean functions and show that sigmoidal nets can be far more efficient than threshold-nets.

2 Equivalence of Activation Functions for Error $e(s,d) = 2^{-s}$

We obtain the following result.

Theorem 2.1 *The following activation functions are equivalent with respect to error $e(s,d) = 2^{-s}$.*

- *the standard sigmoid $\sigma(x) = \frac{1}{1+\exp(-x)}$,*
- *any rational function which is not a polynomial,*
- *any root x^α, provided α is not a natural number,*
- *the logarithm (for any base $b > 1$),*
- *e^x,*
- *the gaussian e^{-x^2},*
- *the radial basis functions $(1+x^2)^\alpha$, $\alpha < 1$, $\alpha \neq 0$*

Notable exceptions from the list of functions equivalent to the standard sigmoid are polynomials, trigonometric polynomials and splines. We do obtain an equivalence to the standard sigmoid by allowing splines of degree s as activation functions for nets of size s. (We will always assume that splines are continuous with a single knot only.)

Theorem 2.2 *Assume that $e(s,d) = 2^{-s}$. Then splines (of degree s for nets of size s) and the standard sigmoid are equivalent with respect to $e(s,d)$.*

Remark 2.1

(a) *Of course, the equivalence of spline-nets and $\{\sigma\}$-nets also holds for* **binary** *input. Since threshold-nets can add and multiply m m-bit numbers with constantly many layers and size polynomial in m (Reif, 1987), threshold-nets can efficiently approximate polynomials and splines.*

Thus, we obtain that $\{\sigma\}$-nets with d layers, size s and Lipschitz-bound L can be simulated by nets of binary thresholds. The number of layers of the simulating threshold-net will increase by a constant factor and its size will increase by a polynomial in $(s+n)\log(L)$, where n is the number of input bits. (The inclusion of n accounts for the additional increase in size when approximately computing a weighted sum by a threshold-net.)

(b) *If we allow size to increase by a polynomial in $s+n$, then threshold-nets and $\{\sigma\}$-nets are actually equivalent with respect to error bound 2^{-s}. This follows, since a threshold function can easily be implemented by a sigmoidal gate (Maass et al.,* 1991*).*

Thus, if we allow size to increase polynomially (in $s+n$) and the number of layers to increase by a constant factor, then $\{\sigma\}$-nets with weights that are at most exponential (in $s+n$) can be simulated by $\{\sigma\}$-nets with weights of size polynomial in s.

$\{\sigma\}$-nets and threshold-nets (respectively nets of linear thresholds) are not equivalent for analog input. The same applies to polynomials, even if we allow polynomials of degree s as activation function for nets of size s:

Theorem 2.3

(a) *Let $sq(x) = x^2$. If a net of linear splines (with d layers and size s) approximates $sq(x)$ over the interval $[-1,1]$, then its approximation error will be at least $s^{-O(d)}$.*

(b) *Let $abs(x) = |x|$. If a polynomial net with d layers and size s approximates $abs(x)$ over the interval $[-1,1]$, then the approximation error will be at least $s^{-O(d)}$.*

We will see in Theorem 2.5 that the standard sigmoid (and hence any activation function listed in Theorem 2.1) is capable of approximating $sq(x)$ and $abs(x)$ with error at most 2^{-s} by constant-layer nets of size polynomial in s. Hence the standard sigmoid is properly stronger than linear splines and polynomials. Finally, we show that *sine* and the standard sigmoid are inequivalent with respect to error 2^{-s}.

Theorem 2.4 *The function $sine(Ax)$ can be approximated by a $\{\sigma\}$-net C_A with d layers, size $s = A^{O(1/d)}$ and error at most $s^{O(-d)}$. On the other hand, every $\{\sigma\}$-net with d layers which approximates $sine(Ax)$ with error at most $\frac{1}{2}$, has to have size at least $A^{\Omega(1/d)}$.*

Below we sketch the proof of Theorem 2.1. The proof itself will actually be more instructive than the statement of Theorem 2.1. In particular, we will obtain a general criterion that allows us to decide whether a given activation function (or class of activation functions) has at least the approximation power of splines.

2.1 Activation Functions with the Approximation Power of Splines

Obviously, any activation function which can efficiently approximate polynomials and the binary threshold will be able to efficiently approximate splines. This follows since a spline can be approximated by the sum $p + t \cdot q$ with polynomials p and q

and a binary threshold t. (Observe that we can approximate a product once we can approximately square: $(x+y)^2/2 - x^2/2 - y^2/2 = x \cdot y$.)

Firstly, we will see that any sufficiently smooth activation function is capable of approximating polynomials.

Definition 2.1 *Let $\gamma : \mathcal{R} \to \mathcal{R}$ be a function. We call γ suitable if and only if there exists real numbers α, β ($\alpha > 0$) and an integer k such that*

(a) *γ can be represented by the power series $\sum_{i=0}^{\infty} a_i(x-\beta)^i$ for all $x \in [-\alpha, \alpha]$. The coefficients are rationals of the form $a_i = \frac{P_i}{Q_i}$ with $|P_i|, |Q_i| \leq 2^{ki}$ (for $i > 1$).*

(b) *For each $i > 2$ there exists j with $i \leq j \leq i^k$ and $a_j \neq 0$.*

Proposition 2.1 *Assume that γ is suitable with parameter k.*

Then, over the domain $[-D, D]$, any degree n polynomial p can be approximated with error ε by a $\{\gamma\}$-net C_p. C_p has 2 layers and size $O(n^{2k})$; its weights are rational numbers whose numerator and denominator are bounded in absolute value by

$$p_{max}(2+D)^{poly(n)} ||\gamma^{(N+1)}||_{[-\alpha,\alpha]} \frac{1}{\varepsilon}.$$

Here we have assumed that the coefficients of p are rational numbers with numerator and denominator bounded in absolute value by p_{max}.

Thus, in order to have at least the approximation power of splines, a suitable activation function has to be able to approximate the binary threshold. This is achieved by the following function class,

Definition 2.2 *Let Γ be a class of activation functions and let $g : [1, \infty] \to \mathcal{R}$ be a function.*

(a). *We say that g is fast converging if and only if*

$$| g(x) - g(x+\varepsilon) | = O(\varepsilon/x^2) \text{ for } x \geq 1, \varepsilon \geq 0,$$

$$0 < \int_1^{\infty} g(u^2)du < \infty \text{ and } | \int_{2^N}^{\infty} g(u^2)du | = O(1/N) \text{ for all } N \geq 1.$$

(b). *We say that Γ is powerful if and only if at least one function in Γ is suitable and there is a fast converging function g which can be approximated for all $s > 1$ (over the domain $[-2^s, 2^s]$) with error 2^{-s} by a $\{\Gamma\}$-net with a constant number of layers, size polynomial in s and Lipschitz-bound 2^s.*

Fast convergence can be checked easily for differentiable functions by applying the mean value theorem. Examples are $x^{-\alpha}$ for $\alpha \geq 1$, $exp(-x)$ and $\sigma(-x)$. Moreover, it is not difficult to show that each function mentioned in Theorem 2.1 is powerful. Hence Theorem 2.1 is a corollary of

Theorem 2.5 *Assume that Γ is powerful.*

(a) *Γ simulates splines with respect to error $e(s,d) = 2^{-s}$.*

(b) *Assume that each activation function in* Γ *can be approximated (over the domain* $[-2^s, 2^s]$*) with error* 2^{-s} *by a spline-net* N_s *of size* s *and with constantly many layers. Then* Γ *is equivalent to splines.*

Remark 2.2 *Obviously,* $1/x$ *is powerful. Therefore Theorem 2.5 implies that constant-layer* $\{1/x\}$*-nets of size* s *approximate* $abs(x) = |x|$ *with error* 2^{-s}*. The degree of the resulting rational function will be polynomial in* s*. Thus Theorem 2.5 generalizes Newman's approximation of the absolute value by rational functions. (Newman, 1964)*

3 Equivalence of Activation Functions for Error s^{-d}

The lower bounds in the previous section suggest that the relaxed error bound $e(s,d) = s^{-d}$ is of importance. Indeed, it will turn out that many non-trivial smooth activation functions lead to nets that simulate $\{\sigma\}$-nets, **provided** the number of input units is counted when determining the size of the net. (We will see in section 4, that linear splines and the standard sigmoid are not equivalent if the number of inputs is **not** counted). The concept of *threshold-property* will be crucial for us.

Definition 3.1 *Let* Γ *be a collection of activation functions. We say that* Γ *has the threshold-property if there is a constant* c *such that the following two properties are satisfied for all* $m > 1$.

(a) *For each* $\gamma \in \Gamma$ *there is a threshold-net* $T_{\gamma,m}$ *with* c *layers and size* $(s+m)^c$ *which computes the binary representation of* $\gamma'(x)$ *where* $|\gamma(x) - \gamma'(x)| \le 2^{-m}$.

The input x *of* $T_{\gamma,m}$ *is given in binary and consists of* $2m+1$ *bits;* m *bits describe the integral part of* x*,* m *bits describe its fractional part and one bit indicates the sign.* $s+m$ *specifies the required number of output bits, i.e.* $s = \lceil \log_2(\sup\{\gamma(x) : -2^{m+1} < x < 2^{m+1}\})\rceil$.

(b) *There is a* Γ*-net with* c *layers, size* m^c *and Lipschitz bound* 2^{m^c} *which approximates the binary threshold over* $D = [-1,1] - [-1/m, 1/m]$ *with error* $1/m$.

We can now state the main result of this section.

Theorem 3.1 *Assume that* $e(s,d) = s^{-d}$.

(a) *Let* Γ *be a class of activation functions and assume that* Γ *has the threshold property. Then,* σ *and* Γ *are equivalent with respect to* e*. Moreover,* $\{\sigma\}$*-nets only require weights and thresholds of absolute value at most* s*. (Observe that* Γ*-nets are allowed to have weights as large as* 2^s*!)*

(b) *If* Γ *and* σ *are equivalent with respect to error* 2^{-s}*, then* Γ *and* σ *are equivalent with respect to error* s^{-d}.

(c) *Additionally, the following classes are equivalent to* $\{\sigma\}$*-nets with respect to* e*. (We assume throughout that all coefficients, weights and thresholds are bounded by* 2^s *for nets of size* s*).*

- *polynomial nets (i.e. polynomials of degree* s *appear as activation function for nets of size* s*),*

- *$\{\gamma\}$-nets, where γ is a suitable function and γ satisfies part (a) of Definition 3.1. (This includes the sine-function.)*
- *nets of linear splines*

The equivalence proof involves a first phase of extracting $O(d \log s)$ bits from the analog input. In a second phase, a binary computation is mimicked. The extraction process can be carried out with error s^{-1} (over the domain $[-1,1] - [-1/s, 1/s]$) once the binary threshold is approximated.

4 Computing boolean functions

As we have seen in Remark 2.1, the binary threshold (respectively linear splines) gains considerable power when *computing boolean functions* as compared to *approximating analog functions*. But sigmoidal nets will be far more powerful when only the number of neurons is counted and the number of input units is disregarded. For instance, sigmoidal nets are far more efficient for "squaring", i.e when computing:

$$M_n = \{(x,y) : x \in \{0,1\}^n, y \in \{0,1\}^{n^2} \text{ and } [x]^2 \geq [y]\} \quad (\text{where } [z] = \sum_i z_i).$$

Theorem 4.1 *A threshold-net computing M_n must have size at least $\Omega(\log n)$. But M_n can be computed by a σ-net with constantly many gates.*

The previously best known separation of threshold-nets and sigmoidal-nets is due to Maass, Schnitger and Sontag (Maass *et al.*, 1991). But their result only applies to threshold-nets with at most two layers; our result holds without any restriction on the number of layers. Theorem 4.1 can be generalized to separate threshold-nets and 3-times differentiable activation functions, but this smoothness requirement is more severe than the one assumed in (Maass *et al.*, 1991).

5 Conclusions

Our results show that good approximation performance (for error 2^{-s}) hinges on two properties, namely efficient approximation of polynomials and efficient approximation of the binary threshold. These two properties are shared by a quite large class of activation functions; i.e. powerful functions. Since (non-polynomial) rational functions are powerful, we were able to generalize Newman's approximation of $| x |$ by rational functions.

On the other hand, for a good approximation performance relative to the relaxed error bound s^{-d} it is already sufficient to efficiently approximate the binary threshold. Consequently, the class of equivalent activation functions grows considerably (but only if the number of input units is counted). The standard sigmoid is distinguished in that its approximation performance scales with the error bound: if larger error is allowed, then smaller weights suffice.

Moreover, the standard sigmoid is actually more powerful than the binary threshold even when computing boolean functions. In particular, the standard sigmoid is able to take advantage of its (non-trivial) smoothness to allow for more efficient nets.

Acknowledgements. We wish to thank R. Paturi, K. Y. Siu and V. P. Roychowdhury for helpful discussions. Special thanks go to W. Maass for suggesting this research, to E. Sontag for continued encouragement and very valuable advice and to J. Lambert for his never-ending patience.

The second author gratefully acknowledges partial support by NSF-CCR-9114545.

References

Arai, W. (1989), Mapping abilities of three-layer networks, *in* "Proc. of the International Joint Conference on Neural Networks", pp. 419-423.

Carrol, S. M., and Dickinson, B. W. (1989), Construction of neural nets using the Radon Transform,*in* "Proc. of the International Joint Conference on Neural Networks", pp. 607-611.

Cybenko, G. (1989), Approximation by superposition of a sigmoidal function, *Mathematics of Control, Signals, and System*, 2, pp. 303-314.

Funahashi, K. (1989), On the approximate realization of continuous mappings by neural networks, *Neural Networks*, 2, pp. 183-192.

Gallant, A. R., and White, H. (1988), There exists a neural network that does not make avoidable mistakes, *in* "Proc. of the International Joint Conference on Neural Networks", pp. 657-664.

Hornik, K., Stinchcombe, M., and White, H. (1989), Multilayer Feedforward Networks are Universal Approximators, *Neural Networks*, 2, pp. 359-366.

Irie, B., and Miyake, S. (1988), Capabilities of the three-layered perceptrons, *in* "Proc. of the International Joint Conference on Neural Networks", pp. 641-648.

Lapades, A., and Farbar, R. (1987), How neural nets work, *in* "Advances in Neural Information Processing Systems", pp. 442-456.

Maass, W., Schnitger, G., and Sontag, E. (1991), On the computational power of sigmoid versus boolean threshold circuits, *in* "Proc. of the 32nd Annual Symp. on Foundations of Computer Science", pp. 767-776.

Newman, D. J. (1964), Rational approximation to $| x |$, *Michigan Math. Journal*, 11, pp. 11-14.

Hecht-Nielson, R. (1989), Theory of backpropagation neural networks, *in* "Proc. of the International Joint Conference on Neural Networks", pp. 593-611.

Poggio, T., and Girosi, F. (1989), A theory of networks for Approximation and learning, *Artificial Intelligence Memorandum*, no 1140.

Reif, J. H. (1987), On threshold circuits and polynomial computation, *in* "Proceedings of the 2nd Annual Structure in Complexity theory", pp. 118-123.

Wei, Z., Yinglin, Y., and Qing, J. (1991), Approximation property of multi-layer neural networks (MLNN) and its application in nonlinear simulation, *in* "Proc. of the International Joint Conference on Neural Networks", pp. 171-176.

Rational Parametrizations of Neural Networks

Uwe Helmke
Department of Mathematics
University of Regensburg
Regensburg 8400 Germany

Robert C. Williamson
Department of Systems Engineering
Australian National University
Canberra 2601 Australia

Abstract

A connection is drawn between rational functions, the realization theory of dynamical systems, and feedforward neural networks. This allows us to parametrize single hidden layer scalar neural networks with (almost) arbitrary analytic activation functions in terms of strictly proper rational functions. Hence, we can solve the uniqueness of parametrization problem for such networks.

1 INTRODUCTION

Nonlinearly parametrized representations of functions $\phi: \mathbb{R} \to \mathbb{R}$ of the form

$$\phi(x) = \sum_{i=1}^{n} c_i \sigma(x - a_i) \qquad x \in \mathbb{R}, \tag{1.1}$$

have attracted considerable attention recently in the neural network literature. Here $\sigma: \mathbb{R} \to \mathbb{R}$ is typically a sigmoidal function such as

$$\sigma(x) = (1 + e^{-x})^{-1}, \tag{1.2}$$

but other choices than (1.2) are possible and of interest. Sometimes more complex representations such as

$$\phi(x) = \sum_{i=1}^{n} c_i \sigma(b_i x - a_i) \tag{1.3}$$

or even compositions of these are considered.

The purpose of this paper is to explore some parametrization issues regarding (1.1) and in particular to show the close connection these representations have with the standard system-theoretic realization theory for rational functions. We show how to define a generalization of (1.1) parametrized by (A, b, c), where A is a matrix over a field, and b and c are vectors. (This is made more precise below). The parametrization involves the (A, b, c) being used to define a rational function. The generalized σ-representation is then defined in terms of the rational function. This connection allows us to use results available for rational functions in the study of neural-network representations such as (1.1). It will also lead to an understanding of the geometry of the space of functions.

One of the main contributions of the paper is to show how in general neural network representations are related to rational functions. In this summary all proofs have been omitted. A complete version of the paper is available from the second author.

2 REALIZATIONS RELATIVE TO A FUNCTION

In this section we explore the relationship between sigmoidal representations of real analytic functions $\phi\colon \mathbb{I} \to \mathbb{R}$ defined on an interval $\mathbb{I} \subset \mathbb{R}$, real rational functions defined on the complex plane $\mathbb{C}$, and the well established realization theory for linear dynamical systems

$$\begin{aligned} \dot{x}(t) &= Ax(t) + bu(t) \\ y(t) &= cx(t) + du(t). \end{aligned}$$

For standard textbooks on systems theory and realization theory we refer to [5, 7].

Let $\mathbb{K}$ denote either the field $\mathbb{R}$ of real numbers or the field $\mathbb{C}$ of complex numbers. Let $\Delta \subset \mathbb{C}$ be an open and simply connected subset of the complex plane and let $\sigma\colon \Delta \to \mathbb{C}$ be an analytic function defined on Δ. For example, σ may be obtained by an analytic continuation of some sigmoidal function $\sigma\colon \mathbb{R} \to \mathbb{R}$ into the domain of holomorphy of the complex plane.

Let $T\colon \mathbb{V} \to \mathbb{V}$ be a linear operator on a finite-dimensional $\mathbb{K}$-vector space $\mathbb{V}$ such that T has all its eigenvalues in Δ. Let $\Gamma \subset \Delta$ be a simple closed curve, oriented in the counter-clockwise direction, enclosing all the eigenvalues of T in its interior. More generally, Γ may consist of a finite number of simple closed curves Γ_k with interiors Δ'_k such that the union of the domains Δ'_k contains all the eigenvalues of T. Then the matrix valued function $\sigma(T)$ is defined as the contour integral [8, p.44]

$$\sigma(T) := \frac{1}{2\pi i} \int_\Gamma \sigma(z)\,(zI - T)^{-1}\,\mathrm{d}z. \tag{2.1}$$

Note that for each linear operator $T\colon \mathbb{V} \to \mathbb{V}$, $\sigma(T)\colon \mathbb{V} \to \mathbb{V}$ is again a linear operator on $\mathbb{V}$.

If we now make the substitution $T := xI + A$ for $x \in \mathbb{C}$ and $A\colon \mathbb{V} \to \mathbb{V}$ $\mathbb{K}$-linear, then

$$\sigma(xI + A) = \frac{1}{2\pi i} \int_\Gamma \sigma(z)\,((z - x)I - A)^{-1}\,\mathrm{d}z$$

becomes a function of the complex variable x, at least as long as Γ contains all the eigenvalues of $xI + A$. Using the change of variables $\xi := z - x$ we obtain

$$\sigma(xI + A) = \frac{1}{2\pi i} \int_{\Gamma'} \sigma(x + \xi)\, (\xi I - A)^{-1}\, \mathrm{d}\xi \tag{2.2}$$

where $\Gamma' = \Gamma - x \subset \Delta$ encircles all the eigenvalues of A.

Given an arbitrary vector $b \in \mathbb{V}$ and a linear functional $c\colon \mathbb{V} \to \mathbb{K}$ we achieve the representation

$$\boxed{c\sigma(xI + A)b = \frac{1}{2\pi i} \int_{\Gamma} \sigma(x + \xi)\, c(\xi I - A)^{-1} b\, \mathrm{d}\xi.} \tag{2.3}$$

Note that in (2.3) the simple closed curve $\Gamma \subset \mathbb{C}$ is arbitrary, as long as it satisfies the two conditions

$$\Gamma \text{ encircles all the eigenvalues of } A \tag{2.4}$$

$$x + \Gamma = \{x + \xi \mid \xi \in \Gamma\} \subset \Delta. \tag{2.5}$$

Let $\phi\colon \mathbb{I} \to \mathbb{R}$ be a real analytic function in a single variable $x \in \mathbb{I}$, defined on an interval $\mathbb{I} \subset \mathbb{R}$.

Definition 2.1 *A quadruple (A, b, c, d) is called a finite-dimensional* σ-realization *of $\phi\colon \mathbb{I} \to \mathbb{R}$ over a field of constants $\mathbb{K}$ if for all $x \in \mathbb{I}$*

$$\phi(x) = c\sigma(xI + A)b + d \tag{2.6}$$

holds, where the right hand side is given by (2.3) and Γ is assumed to satisfy the conditions (2.4)-(2.5). Here $d \in \mathbb{K}$, $b \in \mathbb{V}$, and $A\colon \mathbb{V} \to \mathbb{V}$, $c\colon \mathbb{V} \to \mathbb{K}$ are $\mathbb{K}$-linear maps and $\mathbb{V}$ is a finite dimensional $\mathbb{K}$-vector space.

Definition 2.2 *The* dimension *(or degree) of a σ-realization is* $\dim_{\mathbb{K}} \mathbb{V}$. *The* σ-degree *of ϕ, denoted $\delta_\sigma(\phi)$, is the minimal dimension of all σ-realizations of ϕ. A* minimal σ-realization *is a σ-realization of minimal dimension $\delta_\sigma(\phi)$.*

σ-realizations are a straightforward extension of the system-theoretic notion of a realization of a transfer function. In this paper we will address the following specific questions concerning σ-realizations.

Q1 What are the existence and uniqueness properties of σ-realizations?

Q2 How can one characterize minimal σ-realizations?

Q3 How can one compute $\delta_\sigma(\phi)$?

3 EXISTENCE OF σ-REALIZATIONS

We now consider the question of existence of σ-realizations. To set the stage, we consider the systems theory case $\sigma(x) = x^{-1}$ first. Assume we are given a formal power series

$$\phi(x) = \sum_{i=0}^{N} \frac{\phi_i}{i!} x^i, \quad N \leq \infty, \tag{3.1}$$

and that (A,b,c) is a σ-realization in the sense of definition 2.1. The Taylor expansion of $c(xI+A)^{-1}b$ at 0 is (for A nonsingular)

$$c(xI+A)^{-1}b=\sum_{i=0}^{\infty}(-1)^i cA^{-(i+1)}bx^i. \tag{3.2}$$

Thus

$$\frac{\phi_i}{i!}=(-1)^i cA^{-(i+1)}b, \qquad i=0,\dots,N. \tag{3.3}$$

if and only if the expansions of (3.1) and (3.2) coincide up to order N. Observe [7] that

$$\begin{aligned} & \phi(x)=c(xI+A)^{-1}b \text{ and } \dim\mathbb{V}<\infty \\ \Longleftrightarrow \quad & \phi(x) \text{ is rational with } \phi(\infty)=0. \end{aligned}$$

The possibility of solving (3.3) is now easily seen as follows. Let $\mathbb{V}=\mathbb{R}^{N+1}=\mathrm{Map}(\{0,\dots,N\},\mathbb{R})$ be the finite or infinite $(N+1)$-fold product space of $\mathbb{R}$. (Here $\mathrm{Map}(X,Y)$ denotes the set of all maps from X to Y.) If N is finite let

$$\begin{aligned} A^{-1} &= -\begin{bmatrix} 0 & \cdots & 0 & 1 \\ 1 & \cdots & 0 & 0 \\ & \ddots & \vdots & \vdots \\ 0 & \cdots & 1 & 0 \end{bmatrix} \in \mathbb{R}^{(N+1)\times(N+1)}, \\ b &= (1\,0\,\cdots\,0)^T\in\mathbb{V}, \quad c=\left(\frac{\phi_N}{N!},\phi_0,\phi_1,\frac{\phi_2}{2!},\dots,\frac{\phi_{N-1}}{(N-1)!}\right). \end{aligned} \tag{3.4}$$

For $N=\infty$ we take $A^{-1}\colon\mathbb{R}^{\mathbb{N}}\to\mathbb{R}^{\mathbb{N}}$ as a shift operator

$$\begin{aligned} & A^{-1}\colon\mathbb{R}^{\mathbb{N}}\to\mathbb{R}^{\mathbb{N}} \\ & A^{-1}\colon(x_0,x_1,\dots)\mapsto-(0,x_0,x_1,\dots) \\ \text{and}\quad & b=(1,0,\dots),\quad c=(0,\phi_0,\phi_1,\phi_2/2!,\dots). \end{aligned} \tag{3.5}$$

We then have

Lemma 3.1 *Let $\sigma(x)=\sum_i\frac{\sigma_i}{i!}x^i$ be analytic at $x=0$ and let (A,b,c) be a σ-realization of the formal power series $\phi(x)=\sum_{i=0}^{N}\frac{\phi_i}{i!}x^i$, $N\le\infty$ (i.e. matching of the first $N+1$ derivatives of $\phi(x)$ and $c\sigma(xI+A)b$ at $x=0$). Then*

$$\phi_i=c\sigma^{(i)}(A)b \quad \textit{for } i=0,\dots,N. \tag{3.6}$$

Observe that for $\sigma(x)=x^{-1}$ we have $\sigma^{(i)}(-A)=i!(A^{-1})^{i+1}$ as before. The existence part of the realization question Q1 can now be restated as

Q4 Given $\sigma(x):=\sum_{i=0}^{\infty}\frac{\sigma_i}{i!}x^i$ and a sequence of real numbers $(\phi_0,\dots,\phi_N)$, does there exist an (A,b,c) with

$$\phi_i=c\sigma^{(i)}(A)b,\quad i=0,\dots,N? \tag{3.7}$$

Thus question Q1 is essentially a Loewner interpolation question [1, 3].

Let $\gamma_\ell = cA^\ell b$, $\ell \in \mathbb{N}_0$, and let

$$F = \begin{bmatrix} \sigma_0 & \sigma_1 & \sigma_2 & \cdots \\ \sigma_1 & \sigma_2 & \sigma_3 & \cdots \\ \sigma_2 & \sigma_3 & \sigma_4 & \cdots \\ \vdots & \vdots & \vdots & \ddots \end{bmatrix} = (\sigma_{i+j})_{i,j=0}^{\infty}. \tag{3.8}$$

Write

$$[\gamma] = \begin{bmatrix} \gamma_0 \\ \gamma_1 \\ \gamma_2/2! \\ \gamma_3/3! \\ \vdots \end{bmatrix}, \quad \text{and} \quad [\phi] = \begin{bmatrix} \phi_0 \\ \phi_1 \\ \phi_2 \\ \vdots \end{bmatrix}. \tag{3.9}$$

Then (3.6) (for $N = \infty$) can formally be written as

$$[\phi] = F \cdot [\gamma]. \tag{3.10}$$

Of course, any meaningful interpretation of (3.10) requires that the infinite sums $\sum_{j=0}^{\infty} \frac{\sigma_{i+j}}{j!}\gamma_j$, $i \in \mathbb{N}_0$, exist. This happens, for example, if $\sum_{j=0}^{\infty} \sigma_{i+j}^2 < \infty$, $i \in \mathbb{N}_0$ and $\sum_{j=0}^{\infty} (\gamma_j/j!)^2 < \infty$ exist. We have already seen that every finite or infinite sequence $[\gamma]$ has a realization (A, b, c). Thus we obtain

Corollary 3.2 *A function $\phi(x)$ admits a σ-realization if and only if $[\phi] \in$* image(F).

Corollary 3.3 *Let $H = (\gamma_{i+j})_{i,j=0}^{\infty}$. There exists a finite dimensional σ-realization of $\phi(x)$ if and only if $[\phi] = F[\gamma]$ with* rank $H < \infty$. *In this case $\delta_\sigma(\phi) =$* rank H.

4 UNIQUENESS OF σ-REALIZATIONS

In this section we consider the uniqueness of the representation (2.3).

Definition 4.1 (c.f. [2]) *A system $\{g_1, \ldots, g_n\}$ of continuous functions $g_i\colon \mathbb{I} \to \mathbb{R}$, defined on an interval $\mathbb{I} \subset \mathbb{R}$, is said to satisfy a* Haar* condition of order *n* on $\mathbb{I}$ *if $g_1, \ldots, g_n$ are linearly independent, i.e. For every $c_1, \ldots, c_n \in \mathbb{R}$ with $\sum_{i=1}^{n} c_i g_i(x) = 0$ for all $x \in \mathbb{I}$, then $c_1 = \cdots = c_n = 0$.*

Remark The Haar* condition is implied by the stronger classical Haar condition that

$$\det \begin{bmatrix} g_1(x_1) & \cdots & g_1(x_n) \\ \vdots & & \vdots \\ g_n(x_1) & \cdots & g_n(x_n) \end{bmatrix} \neq 0$$

for all distinct $(x_i)_{i=1}^{n}$ in $\mathbb{I}$. Equivalently, if $\sum_{i=1}^{n} c_i g_i(x)$ has n distinct roots in $\mathbb{I}$, then $c_1 = \cdots = c_n = 0$.

Definition 4.2 *A subset A of $\mathbb{C}$ is called self-conjugate if $a \in A$ implies $\overline{a} \in A$.*

Let $\sigma\colon \mathbb{R} \to \mathbb{R}$ be a continuous function and define $\sigma_{z_i}^{(j)}(x) := \sigma^{(j)}(x + z_i)$. Let

$$\kappa := (\kappa_1, \dots, \kappa_m) \text{ where } \sum_{j=1}^{m} \kappa_j = n, \; \kappa_j \in \mathbb{N}, \; \kappa_j \geq 1, \; j = 1, \dots, m$$

denote a combination of n of size m. For a given combination $\kappa = (\kappa_1, \dots, \kappa_m)$ of n, let $I := \{1, \dots, m\}$ and let $J_i := \{1, \dots, \kappa_i\}$. Let $Z_m := \{z_1, \dots, z_m\}$ and let

$$\sigma(\kappa, Z_m) := \{\sigma_{z_i}^{(j-1)} : i \in I, \, j \in J_i\}. \tag{4.1}$$

Definition 4.3 *If for all $m \leq n$, for all combinations $\kappa = (\kappa_1, \dots, \kappa_m)$ of n of size m, and for any self-conjugate set Z_m of distinct points, $\sigma(\kappa, Z_m)$ satisfies a Haar* condition of order n, then σ is said to be* Haar generating of order n.

Theorem 4.4 (Uniqueness) *Let $\sigma\colon \mathbb{R} \to \mathbb{R}$ be Haar generating of order at least $2n$ on $\mathbb{I}$ and let (A, b, c) and $(\tilde{A}, \tilde{b}, \tilde{c})$ be minimal σ-realizations of order n of functions ϕ and $\tilde{\phi}$ respectively. Then the following equivalence holds*

$$\begin{aligned} & c\sigma(xI + A)b = \tilde{c}\sigma(xI + \tilde{A})\tilde{b} \quad \forall x \in \mathbb{I} \\ & \iff \\ & c(\xi I - A)^{-1}b = \tilde{c}(\xi I - \tilde{A})^{-1}\tilde{b} \quad \forall \xi \in \mathbb{R}. \end{aligned} \tag{4.2}$$

Conversely, if (4.2) holds for almost all order n triples (A, b, c), $(\tilde{A}, \tilde{b}, \tilde{c})$, then $\sigma\colon \mathbb{R} \to \mathbb{R}$ is Haar generating on $\mathbb{I}$ of order $\geq n$.

The following result gives examples of activation functions $\sigma\colon \mathbb{R} \to \mathbb{R}$ which are Haar generating.

Lemma 4.5 *Let $d \in \mathbb{N}_0$. Then 1) The function $\sigma(x) = x^{-d}$ is Haar generating of arbitrary order. 2) The monomial $\sigma(x) = x^d$ is Haar generating of order $d + 1$. 3) The function e^{-x^2} is Haar generating of arbitrary order.*

Remark A simple example of a σ which is not Haar generating of order ≥ 2 is $\sigma(x) = e^x$. In fact, in this case $\sigma(x + z_j) = c_j\sigma(x + z_i)$ for $c_j = e^{z_j - z_i}$, $j = 2, \dots, n$.

Remark The function $\sigma(x) = (1+e^{-x})^{-1}$ is *not* Haar generating of any order ≥ 2. By the periodicity of the complex exponential function, $\sigma(x + 2\pi i) = \sigma(x - 2\pi i)$, $i = \sqrt{-1}$, for all x. Thus the Haar* condition fails for $Z_2 = \{2\pi i, -2\pi i\}$.

In particular, the above uniqueness result fails for the standard sigmoid case. In order to cover this case we need a further definition.

Definition 4.6 *Let $\Omega = \overline{\Omega} \subset \mathbb{C}$ be a self-conjugate subset of $\mathbb{C}$. A function $\sigma\colon \mathbb{R} \to \mathbb{R}$ is said to be* Haar generating of order n on Ω, *if for all $m \leq n$, for all combinations $\kappa = (\kappa_1, \dots, \kappa_m)$ of n of size m, and for any self-conjugate subset $Z_m \subset \Omega$ of distinct points of Ω, $\sigma(\kappa, Z_m)$ satisfies a Haar* condition of order n.*

Of course for $\Omega = \mathbb{C}$, this definition coincides with definition 4.3.

Theorem 4.7 (Local Uniqueness) *Let $\sigma\colon \mathbb{R} \to \mathbb{R}$ be analytic and let $\Omega \subset \mathbb{C}$ be a self-conjugate subset contained in the domain of holomorphy of σ. Let $\mathbb{I}$ be a nontrivial subinterval of $\Omega \cap \mathbb{R}$. Suppose $\sigma\colon \mathbb{R} \to \mathbb{R}$ is Haar generating on Ω of order at least $2n$, $n \in \mathbb{N}$. Then for any two minimal σ-realizations (A, b, c) and $(\tilde{A}, \tilde{b}, \tilde{c})$ of orders at most n with* spect A, spect $\tilde{A} \in \Omega$ *the following equivalence holds:*

$$(4.3) \qquad \begin{array}{c} c\sigma(xI + A)b = \tilde{c}\sigma(xI + \tilde{A})\tilde{b} \quad \forall x \in \mathbb{I} \\ \iff \\ c(\xi I - A)^{-1}b = \tilde{c}(\xi I - \tilde{A})^{-1}\tilde{b} \quad \forall \xi \in \mathbb{R}. \end{array}$$

Lemma 4.8 *Let $\Omega := \{z \in \mathbb{C}\colon |\Im z| < \pi\}$. Then the standard sigmoid function $\sigma(x) = (1 + e^{-x})^{-1}$ is Haar generating on Ω of arbitrary order.*

5 MAIN RESULT

As a consequence of the uniqueness theorems 4.4 and 4.7 we can now state our main result on the existence of minimal σ-realizations of a function $\phi(x)$. It extends a parallel result for standard transfer function realizations, where $\sigma(x) = x^{-1}$.

Theorem 5.1 (Realization) *Let $\Omega \subset \mathbb{C}$ be a self-conjugate subset, contained in the domain of holomorphy of a real meromorphic function $\sigma\colon \mathbb{R} \to \mathbb{R}$. Suppose σ is Haar generating on Ω of order at least $2n$ and assume $\phi(x)$ has a finite dimensional realization (A, b, c) of dimension at most n such that A has all its eigenvalues in Ω.*

1. *There exists a minimal σ-realization (A_1, b_1, c_1) of $\phi(x)$ of degree $\delta_\sigma(\phi) \leq$* $\dim(A, b, c)$. *Furthermore, there exists an invertible matrix S such that*

$$(5.1) \qquad SAS^{-1} = \begin{bmatrix} A_1 & A_2 \\ 0 & A_3 \end{bmatrix}, \quad Sb = \begin{bmatrix} b_1 \\ 0 \end{bmatrix}, \quad cS^{-1} = [c_1, c_2].$$

2. *If (A_1, b_1, c_1) and (A_1', b_1', c_1') are minimal σ-realizations of $\phi(x)$ such that the eigenvalues of A_1 and A_1' are contained in Ω, then there exists a unique invertible matrix S such that*

$$(5.2) \qquad (A_1', b_1', c_1') = (SA_1S^{-1}, Sb_1, c_1S^{-1}).$$

3. *A σ-realization (A, b, c) is minimal if and only if (A, b, c) is controllable and observable; i.e. if and only if (A, b, c) satisfies the generic rank conditions*

$$\operatorname{rank}(b, Ab, \ldots, A^{n-1}b) = n, \qquad \operatorname{rank}\begin{bmatrix} c \\ cA \\ \vdots \\ cA^{n-1} \end{bmatrix} = n$$

for $A \in \mathbb{K}^{n\times n}$, $b \in \mathbb{K}^n$, $c^T \in \mathbb{K}^n$.

Remark The use of the terms "observable" and "controllable" is solely for formal correspondence with standard systems theory. There are no dynamical systems actually under consideration here.

Remark Note that for any σ-realization (A, b, c) of the form $A = \begin{bmatrix} A_{11} & A_{12} \\ 0 & A_{22} \end{bmatrix}$, $b = \begin{bmatrix} b_1 \\ 0 \end{bmatrix}$, $c = [c_1, c_2]$, we have $\sigma(A) = \begin{bmatrix} \sigma(A_{11}) & * \\ 0 & \sigma(A_{22}) \end{bmatrix}$ and thus $c\sigma(xI + A)b = c_1\sigma(xI + A_{11})b_1$. Thus transformations of the above kind always *reduce* the dimension of a σ-realization.

Corollary 5.2 ([9]) *Let* $\sigma(x) = (1 + e^{-x})^{-1}$ *and let* $\phi(x) = \sum_{i=1}^{n} c_i\sigma(x - a_i) = \sum_{i=1}^{n} c_i'\sigma(x - a_i')$ *be two minimal length σ-representations with* $|\Im a_i| < \pi$, $|\Im a_i'| < \pi$, $i = 1, \dots, n$. *Then* $(a_i', c_i') = (a_{p(i)}, c_{p(i)})$ *for a unique permutation* $p\colon \{1, \dots, n\} \to \{1, \dots, n\}$. *In particular, minimal length representation (1.1) with real coefficients a_i and c_i are unique up to a permutation of the summands.*

6 CONCLUSIONS

We have drawn a connection between the realization theory for linear dynamical systems and neural network representations. There are further connections (not discussed in this summary) between representations of the form (1.3) and rational functions of two variables. There are other questions concerning diagonalizable realizations and Jordan forms. Details are given in the full length version of this paper. Open questions include the problem of partial realizations [4, 6].[1]

REFERENCES

[1] A. C. Antoulas and B. D. O. Anderson, On the Scalar Rational Interpolation Problem, *IMA Journal of Mathematical Control and Information*, **3** (1986), pp. 61–88.

[2] E. W. Cheney, *Introduction to Approximation Theory*, Chelsea Publishing Company, New York, 1982.

[3] W. F. Donoghue, Jr, *Monotone Matrix Functions and Analytic Continuation*, Springer-Verlag, Berlin, 1974.

[4] W. B. Gragg and A. Lindquist, On the Partial Realization Problem, *Linear Algebra and its Applications*, **50** (1983), pp. 277–319.

[5] T. Kailath, *Linear Systems*, Prentice-Hall, Englewood Cliffs, 1980.

[6] R. E. Kalman, On Partial Realizations, Transfer Functions, and Canonical Forms, *Acta Polytechnica Scandinavica*, **31** (1979), pp. 9–32.

[7] R. E. Kalman, P. L. Falb and M. A. Arbib, *Topics in Mathematical System Theory*, McGraw-Hill, New York, 1969.

[8] T. Kato, *Perturbation Theory for Linear Operators*, Springer-Verlag, Berlin, 1966.

[9] R. C. Williamson and U. Helmke, Existence and Uniqueness Results for Neural Network Approximations, To appear, IEEE Transactions on Neural Networks, 1993.

[1]This work was supported by the Australian Research Council, the Australian Telecommunications and Electronics Research Board, and the Boeing Commercial Aircraft Company (thanks to John Moore). Thanks to Eduardo Sontag for helpful comments also.

Learning Cellular Automaton Dynamics with Neural Networks

N H Wulff[*] and **J A Hertz**[†]
CONNECT, the Niels Bohr Institute and Nordita
Blegdamsvej 17, DK-2100 Copenhagen Ø, Denmark

Abstract

We have trained networks of $\Sigma-\Pi$ units with short-range connections to simulate simple cellular automata that exhibit complex or chaotic behaviour. Three levels of learning are possible (in decreasing order of difficulty): learning the underlying automaton rule, learning asymptotic dynamical behaviour, and learning to extrapolate the training history. The levels of learning achieved with and without weight sharing for different automata provide new insight into their dynamics.

1 INTRODUCTION

Neural networks have been shown to be capable of learning the dynamical behaviour exhibited by chaotic time series composed of measurements of a single variable among many in a complex system [1, 2, 3]. In this work we consider instead cellular automaton arrays (CA)[4], a class of many-degree-of-freedom systems which exhibits very complex dynamics, including universal computation. We would like to know whether neural nets can be taught to imitate these dynamics, both locally and globally.

One could say we are turning the usual paradigm for studying such systems on its head. Conventionally, one is given the rule by which each automaton updates its state, and the (nontrivial) problem is to find what kind of global dynamical

[*]Present address: NEuroTech A/S, Copenhagen, Denmark

[†]Address until October 1993: Laboratory of Neuropsychology, NIMH, Bethesda MD 20892. email: hertz@nordita.dk

behaviour results. Here we suppose that we are given the history of some CA, and we would like, if possible, to find the rule that generated it.

We will see that a network can have different degrees of success in this task, depending on the constraints we place on the learning. Furthermore, we will be able to learn something about the dynamics of the automata themselves from knowing what level of learning is possible under what constraints.

This note reports some preliminary investigations of these questions. We study only the simplest automata that produce chaotic or complex dynamic behaviour. Nevertheless, we obtain some nontrivial results which lead to interesting conjectures for future investigation.

A CA is a lattice of formal computing units, each of which is characterized by a state variable $S_i(t)$, where i labels the site in the lattice and t is the (digital) time. Every such unit updates itself according to a particular rule or function $f(\ )$ of its own state and that of the other units in its local neighbourhood. The rule is the same for all units, and the updatings of all units are simultaneous.

Different models are characterized by the nature of the state variable (e.g. binary, continuous, vector, etc), the dimensionality of the lattice, and the choice of neighbourhood. In the two cases we study here, the neighbourhoods are of size $N = 3$, consisting of the unit itself and its two immediate neighbours on a chain, and $N = 9$, consisting of the unit itself and its 8 nearest neighbours on a square lattice (the 'Moore neighbourhood'). We will consider only binary units, for which we take $S_i(t) = \pm 1$. Thus, if the neighbourhood (including the unit itself) includes N sites, $f(\ )$ is a Boolean function on the N-hypercube. There are 2^{2^N} such functions.

Wolfram [4] has divided the rules for such automata further into three classes:

1. Class 1: rules that lead to a uniform state.
2. Class 2: rules that lead to simple stable or periodic patterns.
3. Class 3: rules that lead to chaotic patterns.
4. Class 4: rules that lead to complex, long-lived transient patterns.

Rules in the fourth class lie near (in a sense not yet fully understood [5]) a critical boundary between classes 2 and 3. They lead eventually to asymptotic behaviour in class 2 (or possibly 3); what distinguishes them is the length of the transient. It is classes 3 and 4 that we are interested in here.

More specifically, for class 3 we expect that after the (short) initial transients, the motion is confined to some sort of attractor. Different attractors may be reached for a given rule, depending on initial conditions. For such systems we will focus on the dynamics on these attractors, not on the short transients. We will want to know what we can learn from a given history about the attractor characterizing it, about the asymptotic dynamics of the system generally (i.e. about all attractors), and, if possible, about the underlying rule.

For class 4 CA, in contrast, only the transients are of interest. Different initial conditions will give rise to very different transient histories; indeed, this sensitivity is the dynamical basis for the capability for universal computation that has been proved for some of these systems. Here we will want to know what we can learn from a portion of such a history about its future, as well as about the underlying rule.

2 REPRESENTING A CA AS A NETWORK

Any Boolean function of N arguments can be implemented by a $\Sigma-\Pi$ unit of order $P \leq N$ with a threshold activation function, i.e. there exist weights $w^0_{j_1 j_2 \cdots j_P}$ such that

$$f(S_1, S_2 \cdots S_N) = \text{sgn}\left[\sum_{j_1, j_2, \cdots j_P} w^0_{j_1 j_2 \cdots j_P} S_{j_1} S_{j_2} \cdots S_{j_P}\right]. \tag{1}$$

The indices j_k run over the sites in the neighbourhood (1 to N) and zero, which labels a constant formal bias unit $S_0 = 1$. Because the updating rule we are looking for is the same for the entire lattice, the weight $w^0_{j_1 \cdots j_P}$ doesn't depend on i. Furthermore, because of the discrete nature of the outputs, the weights that implement a given rule are not unique; rather, there is a region of weight space for each rule.

Although we could work with other architectures, it is natural to study networks with the same structure as the CA to be simulated. We therefore make a lattice of formal $\Sigma - \Pi$ neurons with short-range connections, which update themselves according to

$$V_i(t+1) = g\left[\sum_{j_1 \cdots j_P} w_{j_1 \cdots j_P} V_{j_1}(t) \cdots V_{j_P}(t)\right], \tag{2}$$

In these investigations, we have assumed that we know *a priori* what the relevant neighbourhood size is, thereby fixing the connectivity of the network. At the end of the day, we will take the limit where the gain of the activation function g becomes infinite. However, during learning we use finite gain and continuous-valued units.

We know that the order P of our $\Sigma - \Pi$ units need not be higher than the neighbourhood size N. However, in most cases a smaller P will do. More precisely, a network with any $P > \frac{1}{2}N$ can in principle (i.e. given the right learning algorithm and sufficient training examples) implement almost all possible rules. This is an asymptotic result for large N but is already quite accurate for $N = 3$, where only two of the 256 possible rules are not implementable by a second-order unit, and $N = 5$, where we found from simple learning experiments that 99.87% of 10000 randomly-chosen rules could be implemented by a third-order unit.

3 LEARNING

Having chosen a suitable value of P, we can begin our main task: training the network to simulate a CA, with the training examples $\{S_i(t) \to S_i(t+1)\}$ taken from a particular known history.

The translational invariance of the CA suggests that weight sharing is appropriate in the learning algorithm. On the other hand, we can imagine situations in which we did not possess *a priori* knowledge that the CA rule was the same for all units, or where we only had access to the automaton state in one neighbourhood. This case is analogous to the conventional time series extrapolation paradigm, where we typically only have access to a few variables in a large system. The difference is that here the accessible variables are binary rather than continuous. In these situations we should or are constrained to learn without each unit having access to error information at other units. In what follows we will perform the training both with and without weight sharing. The differences in what can be learned in the two cases will give interesting information about the CA dynamics being simulated.

Most of our results are for chaotic (class 3) CA. For these systems, this training history is taken after initial transients have died out. Thus many of the 2^N possible examples necessary to specify the rule at each site may be missing from the training set, and it is possible that our training procedure will not result in the network learning the underlying rule of the original system. It might instead learn another rule that coincides with the true one on the training examples. This is even more likely if we are not using weight sharing, because then a unit at one site does not have access to examples from the training history at other sites.

However, we may relax our demand on the network, asking only that it evolve exactly like the original system when it is started in a configuration the original system could be in after transients have died out (i.e. on an attractor of the original system). Thus we are restricting the test set in a way that is "fairer" to the network, given the instruction it has received.

Of course, if the CA has more than one attractor, several rules which yield the same evolution on one attractor need not do so on another one. It is therefore possible that a network can learn the attractor of the training history (i.e. will simulate the original system correctly on a part of the history subsequent to the training sequence) but will not be found to evolve correctly when tested on data from another attractor.

For class 4 automata, we cannot formulate the distinctions between different levels of learning meaningfully in terms of attractors, since the object of interest is the transient portion of the history. Nevertheless, we can still ask whether a network trained on part of the transient can learn the full rule, whether it can simulate the dynamics for other initial conditions, or whether it can extrapolate the training history.

We therefore distinguish three degrees of successful learning:

1. *Learning the rule*, where the network evolves exactly like the original system *from any initial configuration.*
2. *Learning the dynamics*, the intermediate case where the network can simulate the original system exactly after transients, irrespective of initial conditions, despite not having learned the full rule.
3. *Learning to continue the dynamics*, where the successful simulation of the original system is only achieved for the particular initial condition used to generate the training history.

Our networks are recurrent, but because they have no hidden units, they can be trained by a simple variant of the delta-rule algorithm. It can be obtained formally from gradient descent on a modified cross entropy

$$E = \frac{1}{2}\sum_{it}\left[(1+S_i(t))\log\frac{1+S_i(t)}{1+V_i(t)} + (1-S_i(t))\log\frac{1-S_i(t)}{1-V_i(t)}\right]\Theta[-S_i(t)V_i(t)] \quad (3)$$

We used the online version:

$$\Delta w_{j_1 j_2 \cdots j_P} = \eta\Theta[-S_i(t+1)V_i(t+1)][S_i(t+1) - V_i(t+1)]V_{j_1}(t)V_{j_2}(t)\cdots V_{j_P}(t) \quad (4)$$

This is like an extension of the *Adatron* algorithm[6] to $\Sigma-\Pi$ units, but with the added feature that we are using a nonlinear activation function.

The one-dimensional $N = 3$ automata we simulated were the 9 *legal* chaotic ones identified by Wolfram [4]. Using his system for labeling the rules, these are rules 18, 22, 54, 90, 122, 126, 146, 150, and 182. We used networks of order $P = 3$ so that all rules were learnable. (Rule 150 would not have been learnable by a second-order net.) Each network was a chain 60 units long, subjected to periodic boundary conditions.

The training histories $\{S_i(t)\}$ were 1000 steps long, beginning 100 steps after randomly chosen initial configurations. To test for learning the rules, all neighbourhood configurations were checked at every site. To test for learning the dynamics, the CA were reinitialized with different random starting configurations and run 100 steps to eliminate transients, after which new test histories of length 100 steps were constructed. Networks were then tested on 100 such histories. The test set for continuing the dynamics was made simply by allowing the CA that had generated the training set to continue for 100 more steps.

There are no class 4 CA among the one-dimensional $N = 3$ systems. As an example of such a rule, we chose the *Game of Life* which is defined on a square lattice with a neighbourhood size $N = 9$ and has been proved capable of universal computation (see, e.g. [7, 8]). We worked with a lattice of 60×60 units.

The training history for the Game of Life consisted of 200 steps in the transient. The trained networks were tested, as in the case of the chaotic one-dimensional systems, on all possible configurations at every site (learning the rule), on other transient histories generated from different initial conditions (learning the dynamics), and on the evolution of the original system immediately following the training history (learning to continue the dynamics).

4 RESULTS

With weight sharing, it proved possible to learn the dynamics for all 9 of the one-dimensional chaotic rules very easily. In fact, it took no more than 10 steps of the training history to achieve this.

Learning the underlying rules proved harder. After training on the histories of 1000 steps, the networks were able to do so in only 4 of the 9 cases. No qualitative difference in the two groups of patterns is evident to us from looking at their histories (Fig. 1). Nevertheless, we conclude that their ergodic properties must be different, at least quantitatively.

Life was also easy with weight sharing. Our network succeed in learning the underlying rule starting almost anywhere in the long transient.

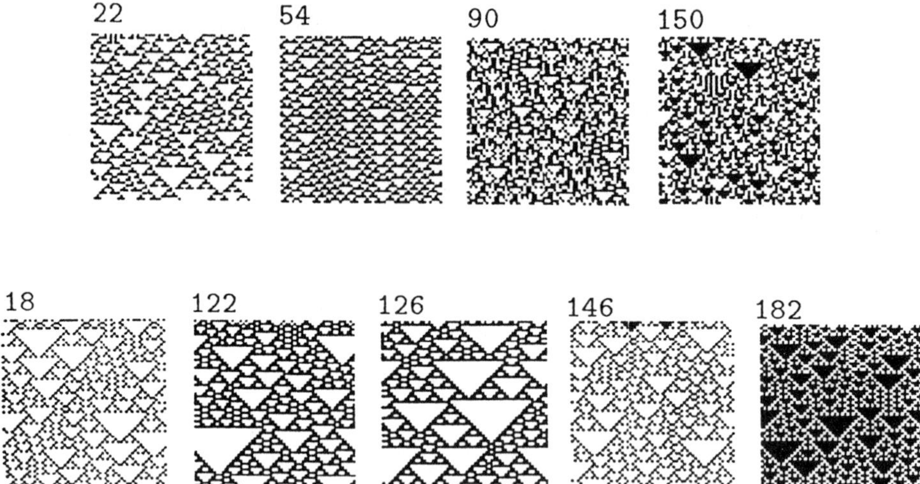

Figure 1: Histories of the 4 one-dimensional rules that could be learned (top) and the 5 that could not (bottom). (Learning with weight sharing.)

Without weight sharing, all learning naturally proved more difficult. While it was possible to learn to continue the dynamics for all the one-dimensional chaotic rules, it proved impossible except in one case (rule 22) to learn the dynamics within the training history of 1000 steps. The networks failed on about 25% of the test histories. It was never possible to learn the underlying rule. Thus, apparently these chaotic states are not as homogeneous as they appear (at least on the time scale of the training period).

Life is also difficult without weight sharing. Our network was unable even to continue the dynamics from histories of several hundred steps in the transient (Fig. 2).

5 DISCUSSION

In previous studies of learning chaotic behaviour in single-variable time series (e.g. [1, 2, 3]), the test to which networks have been put has been to extrapolate the training series, i.e. to continue the dynamics. We have found that this is also possible in cellular automata for all the chaotic rules we have studied, even when only local information about the training history is available to the units. Thus, the CA evolution history *at any site* is rich enough to permit error-free extrapolation.

However, local training data are not sufficient (except in one system, rule 22) to permit our networks to pass the more stringent test of learning the dynamics. Thus, viewed from any single site, the different attractors of these systems are dissimilar enough that data from one do not permit generalization to another.

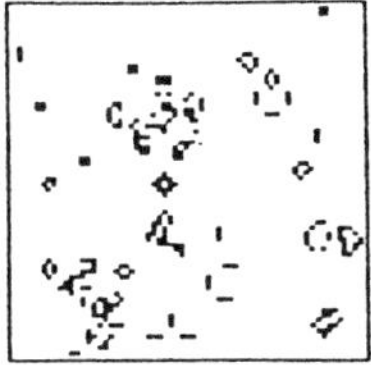

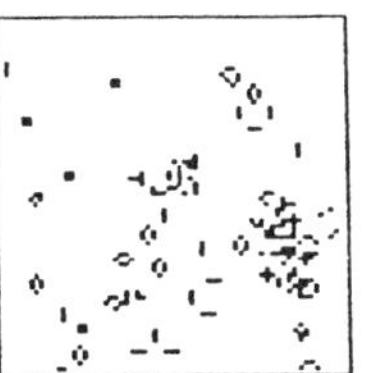

Figure 2: The original Game of Life CA (left) and the network (right), both 20 steps after the end of the training history. (Training done without weight sharing.)

With the access to training data from other sites implied by weight sharing, the situation changes dramatically. Learning the dynamics is then very easy, implying that all possible asymptotic local dynamics that could occur for any initial condition actually do occur *somewhere in the system* in any given history.

Furthermore, with weight sharing, not only the dynamics but also the underlying rule can be learned for some rules. This suggests that these rules are ergodic, in the sense that all configurations occur somewhere in the system at some time. This division of the chaotic rules into two classes according to this global ergodicity is a new finding.

Turning to our class 4 example, Life proves to be impossible without weight sharing, even by our most lenient test, continuing the dynamics. Thus, although one might be tempted to think that the transient in Life is so long that it can be treated operationally as if it were a chaotic attractor, it cannot. For real chaotic attractors, in both in the CA studied here and continuous dynamical systems, networks can learn to continue the dynamics on the basis of local data, while in Life they cannot.

On the other hand, the result that the rule of Life is easy to learn with weight sharing implies that looked at globally, the history of the transient is quite rich. Somewhere in the system, it contains sufficient information (together with the *a priori* knowledge that a second-order network is sufficient) to allow us to predict the evolution from any configuration correctly.

This study is a very preliminary one and raises more questions than it answers. We would like to know whether the results we have obtained for these few simple systems are generic to complex and chaotic CA. To answer this question we will have to study systems in higher dimensions and with larger updating neighbourhoods. Perhaps significant universal patterns will only begin to emerge for large neighborhoods (cf [5]). However, we have identified some questions to ask about these problems.

References

[1] A Lapedes and R Farber, *Nonlinear Signal Processing Using Neural Networks: Prediction and System Modelling*, Tech Rept LA-UR-87-2662, Los Alamos National Laboratory. Los Alamos NM USA

[2] A S Weigend, B A Huberman and D E Rumelhart, *Int J Neural Systems* **1** 193-209 (1990)

[3] K Stokbro, D K Umberger and J A Hertz, *Complex Systems* **4** 603-622 (1991)

[4] S Wolfram, *Theory and Applications of Cellular Automata* (World Scientific, 1986)

[5] C G Langton, pp 12-37 in *Emergent Computation* (S Forrest, ed) MIT Press/North Holland, 1991

[6] J K Anlauf and M Biehl, *Europhys Letters* **10** 687 (1989)

[7] H V McIntosh, *Physica D* **45** 105-121 (1990)

[8] S Wolfram, *Physica D* **10** 1-35 (1984)

Some Estimates of Necessary Number of Connections and Hidden Units for Feed-Forward Networks

Adam Kowalczyk
Telecom Australia, Research Laboratories
770 Blackburn Road, Clayton, Vic. 3168, Australia
(a.kowalczyk@trl.oz.au)

Abstract

The feed-forward networks with fixed hidden units (*FHU-networks*) are compared against the category of remaining feed-forward networks with variable hidden units (*VHU-networks*). Two broad classes of tasks on a finite domain $\mathbf{X} \subset \mathbf{R}^n$ are considered: approximation of every function from an open subset of functions on $\mathbf{X}$ and representation of every dichotomy of $\mathbf{X}$. For the first task it is found that both network categories require the same minimal number of synaptic weights. For the second task and $\mathbf{X}$ in general position it is shown that VHU-networks with threshold logic hidden units can have approximately $1/n$ times fewer hidden units than any FHU-network must have.

1 Introduction

A good candidate artificial neural network for short term memory needs to be: (*i*) easy to train, (*ii*) able to support a broad range of tasks in a domain of interest and (*iii*) simple to implement. The class of feed-forward networks with fixed hidden units (*HU*) and adjustable synaptic weights at the top layer only (shortly: *FHU-networks*) is an obvious candidate to consider in this context. This class covers a wide range of networks considered in the past, including the classical perceptron, higher order networks and non-linear associative mapping. Also a number of training algorithms were specifically devoted to this category (e.g. perceptron, madaline or pseudoinverse) and a number of hardware solutions were investigated for their implementation (e.g. optical devices [8]).

Leaving aside the non-trivial tasks of constructing the domain specific HU for a FHU-network [9] and then optimal loading of specific tasks, in this paper we concentrate on assessing the abilities of such structures to support a wide range of tasks in comparison to more complex feedforward networks with multiple layers of variable HU (*VHU-networks*). More precisely, on a finite domain $\mathbf{X}$ two benchmark tests are considered: approximation of every function from an open subset of functions on $\mathbf{X}$ and representation of every dichotomy of $\mathbf{X}$. Some necessary and sufficient estimates of minimal necessary numbers of adaptable synaptic weights and of HU are obtained and then combined with some sufficient estimates in [10] to provide the final results. In Appendix we present an outline some of our recent results on the extension of the classical Function-Counting Theorem [2] to the multilayer case and discuss some of its implications to assessing network capacities.

2 Statement of the main results

In this paper $\mathbf{X}$ will denote a subset of $\mathbf{R}^n$ of N points. Of interest to us are multilayer feed-forward networks (shortly *FF-networks*), $F_{\mathbf{w}} : \mathbf{X} \to \mathbf{R}$, depending on the k-tuple $\mathbf{w} = (w_1, ..., w_k) \in \mathbf{R}^k$ of *adjustable synaptic weights* to be selected on loading to the network desired tasks. The FF-networks are split into two categories defined above:

- FHU-network with fixed hidden units $\phi_i : \mathbf{X} \to \mathbf{R}$

$$F_{\mathbf{w}}(\mathbf{x}) \stackrel{\text{def}}{=} \sum_{i=1}^{k} w_i \phi_i(\mathbf{x}) \quad (\mathbf{x} \in \mathbf{X}), \tag{1}$$

- VHU-networks with variable hidden units $\psi_{\mathbf{w}'',i} : \mathbf{X} \to \mathbf{R}$ depending on some adjustable synaptic weights $\mathbf{w}''$, where $\mathbf{w} = (\mathbf{w}', \mathbf{w}'') \in \mathbf{R}^{k'} \times \mathbf{R}^{k''} = \mathbf{R}^k$

$$F_{\mathbf{w}}(\mathbf{x}) \stackrel{\text{def}}{=} \sum_{i=1}^{k'} w'_i \psi_{\mathbf{w}'',i}(\mathbf{x}) \quad (\mathbf{x} \in \mathbf{X}). \tag{2}$$

Of special interest are situations where hidden units are built from one or more layers of *artificial neurons*, which, for simplicity, can be thought of as devices computing simple functions of the form

$$(y_1, ..., y_m) \in \mathbf{R}^m \mapsto \sigma(w_{i_1} y_1 + w_{i_2} y_2 + \cdots + w_{i_m} y_m),$$

where $\sigma : \mathbf{R} \to \mathbf{R}$ is a non-decreasing *squashing function*. Two particular examples of squashing functions are (*i*) infinitely differentiable *sigmoid function* $t \mapsto (1 + \exp(-t))^{-1}$ and (*ii*) the *step function* $\theta(t)$ defined as 1 for $t \geq 0$ and $= 0$, otherwise. In the latter case the artificial neuron is called a *threshold logic neuron (ThL-neuron)*.

In the formulation of results below all biases are treated as synaptic weights attached to links from special constant HUs ($\equiv 1$).

2.1 Function approximation

The space $\mathbf{R}^{\mathbf{X}}$ of all real functions on $\mathbf{X}$ has the natural structure of a vector space isomorphic with $\mathbf{R}^N$. We introduce the euclidean norm $||f|| \stackrel{\text{def}}{=} (\sum_{x\in\mathbf{X}} f^2(x))^{1/2}$ on $\mathbf{R}^{\mathbf{X}}$ and denote by $\mathcal{U} \subset \mathbf{R}^{\mathbf{X}}$ an open, non-empty subset. We say that the FF-network $F_{\mathbf{W}}$ can approximate a function f on $\mathbf{X}$ with accuracy $\epsilon > 0$ if $||f - F_{\mathbf{W}}|| < \epsilon$ for a weight vector $\mathbf{w} \in \mathbf{R}^k$.

Theorem 1 *Assume the FF-network $F_{\mathbf{W}}$ is continuously differentiable with respect to the adjustable synaptic weights $\mathbf{w} \in \mathbf{R}^k$ and $k < N$. If it can approximate any function in $\mathcal{U}$ with any accuracy then for almost every function $f \in \mathcal{U}$, if $\lim_{i\to\infty} ||F_{\mathbf{w}(i)} - f|| = 0$, where $\mathbf{w}(1), \mathbf{w}(2), ... \in \mathbf{R}^k$, then $\lim_{i\to\infty} ||\mathbf{w}(i)|| = \infty$.*

In the above theorem "almost every" means with the exception of a subset of the Lebesgue measure 0 on $\mathbf{R}^{\mathbf{X}} \approx \mathbf{R}^N$. The proof of this theorem relies on use of Sard's theorem from differential topology (c.f. Section 3). Note that the above theorem is applicable in particular to the popular "back-propagation" network which is typically built from artificial neurons with the continuously differentiable sigmoid squashing function.

The proof of the following theorem uses a different approach, since the network is not differentiably dependent on its synaptic weights to HUs. This theorem applies in particular to the classical FF-networks built from ThL-neurons.

Theorem 2 *A FF-network $F_{\mathbf{W}}$ must have $\geq N$ HU in the top hidden layer if all units of this layer have a finite number of activation levels and the network can approximate any function in $\mathcal{U}$ with any accuracy.*

The above theorems mean in particular that if we want to achieve an arbitrarily good approximation of any function in $\mathcal{U} \stackrel{\text{def}}{=} \{f : \mathbf{X} \to \mathbf{R} \; ; \; |f(\mathbf{x})| < A\}$, where $A > 0$, and we can use one of VHU-networks of the above type with synaptic weights of *a restricted magnitude only*, then we have to have at least N such weights. However that many weights are necessary and sufficient to achieve the same, with a FHU-network (1) if the functions ϕ_i are linearly independent on $\mathbf{X}$. So variable hidden units give no advantage in this case.

2.2 Implementation of dichotomy

We say that the FF-network $F_{\mathbf{W}}$ can implement a dichotomy $(\mathbf{X}_-, \mathbf{X}_+)$ of $\mathbf{X}$ if there exists $\mathbf{w} \in \mathbf{R}^k$ such that $F_{\mathbf{W}} < 0$ on $\mathbf{X}_-$ and $F_{\mathbf{W}} > 0$ on $\mathbf{X}_+$.

Proposition 3 *A FHU-network $F_{\mathbf{W}}$ can implement every dichotomy of $\mathbf{X}$ if and only if it can exactly compute every function on $\mathbf{X}$. In such a case it must have $\geq N$ HU in the top hidden layer.*

The non-trivial part of the above theorem is necessity in the first part of it, i.e. that being able to implement every dichotomy on $\mathbf{X}$ requires N (fixed) hidden units. In Section 3.3 we obtain this proposition from a stronger result. Note that the above proposition can be deduced from the classical Function-Counting Theorem [2] and also that an equivalent result is proved directly in [3, Theorem 7.2].

We say that the points of a subdomain $\mathbf{X} \subset \mathbf{R}^n$ are in *general position* if every in $\mathbf{R}^n$ contains no more than n points of $\mathbf{X}$. Note that points of every finite subdomain of $\mathbf{R}^n$ are in general position after a sufficiently small perturbation and that the property of being in general position is preserved under sufficiently small perturbations. Note also that the points of a *typical* N-point subdomain $\mathbf{X} \subset \mathbf{R}^n$ are in general position, where "typical" means with the exception of subdomains $\mathbf{X}$ corresponding to a certain subset of Lebesgue measure 0 in the space $(\mathbf{R}^n)^N$ of all N-tuples of points from $\mathbf{R}^n$.

It is proved in [10] that for a subdomain set $\mathbf{X} \subset \mathbf{R}^n$ of N points in general position a VHU-network having $\lceil (N-1)/n \rceil$ (adjustable) ThL-neurons in the first (and the only) hidden layer can implement every dichotomy of $\mathbf{X}$, where the notation $\lceil t \rceil$ denotes the smallest integer $\geq t$. Furthermore, examples are given showing that the above bound is tight. (Note that this paper corrects and gives rigorous proofs of some early results in [1, Lemma 1 and Theorem 1] and also improves [6, Theorem 4].) Combining these results with Proposition 3 we get the following result.

Theorem 4 *Assume that all N points of $\mathbf{X} \subset \mathbf{R}^n$ are in general position. In the class of all FF-networks which can implement every dichotomy on $\mathbf{X}$ there exists a VHU-network with threshold logic HU having a fraction $1/n + O(1/N)$ of the number of the HU that any FHU-network in this class must have. There are examples of $\mathbf{X}$ in general position of any even cardinality $N > 0$ showing that this estimate is tight.*

3 Proofs

Below we identify functions $f : \mathbf{X} \to \mathbf{R}$ with N-tuples of their values at N-points of $\mathbf{X}$ (ordered in a unique manner). Under this identification the FF-networks $F_{\mathbf{w}}$ can be regarded as a transformation

$$\mathbf{w} \in \mathbf{R}^k \rightarrow F_{\mathbf{w}} \in \mathbf{R}^N \tag{3}$$

with the *range* $\mathcal{R}(F_{\mathbf{w}}) \stackrel{\text{def}}{=} \{F_{\mathbf{w}} \ ; \ \mathbf{w} \in \mathbf{R}^k\} \subset \mathbf{R}^N$.

3.1 Proof of Theorem 1.

In this case the transformation (3) is continuously differentiable. Every value of it is singular since $k < N$, thus according to Sard's Theorem [5], $\mathcal{R}(F_{\mathbf{w}}) \subset \mathbf{R}^N$ has Lebesgue measure 0. It is enough to show now that if

$$f \in \mathcal{U} - \mathcal{R}(F_{\mathbf{w}}) \tag{4}$$

and

$$\lim_{i \to \infty} ||F_{\mathbf{w}(i)} - f|| = 0 \quad \text{and} \quad ||\mathbf{w}(i)|| < M, \tag{5}$$

for some $M > 0$, then a contradiction follows. Actually from (5) it follows that f belongs to the topological closure $cl(\mathcal{R}_M)$ of $\mathcal{R}_M \stackrel{\text{def}}{=} \{F_{\mathbf{w}} \ ; \ \mathbf{w} \in \mathbf{R}^k \ \& \ ||\mathbf{w}|| \leq$

$M\}$. However, $\mathcal{R}_M$ is a compact set as a continuous image of a closed ball $\{\mathbf{w} \in \mathbf{R}^k \; ; \; ||\mathbf{w}|| \leq M\}$, so $cl(\mathcal{R}_M) = \mathcal{R}_M$. Consequently $f \in \mathcal{R}_M \subset \mathcal{R}(F_\mathbf{W})$ which contradicts (4). Q.E.D.

3.2 Proof of Theorem 2.

We consider the FF-network (1) for which there exists a finite set $V \subset \mathbf{R}$ of s points such that $\psi_{\mathbf{w}'',i}(\mathbf{x}) \in V$ for every $\mathbf{w}'' \in \mathbf{R}^{k''}$, $1 \leq i \leq k'$ and $\mathbf{x} \in \mathbf{X}$. It is sufficient to show that the set $\mathcal{R}(F_\mathbf{W})$ of all functions computable by $F_\mathbf{W}$ is not dense in $\mathcal{U}$ if $k' < N$. Actually, we can write $\mathcal{R}(F_\mathbf{W})$ as a union

$$\mathcal{R}(F_\mathbf{W}) = \bigcup_{\mathbf{w}'' \in \mathbf{R}^{k''}} L_{\mathbf{w}''} \subset \mathbf{R}^N, \tag{6}$$

where each $L_{\mathbf{w}''} \stackrel{\text{def}}{=} \{\sum_{i=1}^{k'} w'_i \psi_{\mathbf{w}'',i} \; ; \; w'_1, ..., w'_{k'} \in \mathbf{R}\} \subset \mathbf{R}^N$ is a linear subspace of dimension $\leq k' \leq N$ uniquely determined by the vectors $\psi_{\mathbf{w}'',i} \in V^N \subset \mathbf{R}^N$, $i = 1, ..., k'$. However there is a finite number ($\leq s^N$) of different vectors in V^N, thus there is only a finite number ($\leq s^{Nk}$) of different linear subspaces in the family $\{L_{\mathbf{w}''} \; ; \; \mathbf{w}'' \in \mathbf{R}^{k''}\}$. Hence, as $k' < N$, the union (6) is a closed no-where dense subset of $\mathbf{R}^N$ as a finite union of proper linear subspaces (each of which is a closed and nowhere dense subset). Q.E.D.

3.3 Proof of Proposition 3.

We state first a stronger result. We say that a set L of functions on $\mathbf{X}$ is convex if for any couple of functions ϕ_1, ϕ_2 on $\mathbf{X}$ any $\alpha > 0$, $\beta > 0$, $\alpha + \beta = 1$, the function $\alpha\phi_1 + \beta\phi_2$ also belongs to L.

Proposition 5 *Let L be a convex set of functions on $\mathbf{X} = \{\mathbf{x}_1, \mathbf{x}_2, ..., \mathbf{x}_N\}$ implementing every dichotomy of $\mathbf{X}$. Then for each $i \in \{1, 2, ..., N\}$ there exists a function $\phi^i \in L$ such that $\phi^i(\mathbf{x}_i) \neq 0$ and $\phi^i(\mathbf{x}_j) = 0$ for $1 \leq i \neq j \leq N$.*

Proof. We define a transformation $\text{SGN} : \mathbf{R}^\mathbf{X} \to \{-1, 0, +1\}^N$

$$\text{SGN}(\phi) \stackrel{\text{def}}{=} (\text{sgn}(\phi(\mathbf{x}_1)), \text{sgn}(\phi(\mathbf{x}_2)), ..., \text{sgn}(\phi(\mathbf{x}_N))) \in \{-1, 0, +1\}^N,$$

where $\text{sgn}(\xi) \stackrel{\text{def}}{=} -1$ if $\xi < 0$, $\text{sgn}(0) \stackrel{\text{def}}{=} 0$ and $\text{sgn}(\xi) \stackrel{\text{def}}{=} +1$ if $\xi > 0$. We denote by W_k the subset of $\{-1, 0, +1\}^N$ of all points $\mathbf{q} = (q_1, ..., q_N)$ such that $\sum_{i=1}^N |q_i| = k$, for $k = 0, 1, ..., N$.

We show first that convexity of $\mathbf{L}$ implies for $k \in \{1, 2, ..., N\}$ the following

$$W_k \subset \text{SGN}(\mathbf{L}) \quad \Rightarrow \quad W_{k-1} \subset \text{SGN}(\mathbf{L}). \tag{7}$$

For the proof assume $W_k \subset \text{SGN}(L)$ and $\mathbf{q} = (q_1, ..., q_N) \in \{-1, 0, +1\}^N$ is such that $\sum_{i=1}^N |q_i| = k - 1$. We need to show that there exists $\phi \in \mathbf{L}$ such that

$$\text{SGN}(\phi) = \mathbf{q}. \tag{8}$$

The vector $\mathbf{q}$ has at least one vanishing entry, say, without loss of generality, $q_1 = 0$. Let ϕ^+ and ϕ^- be two functions in L such that

$$\mathrm{SGN}(\phi^+) = \mathbf{q}^+ \stackrel{\text{def}}{=} (+1, q_2, ..., q_N),$$
$$\mathrm{SGN}(\phi^-) = \mathbf{q}^- \stackrel{\text{def}}{=} (-1, q_2, ..., q_N).$$

Such ϕ^+ and ϕ^- exist since $\mathbf{q}^+, \mathbf{q}^- \in W_k$. The function

$$\phi \stackrel{\text{def}}{=} (|\phi^+(\mathbf{x}_1)|\phi^- + |\phi^-(\mathbf{x}_1)|\phi^+)/(|\phi^+(\mathbf{x}_1)| + |\phi^-(\mathbf{x}_1)|)$$

belongs to $\mathbf{L}$ as a convex combination of two functions from $\mathbf{L}$ and satisfies (8).

Now note that the assumptions of the proposition imply that $W_N \subset \mathrm{SGN}(\mathbf{L})$. Applying (7) repeatedly we find that $W_1 \subset \mathrm{SGN}(\mathbf{L})$, which means that for every index i, $1 \leq i \leq N$, there exists a function $\phi^i \in \mathbf{L}$ with vanishing all entries but the i-th one. Q.E.D.

Now let us see how Proposition 3 follows from the above result. Sufficiency is obvious. For the necessity we observe that the family $F_{\mathbf{W}}$ of functions on $\mathbf{X}$ is convex being a linear space in the case of a FHU-network (1). Now if this network can compute every dichotomy of $\mathbf{X}$, then each function ϕ^i as in Proposition 5 equals to $F_{\mathbf{W}_i}$ for some $\mathbf{w}_i \in \mathbf{R}^k$. Thus $\mathcal{R}(F_{\mathbf{W}}) = \mathbf{R}^N$ since those functions make a basis of $\mathbf{R}^{\mathbf{X}} \approx \mathbf{R}^N$. Q.E.D.

4 Discussion of results

Theorem 1 combined with observations in [4] allows us to make the following contribution to the recent controversy on relevance/irrelevance of Kolmogorov's theorem on representation of continuous functions $I^n \to \mathbf{R}$, $I \stackrel{\text{def}}{=} [0,1]$ (c.f. [4, 7]), since I^n contains subsets of any cardinality.

> *The FF-networks for approximations of continuous functions on I^n of rising accuracy* have to be complex, *at least in one of the following ways:*
>
> - *involve adjustment of a diverging number of synaptic weights and hidden units, or*
> - *require adjustment of synaptic weights of diverging magnitude, or*
> - *involve selection of "pathological" squashing functions.*

Thus one can only shift complexity from one kind to another, but not eliminate it completely. Although on theoretical grounds one can easily argue the virtues and simplicity of one kind of complexity over the other, for a genuine hardware implementation any of them poses an equally serious obstacle.

For the classes of FF-networks and benchmark tests considered, the networks with multiple hidden layers have no decisive superiority over the simple structures with fixed hidden units unless dimensionality of the input space is significant.

5 Appendix: Capacity and Function-Counting Theorem

The above results can be viewed as a step towards estimation of capacity of networks to memorise dichotomies. We intend to elaborate this subject further now and outline some of our recent results on this matter. A more detailed presentation will be available in future publications.

The capacity of a network in the sense of Cover [2] (*Cover's capacity*) is defined as a maximal N such that for a randomly selected subset $\mathbf{X} \subset \mathbf{R}^n$ of N points with probability 1 the network can implement 1/2 of all dichotomies of $\mathbf{X}$. For a linear perceptron

$$F_{\mathbf{W}}(\mathrm{x}) \stackrel{\text{def}}{=} \sum_{i=1}^{k} w_i x_i \quad (\mathrm{x} \in \mathbf{X}), \tag{9}$$

where $\mathrm{w} \in \mathbf{R}^n$ is the vector of adjustable synaptic weights, the capacity is $2n$,and $2k$ for a FHU-network (1) with suitable chosen hidden units $\phi_1, ..., \phi_k$. These results are based on the so-called Function-Counting Theorem proved for the linear perceptron in the sixties (c.f. [2]). Extension of this result to the multilayer case is still an open problem (c.f. T. Cover's talk on NIPS'92). However, we have recently obtained the following partial result in this direction.

Theorem 6 *Given a continuous probability density on $\mathbf{R}^n$, for a randomly selected subset $\mathbf{X} \subset \mathbf{R}^n$ of N points the FF-network having the first hidden layer built from h ThL-neurons can implement*

$$C(N, nh) \stackrel{\text{def}}{=} 2\sum_{i=0}^{nh} \binom{N-1}{i}, \tag{10}$$

dichotomies of $\mathbf{X}$ with a non-zero *probability. Such a network can be constructed using nh variable synaptic weights between input and hidden layer only.*

For $h = 1$ this theorem reduces to its classical form for which the phrase "with non-zero probability" can be strengthened to "with probability 1" [2].

The proof of the theorem develops Sakurai's idea of utilising the Vandermonde determinant to show the following property of the curve $c(t) \stackrel{\text{def}}{=} (t, t^2, ..., t^{n-1})$, $t > 0$

> (*) *for any subset $\mathbf{X}$ of N points $\mathrm{x}_1 = c(t_1), ..., \mathrm{x}_N = c(t_N)$, $t_1 < t_2 < \cdots < t_N$, any hyperplane in $\mathbf{R}^n$ can intersect no more then n different segments $[\mathrm{x}_i, \mathrm{x}_{i+1}]$ of c.*

The first step of the proof is to observe that the property (*) itself implies that the count (10) holds for such a set X. The second and the crucial step consists in showing that for a sufficiently small $\epsilon > 0$, for any selection of points $\tilde{\mathrm{x}}_1, ..., \tilde{\mathrm{x}}_N \in \mathbf{R}^n$ such that $||\tilde{\mathrm{x}}_i - \mathrm{x}_i|| < \epsilon$ for $i = 1, ..., n$, there exists a curve $\tilde{c}$ passing through these points and satisfying also the property (*).

Theorem 6 implies that in the class of multilayer FF-networks having the first hidden layer built from ThL-neurons only the single hidden layer networks are the most efficient, since the higher layers have no influence on the number of implemented dichotomies (at least for the class of domains $\mathbf{x} \subset \mathbf{R}^n$ considered).

Note that by virtue of (10) and the classical argument of Cover [2] for the class of domains $\mathbf{X}$ as in the Theorem 6 the capacity of the network considered is $2nh$. Thus the following estimates hold.

Corollary 7 *In the class of FF-networks with a fixed number h of hidden units the ratio of the maximal capacity per hidden unit achievable by FHU-network to the maximal capacity per hidden unit achievable by VHU-networks having the ThL-neurons in the first hidden layer only is $2h/2nh = 1/n$. The analogous ratio for capacities per variable synaptic weight (in the class of FF-networks with a fixed number s of variable synaptic weights) is $\leq 2s/2s = 1$.*

Acknowledgement. I thank A. Sakurai of Hitachi Ltd., for helpful comments leading to the improvement of results of the paper. The permission of the Director, Telecom Australia Research Laboratories, to publish this material is gratefully acknowledged.

References

[1] E. Baum. On the capabilities of multilayer perceptrons. *Journal of Complexity*, **4**:193–215, 1988.

[2] T.M. Cover. Geometrical and statistical properties of linear inequalities with applications to pattern recognition. *IEEE Trans. Elec. Comp.*, **EC-14**:326–334, 1965.

[3] R.M. Dudley. Central limit theorems for empirical measures. *Ann. Probability*, **6**:899–929, 1978.

[4] F. Girosi and T. Poggio. Representation properties of networks: Kolmogorov's theorem is irrelevant. *Neural Computation*, **1**:465–469, (1989).

[5] M. Golubitsky and V. Guillemin. *Stable Mapping and Their Singularities.* Springer-Verlag, New York, 1973.

[6] S. Huang and Y. Huang. Bounds on the number of hidden neurons in multilayer perceptrons. *IEEE Transactions on Neural Networks*, **2**:47–55, (1991).

[7] V. Kurkova. Kolmogorov theorem is relevant. *Neural Computation*, 1, 1992.

[8] D. Psaltis, C.H. Park, and J. Hong. Higher order associative memories and their optical implementations. *Neural Networks*, **1**:149–163, (1988).

[9] N. Redding, A. Kowalczyk, and T. Downs. Higher order separability and minimal hidden-unit fan-in. In T. Kohonen *et al.*, editor, *Artificial Neural Networks*, volume **1**, pages 25–30. Elsevier, 1991.

[10] A. Sakurai. n-h-1 networks store no less $n \cdot h + 1$ examples but sometimes no more. In *Proceedings of IJCNN92*, pages III–936–III–941. IEEE, June 1992.

PART VIII

SPEECH AND SIGNAL PROCESSING

Context-Dependent Multiple Distribution Phonetic Modeling with MLPs

Michael Cohen
SRI International
Menlo Park, CA 94025

Horacio Franco
SRI International

Nelson Morgan
Intl. Computer Science Inst.
Berkeley, CA 94704

David Rumelhart
Stanford University
Stanford, CA 94305

Victor Abrash
SRI International

Abstract

A number of hybrid multilayer perceptron (MLP)/hidden Markov model (HMM) speech recognition systems have been developed in recent years (Morgan and Bourlard, 1990). In this paper, we present a new MLP architecture and training algorithm which allows the modeling of context-dependent phonetic classes in a hybrid MLP/HMM framework. The new training procedure smooths MLPs trained at different degrees of context dependence in order to obtain a robust estimate of the context-dependent probabilities. Tests with the DARPA Resource Management database have shown substantial advantages of the context-dependent MLPs over earlier context-independent MLPs, and have shown substantial advantages of this hybrid approach over a pure HMM approach.

1 INTRODUCTION

Hidden Markov models are used in most current state-of-the-art continuous-speech recognition systems. A hidden Markov model (HMM) is a stochastic finite state machine with two sets of probability distributions. Associated with each state is a probability distribution over transitions to next states and a probability distribution over output symbols (often referred to as observation probabilities). When applied to continuous speech, the observation probabilities are typically used to model local speech features such as spectra, and the transition probabilities are used to model the displacement of these features through time. HMMs of individual phonetic segments (phones) can be concatenated to model words and word models can be concatenated, according to a grammar, to model sentences, resulting in a finite state representation of acoustic-phonetic, phonological, and syntactic structure.

The HMM approach is limited by the need for strong statistical assumptions that are unlikely to be valid for speech. Previous work by Morgan and Bourlard (1990) has shown both theoretically and practically that some of these limitations can be overcome by using multilayer perceptrons (MLPs) to estimate the HMM state-dependent observation probabilities. In addition to relaxing the restrictive independence assumptions of traditional HMMs, this approach results in a reduction in the number of parameters needed for detailed phonetic modeling as a result of increased sharing of model parameters between phonetic classes.

Recently, this approach was applied to the SRI-DECIPHER™ system, a state-of-the-art continuous speech recognition system (Cohen et al., 1990), using an MLP to provide estimates of context-independent posterior probabilities of phone classes, which were then converted to HMM context-independent state observation likelihoods using Bayes' rule (Renals et al., 1992). In this paper, we describe refinements of the system to model phonetic classes with a sequence of context-dependent probabilities.

Context-dependent modeling: The realization of individual phones in continuous speech is highly dependent upon phonetic context. For example, the sound of the vowel /ae/ in the words "map" and "tap" is different, due to the influence of the preceding phone. These context effects are referred to as "coarticulation". Experience with HMM technology has shown that using context-dependent phonetic models improves recognition accuracy significantly (Schwartz et al., 1985). This is so because acoustic correlates of coarticulatory effects are explicitly modeled, producing sharper and less overlapping probability density functions for the different phone classes.

Context-dependent HMMs use different probability distributions for every phone in every different relevant context. This practice causes problems that are due to the reduced amount of data available to train phones in highly specific contexts, resulting in models that are not robust and generalize poorly. The solution to this problem used by many HMM systems is to train models at many different levels of context-specificity, including biphone (conditioned only on the phone immediately to the left or right), generalized biphone (conditioned on the broad class of the phone to the left or right), triphone (conditioned on the phone to the left and the right), generalized triphone, and word specific phone. Models conditioned by more specific contexts are linearly smoothed with more general models. The "deleted interpolation" algorithm (Jelinek and Mercer, 1980) provides linear weighting coefficients for the observation probabilities with different degrees of context dependence by maximizing the likelihood of the different models over new, unseen data. This approach cannot be directly extended to MLP-based systems because averaging the weights of two MLPs does not result in an MLP with the average performance. It would be possible to use this approach to average the probabilities that are output from different MLPs; however, since the MLP training algorithm is a discriminant procedure, it would be desirable to use a discriminant or error-based procedure to smooth the MLP probabilities together.

An earlier approach to context-dependent phonetic modeling with MLPs was proposed by Bourlard et al. (1992). It is based on factoring the context-dependent likelihood and uses a set of binary inputs to the network to specify context classes. The number of parameters and the computational load using this approach are not much greater than those for the original context-independent net.

The context-dependent modeling approach we present here uses a different factoring of the desired context-dependent likelihoods, a network architecture that shares the input-to-hidden layer among the context-dependent classes to reduce the number of parameters, and a training procedure that smooths networks with different degrees of context-dependence in order to achieve robustness in probability estimates.

Multidistribution modeling: Experience with HMM-based systems has shown the importance of modeling phonetic units with a sequence of distributions rather than a single distribution. This allows the model to capture some of the dynamics of phonetic segments. The SRI-DECIPHER™ system models most phones with a sequence of three HMM states. Our initial hybrid system used only a single MLP output unit for each HMM phonetic class. This output unit supplied the probability for all the states of the associated phone model.

Our initial attempt to extend the hybrid system to the modeling of a sequence of distributions for each phone involved increasing the number of output units from 69 (corresponding to phone classes) to 200 (corresponding to the states of the HMM phone models). This resulted in an increase in word-recognition error rate by almost 30%. Experiments at ICSI had a similar result (personal communication). The higher error rate seemed to be due to the discriminative nature of the MLP training algorithm. The new MLP, with 200 output units, was attempting to discriminate subphonetic classes, corresponding to HMM states. As a result, the MLP was attempting to discriminate into separate classes acoustic vectors that corresponded to the same phone and, in many cases, were very similar but were aligned with different HMM states. There were likely to have been many cases in which almost identical acoustic training vectors were labeled as a positive example in one instance and a negative example in another for the same output class. The appropriate level at which to train discrimination is likely to be the level of the phone (or higher) rather than the subphonetic HMM-state level (to which these outputs units correspond). The new architecture presented here accomplishes this by training separate output layers for each of the three HMM states, resulting in a network trained to discriminate at the phone level, while allowing three distributions to model each phone. This approach is combined with the context-dependent modeling approach, described in Section 3.

2 HYBRID MLP/HMM

The SRI-DECIPHER™ system is a phone-based, speaker-independent, continuous-speech recognition system, based on semicontinuous (tied Gaussian mixture) HMMs (Cohen et al., 1990). The system extracts four features from the input speech waveform, including 12th-order mel cepstrum, log energy, and their smoothed derivatives. The front end produces the 26 coefficients for these four features for each 10-ms frame of speech.

Training of the phonetic models is based on maximum-likelihood estimation using the forward-backward algorithm (Levinson et al., 1983). Recognition uses the Viterbi algorithm (Levinson et al., 1983) to find the HMM state sequence (corresponding to a sentence) with the highest probability of generating the observed acoustic sequence.

The hybrid MLP/HMM DECIPHER™ system substitutes (scaled) probability estimates computed with MLPs for the tied-mixture HMM state-dependent observation probability densities. No changes are made in the topology of the HMM system.

The initial hybrid system used an MLP to compute context-independent phonetic probabilities for the 69 phone classes in the DECIPHER™ system. Separate probabilities were not computed for the different states of phone models. During the Viterbi recognition search, the probability of acoustic vector Y_t given the phone class q_j, $P(Y_t|q_j)$, is required for each HMM state. Since MLPs can compute Bayesian posterior probabilities, we compute the required HMM probabilities using

$$P(Y_t|q_j) = \frac{P(q_j|Y_t)P(Y_t)}{P(q_j)} \tag{1}$$

The factor $P(q_j|Y_t)$ is the posterior probability of phone class q_j given the input vector Y at time t. This is computed by a backpropagation-trained (Rumelhart et al., 1986) three-layer feed-forward MLP. $P(q_j)$ is the prior probability of phone class q_j and is estimated by counting class occurrences in the examples used to train the MLP. $P(Y_t)$ is common to all states for any given time frame, and can therefore be discarded in the Viterbi computation, since it will not change the optimal state sequence used to get the recognized string.

The MLP has an input layer of 234 units, spanning 9 frames (with 26 coefficients for each) of cepstra, delta-cepstra, log-energy, and delta-log-energy that are normalized to have zero mean and unit variance. The hidden layer has 1000 units, and the output layer has 69 units, one for each context-independent phonetic class in the DECIPHER™ system. Both the hidden and output layers consist of sigmoidal units.

The MLP is trained to estimate $P(q_j|Y_t)$, where q_j is the class associated with the middle frame of the input window. Stochastic gradient descent is used. The training signal is provided by the HMM DECIPHER™ system previously trained by the forward-backward algorithm. Forced Viterbi alignments (alignments to the known word string) for every training sentence provide phone labels, among 69 classes, for every frame of speech. The target distribution is defined as 1 for the index corresponding to the phone class label and 0 for the other classes. A minimum relative entropy between posterior target distribution and posterior output distribution is used as a training criterion. With this training criterion and target distribution, assuming enough parameters in the MLP, enough training data, and that the training does not get stuck in a local minimum, the MLP outputs will approximate the posterior class probabilities $P(q_j|Y_t)$ (Morgan and Bourlard, 1990). Frame classification on an independent cross-validation set is used to control the learning rate and to decide when to stop training as in Renals et al. (1992). The initial learning rate is kept constant until cross-validation performance increases less than 0.5%, after which it is reduced as $1/2^n$ until performance increases no further.

3 CONTEXT-DEPENDENCE

Our initial implementation of context-dependent MLPs models generalized biphone phonetic categories. We chose a set of eight left and eight right generalized biphone phonetic-context classes, based principally on place of articulation and acoustic characteristics. The context-dependent architecture is shown in Figure 1. A separate output layer (consisting of 69 output units corresponding to 69 context-dependent phonetic classes) is trained for each context. The context-dependent MLP can be viewed as a set of MLPs, one for each context, which have the same input-to-hidden weights. Separate sets of context-dependent output layers are used to model context effects in different states of HMM phone models, thereby combining the modeling of multiple phonetic distributions and context-dependence. During training and recognition, speech frames aligned with first states of HMM phones are associated with the appropriate left context output layer, those aligned with last states of HMM phones are associated with the appropriate right context output layer, and middle states of three state models are associated with the context-independent output layer. As a result, since the training proceeds (as before) as if each output layer were part of an independent net, the system learns discrimination between the different phonetic classes within an output layer (which now corresponds to a specific context and HMM-state position), but does not learn discrimination between occurrences of the same phone in different contexts or between the different states of the same HMM phone.

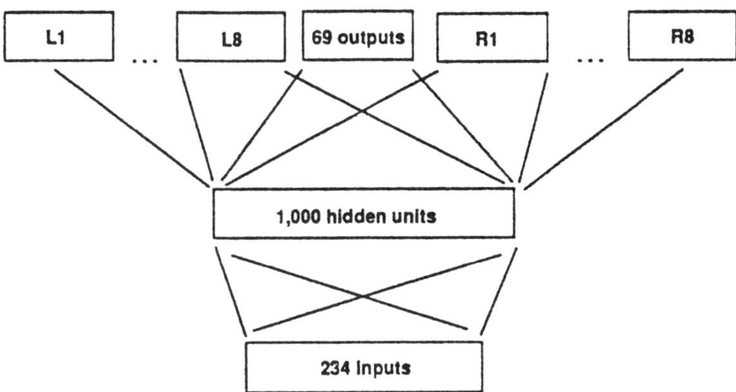

Figure 1: Context-Dependent MLP

3.1 CONTEXT-DEPENDENT FACTORING

In a context-dependent HMM, every state is associated with a specific phone class and context. During the Viterbi recognition search, $P(Y_t | q_j, c_k)$ (the probability of acoustic vector Y_t given the phone class q_j in the context class c_k) is required for each state. We compute the required HMM probabilities using

$$P(Y_t | q_j, c_k) = \frac{P(q_j | Y_t, c_k) P(Y_t | c_k)}{P(q_j | c_k)} \tag{2}$$

where $P(Y_t | c_k)$ can be factored again as

$$P(Y_t | c_k) = \frac{P(c_k | Y_t) P(Y_t)}{P(c_k)} \tag{3}$$

The factor $P(q_j | Y_t, c_k)$ is the posterior probability of phone class q_j given the input vector Y_t and the context class c_k. To compute this factor, we consider the conditioning on c_k in (2) as restricting the set of input vectors only to those produced in the context c_k. If M is the number of context classes, this implementation uses a set of M MLPs (all sharing the same input-to-hidden layer) similar to those used in the context-independent case except that each MLP is trained using only input-output examples obtained from the corresponding context, c_k.

Every context-specific net performs a simpler classification than in the context-independent case because within a context the acoustics corresponding to different phones have less overlap.

$P(c_k|Y_t)$ is computed by a second MLP. A three-layer feed-forward MLP is used which has 1000 hidden units and an output unit corresponding to each context class. $P(q_j|c_k)$ and $P(c_k)$ are estimated by counting over the training examples. Finally, $P(Y_t)$ is common to all states for any given time frame, and can therefore be discarded in the Viterbi computation, since it will not change the optimal state sequence used to get the recognized string.

3.2 CONTEXT-DEPENDENT TRAINING AND SMOOTHING

We use the following method to achieve robust training of context-specific nets:

An initial context-independent MLP is trained, as described in Section 2, to estimate the context-independent posterior probabilities over the N phone classes. After the context-independent training converges, the resulting weights are used to initialize the weights going to the context-specific output layers. Context-dependent training proceeds by backpropagating error only from the appropriate output layer for each training example. Otherwise, the training procedure is similar to that for the context-independent net, using stochastic gradient descent and a relative-entropy training criterion. Overall classification performance evaluated on an independent cross-validation set is used to determine the learning rate and stopping point. Only hidden-to-output weights are adjusted during context-dependent training. We can view the separate output layers as belonging to independent nets, each one trained on a non-overlapping subset of the original training data.

Every context-specific net would asymptotically converge to the context conditioned posteriors $P(q_j|Y_t,c_k)$ given enough training data and training iterations. As a result of the initialization, the net starts estimating $P(q_j|Y_t)$, and from that point it follows a trajectory in weight space, incrementally moving away from the context-independent parameters as long as classification performance on the cross-validation set improves. As a result, the net retains useful information from the context-independent initial conditions. In this way, we perform a type of nonlinear smoothing between the pure context-independent parameters and the pure context-dependent parameters.

4 EVALUATION

Training and recognition experiments were conducted using the speaker-independent, continuous-speech, DARPA Resource Management database. The vocabulary size is 998 words. Tests were run both with a word-pair (perplexity 60) grammar and with no grammar. The training set for the HMM system and for the MLP consisted of the 3990 sentences that make up the standard DARPA speaker-independent training set for the Resource Management task. The 600 sentences making up the Resource Management February 89 and October 89 test sets were used for cross-validation during both the context-independent and context-dependent MLP training, and for tuning HMM system parameters (e.g., word transition weight).

Table 1: Percent Word Error and Parameter Count with Word-Pair Grammar

	CIMLP	CDMLP	HMM	MIXED
Feb91	5.8	4.7	3.8	3.2
Sep92a	10.9	7.6	10.1	7.7
Sep92b	9.5	6.6	7.0	5.7
# Parms	300K	1400K	5500K	6100K

Table 2: Percent Word Error with No Grammar

	CIMLP	CDMLP	HMM	MIXED
Feb91	24.7	18.4	19.3	15.9
Sep92a	31.5	27.1	29.2	25.4
Sep92b	30.9	24.9	26.6	21.5

Table 1 presents word recognition error and number of system parameters for four different versions of the system, for three different Resource Management test sets using the word-pair grammar. Table 2 presents word recognition error for the corresponding tests with no grammar (the number of system parameters are the same as those shown in Table 1).

Comparing context-independent MLP (CIMLP) to context-dependent MLP (CDMLP) shows improvements with CDMLP in all six tests, ranging from a 15% to 30% reduction in word error. The CDMLP system combines multiple-distribution modeling with the context-dependent modeling technique. The CDMLP system performs better than the context-dependent HMM (CDHMM) system in five out of the six tests.

The MIXED system uses a weighted mixture of the logs of state observation likelihoods provided by the CIMLP and the CDHMM (Renals et al., 1992). This system shows the best recognition performance so far achieved with the DECIPHER™ system on the Resource Management database. In all six tests, it performs significantly better than the pure CDHMM system.

5 DISCUSSION

The results shown in Tables 1 and 2 suggest that MLP estimation of HMM observation likelihoods can improve the performance of standard HMMs. These results also suggest that systems that use MLP-based probability estimation make more efficient use of their parameters than standard HMM systems. In standard HMMs, most of the parameters in the system are in the observation distributions associated with the individual states of phone models. MLPs use representations that are more distributed in nature, allowing more sharing of representational resources and better allocation of representational resources based on training. In addition, since MLPs are trained to discriminate between classes, they focus on modeling boundaries between classes rather than class internals.

One should keep in mind that the reduction in memory needs that may be attained by replacing HMM distributions with MLP-based estimates must be traded off against increased computational load during both training and recognition. The MLP computations during training and recognition are much larger than the corresponding Gaussian mixture computations for HMM systems.

The results also show that the context-dependent modeling approach presented here substantially improves performance over the earlier context-independent MLP. In addition, the context-dependent MLP performed better than the context-dependent HMM in five out of the six tests although the CDMLP is a far simpler system than the CDHMM, with approximately a factor of four fewer parameters and modeling of only generalized biphone phonetic contexts. The CDHMM uses a range of context-dependent models including generalized and specific biphone, triphone, and word-specific phone. The fact that context-dependent MLPs can perform as well or better than context-dependent HMMs while using less specific models suggests that they may be more vocabulary-independent, which is useful when porting systems to new tasks. In the near future we will test the CDMLP system on new vocabularies.

The MLP smoothing approach described here can be extended to the modeling of finer context classes. A hierarchy of context classes can be defined in which each context class at one level is included in a broader class at a higher level. The context-specific MLP at a given level in the hierarchy is initialized with the weights of a previously trained context-specific MLP at the next higher level, and then finer context training can proceed as described in Section 3.2.

The distributed representation used by MLPs is exploited in the context-dependent modeling approach by sharing the input-to-hidden layer weights between all context classes. This sharing substantially reduces the number of parameters to train and the amount of computation required during both training and recognition. In addition, we do not adjust the input-to-hidden weights during the context-dependent phase of training, assuming that the features provided by the hidden layer activations are relatively low level and are appropriate for context-dependent as well as context-independent modeling. The large decrease in cross-validation error observed going from context-independent to context-dependent MLPs (30.6% to 21.4%) suggests that the features learned by the hidden layer during the context-independent training phase, combined with the extra modeling power of the context-specific hidden-to-output layers, were adequate to capture the more detailed context-specific phone classes.

The best performance shown in Tables 1 and 2 is that of the MIXED system, which combines CIMLP and CDHMM probabilities. The CDMLP probabilities can also be combined with CDHMM probabilities; however, we hope that the planned extension of our CDMLP system to finer contexts will lead to a better system than the MIXED system without the need for such mixing, therefore resulting in a simpler system.

The context-dependent MLP shown here has more than 1,400,000 weights. We were able to robustly train such a large network by using a cross-validation set to determine when to stop training, sharing many of the weights between context classes, and smoothing context-dependent with context-independent MLPs using the approach described in Section 3.2. In addition, the Ring Array Processor (RAP) special purpose hardware, developed at ICSI (Morgan et al., 1992), allowed rapid training of such large networks on large data sets. In order to reduce the number of weights in the MLP, we are currently exploring alternative architectures which apply the smoothing techniques described here to binary context inputs.

6 CONCLUSIONS

MLP-based probability estimation can be useful for both improving recognition accuracy and reducing memory needs for HMM-based speech recognition systems. These benefits, however, must be weighed against increased computational requirements.

We have presented a new MLP architecture and training procedure for modeling context-dependent phonetic classes with a sequence of distributions. Tests using the DARPA Resource Management database have shown improvements in recognition performance using this new approach, modeling only generalized biphone context categories. These results suggest that sharing input-to-hidden weights between context categories (and not retraining them during the context-dependent training phase) results in a hidden layer representation which is adequate for context-dependent as well as context-independent modeling, error-based smoothing of context-independent and context-dependent weights is effective for training a robust model, and using separate output layers and hidden-to-output weights corresponding to different context classes of different states of HMM phone models is adequate to capture acoustic effects which change throughout the production of individual phonetic segments.

Acknowledgements

The work reported here was partially supported by DARPA Contract MDA904-90-C-5253. Discussions with Herve Bourlard were very helpful.

References

H. Bourlard, N. Morgan, C. Wooters, and S. Renals (1992), "CDNN: A Context Dependent Neural Network for Continuous Speech Recognition," *ICASSP*, pp. 349-352, San Francisco.

M. Cohen, H. Murveit, J Bernstein, P. Price, and M. Weintraub (1990), "The DECIPHER Speech Recognition System," *ICASSP*, pp. 77-80, Alburquerque, New Mexico.

F. Jelinek and R. Mercer (1980), "Interpolated estimation of markov source parameters from sparse data," in *Pattern Recognition in Practice*, E. Gelsema and L. Kanal, Eds. Amsterdam: North-Holland, pp. 381-397.

S. Levinson, L. Rabiner, and M. Sondhi (1983), "An introduction to the application of the theory of probabilistic functions of a Markov process to automatic speech recognition," *Bell Syst. Tech. Journal 62*, pp. 1035-1074.

N. Morgan and H. Bourlard (1990), "Continuous Speech Recognition Using Multilayer Perceptrons with Hidden Markov Models," *ICASSP*, pp. 413-416, Alburquerque, New Mexico.

N. Morgan, J. Beck, P. Kohn, J. Bilmes, E. Allman, and J. Beer (1992), "The Ring Array Processor (RAP): A Multiprocessing Peripheral for Connectionist Applications," *Journal of Parallel and Distributed Computing*, pp. 248-259.

S. Renals, N. Morgan, M. Cohen, and H. Franco (1992), "Connectionist Probability Estimation in the DECIPHER Speech Recognition System," *ICASSP*, pp. 601-604, San Francisco.

D. Rumelhart, G. Hinton, and R. Williams (1986), "Learning Internal Representations by Error Propagation," in *Parallel Distributed Processing: Explorations of the Microstructure of Cognition*, vol 1: Foundations, D. Rumelhart & J. McClelland, Eds. Cambridge: MIT Press.

R. Schwartz, Y. Chow, O. Kimball, S. Roucos, M. Krasner, and J. Makhoul (1985), "Context-dependent modeling for acoustic-phonetic recognition of continuous speech," *ICASSP*, pp. 1205-1208.

Physiologically Based Speech Synthesis

Makoto Hirayama
†ATR Human Information Processing Research Laboratories
2-2, Hikaridai, Seika-cho, Soraku-gun, Kyoto 619-02 Japan

Eric Vatikiotis-Bateson
‡ATR Auditory and Visual Perception Research Laboratories

Kiyoshi Honda‡ **Yasuharu Koike†** **Mitsuo Kawato†***

Abstract

This study demonstrates a paradigm for modeling speech production based on neural networks. Using physiological data from speech utterances, a neural network learns the forward dynamics relating motor commands to muscles and the ensuing articulator behavior that allows articulator trajectories to be generated from motor commands constrained by phoneme input strings and global performance parameters. From these movement trajectories, a second neural network generates PARCOR parameters that are then used to synthesize the speech acoustics.

1 INTRODUCTION

Our group has attempted to model speech production computationally as a process in which linguistic intentions are realized as speech through a causal succession of patterned behavior. Our aim is to gain insight into the cognitive and neurophysiological mechanisms governing this complex skilled behavior as well as to provide plausible models of speech synthesis and possibly recognition based on the physiology of speech production. It is the use of physiological data (EMG) representing

*Also, Laboratory of Parallel Distributed Processing, Research Institute for Electronic Science, Hokkaido University, Sapporo, Hokkaido 060, Japan

motor commands to muscles that distinguishes our modeling effort from those of others who use neural networks for articulation-based synthesis and/or inference of the dynamical constraints on speech motor control (Jordan, 1986, Jordan, 1990, Bailly, Laboissiere, and Schwalz, 1992, Saltzman, 1986, Bengio, Houde, and Jordan, 1992). This paper reports two areas in which implementation of the speech production scheme shown in Figure 1 has progressed. Initially, we concentrated on modeling the dynamics underlying articulation so that phoneme strings can specify motor commands to muscles, which then specify phoneme-specific articulator behavior (Hirayama, Vatikiotis-Bateson, Kawato, and Jordan, 1992). A neural network learned the forward dynamics relating motor commands to muscles and the ensuing articulator behavior associated with prosodically intact, but phonemically simplified, reiterant speech utterances. Then, a cascade neural network (Kawato, Maeda, Uno, and Suzuki, 1990) containing the forward dynamics model along with a suitable smoothness criterion (Uno, Kawato, and Suzuki, 1989) was used to produce continuous motor commands from a sequence of discrete articulatory targets corresponding to the phoneme input string. From this sequence of motor commands, appropriate articulator trajectories were then generated.

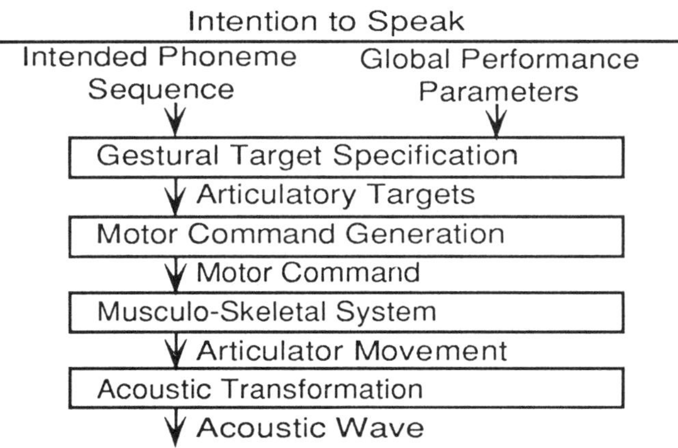

Figure 1: Conceptual scheme of speech production

Although the results of this early work were encouraging, there were two technical limitations obstructing our effort to model real speech. First, using optoelectronic transduction techniques, only simple speech samples whose primary articulators were the lips and jaw could be recorded, hence the use of reiterant *ba*. Without dynamic tongue data, real speech could not be modeled. Also, the reiterant paradigm introduced a degree of rhythmical movement behavior not observed in real speech. The second limitation was that activity of only four muscles and generally only one dimension of articulator motion could be recorded simultaneously. Thus, agonist-antagonist muscle activity was not represented even for this limited set of articulators. Technical improvements in data acquisition and their consequences for the subsequent dynamical modeling of real speech are presented in the next two sections. The second area of progress has been to implement the transform from model- generated articulator trajectories to acoustic output. A neural network is used to acquire the mapping between articulation and acoustics in terms of PARCOR parameters (Itakura and Saito, 1969), which are correlated with vocal tract area functions. Speech signals are then generated using a PARCOR synthesizer from articulator input and appropriate glottal sources (currently, the residual of the PARCOR analysis). The results of this modeling for real and reiterant speech are reported in the final section of the paper.

2 EMPIRICAL DEVELOPMENTS

In order to acquire data more suitable for real speech modeling, two additional experiments were run in which articulator position, EMG and acoustic data were recorded while the same subject produced real and reiterant speech utterances 5-8 seconds long at different speaking rates and styles (e.g., casual *vs.* precise). In the first of these, a sophisticated optoelectronic device, OPTOTRAK (Northern Digital, Inc.), was used because it permitted simultaneous recording of numerous 3D articulator positions for the lips, jaw and head, ten EMG channels, the speech acoustics, and even dynamic tongue-palate contact patterns. These data were used for modeling of the forward dynamics (see Figure 2) and the forward acoustics. Real speech utterances collected with this system were heavily loaded with labial stops, /p,b,m/, and labiodental fricatives, /f,v/, as well as many low vowels /a, ae/. Since surface EMG was used, it was difficult to obtain reliable recordings of jaw opening (anterior belly of the digastric), and closing (medial pterygoid) muscles. More recently, an electromagnetic position traking system, EMMA (Perkell, Cohen, Svirsky, Matthies, Garabieta, and Jackson, 1992), was used to transduce midsagittal motions of the tongue tip and tongue blade as well as the lips, jaw, and head. Data were collected for the same speech utterances used in the OPTOTRAK and original experiments as well as more natural utterances. Reiterant speech was also recorded for *ta*. For this experiment, surface and hooked-wire EMG techniques were combined, which enabled nine orofacial and extrinsic tongue muscles to be recorded for jaw opening and closing, lip opening and closing, and tongue raising and lowering. The most important aspects of the signal processing for modeling the forward dynamics concern the numerical differentiation of articulator position to obtain velocity and acceleration, and the severe low-pass filtering (including rectification and integration) of the EMG to from 2000 Hz to 20-40 Hz. Both of these introduce spatiotemporal distortions, whose effects on the forward dynamics model are currently being examined.

3 MODELING THE FORWARD DYNAMICS

The forward dynamics model was obtained using a 3-layer perceptron with back propagation (Rumelhart, Hinton, and Williams, 1986). Inputs to the network were instantaneous position and velocity for each dimension of articulator motion, and the EMG signals of 9-10 related muscles, which serve as the record of motor commands to muscles; outputs were accelerations for each dimension of motion. Figure 2 shows an example of predicting lip and jaw accelerations from 10 orofacial muscles for the 'natural' test utterance, "Pam put the bobbin in the frying pan and added more puppy parts to the boiling potato soup." As shown by the generalization results in Figure 2, the acquired model produced appropriate acceleration trajectories for real speech utterances, suggesting that utterance complexity is not a limiting factor in this approach.

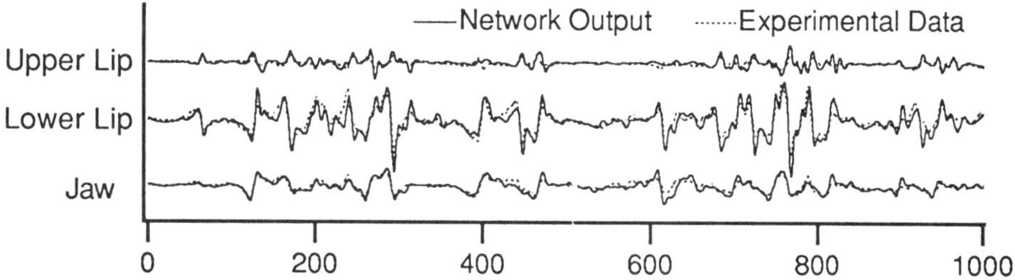

Figure 2: Estimated acceleration over time (5 ms samples) for vertical motion of the three articulators is compared to that of the test sentence: "Pam put the bobbin in the frying pan and added more puppy parts to the boiling potato soup".

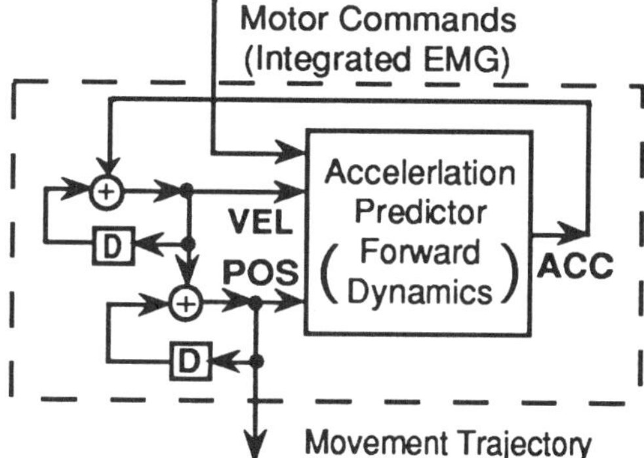

Figure 3: The musculo-skeletal forward dynamics model for producing articulator movement trajectories is implemented as a recurrent network. Continuous motor command (EMG) input drives the network, which uses estimated acceleration at time *tn*, to predict new velocity (integration) and position (double integration) values at the next time step *tn+1*. *D* is a one-sample delay unit. The network is initialized with position and velocity values taken from the test utterance at *t0*.

Network training resulted in a one-step look-ahead predictor of the articulator dynamics, and was connected recurrently as shown in Figure 3. Using only initial values of articulator position and velocity for the first sample and continuous EMG input, estimated acceleration is looped back and summed with the velocities and positions of the input layer to predict their values for each time step. This is perhaps an overly stringent test of the acquired model because errors are cumulative over the entire utterance 5-8 second utterance. Yet the network outputs appropriate articulator trajectories for the entire utterance. Figure 4 shows the generated trajectory for vertical motion of the jaw during reiterant production of *ba* (recorded with the electromagnetometer). While the trajectory generated by the network tends to underestimate movement amplitude and introduce a small DC offset, it preserves the temporal properties of the test utterance very well everywhere except before a phrasal pause. Although good results have been obtained for the analysis

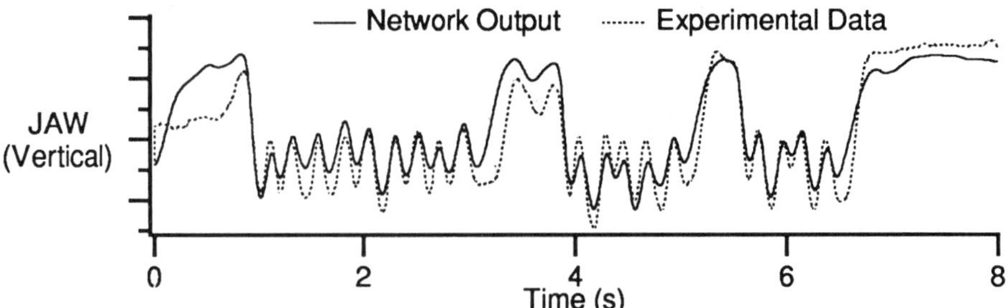

Figure 4: Jaw trajectories, generated by the forward dynamics network are compared with experimental data.

of real speech using the larger sets of articulator and muscle inputs, network complexity has greatly increased. Performance of the full network has been poorer than before in modeling simple reiterant speech, which suggests some form of modularity should be introduced. Also, the addition of tongue data has increased the number of apparent many-to-one mappings between muscle activity and articulator motion. We are now incorporating as a boundary constraint the midsagittal profile of the hard palate and alveolar ridge, against which tongue-tip articulations are made.

4 MODELING THE FORWARD ACOUSTICS

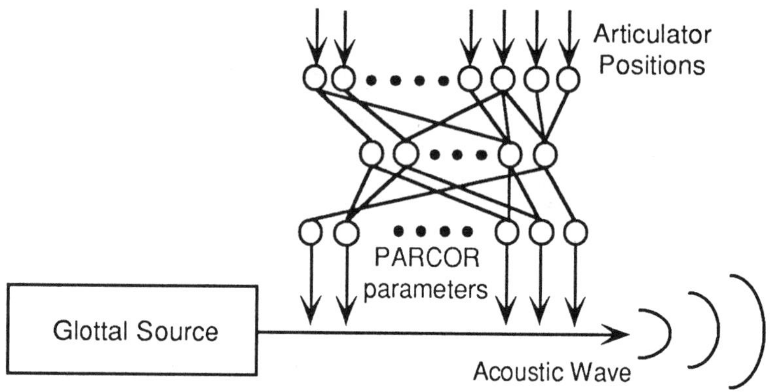

Figure 5: Forward acoustics network.

The final stage of our speech production model entails using a neural network to acquire a model of the relation between articulator motion and the ensuing acoustics. As shown in Figure 5, a 3-layer perceptron, using articulator position as input, was used to learn PARCOR analysis and generate appropriate 16-order PARCOR parameters for subsequent speech synthesis (Itakura and Saito, 1969). We chose PARCOR parameters, rather than more commonly used formant values, because the parameters have some relation to specific cross-sections of the vocal tract – e.g., the first PARCOR corresponds to the cross-sectional area closest to the lips

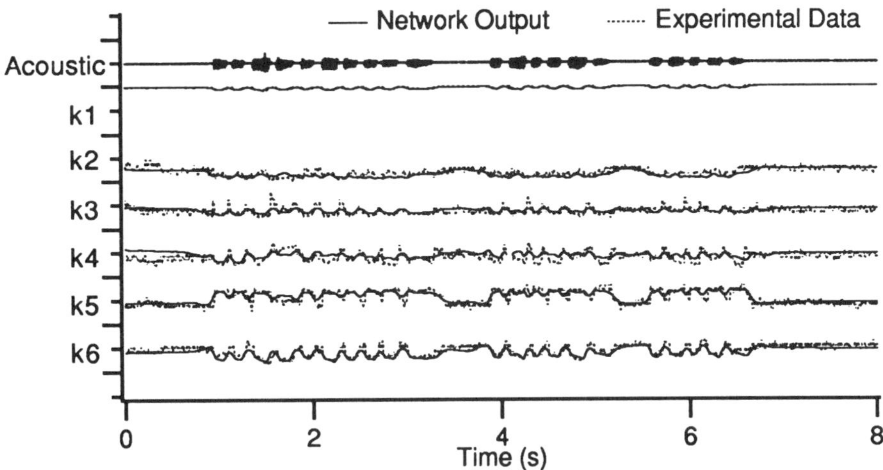

Figure 6: PARCOR parameter values (16-order, 30ms Hanning window at 200Hz) for reiterant *ba* are predicted by the network. Only the first six PARCOR parameters are shown. The range of each parameter is -1 to 1 (small tick beside each wave label indicates 0). The value of *k1* is about 1 during vowels, and network output generally matches the desire wave almost perfectly.

(Wakita, 1973). Also, PARCOR estimation errors do not have the radical consequences that formant estimation errors show. Finally, there is a unique mapping from PARCOR to formant values, but not the reverse (Itakura and Saito, 1969). Figure 6 shows the performance of the PARCOR estimation network for the first 6 parameters out of 16 parameters. Using the learned PARCOR coefficients and a sound source, acoustic signals can be synthesized. Currently, we are investigating various models for controlling sound source as well as prosodic characteristics. However, for this preliminary test of the network's ability to learn PARCOR parameters, the residual signal of PARCOR analysis served as the source waveform. Figure 7 shows an example of the network-learned PARCOR synthesis for reiterant *ba*. In this case, the training result is good as can be seen in the waveform (and frequency spectrum), or by listening the synthesized sound. However, the results have not been as good, so far, for real speech utterances containing a lot of abrupt changes and variability in vocal tract shape. One reason for this may be that learning has not yet converged, because the number articulator input channels is still too limited. So far, we have only two markers on tongue, which is not enough to recover the full vocal tract shape. This situation, hopefully, will improve as data for more tongue positions, or perhaps more functionally motivated placements, are collected. Another reason may be the inherent weakness of PARCOR analysis for modeling dynamic changes in vocal tract shape.

5 SUMMARY

This paper outlines two areas of progress in our effort to develop a computational model of speech production. First, we extended our data acquisition to include more

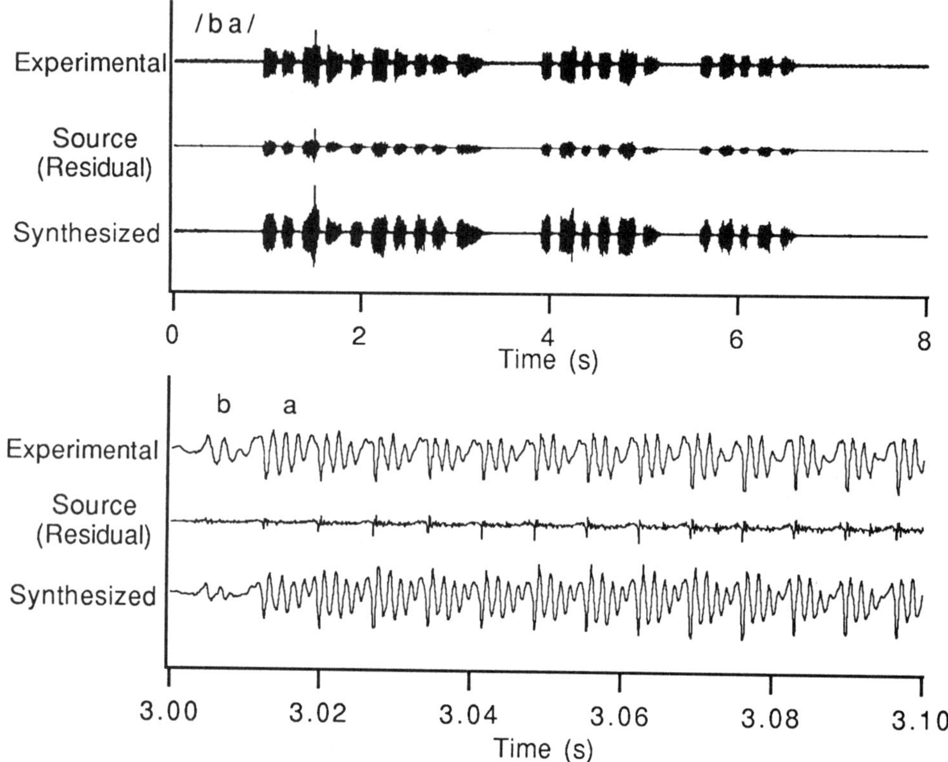

Figure 7: Speech acoustics are synthesized by driving network-learned PARCOR parameters with a glottal source (the residual). The test sentence is reiterant speech using *ba*. Top and bottom graphs differ only in time scale.

muscles and dimensions of motion for more articulators, especially the tongue, so that we could begin modeling the articulatory dynamics of real speech. As hoped, increasing the scope of the data demonstrated the applicability of our network approach to real speech. However, this also increases the size of the network, which has introduced some interesting problems for modeling simple speech samples. We are now considering modifications to the network architecture that will enable adaptive modeling of speech samples, whose complexity (e.g., number of physiological/articulatory components) may vary. Second, we have employed a simple neural network for modeling the articulatory-to-acoustic transform based on PARCOR analysis, whose parameters are correlated with vocal tract shape. Although PARCOR can be used to synthesize speech, its main use for us is as a tool for assessing empirical issues associated with articulatory-acoustic interface.

Acknowledgments

We thank Haskins Laboratories for use of their facilities (NIH grant DC-00121), Vincent Gracco and Kiyoshi Ohsima for muscle insertions, M. I. Jordan for insightful discussion, and Yoh'ichi Toh'kura for continuous encouragement. Further support was provided by HFSP grants to M. Kawato.

References

[1] Bailly, G., Laboissiere, R. and Schwarz, J. L. (1992) Formant trajectories as audible gestures: an alternative for speech synthesis. *Journal of Phonetics*, **19**, 9-23.

[2] Bengio, Y., Houde, J., and Jordan, M. I. (1992) Representations based on articulatory dynamics for speech recognition. Presented at *Neural Networks for Computing*, Snowbird, Utah.

[3] Hirayama, M., Vatikiotis-Bateson, E., Kawato, M., and Jordan, M. I. (1992) Forward dynamics modeling of speech motor control using physiological data. In Moody, J. E., Hanson, S. J., and Lippmann, R. P. (eds.) *Advances in neural information processing systems 4*. San Mateo, CA: Morgan Kaufmann Publishers.

[4] Itakura, F., and Saito, S. (1969) Speech analysis and synthesis by partial correlation parameters. *Proceeding of Japan Acoust. Soc.*, **2-2-6**.

[5] Jordan, M. I. (1986) Serial order: a parallel distributed processing approach. *ICS Report*, **8604**.

[6] Jordan, M. I. (1990) Motor learning and the degrees of freedom problem. In M. Jeannerod (ed.) *Attention and performance XIII*, 796–836, Hillsdale, NJ: Erlbaum.

[7] Kawato, M., Maeda, M., Uno, Y., and Suzuki, R. (1990). Trajectory formation of arm movement by cascade neural-network model based on minimum torque-change criterion. *Biol. Cybern.*, **62**, 275–288.

[8] Perkell, J., Cohen, M., Svirsky, M., Matthies, M., Garabieta, I., and Jackson, M., Electromagnetic midsagittal articulometer systems for transducing speech articulatory movements. *J. Acoust. Soc. Am.*, **92**, 3078–3096.

[9] Rumelhart, D. E., Hinton, G. E., and Williams, R. J. (1986) Learning representations by back-propagating errors. *Nature*, **323**, 533–536.

[10] Saltzman, E. L. (1986) Task dynamic coordination of the speech articulators: A preliminary model. In H. Heuer and C. Fromm (eds.) *Generation and modulation of action patterns*, Berlin: Springer-Verlag.

[11] Uno, Y., Kawato, M., and Suzuki, R. (1989) Formation and control of optimal trajectory in human multijoint arm movement – minimum torque-change model. *Biol. Cybern.*, **61**, 89–101.

[12] Wakita, H. (1973) Direct estimation of the vocal tract shape by inverse filtering of acoustic speech waveforms. *IEEE Trans. Audio Electroacoust.*, **AU-21** 417–427.

Analog Cochlear Model for Multiresolution Speech Analysis

Weimin Liu,* Andreas G. Andreou and Moise H. Goldstein, Jr.
Department of Electrical and Computer Engineering
The Johns Hopkins University, Baltimore, Maryland 21218 USA

Abstract

This paper discusses the parameterization of speech by an analog cochlear model. The tradeoff between time and frequency resolution is viewed as the fundamental difference between conventional spectrographic analysis and cochlear signal processing for broadband, rapid-changing signals. The model's response exhibits a wavelet-like analysis in the scale domain that preserves good temporal resolution; the frequency of each spectral component in a broadband signal can be accurately determined from the inter-peak intervals in the instantaneous firing rates of auditory fibers. Such properties of the cochlear model are demonstrated with natural speech and synthetic complex signals.

1 Introduction

As a non-parametric tool, spectrogram, or short-term Fourier transform, is widely used in analyzing non-stationary signals, such speech. Usually a window is applied to the running signal and then the Fourier transform is performed. The specific window applied determines the tradeoff between temporal and spectral resolutions of the analysis, as indicated by the uncertainty principle [1]. Since only one window is used, this tradeoff is identical for all spectral components in the signal being analyzed. This implies that conventional spectrographic signal representation and its variations are uniform resolution analysis methods. Such is also the case in parametric analysis methods, such as linear prediction coding (LPC).

*Present address: Hughes Network Systems, Inc., 11717 Exploration Lane, Germantown, Maryland 20876 USA

In spectrographic analysis of speech, it is frequently necessary to vary the window length, or equivalently the bandwidth in order to obtain appropriate resolution in time or frequency domain. Such a practice has the effect of changing the duration-bandwidth tradeoff. Broadband (short window) analysis gives better temporal resolution to the extent that vertical voice pitch stripes can be seen; narrowband (long window) can result in better spectral resolution so that the harmonics of the pitch become apparent. A question arises: if the duty of the biological cochlea were to map a signal onto the time-frequency plane, should it be broadband or narrowband?

Neurophysiological data from the study of mammalian auditory periphery suggest that the cochlear filter is effectively broadband with regard to the harmonics in synthetic voiced speech, and a precise frequency estimation of a spectral component, such as a formant, can be determined from the analysis of the temporal patterns in the instantaneous firing rates (IFRs) of auditory nerve fibers (neurograms) [2]. A similar representation was also considered by Shamma [3].

In this paper, we will first have a close look at the spectrogram of speech signals. Then the relevant features of a cochlear model [5, 6] are described and speech processing by the model is presented illustrating good resolution in time and frequency. Careful examination of the model's output reveals that indeed it performs multiresolution analysis.

2 Speech Spectrogram

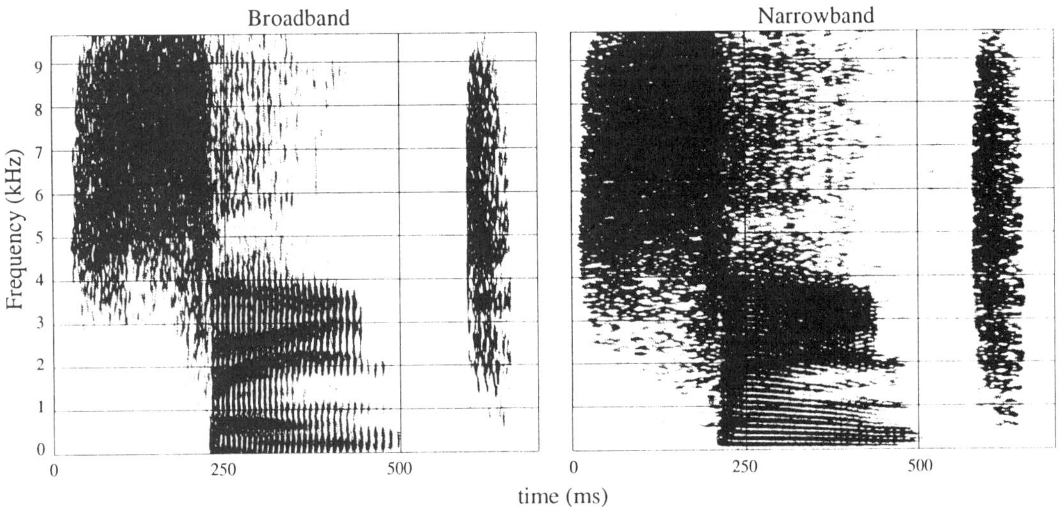

Figure 1: Broadband (6.4ms Hamming window) and narrowband (25.6ms window) spectrograms for the word "saint" spoken by a male speaker.

Figure 1 shows the broadband and narrowband spectrograms of the word "saint" spoken by a male speaker. The broadband spectrogram is usually the choice of speech analysis for several reasons. First, the fundamental frequency is considered of insignificant importance in understanding many spoken languages. Second, broadband reserves good temporal resolution, and meanwhile the representation of formants has been considered adequate. The adequacy of this notion has been seriously challenged, especially for rapidly varying events in real speech [4].

Although the vertical striation in the narrowband spectrogram indicates the pitch period, to accurately estimate the fundamental frequency F_0, it is often desirable to look at the narrowband spectrogram in which harmonics of F_0 are shown. Ideally a speech analysis method should provide multiple resolution so that both formant and harmonic information are represented simultaneously.

To further emphasize this, a synthetic signal of a tone/chirp pair was generated. The synthetic signal (Figure 2) consists of tone and chirp pairs that are separated by 100Hz. There are two 10ms gaps in both the high and low frequency tones; the chirp pair sweeps from 2900Hz-3000Hz down to 200Hz-300Hz in 100ms. The broadband spectrogram clearly shows the temporal gaps but fails to give a clear representation in frequency; the situation is reversed in the narrowband spectrogram.

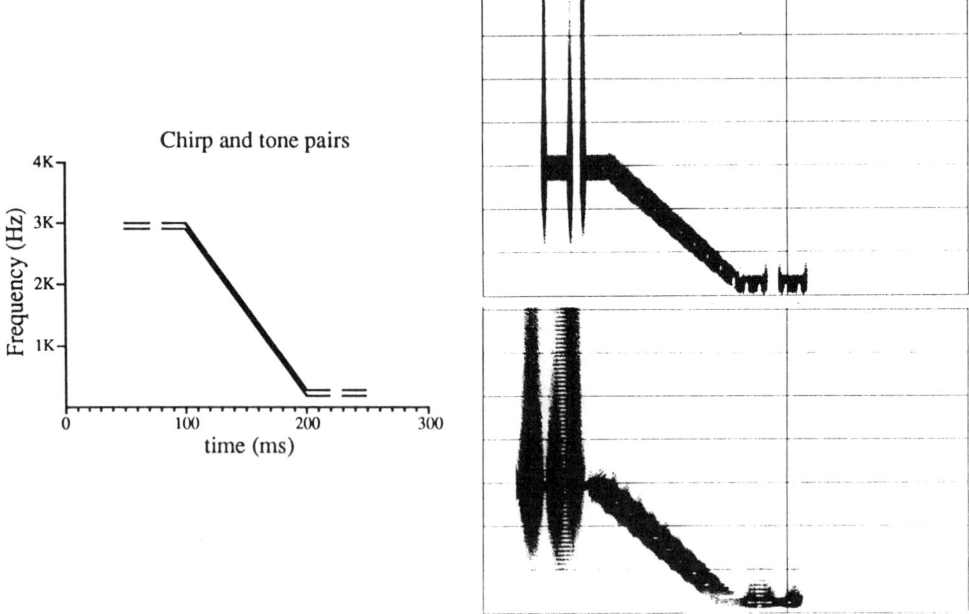

Figure 2: The synthetic tone/chirp pair and its broadband (6.4ms Hamming window) (top) and narrowband (25.6ms window) (bottom) spectrograms.

3 The Analog Cochlear Model

Parameterization of speech using software cochlear models has been pursued by several researchers; please refer to [5, 6] for a literature survey. The alternative to software simulations on engineering workstations, is the analog VLSI [7]. Computationally, analog VLSI models can be more effective compared to software simulations. They are also further constrained by fundamental physical limitations and scaling laws; this may direct the development of more realistic models. The constraints imposed by the technology are: power dissipation, physical extent of computing hardware, density of interconnects, precision and noise limitations in the characteristics of the basic elements, signal dynamic range, and robust behavior and stability. Analog VLSI cochlear models have been reported by Lyon and Mead [10] at Caltech with subsequent work by Lazzaro [11] and Watts [12].

Our model [5] consists of the middle ear, the cochlear filter bank, and hair-cell/synapse modules. All the modules in the model are based on detailed biophysical and physiological studies and it builds on the software simulation and the work in our laboratory by Payton [9]. At the present time the model is implemented both as a software simulation package but also as a set of two analog VLSI chips [6] to minimize the simulation times. Even though the silicon implementation of the model is completely functional, adequate interfaces to standard engineering workstations have not been yet fully developed and therefore here we will focus on results obtained through the software simulations.

The design of the cochlear filter bank structure is the result of the effective bandwidth concept. The filter structure is flexible enough so that an appropriate set of parameters can be found to fit the neurophysiological data. In particular, the cochlear filter bank is tuned so that the model output closely resemble the auditory fibers' instantaneous firing rates (IFR) in response synthetic speech signals [2]. To do so, a fourth order section is used instead of the second order section of our earlier work [5]. Figure 3 shows the response amplitude and group delay of the filter bank that has been calibrated in this manner.

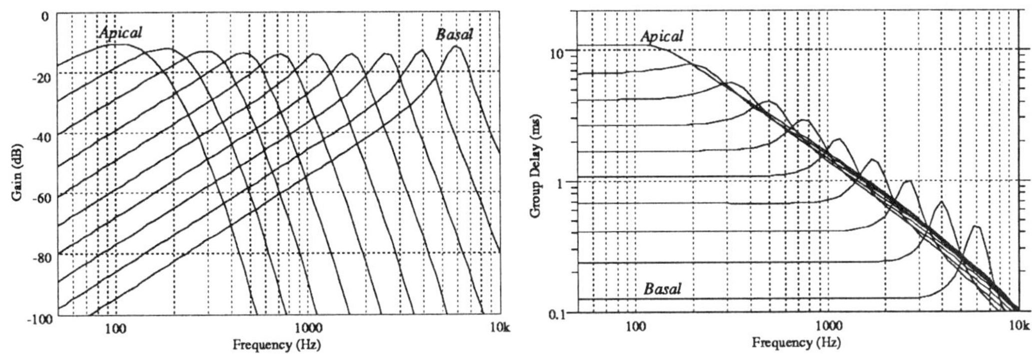

Figure 3: The amplitude and group delay of the cochlear filter bank. The curves that have higher peak frequencies in the amplitude plot and those having smaller group delays are the filter channels representing locations near the base of the cochlea.

The hair cells are the receptor cells for the hearing system. The function of hair cells and synapses in terms of signal processing is more than just rectification; besides the strong compressive nonlinearity in the mechano-electrical transduction, there are also *rapid* and *short-term* additive adaptation properties, as seen in the discharge patterns of auditory nerve fibers. Since the auditory fibers have a limited dynamic range of only 20–30dB, magnitude compression and adaptation become necessary in the transmission of acoustical signals of much wider dynamic range.

A neurotransmitter substance reservoir model, proposed by Smith and Brachman [8], of the hair cell and synapses that characterizes the generation of instantaneous firing rates of nerve fibers has been incorporated in the model. This is computationaly very demanding and the model benefits considerably by the analog VLSI implementation. The circuit output resembles closely the response of mammalian auditory nerve fibers [5].

4 Multiresolution Analysis

The conventional Fourier transform can be considered as a constant- bandwidth analysis scheme, in which the absolute frequency resolution is identical for all frequencies. A wavelet transform, on the other hand, is constant-Q in nature where the relative bandwidth is constant. The cochlear filter that is tuned to fit the experiment data is neither but is more closely related the wavelet transform, even though it required a higher Q at the base than at the apex.

The response of the cochlear model is shown in Figure 4, in the form of a neurogram. Each trace shows the IFR of a channel whose characteristic frequency is indicated on the left. The gross temporal aspects of the neurogram are rather obvious. To obtain insight into the fine time structure of IFRs, additional processing is need. One possible feature that can be extracted is the inter-peak intervals (IPI) in the IFR, which is directly related to the main spectral component in the output. The advantage of such a measure over Fourier transform is that it is not affected by the higher harmonics in the IFR. An autocorrelation and peak-picking operation were performed on the IFR output to capture the inter-peak intervals (IPIs). The procedure was similar to that by Secker-Walker and Searle [2], except that the window lengths of autocorrelation functions directly depend on the channel peak frequency. That is, for high frequency channels, shorter windows were used.

To illustrate the multiresolution nature of cochlear processing, the IPI histogram (Figure 4) across all channels are shown at each response time for the speech input "saint." Both formants and pitch frequencies are clearly shown in the composite IPI histogram.

Similarly, the cochlear model's response to the synthetic tone/chirp pairs is shown in Figure 5. The IPI histogram gives high temporal resolution for high frequencies and high spectral resolution for low frequencies such that the 10ms temporal gap in the high frequency tones and the 100Hz spacing between the two low frequency tones are precisely represented.

However in the high-frequency regions of the IPI histogram, the fact the each trace consists of a pair of tones or chirps is not clearly depicted. This limitation in the spectral resolution is the result of the relatively broad bandwidths in the high-frequency channels of the basilar membrane filter. Undoubtly the information about the 100Hz spacing in the tone/chirp pairs *is* available in the IFRs, which can be estimated from the IFR envelope which exhibits an obvious beat every 10ms (1s/100Hz) in the neurogram. Obtaining the beating information calls for a variable resolution IPI analysis scheme. For speech signals, such analysis may be necessary in pitch frequency estimation when only the IFRs of high characteristic frequencies are available.

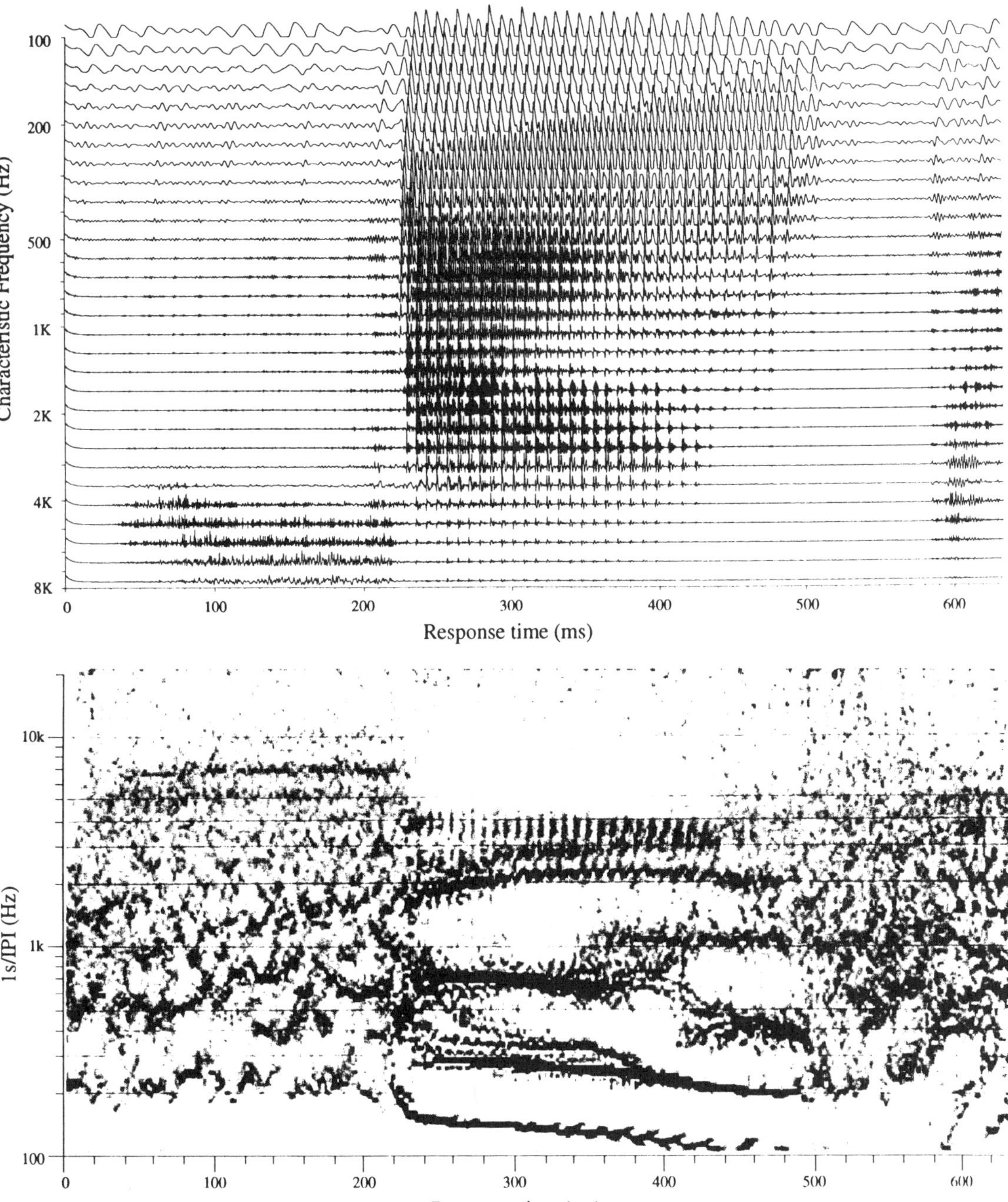

Figure 4: (*Top*) Cochlear model output, in response to "saint," in the form of neurogram. Each trace shows the IFR of one channel. Outputs from different channels are arranged according to their characteristic frequency. (*Bottom*) IPI histograms.

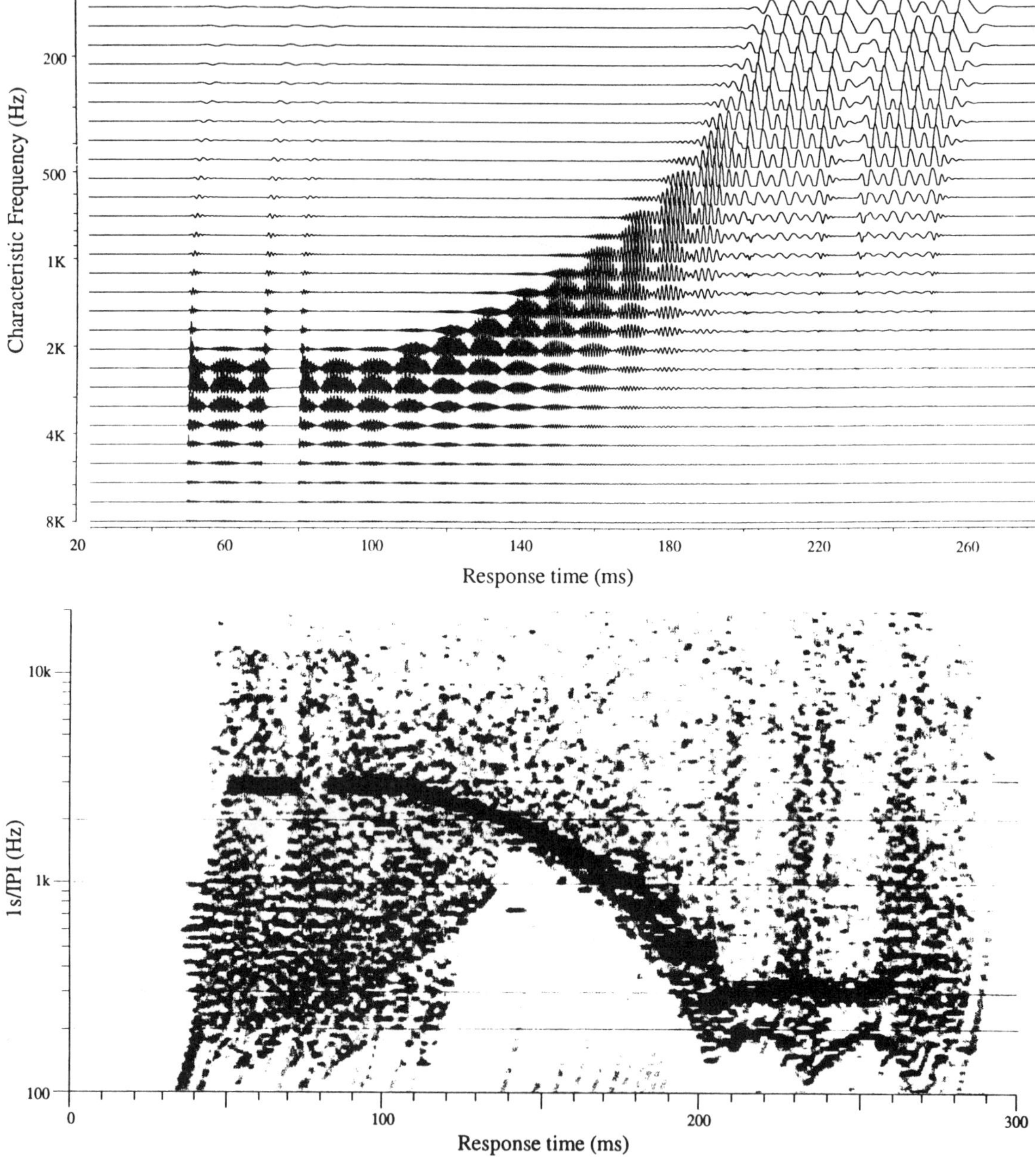

Figure 5: (*Top*) Neurogram: cochlear model response to the tone/chirp pairs. (*Bottom*) IPI histograms.

5 Discussion and Conclusions

We have presented an analog cochlear model that is tuned to match physiological data of mammalian cochleas in response to complex sounds and uses a small number of realistic model parameters. The response of this model has good resolution in time and in frequency, suitable for speech and broadband signal analysis. Both the analysis performed by the cochlear model and at subsequent stages (IPI) is in the *time-domain*. Processing information using temporal representations is pervasive in neural information processing systems. From an engineering perspective, it is advantageous because it results in architectures that can be efficiently implemented in analog VLSI. The cochlear model has been implemented as an analog VLSI system [6] operating in real-time. Appropriate interfaces are also being developed that will enable the silicon model to communicate with standard engineering workstations. Furthermore, refinements of the model may find applications as high-performance front-ends for various speech processing tasks.

References

[1] D. Gabor. (1953) A summary of communication theory. In W. Jackson (ed.), *Communication Theory*, 1-21. London: Butterworths Scientific Pub.

[2] H.E. Secker-Walker and C.L. Searle. (1990) Time-domain analysis of auditory-nerve-fiber firing rates. *J. Acoust. Soc. Am.* 88:1427-1436.

[3] S.A. Shamma. (1985) Speech processing in the auditory system. I: representation of speech sounds in the responses of the auditory-nerve. *J. Acoust. Soc. Am.* 78:1612-1621.

[4] H.F. Siverman and Y.-T. Lee. (1987) On the spectrographic representation of rapidly time-varying speech. *Computer Speech and Language* 2:63-86.

[5] W. Liu, A.G. Andreou and M.H. Goldstein. (1992) Voiced-speech representation by an analog silicon model of the auditory periphery. *IEEE Trans. Neural Networks*, 3(3):477-487.

[6] W. Liu. (1992) *An analog cochlear model: signal representation and VLSI realization* Ph.D. Dissertation, The Johns Hopkins University.

[7] C. A. Mead, (1989) *Analog VLSI and Neural Systems*, Addison–Wesley, Reading MA.

[8] R.L. Smith and M.L. Brachman. (1982) Adaptation in auditory-nerve fibers: a revised model. *Biological Cybernetics* 44:107-120.

[9] K.L Payton. (1988) Vowel processing by a model of the auditory periphery: a comparison to eighth-nerve responses. *J. Acoust. Soc. Am.* 83:155-162.

[10] R.F. Lyon and C.A. Mead. (1988) An analog electronic cochlea. *IEEE Trans. Acoust. Speech, and Signal Process.* 36:1119-1134.

[11] J. Lazzaro and C.A. Mead. (1989) A silicon model of auditory localization. *Neural Computation* 1(1):47-57.

[12] L. Watts. (1992) *Cochlear mechanics: analysis and analog VLSI.* Ph.D. Dissertation, California Institute of Technology.

A Hybrid Linear/Nonlinear Approach to Channel Equalization Problems

Wei-Tsih Lee **John Pearson**
David Sarnoff Research Center
CN5300
Princeton, NJ 08543

Abstract

Channel equalization problem is an important problem in high-speed communications. The sequences of symbols transmitted are distorted by neighboring symbols. Traditionally, the channel equalization problem is considered as a channel-inversion operation. One problem of this approach is that there is no direct correspondence between error probability and residual error produced by the channel inversion operation. In this paper, the optimal equalizer design is formulated as a classification problem. The optimal classifier can be constructed by Bayes decision rule. In general it is nonlinear. An efficient hybrid linear/nonlinear equalizer approach has been proposed to train the equalizer. The error probability of new linear/nonlinear equalizer has been shown to be better than a linear equalizer in an experimental channel.

1 INTRODUCTION

In a typical communication system, a sequence of symbols $\{I_i\}$ are transmitted though a linear time-dispersive channel h(t). Let x(t) be the received signal, it can be written as

$$x(t) = \sum_i I_i h(t-nT) + w(t) \tag{1}$$

where h(t) denotes the elementary pulse waveform, and w(t) represents the random noise with iid Gaussian distribution. In a Quadrature Amplitude Modulation (QAM), symbols $\{I_i\}$ are represented by complex numbers. During the transmission, interferences from neighboring symbols may distort the received signals. It is called Intersymbol Interference (ISI). It mainly because following reasons: nonideal channel which introduces phase or amplitude distortions, phase jitter, and impulse noise. Thus, equalization techniques are used to reduce the ISI.

2 ADAPTIVE LINEAR/RADIAL BASIS FUNCTION APPROACH TO EQUALIZER DESIGN

Traditionally, the channel equalization problem is considered as a channel-inversion operation. The idea is that an equalizer is constructed as to undo the interference from neighboring symbols as they passing through a linear dispersive channel. It can be used to explain different equalizer structures (Zero-forcing, Least mean square, and decision feedback) and their performance [Proakis, 1989]. One problem of this approach is that in general there is no direct correspondence between error probability and residual error produced by the channel inversion operation. In [Gibson, et.al, 1991], authors proposed a classification viewpoint for the equalizer design. They suggested that the optimal equalizer should be a classifier whose decision boundary is constructed according to Bayes decision rule. Compared with the channel inversion approach, the outputs of receiver are used as features for a classifier. The decision is made solely based on the classifier output, hence, on feature distribution. As it is well-known in [Fukunaga, 1978], the optimal decision boundaries can rapidly be computed if the features are Gaussian distributed. However, there is no idea about the structure of the optimal equalizer (classifier)for time-dispersive channel outputs. In next section, we prove that for a linear channel, the optimal equalizer is nonlinear.

2.1 THE OPTIMAL EQUALIZER OF A LINEAR TIME-DISPERSIVE CHANNEL

Let us first consider a two-value equalization problem. Symbols with two possible values {-1, 1} are transmitted. Let the channel be represented in a discrete form as a FIR of $\{h_i\}$, i=0,N-1. The output x_i can be written as

$$x_i = \sum_{j=0}^{N-1} I_{i-j} h_j + w_i \tag{2}$$

The optimal equalizer design is equivalent to the following Bayes decision problem. Given $\{x_i\}$, decide I_i by

$$I_i = \begin{cases} 1 & if \quad P(I_i = 1 | x_i, x_{i+1}, \ldots, x_{i+N-1}) \geq P(I_i = -1 | x_i, x_{i+1}, \ldots, x_{i+N-1}) \\ -1 & if \quad P(I_i = -1 | x_i, x_{i+1}, \ldots, x_{i+N-1}) > P(I_i = 1 | x_i, x_{i+1}, \ldots, x_{i+N-1}) \end{cases} \tag{3}$$

where $P(I_i = 1 | x_i, x_{i+1}, \ldots, x_{i+N-1})$ is the posterior probability of the transmitted symbol I_i being 1 given channel output $\{x_i\}$.

By Bayes theorem, expression(3) can be expanded to the following form:

$$P(I_i = 1 | x_i, \ldots, x_{i+1} x_{i+N-1}) = \frac{P(I_i = 1 x_i, x_{i+1}, \ldots, x_{i+N-1})}{P(x_i, x_{i+1}, \ldots, x_{i+N-1})} \tag{4}$$

$$= \frac{\prod_{j=i}^{i+N-1} \sum_{k_1, k_2, \ldots, k_{i-N+1} \in \{1,-1\}} P(x_j | I_i = 1, \ldots, I_{i-N+1} = k_{i-N+1}) P(I_i = 1, \ldots, I_{i-N+1} = k_{i-N+1})}{P(x_i, x_{i+1}, \ldots, x_{i+N-1})} \tag{5}$$

Since conditional probability $P(x_j | I_i = 1, \ldots, I_{i-N+1} = k_{i-N+1})$ in (5) is a Gaussian distribution, the numerator in (5) is a mixture of Gaussian distribution. Plugging (5) into (3), Bayes decision rule determines the optimal decision boundary as the solution of equality. Since denominator is the same on both sides, it can be ignored. Rearranging the equation, it can be written as summation of exponential functions. The solution of this equation is nonlinear function of $\{x_i\}$. In general, no analytical form can be found. However, it can be solved by numerical methods. Thus, the optimal decision boundary can be determined. The result can be extended to multi-class problems.

Based on the result established above, we provide a theoretical justification of a nonlinear equalizer approach to linear time-dispersive channel. The theoretical comparison of performances of linear and optimal equalizers can be found in [Gibson, et.al, 1991]. They concluded that performance of linear equalizers can not be improved by increasing tap length. This also suggests that a nonlinear equalizer approach is necessary. Another reason for nonlinear equalization approach is due to channels with spectrum hulls [Proakis, 1989]. In this case, the linear equalizer can not achieve the desired performance due to "noise enhancement".

2.2 NONLINEAR EQUALIZER DESIGN PROBLEM

There are several approaches to nonlinear equalizer design. To reduce the Least Mean Square (LMS) error, Voterra-series approach uses high-order product terms of input as new features. The tree-structured linear equalizer method [Gelfand, et.al., 1991] partitions the feature-space, and makes a piecewise linear approximation to the optimal nonlinear equalizer. As reported in [Gelfand, et.al., 1991], the tree-structured linear equalizer approach provides reasonable fast convergence and lower error probability as compared with linear and Voterra series approaches. The problem of this approach is that a lot of training samples are needed to achieve good performance. A neural network approach, MultiLayer Perceptron(MLP) [Gibson, et.al, 1991], trains 3 or 4 layers interconnected Perceptrons to form the nonlinear decision boundary. It is observed in [Gibson, et.al, 1991] that the performance of a MLP equalizer is close to optimal Bayes classifier. However, the training time is long and a fine-turing procedure is used. A nonlinear equalizer approach using radial basis functions is also reported in [Chen, et.al., 1991].

To put equalizers into use, the long training time is unpractical, and a fine-adjusting procedure is not allowed. Hence, it is desired to have an efficient, automatic procedure for nonlinear equalize design. To achieve this goal, we propose a hybrid linear and radial basis functions approach for automatic nonlinear equalizer design.

Although the optimal equalizer should be nonlinear, all these nonlinear design methods require long training time or large amount of training samples. Linear equalizers are not optimal, but with following advantages: easy training, fast convergence. It is also reported that the linear equalizer is relatively robust [Fukunaga, 1978]. Hence, it is desirable to combine the advantages of both linear and nonlinear equalizers. However, the hybrid structure should provide desired properties: fast convergence, automatic training procedure, and low error rate. To satisfy these constraints, we propose a feature-space partitioning approach to hybrid equalizer design.

2.3 FEATURE-SPACE PARTITIONING APPROACH TO HYBRID EQUALIZER DESIGN

To design a hybrid linear/nonlinear equalizer, we adopt the feature-space partitioning concept. The idea is similar to the one developed in [Gelfand, et.al, 1991]. Here, we consider a partitioning method based on geometrical reasoning for equalization problems. The idea is based on the fact that linear equalizers can recover distorted signals, except the cases when strong noise push samples into boundaries where two classes overlaid with each other. We consider the "confused" samples as these samples near decision boundaries. The separation of "confused" samples can be accomplished based on the output values of linear equalizers. If the distance between output value and the closest point in signal constellation [Proakis, 1989] is greater than a threshold, then we consider current sample is "confused". This means that the sample is the one close to decision boundary. To achieve an accurate classification, we classify it by a nonlinear equalizer, which is constructed for separating the samples near Bayes decision boundary.

The hybrid structure consisted of a linear equalizer, followed by a radial basis function (RBS) network, as shown in Fig. 1. A RBS network (Fig.2) is a two-layered network with radial_basis_function nodes in first layer, and a weighted linear combination of outputs of these nodes.

Each feature vector consisted of a collection of consecutive data from the channel. It is assumed that these data are properly time and carrier synchronized [Proakis, 1989]. For the QAM, a complex-valued linear equalizer is adopted. The distance between output value of linear equalizer and the closest point is then computed and compared with threshold as described before. The "confused" samples are classified by a nonlinear RBS equalizer. The output of a RBS network can be written as weighted summation of outputs of nodes as follows:

$$f(x) = \sum_i w_i exp\left(-\frac{\|x - c_i\|}{\sigma^2}\right) \tag{6}$$

where f(x) is the output of network. The output value of each node is computed according to the bell-shaped function centered at c_i. σ^2 is the width of a node. w_i is the weight associated with ith node. In our experiments, the width of all nodes are fixed. The first N training samples are assigned to the centers of N-nodes network. The weights are adjusted according to stochastic gradient decent rule:

$$\Delta w_i = \eta (d_k - f(x_k))\, exp\left(-\frac{\|x_k - c_i\|}{\sigma^2}\right) \tag{7}$$

where η is the learning rate. d_k is the desired output of network

To train a hybrid LE/RBS equalizer, a collection of training samples is used to adjust the parameters of linear equalizer. The training samples for RBS network are collected according to the distance rule described above. They are used to adjust weights of RBS network only.

The classification of a unknown sample follows a similar rule. The output value of the linear equalizer is computed. If the distance between output value and the closest point in signal constellation is smaller than the threshold, then the closest point is considered as the recovered signal. If not, the output of the RBS network is used to classify the sample. The closest point in signal constellation from output of RBS network is then used for sample class. Note, however, that there is a different interpretation for the output of linear and RBS equalizer. The function of linear equalizers can be considered as an approximation of channel inversion. Hence, it is similar to a deconvolution computation [Proakis, 1989]. However, for a RBS network, the output is the summation of weighted local Gaussian functions. For closely located points, the network is asked to give same output by then training procedure. Thus, it is more a classification approach than a deconvolution method.

The approach provides a design method for hybrid LE/RBS equalizer. The linear equaliz-

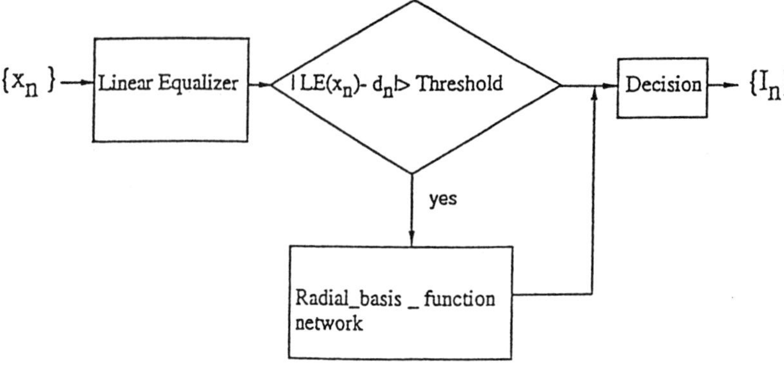

Fig. 1 System Diagram of Hybrid Linear/Nonlinear Equalizer

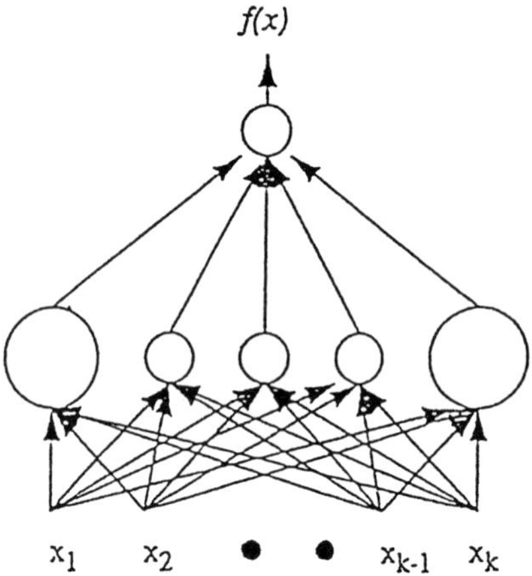

Fig. 2 A Radial_Basis_Function Network

ers perform the channel inversion or partitioning of the feature space, depending on the output value. More complicated tree-structured equalizer [Gelfand, et.al., 1991] can be adopted for this proposes. The nonlinear RBS networks are used for classifying "confused" samples. They can be replaced by MLPs. Hence, the approach provides a general method for designing hybrid structure eqalizers. However, the trade-off between complexity and efficiency of these combinations has to to be considered. For example, a multilayer tree-structured equalizer can divide the space into smaller regions for finer classification. However, the small amount of training samples in practice can be a problem for this method. A MLP network can be used for nonlinear classifier. Nevertheless, convergence time will be a major concern.

3 EXPERIMENT

We have applied our hybrid design method to a 4-QAM system. The channel is modeled by

$$x_{i-1} = 0.406I_i + 0.814I_{i-1} + 0.407I_{i-2} + w_i \tag{8}$$

where $I_i = \{-1-j, -1+j, 1-j, 1+j\}$.

A 7-tapped complex linear equalizer is used for classifying the input. Threshold for nonlinear equalizer is 0.1. We use 4,000training samples and 5,000 testing samples. A 400 nodes RBS network is used for nonlinear equalizer. The first 400 "confused" training samples are used for the center of network. The network is trained according to (6). Learning coefficient η is chosen to be 0.01. The width of a RBS node is 1.0.

Fig. 3 shows the symbol error probability vs. SNR. The error probability is evaluated over 5,000 testing samples. The hybrid LE/RBS network produces nearly 10% reduction of error rate compared with linear equalizer. This shows that a hybrid linear/RBS network equalizer can reduce the error rate by classifying "confused" samples near decision boundaries. No comparison with Bayes classifier has been made. In our experiments, it is observed that the error rate can be reduced further by increasing the number of RBS nodes. This seems imply that a large-size RBS network will in general produce better classification result. However, since there is always a limitation of the computation resources: computation time and memory storage, the performance of the hybrid linear/RBS network is limited, especially in high signal constellation case discussed below.

Equalization in high signal constellation, 16 and 64-QAM, have been tried. The result shows no significant improvement. This can be explained by the increasing of complexity. Recall that the RBS network is to separate the samples near the boundary. To deal with the increasing of number of classes due to high signal constellation, the number of nodes of network must increase proportionally. Since the increasing rate is exponential in terms of number of classes, it implies a straight-forward implementation of RBS network method can not be used for high signal constellation. In [Chen, et.al., 1991], authors suggest a dynamical RBS network with adjustable center location and width. The algorithm runs in batch mode. It is reported that the size of network can be reduced dramatically by the dynamical RBS network method. However, for equalizer application, on-line version of the algorithm is needed.

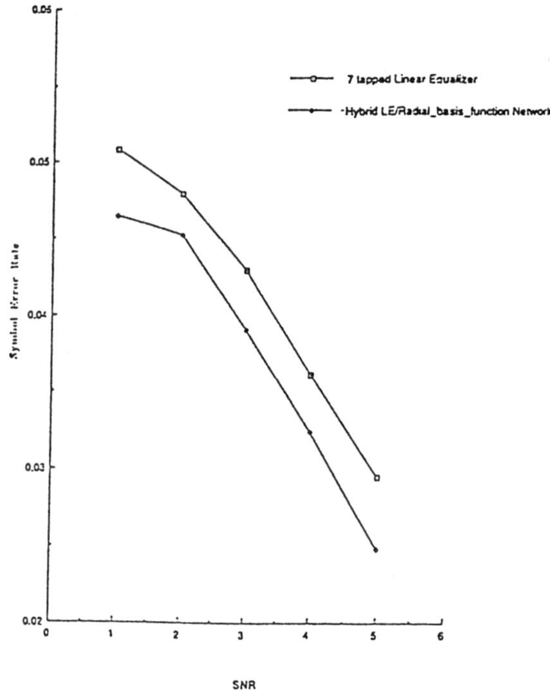

Fig. 3 Error Probability of Hybrid Linear/Radial_Basis_Function Network Equalizer for a Linear Channel $x_{i-1} = 0.406I_i + 0.814I_{i-1} + 0.407I_{i-2} + w_i$ with 4-QAM.

4 CONCLUSION AND DISCUSSION FOR HYBRID LE/RBS EQUALIZER DESIGN

By combining feature-space partitioning and nonlinear equalizers, we have developed a hybrid linear/nonlinear equalization approach. The major contribution of this research is to provide a theoretical justification of nonlinear equalization approach for linear time-dispersive channels. A feature-space partitioning method by linear equalizer is proposed. RBS networks for nonlinear equalizers are integrated into the design to separate the samples near decision boundary. The experiments for 4-QAM equalization have demonstrated the feasibility of the approach. For high signal constellation modulation, a dynamical RBS network method [Chen, et.al., 1991] has been suggested to overcome the problem of increasing complexity.

The hybrid Linear/nonlinear equalization approach combines the strength of linear and nonlinear equalizers. It offers a framework to integrate the deconvolution and classification methods. The approach can be generalized to include complicated partitioning scheme and other nonlinear networks, such as MLP, as well.

More researches need to be conducted to make this approach practical for general use. The relationship between the performance of hybrid equalizer and taps length of linear equalizers, the width and the number of RBS nodes need to be investigated. The on-line version of dynamical RBS network [Chen, et.al., 1991] need to be developed.

Reference:

Proakis, J. G., *Digital Communications*, McGrwa-Hill company, New York, 1989.

Gibson, G.J., Siu, S., Cowan, C.F.N., "The Application of Nonlinear Structures to Reconstruction of Binary Signals," IEEE. Trans. on Signal Processing, vol. 39, No. 8, Aug.,pp. 1877-1884, 1991.

Fukunaga, K., Introduction to Statistical Pattern Recognition, Academic Press, New York, 1978.

Gelfand, S.B., Ravishankar, C.S., and Delp, E.J., "Tree-structured Piecewise Linear Adaptive Equalization," ICC91, 001383, 1386.

Chen, S., Gilbson, G.J., Cowan, C.F.N., and Grant, P.M., "Reconstruction of binary signals using an adaptive radial-basis-function equalizer," Signal Processing, 22, pp. 77-93, 1991.

Chen, S., Cowan, C.F.N., and Grant, P.M., "Orthogonal Least Squares Learning Algorithm for Radial Basis Function Networks," IEEE. Trans. on Neural Networks, vol. 2, no., 2, March, pp.302-309, 1991.

Modeling Consistency in a Speaker Independent Continuous Speech Recognition System

Yochai Konig, Nelson Morgan, Chuck Wooters
International Computer Science Institute
1947 Center Street, Suite 600
Berkeley, CA 94704, USA.

Victor Abrash, Michael Cohen, Horacio Franco
SRI International
333 Ravenswood Ave.
Menlo Park, CA 94025, USA

Abstract

We would like to incorporate speaker-dependent consistencies, such as gender, in an otherwise speaker-independent speech recognition system. In this paper we discuss a Gender Dependent Neural Network (GDNN) which can be tuned for each gender, while sharing most of the speaker independent parameters. We use a classification network to help generate gender-dependent phonetic probabilities for a statistical (HMM) recognition system. The gender classification net predicts the gender with high accuracy, 98.3% on a Resource Management test set. However, the integration of the GDNN into our hybrid HMM-neural network recognizer provided an improvement in the recognition score that is not statistically significant on a Resource Management test set.

1 INTRODUCTION

Earlier work [Bourlard and Morgan, 1991] has shown the ability of Multilayer Perceptrons (MLPs) to estimate emission probabilities for Hidden Markov Models (HMM). As shown in their report, with a few assumptions, an MLP may be viewed as estimating the probability $P(q|x)$ where q is a subword model (or a state of a subword model) and x is the input acoustic speech data. In this hybrid HMM/MLP recognizer, it was shown that these estimates led to improved performance over standard estimation techniques when a fairly simple HMM was used. More recent results have shown improvements using hybrid HMM/MLP probability estimation over a state-of-the-art pure HMM-based system[Cohen *et al.*, 1993; Renals *et al.*, 1992].

Some speaker dependencies exist in common parametric representations of speech, and it is possible that making the dependencies explicit may improve performance for a given speaker (essentially enabling the recognizer to soften the influence of the speaker dependency). The basic problem with modeling and estimating explicitly speaker dependent parameters is the lack of training data. In the limit, the only available information about a new speaker is the utterance to be recognized. This limit is our starting point for this study. Even with this limited information, we can incorporate constraints on analysis that rely on the same speaker producing all the frames in an utterance, thus ensuring consistency. As has been observed for some mainstream Hidden Markov Models (HMM) systems [Murveit *et al.*, 1990], given enough training data, separate phonetic models for male and female speakers can be used to improve performance. Our first attack on consistency, then, is to incorporate gender consistency in the recognition process. In contrast to non-connectionist HMM systems, our proposed architecture attempts to share the gender-independent parameters.

Our study had two steps: first we trained an MLP to estimate the probability of gender. Then, we investigated ways to integrate the gender consistency constraint into our existing MLP-HMM hybrid recognizer, resulting in our GDNN architecture. We will give a short description of some related work, followed by an explanation of the two steps described above. We conclude with some discussion and thoughts about future work.

2 RELATED AND PREVIOUS WORK

Our previous experiments with the Gender-Dependent Neural Network (GDNN) are described in [Abrash *et al.*, 1992; Konig and Morgan, 1992]. Other researchers have worked on related problems. For example Hampshire and Waibel presented the "Meta-Pi" architecture [Hampshire and Waibel, 1990]. The building blocks for the "Meta-Pi" architecture are multiple TDNN's that are trained to recognize the speech of an individual speaker. These building blocks are integrated by another multiple TDNN trained in a Bayesian MAP scheme to maximize the phoneme recognition rate of the overall architecture. The performance of the "Meta-Pi" architecture on a six speaker /b,d,g/ task was comparable to a speaker dependent system on the same task.

Another example of related work is speaker normalization, which attempts to minimize between-speaker variations by transforming the data of a new speaker to that of a reference speaker, and then applying the speaker dependent system for the reference speaker [Huang *et al.*, 1991].

3 THE CLASSIFICATION NET

In order to classify the gender of a new speaker we need features that distinguish between speakers, in contrast to the features that are used for phoneme recognition that are chosen to suppress speaker variations. Given our constraint that the only available information about the new speaker is the sentence to be recognized, we chose features that are a rough estimate of the vocal tract properties and the fundamental frequency of the new speaker. Furthermore, we tried to suppress the linguistic information in our estimate. More specifically, the goal was to build a net that estimates the probability $P(Gender|Data)$. After some experimentation, the first twelve LPC cepstral coefficients were calculated over a 20 msec window every 10 msec (50% overlap) and averaged along each sentence. The sampling rate was 16khz. These features were augmented by an estimate of the fundamental frequency for a total of 13 features per sentence. The MLP had one hidden layer with 24 hidden units. There were two output units, one for each gender. The training set was the 109-speaker DARPA Resource Management corpus. 3500 sentences were used for the training set and 490 in the cross validation set. The size of the test set was 600 sentences, and it was a combination of the DARPA Resource Management speaker-independent Feb89 and Oct89 test sets. The trained MLP predicts the gender for the test set with less than 1.7% error on the sentence level.

4 INCORPORATING GENDER CONSISTENCY INTO OUR HYBRID HMM/MLP RECOGNIZER

4.1 DISCUSSION

Our goal is to find an architecture that shares the gender independent parameters and models the gender dependent parameters. Given our gender consistency constraint we estimate a probability that is explicitly conditioned on gender, as if the phonetic models were simply doubled to permit male and female forms of each phoneme. We can express $P(male, phone|data)$ (which is then divided by priors to get the corresponding data likelihood) by expansion to $P(phone|male, data) \times P(male|data)$. This factorization is realized by two separate MLP's: $P(male|data)$ is estimated by the classification net described above, and $P(phone|male, data)$ is realized by our GDNN described below. For further description on how to factorize probabilities by neural networks see [Morgan and Bourlard, 1992]. The final likelihood for the male case can be expressed as:

$$P(data|phone, male) = \frac{P(phone|male, data) \times P(male|data) \times P(data)}{P(phone|male) \times P(male)} \quad (1)$$

Note that during recognition, $P(data)$ can be ignored. Similarly, a female-assumed probability can be computed for each hypothesized phone. These male and female-assumed probabilities can then be used in separate Viterbi calculations (since we do not permit any hypothesis to switch gender in the midst of an utterance). In other words, dynamic programming is used with the framewise network outputs to evaluate the best hypothesized utterance assuming male gender, and then the same is done for the female case. The case with the lowest cost (highest probability) is then chosen. Note that the output of the classification net only helps in choosing between the sentence recognized according to female gender or male gender.

The critical question is how to estimate $P(phone|gender, data)$. A possible answer is to have two separate nets, one trained only on males, and the other trained only on females. This approach has the potential disadvantages of doubling the number of parameters in the system, and of not sharing the gender independent parameters. We have experimented with a such a net [Konig and Morgan, 1992] and it improved our result over the baseline system.

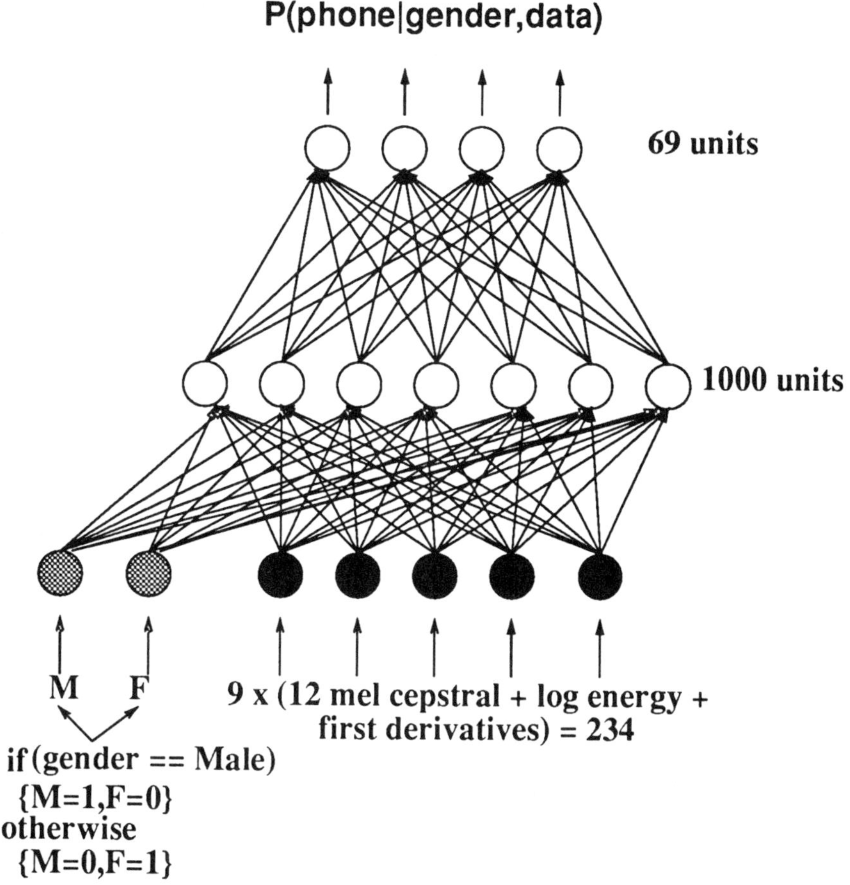

Figure 1: **A Gender Dependent Neural Network(GDNN)**

We present here a hybrid GDNN architecture that has the flexibility to tune itself to each gender. The idea is to have extra binary inputs that specify the gender of the speaker and then the probabilities that the network estimates will be conditioned on the gender. The architecture is shown in figure 1.

4.2 EXPERIMENTS AND RESULTS

We have compared four different architectures. The first architecture is our baseline system, namely, one large net that was trained on all the sentences in the training set. The second uses two separate nets, for males and females. The third is the hybrid GDNN architecture described in figure 1. The fourth architecture is a variant of the third architecture, the difference being that the binary units are connected to the output units instead of to the hidden units. All the nets have 1000 hidden units and 69 output units, including the totally separate male and female nets. While one might think that the consequent doubling of

Table 1: Result Summary

Architecture	*Test Set Word Error*
Baseline	10.6%
Two Separate Nets	10.9%
Hybrid Architecture - Variant(Binary to Output)	10.9%
GDNN Binary to hidden	10.2%

the number of parameters in the system might explain the observed degradation for the performance for the second architecture, we have also experimented with several sizes of male and female separate nets, by changing the number of the hidden units and the number of input frames. None of these experiments resulted in a significant improvement. We used 12 mel-cepstral features and the log-energy along with their first derivatives, so the number of input features per frame was 26. The features were calculated from 20ms of speech, computed every 10 msec (as before). The length of the temporal window (the number of input frames) was 9, so the total number of input features was 234. The training set was the 109-speaker DARPA Resource Management corpus. 3500 sentences were used for the training set and 490 in the cross validation set. The size of the test was the 600 sentences making up the DARPA Feb89 and Oct89 test sets. The results are summarized in table 1, and are achieved using the standard Resource Management wordpair grammar(perplexity = 60) with a simple context-independent HMM recognizer. We should note here that these results are all somewhat worse than our other results published in [Renals *et al.*, 1992; Cohen *et al.*, 1993], as the latter were achieved using SRI's phonological models, and these were done with a single-pronunciation single-state HMM (with each state repeated for a rough duration model).

5 DISCUSSION AND FUTURE WORK

The best results were achieved by the GDNN hybrid architecture that shares the gender-independent parameters while modeling the gender dependent parameters. However the improvement over our baseline is not statistically significant for this test set, although it is consistent with our experiments with other test sets, not reported here. A possible source for further improvement is using a training set with a more balanced representation of gender. In the DARPA Resource Management speaker independent training set there are 2830 sentences uttered by males versus only 1160 sentences uttered by females. Thus, performance may have suffered from an insufficient number of female training sentences. A reasonable extension to this work would be the modeling of additional speaker dependent parameters such as speech rate, accent, etc. Another direction that might be more fruitful is to combine the gender-dependent models in the local estimation of phonemes, and not to do separate Viterbi recognitions for each gender. We are currently examining this latter alternative.

Acknowledgements

Thanks to Steve Renals for his comments along the way. Computations were done on the RAP machine, with support from software guru Phil Kohn, and hardware wiz Jim Beck. Thanks to Hynek Hermansky for advising us about the features for the gender classification net. Thanks to the other members of the speech group at ICSI for their helpful comments. This work was partially funded by DARPA contract MDA904-90-C-5253.

References

[Abrash *et al.*, 1992] V. Abrash, H. Franco, M. Cohen, N. Morgan, and Y. Konig. Connectionist gender adaptation in a hybrid neural network / hidden markov model speech recognition system. In *Proc. Int'l Conf. on Spoken Lang. Processing*, Banff, Canada, October 1992.

[Bourlard and Morgan, 1991] H. Bourlard and N. Morgan. Merging multilayer perceptrons & hidden markov models: Some experiments in continuous speech recognition. In E. Gelenbe, editor, *Artificial Neural Networks: Advances and Applications.* North Holland Press, 1991.

[Cohen *et al.*, 1993] M. Cohen, H. Franco, N. Morgan, D. Rumelhart, and V. Abrash. Context-dependent multiple distribution phonetic modeling. In C.L. Giles, Hanson S.J, and J.D. Cowan, editors, *Advances in Neural Information Processing Systems*, volume 5. Morgan Kaufmann, San Mateo, 1993.

[Hampshire and Waibel, 1990] J.B. Hampshire and A. Waibel. Connectionist architectures for multi-speaker phoneme recognition. In D.S. Touretzky, editor, *Advances in Neural Information Processing Systems 2*, San mateo, CA, 1990. Morgan Kaufman.

[Huang *et al.*, 1991] X.D. Huang, K.F. Lee, and A. Waibel. Connectionist speaker normalization and its application to speech recognition. In *Neural Networks for Siganl Processing, proc. of 1991 IEEE Workshop,*, Princeton, New Jersey, October 1991.

[Konig and Morgan, 1992] Y. Konig and N. Morgan. Gdnn: A gender -dependent neural network for continuous speech recognition. In *Proc. international Joint Conference on Neural Networks*, Baltimore, Maryland, June 1992.

[Morgan and Bourlard, 1992] N. Morgan and H. Bourlard. Factoring neural networks by a statistical method. *Neural Computation*, (4):835–838, 1992.

[Murveit *et al.*, 1990] H. Murveit, M. Weintraub, and M. Cohen. Training set issues in sri's decipher speech recognition system. In *Proc. speech and Natural Language Workshop*, pages 337–340, June 1990.

[Renals *et al.*, 1992] S. Renals, N. Morgan, M. Cohen, H. Franco, and H. Bourlard. Connectionist probability estimation in the decipher speech recognition system. In *Proceedings IEEE Intl. Conf. on Acoustics, Speech, and Signal Processing*, San Francisco, California, March 1992. IEEE.

Transient Signal Detection with Neural Networks: The Search for the Desired Signal

Jose C. Principe and Abir Zahalka

Computational NeuroEngineering Laboratory
Department of Electrical Engineering
University of Florida, CSE 447
Gainesville, FL 32611
principe@synapse.ee.ufl.edu

Abstract

Matched filtering has been one of the most powerful techniques employed for transient detection. Here we will show that a dynamic neural network outperforms the conventional approach. When the artificial neural network (ANN) is trained with supervised learning schemes there is a need to supply the desired signal for all time, although we are only interested in detecting the transient. In this paper we also show the effects on the detection agreement of different strategies to construct the desired signal. The extension of the Bayes decision rule (0/1 desired signal), optimal in static classification, performs worse than desired signals constructed by random noise or prediction during the background.

1 INTRODUCTION

Detection of poorly defined waveshapes in a nonstationary high noise background is an important and difficult problem in signal processing. The matched filter is the optimal linear filter assuming stationary noise [Thomas, 1969]. The application area that we are going to discuss is epileptic spike detection in the electrocorticogram (ECoG), where the matched filtering produce poor results [Barlow and Dubinsky, 1976], [Pola and Romagnoli, 1979] due to the variability of the spike shape and the ever changing background (the brain electric activity). Recently artificial neural networks have been applied to spike detection [Eberhart et al, 1989], [Gabor and

Seydal, 1992], but static neural network architectures were chosen. Here a static multilayer perceptron (MLP) will be augmented with a short term memory mechanism to detect spikes. In the way we utilized the dynamic neural net, the *ANN can be thought of as an extension of the matched filter to nonlinear models*, which we will refer to as *a neural template matcher*. In our implementation, the ANN looks directly at the input signal with a time window larger than the longest spike for the sampling frequency utilized. The input layer of the dynamic network is a delay line, and the data is clocked one sample at a time through the network. The desired signal is "1" following the occurrence of a spike. With this strategy we teach the ANN to produce an output of "1" when a waveform similar to the spike is present within the time window. A spike will be recognized when the ANN output is above a given threshold.

Unlike the matched filter, the ANN does not require a single, explicit waveform for the template (due to the spike shape variability some form of averaging is needed to create the "average" spike shape which is normally a poor compromise). Rather, the ANN will learn the important features of the transient class by training on many sample spikes, refining its approximation with each presentation. Moreover, the ANN using the sigmoid nonlinearity will have to necessarily represent the background activity, since the discriminant function in pattern space is established from information pertaining to all input classes. Therefore, the nonstationary nature of the background can be accommodated during network training and we can expect that the performance of the neural template matcher will be improved with respect to the matched filter.

We will not address here the normalization of the ECoG, nor the issues associated with the learning criterion [Zahalka, 1992]. The purpose of this paper is to delve on the design of the desired signal, and quantify the effect on performance. What should be the shape of the desired sinal for transient detection, when on-line supervised learning is employed? In our approach we decided to construct a desired signal that exists for all time. We shall point out that the existence of a desired signal for every sample will simplify supervised learning, since in principle the conventional backpropagation algorithm [Rumelhart et al, 1986] can be utilized instead of the more time consuming backpropagation through time [Werbos, 1990] or real-time recurrent learning [Williams and Zipzer, 1989]. The simplified learning algorithm may very well be one of the factors which will make ANNs learn on-line as adaptive linear filters do. The main decision regarding the desired signal for spike detection is to decide the value of the desired signal during the background (which for spikes represent 99% of the time), since we decided already that it should be "1" following the spike. Similar problems have been found in speech recognition, when patterns that exist in time need to be learned [Unnikrishnan et al, 1991] [Watrous et al, 1990]. Here we will experimentally compare three desired signals (Figure 1):

Desired signal I- Extrapolating the Bayes rule for static patterns [Makhoul], we will create a target of zero during the background, and a value of 1 following the spike, with a duration equal to the amount of time the spike is in the input window.

Desired signal II- During the background, a random, uniformly distributed (between -0.5 and 0.5), zero mean target signal. Same target as above following the spike.

Desired signal III- During the background the network will be trained as a one step predictor. Same target as above following the spike.

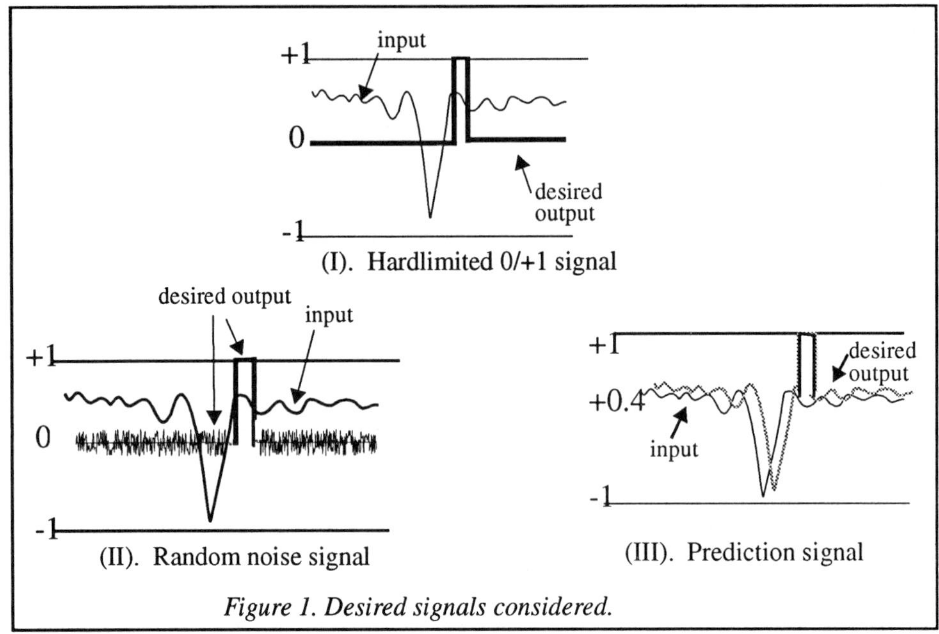

Figure 1. Desired signals considered.

2 NEURAL NETWORK ARCHITECTURE AND TRAINING

One ECoG channel was sampled at 500 Hz (12 bit A/D converter) and was pre-processed for normalization between -1 and 0.4, and DC removal before being presented to the ANN [Zahalka, 1992]. An epileptic spike has a duration between 20 and 70 msec.

The dynamic network used for this application is a time delay neural network (TDNN) consisting of an input layer with 45 taps, 12 hidden processing elements (PEs) and one linear output PE. The input window corresponds to 90 msec, so even the longest spike is fully present in the window during at least 10 samples.

The training set consists of 60 hand picked 2 sec. segments containing one spike each, embedded in 6,860 points of background activity. In principle the data could be streamed on-line to the ANN, provided that we could create also on-line the desired signal. But at this point of the research we preferred to control the segment length and choose well defined spikes to study training issues. The test data set consists of another set (belonging to the same individual) of 49 spikes embedded in 6,970 samples. A spike was defined when the ANN output was above 0.9.

The ANN was trained with the backpropagation algorithm [Rumelhart et al 1986]. The weights were updated after every sample (real-time mode). A momentum term (α=0.9) was used, and 0.1 was added to the sigmoid derivative to speedup learning [Fahlman, 1988]. The training was stopped when the test set performance decreased. The network typically learned in less than 50 presentations of the training set. All the results presented next use the same training/test sets, the same learning and stop criterion and the same network topology.

3 RESULTS

Desired Signal I.

We begin with the most commonly used desired signal for static classification, the hardlimited 0/+1 signal of Figure 1(I), but now extended in time (0 during the background, 1 after the occurrence of the spike). This desired signal has been shown to be optimal in the sense that it is a least square approximation of the *Bayes decision rule [Makhoul, 1991]. However it performs poorly for transient detection* (73% of correct detections and 8% of false positives). We suspect that the problem lies in the different waveshapes present in the background. When an explicit 0 value is given as the desired signal for the background, the network has difficulties extracting common features to all the waves and biases the decision rule. Samples of the network input and the corresponding output are shown in Figure 2(I). Notice that the ANN output gets close to "1" during high amplitude background, and fails to be above 0.9 during small amplitude spikes. In Table 1, the test set performance is better than the training set due to the fact that the spikes chosen for training happen to include more difficult cases.

Table 1. Performance Results.

Desired Signal	Training Set detections	Training Set false positives	Test Set detections	Test Set false positives
0 <--> +1	38/60 = 63%	2/38 = 5%	36/49 = 73%	3/36 = 8%
noise	54/60 = 90%	0/54 = 0%	46/49 = 94%	1/47 = 2%
prediction	50/60 = 83%	1/50 = 2%	45/49 = 92%	2/45 = 4%

Detections mean number of events in agreement between the human expert and the ANN (normalized by the number of spikes in the set).

False positives mean the number of events picked by the ANN, but not considered spikes by the human expert (normalized by the number of ANN detections)

The "random noise" desired signal is shown in Figure 1(II). This signal consists simply of uniformly distributed random values bounded between -0.5 and +0.5 for the nonspike regions and again a value of "+1" after the spikes. This approach is based on the fact that the random number generator will have a zero mean distribution. Therefore, during training over the nonspike regions, the errors backpropagated through the network will normally average out to zero, yielding in practice a "don't care" target for the background. *This effectively should give the least bias to the decision rule.* The net result is that consistent training is only performed over the spike patterns, allowing the network to better learn these patterns and provide improved performance. The results of this configuration are very promising, as can be seen in Table 1 and in Figure 2(II). The "noise" signal performs better than all of the other desired signal configurations examined (94% correct detections and 2% false detections).

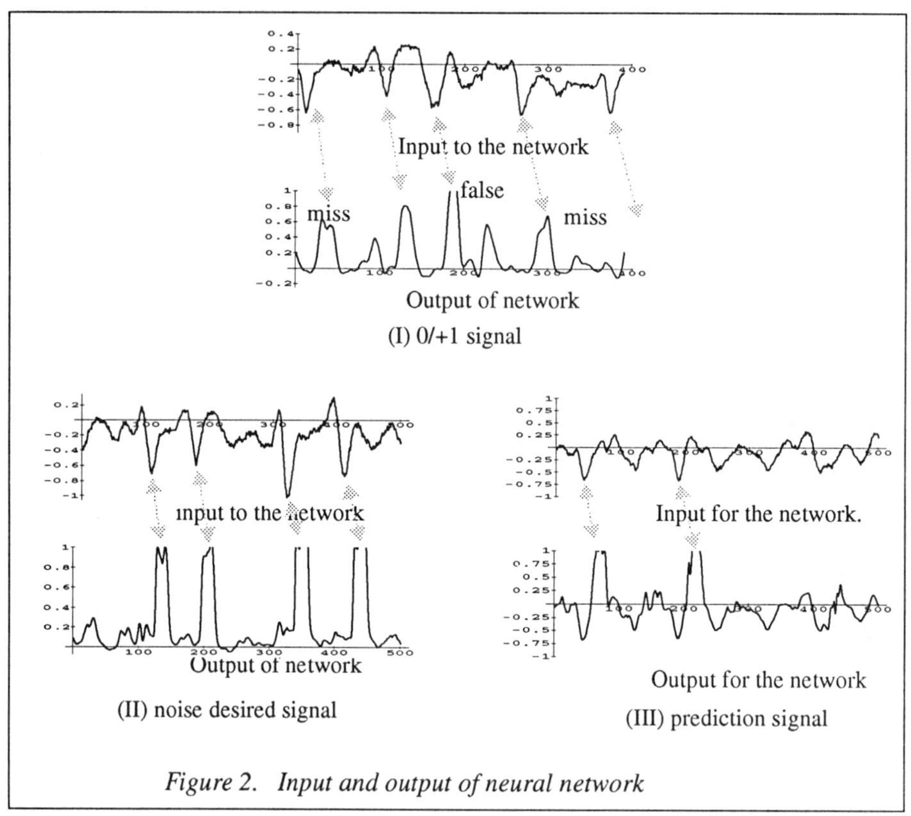

Figure 2. Input and output of neural network

The last signal configuration is the prediction paradigm. The network is performing one-step prediction during the nonspike portions of the signal and a saturation value of "+1" is added to the desired signal after the spike, as in Figure 1(III). The rationale behind such a configuration is that the desired signal is readily available and may require fewer network resources than a target of "0", decreasing the bias in the decision rule for the spike class. The results are given in Table 1, where we see a marked improvement over the hardlimited desired signal (92% correct detection and 4% false positives).

4 COMPARISON WITH MATCHED FILTER

The template for the matched filter was formed by averaging five spikes from the training set. While averaging reduces morphological "crispness," it enhances the robustness of spike shape representation, since the spike shape is variable. The 45 point template is correlated continuously with the time signal from the test set, hence no correction to the nonwhite nature of the ECoG is being done. Performance in both the matched filter and the ANN approach will be dependent upon the threshold levels chosen for detection, which determines the receiver operating characteristic (ROC) for the detector, but requires large data sets to be meaningful. Table 2 shows a partial result, where both detectors are compared in terms of false positives for 90% detection rate and detection rate for 2 false positives. The results presented for the ANN are for the random noise desired signal. In both cases, we see the superiority of the ANN approach.

Table 2. Comparison ANN/Matched filter

90% detection rate		2 false positives	
NN	MF	NN	MF
0 false +'s	21 false +'s	92%	13%

5 CONCLUSIONS

The ultimate conclusion of this experimental work is that neural networks can be used to implement transient detectors, outperforming the conventional matched filter for the detection of spike transients embedded in the ECoG. However, the difficulty in the ANN approach comes in how to setup the training, and the desired signal.

Although the training was not discussed here, we would like to point several issues that are important. *When a cost function that is sensitive to the a priori probability of the classes is used (as the error signal in backpropagation) the proper balance of background versus spike data sizes is relevant for adequate training.* Our results show that at a low spike concentration of 4% (ratio of spike samples over background samples in the training set), the network never learns the waveform and always outputs the value chosen to represent the background. For our application, these problems disappear at an 18% concentration level.

Another important issue is the selection of the class exemplars for training. *Transient detection is a one class classification problem (A versus the universe)*, rather than a two class classification problem. It is not possible to cover appropriately the unconstrained background with examples, and even when a large number of background waves is utilized (in our case 80% of the training samples belonged to the background) the training produced bad results. We found out that only the waves similar in shape to the spikes are important to bound the spike class in feature space. As a solution, we *included in the training set the false positives*, i.e. waves that the system detects as spikes but the human expert classifies as background, to improve the detection agreement with the human [Zahalka, 1992].

The issues regarding the choice of the desired signal are also important. We found experimentally that the best desired signal for our case is the one that uses random noise during the background. We can not, at this point, explain this result theoretically. This desired signal is also the one that uses fewer network resources (i. e. number of hidden units) without degrading the performance [Zahalka, 1992]. *This result came as a surprise since the 0/1 signal has been shown to be optimal for static patterns in the sense that makes the classifier approximate the Bayes decision rule.* The explanation may be simply a matter of local minima in the performance surface of the network trained with the 0/1 desired signal, but it may also reflect deeper causes. With the 0/1 desired signal, the network weights are updated equally with the information of the background waveforms and with the information regarding the spikes. The training paradigm should emphasize the spikes, since the spikes are the waves we are interested in. Moreover, since the background class is unconstrained, many more degrees of freedom are necessary to represent well the background. When not enough hidden units are available, the network biases the discriminant function, and the performance is poor. In the prediction paradigm the background is selected as the desired signal and the required number of hidden nodes to predict the next sample is much smaller (actually only three hidden nodes are sufficient to keep the reported performance [Zahalka, 1992]). The network resources naturally self organize as two template matching nodes and one prediction node. However, we have found out that the signal has to be properly normalized in the sense that the target for the spike ("1") must be outside the range of the input signal voltages (that is the reason we normalize the input signal between -1 and 0.4). From a classification point of view we "do not care" what the net output is provided it is far from the target of "1". The random noise target with zero mean achieves this goal very easily, because the error gradient during the background averages out to zero. Therefore the weights reflect primarily the information containing in the shape of the spike. We found out that only two hidden nodes are sufficient to keep the reported performance. [Zahalka, 1992]. It seems that the theory of time varying signal classification with neural networks is not a straight forward extension of the static classification case, and requires further theoretical analysis.

An implication of this work regards the role of supervised learning in biological neural networks. This work shows that during non-interesting events, there is no need to provide a target to the neural assembly (noise, which is so readily available in biological systems, suffices). Re-enforcement stimulus are only needed during or after relevant events, which is compatible with the information processing models of the olfactory bulb [Freeman and DiPrisco, 1989]. Therefore, looking at learning and adaptation in biological systems as a signal detection instead of a classification problem seems promising.

Acknowledgments

This work has been partially supported by NSF grants ECS-9208789 and DDM-8914084.

References

Barlow J. S. and Dubinsky J., (1976) "Some Computer Approaches to Continuous

Automatic Clinical EEG Monitoring," in *Quantitative Analytic Studies in Epilepsy,* Raven Press, New York, 309-327.

Eberhart R., Dobbins R., Weber W., (1989) "Casenet: a neural network tool for EEG waveform classifiaction", *Proc IEEE Symp. Comp. Based Medical Systems*, Minneapolis, 60-68, 1989.

Fahlman S.,(1988) "Faster learning variations on backpropagation: an empirical study", *Proc. 1988 Connectionist Summer School*, Morgan Kaufmann, 38-51.

Freeman W., DiPrisco V., (1986) "EEG spatial pattern differences with discriminated odors manifest chaotic and limit cycle attractors in olfactory bulb of rabbits", in *Brain Theory,* Ed. Palm and Aertsen, Springer, 97-120.

Gabor A., Seydal M., (1992) "Automated interictal EEG spike detection using artifical neural networks", *Electroenc. Clin. Neurophysiol.*, (83), 271-280.

Makhoul J., (1991) "Pattern recognition properties of neural networks",*Proc. 1991 IEEE Workshop Neural Net. in Sig. Proc.*, 173-187, Princeton.

Pola P. and Romagnoly O., (1979) "Automatic analysis of interictal epileptic activity related to its morphological aspects", *Electroenceph. Clin. Neurophysiol.*, #46, 227-231.

Rumelhart,D.E., Hinton,G.E. and Williams,R.J. (1986) "Learning internal representations by error propagation. in *Parallel Distributed Processing* (Rumelhart, McClelland, eds.), ch. 8, Cambridge, MA.

Thomas J., (1969) "*An Introduction to statistical Communication Theory*", Wiley.

Watrous R., Ladendorf B., Kuhn G., (1990) "Complete gradient optimization of a recurrent network applied to b,d,g discrimination", *J. Acoust. Soc. Am.* 87 (3), 1301-1309.

Werbos, P.J. (1990) "Backpropagation through time: what it does and how to do it", *Proc. IEEE*, vol 78, no10, 1550-1560.

Williams,R.J. and Zipser, D. (1989) "A learning algorithm for continually running fully recurrent neural networks. in *Neural Computation, vol. 1 (2).*

Unikrishnan K., Hopfield J., Tank D., (1991) "Connected-Digit Speaker-dependent speech recognition using a neural network with time delayed connections", *IEEE Trans. Sig Proc.*, vol 39, #3, 698-713.

Zalahka A., (1992) "Signal detection with neural networks: an application to the recognition of epileptic spikes", *Master Thesis*, University of FLorida.

Performance Through Consistency: MS-TDNN's for Large Vocabulary Continuous Speech Recognition

Joe Tebelskis and Alex Waibel
School of Computer Science
Carnegie Mellon University
Pittsburgh, PA 15213

Abstract

Connectionist speech recognition systems are often handicapped by an inconsistency between training and testing criteria. This problem is addressed by the Multi-State Time Delay Neural Network (MS-TDNN), a hierarchical phoneme and word classifier which uses DTW to modulate its connectivity pattern, and which is directly trained on word-level targets. The consistent use of word accuracy as a criterion during both training and testing leads to very high system performance, even with limited training data. Until now, the MS-TDNN has been applied primarily to small vocabulary recognition and word spotting tasks. In this paper we apply the architecture to large vocabulary continuous speech recognition, and demonstrate that our MS-TDNN outperforms all other systems that have been tested on the CMU Conference Registration database.

1 INTRODUCTION

Neural networks hold great promise in the area of speech recognition. But in order to fulfill their promise, they must be used "properly". One obvious condition of "proper" use is that both training and testing should use a consistent error criterion. Unfortunately, in speech recognition, this obvious condition is often violated: networks are frequently trained using phoneme-level criteria (phoneme classification or acoustic prediction), while the testing criterion is word recognition accuracy. If phoneme recognition were perfect, then word recognition would also be perfect; but of course this is not the case, and the errors which are inevitably made are optimized for the wrong criterion, resulting in suboptimal word recognition accuracy.

The Multi-State Time Delay Neural Network (MS-TDNN) has recently been proposed as a solution to this problem [1]. The MS-TDNN is a hierarchically structured classifier which consistently uses word accuracy as a criterion for both training and testing. It has so far yielded excellent results on small vocabulary recognition [1, 2, 3] and a word spotting task [4]. In the present paper, we review the MS-TDNN architecture, discuss its application to large vocabulary continuous speech recognition, and present some favorable experimental results on this task.

2 RESOLVING INCONSISTENCIES: MS-TDNN ARCHITECTURE

In this section we motivate the design of our MS-TDNN by showing how a series of intermediate designs resolve successive inconsistencies.

The preliminary system architecture, shown in Figure 1(a), simply consists of a phoneme classifier, in this case a TDNN, whose outputs are copied into a DTW matrix, in which continuous speech recognition is performed. Many existing systems are based on this type of approach. While this is fine for bootstrapping purposes, the design is ultimately suboptimal because the training criterion is inconsistent with the testing criterion: phoneme classification is not word classification.

To address this inconsistency we must train the network explicitly to perform word classification. To this end, we define a word layer with one unit for each word in the vocabulary; the idea is illustrated in Figure 1(b) for the word "cat". We correlate the activation of the word unit with the associated DTW score by establishing connections from the DTW alignment path to the word unit. Also, we give the phonemes within a word independently trainable weights, to enhance word discrimination (for example, to discriminate "cat" from "mat" it may be useful to give special emphasis to the first phoneme); these weights are tied over all frames in which the phoneme occurs. Thus a word unit is an ordinary unit, except that its connectivity to the preceding layer is determined dynamically, and its net input should be normalized by the total duration of the word. The word unit is trained on a target of 1 or 0, depending if the word is correct or incorrect for the current segment of speech, and the resulting error is backpropagated through the entire network. Thus, word discrimination is treated very much like phoneme discrimination.

Although network (b) resolves the original inconsistency, it now suffers from a secondary one – namely, that the weights leading to a word unit are used during training but ignored during testing, since DTW is still performed entirely in the DTW layer. We resolve this inconsistency by "pushing down" these weights one level, as shown in Figure 1(c). Now the phoneme activations are no longer directly copied into the DTW layer, but instead are modulated by a weight and bias before being stored there (DTW units are linear); and the word unit has constant weights, and no bias. During word-level training, error is still backpropagated from targets at the word level, but biases and weights are modified only at the DTW level and

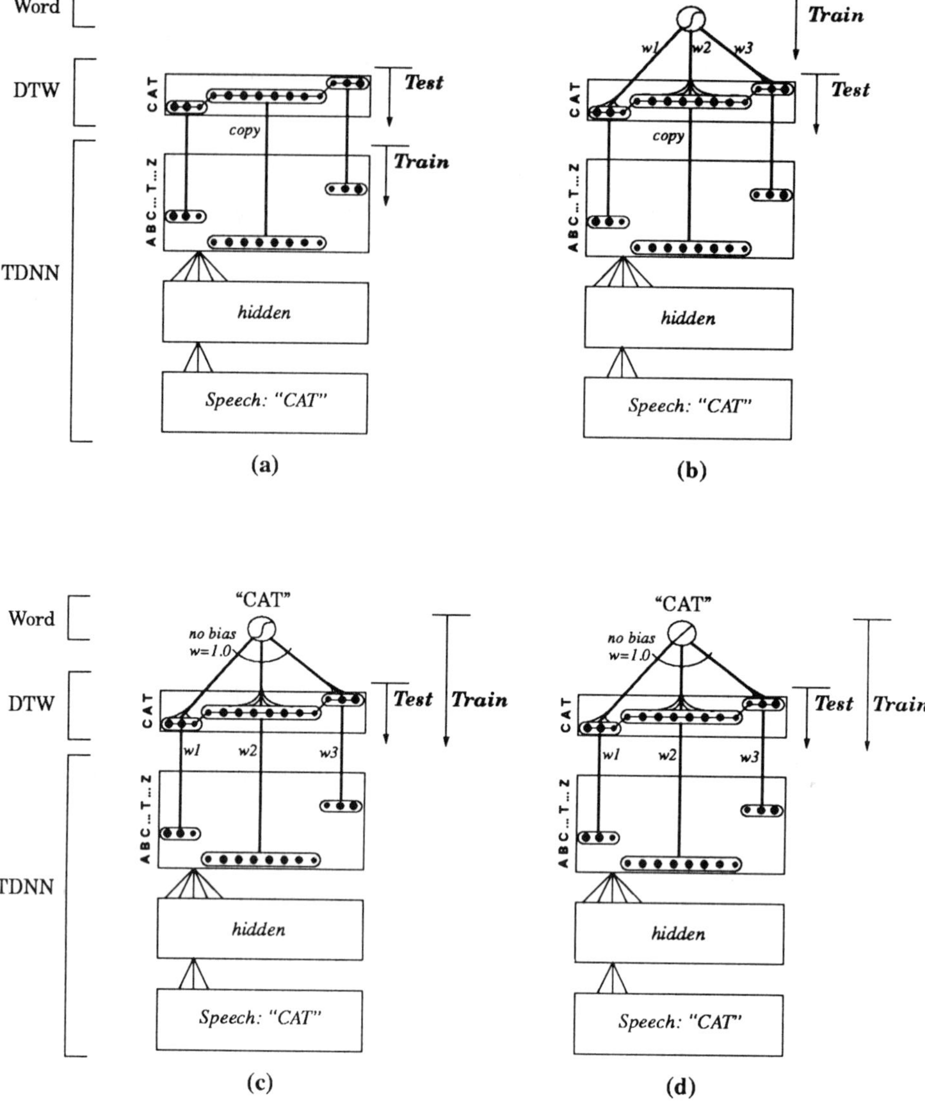

Figure 1: Resolving inconsistencies: (a) TDNN+DTW. (b) Adding word layer. (c) Pushing down weights. (d) Linear word units, for continuous speech recognition.

below. Note that this transformed network is not exactly equivalent to the previous one, but it preserves the properties that there are separate learned weights associated with each phoneme, and there is an effective bias for each word.

Network (c) is still flawed by a minor inconsistency, arising from its sigmoidal word unit. The problem does not exist for isolated word recognition, since any monotonic function (sigmoidal or otherwise) will correlate the highest word activation with the highest DTW score. However, for continuous speech recognition, which concatenates words into a sentence, the optimal sum of sigmoids may not correspond to the optimal sigmoid of a sum, leading to an inconsistency between word and sentence recognition. Linear word units, as shown in (d), resolve this problem; in practice we have found that linear word units perform slightly better than sigmoidal word units.

The resulting architecture is called a "Multi-State TDNN" because it integrates the DTW alignment of multiple states into a TDNN to perform word classification. While an MS-TDNN for small vocabulary recognition can be based on word models with non-shared states [4], a large vocabulary MS-TDNN must be based on shared units of speech, such as phonemes. In our system, the TDNN (first three layers) is shared by all words in the vocabulary, while each word requires only one non-shared weight and bias for each of its phonemes. Thus the number of parameters in the MS-TDNN remains moderate even for a large vocabulary, and it can make the most of limited training data. Moreover, new words can be added to the vocabulary without retraining, by simply defining a new DTW layer for each new word, with incoming weights and biases initialized to 1.0 and 0.0, respectively.

Given constant weights under the word layer, word level training is really just another way of viewing DTW level training; but the former is conceptually simpler because there is a single binary target for each word, which makes word level discrimination very straightforward. For a large vocabulary, discriminating against all incorrect words would be very expensive, so we discriminate against only a small number of close matches (typically 1).

Word level training yields better word classification than phoneme level training. In one experiment, for example, we bootstrapped our system with phoneme level training (as shown in Figure 1a), and found that word recognition accuracy asymptoted at 71% on a test set. We then continued training from the word level (as shown in Figure 1d), and found that word accuracy improved to 81% on the test set. It is worth noting that in an intermediate experiment, even when we held the DTW layer's incoming weights and biases constant (at 1.0 and 0.0 respectively), thus adding no new trainable parameters to the system, we found that word level training still improved the word accuracy from 71% to 75% on the test set, as a consequence of word-level discrimination.

3 BALANCING THE TRAINING SET

The MS-TDNN must be first bootstrapped with phoneme level training. In our early experiments we had difficulty bootstrapping the TDNN, not only because our training set was unbalanced, but also because the vast majority of phonemes were being trained on a target of 0, so that the negative training was overwhelming and

	N	O	N	A	T	Y	E	T
A	○	○	○	●	○	○	○	○
E	○	○	○	○	○	○	●	○
O	○	●	○	○	○	○	○	○
N	●	○	●	○	○	○	○	○
T	○	○	○	○	●	○	○	●
Y	○	○	○	○	○	●	○	○
Z	○	○	○	○	○	○	○	○

Scale backprop error by:

	N	O	N	A	T	Y	E	T
A	-1/7	-1/7	-1/7	**1.0**	-1/7	-1/7	-1/7	-1/7
E	-1/7	-1/7	-1/7	-1/7	-1/7	-1/7	**1.0**	-1/7
O	. . . .							
N	**1/2**	-1/6	**1/2**	-1/6	-1/6	-1/6	-1/6	-1/6
T	-1/6	-1/6	-1/6	-1/6	**1/2**	-1/6	-1/6	**1/2**
Y	. . . .							
Z	-1/8	-1/8	-1/8	-1/8	-1/8	-1/8	-1/8	-1/8

Figure 2: Balancing the training set: "No not yet".

defeating the positive training. In order to address these problems, we normalized the amount of error backpropagated from each phoneme unit so that the relative influence of positive and negative training was balanced out over the entire training set.

This apparently novel technique is illustrated in Figure 2. Given the utterance "No not yet", for example, we observe that there are two frames each of "N" and "T", one frame of several other phonemes, and zero of others. Based on these counts, we compute a backpropagation scaling factor for each phoneme in each frame, as shown in the bottom half of the figure.

We found that this technique was indispensible when bootstrapping with the squared error criterion, $E = \sum(T_i - Y_i)^2$. In subsequent experiments, we found that it was still somewhat helpful but no longer necessary when training with the McClelland error function, $E = -\sum log(1 - (T_i - Y_i)^2)$, or with the Cross Entropy error function, $E = -\sum(T_i log Y_i) + (1 - T_i) log(1 - Y_i)$. We attribute this difference to the fact that the sum squared error function is merely a quadratic error function, whereas the latter two functions tend towards infinite error as the difference between the target and actual activation approaches its maximum value, compensating more forcefully for the flat behavior encouraged by all the negative training.

4 EXPERIMENTAL RESULTS

We have trained and tested our MS-TDNN on two recordings of 200 English sentences from the CMU Conference Registration database, recorded by one male speaker using a close-speaking microphone. Our speaker-dependent testing results

Table 1: Comparison of speech recognition systems applied to the CMU Conference Registration Database. HMM-n = HMM with n mixture densities [5]. LPNN = Linked Predictive Neural Network [6]. HCNN = Hidden Control Neural Network [7]. LVQ = Learned Vector Quantization [8]. TDNN corresponds to MS-TDNN without word-level training. (Perplexity 402(a) used only 41 test sentences; 402(b) used 204 test sentences.)

System	perplexity 7	111	402(a)	402(b)
HMM-1		55%		
HMM-5	96%	71%	58%	
HMM-10	97%	75%	66%	
LPNN	97%	60%	41%	
HCNN		75%		
LVQ	98%	84%	74%	61%
TDNN	98%	78%	72%	64%
MS-TDNN	**98%**	**82%**	**81%**	**70%**

are given in Table 1, along with comparative results from several other systems. It can be seen that the MS-TDNN has outperformed all other systems that have been compared on this database. This particular MS-TDNN used 16 melscale spectral input units, 20 hidden units, 120 phoneme units (40 phonemes with a 3-state model), 5,487 DTW units, and 402 word units, with 3 and 5 delays respectively in the first two layers of weights, giving a total of 24,074 weights; it used symmetric (-1..1) unit activations and inputs, and linear DTW units and word units. Word level training was performed using the Classification Figure of Merit (CFM) error function, $E = (1 + (Y_{\bar{c}} - Y_c))^2$, in which the correct word (with activation Y_c) is explicitly discriminated from the best incorrect word (with activation $Y_{\bar{c}}$); CFM was somewhat better than MSE for word level training, although the opposite was true for phoneme level training. Negative word level training was performed only if the two words were sufficiently confusable, in order to avoid disrupting the network on behalf of words that had already been well-learned.

More recently we have begun experiments on the speaker independent Resource Management database, containing nearly 4000 training sentences. To date we have primarily focused on bootstrapping the phoneme level TDNN on this database, without doing much word level training; but early experiments suggest we may reasonably expect another 4% improvement from word level training. Our preliminary results are shown in Table 2, compared against two other systems: an early version of Sphinx [9], and a simple but large MLP which has been trained as a phoneme classifier [10]. Each of these systems uses context independent phoneme models, with multiple states per phoneme, and includes differenced coefficients in its input representation. It can be seen that our TDNN outperforms this version of Sphinx while using a comparable number of parameters, but is outperformed by the MLP which has an order of magnitude more parameters. (We note that the MLP also uses phonological models to enhance its performance, and uses online training with ran-

Table 2: Context-independent systems applied to the Resource Management database.

System	parameters	perplexity 60	1000
Early Sphinx	35,000	76%	36%
MLP (ICSI-SRI)	300,000	94%	75%
TDNN	42,000	79%	43%
MS-TDNN	75,000	(+4%)	-

dom sampling rather than updating the weights after each sentence.) In any case, we suggest that the MLP might further improve its performance by incorporating word level training.

5 REMAINING INCONSISTENCIES

While the MS-TDNN was designed for consistency, it is not yet entirely consistent. For example, the MS-TDNN's training algorithm assumes that the network connectivity is fixed; but in fact the connectivity at the word level varies, depending on the DTW alignment path during the current iteration. We presume that this is a negligible factor, however, by the time the training has asymptoted and the segmentation has stabilized.

A more serious inconsistency arises during discriminative training. In our MS-TDNN, negative training is performed at known word boundaries; this is inconsistent because word boundaries are in fact unknown during testing. It would be better to discriminate against words found by a free alignment, as suggested by Hild [3]. Unfortunately this is an expensive operation, and it proved impractical for our system.

6 CONCLUSION

We have shown that the performance of a connectionist speech recognition system can be improved by resolving inconsistencies in its design. Specifically, by introducing word level training into a TDNN phoneme classifier (thus defining an MS-TDNN), the training and testing criteria become consistent, enhancing the system's word recognition accuracy. We applied our MS-TDNN architecture to the task of large vocabulary continuous speech recognition, and found that it outperforms all other systems that have been evaluated on the CMU Conference Registration database. In addition, preliminary results suggest that the MS-TDNN may perform well on the large vocabulary Resource Management database, using a relatively small number of free parameters. Our future work will focus on this investigation.

Acknowledgements

The authors gratefully acknowledge the support of DARPA and the National Science Foundation.

References

[1] P. Haffner, M. Franzini, and A. Waibel. Integrating Time Alignment and Connectionist Networks for High Performance Continuous Speech Recognition. In *Proc. International Conference on Acoustics, Speech, and Signal Processing (ICASSP)*, 1991.

[2] P. Haffner. Connectionist Word-Level Classification in Speech Recognition. In *Proc. ICASSP*, 1992.

[3] H. Hild and A. Waibel. Connected Letter Recognition with a Multi-State Time Delay Neural Network. In *Advances in Neural Information Processing Systems 5*, Morgan Kaufmann Publishers, 1993.

[4] T. Zeppenfeld and A. Waibel. A Hybrid Neural Network, Dynamic Programming Word Spotter. In *Proc. ICASSP*, 1992.

[5] O. Schmidbauer. An LVQ Based Reference Model for Speaker-Independent and -Adaptive Speech Recognition. Technical Report, Carnegie Mellon University, 1991.

[6] J. Tebelskis, A. Waibel, B. Petek, and O. Schmidbauer. Continuous Speech Recognition using Linked Predictive Neural Networks. In *Proc. ICASSP*, 1991.

[7] B. Petek and J. Tebelskis. Context-Dependent Hidden Control Neural Network Architecture for Continuous Speech Recognition. In *Proc. ICASSP*, 1992.

[8] O. Schmidbauer and J. Tebelskis. An LVQ Based Reference Model for Speaker Adaptive Speech Recognition. In *Proc. ICASSP*, 1992.

[9] K. F. Lee. Large Vocabulary Speaker-Independent Continuous Speech Recognition: The SPHINX System. PhD Thesis, Carnegie Mellon University, 1988.

[10] M. Cohen, H. Franco, N. Morgan, D. Rumelhart, and V. Abrash. Context-Dependent Multiple Distribution Phonetic Modeling with MLP's. In *Advances in Neural Information Processing Systems 5*, Morgan Kaufmann Publishers, 1993.

A Hybrid Neural Net System for State-of-the-Art Continuous Speech Recognition

G. Zavaliagkos
Northeastern University
Boston MA 02115

Y. Zhao
BBN Systems and Technologies
Cambridge, MA 02138

R. Schwartz
BBN Systems and Technologies
Cambridge, MA 02138

J. Makhoul
BBN Systems and Technologies
Cambridge, MA 02138

Abstract

Untill recently, state-of-the-art, large-vocabulary, continuous speech recognition (CSR) has employed Hidden Markov Modeling (HMM) to model speech sounds. In an attempt to improve over HMM we developed a hybrid system that integrates HMM technology with neural networks. We present the concept of a "Segmental Neural Net" (SNN) for phonetic modeling in CSR. By taking into account all the frames of a phonetic segment simultaneously, the SNN overcomes the well-known conditional-independence limitation of HMMs. In several speaker-independent experiments with the DARPA Resource Management corpus, the hybrid system showed a consistent improvement in performance over the baseline HMM system.

1 INTRODUCTION

The current state of the art in continuous speech recognition (CSR) is based on the use of hidden Markov models (HMM) to model phonemes in context. Two main reasons for the popularity of HMMs are their high performance, in terms of recognition accuracy, and their computational efficiency However, the limitations of HMMs in modeling the speech signal have been known for some time. Two such limitations are (a) the conditional-independence assumption, which prevents a HMM from taking full advantage of the correlation that exists among the frames of a phonetic segment, and (b) the awkwardness with which segmental features can be incorporated into HMM systems. We have developed the concept of Segmental Neural Nets (SNN) to overcome the two HMM limitations just mentioned for phonetic modeling in speech. A segmental neural net is a neural network that attempts to recognize a complete phonetic segment as a single unit, rather than a sequence of conditionally independent frames.

Neural nets are known to require a large amount of computation, especially for training. Also, there is no known efficient search technique for finding the best scoring segmentation with neural nets in continuous speech. Therefore, we have developed a hybrid SNN/HMM system that is designed to take full advantage of the good properties of both methods. The two methods are integrated through a novel use of the N-best (multiple hypotheses) paradigm developed in conjunction with the BYBLOS system at BBN [1].

2 SEGMENTAL NEURAL NET MODELING

There have been several recent approaches to the use of neural nets in CSR. The SNN differs from these approaches in that it attempts to recognize each phoneme by using all the frames in a phonetic segment simultaneously to perform the recognition. By looking at a whole phonetic segment at once, we are able to take advantage of the correlation that exists among frames of a phonetic segments, thus ameliorating the limitations of HMMs.

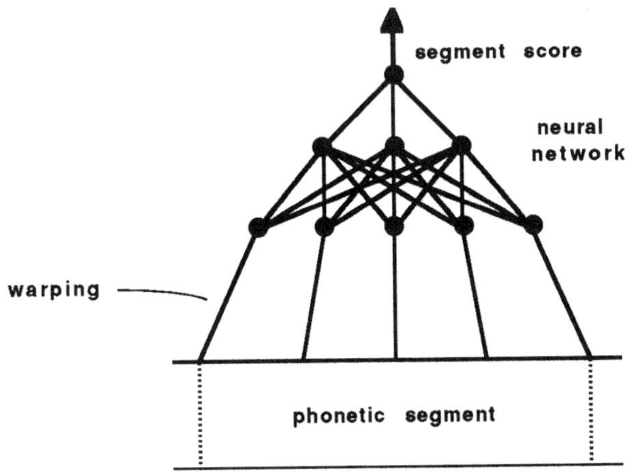

Figure 1: The SNN model samples the frames and produces a single segment score.

The structure of a typical SNN is shown in Figure 1. The input to the network is a fixed length representation of the speech segment. This input is scored by the network. If the network was trained to minimize a mean square error (MSE) or a relative entropy distortion measure, the output of the network will be an estimate of the posterior probability $P(C|x)$ of the phonetic class C given the segment x [2, 3]. This property of the SNN allows a natural extension to CSR: We segment the utterance into phonetic segments, and score each one of them seperately. The score of the utterance is simply the product of the scores of the individual segments.

The procedure described above requires the availability of some form of phonetic segmentation of the speech. We describe in Section 3 how we use the HMM to obtain likely candidate segmentations. Here, we shall assume that a phonetic segmentation has been made available and each segment is represented by a sequence of frames of speech features. The actual number of such frames in a phonetic segment is variable. However, for input to the neural network, we need a fixed length representation. Therefore, we have to convert the variable number of frames in each segment to a fixed number of frames. We have considered two approaches to cope with this problem: time sampling and Discrete Cosine Transform (DCT).

In the first approach, the requisite time warping is performed by a quasi-linear sampling of the feature vectors comprising the segment to a fixed number of frames (5 in our system). For example, in a 17-frame phonetic segment, we use frames 1, 5, 9, 13, and 17 as input to the SNN. The second approach uses the Discrete Cosine Transform (DCT). The DCT can be used to represent the frame sequence of a segment as follows. Consider the sequence of cepstral features across a segment as a time sequence and take its DCT. For an m frame segment, this transform will result in a set of m DCT coefficients for each feature. Truncate this sequence to its first few coefficients (the more coefficients , the more precise the representation). To keep the number of features the same as in the quasi-linear sampling, we use only five coefficients. If the input segment has less than five frames, we initially interpolate in time so that a five-point DCT is possible. Compared to the quasi-linear sampling, DCT has the advantage of using information from all input frames.

Duration: Because of the time warping function, the SNN score for a segment is independent of the duration of the segment. In order to provide duration information to the SNN, we constructed a simple durational model. For each phoneme, a histogram was made of segment durations in the training data. This histogram was then smoothed by convolving with a triangular window, and probabilities falling below a floor level were reset to that level. The duration score was multiplied by the neural net score to give an overall segment score.

3 THE N-BEST RESCORING PARADIGM

Our hybrid system is based on the N-best rescoring paradigm [1], which allows us to design and test the SNN with little regard to the usual problem of searching for the segmentation when dealing with a large vocabulary speech recognition system.

Figure 2 illusrates the hybrid system. Each utterance is decoded using the BBN BYBLOS system [4]. The decoding is done in two steps: First the N-best recognition is performed, producing a list of the candidate N best-scoring sentence hypotheses. In this stage, a relatively simple HMM is used for computation purposes. The length of the N-best list is chosen to be long enough to almost always include the correct answer. The second step is the HMM rescoring, where a more sophisticated HMM is used. The recognition process may stop at this stage, selecting the top scoring utterance of the list (HMM 1-best output).

To incorporate the SNN in the N-best paradigm, we use the HMM system to generate a segmentation for each N-best hypothesis, and the SNN to generate a score for the hypothesis using the HMM segmentation. The N-best list may be reordered based on

SNN scores alone. In this case the recognition process stops by selecting the top scoring utterance of the rescored list (NN 1-best output).

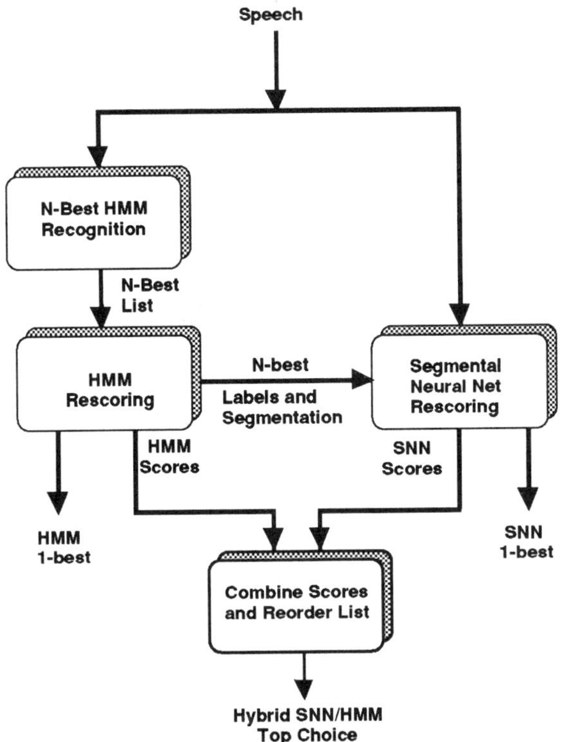

Figure 2: Schematic diagram of the hybrid SNN/HMM system

The last stage in the hybrid system is to combine several scores for each hypothesis, such as SNN score, HMM score, grammar score, and the hypothesized number of words and phonemes. (The number of words and phonemes are included because they serve the same purpose as word and phoneme insertion penalties in a HMM CSR system.) We form a composite score by taking a linear combination of the individual scores. The linear combination is determined by selecting the weights that give the best performance over a development test set. These weights can be chosen automatically [5]. After we have rescored the N-Best list, we can reorder it according to the new composite scores. If the CSR system is required to output just a single hypothesis, the highest scoring hypothesis is chosen (hybrid SNN/HMM top choice in Figure 2).

4 SNN TRAINING

The training of the phonetic SNNs is done in two steps. In the first training step, we segment all of the training utterances into phonetic segments using the HMM models and the utterance transcriptions. Each segment then serves as a positive example of the SNN output corresponding to the phonetic label of the segment and as a negative example for all the other phonetic SNN outputs (we are using a total of 53 phonetic outputs). We call this training method *1-best training*.

The SNN is trained using the log-error distortion measure [6], which is an extension of the relative entropy measure to an M-class problem. To ensure that the outputs are in fact probabilities, we use a sigmoidal nonlinearity to restrict their range in $[0, 1]$ and an output normalization layer to make them sum to one. The models are initialized by removing the sigmoids and using the MSE measure. Then we reinstate the sigmoids and proceed with four iterations of a quasi-Newton [7] error minimization algorithm. For the adopted error measure, when the neural net non-linearity is the usual sigmoid function, there exists a unique minimum for single-layer nets [6].

The 1-best training described has one drawback: the training does not cover all the cases that the network will be required to encounter in the N-best rescoring paradigm. With 1-best training, given the correct segmentation, we train the network to discriminate between correct and incorrect labeling. However, the network will also be used to score N-best hypotheses with incorrect segmentation. Therefore, it is important to train based on the N-best lists in what we call N-best training. During N-best training, we produce the N-best lists for all of the training sentences, and we then train positively with all the correct hypotheses and negatively on the "misrecognized" parts of the incorrect hypothesis.

4.1 Context Modelling

Some of the largest gains in accuracy for HMM CSR systems have been obtained with the use of context (i.e., phonetic identity of neighboring segments). Consequently, we implemented a version of the SNN that provided a simple model of left-context. In addition to the SNN previously described, which only models a segment's phonetic identity and makes no reference to context, we trained 53 additional left-context networks. Each of these 53 networks were identical in structure to the context-independent SNN. In the recognition process, the segment score is obtained by combining the output of the context-independent SNN with the corresponding output of the SNN that models the left-context of the segment. This combination is a weighted average of the two network values, where the weights are determined by the number of occurrences of the phoneme in the training data and the number of times the phoneme has its present context in the training data.

4.1.1 Regularization Techniques for Context Models

During neural net training of context models, a decrease of the distortion on the training set often causes an increase of the distortion on the test set. This problem is called overtraining, and it typically occurs when the number of training samples is on the order of the number of the model parameters. Regularization provides a class of smoothing techniques to ameliorate the overtraining problem. Instead of minimizing the distortion measure alone, we are minimizing the following objective function:

$$Distortion\_measure + \frac{\lambda_1}{N_d^{\eta_1}}||\vec{W}||^2 + \frac{\lambda_2}{N_d^{\eta_2}}||\vec{W} - \vec{W}_0||^2 \quad (1)$$

where $\vec{W}_0$ is the set of weights corresponding to the context-independent model, N_d is the number of data points, and $\lambda_1, \lambda_2, \eta_1, \eta_2$ are smoothing parameters. The first regularization term is used to control the excursion of the weights in general and the other to control the degree to which the context-dependent model is allowed to deviate from the corresponding context-independent model (to achieve this first we initialize the context-dependent models with the context-independent model). In our initial experiments, we used values of $\lambda_1 = \lambda_2 = 1.0$, $\eta_1 = 1$, $\eta_2 = 2$.

When there are very few training data for a particular context model, the regularization terms in (1) prevail, constraining the model parameters to remain close to their initial estimates. The regularization term is gradually turned off with the presence of more data. What we accomplish in this way is an automatic mechanism that controls overtraining.

4.2 Elliptical Basis Functions

Our efforts to use multi-layer structures has been rather unsuccessful so far. The best improvement we got was a mere 5% reduction in error rate over the single-layer performance, but with a 10-fold increase in both number of parameters and computation time. We suspect that our training is getting trapped in bad local minima. Due to the above considerations, we considered an alternative multi-layer structure, the Elliptical Basis Function (EBF) network. EBFs are natural extensions of Radial Basis Functions, where a full covariance matrix is introduced in the basis functions. As many researchers have suggested, EBF networks provide modelling capabilities that are as powerful as multi-layer perceptrons. An advantage of EBF is that there exist well established techniques for estimating the elliptical basis layer. As a consequence, the problem of training an EBF network can be reduced to a one-layer problem, i.e., training the second layer only.

Our approach with EBF is to initialize them with Maximum Likelihood (ML). ML training allows us to use very detailed context models, such as triphones. The next step, which is not yet implemented, is to either proceed with discriminative NN training, or use a nonlinearity at the outout layer and treat the second layer as a single-layer feedforward model, or both.

5 EXPERIMENTAL CONDITIONS AND RESULTS

Experiments to test the performance of the hybrid system were performed on the speaker-independent (SI) portion of the DARPA 1000-word Resource Management speech corpus. The training set consisted of utterances from 109 speakers, 2830 utterances from male speakers and 1160 utterances from female speakers. We have tested our system with 5 different test sets. The Feb '89 set was used as a cross-validation set for the SNN system. Feb '89 and Oct '89 were used as development sets whenever the weights for the combination of two or more models were to be estimated. Feb '91 and the two Sep '92 sets were used as independent test sets.

Both the NN and the HMM systems had 3 separate models made from male, female, and combined data. During recognition all 3 models were used to score the utterances, and the recognition answer was decided by a 3-way gender selection: For each utterance, the model that produced the highest score was selected. The HMM used was the February '91 version of the BBN BYBLOS system.

In the experiments, we used SNNs with 53 outputs, each representing one of the phonemes in our system. The SNN was used to rescore N-best lists of length N = 20. The input to the net is a fixed number of frames of speech features (5 frames in our system). The features in each 10-ms frame consist of 16 scalar values: power, power difference, and 14 mel-warped cepstral coefficients. For the EBF, the differences of the cepstral parameters were used also.

Table 1: SNN development on February '89 test set

		Word Error (%)
	Original SSN (MSE)	13.7
+	Log-Error Criterion	11.6
+	N-Best training	9.0
+	Left Context	7.4
+	Regularization	6.6
+	word,phoneme penalties	5.7
	EBF	4.9

Table 1 shows the word error rates at the various stages of development. All the experiments mentioned below used the Feb '89 test set. The original 1-layer SNN was trained using the 1-best training algorithm and the MSE criterion, and gave a word error rate of 13.7%. The incorporation of the duration and the adoption of the log-error training criterion both resulted in some improvement, bringing the error rate down to 11.6%. With N-best training the error rate dropped to 9.0%; adding left context models reduced the word error rate down to 7.4%. When the the context models were trained with the regularization criterion the error rate dropped to 6.6%. All of the above results were obtained using the mean NN score (NN score divided by the number of segments). When we used word and phone penalties, the performance was even better, a 5.7% word error rate. For the same conditions, the performance for the EBF system was 4.9% word error rate. We should mention that the implementation of training with regularization was not complete at the time the hybrid system was tested on the September 92 test, so we will exclude it from the NN results presented below.

The final hybrid system included the HMM, the SNN and EBF models, and Table 2 summarizes its performance (in this table, NN stands for the combination of SNN and EBF). We notice that with the exception of of the Sep '92 test sets the word error of the HMM was roughly around 3.5%(3.8, 3.7 and 3.4%). For the same test sets, the NN had a word error slightly higher than 4.0%, and the hybrid NN/HMM system a word error rate of 2.7%. We are very happy to see the performance of our neural net approaching the performance of the HMM. It is also worthwhile to mention that the performance of the hybrid system for Feb '89, Oct '89 and Feb '91 is the best performance reported so far for these sets.

Special mention has to be made for the Sep '92 test sets. These test sets proved to be radically different than the previous released RM tests, resulting in almost a doubling of the HMM word error rate. The deterioration in performance of the hybrid system was bigger, and the improvement due to the hybrid system was less than 10% (compared to an improvement of $\approx$ 25% for the other 3 sets). We have all been baffled by these unexpected results, and although we are continuously looking for an explanation of this

System	Word Error % Feb '89	Oct '89	Feb '91	Sep '92
HMM	3.7	3.8	3.4	6.0
NN	4.0	4.2	4.1	7.4
NN+HMM	2.7	2.7	2.7	5.5

Table 2: Hybrid Neural Net/HMM system.

strange behaviour our efforts have not yet been successful.

6 CONCLUSIONS

We have presented the Segmental Neural Net as a method for phonetic modeling in large vocabulary CSR systems and have demonstrated that, when combined with a conventional HMM, the SNN gives a significant improvement over the performance of a state-of-the-art HMM CSR system. The hybrid system is based on the N-best rescoring paradigm which, by providing the HMM segmentation, drastically reduces the computation for our segmental models and provides a simple way of combining the best aspects of two systems. The improvements achieved from the use of a hybrid system vary from less than 10% to about 25% reduction in word error rate, depending on the test set used.

References

[1] R. Schwartz and S. Austin, "A Comparison of Several Approximate Algorithms for Finding Multiple (N-Best) Sentence Hypotheses," *IEEE Int. Conf. Acoustics, Speech and Signal Processing*, Toronto, Canada, May 1991, pp. 701-704.

[2] A. Barron, "Statistical properties of artificial neural networks," *IEEE Conf. Decision and Control*, Tampa, FL, pp. 280-285, 1989.

[3] H. Gish, "A probabilistic approach to the understanding and training of neural network classifiers," *IEEE Int. Conf. Acoust., Speech, Signal Processing*, April 1990.

[4] M. Bates et. all, "The BBN/HARC Spoken Language Understanding System" *IEEE Int. Conf. Acoust., Speech,Signal Processing*, Apr 1992, Minneapolis, MI, Apr. 1993

[5] M. Ostendorf et. all, "Integration of Diverse Recognition Methodologies Through Reevaluation of N-Best Sentence Hypotheses," *Proc. DARPA Speech and Natural Language Workshop*, Pacific Grove, CA, Morgan Kaufmann Publishers, February 1991.

[6] A. El-Jaroudi and J. Makhoul, "A New Error Criterion for Posterior Probability Estimation with Neural Nets," *International Joint Conference on Neural Networks*, San Diego, CA, June 1990, Vol III, pp. 185-192.

[7] D. Luenberger, *Linear and Nonlinear Programming*, Addison-Wesley, Massachusetts, 1984.

[8] R. Schwartz et. all, "Improved Hidden Markov Modeling of Phonemes for Continuous Speech Recognition," *IEEE Int. Conf. Acoustics, Speech and Signal Processing*, San Diego, CA, March 1984, pp. 35.6.1–35.6.4.

Connected Letter Recognition with a Multi-State Time Delay Neural Network

Hermann Hild and **Alex Waibel**
School of Computer Science
Carnegie Mellon University
Pittsburgh, PA 15213-3891, USA

Abstract

The Multi-State Time Delay Neural Network (MS-TDNN) integrates a nonlinear time alignment procedure (DTW) and the high-accuracy phoneme spotting capabilities of a TDNN into a connectionist speech recognition system with word-level classification and error backpropagation. We present an MS-TDNN for recognizing continuously spelled letters, a task characterized by a small but highly confusable vocabulary. Our MS-TDNN achieves 98.5/92.0% word accuracy on speaker dependent/independent tasks, outperforming previously reported results on the same databases. We propose training techniques aimed at improving sentence level performance, including free alignment across word boundaries, word duration modeling and error backpropagation on the sentence rather than the word level. Architectures integrating submodules specialized on a subset of speakers achieved further improvements.

1 INTRODUCTION

The recognition of spelled strings of letters is essential for all applications involving proper names, addresses or other large sets of special words which due to their sheer size can not be in the basic vocabulary of a recognizer. The high confusability of the English letters makes the seemingly easy task a very challenging one, currently only addressed by a few systems, e.g. those of R. Cole et. al. [JFC90, FC90, CFGJ91] for isolated spoken letter recognition. Their connectionist systems first find a broad phonetic segmentation, from which a letter segmentation is derived, which is then

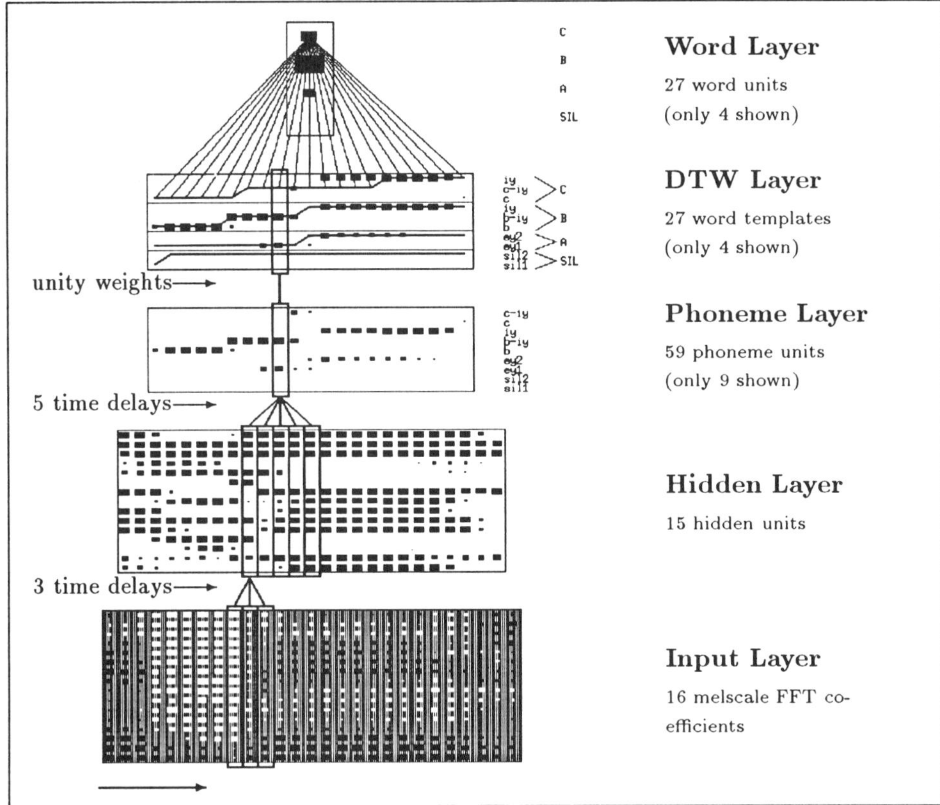

Figure 1: The MS-TDNN recognizing the excerpted word 'B'. Only the activations for the words 'SIL', 'A', 'B', and 'C' are shown.

classified by another network. In this paper, we present the MS-TDNN as a connectionist speech recognition system for connected letter recognition. After describing the baseline architecture, training techniques aimed at improving sentence level performance and architectures with gender-specific subnets are introduced.

Baseline Architecture. Time Delay Neural Networks (TDNNs) can combine the robustness and discriminative power of Neural Nets with a time-shift invariant architecture to form high accuracy phoneme classifiers [WHH+89]. The Multi-State TDNN (MS-TDNN) [HFW91, Haf92, HW92], an extension of the TDNN, is capable of classifying words (represented as sequences of phonemes) by integrating a nonlinear time alignment procedure (DTW) into the TDNN architecture. Figure 1 shows an MS-TDNN in the process of recognizing the excerpted word 'B', represented by 16 melscale FFT coefficients at a 10-msec frame rate. The first three layers constitute a standard TDNN, which uses sliding windows with time delayed connections to compute a score for each phoneme (state) for every frame, these are the activations in the "Phoneme Layer". In the "DTW Layer", each word to be recognized is modeled by a sequence of phonemes. The corresponding activations are simply copied from the Phoneme Layer into the word models of the DTW Layer, where an optimal alignment path is found for each word. The activations along these paths are then collected in the word output units. All units in the DTW and Word Layer are linear and have no biases. 15 (25 to 100) hidden units per frame were used for speaker-dependent (-independent) experiments, the entire 26 letter network has approximately 5200 (8600 to 34500) parameters.

Training starts with "bootstrapping", during which only the front-end TDNN is used with fixed phoneme boundaries as targets. In a second phase, training is performed with word level targets. Phoneme boundaries are freely aligned within given word boundaries in the DTW layer. The error derivatives are backpropagated from the word units through the alignment path and the front-end TDNN.
The choice of sensible objective functions is of great importance. Let $Y = (y_1, \ldots, y_n)$ the output and $T = (t_1, \ldots, t_n)$ the target vector. For training on the phoneme level (bootstrapping), there is a target vector T for each frame in time, representing the correct phoneme j in a "1-out-of-n" coding, i.e. $t_i = \delta_{ij}$. To see why the standard *Mean Square Error* ($MSE = \sum_{i=1}^{n} (y_i - t_i)^2$) is problematic for "1-out-of-n" codings for large n ($n = 59$ in our case), consider for example that for a target $(1.0, 0.0, \ldots, 0.0)$ the output vector $(0.0, \ldots, 0.0)$ has only half the error than the more desirable output $(1.0, 0.2, \ldots, 0.2)$. To avoid this problem, we are using

$$E_{McClelland}(T, Y) = \sum_{i=1}^{n} log(1 - (y_i - t_i)^2)$$

which (like cross entropy) punishes "outliers" with an error approaching infinity for $|t_i - y_i|$ approaching 1.0. For the word level training, we have achieved best results with an objective function similar to the "Classification Figure of Merit (CFM)" [HW90], which tries to maximize the distance $d = y_c - y_{hi}$ between the correct score y_c and the highest incorrect score y_{hi} instead of using absolute target values of 1.0 and 0.0 for correct and incorrect word units:

$$E_{CFM}(T, Y) = f(y_c - y_{hi}) = f(d) = (1 - d)^2$$

The philosophy here is not to "touch" any output unit not directly related to correct classification. We found it even useful to apply error backpropagation only in the case of a wrong or too narrow classification, i.e. if $y_c - y_{hi} < \delta_{safety\_margin}$.

2 IMPROVING CONTINUOUS RECOGNITION

2.1 TRAINING ACROSS WORD BOUNDARIES

A proper treatment of word[1] boundaries is especially important for a short word vocabulary, since most phones are at word boundaries. While the phoneme boundaries within a word are freely aligned by the DTW during "word level training", the word boundaries are fixed and might be error prone or suboptimal. By extending the alignment one phoneme to the left (last phoneme of previous word) and the right (first phoneme of next word), the word boundaries can be optimally adjusted

[1] In our context, a "word" consists of one spelled letter, and a "sentence" is a continuously spelled string of letters.

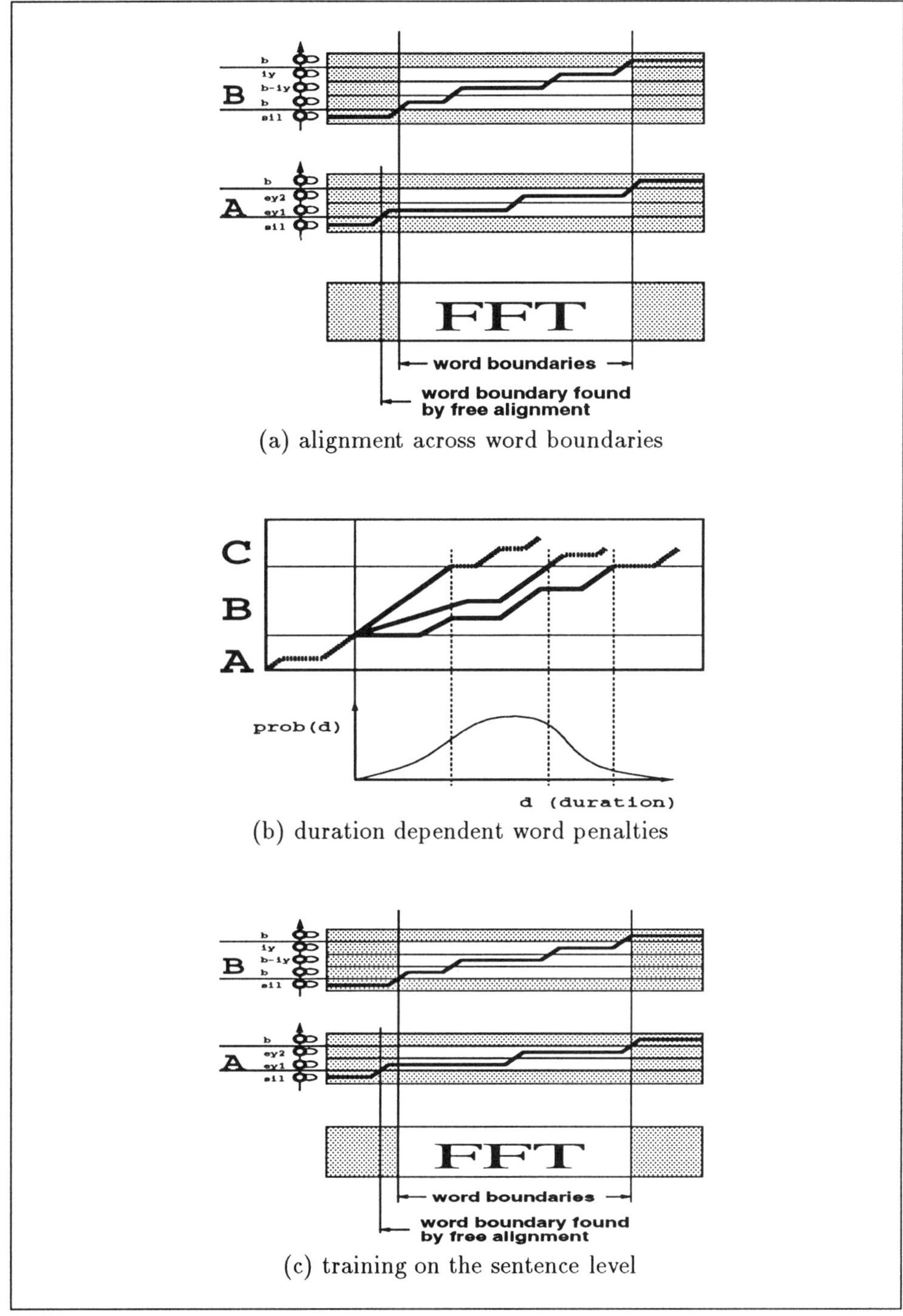

(a) alignment across word boundaries

(b) duration dependent word penalties

(c) training on the sentence level

Figure 2: Various techniques to improve sentence level recognition performance

in the same way as the phoneme boundaries within a word. Figure 2(a) shows an example in which the word to recognize is surrounded by a silence and a 'B', thus the left and right context (for all words to be recognized) is the phoneme 'sil' and 'b', respectively. The gray shaded area indicates the extension necessary to the DTW alignment. The diagram shows how a new boundary for the beginning of the word 'A' is found. As indicated in figure 3, this techniques improves continuous recognition significantly, but it doesn't help for excerpted words.

2.2 WORD DURATION DEPENDENT PENALIZING OF INSERTION AND DELETION ERRORS

In "continuous testing mode", instead of looking at word units the well-known "One Stage DTW" algorithm [Ney84] is used to find an optimal path through an unspecified sequence of words. The short and confusable English letters cause many word insertion and deletion errors, such as "T E" vs. "T" or "O" vs. "O O", therefore proper duration modeling is essential.
As suggested in [HW92], minimum phoneme duration can be enforced by "state duplication". In addition, we are modeling a duration and word dependent penalty $Pen_w(d) = log(k + prob_w(d))$, where the pdf $prob_w(d)$ is approximated from the training data and k is a small constant to avoid zero probabilities. $Pen_w(d)$ is added to the accumulated score AS of the search path, $AS = AS + \lambda_w * Pen_w(d)$, whenever it crosses the boundary of a word w in Ney's "One Stage DTW" algorithm, as indicated in figure 2(b). The ratio λ_w, which determines the degree of influence of the duration penalty, is another important degree of freedom. There is no straightforward mathematically exact way to compute the effect of a change of the "weight" λ_w to the insertion and deletion rate. Our approach is a (pseudo) gradient descent, which changes λ_w proportional to $E(w) = (\#ins_w - \#del_w)/\#w$, i.e. we are trying to maximize the relative balance of insertion and deletion errors.

2.3 ERROR BACKPOPAGATION AT THE SENTENCE LEVEL

Usually the MS-TDNN is trained to classify excerpted words, but evaluated on continuously spoken sentences. We propose a simple but effective method to extend training on the sentence level. Figure 2(c) shows the alignment path of the sentence "C A B", in which a typical error, the insertion of an 'A', occurred. In a forced alignment mode (i.e. the correct sequence of words is enforced), positive training is applied along the correct path, while the units along the incorrect path receive negative training. Note that the effect of positive and negative training is neutralized if the paths are the same, only differing parts receive non-zero error backpropagation.

2.4 LEARNING CURVES

Figure 3 demonstrates the effect of the various training phases. The system is bootstrapped (a) during iteration 1 to 130. Word level training starts (b) at iteration 110. Word level training with additional "training across word boundaries" (c) is started at iteration 260. Excerpted word performance is not improved after (c), but continuous recognition becomes significantly better, compare (d) and (e). In (d), sentence level training is started directly after iteration 260, while in (e) sentence level training is started after additional "across boundaries (word level) training".

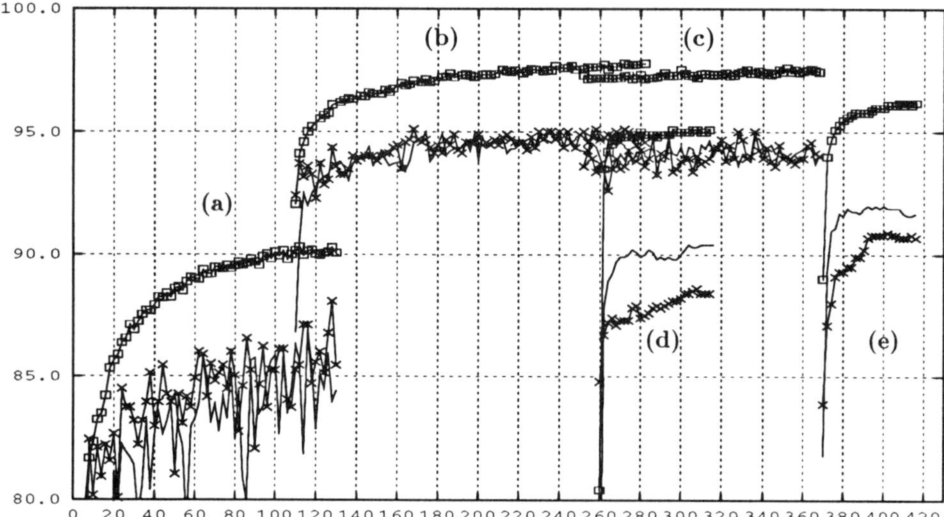

Figure 3: Learning curves (a = bootstrapping, b,c = word level (excerpted words), d,e = sentence level training (continuous speech)) on the training (□), crossvalidation (-) and test set (x) for the speaker-independent RM Spell-Mode data.

3 GENDER SPECIFIC SUBNETS

A straightforward approach to building a more specialized system is simply to train two entirely individual networks for male and female speakers only. During training, the gender of a speaker is known, during testing it is determined by an additional "gender identification network", which is simply another MS-TDNN with two output units representing male and female speakers. Given a sentence as input, this network classifies the speaker's gender with approx. 99% correct. The overall modularized network improved the word accuracy from 90.8% (for the "pooled" net, see table 1) to 91.3%. However, a hybrid approach with specialized gender-specific connections at the lower, input level and shared connections for the remaining net worked even better. As depicted in figure 4, in this architecture the gender identification network selects one of the two gender-specific bundles of connections between the input and hidden layer. This technique improved the word accuracy to 92.0%. More experiments with speaker-specific subnetworks are reported in [HW93].

4 EXPERIMENTAL RESULTS

Our MS-TDNN achieved excellent performance on both speaker dependent and independent tasks. For **speaker dependent** testing, we used the "CMU Alph-Data", with 1000 sentences (i.e. a continuously spelled string of letters) from each of 3 male and 3 female speakers. 500, 100, and 400 sentences were used as train-

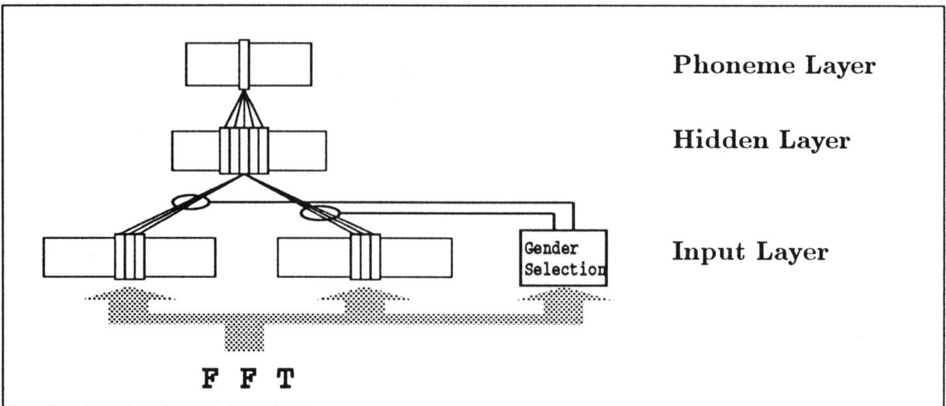

Figure 4: A network architecture with gender-specific and shared connections. Only the front-end TDNN is shown.

ing, cross-validation and test set, respectively. The DARPA Resource Management Spell-Mode Data were used for **speaker independent** testing. This data base contains about 1700 sentences, spelled by 85 male and 35 female speakers. The speech of 7 male and 4 female speakers was set aside for the test set, one sentence from all 109 and all sentences from 6 training speakers were used for crossvalidation. Table 1 summarizes our results. With the help of the training techniques described above we were able to outperform previously reported [HFW91] speaker dependent results as well as the HMM-based SPHINX System.

5 SUMMARY AND FUTURE WORK

We have presented a connectionist speech recognition system for high accuracy connected letter recognition. New training techniques aimed at improving sentence level recognition enabled our MS-TDNN to outperform previous systems of its own kind as well as a state-of-the art HMM-based system (SPHINX). Beyond the gender specific subnets, we are experimenting with an MS-TDNN which maintains several "internal speaker models" for a more sophisticated speaker-independent system. In the future we will also experiment with context dependent phoneme models.

Acknowledgements

The authors gratefully acknowledge support by the National Science Foundation and DARPA. We wish to thank Joe Tebelskis for insightful discussions, Arthur McNair for keeping our machines running, and especially Patrick Haffner. Many of the ideas presented have been developed in collaboration with him.

References

[CFGJ91] R. A. Cole, M. Fanty, Gopalakrishnan, and R. D.T. Janssen. Speaker-Independent Name Retrival from Spellings Using a Database of 50,000 Names.

Speaker Dependent (CMU Alph Data) 500/2500 train, 100/500 crossvalidation, 400/2000 test sentences/words			
speaker	SPHINX[HFW91]	MS-TDNN[HFW91]	our MS-TDNN
mjmt	96.0	97.5	**98.5**
mdbs	83.9	89.7	**91.1**
maem	–	–	**94.6**
fcaw	–	–	**98.8**
flgt	–	–	**86.9**
fee	–	–	**91.0**

Speaker Independent (Resource Management Spell-Mode) 109 (ca. 11000) train, 11 (ca. 900) test speaker (words).			
SPHINX[HH92]		our MS-TDNN	
	+ Senone		gender specific
88.7	90.4	**90.8**	**92.0**

Table 1: Word accuracy (in % on the test sets) on speaker dependent and speaker independent connected letter tasks.

In *Proceedings of the International Conference on Acoustics, Speech and Signal Processing*, Toronto, Ontario, Canada, May 1991. IEEE.

[FC90] M. Fanty and R. Cole. Spoken letter recognition. In *Proceedings of the Neural Information Processing Systems Conference NIPS*, Denver, November 1990.

[Haf92] P. Haffner. Connectionist Word-Level Classification in Speech Recognition. In *Proc. IEEE International Conference on Acoustics, Speech, and Signal Processing*. IEEE, 1992.

[HFW91] P. Haffner, M. Franzini, and A. Waibel. Integrating Time Alignment and Neural Networks for High Performance Continuous Speech Recognition. In *Proc. Int. Conf. on Acoustics, Speech, and Signal Processing*. IEEE, 1991.

[HH92] M.-Y. Hwang and X. Huang. Subphonetic Modeling with Markov States - Senone. In *Proc. IEEE International Conference on Acoustics, Speech, and Signal Processing*, pages I33 – I37. IEEE, 1992.

[HW90] J. Hampshire and A. Waibel. A Novel Objective Function for Improved Phoneme Recognition Using Time Delay Neural Networks. *IEEE Transactions on Neural Networks*, June 1990.

[HW92] P. Haffner and A. Waibel. Multi-state Time Delay Neural Networks for Continuous Speech Recognition. In *NIPS(4)*. Morgan Kaufman, 1992.

[HW93] H. Hild and A. Waibel. Multi-Speaker/Speaker-Independent Architectures for the Multi-State Time Delay Neural Network. In *Proc. IEEE International Conference on Acoustics, Speech, and Signal Processing*. IEEE, 1993.

[JFC90] R.D.T. Jansen, M. Fanty, and R. A. Cole. Speaker-independent Phonetic Classification in Continuous English Letters. In *Proceedings of the IJCNN 90, Washington D.C.*, July 1990.

[Ney84] H. Ney. The Use of a One-Stage Dynamic Programming Algorithm for Connected Word Recognition. In *IEEE Transactions on Acoustics, Speech, and Signal Processing*, pages 263–271. IEEE, April 1984.

[WHH+89] A. Waibel, T. Hanazawa, G. Hinton, K. Shikano, and K. Lang. Phoneme Recognition Using Time-Delay Neural Networks. *IEEE, Transactions on Acoustics, Speech and Signal Processing*, March 1989.

PART IX

APPLICATIONS

Recognition-based Segmentation of On-line Hand-printed Words

M. Schenkel*, H. Weissman, I. Guyon, C. Nohl, D. Henderson
AT&T Bell Laboratories, Holmdel, NJ 07733
* Swiss Federal Institute of Technology, CH-8092 Zürich

Abstract

This paper reports on the performance of two methods for recognition-based segmentation of strings of on-line hand-printed capital Latin characters. The input strings consist of a time-ordered sequence of X-Y coordinates, punctuated by pen-lifts. The methods were designed to work in "run-on mode" where there is no constraint on the spacing between characters. While both methods use a neural network recognition engine and a graph-algorithmic post-processor, their approaches to segmentation are quite different. The first method, which we call *INSEG* (for input segmentation), uses a combination of heuristics to identify particular pen-lifts as tentative segmentation points. The second method, which we call *OUTSEG* (for output segmentation), relies on the empirically trained recognition engine for both recognizing characters and identifying relevant segmentation points.

1 INTRODUCTION

We address the problem of writer independent recognition of hand-printed words from an 80,000-word English dictionary. Several levels of difficulty in the recognition of hand-printed words are illustrated in figure 1. The examples were extracted from our databases (table 1). Except in the cases of boxed or clearly spaced characters, segmenting characters independently of the recognition process yields poor recognition performance. This has motivated us to explore recognition-based segmentation techniques.

Table 1: **Databases used for training and testing.** *DB2* contains words one to five letters long, but only four and five letter words are constrained to be legal English words. *DB3* contains legal English words of any length from an 80,000 word dictionary.

uppercase database	data nature	pad used	training set size	test set size	approx. # of donors
DB1	boxed letters	AT&T	9000	1500	250
DB2	short words	Grid	8000	1000	400
DB3	English words	Wacom	-	600	25

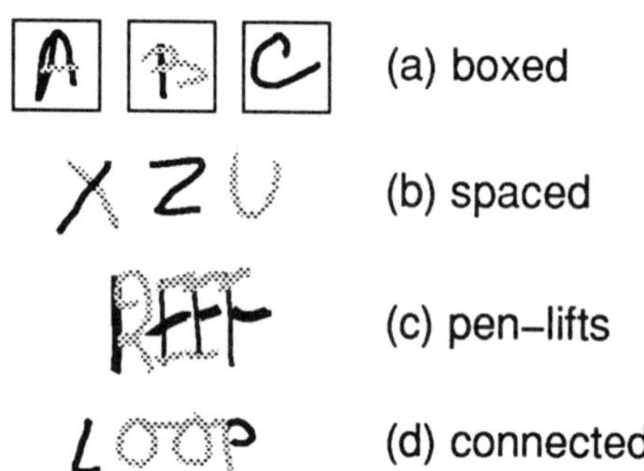

Figure 1: **Examples of styles that can be found in our databases:** (a) *DB*1; (b) *DB*2; (c), (d) *DB*2 and *DB*3. The line thickness or darkness is alternated at each pen-lift.

The basic principle of recognition-based segmentation is to present to the recognizer many "tentative characters". The recognition scores ultimately determine the string segmentation. We have investigated two different recognition-based segmentation methods which differ in their definition of the tentative characters, but have very similar recognition engines.

The data collection device provides pen trajectory information as a sequence of (x, y) coordinates at regular time intervals (10-15 ms). We use a preprocessing technique which preserves this information by keeping a finely sampled sequence of feature vectors along the pen trajectory (Guyon et al. 1991, Weissman et al. 1992). The recognizer is a Time Delay Neural Network ($TDNN$) (Lang and Hinton 1988, Waibel et al. 1989, Guyon et al. 1991). There is one output per class, in this case 26 outputs, providing a score for all the capital letters of the Latin alphabet.

The critical step in the segmentation process is the postprocessing which disentangles various word hypotheses using the character recognition scores provided by the $TDNN$. For this purpose, we use conventional dynamic programming algorithms. In addition we use a dictionary that checks the solution and returns a list of similar legal words. The best word hypotheses, subject to this list, is again chosen by dynamic programming algorithms.

Recognition-based segmentation relies on the recognizer to give low confidence scores for wrong tentative characters corresponding to a segmentation mistake. Recognizers trained only on valid characters usually perform poorly on such a task.

We use "segmentation-driven training" techniques which allow the training of wrong tentative characters, produced by the segmentation engine itself, as negative examples. This additional training has reduced our error rates by more than a factor of two.

In section 2 we describe the *INSEG* method which uses tentative characters delineated by heuristic segmentation points. It is expected to be most appropriate for hand-printed capital letters since nearly all writers separate these letters by pen-lifts. This method was inspired by a similar technique used for Optical Character Recognition (OCR) (Burges et al. 1992). In section 3 we present an alternative method, *OUTSEG*, which expects the recognition engine to learn empirically (learning by examples) both to recognize characters and to identify relevant segmentation points. This second method bears similarities with the OCR methods proposed by Matan et al. (1991) or Keeler et al. (1991). In section 4 we compare the two methods and present experimental results.

2 SEGMENTATION IN INPUT SPACE

Figure 2 shows the different steps of the *INSEG* process. Module 1 is used to define "tentative characters" delineated by "tentative cuts" (spaces or pen-lifts). The tentative characters are then handed to module 2 which performs the preprocessing and the scoring of the characters with a *TDNN*. The recognition results are then gathered into an interpretation graph. In module 3 the best path through that graph is found with the Viterbi algorithm.

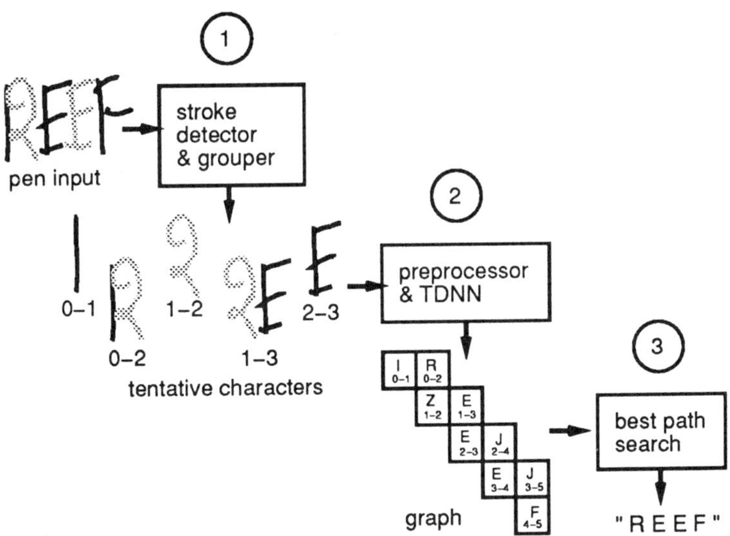

Figure 2: **Processing steps of the *INSEG* method.**

In figure 3 we show a simplified representation of an interpretation graph built by our system. Each tentative character (denoted $\{i, j\}$) has a double index: the tentative cut i at the character starting point and the tentative cut j at the character end point. We denote by $X\{i, j\}$ the node associated to the score of letter X for the tentative character $\{i, j\}$. A path through the graph starts at a node $X\{0, .\}$ and ends at a node $Y\{., m\}$, where 0 is the word starting point and m the last pen-lift. In between, only transitions of the kind $X\{., i\} \rightarrow Y\{i, .\}$ are allowed to prevent character overlapping.

To avoid searching through too complex a graph, we need to perform some pruning. The spatial relationship between strokes is used to discard unlikely tentative cuts. For instance, strokes with a large horizontal overlap are bundled. The remaining tentative characters are then grouped in different ways to form alternative tentative characters. Tentative characters separated by a large horizontal spatial interval are never considered for grouping.

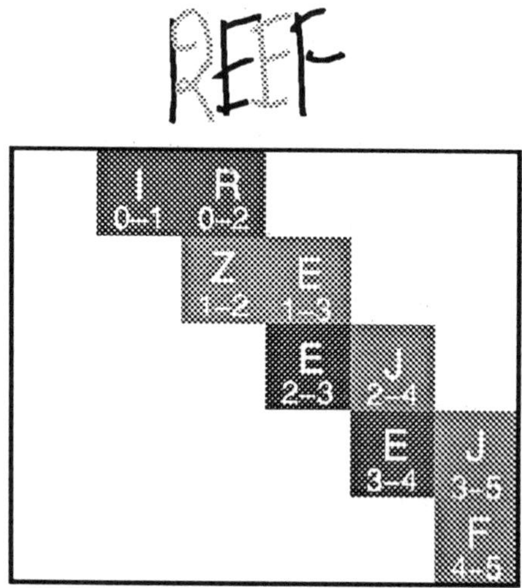

Figure 3: **Graph obtained with the input segmentation method.** The grey shading in each box indicates the recognition scores (the darker, the stronger the recognition score and the higher the recognition confidence).

In table 2 we present the results obtained with the $TDNN$ recognizer used by Guyon et al. (1991), with 4 convolutional layers and 6,252 weights. Characters are preprocessed individually, which provides the network with a fixed dimension input.

3 SEGMENTATION IN OUTPUT SPACE

In contrast with $INSEG$, the $OUTSEG$ method does not rely on human designed segmentation hints: the neural network learns both recognition and segmentation features from examples.

Tentative characters are produced simply in that a window is swept over the input sequence in small steps. At each step the content of the window is taken to be a tentative character. Successive characters usually overlap considerably.

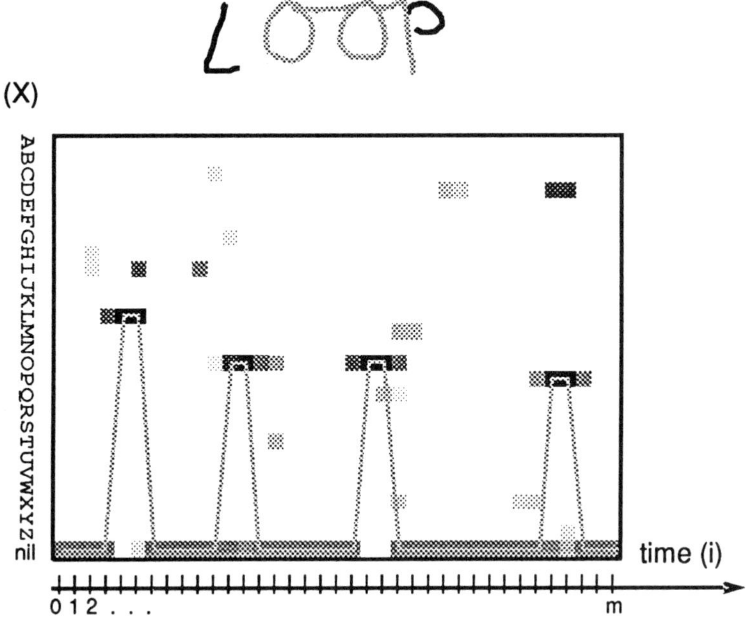

Figure 4: *TDNN* **outputs of the** *OUTSEG* **system.**
The grey curve indicates the best path through the graph, using duration modeling. The word "LOOP" was correctly recognized in spite of the ligatures which prevent segmentation on the basis of pen-lifts.

In figure 4, we show the outputs of our *TDNN* recognizer when the word "LOOP" is processed. The main matrix is a simplified representation of our interpretation graph. Tentative character numbers i ($i \in \{1, 2, ..., m\}$), run along the time direction. Each column contains the scores of all possible interpretations X ($X \in \{A, B, C, ..., Z, nil\}$) of a given tentative character. The bottom line is the nil interpretation score which approximates the probability that the present input is not a character (meaningless character): $P(nil\{i\}|input) = 1 - (P(A\{i\}|input) + P(B\{i\}|input) + ... + P(Z\{i\}|input))$

The connections between nodes reflect a model of character durations. A simple way of enforcing duration is to allow only the following transitions:

$$\begin{aligned} X\{i\} &\rightarrow X\{i+1\}, \\ nil\{i\} &\rightarrow nil\{i+1\}, \\ X\{i\} &\rightarrow nil\{i+1\}, \\ nil\{i\} &\rightarrow X\{i+1\}, \end{aligned}$$

where X stands for a certain letter. A character interpretation can be followed by the same interpretation but cannot be followed immediately by another character interpretation: they must be separated by *nil*. This permits distinguishing between letter duration and letter repetition (such as the double "O" in our example). The best path in the graph is found by the Viterbi algorithm.

In fact, this simple pattern of connections corresponds to a Markov model of duration, with exponential decay. We implemented a slightly fancier model which allows the generation of any duration distribution (Weissman et al. 1992) to help prevent character omission or insertion. In our experiments, we selected two Poisson distributions to model character and the *nil*-class duration respectively.

We use a $TDNN$ recognizer with 3 layers and 10,817 weights. The sequence of recognition scores is obtained by sweeping the neural network over the input. Because of the convolutional structure of the $TDNN$, there are many identical computations between two successive calls of the recognizer and only about one sixth of the network connections have to be reevaluated for each new tentative character. As a consequence, although the $OUTSEG$ system processes many more tentative characters than the $INSEG$ system does, the overall computation time is about the same.

4 COMPARISON OF RESULTS AND CONCLUSIONS

Table 2: **Comparison of the performance of the two segmentation methods using a $TDNN$ recognizer.**

	Error without dictionary		*Error with dictionary*	
on $DB2$	% char.	% word	% char.	% word
$INSEG$	9	18	8.5	15
$OUTSEG$	10	21	8	17
on $DB3$	% char.	% word	% char.	% word
$INSEG$	8	33	5	13
$OUTSEG$	11	48	7	21

We summarize in table 2 the results obtained with our two segmentation methods. To complement the results obtained with database $DB2$, we used (without retraining) database $DB3$ as a control, containing words of any length from the English dictionary. In our current versions, $INSEG$ performs better than $OUTSEG$. The $OUTSEG$ method can handle connected letters (such as in the example of the word "LOOP" in figure 4), while the $INSEG$ method, which relies on pen lifts, cannot. But, we discovered that very few people did not separate their characters by pen lifts in the data we collected. On the other hand, an advantage of the $INSEG$ method is that it can easily be used with recognizers other than the $TDNN$, whereas the $OUTSEG$ method relies heavily on the convolutional structure of the $TDNN$ for computational efficiency.

For comparison, we substituted two other neural network recognizers to the $TDNN$. These networks use alternative input representations. The $OCR-net$ was designed for Optical Character Recognition (Le Cun et al. 1989) and uses pixel map inputs.

Its first layer performs local line orientation detection. The $orientation - net$ has an architecture similar to that of the $OCR - net$, but its first layer is removed and local line orientation information, directly extracted from the pen trajectory, is transmitted to the second layer (Weissbuch and Le Cun 1992). Without a dictionary, the $OCR - net$ has an error rate more than twice that of the $TDNN$ but the $orientation - net$ performs similarly. With dictionary the $orientation - net$ has a 25% lower error rate than the $TDNN$. This improvement is attributed to better second and third best recognition choices, which facilitates dictionary use.

Our best results to date (tables 3) were obtained with the $INSEG$ method, using two recognizers combined with a voting scheme: the $TDNN$ and the $orientation - net$. For comparison purposes we mention the results obtained by a commercial recognizer on the same data. One should notice that our dictionary is the same as the one from which the data was drawn and is probably a larger dictionary than the one used by the commercial system. Our results are substantially better than those of the commercial system. On an absolute scale they are quite satisfactory if we take into account that the test data was not cleaned at all and that more than 20% of the errors have been identified to be patterns written in cursive, misspelled or totally illegible.

We expect the $OUTSEG$ method to work best for cursive handwriting, which does not exhibit trivial segmentation hints, but we do not have any direct evidence to support this expectation as yet. Rumelhart (1992) had success with a version of $OUTSEG$. Work is in progress to extend the capabilities of our systems to cursive writing.

Table 3: **Performance of our best system.** For comparison, we mention in parenthesis the performances obtained by a commercial recognizer on the same data. The performance of the commercial system with dictionary (marked with a *) are penalized because $DB2$ and $DB3$ include words not contained in its dictionary.

	Error without dictionary		*Error with dictionary*	
Method	% char.	% word	% char.	% word
$DB2$	7 (18)	13 (29)	7 (17*)	10 (32*)
$DB3$	6 (20)	23 (61)	5 (18*)	11 (49*)

Acknowledgments

We wish to thank the entire Neural Network group at Bell Labs Holmdel for their supportive discussions. Helpful suggestions with the editing of this paper by L. Jackel and B. Boser are gratefully acknowledged. We are grateful to Anne Weissbuch, Yann Le Cun and Jan Ben for giving us their Neural Networks to try on our $INSEG$ method. We are indebted to Howard Page for providing comparison figures with the commercial recognizer. The experiments were performed with the neural network simulators of B. Boser, Y. Le Cun and L. Bottou who we thank for their help and advice.

References

I. Guyon, P. Albrecht, Y. Le Cun, J. Denker and W. Hubbard. Design of a neural network character recognizer for a touch terminal. *Pattern Recognition*, 24(2), 1991.

H. Weissman, M. Schenkel, I. Guyon, C. Nohl and D. Henderson. Recognition-based Segmentation of On-line Run-on Handprinted Words: Input vs. Output Segmentation. Submitted to Pattern Recognition, October 1992.

K. J. Lang and G. E. Hinton. A time delay neural network architecture for speech recognition. Technical Report CMU-cs-88-152, Carnegie-Mellon University, Pittsburgh PA, 1988.

A. Waibel, T. Hanazawa, G. Hinton, K. Shikano and K. Lang. Phoneme recognition using time-delay neural networks. *IEEE Transactions on Acoustics, Speech and Signal Processing*, 37:328–339, March 1989.

C. J. C. Burges, O. Matan, Y. Le Cun, D. Denker, L. D. Jackel, C. E. Stenard, C. R. Nohl and J. I. Ben. Shortest path segmentation: A method for training neural networks to recognize character strings. In *IJCNN'92*, volume 3, Baltimore, 1992. IEEE.

O. Matan, C. J. C. Burges, Y. Le Cun and J. Denker. Multi-digit recognition using a Space Dispacement Neural Network. In J. E. Moody et al., editor, *Advances in Neural Information Processing Systems 4*, Denver, 1992. Morgan Kaufmann.

J. Keeler, D. E. Rumelhart and W-K. Leow. Integrated segmentation and recognition of hand-printed numerals. In R. Lippmann et al., editor, *Advances in Neural Information Processing Systems 3*, pages 557–563, Denver, 1991. Morgan Kaufmann.

Y. Le Cun, L.D. Jackel, B. Boser, J.S. Denker, H.P. Graf, I. Guyon, D. Henderson, R.E. Howard and W. Hubbard. Handwritten digit recognition: Application of neural network chips and automatic learning. *IEEE Communications Magazine*, pages 41–46, November 1989.

A. Weissbuch and Y. Le Cun. Private communication. 1992.

D. Rumelhart et al. Integrated segmentation and recognition of cursive handwriting. In *Third NEC symposium Computational Learning and Cognition*, Princeton, New Jersey, 1992 (to appear).

Planar Hidden Markov Modeling: from Speech to Optical Character Recognition

Esther Levin and Roberto Pieraccini
ATT Bell Laboratories
600 Mountain Ave.
Murray Hill, NJ 07974

Abstract

We propose in this paper a statistical model (planar hidden Markov model - PHMM) describing statistical properties of images. The model generalizes the single-dimensional HMM, used for speech processing, to the planar case. For this model to be useful an efficient segmentation algorithm, similar to the Viterbi algorithm for HMM, must exist. We present conditions in terms of the PHMM parameters that are sufficient to guarantee that the planar segmentation problem can be solved in polynomial time, and describe an algorithm for that. This algorithm aligns optimally the image with the model, and therefore is insensitive to elastic distortions of images. Using this algorithm a joint optimal segmentation and recognition of the image can be performed, thus overcoming the weakness of traditional OCR systems where segmentation is performed independently before the recognition leading to unrecoverable recognition errors.

The PHMM approach was evaluated using a set of isolated hand-written digits. An overall digit recognition accuracy of 95% was achieved. An analysis of the results showed that even in the simple case of recognition of isolated characters, the elimination of elastic distortions enhances the performance significantly. We expect that the advantage of this approach will be even more significant for tasks such as connected writing recognition/spotting, for which there is no known high accuracy method of recognition.

1 Introduction

The performance of traditional OCR systems deteriorate very quickly when documents are degraded by noise, blur, and other forms of distortion. The main reason for such deterioration is that in addition to the intra-class character variability caused by distortion, the segmentation of the text into words and characters becomes a nontrivial task. In most of the traditional systems, such segmentation is done *before* recognition, leading to many recognition errors, since recognition algorithms cannot usually recover from errors introduced in the segmentation phase. Moreover, in many cases the segmentation is ill-defined, since many plausible segmentations might exist, and only grammatical and linguistic analysis can find the "right " one. To address these problems, an algorithm is needed that can :

- be tolerant to distortions leading to intra-class variability

- perform segmentation together with recognition, thus jointly optimizing both processes, while incorporating grammatical/linguistic constraints.

In this paper we describe a planar segmentation algorithm that has the above properties. It results from a direct extension of the Viterbi (Forney, 1973) algorithm, widely used in automatic speech recognition, to two-dimensional signals.

In the next section we describe the basic hidden Markov model and define the segmentation problem. In section 3 we introduce the planar HMM that extends the HMM concept to model images. The planar segmentation problem for PHMM is defined in section 4. It was recently shown (Kearns and Levin, 1992) that the planar segmentation problem is NP-hard, and therefore, in order to obtain an effective planar segmentation algorithm, we propose to constrain the parameters of the PHMM. We show sufficient conditions in terms of PHMM parameters for such algorithm to exist and describe the algorithm. This approach differs from the one taken in references (Chellappa and Chatterjee, 1985) and (Derin and Elliot, 1987), where instead of restricting the problem, a suboptimal solution to the general problem was found. Since in (Kearns and Levin, 1992) it was also shown that planar segmentation problem is hard to approximate, such suboptimal solution doesn't have any guaranteed bounds. The segmentation algorithm can now be used effectively not only for aligning isolated images, but also for joint recognition/segmentation, eliminating the need of independent segmentation that usually leads to unrecoverable errors in recognition. The same algorithm is used for estimation of the parameters of the model given a set of example images. In section 5, results of isolated hand-written digit recognition experiments are presented. The results indicate that even in the simple case of isolated characters, the elimination of planar distortions enhances the performance significantly. Section 6 contains the summary of this work.

2 Hidden Markov Model

The HMM is a statistical model that is used to describe temporal signals $G=\{g(t): 1 \le t \le T, g \in \mathbf{G} \subset \mathbf{R}^n\}$ in speech processing applications (Rabiner, 1989; Lee *et al.*, 1990; Wilpon *et al.*, 1990; Pieraccini and Levin, 1991). The HMM is a composite statistical source comprising a set $\mathbf{s}=\{1, \cdots, T_R\}$ of T_R sources called states. The i-th state, $i \in \mathbf{s}$, is characterized by its probability distribution $P_i(g)$ over $\mathbf{G}$. At each time t only one of the states is active, emitting the observable $g(t)$. We denote by $s(t)$, $s(t) \in \mathbf{s}$ the random variable corresponding to the active state at time t. The joint probability distribution (for real-valued g) or discrete probability mass (for g being a discrete variable) $P(s(t), g(t))$ for $t>1$ is characterized by the following property:

$$P(s(t),g(t) \mid s(1:t-1),g(1:t-1)) = P(s(t) \mid s(t-1))\, P(g(t) \mid s(t)) \equiv \tag{1}$$
$$= P(s(t) \mid s(t-1))\, P_{s(t)}(g(t)),$$

where $s(1:t-1)$ stands for the sequence $\{s(1), \cdots s(t-1)\}$, and $g(1:t-1)=\{g(1), \ldots, g(t-1)\}$. We denote by a_{ij} the transition probability $P(s(t)=j \mid s(t-1)=i)$, and by π_i, the probability of state i being active at $t=1$, $\pi_i = P(s(1)=i)$. The probability of the entire sequence of states $S \equiv s(1:T)$ and observations $G=g(1:T)$ can be expressed as

$$P(G,S) = \pi_{s(1)} P_{s(1)}(g(1)) \prod_{t=2}^{T} a_{s(t-1)s(t)}\, P_{s(t)}(g(t)). \tag{2}$$

The interpretation of equations (1) and (2) is that the observable sequence G is generated in two stages: first, a sequence S of T states is chosen according to the Markovian distribution parametrized by $\{a_{ij}\}$ and $\{\pi_i\}$; then each one of the states $s(t)$, $1 \le t \le T$, in S generates an observable $g(t)$ according to its own memoryless distribution $P_{s(t)}$, forming the observable sequence G. This model is called a *hidden* Markov model, because the state sequence S is not given, and only the observation sequence G is known. A particular case of this model, called a *left-to-right* HMM, where $a_{ij}=0$ for $j<i$, and

$\pi_1 = 1$, is especially useful for speech recognition. In this case each state of the model represents an unspecified acoustic unit, and due to the "left-to-right" structure, the whole word is modeled as a concatenation of such acoustic units. The time spent in each of the states is not fixed, and therefore the model can take into account the duration variability between different utterances of the same word.

The segmentation problem of HMM is that of estimating the most probable state sequence $\hat{S}$, given the observation G,

$$\hat{S} = \underset{S}{argmax}\, P(S \mid G) = \underset{S}{argmax}\, P(G,S). \tag{3}$$

The problem of finding $\hat{S}$ through exhaustive search is of exponential complexity, since there exist T^{T_R} possible state sequences, but it can be solved in polynomial time using a dynamic programming approach (i.e. Viterbi algorithm). The segmentation plays a central role in all HMM-based speech recognizers, since for connected speech it gives the segmentation into words or sub-word units, and performs a recognition simultaneously, in an optimal way. This is in contrast to sequential systems, in which the connected speech is first segmented into words/subwords according to some rules, and than the individual segments are recognized by computing the appropriate likelihoods, and where many recognition errors are caused by unrecoverable segmentation errors. Higher-level syntactical knowledge can be integrated into decoding process through transition probabilities between the models. The segmentation is also used for estimating the HMMs parameters using a corpus of a training data.

3 The Two-Dimensional Case: Planar HMM

In this section we describe a statistical model for planar image $G = \{g(x,y):(x,y) \in L_{X,Y},\ g \in \mathbf{G}\}$. We call this model "Planar HMM" (PHMM) and design it to extend the advantages of conventional HMM to the two-dimensional case.

The PHMM is a composite source, comprising a set $\mathbf{s} = \{(\tilde{x},\tilde{y}),\ 1 \le \tilde{x} \le X_R,\ 1 \le \tilde{y} \le Y_R\}$ of $N = X_R Y_R$ states. Each state in $\mathbf{s}$ is a stochastic source characterized by its probability density $P_{\tilde{x},\tilde{y}}(g)$ over the space of observations $g \in \mathbf{G}$. It is convenient to think of the states of the model as being located on a rectangular lattice where each state corresponds to a pixel of the corresponding reference image. Similarly to the conventional HMM, only one state is active in the generation of the (x,y)-th image pixel $g(x,y)$. We denote by $s(x,y) \in \mathbf{s}$ the active state of the model that generates $g(x,y)$. The joint distribution governing the choice of active states and image values has the following Markovian property:

$$\begin{aligned} P(g(x,y), s(x,y) \mid g(1{:}X, 1{:}y-1), g(1{:}x-1,y), s(1{:}X, 1{:}y-1), s(1{:}x-1,y)) = \\ = P(g(x,y) \mid s(x,y))\, P(s(x,y) \mid s(x-1,y), s(x,y-1)) = \\ = P_{s(x,y)}(g(x,y))\, P(s(x,y) \mid s(x-1,y), s(x,y-1)) = \end{aligned} \tag{4}$$

where $g(1{:}X,y-1) \equiv \{g(x,y) : (x,y) \in R_{X,y-1}\}$, $g(1{:}x-1,y) \equiv \{g(1,y), \cdots, g(x-1,y)\}$, and $s(1{:}X, 1{:}y-1)$, $s(1{:}x-1,y)$ are the active states involved in generating $g(1{:}X,y-1)$, $g(1{:}x-1,y)$, respectively, and $R_{X,y-1}$ is an axis parallel rectangle between the origin and the point $(X,y-1)$. Similarly to the one-dimensional case, it is useful to define a *left-to-right bottom-up* PHMM where $P(s(x,y)=(m,n) \mid s(x-1,y)=(i,j), s(x,y-1)=(k,l)) \neq 0$ only when $i \le m$ and $l \le n$, that does not allow for "fold overs" in the state image. The Markovian property (4) allows the left-to-right bottom-up PHMM to model elastic distortions among different realizations of the same image, similarly to the way the Markovian property in left-to-right HMM handles temporal alignment. We have chosen this definition (4) of Markovian property rather than others (see for example Derin and Kelly, 1989) since it leads to the formulation of a segmentation problem which is similar to the planar alignment defined in (Levin and Pieraccini, 1992).

Using property (4), the joint likelihood of the image $G = g(1{:}X, 1{:}Y)$ and the state image $S = s(1{:}X, 1{:}Y)$ can be written as

$$P(G,S) = \prod_{x=1}^{X} \prod_{y=1}^{Y} P_{s(x,y)}(g(x,y)) \tag{5}$$

$$\pi_{s(1,1)} \prod_{x=2}^{X} \overset{H}{a}_{s(x-1,1),s(x,1)} \prod_{y=2}^{Y} \overset{V}{a}_{s(1,y-1),s(1,y)} \prod_{y=2}^{Y} \prod_{x=2}^{X} A_{s(x-1,y),s(x,y-1),s(x,y)},$$

where:

$$A_{(i,j),(k,l),(m,n)} \equiv P(\, s(x,y) = (m,n) \mid s(x-1,y) = (i,j),\, s(x,y-1) = (k,l)\,),$$

$$\overset{H}{a}_{(i,j),(m,n)} \equiv P(\, s(x,1) = (m,n) \mid s(x-1,1) = (i,j)\,),$$

$$\overset{V}{a}_{(k,l),(m,n)} \equiv P(\, s(1,y) = (m,n) \mid s(1,y) = (k,l)\,),$$

and

$$\pi_{ij} \equiv P(\, s(1,1) = (i,j)\,)$$

denote the generalized transition probabilities of PHMM. Similarly to HMM, (5) suggests that an image G is generated by the PHMM in two successive stages: in the first stage the state matrix S is generated according to the Markovian probability distribution parametrized by $\{A\}$, $\{\overset{H}{a}\}$, $\{\overset{V}{a}\}$, and $\{\pi\}$. In the second stage, the image value in the (x,y)-th pixel is produced independently from other pixels according to the distribution of the $s(x,y)$-th state $P_{s(x,y)}(g)$. As in HMM, the state matrix S in most of the applications is not known, only G is observed.

4 Planar Segmentation Problem

The segmentation problem of PHMM is that of finding the state matrix $\hat{S}$ that best explains the observable image G and defines an optimal alignment of the image to the model. Solving this problem eliminates the sensitivity to intra-class elastic distortions and allows for simultaneous segmentation/recognition of images similarly to the one-dimensional case. $\hat{S}$ can be estimated as in (3) by $\hat{S} = \underset{S}{argmax}\, P(G,S)$. If we approach this maximization by exhaustive search, the computational complexity is exponential, since there are $(X_R Y_R)^{XY}$ different state matrices. Since the segmentation problem is NP-hard (Kearns and Levin, 1992), we suggest to simplify the problem by constraining the parameters of the PHMM, so that efficient segmentation algorithm can be found. In this section we present conditions in terms of the generalized transition probabilities of PHMM that are sufficient to guarantee that the most likely state image $\hat{S}$ can be computed in polynomial time, and describe an algorithm for doing that.

For the problem of finding $\hat{S}$ to be solved in polynomial time, there should exist a grouping of the set $\mathbf{s}$ of states of the model into N_G mutually exclusive[1] subsets of states γ_p, $\mathbf{s} = \bigcup_{p=1}^{N_G} \gamma_p$. The generalized transition probabilities should satisfy the two following constraints with respect to such grouping:

$$A_{(i,j),(k,l),(m,n)} \neq 0 \;\; ; \;\; \overset{H}{a}_{(i,j),(m,n)} \neq 0 \tag{6}$$

only if there exists p, $1 \le p \le N_G$, such that (i,j), $(m,n) \in \gamma_p$.

$$A_{(i,j),(k,l),(m,n)} = A_{(i,j),(k_1,l_1),(m,n)} \;\; ; \;\; \overset{V}{a}_{(k,l),(m,n)} = \overset{V}{a}_{(k_1,l_1),(m,n)} \tag{7}$$

[1] It is possible to drop the mutually exclusiveness constraints by duplicating states, but then we have to ensure that the number of subsets, N_G, should be polynomial in the dimensions of the model X_R, Y_R.

if there exists p, $1 \le p \le N_G$, such that $(k,l), (k_1,l_1) \in \gamma_p$.

Condition (6) means that the the left neighbor (i,j) of the state (m,n) in the state matrix S must be a member of the same subset γ_p as (m,n). Condition (7) means that the value of transition probability $A_{(i,j),(k,l),(m,n)}$ does not depend explicitly on the identity (k,l) of the bottom neighboring state, but only on the subset γ_p to which (k,l) belongs.

Under (6) and (7) the most likely state matrix $\hat{S}$ can be found using an algorithm described in (Levin and Pieraccini, 1992). This algorithm makes use of the Viterbi procedure at two different levels. In the first stage optimal segmentation is computed for each subset γ_p with each image raw using Viterbi. Then global segmentation is found, through Viterbi, by combining optimally the segmentations obtained in the previous stage.

Although conditions (6),(7) are hard to check in practice since any possible grouping of the states has to be considered, they can be effectively used in constructive mode, i.e., chosing one particular grouping, and then imposing the constraints (6) and (7) on the generalized transition probabilities with respect to this grouping. For example, if we choose $\gamma_p = \{(\tilde{x},\tilde{y}) \mid 1 \le \tilde{x} \le X_R, \tilde{y} = p\}$, $1 \le p \le Y_R$, then the constraints (6),(7) become:

$$A_{(i,j),(k,l),(m,n)} \neq 0, \ \overset{H}{a}_{(i,j),(m,n)} \neq 0 \ \text{ only for } j = n , \tag{8}$$

and,

$$A_{(i,j),(k,l),(m,n)} = A_{(i,j),(k_1,l),(m,n)}, \ \overset{V}{a}_{(k,l),(m,n)} = \overset{V}{a}_{(k_1,l),(m,n)} \ \text{ for } 1 \le k_1, k \le X_R . \tag{9}$$

Note that constraints (6), (7) break the symmetry between the roles of the two coordinates. Other sets of conditions can be obtained from (6) and (7) by coordinate transformation. For example, the roles of the vertical and the horizontal axes can be exchanged. A grouping and constraints set chosen for a particular application should reflect the geometric properties of the images.

5 Experimental Results

The PHMM approach was tested on a writer-independent isolated handwritten digit recognition application. The data we used in our experiments was collected from 12 subjects (6 for training and 6 for test). Each subject was asked to write 10 samples of each digit. Samples were written in fixed-size boxes, therefore naturally size-normalized and centered. Each sample in the database was represented by a 16×16 binary image.

Each character class (digit) was represented by a single PHMM, satisfying (6) and (7). Each PHMM had a *strictly* left-to-right bottom-up structure, where the state matrix S was restricted to contain every state of the model, i.e., states could not be skipped. All models had the same number of states. Each state was represented by its own binary probability distribution, i.e., the probability of a pixel being 1 (black) or 0 (white). We estimated these probabilities from the training data with the following generalization of the Viterbi training algorithm (Jelinek, 1976). For the initialization we uniformly divided each training image into regions corresponding to the states of its model. The initial value of $P_i(g=1)$ for the i-th state was obtained as a frequency count of the black pixels in the corresponding region over all the samples of the same digit. Each iteration of the algorithm consisted of two stages: first, the samples were aligned with the corresponding model, by finding the best state matrix $\hat{S}$. Then, a new frequency count for each state was used to update $P_i(1)$, according to the obtained alignment. We noticed that the training procedure converged usually after 2-4 iterations, and in all the experiments the algorithm was stopped at the 10th iteration. The recognition was performed by assigning the test sample to the class k for which the alignment likelihood was maximal.

Table 1 shows the number of errors in the recognition of the training set and the test set for different sizes of the models.

Number of states $X_R = Y_R$	Recognition Errors	
	Training	Test
6	78	82
8	36	50
9	35	48
10	26	32
11	21	38
12	18	42
16	36	64

Table 1: Number of errors in the recognition of the training set and the test set for different size of the models (out of 600 trials in both cases)

It is worth noting the following two points. First, the test error shows a minimum for $X_R = Y_R = 10$ of 5%. By increasing or decreasing the number of states this error increases. This phenomenon is due to the following:

1. The typical under/over parametrization behavior.
2. Increasing the number of states closer to the size of the modeled images reduces the flexibility of the alignment procedure, making this a trivial uniform alignment when $X_R = Y_R = 16$.

Also, the training error decreases monotonically with increasing number of states up to $X_R = Y_R = 16$. This is again typical behavior for such systems, since by increasing the number of states, the number of model parameters grows, improving the fit to the training data. But when the number of states equals the dimensions of the sample images, $X_R = Y_R = 16$, there is a sudden significant increase in the training error. This behavior is consistent with point (2) above.

Fig. 1 shows three sets of models with different numbers of states. The states of the models in this figure are represented by squares, where the grey level of the square encodes the probability $P(g=1)$. The (6×6) state models have a very coarse representation of the digits, because the number of states is so small. The (10×10) state models appear much sharper than the (16×16) state models, due to their ability to align the training samples.

This preliminary experiment shows that eliminating elastic distortions by the alignment procedure discussed above plays an important role in the task of isolated character recognition, improving the recognition accuracy significantly. Note that the simplicity of this task does not stress the full power of the PHMM representation, since the data was isolated, size-normalized, and centered. On this task, the achieved performance is comparable to that of many other OCR systems. We expect that in harder tasks, involving connected text, the advantage of the proposed method will enhance the performance. Recently, this approach is being successfully applied to the task of recognition of noisy degraded printed messages (Agazzi *et al.*, 1993).

6 Summary and Discussion

In this paper we describe a planar hidden Markov model and develop a planar segmentation algorithm that generalizes the Viterbi procedure widely used in speech recognition. This algorithm can be used to perform joint optimal recognition/segmentation of images incorporating some grammatical constraints and tolerating intra-class elastic distortions. The PHMM approach was tested on an isolated, hand-written digit recognition application. An analysis of the results indicate that even in a simple case of isolated characters, the elimination of elastic distortions enhances recognition performance significantly. We expect that the advantage of this approach will be even more valuable in harder tasks, such as cursive writing recognition/spotting, for which an effective solution using the current available techniques has not yet been found.

Figure 1: Three sets of models with 6×6, 10×10, and 16×16 states.

References

O. E. Agazzi, S. S. Kuo, E. Levin, R. Pieraccini, " Connected and Degraded Text Recognition Using Planar Hidden Markov Models," *Proc. Of Int. COnference on Acoustics Speech and Signal Processing*, April 1993.

R. Chellappa, S. Chatterjee, "Classification of textures Using Gaussian Markov Random Fields," *IEEE Transactions on ASSP* , Vol. 33, No. 4, pp. 959-963, August 1985.

H. Derin, H. Elliot, "Modeling and Segmentation of Noisy and Textured Images Using Gibbs Random Fields," *IEEE Transactions on PAMI* , Vol. 9, No. 1 pp. 39-55, January 1987.

H. Derin, P. A. Kelly, 'Discrete-Index Markov-Type Random Processes,' in IEEE Proceedings, vol 77, #10, pp.1485-1510, 1989

G.D. Forney, "The Viterbi algorithm," *Proc. IEEE,* Mar. 1973.

F. Jelinek, "Continuous Speech Recognition by Statistical Methods," *Proceedings of IEEE*, vol. 64, pp. 532-556, April 1976.

M. Kearns, E. Levin, *Unpublished*, 1992.

C.-H. Lee, L. R. Rabiner, R. Pieraccini, J. G. Wilpon, "Acoustic Modeling for Large Vocabulary Speech Recognition," *Computer Speech and Language*, 1990, No. 4, pp. 127-165.

E. Levin, R. Pieraccini, "Dynamic Planar Warping and Planar Hidden Markov Modeling: from Speech to Optical Character Recognition," submitted to *IEEE Trans. on PAMI,* 1992.

R. Pieraccini, E. Levin, "Stochastic Representation of Semantic Structure for Speech Understanding," *Proceedings of EUROSPEECH 91*, Vol.2, pp. 383-386, Genova, September 1991.

L.R. Rabiner, "A Tutorial on Hidden Markov Models and Selected Applications in Speech Recognition," *Proc. IEEE*, Feb. 1989.

J. G. Wilpon, L. R. Rabiner, C.-H. Lee, E. R. Goldman, "Automatic Recognition of Keywords in Unconstrained Speech Using Hidden Markov Models," *IEEE Trans. on ASSP*, Vol. 38, No. 11, pp 1870-1878, November 1990.

Forecasting Demand for Electric Power

Jen-Lun Yuan and Terrence L. Fine
School of Electrical Engineering
Cornell University
Ithaca, NY 14853

Abstract

We are developing a forecaster for daily extremes of demand for electric power encountered in the service area of a large midwestern utility and using this application as a testbed for approaches to input dimension reduction and decomposition of network training. Projection pursuit regression representations and the ability of algorithms like SIR to quickly find reasonable weighting vectors enable us to confront the vexing architecture selection problem by reducing high-dimensional gradient searchs to fitting single-input single-output (SISO) subnets. We introduce dimension reduction algorithms, to select features or relevant subsets of a set of many variables, based on minimizing an index of level-set dispersions (closely related to a projection index and to SIR), and combine them with backfitting to implement a neural network version of projection pursuit. The performance achieved by our approach, when trained on 1989, 1990 data and tested on 1991 data, is comparable to that achieved in our earlier study of backpropagation trained networks.

1 Introduction

Our work has the intertwined goals of:

(i) contributing to the improvement of the short-term electrical load (demand) forecasts used by electric utilities to buy and sell power and ensure that they can meet demand;

(ii) reducing the computational burden entailed in gradient–based training of neural networks and thereby enabling the exploration of architectures;

(iii) improving prospects for good statistical generalization by use of rational methods for reducing complexity through the identification of good small subsets of variables drawn from a large set of candidate predictor variables (feature selection);

(iv) benchmarking backpropagation and neural networks as an approach to the applied problem of load forecasting.

Our efforts proceed in the context of a problem suggested by the operational needs of a particular electric utility to make daily forecasts of short–term load or demand. Forecasts are made at midday (1 p.m.) on a weekday t (Monday - Thursday), for the next evening peak $e(t)$ (occuring usually about 8 p.m. in the winter), the daily minimum $d(t+1)$ (occuring about 4 a.m. the next morning) and the morning peak $m(t+1)$ (about noon). In addition, on Friday we are to forecast these three variables for the weekend through the Monday morning peak. These daily extremes of demand are illustrated in an excerpt from our hourly load data plotted in Figure 1.

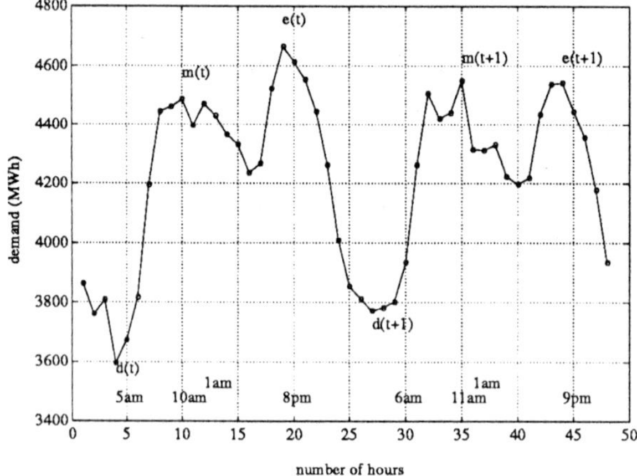

Figure 1: Hourly demand for two consecutive days showing the intended forecasting variables.

In this paper, we focus on forecasting these extremal demands up to three days ahead (e.g. forecasting on Fridays). Neural network–based forecasters are developed which parallel the recently proposed method of slicing inverse regression (SIR) (Li [1991]) and then use backfitting (Hastie and Tibshirani [1990]) to implement a training algorithm for a projection pursuit model (Friedman [1987], Huber [1985]) that can be implemented with a single hidden layer network. Our data consists of hourly integrated system demand (MWH) and hourly temperatures measured at three cities in the service area of a large midwestern utility during 1989-91. We use 1989 and 1990 for a training set and test over the whole of 1991, with the exception of holidays that occur so infrequently that we have no training base.

2 Baseline Performance

2.1 Previous Work on Load Forecasting

Since demand is a process which does not have a known physical or mathematical model, we do not know the best achievable forecasting performance, and we are led to making comparisons with methods and results reported elsewhere. There is a substantial literature on short-term load forecasting, with Gross et al. [1987] and Willis et al. [1984] providing good reviews of approaches based upon such statistical methods as linear least squares regression and Box-Jenkins and ARMAX time series models. Many utilities rely upon the seemingly seat-of-the-pants estimates produced by individuals who have been long employed at this task and who extrapolate from a large historical data base. In the past few years there have been several efforts to employ neural networks trained through backpropagation. In two such recent studies conducted at the Univ. of Washington an average peak error of 2.04% was reported by Damborg et al. [1990] and an hourly load error of about 2.2% was given by Connor et al. [1991]. However, the accuracies reported in the literature are difficult to compare with since utilities are exposed to different operating conditions (e.g., weather, residential/industrial balance). To provide a benchmark for the error performance achieved by our method, we evaluated three basic forecasting models on our data. These methods are based on a pair of features made plausible by the scatter plots shown in Figure 2.

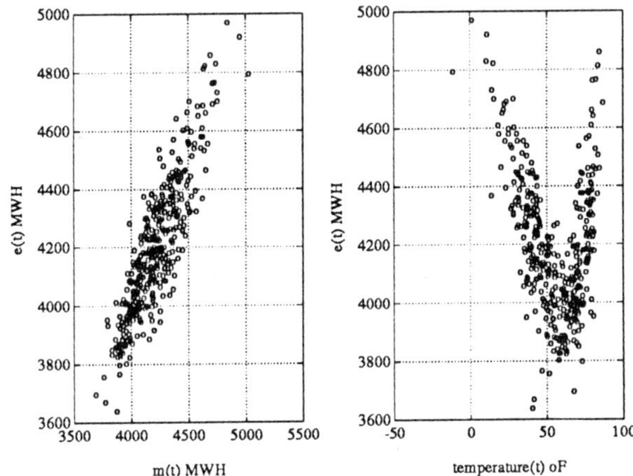

Figure 2: Evening peaks (Tue.-Fri.,1989-90) vs. morning peaks and temperatures.

2.2 Feature Selection and Homogeneous Data Types

Demand depends on predictable calendar factors such as the season, day-of-the-week and time-of-day considerations. We grouped separately Mondays, Tuesdays through Fridays, Saturdays, and Sundays, as well as holidays. In contrast to all of the earlier work on this problem, we ignored seasonal considerations and let the network and training algorithm adjust as needed. The advantage of this was the ability to form larger training data sets. We thus constructed twelve networks, one

type	m(t+1)	e(t)	d(t+1)
Monday	m(t-3)	m(t)	d(t-3)
Tue.-Fri.	m(t-1)	m(t)	d(t-1)
Saturday	m(t-1)	m(t-1)	d(t-1)
Sunday	m(t-2)	m(t-2)	d(t- 2)

Table 1: Most recent peaks of a two-feature set

type	m(t+1)			e(t)			d(t+1)		
	LLS	LOESS	BP	LLS	LOESS	BP	LLS	LOESS	BP
Monday	3.78	2.45	2.42	1.73	2.43	1.59	4.40	3.30	2.69
Tue.-Fri.	3.01	2.44	1.98	1.89	3.04	1.65	3.29	3.81	2.49
Saturday	3.37	2.60	2.36	4.54	3.76	3.10	3.48	3.25	2.06
Sunday	4.83	3.28	3.79	4.89	2.74	3.81	4.26	2.44	3.03

Table 2: Forecasting accuracies (percentage absolute error) for three basic methods

for each pair consisting of one of these four types of days and one of the three daily extremes to be forecast. Demand also depends heavily upon weather which is the primary random factor affecting forecasts. This dependency can be seen in the scatter plots of current demand vs. previous demand and temperature in Figure 2, particularly in the projection onto the 'current demand–temperature' plane which shows a pronounced "U"-shaped nonlinearity. A two-feature set consisting of the most recent peaks and average temperatures over the three cities and the preceding six hours is employed for testing all three models (Table 1).

2.3 Benchmark Results

The three basic forecasting models using the two-featured set are:

1) linear regression model fitted to the data in Figure 2;

2) demand vs. temperature models which roughly model the "U-shaped" nonlinear relationship, (LOESS with .5 span was employed for scatter plot smoothing);

3) backpropagation trained neural networks using 5 logistic nodes in a single hidden layer.

The test set errors are given in Table 2. Note that among these three models, BP-trained neural networks gives superior test set performance on all but Sundays. These models all give results comparable to those obtained in our earlier work on forecasting demands for Tuesday-Friday using autoregressive neural networks (Yuan and Fine [1992]).

3 Projection Pursuit Training

Satisfactory forecasting performance of the neural networks described above relies on the appropriate choice of feature sets and network architectures. Unfortunately, BP can only address the problem of appropriate architecture and relevant feature sets through repeated time–consuming experiments. Modeling of high–dimensional input features using gradient search requires extensive computation. We were thus prompted to look at other network structures and at training algorithms that could make it easier to explore architecture and training problems. Our initial attempt combined the dimension reduction algorithm of SIR (Li [1991]), currently replaced by an algorithm of our devising sketched in Section 4, and backfitting (Hastie et.al [1990]) to implement a neural network version of projection pursuit regression (PPR).

3.1 The Algorithm

A general nonlinear regression model for a forecast variable y in terms of a vector x of input variables and model noise ϵ, independent of x, is given by

$$y = f(\beta_1' x, \beta_2' x, .., \beta_k' x, \epsilon) \qquad (*).$$

A least mean square predictor is the conditional expectation $E(y|x)$. The projection pursuit model/approximation of this conditional expectation is given in terms of a family of SISO functions $\Xi_1, \Xi_2, .., \Xi_k$ by

$$E(y|x) = \sum_{i=1}^{k} \Xi_i(\beta_i' x) + \beta_0.$$

A single hidden layer neural network can approximate this representation by introducing subnets whose summed outputs approximate the individual Ξ_j.

We train such a 'projection pursuit network' with nodes partitioned into subnets, representing the Ξ_i, by training the subnets individually in rotation. In this we follow the statistical regression notion of backfitting. The subnet Ξ_i is trained to predict the residuals resulting from the difference between the weighted outputs of the other $k-1$ subnets and the true value of the demand variable. After a number of training cycles one then proceeds to the next subnet and repeats the process. The inputs to each subnet Ξ_i are the low–dimensional projections $\beta_i' x$ of the regression model. One termination criteria for determining the number of subnets k is to stop adding subnets when the projection appears to be normally distributed; results of Diaconis and Freedman point out that 'most' projections will be so distributed and thus are 'uninteresting'. The directions β_i can be found by minimizing some projection index which defines interesting projections that deviates from Gaussian distributions (e.g., Friedman [1987]). Each β_i determines the weights connecting the input to subnet Ξ_i.The whole projection pursuit regression process is simplified by decoupling the direction β search from training the SISO subnets. Albeit, its success depends upon an ability to rapidly discern the significant directions β_i.

3.2 Implementations

There are several variants in the implementation of projection pursuit training algorithms. General PPR procedure can be implemented in one stage by computa-

type	m(t+1)	e(t)	d(t+1)
Monday	2.35/3.45	1.25/1.60	2.76/3.49
Tue.-Fri.	2.37/2.83	1.65/1.66	2.15/2.66
Saturday	2.67/3.16	2.78/3.96	2.57/3.04
Sunday	3.15/5.38	2.63/3.67	2.29/3.61

Table 3: Forecasting performance (training/testing percentage error) of projection pursuit trained networks

tionally intensive numerical methods, or in a two–stage heuristic (finding β_i, then Ξ_i) as proposed here. It can be implemented with or without backfitting after the PPR phase is done. Intrator [1992] has recently suggested incorporating the projection index into the objective function and then running an overall BPA. Other variants in training each Ξ_i net include using nonparametric smoothing techniques such as LOESS or kernel methods. BP training can then be applied only in the last stage to fit the smoothed curves so obtained. The complexity of each subnet is then largely determined by the smoothing parameters, like window sizes, inherent in most nonparametric smoothing techniques. Another practical advantage of this process is that one can incorporate easily fixed functions of a single variable (e.g. linear nodes or quadratic nodes) when one's prior knowledge of the data source suggests that such components may be present. Our current implementation employs the two-stage algorithm with simple (either one or two nodes) logistic Ξ_i subnets. Each SISO Ξ_i net runs a BP algorithm to fit the data. The directions β_i are calculated based on minimizing a projection index (dispersion of level–sets, described in Section 4) which can be executed in a direct fashion. One can encourage the convergence of backfitting by using a relaxation parameter (like a momentum parameter in BPA) to control the amount updated in the current direction. Training (fitting) of each (SISO) Ξ_i net can be carried out more efficiently than running BP based on high–dimensional inputs, for example, it is less expensive to evaluate the Hessian matrices in a Ξ_i net than in a full BPA networks.

3.3 Forecasting Results

Experimental results were obtained using the two-component feature data sets which gave the earlier baseline performance. To calibrate the performance we employed in all twelve projection pursuit trained networks an uniform architecture of three subnets (a $(1, 2, 2)$-logistic network), matching the 5 nodes of the BP network of Section 2.The number of backfitting cycles was set to 20 with a relaxation parameter $\omega = 0.1$. BPA was employed for fitting each $\Xi_i$net. The training/testing percentage absolute errors are given in Table 3. The limited data sets in the cases of individual days (Monday, Saturday, Sunday) led to failure in generalization that could have been prevented by using one or two, rather than three, subnets.

4 Dimension Reduction

4.1 Index of Level–Set Dispersion

A key step in the projection pursuit training algorithm is to find for each Ξ_i net the projection direction β_i, an instance of the important problem of economically choosing input features/variables in constructing a forecasting model. In general, the fewer the number of input features, the more likely are the results to generalize from training set performance to test set performance- reduction in variance at the possible expense of increase in bias. Our controlled size subnet projection pursuit training algorithm deals with part of the complexity problem, provided that the input features are fixed. We turn now to our approach to finding input features or search directions based on minimizing an index of dispersion of level–sets. Li [1991] proposed taking an inverse ('slicing the y's') point of view to estimate the directions β_i. The justification provided for this so–called slicing inverse regression (SIR) method, however, requires that the input or feature vector x be elliptically symmetrically distributed, and this is not likely to be the case in our electric load forecasting problem. The basic idea behind minimizing dispersion of level–sets is that from Eq. (*) we see that a fixed value of y, and small noise ϵ, implies a highly constrained set of values for $\beta_1'x, ..., \beta_k'x$, while leaving unconstrained the components of x that lie in the subspace $B^\perp$ orthogonal to that space B spanned by the β_i. Hence, if one has a good number of *i.i.d.* observations sharing a similar value of the response y, then there should be more dispersion of input vectors projected into $B^\perp$ than along the projections into B. We implement this by quantizing the observed y values into, say, H slices, with L_h denoting the h_th level–set containing those inputs with y-value in the h_th slice, and $\bar{x_h}$ is their sample mean. The β are then picked as the the eigenvector associated with the smallest eigenvalue of the centered covariance matrix:

$$\sum_{h=1}^{H} \sum_{x_i \in L_h} (x_i - \bar{x_h})(x_i - \bar{x_h})'.$$

4.2 Implementations

In practical implementations, one may discard both extremes of the family of H level sets (trimming) to avoid large response values when it is believed that they may correspond to large magnitudes of input components. One should also standardize initially the input data to a unit sample covariance matrix. Otherwise, our results will reflect the distribution of x rather than the functional relationship of Eq. (*). We have applied this projection index both in finding the β_i during projection pursuit training and in reducing a high–dimensional feature set to a low–dimensional feature set. We have implemented such a feature selection scheme for forecasting the Monday - Friday evening peaks.The initial feature set consists of thirteen hourly loads from 1am to 1pm, thirteen hourly temperatures from 1am to 1pm and the temperature around the peak times. Three eigenvectors of the centered covariance matrix were chosen, thereby reducing a 27–dimensional feature set to a 3–dimensional one. We then ran a standard BPA on this reduced featured set and tested on the 1991 data. We obtained a percentage absolute error of 1.6% (rms error about 100 MWH), which is as good as all of our previous efforts.

Acknowledgements

Partial support for this research was provided by NSF Grant No. ECS–9017493.

We wish to thank Prof. J. Hwang, Mathematics Department, Cornell, for initial discussions of SIR and are grateful to Dr. P.D. Yeshakul, American Electric Service Corp., for providing the data set and instructing us patiently in the lore of short–term load forecasting.

References

Connor, J., L. Atlas, R.D. Martin [1991], Recurrent networks and NARMA modeling, NIPS 91.

Damborg, M., M.El-Sharkawi, R. Marks II [1990], Potential of artificial neural networks in power system operation, *Proc. 1990 IEEE Inter.Symp. on Circuits and Systems*, **4**, 2933–2937.

Friedman, J. [1987], Exploratory projection pursuit, *J. Amer. Stat. Assn.*, **82**, 249-266.

Gross,G., F. Galiana [1987], Short–term load forecasting, *Proc. IEEE,* **75**, 1558–1573.

Hastie, T., R. Tibshirani [1990], *Generalized Additive Models,*Chapman and Hall.

Huber, P. [1985], Projection pursuit, *The Annals of Statistics,***13**, 435-475.

Intrator, N. [1992] Combinining exploratory projection pursuit and projection pursuit regression with applicatons to neural networks, To appear in *Neural Computation.*

Li, K.-C. [1991] Slicing inverse regression for dimension reduction, *Journal of American Statistical Assoc.*, **86**.

Willis, H.L., J.F.D. Northcote–Green [1984], Comparison tests of fourteen load forecasting methods, *IEEE Trans. on Power Apparatus and Systems,* **PAS–103**, 1190–1197.

Yuan, J–L., T.L.Fine [1992], Forecasting demand for electric power using autoregressive neural networks, *Proc. Conf. on Info. Sci. and Systems,* Princeton, NJ.

Hidden Markov Models in Molecular Biology: New Algorithms and Applications

Pierre Baldi *
Jet Propulsion Laboratory
California Institute of Technology
Pasadena, CA 91109

Yves Chauvin †
Net-ID, Inc.
8, Cathy Place
Menlo Park, CA 94305

Tim Hunkapiller
Division of Biology
California Institute of Technology

Marcella A. McClure
Department of Evolutionary Biology
University of California, Irvine

Abstract

Hidden Markov Models (HMMs) can be applied to several important problems in molecular biology. We introduce a new convergent learning algorithm for HMMs that, unlike the classical Baum-Welch algorithm is smooth and can be applied on-line or in batch mode, with or without the usual Viterbi most likely path approximation. Left-right HMMs with insertion and deletion states are then trained to represent several protein families including immunoglobulins and kinases. In all cases, the models derived capture all the important statistical properties of the families and can be used efficiently in a number of important tasks such as multiple alignment, motif detection, and classification.

*and Division of Biology, California Institute of Technology.
†and Department of Psychology, Stanford University.

1 INTRODUCTION

Hidden Markov Models (e.g., Rabiner, 1989) and the more general EM algorithm in statistics can be applied to the modeling and analysis of biological primary sequence information (Churchill (1989), Lawrence and Reilly (1990), Baldi et al. (1992), Cardon and Stormo (1992), Haussler et al. (1992)). Most notably, as in speech recognition applications, a family of evolutionarily related sequences can be viewed as consisting of different utterances of the same prototypical sequence resulting from a common underlying HMM dynamics. A model trained from a family can then be used for a number of tasks including multiple alignments and classification. The multiple alignment is particularly important since it reveals the highly conserved regions of the molecules with functional and structural significance even in the absence of any tertiary information. The multiple alignment is also an essential tool for proper phylogenetic tree reconstruction and other important tasks. Good algorithms based on dynamic programming exist for the alignment of two sequences. However they scale exponentially with the number of sequences and the general multiple alignment problem is known to be NP-complete. Here, we briefly present a new algorithm and its variations for learning in HMMs and the results of some of the applications of this approach to new protein families.

2 HMMs FOR BIOLOGICAL PRIMARY SEQUENCES

A HMM is characterized by a set of states, an alphabet of symbols, a probability transition matrix $T = (t_{ij})$ and a probability emission matrix e_{ij}. As in speech applications, we are going to consider left-right architectures: once a given state is left it can never be visited again. Common knowledge of evolutionary mechanisms suggests the choice of three types of states (in addition to the start and to the end state): the main states $m_1, ..., m_N$, the delete states $d_1, ..., d_{N+1}$ and the insert states $i_1, ..., i_{N+1}$. N is the length of the model which is usually chosen equal to the average length of the sequences in the family and, if needed, can be adjusted in later stages. The details of a typical architecture are given in Figure 1. The alphabet has 4 letters in the case of DNA or RNA sequences, one symbol per nucleotide, and 20 letters in the case of proteins, one symbol per amino acid. Only the main and insert states emit letters, while the delete states are of course mute. The linear sequence of state transitions $start \rightarrow m_1 \rightarrow m_2 \rightarrow ... \rightarrow m_N \rightarrow end$ is the backbone of the model and correponds to the path associated with the prototypical sequence in the family under consideration. Insertions and deletions are defined with respect to this backbone. Insertions and deletions are treated symmetrically except for the loops on the insert states needed to account for multiple insertions. The adjustable parameters of the HMM provide a natural way of incorporating variable gap penalties. A number of other architectures are also possible.

3 LEARNING ALGORITHMS

Learning from examples in HMMs is typically accomplished using the Baum-Welch algorithm. In the Baum-Welch algorithm, the expected number n_{ij} (resp. m_{ij}) of $i \rightarrow j$ transitions (resp. emissions of letter j from state i) induced by the data are calculated using the forward-backward procedure. The transition and emission

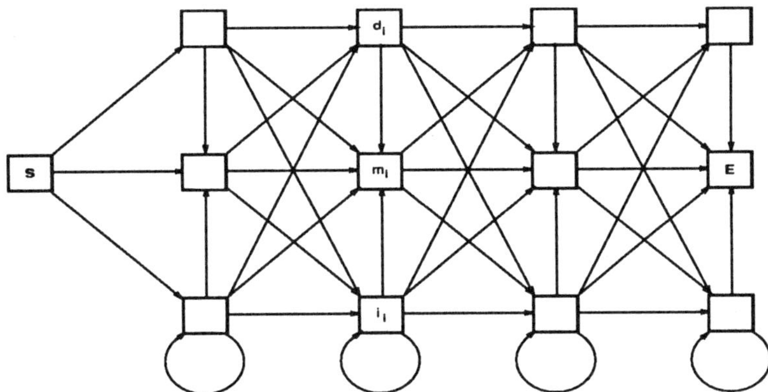

Figure 1: The basic left-right HMM architecture. S and E are the start and end states.

probabilities are then reset to the observed frequencies by

$$t_{ij}^{+} = \frac{n_{ij}}{n_i} \text{ and } e_{ij}^{+} = \frac{m_{ij}}{m_i} \tag{1}$$

where $n_i = \sum_j n_{ij}$ and $m_i = \sum_j m_{ij}$. It is clear that this algorithm can lead to abrupt jumps in parameter space and that the procedure cannot be used for on-line learning (after each training example). This is even more so if, in order to save some computations, the Viterbi approximation is used to estimate likelihoods and transition and emission statistics by computing only the most likely paths as opposed to the forward-bacward procedure where all possible paths are examined.

A new algorithm for HMM learning which is smooth and can be used on-line or in batch mode, with or without the Viterbi approximation, can be defined as follows. First, we use a Boltzmann-Gibbs representation for the parameters. For each t_{ij} (resp. e_{ij}) we define a new parameter w_{ij} (resp. v_{ij}) by

$$t_{ij} = \frac{e^{w_{ij}}}{\sum_k e^{w_{ik}}} \text{ and } e_{ij} = \frac{e^{v_{ij}}}{\sum_k e^{v_{ik}}} \tag{2}$$

Normalisation constraints are naturally enforced by this representation throughout learning with the added advantage that none of the parameters can reach the absorbing value 0. After computing on-line or in batch mode the statistics n_{ij} and m_{ij} using the forward-backward procedure (or the usual Viterbi approximation), the update equations are particularly simple and given by

$$\Delta w_{ij} = \eta(\frac{n_{ij}}{n_i} - t_{ij}) \text{ and } \Delta v_{ij} = \eta(\frac{m_{ij}}{m_i} - e_{ij}) \tag{3}$$

where η is the learning rate. In Baldi et al. (1992) a proof is given that this algorithm must converge to a maximum of the product of the likelihoods of the training sequences. In the case of an on-line Viterbi approximation, the optimal path associated with the current training sequence is first computed. The update equations are then given by

$$\Delta w_{ij} = \eta(t_{ij}^{t} - t_{ij}) \text{ and } \Delta v_{ij} = \eta(t_{ij}^{e} - e_{ij}) \tag{4}$$

Here, for a fixed state i, t_{ij}^t and t_{ij}^e are the target transition and emission values: $t_{ij}^t = 1$ every time the transition $s_i \rightarrow s_j$ is part of the Viterbi path of the corresponding training sequence sequence and 0 otherwise and similarly for t_{ij}^e.

After training, the model derived can be used for a number of tasks. First, by computing for each sequence its most likely path through the model using the Viterbi algorithm, multiple sequences can be aligned to each other in time $O(KN^2)$, linear in the number K of sequences. The model can also be used for classification and data base searches. The likelihood of any sequence (randomly generated or taken from any data base) can be calculated and compared to the likelihood of the sequences in the family being modeled. Additional applications are discussed in Baldi et al. (1992).

4 EXPERIMENTS AND RESULTS

The previous approach has been applied to a number of protein families including globins, immunoglobulins, kinases, aspartic acid proteases and G-coupled receptor proteins. The first application and alignment of the globin family using HMMs (trained with the Viterbi approximation of the Baum-Welch algorithm, and a number of additional heuristics) was given by Haussler et al. (1992). Here, we briefly describe some of our results on the immunoglobulin and the kinase families [1].

4.1 IMMUNOGLOBULINS

Immunoglobulins or antibodies are proteins produced by B cells that bind with specificity to foreign antigens in order to neutralize them or target their destruction by other effector cells (e.g., Hunkapiller & Hood, 1989). The set of sequences used in our experiments consists of immunoglobulins V region sequences from the Protein Identification Resources (PIR) data base. It corresponds to 294 sequences, with minimum length 90, average length 117 and maximum length 254. The variation in length resulted from including any sequence with a V region, including those that also included signal or leader sequences, germline sequences that did not include the J segment, and some that contained the C region as well. Seventy seqences contained one or more special characters indicating an ambiguous amino acid determination and were removed.

For the immunoglobulins variable V regions, we have trained a model of length 117 using a random subset of 150 sequences. Figure 2 displays the alignment corresponding to the first 20 sequences in this random subset. Letters emitted from the main states are upper case and letters emitted from insertion states are lower case. Dashes represent deletions or accomodate for insertions. As can be observed, the algorithm has been able to detect all the main regions of highly conserved residues. Most importantly, the cysteine residues towards the beginning and the end responsible for the disulphide bonds which holds the chains together are perfectly aligned and marked. The only exception is the fifth sequence from the bottom which has a serine residue in its terminal portion. It is also important to remark that some

[1] Recently, Hausssler et al. have also independently applied their approach to the kinase family (Haussler, private communication).

```
PH0106    mklpvrllvlmfwipasssDvVMTQTPLSLpvSLGDQASISCRSSQSLVHSngnTYLNWYLQ--KAGQS-
B27563    ----------------------LQQPGAELv-KPGASVKLSCKASGYTFTN---YWIHWVKQ--RPGRGL
MHMS76    ------------------------ESGGGLv-QPGGSMKLSCVASGFTFSN---YWMNWVRQ--SPEKGL
D28035    mefglswiflvailkgvqcEvRLVESGGDLv-EPGGSLRVSCEVSGFIFSK---AWMNWVRQ--APGKGL
D24672    ---------------------------------------ISCKASGYTFTN---YGMNWVKQ--APGKGL
PH0100    -------------------LvQLQQSGPVLv-KPGTSMKISCKTSGYSFTG---YTMSWVRQ--SHGKSL
B27888    -------------------EvMLVESGGGLa-KPGGSLKLSCTTSGFTFSI---HAMSWVRQ--TPEKRL
PL0160    -------------------QvQLQQSGPGLv-KPSQTLSLTCAISGDSVSSns-AAWNWIRQ--SPSRGL
E28833    -------------------DvVMTQTPLSLpvSLGDQASISCRSSQSLVRSngnTYLHWYLQ--KPGQP-
D30539    -------------------EvKLVESGGGLv-QSGGSLRLSCATSGFTFSD---FYMEWVRQ--PPGKSL
C30560    -------------------QvHLQQSGAELv-KPGASVKISCKASGYTFTS---YWMNWVKQ--RPGQGL
AVMSX4    -------------------EvKLLESGGGLv-QPGGSLKLSCAASGFDFSR---YWMSWVRQ--APGKGL
C30540    -------------------EvKLVESGGGLv-QPGGSLRLSCATSGFTFSD---FYMEWVRQ--PPGKRL
PL0123    -------------------EvQLVESGGGLv-QPGGSLRLSCAASGFTFSS---YWMSWVRQ--APGKGL
H36005    -------------------EvQLVESGGGLv-KPGGSLRLSCAASGFTFSN---AWMNWVRQ--APGKGL
PH0097    -------------------DvKLVESGGGLv-KPGGSLKLSCAASGFTFSS---YIMSWVRQ--TPEKRL
I37267    gsimg---------------vQLQQSGPELv-KPGASVKISCKTSGYTFTE---YTMHWVKQ--SHGKSL
A25114    -------------------DvHLQESGPGLv-KPSQSLSLTCSVTGYSITRg--YNWNWIRR--FPGNKL
D2HUWA    -------------------RlQLQESGPGLv-KPSETLSLTCIVSGGPIRRtg-YYWGWIRQ--PPGKGL
A30539    -------------------EvKLVESGGGLv-QPGGSLRLSCATSGFTFSD---FYMEWVRQ--PPGKRL
...................................................*............................

PH0106    -p-KLLI-YKV---SNR-FSGVPDRFSGSG--SGTDFTLKISRVEAEDLGIYFCSQ--------------
B27563    E-WIGRI-DPNSGGTKY-NEKFKNKATLTINKPSNTAYMQLSSLTSDDSAVYYCARGYDYSYY-------
MHMS76    E-WVAEIrLKSGYATHY-AESVKGRFTISRDDSKSSVYLQMNNLRAEDTGIYYCTRPGV-----------
D28035    Q-WVGQIkNKVDGGTIDYAAPVKGRFIISRDDSKSTVYLQMNRLKIEDTAVYYCVGNYTGT---------
D24672    K-WMGWI-NTYTGEPTY-ADDFKGRFAFSLETSASTAYLQINNLKNEDTATYFCARGSSYDYY-------
PH0100    E-WIGLI-IPSNGGTNY-NQKFKDKASLTVDKSSSTAYMELLSLTSEDSAVYYCARPSYYGSRnyy----
B27888    E-WVAAI-SSGGSYTFY-PDSVKGRFTISRDNAKNTLYLQINSLRSEDTAIYYCAREEGLRLDdy-----
PL0160    E-WLGRT-YYRSKWYNDYAVSVKSRITINPDTSKNQFSLQLNSVTPEDTAVYYCARELGDA---------
E28833    -p-KLLI-YKV---SNR-VSGVPDRFSGSG--SGTDFTLKISRVEAEDLGVYFCSQSTHV----------
D30539    E-WIAASrNEANDYTTEYSASVKGRFIVSRDTSQSILYLQMIALRAEDTAIYYCSRDYYGSSYw------
C30560    E-WIGEI-DPSNSYTNN-NQKFKNKATLTVDKSSNTAYMQLSSLTSEDSAVYYCARWGTGSSWg------
AVMSX4    E-WIGEI-NPDSSTINY-TPSLKDKFIISRDNAKNTLYLQMSKVRSEDTALYYCARLHYYGY--------
C30540    E-WIAASrNKAHDYTTEYSASVKGRFIVSRDTSQSILYLQMNALRAEDTAIYYCARDADYGSSshw----
PL0123    E-WVANI-KQDGSEKYY-VDSVKGRFTISRDNAKNSLYLQMNSLRAEDTAVYYCAR--------------
H36005    E-WVGRIkSKTDGGTTDYAAPVKGRFTISRDDSKNTLYLQMNSLKTEDTAVYYCTTDRGGSSQ-------
PH0097    E-WVATI-SSGGRYTYY-SDSVKGRFTISRDNAKNTLYLQMSSLRSEDTAMYYSTASGDS----------
I37267    E-WIGGI-NPNNGGTSY-NQKFKGKATLTVDKSSSTAYMELRSLTSEDSAVYYCARRGLTTVVaksy---
A25114    E-WMGYI-NYDGS-NNY-NPSLKNRISVTRDTSKNQFFLKMNSVTTEDTATYYCARLIPFSDGyyedyy-
D2HUWA    E-WIGGV-YYTGS-IYY-NPSLRGRVTISVDTSRNQFSLNLRSMSAADTAMYYCARGNPPPYYdigtgsd
A30539    E-WIAASrNKANDYTTEYSASVKGRFIVSRDTSQSILYLQMNALRAEDTAIYYCARDYYGSSYvw-----
...............................................................*................

PH0106    ----------------tthvpptfgggtkleikr-
B27563    -AMDYWGQGTSVTVSS-------------------
MHMS76    --PDYWGQGTTLTVSS-------------------
D28035    --VDYWGQGTLVTVSS-------------------
D24672    -AMDYWGQGTSVTVSS-------------------
PH0100    -AMDYWGQGTSVTVSSak-----------------
B27888    -AMDYWGQGTSVTVS--------------------
PL0160    --FDIWGQGTMVTVSS-------------------
E28833    -----------------------------------
D30539    -YFDVWGAGTTVTVSS-------------------
C30560    -WFAYWGQGTLVTVSA-------------------
AVMSX4    --AAYWGQGTLVTVSAe------------------
C30540    -YFDVWGAGTTVTVSS-------------------
PL0123    -----------------------------------
H36005    --GDYWGQGTLVTVSS-------------------
PH0097    --FDYWGQGTTLTVSSak-----------------
I37267    -YFDYWGQGTTLTVSS-------------------
A25114    -AMDYWGQGT-------------------------
D2HUWA    dGIDVWGQGTTVHVSS-------------------
A30539    -YFDVWGAGTTVTVSS-------------------
.............................................
```

Figure 2: Immunoglobulin alignment.

of the sequences in the family have some sort of "header" (leader signal peptide) whereas the others do not. We did not remove the headers prior to training and used the sequences as they were given to us. The model was able to detect and accomodate these "headers" by treating them as initial inserts as can be seen from the alignment of two of the sequences.

4.2 KINASES

Eukaryotic protein kinases constitute a very large family of proteins that regulate the most basic of cellular processes through phosphorylation. They have been termed the "transistors" of the cell (Hunter (1987)). We have used the sequences available in the kinase data base maintained at the Salk Institute. Our basic set consists of 224 sequences, with minimum length 156, average length 287, and maximal length 569. Only one sequence containing a special symbol (X) was discarded. In one experiment, we trained a model of length 287 using a random subset of 150 kinase sequences. Figure 3 displays the corresponding alignment for a subset of 12 phylogenetically representative sequences. These include serine/threonine, tyrosine and dual specificity kinases from mammals, birds, fungi and retroviruses and herpes viruses. The percentage of identical residues within the kinase data sets ranges from 8-30%, suggesting that only those residues involved in catalysis are conserved among these highly divergent sequences. All the 12 characteristic catalytic domains or subdomains described in Hanks and Quinn (1991) are easily recognizable and marked. Additional highly conserved positions can also be observed consistent with previously constructed multiple alignments. For instance, the initial hydrophobic consensus Gly-X-Gly-XX-Gly together with the Lys located 15 or 20 residues downstream are part of the ATP/GTP binding site. The carboxyl terminus is characterized by the presence of an invariant Arg residue. Conserved residues in proximity to the acceptor amino acid are found in the VIb (Asp), VII (Asp-Phe-Gly) and VIII domains (Ala-Pro-Glu). In Figure 4, the entropy of the emission distribution of each main state is plotted: motifs are easily detectable and correspond to positions with very low entropy.

5 DISCUSSION

HMMs are emerging as a powerful, adaptive, and modular tool for computational biology. Here, they have been used, together with a new learning algorithm, to model families of proteins. In all cases, the models derived capture all the important statistical properties of the families. Additional results and potential applications, such as phylogenetic tree reconstruction, classification, and superfamily modeling, are discussed in Baldi et al. (1992).

References

Baldi, P., Chauvin, Y., Hunkapiller, T. and McClure, M. A. (1992) Adaptive Algorithms for Modeling and Analysis of Biological Primary Sequence Information. Technical Report.

Cardon, L. R. and Stormo, G. D. (1992) Expectation Maximization Algorithm for Identifying Protein-binding Sites with Variable Lengths from Unaligned DNA

```
CD28    anYKR--LEKVGEGTYGVVYKALDLrpg--QGQRVVALK------KIRLESEDEGVPSTAIREISLLKEL-K-DDNIVRLYDIVH
MLCK    --FSMnsKEALGGGKFGAVCTCTEK-----STGLKLAAK---VI-KKQTPKDKE----MVMLEIEVMNQL-N-HRNLIQLYAAIE
PSKH    akYDI--KALIGRGSFSRVVRVEHR-----ATRQPYAIK---MIETKYREGRE-----VCESELRVLRRV-R-HANIIQLVEVFE
CAPK    dqFER--IKTLGTGSFGRVMLVKHM-----ETGNHYAMK---ILDKQKVVKLKQIE--HTLNEKRILQAV-N-FPFLVKLEFSFK
WEE1    trFRN--VTLLGSGEFSEVFQVEDPv----EKTLKYAVK---KL-KVKFSGPKERN--RLLQEVSIQRALkG-HDHIVELMDSWE
CSRC    esLRL--EVKLGQGCFGEVWMGTWN------GTTRVAIK---TLKPGNMSPE------AFLQEAQVMKKL-R-HEKLVQLYAVVS
EGFR    teFKK--IKVLGSGAFGTVYKGLWIpege-KVKIPVAIK---ELREATSPKANK----EILDEAYVMASV-D-NPHVCRLLGICL
PDGF    dqLVL--GRTLGSGAFGQVVEATAHglshsQATMKVAVK---MLKSTARSSEKQ----ALMSELY--GDL--v-DYLHRNKHTFL
VFES    edLVL--GEQIGRGNFGEVFSGRLR-----ADNTLVAVK---SCRETLPPDIKA----KFLQEAKILKQY-S-HPNIVRLIGVCT
RAF1    seVML--STRIGSGSFGTVYKGKWH--------GDVAVK---ILKVVDPTPEQFQ---AFRNEVAVLRKT-R-HVNILLFMGYMT
CMOS    eqVCL--LQRLGAGGFGSVYKATYR-------GVPVAIKQvNKCTKNRLASRR-----SFWAELNV-ARL-R-HDNIVRVVAAST
HSVK    mgFTI--HGALTPGSEGCVFDSSHP-----DYPQRVIVK------AGWYT--------STSHEARLLRRL-D-HPAILPLLDLHV
.....................*..*.*...................*.......................*......................
.......................I.....................II......................III..............IV.....

CD28    SDAHk---------LY-L-V-FEFLDL-DLKRYMEGIpkd---------------------------------------------
MLCK    TPHE----------IV-L-F-MEYIEGGELFERIVDE------------------------------------------------
PSKH    TQER----------VY-M-V-MELATGGELFDRIIAK------------------------------------------------
CAPK    DNSN----------LY-M-V-MEYVPGGEMFSHLRRI------------------------------------------------
WEE1    HGGF----------LY-M-Q-VELCENGSLDRFLEEQgql---------------------------------------------
CSRC    -EEP----------IY-I-V-TEYMSKGSLLDFLKGE------------------------------------------------
EGFR    -TST----------VQ-L-I-TQLMPFGCLLDYVREH------------------------------------------------
PDGF    -QRHsnkhcppsaeLYs-n-a--LPVGFSLPSHLNLTgesdggymdmskdesidyvpmldmkgdikyadiespsymapydnyvps
VFES    QKQP----------IY-I-V-MELVQGGDFLTFLRTE------------------------------------------------
RAF1    -KDN----------LA-I-V-TQWCEGSSLYKHLHVQ------------------------------------------------
CMOS    RTPAgsnsl-----GT-I-I-MEFGGNVTLHQVIYGAaghpegdagephcrtg--------------------------------
HSVK    VSGV----------TC-L-V-LPKYQA-DLYTYLSRR------------------------------------------------
.............................................................................................
.................................V...........................................................

CD28    ---------------QP-LGADIVKKFMMQ-LCKGIAYCHSHRILHRDLKPQNLL-INKDG---N-LKLGDFGLARAFGVPLRAY
MLCK    --------------DYH-LTEVDTMVFVRQ-ICDGILFMHKMRVLHLDLKPENILcVNTTG---HlVKIIDFGLARRYNPNEKL-
PSKH    ---------------GS-FTERDATRVLQM-VLDGVRYLHALGITHRDLKPENLL-YYHPGtdsK-IIITDFGLASARKKGDDCL
CAPK    ---------------GR-FSEPHARFYAAQ-IVLTFEYLHSLDLIYRDLKPENLL-IDQQG---Y-IQVTDFGFAKRVKGRT---
WEE1    ---------------SR-LDEFRVWKILVE-VALGLQFIHHKNYVHLDLKPANVM-ITFEG---T-LKIGDFGMASVWPVPRG--
CSRC    --------------MGKyLRLPQLVDMAAQ-IASGMAYVERMNYVHRDLRAANIL-VGENL---V-CKVADFGLARLIEDNEYTA
EGFR    --------------KDN-IGSQYLLNWCVQ-IAKGMNYLEDRRLVHRDLAARNVL-VKTPQ---H-VKITDFGLAKLLGAEEKEY
PDGF    apertyratlinds-PV-LSYTDLVGFSYQ-VANGMDFLASKNCVHRDLAARNVL-ICEGK---L-VKICDFGLARDIMRDSNYI
VFES    --------------GAR-LRMKTLLQMVGD-AAAGMEYLESKCCIHRDLAARNCL-VTEKN---V-LKISDFGMSREAADGIYAA
RAF1    --------------ETK-FQMFQLIDIARQ-TAQGMDYLHAKNIIHRDMKSNNIF-LHEGL---T-VKIGDFGLATVKSRWSGSQ
CMOS    ---------------GQ-LSLGKCLKYSLD-VVNGLLFLHSQSIVHLDLKPANIL-ISEQD---V-CKISDFGCSEKLEDLLCFQ
HSVK    --------------LNP-LGRPQIAAVSRQ-LLSAVDYIHRQGIIHRDIKTENIF-INTPE---D-ICLGDFGAACFVQGSRSSP
.......................................................*....*.................*.*............
...............................VIa.......................VIb.................VII.............

CD28    ---THEIVTLWYRAPEVLLgGK---QYSTGVDTWSIGCIFAEMCNRKP---------------IFSGDSE-----IDQIFKIFRV
MLCK    ---KVNFGTPEFLSPEVVN-YD---QISDKTDMWSLGVITYMLLSGLS---------------PFLGDDD-----TETLNNVLSG
PSKH    M--KTTCGTPEYIAPEVLV-RK---PYTNSVDMWALGVIAYILLSGTM---------------PFEDDNR-----TRLYRQILRG
CAPK    ---WTLCGTPEYLAPEIIL-SK---GYNKAVDWWALGVLIYEMAAGYP---------------PFFADQP-----IQIYEKIVSG
WEE1    ---MEREGDCEYIAPEVLA-NH---LYDKPADIFSLGITVFEAAANIV--------------LPDNGQSW-----Q----KLRSG
CSRC    R--QGAKFPIKWTAPEAAL-YG---RFTIKSDVWSFGILLTELTTKGR--------------VPYPGMVN-----REVLDQVERG
EGFR    H-AEGGKVPIKWMALESIL-HR---IYTHQSDVWSYGVTVWELMTFGS--------------KPYDGIPA-----SEISSILEKG
PDGF    S-KGSTYLPLKWMAPESIF-NS---LYTTLSDVWSFGILLWEIFTLGG--------------TPYPELPM----NDQFYNAIKRG
VFES    S-GGLRQVPVKWTAPEALN-YG---RYSSESDVWSFGILLWETFSLGA--------------SPYPNLSN-----QQTREFVEKG
RAF1    Q-VEQPTGSVLWMAPEVIR-MQdnnPFSFQSDVYSYGIVLYELMTGEL---------------PYS---R-----DQIIFMVGRG
CMOS    TpSYPLGGTYTHRAPELLK-GE---GVTPKADIYSFAITLWQMTTKQA---------------PYSGERQ-----HILYAVVAYD
HSVK    F-PYGIAGTIDTNAPEVLA-GD---PYTTTVDIWSAGLVIFETAVHNA-------------------------------------
......................**...............*....*................................................
.....................VIII................IX........................................X.........

CD28    ---LGTPNEAIwpdivylpdfkpsfpqwrrkdlsqvvpsLDPRGIDLLDKLLAYDPINRISARRAAIHPYFQES--------
MLCK    nwyFDEETFEA----------------------------VSDEAKDFVSNLIVKEQGARMSAAQCLAHPWLNNL--------
PSKH    kysYSGEPWPS----------------------------VSNLAKDFIDRLLTVDPGARMTALQALRHPWVVSM--------
CAPK    ---KVR-FPSH----------------------------FSSDLKDLLRNLLQVDLTKRFGNLKDGVNDIKNHK--------
WEE1    ---DLSDAPRLsstdngssltsssretpansii------GQGGLDRVVEWMLSPEPRNRPTIDQILATD--EVCWV------
CSRC    ---YRMPCPPE----------------------------CPESLHDLMCQCWRRDPEERPTFEYLQAFLEDYFT--------
EGFR    ---ERLPQPPI----------------------------CTIDVYMIMVKCWMIDADSRPKFRELIIEFSKMAR--------
PDGF    ---YRMAQPAH----------------------------ASDEIYEIMQKCWEEKFETRPPFSQLVLLLERLLGEGykkky-
VFES    ---GRLPCPEL----------------------------CPDAVFRLMEQCWAYEPGQRPSFSAIYQEL-------------
RAF1    ---YASPDLSKlykn------------------------CPKAMKRLVADCVKKVKEERPLFPQILSSIELLQH--------
CMOS    ---LRPSLSAAvfedsl----------------------PGQRLGDVIQRCWRPSAAQRPSARLLLVDLTSLKA--------
HSVK    ----------------------------------------------------------------------------------
..................................................................*.......................
.................................................................XI.......................
```

Figure 3: Kinase alignment of 12 representative sequences.

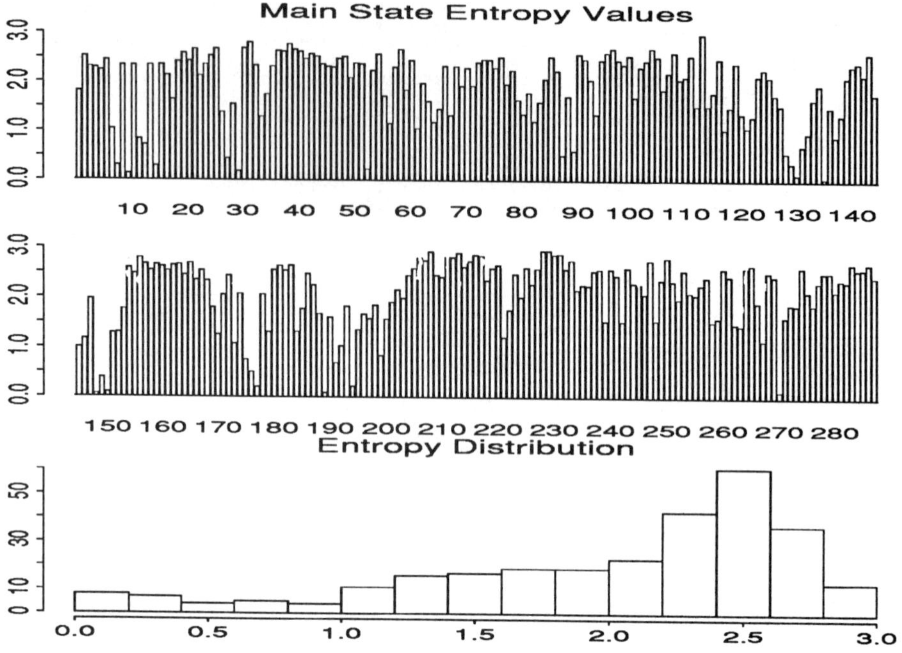

Figure 4: Kinase emission entropy plot and distribution.

Fragments. Journal of Molecular Biology, **223**, 159-170.

Churchill, G. A. (1989) Stochastic Models for Heterogeneous DNA Sequences. Bulletin of Mathematical Biology, **51**, 1, 79-94.

Hanks, S. K., Quinn, A. M. (1991) Protein Kinase Catalytic Domain Sequences Database: Identification of Conserved Features of Primary Structure and Classification of Family Members. Methods in Enzymology, **200**, 38-62.

Haussler, D., Krogh, A., Mian, S. and Sjolander, K. (1992) Protein Modeling using Hidden Markov Models. Computer and Information Sciences Technical Report (UCSC-CRL-92-93), University of California, Santa Cruz.

Hunkapiller, T. and Hood, L. (1989) Diversity of the Immunoglobulin Gene Superfamily. Advances in Immunology, **44**, 1-63, Academic Press, Inc.

Hunter, T. (1987) A Thousand and One Protein Kinases. Cell, **50**, 823-829.

Lawrence, C. E. and Reilly, A. A. (1990) An Expectation Maximization (EM) Algorithm for the Identification and Characterization of Common Sites in Unaligned Biopolymer Sequences. Proteins: Struct. Funct. Genet., **7**, 41-51.

Rabiner, L. R. (1989) A Tutorial on Hidden Markor Models and Selected Applications in Speech Recognition. Proceedings of the IEEE, **77**, 2, 257-286.

A Neural Network that Learns to Interpret Myocardial Planar Thallium Scintigrams

Charles Rosenberg, Ph.D.[*]
Department of Computer Science
Hebrew University
Jerusalem, Israel

Jacob Erel, M.D.
Department of Cardiology
Sapir Medical Center
Meir General Hospital
Kfar Saba, Israel

Henri Atlan, M.D., PhD.
Department of Biophysics and Nuclear Medicine
Hadassah Medical Center
Jerusalem, Israel

Abstract

The planar thallium-201 myocardial perfusion scintigram is a widely used diagnostic technique for detecting and estimating the risk of coronary artery disease. Neural networks learned to interpret 100 thallium scintigrams as determined by individual expert ratings. Standard error back-propagation was compared to standard LMS, and LMS combined with one layer of RBF units. Using the "leave-one-out" method, generalization was tested on all 100 cases. Training time was determined automatically from cross-validation performance. Best performance was attained by the RBF/LMS network with three hidden units per view and compares favorably with human experts.

1 Introduction

Coronary artery disease (CAD) is one of the leading causes of death in the Western World. The planar thallium-201 is considered to be a reliable diagnostic tool in the detection of

[*]Current address: Geriatrics, Research, Educational and Clinical Center, VA Medical Center, Salt Lake City, Utah.

CAD. Thallium is a radioactive isotope that distributes in mammalian tissues after intervenous administration and is imaged by a gamma camera. The resulting scintigram is visually interpreted by the physician for the presence or absence of defects — areas with relatively lower perfusion levels. In myocardial applications, thallium is used to measure myocardial ischemia and to differentiate between viable and non-viable (infarcted) heart muscle (Pohost and Henzlova, 1990).

Diagnosis of CAD is based on the comparison of two sets of images, one set acquired immediately after a standard effort test (BRUCE protocol), and the second following a delay period of four hours. During this delay, the thallium redistributes in the heart muscle and spontaneously decays. Defects caused by scar tissue are relatively unchanged over the delay period (fixed defect), while those caused by ischemia are partially or completely filled-in (reversible defect) (Beller, 1991; Datz et al., 1992).

Image interpretation is difficult for a number of reasons: the inherent variability in biological systems which makes each case essentially unique, the vast amount of irrelevant and noisy information in an image, and the "context-dependency" of the interpretation on data from many other tests and clinical history. Interpretation can also be significantly affected by attentional shifts, perceptual abilities, and mental state (Franken Jr. and Berbaum, 1991; Cuarón et al., 1980).

While networks have found considerable application in ECG processing (e.g. (Artis et al., 1991)) and clinical decision-making (Baxt, 1991b; Baxt, 1991a), they have thus far found limited application in the field of nuclear medicine. Non-cardiac imaging applications include the grading of breast carcinomas (Dawson et al., 1991) and the discrimination of normal vs. Alzheimer's PET scans (Kippenhan et al., 1990). Of the studies dealing specifically with cardiac imaging, neural networks have been applied to several problems in cardiology including the identification of stenosis (Porenta et al., 1990; Cios et al., 1989; Cios et al., 1991; Cianflone et al., 1990; Fujita et al., 1992). These studies encouraged us to explore the use of neural networks in the interpretation of cardiac scintigraphy.

2 Methods

We trained one network consisting of a layer of gaussian RBF units in an unsupervised fashion to discover features in circumferential profiles in planar thallium scintigraphy. Then a second network was trained in a supervised way to map these features to physician's visual interpretations of those images using the delta rule (Widrow and Hoff, 1960). This architecture was previously found to compare favorably to other network learning algorithms (2-layer backpropagation and single-layer networks) on this task (Rosenberg et al., 1993; Erel et al., 1993).

In our experiments, all of the input vectors representing single views $\vec{I}$ were first normalized to unit length $\vec{V} = \frac{\vec{I}}{\|\vec{I}\|}$. The activation value of a gaussian unit, O_j, is then given by:

$$net_j = \sum_i (w_{ij} - v_i)^2 \quad (1)$$

$$O_j = exp(-\frac{net_j}{\omega}) \quad (2)$$

where j is an index to a gaussian unit and i is an input unit index. The width of the gaussian,

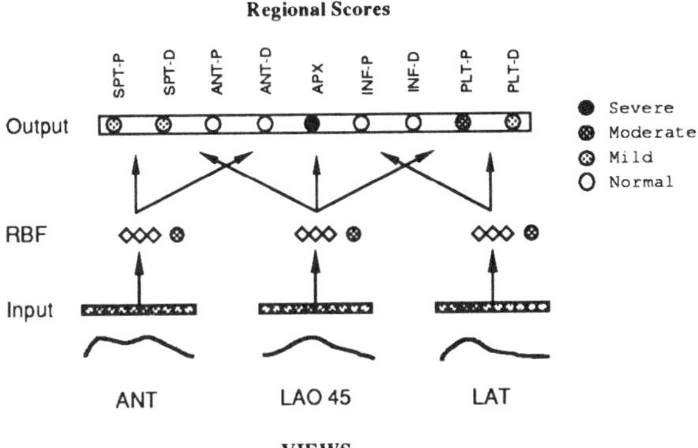

Figure 1: The network architecture. The first layer (Input) encoded the three circumferential profiles representing the three views, anterior (ANT), left lateral oblique (LAO), and left lateral (LAT). The second layer consisted of radial basis function (RBF) units, the third layer, semi-linear units trained in a supervised fashion. The outputs of the network corresponded to the visual scores as given by the expert observer. An additional unit per view encoded the scaling factor of the input patterns lost as a result of input normalization.

given by ω, was fixed at 0.25 for all units[1].

The gaussian units were trained using a competitive learning rule which moves the center of the unit closest to the current input pattern (O_{max}, i.e. the "winner") closer to the input pattern[2]:

$$\Delta w_{i,winner} = \eta(v_i - w_{i,winner}) \quad (3)$$

2.1 Data Acquisition and Selection

Scintigraphic images were acquired for each of three views: anterior (ANT), left lateral oblique (LAO 45), and left lateral (LAT) for each patient case. Acquisition was performed twice, once immediately following a standard effort test and once following a delay period of four hours. Each image was pre-processed to produce a circumferential profile (Garcia et al., 1981; Francisco et al., 1982)[3], in which maximum pixel counts within each of 60, 6° contiguous segmental regions are plotted as a function of angle (Garcia, 1991). Preprocessing involved positioning of the region of interest (ROI), interpolative background subtraction, smoothing and rotational alignment to the heart's apex (Garcia, 1991).

[1]We have considered applying the learning rule to the unit widths (ω) as well as the RBF weights, however we have not as yet pursued this possibility.

[2]Following Rumelhart and Zipser (Rumelhart and Zipser, 1986), the other units were also pulled towards the input vector, although to a much smaller extent than the winner. We used a ratio of 1 to 100.

[3]The profiles were generated using the Elscint CTL software package for planar quantitative thallium-201 based on the Cedars-Sinai technique (Garcia et al., 1981; Maddahi et al., 1981; Areeda et al., 1982).

Lesion	mild	moderate	severe	Total
single	12	5	0	17
multiple	16	16	11	43
Total	28	21	11	60

Table 1: Distribution of Abnormal Cases as Scored by the Expert Observer. Defects occurring in any combination of two or more regions (even the proximal and distal subregions of a single area) were treated as one multiple defect. The severity level of multiple lesions was based on the most severe lesion present.

Cases were pre-selected based on the following criteria (Beller, 1991):

- **Insufficient exercise.** Cases in which the heart rate was less than 130 b.p.m. were eliminated, as this level of stress is generally deemed insufficient to accurately distinguish normal from abnormal conditions.
- **Positional abnormalities.** In a few cases, the "region of interest" was not positioned or aligned correctly by the technician.
- **Increased lung uptake.** Typically in cases of multi-vessel disease, a significant proportion of the perfusion occurs in the lungs as well as in the heart, making it more difficult to determine the condition of the heart due to the partially overlapping positions of the heart and lungs.
- **Breast artifacts.**

Cases were selected at random between August, 1989 and March, 1992. Approximately a third of the cases were eliminated due to insufficient heart rate, 4-5% due to breast artifacts, 4% due to lung uptake, and 1-2% due to positional abnormalities. A set of one hundred usable cases remained.

2.2 Visual Interpretation

Each case was visually scored by a single expert observer for each of nine anatomical regions generally accepted as those that best relate to the coronary circulation: *Septal: proximal* and *distal*, *Anterior: proximal* and *distal*, *Apex*, *Inferior: proximal* and *distal*, and *Posterior-Lateral: proximal* and *distal*. Scoring for each region was from *normal* (1) to *severe* (4), indicating the level of the observed perfusion deficit.

Intra-observer variability was examined by having the observer re-interpret 17 of the cases a second time. The observer was unable to remember the cases from the first reading and could not refer to the previous scores.

Exact matches were obtained on 91.5% of the regions; only 8 of the 153 total regions (5%) were labeled as a defect (mild, moderate or severe) on one occasion and not on the other. All differences, when they occurred, were of a single rating level[4].

[4]In contrast, measured *inter*-observer variability was much higher. A set of 13 cases was individ-

2.3 The Network Model

The input units of the network were divided into 3 groups of 60 units each, each group representing the circumferential profile for a single view. A set of 3 RBF units were assigned to each input group. Then a second layer of weights was trained using the delta rule to reproduce the target visual scores assigned by the expert observer. The categorical visual scores were translated to numerical values to make the data suitable for network learning: *normal* = 0.0, *mild defect* = 0.3, *moderate defect* = 0.7, and *severe defect* = 1.0.

In order to make efficient use of the available data, we actually trained 100 identical networks; each network was trained on a subset of 99 of the 100 cases and tested on the remaining one. This procedure, sometimes referred to as the "leave-one-out" or "jack-knife" method, enabled us to determine the generalization performance for each case. This procedure was followed for both the RBF and the delta rule training[5]. Training of a single network took only a few minutes of Sun 4 computer time.

3 Results

Because of the larger numbers of confusions between normal and mild regions in both the inter- and intra-observer scores, disease was defined as moderate or severe defects. The threshold value dividing the output values of the network into these two sets was varied from 0 to 1 in 0.01 step increments. The number of agreements between the expert observer and the network were computed for each threshold value. The resulting scores, accumulated over all threshold values, were plotted as a Receiver Operating Characteristic (ROC) curve.

Best performance (percent correct) was achieved with a threshold value of 0.28, which yielded an overall accuracy of 88.7% (798/900 regions) on the stress data. However, this value of the threshold heavily favored specificity over sensitivity due to the preponderance of normal regions in the data. Using the decision threshold which maximized the sum of sensitivity and specificity, 0.10, accuracy dropped to 84.9% (764/900) but sensitivity improved to 0.771 (121/157), and specificity was 0.865 (643/743).

3.1 Distinguishing Fixed vs. Reversible Defects

In order to take into account the delayed distribution as well as the stress set of images, the network was essentially duplicated: one network processed the stress data, and the other,

ually interpreted by 3 expert observers in a previous experiment (Rosenberg et al., 1993). Percent agreement (exact matches) between the observers was 82% (288/351). Of the 63 mis-matches, 5 or about 8% of the regions were of 2 levels of severity. There were no differences of 3 levels of severity. Approximately two-thirds of the disagreements were between normal and mild regions. These results indicate that the single observer data employed in the present study are more reliable than the mixed consensus and individual scores used previously.

[5]Details of network learning were as follows: Each of the 100 networks was initialized and trained in the same way. RBF-to-output unit weights were initialized to small random values between 0.5 and -0.5. Input-to-RBF unit weights were first randomized and then normalized so that the weight vectors to each RBF unit were of unit length. Unsupervised, competitive training of the RBF units continued for 100 "epochs" or complete sweeps through the set of 99 cases: 20 epochs with a learning rate (η) of 0.1 followed by 80 epochs at 0.01 without momentum (α). Supervised training using a learning rate of 0.05 and momentum 0.9, was terminated based on cross-validation testing after 200 epochs. Further training led to over-training and poorer generalization.

the redistribution data. (For details, see (Erel et al., 1993).)

The combined network exhibited only a limited ability to distinguish between scar and ischemia. Performance on scar detection was good (sens. 0.728 (75/103), spec. 0.878 (700/797)), but the sensitivity of the network on ischemia detection was only 0.185 (10/54). This result may be explained, at least in part, by the much smaller number of ischemic regions included in the data set as compared with scars (54 versus 103).

4 Conclusions and Future Directions

We suspect that our major limitation is in defect sampling. In order that a statistical system (networks or otherwise) generalize well to new cases, the data used in training must be representative of the full population of data likely to be sampled. This is unlikely to happen when the number of positive cases is on the order of 50, as was the case with ischemia, since each possible defect location, *plus* all the possible combinations of locations must be included.

A variant of backpropagation, called competitive backpropagation, has recently been developed which is claimed to generalize appropriately in the presence of multiple defects (Cho and Reggia, 1993). Weights in this network are constrained to take on positive values, so that diagnoses made by the system add constructively. In a standard backpropagation network, multiple diseases can cancel each other out, due to complex interactions of both positive and negative connection strengths. We are currently planning to investigate the application of this learning algorithm to the problem of ischemia detection.

Other improvements and extensions include:

- **Elicit confidence ratings.** Expert visual interpretations could be augmented by degree of confidence ratings. Highly ambiguous cases could be reduced in importance or eliminated. The ratings could also be used as additional targets for the network[6]: cases indicated by the network with low levels of confidence would require closer inspection by a physician. Initial results are promising in this regard.
- **Provide additional information.** We have not yet incorporated clinical history, gender, and examination EKG. Clinical history has been found to have a profound impact on interpretation of radiographs (Doubilet and Herman, 1981). The inclusion of these variables should allow the network to approximate more closely a complete diagnosis, and boost the utility of the network in the clinical setting.
- **Add constraints.** Currently we do not utilize the angles that relate the three views. It may be possible to build these angles in as constraints and thereby cut down on the number of free network parameters.
- **Expand application.** Besides planar thallium, our approach may also be applied to non-planar 3-D imaging technologies such as SPECT and other nuclear agents or stress-inducing modalities such as dipyridamole. Preliminary results are promising in this regard.

[6] See (Tesauro and Sejnowski, 1988) for a related idea.

Acknowledgements

The authors wish to thank Mr. Haim Karger for technical assistance, and the Departments of Computer Science and Psychology at the Hebrew University for computational support. We would also like to thank Drs. David Shechter, Moshe Bocher, Roland Chisin and the staff of the Department of Medical Biophysics and Nuclear Medicine for their help, both large and small, and two anonymous reviewers. Terry Sejnowski suggested our use of RBF units.

References

Areeda, J., Train, K. V., Garcia, E. V., Maddahi, J., Rosanki, A., Waxman, A., and Berman, D. (1982). Improved analysis of segmental thallium-201 myocardial scintigrams: Quantitation of distribution, washout, and redistribution. In Esser, P. D., editor, *Digital Imaging*. Society of Nuclear Medicine, New York.

Artis, S., Mark, R., and Moody, G. (1991). Detection of atrial fibrillation using artificial neural networks. In *Computers in Cardiology*, pages 173–176, Venice, Italy. IEEE, IEEE Computer Society Press.

Baxt, W. (1991a). Use of an artificial neural network for data analysis in clinical decision-making: The diagnosis of acute coronary occlusion. *Neural Computation*, 2:480–489.

Baxt, W. (1991b). Use of an artificial neural network for the diagnosis of myocardial infarction. *Annals of Internal Medicine*, 115:843–848.

Beller, G. A. (1991). Myocardial perfusion imaging with thallium-201. In Marcus, M. L., Schelbert, H. R., Skorton, D. J., and Wolf, G. L., editors, *Cardiac Imaging*. W. B. Sanders.

Cho, S. and Reggia, J. (1993). Multiple disorder diagnosis with adaptive competitive neural networks. *Artificial Intelligence in Medicine*. To appear.

Cianflone, D., Carandente, O., Fragasso, G., Margononato, A., Meloni, C., Rossetti, E., Gerundini, P., and Chiechia, S. L. (1990). A neural network based model of predicting the probability of coronary lesion from myocardial perfusion SPECT data. In *Proceedings of the 37th Annual Meeting of the Society of Nuclear Medicine*, page 797.

Cios, K. J., Goodenday, L. S., Merhi, M., and Langenderfer, R. (1989). Neural networks in detection of coronary artery disease. In *Computers in Cardiology Conference*, pages 33–37, Jerusalem, Israel. IEEE, IEEE Computer Society Press.

Cios, K. J., Shin, I., and Goodenday, L. S. (1991). Using fuzzy sets to diagnose coronary artery stenosis. *Computer*, pages 57–63.

Cuarón, A., Acero, A., Cárdena, M., Huerta, D., Rodríguez, A., and de Garay, R. (1980). Interobserver variability in the interpretation of myocardial images with Tc-99m-labeled diphosponate and pyrophosphate. *Journal of Nuclear Medicine*, 21(1):1–9.

Datz; F., Gabor, F., Christian, P., Gullber, G., Menzel, C., and Morton, K. (1992). The use of computer-assisted diagnosis in cardiac-perfusion nuclear medicine studies: A review. *Journal of Digital Imaging*, 5(4):1–14.

Dawson, A., Austin, R., and Weinberg, D. (1991). Nuclear grading of breast carcinoma by image analysis. *American Journal of Clinical Pathology*, 95(4):S29–S37.

Doubilet, P. and Herman, P. (1981). Interpretation of radiographs: Effect of clinical history. *American Journal of Roentgenology*, 137:1055–1058.

Erel, J., Rosenberg, C., and Atlan, H. (1993). Neural network for automatic interpretation of thallium scintigrams. In preparation.

Francisco, D. A., Collins, S. M., and et al., R. T. G. (1982). Tomographic thallium-201 myocardial perfusion scintigrams after maximal coronary artery vasodiliation with intravenous dipyridamole: Comparison of qualitative and quantitative approaches. *Circulation*, 66(2).

Franken Jr., E. A. and Berbaum, K. S. (1991). Perceptual aspects of cardiac imaging. In Marcus, M. L., Schelbert, H. R., Skorton, D. J., and Wolf, G. L., editors, *Cardiac Imaging*. W. B. Sanders.

Fujita, H., Katafuchi, T., Uehara, T., and Nishimura, T. (1992). Application of artificial neural network to computer-aided diagnosis of coronary artery disease in myocardial SPECT bull's-eye images. *The Journal of Nuclear Medicine*, 33(2):272–276.

Garcia, E. V. (1991). Physics and instrumentation of radionuclide imaging. In Marcus, M. L., Schelbert, H. R., Skorton, D. J., and Wolf, G. L., editors, *Cardiac Imaging*. W. B. Sanders.

Garcia, E. V., Maddahi, J., Berman, D. S., and Waxman, A. (1981). Space-time quantitation of thallium-201 myocardial scintigraphy. *Journal of Nuclear Medicine*, 22:309–317.

Kippenhan, J., Barker, W., Pascal, S., and Duara, R. (1990). A neural-network classifier applied to PET scans of normal and Alzheimer's disease (AD) patients. In *The Proceedings of the 37th Annual Meeting of the Society of Nuclear Medicine*, volume 31, Washington, D.C.

Maddahi, J., Garcia, E. V., Berman, D. S., Waxman, A., Swan, H. J. C., and Forrester, J. (1981). Improved noninvasive assessment of coronary artery disease by quantitative analysis of regional stress myocardial distribution and washout of thallium-201. *Circulation*, 64:924–935.

Pohost, G. M. and Henzlova, M. J. (1990). The value of thallium-201 imaging. *New England Journal of Medicine*, 323(3):190–192.

Porenta, G., Kundrat, S., Dorffner, G., Petta, P., Duit, J., and r, H. S. (1990). Computer based image interpretations of thallium- 201 scintigrams: Assessment of coronary artery disease using the parallel distributed processing approach. In *Proceedings of the 37th Annual Meeting of the Society of Nuclear Medicine*, page 825.

Rosenberg, C., Erel, J., and Atlan, H. (1993). A neural network that learns to interpret myocardial planar thallium scintigrams. *Neural Computation*. To appear.

Rumelhart, D. and Zipser, D. (1986). Feature discovery by competitive learning. In Rumelhart, D. and McClelland, J., editors, *Parallel Distributed Processing*, volume 1, chapter 5, pages 151–193. MIT Press, Cambridge, Mass.

Tesauro, G. and Sejnowski, T. J. (1988). A parallel network that learns to play backgammon. Technical Report CCSR-88-2, University of Illinois at Urbana-Champaign Center for Complex Systems Research.

Widrow, B. and Hoff, M. (1960). Adaptive switching circuits. In *1960 IRE WESCON Convention Record*, volume 4, pages 96–104. IRE, New York.

PART X

IMPLEMENTATIONS

An Analog VLSI Chip for Radial Basis Functions

Janeen Anderson **John C. Platt** **David B. Kirk***
Synaptics, Inc.
2698 Orchard Parkway
San Jose, CA 95134

Abstract

We have designed, fabricated, and tested an analog VLSI chip which computes radial basis functions in parallel. We have developed a synapse circuit that approximates a quadratic function. We aggregate these circuits to form radial basis functions. These radial basis functions are then averaged together using a follower aggregator.

1 INTRODUCTION

Radial basis functions (RBFs) are a method for approximating a function from scattered training points [Powell, 1987]. RBFs have been used to solve recognition and prediction problems with a fair amount of success [Lee, 1991] [Moody, 1989] [Platt, 1991]. The first layer of an RBF network computes the distance of the input to the network to a set of stored memories. Each basis function is a non-linear function of a corresponding distance. The basis functions are then added together with second-layer weights to produce the output of the network. The general form of an RBF is

$$y_i = \sum_j h_{ij} \phi_j \left(||\vec{I} - \vec{c}_j|| \right), \tag{1}$$

where y_i is the output of the network, h_{ij} is the second-layer weight, ϕ_j is the non-linearity, $\vec{c}_j$ is the jth memory stored in the network and $\vec{I}$ is the input to

*Current address: Caltech Computer Graphics Group, Caltech 350-74, Pasadena, CA 92115

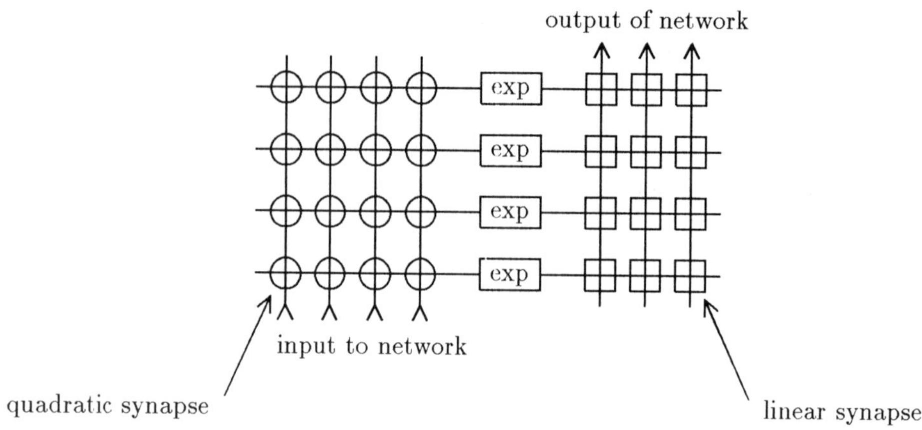

Figure 1: The architecture of a Gaussian RBF network.

the network. Many researchers use Gaussians to create basis functions that have a localized effect in input space [Poggio, 1990][Moody, 1989]:

$$y_i = \sum_j h_{ij} \exp\left(-\frac{1}{2\sigma^2}\sum_k (I_k - c_{jk})^2\right). \tag{2}$$

The architecture of a Gaussian RBF network is shown in figure 1.

RBFs can be implemented either via software or hardware. If high speed is not necessary, then computing all of the basis functions in software is adequate. However, if an application requires many inputs or high speed, then hardware is required.

RBFs use a lot of operations more complex than simply multiplication and addition. For example, a Gaussian RBF requires an exponential for every basis function. Using a partition of unity requires a divide for every basis function. Analog VLSI is an attractive way of computing these complex operations very quickly: we can compute all of the basis functions in parallel, using a few transistors per synapse.

This paper discusses an analog VLSI chip that computes radial basis functions. We discuss how we map the mathematical model of an RBF into compact analog hardware. We then present results from a test chip that was fabricated. We discuss possible applications for the hardware architecture and future theoretical work.

2 MAPPING RADIAL BASIS FUNCTIONS INTO HARDWARE

In order to create an analog VLSI chip, we must map the idea of radial basis functions into transistors. In order to create a high-density chip, the mathematics of RBFs must be modified to be computed more naturally by transistor physics. This section discusses the mapping from Gaussian RBFs into CMOS circuitry.

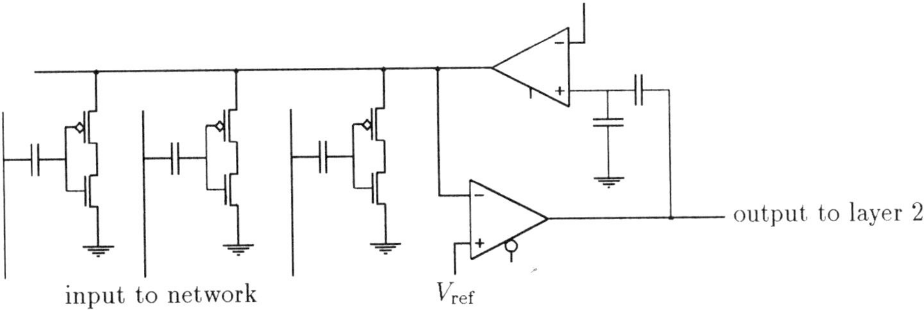

Figure 2: Circuit diagram for first-layer neuron, showing three Gaussian synapses and the sense amplifier.

2.1 Computing Quadratic Distance

Ideally, the first-layer synapses in figure 1 would compute a quadratic distance of the input to a stored value. Quadratics go to infinity for large values of their input, hence are hard to build in analog hardware and are not robust against outliers in the input data. Therefore, it is much more desirable to use a saturating non-linearity: we will use a Gaussian for a first-layer synapse, which approximates a quadratic near its peak.

We implement the first-layer Gaussian synapse using an inverter (see figure 2). The current running through each inverter from the voltage rail to ground is a Gaussian function of the inverter's input, with the peak of the Gaussian occurring halfway between the voltage rail and ground [Mead, 1980][Mead, 1992].

To adjust the center of the Gaussian, we place a capacitor between the input to the synapse and the input of the inverter. The inverter thus has a floating gate input. We adjust the charge on the floating gate by using a combination of tunneling and non-avalanche hot electron injection [Anderson, 1990] [Anderson, 1992].

All of the Gaussian synapses for one neuron share a voltage rail. The sense amplifier holds that voltage rail at a particular voltage, V_{ref}. The output of the sense amplifier is a voltage which is linear in the total current being drawn by the Gaussian synapses. We use a floating gate in the sense amplifier to ensure that the output of the sense amplifier is known when the input to the network is at a known state. Again, we adjust the floating gate via tunneling and injection.

Figure 3 shows the output of the sense amplifier for four different neurons. The data was taken from a real chip, described in section 3. The figure shows that the top of a Gaussian approximates a quadratic reasonably well. Also, the width and heights of the outputs of each first-layer neuron match very well, because the circuit is operated above threshold.

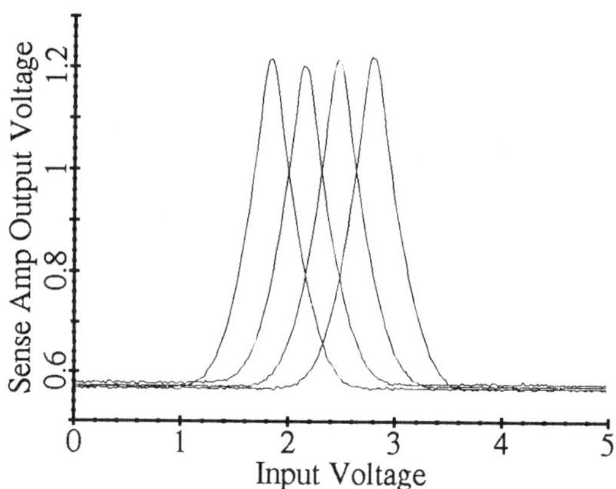

Figure 3: Measured output of set of four first-layer neurons. All of the synapses of each neuron are programmed to peak at the same voltage. The x-axis is the input voltage, and the y-axis is the voltage output of the sense amplifier

2.2 Computing the Basis Function

To compute a Gaussian basis function, the distance produced by the first layer needs to be exponentiated. Since the output of the sense amplifier is a voltage negatively proportional to the distance, a subthreshold transistor can perform this exponentiation.

However, subthreshold circuits can be slow. Also, the choice of a Gaussian basis function is somewhat arbitrary [Poggio, 1990]. Therefore, we choose to adjust the sense amplifier to produce a voltage that is both above and below threshold. The basis function that the chip computes can be expressed as

$$S_j = \sum_k \text{Gaussian}(I_k - c_{jk}); \tag{3}$$

$$\phi_j = \begin{cases} (S_j - \theta)^2, & \text{if } S_j > \theta; \\ 0, & \text{otherwise.} \end{cases} \tag{4}$$

where θ is a threshold that is set by how much current is required by the sense amplifier to produce an output equal to the threshold voltage of a N-type transistor.

Equations 3 and 4 have an intuitive explanation. Each first-layer synapse votes on whether its input matched its stored value. The sum of these votes is S_j. If the sum S_j is less than a threshold θ, then the basis function ϕ_j is zero. However, if the number of votes exceeds the threshold, then the basis function turns on. Therefore, one can adjust the dimensionality of the basis function by adjusting θ: the dimensionality is $\lceil N - \theta - 1 \rceil$, where N is the number of inputs to the network.

Figure 4 shows how varying θ changes the basis function, for $N = 2$. The input to the network is a two-dimensional space, represented by location on the page. The value of the basis function is represented by the darkness of the ink. Setting $\theta = 1$ yields the basis function on the left, which is a fuzzy 0-dimensional point. Setting $\theta = 0$ yields the basis function on the right, which is a union of fuzzy 1-dimensional lines.

Figure 4: Examples of two simulated basis functions with differing dimensionality.

Having an adjustable dimension for basis functions is useful, because it increases the robustness of the basis function. A Gaussian radial basis function is non-zero only when all elements of the input vector roughly match the center of the Gaussian. By using a hardware basis function, we can allow certain inputs not to match, while still turning on the basis function.

2.3 Blending the Basis Functions

To make the blending of the basis functions easier to implement in analog VLSI, we decided to use an alternative method for basis function combination, called the partition of unity [Moody, 1989]:

$$y_i = \frac{\sum_j h_{ij}\phi_j}{\sum_j \phi_j}. \tag{5}$$

The partition of unity suggests that the second layer should compute a weighted average of first-layer outputs, not just a weighted sum. We can compute a weighted average reasonably well with a follower aggregator used in the linear region [Mead, 1989].

Equations 4 and 5 can both be implemented by using a wide-range amplifier as a synapse (see figure 5). The bias of the amplifier is the output of the sense amplifier. That way, the above-threshold non-linearity of the bias transistor is applied to the output of the first layer and implements equation 4. The amplifier then attempts to drag the output of the second-layer neuron towards a stored value h_{ij} and implements equation 5. We store the value on a floating gate, using tunneling and injection.

The follower aggregator does not implement equation 5 perfectly: the amplifiers saturate, hence introduce a non-linearity. A follower aggregator implements

$$\sum_j \tanh(\alpha(h_{ij} - y_i))\phi_j = 0. \tag{6}$$

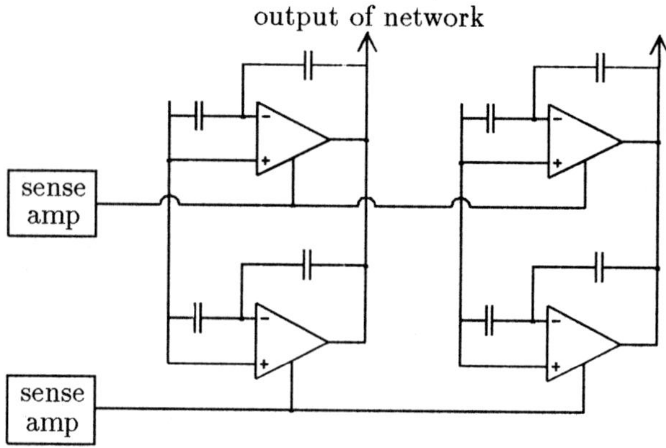

Figure 5: Circuit diagram for second-layer synapses.

We use a capacitive divider to increase the linear range (decrease α) of the amplifiers. However, the non-linearity of the amplifiers may be beneficial, because it reduces the effect of outliers in the stored h_{ij} values.

3 RESULTS

We fabricated the chip in 2 micron CMOS. The current version of the chip has 8 inputs, 159 basis functions and 4 outputs. The chip size is 2.2 millimeters by 9.6 millimeters

The core radial basis function circuitry works end-to-end. By measuring the output of the sense amplifier, we can measure the response of the first layer, which is shown in figure 3. Experiments show that the average width of the first-layer Gaussians is 0.350 volts, with a standard deviation of 23 millivolts. The centers of the first-layer Gaussians can be programmed more accurately than 15 millivolts, which is the resolution of the test setup for this chip. Further experiments show that the second-layer followers are linear to within 4% over 5 volts. Due to one mis-sized transistor, programming the second layer accurately is difficult.

We have successfully tested the chip at 90 kHz, which is the speed limit of the current test setup. We have not yet tested the chip at its full speed. The static power dissipation of the chip is 2 milliwatts.

Figure 6 shows an example of real end-to-end output of the chip. All synapses for each first-layer neuron are programmed to the same value. The first-layer neurons are programmed to a ramp: each neuron is programmed to respond to a voltage 32 millivolts higher than the previous neuron. The second layer neurons are programmed to values shown by y-values of the dots in figure 6. The output of the chip is shown as the solid line in figure 6. The output is measured as all of the inputs to the chip are swept simultaneously. The chip splines and smooths out the noisy stored second-layer values. Notice that the stored second-layer values are low for inputs near 2.5 V: the output of a chip is correspondingly lower.

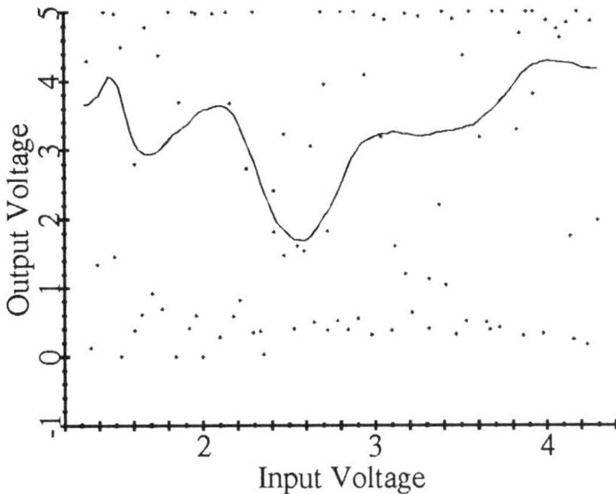

Figure 6: Example of end-to-end output measured from the chip.

4 FUTURE WORK

The mathematical model of the hardware network suggests interesting theoretical future work. There are two novel features of this model: the variable dimensionality of the basis functions, and the non-linearity in the partition of unity. More simulation work needs to be done to see how much of an benefit these features yield.

The chip architecture discussed in this paper is suitable for many medium-dimensional function mapping problems where radial basis functions are appropriate. For example, the chip is useful for high speed control, optical character recognition, and robotics.

One application of the chip we have studied further is the antialiasing of printed characters, with proportional spacing, multiple fonts, and arbitrary scaling. Each antialiased pixel has an intensity which is the integral of the character's partial coverage of that pixel convolved with some filter. The chip could perform a function interpolation for each pixel of each character. The function being interpolated is the intensity integral, based on the subpixel coverage as convolved with the antialiasing filter kernel. Figure 7 shows the results of the anti-aliasing of the character using a simulation of the chip.

5 CONCLUSIONS

We have described a multi-layer analog VLSI neural network chip that computes radial basis functions in parallel. We use inverters as first-layer synapses, to compute Gaussians that approximate quadratics. We use follower aggregators as second-layer neurons, to compute the basis functions and to blend the basis functions using a partition of unity. Preliminary experiments with a test chip shows that the core radial basis function circuitry works. In the future, we will explore the new basis function model suggested by the hardware and further investigate applications of the chip.

Figure 7: Three images of the letter "a". The image on the left is the high resolution anti-aliased version of the character. The middle image is a smaller version of the left image. The right image is the chip simulation, trained to be close to the middle image, by using the left image as the training data.

Acknowledgements

We would like to thank Federico Faggin and Carver Mead for their good advice. Thanks to John Lazzaro who gave us a new version of Until, a graphics editor. We would also like to thank Steven Rosenberg and Bo Curry of Hewlett-Packard Laboratories for their suggestions and support.

References

Anderson, J., Mead, C., 1990, MOS Device for Long-Term Learning, U. S. Patent 4,935,702.

Anderson, J., Mead, C., Allen, T., Wall, M., 1992, Adaptable MOS Current Mirror, U. S. Patent 5,160,899.

Lee, Y., 1991, Handwritten Digit Recognition Using k Nearest-Neighbor, Radial Basis Function, and Backpropagation Neural Networks, *Neural Computation,* vol. 3, no. 3, 440–449.

Mead, C., Conway, L., 1980, Introduction to VLSI Systems, Addison-Wesley, Reading, MA.

Mead, C., 1989, Analog VLSI and Neural Systems, Addison-Wesley, Reading, MA.

Mead, C., Allen, T., Faggin, F., Anderson, J., 1992, Synaptic Element and Array, U. S. Patent 5,083,044.

Moody, J., Darken, C., 1989, Fast Learning in Networks of Locally-Tuned Processing Units, *Neural Computation,* vol. 1, no. 2, 281–294.

Platt, J., 1991, Learning by Combining Memorization and Gradient Descent, *In:* Advances in Neural Information Processing 3, Lippman, R., Moody, J., Touretzky, D., eds., Morgan-Kaufmann, San Mateo, CA, 714–720.

Poggio, T., Girosi, F., 1990, Regularization Algorithms for Learning That Are Equivalent to Multilayer Networks, *Science,* vol. 247, 978–982.

Powell, M. J. D., 1987, Radial Basis Functions for Multivariable Interpolation: A Review, *In:* Algorithms for Approximation, J. C. Mason, M. G. Cox, eds., Clarendon Press, Oxford.

Generic Analog Neural Computation — The EPSILON Chip

Stephen Churcher
Dept. of Elec. Engineering
University of Edinburgh
King's Buildings
Edinburgh, EH9 3JL

Donald J. Baxter
Dept. of Elec. Engineering
University of Edinburgh
King's Buildings
Edinburgh, EH9 3JL

Alister Hamilton
Dept. of Elec. Engineering
University of Edinburgh
King's Buildings
Edinburgh, EH9 3JL

Alan F. Murray
as above

H. Martin Reekie
as above

Abstract

An analog CMOS VLSI neural processing chip has been designed and fabricated. The device employs "pulse-stream" neural state signalling, and is capable of computing some 360 million synaptic connections per second. In addition to basic characterisation results, the performance of the chip in solving "real-world" problems is also demonstrated.

1 INTRODUCTION

Inspired by biology, and borne out of a desire to perform analogue computation with fundamentally *digital* fabrication processes, the so-called "pulse-stream" arithmetic system has been steadily evolved and improved since its inception in 1986 (Murray1990a, Murray1989a). In addition to this continuous development at Edinburgh, many other research groups around the world (most notably Meador *et al* (Meador1990a)) have experimented with their own pulse-firing neural circuits.

In pulsed implementations, each neural state is represented by some variable attribute (e.g. the width of fixed frequency pulses, or the rate of fixed width pulses) of a train (or "stream") of pulses. The neuron design therefore reduces to a form of oscillator. Each neuron is fed by a column of synapses, which multiply incoming neural states by the synaptic weights. In contrast with the original circuits of Murray and Smith (Murray1987a), the synapse design which will be discussed herein utilises *analog* circuit techniques to perform the multiplication of neural state by synaptic weight.

This paper describes the Edinburgh Pulse-Stream Implementation of a Learning Oriented Network (EPSILON) chip. EPSILON was developed as a flexible neural processor, capable of addressing a variety of applications. The main design criteria were as follows :

- That it be large enough to be of use in practical problems.
- It should be capable of implementing networks of arbitrary size and architecture.
- It must be able to act as both a "slave" accelerator to a conventional computer, *and* as an "autonomous" processor.

As will be seen, these constraints resulted in a chip which could realise only a single layer of synaptic weights, but which could be *cascaded* to form large, useful networks for solving real-world problems.

The remaining sections of this paper describe the attributes of pulse-coded neural systems in general, before detailing the circuits which were employed on EPSILON. Finally, results from a vowel recognition application are presented, in order to illustrate the performance of EPSILON when applied to real tasks.

2 PULSE CODED NEURAL SYSTEMS

As already mentioned, EPSILON is a pulse coded analog neural processing chip. In such implementations, neural states are encoded as *digital* pulses. The states themselves may then be represented either by varying the *width* of the pulses (pulse width modulation — PWM), or by varying the *rate* of the pulses (pulse frequency modulation — PFM). The arguments for using pulses in this way are strong. Firstly, they provide a very effective and robust method for communicating states both on- and between-chip, since pulses are extremely resistant to noise. Secondly, the use of pulses to represent states renders interfacing to digital circuits and computer peripherals straightforward. Finally, pulsed signalling leads to simplification of artihmetic circuits (i.e. synapses), resulting in much higher inter-connection densities.

Unfortunately, pulse-based systems do have drawbacks. In common with all analog circuits, the synaptic computing elements have limited precision (usually equivalent to about 7 bits), and their performance is subject to the vagaries of fabrication process variations. This results in a situation whereby supposedly "matched" circuits vary markedly in their characteristics. Furthermore, the switching which is inherent in any pulsed circuit results in increased levels of system noise, most usually in the form of power supply transients. An additional problem with pulse frequency modulation (PFM) systems is that computation rates are dependent on the data; this is an important consideration in speed-critical applications.

3 THE EPSILON DESIGN

This section describes the circuits which were used in the EPSILON design. The operating principles of each circuit are discussed, and characterisation results presented. In accordance with the demerits mentioned in the previous section, all circuits were designed to be tolerant to noise and process variations, to *cause* as little noise as possible themselves, and to be easy to "set up" in practice. Finally, the specification of the EPSILON chip is presented.

3.1 SYNAPSE

The synapse design was based on the standard transconductance multiplier circuit, which had previously been the basis for monolithic analogue transversal filters for use in signal processing applications (Denyer1981a). Such multipliers use MOS transistors in their *linear* region of operation to generate output currents proportional to a product of two input voltages. This concept was adapted for use in pulsed neural networks by fixing one of the input voltages, and using a neural state to gate the output current. In this manner, the synaptic weight controls the magnitude of the output current, which is multiplied by the incoming neural pulses. The resultant charge packets are subsequently integrated to yield the total post-synaptic activity voltage.

Figure 1 shows the basic pulsed multiplier cell, where M1 and M2 form the transconductance multiplier, and M3 is the output pulse transistor. By ensuring that the drain-source voltages for M1 and M2 are the same and constant (the differential amplifier and transistors M4 and M5 are used to satisfy this constraint), non-linearities in the transistor responses can be cancelled out, such that I_{OUT} is linearly dependent on the difference of V_{GS1} and V_{GS2} (Murray1992a). Multiplication is achieved by pulsing this current by the neural state, V_j. An "instantaneous" representation of the aggregated post-synaptic activity is given by the output voltage, V_{OUT}; this must subsequently be integrated in order to provide an activity input to a neuron.

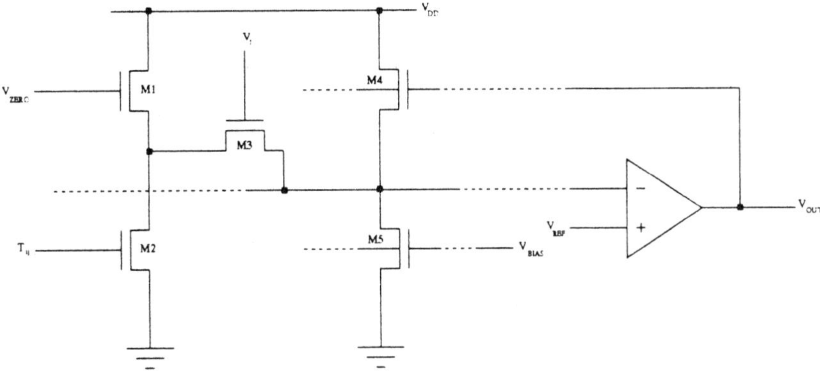

Figure 1: Transconductance Multiplier Synapse

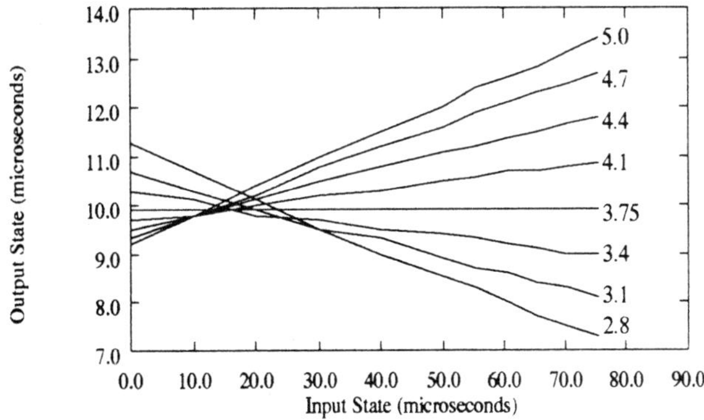

Figure 2: Synapse Characterisation Results

Results from characterisation tests of the synapse are presented in Figure 2, which shows output state against input state, for different synaptic weight voltages. As seen from the Figure, the linearity of the synapses, with respect to input state, is very high. The variation of synapse response with synaptic weight voltage is also fairly uniform. The graphs depict mean performance over all the synaptic columns in all the chips tested. The associated standard deviations were more or less constant, representing a variation of approximately ± 300 *ns* in the values of the output pulse widths. The effects of intra- and inter-chip process mismatches would therefore seem to be well contained by the circuit design. The "zero point" in the synaptic weight range was set at 3.75 *V* and, as can be seen from the Figure, each graph shows an offset problem when the input neural state is zero. This was attributable to an imbalance in the operating conditions of the transistors in the synapse, induced by the non-ideal nature of the power supplies (i.e. the non-zero sheet resistance of the power supply tracks), resulting in an offset in the input voltage to the post-synaptic integrator. This problem is easily obviated in practice, by employing three synapses per column to cancel the offset.

3.2 NEURONS

In order to reflect the diversity of neural network forms, and possible applications, two different neuron designs were included on the EPSILON chip. The first, a *synchronous* pulse width modulation neuron was designed with vision applications in mind. This circuit could guarantee network computation times, thereby eliminating the data dependency inherent in pulse frequency systems. The second neuron design used *asynchronous* pulse frequency modulation; the asynchronous nature of these circuits is advantageous in feedback and recurrent neural architectures, where temporal characteristics are important. As with the synapse, both circuits were designed to minimise transient noise injection, and to be tolerant of process variations.

3.2.1 Pulse Width Modulation

As already stated, this system retains all the advantages of using pulses for communication/calculation, whilst being able to *guarantee* a maximum network evaluation time. In the first instance, the main disadvantage with this technique appeared to be its synchronous nature - neurons would all be switching together causing larger power supply transients than in an asynchronous system. This problem has, however, been circumvented via a "double-sided" pulse modulation scheme, which will be more fully explained later.

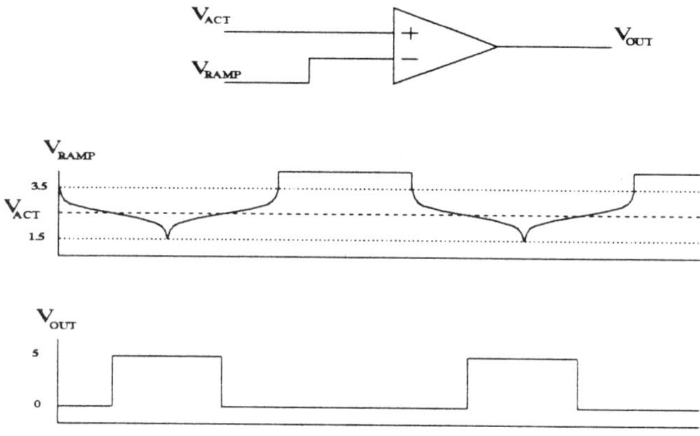

Figure 3: Pulse-Width Modulation Neuron

The operation of the pulse-width modulation neuron is illustrated in Figure 3. The neuron itself is nothing more elaborate than a 2-stage comparator, with an inverter output driver stage. The inputs to the circuit are the integrated post-synaptic activity voltage, V_{ACT}, and a reference voltage, V_{RAMP}, which is generated off-chip and is globally distributed to all neurons in parallel. As seen from the waveforms in Figure 3, the output of the neuron changes state whenever the reference signal crosses the activity voltage level. An output pulse, which is some function of the input activation, is thus generated. The transfer function is entirely dependent on the shape of the reference signal - when this is generated by a RAM look-up table, the function can become completely arbitrary and hence user programmable. Figure 3 shows the signal which should be applied if a *sigmoidal* transfer characteristic is desired. Note that the sigmoid signals are "on their sides" - this is because the input (or independent variable) is on the vertical axis rather than the horizontal axis, as would normally be expected. The use of a "double-sided" ramp for the reference signal was alluded to earlier - this mechanism generates a pulse which is symmetrical about the mid-point of the ramp, thereby greatly reducing the likelihood of coincident edges. This edge-asynchronicity obviates the problem of larger switching transients on the power supplies. Furthermore, because the analogue element (i.e. the ramp voltage) is effectively removed from the chip, and the circuit itself merely functions as a digital block, the system is immune to process variations.

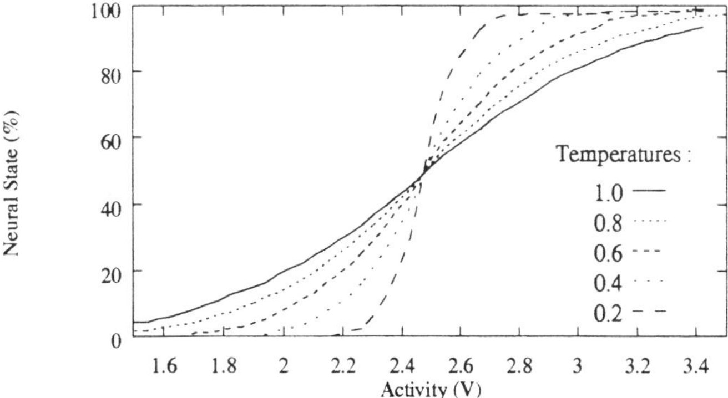

Figure 4: PWM Neuron Performance

Figure 4 shows plots of output state (measured as a percentage of a maximum possible 20 μs pulse) versus input activity voltage, for five different sigmoid "temperatures", averaged over all the neurons on one chip. As can be seen, the fidelity of the sigmoids is extremely high, and it should be noted that all the curves are symmetrical about their midpoints — something which is difficult to achieve using standard analog circuits.

3.2.2 Pulse Frequency Modulation

The second neuron design which was included in EPSILON used pulse frequency encoding of the neural state. Although hampered by data dependent calculation times, its wholly asynchronous nature makes it ideal for neural network architectures which embody temporal characteristics i.e. feedback networks, and recurrent networks.

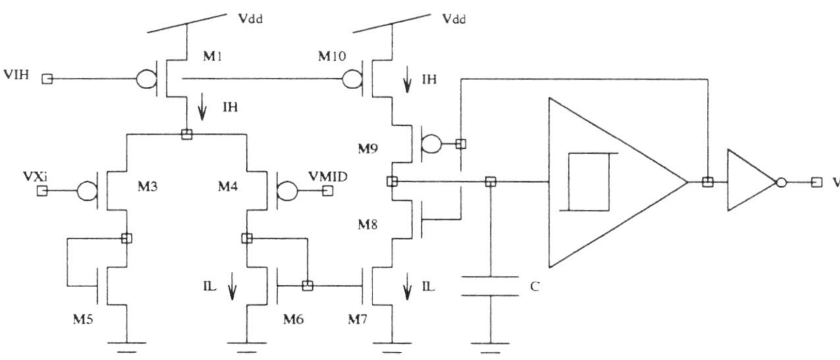

Figure 5: Pulse Frequency Modulation Neuron

The neuron design is illustrated in Figure 5, and is basically a Voltage Controlled Oscillator (VCO) with a variable gain sigmoidal transfer characteristic. Oscillation is achieved via the hysteretic charge and discharge of capacitor C, by the currents IH and IL respectively. The output pulse width is constant, and is set by IH, whilst the inter-pulse spacing (and hence output frequency) is controlled by IL. IL itself is determined by the activity voltage, VXI, via the differential stage constituted by transistors M3 to M6. It is this latter which gives the VCO its sigmoidal characteristic, and gain variations may be achieved by injecting and removing additional current at appropriate points in this stage (note that the circuitry for this has been omitted from Figure 5, for the sake of clarity).

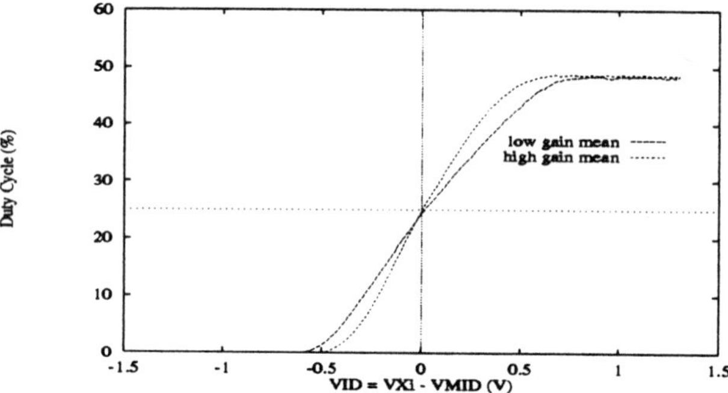

Figure 6: PFM Neuron Performance

The characterisation results for the VCO are presented in Figure 6. The Figure shows plots of output percentage duty cycle versus input differential voltage, for different values of sigmoid gain. Note that the curves are fair approximations to sigmoids, although, in contrast with the pulse width modulation neuron, they are *not* symmetrical about their mid-points. It can also be seen that the range of possible sigmoid gains is smaller than the range available with the PWM system, although this is not a crucial factor in many applications.

3.3 EPSILON SPECIFICATION

The circuits described in the previous section were combined to form the EPSILON chip. This was subsequently fabricated by European Silicon Structures (ES2) using their ECPD15 (i.e. 1.5 μm, double metal, single poly CMOS). As already stated, each chip was capable of implementing a single layer of synaptic connections, and could accept inputs as either analog voltages (for direct interface to sensors) or as pulses (for communication with other chips, and with digital systems). The full specification is given in Table 1.

4 APPLICATION — VOWEL RECOGNITION

After the device characterisation experiments had been completed, EPSILON was used to implement a multi-layer perceptron (MLP) for speech data classification. The MLP had 54 inputs, 27 hidden units, and 11 outputs, and the task was to classify 11 different vowel sounds spoken by each of 33 speakers. The input vectors were formed by the analog outputs of 54 band-pass filters.

The MLP was initially trained on a SPARC station, using a subset of 22 patterns. Learning (using the Virtual Targets algorithm, with 0 % noise (Murray1991a)) proceeded until the maximum bit error in the output vector was ≤ 0.3, at which point the weight set was

Table 1: EPSILON Specifications

EPSILON Specification	
No. of State Input Pins	30
No. of Actual State Inputs	120, Muxed in Banks of 30
Input Modes	Analog, PW, or PF
No. of State Outputs	30, Directly Pinned Out
Output Modes	PW or PF
No. of Synapses	3600
No. of Weight Load Channels	2
Weight Load Time	3.6 *ms*
Weight Storage	Dynamic
Maximum Speed (cps)	360 *Mcps*
Technology	1.5 μm, Double Metal CMOS
Die Size	9.5 *mm* x 10.1 *mm*
Maximum Power Dissipation	350 *mW*

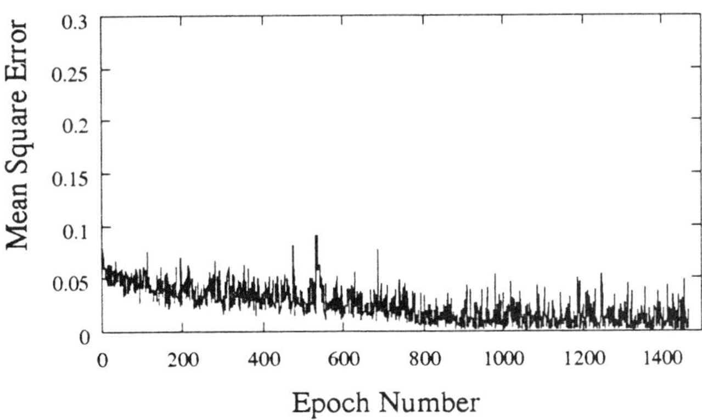

Figure 7: EPSILON Under Training

downloaded to EPSILON. Training was then restarted under the same regime as before (using the same "stop" criterion), although this time EPSILON was used to evaluate the "forward pass" phases of the network. Figure 7 shows the evolution of mean square error with number of epochs during this period; at the end of training, EPSILON could correctly identify all 22 training patterns.

Subsequent to this, 176 "unseen" test patterns were presented to the EPSILON network, with the result that 65.34 % of these vectors were correctly classified. This compared very favourably with similar generalisation experiments which were carried out on a SPARC : in this case, the best result obtained was 67.61 %.

5 CONCLUSIONS

In conclusion, a large analog VLSI neural chip, composed of process tolerant circuits, with useful characteristics has been fabricated. Although not a *self*-learning device, it has been proved that EPSILON will support learning, and can be applied successfully to real-world problems. Indeed, when correctly trained, the performance of the EPSILON chip has been shown to be comparable with that of software simulations on a SPARC station.

Work is currently under way to apply EPSILON to computer vision tasks; more specifically, it it will be used to implement an MLP which is capable of recognising regions in segmented images of natural scenes. Furthermore, the success of the learning experiments has given us sufficient confidence to undertake the development of a self-learning analog neural chip. It is envisaged that this will employ EPSILON-type circuits, and will implement the Virtual Targets (Murray1991a) training algorithm; the design of a small prototype is currently nearing completion.

Acknowledgements

The authors would like to thank the Science and Engineering Research Council for their continued funding of this work. In addition, Stephen Churcher and Donald Baxter are grateful to British Aerospace PLC and Thorn-EMI CRL respectively for sponsorship and technical support during the course of their PhD's.

Lionel Tarassenko (Dept. of Engineering Science, University of Oxford) must also be thanked for his invaluable comments, and for supplying the vowel database.

References

Murray1990a.
A. F. Murray, D. Baxter, Z. Butler, S. Churcher, A. Hamilton, H. M. Reekie, and L. Tarassenko, "Innovations in Pulse Stream Neural VLSI : Arithmetic and Communications", *IEEE Workshop on Microelectronics for Neural Networks, Dortmund 1990*, pp. 8-15, 1990.

Murray1989a.
A. F. Murray, "Pulse Arithmetic in VLSI Neural Networks", *IEEE MICRO*, vol. 9, no. 6, pp. 64-74, 1989.

Meador1990a.
J. Meador, A. Wu, C. Cole, N. Nintunze, and P. Chintrakulchai, "Programmable Impulse Neural Circuits", *IEEE Transactions on Neural Networks*, vol. 2, no. 1, pp. 101-109, 1990.

Murray1987a.
A. F. Murray and A. V. W. Smith, "Asynchronous Arithmetic for VLSI Neural Systems", *Electronics Letters*, vol. 23, no. 12, pp. 642-643, June, 1987.

Denyer1981a.
P. B. Denyer and J. Mavor, "MOST Transconductance Multipliers for Array Applications", *IEE Proc. Pt. 1*, vol. 128, no. 3, pp. 81-86, June 1981.

Murray1992a.
A.F. Murray, A. Hamilton, D.J. Baxter, S. Churcher, H.M. Reekie, and L. Tarassenko, "Integrated Pulse-Stream Neural Networks - Results, Issues and Pointers", *IEEE Trans. Neural Networks*, pp. 385-393, 1992.

Murray1991a.
A. F. Murray, "Analog VLSI and Multi-Layer Perceptrons - Accuracy, Noise and On-Chip Learning", *Proc. Second International Conference on Microelectronics for Neural Networks, Munich (Germany)*, pp. 27-34, 1991.

Visual Motion Computation in Analog VLSI using Pulses

Rahul Sarpeshkar, Wyeth Bair and Christof Koch
Computation and Neural Systems Program
California Institute of Technology
Pasadena, CA 91125.

Abstract

The real time computation of motion from real images using a single chip with integrated sensors is a hard problem. We present two analog VLSI schemes that use pulse domain neuromorphic circuits to compute motion. Pulses of variable width, rather than graded potentials, represent a natural medium for evaluating temporal relationships. Both algorithms measure speed by timing a moving edge in the image. Our first model is inspired by Reichardt's algorithm in the fly and yields a non-monotonic response vs. velocity curve. We present data from a chip that implements this model. Our second algorithm yields a monotonic response vs. velocity curve and is currently being translated into silicon.

1 Introduction

Analog VLSI chips for the real time computation of visual motion have been the focus of much active research because of their importance as sensors for robotic applications. Correlation schemes such as those described in (Delbrück, 1993) have been found to be more robust than gradient schemes described in (Tanner and Mead, 1986), because they do not involve noise-sensitive operations like spatial-differentiation and division. A comparison of four experimental schemes may be found in (Horiuchi et al., 1992). In spite of years of work, however, there is still no motion chip that robustly computes motion under all environmental conditions.

Motion algorithms operating on higher level percepts in an image such as zero-crossings (edges) are more robust than those that operating on lower level percepts in an image such as raw image intensity values (Marr and Ullman, 1981). Our work demonstrates how, if the edges in an image are identified, it is possible to compute motion, quickly and easily, by using pulses. We compute the velocity at each point in the image. The estimation of the flow-field is of tremendous importance in computations such as time-to-contact, figure-ground-segregation and depth-from-motion. Our motion scheme is well-suited to typical indoor environments that tend to have a lot of high-contrast edges. The much harder problem of computing motion in low-contrast, high-noise outdoor environments still remains unsolved.

We present two motion algorithms. Our first algorithm is a "delay-and-correlate" scheme operating on spatial edge features and is inspired by work on fly vision (Hassenstein and Reichardt, 1956). It yields a non-monotonic response vs. velocity curve. We present data from a chip that implements it. Our second algorithm is a "facilitate-and-trigger" scheme operating on temporal edge features and yields a monotonic response vs. velocity curve. Work is under way to implement our second algorithm in analog VLSI.

2 The Delay-and-Correlate Scheme

Conceptually, there are two stages of computation. First, the zero-crossings in the image are computed and then the motion of these zero-crossings is detected. The zero-crossing circuitry has been described in (Bair and Koch, 1991). We concentrate on describing the motion circuitry.

A schematized version of the chip is shown in Figure 1a. Only four photoreceptors in the array are shown. The 1-D image from the array of photoreceptors is filtered with a spatial bandpass filter whose kernel is composed of a difference of two exponentials (implemented with resistive grids). The outputs of the bandpass filter feed into edge detection circuitry that output a bit indicating the presence or absence of an edge between two adjacent pixels. The edges on the chip are separated into two polarities, namely, right-side-bright (R) and left-side-bright (L), which are kept separate throughout the chip, including the motion circuitry. For comparison, in biology, edges are often separated into light-on edges and light-off edges. The motion circuits are sensitive only to the motion of those edges from which they receive inputs. They detect the motion of a zero-crossing from one location to an adjacent location using a Reichardt scheme as shown in Figure 1b. Each motion detecting unit receives two zero-crossing inputs ZC_n and ZC_{n+2}[1]. The ON-cells detect the onset of zero-crossings (a rising voltage edge) by firing a pulse. The units marked with D's delay these pulses by an amount D, controlled externally. The correlation units marked with X's logically AND a delayed version of a pulse from one location with an undelayed version of a pulse from the adjacent location. The output from the left correlator is sensitive to motion from location $n+2$ to location n since the motion delay is compensated by the built-in circuit delay. The outputs of the two correlators are subtracted to yield the final motion signal. Figure 2a shows the circuit details. The boxes labelled with pulse symbols represent axon circuits. The

[1] ZC_{n+1} could have been used as well. ZC_{n+2} was chosen due to wiring constraints and because it increases the baseline distance for computing motion.

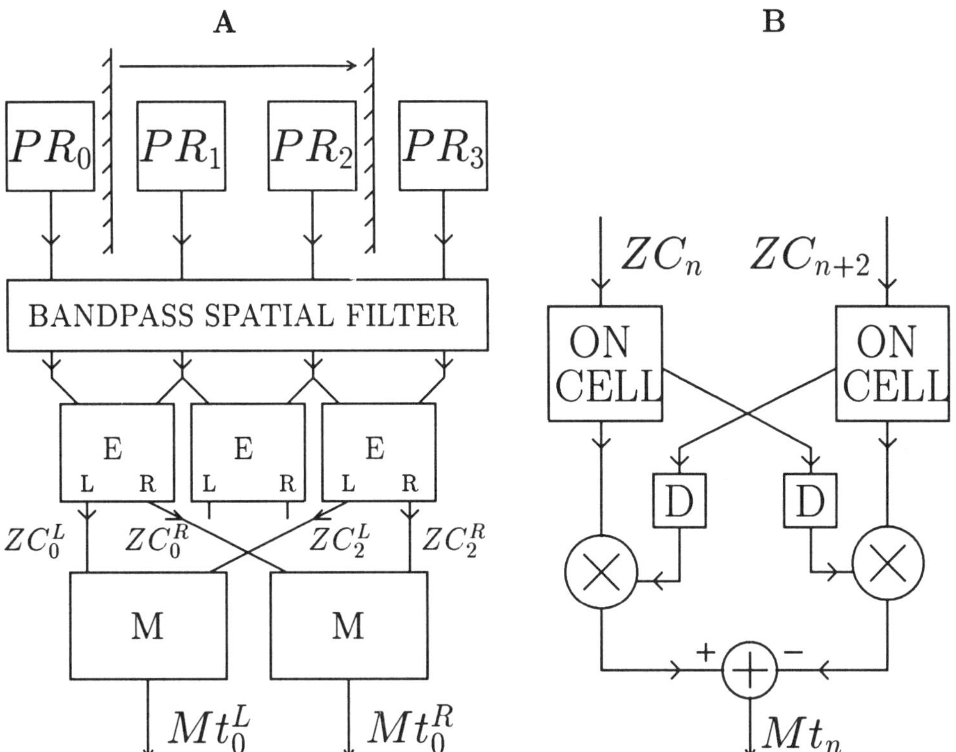

Figure 1—(A) The bandpass filtered photoreceptor signal is fed to the edge detectors marked with E's. The motion of these edges is detected by the motion detecting units marked with M's. (B) A single motion detecting unit, corresponding to a "M" unit in fig. A, has a Reichardt-like architecture.

axon circuits generate a single pulse of externally controlled width, P, in response to a sharp positive transition in their input, but remain inactive in response to a negative transition. In order to generate pulses that are delayed from the onset of a zero-crossing, the output of one axon circuit, with pulse width parameter D, is coupled via an inverter to the input of another axon circuit, with pulse width parameter P. The multiplication operation is implemented by a simple logical AND. The subtraction operation is implemented by a subtraction of two currents. An off-chip sense amplifier converts the bidirectional current pulse outputs of the local motion detectors into active-low or active-high voltage pulses. The axon circuit is shown in Figure 2b. Further details of its operation may be found in (Sarpeshkar et al., 1992).

Figure 3a shows how the velocity tuning curve is obtained. If the image velocity, v, is positive, and Δx is the distance between adjacent zero-crossing locations, then it can be shown that the output pulse width for the positive-velocity half of the motion detector, t_p, is

$$t_p = u\Theta(u), \tag{1}$$

where

$$u = P - \mid \frac{\Delta x}{v} - D \mid, \tag{2}$$

and $\Theta(,)$ is the unit step function. If v is negative, the same eqns. apply for the negative-velocity half of the motion detector except that the signs of Δx and t_p are reversed.

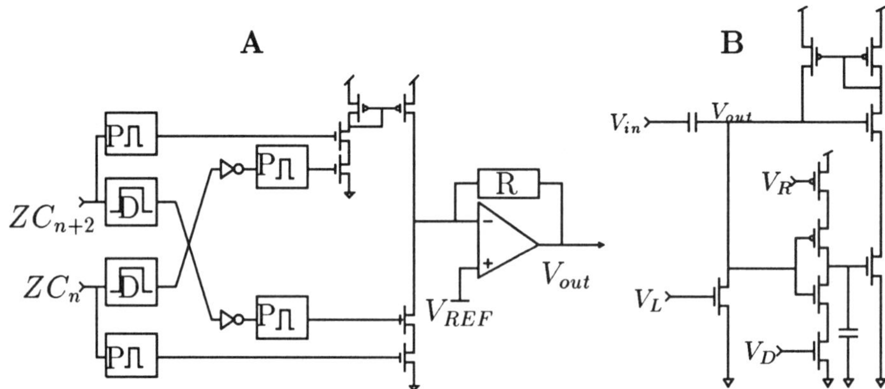

Figure 2—(A) The circuitry implementing the Reichardt scheme of Figure 1b, is shown. The boxes labelled P and D represent axon circuits of pulse width parameter P and D, respectively. (B) The circuit details of an axon circuit that implements an ON-cell of Figure 1b are shown. The input and output are V_{in} and V_{out} respectively. The circuit was designed to mimic the behavior of sodium and leak conductances at the node of Ranvier in an axon fiber. The pulse width of the output pulse, the refractory period following its generation, and the threshold height of the input edge needed to trigger the pulse are determined by the values of bias voltages V_D, V_R and V_L respectively.

Experimental Data

Figure 4a shows the outputs of motion detectors between zero-crossings 3 and 5, 7 and 9, and 11 and 13, denoted as Mt_3, Mt_7, and Mt_{11}, respectively. For an edge passing from left to right, the outputs Mt_{11}, Mt_7 and Mt_3 are excited in this order, and they each report a positive velocity (active high output that is above V_{REF}). For an edge passing from right to left, the outputs Mt_3, Mt_7 and Mt_{11} are excited in this order and they each report a negative velocity (active low output that is below V_{REF}). Note that the amplitudes of these pulses contain no speed information and only signal the direction of motion. Figure 4b shows that the output Mt_3 is tuned to a particular velocity. As the rotational frequency of a cylinder with a painted edge is decreased from a velocity corresponding to a motor voltage of - 6.1V to a velocity corresponding to a motor voltage of -1.3V, the output pulse width increases, then decreases again, as the optimal velocity is traversed through. A similar tuning curve is observed for positive motor voltages. If the distance from the surface of the spinning cylinder to the center of the lens is o, the distance from the center of the lens to the chip is i, the radius of the spinning cylinder is R, and its frequency

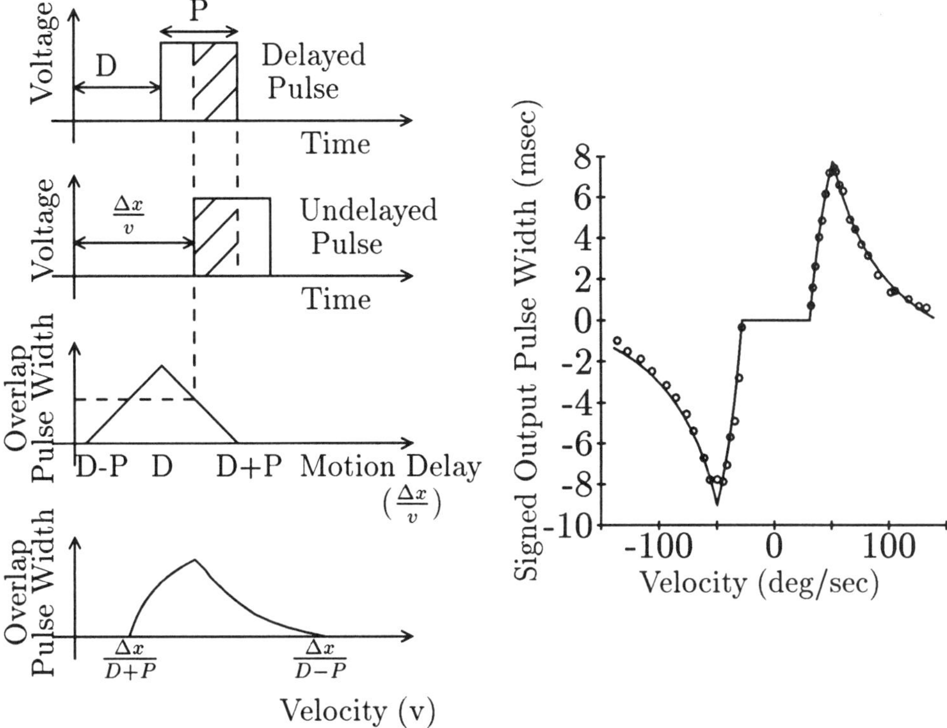

Figure 3—(a) The figure shows how the overlap between the delayed and undelayed pulses gives rise to velocity tuning for motion in the preferred direction. (b) The figure shows experimental data (circles) and a theoretical fit (line) for the motion unit Mt_3's output response vs. angular velocity.

of rotation is f, then the velocity, v, of the moving edge as seen by the chip is given by

$$v = 2\pi f R \frac{i}{o}. \tag{3}$$

The angular velocity, ω, of the moving edge, is

$$\omega = \frac{2\pi f R}{o} = \frac{v}{i}. \tag{4}$$

Figure 3b shows the output pulse width of Mt_3 plotted against the angular velocity of the edge (ω). The data are fit by a curve that computes t_p vs. ω from (1)-(4), using measured values of $\Delta x = 180\ \mu$m, $o = 310$ mm, $i = 17$ mm, and $R = 58$ mm.

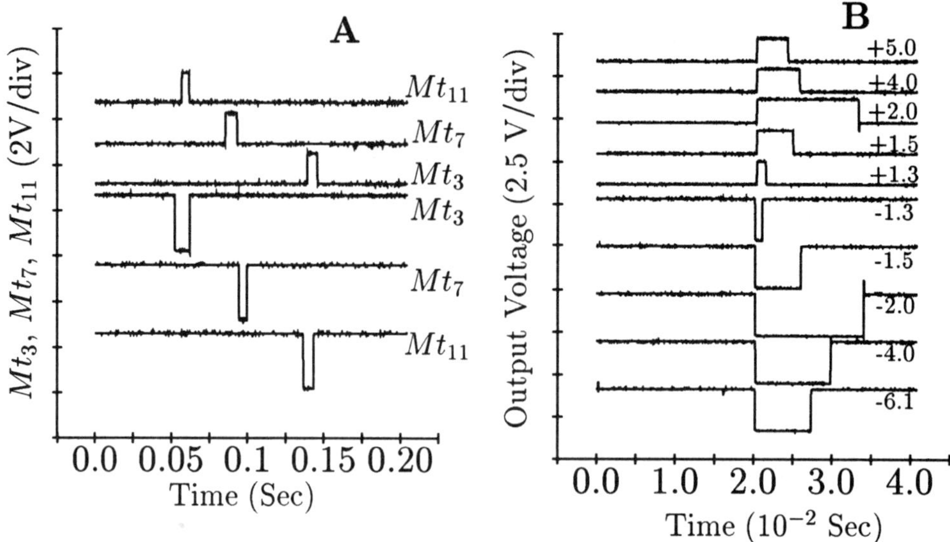

Figure 4—(A) The chip output waveforms are active-high when the motion is in a direction such that motion detectors 11, 7 and 3 are stimulated in that order. In the opposite direction (3 → 7 → 11), the output waveforms are active-low. (B) The figure demonstrates the tuned velocity behavior of the motion unit Mt_3 for various motor voltages (in V). Large positive voltages correspond to fast motion in one direction and large negative voltages correspond to fast motion in the opposite direction.

3 The Facilitate-and-Trigger Scheme

Although the delay-and-correlate scheme works well, the output yields ambiguous motion information due to its non-monotonic velocity dependence, i.e., we don't know if the output is small because the velocity is too slow or because it is too fast. This problem may be solved by aggregating the outputs of a series of motion detectors with overlapping tuning curves and progressively larger optimal velocities. This solution is plausible in physiology but expensive in VLSI. We were thus motivated to create a new motion detector that possessed a monotonic velocity tuning curve from the outset.

Figure 5a shows the architecture of such a motion detecting unit: The need for computing spatial edges is obviated by having a photoreceptor sensitive to temporal features caused by moving edges, i.e., sharp light onsets/offsets (Delbrück, 1993). Each ON-cell fires a pulse in response to the onset of a temporal edge. The pulses are fed to the facilitatory (F) and trigger (T) inputs of motion detectors tuned for motion in the left or right directions. The facilitatory pulse defines a time window of externally controlled width F, within which the output motion pulse may be activated by the trigger pulse. Thus, the rising edge of the trigger pulse must occur within the time window set by the facilitatory pulse in order to create a motion output. If this condition is satisfied, the output motion pulse is triggered (begins) at the start of the trigger pulse and ends at the end of the facilitatory pulse; its width, thus, encodes the arrival time difference between the onset pulses at adjacent locations due to the motion delay. Each half of the motion detector only responds to motion in the direction that corresponds to F *before* T. Figure 5c shows that the velocity tuning in this scheme is monotonic. It can be shown that the output pulse width for the positive half of the motion detector, t_p, is given by

$$t_p = u\Theta(u), \tag{5}$$

where u is given by,

$$u = F - \frac{\Delta x}{v}. \tag{6}$$

The dead zone near the origin may be made as small as needed by increasing the width of the facilitatory pulse. Figure 5b shows a compact circuit that

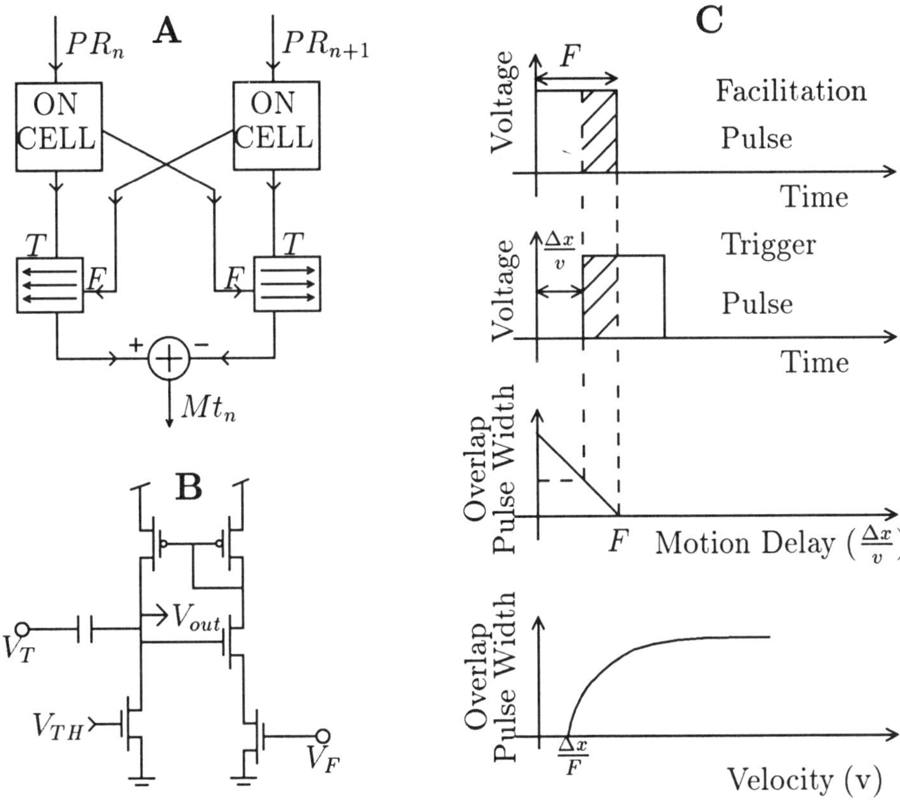

Figure 5—(A) The motion detecting unit uses a facilitate-and-trigger paradigm instead of a delay-and-correlate paradigm as a basis for its operation. (B) A compact circuit implements the motion detecting unit. V_T is the trigger input, V_F is the facilitatory input, V_{out} is the output and V_{TH} is a bias voltage. (C) The output response has a monotonic dependence on velocity.

implements the facilitate-and-trigger scheme. The ON-cell, subtraction and sense-amplifier circuitry are implemented as in the Reichardt scheme.

The facilitate-and-trigger approach requires a total of 32 transistors per motion unit compared with a total of 64 in the delay-and-correlate approach, needs one parameter to be controlled (F) rather than two (D and P), and yields monotonic tuning from the outset. We, therefore, believe that it will prove to be the superior of the two approaches.

4 Conclusions

The evaluations of onsets, delays and coincidences, required for computing motion are implemented very naturally with pulses rather than by graded potentials as in all other motion chips, built so far. Both of our motion algorithms time the motion of image features in an efficient fashion by using pulse computation.

Acknowledgements

Many thanks to Carver Mead for his encouragement, support and use of lab facilities. We acknowledge useful discussions with William Bialek, Nicola Franceschini and Tobias Delbrück. This work was supported by grants from the Office of Naval Research and the California Competitive Technologies Program. Chip fabrication was provided by MOSIS.

References

W. Bair, and C. Koch, "An Analog VLSI Chip for Finding Edges from Zero-crossings.", In *Advances in Neural Information Processing Systems Vol. 3*, R. Lippman, J. Moody, D. Touretzky, eds., pp. 399-405, Morgan Kaufmann, San Mateo, CA, 1991.

T. Delbrück, "Investigations of Analog VLSI Visual Transduction and Motion Processing", PhD. thesis, Computation and Neural Systems Program, Caltech, Pasadena, CA, 1993.

B. Hassenstein and W. Reichardt, "Systemtheoretische Analyse der Zeit, Reihenfolgen, und Vorzeichenauswertung bei der Bewegungsperzepion des Rüsselkäfers *Chlorophanus*", *Z. Naturforsch.* **11b:** pp. 513-524, 1956.

T. Horiuchi, W. Bair, A. Moore, B. Bishofberger, J. Lazzaro, C. Koch, "Computing Motion Using Analog VLSI Vision Chips: an Experimental Comparison among Different Approaches", Intl. Journal of Computer Vision, **8**, pp. 203-216, 1992.

D. Marr and S. Ullman, "Directional Selectivity and its Use in Early Visual Processing", *Proc. R. Soc. Lond B* **211**, pp. 151-180, 1981.

R. Sarpeshkar, L. Watts, C. Mead, "Refractory Neuron Circuits", Internal Lab Memorandum, Physics of Computation Laboratory, Pasadena, CA, 1992.

J. Tanner and C. Mead, "An Integrated Optical Motion Sensor", *VLSI Signal Processing II*, S-Y Kung, R.E. Owen, and J.G. Nash, eds., 59-76, IEEE Press, NY, 1986.

Analog VLSI Implementation of Multi-dimensional Gradient Descent

David B. Kirk, Douglas Kerns, Kurt Fleischer, Alan H. Barr
California Institute of Technology
Beckman Institute 350-74
Pasadena, CA 91125
E-mail: dk@egg.gg.caltech.edu

Abstract

We describe an analog VLSI implementation of a multi-dimensional gradient estimation and descent technique for minimizing an on-chip scalar function $f()$. The implementation uses noise injection and multiplicative correlation to estimate derivatives, as in [Anderson, Kerns 92]. One intended application of this technique is setting circuit parameters on-chip automatically, rather than manually [Kirk 91]. Gradient descent optimization may be used to adjust synapse weights for a backpropagation or other on-chip learning implementation. The approach combines the features of continuous multi-dimensional gradient descent and the potential for an annealing style of optimization. We present data measured from our analog VLSI implementation.

1 Introduction

This work is similar to [Anderson, Kerns 92], but represents two advances. First, we describe the extension of the technique to multiple dimensions. Second, we demonstrate an implementation of the multi-dimensional technique in analog VLSI, and provide results measured from the chip. Unlike previous work using noise sources in adaptive systems, we use the noise as a means of estimating the gradient of a function $f(\underline{y})$, rather than performing an annealing process [Alspector 88]. We also estimate gradients continuously in position and time, in contrast to [Umminger 89] and [Jabri 91], which utilize discrete position gradient estimates.

It is interesting to note the existence of related algorithms, also presented in this volume [Cauwenberghs 93] [Alspector 93] [Flower 93]. The main difference is that our implementation operates in continuous time, with continuous differentiation and integration operators. The other approaches realize the integration and differentiation processes as discrete addition and subtraction operations, and use unit perturbations. [Cauwenberghs 93] provides a detailed derivation of the convergence and scaling properties of the discrete approach, and a simulation. [Alspector 93] provides a description of the use of the technique as part of a neural network hardware architecture, and provides a simulation. [Flower 93] derived a similar discrete algorithm from a node perturbation perspective in the context of multi-layered feed-forward networks. Our work is similar in spirit to [Dembo 90] in that we don't make any explicit assumptions about the "model" that is embodied in the function $f()$. The function may be implemented as a neural network. In that case, the gradient descent is on-chip learning of the parameters of the network.

We have fabricated a working chip containing the continuous-time multi-dimensional gradient descent circuits. This paper includes chip data for individual circuit components, as well as the entire circuit performing multi-dimensional gradient descent and annealing.

2 The Gradient Estimation Technique

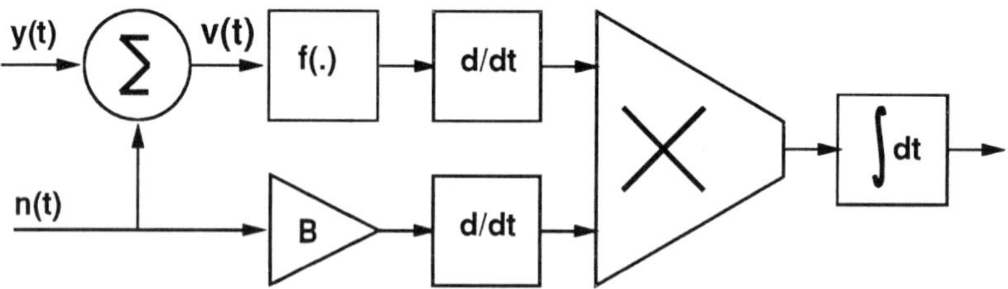

Figure 1: Gradient estimation technique from [Anderson, Kerns 92]

Anderson and Kerns [Anderson, Kerns 92] describe techniques for one-dimensional gradient estimation in analog hardware. The gradient is estimated by correlating (using a multiplier) the output of a scalar function $f(v(t))$ with a noise source $n(t)$, as shown in Fig. 1. The function input $y(t)$ is additively "contaminated" by the noise $n(t)$ to produce $v(t) = y(t) + n(t)$. A scale factor B is used to set the scale of the noise to match the function output, which improves the signal-to-noise ratio. The signals are "high-pass" filtered to approximate differentiation (shown as d/dt operators in Fig. 1) directly before the multiplication. The results of the multiplication are "low-pass" filtered to approximate integration.

The gradient estimate is integrated over time, to smooth out some of the noise and to damp the response. This smoothed estimate is compared with a "zero" reference, using an amplifier A, and the result is fed back to the input, as shown in Fig. 2. The contents of Fig. 1 are represented by the "Gradient Estimation" box in Fig. 2.

We have chosen to implement the multi-dimensional technique in analog VLSI. We

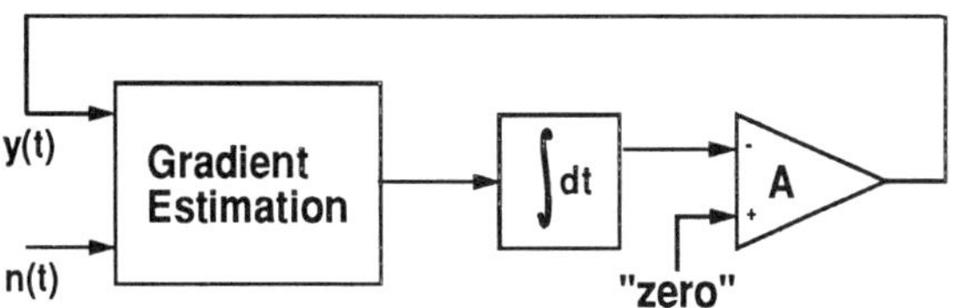

Figure 2: Closing the loop: performing gradient descent using the gradient estimate.

will not reproduce here the one-dimensional analysis from [Anderson, Kerns 92], but summarize some of the more important results, and provide a multi-dimensional derivation. [Anderson 92] provides a more detailed theoretical discussion.

3 Multi-dimensional Derivation

The multi-dimensional gradient descent operation that we are approximating can be written as follows:

$$\underline{y}'(t) = -k\nabla f(\underline{y}(t)) \tag{1}$$

where $\underline{y}$ and $\underline{y}'$ are vectors, and the solution is obtained continuously in time t, rather than at discrete t_i. The circuit described in the block diagram in Fig. 1 computes an approximation to the gradient:

$$\nabla f = \frac{\partial f}{\partial y_i} \approx \int \left(\frac{d}{dt} f\left(\underline{y}(t) + \underline{n}(t)\right) n_i'(t) \right) dt \tag{2}$$

We approximate the operations of differentiation and integration in time by realizable high-pass and low-pass filters, respectively. To see that Eq. 2 is valid, and that this result is useful for approximating Eq. 1, we sketch an N-dimensional extension of [Anderson 92]. Using the chain rule,

$$\frac{d}{dt} f\left(\underline{y}(t) + \underline{n}(t)\right) = \sum_j \left(y_j'(t) + n_j'(t)\right) \frac{\partial f}{\partial y_j} \tag{3}$$

Assuming $n_j'(t) \gg y_j'(t)$, the rhs is approximated to produce

$$\frac{d}{dt} f\left(\underline{y}(t) + \underline{n}(t)\right) = \sum_j n_j'(t) \frac{\partial f}{\partial y_j} \tag{4}$$

Multiplying both sides by $n_i'(t)$, and taking the expectation integral operator $E[\,]$ of each side,

$$E\left[n_i'(t) \frac{d}{dt} f\left(\underline{y}(t) + \underline{n}(t)\right) \right] = E\left[n_i'(t) \sum_j n_j'(t) \frac{\partial f}{\partial y_j} \right] \tag{5}$$

If the noise sources $n_i(t)$ and $n_j(t)$ are uncorrelated, $n_i'(t)$ is independent of $n_j'(t)$ when $i \neq j$, and the sum on the right has a contribution only when $i = j$,

$$E\left[n_i'(t) \frac{d}{dt} f\left(\underline{y}(t) + \underline{n}(t)\right) \right] = E\left[n_i'(t) n_i'(t) \frac{\partial f}{\partial y_i} \right] \tag{6}$$

$$E\left[n_i'(t)\frac{d}{dt}f\left(\underline{y}(t)+\underline{n}(t)\right)\right]\approx\alpha\frac{\partial f}{\partial y_i}=\alpha\nabla f \tag{7}$$

The expectation operator $E[\,]$ can be used to smooth random variations of the noise $n_i(t)$. So, we have

$$\nabla f=\frac{\partial f}{\partial y_i}\approx\frac{1}{\alpha}E\left[n_i'(t)\frac{d}{dt}f\left(\underline{y}(t)+\underline{n}(t)\right)\right] \tag{8}$$

Since the descent rate k is arbitrary, we can absorb α into k. Using equation 8, we can approximate the gradient descent technique as follows:

$$y_i'(t)\approx-\hat{k}\;E\left[n_i'(t)\frac{d}{dt}f\left(\underline{y}(t)+\underline{n}(t)\right)\right] \tag{9}$$

4 Elements of the Multi-dimensional Implementation

We have designed, fabricated, and tested a chip which allows us to test these ideas. The chip implementation can be decomposed into six distinct parts:

noise source(s): an analog VLSI circuit which produces a noise function. An independent, correlation-free noise source is needed for each input dimension, designated $n_i(t)$. The noise circuit is described in [Alspector 91].

target function: a scalar function $f(y_1, y_2, \cdots, y_N)$ of N input variables, bounded below, which is to be minimized [Kirk 91]. The circuit in this case is a 4-dimensional variant of the bump circuit described in [Delbrück 91]. In the general case, this $f()$ can be any scalar function or error metric, computed by some circuit. Specifically, the function may be a neural network.

input signal(s): the inputs $y_i(t)$ to the function $f()$. These will typically be on-chip values, or real-world inputs.

multiplier circuit(s): the multiplier computes the correlation between the noise values and the function output. Offsets in the multiplication appear as systematic errors in the gradient estimate, so it is important to compensate for the offsets. Linearity is not especially important, although monotonicity is critical. Ideally, the multiplication will also have a "tanh-like" character, limiting the output range for extreme inputs.

integrator: an integration over time is approximated by a low-pass filter

differentiator: the time derivatives of the noise signals and the function are approximated by a high-pass filter.

The N inputs, $y_i(t)$, are additively "contaminated" with the noise signals, $n_i(t)$, by capacitive coupling, producing $v_i(t) = y_i(t) + n_i(t)$, the inputs to the function $f()$. The function output is differentiated, as are the noise functions. Each differentiated noise signal is correlated with the differentiated function output, using the multipliers. The results are low-pass filtered, providing N partial derivative estimates, for the N input dimensions, shown for 4 dimensions in Fig. 3.

The function $f()$ is implemented as an 4-dimensional extension of Delbrück's [Delbrück 91] bump circuit. Details of the N-dimensional bump circuit can be found in [Kirk 93]. For learning and other applications, the function $f()$ can implement some other error metric to be minimized.

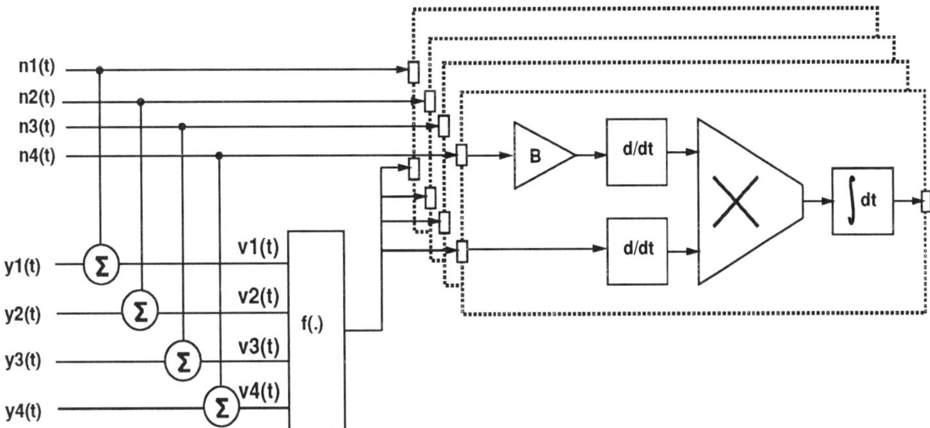

Figure 3: Block diagram for a 4-dimensional gradient estimation circuit.

5 Chip Results

We have tested chips implementing the gradient estimation and gradient descent techniques described in this paper. Figure 4 shows the gradient estimate, without the closed loop descent process. Figure 5 shows the trajectories of two state variables during the 2D gradient descent process. Figure 6 shows the gradient descent process in operation on a 2D bump surface, and Fig. 7 shows how, using appropriate choice of noise scale, we can perform annealing using the gradient estimation hardware.

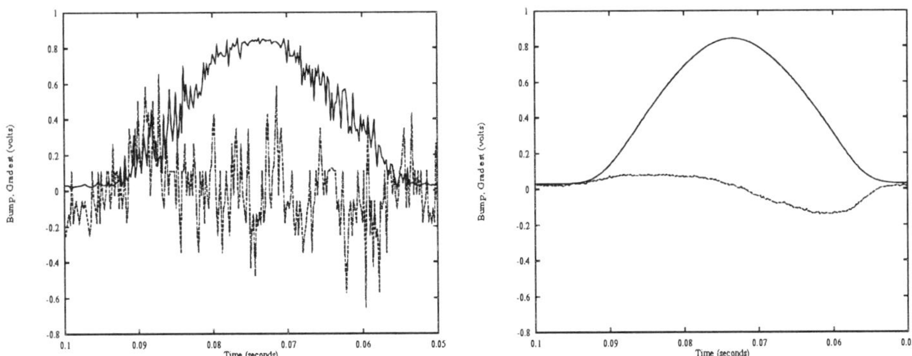

Figure 4: Measured Chip Data: 1D Gradient Estimate. Upper curves are 1D bump output as the input $y(t)$ is a slow triangle wave. Lower curves are gradient estimates. (left) raw data, and (right) average of 1024 runs.

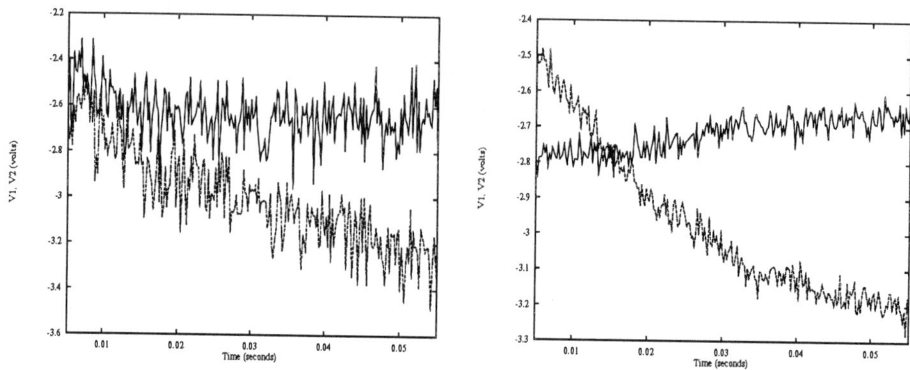

Figure 5: Measured Chip Data: 2D Gradient Descent. The curves above show the function optimization by gradient descent for 2 variables. Each curve represents the path of one of the state variables $\underline{y}(t)$ from some initial values to the values for which the function $f()$ is minimized. (left) raw data, and (right) average of 8 runs.

6 Conclusions

We have implemented an analog VLSI structure for performing continuous multi-dimensional gradient descent, and the gradient estimation uses only local information. The circuitry is compact and easily extensible to higher dimensions. This implementation leads to on-chip multi-dimensional optimization, such as is needed to perform on-chip learning for a hardware neural network. We can also perform a kind of annealing by adding a schedule to the scale of the noise input. Our approach also has some drawbacks, however. The gradient estimation is sensitive to the input offsets in the multipliers and integrators, since those offsets result in systematic errors. Also, the gradient estimation technique adds noise to the input signals.

We hope that with only small additional circuit complexity, the performance of analog VLSI circuits can be greatly increased by permitting them to be intrinsically adaptive. On-chip implementation of an approximate gradient descent technique is an important step in this direction.

Acknowledgements

This work was supported in part by an AT&T Bell Laboratories Ph.D. Fellowship, and by grants from Apple, DEC, Hewlett Packard, and IBM. Additional support was provided by NSF (ASC-89-20219), as part of the NSF/DARPA STC for Computer Graphics and Scientific Visualization. All opinions, findings, conclusions, or recommendations expressed in this document are those of the author and do not necessarily reflect the views of the sponsoring agencies.

References

[Alspector 93] Alspector, J., R. Meir, B. Yuhas, and A. Jayakumar, "A Parallel Gradient

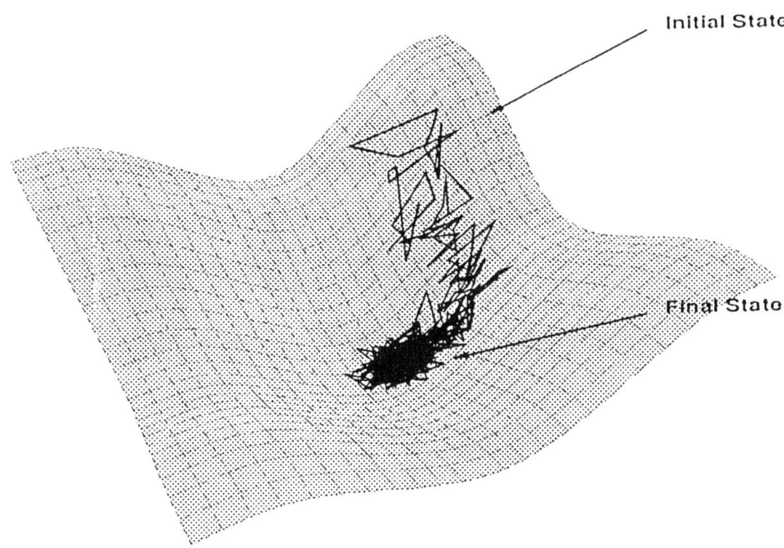

Figure 6: Measured Chip Data: 2D Gradient Descent. Here we see the results for 2D gradient descent on a 2D bump surface. Both the bump surface and the descent path are actual data measured from our chips.

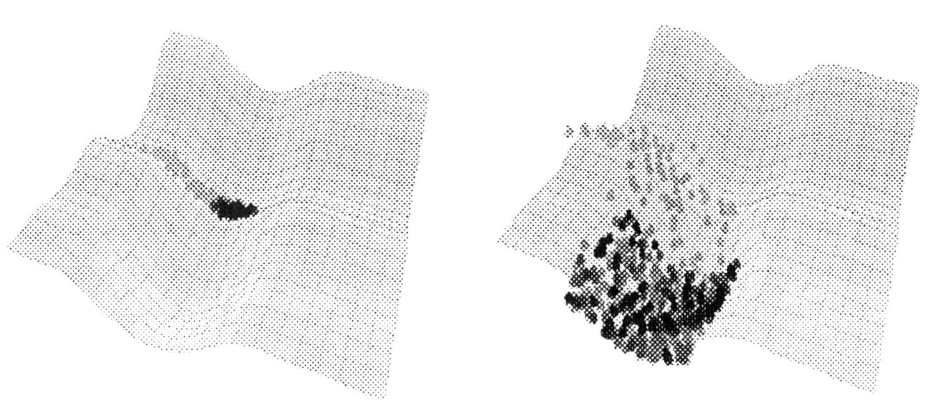

Figure 7: Measured Chip Data: 2D Gradient Descent and Annealing. Here we see the effects of varying the amplitude of the noise. The dots represent points along the optimization path. At left, with small magnitude noise, the process descends to a local minimum. At right, with larger magnitude, the descent process escapes to the global minimum. A schedule of gradually decreasing noise amplitude could reduce the probability of getting caught in undesirable local minima, and increase the probability of converging to a small region near a more desirable minimum, or even the global minimum.

Descent Method for Learning in Analog VLSI Neural Networks," in *Advances in Neural Information Processing Systems*, Vol. 5, Morgan Kaufman, San Mateo, CA, 1993.

[Alspector 91] Alspector, J., J. W. Gannett, S. Haber, M. B. Parker, and R. Chu, "A VLSI–Efficient Technique for Generating Multiple Uncorrelated Noise Sources and Its Application to Stochastic Neural Networks," IEEE Transactions on Circuits and Systems, Vol.38, no.1, pp.109–123, January, 1991.

[Alspector 88] Alspector, J., B. Gupta, and R. B. Allen, "Performance of a stochastic learning microchip," in *Advances in Neural Information Processing Systems, vol. I,* Denver Colorado, Nov. 1988. D. S. Touretzky, ed., Morgan Kauffman Publishers, 1989, pp. 748–760.

[Anderson, Kerns 92] Anderson, Brooke P., and Douglas Kerns, "Using Noise Injection and Correlation in Analog Hardware to Estimate Gradients," submitted to IEEE Transactions on Circuits and Systems I: Fundamental Theory and Applications.

[Anderson 92] Anderson, Brooke P., "Low-pass Filters as Expectation Operators for Multiplicative Noise," submitted to IEEE Transactions on Circuits and Systems I: Fundamental Theory and Applications.

[Cauwenberghs 93] Cauwenberghs, Gert, "A Fast Stochastic Error-Descent Algorithm for Supervised Learning and Optimization," in *Advances in Neural Information Processing Systems*, Vol. 5, Morgan Kaufman, San Mateo, CA, 1993.

[Delbrück 91] Delbrück, Tobias, " 'Bump' Circuits for Computing Similarity and Dissimilarity of Analog Voltages," Proceedings of International Joint Conference on Neural Networks, July 8-12, 1991, Seattle Washington, pp I-475–479. (Extended version as Caltech Computation and Neural Systems Memo Number 10.)

[Dembo 90] Dembo, A., and T. Kailath, "Model-Free Distributed Learning," IEEE Transactions on Neural Networks, Vol. 1, No. 1, pp. 58-70, 1990.

[Flower 93] Flower, B., and M. Jabri, "Summed Weight Neuron Perturbation: An $\mathcal{O}(n)$ Improvement over Weight Perturbation," in *Advances in Neural Information Processing Systems*, Vol. 5, Morgan Kaufman, San Mateo, CA, 1993.

[Jabri 91] Jabri, M., S. Pickard, P. Leong, Z. Chi, and B. Flower, "Architectures and Implementations of Right Ventricular Apex Signal Classifiers for Pacemakers," IEEE Neural Information Processing Systems 1991 (NIPS 91), Morgan Kaufman, San Diego, 1991.

[Kerns 92] Kerns, Douglas, "A Compact Noise Source for VLSI Applications," submitted to IEEE Transactions on Circuits and Systems I: Fundamental Theory and Applications.

[Kirk 91] Kirk, David, Kurt Fleischer, and Alan Barr, "Constrained Optimization Applied to the Parameter Setting Problem for Analog Circuits," IEEE Neural Information Processing Systems 1991 (NIPS 91), Morgan Kaufman, San Diego, 1991.

[Kirk 93] Kirk, David, "Accurate and Precise Computation using Analog VLSI, with Applications to Computer Graphics and Neural Networks," Ph.D. Thesis, California Institute of Technology, Caltech-CS-TR-93-??, June, 1993.

[Mead 89] Mead, Carver, "Analog VLSI and Neural Systems," Addison-Wesley, 1989.

[Platt 89] Platt, John, "Constrained Optimization for Neural Networks and Computer Graphics," Ph.D. Thesis, California Institute of Technology, Caltech-CS-TR-89-07, June, 1989.

[Umminger 89] Umminger, Christopher B., and Steven P. DeWeerth, "Implementing Gradient Following in Analog VLSI," Advanced Research in VLSI, MIT Press, Boston, 1989, pp. 195-208.

An Object-Oriented Framework for the Simulation of Neural Nets

A. Linden **Th. Sudbrak** **Ch. Tietz** **F. Weber**
German National Research Center for Computer Science
D-5205 Sankt Augustin 1, Germany

Abstract

The field of software simulators for neural networks has been expanding very rapidly in the last years but their importance is still being underestimated. They must provide increasing levels of assistance for the design, simulation and analysis of neural networks. With our object-oriented framework (SESAME) we intend to show that very high degrees of transparency, manageability and flexibility for complex experiments can be obtained. SESAME's basic design philosophy is inspired by the natural way in which researchers explain their computational models. Experiments are performed with networks of building blocks, which can be extended very easily. Mechanisms have been integrated to facilitate the construction and analysis of very complex architectures. Among these mechanisms are the automatic configuration of building blocks for an experiment and multiple inheritance at run-time.

1 Introduction

In recent years a lot of work has been put into the development of simulation systems for neural networks [1, 2, 3, 4, 5, 6, 7, 9, 10, 11, 12]. Unfortunately their importance has been largely underestimated. In future, software environments will provide increasing levels of assistance for the design, simulation and analysis of neural networks as well as for other pattern and signal processing architectures. Yet large improvements are still necessary in order to fulfill the growing demands of the research community. Despite the existence of at least 100 software simulators, only very few of them can deal with, e. g. multiple learning paradigms and applications, very large experiments.

In this paper we describe an object oriented framework for the simulation of neural networks and try to illustrate its flexibility, transparency and extendability. The prototype called SESAME has been implemented using C++ (on UNIX workstations running X-Windows) and currently consists of about 39.000 lines of code, implementing over 80 classes for neural network algorithms, pattern handling, graphical output and other utilities.

2 Philosophy of Design

The main objective of SESAME is to allow for arbitrary combinations of different learning and pattern processing paradigms (e. g. supervised, unsupervised, self-supervised or reinforcement learning) and different application domains (e. g. pattern recognition, vision, speech or control). To some degree the design of SESAME has been based on the observation that many researchers explain their neural information processing systems (NIPS) with block-diagrams. Such a block diagram consists of a group of primitive elements (building blocks). Each building block has inputs and outputs and a functional relationship between them. Connections describe the flow of data between the building blocks. Scripts related to the building blocks specify the flow of control. Complex NIPS are constructed from a library of building blocks (possibly themselves whole NIPS), which are interconnected via uniform communication links.

3 SESAME Design and Features

All building blocks share a list of common components. They all have *insites* and *outsites* that build the endpoints of communication links. *Datafields* contain the data (e. g. weight matrices or activation vectors) which is sent over the links. *Action functions* process input from the insites, update the internal state and compute appropriate outputs, e. g. performing weight updates and propagating activation or error vectors. *Command functions* provide a uniform user interface for all building blocks. *Scripts* control the execution of action or command functions or other scripts. They may contain conditional statements and loops as control structures. Furthermore a *symbol table* allows run-time access to parameters of the building block as learning rates, sizes, data ranges etc. Many other internal data structures and routines are provided for the *administration* and maintainance of building blocks.

The description of an experiment may be divided into the functional description of the building blocks (which can be done either in C++ or in the high-level description language, see below), the connection topology of the building blocks used, the control flow defined by scripts and a set of parameters for each of the building blocks.

Design Highlights

3.1 User Interface

The user interface is text oriented and may be used interactively as well as script driven. This implies that any command that the user may choose interactively can also be used in a command file that is called non-interactively. This allows the easy adaption of arbitrary user interface structures from a primitive batch interface for large offline simulatiors to a fancy graphical user interface for online experiments.

Another consequence is that experiments are specified in the same command language that is used for the user interface. The user may thus easily switch from description files from previously saved experiments to the interactive manipulation of already loaded ones. Since the complete structure of an experiment is accessible at runtime, this not only means manipulation of parameters but also includes any imaginable modification of the experiment topology. The experienced user can, for example, include new building blocks for experiment observation or statistical evaluation and connect them to any point of the communication structure. Deletion of building blocks is possible, as well as modifying control scripts. The complete state of the experiment (i. e. the current values of all relevant data) can be saved for later experiments.

3.2 Hierarchies

In SESAME we distinguish two kinds of building blocks: *terminal* and *non-terminal* blocks. Non-terminal building blocks are used to structure a complex experiment into hierarchies of abstract building blocks containing substructures of an experiment that may themselves contain hierarchies of substructures. Terminal building blocks provide the data structures and primitive functions that are used in scripts (of non-terminal blocks) to compose the network algorithms. A non-terminal building block hides its internal structure and provides abstract sites and scripts as an interface to its internals. Therefore it appears as a terminal building block to the outside and may be used as such for the construction of an experiment. This construction is equivalent to the building of a single non-terminal building block (the *Experiment*) that encloses the complete experiment structure.

3.3 Construction of New Building Blocks

The functionality of SESAME can be extended using two different approaches. New terminal building blocks can be programmed deriving from existing C++ classes or new non-terminal building blocks may be assembled by using previously defined building blocks:

3.3.1 Programming New Terminal Building Blocks

Terminal building blocks can be designed by derivation from already existing C++ classes. The complete administration structure and possible predefined properties are inherited from the parent classes. In order to add new properties — e. g. new action functions, symbols, datafields, insites or outsites — a set of basic operations is being provided by the framework. One should note that new algorithms and structures can be added to a class without any changes to the framework of SESAME.

3.3.2 Composing New Non-Terminal Building Blocks

Non-terminal building blocks can be combined from libraries of already designed terminal or non-terminal blocks. See for an example fig. ??, where a set of building blocks build a multilayer net which can be collapsed into one building block and reused in other contexts. Here insites and outsites define an interface between building blocks on adjacent levels of the experiment hierarchy. The flow of data inside the new building block is controlled by scripts that call action functions or scripts of its components. Such an abstract building block may be saved in a library for reuse. Even whole experiments can be collapsed to one building block leaving a lot of possibilities for the experimenter to cope with very large and complicated experiments.

3.3.3 Deriving New Non-Terminal Building Blocks

A powerful mechanism for organizing very complex experiments and allowing high degrees of flexibility and reuse is offered by the concept of inheritance. The basic mechanism executes the description of the parent building block and thereafter the description of the refinements for the derived block. All this may be done interactively, thus additional refinements can be added at runtime. Even the set of formal parameters of a block may be inherited and/or refined. Multiple inheritance is also possible.

For an example consider a general function approximator which may be used at many points in a more complex architecture. It can be implemented as an abstract base building block, only supplying basic structure as input and output and basic operations as "propagate input" and "train". Derivations of it then implement the algorithm and structure actually used. Statistical routines, visualization facilities, pattern handling and other utilities can be added as further specializations to a basic function approximator.

3.3.4 Parameters and Generic Building Blocks

A building block may also define formal parameters that allow the user to configure it at the time of its instantiation or inclusion into some other non-terminal building block. Thus non-terminal building blocks can be generic. They may be parameterized with types for interior building blocks, names of scripts etc. With this mechanism a multilayer net can be created with an arbitrary type of node or weight layers.

3.4 Autoconfiguration

When a user defines an experiment, only parameters that are really important must be specified. Redundant parameters, that depend on other paremeters of other building blocks, can often be determined automatically. In SESAME this is done via a constraint satisfaction process. Not only does this mechanism avoid specification of redundant information and check experiment parameters for consistency, but it also enables the construction of generic structures. Communication links between outsites and insites of building blocks check data for matching types. Building blocks impose additional constraints on the data formats of their own sites. Constraints are formed upon information about the base types, dimensions, sizes and ranges of the data sent between the sites. The primary source of information are the parameters given to the building blocks at the time of their instantiation. After building the whole experiment, a propagation mechanism iteratively tries to complete missing information in order to satisfy all constraints. Thus information which is determined in one building block of the experiment may spread all over the experiment topology. As an example one can think of a building block which loads patterns from a file. The dimensionality of these patterns may be used automatically to configure building blocks holding weight layers for a multilayer network.

This autoconfiguration can be considered as finding the unique solution of set of equations where three cases may occur: inconsistency (contradiction between two information sources at one site), deadlock (insufficient information for a site) or success (unique solution). Inconsistencies are a proof of an erroneous design. Deadlocks indicate that the user has missed something.

3.5 Experiment Observation

Graphical output, file I/O or statistical analysis are usually not performed within the normal building blocks which comprise the network algorithms. These features are built into specialized utility building blocks that can be integrated at any point of the experiment topology, even during experiment runs.

4 Classes of Building Blocks

SESAME supports a rich taxonomy of building blocks for experiment construction:

For neural networks one can use building blocks for complete *node* and *weight* layers to construct multilayer networks. This granulation was chosen to allow for a more efficient way of computation than with building blocks that contain single neurons only. This level of abstraction still captures enough flexibility for many paradigms of NIPS. However, terminal building blocks for complete classes of neural nets are also provided if efficiency is first demand.

Mathematical building blocks perform arithmetic, trigonometric or more general mathematical transformations, as scaling and normalization. Building blocks for *coding* provide functionality to encode or decode patterns.

Utility building blocks provide access to the filesystem, where not only input or output files can be dealt with but also other UNIX processes by means of pipes. Others simply store structured or unstructured patterns to make them randomly accessible.

Graphical building blocks can be used to display any kind of data no matter if weight matrices, activation or error vectors are involved. This is a consequence of the abstract view of combining building blocks with different functionality but a uniform data interface. There are special building blocks for *analysis* which allow for clustering, averaging, error analysis, plotting and other statistical evaluations.

Finally simulations (cartpole, robot-arms etc.) can also be incorporated into building blocks. Real-world applications or other software packages can be accessed via specialized interface blocks.

5 Examples

Some illustrative examples for experiments can be found in [?] and many additional and more complex examples in the SESAME documentation. The full documentation as well as the software are available via ftp (see below).

Here we sketch only briefly, how paradigms and applications from different domains can be easily glued together as a natural consequence of the design of SESAME. Figure ?? shows part of an experiment in which a robot arm is controlled via a modified Kohonen feature map and a potential field path planner. The three building blocks, *workspace*, *map* and *planner* form the main part of the experiment. *Workspace* contains the simulation for the controlled robot arm and its graphical display and *map* contains the feature map that is used to transform the map coordinates proposed by *planner* to robot arm configurations. The map has been trained in another experiment to map the configuration space of the robot arm and the planner may have stored the positions of obstacles with respect to the map coordinates in still another experiment. The configuration and obstacle map have been saved as the results of the earlier experiments and are reused here. The *map* was taken from a library that contains different flavors of feature maps in form of non-terminal building blocks and hides the details of its complicated inner structure. The *Views* help to visualize the experiment and the *Buffers* are used to provide start values for the experiment runs. A *Subtractor* is shown that generates control inputs for the *workspace* by simply performing vector subtraction on subsequently proposed state vectors for the robot arm simulation.

6 Epilogue

We designed an object-oriented neural network simulator to cope with the increasing demands imposed by the current lines of research. Our implementation offers a high degree of flexibility for the experimental setup. Building blocks may be combined to build complex experiments in short development cycles. The simulator framework provides mechanisms to detect errors in the experiment setup and to provide parameters for generic subexperiments. A prototype was built, that is in use as our main research tool for neural network experiments and is constantly refined. Future developments are still necessary, e. g. to provide a graphical interface and more elegant mechanisms for the reuse of predefined building blocks. Further research issues are the parallelization of SESAME and the compilation of experiment parts to optimize their performance.

The software and its preliminary documentation can be obtained via ftp at `ftp.gmd.de` in the directory `gmd/as/sesame`. Unfortunately we cannot provide professional support at this moment.

Acknowledgments go to the numerous programmers and users of SESAME for all the work, valuable discussions and hints.

References

[1] B. Angeniol and P. Treleaven. The PYGMALION neural network programming environment. In R. Eckmiller, editor, *Advanced Neural Computers*, pages 167 – 175, Amsterdam, 1990. Elsevier Science Publishers B. V. (North-Holland).

[2] N. Goddard, K. Lynne, T. Mintz, and L. Bukys. Rochester connectionist simulator. Technical Report TR-233 (revised), Computer Science Dept, University of Rochester, 1989.

[3] G. L. Heileman, H. K. Brown, and Georgiopoulos. Simulation of artificial neural network models using an object-oriented software paradigm. In *Proceedings of the International Joint Conference on Neural Networks*, pages II–133 – II–136, Washington, DC, 1990.

[4] NeuralWare Inc. Neuralworks professional ii user manual. 1989.

[5] T. T. Kraft. ANSpec tutorial workbook. San Diego, CA, 1990.

[6] T. Lange, J.B. Hodges, M. Fuenmayor, and L. Belyaev. Descartes: Development environment for simulating hybrid connectionist architectures. In *Proceedings of the Eleventh Annual Conference of the Cognitive Science Society, Ann Arbor, MI, August 1989*, 1989.

[7] A. Linden and C. Tietz. Combining multiple neural network paradigms and applications using SESAME. In *Proceedings of the Internation Joint Conference on Neural Networks IJCNN – Baltimore*. IEEE, 1992.

[8] Y. Miyata. A user's guide to SunNet version 5.6 – a tool for constructing, running, and looking into a PDP network. 1990.

[9] J. M. J. Murre and S. E. Kleynenberg. The MetaNet network environment for the development of modular neural networks. In *Proceedings of the International Neural Network Conference, Paris, 1990*, pages 717 – 720. IEEE, 1990.

[10] M.A. Wilson, S.B. Upinder, J.D. Uhley, and J.M. Bower. GENESIS: A system for simulating neural networks. In David S. Touretzky, editor, *Advances in Neural Information Processing Systems I*, pages 485–492. Morgan Kaufmann, 1988. Collected papers of the IEEE Conference on Neural Information Processing Systems – Natural and Synthetic, Denver, CO, November 1988.

[11] A. Zell, N. Mache, T. Sommer, and T. Korb. Recent developments of the snns neural network simulator. In *SPIE Conference on Applications of Artificial Neural Networks*. Universit"at Stuttgart, April 1991.

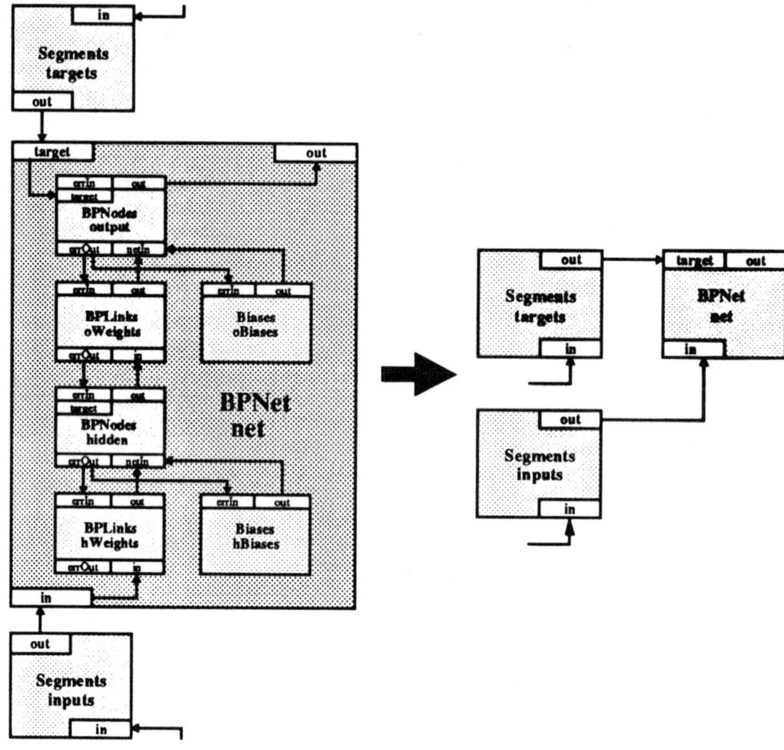

Figure 1: Integration of several terminal building blocks into a non-terminal building block with the Backpropagation example.

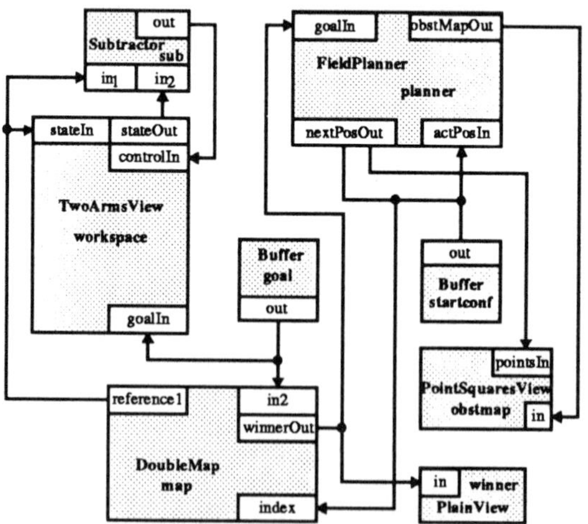

Figure 2: Robot arm control with a hybrid controller

Attractor Neural Networks with Local Inhibition: from Statistical Physics to a Digital Programmable Integrated Circuit

E. Pasero
Dipartimento di Elettronica
Politecnico di Torino
I-10129 Torino, Italy

R. Zecchina
Dipartimento di Fisica Teorica e INFN
Universitá di Torino
I-10125 Torino, Italy

Abstract

Networks with local inhibition are shown to have enhanced computational performance with respect to the classical Hopfield-like networks. In particular the critical capacity of the network is increased as well as its capability to store correlated patterns. Chaotic dynamic behaviour (exponentially long transients) of the devices indicates the overloading of the associative memory. An implementation based on a programmable logic device is here presented. A 16 neurons circuit is implemented whit a XILINK 4020 device. The peculiarity of this solution is the possibility to change parts of the project (weights, transfer function or the whole architecture) with a simple software download of the configuration into the XILINK chip.

1 INTRODUCTION

Attractor Neural Networks endowed with local inhibitory feedbacks, have been shown to have interesting computational performances[1]. Past effort was concentrated in studying a variety of synaptic structures or learning algorithms, while less attention was devoted to study the possible role played by different dynamical schemes. The definition of relaxation dynamics is the central problem for the study of the associative and computational capabilities in models of attractor neural networks and might be of interest also for hardware implementation in view of the constraints on the precision of the synaptic weights.

In this paper, we give a brief discussion concerning the computational and physical role played by local inhibitory interactions which lead to an effective non-monotonic transfer function for the neurons. In the last few years others models characterized by non-monotonic neurons have been proposed[2,3].

For Hebbian learning we show, numerically, that the critical capacity increases with respect to the Hopfield case and that such result can be interpreted in terms of a twofold task realized by the dynamical process. By means of local inhibition, the system dynamically selects a subspace (or subnetwork) of minimal static noise with respect to the recalled pattern; at the same time, and in the selected subspace, the retrieval of the memorized pattern is performed. The dynamic behaviour of the network, for deterministic sequential updating, range from fixed points to chaotic evolution, with the storage ratio as control parameter, the transition appearing in correspondence to the collapse of the associative performance. Resorting to two simplified versions of the model, we study the problem of their optimal performance by the replica method; in particular the role of non-monotonic functions and of subspaces dynamical selection are discussed.

In a second part of the work, the implementation of the discussed model by means of a XILINK programmable gate array is discussed. The circuit implements a 16-32 neurons network in which the analogical characteristics (such as a capacitive decay) are emulated by digital solutions. As expected, the limited resolution of the weghts does not represent a limit for the performance of the network.

2 THE MODEL: theory and performance

We study an attractor neural network composed of N three state $\pm 1, 0$ formal neurons. The ± 1 values code for the patterns (the patterns are indeed binary) and are thus used during the learning phase, while the 0-state is a *don't care* state, not belonging to the patterns code, which has only a dynamical role. The system is assumed to be fully connected and its evolution is governed by sequential or parallel updating of the following equations

$$S_i = \begin{cases} sgn(h_i) & if \quad |h_i| \leq \gamma \\ 0 & if \quad |h_i| > \gamma \end{cases} \tag{1}$$

$$h_i(t+1) = \lambda h_i(t) + \sum_{j=1}^{N} J_{ij} S_j(t) \qquad i = 1, ..., N \tag{2}$$

where γ is a dynamic threshold of the local inhibitory feedback (typically we take $\gamma(t) = \frac{1}{N}\sum_i |h_i(t-1)|$), the $\{J_{ij}\}$ are the *synaptic* conductances and λ is a capacitive decay factor of the input potential ($\lambda = e^{\frac{1}{\tau}}$, where $\tau = RC$).

The performance of the network are described in terms of two parameters which have both a dynamical and a computational simple interpretation. In particular we define the **retrieval activity** as the fraction of neurons which are not not in the zero state

$$a = \frac{1}{N} \sum_i S_i^2, \tag{3}$$

while the parameter that defines the retrieval quality is the **scaled overlap**

$$m^\mu = \frac{1}{Na} \sum_i \xi_i^\mu S_i. \tag{4}$$

where the $\{\xi_i^\mu = \pm 1,\ i = 1, N; \mu = 1, P\}$ are the memorized binary patterns. The scaled overlap can be thought simply as the overlap computed in the subspace M of the *active* neurons, $M \equiv \{i \ / \ S_i \neq 0,\ i = 1, N\}$.

Given a set of P random independent binary patterns $\{\xi_i^\mu\}$, the Hebb-Hopfield learning rule corresponds to fix the synaptic matrix J_{ij} by the additive relation $J_{ij} = \frac{1}{N} \sum_{\mu=1}^{P} \xi_i^\mu \xi_j^\mu$ (with $J_{ii} = 0$). The effect of the dynamical process defined by (1) and (2) is the selection of subspaces M of active neurons in which the static noise is minimized (such subspaces will be hereafter referred to as *orthogonal* subspaces). Before entering in the description of the results, it is worthwhile to remember that, in Hopfield-like attractor neural networks, the mean of cross correlation fluctuations produce in the local fields of the neurons a static noise, referred to as cross-talk of the memories. Together with temporal correlations, the static noise is responsible of the phase transition of the neural networks from associative memory to spin-glass. More precisely, when the Hopfield model is in a fixed point ξ^σ which belongs to the set of memories, the local fields are given by $h_i \xi_i^\sigma = 1 + R_i^\sigma$ where $R_i^\sigma = \frac{1}{N} \sum_{\mu \neq \sigma} \sum_{j \neq i} \xi_i^\mu \xi_j^\mu \xi_i^\sigma \xi_j^\sigma$ is the static noise (gaussian distribution with 0 mean and variance $\sqrt{\alpha}$).

The preliminary performance study of the model under discussion have revealed several new basic features, in particular: (i) the critical capacity, for the Hebb learning rule, results increased up to $\alpha_c \approx 0.33$ (instead of 0.14[4]); (ii) the mean cross correlation fluctuations computed in the selected subspaces is minimized by the dynamical process in the region $\alpha < \alpha_c$; (iii) in correspondence to the associative transition the system goes through a dynamic transition from fixed points to chaotic trajectories.

The quantitative results concerning associative performance, are obtained by means of extended simulations. A typical simulation takes the memorized patterns as initial configurations and lets the system relax until it reaches a stationary point. The quantity describing the performance of the network as an associative memory is the mean scaled overlap m between the final stationary states and the memorized patterns, used as initial states. As the number of memorized configurations grows, one observes a threshold at $\alpha = \alpha_c \approx 0.33$ beyond which the stored states become unstable. (numerical results were performed for networks of size up to $N = 1000$). We observe that since the recall of the patterns is performed with no errors (up to

$\alpha \approx 0.31$), also the number of stored bits in the synaptic matrix results increased with respect to the Hopfield case.

The typical size of the sub-networks D_M, like the network capacity, depends on the threshold parameter γ and on the kind of updating: for $\gamma(t) = \frac{1}{N}\sum_i |h_i(t-1)|$ and parallel updating we find $D_M \simeq N/2$ ($\alpha_c = 0.33$).

The static noise reduction corresponds to the minimization of the mean fluctuation of the cross correlations (cross talk) in the subspaces, defined by

$$C = \frac{1}{P}\sum_{\sigma}\sum_{\mu\neq\sigma}\left(\frac{1}{aN}\sum_{i=1}^{N}\xi_i^{\mu}\xi_i^{\sigma}\epsilon_i^{\sigma}\right)^2 = \frac{1}{P}\sum_{\sigma}\sum_{\mu\neq\sigma}\left(\frac{1}{aN}\sum_{i\in M}\xi_i^{\mu}\xi_i^{\sigma}\right)^2 \qquad (5)$$

where $\epsilon_i^{\sigma} = 1$ if $i \in M$ in pattern σ and zero otherwise, as a function of α. Under the dynamical process (1) and (2), C does not follow a statistical law but undergoes a minimization that qualitatively explains the increase in the storage capacity. For $\alpha < \alpha_c$, once the system has relaxed in a stationary subspace, the model becomes equivalent (in the subspace) to a Hopfield network with a static noise term which is no longer random. The statistical mechanics of the combinatorial task of minimizing the *noise-energy* term (5) can be studied analytically by the replica method; the results are of general interest in that give an upper bound to the performance of networks endowed with Hebb-like synaptic matrices and with the possibility selecting optimal subnetworks for retrieval dynamics of the patterns[8].

As already stated, the behaviour of the neural network as a dynamical system is directly related to its performance as an associative memory. The system shows an abrupt transition in the dynamics, from fixed points to chaotic exponentially long transients, in correspondence to the value of the storage ratio at which the memorized configurations become unstable. The only (external) control parameter of the model as a dynamical system is the storage ratio $\alpha = P/N$. Dynamic complex behaviour appears as a clear signal of saturation of the attractor neural network and does not depend on the symmetry of the couplings.

As a concluding remark concerning this short description of the network performance, we observe that the dynamic selection of subspaces seems to take advantage of finite size effects allowing the storage of correlated patterns also with the simple Hebb rule. Analytical and numerical work is in progress on this point, devoted to clarify the performance with spatially correlated patterns[5].

Finally, we end this theoretical section by addressing the problem of optimal performance for a different choice of the synaptic weights. In this direction, it is of basic interest to understand whether a dynamical scheme which allows for dynamic selection of subnetworks provides a neural network model with enhanced optimal capacity with respect to the classical spin models. Assuming that nothing is known about the couplings, one can consider the J_{ij} as dynamical variables and study the fractional volume in the space of interactions that makes the patterns fixed points of the dynamics. Following Gardner and Derrida[6], we describe the problem in terms of a cost-energy function and study its statistical mechanics: for a generic choice of the $\{J_{ij}\}$, the cost function E_i is defined to be the number of patterns such that a given site i is wrong (with respect to (1))

$$E_i(\{J_{ij}\},\{\epsilon_i^\mu\}) = \sum_{\mu=1}^{P}\left[\epsilon_i^\mu\left(\Theta(h_i^\mu\xi_i^\mu+\gamma)-\Theta(h_i^\mu\xi_i^\mu)\right)+(1-\epsilon_i^\mu)\Theta(\gamma^2-h_i^{\mu 2})\right] \quad (6)$$

where Θ is the step function, the $h_i^\mu = \frac{1}{\sqrt{N}}\sum_j J_{ij}\xi_j^\mu\epsilon_j^\mu$ are the local fields, γ is the threshold of the inhibitory feedback and with $\epsilon_i^\mu = \{0,1\}$ being the variables that identify the subspace M ($\epsilon_i^\mu = 1$ if $i \in M$ and zero otherwise).

In order to estimate the optimal capacity, one should perform the replica theory on the following partition function

$$Z = \mathrm{Tr}_{\{\epsilon_i^\mu/\sum_i\epsilon_i^\mu=aN\}}\int\prod_{i\neq j} dJ_{ij}\delta(\sum_{j(\neq i)} J_{ij}^2 - N)\mathrm{e}^{-\beta\sum_i E_i} \quad (7)$$

Since the latter task seems unmanageable, as a first step we resort to two simplified version of the model which, separately, retain its main characteristics (subspaces and non-monotonicity); in particular:

(i) we assume that the $\{\epsilon_i^\mu\}$ are quenched random variables, distributed according to $P(\epsilon_i^\mu) = (1-A)\delta(\epsilon_i^\mu) + A\delta(\epsilon_i^\mu - 1)$, $A \in [0,1]$;

(ii) we consider the case of a two-state (±1) non-monotonic transfer function.

For lack of space, here we list only the final results. The expressions of the R.S. critical capacity for the models are, respectively:

$$\alpha_c^{R.S.}(\gamma;A) = \left\{2(1-A)\int_0^\gamma D\zeta(\gamma-\zeta)^2 + \frac{A}{2} + A\int_\gamma^\infty D\zeta(\gamma-\zeta)^2\right\}^{-1} \quad (8)$$

$$\alpha_c^{R.S.}(\gamma) = \left\{\int_0^{\frac{\gamma}{2}} D\zeta\zeta^2 + \int_{\frac{\gamma}{2}}^\infty D\zeta(\gamma-\zeta)^2\right\}^{-1} \quad (9)$$

where $D\zeta = \frac{1}{\sqrt{2\pi}}\mathrm{e}^{\frac{-\zeta^2}{2}}d\zeta$ (for (9) see also Ref.[4]).

The values of critical capacity one finds are much higher than the monotonic perceptron capacity ($\alpha_c = 2$). Unfortunately, the latter results are not reliable in that the stability analysis shows that the RS solution are unstable. Replica symmetry breaking is thus required. All the details concerning the computation with one step in replica symmetry breaking of the critical capacity and stabilities distribution can be found in Ref.[9]. Here we just quote the final quantitative result concerning optimal capacity for the non-monotonic two-state model: numerical evaluation of the saddle-point equations (for unbiased patterns) gives $\alpha_c(\gamma^{opt}) \approx 4.8$ with $\gamma^{opt} \approx 0.8$, the corresponding R.S. value from (9) being $\alpha_c^{R.S.} \approx 10.5$.

3 HARDWARE IMPLEMENTATION: a digital programmable integrated circuit

The performance of the network discussed in the above section points out the good behavior of the *dynamical* approach. Our goal is now to investigate the performance of this system with special hardware. Commercial neural chips[9] and[10] are not feasible: the featu res of our net require non monotonic transfer characteristic due to local inhibitions. These aspects are not allowed in traditional networks. The implementation of a full custom chip is, on the other side, an hasty choice. The model is still being studied: new developments must be expected in the next future. Therefore we decided to build a prototype based on programmable logic circuits. This solution allows us to implement the circuit in a short time not to the detriment of the performance. Moreover the same circuit will be easily updated to the next evolutions. After an analysis of the existing logic circuits we decided to use the FPGAs devices[11]. The reasons are that we need a large quantity of internal registers, to represent both synapses and capacitors, and the fastest interconnections. Xilinx 4000 family[12] offers us the most interesting approach: up tp 20000 gates are programmable and up to 28 K bit of Ram are available. Moreover a 3 ns propagation delay between internal blocks allow to implement very fast systems. We decided to use a XC4020 circuit with 20000 equivalent gates. Main problems related to the implementation of our model are the following: (a) number of neurons, (b) number of connections and (c) computation time parameters. (a) and (b) are obviously related to the logic device we have at our disposal. The number of gates we can use to implement the transfer function of our non monotonic neurons are mutually exclusive with the number of bits we decide to assign to the weights. The 20000 gates must be divided between logic gates and Ram cells. The parameter (c) depends on our choices in implementing the neural network. We can decide to connect the logic blocks in a sequential or in a parallel way. The global propagation time is the sum of the propagation delays of each logic block, from the the input to the output. Therefore if we put more blocks in parallel we don't increase the propagation delay and the time performance is better. Unfortunately the parallel solution clashes with the limitations of available logic blocks of our device. Therefore we decided to design two chips: the first circuit can implement 16 neurons in a faster parallell implementation and the second circuit allow us to use 32 (or more) neurons in a slower serial approach. Here we'll describe the fastest implementation.

Figure 1 shows the 16 neurons of the neural chip. Each neuron, described in figure 2, performs a sequential sum and multiplication of the outputs of the other 15 neurons by the synaptic values stored inside the internal Ram. A special circuit implements the activation function described in the previuos section. All the neurons perform these operations in a parallel way: 15 clock pulses are sufficient to perform the complete operation for the system. Figure 2 shows the circuit of the neuron. T1 is a Ram where the synapses Tij are stored after the training phase. M1 and A1 perform sums and multiplications according to our model. D1 simulates the λ decay factor: every 15 clock cycles, which correspond to a complete cycle of sum and multiplication for all the 16 neurons, this circuit decreases the input of the neuron of a factor λ. The activation function (1) is realized by F1. Such circuit emulates a three levels logic, based on -1, 0 and +1 values by using two full adder blocks. Limitation due to the electrical characteristic of the circuit, impose a maximum clock cycle of 20 MHz . The 16 neurons version of the chip takes from 4 to 6 complete computations to gain stability and every computation is 16 clock cycles long. Therefor e the network gives a stable state after 3 μs at maximum. The second version of this circuit allows to use more neurons at a lower speed. We used the Xilinx device to implement one neuron while the synapses and the capacitors are stored in an external fast memory. The single neuron is time multiplexed in order to emulate a large number identical devices. At each step, both synapses and state variables are downloaded and uploaded from an external memory. This solution is obviously slower than the first one but a larger number of nerons can be implemented. A 32 neurons version takes about 6 μs to reach a stable configuration.

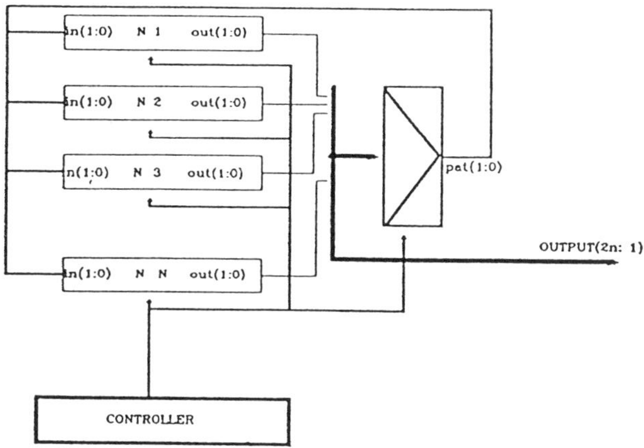

Figure 1 - Neural Chip

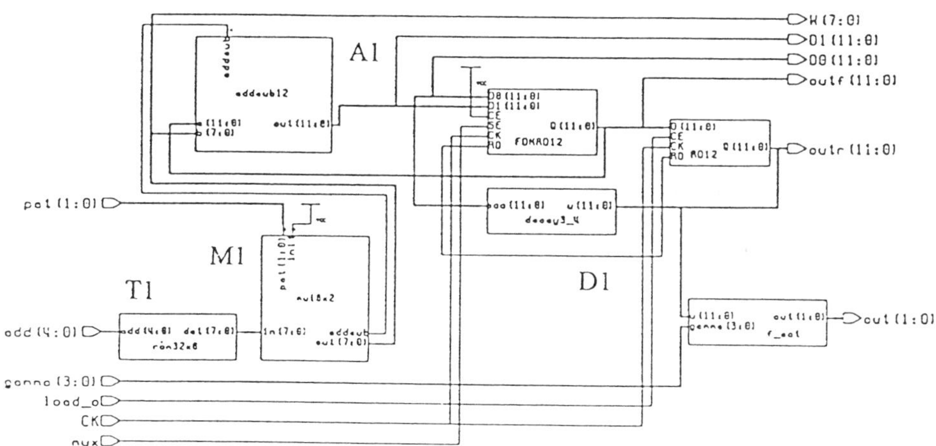

Figure 2 - Neuron

4 CONCLUSION

A modified approach to attractor neural networks and its implementation on a XILINK XC4020 FPGA was discussed. The chip is now under test. Six μs are sufficient for the relaxation of the system in a stable state, and the recognition of an input pattern is thus quite fast. A next step will be the definition of a multiple chip system endowed with more than 32 neurons, with the weights stored in an external fast memory.

Acknowledgements

This work was partially supported by the *Annethe*-INFN Italian project and by *Progetto finalizzato sistemi informatici e calcolo parallelo* of CNR under grant N. 91.00884.PF69.

References

[1] R. Zecchina, "Computational and Physical Role of Local Inhibition in Attractor Neural Networks: a Simple Model," *Parallel Architectures and Neural Networks*, edt. E.R. Caianiello, World Scientific (1992).

[2] M. Morita, S. Yoshizawa, H. Nakano, "Analysis and Improvement of the Dynamics of Autocorrelated Associative Memory," *IEICE Trans.* **J73-D-II**, 232 (1990).

[3] K. Kobayashi, "On the Capacity of a Neuron with a Non-Monotone Output Function," *Network*, **2**, 237 (1991).

[4] D.J. Amit, M. Gutfreund, H. Sompolinsky, "Storing Infinite Numbers of Patterns in a Spin-Glass Model of Neural Networks," *Phys. Rev. Lett.*, **55**, 1530 (1985).

[5] G. Boffetta, N. Brunel, R. Monasson, R. Zecchina, in preparation (1993).

[6] E. Gardner, B. Deridda, "Optimal Storage Properties of Neural Network Models," *J. Phys.*, **A21**, 271 (1988).

[7] G. Boffetta, R. Monasson, R. Zecchina, "Symmetry Breaking in Non-Monotonic Neural Networks," in preparation (1992).

[8] N. Brunel, R. Zecchina, "Statistical Mechanics of Optimal Memory Retrieval in the Space of Dynamic Neuronal Activities," preprint (1993).

[9] "An electrical Trainable Artificial Neural Network", proceedings of IJCNN, 1989, S. Diego.

[10] M. Dzwonczyk, M.Leblanc, "INCA: An Integrated Neurocomputing Architecture", proceedings of AIAA Computing in Aerospace, October 1991

[11] W.R. Moore, W. Luk, "FPGAs", Abingdon EE-CS Books, 1991

[12] "The XC4000 Data Book", Xilinx, 1991

Hybrid Circuits of Interacting Computer Model and Biological Neurons

Sylvie Renaud-LeMasson*
Department of Physics
Brandeis University
Waltham, MA 02254

Gwendal LeMasson#
Department of Biology
Brandeis University
Waltham, MA 02254

Eve Marder
Department of Biology
Brandeis University
Waltham, MA 02254

L.F. Abbott
Department of Physics
Brandeis University
Waltham, MA 02254

Abstract

We demonstrate the use of a digital signal processing board to construct hybrid networks consisting of computer model neurons connected to a biological neural network. This system operates in real time, and the synaptic connections are realistic effective conductances. Therefore, the synapses made from the computer model neuron are integrated correctly by the postsynaptic biological neuron. This method provides us with the ability to add additional, completely known elements to a biological network and study their effect on network activity. Moreover, by changing the parameters of the model neuron, it is possible to assess the role of individual conductances in the activity of the neuron, and in the network in which it participates.

*Present address, IXL, Université de Bordeaux 1-Enserb, CNRSURA 846, 351 crs de la Liberation, 33405 Talence Cedex, France.

#Present address, LNPC, CNRS, Université de Bordeaux 1, Place de Dr. Peyneau, 33120 Arcachon, France

1 INTRODUCTION

A primary goal in neuroscience is to understand how the electrical properties of individual neurons contribute to the complex behavior of the networks in which they are found. However, the experimentalist wishing to assess the contribution of a given neuron or synapse in network function is hampered by lack of adequate tools. For example, although pharmacological agents are often used to block synaptic connections within a network (Eisen and Marder, 1982), or individual currents within a neuron (Tierney and Harris-Warrick, 1992), it is rarely possible to do precise pharmacological dissections of network function. Computational models of neurons and networks (Koch and Segev, 1989) allow the investigator the control over parameters not possible with pharmacology. However, because realistic computer models are always based on inadequate biophysical data, the investigator must always be concerned that the simulated system may differ from biological reality in a critical way. We have developed a system that allows us to construct hybrid networks consisting of a model neuron interacting with a biological neural network. This allows us to work with a real biological system while retaining complete control over the parameters of the model neuron.

2 THE MODEL NEURON

Biophysical data describing the ionic currents of the Lateral Pyloric (LP) neuron of the crab stomatogastric ganglion (STG) (Golowasch and Marder, 1992) were used to construct an isopotential model LP neuron using MAXIM. MAXIM is a software package that runs on MacIntosh systems and provides a graphical modeling tool for neurons and small neural networks (LeMasson, 1993). The model LP neuron used uses Hodgkin-Huxley type equations and contains a fast Na^+ conductance, a Ca^+ conductance, a delayed rectifier K^+ conductance, a transient outward current (i_A) and a hyperpolarization-activated current (i_h), as well as a leak conductance. This model is similar to that reported in Buchholtz et al. (1992) but because the raw data were refit using MAXIM, details are slightly different.

3 ARTIFICIAL SYNAPSES

Artificial chemical synapses are produced by the same method used in Sharp et al. (1993). An axoclamp in discontinuous current clamp (DCC) mode is used to record the membrane potential and inject current into the biological neurons (Fig. 1). The presynaptic membrane potential is used to control current injection into the postsynaptic neuron simulating a conductance change (rather than an injected current as in Yarom et al.). The synaptic current injected into the postsynaptic neuron depends on the programmed synaptic conductance and an investigator-determined reversal potential. The investigator also specifies the threshold and the function relating "transmitter release" to presynaptic membrane potential, as well as the time course of the synaptic conductance.

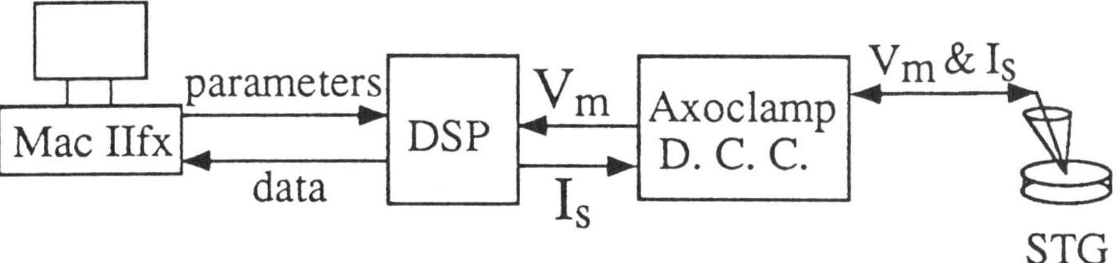

Figure 1: Schematic diagram of the system used to establish hybrid circuits.

4 HARDWARE

Our system uses a Digital Signal Processor (DSP) board with built-in A/D and D/A 16 bit-precision converters (Spectral Innovations MacDSP256KNI), with DSP32C (AT&T) mounted in a Macintosh II fx (MAC) computer. A block diagram of the system is shown Fig. 1. The parameters describing the membrane and synaptic conductances of the model neuron are stored in the MAC and are transferred to the DSP board RAM (256x32K) through the standard NuBus interface. The DSP translates the parameter files into look-up tables via a polynomial fitting procedure. The differential equations of the LP model and the artificial synapses are integrated by the DSP board, taking advantage of its optimized arithmetic functions and data access. In this system, the computational model runs on the DSP board, and the Mac IIfx functions to store and display data on the screen.

The computational speed of this system depends on the integration time step and the complexity of the model (the number of differential equations implemented in the model). For the results shown here, the integration time step was 0.7 msec, and under the conditions described below, 10-15 differential equations were used. The current system is limited to two real neurons and one model neuron because the DSP board has only two input and two output channels. A later generation system with more input and output channels and additional speed will increase the number of neurons and connections that can be created. During any one time step, the membrane potential of the model neuron is computed, the synaptic currents are determined, and a voltage command is exported to the Axoclamp instructing it to inject the appropriate current into the biological neuron (typically a few nA). During each time step the Axoclamp is used to measure the membrane potential of the biological neurons (typically between -80mV and 0mV) used to compute the value of the synaptic inputs to the model neuron. The computed and measured membrane potentials are periodically (every 500 time steps) sent to the computer main memory to be displayed and recorded.

To make this system run in real time, it is necessary to maintain perfect timing among all the components. Therefore in every experiment we first determine the minimum time step needed to do the integration depending on the complexity of the model being implemented. For complex models we used the internal clock of the MacII to drive the board. Under some conditions it was preferable to drive the board with an external clock. It is critical that the Axoclamp sampling rate be more than twice the board time step if the two are not synchronized. In our experiments, the Axoclamp switching

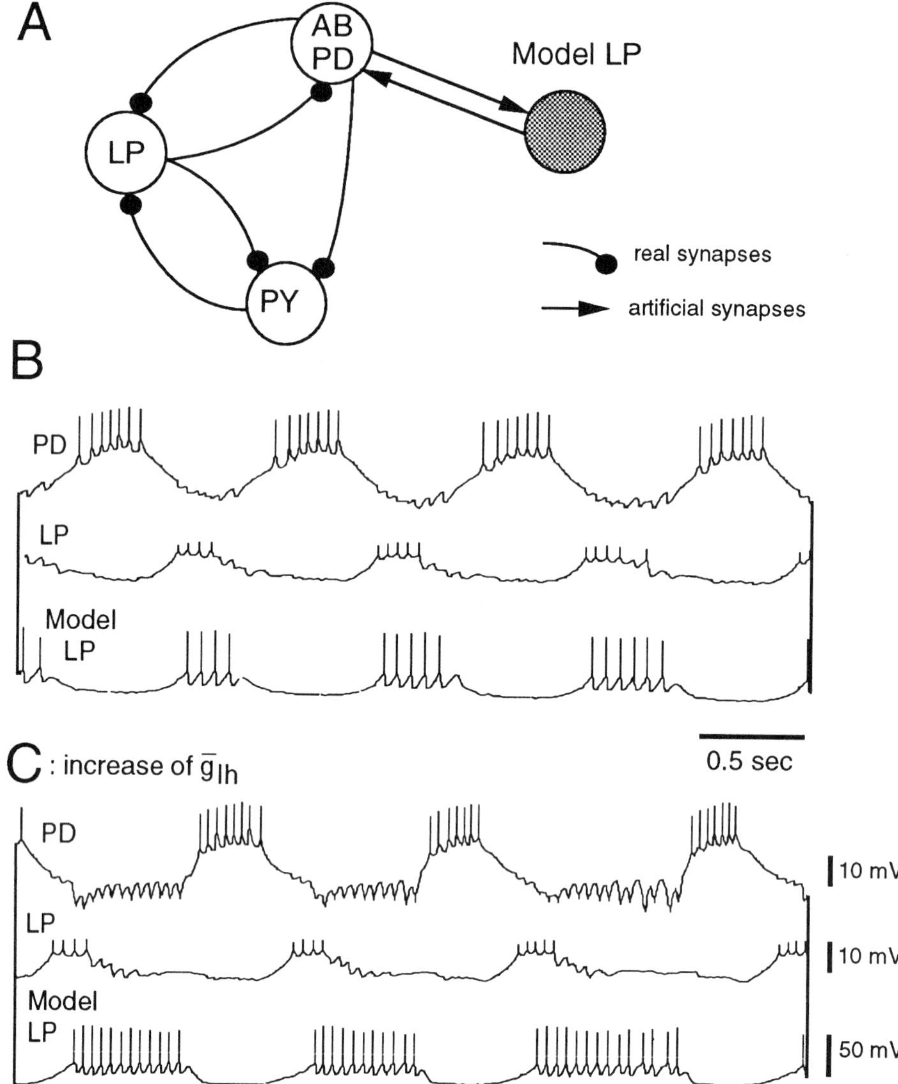

Figure 2: Hybrid network consisting of a model LP neuron connected to a PD neuron of a biological stomatogastric ganglion. A: Simplified connectivity diagram of the pyloric circuit of the stomatogastric ganglion. The AB/PD group consists of one AB neuron electrically coupled to two PD neurons. All chemical synapses are inhibitory. B: Simultaneous intracellular recordings from two biological neurons (PD and LP) and a plot of the membrane potential of the model LP neuron connected to the circuit. The parameters of the synaptic connections and the model LP neuron were adjusted so that the model LP neuron fired in the same time in the pyloric cycle as the biological LP neuron. C: Same recording configuration as B, but maximal conductance of i_h in the model neuron was increased.

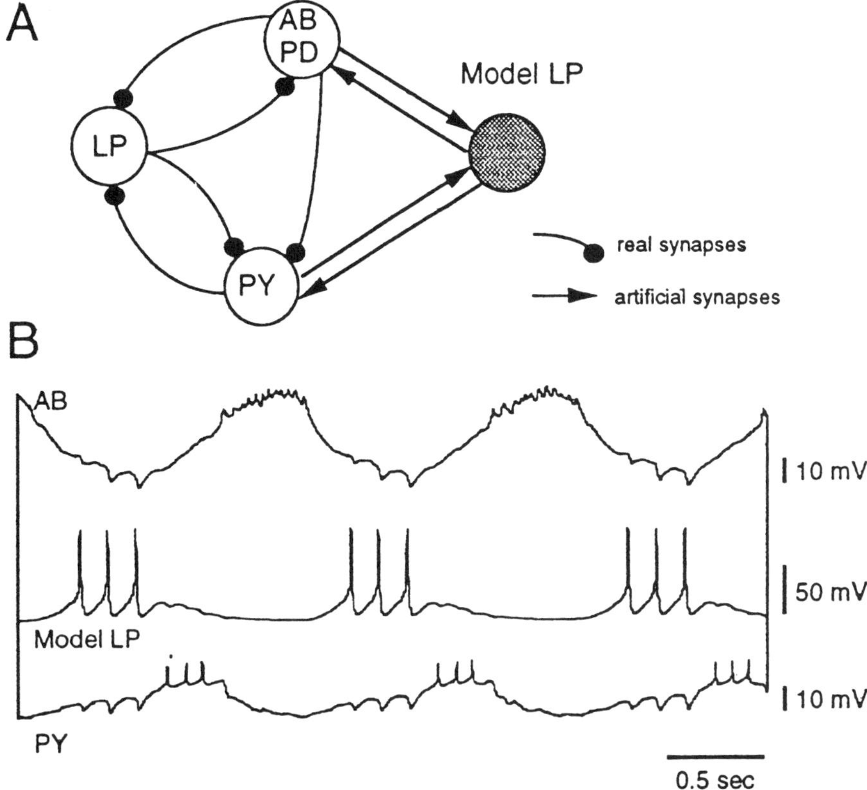

Figure 3: Hybrid network in which the model LP neuron is connected to two different biological neurons. A: Connectivity diagram showing the pattern of synaptic connections shown in part B. B: Simultaneous recordings from the biological AB neuron, the model LP neuron, and a biological PY neuron.

circuit was running about three times faster than the board time step. However, if experimental conditions force a slower Axoclamp sampling rate, then it will be important to synchronize the Axoclamp clock with the board.

5 RESULTS

The STG of the lobster, *Panulirus interruptus* contains one LP neuron, two Pyloric Dilator (PD) neurons, one Anterior Burster (AB), and eight Pyloric (PY) neurons (Eisen and Marder, 1982; Harris-Warrick et al., 1992). The connectivity among these neurons is known, and is shown in Figure 2A. The PD and LP neurons fire in alternation, because of the reciprocal inhibitory connections between them. Figure 2B shows a model LP neuron connected with reciprocal inhibitory synapses to a biological PD neuron. The parameters controlling the threshold, activation curve, time course, and reversal potential of the model neuron were adjusted until the model neuron fired at the same time within the rhythmic pyloric cycle as the biological LP neuron (Fig. 2B). Once these parameters were set, it was then possible to ask what effect changing the membrane properties of the model neuron had on emergent network activity. Figure 2C shows the result of increasing the maximal conductance of one of the currents in the model LP neuron, i_h. Note that increasing this current increased the number of LP action potentials per burst. The increased activity in the LP neuron delayed the onset of the next burst in the PD neurons because of the inhibitory synapse between the model LP neuron and the biological PD neuron, and the cycle period therefore also increased. Another effect seen in this example, is that the increased conductance of i_h in the LP neuron delayed the onset of the model LP neuron's firing relative to that of the biological LP neuron.

In the experiment shown in Figure 3 we created reciprocal inhibitory connections between the model LP neuron and two biological neurons, the AB and a PY (Fig. 3A). (The action potentials in the AB neuron are highly attenuated by the cable properties of this neuron). This example shows clearly the unitary inhibitory postsynaptic potentials (IPSPs) in the biological neurons resulting from the model LP's action potentials. During each burst of LP action potentials the IPSPs in the AB neuron increase considerably in amplitude, although the AB neuron's membrane potential is moving towards the reversal potential of the IPSPs. This occurs presumably because the conductance of the AB neuron is higher right at the end of its burst, and decreases as it hyperpolarizes. The same burst of LP action potentials evokes IPSPs in the PY neuron that increase in amplitude, here presumably because the PY neuron is depolarizing and increasing the driving force on the artificial chemical synapse. These recordings demonstrate that although the same function is controlling the synaptic "release" properties in the model LP neuron, the actual change in membrane potential evoked by action potentials in the LP neuron is affected by the total conductance of the biological neurons.

6 CONCLUSIONS

The ability to connect a realistic model neuron to a biological network offers a unique opportunity to study the effects of individual currents on network activity. It also provides realistic, two-way interactions between biological and computer-based networks. As well as providing an important new tool for neuroscience, this represents an exciting new direction in biologically-based computing.

7 ACKNOWLEDGMENTS

We thank Ms. Joan McCarthy for help with manuscript preparation. Research supported by MH 46742, the Human Science Frontier Program, and NSF DMS-9208206.

8 REFERENCES

Buchholtz, F., Golowasch, J., Epstein, I.R., and Marder, E. (1992) Mathematical model of an identified stomatogastric ganglion neuron. *J. Neurophysiology* 67:332-340.

Eisen, J.S., and Marder, E. (1982) Mechanisms underlying pattern generation in lobster stomatogastric ganglion as determined by selective inactivation of identified neurons. III. Synaptic connections of electrically coupled pyloric neurons. *J. Neurophysiology* 48:1392-1415.

Golowasch, J. and Marder, E. (1992) Ionic currents of the lateral pyloric neuron of the stomatogastric ganglion of the crab. *J. Neurophysiology* 67:318-331.

Harris-Warrick, R.M., Marder, E., Selverston, A.I., and Maurice, M., eds. (1992) *Dynamic Biological Networks.* Cambridge, MA: MIT Press.

Koch, C., and Segev, I., eds. (1989) *Methods in Neuronal Modeling.* Cambridge, MA: MIT press.

LeMasson, G. (1993) Maxim: A software system for simulating single neurons and neural networks, in preparation.

Sharp, A.A., O'Neil, M.B., Abbott, L.F. and Marder, E. (1993) The dynamic clamp: Computer-generated conductances in real neurons. *J. Neurophysiology*, in press.

Yarom, Y. (1992) Rhythmogenesis in a hybrid system interconnecting an olivary neuron to an network of coupled oscillators. *Neuroscience* 44:263-275.

Silicon Auditory Processors as Computer Peripherals

John Lazzaro, John Wawrzynek
CS Division
UC Berkeley
Evans Hall
Berkeley, CA 94720
lazzaro@cs.berkeley.edu, johnw@cs.berkeley.edu

M. Mahowald*, Massimo Sivilotti†, Dave Gillespie‡
California Institute of Technology
Pasadena, CA 91125

Abstract

Several research groups are implementing analog integrated circuit models of biological auditory processing. The outputs of these circuit models have taken several forms, including video format for monitor display, simple scanned output for oscilloscope display and parallel analog outputs suitable for data-acquisition systems. In this paper, we describe an alternative output method for silicon auditory models, suitable for direct interface to digital computers.

* Present address: M. Mahowald, MRC Anatomical Neurophamacology Unit, Mansfield Rd, Oxford OX1 3TH England. mam@vax.oxford.ac.uk

† Present address: Mass Sivilotti, Tanner Research, 180 North Vinedo Avenue, Pasadena, CA 91107. mass@tanner.com

‡ Present address: Dave Gillespie, Synaptics, 2698 Orchard Parkway, San Jose CA, 95134. daveg@synaptics.com

1. INTRODUCTION

Several researchers have implemented computational models of biological auditory processing, with the goal of incorporating these models into a speech recognition system (for a recent review, see (Jankowski, 1992)). These projects have shown the promise of the biological approach, sometimes showing clear performance advantages over traditional methods.

The application of these computational models is limited by their large computation and communication requirements. Analog VLSI implementations of these neural models may relieve this computational burden; several VLSI research groups have efforts in this area, and working integrated circuit models of many popular representations presently exist. A review of these models is presented in (Lazzaro, 1991). In this paper, we present an interface method (Mahowald, 1992; Sivilotti, 1991) that addresses the communications issues between analog VLSI auditory implementations and digital processors.

2. COMMUNICATIONS IN NEURAL SYSTEMS

Biological neurons communicate long distances using a pulse representation. Communications engineers have developed several schemes for communicating on a wire using pulses as atomic units. In these schemes, maximally using the communications bandwidth of a wire implies the mean rate of pulses on the wire is a significant fraction of the maximum pulse rate allowed on the wire.

Using this criterion, neural systems use wires very inefficiently. In most parts of the brain, most of the wires are essentially inactive most of the time. If neural systems are not organized to fully utilize the available bandwidth of each wire, what does neural communication optimize? Evidence suggests that energy conservation is an important issue for neural systems. A simple strategy for energy conservation is the reduction of the total number of pulses in the representation. Many possible coding strategies satisfy this energy requirement.

The strategies observed in neural systems share another common property. Neural systems often implement a class of computations in a manner that produces an energy-efficient output encoding as an additional byproduct. The energy-efficient coding is not performed simply for communication and immediately reversed upon receipt, but is an integral part of the new representation. In this way, energy-efficient neural coding is intrinsically different from engineering data compression techniques.

Temporal adaptation, lateral inhibition, and spike correlations are examples of neural processing methods that perform interesting computations while producing an energy-efficient output code. These representational principles are the foundation of the neural computation and communication method we advocate in this paper. In this method, the output units of a chip are spiking neuron circuits that use energy-efficient coding methods. To communicate this code off a chip, we use a distinctly non-biological approach.

3. THE EVENT-ADDRESS PROTOCOL

The unique characteristics of energy-efficient codes define the remaining off-chip communications problem. In the spiking neuron protocol, the height and width of the spike carries no information; the neuron imparts new information only at the moment a spike begins. This moment occurs asynchronously; there is no global clock synchronizing the output units. One way of completely specifying the information in the output units is an event list, a tabulation of the precise time each output unit begins a new spike. We can use this specification as a basis for an off-chip communications system, that sends an event-list message off-chip at the moment an output neuron begins a new spike. An event-list message includes the identification of the output unit, and the time of firing. A performance analysis of this protocol can be found in (Lazzaro *et al.*, 1992).

Note that an explicit timestamp for each entry in the event list is not necessary, if communication latency between the sending chip and the receiver is a constant. In this case, the sender simply communicates, upon onset of a spike from an output, the identity of the output unit; the receiver can append a locally generated timestamp to complete the event. If simplified in this manner, we refer to the event-list protocol as the event-address protocol.

We have designed a working system that computes a model of auditory nerve response, in real time, using analog VLSI processing. This system takes as input an analog sound source, and uses the event-list representation to communicate the model output to the host computer.

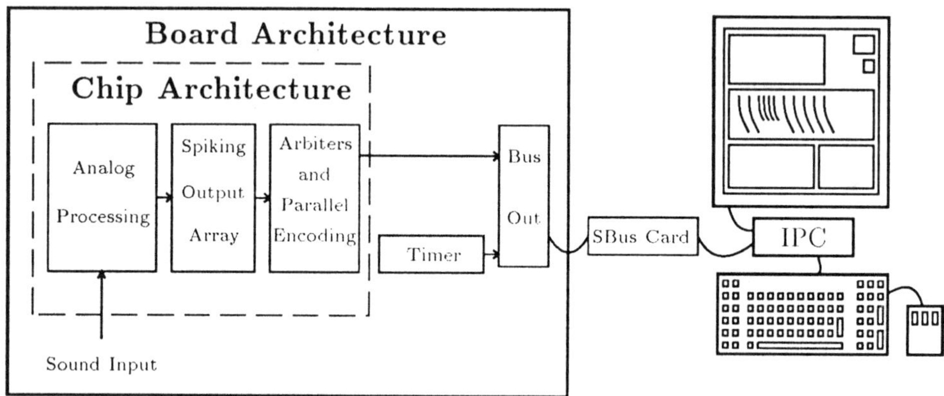

Figure 1. System block diagram, showing chip architecture, board architecture, and the host computer (Sun IPC).

4. SYSTEMS IMPLEMENTATION

Figure 1 is a block diagram of this system. A single VLSI chip computes the auditory model response; an array of spiking neuron circuits is the final representation of the model. This chip also implements the event-address protocol, using asynchronous arbitration circuits. The chip produces a parallel binary encoding of the model output, as an asynchronous stream of event addresses. These on-chip operations are shown inside the dashed rectangle in Figure 1, labelled **Chip Architecture**.

Additional digital processing completes the custom hardware in the system. This hardware transforms the event-address protocol into an event-list protocol, by adding a time marker for each event (16 bit time markers with 20μs resolution). In addition, the hardware implements the bus interface to the host computer, in conjunction with a commercial interface board. The commercial interface board supports 10 MBytes/second asynchronous data transfers between our custom hardware and the host computer, and includes 8 KBytes of data buffers. Our display software produces a real-time graphical display of the auditory model response, using the X window system.

5. VLSI CIRCUIT DETAILS

Figure 2 shows a block diagram of the chip. The analog input signal connects to circuits that perform analog processing, that are fully described and referenced in (Lazzaro *et al.*, 1993). The output of this analog processing is represented by 150 spiking neurons, arranged in a 30 by 5 array. These are the output units of the chip; the event-address protocol communicates the activity of these units off chip. At the onset of a spike from an output unit, the array position of the spiking unit, encoded as a binary number, appears on the output bus. The asynchronous output bus is shown in Figure 2 as the data signals marked **Encoded X Output** (column position) and **Encoded Y Output** (row position), and the acknowledge and request control signals A_c and R_c.

We implemented the event-address protocol as an asynchronous arbitration protocol in two dimensions. In this scheme, an output unit can access two request lines, one associated with its row and one associated with its column. Using a wire-OR signalling protocol, any output unit on a particular row or column may assert the request line. Each request line is paired with an acknowledge line, driven by the arbitration circuitry outside the array. Row and column wires for acknowledge and request are explicitly shown in Figure 2, as the lines that form a grid inside the output unit array.

At the onset of a spike, an output unit asserts its row request line, and waits for a reply on its row acknowledge line. An asynchronous arbitration system, marked in Figure 2 as **Y Arbitration Tree**, assures only one output row is acknowledged. After row acknowledgement, the output unit asserts its column request line, and waits for a reply on its column acknowledge line. The arbitration system is shown in detail in Figure 2; four two-input arbiter circuits, shown as rectangles marked with the letter A, are connected as a tree to arbitrate among the 5 column inputs.

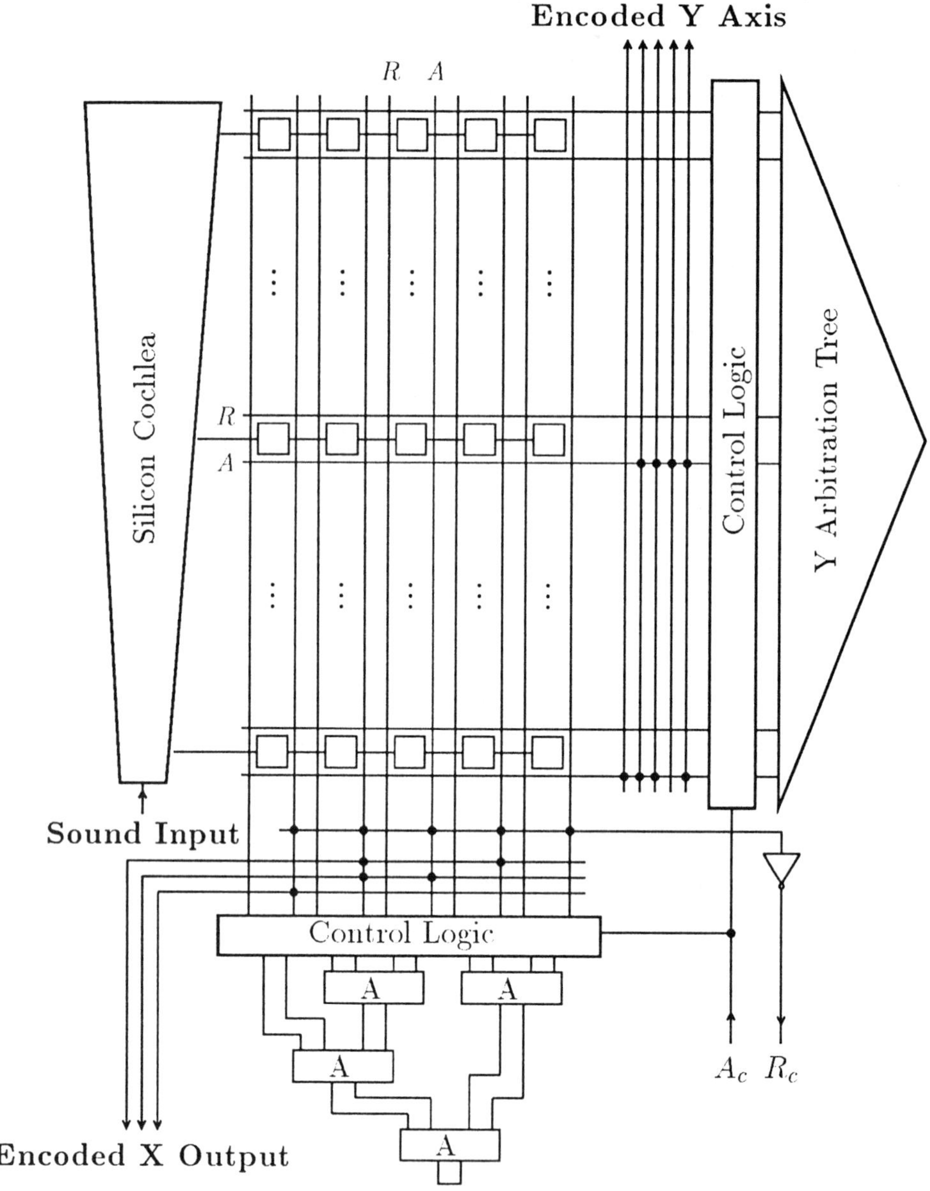

Figure 2. Block diagram of the chip. See text for details.

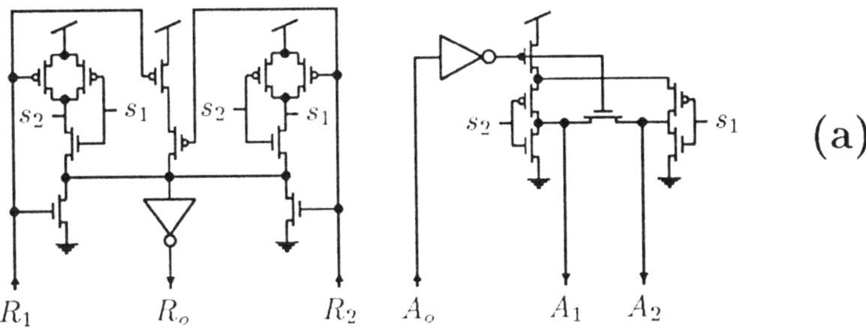

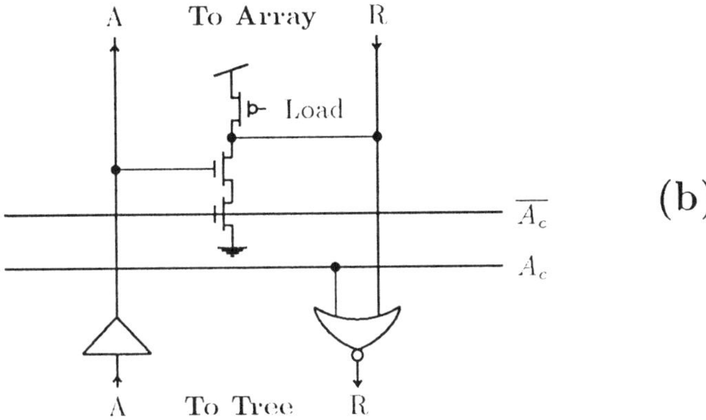

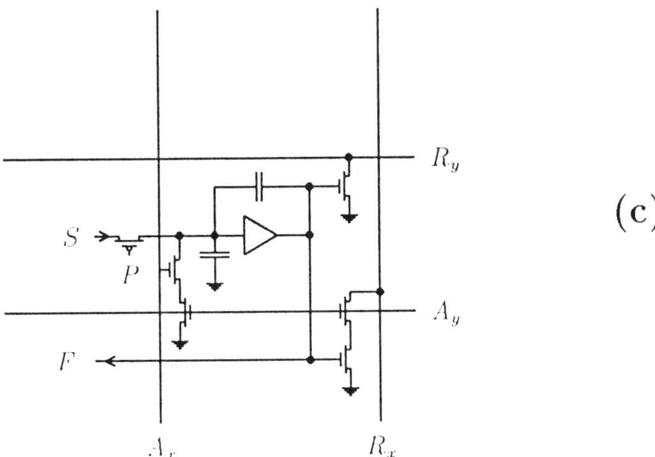

Figure 3. Diagrams of communication circuits in the chip. **(a)** Two-input arbiter circuit. **(b)** Control logic to interface arbitration logic and output unit array. **(c)** Output unit circuit.

Upon the arrival of both row and column acknowledgements, the output unit releases both row and column request lines. Static latches, shown in Figure 2 as the rectangles marked **Control Logic**, retain the state of the row and column request lines.

Binary encoders transform the row and column acknowledge lines into the output data bus. Another column encoder senses the acknowledgement of any column, and asserts the bus control output R_c. When the external device has secured the data, it responds by asserting the A_c signal. The A_c signal clears the static latches in the **Control Logic** blocks and resets R_c. When A_c is reset, the data transfer is complete, and the chip is ready for the next communication event.

Figure 3 shows the details of the communications circuits of Figure 2. Figure 3(a) shows the two-input arbiter circuit used to create the binary arbitration trees in Figure 3. This digital circuit takes as input two request signals, R_1 and R_2, and produces the associated acknowledge signals A_1 and A_2. The acknowledgement of a request precludes the acknowledgement of a second request. The circuit asserts an acknowledge signal until its associated request is released.

R_o is an auxiliary output signal indicating either R_1 or R_2 has been asserted; A_o is an auxiliary input signal that enables the A_1 and A_2 outputs. The auxiliary signals allow the two-input arbiter to function as an element in arbitration trees, as shown in Figure 2; the R_o and A_o signals of one level of arbitration connect to the R_k and A_k signals at the next level of arbitration. In two-input operation, the R_o and A_o signals are connected together, as shown in the root arbiter in Figure 2.

Figure 3(b) shows the circuit implementation of the **Control Logic** blocks in Figure 2; this circuit is repeated for each row and column connection. This circuit interfaces the output bus control input A_c with the arbitration circuitry. If output communication is not in progress, A_c is at ground, and $\overline{A}_c$ is at V_{dd}.

The PFET transistor marked as **Load** acts as a static pullup to the array request line (R); output units pull this line low to assert a request. The NOR gate inverts the array request line, and routes it to the arbitration tree. When a pending request is acknowledged by the tree acknowledge line, the two NFET transistors act to latch the array request line. The assertion of A_c releases the array request line and disables the arbitration tree request input; these actions reset all state in the communications system. When A_c is released, the system is ready to communicate a new event.

Figure 3(c) shows the circuit implementation of a unit in the output array. In this implementation, each output unit is a two-stage low-power axon circuit (Lazzaro, 1992). The first axonal stage receives the cochlear input; this axon stage is not shown in Figure 3(c). The first stage couples into the second stage, shown in Figure 3(c), via the S and F wires.

To understand the operation of this circuit, we consider the transmission of a single spike. Initially, we assume the request lines R_x and R_y are held high by the static pullup PFET transistors shown in Figure 3(b); in addition, we assume the acknowledge lines A_x and A_y are at ground, and the noninverting buffer input voltage is at ground.

When the first axonal stage fires, the S signal changes from ground potential to V_{dd}. At this point the buffer input voltage begins to increase, at a rate determined by the analog control voltage P. When the switching threshold of the buffer is reached, the buffer output voltage F swings to V_{dd}; capacitive feedback ensures a reliable switching transition. At this point, the output unit pulls the request line R_y low, and the communications sequence begins.

The Y arbitration logic replies to the R_y request by asserting the A_y line. When both F and A_y are asserted, the output unit pulls the request line R_x low. The X arbitration logic replies to the R_x request by asserting the A_x line. The assertion of both A_x and A_y resets the buffer input voltage to ground. As a result, the F line swings to ground potential, the output unit releases the R_x and R_y lines, and the first axon stage is enabled. At this point, the latch circuit of Figure 3(b) maintains the state of the R_x and R_y lines, until it is cleared by the off-chip acknowledge signal.

Acknowledgements

Research and prototyping of the event-address interface took place in Carver Mead's laboratory at Caltech; we are grateful for his insights, encouragement, and support. The Caltech-based research was funded by the ONR, HP, and the Systems Development Foundation. Research and prototyping of the auditory-nerve demonstration chip and system took place at UC Berkeley, and was funded by the NSF (PYI award MIPS-895-8568), AT&T, and the ONR (URI-N00014-92-J-1672).

References

Jankowski, C. R. (1992). "A Comparison of Auditory Models for Automatic Speech Recognition," S.B. Thesis, MIT Dept of Electrical Engineering and Computer Science.

Lazzaro, J. P. (1991). "Biologically-based auditory signal processing in analog VLSI," *IEEE Asilomar Conference on Signals, Systems, and Computers.*

Lazzaro, J. P. (1992). "Low-power silicon spiking neurons and axons," *IEEE International Symposium on Circuits and Systems*, San Diego, CA, p. 2220–2224.

Lazzaro, J., Wawrzynek, J., Mahowald, M., Sivilotti, M., and Gillespie, D. (1993). "Silicon auditory processors as computer peripherals," *IEEE Transactions of Neural Networks,* May (in press).

Mahowald, M. (1992). Ph.D. Thesis, Computation and Neural Systems, California Institute of Technology.

Sivilotti, M. (1991). "Wiring considerations in analog VLSI systems, with applications to field-programmable networks," Computer Science Technical Report (Ph. D. Thesis), California Insitute of Technology.

Object-Based Analog VLSI Vision Circuits

Christof Koch
Computation and Neural Systems
California Institute of Technology
Pasadena, CA

Bimal Mathur, Shih-Chii Liu
Rockwell International Science Center
Thousand Oaks, CA

John G. Harris
MIT Artificial Intelligence Laboratory
Cambridge, MA

Jin Luo, Massimo Sivilotti
Tanner Research, Inc.
Pasadena, CA

Abstract

We describe two successfully working, analog VLSI vision circuits that move beyond pixel-based early vision algorithms. One circuit, implementing the *dynamic wires* model, provides for dedicated lines of communication among groups of pixels that share a common property. The chip uses the dynamic wires model to compute the arclength of visual contours. Another circuit labels all points inside a given contour with one voltage and all other with another voltage. Its behavior is very robust, since small breaks in contours are automatically sealed, providing for *Figure-Ground* segregation in a noisy environment. Both chips are implemented using networks of resistors and switches and represent a step towards object level processing since a single voltage value encodes the property of an ensemble of pixels.

1 CONTOUR-LENGTH CHIP

Contour length computation is useful for further processing such as structural saliency (Shaashua and Ullman, 1988), which is thought to be an important stage before object recognition. This computation is impossible on an analog chip if we

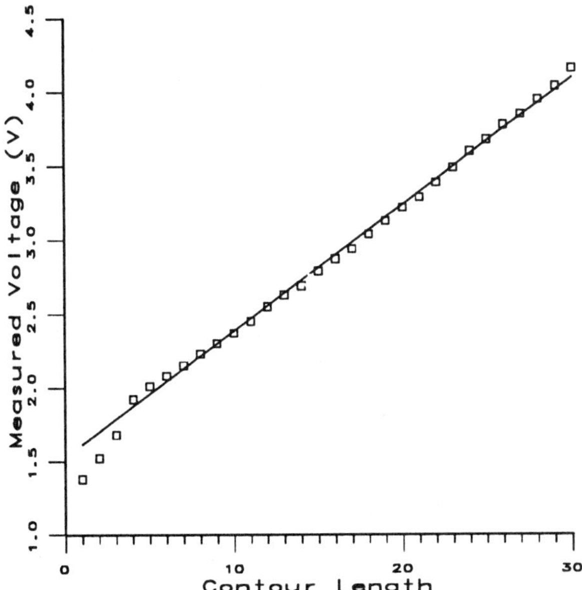

Figure 1: Figure 1: Plot of measured voltage vs. contour length from 30 different contours scanned into the contour length chip. The voltage is a linear function of contour length.

are restricted to pure pixel- or image-based operations. The *dynamic wire* methodology provides dedicated lines of communication among groups of pixels of an image which share common properties (Liu and Harris, 1992). In simple applications, object regions can be grouped together to compute the area or the center of mass of each object. Alternatively, object boundaries may be used to compute curvature or contour length. These ideas are not limited to sets of simple electrical wires; resistive networks can also be configured on the fly. The problem of smoothing object contours using resistive dynamic wires has been previously studied (Liu and Harris, 1992).

In the contour-length application, pixels along image contours are electrically connected by a reconfigurable dynamic wire. The first step of processing requires that each contour choose an arbitrary but unique *leader* pixel. The top of Fig. 2 shows several examples of contours and indicates which pixels where chosen as leaders by the chip. The leader is responsible for connecting a shunting resistor between the shared dynamic wire and ground. If each pixel on the contour supplies a constant amount of current to the dynamic wire, all of the current must flow through the shunting resistor. Therefore, the voltage on the wire will encode the contour length. Fig. 1 shows the linear relationship between the measured voltage and the contour length. The bottom half of Fig. 2 shows the length of several example contours using an intensity coding. The brighter contours indicate a higher voltage and therefore a longer contour. The contour length chip was fabricated through MOSIS using 2μm CMOS technology. The prototype 2x2 mm^2 chip contains an a 7x7 pixel array.

Figure 2: Four binary contour images were scanned into the contour-length chip and are shown in the top figure. The highlighted pixel in each contour was chosen by the chip to be the leader. The bottom figure shows the measured voltages (indicated by intensity) from the contour-length chip for the four images are shown. Since the intensity of each pixel encodes its length, the longer contours are brighter.

The most challenging aspect of the design of the contour-length chip is the circuitry to uniquely select a pixel from each contour to be the leader. The leader is selected by entering all the pixels along each contour in a competition. The winner of this competition will be the leader. This competition requires each node to charge up its own capacitor once a reset line has been triggered. The first node that charges its capacitor above the trip point of a digital inverter will pull down a global precharge wire which connects all the pixels along the contour. This wire will in turn latch the states of the winner and losers. One of the pixels will normally toggle first because of the inherent offsets and component mismatches in silicon.

2 FIGURE-GROUND CHIP

Ullman (1984) proposed that a visual routine is used in human vision to determine if a specified point in the visual field is inside or outside of one (or more) closed visual contours. We describe such a chip that labels all points inside a given—possibly incomplete and broken—contour. We assume that the presence of an edge in the image causes switches at the corresponding grid point within a rectangular resistive network to open (Fig. 3). A closed edge contour will then correspond to a series of open switches on this grid. We assume that the visual contour will always encompass the central grid point in the array. At this point, the resistive grid is connected to the battery V_{fig}, while the periphery of the array is grounded to V_{gnd}. If the voltage at all other grid points is left floating and the contour is complete, that is, the central grid point is completely isolated from the periphery of the chip by a series of open grid points, the voltage at all points inside the contour rises to V_{fig}, while the voltage at grid points outside the contour will settle to V_{gnd}. Thus, the *figure* will be labeled by one voltage level and *ground* by another.

Contours in real images are frequently incomplete, but instead have broken segments of one or more pixels. This will enable the current to flow through these holes in the contour, smearing out the voltage level between inside and outside. We exploit a property of Mead's (1989) Hres circuit, used to implement the resistances, to achieve contour completion. While the current flowing through Hres is linear in the voltage gradient for small voltage differences, it saturates for large voltage gradients. At those locations where the contour is broken, the saturating resistances limit the current flow, preventing smoothing of the voltage profile to occur.

Figure 4 shows the responses of the Figure-Ground chip to different input patterns collected with a fixed bias: $V_{fig} = 3.5\ V$ and $V_{gnd} = 2\ V$. The two-dimensional data is presented as pairs of images. The input patterns are located on the left while the corresponding voltage outputs are presented next to the input on the right. The black-white patterns are used to represent the binary input data encoding object boundaries. Thus, at all locations marked in black, the associated switches shown in Fig. 1a are opened. The gray-scale on the right denotes output voltage levels, where the darkest value corresponds to V_{fig} and the brightest to V_{gnd}. The center pixel of the view field is always set to V_{fig}. Notice that at every node where a boundary input signal (in black) appears and the switches are opened, the output voltage at that node is tied to V_{gnd}. This can be seen best in (e; white outline). To evaluate the ability of our circuit to perform Figure-Ground segregation in the presence of breaks in the contour, more and wider breaks are introduced into a simple square

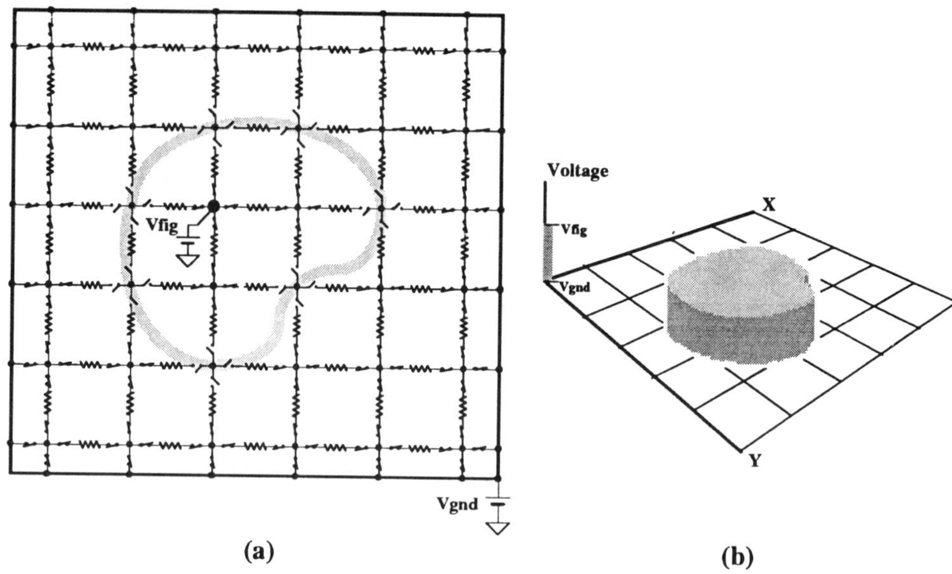

Figure 3: (**a**) The Figure-Ground network is made up of resistors and switches. The input to the chip is a binary edge map. At every grid point in the rectangular array where edges have been found, four switches are opened, isolating that node from its four neighbors (the shaded edge contour corresponds to a series of isolated nodes). We assume that the central point in the array is always enclosed by the contour. This point is connected to a voltage source V_{fig}, while the periphery is connected to the voltage V_{gnd}. If the contour is unbroken, the voltage at each interior point will then rise to V_{fig}, while all outside grid points will settle to V_{gnd}. Thus, the object is rapidly segregated from the background. If the contour is not complete, the saturating resistors (indicated with simple resistors) will limit the current flowing through these holes in the contour and partially seal off the boundary. (**b**) represents a conceptual view of how an object (figure) is segregated from the background in the two-dimensional view field, in terms of two distinct voltage levels (V_{fig} labels the object and V_{gnd} labels the background). The circuit has 48 by 48 nodes on a 4.6 by 6.8 mm^2 die size and was implemented using MOSIS 2 μm CMOS technology.

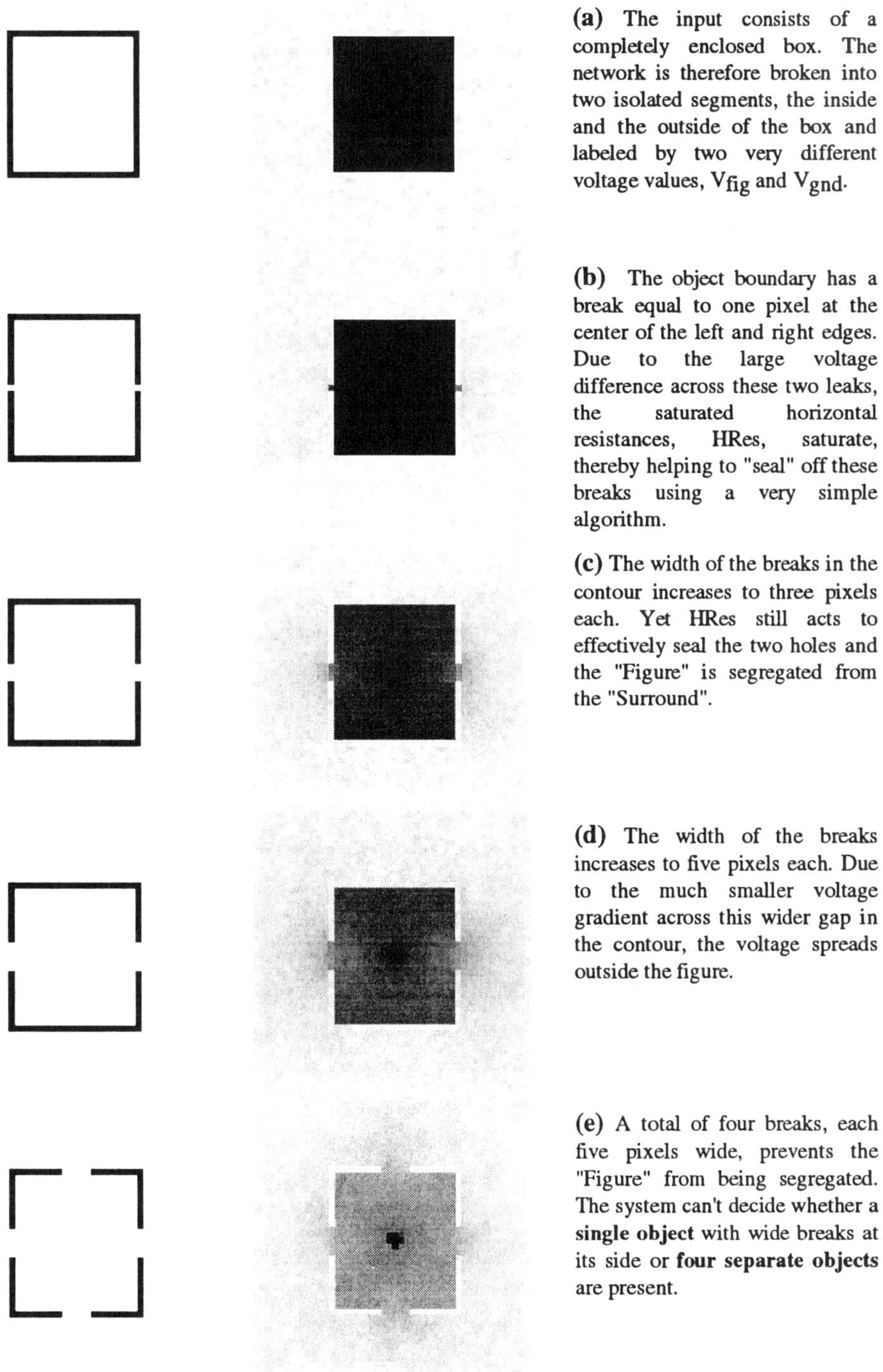

(a) The input consists of a completely enclosed box. The network is therefore broken into two isolated segments, the inside and the outside of the box and labeled by two very different voltage values, V_{fig} and V_{gnd}.

(b) The object boundary has a break equal to one pixel at the center of the left and right edges. Due to the large voltage difference across these two leaks, the saturated horizontal resistances, HRes, saturate, thereby helping to "seal" off these breaks using a very simple algorithm.

(c) The width of the breaks in the contour increases to three pixels each. Yet HRes still acts to effectively seal the two holes and the "Figure" is segregated from the "Surround".

(d) The width of the breaks increases to five pixels each. Due to the much smaller voltage gradient across this wider gap in the contour, the voltage spreads outside the figure.

(e) A total of four breaks, each five pixels wide, prevents the "Figure" from being segregated. The system can't decide whether a **single object** with wide breaks at its side or **four separate objects** are present.

Figure 4

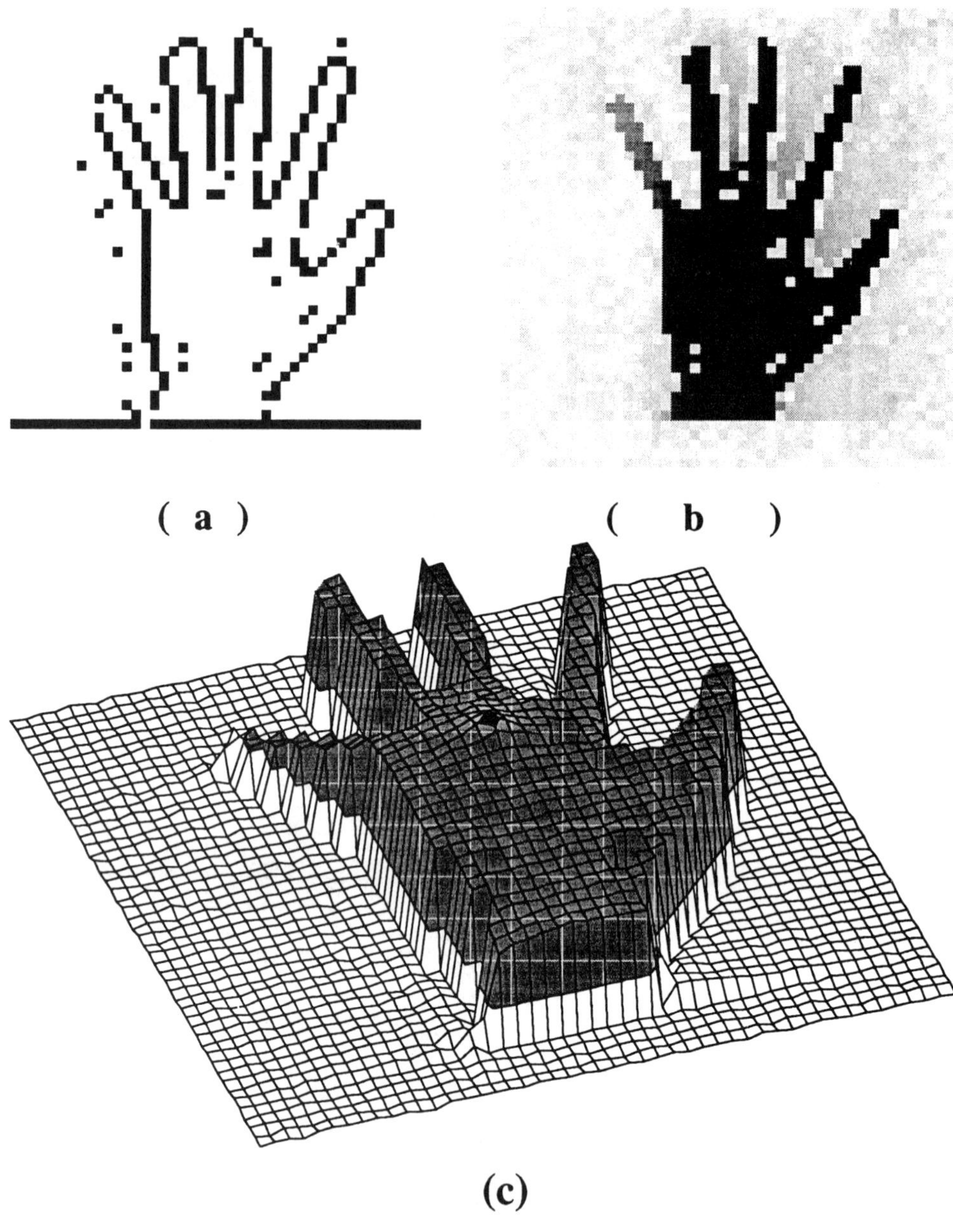

Figure 5: The Figure-Ground response to a noisy and incomplete contour outlining a hand (the binary image shown in **(a)** is scanned in from off-chip). The output voltage is shown as intensity in **(b)** and as a 3-D plot in **(c)**. The center node is tied to 3.5 V and marked as black in **(c)**. The shaded area labels all pixels whose voltage is above 2.4 V. Notice the voltage decay along the little finger, due to an incomplete contour at the finger tip.

contour. The box and break points on the sides are center-row symmetrical and the breaks are respectively one, three and five pixels wide. In (e), two additional, five pixel wide breaks have been included. For small enough breaks, our circuit has an excellent boundary-completion capabilities. This is important for machine vision, since real images rarely have complete boundaries.

The performance of the chip is illustrated in Fig. 4. If the contour is unbroken, the voltage inside the figure rises to V_{fig}, segregating it from the surround. If a small gap appears in the contour, it can be partially sealed off by the action of the saturating resistance Hres, which limits the current flowing through this gap, inhibiting full voltage equalization from occurring. As the break in the contour becomes larger, the voltage gradient across the *illusionary contour* between the upper and the lower part of the figure becomes smaller and smaller. If Hres is set to a low conductance, the gradient becomes larger again (Fig. 5c); now, however, the chip fails to discriminate between very small and large gaps. Note that inside and outside are strictly defined only for a closed contour. Thus, it is somewhat arbitrary at what distance two edges are considered to be part of the same or separate contours (e.g., Fig. 5). If the output voltage is thresholded at 3.0 V (in the case of Fig. 5b), the contour with one or two pixel breaks would be considered a single Figure, while the two larger breaks would not be.

3 CONCLUSION

Most analog vision chips are restricted to work either at the local, pixel-level or the global, image-level. The dynamic wire and figure-ground chips discussed in this paper allow data-dependent neighborhoods to form. With these configured neighborhoods, analog chips can now perform object-level processing.

Acknowledgements

This Work is supported by the National Science Foundation, the Office of Naval Research and Rockwell International Science Center. We thank MOSIS for all chip fabrication. JGH is supported by an NSF postdoctoral fellowship.

References

Liu, S. and Harris, J.G. (1992), Dynamic wires: an analog VLSI model for object processing, *Internat. Journal of Comp. Vision.* **8**: pp. 231-239.

Luo, J., Koch, C. and Mathur, B. (1992), Figure-Ground segregation using an analog VLSI Chip, *IEEE Micro*, Vol. 12 46-57, 1992.

Shaashua, A. and Ullman, S. (1988), Structural saliency: The detection of globally salient structures using a locally connected network. In *Proceedings of the IEEE Computer Vision and Pattern Recognition Conference.*

Ullman, S. (1984), Visual routines, *Cognition*, Vol. 18, pp. 97-159, 1984.

A Parallel Gradient Descent Method for Learning in Analog VLSI Neural Networks

J. Alspector R. Meir* B. Yuhas A. Jayakumar D. Lippe†
Bellcore
Morristown, NJ 07962-1910

Abstract

Typical methods for gradient descent in neural network learning involve calculation of derivatives based on a detailed knowledge of the network model. This requires extensive, time consuming calculations for each pattern presentation and high precision that makes it difficult to implement in VLSI. We present here a perturbation technique that *measures*, not *calculates*, the gradient. Since the technique uses the actual network as a measuring device, errors in modeling neuron activation and synaptic weights do not cause errors in gradient descent. The method is parallel in nature and easy to implement in VLSI. We describe the theory of such an algorithm, an analysis of its domain of applicability, some simulations using it and an outline of a hardware implementation.

1 Introduction

The most popular method for neural network learning is back-propagation (Rumelhart, 1986) and related algorithms that calculate gradients based on detailed knowledge of the neural network model. These methods involve calculating exact values of the derivative of the activation function. For analog VLSI implementations, such techniques require impossibly high precision in the synaptic weights and precise modeling of the activation functions. It is much more appealing to *measure* rather than *calculate* the gradient for analog VLSI implementation by perturbing either a

*Present address: Dept. of EE; Technion; Haifa, Israel
†Present address: Dept. of EE; MIT; Cambridge, MA

single weight (Jabri, 1991) or a single neuron (Widrow, 1990) and measuring the resulting change in the output error. However, perturbing only a single weight or neuron at a time loses one of the main advantages of implementing neural networks in analog VLSI, namely, that of computing weight changes in parallel. The one-weight-at-a-time perturbation method has the same order of time complexity as a serial computer simulation of learning. A mathematical analysis of the possibility of model free learning using parallel weight perturbations followed by local correlations suggests that random perturbations by additive, zero-mean, independent noise sources may provide a means of parallel learning (Dembo, 1990). We have previously used such a noise source (Alspector, 1991) in a different implementable learning model.

2 Gradient Estimation by Parallel Weight Perturbation

2.1 A Brownian Motion Algorithm

One can estimate the gradient of the error $E(\mathbf{w})$ with respect to any weight w_1 by perturbing w_1 by δw_1 and measuring the change in the output error δE as the entire weight vector $\mathbf{w}$ except for component w_1 is held constant.

$$\frac{\delta E}{\delta w_1} = \frac{E(\mathbf{w}+\delta \mathbf{w_1}) - E(\mathbf{w})}{\delta w_1} \tag{1}$$

This leads to an approximation to the true gradient $\frac{\partial E}{\partial w_1}$:

$$\frac{\partial E}{\partial w_1} = \frac{\delta E}{\delta w_1} + O([\delta w_1]) \tag{2}$$

For small perturbations, the second (and higher order) term can be ignored. This method of perturbing weights one-at-a-time has the advantage of using the correct physical neurons and synapses in a VLSI implementation but has time complexity of $O(W)$ where W is the number of weights.

Following (Dembo, 1990), let us now consider perturbing all weights simultaneously. However, we wish to have the perturbation vector $\delta\mathbf{w}$ chosen uniformly on a hypercube. Note that this requires only a random sign multiplying a fixed perturbation and is natural for VLSI. Dividing the resulting change in error by any single weight change, say δw_1, gives

$$\frac{\delta E}{\delta w_1} = \frac{E(\mathbf{w}+\delta \mathbf{w}) - E(\mathbf{w})}{\delta w_1} \tag{3}$$

which by a Taylor expansion is

$$\frac{\delta E}{\delta w_1} = \frac{\sum_{i=1}^{W} \frac{\partial E}{\partial w_i}\delta w_i}{\delta w_1} + O([\delta w_1]) \tag{4}$$

leading to the approximation (ignoring higher order terms)

$$\frac{\delta E}{\delta w_1} = \frac{\partial E}{\partial w_1} + \sum_{i>1}^{W} \left(\frac{\partial E}{\partial w_i}\right)\left(\frac{\delta w_i}{\delta w_1}\right). \tag{5}$$

An important point of this paper, emphasized by (Dembo, 1990) and embodied in Eq. (5), is that the last term has expectation value zero for random and independently distributed δw_i since the last expression in parentheses is equally likely to be $+1$ as -1. Thus, one can approximately follow the gradient by perturbing all weights at the same time. If each synapse has access to information about the resulting change in error, it can adjust its weight by assuming it was the only weight perturbed. The weight change rule

$$\Delta w_i = -\eta \frac{\delta E}{\delta w_i}, \tag{6}$$

where η is a learning rate, will follow the gradient on the average but with the considerable noise implied by the second term in Eq. (5). This type of stochastic gradient descent is similar to the random-direction Kiefer-Wolfowitz method (Kushner, 1978), which can be shown to converge under suitable conditions on η and δw_i. This is also reminiscent of Brownian motion where, although particles may be subject to considerable random motion, there is a general drift of the ensemble of particles in the direction of even a weak external force. In this respect, there is some similarity to the directed drift algorithm of (Venkatesh, 1991), although that work applies to binary weights and single layer perceptrons whereas this algorithm should work for any level of weight quantization or precision - an important advantage for VLSI implementations - as well as any number of layers and even for recurrent networks.

2.2 Improving the Estimate by Multiple Perturbations

As was pointed out by (Dembo, 1990), for each pattern, one can reduce the variance of the noise term in Eq. (5) by repeating the random parallel perturbation many times to improve the statistical estimate. If we average over P perturbations, we have

$$\frac{\delta E}{\delta w_1} = \frac{1}{P}\sum_{p=1}^{P} \frac{\delta E}{\delta w_1^p} = \frac{\partial E}{\partial w_1} + \frac{1}{P}\sum_{p=1}^{P}\sum_{i>1}^{W} \left(\frac{\partial E}{\partial w_i}\right)\left(\frac{\delta w_i^p}{\delta w_1^p}\right) \tag{7}$$

where p indexes the perturbation number. The variance of the second term, which is a noise, ν, is

$$< \nu^2 > = \frac{1}{P^2} \sum_{p,p'=1}^{P} \sum_{i,i'>1}^{W} \left(\frac{\partial E}{\partial w_i}\right)\left(\frac{\partial E}{\partial w_{i'}}\right)\left\langle \left(\frac{\delta w_i^p}{\delta w_1^p}\right)\left(\frac{\delta w_{i'}^{p'}}{\delta w_1^{p'}}\right)\right\rangle \tag{8}$$

where the expectation value, $<>$, leads to the Kronecker delta function, $\delta_{ii'}^{pp'}$. This reduces Eq. (8) to

$$< \nu^2 > = \frac{1}{P^2} \sum_{p=1}^{P} \sum_{i>1}^{W} \left(\frac{\partial E}{\partial w_i} \right)^2 . \tag{9}$$

The double sum over perturbations and weights (assuming the gradient is bounded and all gradient directions have the same order of magnitude) has magnitude $O(PW)$ so that the variance is $O(\frac{W}{P})$ and the standard deviation is

$$< (\nu^2) >^{\frac{1}{2}} = O\left(\left(\frac{W}{P} \right)^{\frac{1}{2}} \right). \tag{10}$$

Therefore, for a fixed variance in the noise term, it may be necessary to have a number of perturbations of the same order as the number of weights. So, if a high precision estimate of the gradient is needed throughout learning, it seems as though the time complexity will still be $O(W)$ giving no advantage over single perturbations. However, one or a few of the gradient derivatives may dominate the noise and reduce the effective number of parameters. One can also make a qualitative argument that early in learning, one does not need a precise estimate of the gradient since a general direction in weight space will suffice. Later, it will be necessary to make a more precise estimate for learning to converge.

2.3 The Gibbs Distribution and the Learning Problem

Note that the noise of Eq. (7) is gaussian since it is composed of a sum of random sign terms which leads to a binomial distribution and is gaussian distributed for large P. Thus, in the continuous time limit, the learning problem has Langevin dynamics such that the time rate of change of a weight w_k is,

$$\frac{dw_k}{dt} = -\eta \frac{\delta E}{\delta w_k} = -\eta \frac{\partial E}{\partial w_k} + \nu_k, \tag{11}$$

and the learning problem converges in probability (Zinn-Justin, 1989), so that asymptotically $Pr(\mathbf{w}) \propto \exp[-\beta E(\mathbf{w})]$ where β is inversely proportional to the noise variance.

Therefore, even though the gradient is noisy, one can still get a useful learning algorithm. Note that we can "anneal" ν_k by a variable perturbation method. Depending on the annealing schedule, this can result in a substantial speedup in learning over the one-weight-at-a-time perturbation technique.

2.4 Similar Work in these Proceedings

Coincidentally, there were three other papers with similar work at NIPS*92. This algorithm was presented with different approaches by both (Flower, 1993) and (Cauwenberghs, 1993). [1] A continuous time version was implemented in VLSI but not on a neural network by (Kirk, 1993).

[1] We note that (Cauwenberghs, 1993) shows that multiple perturbations are not needed for learning if Δw is small enough and he does not study them. This does not agree with our simulations (following)

3 Simulations

3.1 Learning with Various Perturbation Iterations

We tried some simple problems using this technique in software. We used a standard sigmoid activation function with unit gain, a fixed size perturbation of .005 and random sign. The learning rate, η, was .1 and momentum, α, was 0. We varied the number of perturbation iterations per pattern presentation from 1 to 128 (2^l where l varies from 0 to 7). We performed 10 runs for each condition and averaged the results. Fig. 1a shows the average learning curves for a 6 input, 12 hidden, 1 output unit parity problem as the number of perturbations per pattern presentation is varied. The symbol plotted is l.

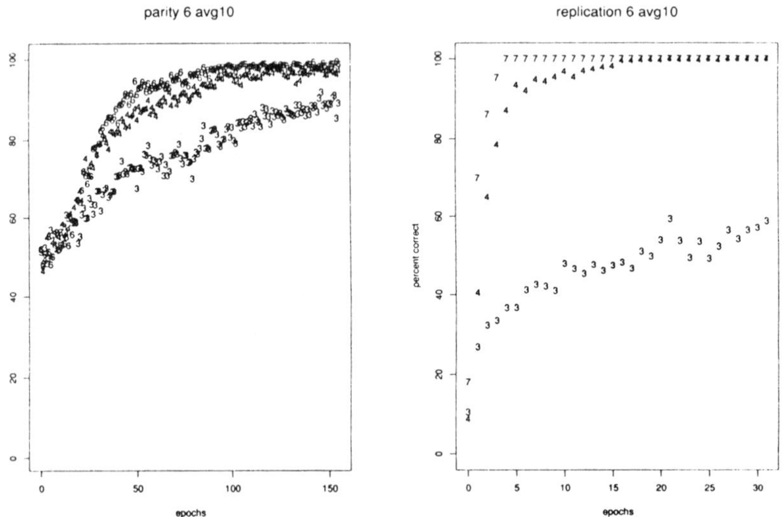

Figure 1. Learning curves for 6-12-1 parity and 6-6-6 replication.

There seems to be a critical number of perturbations, P_c, about 16 ($l = 4$) in this case, below which learning slows dramatically.

We repeated the measurements of Fig. 1a for different sizes of the parity problem using a N-2N-1 network. We also did these measurements on a different problem, replication or identity, where the task is to replicate the bit pattern of the input on the output. We used a N-N-N network for this task so that we have a comparison with the parity problem as N varies for roughly the same number of weights ($2N^2 + 2N$) in each network. The learning curves for the 6-6-6 problem are plotted in Fig. 1b. The critical value also seems to be 16 ($l = 4$).

perhaps because we do not decrease δw and η as learning proceeds. He did not check this for large problems as we did. In an implementation, one will not be able to reduce δw too much so that the effect on the output error can be measured. It is also likely that multiple perturbations can be done more quickly than multiple pattern presentations, if learning speed is an issue. He also notes the importance of correlating with the change in error rather than the error alone as in (Dembo, 1990).

3.2 Scaling of the Critical Value with Problem Size

To determine how the critical value of perturbation iterations scales, we tried a variety of problems besides the N-N-N replication and N-2N-1 parity. We added N-2N-N replication and N-N-1 parity to see how more weights affect the same problem. We also did N-N-N/2 edge counting, where the output is the number of sign changes in an ordered row of N inputs. Finally we did N-2N-N and N-N-N hamming where the output is the closest hamming code for N inputs. We varied the number of perturbation iterations so that p = 1,2,5,10,20,50,100,200,400.

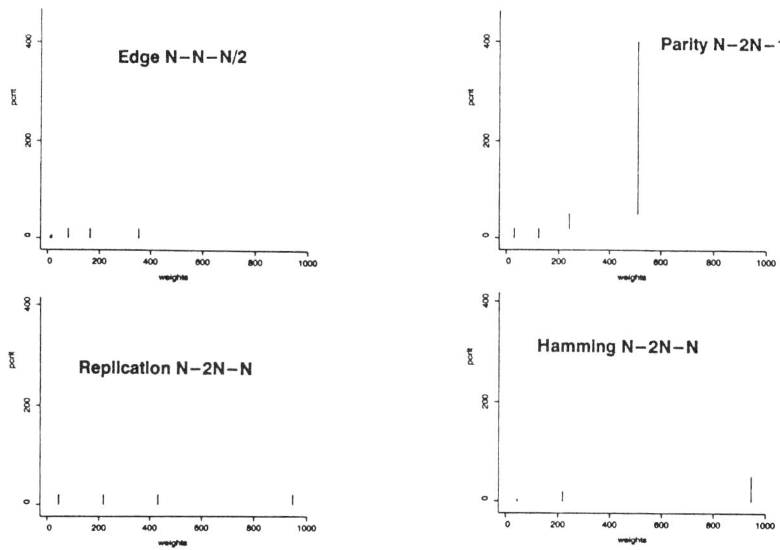

Figure 2. Critical value scaling for different problems.

Fig. 2 gives a feel for the effective scale of the problem by plotting the critical value of the number of perturbation iterations as a function of the number of weights for some of the problems we looked at. Note that the required number of iterations is not a steep function of the network size except for the parity problem. We speculate that the scaling properties are dependent on the shape of the error surface. If the derivatives in Eq. 9 are large in all dimensions (learning on a bowl-shaped surface), then the effective number of parameters is large and the variance of the noise term will be on the order of the number of weights, leading to a steep dependence in Fig. 2. If, however, there are only a few weight directions with significantly large error derivatives (learning on a taco shell), then the noise will scale at a slower rate than the number of weights leading to a weak dependence of the critical value with problem size. This is actually a nice feature of parallel perturbative learning because it means learning will be noisy and slow in a bowl where it's easy, but precise and fast in a taco shell where it's hard.

The critical value is required for convergence at the end of learning but not at the start. This means it should be possible to anneal the number of perturbation iterations to achieve an additional speedup over the one-weight-at-a-time perturbation technique. We would also like to understand how to vary δw and η as learning proceeds. The stochastic approximation literature is likely to serve as a useful guide.

3.3 Computational Geometry of Stochastic Gradient Descent

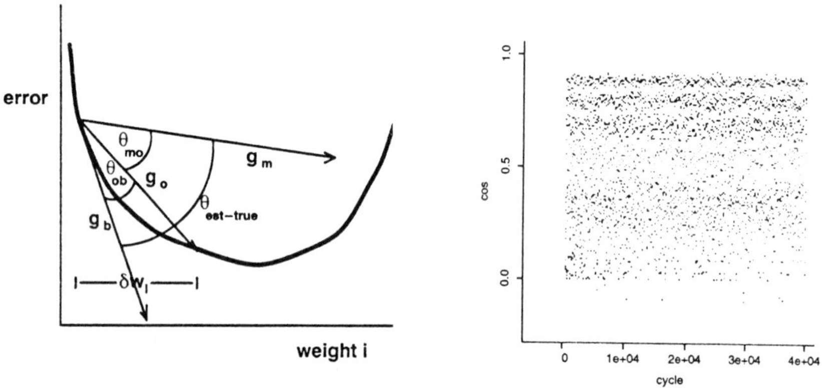

Figure 3. Computational Geometry of Stochastic Gradient Descent.

Fig. 3a shows some relevant gradient vectors and angles in the learning problem. For a particular pattern presentation, the true gradient, g_b, from a back-propagation calculation is compared with the one-weight-at-a-time gradient, g_o, from a perturbation, δw_i, in one weight direction. The gradient from perturbing all weights, g_m, adds a noise vector to g_o. By taking the normalized dot product between g_m and g_b, one obtains the direction cosine between the estimated and the true gradient direction. This is plotted in Fig. 3b for the 10 input N-N-1 parity problem for all nine perturbation values. The shaded bands increase in *cos* (decrease in angle) as the number of perturbations goes from 1 to 400. Note that the angles are large but that learning still takes place. Note also that the dot product is almost always positive except for a few points at low perturbation numbers. Incidentally, by looking at plots of the true to one-weight-at-a-time angles (not shown), we see that the large angles are due almost entirely to the parallel perturbative noise term and not to the stepsize, δw.

4 Outline of an analog implementation

Fig. 4 shows a diagram of a learning synapse using this perturbation technique. Note that its only inputs are a single bit representing the sign of the perturbation and a broadcast signal representing the change in the output error. Multiple perturbations can be averaged by the summing buffer and weight is stored as charge on a capacitor or floating gate device.

An estimate of the power and area of an analog chip implementation gives the following: Using a standard 1.2μm, double poly technology, the synapse with about 7 to 8 bits of resolution and which includes a 0.5 pf storage capacitor, weight refresh (Hochet, 1989) and update circuitry can be fabricated with an area of about 1600 μm^2 and with a power dissipation of about 100 μW with continuous self-refresh. This translates into a chip of about 22000 synapses at 2.2 watts on a 36 mm^2 die core. It is likely that the power requirements can be greatly reduced with a more relaxed refresh technique or with a suitable non-volatile analog storage technology.

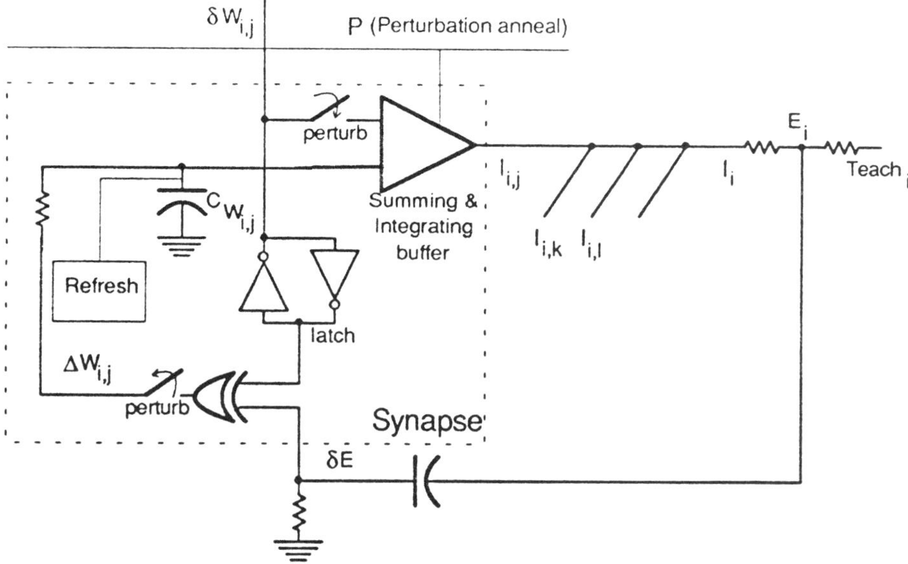

Figure 4. Diagram of perturbative learning synapse.

We intend to use our noise generation technique (Alspector, 1991) to provide uncorrelated perturbations potentially to thousands of synapses. Note also that the error signal can be generated by a simple resistor or a comparator followed by a summer. The difference signal can be generated by a simple differentiator.

5 Conclusion

We have analyzed a parallel perturbative learning technique and shown that it should converge under the proper conditions. We have performed simulations on a variety of test problems to demonstrate the scaling behavior of this learning algorithm. We are continuing work to understand speedups possible in an analog VLSI implementation. Finally, we describe such an implementation. Future work will involve applying this technique to learning in recurrent networks.

Acknowledgment

We thank Barak Pearlmutter for valuable and insightful discussions and Gert Cauwenberghs for making an advance copy of his paper available. This work has been partially supported by AFOSR contract F49620-90-C-0042, DEF.

References

J. Alspector, J. W. Gannett, S. Haber, M.B. Parker, and R. Chu, "A VLSI-Efficient Technique for Generating Multiple Uncorrelated Noise Sources and Its Application to Stochastic Neural Networks", *IEEE Trans. Circuits and Systems*, **38**, 109, (Jan., 1991).

J. Alspector, A. Jayakumar, and S. Luna, "Experimental Evaluation of Learning in a Neural Microsystem" in *Advances in Neural Information Processing Systems 4*, J. E. Moody, S. J. Hanson, and R. P. Lippmann (eds.) San Mateo,CA: Morgan-Kaufmann Publishers (1992), pp. 871-878.

G. Cauwenberghs, "A Fast Stochastic Error-Descent Algorithm for Supervised Learning and Optimization," in *Advances in Neural Information Processing Systems,* San Mateo, CA: Morgan Kaufman Publishers, vol. **5**, 1993.

A. Dembo and T. Kailath, "Model-Free Distributed Learning", *IEEE Trans. Neural Networks* **B1**, (1990) pp. 58-70.

B. Flower and M. Jabri, "Summed Weight Neuron Perturbation: An $\mathcal{O}(n)$ Improvement over Weight Perturbation," in *Advances in Neural Information Processing Systems,* San Mateo, CA: Morgan Kaufman Publishers, vol. **5**, 1993.

B. Hochet, "Multivalued MOS memory for Variable Synapse Neural Network", *Electronics Letters*, vol 25, no 10, (May 11, 1989) pp. 669-670.

M. Jabri and B. Flower, "Weight Perturbation: An Optimal Architecture and Learning Technique for Analog VLSI Feedforward and Recurrent Multilayer Networks", *Neural Computation* **3** (1991) pp. 546-565.

D. Kirk, D. Kerns, K. Fleischer, and A. Barr, "Analog VLSI Implementation of Gradient Descent," in *Advances in Neural Information Processing Systems,* San Mateo, CA: Morgan Kaufman Publishers, vol. **5**, 1993.

H.J. Kushner and D.S. Clark, "Stochastic Approximation Methods for Constrained and Unconstrained Systems", p. 58 ff., Springer-Verlag, New York, (1978).

D. E. Rumelhart, G. E. Hinton, and R. J. Williams, "Learning Internal Representations by Error Propagation", in *Parallel Distributed Processing: Explorations in the Microstructure of Cognition. Vol. 1: Foundations*, D. E. Rumelhart and J. L. McClelland (eds.), MIT Press, Cambridge, MA (1986), p. 318.

S. Venkatesh, "Directed Drift: A New Linear Threshold Algorithm for Learning Binary Weights On-Line", *Journal of Computer Science and Systems*, (1993), in press.

B. Widrow and M. A. Lehr, "30 years of Adaptive Neural Networks. Perceptron, Madaline, and Backpropagation", *Proc. IEEE* **78** (1990) pp. 1415-1442.

J. Zinn-Justin, "Quantum Field Theory and Critical Phenomena", p. 57 ff., Oxford University Press, New York, (1989).

PART XI

COGNITIVE SCIENCE

Harmonic Grammars for Formal Languages

Paul Smolensky
Department of Computer Science &
Institute of Cognitive Science
University of Colorado
Boulder, Colorado 80309-0430

Abstract

Basic connectionist principles imply that grammars should take the form of systems of parallel soft constraints defining an optimization problem the solutions to which are the well-formed structures in the language. Such *Harmonic Grammars* have been successfully applied to a number of problems in the theory of natural languages. Here it is shown that formal languages too can be specified by Harmonic Grammars, rather than by conventional serial re-write rule systems.

1 HARMONIC GRAMMARS

In collaboration with Géraldine Legendre, Yoshiro Miyata, and Alan Prince, I have been studying how symbolic computation in human cognition can arise naturally as a higher-level virtual machine realized in appropriately designed lower-level connectionist networks. The basic computational principles of the approach are these:

(1) a. When analyzed at the lower level, mental representations are distributed patterns of connectionist activity; when analyzed at a higher level, these same representations constitute symbolic structures. The particular symbolic structure $\mathtt{s}$ is characterized as a set of *filler/role bindings* $\{\mathtt{f}_i/r_i\}$, using a collection of structural roles $\{r_i\}$ each of which may be occupied by a filler $\mathtt{f}_i$—a constituent symbolic struc-

ture. The corresponding lower-level description is an activity vector $\mathbf{s} = \sum_i \mathbf{f}_i \otimes \mathbf{r}_i$. These *tensor product representations* can be defined recursively: fillers which are themselves complex structures are represented by vectors which in turn are recursively defined as tensor product representations. (Smolensky, 1987; Smolensky, 1990).

b. When analyzed at the lower level, mental processes are massively parallel numerical activation spreading; when analyzed at a higher level, these same processes constitute a form of symbol manipulation in which entire structures, possibly involving recursive embedding, are manipulated in parallel. (Dolan and Smolensky, 1989; Legendre et al., 1991a; Smolensky, 1990).

c. When the lower-level description of the activation spreading processes satisfies certain mathematical properties, this process can be analyzed on a higher level as the construction of that symbolic structure including the given input structure which *maximizes Harmony* (equivalently, minimizes 'energy'. The Harmony can be computed either at the lower level as a particular mathematical function of the numbers comprising the activation pattern, or at the higher level as a function of the symbolic constituents comprising the structure. In the simplest cases, the core of the Harmony function can be written at the lower, connectionist level simply as the quadratic form $H = \mathbf{a}^T\mathbf{W}\mathbf{a}$, where $\mathbf{a}$ is the network's activation vector and $\mathbf{W}$ its connection weight matrix. At the higher level, $H = \sum_{c_1,c_2} H_{c_1;\,c_2}$; each $H_{c_1;\,c_2}$ is the Harmony of having the two symbolic constituents c_1 and c_2 in the same structure (the c_i are constituents *in particular structural roles*, and may be the same). (Cohen and Grossberg, 1983; Golden, 1986; Golden, 1988; Hinton and Sejnowski, 1983; Hinton and Sejnowski, 1986; Hopfield, 1982; Hopfield, 1984; Hopfield, 1987; Legendre et al., 1990a; Smolensky, 1983; Smolensky, 1986).

Once Harmony (connectionist well-formedness) is identified with grammaticality (linguistic well-formedness), the following results (1c) (Legendre et al., 1990a):

(2) a. The explicit form of the Harmony function can be computed to be a sum of terms each of which measures the well-formedness arising from the coexistence, within a single structure, of a pair of constituents in their particular structural roles.

b. A (descriptive) grammar can thus be identified as a set of *soft rules* each of the form:

> If a linguistic structure S simultaneously contains constituent c_1 in structural role r_1 and constituent c_2 in structural role r_2, then add to $H(S)$, the Harmony value of S, the quantity $H_{c_1,r_1;\,c_2,r_2}$ (which may be positive or negative).

A set of such soft rules (or "constraints," or "preferences") defines a *Harmonic Grammar.*

c. The constituents in the soft rules include both those that are given in the input and the "hidden" constituents that are assigned to the input by the grammar. The problem for the parser (computational grammar) is to construct that structure S, containing both input and "hidden" constituents, with the highest overall Harmony $H(S)$.

Harmonic Grammar (HG) is a formal development of conceptual ideas linking Harmony to linguistics which were first proposed in Lakoff's *cognitive phonology* (Lakoff, 1988; Lakoff, 1989) and Goldsmith's *harmonic phonology* (Goldsmith, 1990; Goldsmith, in press). For an application of HG to natural language syntax/semantics, see (Legendre et al., 1990a; Legendre et al., 1990b; Legendre et al., 1991b; Legendre et al., in press). Harmonic Grammar has more recently evolved into a non-numerical formalism called *Optimality Theory* which has been successfully applied to a range of problems in phonology (Prince and Smolensky, 1991; Prince and Smolensky, in preparation). For a comprehensive discussion of the overall research program see (Smolensky et al., 1992).

2 HGs FOR FORMAL LANGUAGES

One means for assessing the expressive power of Harmonic Grammar is to apply it to the specification of formal languages. Can, e.g., any Context-Free Language (CFL) L be specified by an HG? Can a set of soft rules of the form (2b) be given so that a string $s \in L$ iff the maximum-Harmony tree with s as terminals has, say, $H \geq 0$? A crucial limitation of these soft rules is that each may only refer to a *pair* of constituents: in this sense, they are only *second order*. (It simplifies the exposition to describe as "pairs" those in which both constituents are the same; these actually correspond to first order soft rules, which also exist in HG.)

For a CFL, a tree is well-formed iff all of its *local trees* are—where a local tree is just some node and all its children. Thus the HG rules need only refer to pairs of nodes which fall in a single local tree, i.e., parent-child pairs and/or sibling pairs. The H value of the entire tree is just the sum of all the numbers for each such pair of nodes given by the soft rules defining the HG.

It is clear that for a general context-free grammar (CFG), pairwise evaluation doesn't suffice. Consider, e.g., the following CFG fragment, G_0 : $A \rightarrow B\ C$, $A \rightarrow D\ E$, $F \rightarrow B\ E$, and the ill-formed local tree $(A\ ;\ (B\ E))$ (here, A is the parent, B and E the two children). Pairwise well-formedness checks fail to detect the ill-formedness, since the first rule says B can be a left child of A, the second that E can be a right child of A, and the third that B can be a left sibling of E. The ill-formedness can be detected only by examining *all three* nodes simultaneously, and seeing that this triple is not licensed by any single rule.

One possible approach would be to extend HG to rules higher than second order, involving more than two constituents; this corresponds to H functions of degree higher than 2. Such H functions go beyond standard connectionist networks with pairwise connectivity, requiring networks defined over hypergraphs rather than ordinary graphs. There is a natural alternative, however, that requires no change at all in HG, but instead adopts a special kind of grammar for the CFL. The basic trick is a modification of an idea taken from Generalized Phrase Structure Grammar (Gazdar et al., 1985), a theory that adapts CFGs to the study of natural languages.

It is useful to introduce a new normal form for CFGs, *Harmonic Normal Form*

(HNF). In HNF, all rules of are three types: $A[i] \rightarrow B\ C$, $A \rightarrow a$, and $A \rightarrow A[i]$; and there is the further requirement that there can be only one branching rule with a given left hand side—the *unique branching condition.* Here we use lowercase letters to denote terminal symbols, and have two sorts of non-terminals: general symbols like A and *subcategorized* symbols like $A[1], A[2], ..., A[i]$. To see that every CFL L does indeed have an HNF grammar, it suffices to first take a CFG for L in Chomsky Normal Form, and, for each (necessarily binary) branching rule $A \rightarrow B\ C$, (i) replace the symbol A on the left hand side with $A[i]$, using a different value of i for each branching rule with a given left hand side, and (ii) add the rule $A \rightarrow A[i]$.

Subcategorizing the general category A, which may have several legal branching expansions, into the specialized subcategories $A[i]$, each of which has only one legal branching expansion, makes it possible to determine the well-formedness of an entire tree simply by examining each parent/child pair separately: an entire tree is well-formed iff every parent/child pair is. The unique branching condition enables us to evaluate the Harmony of a tree simply by adding up a collection of numbers (specified by the soft rules of an HG), one for each node and one for each link of the tree. Now, any CFL L can be specified by a Harmonic Grammar. First, find an HNF grammar G_{HNF} for L; from it, generate a set of soft rules defining a Harmonic Grammar G_H via the correspondences:

G_{HNF}	G_H
a	R_a: If a is at any node, add -1 to H
A	R_A: If A is at any node, add -2 to H
$A[i]$	$R_{A[i]}$: If $A[i]$ is at any node, add -3 to H
start symbol S	R_{root}: If S is at the root, add $+1$ to H
$A \rightarrow \alpha$ ($\alpha = a$ or $A[i]$)	If α is a left child of A, add $+2$ to H
$A[i] \rightarrow B\ C$	If B is a left child of $A[i]$, add $+2$ to H
	If C is a right child of $A[i]$, add $+2$ to H

The soft rules R_a, R_A, $R_{A[i]}$ and R_{root} are first-order and evaluate tree nodes; the remaining second-order soft rules are *legal domination* rules evaluating tree links.

This HG assigns $H = 0$ to any legal parse tree (with S at the root), and $H < 0$ for any other tree; thus $s \in L$ iff the maximal-Harmony completion of s to a tree has $H \geq 0$.

Proof. We evaluate the Harmony of any tree by conceptually breaking up its nodes and links into pieces each of which contributes either $+1$ or -1 to H. In legal trees, there will be complete cancellation of the positive and negative contributions; illegal trees will have uncancelled -1s leading to a total $H < 0$.

The decomposition of nodes and links proceeds as follows. Replace each (undirected) link in the tree with a pair of directed links, one pointing up to the parent, the other down to the child. If the link joins a legal parent/child pair, the corresponding legal domination rule will contribute $+2$ to H; break this $+2$ into two contributions of $+1$, one for each of the directed links. We similarly break up the non-terminal nodes into sub-nodes. A non-terminal node labelled

$A[i]$ has two children in legal trees, and we break such a node into three sub-nodes, one corresponding to each downward link to a child and one corresponding to the upward link to the parent of $A[i]$. According to soft rule $R_{A[i]}$, the contribution of this node $A[i]$ to H is -3; this is distributed as three contributions of -1, one for each sub-node. Similarly, a non-terminal node labelled A has only one child in a legal tree, so we break it into two sub-nodes, one for the downward link to the only child, one for the upward link to the parent of A. The contribution of -2 dictated by soft rule R_A is similarly decomposed into two contributions of -1, one for each sub-node. There is no need to break up terminal nodes, which in legal trees have only one outgoing link, upward to the parent; the contribution from R_a is already just -1.

We can evaluate the Harmony of any tree by examining each node, now decomposed into a set of sub-nodes, and determining the contribution to H made by the node and its *outgoing* directed links. We will not double-count link contributions this way; half the contribution of each original undirected link is counted at each of the nodes it connects.

Consider first a non-terminal node n labelled by $A[i]$; if it has a legal parent, it will have an upward link to the parent that contributes $+1$, which cancels the -1 contributed by n's corresponding sub-node. If n has a legal left child, the downward link to it will contribute $+1$, cancelling the -1 contributed by n's corresponding sub-node. Similarly for the right child. Thus the total contribution of this node will be 0 if it has a legal parent and two legal children. For each *missing* legal child or parent, the node contributes an uncancelled -1, so the contribution of this node n in the general case is:

(3) H_n = -(the number of missing legal children and parents of node n)

The same result (3) holds of the non-branching non-terminals labelled A; the only difference is that now the only child that could be missing is a legal left child. If A happens to be a legal start symbol in root position, then the -1 of the sub-node corresponding to the upward link to a parent is cancelled not by a legal parent, as usual, but rather by the $+1$ of the soft rule R_{root}. The result (3) still holds even in this case, if we simply agree to count the root position itself as a legal parent for start symbols. And finally, (3) holds of a terminal node n labelled a; such a node can have no missing child, but might have a missing legal parent.

Thus the total Harmony of a tree is $H = \sum_n H_n$, with H_n given by (3). That is, H is the *minus* the total number of missing legal children and parents for all nodes in the tree. Thus, $H = 0$ if each node has a legal parent and all its required legal children, otherwise $H \leq 0$. Because the grammar is in Harmonic Normal Form, a parse tree is legal iff every every node has a legal parent and its required number of legal children, where "legal" parent/child dominations are defined only pairwise, in terms of the parent and one child, blind to any other children that might be present or absent. Thus we have established the desired result, that the maximum-Harmony parse of a string s has $H \geq 0$ iff $s \in L$.

We can also now see how to understand the soft rules of G_H, and how to generalize beyond Context-Free Languages. The soft rules say that each node makes a negative contribution equal to its valence, while each link makes a positive contribution equal to its valence (2); where the "valence" of a node (or link) is just the number of links (or nodes) it is attached to in a legal tree. The negative contributions of the nodes are made any time the node is present; these are cancelled by positive contributions from the links only when the link constitutes a legal domination, sanctioned by the grammar.

So in order to apply the same strategy to unrestricted grammars, we will simply set the magnitude of the (negative) contributions of nodes equal to their valence, as determined by the grammar. □

We can illustrate the technique by showing how HNF solves the problem with the simple three-rule grammar fragment G_0 introduced early in this section. The corresponding HNF grammar fragment G_{HNF} given by the above construction is $A[1] \rightarrow B\ C$, $A \rightarrow A[1]$, $A[2] \rightarrow D\ E$, $A \rightarrow A[2]$, $F[1] \rightarrow B\ E$, $F \rightarrow F[1]$. To avoid extraneous complications from adding a start node above and terminal nodes below, suppose that both A and F are valid start symbols and that B, C, D, E are terminal nodes. Then the corresponding HG G_H assigns to the ill-formed tree $(A\ ;\ (B\ E))$ the Harmony -4, since, according to G_{HNF}, B and E are both missing a legal parent and A is missing two legal children. Introducing a now-necessary subcategorized version of A helps, but not enough: $(A\ ;\ (A[1]\ ;\ (B\ E)))$ and $(A\ ;\ (A[2]\ ;\ (B\ E)))$ both have $H = -2$ since in each, one leaf node is missing a legal parent (E and B, respectively), and the $A[i]$ node is missing the corresponding legal child. But the correct parse of the string $B\ E$, $(F\ ;\ (F[1]\ ;\ (B\ E)))$, has $H = 0$.

This technique can be generalized from context-free to unrestricted (type 0) formal languages, which are equivalent to Turing Machines in the languages they generate (e.g., (Hopcroft and Ullman, 1979)). The ith production rule in an unrestricted grammar, $R_i : \alpha_1\alpha_2\cdots\alpha_{n_i} \rightarrow \beta_1\beta_2\cdots\beta_{m_i}$ is replaced by the two rules: $R_i' : \alpha_1\alpha_2\cdots\alpha_{n_i} \rightarrow \Gamma[i]$ and $R_i'' : \Gamma[i] \rightarrow \beta_1\beta_2\cdots\beta_{m_i}$, introducing new non-terminal symbols $\Gamma[i]$. The corresponding soft rules in the Harmonic Grammar are then: "If the kth parent of $\Gamma[i]$ is α_k, add $+2$ to H" and "If β_k is the kth child of $\Gamma[i]$, add $+2$ to H"; there is also the rule $R_{\Gamma[i]}$: "If $\Gamma[i]$ is at any node, add $-n_i - m_i$ to H." There are also soft rules R_a, R_A, and R_{root}, defined as in the context-free case.

Acknowledgements

I am grateful to Géraldine Legendre, Yoshiro Miyata, and Alan Prince for many helpful discussions. The research presented here has been supported in part by NSF grant BS-9209265 and by the University of Colorado at Boulder Council on Research and Creative Work.

References

Cohen, M. A. and Grossberg, S. (1983). Absolute stability of global pattern formation and parallel memory storage by competitive neural networks. *IEEE Transactions on Systems, Man, and Cybernetics*, 13:815–825.

Dolan, C. P. and Smolensky, P. (1989). Tensor Product Production System: A modular architecture and representation. *Connection Science*, 1:53–68.

Gazdar, G., Klein, E., Pullum, G., and Sag, I. (1985). *Generalized Phrase Structure Grammar.* Harvard University Press, Cambridge, MA.

Golden, R. M. (1986). The "Brain-State-in-a-Box" neural model is a gradient descent algorithm. *Mathematical Psychology*, 30–31:73–80.

Golden, R. M. (1988). A unified framework for connectionist systems. *Biological Cybernetics*, 59:109–120.

Goldsmith, J. A. (1990). *Autosegmental and Metrical Phonology.* Basil Blackwell, Oxford.

Goldsmith, J. A. (In press). Phonology as an intelligent system. In Napoli, D. J. and Kegl, J. A., editors, *Bridges between Psychology and Linguistics: A Swarthmore Festschrift for Lila Gleitman.* Cambridge University Press, Cambridge.

Hinton, G. E. and Sejnowski, T. J. (1983). Analyzing cooperative computation. In *Proceedings of the Fifth Annual Conference of the Cognitive Science Society*, Rochester, NY. Erlbaum Associates.

Hinton, G. E. and Sejnowski, T. J. (1986). Learning and relearning in Boltzmann machines. In Rumelhart, D. E., McClelland, J. L., and the PDP Research Group, editors, *Parallel Distributed Processing: Explorations in the Microstructure of Cognition, Volume 1: Foundations*, chapter 7, pages 282–317. MIT Press/Bradford Books, Cambridge, MA.

Hopcroft, J. E. and Ullman, J. D. (1979). *Introduction to Automata Theory, Languages, and Computation.* Addison-Wesley, Reading, MA.

Hopfield, J. J. (1982). Neural networks and physical systems with emergent collective computational abilities. *Proceedings of the National Academy of Sciences, USA*, 79:2554–2558.

Hopfield, J. J. (1984). Neurons with graded response have collective computational properties like those of two-state neurons. *Proceedings of the National Academy of Sciences, USA*, 81:3088–3092.

Hopfield, J. J. (1987). Learning algorithms and probability distributions in feed-forward and feed-back networks. *Proceedings of the National Academy of Sciences, USA*, 84:8429–8433.

Lakoff, G. (1988). A suggestion for a linguistics with connectionist foundations. In Touretzky, D., Hinton, G. E., and Sejnowski, T. J., editors, *Proceedings of the Connectionist Models Summer School*, pages 301–314, San Mateo, CA. Morgan Kaufmann.

Lakoff, G. (1989). Cognitive phonology. Paper presented at the UC-Berkeley Workshop on Rules and Constraints.

Legendre, G., Miyata, Y., and Smolensky, P. (1990a). Harmonic Grammar—A formal multi-level connectionist theory of linguistic well-formedness: Theoretical foundations. In *Proceedings of the Twelfth Annual Conference of the Cognitive Science Society*, pages 388–395, Cambridge, MA. Lawrence Erlbaum.

Legendre, G., Miyata, Y., and Smolensky, P. (1990b). Harmonic Grammar—A formal multi-level connectionist theory of linguistic well-formedness: An application. In *Proceedings of the Twelfth Annual Conference of the Cognitive Science Society*, pages 884–891, Cambridge, MA. Lawrence Erlbaum.

Legendre, G., Miyata, Y., and Smolensky, P. (1991a). Distributed recursive structure processing. In Touretzky, D. S. and Lippman, R., editors, *Advances in Neural Information Processing Systems 3*, pages 591–597, San Mateo, CA. Morgan Kaufmann. Slightly expanded version in Brian Mayoh, editor, *Scandinavian Conference on Artificial Intelligence—91*, pages 47–53. IOS Press, Amsterdam.

Legendre, G., Miyata, Y., and Smolensky, P. (1991b). Unifying syntactic and semantic approaches to unaccusativity: A connectionist approach. In Sutton, L. and Johnson (with Ruth Shields), C., editors, *Proceedings of the Seventeenth Annual Meeting of the Berkeley Linguistics Society*, pages 156–167, Berkeley, CA.

Legendre, G., Miyata, Y., and Smolensky, P. (In press). Can connectionism contribute to syntax? Harmonic Grammar, with an application. In Deaton, K., Noske, M., and Ziolkowski, M., editors, *Proceedings of the 26th Meeting of the Chicago Linguistic Society*, Chicago, IL.

Prince, A. and Smolensky, P. (1991). Notes on connectionism and Harmony Theory in linguistics. Technical report, Department of Computer Science, University of Colorado at Boulder. Technical Report CU-CS-533-91.

Prince, A. and Smolensky, P. (In preparation). Optimality Theory: Constraint interaction in generative grammar.

Smolensky, P. (1983). Schema selection and stochastic inference in modular environments. In *Proceedings of the National Conference on Artificial Intelligence*, pages 378–382, Washington, DC.

Smolensky, P. (1986). Information processing in dynamical systems: Foundations of Harmony Theory. In Rumelhart, D. E., McClelland, J. L., and the PDP Research Group, editors, *Parallel Distributed Processing: Explorations in the Microstructure of Cognition. Volume 1: Foundations*, chapter 6, pages 194–281. MIT Press/Bradford Books, Cambridge, MA.

Smolensky, P. (1987). On variable binding and the representation of symbolic structures in connectionist systems. Technical report, Department of Computer Science, University of Colorado at Boulder. Technical Report CU-CS-355-87.

Smolensky, P. (1990). Tensor product variable binding and the representation of symbolic structures in connectionist networks. *Artificial Intelligence*, 46:159–216.

Smolensky, P., Legendre, G., and Miyata, Y. (1992). Principles for an integrated connectionist/symbolic theory of higher cognition. Technical report, Department of Computer Science, University of Colorado at Boulder. Technical Report CU-CS-600-92.

Analogy--Watershed or Waterloo? Structural alignment and the development of connectionist models of analogy

Dedre Gentner
Department of Psychology
Northwestern University
2029 Sheridan Rd.
Evanston, IL 60208

Arthur B. Markman
Department of Psychology
Northwestern University
2029 Sheridan Rd.
Evanston, IL 60208

ABSTRACT

Neural network models have been criticized for their inability to make use of compositional representations. In this paper, we describe a series of psychological phenomena that demonstrate the role of structured representations in cognition. These findings suggest that people compare relational representations via a process of structural alignment. This process will have to be captured by any model of cognition, symbolic or subsymbolic.

1.0 INTRODUCTION

Pattern recognition is central to cognition. At the perceptual level, we notice key features of the world (like symmetry), recognize objects in front of us and identify the letters on a printed page. At a higher level, we recognize problems we have solved before and determine similarities—including analogical similarities—between new situations and old ones. Neural network models have been successful at capturing sensory pattern recognition (e.g., Sabourin & Mitiche, 1992). In contrast, the determination of higher level similarities has been well modeled by symbolic processes (Falkenhainer, Forbus, & Gentner, 1989). An important question is whether neural networks can be extended to high-level similarity and pattern recognition.

In this paper, we will summarize the constraints on cognitive representations suggested by the psychological study of similarity and analogy. We focus on three themes: (1) structural alignment; (2) structural projection; and (3) flexibility.

2.0 STRUCTURAL ALIGNMENT IN SIMILARITY

Extensive psychological research has examined the way people compare pairs of items to determine their similarity. Mounting evidence suggests that the similarity of two complex items depends on the degree of match between their component objects (common and distinctive *attributes*) and on the degree of match between the *relations* among the component objects. Specifically, there is evidence that (1) similarity involves structured pattern matching, (2) similarity involves structured pattern completion, (3) comparing the same item with different things can highlight different aspects of the item and (4) even comparisons of a single pair of items may yield multiple interpretations. We will examine these four claims in the following sections.

2.1 SIMILARITY INVOLVES STRUCTURED PATTERN MATCHING

The central idea underlying structured pattern matching is that similarity involves an alignment of relational structure. For example, in Figure 1a, configuration A is clearly more similar to the top configuration than configuration B, because A has similar objects taking part in the same relation (*above*), while B has similar objects taking part in a different relation (*next-to*). This determination can be made regardless of whether the objects taking part in the relations are similar. For example, in Figure 1b configuration A is also more similar to the top configuration than is configuration B, because A shares a relation with the top configuration, while B does not. As a check on this intuition, 10 subjects were asked to tell us which configuration (A or B) went best with the top configuration for the triads in Figures 1a and 1b. All 10 subjects chose configuration A for both triads. This example demonstrates that relations (such as the common *above* relation) are important in similarity processing.

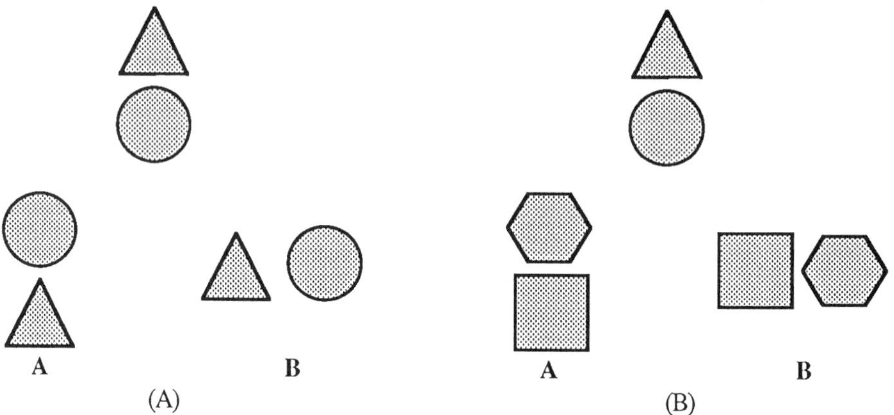

Figure 1. Examples of structural alignment in perception.

The importance of relations was also demonstrated by Palmer (1978) who asked subjects to rate the similarity of pairs of configurations like those in Figure 2. The pair in Figure 2a shares the global property that both are open figures, while the pair in Figure 2b does not. As would be expected if subjects attend to relations when determining similarity, higher similarity ratings were given to pairs like the one in Figure 2a than to pairs like the one in Figure 2b. This finding can only be explained by appealing to structural similarity, because both pairs of configurations share the same number of local line segments. Consistent with this result, Palmer also found that subjects were faster to say that the items in Figure 2b are different than that the items in Figure 2a are different. A similar result was obtained by Lockhead and King (1977).

Figure 2. Structured pattern matching in a study by Palmer (1978).

Further research suggests that common bindings between relations and the items they relate are also central to similarity. For example, Clement and Gentner (1991) presented subjects with pairs of analogous stories. One story described organisms called Tams that ate rocks, while the other described robots that collected data on a planet. In each story, one matching fact also had a matching causal antecedent. For example, *the Tams' exhausting the minerals on the rock CAUSED them to* ***move to another rock***, while *the robots' exhausting the data on a planet CAUSED them to* ***move to another planet***. A second matching fact did not have a matching causal antecedent. For example, ***the Tams' underbelly could not function on a new rock*** and the ***robots' probe could not function on a new planet***, but the causes of these facts did not match. Subjects were asked which of the two pairs of key facts (shown in bold) was more important to the stories. Subjects selected the pair that had the matching causal antecedent, suggesting that their mappings preserved the relational connections in the stories.

2.2 STRUCTURED PATTERN COMPLETION

Pattern completion has long been a central feature of neural network models (Anderson, Silverstein, Ritz, & Jones, 1977; Hopfield, 1982). For example, in the BSB model of Anderson et al., vectors in which some units are below their maximum value are filled in by completing a pattern based on the vector similarities of the current activation pattern to previously learned patterns.

The key issue here is the kind of information that guides pattern completion in humans. Data from psychological studies suggests that subjects' pattern matching ability is controlled by structural similarities rather than by geometric similarities. For example, Medin and Goldstone presented subjects with pairs of objects like those in Figure 3 (Medin, Goldstone & Gentner, in press). The left-hand figure in both pairs is somewhat ambiguous, but the right-hand figure is not. Subjects who were asked to list the commonalities of the pair in Figure 3a said that both figures had three prongs, while subjects who were asked to list the commonalities of the pair in Figure 3b said that both figures had four prongs. This finding was obtained for 15 of 16 triads tested, and suggests that subjects were mapping the structure from the unambiguous figure onto the ambiguous one. Of course, in order for the mapping to take place, the underlying structure of the figures has to be readily alignable, and there must be ambiguity in the target figure. In the pair in Figure 3c, the left hand item cannot be viewed as having four prongs, and so this mapping is not made.

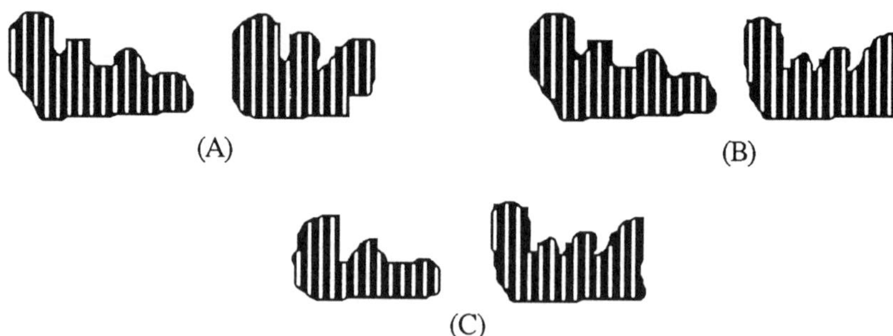

Figure 3: Example of structured pattern completion.

Structured pattern completion also occurs in conceptual structures. Clement and Gentner (1991) extended the study described above by deleting the key matching facts from one of the stories (e.g., the **bold** facts from the robot story). Subjects read both stories, then predicted one new fact about the robot story. Subjects were free to predict anything at all, but 50% of the subjects predicted the fact with the matching causal antecedent, while only 28% of the subjects predicted the fact with no matching causal antecedent. By comparison, a control group that made predictions about the target story without seeing the base predicted both facts at the same rate (about 5%). This finding underlines the importance of connectivity in pattern completion. People's predictions were determined not just by the local information, but by whether it was connected to matching information. Thus, pattern completion is structure-sensitive.

2.3 DIFFERENT COMPARISONS-DIFFERENT INTERPRETATIONS

Comparison is flexible. When an item takes part in many comparisons, it may be interpreted differently in each comparison. For example, in Figure 3a, the left figure is interpreted as having 3 prongs, while in Figure 3b, it is interpreted as having 4 prongs. Similarly, the comparison 'My surgeon is a butcher' conveys a clumsy surgeon, but 'Genghis Khan was a butcher' conveys a ruthless killer (Glucksberg and Keysar, 1992).

This type of flexibility is also evident in an example presented by Spellman and Holyoak (1992). They pointed out that some politicians likened the Gulf War to World War II, implying that the United States was acting as the world's policeman to stop a tyrant. Other politicians compared Operation Desert Storm to Vietnam, implying that the United States entered into a potentially endless conflict between two other nations. Clearly, different comparisons highlighted different features of the Gulf War.

2.4 SAME COMPARISON-DIFFERENT INTERPRETATIONS

Even a single comparison can yield more than one distinct interpretation. This situation may arise when the items are richly represented, with many different clusters of knowledge. It can also arise when the comparison permits more than one alignment, as when the similarities of the objects in an item suggest different correspondences than do the relational similarities (i.e. components are *cross-mapped* (Gentner & Toupin, 1986)).

Markman and Gentner (in press) presented subjects with pairs of scenes like those depicting the perceptual higher order relation *monotonic increase in size* shown in Figure 4. In Figure 4, the circle with the arrow over it in the left-hand figure is the largest circle in the array. It is cross-mapped, since it is the same size as the middle circle in the right-hand figure, but plays the same relational role as the left (largest) circle. Subjects were given a mapping task in which they were asked to point to the object in the right-hand figure that went with with the cross-mapped circle in the left-hand figure. In this task, subjects chose the circle that looked most similar 91% of the time. However, a second group of subjects, who rated the similarity of the pair before doing this mapping, selected the object playing the same relational role 61% of the time. In both tasks, when subjects were asked whether there were any other good choices, they generally described the other possible mapping. These results show that the same comparison can be aligned in different ways, and that similarity comparisons promote structural alignment.

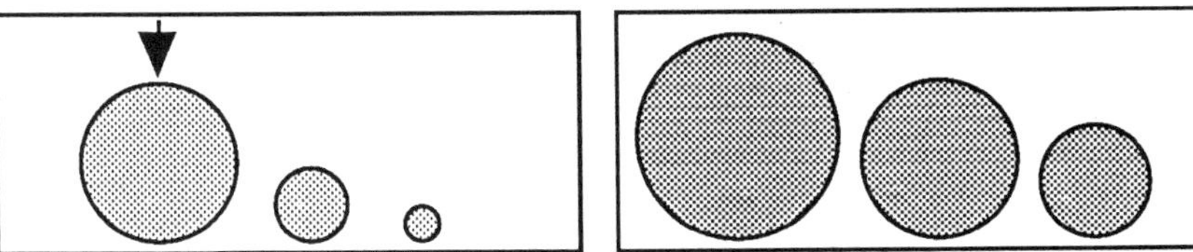

Figure 4: Stimuli with a cross-mapping from Markman and Gentner (in press).

Goldstone (personal communication) has demonstrated that, not only are comparisons flexible, but subjects can attend to attribute and relation matches selectively. He presented subjects with triads like the one in Figure 5. Subjects were asked to choose either the bottom figure with the most attribute similarity to the top one, or the bottom figure with the most relational similarity to the top one. In this study, and other pilot studies, subjects were highly accurate at both task, suggesting flexibility to attend to different kinds of similarity.

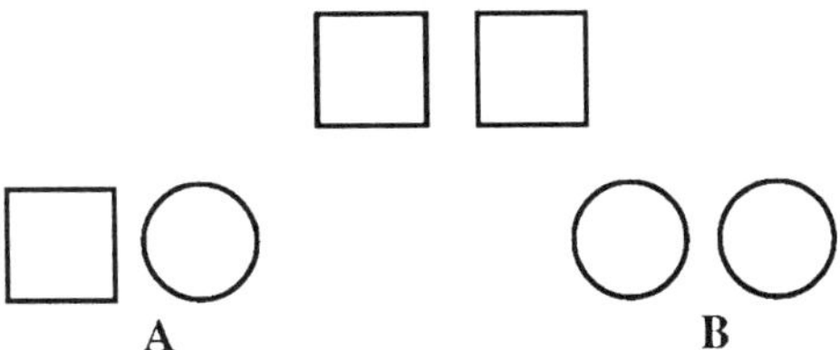

Figure 5: Sample stimuli from study by Goldstone.

Similar flexibility can also be found in stimuli with conceptual relations. Gentner (1988) presented children with *double metaphors* that can have two meanings, one based on attribute similarities and a second based on relational similarities. For example, the metaphor 'Plant stems are like drinking straws' can mean that both are round and skinny, or that both transport fluids from low places to high places. Gentner found that young children (age 5-6) made the attribute-based interpretation, while older children (age 9-10) and adults could make either interpretation (but preferred the relation-based interpretation).

There are limits to this flexibility. People prefer to make structurally consistent mappings (Gentner, 1983). For example, Spellman and Holyoak (1992) told subjects to map Operation Desert Storm onto World War II. When they asked subjects to find a correspondence for George Bush given that Saddam Hussein corresponded to Hitler, subjects generally chose either FDR or Churchill. Then, subjects were asked to make a mapping for the United States in 1991. Interestingly, subjects who mapped Bush to FDR almost always mapped the US in 1991 to the US during World War II. In contrast, subjects who mapped Bush to Churchill almost always mapped the US in 1991 to Britain during World War II. Thus, subjects maintained structurally consistent mappings.

This type of flexibility adds significant complexity to the comparison process, because a system cannot simply be trained to search for relational correspondences or be taught to prefer only attribute matches. Rather, the comparison process must determine both attribute and relation matches and must be able to keep different mappings distinct from each other.

2.5 SUMMARY OF EMPIRICAL EVIDENCE

These findings suggest that comparisons of both perceptual and conceptual materials involve structural alignment. Further, structural alignment promotes structure sensitive pattern completion. Finally, comparisons allow for multiple interpretations of a single item in different comparisons or multiple interpretations of a single comparison. Any model of human cognition that involves comparison must exhibit these properties.

3.0 IMPLICATIONS FOR COGNITIVE MODELS

Many of the questions concerning the adequacy of connectionist models and neural networks for high-level cognitive tasks have centered on linguistic processing and the crucial role of compositional relational structures in sentence comprehension (Fodor & McLaughlin, 1990; Fodor & Pylyshyn, 1988). Recent work has addressed this problem by examining ways to represent hierarchical structure in connectionist models, implementing stacks and binary trees to model variable binding and recursive sentence processing (e.g., Elman, 1990; Pollack, 1990; Smolensky, 1990; see also Quinlan, 1991 for a review). It is too soon to tell how successful these methods will be, or whether they can be extended to the general case of structural alignment.

The results summarized here underline the need for representations that permit structural alignment. How should this be done? As van Gelder (1990) discusses, symbolic systems traditionally use *concatenative* representation, in which symbol names are concatenated to build a compositional representation. For example, a circle above a triangle could be represented by the assertion **above**(circle,triangle). Such symbolic representations have been used to model the analogy and similarity phenomena described here with some success (Falkenhainer, et al., 1989). Van Gelder (1990) suggests a weaker criterion of *functional compositionality*. In functionally compositional representations, tokens for the symbols are not directly present in the representation, but they can be extracted from the representation via some process. Van Gelder suggests that the natural representation used by neural networks is functionally compositional. Analogously, the question of whether connectionist models can model the phenomena described here should be couched in terms of *functional alignability*: whether the representations can be decomposed and aligned, rather than whether the structure is transparently present.

Along this track, an intriguing question is whether the surface form of functionally compositional representations will be similar to the degree that the structures they represent are similar. If so, the alignment process could take place simply by comparing activation vectors. As yet, there are no networks that exhibit this behavior. Further, given the evidence that geometric representations are insufficient to model human similarity comparisons (see Tversky (1977) for a review), we are pessimistic about the prospects that this type of model will be developed.

In conclusion, substantial psychological evidence suggests that determining the similarity of two items requires a flexible alignment of structured representations. We suspect that connectionist models of cognitive processes that involve comparisons will have to exhibit concatenative compositionality in order to capture the flexibility inherent in comparisons. However, we leave open the possibility that systems exhibiting functional alignability will be successful.

Acknowledgments

This research was sponsored by ONR grant BNS-87-20301. We thank Jon Handler, Ed Wisniewski, Phil Wolff and the whole Similarity and Analogy group for comments on this work. We also thank Laura Kotovsky, Catherine Kreiser and Russ Poldrack for running the pilot studies described above.

References

Anderson, J. A., Silverstein, J. W., Ritz, S. A., & Jones, R. S. (1977). Distinctive features, categorical perception and probability learning: Some applications of a neural model. Psychological Review, 84, 413-451.

Clement, C. A., & Gentner, D. (1991). Systematicity as a selection constraint in analogical mapping. Cognitive Science, 15, 89-132.

Elman, J.L. (1990). Finding structure in time. Cognitive Science, 14(2), 179-212.

Falkenhainer, B., Forbus, K. D., & Gentner, D. (1989). The structure-mapping engine: Algorithm and examples. Artificial Intelligence, 41(1), 1-63.

Fodor, J., & McLaughlin, B. (1990). Connectionism and the problem of systematicity: Why Smolensky's solution doesn't work. Cognition, 35, 183-204.

Fodor, J. A., & Pylyshyn, Z. W. (1988). Connectionism and cognitive architecture: A critical analysis. Cognition, 28, 3-71.

Gentner, D. (1983). Structure mapping: A theoretical framework for analogy. Cognitive Science, 7, 155-170.

Gentner, D. (1988). Metaphor as structure mapping: The relational shift. Child Development, 59, 47-59.

Gentner, D., & Toupin, C. (1986). Systematicity and surface similarity in the development of analogy. Cognitive Science, 10, 277-300.

Glucksberg, S. & Keysar, B. (1990). Understanding metaphorical comparisons: Beyond similarity. Psychological Review, 97(1), 3-18.

Hopfield, J. J. (1982). Neural networks and physical systems with emergent collective computational abilities. Proceedings of the National Academy of Sciences, 79, 2554-2558.

Lockhead, G. R., & King, M. C. (1977). Classifying integral stimuli. Journal of Experimental Psychology: Human Perception and Performance, 3(3), 436-443.

Markman, A. B., & Gentner, D. (in press). Structural alignment during similarity comparisons. Cognitive Psychology.

Medin, D. L., Goldstone, R. L., & Gentner, D. (in press). Respects for similarity. Psychological Review.

Palmer, S. E. (1978). Structural aspects of visual similarity. Memory and Cognition, 6(2), 91-97.

Pollack, J. B. (1990). Recursive distributed representations. Artificial Intelligence, 46(1-2), 77-106.

Quinlan, P.T. (1991). Connectionism and Psychology: A psychological perspective on new connectionist research. Chicago: The University of Chicago Press.

Sabourin, M. & Mitiche, A. (1992). Optical character recognition by a neural network. Neural Networks, 5(5), 843-852.

Smolensky, P. (1990). Tensor product variable binding and the representation of symbolic structures in connectionist systems. Artificial Intelligence, 46, 159-216.

Spellman, B. A., & Holyoak, K. J. (1992). If Saddam is Hitler then who is George Bush? Analogical mapping between systems of social roles. Journal of Personality and Social Psychology, 62(6), 913-933.

Tversky, A. (1977). Features of similarity. Psychological Review, 84(4), 327-352.

van Gelder, T. (1990). Compositionality: A connectionist variation on a classical theme. Cognitive Science, 14(3), 355-384.

A Connectionist Symbol Manipulator That Discovers the Structure of Context-Free Languages

Michael C. Mozer and Sreerupa Das
Department of Computer Science &
Institute of Cognitive Science
University of Colorado
Boulder, CO 80309–0430

Abstract

We present a neural net architecture that can discover hierarchical and recursive structure in symbol strings. To detect structure at multiple levels, the architecture has the capability of reducing symbols substrings to single symbols, and makes use of an external stack memory. In terms of formal languages, the architecture can learn to parse strings in an LR(0) context-free grammar. Given training sets of positive and negative exemplars, the architecture has been trained to recognize many different grammars. The architecture has only one layer of modifiable weights, allowing for a straightforward interpretation of its behavior.

Many cognitive domains involve complex sequences that contain hierarchical or recursive structure, e.g., music, natural language parsing, event perception. To illustrate, "the spider that ate the hairy fly" is a noun phrase containing the embedded noun phrase "the hairy fly." Understanding such multilevel structures requires forming *reduced descriptions* (Hinton, 1988) in which a string of symbols or states ("the hairy fly") is reduced to a single symbolic entity (a noun phrase). We present a neural net architecture that learns to encode the structure of symbol strings via such reduction transformations.

The difficult problem of extracting multilevel structure from complex, extended sequences has been studied by Mozer (1992), Ring (1993), Rohwer (1990), and Schmidhuber (1992), among others. While these previous efforts have made some

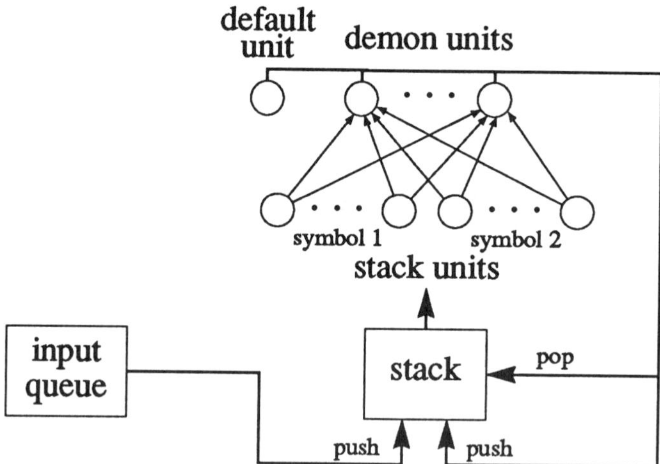

Figure 1: The demon model.

progress, no one has claimed victory over the problem. Our approach is based on a new perspective—one of symbolic reduction transformations—which affords a fresh attack on the problem.

1 A BLACKBOARD ARCHITECTURE

Our inspiration is a blackboard style architecture that works as follows. The input, a sequence of symbols, is copied onto a *blackboard*—a scratch pad memory—one symbol at a time. A set of *demons* watch over the blackboard, each looking for a specific pattern of symbols. When a demon observes its pattern, it *fires*, causing the pattern to be replaced by a symbol associated with that demon, which we'll call its *identity*. This process continues until the entire input string has been read or no demon can fire. The sequence of demon firings and the final blackboard contents specify the structure of the input.

The model we present is a simplified version of this blackboard architecture. The blackboard is implemented as a stack. Consequently, the demons have no control over *where* they write or read a symbol; they simply push and pop symbols from the stack. The other simplification is that the demon firing is based on template matching, rather than a more sophisticated form of pattern matching.

The demon model is sketched in Figure 1. An *input queue* holds the input string to be parsed, which is gradually transferred to the stack. The top k stack symbols are encoded in a set of *stack units*; in the current implementation, $k = 2$. Each demon is embodied by a special processing unit which receives input from the stack units. The weights of each *demon unit* specify a pair of symbols, which the demon unit matches against the two stack symbols. If there is a match, the demon unit pops the top two stack symbols and pushes its identity. If no demon unit matches, an additional unit, called the *default unit*, becomes active. The default unit is responsible for transferring a symbol from the input queue onto the stack.

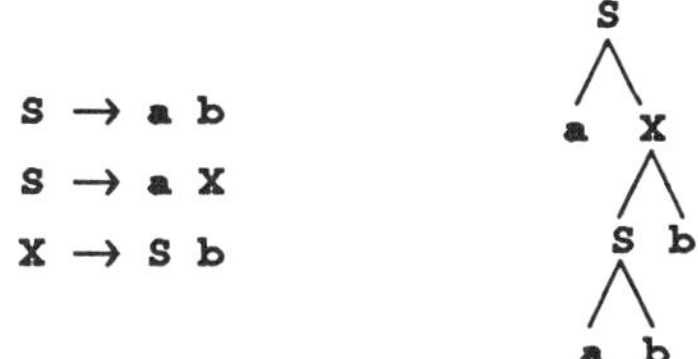

Figure 2: The rewrite rules defining a grammar that generates strings of the form $a^n b^n$ and a parse tree for the string aabb.

2 PARSING CONTEXT-FREE LANGUAGES

Each demon unit reduces a pair of symbols to a single symbol. We can express the operation of a demon as a rewrite rule of the form X → a b, where the lower case letters denote symbols in the input string and upper case letters denote the demon identities, also symbols in their own right. The above rule specifies that when the symbols a and b appear on the top of the stack, in that order, the X demon unit should fire, erasing those two symbols and replacing them with an X. Demon units can respond to internal symbols (demon identities) instead of input symbols, allowing internal symbols on the right hand side of the rule. Demon units can also respond to individual input symbols, achieving rules of the form X → a.

Multiple demon units can have the same identity, leading to rewrite rules of a more general form, e.g., X → a b | Y c | d Z | a. This class of rewrite rules can express a subset of context-free grammars. Figure 2 shows a sample grammar that generates strings of the form $a^n b^n$ and a parse tree for the input string aabb. The demon model essentially constructs such parse trees via the sequence of reduction operations.

That each rule has only one or two symbols on the right hand side imposes no limitation on the class of grammars that can be recognized. However, the demon model does require certain knowledge about the grammars to be identified. First, the maximum number of rewrite rules and the maximum number of rules having the same left-hand side must be specified in advance. This is because the units have to be allocated prior to learning. Second, the LR-class of the grammar must be given. To explain, any context-free grammar can be characterized as LR(n), which indicates that the strings of the grammar can be parsed from left to right with n symbols of look ahead on the input queue. The demon model requires that n be specified in advance. In the present work, we examine only LR(0) grammars, but the architecture can readily be generalized to arbitrary n.

Giles et al. (1990), Sun et al. (1990), and Das, Giles, and Sun (1992) have previously explored the learning of context-free grammars in a neural net. Their approach was based on the automaton perspective of a recognizer, where the primary interest was to learn the dynamics of a pushdown automaton. There has also been significant work in context-free grammar inference using symbolic approaches. In general, these approaches require a significant amount of prior information about the grammar and, although theoretically sound, have not proven terribly useful in practice. A promising exception is the recent proposal of Stolcke (1993).

3 CONTINUOUS DYNAMICS

So far, we have described the model in a discrete way: demon firing is all-or-none and mutually exclusive, corresponding to the demon units achieving a unary representation. This may be the desired behavior following learning, but neural net learning algorithms like back propagation require exploration in continuous state and weight spaces and therefore need to allow partial activity of demon units. The continuous activation dynamics follow.

Demon unit i computes the distance between its weights, $\mathbf{w}_i$, and the input, $\mathbf{x}$: $dist_i = b_i|\mathbf{w}_i - \mathbf{x}|^2$, where b_i is an adjustable bias associated with the unit. The activity of unit i, denoted s_i, is computed via a normalized exponential transform (Bridle, 1990; Rumelhart, in press),

$$s_i = \frac{e^{-dist_i}}{\sum_j e^{-dist_j}},$$

which enforces a competition among the units. A special unit, called the default unit, is designed to respond when none of the demons fire strongly. Its activity, s_{def}, is computed like that of any demon unit with $dist_{def} = b_{def}$.

4 CONTINUOUS STACK

Because demon units can be partially active, stack operations need to be performed partially. This can be accomplished with a *continuous stack* (Giles et al., 1990). Unlike a discrete stack where an item is either present or absent, items can be present to varying degrees. Each item on the stack has an associated *thickness*, a scalar in the interval $[0, 1]$ indicating what fraction of the item is present (Figure 3).

To understand how the thickness plays a role in processing, we digress briefly and explain the encoding of symbols. Both on the stack and in the network, symbols are represented by numerical vectors that have one component per symbol. The vector representation of some symbol X, denoted $\mathbf{r}_X$, has value 1 for the component corresponding to X and 0 for all other components. If the symbol has thickness t, the vector representation is $t\mathbf{r}_X$.

Although items on the stack have different thicknesses, the network is presented with *composite symbols* having thickness 1.0. Composite symbols are formed by combining stack items. For example, in Figure 3, composite symbol 1 is defined as the vector $.2\mathbf{r}_X + .5\mathbf{r}_Z + .3\mathbf{r}_Y$. The input to the demon network consists of the top two composite symbols on the stack.

The advantages of a continuous stack are twofold. First, it is required for network learning; if a discrete stack were used, a small change in weights could result in a big (discrete) change in the stack. This was the motivation underlying the continuous stack used by Giles et al. Second, the continuous stack is differentiable and hence allows us to back propagate error through the stack during learning. While we have summarized this point in one sentence, the reader must appreciate the fact that it is no small feat! Giles et al. did not consider back propagation through the stack.

Each time step, the network performs two operations on the stack:

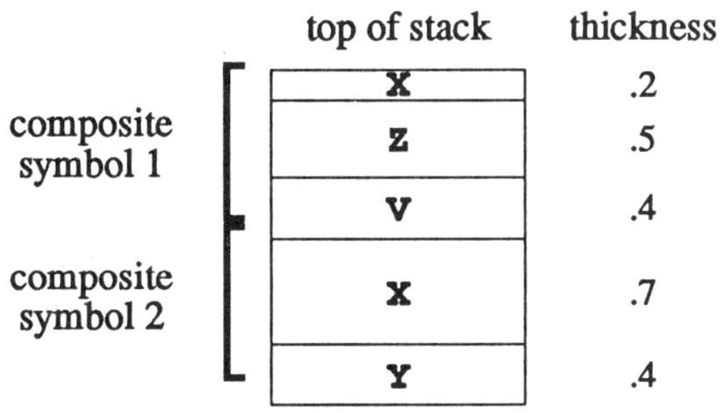

	top of stack	thickness
composite symbol 1	X	.2
	Z	.5
	V	.4
composite symbol 2	X	.7
	Y	.4

Figure 3: A continuous stack. The symbols indicate the contents; the height of a stack entry indicates its thickness, also given by the number to the right. The top composite symbol on the stack is a combination of the items forming a total thickness of 1.0; the next composite symbol is a combination of the items making up the next 1.0 units of thickness.

Pop. If a demon unit fires, the top two composite symbols should be popped from the stack (to be replaced by the demon's identity). If no demon unit fires, in which case the default unit becomes active, the stack should remain unchanged. These behaviors, as well as interpolated behaviors, are achieved by multiplying by s_{def} the thickness of any portion of a stack item contributing to the top two composite symbols. Remember that s_{def} is 0 when one or more demon units are strongly active, and is 1 when the default unit is fully active.

Push. The symbol written onto the stack is the composite symbol formed by summing the identity vectors of the demon units, weighted by their activities: $\sum_i s_i \mathbf{r}_i$, where $\mathbf{r}_i$ is the vector representing demon i's identity. Included in this summation is the default unit, where $\mathbf{r}_{def}$ is defined to be the composite symbol over thickness s_{def} of the input queue. (After a thickness of s_{def} is read from the input queue, it is removed from the queue.)

5 TRAINING METHODOLOGY

The system is trained on positive and negative examples of a context-free grammar. Its task is to classify each input string as grammatical or not. Because the grammars can always be written such that the root of the parse tree is the symbol S (e.g., Figure 2), the stack should contain just S upon completion of processing of a positive example. For a negative example, the stack should contain anything but S.

These criteria can be translated into an objective function as follows. If one assumes a Gaussian noise distribution over outputs, the probability that the top of the stack contains the symbol S following presentation of example i is

$$p_i^{root} \propto e^{-|\mathbf{c}_i - \mathbf{r}_S|^2},$$

where $\mathbf{c}_i$ is the vector representing the top composite symbol on the stack; and the probability that the total thickness of the stack is 1 (i.e., the stack contains exactly one item) is

$$p_i^{thick} \propto e^{-\Phi(T_i-1)^2},$$

where T_i is the total thickness of the stack and Φ is a constant. For a positive example, the objective function should be greatest when there is a high probability of S being on the stack and a high probability of it being the sole item on the stack; for a negative example, the objective function should be greatest when either event has a low probability. We thus obtain a likelihood objective function whose logarithm the learning procedure attempts to maximize:

$$L = \prod_{i \in \text{pos example}} p_i^{root} p_i^{thick} \prod_{i \in \text{neg example}} (1 - p_i^{root} p_i^{thick}).$$

Training sets were generated by hand, with a preference for shorter strings. Positive examples were generated from the grammar; negative examples were either randomly generated or were formed by perturbing a grammatical string. In most training sets, there were roughly 3-5 times as many negative examples as positive. One might validly be concerned that we introduced some bias in our selection of examples. If so, it was not deliberate. In the initial experiments reported below, our goal was primarily to demonstrate that under some conditions, the network could actually induce the grammar. In the next phase of our research, we plan a systematic investigation of the number and nature of examples required for successful learning.

The total number of demon units and the (fixed) identity of each was specified in advance of learning. For the grammar in Figure 2, we provided at least two S demons and one X demon. Any number of demons beyond the minimum did not affect performance. The initial weights $\{w_{ij}\}$ were selected from a uniform distribution over the interval $[.45, .55]$. The b_i were initialized to 1.0.

Before an example is presented, the stack is reset to contain only a single symbol, the null symbol with vector representation **0** and infinite thickness. The example string is placed in the input queue. The network is then allowed to run for $2l-1$ time steps, which is exactly the number of steps required to process any grammatical string of length l. One can intuit this fact by considering that it takes two operations to process each symbol, one to transfer the symbol from the input queue to the stack, and another to reduce the symbol.

The derivative of the objective function is computed with respect to the weight parameters using a form of back propagation through time (Rumelhart, Hinton, & Williams, 1986). This involves "unfolding" the architecture in time and back propagating through the stack. Weights are then updated to perform gradient ascent in the log likelihood function.

6 RESULTS AND DISCUSSION

We have successfully trained the architecture on a variety of grammars, including those shown in Table 1. In each case, the network discriminates positive and negative examples perfectly on the training set. For the first three grammars, additional (longer) strings were used to test network generalization performance. In each case, generalization performance was 100%.

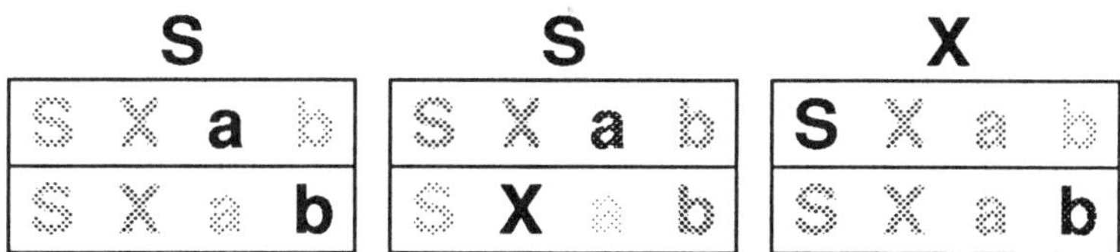

Figure 4: Sample weights for $a^n b^n$. Weights are organized by demon unit, whose identities appear above the rectangles. The top and bottom halves of the rectangle represents connections from composite symbols 1 and 2, respectively. The darker the shading is of a symbol in a rectangle, the larger the connection strength is from the input unit representing that symbol to the demon unit. The weights clearly indicate the three rewrite rules of the grammar.

Table 1: Grammars successfully learned by the demon model

grammar name	*rewrite rules*
$a^n b^n$	S → a b | a X X → S b
parenthesis balancing	S → ( ) | (X | S S X → S)
postfix	S → Y X | S X X → Y + | S + Y → a | b
pseudo natural language	S → NP VP NP → d NP_2 | NP_2 NP_2 → n | a n VP → v NP

Due to the simplicity of the architecture—the fact that there is only one layer of modifiable weights—the learned weights can often be interpreted as symbolic rewrite rules (Figure 4). It is a remarkable achievement that the numerical optimization framework of neural net learning can be used to discover symbolic rules (see also Mozer & Bachrach, 1991).

The first three grammars were successfully learned by the model of Giles et al. (1990), although the analysis required to interpret the weights is generally more cumbersome and tentative. The last grammar could not be learned by their model (Das et al., 1992).

When more demon units are provided to the model than are required for the domain, the weights tend to be less interpretable, but generalization performance is just as good. (Of course, this result can hold for only a limited range of network sizes.) The model also does well with very small training sets (e.g., three positive, three negative examples for $a^n b^n$). This is no doubt because the architecture imposes strong biases on the learning process. We performed some preliminary experiments with staged training in which the length of strings in the training set was increased gradually, allowing the model to first learn simple cases and then move on to more difficult cases. This substantially improved the training time and robustness.

Although the current version of the model is designed for LR(0) context-free grammars, it can be extended to LR(n) by including connections from the first n composite symbols in the input queue to the demon units. However, our focus is not necessarily on building the theoretically most powerful formal language recognizer and learning system; rather, our primary interest has been on integrating symbol manipulation capabilities into a neural network architecture. In this regard, the model makes a clear contribution. It has the ability represent a string of symbols with a single symbol, and to do so iteratively, allowing for the formation of hierarchical and recursive structures. This is the essence of symbolic information processing, and, in our view, a key ingredient necessary for structure learning.

Acknowledgements

This research was supported by NSF Presidential Young Investigator award IRI-9058450 and grant 90-21 from the James S. McDonnell Foundation. Our thanks to Paul Smolensky, Lee Giles, and Jürgen Schmidhuber for helpful comments regarding this work.

References

Bridle, J. (1990). Training stochastic model recognition algorithms as networks can lead to maximum mutual information estimation of parameters. In D. S. Touretzky (Ed.), *Advances in neural information processing systems 2* (pp. 211–217). San Mateo, CA: Morgan Kaufmann.

Das, S., Giles, C. L., & Sun, G. Z. (1992). Learning context-free grammars: Capabilities and limitations of neural network with an external stack memory. In *Proceedings of the Fourteenth Annual Conference of the Cognitive Science* (pp. 791–795). Hillsdale, NJ: Erlbaum.

Giles, C. L., Sun, G. Z., Chen, H. H., Lee, Y. C., & Chen, D. (1990). Higher order recurrent networks and grammatical inference. In D. S. Touretzky (Ed.), *Advances in neural information processing systems 2* (pp. 380–387). San Mateo, CA: Morgan Kaufmann.

Hinton, G. E. (1988). Representing part–whole hierarchies in connectionist networks. *Proceedings of the Eighth Annual Conference of the Cognitive Science Society.*

Mozer, M. C. (1992). The induction of multiscale temporal structure. In J. E. Moody, S. J. Hanson, & R. P. Lippman (Eds.), *Advances in neural information processing systems IV* (pp. 275–282). San Mateo, CA: Morgan Kaufmann.

Mozer, M. C., & Bachrach, J. (1991). SLUG: A connectionist architecture for inferring the structure of finite-state environments. *Machine Learning*, 7, 139–160.

Ring, M. (1993). Learning sequential tasks by incrementally adding higher orders. *This volume.*

Rohwer, R. (1990). The 'moving targets' training algorithm. In D. S. Touretzky (Ed.), *Advances in neural information processing systems 2* (pp. 558–565). San Mateo, CA: Morgan Kaufmann.

Rumelhart, D. E., Hinton, G. E., & Williams, R. J. (1986). Learning internal representations by error propagation. In D. E. Rumelhart & J. L. McClelland (Eds.), *Parallel distributed processing: Explorations in the microstructure of cognition. Volume I: Foundations* (pp. 318–362). Cambridge, MA: MIT Press/Bradford Books.

Rumelhart, D. E. (in press). Connectionist processing and learning as statistical inference. In Y. Chauvin & D. E. Rumelhart (Eds.), *Backpropagation: Theory, architectures, and applications.* Hillsdale, NJ: Erlbaum.

Schmidhuber, J. (1992). Learning unambiguous reduced sequence descriptions. In J. E. Moody, S. J. Hanson, & R. P. Lippman (Eds.), *Advances in neural information processing systems IV* (pp. 291–298). San Mateo, CA: Morgan Kaufmann.

Stolcke, A., & Omohundro, S. (1993). Hidden markov model induction by Bayesian model merging. *This volume.*

Sun, G. Z., Chen, H. H., Giles, C. L., Lee, Y. C., & Chen, D. (1990). Connectionist pushdown automata that learn context-free grammars. In *Proceedings of the International Joint Conference on Neural Networks* (pp. I-577). Hillsdale, NJ: Erlbaum Associates.

Network Structuring And Training Using Rule-based Knowledge

Volker Tresp
Siemens AG
Central Research
Otto-Hahn-Ring 6
8000 München 83, Germany

Jürgen Hollatz*
Institut für Informatik
TU München
Arcisstraße 21
8000 München 2, Germany

Subutai Ahmad
Siemens AG
Central Research
Otto-Hahn-Ring 6
8000 München 83, Germany

Abstract

We demonstrate in this paper how certain forms of rule-based knowledge can be used to prestructure a neural network of normalized basis functions and give a probabilistic interpretation of the network architecture. We describe several ways to assure that rule-based knowledge is preserved during training and present a method for complexity reduction that tries to minimize the number of rules and the number of conjuncts. After training the refined rules are extracted and analyzed.

1 INTRODUCTION

Training a network to model a high dimensional input/output mapping with only a small amount of training data is only possible if the underlying map is of low complexity and the network, therefore, can be of low complexity as well. With increasing

*Mail address: Siemens AG, Central Research, Otto-Hahn-Ring 6, 8000 München 83.

network complexity, parameter variance increases and the network prediction becomes less reliable. This predicament can be solved if we manage to incorporate prior knowledge to bias the network as it was done by Röscheisen, Hofmann and Tresp (1992). There, prior knowledge was available in the form of an algorithm which summarized the engineering knowledge accumulated over many years. Here, we consider the case that prior knowledge is available in the form of a set of rules which specify knowledge about the input/output mapping that the network has to learn. This is a very common occurrence in industrial and medical applications where rules can be either given by experts or where rules can be extracted from the existing solution to the problem.

The inclusion of prior knowledge has the additional advantage that if the network is required to extrapolate into regions of the input space where it has not seen any training data, it can rely on this prior knowledge. Furthermore, in many on-line control applications, the network is required to make reasonable predictions right from the beginning. Before it has seen sufficient training data it has to rely primarily on prior knowledge.

This situation is also typical for human learning. If we learn a new skill such as driving a car or riding a bicycle, it would be disastrous to start without prior knowledge about the problem. Typically, we are told some basic rules, which we try to follow in the beginning, but which are then refined and altered through experience. The better our initial knowledge about a problem, the faster we can achieve good performance and the less training is required (Towel, Shavlik and Noordewier, 1990).

2 FROM KNOWLEDGE TO NETWORKS

We consider a neural network $y = \mathcal{NN}(\mathbf{x})$ which makes a prediction about the state of $y \in \Re$ given the state of its input $\mathbf{x} \in \Re^n$. We assume that an expert provides information about the same mapping in terms of a set of rules. The premise of a rule specifies the conditions on $\mathbf{x}$ under which the conclusion can be applied. This region of the input space is formally described by a basis function $b_i(\mathbf{x})$. Instead of allowing only binary values for a basis function (1: premise is valid, 0: premise is not valid), we permit continuous positive values which represent the certainty or weight of a rule given the input.

We assume that the conclusion of the rule can be described in form of a mathematical expression, such as *conclusion*$_i$*: the output is equal to* $w_i(\mathbf{x})$ where $w_i(\mathbf{x})$ is a function of the input (or a subset of the input) and can be a constant, a polynomial or even another neural network.

Since several rules can be active for a given state of the input, we define the output of the network to be a weighted average of the conclusions of the active rules where the weighting factor is proportional to the activity of the basis function given the input

$$y(\mathbf{x}) = \mathcal{NN}(\mathbf{x}) = \frac{\sum_i w_i(\mathbf{x})\, b_i(\mathbf{x})}{\sum_j b_j(\mathbf{x})}. \quad (1)$$

This is a very general concept since we still have complete freedom to specify the form of the basis function $b_i(\mathbf{x})$ and the conclusion $w_i(\mathbf{x})$. If $b_i(\mathbf{x})$ and $w_i(\mathbf{x})$ are described by neural networks themselves, there is a close relationship with the adaptive mixtures of local experts (Jacobs, Jordan, Nowlan and Hinton, 1991). On the other hand, if we assume that the basis function can be approximated by a multivariate Gaussian

$$b_i(\mathbf{x}) = \kappa_i \; exp[-\frac{1}{2}\sum_j \frac{(x_j - \mu_{ij})^2}{\sigma_{ij}^2}], \tag{2}$$

and if the w_i are constants, we obtain the network of normalized basis functions which were previously described by Moody and Darken (1989) and Specht (1990).

In some cases the expert might want to formulate the premise as simple logical expressions. As an example, the rule

$$IF \;\; [((x_1 \approx a) \; AND \; (x_4 \approx b)] \; OR \; (x_2 \approx c) \;\; THEN \;\; y = d \times x^2$$

is encoded as

$$premise_i: \quad b_i(\mathbf{x}) = exp[-\frac{1}{2}\frac{(x_1 - a)^2 + (x_4 - b)^2}{\sigma^2}] + exp[-\frac{1}{2}\frac{(x_2 - c)^2}{\sigma^2}]$$

$$conclusion_i: \quad w_i(\mathbf{x}) = d \times x^2.$$

This formulation is related to the fuzzy logic approach of Tagaki and Sugeno (1992).

3 PRESERVING THE RULE-BASED KNOWLEDGE

Equation 1 can be implemented as a network of normalized basis functions $\mathcal{NN}^{init}$ which describes the rule-based knowledge and which can be used for prediction. Actual training data can be used to improve network performance. We consider four different ways to ensure that the expert knowledge is preserved during training.

Forget. We use the data to adapt $\mathcal{NN}^{init}$ with gradient descent (we typically adapt all parameters in the network). The sooner we stop training, the more of the initial expert knowledge is preserved.

Freeze. We freeze the parameters in the initial network and introduce a new basis function whenever prediction and data show a large deviation. In this way the network learns an additive correction to the initial network.

Correct. Whereas normal weight decay penalizes the deviation of a parameter from zero, we penalize a parameter if it deviates from its initial value q_j^{init}

$$E_P = \frac{1}{2}\alpha_j \sum_j (q_j - q_j^{init})^2 \tag{3}$$

where the q_j is a generic network parameter.

Internal teacher. We formulate a penalty in terms of the mapping rather than in terms of the parameters

$$E_P = \frac{1}{2}\alpha \int (\mathcal{NN}^{init}(\mathbf{x}) - \mathcal{NN}(\mathbf{x}))^2 d\mathbf{x}.$$

This has the advantage that we do not have to specify priors on relatively unintuitive network parameters. Instead, the prior directly reflects the certainty that we associate with the mapping of the initialized network which can often be estimated. Röscheisen, Hofmann and Tresp (1992) estimated this certainty from problem specific knowledge. We can approximate the integral in Equation 3 numerically by Monte-Carlo integration which leads to a training procedure where we adapt the network with a mixture of measured training data and training data artificially generated by $\mathcal{NN}^{init}(\mathbf{x})$ at randomly chosen inputs. The mixing proportion directly relates to the weight of the penalty, α (Röscheisen, Hofmann and Tresp, 1992).

4 COMPLEXITY REDUCTION

After training the rules can be extracted again from the network but we have to ensure that the set of rules is as concise as possible, otherwise the value of the extracted rules is limited. We would like to find the smallest number of rules that can still describe the knowledge sufficiently. Also, the network should be encouraged to find rules with the smallest number of conjuncts, which in this case means that a basis function is only dependent on a small number of input dimensions.

We suggest the following pruning strategy for Gaussian basis functions.

1. *Prune basis functions.* Evaluate the relative weight of each basis function at its center $\omega_i = b_i(\mu_i)/\sum_j b_j(\mu_i)$ which is a measure of its importance in the network. Remove the unit with the smallest ω_i. Figure 1 illustrates the pruning of basis functions.

2. *Prune conjuncts.* Successively, set the largest σ_{ij} equal to infinity, effectively removing input j from basis function i.

Sequentially remove basis functions and conjuncts until the error increases above a threshold. Retrain after a unit or a conjunct is removed.

5 A PROBABILISTIC INTERPRETATION

One of the advantages of our approach is that there is a probabilistic interpretation of the system. In addition, if the expert formulates his or her knowledge in terms of probability distributions then a number of useful properties can be derived (it is natural here to interpret probability as a subjective degree of belief in an event.). We assume that the system can be in a number of states s_i which are unobservable. Formally, each of those hidden states corresponds to a rule. The prior probability that the system is in state s_i is equal to $P(s_i)$. Assuming that the system is in state s_i there is a probability distribution $P(\mathbf{x}, y|s_i)$ that we measure an input vector $\mathbf{x}$ and an output y and

$$P(\mathbf{x}, y) = \sum_i P(\mathbf{x}, y|s_i)\, P(s_i) = \sum_i P(y|\mathbf{x}, s_i)\, P(\mathbf{x}|s_i)\, P(s_i). \tag{4}$$

For every rule the expert specifies the probability distributions in the last sum. Let's consider the case that $P(\mathbf{x}, y|s_i) = P(\mathbf{x}|s_i)\, P(y|s_i)$ and that $P(\mathbf{x}|s_i)$ and $P(y|s_i)$ can be approximated by Gaussians. In this case Equation 4 describes a Gaussian mixture model. For every rule, the expert has to specify

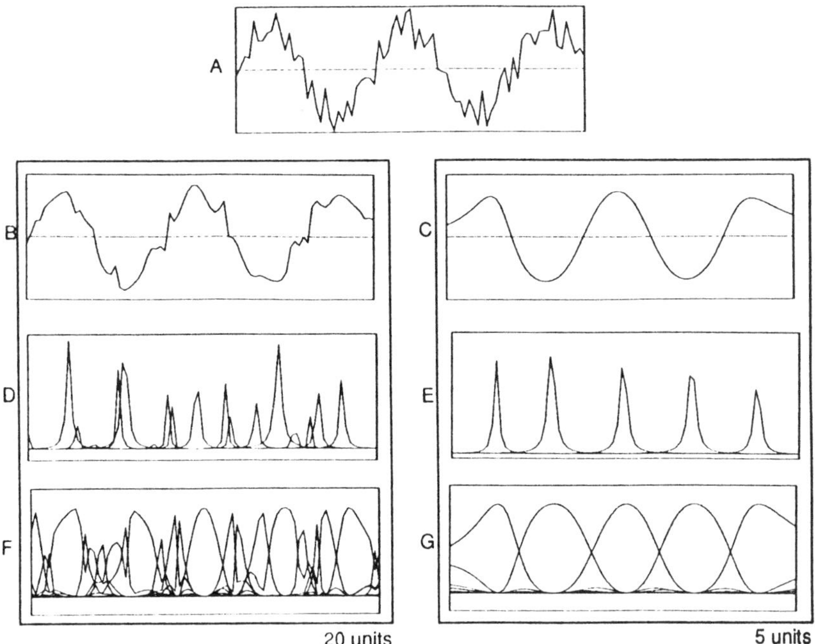

Figure 1: 80 values of a noisy sinusoid (A) are presented as training data to a network of 20 (Cauchy) basis functions, $(b_i(\mathbf{x}) = \kappa_i\ [1+\sum_j (x_j - \mu_{ij})^2/\sigma_{ij}^2]^{-2})$. (B) shows how this network also tries to approximate the noise in the data. (D) shows the basis functions $b_i(\mathbf{x})$ and (F) the normalized basis functions $b_i(\mathbf{x})/\sum_j b_j(\mathbf{x})$. Pruning reduces the network architecture to 5 units placed at the extrema of the sinusoid (basis functions: E, normalized basis functions: G). The network output is shown in (C).

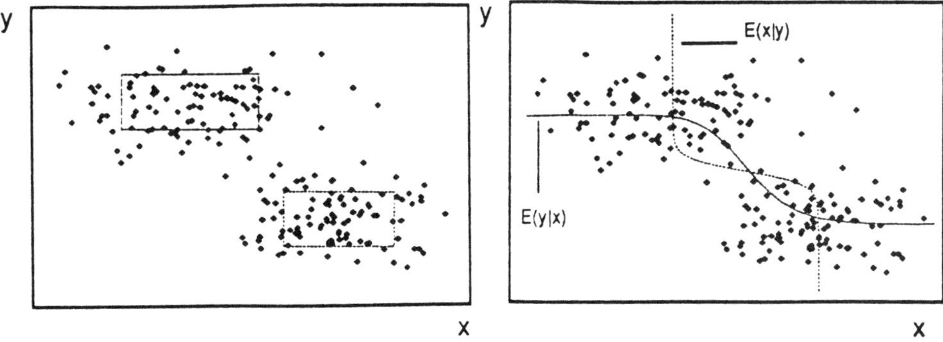

Figure 2: Left: The two rectangles indicate centers and standard deviations of two Gaussians that approximate a density. Right: the figure shows the expected values $\mathcal{E}(y|x)$ (continuous line) and $\mathcal{E}(x|y)$ (dotted line).

- $P(s_i)$, the probability of the occurrence of state s_i (the overall weight of the rule),
- $P(\mathbf{x}|s_i) = N_i(\mathbf{x}; \mu_i, \Sigma_i)$, the probability that an input vector $\mathbf{x}$ occurs, given that the system is in state s_i, and
- $P(y|s_i) = N_i^y(y; w_i, \sigma_i^y)$, the probability of output y given state s_i.

The evidence for a state given an input $\mathbf{x}$ becomes

$$P(s_i|\mathbf{x}) = \frac{P(\mathbf{x}|s_i)P(s_i)}{\sum_j P(\mathbf{x}|s_j)P(s_j)}$$

and the expected value of the output

$$\mathcal{E}(y|\mathbf{x}) = \frac{\sum_i \int y \; P(y|\mathbf{x}, s_i) \; dy \; P(\mathbf{x}|s_i)P(s_i)}{\sum_j P(\mathbf{x}|s_j)P(s_j)}, \tag{5}$$

where, $P(\mathbf{x}|s_i) = \int P(\mathbf{x}, y|s_i) \; dy$. If we substitute $b_i(\mathbf{x}) = P(\mathbf{x}|s_i)P(s_i)$ and $w_i(\mathbf{x}) = \int y \; P(y|\mathbf{x}, b_i) \; dy$ we can calculate the expected value of y using the same architecture as described in Equation 1.

Subsequent training data can be employed to improve the model. The likelihood of the data $\{\mathbf{x^k}, y^k\}$ becomes

$$L = \prod_k \sum_i P(\mathbf{x^k}, y^k|s_i) \; P(s_i)$$

which can be maximized using gradient descent or EM. These adaptation rules are more complicated than supervised learning since according to our model the data generating process also makes assumptions about the distributions of the data in the input space.

Equation 4 gives an approximation of the joint probability density of input and output. Input and output are formally equivalent (Figure 2) and, in the case of Gaussian mixtures, we can easily calculate the optimal output given just a subset of inputs (Ahmad and Tresp, 1993).

A number of authors used clustering and Gaussian approximation on the input space alone and resources were distributed according to the complexity of the input space. In this method, resources are distributed according to the complexity of both input and output space.[1]

6 CLASSIFICATION

A conclusion now specifies the correct class. Let $\{b_{ik}|i = 1...N_k\}$ denote the set of basis functions whose conclusion specifies $class_k$. We set $w_{ij}^k = \delta_{kj}$, where w_{ij}^k is the weight from basis function b_{ij} to the kth output and δ_{kj} is the Kronecker symbol. The kth output of the network

$$y_k(\mathbf{x}) = \mathcal{NN}_k(\mathbf{x}) = \frac{\sum_{ij} w_{ij}^k b_{ij}(\mathbf{x})}{\sum_{lm} b_{lm}(\mathbf{x})} = \frac{\sum_i b_{ik}(\mathbf{x})}{\sum_{lm} b_{lm}(\mathbf{x})}. \tag{6}$$

[1]Note, that a probabilistic interpretation is only possible if the integral over a basis function is finite, i.e. all variances are finite.

specifies the certainty of $class_k$, given the input. During training, we do *not* adapt the output weights w_{ij}^k. Therefore, the outputs of the network are always positive and sum to one.

A probabilistic interpretation can be found if we assume that $P(\mathbf{x}|class_k)P(class_k) \approx \sum_i b_{ik}(\mathbf{x})$. We obtain,

$$P(class_k|\mathbf{x}) = \frac{P(\mathbf{x}|class_k)P(class_k)}{\sum_l P(\mathbf{x}|class_l)P(class_l)}$$

and recover Equation 6. If the basis functions are Gausssians, again we obtain a Gaussian mixture learning problem and, as a special case (one unit per class), a Gaussian classifier.

7 APPLICATIONS

We have validated our approach on a number of applications including a network that learned how to control a bicycle and an application in the legal sciences (Hollatz and Tresp, 1992). Here we present results for a well known data set, the Boston housing data (Breiman *et al.,* 1981), and demonstrate pruning and rule extraction. The task is to predict the housing price in a Boston neighborhood as a function of 13 potentially relevant input features. We started with 20 Gaussian basis functions which were adapted using gradient descent. We achieved a generalization error of 0.074. We then pruned units and conjuncts according to the procedure described in Section 4. We achieved the best generalization error (0.058) using 4 units (this is approximately 10% better than the result reported for CART in Breiman *et al.*, 1981). With only two basis functions and 3 conjuncts, we still achieved reasonable prediction accuracy (generalization error of 0.12; simply predicting the mean results in a generalization error of 0.28). Table 1 describes the final network. Interestingly, our network was left with the input features which CART also considered the most relevant.

The network was trained with normalized inputs. If we translate them back into real world values, we obtain the rules:

Rule$_{14}$: IF the number of rooms (RM) is approximately 5.4 (0.62 corresponds to 5.4 rooms which is smaller than the average of 6.3) AND the pupil/teacher value is approximately 20.2 (0.85 corresponds to 20.2 pupils/teacher which is higher than the average of 18.4) THEN the value of the home is approximately $14000 (0.528 corresponds to $14000 which is lower than the average of $22500).

Table 1: Network structure after pruning.

	conclusion	feature j	CART rating	center: μ_{ij}	width: σ_{ij}
Unit#: $i = 14$	$w_i = 0.528$	RM	second	0.62	0.21
$\kappa_i = 0.17$		P/T	third	0.85	0.35
Unit#: $i = 20$	$w_i = 1.6$	LSTAT	most important	0.06	0.24
$\kappa_i = 0.83$					

$Rule_{20}$: IF the percentage of lower-status population (LSTAT) is approximately 2.5% (0.06 corresponds to 2.5% which is lower than the average of 12.65%), THEN the value of the home is approximately \$34000 (1.6 corresponds to \$34000 which is higher than the average of \$22500).

8 CONCLUSION

We demonstrated how rule-based knowledge can be incorporated into the structuring and training of a neural network. Training with experimental data allows for rule refinement. Rule extraction provides a quantitative interpretation of what is "going on" in the network, although, in general, it is difficult to define the domain where a given rule "dominates" the network response and along which boundaries the rules partition the input space.

Acknowledgements

We acknowledge valuable discussions with Ralph Neuneier and his support in the Boston housing data application. V.T. was supported in part by a grant from the Bundesminister für Forschung und Technologie and J. H. by a fellowship from Siemens AG.

References

S. Ahmad and V. Tresp. Some solutions to the missing feature problem in vision. This volume, 1993.

L. Breiman *et al.*. *Classification and regression trees.* Wadsworth and Brooks, 1981.

R. A. Jacobs, M. I. Jordan, S. J. Nowlan and G. E. Hinton. Adaptive mixtures of local experts. *Neural Computation,* Vol. 3, pp. 79-87, 1991.

J. Hollatz and V. Tresp. A Rule-based network architecture. *Artificial Neural Networks II,* I. Aleksander, J. Taylor, eds., Elsevier, Amsterdam, 1992.

J. Moody and C. Darken. Fast learning in networks of locally-tuned processing units. *Neural Computation*, Vol. 1, pp. 281-294, 1989.

M. Röscheisen, R. Hofmann and V. Tresp. Neural control for rolling mills: incorporating domain theories to overcome data deficiency. In: *Advances in Neural Information Processing Systems 4,* 1992.

D. F. Specht. Probabilistic neural networks. *Neural Networks,* Vol. 3, pp. 109-117, 1990.

T. Takagi and M. Sugeno. Fuzzy identification of systems and its applications to modeling and control. *IEEE Transactions on Systems, Man and Cybernetics,* Vol. 15, No. 1, pp. 116-132, 1985.

G. G. Towell, J. W. Shavlik and M. O. Noordewier. Refinement of approximately correct domain theories by knowledge-based neural networks. In *Proceedings of the Eights National Conference on Artificial Intelligence,* pp. 861-866, MA, 1990.

A dynamical model of priming and repetition blindness

Daphne Bavelier
Laboratory of Neuropsychology
The Salk Institute
La Jolla, CA 92037

Michael I. Jordan
Department of Brain and Cognitive Sciences
Massachusetts Institute of Technology
Cambridge MA 02139

Abstract

We describe a model of visual word recognition that accounts for several aspects of the temporal processing of sequences of briefly presented words. The model utilizes a new representation for written words, based on dynamic time warping and multidimensional scaling. The visual input passes through cascaded perceptual, comparison, and detection stages. We describe how these dynamical processes can account for several aspects of word recognition, including repetition priming and repetition blindness.

1 INTRODUCTION

Several psychological phenomena show that the construction of organized and meaningful representations of the visual environment requires establishing separate representations (termed episodic representations) for the different objects viewed. Three phenomena in the word recognition literature suggest that the segregation of the visual flow into separate episodic representations can be characterized in terms of specific temporal constraints. We developed a model to explore the nature of these constraints.

2 DESCRIPTION OF THE BEHAVIORAL DATA

In a typical priming experiment, subjects are presented with a first word, termed the "prime," and then asked to name or make a judgment to a second word, termed the "target." The performance of subjects is compared in conditions in which the target and prime are related versus conditions in which they are unrelated.

When the prime is presented fast enough so that it cannot be identified (about 40 ms), subjects' performance on the target is facilitated when the prime and the target are identical compared to the case in which they are unrelated. This effect, known as "**masked priming**," is very short lasting, appearing only within trials, and lasting on the order of 100 ms (Humphreys, Evett, Quinlan & Besner, 1987).

If the prime, however, is presented for a period such that it is just identifiable (about 100 ms), subjects' performance on the target is hindered when prime and target are identical (Kanwisher, 1987; Humphreys et al., 1987). This effect, known as "**repetition blindness**," is conditional on the conscious identification of the prime. The size of the effect decreases as the duration between the two items increases. Repetition blindness is observed only within trials and vanishes for inter-stimulus durations on the order of 500 ms.

When the prime is presented long enough to be easily identifiable (about 250 ms or more), subjects' performance on the target is once again facilitated when prime and target are identical (Salasoo, Shiffrin & Feustel, 1985). This effect, known as "**classical repetition priming**," is long lasting, being observed not only within trials, but between trials and even between sessions. In certain experimental conditions, it has been observed to last up to a year.

These results implicate two factors influencing word recognition: the time of presentation and whether or not the prime has been identified. We have developed a model that captures the rather non-intuitive result that as the time of presentation of the prime increases, recall of the target is first facilitated, then inhibited and then facilitated again. The two main features of the model are the dynamical properties of the word representations and the dependence of the detection processes for each word on previous conscious identification of that word.

3 REPRESENTATION

The representation that we developed for our model is a vector space representation that allows each word to be represented by a fixed-length vector, even though the words are of different length. We developed an algorithmic method for finding the word representations that avoids some of the difficulties with earlier proposals (cf. Pinker & Prince, 1988).

The algorithm proceeds in three stages. First, *dynamic programming* (Bellman, 1957) is used to compute an inter-word similarity matrix. The transition costs in the dynamic programming procedure were based on empirically-determined values of visual similarity between individual letters (Townsend, 1971). Interestingly, we found that dynamic programming solutions naturally capture several factors that are known to be important in human sensitivity to orthographic similarity (for example, orthographic priming increases as a function of the number of letters shared between the prime and the target in a nonlinear manner, shared end-letters are more important than shared middle-letters, and relative letter position determines orthographic similarity (Humphreys et al., 1987)).

After the dynamic programming stage, *multidimensional scaling* (Torgerson, 1958) is used to convert the inter-word similarity matrix into a vector space representation in which distance correlates with similarity.

Next, word vectors are normalized by projecting them onto a semi-hypersphere. This gives the origin of the vector space a meaning, allowing us to use vector magnitude to represent signal energy.

This representation also yielded natural choices for the "blank" stimulus and the "mask" stimulus. The "blank" was taken to be the origin of the space and the "mask" was taken to be a vector on the far side of the hypersphere. In the dynamical model that we describe below, vectors that are far apart have maximally disruptive effects on each other. A distant stimulus causes the state to move rapidly away from a particular word vector, thus interfering maximally with its processing.

4 PROCESSING

4.1 FORMALIZATION OF THE PROBLEM AS A SIGNAL DETECTION PROBLEM

We formalize the problem of visual word recognition as a problem of detecting significant fluctuations of a multidimensional signal embedded in noise. This can be viewed as a maximum likelihood detection problem in which the onsets and durations of the signal are not known a priori. Our model has two main levels of processing: a perceptual stage and a detection stage.

Perceptual Stage

The perceptual stage is a bank of noisy linear filters. Let W_i denote the n-dimensional word vector presented at time t, with components $W_{i,k}$. The word vector is corrupted with white noise $\epsilon[t]$ to form the input $u_k[t]$:

$$u_k[t] = W_{i,k} + \epsilon[t],$$

and this input is filtered:

$$r_k[t] = -a_0 r_k[t-1] - a_1 r_k[t-2] + b u_k[t] + \eta[t],$$

in the presence of additional white noise $\eta[t]$.

Detection Stages

The first detection stage in the model is a linear filter whose inverted impulse response is matched to the impulse response of the perceptual filter:

$$s_k[t] = -c_0 s_k[t-1] - c_1 s_k[t-2] + d r_k[t].$$

Such a filter is known as a *matched filter*, and is known to have optimality properties that make it an effective preprocessor for a system that utilizes thresholds for making decisions (van Trees, 1968). The output of the matched filter is projected onto each of the words in the lexicon to form scalar "word activation" signals $x_i[t]$ that can be compared to thresholds:

$$x_i[t] = \sum_{k=1}^{n} W_{i,k} s_k[t].$$

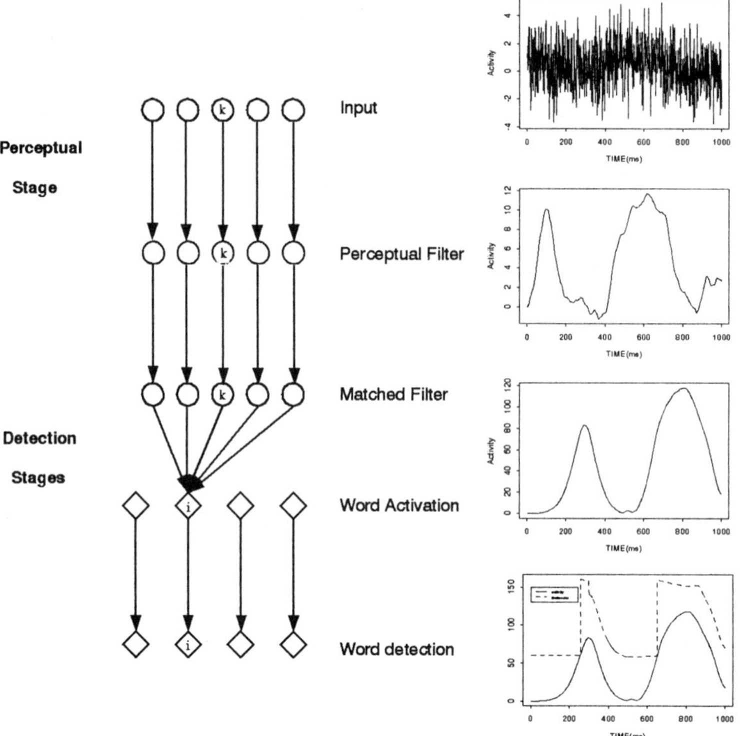

Figure 1: The processing stages of the model. The figures on the right show the signals in the model projected onto the vector for the word *bring*. *Bring* was presented for 100 ms, followed by a 300 ms blank, followed by a second presentation of *bring* for 300 ms.

The decision process is a simple binary decision based on a variable *baseline* $\mu_i[t]$ and a variable *threshold* $\theta_i[t]$:

$$y_i = \begin{cases} 1 & \text{if } x_i[t] - \mu_i[t] > \theta_i[t] \\ 0 & \text{otherwise} \end{cases}$$

4.2 DETECTION DYNAMICS

The problem of detecting signals that may overlap in time and have unknown onsets and unknown durations requires the system to focus on *fluctuations* rather than the absolute heights of the activation curves. Moreover, the test for significance of a fluctuation must be dependent on the state of the detection mechanism and the state of the filters. Our significance test utilizes two time-varying quantities to capture this state-dependence: the baseline μ and the threshold θ.

The baseline $\mu_i[t]$ varies as follows. On time steps for which the fluctuations are subthreshold ($y_i[t] = 0$, for all i), each baseline simply tracks the most recent minimum value of the corresponding word activation signal:

$$\mu_i[t] = \begin{cases} \mu_i[t-1] & \text{if } x_i[t] > \mu_i[t] \\ x_i[t] & \text{otherwise} \end{cases}$$

When a fluctuation passes threshold ($y_i[t] = 1$, for some i), the word i is "detected," and the baselines of all words are increased:

$$\mu_k[t] = \mu_k[t-1] + \xi\phi(i,k),$$

where $\phi(i,k)$ is the angle between W_i and W_k and ξ is a positive scaling parameter. This rule prevents multiple detections during a single presentation and it prevents the neighbors of a detected word from being detected due to their overlap with the detected word.

The threshold θ_i is subject to first-order dynamics that serve to increase or decrease the threshold as a function of the recent activation history of the word (a rudimentary form of adaptation):

$$\theta_i[t] = \alpha\theta_i[t-1] + (1-\alpha)\theta_i^0 - \beta(x_i[t] - \mu_i[t])_+,$$

where α and β are positive numbers. This rule has the effect of decreasing the threshold if the activation of the word is currently above its baseline, and increasing the threshold toward its nominal value θ_i^0 otherwise.

4.3 PARAMETERS

The parameters in the model were determined from the behavioral data and from the structural assumptions of the model in the following manner. The dynamics of the perceptual filter were determined by the time constants of masked priming, as given by the behavioral data. This choice also fixed the dynamics of the matched filter, since the matched filter was tied to the dynamics of the perceptual filter. The dynamics of the baseline μ (i.e., the value ξ) were determined by the constraint that a long presentation of a word not lead to multiple detections of the word. Finally, the dynamics of the threshold θ were determined by the dynamics of classical repetition priming as given by the behavioral data. Note that the behavioral data on repetition blindness were not used in adjusting the parameters of the model.

5 ACCOUNTS OF THE THREE BASIC PHENOMENA

5.1 MASKED PRIMING

The facilitation observed in masked priming is due to temporal superposition in the perceptual filter and the matched filter. At the time scale at which masked priming is observed, the activation due to the first critical word (C1) overlaps with the activation due to the second critical word (C2) (see Figure 2A), leading to a larger word activation value when C1 and C2 are identical than when they are different.

5.2 REPETITION BLINDNESS

The temporal superposition that leads to masked priming is also responsible for repetition blindness (see Figure 3). The temporal overlap from the filtering dynamics

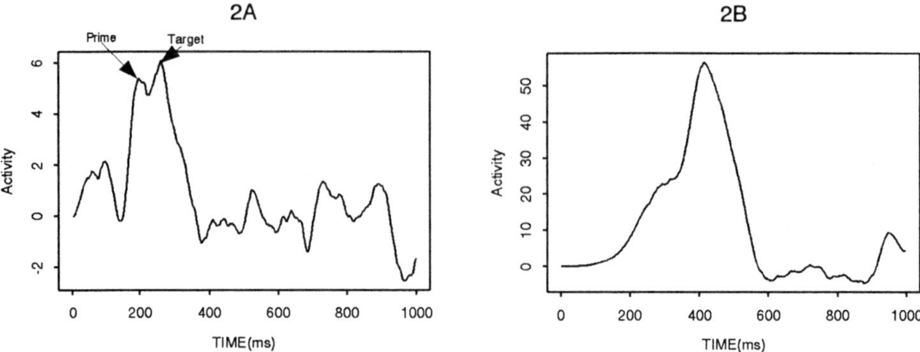

Figure 2: Activation curves at the perceptual level (A) and the matched filter level (B) for the word *bring* during the presentation of the sequence *bring*, *character*, *bring*. Each word was presented for 40 ms.

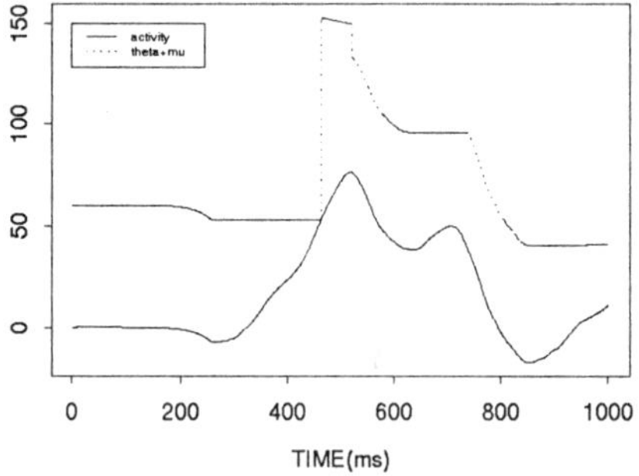

Figure 3: Activation curves for the word *bring* during the presentation of the sequence *bring*, *character*, *bring*. Each word was presented for 100 ms.

will prevent the baseline μ from getting reset to a sufficiently small value to allow a second detection. That is, repetition blindness arises because the fluctuation due to the brief presentation of C2 is not judged significant against the background of the recent detection of the word. Note that such a failure to detect the second occurrence will happen only when C1 has been correctly detected, because only then will the baseline be increased. This dependence of repetition blindness on explicit detection of the first occurrence also characterizes the behavioral data (Kanwisher, 1987).

5.3 CLASSICAL REPETITION PRIMING

The facilitation observed in classical repetition priming is due to the dynamics of the threshold θ. The value of θ decreases during significant increases in the activation of a word; hence a smaller fluctuation in activation is needed for the next occurrence

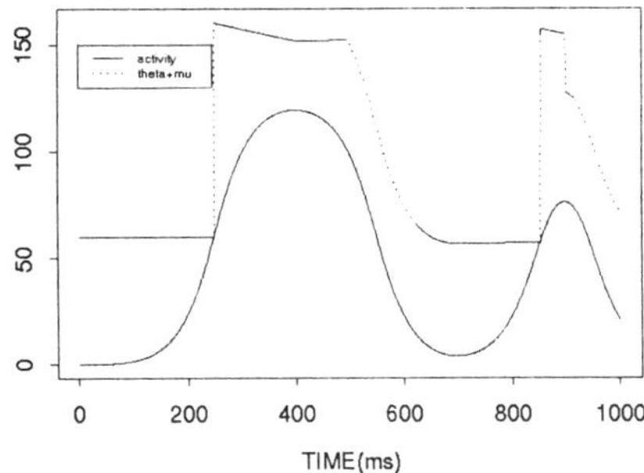

Figure 4: Activation curves for the word *bring* during the presentation of the word *bring* for 300ms, followed by a 300ms blank, followed by *bring* again for 100ms.

to be detected (see Figure 4).

6 OTHER DATA ACCOUNTED FOR BY THE MODEL

The model captures most of the specific characteristics of the three basic phenomena that we have reviewed. For example, it accounts for the finding of masked priming between orthographic neighbors (Humphreys, et al., 1987). This effect arises in the model because a distributed representation is used for the words. The model also captures the finding that the size of repetition blindness decreases as the interval between the critical stimuli increases (this is due to the fact that the baseline is reset to increasingly lower values as the inter-stimulus interval increases), as well as the fact that the size of repetition blindness decreases as the duration of presentation of C2 increases (because the activation for C2 continues to increase while the baseline remains fixed). Similarly, the model accounts for the finding that the manifestation of repetition blindness is dependent on the conscious identification of the first occurrence, as well the finding of repetition blindness between orthographic neighbors (Kanwisher, 1987). Specifics of classical repetition priming, such as the finding that priming is restricted to a word identity, and the fact that its size increases with the number of repetitions and diminishes as the lag between repetitions increases (Salasoo, Shiffrin & Feustel, 1985), are also captured by the model.

The model also accounts for other behavioral phenomena described in the literature on word recognition. Our vector space representation allows us to account naturally for the fact that the final words in a list are recalled better than the middle words in the list (the "recency" effect). This occurs because dissimilar words tend to have large angle between them (and therefore "inhibit" each other dynamically), whereas the "blank" is at the origin of the space and is relatively "close" to all of the words. The residual activation for a presented word therefore tends to be stronger if followed by a blank than by a dissimilar word. The model also captures certain of the effects of pattern masks on word recognition. For example, "forward" masking, a condition in which the mask precedes the word to be detected, is known to be less disruptive than "backward" masking, a condition in which the mask follows the word to be detected. This occurs in the model because of the dynamics of the baselines: preceding a word with a mask tends to reset its baseline to lower values and therefore renders the test for significance relatively more sensitive.

7 CONCLUSIONS

From the point of view of the current model, the fact that the detection of repeated items is enhanced, then suppressed, then once again enhanced as the duration of the items is increased finds a natural explanation in the nature of the signal processing task that the word recognition system must solve. The signals that arrive in temporal sequence for perceptual processing have unknown onset times, unknown durations, and are corrupted by noise. The fact that signals have unknown onset times and can superimpose implies that the system must detect *fluctuations* in signal strength rather than absolute values of signal strength. The presence of noise, inevitable given the neural hardware and the complex multidimensional nature of the signal, implies that the system must detect *significant fluctuations* and must incorporate information about recent events into its significance tests. The real-time constraints of this detection task and the need to guard against errors imply that certain of the fluctuations will be missed, a fact that will result in "blindness" to repeated items at certain time scales.

Acknowledgments

This research was funded by the McDonnell-Pew Centers for Cognitive Neuroscience at UCSD and MIT, by a grant from the McDonnell-Pew Foundation to Michael I. Jordan, and by NIDCD Grant 5RO1-DC-00128 to Helen Neville.

References

Humphreys, G. W., Evett, L. J., Quinlan, P. T., & Besner, D. (1987). Orthographic priming. In M. Coltheart (Ed.), *Attention and Performance XII* (pp. 105-125). Hillsdale, NJ: Erlbaum.

Kanwisher, N. (1987). Repetition blindness: Type recognition without token individuation. *Cognition, 27*, 117-143.

Pinker, S. & Prince, A. (1988). On language and connectionism: Analysis of a parallel distributed processing model of language acquisition. Cognition, 28, 73-193.

Salasoo, A., Shiffrin, R. M., & Feustel, T. C. (1985). Building Permanent Memory Codes: Codification and Repetition Effects in Word Identification. *Journal of Experimental Psychology: General, 114*, 50-77.

Torgerson, W. S. (1958). Theory and Methods of Scaling. J. Wiley & Sons: New York.

Townsend, J. T. (1971). Theoritical analysis of an alphabetic confusion matrix. *Perception and Psychophysics, 9*, 40-50. (see also 449-454).

Van Trees, F. (1968). *Detection, Estimation and Modulation Theory*, Part I. New York: Wiley.

A Knowledge-Based Model of Geometry Learning

Geoffrey Towell
Siemens Corporate Research
755 College Road East
Princeton, NJ 08540

towell@learning.siemens.com

Richard Lehrer
Educational Psychology
University of Wisconsin
1025 West Johnson St.
Madison, WI 53706
lehrer@vms.macc.wisc.edu

Abstract

We propose a model of the development of geometric reasoning in children that explicitly involves learning. The model uses a neural network that is initialized with an understanding of geometry similar to that of second-grade children. Through the presentation of a series of examples, the model is shown to develop an understanding of geometry similar to that of fifth-grade children who were trained using similar materials.

1 Introduction

One of the principal problems in instructing children is to develop sequences of examples that help children acquire useful concepts. In this endeavor it is often useful to have a model of how children learn the material, for a good model can guide an instructor towards particularly effective examples. In short, good models of learning help a teacher maximize the utility of the example presented.

The particular problem with which we are concerned is learning about conventional concepts in geometry, like those involved in identifying, and recognizing similarities and differences among, shapes. This is a difficult subject to teach because children (and adults) have a complex set of informal rules for geometry (that are often at odds with conventional rules). Hence, instruction must supplant this informal geometry with a common formalism. To be efficient in their instruction, teachers need a model of geometric learning which, at the very least:

1. can represent children's understanding of geometry prior to instruction,
2. can describe how understanding changes as a result of instruction,
3. can predict the effect of differing instructional sequences.

In this paper we describe a neural network based model that has these properties.

An extant model of geometry learning, the ''van Hiele model'' [6] represents children's understanding as purely perceptual -- appearances dominate reasoning. However, our research suggests that children's reasoning is better characterized as a mix of perception and rules. Moreover, unlike the model we propose, the van Hiele model can neither be used to test the effectiveness of instruction prior to trying that instruction on children nor can it be used to describe how understanding changes as a result of a specific type of instruction.

Briefly, our model uses a set of rules derived from interviews with first and second grade children [1, 2], to produce a stereotypical informal conception of geometry. These rules, described in more detail in Section 2.1, give our model an explicit representation of pre-instructional geometry understanding. The rules are then translated into a neural network using the KBANN algorithm [3]. As a neural network, our model can test the effect of differing instructional sequences by simply training two instances with different sets of examples. The experiments in Section 3 take advantage of this ability of our model; they show that it is able to accurately model the effect of two different sets of instruction.

2 A New Model

This section describes the initial state of our model and its implementation as a neural network. The initial state of the model is intended to reproduce the decision processes of a typical child prior to instruction. The methodology used to derive this information and a brief description of this information both are in the first subsection. In addition, this subsection contains a small experiment that shows the accuracy of the initial state of the model. In the next subsection, we briefly describe the translation of those rules into a neural network.

2.1 The initial state of the model

Our model is based upon interviews with children in first and second grade [1, 2]. In these interviews, children were presented with sets of three figures such as the triad in Figure 1. They were asked which pair of the three figures is the most similar and why they made their decision. These interviews revealed that, prior to instruction, children base judgments of similarity upon the seven attributes in Table 1.

For the triad discrimination task, children find ways in which a pair is similar that is not shared by the other two pairs. For instance, B and C in Figure 1.2 are both *pointy* but A is not. As a result, the modal response of children prior to instruction is that {B C} is the most similar pair. This decision making process is described by the rules in Table 2.

In addition to the rules in Table 2, we include in our initial model a set of rules that describe templates for standard geometric shapes. This addition is based upon interviews with children which suggest that they know the names of shapes such as triangles and squares, and that they associate with each name a small set of templates. Initially, children treat these shape names as having no more importance than any of the attributes in Table 1. So, our model initial treats shape names exactly as one of those attributes. Over time children learn that the names of shapes are very important because they are diagnostic (the name indicates properties). Our hope was that the model would make a similar transition so that the shape names would become sufficient for similarity determination.

Note that the rules in Table 2 do not always yield a unique decision. Rather, there are

Table 1: Attributes used by children prior to instruction.

Attribute name	*Possible values*	*Attribute name*	*Possible values*
Tilt	0, 10, 20, 30, 40	Slant	yes, no
Area	small, medium, large	Shape	skinny, medium, fat
Pointy	yes, no	Direction	$\leftarrow, \rightarrow, \uparrow, \downarrow$
2 long & short	yes, no		

Table 2: Rules for similarity judgment in the triad discrimination task.

```
1. IF fig-val(fig1?, att?) = fig-val(fig2?, att?) THEN
   same-att-value(fig1?, fig2?, att?).
2. IF not(same-att-value(fig1?, fig3?, att?)) AND fig1? ≠ fig3?
   AND fig2? ≠ fig3? THEN unq-sim(fig1?, fig2?, att?).
3. IF c(unq-sim(fig1?, fig2?, att?)) >
   c(unq-sim(fig1?, fig2?, att?)) AND
   c(unq-sim(fig1?, fig3?, att?)) > c(unq-sim(fig2?, fig3?, att?))
   AND fig1? ≠ fig3? AND fig2?≠ fig3? THEN
   most-similar(fig1?, fig2?).
```

Labels followed by a '?' indicate variables.
fig-val(fig?, att?) returns the value of att? in fig?
c() counts the number of instances.

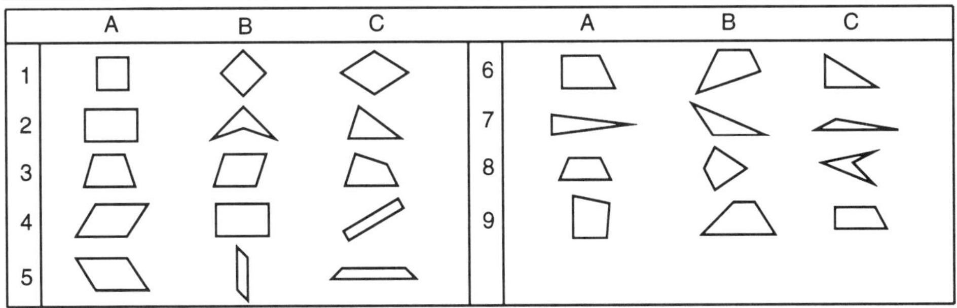

Figure 1: Triads used to test learning.

triads for which these rules cannot decide which pair is most similar. This is not often the case for a particular child, who usually finds one attribute more salient than another. Yet, frequently when the rules cannot uniquely identify the most similar pair, a classroom of children is equally divided. Hence, the model may not accurately predict an individual response, but is it usually correct at identifying the modal responses.

To verify the accuracy of the initial state of our model, we used the set of nine testing triads shown in Figure 1 which were developed for the interviews with children. As shown in Table 3, the model matches very nicely responses obtained from a separate sample of 48 second grade children. Thus, we believe that we have a valid point from which to start.

2.2 The translation of rule sets into a neural network

We translate rules sets into neural networks using the KBANN algorithm [3] which uses a set of hierarchically-structured rules in the form of propositional Horn clauses to set the topology and initial weights of an artificial neural network. Because the rules in Table 2 are

Table 3: Initial responses by the model.

Triad Number	1	2	3	4	5	6	7	8	9
Initial Model	BC	BC	AC	AC	BC	AB/BC	AC	**AB/BC**	AC/BC
Second Grade Children	BC	BC	AC	AC	BC	AB/BC	AC	**AB**	AC/BC

Answers in the "initial model" row indicate the responses generated by the initial rules. More than response in a column indicates that the rules could not differentiate among two pairs.

Answers in the "second grade" row are the modal responses of second grade children. More than one answer in a column indicates that equal numbers of children judged the pairs most similar.

Table 4: Properties used to describe figures.

Property name	*values*	*Property name*	*values*
Convex	Yes No	# Pairs Equal Opposite Angles	0 1 2 3 4
# Sides	3 4 5 6 8	# Pairs Opposite Sides Equal	0 1 2 3 4
# Angles	3 4 5 6 8	# Pairs Parallel Sides	0 1 2 3 4
All Sides Equal	Yes No	Adjacent Angles = 180	Yes No
# Right Angles	0 1 2 3 4	# Lines of Symmetry	0 1 2 3 4 5 6 8
All Angles Equal	Yes No	# Equal Sides	0 2 3 4 5 6 8
# Equal Angles	0 2 3 4 5 6 8		

not in propositional form, they must be expanded before they can be accepted by KBANN. The expansion turns a simple set of three rules into an ugly set of approximately 100 rules.

Figure 2 is a high-level view of the structure of the neural network that results from the rules. In this implementation we present all three figures at the same time and all decisions are made in parallel. Hence, the rules described above must be repeated at least three times. In the neural network that results from the rule translation, these repeated rules are not independent. Rather they are linked so that modifications of the rules are shared across every pairing. Thus, the network cannot learn a rule which applies only to one pair.

Finally, the model begins with the set of 13 properties listed in Table 4 in addition to the attributes of Table 1. (Note that we use "attribute" to refer to the informal, visual features in Table 1 and "property" to refer to the symbolic features in Table 4.) As a result, each figure is described to the model as a 74 position vector (18 positions encode the attributes; the remaining 56 positions encode the properties).

3 An Experiment Using the Model

One of the points we made in the introduction is that a useful model of geometry learning should be able to predict the effect of instruction. The experiment reported in this section tests this facet of our model. Briefly, this experiment trains two instances of our model using different sets of data. We then compare the instances to children who have been trained using a set of problems similar to one of those used to train the model. Our results show that the two instances learn quite different things. Moreover, the instance trained with material similar to the children predicts the children's responses on test problems with a high level of accuracy.

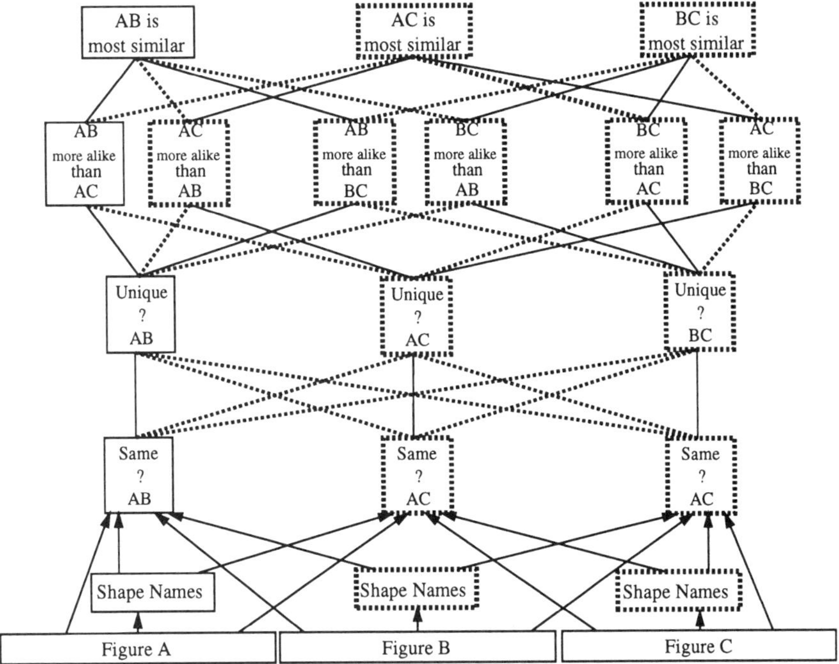

Boxes indicate one or more units.
Dashed boxes indicate units associated with duplicated rules
Dashed lines indicate one or more negatively weighted links.
Solid lines indicate one or more positively weighted links.

Figure 2: The structure of the neural network for our model.

3.1 Training the model

For this experiment, we developed two sets of training shapes. One set contains every polygon in a fifth-grade math textbook [4] (Figure 3). The other set consists of 81 items which might be produced by a child using a modified version of LOGO (Figure 4). Here we assume that one of the effects of learning geometry with a tool like LOGO is simply to increase the extent and range of possible examples. A collection of 33 triads were selected from each set to train the model.[1] Training consisted of repeated presentations of each of the 33 triads until the network correctly identified the most similar pair for each triad.

3.2 Tests of the model

In this section, we test the ability of the model to accurately predict the effects of instruction. We do this by comparing the two trained instances of the model to the modal responses of fifth graders who had used LOGO for two weeks. In those two weeks, the children had generates many (but not all) of the figures in Figure 4. Hence, we expected that the instance

[1] In choosing the same number of triads for each training set, we are being very generous to the textbook. In reality, not only do children see more figures when using LOGO, they are also able to make many more contrasts between figures. Hence, it might be more accurate to make the LOGO training set much larger than the textbook training set.

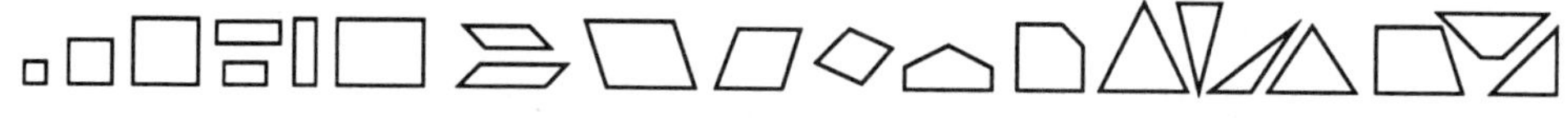

Figure 3: Representative textbook shapes.

Figure 4: Representative shapes encountered using a modified version of LOGO.

of the model trained using triads drawn from Figure 4 would better predict the responses of these children than the other instance of the model.

Clearly, the results in Table 5 verify our expectations. The LOGO-trained model agrees with the modal responses of children on an average of six examples while the textbook-trained model agrees on an average of three examples. The respective binomial probabilities of six and three matches is 0.024 and 0.249. These probabilities suggest that the match between the LOGO-trained model and the children is unlikely to have occurred by chance. On the other hand, the instance of the model trained by the textbook examples has the most probable outcome from simply random guessing. Thus, we conclude that the LOGO-trained model is a good predictor of children's learning when using LOGO.

In addition, whereas the textbook-trained model was no better than chance at estimating the conventional response, the LOGO-trained model matched convention on an average of seven triads. Interestingly, on both triads where the LOGO-trained model did not match convention, it could not due to lack of appropriate information. For triad 3, convention matches the trapezoid with the parallelogram rather than either of these with the quadrilateral because the trapezoid and the parallelogram both have some pairs of parallel lines. The model, however, has only information about the number of pairs of parallel lines. On the basis of this feature, the three figures are equally dissimilar. For triad 7, the other triad for which the LOGO-trained model did not match convention, the conventional paring matches two obtuse triangles. However, the model has no information about angles other than number and number of right angles. Hence, it could not possibly get this triad correct (at least not for the right reason). We expect that correcting these minor weaknesses will improve the model's ability to make the conventional response.

Table 5: Responses after learning by trained instances of the model and children.

Triad Number	1	2	3	4	5	6	7	8	9
Textbook Trained	AB/BC	BC	AC	AC	BC	AB	AC	AB	AC
LOGO Trained	AB/BC	AB	??	BC	AB	AB	AB	AB	BC
Fifth Grade Children	AB/BC	AB	AC/AB	BC	AB	AB/BC	AC	AB/BC	BC
Convention	AB	AB	AB	BC	AB	AB	BC	AB	BC

Responses by the model are the modal responses over 500 trials.
?? indicates that the model was unable to select among the pairings.

The success of our model in the prediction experiment lead us to investigate the reasons underlying the answers generated by its two instances. In so doing we hoped to gain an understanding of the networks' reasoning processes. Such an understanding would be invaluable in the design of instruction for it would allow the selection of examples that fill specific learning deficits. Unfortunately, trained neural networks are often nearly impossible to comprehend. However, using tools such as those described by Towell and Shavlik [5], we believe that we developed a reasonably clear understanding of the effects of each set of training examples.

The LOGO-trained model made comprehensive adjustments of its initial conditions. Of the eight attributes, it attends to only size and 2 long & short after training. While learning to ignore most of the attributes, the model also learned to pay attention to several of the properties. In particular, number of angles, number of sides, all angles, equal, all sides equal, and number of pairs of opposite sides parallel, all were important to the network after training. Thus, the LOGO-trained instance of the model made a significant transition in its basis for geometric reasoning. Sadly, in making this transition, the declarative clarity of the initial rules was lost. Hence, it is impossible to precisely state the rules that the trained model used to make its final decisions.

By contrast, the textbook-trained instance of the model failed to learn that most of the attributes were unimportant. Instead, the model simply learned that several of the properties were also important. As a result, reasons for answers on the test set often seemed schizophrenic. For instance, in responding BC on test triad 2, the network attributed the decision to similarities in: area, pointiness, point-direction, number of sides, number of angles, number of right angle and all angles equal. Given this combination, it is not surprising that the example is answered incorrectly. This result suggests that typical textbooks may accentuate the importance of conventional properties, but they provide little grist for abandoning the mill of informal attributes.

3.3 Discussion

This experiment demonstrated the utility of our model in several ways. First, it showed that the model is sensitive to differences in training set. Of itself, this is neither a surprising nor interesting conclusion. What is important about the difference in learning is that the model trained in a manner similar to a classroom of fifth grade children made responses to the test set that we quite similar to those of fifth grade children.

In addition to making different responses to the test set, the two trained instances of the model appeared to learn different things. In particular, the LOGO-trained instance essentially replaced its initial knowledge with something much more like the formal geometry. On the other hand, the textbook-trained instance simply added several concepts from formal geometry to the informal concept with which it was initialized. An improved transition from informal to formal geometry is one of the advantages claimed for LOGO based instruction [2]. Hence, the difference between the two instances of the model agrees with observation of children.

This result suggests that our model is able to predict the effect of differing instructional sequences. A further experiment of this hypothesis would be to use our model to design a set of instruction materials. This could be done by starting with an apparently good set of materials, training the model, examining its deficiencies and revising the training materials appropriately. Our hypothesis is that a set of materials so constructed would be superior to the materials normally used in classrooms. Testing of this hypothesis is one of our major directions for future research.

4 Conclusions

In this paper we have described a model of the initial stages of geometry learning by elementary school children. This model is initialized using a set of rules based upon interviews with first and second grade children. This set of rules is shown to accurately predict the responses of second grade children on a hard set of similarity determination problems.

Given that we have a valid starting point for our model, we test it by training those rules, after re-representing them in a neural network, with two different sets of training materials. Each instance of the model is analyzed in two ways. First, they are compared, on an independent set of testing examples, to fifth grade children who had been trained using materials similar to one of the model's training sets. This comparison showed that the model trained with materials similar to the children accurately reproduced the responses of the children. The second analysis involved examining the model after training to determine what it had learned. Both instances of the model learned to attend to the properties that were not mentioned in the initial rules. The model trained with the richer (LOGO-based) training set also learned that the informal attributes were relatively unimportant. Conversely, the model trained with the textbook-based training examples merely added information about properties to the pre-existing information. Therefore, we believe that the model we have described is has the potential to become a valuable tool for teachers.

References

[1] R. Lehrer, W. Knight, M. Love, and L. Sancilio. Software to link action and description in pre-proof geometry. Presented at the Annual Meeting of the American Educational Research Association, 1989.

[2] R. Lehrer, L. Randle, and L. Sancilio. Learning preproof geometry with LOGO. *Cognition and Instruction*, 6:159--184, 1989.

[3] M. O. Noordewier, G. G. Towell, and J. W. Shavlik. Training knowledge-based neural networks to recognize genes in DNA sequences. In *Advances in Neural Information Processing Systems*, volume 3, pages 530--536, Denver, CO, 1991. Morgan Kaufmann.

[4] M. A. Sobel, editor. *Mathematics*. McGraw-Hill, New York, 1987.

[5] G. G. Towell and J. W. Shavlik. Interpretation of artificial neural networks: Mapping knowledge-based neural networks into rules. In *Advances in Neural Information Processing Systems*, volume 4, pages 977--984, Denver, CO, 1991. Morgan Kaufmann.

[6] P. M. van Hiele. *Structure and Insight*. Academic Press, New York, 1986.

Word Space

Hinrich Schütze
Center for the Study of Language and Information
Ventura Hall
Stanford, CA 94305-4115

Abstract

Representations for semantic information about words are necessary for many applications of neural networks in natural language processing. This paper describes an efficient, corpus-based method for inducing distributed semantic representations for a large number of words (50,000) from lexical coccurrence statistics by means of a large-scale linear regression. The representations are successfully applied to word sense disambiguation using a nearest neighbor method.

1 Introduction

Many tasks in natural language processing require access to semantic information about lexical items and text segments. For example, a system processing the sound sequence: /rέkənaisbí:tʃ/ needs to know the topic of the discourse in order to decide which of the plausible hypotheses for analysis is the right one: e.g. "wreck a nice beach" or "recognize speech". Similarly, a mail filtering program has to know the topical significance of words to do its job properly.

Traditional semantic representations are ill-suited for artificial neural networks since they presume a varying number of elements in representations for different words which is incompatible with a fixed input window. Their localist nature also poses problems because semantic similarity (for example between *dog* and *cat*) may be hidden in inheritance hierarchies and complicated feature structures. Neural networks perform best when similarity of targets corresponds to similarity of inputs; traditional symbolic representations do not have this property. Microfeatures have been widely used to overcome these problems. However, microfeature representations have to be encoded by hand and don't scale up to large vocabularies.

This paper presents an efficient method for deriving vector representations for words from lexical cooccurrence counts in a large text corpus. Proximity of vectors in the space (measured by the normalized correlation coefficient) corresponds to semantic similarity. Lexical coocurrence can be easily measured. However, for a vocabulary of 50,000 words, there are 2,500,000,000 possible coocurrence counts to keep track of. While many of these are zero, the number of non-zero counts is still huge. On the other hand, in any document collection most of these counts are small and therefore unreliable. Therefore, **letter fourgrams** are used here to bootstrap the representations. Cooccurrence statistics are collected for 5,000 selected fourgrams. Since each of the 5000 fourgrams is frequent, counts are more reliable than cooccurrence counts for rare words. The 5000-by-5000 matrix used for this purpose is manageable. A vector for a lexical item is computed as the sum of fourgram vectors that occur close to it in the text. This process of **confusion** yields representations of words that are fine-grained enough to reflect semantic differences between the various case and inflectional forms a word may have in the corpus.

The paper is organized as follows. Section 2 discusses related work. Section 3 describes the derivation of the vector representations. Section 4 performs an evaluation. The final section concludes.

2 Related Work

Two kinds of semantic representations commonly used in connectionism are microfeatures (e.g. Waltz and Pollack 1985, McClelland and Kawamoto 1986) and localist schemes in which there is a separate node for each word (e.g. Cottrell 1989). Neither approach scales up well enough in its original form to be applicable to large vocabularies and a wide variety of topics. Gallant (1991), Gallant et al. (1992) present a less labor-intensive method based on microfeatures, but the features for core stems still have to be encoded by hand for each new document collection. The derivation of the *Word Space* presented here is fully automatic. It also uses feature vectors to represent words, but the features cannot be interpreted on their own. Vector similarity is the only information present in Word Space: semantically related words are close, unrelated words are distant. The emphasis on semantic similarity rather than decomposition into interpretable features is similar to Kawamoto (1988). Scholtes (1991) uses a two-dimensional Kohonen map to represent semantic similarity. While a Kohonen map can deal with non-linearities (in contrast to the singular value decomposition used below), a space of much higher dimensionality is likely to capture more of the complexity of semantic relatedness present in natural language. Scholtes' idea to use n-grams to reduce the number of initial features for the semantic representations is extended here by looking at n-gram coocurrence statistics rather than occurrence in documents (cf. (Kimbrell 1988) for the use of n-grams in information retrieval).

An important goal of many schemes of semantic representation is to find a limited number of semantic classes (e.g. classical thesauri such as Roget's, Crouch 1990, Brown et al. 1990). Instead, a multidimensional space is constructed here, in which each word has its own individual representation. Any clustering into classes introduces artificial boundaries that cut off words from part of their semantic neighbor-

```
governor quits knights of columbus over bishop's abortion gag rule
GOVE    _QUI    NIGH       OLUM            SHOP  ABOR        _RUL
  VERN   QUIT       HTS_     LUMB            HOP_  BORT         RULE
   ERNO                                              ORTI         ULE_
    RNOR                                              RTIO
```

Figure 1: A line from the New York Times with selected fourgrams.

hood. In large classes, there will be members "from opposite sides of the class" that are only distantly related. So any class size is problematic, since words are either separated from close neighbors or lumped together with distant terms. Conversely, a multidimensional space does not make such an arbitrary classification necessary.

3 Derivation of the Vector Representations

Fourgram selection. There are about 600,000 possible fourgrams if the empty space, numbers and non-alphanumeric characters are included as "special letters". Of these, 95,000 occurred in 5 months of the New York Times. They were reduced to 5000 by first deleting all rare ones (frequency less than 1000) and then redundant and uninformative fourgrams as described below.

If there is a group of fourgrams that occurs in only one word, all but one is deleted. For instance, the fourgrams BAGH, AGHD, GHDA, HDAD tend to occur together in *Baghdad*, so three of them will be deleted. The rationale for this move is that cooccurrence information about one of the fourgrams can be fully derived from each of the others, so that an index in the matrix would be wasted if more than one of them was included. The relative frequency of one fourgram occurring after another was calculated with fivegrams. For instance, the relative frequency of AGHD following BAGH is the frequency of the fivegram BAGHD divided by the frequency of the fourgram BAGH.

Most fourgrams occur predominantly in three or four stems or words. Uninformative fourgrams are sequences such as RETI or TION that are part of so many different words (*resigned*, *residents*, *retirements*, *resisted*, ...; *abortion*, *desperation*, *construction*, *detention*, ...) that knowledge about coocurrence with them carries almost no semantic information. Such fourgrams are therefore useless and are deleted. Again, fivegrams were used to identify fourgrams that occurred frequently in many stems.

A set of 6290 fourgrams remained after these deletions. To reduce it to the required size of 5000, the most frequent 300 and the least frequent 990 were also deleted. Figure 1 shows a line from the New York Times and which of the 5000 selected fourgrams occurred in it.

Computation of fourgram vectors. The computation of word vectors described below depends on fourgram vectors that accurately reflect semantic similarity in the sense of being used to describe the same contents. Consequently, one needs to be able to compare the sets of contexts two fourgrams occur in. For this purpose, a **collocation matrix** for fourgrams was collected such that the entry $a_{i,j}$

counts the number of times that fourgram i occurs at most 200 fourgrams to the left of fourgram j. Two columns in this matrix are similar if the contexts the corresponding fourgrams are used in are similar. The counts were determined using five months of the New York Times (June – October 1990). The resulting collocation matrix is dense: only 2% of entries are zeros, because almost any two fourgrams cooccur. Only 10% of entries are smaller than 10, so that culling small counts would not increase the sparseness of the matrix. Consequently, any computation that employs the fourgram vectors directly would be inefficient. For this reason, a singular value decomposition was performed and 97 singular values extracted (cf. Deerwester et al. 1990) using an algorithm from SVDPACK (Berry 1992). Each fourgram can then be represented by a vector of 97 real values. Since the singular value decomposition finds the best least-square approximation of the original space in 97 dimensions, two fourgram vectors will be similar if their original vectors in the collocation matrix are similar. The reduced fourgram vectors can be efficiently used for confusion as described in the following section.

Computation of word vectors. We can think of fourgrams as highly ambiguous terms. Therefore, they are inadequate if used directly as input to a neural net. We have to get back from fourgrams to words. For the experiment reported here, cooccurrence information was used for a second time to achieve this goal: in this case coocurrence of a target word with any of the 5000 fourgrams. For each of the selected words (see below), a context vector was computed for every position at which it occurred in the text. A context vector was defined as the sum of all defined fourgram vectors in a window of 1001 fourgrams centered around the target word. The context vectors were then normalized and summed. This sum of vectors is the vector representation of the target word. It is the **confusion** of all its uses in the corpus. More formally, if $C(w)$ is the set of positions in the corpus at which w occurs and if $\varphi(f)$ is the vector representation for fourgram f, then the vector representation $\tau(w)$ of w is defined as: (the dot stands for normalization)

$$\tau(w) = \sum_{i \in C(w)} \Big(\sum_{f \text{ close to } i}^{\bullet} \varphi(f) \Big)$$

The treatment of words is case-sensitive. The following terminology will be used: a *surface form* is the string of characters as it occurs in the text; a *lemma* is either lower case or upper case: all letters are lower case with the possible exception of the first; *word* is used as a case-insensitive term. So every word has exactly two lemmas. A lemma of length n has up to 2^n surface forms. Almost every lower case lemma can be realized as an upper case surface form. But upper case lemmas are hardly ever realized as lower case surface forms.

The confusion vectors were computed for all 54366 lemmas that occurred at least 10 times in 18 months of the New York Times News Service (May 1989 – October 1990, about 50 million words). Table 1 lists the percentage of lower case and upper case lemmas, and the distribution of lemmas with respect to words.

lemmas	number	percent
lower case	32549	60%
upper case	21817	40%
total	54366	100%

words	number	percent
lower case lemma only	23766	52%
upper case lemma only	13034	29%
both lemmas	8783	19%
total	45583	100%

Table 1: The distribution of lower and upper case in words and lemmas.

word	nearest neighbors
burglar	burglars thief rob mugging stray robbing lookout chase crate thieves
disable	deter intercept repel halting surveillance shield maneuvers
disenchantment	disenchanted sentiment resentment grudging mindful unenthusiastic
domestically	domestic auto/-s importers/-ed threefold inventories drastically cars
Dour	melodies/-dic Jazzie danceable reggae synthesizers Soul funk tunes
grunts	heap into ragged goose neatly pulls buzzing rake odd rough
kid	dad kidding mom ok buddies Mom Oh Hey hey mama
S.O.B.	Confessions Jill Julie biography Judith Novak Lois Learned Pulitzer
Ste.	dry oyster whisky hot filling rolls lean float bottle ice
workforce	jobs employ/-s/-ed/-ing attrition workers clerical labor hourly
keeping	hoping bring wiping could some would other here rest have

Table 2: Ten random and one selected word and their nearest neighbors.

4 Evaluation

Table 2 shows a random sample of 10 words and their ten nearest neighbors in Word Space (or less depending on how many would fit in the table). The neighbors are listed in order of proximity to the head word. *burglar*, *disenchantment*, *kid*, and *workforce* are closely related to almost all of their nearest neighbors. The same is true for *disable*, *domestically*, and *Dour*, if we regard as the goal to come up with a characterization of semantic similarity in a corpus (as opposed to the language in general). In the New York Times, the military use of *disable* dominates, Iraq's military, oil pipelines and ships are disabled. Similarly, *domestic* usually refers to the domestic market, and only one person named *Dour* occurs in the newspaper: the Senegalese jazz musician Youssou N'Dour. So these three cases can also be counted as successes. The topic/content of *grunts* is moderately well characterized by other objects like *goose* and *rake* that one would also expect on a farm. Finally, little useful information can be extracted for *S.O.B.* and *Ste.* *S.O.B.* mainly occurs in articles about the bestseller "Confessions of an S.O.B." Since it is not used literally, its semantics don't come out very well. The neighbors of *Ste* are for the most part words associated with water, because the name of the river "Ste.-Marguerite" in Quebec (popular for salmon fishing) is the most frequent context for *Ste*. Since the significance of *Ste* depends heavily on the name it occurs in, its usefulness as a contributor of semantic information is limited, so its poor characterization should probably not be seen as problematic. The word *keeping* has been added to the table to show that the vector representations of words that can be used in a wide variety of contexts are not interesting.

Table 3 shows that it is important for many words to make a distinction between

word	nearest neighbors
pinch (.41)	outs pitch Cone hitting Cary strikeout Whitehurst Teufel Dykstra mound
Pinch	unsalted grated cloves pepper teaspoons coarsely parsley Combine cumin
kappa (.49)	casein protein/-s synthesize liposomes recombinant enzymes amino dna
Kappa	Phi Wesleyan graduate cum dean graduating nyu Amherst College Yale
roe (.54)	cod squid fish salmon flounder lobster haddock lobsters crab chilled
Roe	Wade v overturn/-ing uphold/-ing abortion Reproductive overrule
completion (.73)	complete/-d/-s/-ing complex phase/-s uncompleted incomplete
completions	touchdown/-s interception/-s td yardage yarder tds fumble sacked
ok (.60)	d me I m wouldn t crazy you ain anymore
oks	approve/-s/-d/-ing Senate Waxman bill appropriations omnibus
triad (.52)	warhead/-s ballistic missile/-s ss bombers intercontinental silos
triads	Triads Organized Interpol Cosa Crips gangs trafficking smuggling

Table 3: Words for which case or inflection matter.

word	senses	% correct			
		1	2	3	sum
capital/s	goods/seat of government	96	92		95
interest/s	special attention/financial	94	92		93
motion/s	movement/proposal	92	91		92
plant/s	factory/living being	94	88		92
ruling	decision/to exert control	90	91		90
space	area, volume/outer space	89	90		90
suit/s	legal action/garments	94	95		95
tank/s	combat vehicle/receptacle	97	85		95
train/s	railroad cars/to teach	94	69		89
vessel/s	ship/blood vessel/hollow utensil	93	91	86	92

Table 4: Ten disambiguation experiments using the vector representations.

lower case and upper case and between different inflections. The normalized correlation coefficient between the two case/inflectional forms of the word is indicated in each example.

Word sense disambiguation. Word sense disambiguation is a task that many semantic phenomena bear on and therefore well suited to evaluate the quality of semantic representations. One can use the vector representations for disambiguation in the following way. The context vector of the occurrence of an ambiguous word is defined as the sum of all word vectors ocurring in a window around it. The set of context vectors of the word in the training set can be clustered. The clustering programs used were AutoClass (Cheeseman et al. 1988) and Buckshot (Cutting et al. 1992). The clusters found (between 2 and 13) were assigned senses by inspecting a few of its members (10–20). An occurrence of an ambiguous word in the test set was then disambiguated by assigning the sense of the training cluster that was closest to its context vector. Note that this method is unsupervised in that the structure of the "sense space" is analyzed automatically by clustering. See Schütze (1992) for a more detailed description.

Table 4 lists the results for ten disambiguation experiments that were performed using the above algorithm. Each line shows the ambiguous words, its major senses and the success rate of disambiguation for the individual senses and all major senses together. Training and test sets were taken from the New York Times newswire and were disjoint for each word. These disambiguation results are among the best reported in the literature (e.g. Yarowsky 1992). Apparently, the vector representations respect fine sense distinctions.

An interesting question is to what degree the vector representations are distributed. Using the algorithm for disambiguation described above, a set of contexts of *suit* was clustered and applied to a test text. When the first 30 dimensions were used for clustering the training set, the error rate was 9% in the test set. When only the odd dimensions were used (1,3,5,...,27,29) the error was 14%. With only the even dimensions (2,4,6,...,28,30), 13% of occurrences in the test set were misclassified. This graceful degradation indicates that the vector representations are distributed.

5 Discussion and Conclusion

The linear dimensionality reduction performed here could be a useful preprocessing step for other applications as well. Each of the fourgram features carries a small amount of information. Neglecting individual features degrades performance, but there are so many that they cannot be used directly as input to a neural network. The word sense disambiguation results suggest that no information is lost when only axes of variations extracted by the singular value decomposition are considered instead of the original 5000-dimensional fourgram vectors. Schütze (Forthcoming) uses the same methodology for the derivation of **syntactic** representations for words (so that verbs and nouns occupy different regions in syntactic word space). Problems in pattern recognition often have the same characteristics: uniform distribution of information over all input features or pixels and a high-dimensional input space that causes problems in training if the features are used directly. A singular value decomposition could be a useful preprocessing step for data of this nature that makes neural nets applicable to high-dimensional problems for which training would otherwise be slow if possible at all.

This paper presents Word Space, a new approach to representing semantic information about words derived from lexical cooccurrence statistics. In contrast to microfeature representations, these semantic representations can be summed for a given context to compute a representation of the topic of a text segment. It was shown that semantically related words are close in Word Space and that the vector representations can be used for word sense disambiguation. Word Space could therefore be a promising input representation for applications of neural nets in natural language processing such as information filtering or language modeling in speech recognition.

Acknowledgements

I'm indebted to Mike Berry for SVDPACK, to NASA and RIACS for AutoClass and to the San Diego Supercomputer Center for computing resources. Thanks to Martin Kay, Julian Kupiec, Jan Pedersen, Martin Röscheisen, and Andreas Weigend for help and discussions.

References

Berry, M. W. 1992. Large-scale sparse singular value computations. *The International Journal of Supercomputer Applications* 6(1):13–49.

Brown, P. F., V. J. D. Pietra, P. V. deSouza, J. C. Lai, and R. L. Mercer. 1990. Class-based n-gram models of natural language. Manuscript, IBM.

Cheeseman, P., J. Kelly, M. Self, J. Stutz, W. Taylor, and D. Freeman. 1988. AutoClass: A Bayesian classification system. In *Proceedings of the Fifth International Conference on Machine Learning.*

Cottrell, G. W. 1989. *A Connectionist Approach to Word Sense Disambiguation.* London: Pitman.

Crouch, C. J. 1990. An approach to the automatic construction of global thesauri. *Information Processing & Management* 26(5):629–640.

Cutting, D., D. Karger, J. Pedersen, and J. Tukey. 1992. Scatter-gather: A cluster-based approach to browsing large document collections. In *Proceedings of SIGIR'92.*

Deerwester, S., S. T. Dumais, G. W. Furnas, T. K. Landauer, and R. Harshman. 1990. Indexing by latent semantic analysis. *Journal of the American Society for Information Science* 41(6):391–407.

Gallant, S. I. 1991. A practical approach for representing context and for performing word sense disambiguation using neural networks. *Neural Computation* 3(3):293–309.

Gallant, S. I., W. R. Caid, J. Carleton, R. Hecht-Nielsen, K. P. Qing, and D. Sudbeck. 1992. HNC's matchplus system. In *Proceedings of TREC.*

Kawamoto, A. H. 1988. Distributed representations of ambiguous words and their resolution in a connectionist network. In S. L. Small, G. W. Cottrell, and M. K. Tanenhaus (Eds.), *Lexical Ambiguity Resolution: Perspectives from Psycholinguistics, Neuropsychology, and Artificial Intelligence.* San Mateo CA: Morgan Kaufmann.

Kimbrell, R. E. 1988. Searching for text? Send an N-gram! *Byte Magazine* May:297–312.

McClelland, J. L., and A. H. Kawamoto. 1986. Mechanisms of sentence processing: Assigning roles to constituents of sentences. In J. L. McClelland, D. E. Rumelhart, and the PDP Research Group (Eds.), *Parallel Distributed Processing. Explorations in the Microstructure of Cognition. Volume 2: Psychological and Biological Models,* 272–325. Cambridge MA: The MIT Press.

Scholtes, J. C. 1991. Unsupervised learning and the information retrieval problem. In *Proceedings of the International Joint Conference on Neural Networks.*

Schütze, H. 1992. Dimensions of meaning. In *Proceedings of Supercomputing '92.*

Schütze, H. Forthcoming. Sublexical tagging. In *Proceedings of the IEEE International Conference on Neural Networks.*

Waltz, D. L., and J. B. Pollack. 1985. A strongly interactive model of natural language interpretation. *Cognitive Science* 9:51–74.

Yarowsky, D. 1992. Word-sense disambiguation using statistical models of Roget's categories trained on large corpora. In *Proceedings of Coling-92.*

Perceiving Complex Visual Scenes: An Oscillator Neural Network Model that Integrates Selective Attention, Perceptual Organisation, and Invariant Recognition

Rainer Goebel
Department of Psychology
University of Braunschweig
Spielmannstr. 19
W-3300 Braunschweig, Germany

Abstract

Which processes underly our ability to quickly recognize familiar objects within a complex visual input scene? In this paper an implemented neural network model is described that attempts to specify how selective visual attention, perceptual organisation, and invariance transformations might work together in order to segment, select, and recognize objects out of complex input scenes containing multiple, possibly overlapping objects. Retinotopically organized feature maps serve as input for two main processing routes: the 'where-pathway' dealing with location information and the 'what-pathway' computing the shape and attributes of objects. A location-based attention mechanism operates on an early stage of visual processing selecting a contigous region of the visual field for preferential processing. Additionally, location-based attention plays an important role for invariant object recognition controling appropriate normalization processes within the what-pathway. Object recognition is supported through the segmentation of the visual field into distinct entities. In order to represent different segmented entities at the same time, the model uses an oscillatory binding mechanism. Connections between the where-pathway and the what-pathway lead to a flexible cooperation between different functional subsystems producing an overall behavior which is consistent with a variety of psychophysical data.

1 INTRODUCTION

We are able to recognize a familiar object from many different viewpoints. Additionally, an object normally does not appear in isolation but in combination with other objects. These varying viewing conditions produce very different retinal neural representations. The task of the visual system can be considered as a transformation process forming high-level object representations which are invariant with respect to different viewing conditions. Selective attention and perceptual organisation seem to play an important role in this transformation process.

1.1 LOCATION-BASED VS OBJECT-BASED ATTENTION

Neisser (1967) assumed that visual processing is done in two stages: an early stage that operates in parallel across the entire visual field, and a later stage that can only process information from a limited part of the field at any one time. Neisser (1967) proposed an *object-based approach* to selective attention: the first, 'preattentive', stage segments the whole field into seperate objects on the basis of Gestalt principles; the second stage, focal attention, *selects one of these objects* for detailed analysis.

Other theories stress the *location-based* nature of visual attention: a limited contigous *region* is filtered for detailed analysis (e.g., Posner et al., 1980). There exists a number of models of location-based attention (e.g., Hinton & Lang, 1985; Mozer, 1991; Sandon, 1990) and a few models of object-based attention using whole object knowledge (e.g., Fukushima, 1986). Our model attempts to integrate both approaches: location-based attention - implemented as a 'spotlight' - operates on an early stage of visual processing selecting a contigous region for detailed processing. However, the position and the size of the attentional window is determined to a large extent from the results of a segmentation process operating at different levels within the system.

1.2 DYNAMIC BINDING

The question of how groupings can be represented in a neural network is known as the binding problem. It occurs in many variations, e.g., as the problem of how to represent multiple objects simultaneously but sufficiently distinct that confusions ('illusory conjunctions') at later processing stages are avoided.

An interesting solution of the binding problem is based on ideas proposed by Milner (1974) and von der Malsburg (1981). In contrast to most connectionist models assuming that only the *average output activity* of neurons encodes important information, they suggest that the *exact timing* of neuronal activity (the firing of individual neurons or the 'bursting' of cell groups) plays an important role for information processing in the brain. The central idea is that stimulated units do not respond with a constant output but with *oscillatory behavior* which can be exploited to represent feature linkings. A possible solution for representing multiple objects might be that the parts of one object are bound together through synchronized (phase-locked) oscillations and separated from other objects through an uncorellated phase relation. Recent empirical findings (Eckhorn et al., 1988; Gray & Singer, 1989) provide some evidence that the brain may indeed use phase-locked oscillations as a means for representing global object properties.

2 THE MODEL

2.1 SYSTEM DYNAMICS

In order to establish dynamic binding via phase-locked oscillations the units of the model must be able to exhibit oscillatory behavior. Stimulated from the empirical findings mentioned earlier, a rapidly growing number of work has studied populations of oscillating units (e.g., Eckhorn et al., 1990; Sompolinsky et al., 1990). There exists also a number of models using phase-locked oscillations in order to simulate various aspects of perceptual organisation (e.g., Schillen & König, 1991; Mozer, Zemel, Behrmann & Williams, 1992). We defined computationally simple model neurons which allow to represent independently an activation value and a period value. Such a model neuron possesses two types of input areas: the *activation gate* (a-gate) and the *period-gate* (p-gate) which allow the model neurons to communicate via two types of connections (cf. Eckhorn et al., 1990; they distinguish between 'feeding' and 'linking' connections). We make the following definitions:

- w^a_{ij}: weight from model neuron j to the a-gate of model neuron i.
- w^p_{ij}: weight from model neuron j to the p-gate of model neuron i.
- $\xi_i(t)$: internal time-keeper of unit i
- T: globally defined period length
- $T_i(N)$: period length of unit i (Nth oscillation)

Each model neuron possesses an internal time-keeper $\xi_i(t)$ counting the number of bins elapsed since the last firing point. A model neuron is refractory until the time-keeper reaches the value T_i (e.g., $T_i = T = 8$). Then it may emit an activation value and resets the time-keeper. Depending on the stimulation received at the p-gate (see below) a model neuron fires either if $\xi = T - 1$ or $\xi = T$. This variation of the individual period length T_i is the only possibility for a unit to change its phase relation to other units. The value of the globally defined period length T determines directly how many objects may be represented 'simultaneously'.
The activation value a_i at the internal time ξ is determined as follows:

$$net_i(\xi = T_i) = \sum_{\xi=1}^{T_i} \sum_{j=1}^{n} w^a_{ij} a_j(\xi) \tag{1}$$

$$a_i(\xi) = \begin{cases} (1-\tau) a_i(\xi - T_i) + \tau\,\sigma(net_i(\xi) + b_i) & \text{if } \xi = T_i \\ 0 & \text{otherwise} \end{cases} \tag{2}$$

where $\sigma(x)$ is the logistic (sigmoidal) function. If we consider an extreme case with $T = 1$ we obtain the following equations:

$$net_i(t) = \sum_{j=1}^{n} w^a_{ij} a_j \tag{3}$$

$$a_i(t) = (1 - \tau)a_i(t-1) + \tau\,\sigma(net_i(t) + b_i) \tag{4}$$

This derivation allows us to study the same network as a conventional connectionist network ($T = 1$) with a 'non-oscillatory' activation function to which we can add a dynamic binding mechanism by simply setting $T > 1$. In the latter case the input at the p-gate determines the length of the current period as either $T_i = T - 1$ or $T_i = T$. The decision to shift the phase relation to other neurons should be done in such a way that the 'belongingness constraints' imposed by the connectivity pattern of the p-weights w^p_{ij} is maximized, e.g., if two units are positively p-coupled they should oscillate in phase, if they are negatively p-coupled they should oscillate out of phase. The decision whether a unit fires at $T - 1$ or T depends on two values, the stimulation received during the refractory period $1 \leq \xi < T_i(N-1)$ and on the stimulation received at the last firing point $\xi = T_i(N-1)$. These values behave as two opposite forces g_i determining the probability $P_i^<$ of shortening the next period:

$$g_i^1 = \sum_{j=1}^{n} w^p_{ij} a_j(\xi) \qquad \text{if } \xi = T_i \tag{5}$$

$$g_i^2 = \sum_{\xi=1}^{T_i-1} \sum_{j=1}^{n} \frac{1}{T_i - \xi + 2} w^p_{ij} a_j(\xi) \qquad \text{if } 1 \leq \xi < T_i \tag{6}$$

$$P_i^< = r + \frac{1 - 2r}{1 + e^{(g_i^1 - g_i^2)}} \tag{7}$$

If the value of $g_i^1 - g_i^2$ is large (e.g., there are many positively p-coupled units firing at the same time) it is unlikely that the unit shortens its next period length. If instead the value of $g_i^2 - g_i^1$ is large (e.g., there are many positively coupled neurons firing just before the considered unit) it is likely that the unit will shorten its next period. There exists also a small overall noise level $r = 0.01$ which allows for symmetry breaking (e.g., if two strongly negatively coupled neurons are accidentally phase-locked).

2.2 THE INPUT MODULE

Figure 1 shows an overview of the architecture of the model, called HOTSPOT. An input is presented to the model by clamping on units at the model-retina consisting of two layers with 15x25 units. Each layer is meant to correspond to a different color-sensitive ganglion cell type. The retinal representation is then analyzed within different retinotopically organized feature maps (4 oriented line segments and 2 unoriented color blobs) as a simplified representation of an early visual processing stage (corresponding roughly to V1). A lateral connectivity pattern of p-weights within and between these feature maps computes initial feature linkings consistent with the findings of Eckhorn et al., (1988) and Gray and Singer (1989). Each feature map also projects to a second feature-specific layer. The weights between those layers compute the saliency at each position of a particular feature type. These saliency values are finally integrated within the *saliency map*. The retinotopic feature maps project to both the *what pathway*, corresponding roughly to the occipito-temporal processing stream and the *where-pathway*, corresponding to the occipito-parietal stream (e.g., Ungerleider & Mishkin, 1982).

2.3 THE SPOTLIGHT-LAYER

The *spotlight-layer* receives bottom-up input from the feature maps via the saliency map and top-down input from the *spotlight-control module*. Based on these sources of stimulation, the spotlight layer computes a circular region of activity representing the current focus of spatial attention. The spotlight-layer corresponds roughly to the pulvinar nucleus of the thalamus. The spotlight-layer gates the flow of information within the what-pathway.

2.4 THE WHAT-PATHWAY: FROM FEATURES TO OBJECTS

Processing within the what-pathway includes spatial selection, invariance transformation, complex grouping, object-based selection and object recognition.

2.4.1 The Invariance Module

The task of the Invariance module is to retain the spatial arrangement of the features falling within the attentional spotlight while abstracting at the same time the *absolute retinal position* of the attended information. This goal is achieved in several stages along the what-pathway for each feature type. The basic idea is that each neuron connects to several neurons at the next layer. If a certain position is not attended its 'standard' way may be 'open'. If, however, a position is attended, the decision which way is currently gated for a neuron depends on the position and width of the attentional spotlight. Special control layers compute explicitly whether a certain absolute position falls within one of 5 horizontal and 5 vertical regions of the spotlight (e.g., the horizontal regions are 'far left', 'near left', 'center', 'near right', 'far right'). These layers gate the feedforward-synapses within the what-pathway. Finally, the selected information reaches the *invariance-output layers* which have a 7x7 resolution for each feature type. Recently Olshausen, Anderson and Van Essen (1992) proposed a strikingly similar approach for forming invariant representations.
Despite invariance transformations the representation of an object at the invariance-output layers may not be exactly the same as in previous experiences. Therefore the model uses additional processes contributing to invariant object recognition, most importantly the extraction of global features and the exploitation of population codes for the length, position and orientation of features. This also establishes a limited kind of rotation invariance. The selection of information within the what-pathway is consistent with findings from Moran & Desimone (1985): unattended information is excluded from further processing only, if it would stimulate the same population of neurons at the next stage as the selected information.

2.4.2 The Object-Recognition-Module

The output of the Invariance Module, the *perceptual-code stage*, feeds to the *object-recognition layer* and receives recurrent connections from that layer terminating both on the a-gate and the p-gate of its units. These connections are trained using the back-propagation learning rule ($T = \tau = 1$). The recurrent loop establishes an interactive recognition process allowing to recognize distorted patterns through the completion of missing information and the suppression of noise.
At the perceptual-code stage perceptual organisation continues based on the initial feature linkings computed within the elementary feature maps. The p-weight pattern

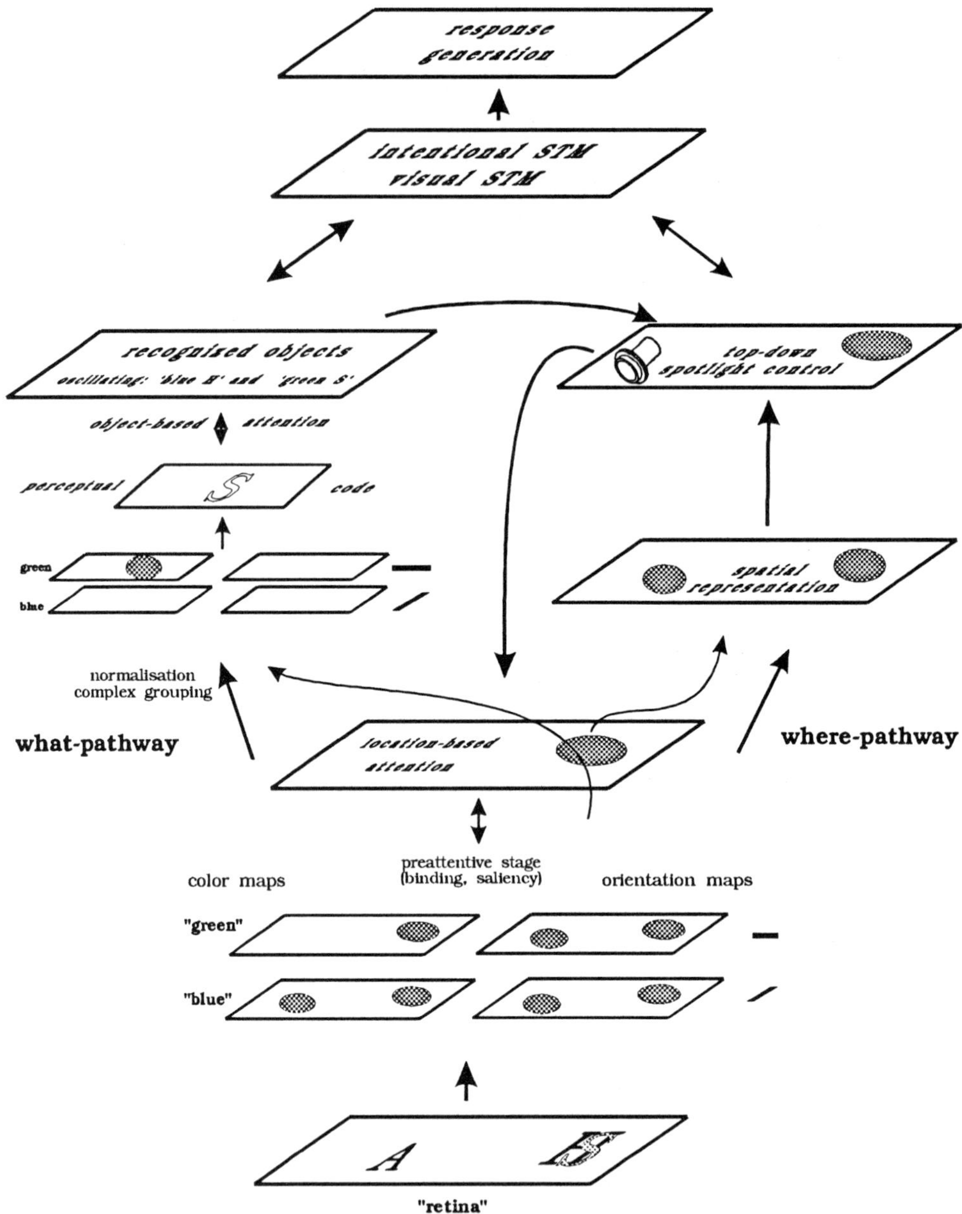

Figure 1: The architecture of HOTSPOT

within the perceptual-code stage implements a set of Gestalt principles such as spatial proximity, similarity and continuity of contour. In additon, acquired shape knowledge is another force acting on the perceptual-code stage in order to bind or separate global features. *Object-based attention* may select one of multiple oscillating objects. For determining a specific object it may use whole-object knowledge (e.g., 'select the letter H'), spatial cues (e.g., 'select the right object') or color cues (e.g., 'select the green object') as well as a combined cue. If the selected object does not use the whole resolution of the perceptual-code stage, commands are sent to the where-pathway in order to adjust the spotlight accordingly.

2.5 THE WHERE-PATHWAY

The where-pathway consists of the *saliency map*, the *spotlight-control module*, the *disengagement layer* and the *spatial-representation layer.* The spotlight-control module performs relative movements and size changes of the attentional spotlight which are demanded by the saliency map, object-based selection or commands from a short-term store holding task instructions. If the current position of the spotlight is not changed for some time, the disengagement layer inhibits the corresponding position at the saliency map. The *spatial-representation layer* contains a coarsely tuned representation of all active retinal positions. If no position within the visual field is particularly salient, this layer determines possible target positions for spatial attention.

If the model knows "where what is" this knowledge is transferred to the *visual short-term memory* where a sequence of 'location-object couplings' can be stored.

3 CONCLUSION

In this paper an oscillator neural network model was presented that integrates location-based attention, perceptual organisation, and invariance transformations. It was outlined how the cooperation between these mechanisms allow the model to segment, select and recognize objects within a complex input scene. The model was successfully applied to simulate a wide variety of psychophysical data including texture segregation, visual search, hierarchical segmentation and recognition. A typical 'processing cycle' of the model consists of an initial segmentation of the visual field with a broadly tuned spotlight. Then a segmented, but not necessarily recognizable, entity may be selected due to its saliency or by object-based attention. This selection in turn induces movements of the location-based attention mechanism until the selected entity is surrounded by the spotlight. Since in this case appropriate invariance transformations are computed the selected object is optimally recognized. Some predictions of the model concerning the object-based nature of selective attention are currently experimentally tested. HOTSPOT indicates a promising way towards a deeper understanding of complex visual processing by bringing together both neurobiological and psychophysical findings in a fruitful way.

Acknowledgements

I am grateful to Reinhard Eckhorn, Peter König, Michael Mozer, Werner X. Schneider, Wolf Singer and Dirk Vorberg for valuable discussions.

References

Eckhorn, R, Bauer, R, Jordan, W., Brosch, M., Kruse, W., Munk, M. & Reitboeck, H.J. (1988) Coherent Oscillations: A mechanism of feature linking in the visual cortex? *Biological Cybernetics*, **60**, 121-130

Eckhorn, R., Reitboeck, H. J., Arndt, M., & Dicke, P. (1990). Feature linking via synchronization among distributed assemblies: The simulation of results from cat visual cortex. *Neural Computation, 2*, 293-307.

Fukushima, K. (1986). A neural network model for selective attention in visual pattern recognition. *Biological Cybernetics, 55*, 5-15.

Gray, M. C. & Singer, W. (1989). Stimulus-specific neuronal oscillations in orientation columns of cat visual cortex. *PNAS USA*, **86**, 1698-1702.

Hinton, G.E, Lang, K.J. (1985). Shape Recognition and Illusory Conjunctions. Proceedings of the 9th IJCAI - Los Angeles, 1, 252-259.

Milner, P.M. (1974). A model for visual shape recognition. *Psych. Rev.*, **81**, 521-535.

Moran, J. & Desimone, R. (1985). Selective attention gates visual processing in the extrastriate cortex. *Science*, **229**, 782-784.

Mozer, M. C. (1991). *The perception of multiple objects: a connectionist approach.* MIT Press / Bradford Books.

Mozer, M. C., Zemel, R. S., & Behrmann, M., Williams, C.K.I. (1992). Learning to segment images using dynamic feature binding. *Neural Computation*, **4**, 650-665.

Neisser, U. (1967). *Cognitive Psychology.* New York: Appleton-Century-Crofts.

Olshausen, B., Anderson, Ch., & Van Essen, D. (1992), A neural model of visual attention and invariant pattern recognition. CNS Memo 18, CalTech.

Posner, M. I., Snyder, C. R. R., & Davidson, B.J. (1980). Attention and the detection of signals. *Journal of Experimental Psychology: General, 109*, 160-174.

Sandon, P. (1990). Simulating visual attention. *Journal of Cog. Neurosc.*, **2**, 213-231.

Schillen, Th. B. & König, P. (1991). Stimulus-dependent assembly formation of oscillatory responses: II. Desynchronization. *Neural Computation, 3*, 167-178.

Sompolinsky, H., Golomb, D., & Kleinfeld, D. (1990). Global processing of visual stimuli in a neural network of coupled oscillators. *Proc. Natl. Acad. Sci. USA*, **87**, 7200-7204.

Ungerleider, L. G., & Mishkin, M. (1982). Two cortical visual systems. In D. J. Ingle, M. A. Goodale, & R. J. W. Mansfield (Eds.), *Analysis of visual behavior.* Cambridge, MA: MIT Press.

Van Essen (1985). Functional organization of primate visual cortex. In A. Peters & E. G. Jones (Eds.)., *Cerebral cortex, vol. 3.* New York: Plenum Press.

Von der Malsburg, C. (1981) The correlation theory of brain function. Internal Report 81-2, Dept. of Neurobiology, MPI for Biophysical Chemistry.

PART XII

Computational and Theoretical Neurobiology

Mapping Between Neural and Physical Activities of the Lobster Gastric Mill

Kenji Doya **Mary E.T. Boyle** **Allen I. Selverston**

Department of Biology
University of California, San Diego
La Jolla, CA 92093-0322

Abstract

A computer model of the musculoskeletal system of the lobster gastric mill was constructed in order to provide a behavioral interpretation of the rhythmic patterns obtained from isolated stomatogastric ganglion. The model was based on Hill's muscle model and quasi-static approximation of the skeletal dynamics and could simulate the change of chewing patterns by the effect of neuromodulators.

1 THE STOMATOGASTRIC NERVOUS SYSTEM

The crustacean stomatogastric ganglion (STG) is a circuit of 30 neurons that controls rhythmic movement of the foregut. It is one of the best elucidated neural circuits. All the neurons and the synaptic connections between them are identified and the effects of neuromodulators on the oscillation patterns and neuronal characteristics have been extensively studied (Selverston and Moulins 1987, Harris-Warrick et al. 1992). However, STG's function as a controller of ingestive behavior is not fully understood in part because of our poor understanding of the controlled object: the musculoskeletal dynamics of the foregut. We constructed a mathematical model of the gastric mill, three teeth in the stomach, in order to predict motor patterns from the neural oscillation patterns which are recorded from the isolated ganglion.

The animal we used was the Californian spiny lobster (*Panulirus interruptus*), which

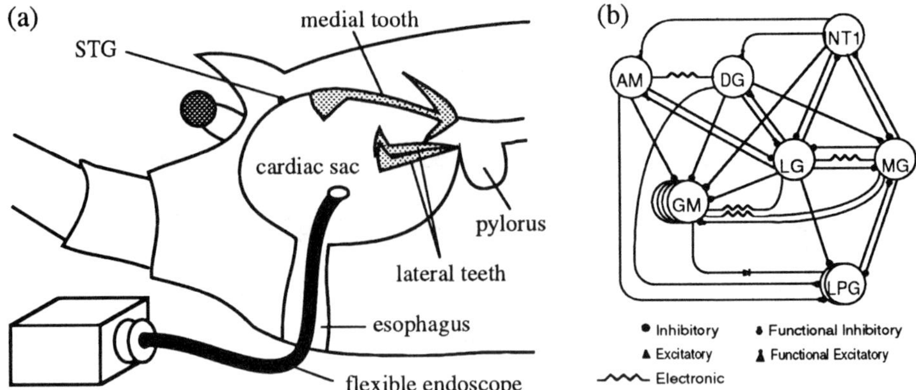

Figure 1: The lobster stomatogastric system. (a) Cross section of the foregut (objects are not to scale). (b) The gastric circuit.

is available locally. The stomatogastric nervous system controls four parts of the foregut: esophagus, cardiac sac (stomach), gastric mill, and pylorus (entrance to the intestine) (Figure 1.a). The gastric mill is composed of one medial tooth and two lateral teeth. These grind large chunks of foods (mollusks, algae, crabs, sea urchins, etc.) into smaller pieces and mix them with digestive fluids. The chewing period ranges from 5 to 10 seconds. Several different chewing patterns have been analyzed using an endoscope (Heinzel 1988a, Boyle et al. 1990). Figure 2 shows two of the typical chewing patterns: "cut and grind" and "cut and squeeze".

The STG is located in the opthalmic artery which runs from the heart to brain over the dorsal surface of the stomach. When it is taken out with two other ganglia (the esophageal ganglion and the commissural ganglion), it can still generate rhythmic motor outputs. This isolated preparation is ideal for studying the mechanism of rhythmic pattern generation by a neural circuit. From pairwise stimulus and response of the neurons, the map of synaptic connections has been established. Figure 1 (b) shows a subset of the STG circuit which controls the motion of the gastric mill. It consists of 11 neurons of 7 types. GM and DG neurons control the medial tooth and LPG, MG, and LG neurons control the lateral teeth. A question of interest is how this simple neural network is utilized to control the various movement patterns of the gastric mill, which is a fairly complex musculoskeletal system.

The oscillation pattern of the isolated ganglion can be modulated by perfusing it with of several neuromodulators, e.g. proctolin, octopamine (Heinzel and Selverston 1988), CCK (Turrigiano 1990), and pilocarpine (Elson and Selverston 1992). However, the behavioral interpretation of these different activity patterns is not well understood. The gastric mill is composed of 7 ossicles (small bones) which is loosely suspended by more than 20 muscles and connective tissues. That makes it is very difficult to intuitively estimate the effect of the change of neural firing patterns in terms of the teeth movement. Therefore we, decided to construct a quantitative model of the musculoskeletal system of the gastric mill.

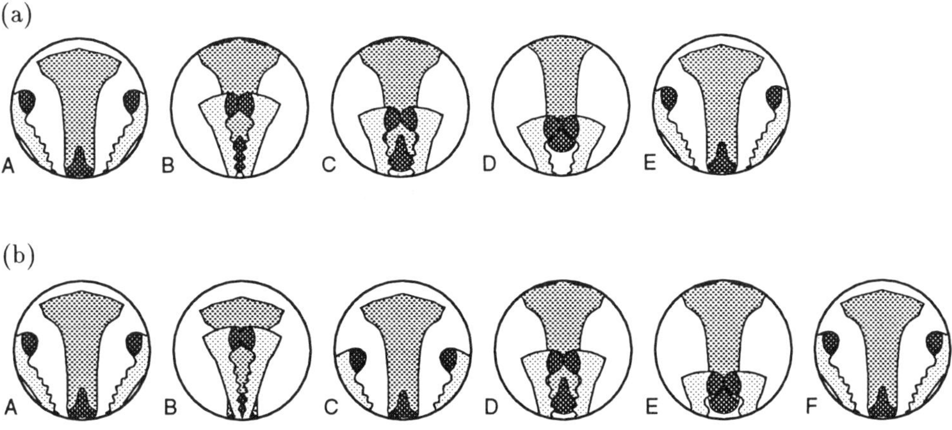

Figure 2: Typical chewing patterns of the gastric mill. (a) cut and grind. (b) cut and squeeze.

2 PHYSIOLOGICAL EXPERIMENTS

In order to design a model and determine its parameters, we performed anatomical and physiological experiments described below.

Anatomical experiments: The carapace and the skin above the stomach mill was removed to expose a dorsal view of the ossicles and the muscles which control the gastric mill. Usually, the gastric mill was quiescent without any stimuli. The positions of the ossicles and the lengths of the muscles at the resting state was measured. After the behavioral experiments mentioned below, the gastric mill was taken out and the size of the ossicles and the positions of the attachment points of the muscles were measured.

Behavioral experiments: With the carapace removed and the gastric mill exposed, one video camera was used to record the movement of the ossicles and the muscles. Another video camera attached to a flexible endoscope was used to record the motion of the teeth from inside the stomach. In the resting state, muscles were stimulated by a wire electrode to determine the behavioral effects. In order to induce chewing, neuromodulators such as proctolin and pilocarpine were injected into the artery in which STG is located.

Single muscle experiments: The gm1, the largest of the gastric mill muscles, was used to estimate the parameters of the muscle model mentioned below. It was removed without disrupting the carapace or ossicle attachment points and fixed to a tension measurement apparatus. The nerve fiber *aln* that innervates gm1 was stimulated using a suction electrode. The time course of isometric tension was recorded at different muscle lengths and stimulus frequencies. The parameters obtained from the gm1 muscle experiment were applied to other muscles by considering their relative length and thickness.

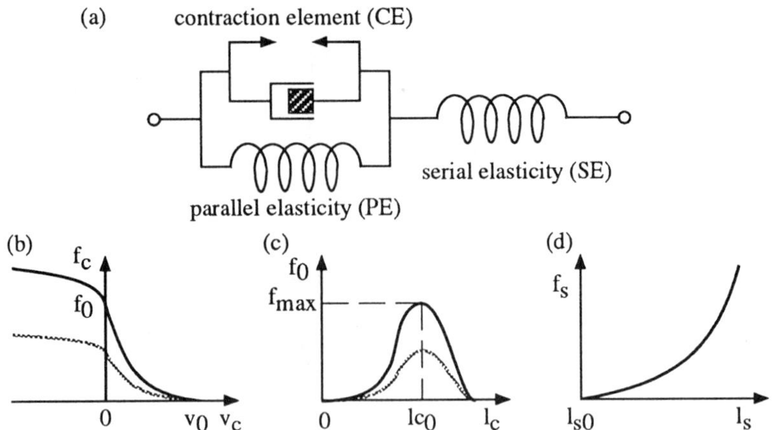

Figure 3: The Hill-based muscle model.

3 MODELING THE MUSCULOSKELETAL SYSTEM

3.1 MUSCULAR DYNAMICS

There are many ways to model muscles. In the simplest models, the tension or the length of a muscle is regarded as an instantaneous function of the spike frequency of the motor nerve. In some engineering approaches, a muscle is considered as a spring whose resting length and stiffness are modulated by the nervous input (Hogan 1984). Since these models are a linear static approximation of the nonlinear dynamical characteristics of muscles, their parameters must be changed to simulate different motor tasks (Winters90). Molecular models (Zahalak 1990), which are based on the binding mechanisms of actin and myosin fibers, can explain the widest range of muscular characteristics found in physiological experiments. However, these complex models have many parameters which are difficult to estimate.

The model we employed was a nonlinear macroscopic model based on A. V. Hill's formulation (Hill 1938, Winters 1990). The model is composed of a contractile element (CE), a serial elasticity (SE), and a parallel elasticity (PE) (Figure 3.a). This model is based on empirical data about nonlinear characteristics of muscles and its parameters can be determined by physiological experiments.

The output force f_c of the CE is a function of its length l_c and its contraction speed $v_c = -dl_c/dt$ (Figure 3.b)

$$\frac{f_c}{f_0} = \begin{cases} \frac{v_0 - v_c}{v_0 + v_c/\alpha} & v_c \geq 0 \text{ (contraction)}, \\ 1 + \beta(1 - \frac{\beta v_0 + v_c}{\beta v_0 - v_c/\alpha}) & v_c < 0 \text{ (extension)}, \end{cases} \tag{1}$$

where f_0 is the isometric output force (at $v_c = 0$) and v_0 is the maximal contraction velocity. The parameters of the f-v curve were $\alpha = 0.25$ and $\beta = 0.3$. The isometric force f_0 was given as the function of CE length l_c and the activation level $a(t)$ of the muscle (Figure 3.c)

$$f_0(l_c, a(t)) = \begin{cases} f_{max}\frac{1}{1-\gamma}\left(\frac{l_c}{l_{c0}}\right)^2\left(\frac{l_c}{l_{c0}} - \gamma\right)a(t) & 0 < l_c < \gamma, \\ 0 & \text{otherwise,} \end{cases} \tag{2}$$

where l_{c0} is the resting length of the CE and $\gamma = 1.5$.

The SE was modeled as an exponential spring (Figure 3.d)

$$f_s(l_s) = \begin{cases} k_1(\exp[k_2\frac{l_s - l_{s0}}{l_{s0}}] - 1) & l_s \geq l_{s0}, \\ 0 & l_s < l_{s0}, \end{cases} \tag{3}$$

where f_s is the output force, l_{s0} is the resting length, and k_1 and k_2 are stiffness parameters. The PE was supposed to have the same exponential elasticity (3).

In the simulations, the CE length l_c was taken as the state variable. The total muscle length $l_m = l_c + l_s$ is given by the skeletal model and the muscle activation $a(t)$ is given by the the activation dynamics described below. The SE length is given from $l_s = l_m - l_c$ and then the output force $f_s(l_s) = f_c + f_p = f_m$ is given by (3). The contraction velocity $v_c = -\frac{dl_c}{dt}$ is derived from the inverse of (1) at $f_c = f_s(l_s) - f_p(l_c)$ and then integrated to update the CE length l_c.

The activation level $a(t)$ of a muscle is determined by the free calcium concentration in muscle fibers. Since we don't have enough data about the calcium dynamics in muscle cells, the activation dynamics was crudely approximated by the following equations.

$$\tau_a \frac{da(t)}{dt} = -a(t) + e(t), \quad \text{and} \quad \tau_e \frac{de(t)}{dt} = -e(t) + n(t)^2, \tag{4}$$

where $n(t)$ is the normalized firing frequency of the nerve input and $e(t)$ is the electric activity of the muscle fibers. The nonlinearity in the nervous input represents strong facilitation of the postsynaptic potential (Govind and Lingle 1987).

We incorporated seven of the gastric mill muscles: gm1, gm2, gm3a, gm3c, gm4, gm6b, and gm9a (Maynard and Dando 1974). The muscles gm1, gm2, gm3a, and gm3c are extrinsic muscles that have one end attached to the carapace and gm4, gm6b, and gm9a are intrinsic muscles both ends of which are attached of the ossicles. Three connective tissues were also incorporated and regarded as muscles without contraction elements. See Figure 4 for the attachment of these muscles and tissues to the ossicles.

3.2 SKELETAL DYNAMICS

The medial tooth was modeled as three rigid pieces P_1, P_2 and P_3. P_1 is the base of the medial tooth. P_2 is the main body of the medial tooth. P_3 forms the cusp and the V-shaped lever on the dorsal side. The lateral tooth was modeled as two rigid pieces P_4 and P_5. P_4 is a L-shaped plate with a cusp at the angle and is connected to P_3 at the dorsal end. P_5 is a rod that is connected to P_4 near the root of the cusp (Figure 4).

We assumed that the motion is symmetric with respect to the midline. Therefore the motion of the medial tooth was two-dimensional and only the left one of the

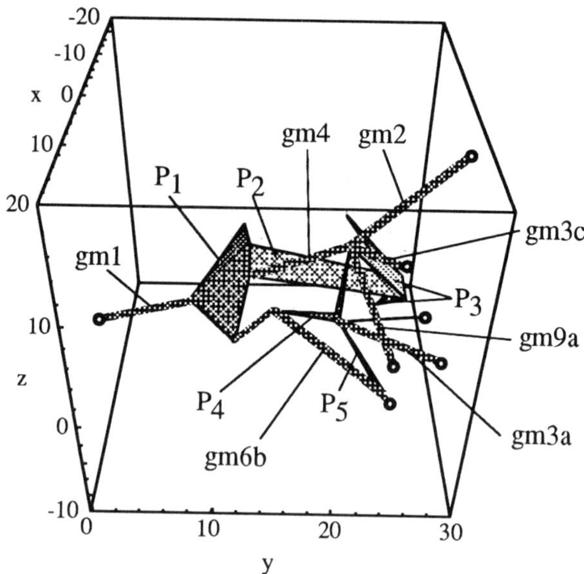

Figure 4: The design of the gastric mill model. Ossicle P_1 stands for the ossicles I and II, P_2 for VII, P_3 for VI, P_4 for III, IV, and V, P_5 for XIV in the standard description by Maynard and Dando (1974).

two lateral teeth was considered. The coordinate system was taken so that x-axis points to the left, y-axis backward, and z-axis upward. The rotation angles of the ossicles around x, y, and z axes ware represented as θ, ϕ, and ψ respectively. The configuration of the ossicles was determined by a 10 dimensional vector

$$\Theta = (y_0, z_0, \theta_1, \theta_2, \theta_3, \theta_4, \phi_4, \psi_4, \theta_5, \phi_5), \tag{5}$$

where (y_0, z_0) represents the position of the joint between P_1 and P_2 and $(\theta_1, \theta_2, \theta_3)$ represents the rotation angle of P_1, P_2 and P_3 in the y-z plane. The rotation angles of P_4 and P_5 were represented as $(\theta_4, \phi_4, \psi_4)$ and (θ_5, ϕ_5) respectively. P_5 has only two degrees of rotation freedom since it is regarded as a rod.

We employed a quasi-static approximation. The configuration of the ossicles Θ was determined by the static balance of force. Now let L_m and F_m be the vectors of the muscle lengths and forces. Then the balance of the generalized forces in the Θ space (force for translation and torque for rotation) is given by

$$T_m(\Theta, F_m) + T_e = 0, \tag{6}$$

where T_m and T_e represent the generalized forces from muscles and external loads. The muscle force in the Θ space is given by

$$T_m(\Theta, F_m) = J(\Theta)^T F_m, \tag{7}$$

where $J(\Theta) = \partial L_m / \partial \Theta$ is the Jacobian matrix of the mapping $\Theta \mapsto L_m$ determined by the ossicle kinematics and the muscle attachment. Since it is very difficult to obtain a closed form solution of (6), we used a gradient descent equation

$$\frac{d\Theta}{dt} = -\varepsilon(T_m(\Theta, F_m) + T_e) = -\varepsilon(J(\Theta)^T F_m + T_e) \tag{8}$$

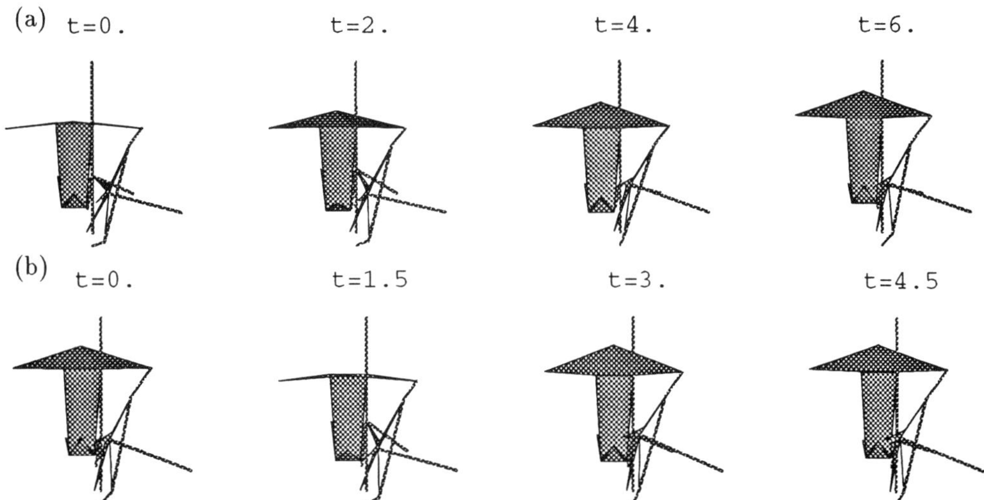

Figure 5: Chewing patterns predicted from oscillation patterns of isolated STG. (a) spontaneous pattern. (b) proctolin induced pattern.

to find the approximate solution of $\Theta(t)$. This is equivalent to assuming a viscosity term $\varepsilon^{-1}d\Theta/dt$ in the motion equation.

4 SIMULATION RESULTS

The musculoskeletal model is a 17-th order differential equation system and was integrated by Runge-Kutta method with a time step 1ms. Figure 5 shows examples of motion patterns predicted by the model. The motoneuron output of spontaneous oscillation of the isolated ganglion was used in (a) and the output under the effect of proctolin was used in (b). It has been reported in previous behavioral studies (Heinzel 1988b) that the dose of proctolin typically evokes "cut and grind" chewing pattern. The trajectory (b) predicted from the proctolin induced rhythm has a larger forward movement of the medial tooth while the lateral teeth are closed, which qualitatively agrees with the behavioral data.

5 DISCUSSION

The motor pattern generated by the model is considerably different from the chewing patterns observed in the intact animal using an endoscope. This is partly because of crude assumptions in model construction and errors in parameter estimation. However, this difference may also be due to the lack of sensory feedback in the isolated preparation. The future subject of this project is to refine the model so that we can reliably predict the motion from the neural outputs and to combine it with models of the gastric network (Rowat and Selverston, submitted) and sensory receptors. This will enable us to study how a biological control system integrates central pattern generation and sensory feedback.

Acknowledgements

We thank Mike Beauchamp for the gm1 muscle data. This work was supported by the grant from Office of Naval Research N00014-91-J-1720.

References

Boyle, M. E. T., Turrigiano, G. G., and Selverston, A. I. 1990. An endoscopic analysis of gastric mill movements produced by the peptide cholecystokinin. *Society for Neuroscience Abstracts* **16**, 724.

Elson, R. C. and Selverston, A. I. 1992. Mechanisms of gastric rhythm generation in the isolated stomatogastric ganglion of spiny lobsters: Bursting pacemaker potentials, synaptic interactions and muscarinic modulation. *Journal of Neurophysiology* **68**, 890–907.

Govind, C. K. and Lingle, C. J. 1987. Neuromuscular organization and pharmacology. In Selverston, A. I. and Moulins, M., editors, *The Crustacean Stomatogastric System*, pages 31–48. Springer-Verlag, Berlin.

Harris-Warrick, R. M., Marder, E., Selverston, A. I., and Moulins, M. 1992. *Dynamic Biological Networks — The Stomatogastric Nervous System.* MIT Press, Cambridge, MA.

Heinzel, H. G. 1988. Gastric mill activity in the lobster. I: Spontaneous modes of chewing. *Journal of Neurophysiology* **59**, 528–550.

Heinzel, H. G. 1988. Gastric mill activity in the lobster. II: Proctolin and octopamine initiate and modulate chewing. *Journal of Neurophysiology* **59**, 551–565.

Heinzel, H. G. and Selverston, A. I. 1988. Gastric mill activity in the lobster. III: Effects of proctolin on the isolated central pattern generator. *Journal of Neurophysiology* **59**, 566–585.

Hill, A. V. 1938. The heat of shortening and the dynamic constants of muscle. *Proceedings of the Royal Sciety of London, Series B* **126**, 136–195.

Hogan, N. 1984. Adaptive control of mechanical impedance by coactivation of antagonist muscles. *IEEE Transactions on Automatic Control* **29**, 681–690.

Maynard, D. M. and Dando, M. R. 1974. The structure of the stomatogastric neuromuscular system in callinectes sapidus, homarus americanus and panulirus argus (decapoda crustacea). *Philosophical Transactions of Royal Society of London, Biology* **268**, 161–220.

Rowat, P. F. and Selverston, A. I. Modeling the gastric mill central pattern generator of the lobster with a relaxation-oscillator network. submitted.

Selverston, A. I. and Moulins, M. 1987. *The Crustacean Stomatogastric System.* Springer-Verlag, New York, NY.

Turrigiano, G. G. and Selverston, A. I. 1990. A cholecystokinin-like hormone activates a feeding-related neural circuit in lobster. *Nature* **344**, 866–868.

Winters, J. M. 1990. Hill-based muscle models: A systems engineering perspective. In Winters, J. M. and Woo, S. L.-Y., editors, *Multiplie Muscle Systems: Biomechanics and Movement Organization*, chapter 5, pages 69–93. Springer-Verlag, New York, NY.

Zahalak, G. I. 1990. Modeling muscle mechanics (and energetics). In Winters, J. M. and Woo, S. L.-Y., editors, *Multiplie Muscle Systems: Biomechanics and Movement Organization*, chapter 1, pages 1–23. Springer-Verlag, New York, NY.

A Neural Model of Descending Gain Control in the Electrosensory System

Mark E. Nelson
Beckman Institute
University of Illinois
405 N. Mathews
Urbana, IL 61801

Abstract

In the electrosensory system of weakly electric fish, descending pathways to a first-order sensory nucleus have been shown to influence the gain of its output neurons. The underlying neural mechanisms that subserve this descending gain control capability are not yet fully understood. We suggest that one possible gain control mechanism could involve the regulation of total membrane conductance of the output neurons. In this paper, a neural model based on this idea is used to demonstrate how activity levels on descending pathways could control both the gain and baseline excitation of a target neuron.

1 INTRODUCTION

Certain species of freshwater tropical fish, known as weakly electric fish, possess an active electric sense that allows them to detect and discriminate objects in their environment using a self-generated electric field (Bullock and Heiligenberg, 1986). They detect objects by sensing small perturbations in this electric field using an array of specialized receptors, known as electroreceptors, that cover their body surface. Weakly electric fish often live in turbid water and tend to be nocturnal. These conditions, which hinder visual perception, do not adversely affect the electric sense. Hence the electrosensory system allows these fish to navigate and capture prey in total darkness in much the same way as the sonar system of echolocating bats allows them to do the same. A fundamental difference between bat echolocation and fish "electrolocation" is that the propagation of the electric field emitted by the fish is essentially instantaneous when considered on the time scales that characterize nervous system function. Thus rather than processing echo delays as bats do, electric fish extract information from instantaneous amplitude and phase modulations of their emitted signals.

The electric sense must cope with a wide range of stimulus intensities because the magnitude of electric field perturbations varies considerably depending on the size, distance and impedance of the object that gives rise to them (Bastian, 1981a). The range of intensities that the system experiences is also affected by the conductivity of the surrounding water, which undergoes significant seasonal variation. In the electrosensory system, there are no peripheral mechanisms to compensate for variations in stimulus intensity. Unlike the visual system, which can regulate the intensity of light arriving at photoreceptors by adjusting pupil diameter, the electrosensory system has no equivalent means for directly regulating the overall stimulus strength experienced by the electroreceptors, [1] and unlike the auditory system, there are no efferent projections to the sensory periphery to control the gain of the receptors themselves. The first opportunity for the electrosensory system to make gain adjustments occurs in a first-order sensory nucleus known as the electrosensory lateral line lobe (ELL).

In the ELL, primary afferent axons from peripheral electroreceptors terminate on the basal dendrites of a class of pyramidal cells referred to as E-cells (Maler et al., 1981; Bastian, 1981b), which represent a subset of the output neurons for the nucleus. These pyramidal cells also receive descending inputs from higher brain centers on their apical dendrites (Maler et al., 1981). One noteworthy feature is that the descending inputs are massive, far outnumbering the afferent inputs in total number of synapses. Experiments have shown that the E-cells, unlike peripheral electroreceptors, maintain a relatively constant response amplitude to electrosensory stimuli when the overall electric field normalization is experimentally altered. This automatic gain control capability is lost, however, when descending input to the ELL is blocked (Bastian, 1986ab). The underlying neural mechanisms that subserve this descending gain control capability are not yet fully understood, although it is known that GABAergic inhibition plays a role (Shumway & Maler, 1989). We suggest that one possible gain control mechanism could involve the regulation of total membrane conductance of the pyramidal cells. In the next section we present a model based on this idea and show how activity levels on descending pathways could regulate both the gain and baseline excitation of a target neuron.

2 NEURAL CIRCUITRY FOR DESCENDING GAIN CONTROL

Figure 1 shows a schematic diagram of neural circuitry that could provide the basis for a descending gain control mechanism. This circuitry is inspired by the circuitry found in the ELL, but has been greatly simplified to retain only the aspects that

[1] In principle, this could be achieved by regulating the strength of the fish's own electric discharge. However, these fish maintain a remarkably stable discharge amplitude and such a mechanism has never been observed.

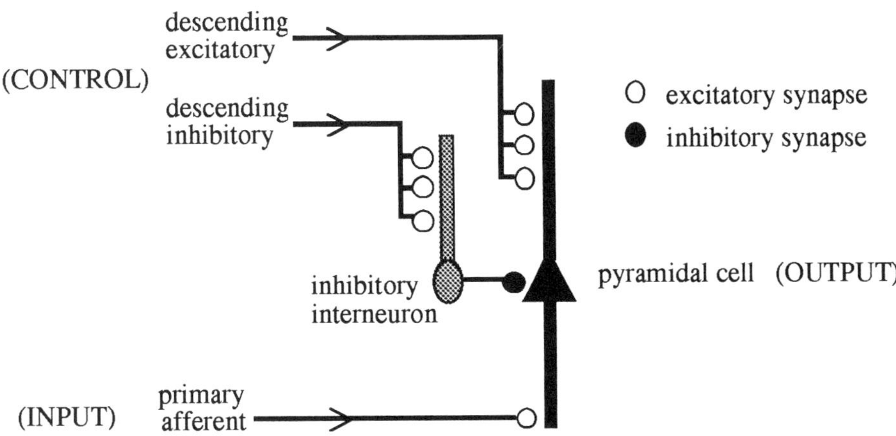

Figure 1: Neural circuitry for descending gain control. The gain of the pyramidal cell response to an input signal arriving on its basilar dendrite can be controlled by adjusting the tonic levels of activity on two descending pathways. A descending excitatory pathway makes excitatory synapses (open circles) directly on the pyramidal cell. A descending inhibitory pathway acts through an inhibitory interneuron (shown in gray) to activate inhibitory synapses (filled circles) on the pyramidal cell.

are essential for the proposed gain control mechanism. The pyramidal cell receives afferent input on a basal dendrite and control inputs from two descending pathways. One descending pathway makes excitatory synaptic connections directly on the apical dendrite of the pyramidal cell, while a second pathway exerts a net inhibitory effect on the pyramidal cell by acting through an inhibitory interneuron. We will show that under appropriate conditions, the gain of the pyramidal cell's response to an input signal arriving on its basal dendrite can be controlled by adjusting the tonic levels of activity on the two descending pathways. At this point it is worth pointing out that the spatial segregation of input and control pathways onto different parts of the dendritic tree is not an essential feature of the proposed gain control mechanism. However, by allowing independent experimental manipulation of these two pathways, this segregation has played a key role in the discovery and subsequent characterization of the gain control function in this system (Bastian, 1986ab).

The gain control function of the neural circuitry show in Figure 1 can best be understood by considering an electrical equivalent circuit for the pyramidal cell. The equivalent circuit shown in Figure 2 includes only the features that are necessary to understand the gain control function and does not reflect the true complexity of ELL pyramidal cells, which are known to contain many different types of voltage-dependent channels (Mathieson & Maler, 1988). The passive electrical properties of the circuit in Figure 2 are described by a membrane capacitance C_m, a leakage conductance $g_{\ell eak}$, and an associated reversal potential $E_{\ell eak}$. The excitatory descending pathway directly activates excitatory synapses on the pyramidal cell, giving rise to an excitatory synaptic conductance g_{ex} with a reversal potential E_{ex}.

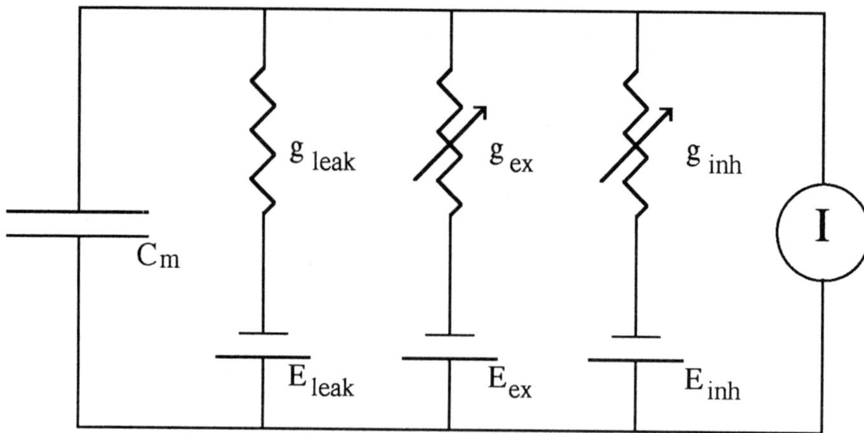

Figure 2: Electrical equivalent circuit for the pyramidal cell in the gain control circuit. The excitatory and inhibitory conductances, g_{ex} and g_{inh}, are shown are variable resistances to indicate that their steady-state values are dependent on the activity levels of the descending pathways.

The inhibitory descending pathway acts by exciting a class of inhibitory interneurons which in turn activate inhibitory synapses on the pyramidal cell with inhibitory conductance g_{inh} and reversal potential E_{inh}. In this model, the excitatory and inhibitory conductances g_{ex} and g_{inh} represent the population conductances of all the individual excitatory and inhibitory synapses associated with the descending pathways. Although individual synaptic events give rise to a *time-dependent* conductance change (which is often modeled by an α function), we consider the regime in which the activity levels on the descending pathways, the number of synapses involved, and the synaptic time constants are such that the summed effect can be well described by a single *time-invariant* conductance value for each pathway. The input signal (the one under the influence of the gain control mechanism) is modeled in a general form as a time-dependent current I(t). This current can represent either the synaptic current arising from activation of synapses in the primary afferent pathway, or it can represent direct current injection into the cell, such as might occur in an intracellular recording experiment.

The behavior of the membrane potential $V(t)$ for this model system is described by

$$C_m \frac{dV(t)}{dt} + g_{\ell\mathrm{eak}}(V(t) - E_{\ell\mathrm{eak}}) + g_{\mathrm{ex}}(V(t) - E_{\mathrm{ex}}) + g_{\mathrm{inh}}(V(t) - E_{\mathrm{inh}}) = I(t) \quad (1)$$

In the absence of an input signal ($I = 0$), the system will reach a steady-state ($dV/dt = 0$) membrane potential V_{ss} given by

$$V_{ss}(I = 0) = \frac{g_{\ell\mathrm{eak}}\mathrm{E}_{\ell\mathrm{eak}} + g_{\mathrm{ex}}\mathrm{E}_{\mathrm{ex}} + g_{\mathrm{inh}}\mathrm{E}_{\mathrm{inh}}}{g_{\ell\mathrm{eak}} + g_{\mathrm{ex}} + g_{\mathrm{inh}}} \quad (2)$$

If we consider the input $I(t)$ to give rise to fluctuations in membrane potential $U(t)$ about this steady state value

$$U(t) = V(t) - V_{ss} \tag{3}$$

then (1) can be rewritten as

$$C_m \frac{dU(t)}{dt} + g_{tot} U(t) = I(t) \tag{4}$$

where g_{tot} is the total membrane conductance

$$g_{tot} = g_{leak} + g_{ex} + g_{inh} \tag{5}$$

Equation (4) describes a first-order low-pass filter with a transfer function $G(s)$, from input current to output voltage change, given by

$$G(s) = \frac{R_{tot}}{\tau s + 1} \tag{6}$$

where s is the complex frequency ($s = i\omega$), R_{tot} is the total membrane resistance ($R_{tot} = 1/g_{tot}$), and τ is the RC time constant

$$\tau = R_{tot} C_m = \frac{C_m}{g_{tot}} \tag{7}$$

The frequency dependence of the response gain $|G(i\omega)|$ is shown in Figure 3. For low frequency components of the input signal ($\omega\tau << 1$), the gain is inversely proportional to the total membrane conductance g_{tot}, while at high frequencies ($\omega\tau >> 1$), the gain is independent of g_{tot}. This is due to the fact that the impedance of the RC circuit shown in Figure 2 is dominated by the resistive components at low frequencies and by the capacitive component at high frequencies. Note that the RC time constant τ, which characterizes the low-pass filter cutoff frequency, varies inversely with g_{tot}. For components of the input signal below the cutoff frequency, gain control can be accomplished by regulating the total membrane conductance.

In electrophysiological terms, this mechanism can be thought of in terms of regulating the input resistance of the neuron. As the total membrane conductance is increased, the input resistance is decreased, meaning that a fixed amount of current injection will cause a smaller change in membrane potential. Hence increasing the total membrane conductance decreases the response gain.

In our model, we propose that regulation of total membrane conductance occurs via activity on descending pathways that activate excitatory and inhibitory synaptic conductances. For this proposed mechanism to be effective, these synaptic conductances must make a significant contribution to the total membrane conductance of the pyramidal cell. Whether this condition actually holds for ELL pyramidal cells has not yet been experimentally tested. However, it is not an unreasonable assumption to make, considering recent reports that synaptic background activity can have

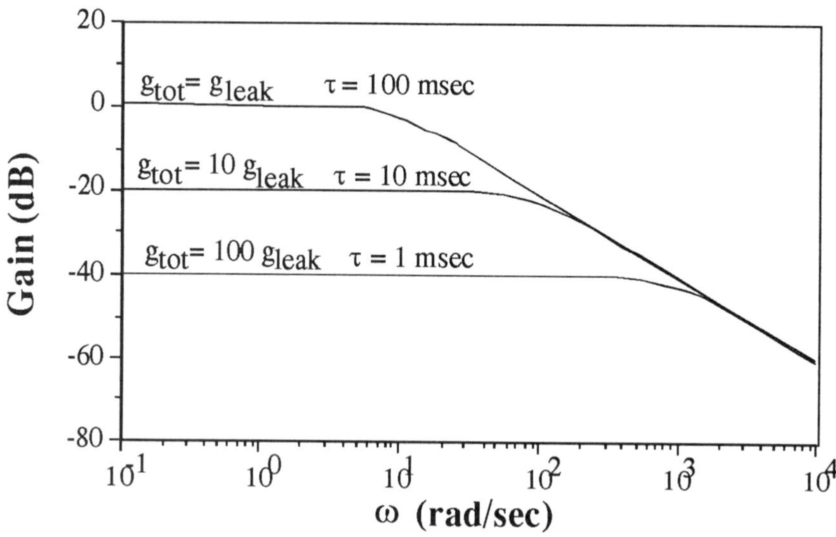

Figure 3: Gain as a function of frequency for three different values of total membrane conductance g_{tot}. At low frequencies, gain is inversely proportional to g_{tot}. Note that the time constant τ, which characterizes the low-pass cutoff frequency, also varies inversely with g_{tot}. Gain is normalized to the maximum gain: $G_{max} = \frac{1}{g_{leak}}$; $Gain(dB) = 20\log_{10}(\frac{G}{G_{max}})$.

a significant influence on the total membrane conductance of cortical pyramidal cells (Bernander et al., 1991) and cerebellar Purkinje cells (Rapp et al., 1992).

3 CONTROL OF BASELINE EXCITATION

If the only functional goal was to achieve regulation of total membrane conductance, then synaptic background activity on a single descending pathway would be sufficient and there would be no need for the paired excitatory and inhibitory control pathways shown in Figure 1. However, the goal of gain control is regulate the total membrane conductance while holding the baseline level of excitation constant. In other words, we would like to be able to change the sensitivity of a neuron's response without changing its spontaneous level of activity (or steady-state resting potential if it is below spiking threshold). By having paired excitatory and inhibitory control pathways, as shown in Figure 1, we gain the extra degree-of-freedom necessary to achieve this goal.

Equation (2) provided us with a relationship between the synaptic conductances in our model and the steady-state membrane potential. In order to change the gain of a neuron, without changing its baseline level of excitation, the excitatory and inhibitory conductances must be adjusted in a way that achieves the desired total membrane conductance g_{tot} and maintains a constant V_{ss}. Solving equations (2) and (5) simultaneously for g_{ex} and g_{inh}, we find

$$g_{ex} = \frac{g_{\text{tot}}(V_{\text{ss}} - E_{\text{inh}}) - g_{\ell\text{eak}}(E_{\ell\text{eak}} - E_{\text{inh}})}{(E_{\text{ex}} - E_{\text{inh}})} \tag{8}$$

$$g_{inh} = \frac{g_{\text{tot}}(V_{\text{ss}} - E_{\text{ex}}) - g_{\ell\text{eak}}(E_{\ell\text{eak}} - E_{\text{ex}})}{(E_{\text{inh}} - E_{\text{ex}})} \tag{9}$$

For example, consider a case where the reversal potentials are $E_{\ell eak} = -70$ mV, $E_{ex} = 0$ mV, and $E_{inh} = -90$ mV. Assume want to find values of the steady-state conductances, g_{ex} and g_{inh}, that would result in a total membrane conductance that is twice the leakage conductance (i.e. $g_{tot} = 2g_{\ell eak}$) and would produce a steady-state depolarization of 10 mV (i.e. $V_{ss} = -60$ mV). Using (8) and (9) we find the required synaptic conductance levels are $g_{ex} = \frac{4}{9}g_{\ell eak}$ and $g_{inh} = \frac{5}{9}g_{\ell eak}$.

4 DISCUSSION

The ability to regulate a target neuron's gain using descending control signals would provide the nervous system with a powerful means for implementing adaptive signal processing algorithms in sensory processing pathways as well as other parts of the brain. The simple gain control mechanism proposed here, involving the regulation of total membrane conductance, may find widespread use in the nervous system. Determining whether or not this is the case, of course, requires experimental verification. Even in the electrosensory system, which provided the inspiration for this model, definitive experimental tests of the proposed mechanism have yet to be carried out. Fortunately the model provides a straightforward experimentally testable prediction, namely that if activity levels on the presumed control pathways are changed, then the input resistance of the target neuron will reflect those changes. In the case of the ELL, the prediction is that if descending pathways were silenced while monitoring the input resistance of an E-type pyramidal cell, one would observe an increase in input resistance corresponding to the elimination of the descending contributions to the total membrane conductance.

We have mentioned that the gain control circuitry of Figure 1 was inspired by the neural circuitry of the ELL. For those familiar with this circuitry, it is interesting to speculate on the identity of the interneuron in the inhibitory control pathway. In the gymnotid ELL, there are at least six identified classes of inhibitory interneurons. For the proposed gain control mechanism, we are interested in the identifying those that receive descending input and which make inhibitory synapses onto pyramidal cells. Four of the six classes meet these criteria: granule cell type 2 (GC2), polymorphic, stellate, and ventral molecular layer neurons. While all four classes may participate to some extent in the gain control mechanism, one would predict, based on cell number and synapse location, that GC2 (as suggested by Shumway & Maler, 1989) and polymorphic cells would make the dominant contribution. The morphology of GC2 and polymorphic neurons differs somewhat from that shown in Figure 1. In addition to the apical dendrite, which is shown in the figure, these neurons also have a basal dendrite that receives primary afferent input. GC2 and polymorphic neurons are excited by primary afferent input and thus provide additional inhibition to pyramidal cells when afferent activity levels increase. This can be viewed as providing a feedforward component to the automatic gain control mechanism.

In this paper, we have confined our analysis to the effects of tonic changes in descending activity. While this may be a reasonable approximantion for certain experimental manipulations, it is unlikely to be a good representation of the dynamic patterns that occur under natural conditions, particularly since the descending pathways form part of a feedback loop that includes the ELL output neurons. The full story in the electrosensory system will undoubtably be much more complex. For example, there is already experimental evidence demonstrating that, in addition to gain control, descending pathways influence the spatial and temporal filtering properties of ELL output neurons (Bastian, 1986ab; Shumway & Maler, 1989).

Acknowledgements

This work was supported by NIMH 1-R29-MH49242-01. Thanks to Joe Bastian and Lenny Maler for many enlightening discussions on descending control in the ELL.

References

Bastian, J. (1981a) Electrolocation I: An analysis of the effects of moving objects and other electrical stimuli on the electroreceptor activity of *Apteronotus albifrons.* J. Comp. Physiol. **144**, 465-479.

Bastian, J. (1981b) Electrolocation II: The effects of moving objects and other electrical stimuli on the activities of two categories of posterior lateral line lobe cells in *Apteronotus albifrons.* J. Comp. Physiol. **144**, 481-494.

Bastian, J. (1986a) Gain control in the electrosensory system mediated by descending inputs to the electrosensory lateral line lobe. J. Neurosci. **6**, 553-562.

Bastian, J. (1986b) Gain control in the electrosensory system: a role for the descending projections to the electrosensory lateral line lobe. J. Comp. Physiol. **158**, 505-515.

Bernander, O., Douglas, R.J., Martin, K.A.C. & Koch, C. (1991) Synaptic background activity influences spatiotemporal integration in single pyramidal cells. Proc. Natl. Acad. Sci. USA **88**, 11569-11573.

Bullock, T.H. & Heiligenberg, W., eds. (1986) *Electroreception.* Wiley, New York.

Maler, L., Sas, E. and Rogers, J. (1981) The cytology of the posterior lateral line lobe of high frequency weakly electric fish (Gymnotidei): Dendritic differentiation and synaptic specificity in a simple cortex. J. Comp. Neurol. **195**, 87-140.

Mathieson, W.B. & Maler, L. (1988) Morphological and electrophysiological properties of a novel *in vitro* preparation: the electrosensory lateral line lobe brain slice. J. Comp. Physiol. **163**, 489-506.

Rapp, M., Yarom, Y. & Segev, I. (1992) The impact of parallel fiber background activity on the cable properties of cerebellar Purkinje Cells. Neural Comp. **4**, 518-533.

Shumway, C.A. & Maler, L.M. (1989) GABAergic inhibition shapes temporal and spatial response properties of pyramidal cells in the electrosensory lateral line lobe of gymnotiform fish J. Comp. Physiol. **164**, 391-407.

Using hippocampal 'place cells' for navigation, exploiting phase coding

Neil Burgess, John O'Keefe and Michael Recce
Department of Anatomy, University College London,
London WC1E 6BT, England.
(e-mail: n.burgess@ucl.ac.uk)

Abstract

A model of the hippocampus as a central element in rat navigation is presented. Simulations show both the behaviour of single cells and the resultant navigation of the rat. These are compared with single unit recordings and behavioural data. The firing of CA1 place cells is simulated as the (artificial) rat moves in an environment. This is the input for a neuronal network whose output, at each theta (θ) cycle, is the next direction of travel for the rat. Cells are characterised by the number of spikes fired and the time of firing with respect to hippocampal θ rhythm. 'Learning' occurs in 'on-off' synapses that are switched on by simultaneous pre- and post-synaptic activity. The simulated rat navigates successfully to goals encountered one or more times during exploration in open fields. One minute of random exploration of a $1m^2$ environment allows navigation to a newly-presented goal from novel starting positions. A limited number of obstacles can be successfully avoided.

1 Background

Experiments have shown the hippocampus to be crucial to the spatial memory and navigational ability of the rat (O'Keefe & Nadel, 1978). Single unit recordings in freely moving rats have revealed 'place cells' in fields CA3 and CA1 of the hippocampus whose firing is restricted to small portions of the rat's environment (the corresponding 'place fields') (O'Keefe & Dostrovsky, 1971), see Fig. 1a. In addition cells have been found in the dorsal pre-subiculum whose primary behavioural

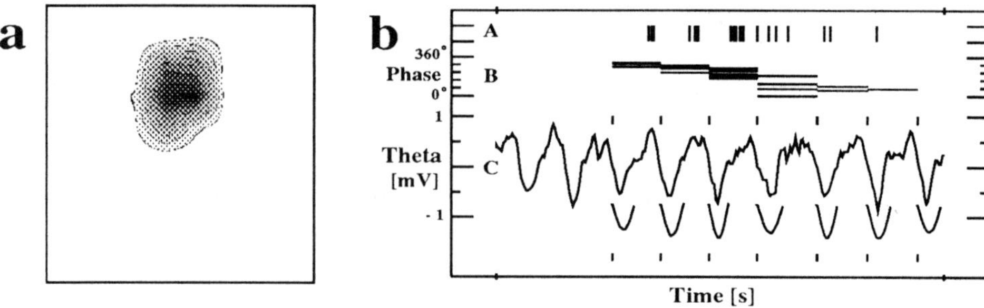

Figure 1: a) A typical CA1 place field, max. rate (over $1s$) is 13.6 spikes/s. b) One second of the EEG θ rhythm is shown in **C**, as the rat runs through a place field. **A** shows the times of firing of the place cell. Vertical ticks immediately above and below the EEG mark the positive to negative zero-crossings of the EEG, which we define as $0°$ (or $360°$) of phase. **B** shows the phase of θ at which each spike was fired (O'Keefe & Recce, 1992).

correlate is 'head-direction' (Taube et al., 1990). Both are suggestive of navigation.

Temporal as well as spatial aspects of the electrophysiology of the hippocampal region are significant for a model. The hippocampal EEG 'θ rhythm' is best characterised as a sinusoid of frequency $7-12Hz$ and occurs whenever the rat is making displacement movements. Recently place cell firing has been found to have a systematic phase relationship to the local EEG (O'Keefe & Recce, 1992), see §3.1 and Fig. 1b. Finally, the θ rhythm has been found to modulate long-term potentiation of synapses in the hippocampus (Pavlides et al., 1988).

2 Introduction

We are designing a model that is consistent with both the data from single unit recording and the behavioural data that are relevant to spatial memory and navigation in the rat. As a first step this paper examines a simple navigational strategy that could be implemented in a physiologically plausible way to enable navigation to previously encountered reward sites from novel starting positions. We assume the firing properties of CA1 place cells, which form the input for our system.

The simplest map-based strategies (as opposed to route-following ones) are based on defining a surface over the whole environment, on which gradient ascent leads to the goal (e.g. delayed reinforcement or temporal difference learning). These tend to have the problem that, to build up this surface, the goal must be reached many times, from different points in the environment (by which time the rat has died of old age). Further, a new surface must be computed if the goal is moved. Specific problems are raised by the properties of rats' navigation: (i) the position of CA1 place fields is independent of goal position (Speakman & O'Keefe, 1990); (ii) high firing rates in place cells are restricted to limited portions of the environment; (iii) rats are able to navigate after a brief exploration of the environment, and (iv) can take novel short-cuts or detours (Tolman, 1948).

To overcome these problems we propose that a more diffuse representation of position is rapidly built up downstream of CA1, by cells with larger firing fields than in CA1. The patterns of activation of this group of cells, at two different locations in the environment, have a correlation that decreases with the separation of the two locations (but never reaches zero, as is the case with small place fields). Thus the overlap between the pattern of activity at any moment and the pattern of activity at the goal location would be a measure of nearness to the goal. We refer to these cells as 'subicular' cells because the subiculum seems a likely site for them, given single unit recordings (Barnes et al., 1990) showing spatially consistent firing over large parts of the environment.

We show that the output of these subicular cells is sufficient to enable navigation in our model. In addition the model requires: (i) 'goal' cells (see Fig. 4a) that fire when a goal is encountered, allowing synaptic connections from subicular cells to be switched on, (ii) phase-coded place cell firing, (iii) 'head-direction' cells, and (iv) synaptic change that is modulated by the phase of the EEG. The relative firing rates of groups of goal cells code for the direction of objects encountered during exploration, in the same way that cells in primate motor cortex code for the direction of arm movements (Georgopoulos et al., 1988).

3 The model

In our simulation a rat is in constant motion (speed $30cm/s$) in a square environment of size $L \times L$ ($L \leq 150cm$). Food or obstacles can be placed in the environment at any time. The rat is aware of any objects within $6cm$ (whisker length) of its position. It bounces off any obstacles (or the edge of the environment) with which it collides. The θ frequency is taken to be $10Hz$ (period $0.1s$) and we model each θ cycle as having 5 different phases. Thus the smallest timestep (at which synaptic connections and cell firing rates are updated) is $0.02s$. The rat is either 'exploring' (its current direction is a random variable within 30° of its previous direction), or 'searching' (its current direction is determined by the goal cells, see below). Synaptic and cell update rules are the same during searching or exploring.

3.1 The phase of CA1 place cell firing

When a rat on a linear track runs through a place field, the place cell fires at successively earlier phases of the EEG θ rhythm. A cell that fires at phase 360° when the rat enters the place field may fire as much as 355° earlier in the θ cycle when exiting the field (O'Keefe & Recce, 1992), see Fig. 1b.

Simulations below involve 484 CA1 place cells with place field centres spread evenly on a grid over the whole environment. The place fields are circular, with diameters $0.25L$, $0.35L$ or $0.4L$ (as place fields appear to scale with the size of an environment; Muller & Kubie, 1987). The fraction of cells active during any $0.1s$ interval is thus $\pi(0.125^2 + 0.175^2 + 0.2^2)/3 = 9\%$. When the rat is in a cell's place field it fires 1 to 3 spikes depending on its distance from the field centre, see Fig. 2b.

When the (simulated) rat first enters a place field the cell fires 1 spike at phase 360° of the θ rhythm; as the rat moves through the place field, its phase of firing shifts backwards by 72° every time the number of spikes fired by the cell changes

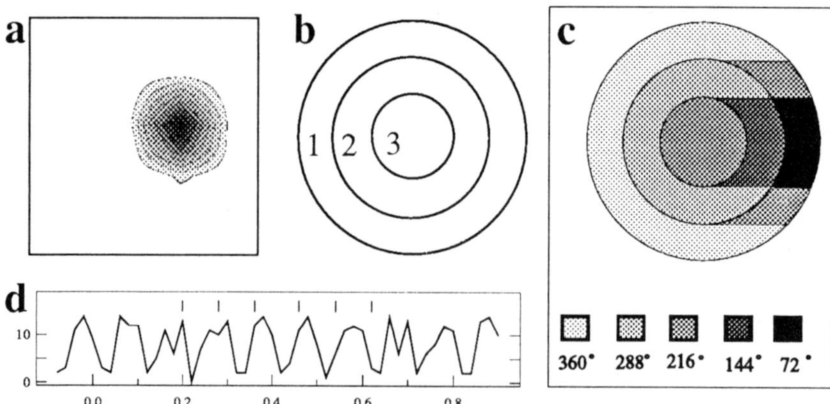

Figure 2: a) Firing rate map of a typical place cell in the model (max. rate 11.6 spikes/s); b) Model of a place field; the numbers indicate the number of spikes fired by the place cell when the rat is in each ring. c) The phase at which spikes would be fired during all possible straight trajectories of the rat through the place field *from left to right.* d) The total number of spikes fired in the model of CA1 versus time, the phase of firing of one place cell (as the rat runs through the centre of the field) is indicated be vertical ticks above the graph.

(i.e. each time it crosses a line in Fig. 2b). Thus each theta cycle is divided into 5 timesteps. No shift results from passing through the edge of the field, whereas a shift of 288° ($0.08s$) results from passing through the middle of the field, see Fig. 2c. The consequences for the model in terms of which place cells fire at different phases within one θ cycle are shown in Fig. 3. The cells that are active at phase 360° have place fields centred ahead of the position of the rat (i.e. place fields that the rat is entering), those active at phase 0° have place fields centred behind the rat. If the rat is simultaneously leaving field A and entering field B then cell A fires before cell B, having shifted backwards by up to $0.08s$. The total number of spikes fired at each phase as the rat moves about implies that the envelope of all the spikes fired in CA1 oscillates with the θ frequency. Fig. 2d shows the shift in the firing of one cell compared to the envelope (cf. Fig. 1b).

3.2 Subicular cells

We simulate 6 groups of 80 cells (480 in total); each subicular cell receives one synaptic connection from a random 5% of the CA1 cells. These connections are either on or off (1 or 0). At each timestep ($0.02s$) the 10 cells in each group with the greatest excitatory input from CA1 fire between 1 and 5 spikes (depending on their relative excitation). Fig. 3c shows a typical subicular firing rate map. The consequences of phase coding in CA1 (Figs. 3a and b) remain in these subicular cells as they are driven by CA1: the net firing field of all cells active at phase 360° of θ is peaked *ahead* of the rat.

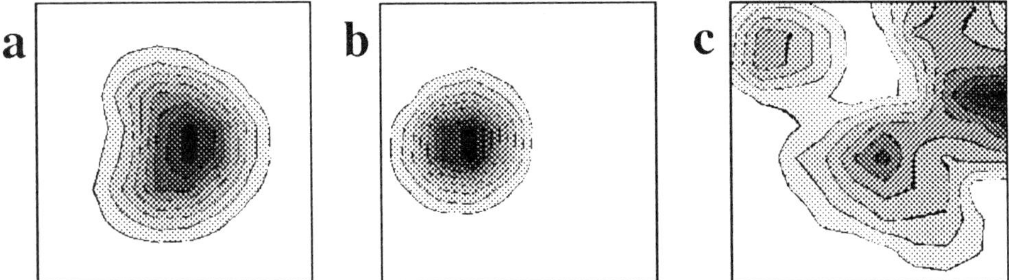

Figure 3: Net firing rate map of all the place cells that were active at the 360° (a) and 72° (b) phases of θ as the rat ran through the centre of the environment from left to right. c) Firing rate map of a typical 'subicular' cell in the model; max. rate (over $1.0s$) is 46.4 spikes/s. Barnes et al. (1990) found max. firing rates (over $0.1s$) of 80 spikes/s (mean 7 spikes/s) in the subiculum.

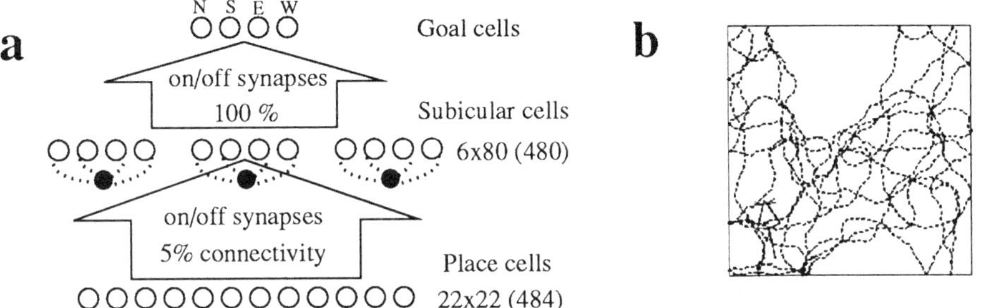

Figure 4: a) Connections and units in the model; interneurons shown between the subicular cells indicate competitive dynamics, but are not simulated explicitly. b) The trajectory of 90 seconds of 'exploration' in the central $126 \times 126cm^2$ of the environment. The rat is shown in the bottom left hand corner, to scale.

3.2.1 Learning

The connections are initialised such that each subicular cell receives on average one 'on' connection. Subsequently a synaptic connection can be switched on only during phases 180° to 360° of θ. A synapse becomes switched on if the pre-synaptic cell is active, and the post-synaptic cell is above a threshold activity (4 spikes), in the same timestep ($0.02s$). Hence a subicular firing field is rapidly built up during exploration, as a superposition of CA1 place fields, see Fig 3c.

3.3 Goal cells

The correlation between the patterns of activity of the subicular cells at two different locations in the environment decreases with the separation of the two locations. Thus if synaptic connections to a goal cell were switched on when the rat encountered food then a firing rate map of the goal cell would resemble a cone covering the entire environment, peaked at the food site, i.e. the firing rate would indicate

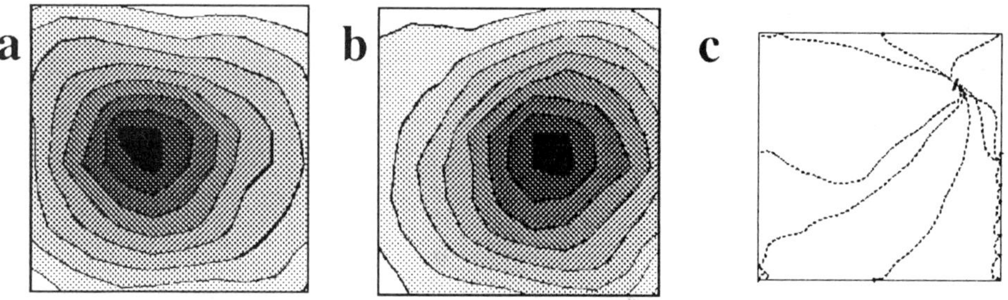

Figure 5: Goal cell firing fields, a) West, b) East, of 'food' encountered at the centre of the environment. c) Trajectories to a goal from 8 novel starting positions. All figures refer to encountering food immediately after the exploration in Fig. 4b. Notice that much of the environment was never visited during exploration.

the closeness of the food during subsequent movement of the rat. The scheme we actually use involves groups of goal cells continuously estimating the distance to 4 points displaced from the goal site in 4 different directions.

Notice that when a freely moving rat encounters an interesting object a fair amount of 'local investigation' takes place (sniffing, rearing, looking around and local exploration). During the local investigation of a small object the rat crosses the location of the object in many different directions. We postulate groups of goal cells that become excited strongly enough to induce synaptic change in connections from subicular cells whenever the rat encounters a specific piece of food and is heading in a particular direction. This supposes the joint action of an object classifier and of head-direction cells; head-direction cells corresponding to different directions being connected to different goal cells. Since synaptic change occurs only at the 180° to 360° phases of θ, and the net firing rate map of all the subicular cells that are active at phase 360° during any θ cycle is peaked ahead of the rat, goal cells have firing fields that are peaked a little bit away from the goal position. For example, goal cells whose subicular connections are changed when the rat is heading east have firing rate fields that are peaked to the east of the goal location, see Fig. 5.

Local investigation of a food site is modelled by the rat moving $12cm$ to the north, south, east and west and occurs whenever food is encountered. Navigation is restricted to the central $126 \times 126cm^2$ portion of the $150 \times 150cm^2$ environment (over which firing rate maps are shown) to leave room for this. There are 4 goal cells for every piece of food found in the environment, (GC_north, GC_south, GC_east, GC_west), see Fig. 4a. Initially the connections from all subicular cells are off; they are switched on if the subicular cell is active and the rat is at the particular piece of food, travelling in the right direction. When the rat is searching, goal cells simply fire a number of spikes (in each $0.02s$ timestep) that is proportional to their net excitatory input from the subicular cells.

3.4 Maps and navigation

When the rat is to the north of the food, GC_north fires at a higher rate than GC_south. We take the firing rate of GC_north to be a 'vote' that the rat is north

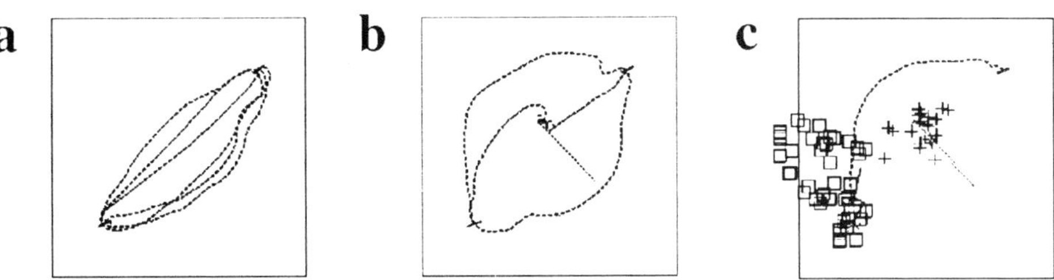

Figure 6: a) Trajectory of rat with alternating goals. b) an obstacle is interposed; the rat collides with the obstacle on the first run, but learns to avoid the collision site in the 2 subsequent runs. c) Successive predictions of goal (box) and obstacle (cross) positions generated as the rat ran from one goal site to the other; the predicted positions get more accurate as the rat gets closer to the object in question.

of the goal. Similarly the firing rate of GC_south is a vote that the rat is south of the goal: the resultant direction (the vector sum of directions north, south, east and west, weighted by the firing rates of the corresponding cells) is an estimate of the direction of the rat from the food (cf.Georgopoulos et al., 1988). Since the firing rate maps of the 4 goal cells are peaked quite close to the food location, their net firing rate increases as the food is approached, i.e. it is an estimation of how close the food is. Thus the firing rates of the 4 goal cells associated with a piece of food can be used to predict its approximate position relative to the rat (e.g. $70cm$ northeast), as the rat moves about the environment (see Fig. 6c).

We use groups of goal cells to code for the locations at which the rat encountered any objects (obstacles or food), as described above. A new group of goal cells is recruited every time the rat encounters a new object, or a new ($6cm$) part of an extended object. The output of the system acts as a *map* for the rat, telling it where everything is relative to itself, as it moves around. The process of *navigation* is to decide which way to go, given the information in the map. When there are no obstacles in the environment, navigation corresponds to moving in the direction indicated by the group of goal cells corresponding to a particular piece of food. When the environment includes many obstacles the task of navigation is much harder, and there is not enough clear behavioural data to guide modelling.

We do not model navigation at a neuronal level, although we wish to examine the navigation that would result from a simple reading of the 'map' provided by our model. The rules used to direct the simulated rat are as follows: (i) every $0.1s$ the direction and distance to the goal (one of the pieces of food) are estimated; (ii) the direction and distance to all locations at which an obstacle was encountered are estimated; (iii) obstacle locations are classified as 'in-the-way' if (a) estimated to be within $45°$ of the goal direction, (b) closer than the goal and (c) less than $L/2$ away; (iv) the current direction of the rat becomes the vector sum of the goal direction (weighted by the net firing rate of the corresponding 4 goal cells) minus the directions to any in-the-way obstacles (weighted by the net firing rate of the 'obstacle cells' and by the similarity of the obstacle and goal directions).

4 Performance

The model achieves latent learning (i.e. the map is constructed independently of knowledge of the goal, see e.g. Tolman, 1948). A piece of food encountered only once, after exploration, can be returned to, see Fig. 5c. Notice that a large part of the environment was never visited during exploration (Fig. 4b). Navigation is equally good after exploration in an environment containing food/obstacles from the beginning. If the food is encountered only during the earliest stages of exploration (before a stable subicular representation is built up) then performance is worse. Multiple goals and a small number of obstacles can be accommodated, see Fig. 6. Notice that searching also acts as exploration, and that synaptic connections can be switched at any time: all learning is incremental, but saturates when all the relevant synapses have been switched on. Performance does not depend crucially on the parameter values, used although it is worse with fewer cells, and smaller environments require less exploration before reliable navigation is possible (e.g. $60s$ for a $1m^2$ box). Quantitative analysis will appear in a longer paper.

References

Barnes C A, McNaughton B L, Mizumori S J Y, Leonard B W & Lin L-H (1990) 'Comparison of spatial and temporal characteristics of neuronal activity in sequential stages of hippocampal processing', *Progress in Brain Research* **83** 287-300.

Georgopoulos A P, Kettner R E & Schwartz A B (1988) 'Primate motor cortex and free arm movements to visual targets in three-dimensional space. II. Coding of the direction of movement by a neuronal population', *J. Neurosci.* **8** 2928-2937.

Muller R U & Kubie J L (1987) 'The effects of changes in the environment on the spatial firing of hippocampal complex-spike cells', *J. Neurosci.* **7** 1951-1968.

O'Keefe J & Dostrovsky J (1971) 'The hippocampus as a spatial map: preliminary evidence from unit activity in the freely moving rat', *BrainRes.* **34** 171-175.

O'Keefe J & Nadel L (1978) *The hippocampus as a cognitive map*, Clarendon Press, Oxford.

O'Keefe J & Recce M (1992) 'Phase relationship between hippocampal place units and the EEG theta rhythm', *Hippocampus,* to be published.

Pavlides C, Greenstein Y J, Grudman M & Winson J (1988) 'Long-term potentiation in the dentate gyrus is induced preferentially on the positive phase of θ-rhythm', *Brain Res.* **439** 383-387.

Speakman A S & O'Keefe J (1990) 'Hippocampal complex spike cells do not change their place fields if the goal is moved within a cue controlled environment', *European Journal of Neuroscience* **2** 544-555.

Taube J S, Muller R U & Ranck J B Jr (1990) 'Head-direction cells recorded from the postsubiculum in freely moving rats. I. Description & quantitative analysis', *J. Neurosci.* **10** 420-435.

Tolman E C (1948) 'Cognitive Maps in rats and men', *Psychological Review* **55** 189-208.

Adaptive Stimulus Representations: A Computational Theory of Hippocampal-Region Function

Mark A. Gluck **Catherine E. Myers**
Center for Molecular and Behavioral Neuroscience
Rutgers University, Newark, NJ 07102
gluck@pavlov.rutgers.edu *myers@pavlov.rutgers.edu*

Abstract

We present a theory of cortico-hippocampal interaction in discrimination learning. The hippocampal region is presumed to form new stimulus representations which facilitate learning by enhancing the discriminability of predictive stimuli and compressing stimulus-stimulus redundancies. The cortical and cerebellar regions, which are the sites of long-term memory, may acquire these new representations but are not assumed to be capable of forming new representations themselves. Instantiated as a connectionist model, this theory accounts for a wide range of trial-level classical conditioning phenomena in normal (intact) and hippocampal-lesioned animals. It also makes several novel predictions which remain to be investigated empirically. The theory implies that the hippocampal region is involved in even the simplest learning tasks; although hippocampal-lesioned animals may be able to use other strategies to learn these tasks, the theory predicts that they will show consistently different patterns of transfer and generalization when the task demands change.

1 INTRODUCTION

It has long been known that the hippocampal region (including the entorhinal cortex, subicular complex, hippocampus and dentate gyrus) plays a role in learning and memory. For example, the hippocampus has been implicated in human declarative memory (Scoville & Millner, 1957; Squire, 1987) while hippocampal damage in animals impairs such seemingly disparate abilities as spatial mapping (O'Keefe & Nadel, 1978), contextual sensitivity (Hirsh, 1974; Winocur, Rawlins & Gray, 1987; Nadel & Willner, 1980), temporal processing (Buszaki, 1989; Akase, Alkon & Disterhoft, 1989), configural association (Sutherland & Rudy, 1989) and the flexible use of representations in novel situations (Eichenbaum & Buckingham, 1991). Several theories have characterized hippocampal function in terms of one or more of these abilities. However, a theory which can predict the full range of deficits after hippocampal lesion has been elusive.

This paper attempts to provide a functional interpretation of a hippocampal-region role in associative learning. We propose that one function of the hippocampal region is to construct new representations which facilitate discrimination learning. We argue that this representational function is sufficient to derive and unify a wide range of trial-level conditioned effects observable in the intact and lesioned animal.

2 A THEORY OF CORTICO-HIPPOCAMPAL INTERACTION

Psychological theories have often found it useful to characterize stimuli as occupying points in an internal representation space (c.f. Shepard, 1958; Nosofsky, 1984). Connectionist theories can be interpreted in a similar geometric framework. For example, in a connectionist network (see Figure 1A) a stimulus input such as a tone is recoded in the network's internal layer as a pattern of activations. A light input will activate a different pattern of activations in the internal layer nodes (Figure 1B). These internal layer activations can be viewed as a representation of the stimulus inputs, and can be plotted in multi-dimensional internal representation space (Figure 1C). Learning to classify stimulus inputs corresponds to finding an appropriate partition of representation space. In the connectionist model, the lower layer of network weights determine the representation while the upper layer of network weights determine the classification.

Our basic premise is that the hippocampal region has the ability to modify stimulus representations to facilitate classification, and that its representations are biased by two constraints. The first constraint, predictive differentiation, is a bias to differentiate the representations of stimuli which are to be classified differently. Predictive differentiation increases the representational resources (i.e., hidden units) devoted to representing stimulus features which are especially predictive of how a stimulus is to be classified. For example, if red stimuli alone should evoke a response, then many representational

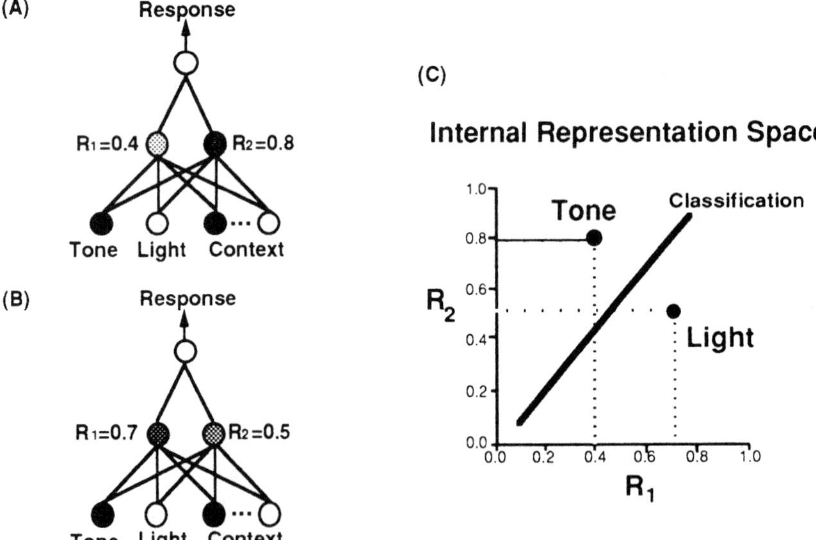

Figure 1: Stimulus representations. The activations of the internal layer nodes in a connectionist network constitute a representation of the network's stimulus inputs. (A) Internal representation for an example tone stimulus. (B) Internal representation for an example light stimulus. (C) Translation of these representations into points in an internal representation space, with one dimension encoding the activation level of each internal node. Classifying stimuli corresponds to partitioning representation space so that representations of stimuli which ought to be classified together lie in the same partition. Classification is easier if the representations of stimuli to be classified together are clustered while representations of stimuli to be classified differently are widely separated in this space.

resources should be devoted to encoding color. The second constraint, redundancy compression, reduces the resources allocated to represent features which are redundant or irrelevant in predicting the desired response. These two constraints are by nature complementary, given a finite amount of representational resources. Compressing redundant features frees resources to encode more predictive features. Conversely, increasing the resources allocated to predictive features forces compression of the remaining (less predictive) features.

This proposed hippocampal-region function may be modelled by a predictive autoencoder (on the right in Figure 2). An autoencoder (Hinton, 1989) learns to map from stimulus inputs, through an internal layer, to an output which is a reproduction of those inputs. This is also known as **stimulus-stimulus learning**. To do this, the network must have access to some multi-layer learning algorithm such as error backpropagation (Rumelhart, Hinton & Williams, 1986). When the internal layer is narrower than the input and output layers, the system develops a recoding in the internal layer which takes advantage of redundancies in the inputs. A predictive autoencoder has the further constraint that it must also output a classification response to the inputs. This is also known as **stimulus-response learning**. The internal layer recoding must therefore also emphasize stimulus features which are especially predictive of this classification. Therefore, a predictive autoencoder learns to form internal representations constrained by both predictive differentiation and redundancy compression, and is thus an example of a mechanism for implementing the two representational biases described above.

The cerebral and cerebellar cortices form the sites of long term memory in this theory, but are not themselves directly able to form new representations. They can, however, acquire new representations formed in the hippocampal region. A simplified model of one such cerebellar region is shown on the left in Figure 2. This network does not have access to multi-layer learning which would allow it to independently form new internal representations by itself. Instead, the two layers of weights in this network evolve independently. The bottom layer of weights is trained so that the current input pattern generates an internal representation equivalent to that developed in the hippocampal model. Independently and simultaneously, weights in the cortical network top layer are trained to map from this evolving representation to the classification response. Because the cortical networks are not creating new representations, but only learning two independent single-layer mappings, they can use a much simpler learning rule than the hippocampal model. One such algorithm is the LMS learning rule (Widrow & Hoff, 1960), which can instantiate the Rescorla-Wagner (1972) model of classical conditioning.

Cortical (Cerebellar) Network   Hippocampal-System Model

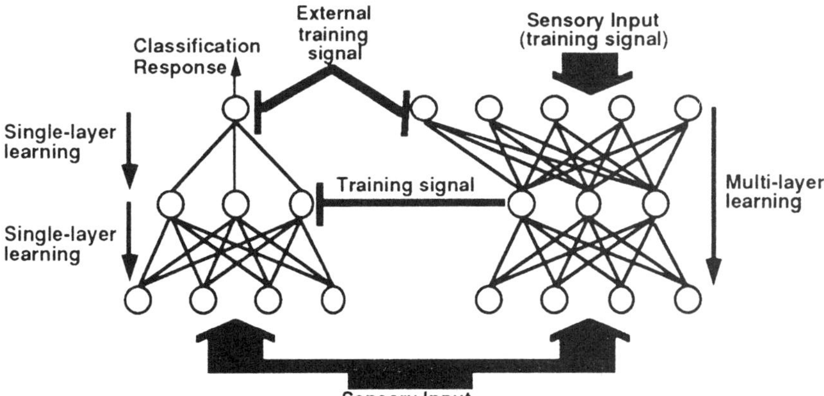

Figure 2. The cortico-hippocampal model: new representations developed in the hippocampal model can be acquired by cortical networks which are incapable of developing such representations by themselves.

3 MODELLING HIPPOCAMPAL INVOLVEMENT IN CLASSICAL CONDITIONING

A popular experimental paradigm for the study of associative learning in animals is classical conditioning of the rabbit eyeblink response (see Gormezano, Kehoe & Marshall, 1983, for review). A puff of air delivered to the eye elicits a blink response in the rabbit. If a previously neutral stimulus, such as a tone or light (called the **conditioned stimulus**), is repeatedly presented just before the airpuff, the animal will develop a blink response to this stimulus -- and time the response so that the lid is maximally closed just when the airpuff is scheduled to arrive. Ignoring the many temporal factors -- such as the interval between stimuli or precise timing of the response -- this reduces to a classification problem: learning which stimuli accurately predict the airpuff and should therefore evoke a response.

During a training trial, both the hippocampal and cortical networks receive the same input pattern. This pattern represents the presence or absence of all stimulus cues -- both conditioned stimuli and background contextual cues. Contextual cues are always present, but may change slowly over time. The hippocampus is trained incrementally to predict the current values of all cues -- including the US. The evolving hippoocampal internal layer representation is provided to the cortical network, which concurrently learns to reproduce this representation and to associate this evolving internal representation with a prediction of the US. This cortical network prediction is interpreted as the system's response.

The complete (intact) cortico-hippocampal model of Figure 2 can be shown to produce conditioned behavior comparable to that of normal (intact) animals. Hippocampal lesions can be simulated by disabling the hippocampal model. This eliminates the training signal which the cortical model would otherwise use to construct internal layer representations. As a result, the lower layer of cortical network weights remains fixed. The lesioned model's cortical network can still modify its upper layer of weights to learn new discriminations for which its current (now fixed) internal representation is sufficient.

4 BEHAVIORAL RESULTS

A stimulus discrimination task involves learning that one stimulus A predicts the airpuff but a second stimulus B does not. The notation <A+, B-> is used to indicate a series of training trials intermixing A+ (A preceeds the airpuff), B- (B does not preceed the airpuff) and context-alone presentations. Figure 3A shows the appropriate development of responses to A but not to B during this task. Both the intact and lesioned systems can acquire this discrimination. In fact, the lesioned system learns somewhat faster: it is only learning a classification, since its representation is fixed and (for this simple task) generally sufficient. In the intact system, by contrast, the hippocampal model is developing a new representation and transferring it to the cortical network The cortical network must then learn classifications based on this changing representation. This will be slower than learning based on a fixed representation. This paradox of discrimination facilitation after hippocampal lesion has often been reported in the animal literature (Schmaltz & Theios, 1972; Eichenbaum, Fagan, Mathews & Cohen, 1988); one previous interpretation has been to suggest that the hippocampal region is somehow "unneccessary for" or even "inhibitory to" simple discrimination learning. Our model suggests a different interpretation: the intact system learns more slowly because it is actually learning more than the lesioned system. The intact system is learning not only how to map from stimuli to responses, it is also developing new stimulus representations which enhance the differentiation among representations of predictive stimulus features while compressing the representations of redundant and irrelevant stimulus features.

The benefit of this re-representation can most readily be seen when the task demands suddenly change. For example, suppose the task valences shift from <A+, B-> to <A-, B+>. The representation developed during the first training phase, which maximally differentiated features distinguishing stimulus A from B, will still be useful in the second training phase. Only the classification needs to be relearned. Figure 3B shows that the intact system can learn the reversed task slightly more quickly than it learned the original task. Successive reversals are expected to be even more facilitated, as the representations of A and B grow ever more distinct (see Sutherland & Mackintosh, 1971, for a review of the relevant empirical data). In contrast, the lesioned system is severely impaired in the reversal task (Figure 3B). In the lesioned system, with a fixed representation, all the information is contained in the upper classificatory layer of weights. This information must be unlearned before the reversal task can be learned. Consistent with the model's behavior, empirical studies of hippocampal-lesioned animals show strong impairment at reversal learning (Berger & Orr, 1983).

The simplest evidence for redundancy compression likewise occurs during a transfer task. During unreinforced pre-exposure to a stimulus cue A, the presence or absence of A is irrelevant in terms of predicting US arrival (since a US never comes). Our theory expects that the representation of A will therefore become compressed with the representations of of the background contextual cues. In a subsequent training phase in which A does predict the US, the system must learn to respond to a feature it previously learned to ignore. The representation of A must now be re-differentiated from the context. Our theory therefore expects that learning to respond to A will be slowed, relative to learning

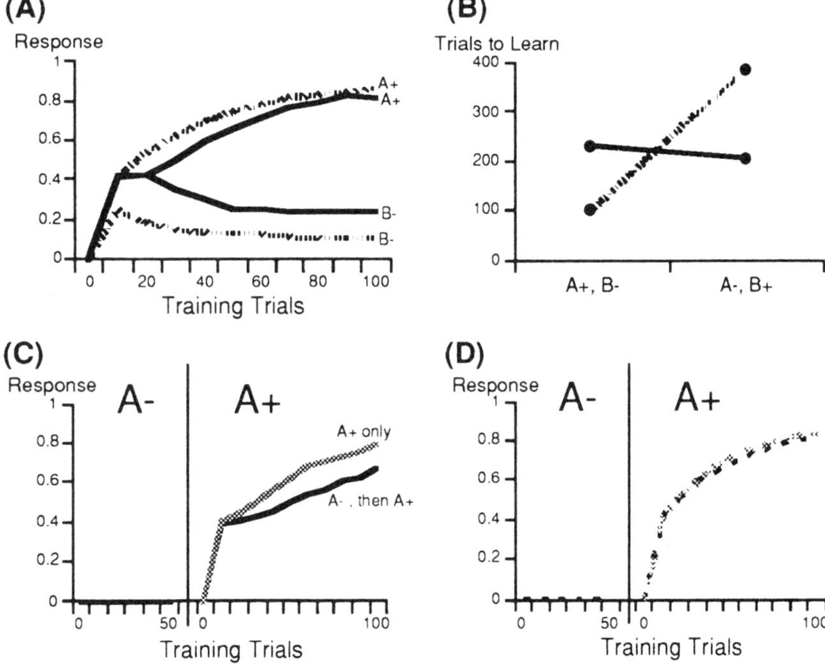

Figure 3. Behavioral results. Solid line = intact system, dashed line = lesioned system (A) Discrimination learning <A+, B-> in intact and lesioned models; lesioned model learns slightly faster. (B) Discrimination reversal (<A+, B-,> then <A-, B+>) Intact system shows facilitation on successive reversals, lesioned system is severely impaired. (C) Latent inhibition (A- impairs A+) in the intact model; (D) No latent inhibition in the lesioned model. All results shown are consistent with empirical data (see text for references).

without pre-exposure to A (Figure 3C). This effect occurs in animals and is known as latent inhibition (Lubow, 1973).

In this theory, latent inhibition arises from hippocampal-dependent recodings. In the lesioned system, there is no stimulus-stimulus learning during the pre-exposure phase, and no redundancy compression in the (fixed) internal representation. Therefore, unreinforced pre-exposure does not slow the learning of a response to A (Figure 3D). Empirical studies have shown that hippocampal lesions also eliminate latent inhibition in animals (Solomon & Moore, 1975).

Incidentally, a standard feedforward backpropagation network, with the same architecture as the cortical network, but with access to a multi-layer learning algorithm, fails to show latent inhibition. Such a network can form representations in its internal layer, but unlike the hippocampal model it does not perform stimulus-stimulus learning. Therefore, there is no effect of unreinfored pre-exposure of a stimulus, and no latent inhibition effect (simulations not shown).

This cortico-hippocampal theory can account for many other effects of hippocampal lesions (see Gluck & Myers, 1992, 1993 / in press): including increased stimulus generalization and elimination of sensory preconditioning. It also provides an interpretation of the observation that hippocampal disruption can damage learning more than complete hippocampal removal (Solomon, Solomon, van der Schaaf & Perry, 1983): if the training signals from the hippocampus are "noisy", the cortical network will acquire a distorted and continuously changing internal representation. In general, this will make classification learning harder than in the lesioned system where the internal representation is simply fixed.

The theory also makes several novel and testable predictions. For example, in the intact animal, training to discriminate two highly similar stimuli is facilitated by pre-training on an easier version of the same task -- even if the hard task is a reversal of the easy task (Mackintosh & Little, 1970). The theory predicts that this effect arises from predictive differentiation during the pre-training phase, and therefore should be eliminated after hippocampal lesion. Another effect observed in intact animals is compound preconditioning: discrimination of two stimuli A and B is impaired by pre-exposure to the compound AB (Lubow, Rifkin & Alek, 1976). The theory attributes this effect to redundancy compression in the pre-exposure phase, and therefore again predicts that the effect should disappear in the hippocampal-lesioned animal.

5 CONCLUSIONS

There are many hippocampal-dependent phenomena which the model, in its present form, does not address. For example, the model does not consider real-time temporal effects, or operant choice behavior. Because it is a trial-level model, it does not address the issue of a consolidation period during which memories gradually become independent of the hippocampus. We have also not considered here the physiological mechanisms or structures within the hippocampal region which might implement the proposed hippocampal function. Finally, the model would require extensions before it could apply to such high-level behaviors as spatial navigation, human declarative memory, and working memory -- all of which are known to be disrupted by hippocampal lesions.

Despite the theory's restricted scope, it provides a simple and unified account of a wide range of trial-level conditioning data. It also makes several novel predictions which remain to be investigated in lesioned animals. The theory suggests that the effects of hippocampal damage may be especially informative in studies of two-phase transfer tasks. In these paradigms, both intact and hippocampal-lesioned animals are expected to behave similarly on a simple initial learning task, but exhibit different behaviors on a subsequent transfer or generalization task.

REFERENCES

Akase, E., Alkon, D., & Disterhoft, J. (1989). Hippocampal lesions impair memory of short-delay conditioned eye blink in rabbits. Behavioral Neuroscience, 103(5), 935-943.

Berger, T. W., & Orr, W. B. (1983). Hippocampectomy selectively disrupts discrimination reversal learning of the rabbit nictitating membrane response. Behavioral Brain Research, 8, 49-68.

Buszaki, G. (1989). Two-stage model of memory trace formation: A role for "noisy" brain states. Neuroscience, 31(3), 551-570.

Eichenbaum, H., & Buckingham, J. (1991). Studies on hippocampal processing: Experiment, theory, and model. In M. Gabriel & J. Moore (Eds.), Neurocomputation and learning: Foundations of adaptive networks Cambridge, MA: M.I.T. Press.

Eichenbaum, H., Fagan, A., Mathews, P., & Cohen, N. (1988). Hippocampal system dysfunction and odor discrimination learning in rats: Impairment or facilitation depending on representational demands. Behavioral Neuroscience, 102(3), 331-339.

Gluck, M. & Myers, C. (1992). Hippocampal-system function in stimulus representation and generalization: A computational theory. Proceedings 14th Annual Conference of the Cognitive Science Society, Bloomington, IN, 390-395.

Gluck, M., & Myers, C. (1993 / in press). Hippocampal mediation of stimulus representation: A computational theory, Hippocampus.

Gormezano, I., Kehoe, E. K., & Marshal, B. S. (1983). Twenty years of classical conditioning research with the rabbit. Progress in Psychobiology and Physiological Psychology, 10, 197-275.

Hinton, G. E. (1989). Connectionist learning procedures. Artificial Intelligence, 40, 185-234.

Hirsh, R. (1974). The hippocampus and contextual retrieval of information from memory: A theory. Behavioral Biology, 12, 421-444.

Lubow, R. E. (1973). Latent inhibition. Psychological Bulletin, 79, 398-407.

Lubow, R., Rifkin, B., & Alek, M. (1976). The context effect: The relationship between stimulus pre-exposure and environmental pre-exposure determines subsequent learning. Journal of Experimental Psychology: Animal Behavior Processes, 2(1), 38-47.

Mackintosh, N. & Little, L. (1970). An analysis of transfer along a continuum. Canad. J. Psychol. / Rev. Canad. Psychol., 24(5), 362-369.

Nadel, L., & Willner, J. (1980). Context and conditioning: A place for space. Physiological Psychology, 8, 218-228.

Nosofsky, R. M. (1974). Choice, similarity, and the context theory of classification. Journal of Experimental Psychology: Learning, Memory and Cognition, 10, 104-114.

O'Keefe, J., & Nadel, L. (1978). The Hippocampus as a Cognitive Map. Oxford, UK: Claredon University Press.

Rescorla, R. A., & Wagner, A. R. (1972). A theory of Pavlovian conditioning: Variations in the effectiveness of reinforcement and non-reinforcement. In A. H. Black & W. F. Prokasy (Eds.), Classical Conditioning II: Current Research and Theory New York: Appleton-Century-Crofts.

Rumelhart, D. E., Hinton, G. E., & Williams, R. J. (1986). Learning internal representations by error propagation. In D. Rumelhart & J. McClelland (Eds.), Parallel Distributed Processing: Explorations in the Microstructure of Cognition (Vol. 1: Foundations) (pp. 318-362). Cambridge, MA: MIT Press.

Schmaltz, L. W., & Theios, J. (1972). Acquisition and extinction of a classically conditioned response in hippocampectomized rabbits (Oryctolagus cuniculus). Journal of Comparative and Physiological Psychology, 79, 328-333 .

Scoville, W. B., & Milner, B. (1957). Loss of recent memory after bilateral hippocampal lesions. Journal of Neurology, Neurosurgery, & Psychiatry, 20, 11-21.

Shepard, R. N. (1958). Stimulus and response generalization: Deduction of the generalization gradient from a trace model. Psychological Review, 65, 242-256.

Solomon, P. R., & Moore, J. W. (1975). Latent inhibition and stimulus generalization of the classically conditioned nictitating membrane response in rabbits (Oryctolagus cuniculus) following dorsal hippocampal ablation. Journal of Comparative and Physiological Psychology, 89, 1192-1203.

Solomon, P., Solomon, S., van der Schaaf, E. & Perry, H. (1983). Altered activity in the hippocampus is more detrimental to classical conditioning than removing the structure. Science, 220, 329-331.

Squire, L. R. (1987). Memory and brain. New York: Oxford University Press.

Sutherland, N. & Mackintosh, N. (1971). Mechanisms of Animal Discrimination Learning. New York: Academic Press.

Sutherland, R. J., & Rudy, J. W. (1989). Configural association theory: The role of the hippocampal formation in learning, memory, and amnesia. Psychobiology, 17 (2), 129-144.

Widrow, B., & Hoff, M. (1960). Adaptive switching circuits. Institute of Radio Engineers, Western Electronic Show and Convention, Convention Record, 4, 96-194.

Winocur, G., Rawlins, J. & Gray, J. R. (1987). The hippocampus and conditioning to contextual cues. Behavioral Neuroscience, 101, 617-625.

Statistical Modeling of Cell-Assemblies Activities in Associative Cortex of Behaving Monkeys

Itay Gat and Naftali Tishby
Institute of Computer Science and
Center for Neural Computation
Hebrew University, Jerusalem 91904, Israel *

Abstract

So far there has been no general method for relating extracellular electrophysiological measured activity of neurons in the associative cortex to underlying network or "cognitive" states. We propose to model such data using a multivariate Poisson Hidden Markov Model. We demonstrate the application of this approach for temporal segmentation of the firing patterns, and for characterization of the cortical responses to external stimuli. Using such a statistical model we can significantly discriminate two behavioral modes of the monkey, and characterize them by the different firing patterns, as well as by the level of coherency of their multi-unit firing activity.

Our study utilized measurements carried out on behaving Rhesus monkeys by M. Abeles, E. Vaadia, and H. Bergman, of the Hadassa Medical School of the Hebrew University.

1 Introduction

Hebb hypothesized in 1949 that the basic information processing unit in the cortex is a cell-assembly which may include thousands of cells in a highly interconnected network[1]. The cell-assembly hypothesis shifts the focus from the single cell to the

* {itay,tishby}@cs.huji.ac.il

complete network activity. This view has led several laboratories to develop technology for simultaneous multi-cellular recording from a small region in the cortex[2, 3]. There remains, however, a large discrepancy between our ability to construct neural-network models and their correspondence with such multi-cellular recordings. To some extent this is due to the difficulty in observing simultaneous activity of any significant number of individual cells in a living nerve tissue. Extracellular electrophysiological measurements have so far obtained simultaneous recordings from just a few randomly selected cells (about 10), a negligibly small number compared to the size of the hypothesized cell-assembly. It is quite remarkable therefore, that such local measurements in the associative cortex have yielded so much information, such as synfire chains [2], multi-cell firing correlation[6], and statistical correlation between cell activity and external behavior. However, such observations have so far relied mostly on the accumulated statistics of cell firing over a large number of repeated experiments, to obtain any statistically significant effect. This is due to the very low firing rates (about 10Hz) of individual cells in the associative cortex, as can be seen in figure 1.

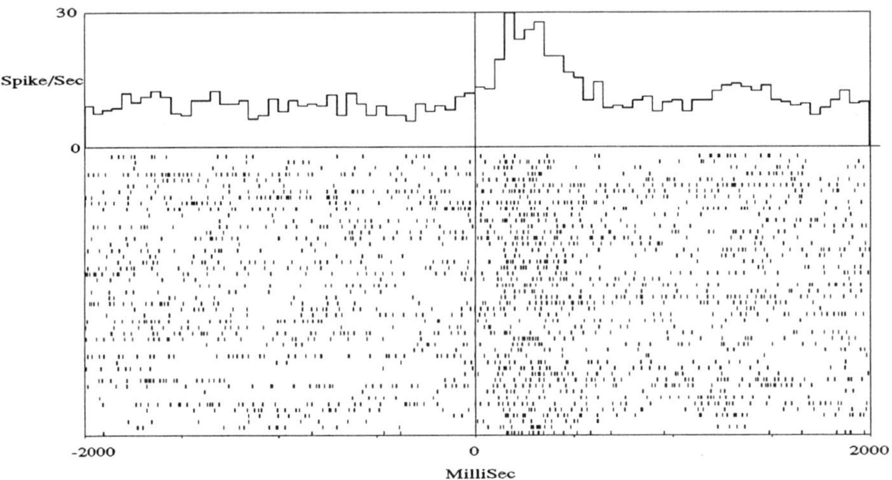

Figure 1: An example of firing times of a single unit. Shown are 48 repetitions of the same trial, aligned by the external stimulus marker, and drawn horizontally one on top of another. The accumulated histogram estimates the firing rate in 50msec bins, and exhibits a clear increase of activity right after the stimulus.

Clearly, simultaneous measurements of the activity of 10 units contain more information than single unit firing and pairwise correlations. The goal of the present study is to develop and evaluate a statistical method which can better capture the multi- unit nature of this data, by treating it as a vector stochastic process. The firing train of each of these units is conventionally modeled as a Poisson process with a time-dependent average firing rate[2]. Estimating the firing rate parameter requires careful averaging over a sliding window. The size of this window should be long enough to include several spikes, and short enough to capture the variability.

Within such a window the process is characterized by a vector of average rates, and possibly higher order correlations between the units.

The next step, in this framework, is to collect such vector-frames into statistically similar clusters, which should correspond to similar network activity, as reflected by the firing of these units. Furthermore, we can facilitate the well-established formulation of Hidden-Markov-Models[7] to estimate these "hidden" states of the network activity, similarly to the application of such models to other stochastic data, e.g. speech. The main advantage of this approach is its ability to characterize statistically the multi-unit process, in an unsupervised manner, thus allowing for finer discrimination of individual events. In this report we focus on the statistical discrimination of two behavioral modes, and demonstrate not only their distinct multi-unit firing patterns, but also the fact that the *coherency level* of the firing activity in these two modes is significantly different.

2 Origin of the data

The data used for the present analysis was collected at the Hadassa Medical School, by recording from a Rhesus monkey *Macaca Mulatta* who was trained to perform a spatial delayed release task. In this task the monkey had to remember the location from which a stimulus was given and after a delay of 1-32 seconds, respond by touching that location. Correct responses were reinforced by a drop of juice. After completion of the training period, the monkey was anesthetized and prepared for recording of electrical activity in the frontal cortex. After the monkey recovered from the surgery the activity of the cortex was recorded, while the monkey was performing the previously learned routine. Thus the recording does not reflect the learning process, but rather the cortical activity of the well trained monkey while performing its task. During each of the recording sessions six microelectrodes were used simultaneously. With the aid of two pattern detectors and four window-inscriminates, the activity of up to 11 single units (neurons) was concomitantly recorded. The recorded data contains the firing times of these units, the behavioral events of the monkey, and the electro-occulogram (EOG)[5, 2, 4].

2.1 Behavioral modes

To understand the results reported here it is important to focus on the behavioral aspect of these experiments. The monkey was trained to perform a spatial delayed response task during which he had to alternate between two behavioral modes. The monkey initiated the trial, by pressing a central key, and a fixation light was turned on in front of it. Then after 3-6 seconds a visual stimulus was given either from the left or from the right. The stimulus was presented for 100 millisec. After a delay the fixation light was dimmed and the monkey had to touch the key from which the visual stimulus came ("Go" mode), or keep his hand on the central key regardless of the external stimulus ("No-Go" mode). For the correct behavior the monkey was rewarded with a drop of juice. After 4 correct trials all the lights in front of the monkey blinked (this is called "switch" henceforth), signaling the monkey to change the behavioral mode - so that if started in the "Go" mode he now had to switch to "No-Go" mode, or vice versa.

There is a clear statistical indication, based on the accumulated firing histograms, that the firing patterns are different in these two modes. One of our main experimental results so far is a more quantitative analysis of this observation, both in terms of the firing patterns directly, and by using a new measure of the *coherency level* of the firing activity.

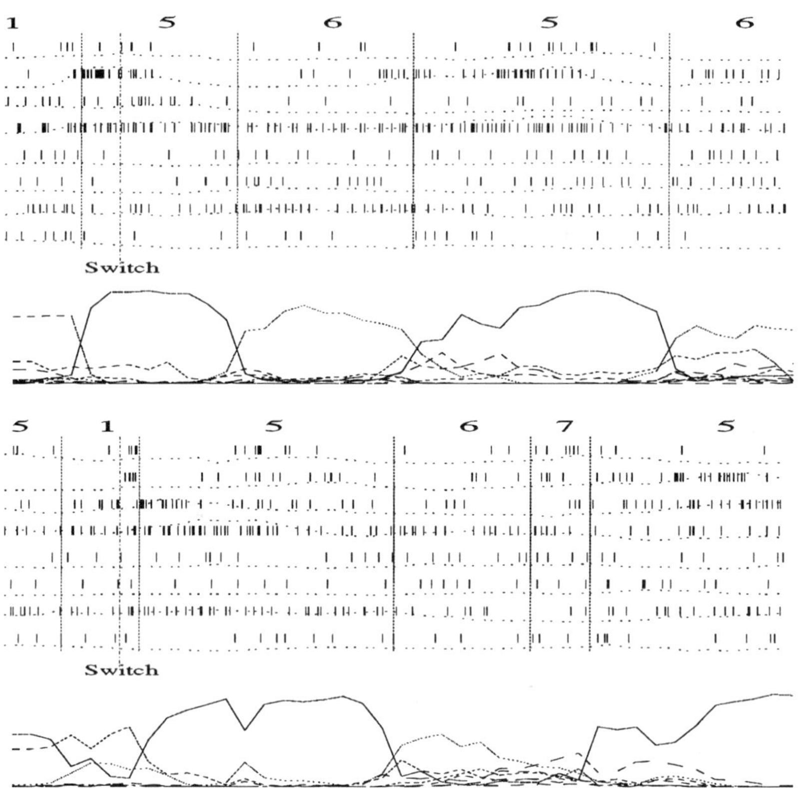

Figure 2: Multi-unit firing trains and their statistical segmentation by the model. Shown are 4 sec. of activity, in two trials, near the "switch". Estimated firing rates for each channel are also plotted on top of the firing spikes. The upper example is taken from the training data, while the lower is outside of the training set. Shown are also the association probabilities for each of the 8 states of the model. The monkey's cell-assembly clearly undergoes the state sequence "1", "5", "6", "5" in both cases. Similar sequence was observed near the same marker in many (but not all) other instances of the same event during that measurement day.

2.2 Method of analysis

As was indicated before, most of the statistical analysis so far was done by accumulating the firing patterns from many trials, aligned by external markers. This supervised mode of analysis can be understood from figure 1, where 48 different

"Go" firing trains of a single unit are aligned by the marker. There is a clear increase in the accumulated firing rate following the marker, indicating a response of this unit to the stimulus. In contrast, we would like to obtain, in an unsupervised *self organizing* manner, a statistical characterization of the *multi-unit* firing activity around the marked stimuli, as well as in other *unobserved* cortical processes. We claim to achieve this goal through characteristic sequences of Markov states.

3 Multivariate Poisson Hidden Markov Model

The following statistical assumptions underlie our model. Channel firing is distributed according to a Poisson distribution. The distances between spikes are distributed exponentially and their number in each frame, n, depends only on the mean firing rate λ, through the distribution

$$P_\lambda(n) = \frac{e^{-\lambda}\lambda^n}{n!} \ . \tag{1}$$

The estimation of the parameter λ is performed in each channel, within a sliding window of $500ms$ length, every $100ms$. These overlapping windows introduce correlations between the frames, but generate less noisy, smoother, firing curves. These curves are depicted on top of the spike trains for each unit in figure 2.

The multivariate Poisson process is taken as a Maximum Entropy distribution with i.i.d. Poisson prior, subject to pairwise channel correlations as additional constraints, yielding the following parametric distribution

$$P_\Lambda(n_1, n_2, ..., n_d) = \prod_{i=1}^{d} P_{\lambda_i}(n_i) \ \exp[-\sum_{ij} \lambda_{ij}(n_i - \lambda_i)(n_j - \lambda_j) - \lambda_0] \ . \tag{2}$$

The λ_{ij} are additional Lagrange multipliers, determined by the observed pairwise correlation $E[(n_i - \lambda_i)(n_j - \lambda_j)]$, while λ_0 ensures the normalization. In the analysis reported here the pairwise correlation term has not been implemented.

The statistical distance between a frame and the cluster centers is determined by the probability that this frame is generated by the centroid distribution. This probability is asymptotically fixed by the empirical information divergence (KL distance) between the processes[8, 9]. For 1-dimensional Poisson distributions the divergence is simply given by

$$D[p_1|p_2] = \sum_x p_1(x) \log \frac{p_1(x)}{p_2(x)} = \lambda_2 - \lambda_1 + \lambda_1 \log \frac{\lambda_1}{\lambda_2} \ . \tag{3}$$

The uncorrelated multi-unit divergence is simply the sum of divergences for all the units. Using this measure, we can train a multivariate Poisson Hidden Markov Model, where each state is characterized by such a vector Poisson process. This is a special case of a method called *distributional clustering*, recently developed in a more general setup[10].

The clustering provides us with the desired statistical segmentation of the data into states. The probability of a frame, x_t, to belong to a given state, S_j, is determined by the probability that the vector firing pattern is generated by the state centroid's distribution. Under our model assumptions this probability is a function solely of the empirical divergences, Eq.(3), and is given by

$$P(x_t \in S_j) = \frac{e^{-\beta D[x_t|S_j]}}{\sum_i e^{-\beta D[x_t|S_i]}} , \tag{4}$$

where β determines the "cluster-hardness". These state probability curves are plotted in figure 2 in correspondence with the spike trains. The most probable state at each instance determines the most likely segmentation of the data, and the frames are labeled by this most probable state number. These labels are also shown on top of the spike trains in figure 2.

4 Experimental results

We used about 6000 seconds of recordings done during a single day. It is important to note that this was an exceptionally good day in terms of the measurement quality. During that period the monkey performed 60 repetitions of his trained routine, in sets of 4 trials of "Go" mode, followed by 4 trials in the "No-Go" mode. We selected the 8 most active recorded units for our modeling. The training of the models was done on the first 4000 seconds of recording, 2000 seconds for each mode, while the rest was used for testing.

4.1 The nature of the segmentation

Any method can segment the data in some way, but the point is to obtain reliable predictions using this segmentation. As always, there is some arbitrariness in the choice of the number of states (or clusters), which ideally is determined by the data. Here we tested only 8 and 15 states, and in most cases 8 were sufficient for our purposes. Since we used "fuzzy", or "soft" clustering, each frame has some probability of belonging to any of the clusters. Although in most cases the most likely state is clearly defined, the complete picture is seen only from the complete association distribution. Notice, e.g., in the lower segment of figure 2, where a most likely state "7" "pops up" between states "6" and "5", but is clearly not significant, as seen from the corresponding probability curve.

4.2 Characterization of events by state-sequences

The first test of the segmentation is whether it is correlated with the external markers in any way. Since the markers were not used in any way during the training of the model (clustering), such correlations is a valid test of consistency. Moreover, one would like this correspondence to the markers to hold also outside of the training data. An exhaustive statistical examination of this question has not been made, as yet, but we could easily find many instances of similar state sequences near the same external marker, both within and outside of the training data. In figure 2 we bring a typical example to this effect. The next step is to train small left-to-right Markov models to spot these events more reliably.

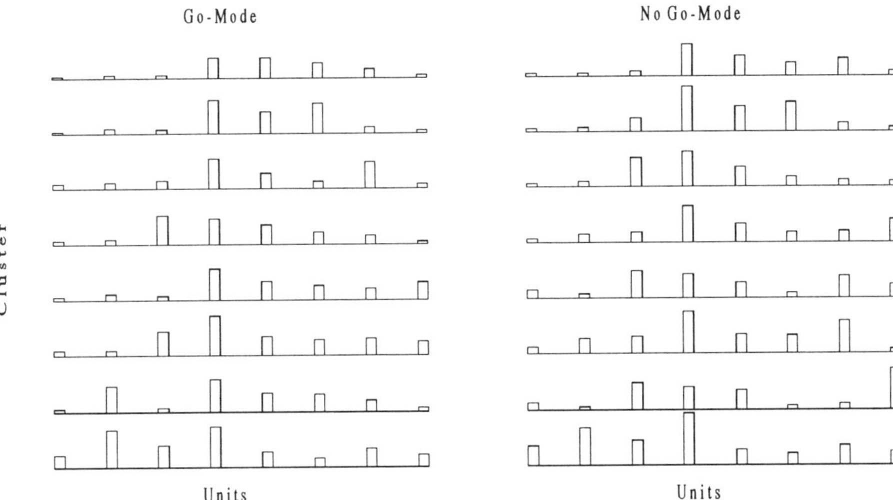

Figure 3: Average firing rates for each unit in each state, for the "Go" and "No-Go" modes. Notice that while no single unit clearly discriminates the two modes, their overall statistical discrimination is big enough that on average 100 frames are enough to determine the correct mode, more than 95% of the time.

4.3 Statistical Inference of "Go" and "No-Go" modes

Next we examined the statistical difference between models trained on the "Go" vs. "No-Go" modes. Here we obtained a highly significant difference in the cluster centroid's distributions, as shown in figure 3. The average statistical divergence between different clusters within each mode were 9.18 and 9.52 (natural logarithm),in "Go" and "No-Go" respectively, while in between those modes the divergence was more than 35.

4.4 Behavioral mode and the network firing coherency

In addition to the clearly different cluster centers in the two modes, there is another interesting and unexpected difference. We would like to call this *firing coherency level*, and it characterize the spread of the data around the cluster centers. The average divergence between the frames and their most likely state is consistently much higher in the "No-Go" mode than in the "Go" mode (figure 4). This is in agreement with the assumption that correct performance of the "No-Go" paradigm requires little attention, and therefore the brain may engage in a variety of processes.

Acknowledgments

Special thanks are due to Moshe Abeles for his continuous encouragement and support, and for his important comments on the manuscript. We would also like to thank Hagai Bergman, and Eilon Vaadia for sharing their data with us, and for numerous stimulating and encouraging discussions of our approach. This research was supported in part by a grant from the Unites States Israeli Binational Science Foundation (BSF).

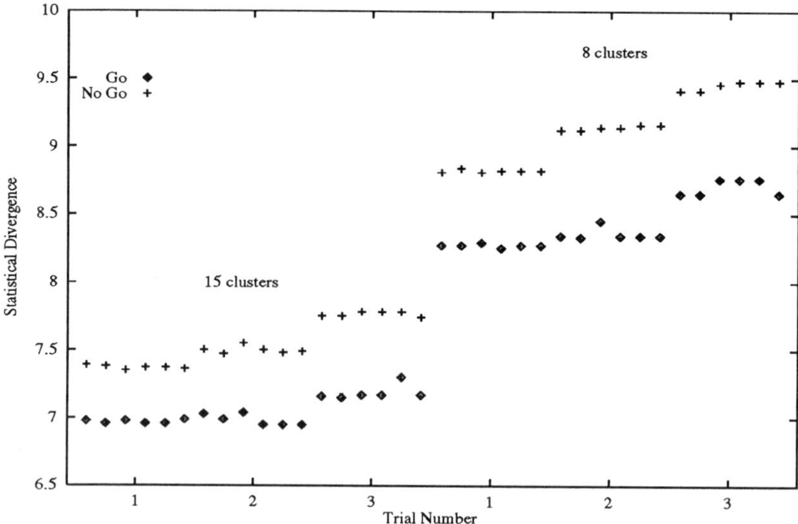

Figure 4: Firing coherency in the two behavioral modes at different clustering trials. The "No-Go" average divergence to the cluster centers is systematically higher than in the "Go" mode. The effect is shown for both 8 and 15 states, and is even more profound with 8 states.

References

[1] D. O. Hebb, *The Organization of Behavior*, Wiley, New York (1949)

[2] M. Abeles, *Corticonics*, (Cambridge University Press, 1991)

[3] J. Kruger, *Simultaneous Individual Recordings From Many Cerebral Neurons: Techniques and Results*, Rev. Phys. Biochem. Pharmacol.: 98:pp. 177-233 (1983)

[4] M. Abeles, E. Vaadia, H. Bergman, *Firing patterns of single unit in the prefrontal cortex and neural-networks models.*, Network 1 (1990)

[5] M. Abeles, H. Bergman, E. Margalit and E. Vaadia, *Spatio Temporal Firing Patterns in the Frontal Cortex of Behaving Monkeys.*, Hebrew University preprint (1992)

[6] E. Vaadia, E. Ahissar, H. Bergman, and Y. Lavner, *Correlated activity of neurons: a neural code for higher brain functions* in: J.Kruger (ed), Neural Cooperativity pp. 249-279, (Springer-Verlag 1991).

[7] A. B. Poritz, *Hidden Markov Models: A Guided tour*,(ICASSP 1988 New York).

[8] T.M. Cover and J.A. Thomas, *Information Theory*, (Wiley, 1991).

[9] J. Ziv and N. Merhav, *A Measure of Relative Entropy between Individual Sequences*, Technion preprint (1992)

[10] N. Tishby and F. Pereira, *Distributional Clustering*, Hebrew University preprint (1993).

Deriving Receptive Fields Using An Optimal Encoding Criterion

Ralph Linsker
IBM T. J. Watson Research Center
P. O. Box 218, Yorktown Heights, NY 10598

Abstract

An information-theoretic optimization principle ('infomax') has previously been used for unsupervised learning of statistical regularities in an input ensemble. The principle states that the input-output mapping implemented by a processing stage should be chosen so as to maximize the average mutual information between input and output patterns, subject to constraints and in the presence of processing noise. In the present work I show how infomax, when applied to a class of nonlinear input-output mappings, can under certain conditions generate optimal filters that have additional useful properties: (1) Output activity (for each input pattern) tends to be concentrated among a relatively small number of nodes. (2) The filters are sensitive to higher-order statistical structure (beyond pairwise correlations). If the input features are localized, the filters' receptive fields tend to be localized as well. (3) Multiresolution sets of filters with subsampling at low spatial frequencies – related to pyramid coding and wavelet representations – emerge as favored solutions for certain types of input ensembles.

1 INTRODUCTION

In unsupervised network learning, the development of the connection weights is influenced by statistical properties of the ensemble of input vectors, rather than by the degree of mismatch between the network's output and some 'desired' output. An implicit goal of such learning is that the network should transform the input so that salient features present in the input are represented at the output in a more useful form. This is often done by reducing the input dimensionality in a way that preserves the high-variance components of the input (e.g., principal component analysis, Kohonen feature maps).

The principle of maximum information preservation ('infomax') is an unsupervised learning strategy that states (Linsker 1988): From a set of allowed input-output mappings (e.g., parametrized by the connection weights), choose a mapping that maximizes the (ensemble-averaged) Shannon information that the output vector conveys about the input vector, in the presence of noise. Such a mapping maximizes the ensemble-averaged mutual information (MI) between input and output.

This paper (a) summarize earlier results on infomax solutions for linear networks, (b) identifies some limitations of these solutions (ways in which very different filter sets are equally optimal from the infomax standpoint), and (c) shows how, by adding a small nonlinearity to the network, one can remove these limitations and at the same time improve the utility of the output representations. We show that infomax, acting on the modified network, tends to favor sparsely coded representations and (depending on the input ensemble) sets of filters that span multiple resolution scales (related to wavelets and 'pyramid coding').

2 INFOMAX IN LINEAR NETWORKS

For definiteness and brevity, we consider a linear network having a particular type of noise model and input statistical properties. For a more detailed discussion of related models see (Linsker 1989).

Since the computation of the MI (which involves the output entropy) is in general intractable for continuous-valued output vectors, previous work (and the present paper) makes use of a surrogate MI, which we will call the 'as-if-Gaussian' MI. This quantity is, by definition, computed as though the output vectors comprised a multivariate Gaussian distribution having the same mean and covariance as the actual distribution of output vectors. Although expedient, this substitution has lacked a principled justification. The Appendix shows that, under certain conditions, using this 'surrogate MI' (and not the full MI) is indeed appropriate and justified.

Denote the input vector by $S \equiv \{S_i\}$ (S_i is the activity at input node i), the output vector by $Z \equiv \{Z_n\}$, the matrix of connection weights by $C \equiv \{C_{ni}\}$, noise at the input nodes by $N \equiv \{N_i\}$, and noise at the output nodes by $\nu \equiv \{\nu_n\}$. Then our processing model is, in matrix form, $Z = C(S+N)+\nu$. Assume that N and ν are Gaussian random variables, $\langle S\rangle = \langle N\rangle = \langle \nu\rangle = 0$, $\langle SN^T\rangle = \langle S\nu^T\rangle = \langle N\nu^T\rangle = 0$, and, for the covariance matrices, $\langle SS^T\rangle = Q$, $\langle NN^T\rangle = \eta I$, $\langle \nu\nu^T\rangle = \beta I'$. (Angle brackets denote an ensemble average, superscript T denotes transpose, and I and I' denote unit matrices on the input and output spaces, respectively.) In general, MI $= H_Z - \langle H_{Z|S}\rangle$ where H_Z is the output entropy and $H_{Z|S}$ is the entropy of the output for given S. Replacing MI by the 'as-if-Gaussian' MI means replacing H_Z by the expression for the entropy of a multivariate Gaussian distribution, which is (apart from an irrelevant constant term) $H_Z^G = (1/2)\ln\det Q'$, where $Q' \equiv \langle ZZ^T\rangle = CQC^T + \eta CC^T + \beta I'$ is the output covariance. Note that, when S is fixed, $Z = CS + (CN+\nu)$ is a Gaussian distribution centered on CS, so that we have $\langle H_{Z|S}\rangle = (1/2)\ln\det Q''$ where $Q'' = \langle (CN+\nu)(CN+\nu)^T\rangle = \eta CC^T + \beta I'$. Therefore the 'as-if-Gaussian' MI is

$$\mathrm{MI}' = (1/2)[\ln\det Q' - \ln\det Q'']. \tag{1}$$

The variance of the output at node n (prior to adding noise ν_n) is $V_n = \langle [C(S+N)]_n^2 \rangle = (CQC^T + \eta CC^T)_{nn}$. We will constrain the dynamic range of each output node (limiting the number of output values that can be discriminated from one another in the presence of output noise) by requiring that $V_n = 1$ for each n. Subject to this constraint, we are to find a matrix C that maximizes MI$'$. For a local Hebbian algorithm that accomplishes this maximization, see (Linsker 1992). Here, in order to proceed analytically, we consider a special case of interest.

Suppose that the input statistics are shift-invariant, so that the covariance $\langle S_i S_j \rangle$ is a function of $(j-i)$. We then use a shift-invariant filter Ansatz, $C_{ni} \equiv C(i-n)$. Infomax then determines the optimal filter gain as a function of spatial frequency; i.e., the magnitude of the Fourier components $c(k)$ of $C(i-n)$. The derivation is summarized below.

Denote by $q(k)$, $q'(k)$, and $q''(k)$ the Fourier transforms of $Q(j-i)$, $Q'(m-n)$, and $Q''(m-n)$ respectively. Since $Q' = CQC^T + \eta CC^T + \beta I'$, therefore $q'(k) = [q(k)+\eta) \mid c(k) \mid^2 + \beta$. Similarly, $q''(k) = \eta \mid c(k) \mid^2 + \beta$. We obtain $\mathrm{MI}' = (1/2)\Sigma_k[\ln q'(k) - \ln q''(k)]$. Each node's output variance V_n is equal to $V = (1/K)\Sigma_k[q(k)+\eta] \mid c(k) \mid^2$ where K is the number of terms in the sum over k.

To maximize MI$'$ subject to the constraint on V we use the Lagrange multiplier method; that is, we maximize $\mathrm{MI}'' \equiv \mathrm{MI}' + \mu(V-1)$ with respect to each $\mid c(k) \mid^2$. This yields an equation for each k that is quadratic in $\mid c(k) \mid^2$. The unique solution is

$$(\eta/\beta) \mid c(k) \mid^2 = -1 + \frac{q(k)}{2[q(k)+\eta]}\{1 + [1 - \frac{2\eta K}{\mu\beta q(k)}]^{1/2}\} \tag{2}$$

if the RHS is positive, and zero otherwise. The Lagrange multiplier $\mu(<0)$ is chosen so that the $\{\mid c(k) \mid\}$ satisfy $V = 1$.

Starting from a differently-stated goal (that of reducing redundancy subject to a limit on information loss), which turns out to be closely related to infomax, (Atick & Redlich 1990a) found an expression for the optimal filter gain that is the same as that of Eq. 2 except for the choice of constraint.

Filter properties found using this approach are related to those found in early stages of biological sensory processing. Smoothing and bandpass (contrast-enhancing) filters emerge as infomax solutions (Linsker 1989, Atick & Redlich 1990a) in certain cases, and good agreement with retinal contrast sensitivity measurements has been found (Atick & Redlich 1990b).

Nonetheless, the value of the infomax solution Eq. 2 is limited in two important ways. First, the phases of the $\{c(k)\}$ are left undetermined. Any choice of phases is equally good at maximizing MI$'$ in a linear network. Thus the real-space response function $C(i-n)$, which determines the receptive field properties of the output nodes, is nonunique (and indeed may be highly nonlocalized in space).

Second, it is useful to extend the solution Ansatz to allow a number of different filter types $a = 1, \ldots, A$ at each output site, while continuing to require that each type satisfy the shift-invariance condition $C_{ni}(a) \equiv C(i-n;a)$. For example, one may want to model a topographic 'retinocortical' mapping in which each patch of cortex (each 'site') contains multiple filter types, yet each patch carries out the same set of processing functions on its input. For this Ansatz, one again obtains Eq. 2 (derivation omitted here), but with $|\, c(k)\, |^2$ on the LHS replaced by $\Sigma_a \rho(a) |\, c(k;a)\, |^2$, where $c(k;a)$ is the F.T. of $C(i-n;a)$, and $\rho(a)$ is the fraction of the total number of filters (at each site) that are of type a. The partitioning of the overall (sum-squared) gain among the multiple filter types is thus left undetermined.

The higher-order statistical structure of the input (beyond covariance) is not being exploited by infomax in the above analysis, because (1) the network is linear and (2) only pairwise correlations among the output activities enter into MI$'$. We shall show that if we make the network even mildly nonlinear, MI$'$ is no longer independent of the choice of phases or of the partitioning of gain among multiple filter types.

3 NETWORK WITH WEAK NONLINEARITY

We consider the weakly nonlinear input-output relation $Z_n = U_n + \epsilon U_n^3 + \Sigma_i C_{ni} N_i + \nu_n$, where $U_n \equiv \Sigma_i C_{ni} S_i$, for small ϵ. This differs from the linear network analyzed above by the term in U_n^3. (For simplicity, terms nonlinear in the noise are not included.) The cubic term increases the signal-to-noise ratio selectively when U_n is large in absolute value. We maximize MI$'$ as defined in Eq. 1.

Heuristically, the new term will cause infomax to favor solutions in which some output nodes have large (absolute) activity values, over solutions in which all output nodes have moderate activities. The output layer can thus encode information about the input vector (e.g., signal the presence of a feature) via the high activity of a small number of nodes, rather than via the particular activity values of many nodes. This has several (interrelated) potential advantages. (1) The concentration of activity among fewer nodes is a type of sparse coding. (2) The resulting output representation may be more resistant to noise. (3) The presence of a feature can be signaled to a later processing stage using fewer connections. (4) Since the particular nodes that have high activity depend upon the input vector, this type of mapping transforms a set of continuous-valued inputs at each site into a partially place-coded representation. A model of this sort may thus be useful for understanding better the formation of place-coded representations in biological systems.

3.1 MATHEMATICAL DETAILS

This section may be skipped without loss of continuity. In matrix form, $U \equiv CS$, $W_n \equiv U_n^3$ for each n, and $Z = U + \epsilon W + CN + \nu$. Keeping terms through first order in ϵ, the output covariance is $Q' \equiv \langle ZZ^T \rangle = CQC^T + \eta CC^T + \beta I' + \epsilon F$, where $F \equiv \langle WU^T \rangle + \langle UW^T \rangle$. [As an aside, $F_{nm} = \langle U_n U_m (U_n^2 + U_m^2) \rangle$ resembles the covariance $\langle U_n U_m \rangle$, except that presentations having large $U_m^2 + U_n^2$ are given greater weight in the ensemble average.] For shift-invariant input statistics and one filter type $C_{ni} \equiv C(i-n)$, taking the Fourier transform yields $q'(k) = [q(k)+\eta] |\, c(k;a)\, |^2 + \beta + \epsilon f(k)$ where $f(k)$ is the F.T. of $F(m-n) \equiv F_{nm}$. So $\ln\det Q' = \Sigma_k \ln q'(k) = \Sigma \ln\{[q(k)+\eta]\,|\, c(k)\, |^2 + \beta\} + \epsilon \Sigma g(k)$ where $g(k) \equiv [f(k)/\{[q(k)+\eta] |\, c(k;a)\, |^2 + \beta\}]$. Using a Lagrange multiplier as before, the quantity to be maximized is MI$'' =$

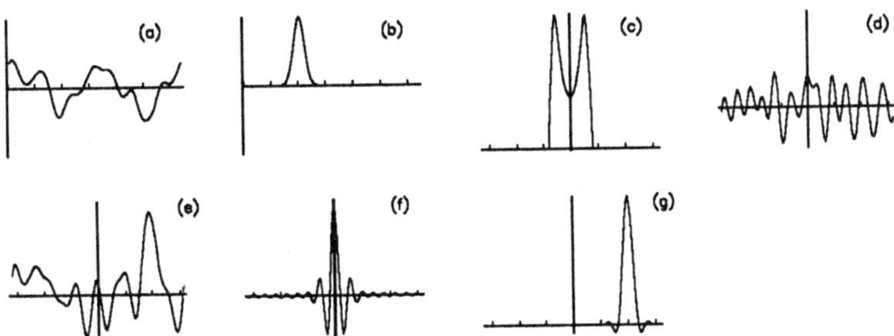

Figure 1: Breaking of phase degeneracy. See text for discussion.

$\mathrm{MI}''(\epsilon = 0) + (\epsilon/2)\Sigma g(k)$.

Now suppose there are multiple filter types $a = 1, \ldots, A$ at each output site. For each k define $d(k)$ to be the $A \times A$ matrix whose elements are: $d(k)_{ab} \equiv [q(k) + \eta]c(k;a)c^*(k;b) + [\beta/\rho(a)]\delta_{ab}$ where δ_{ab} is the Kronecker delta. Also define $f(k)$ to be the $A \times A$ matrix each of whose elements $f(k)_{ab}$ is the F.T. of $F(m-n;a,b)$ where $F(m-n;a,b) = \langle U_n(a)W_m(b)\rangle + \langle W_n(a)U_m(b)\rangle$. Then the $O(\epsilon)$ part of MI$''$ is: $(\epsilon/2)\Sigma_k \mathrm{Tr}\{[d(k)]^{-1}f(k)\}$. Note that $[d(k)]^{-1}$ is the inverse of the matrix $d(k)$, and that 'Tr' denotes the trace. [Outline of derivation: In the basis defined by the Fourier harmonics, Q' is block diagonal (one $A \times A$ block for each k). So $\ln\det Q' = \Sigma_k \ln\det q'(k)$ where each $q'(k)$ is an $A \times A$ matrix of the form $q_1'(k) + \epsilon q_2'(k)$. Expanding $\ln\det q'(k)$ through $O(\epsilon)$ yields the stated result.]

The infomax calculation to lowest order in ϵ [i.e., $O(\epsilon^0)$] is the same as for the linear network. Here, for simplicity, we determine the sum-squared gain, $\Sigma_a\rho(a)\mid c(k;a)\mid^2$, as in the linear case; then seek to maximize the new term, of $O(\epsilon)$, subject to this constraint on the value of the sum-squared gain. How the nonlinear term breaks phase and gain-apportionment degeneracies is of interest here; a small $O(\epsilon)$ correction to the sum-squared gain is not.

4 ILLUSTRATIVE RESULTS

Two examples will show how adding the nonlinear perturbative term to the network's output breaks a degeneracy among different filter solutions. In each case the input space is a one-dimensional 'retina' with wraparound.

4.1 BREAKING THE PHASE DEGENERACY

In this example (see Figure 1) there is one filter type at each output site. We consider two types of input ensembles: (1) Each input vector (Fig. 1a shows one example) is drawn from a multivariate Gaussian distribution (so there is no higher-order statistical structure beyond pairwise correlations). The input covariance matrix $Q(j-i)$ is a Gaussian function of the distance between the sites. (2) Each input vector is a random sum of Gaussian 'bumps': $S_i = \Sigma_j a_j [s(i-j) - s_0]$ where $s(i-j)$ is a Gaussian (shown in Fig. 1b for j=20; there are 64 nodes in all); s_0 is the mean value of $s(i-j)$; and each a_j is independently and randomly chosen (with constant probability) to be 1 or 0. This ensemble does have higher-order structure, with each input presentation being characterized by the presence of localized features (the bumps) at particular locations.

The infomax solution for $|\ c(k)\ |^2$ is plotted versus spatial frequency k in Fig. 1c for a particular choice of noise parameters (η, β). As stated earlier, MI′ for a linear network is indifferent to the phases of the Fourier components $\{c(k)\}$. A particular random choice of phases produces the real-space filter $C(i-n)$ shown in Fig. 1d, which spans the entire 'retina.' Setting all phases to zero produces the localized filter shown in Fig. 1f. If the Gaussian 'bump' of Fig. 1b is presented as input to a network of filters each of which is a shifted version of Fig. 1d, the linear response of the network (i.e., the convolution of the 'bump' with the filter) is shown in Fig. 1e. Replacing the filter of Fig. 1d by that of Fig. 1f, but keeping the input the same, produces the output response shown in Fig. 1g.

The cubic nonlinearity causes MI′ to be larger for the filter of Fig. 1f than for that of Fig. 1d. Heuristically, if we focus on the diagonal elements of the output covariance Q', the nonlinear term is $2\epsilon\langle U_n^4 \rangle$. Maximizing MI′ favors increasing this term (subject to a constraint on output variance) hence favors filter solutions for which the U_n distribution is non-Gaussian with a preponderance of large values. Projection pursuit methods also use a measure of the non-Gaussianity of the output distribution to construct filters that extract 'interesting' features from high-dimensional data (cf. Intrator 1992).

4.2 BREAKING THE PARTITIONING DEGENERACY FOR MULTIPLE FILTER TYPES

In this example (see Fig. 2), the input ensemble comprises a set of self-similar patterns (each is a sine-Gabor 'ripple' as in Fig. 2a) that are related by translation and dilation (scale change over a factor of 80). Figure 2b shows the input power spectrum vs. k; the scaling region goes as $1/k$. Figure 2c shows the infomax solution for the gain $|\ c(k;a)\ |$ vs. k when there is just one filter type. When the input SNR is large (as in the scaling region) the infomax filters 'whiten' the output; note the flat portion of the output power spectrum (Fig. 2d). [We modify the infomax solution by extending the power-law form of $|\ c(k)\ |$ to low k (dotted line in Figs. 2c,d). This avoids artifacts resulting from the rapid increase in $|\ c(k)\ |$, which is in turn caused by our having omitted low-k patterns from the input ensemble for reasons of numerical efficiency.] The dotted envelope curve in Figure 2e shows the sum-squared gain $\Sigma_a \rho(a)\ |\ c(k)\ |^2$ when multiple filter types a are allowed. The quantity plotted is just the square of that shown in Fig. 2c, but on a linear rather than log-log plot (note values greater than 5 are cut off to save space).

The network nonlinearity has the following effect. We first allow two filter types to share the overall gain. Optimizing MI′ over various partitionings, we find that infomax favors a crossover between filter types at $k \approx 400$. Allowing three, then four, filter types produces additional crossovers at lower k. For an Ansatz in which each filter's share of the sum-squared gain is tapered linearly near its cutoff frequencies, the best solution found for each $\rho(a) \mid c(k) \mid^2$ is shown in Fig. 2e (semilog plot vs. k). Figure 2f plots the corresponding $\mid c(k;a) \mid$ vs. k on a linear scale. Note that the three lower-k filters appear roughly self-similar. (The peak in the highest-k filter is an artifact due to the cutoff of the input ensemble at high k.) The four real-space filters $C(i-n;a)$ are plotted vs. $(i-n)$ in Fig. 2g [phases chosen to make $C(i-n;a)$ antisymmetric].

The resulting filters span multiple resolution scales. The density $\rho(a)$ is less for the lower-frequency filters (spatial subsampling). When more filter types are allowed, the increase in MI′ becomes progressively less. Although in our model the filters are present with density ρ at each output site, a similar MI′ is obtained if one spaces adjacent filters of type a by a distance $\propto 1/\rho(a)$. The resulting arrangement of filters resembles the 'tiling' of the joint space and spatial-frequency domain that is used in wavelet and 'pyramid coding' approaches to image processing. [The infomax filters overlap, rather than disjointly tiling the (x,k) domain.]

Using the infomax method, the region of (x,k) space spanned by an optimal filter has an aspect ratio that depends upon the relative distances – along the x and k axes – over which the input feature is 'coherent' (possesses higher-order correlations). One may thus be able to use infomax to predict relationships between statistical measures of coherence in natural scenes and observed (x,k) aspect ratios for, e.g., orientation-selective cells. See (Field 1989) for a discussion of this issue that is not based on infomax.

5 APPENDIX: HEURISTIC JUSTIFICATION FOR USING A SURROGATE, 'AS-IF-GAUSSIAN,' MUTUAL INFORMATION

The mutual information between input S and output Z is MI $= \int dSdZ P_{SZ} \ln(P_{SZ}/P_S P_Z) = \int dS P_S \mathrm{KD}(P_{Z|S};P_Z)$ where $\mathrm{KD}(P_{Z|S};P_Z) = \int dZ P_{Z|S} \ln(P_{Z|S}/P_Z)$ is a Kullback divergence. So, maximizing MI means maximizing the average (over S) of $\mathrm{KD}(P_{Z|S};P_Z)$.

What does the KD represent? Suppose that the network has somehow learned the distribution P_Z. Before being presented with a particular input S, the network 'expects' an output vector drawn from P_Z. The actual output response to S, however, is a vector drawn from $P_{Z|S}$. The KD measures the 'surprise' (i.e., the amount of information gained) upon seeing the actual distribution $P_{Z|S}$ when one expected P_Z. Infomax maximizes this average 'surprise.'

However, the network cannot in general have access to the full distribution P_Z, which contains far too much information (including all higher-order statistics) to be stored in the connections and nodes of the network. Let us suppose for definiteness that the system remembers only the mean and the covariance matrix of Z. Define P_Z^G to be the multivariate Gaussian distribution that has the same mean and covariance as P_Z. Then we may think of the system as a priori 'expecting' the output vector to be drawn from the distribution P_Z^G.

We accordingly modify the principle so that we maximize the average (over S) of $\mathrm{KD}(P_{Z|S};P_Z^G)$ (note the superscript G). This equals

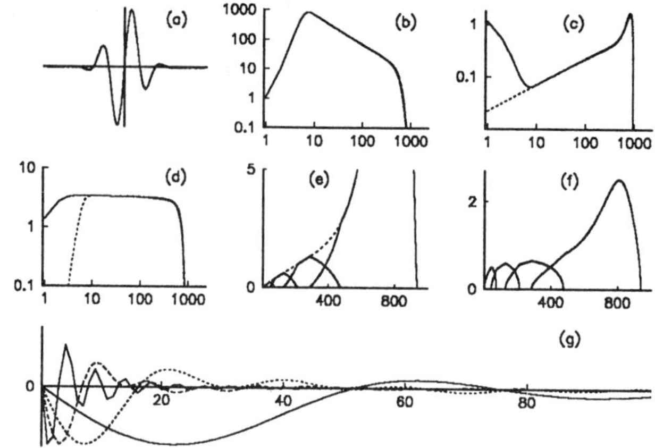

Figure 2: Partitioning among multiple filter types. See text.

$\int dSP_S \int dZP_{Z|S} \ln(P_{Z|S}/P_Z^G) = \langle -H_{Z|S} \rangle_S - \int dZP_Z \ln P_Z^G$ (where H denotes entropy). Using a property of the Gaussian distribution, we have $-\int dZP_Z \ln P_Z^G = -\int dZP_Z^G \ln P_Z^G = H_Z^G$. We conclude that the average of KD equals $H_Z^G - \langle H_{Z|S} \rangle_S$, which is exactly equal to the surrogate 'as-if-Gaussian' MI defined preceding Eq. 1. This argument provides a principled justification for using the surrogate MI, when the system has stored information about the output vectors' mean and covariance, but not about higher-order statistics.

References

J. J. Atick & A. N. Redlich. (1990a) Towards a theory of early visual processing. *Neural Computation* **2**:308-320.

J. J. Atick & A. N. Redlich. (1990b) Quantitative tests of a theory of retinal processing: contrast sensitivity curves. Inst. Adv. Study IASSNS-HEP-90/51.

D. J. Field. (1989) What the statistics of natural images tell us about visual coding. In *Proc. SPIE* **1077**:269-276.

N. Intrator. (1992) Feature extraction using an unsupervised neural network. *Neural Computation* **4**:98-107.

R. Linsker. (1988) Self-organization in a perceptual network. *Computer* **21**(3):105-117.

R. Linsker. (1989) An application of the principle of maximum information preservation to linear systems. In D. S. Touretzky (ed.), *Advances in Neural Information Processing Systems 1*, 186-194. San Mateo, CA: Morgan Kaufmann.

R. Linsker. (1992) Local synaptic learning rules suffice to maximize mutual information in a linear network. *Neural Computation* **4**(5):691-702.

Biologically Plausible Local Learning Rules for the Adaptation of the Vestibulo-Ocular Reflex

Olivier Coenen* **Terrence J. Sejnowski**
Computational Neurobiology Laboratory
Howard Hughes Medical Institute
The Salk Institute
P.O.Box 85800
San Diego, CA 92186-5800

Stephen G. Lisberger
Department of Physiology
W.M. Keck Foundation Center
for Integrative Neuroscience
University of California,
San Fransisco, CA, 94143

Abstract

The vestibulo-ocular reflex (VOR) is a compensatory eye movement that stabilizes images on the retina during head turns. Its magnitude, or gain, can be modified by visual experience during head movements. Possible learning mechanisms for this adaptation have been explored in a model of the oculomotor system based on anatomical and physiological constraints. The local correlational learning rules in our model reproduce the adaptation and behavior of the VOR under certain parameter conditions. From these conditions, predictions for the time course of adaptation at the learning sites are made.

1 INTRODUCTION

The primate oculomotor system is capable of maintaining the image of an object on the fovea even when the head and object are moving simultaneously. The vestibular organs provide information about the head velocity with a short delay of 14 ms but visual signals from the moving object are relatively slow and can take 100 ms to affect eye movements. The gain, G, of the VOR, defined as minus the eye velocity over the head velocity $(-\dot{e}/\dot{h})$, can be modified by wearing magnifying or diminishing glasses (figure 1). VOR adaptation, absent in the dark, is driven by the combination of image slip on the retina and head turns.

*University of California, San Diego. Dept. of Physics. La Jolla, CA, 92037. Email address: olivier@helmholtz.sdsc.edu

During head turns on the first day of wearing magnifying glasses, the magnified image of an object slips on the retina. After a few days of adaptation, the eye velocity and hence the gain of the VOR increases to compensate for the image magnification.

We have constructed a model of the VOR and smooth pursuit systems that uses biologically plausible local learning rules that are consistent with anatomical pathways and physiological recordings. The learning rules in the model are local in the sense that the adaptation of a synapse depends solely on signals that are locally available. A similar model with different local learning rules has been recently proposed (Quinn *et al.*, Neuroscience 1992).

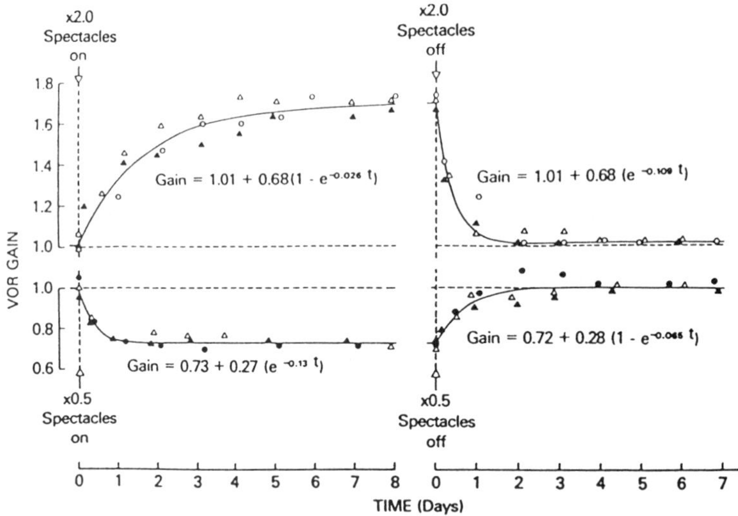

Figure 1: Time course of the adapting VOR and its recovery of gain in monkeys exposed to the long-term influence of magnifying (upper curves) and diminishing (lower curves) spectacles. Different symbols obtained from different animals, demonstrating the consistency of the adaptive change. From Melvill Jones (1991), selected from Miles and Eighmy (1980).

2 THE MODEL

Feedforward and recurrent models of the VOR have been proposed (Fujita, 1982; Galiana, 1986; Kawato and Gomi, 1992; Quinn et al., 1992; Arnold and Robinson, 1992; Lisberger and Sejnowski, 1992). In this paper we study a static and linear version of a previously studied recurrent network model of the VOR and smooth pursuit system (Lisberger, 1992; Lisberger and Sejnowski, 1992; Viola, Lisberger and Sejnowski, 1992). The time delays and time constants associated with nodes in the network were eliminated so that the time course of the VOR plasticity could be more easily analyzed (figure 2).

The model describes the system ipsilateral to one eye. The visual error, which carries the image retinal slip velocity signal, is a measure of the performance of both the VOR and smooth pursuit system as well as the main error signal for learning. The value at each node represents changes in its firing rate from its resting firing rate. The transformation from the rate of firing of premotor signal (N) to eye velocity is represented in the model by a gain

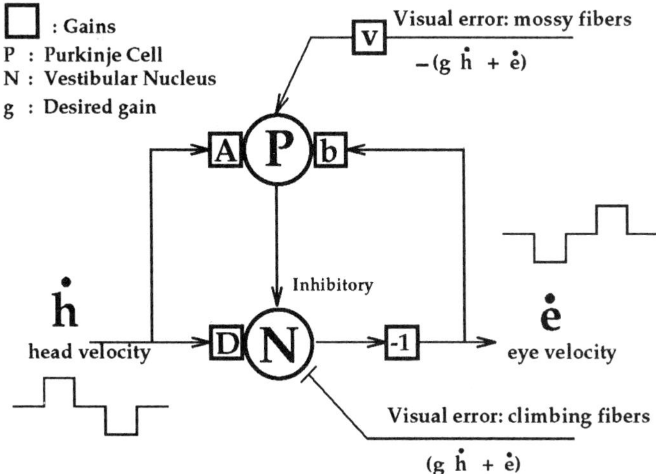

Figure 2: **Diagram of the VOR and smooth pursuit model.** The input and output of the model are, respectively, head velocity and eye velocity. The model has three main parts: the node P represents an ensemble of Purkinje cells from the ventral paraflocculus of the cerebellum, the node N represents an ensemble of flocculus-target neurons in the vestibular nucleus, and the visual inputs which provide the visual error signals in the mossy and climbing fibers. The capital letter gains A and D, multiplying the input signals to the nodes, are modified according to their learning rules. The lower case letters b, v, and g are also multiplicative gains, but remain constant during adaptation. The traces represent head and eye velocity modulation in time. The visual error signal in the climbing fibers drives learning in node N but does not constitute one of its inputs in the present model.

of -1. The gain of the VOR in this model is given by $\frac{D-A}{1-b}$. We have not modeled the neural integrator that converts eye velocity commands to eye position signals that drive the motoneurons.

3 LEARNING RULES

We have adopted the learning rules proposed by Marr (1969), Albus (1971) and Ito (1970) for adaptation in the cerebellum and by Lisberger (1988), Miles and Lisberger (1981) for plasticity in the brain stem (figure 3). These are variations of the delta rule and depend on an explicit representation of the error signal at the synapses.

Long term depression at mossy fiber synapses on Purkinje cells has been observed *in vitro* under simultaneous stimulation of climbing fibers and mossy fibers (Ito, Sakurai and Tongroach, 1982). In addition, we have included a learning mechanism for potentiation of mossy fiber head velocity inputs under concurrent mossy fiber visual and head velocity inputs. Although the climbing fiber inputs to the cerebellum were not directly represented in this model (figure 2), the image velocity signal carried by the mossy fibers to P was used in the model to achieve the same result.

There is good indirect evidence that learning also occurs in the vestibular nucleus. We have adopted the suggestion of Lisberger (1988) that the effectiveness of the head velocity input to some neurons in the vestibular nucleus may be modified by head velocity input in

$$\Delta = \begin{array}{c}\text{Learning}\\ \text{Rate}\end{array} \times \left(\begin{array}{c}\text{Input}\\ \text{Signal}\end{array}\right) \times \left(\begin{array}{c}\text{Error}\\ \text{Signal}\end{array}\right)$$

Cerebellum (P):

$$\begin{aligned}
\dot{A} &= \eta_A \times \left(\begin{array}{c}\text{Head}\\ \text{Velocity}\end{array}\right) \times \left(\begin{array}{c}\text{Mossy fiber}\\ \text{Visual signal}\end{array}\right)\\
&= \eta_A \times \dot{h} \times -v(g\dot{h} + \dot{e})\\
&= \eta_A \times \dot{h} \times -v[(g - D)\dot{h} + P]\\
&\propto \dot{h}^2
\end{aligned}$$

Vestibular nucleus (N):

$$\begin{aligned}
\dot{D} &= \eta_D \times \left(\begin{array}{c}\text{Head}\\ \text{Velocity}\end{array}\right) \times \left(\begin{array}{c}\text{Climbing fiber}\\ \text{Visual signal}\end{array} - \begin{array}{c}\text{Purkinje}\\ \text{Signal}\end{array}\right)\\
&= \eta_D \times \dot{h} \times [(1 - q)(g\dot{h} + \dot{e}) - qP]\\
&= \eta_D \times \dot{h} \times [(1 - q)(g - D)\dot{h} + (1 - 2q)P]\\
&\propto \dot{h}^2
\end{aligned}$$

where

$$P = \frac{A - bD - (g - D)v}{1 - b + v}\dot{h}$$

Figure 3: **Learning rules for the cerebellum and vestibular nucleus.** The gains A and D change according to the correlation of their input signal and the error signal to the node, as shown for Δ at the top. The parameter q determines the proportion of learning from Purkinje cell inputs compared to learning from climbing fiber inputs. When $q = 1$, only Purkinje cell inputs drive the adaptation at node N; if $q = 0$, learning occurs solely from climbing fiber inputs.

association with Purkinje cells firing. We have also added adaptation from pairing the head velocity input with climbing fiber firing. The relative effectiveness of these two learning mechanisms is controlled by the parameter q (figure 3).

Learning for gain D depends on the interplay between several signals. If the VOR gain is too small, a rightward head turn P (positive value for head velocity) results in too small a leftward eye turn (a negative value for eye velocity). Consequently, the visual scene appears to move to the left (negative image slip). P then fires below its resting level (negative) and its inhibitory influence on N decreases so that N increases its firing rate (figure 4 bottom left). This corrects the VOR gain and increases gain D according to figure 3. Concurrently, the climbing fiber visual signal is above resting firing rate (positive) which also leads to an increase in gain D.

Since the signal passing through gain A has an inhibitory influence via P onto N, decreasing gain A has the opposite effect on the eye velocity as decreasing gain D. Hence, if the VOR is too small we expect gain A to decrease. This is what happens during the early phase of learning (figure 4 top left).

4 RESULTS

Finite difference equations of the learning rules were used to calculate changes in gains A and D at the end of each cycle during our simulations. A cycle was defined as one biphasic

Desired gain $g = 1.6$

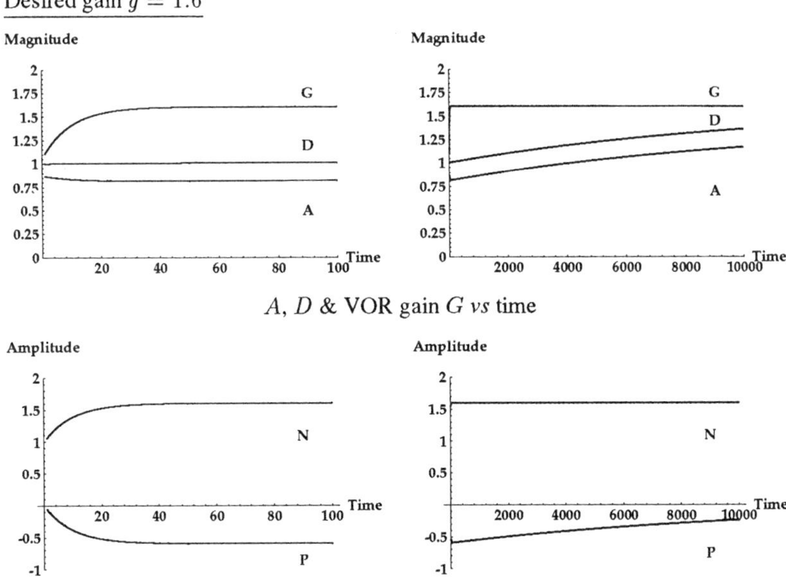

P & N responses to a head turn during learning *vs* time

Figure 4: **Simulation of change in gain from 1.0 to 1.6.** Top: Short-term (left) and long-term (right) adaptation of the gains A, D and G. Bottom: Changes on two time scales of P and N responses to a head turn of amplitude 1 during learning. The parameters were $v = 1.0$, $b = .88$, $r = \frac{\eta_A}{\eta_D} = 10.$, and $q = .01$.

head velocity input as shown in figure 2. We assumed that the learning rates were so small that the changes in gains, and hence in the node responses, were negligibly small during each iteration. This allowed the replacement of $A(t)$ and $D(t)$ by their values obtained on the previous iteration for the calculations of $\dot{A}$ and $\dot{D}$. The period of the iteration as well as the amplitude of the head velocity input were chosen so that the integral of the head velocity squared over one iteration equaled 1.

For the simulations shown in figure 4 the gain G of the VOR increased monotonically from 1 to reach the desired value 1.6 within 60 time steps. This rapid adaptation was mainly due to a rapid decrease in A, as expected from the local learning rule (figure 3), since the learning rate η_A was greater than the learning rate η_D. Over a longer time period, learning was transferred from A to D: D increased from 1 to reach its final value 1.6 while the VOR gain stayed constant. Transfer of learning occurs when P fires in conjunction with a head turn. P can have an elevated firing rate even though the visual error signal is zero (that is, even if the VOR gain G has reached the desired gain g) because of the difference between its two other inputs: the head velocity input through A and the eye velocity feedback input through b. It is only when these two inputs become equal in amplitude that P firing goes to zero. It can be shown that when learning settles (when $\dot{D}$ and $\dot{A}$ equal zero) $D = g$, $A = bg$, and $P = 0$. With these values for A and D, the two other inputs to P are indeed equal in amplitude: one equals $A\dot{h}$, while the other equals $b(-1)D\dot{h}$. During the later part of learning, gain A is driven in the opposite direction (increase) than during the earlier part (decrease). This comes from a sign reversal of the visual error input to P. After the first 60 time steps, the gain has reached the desired gain due to a rapid decrease in A, this means that any subsequent increase in D, due to transfer of learning as explained above, will cause the gain of the VOR G to become larger than the desired gain g, hence the visual error changes sign. In order to compensate for this small error, gain A increases promptly, keeping G very close to the desired gain. This process goes on until A and D reach their equilibrium values stated above.

The short and long-term changes in P and N responses to a velocity step are also shown. As the firing of P decreased with the adaptation of A, the firing rate of N increased to the right level.

5 OVERSHOOT OF THE VOR GAIN G

In this section we show that for some ranges of the learning parameters, the gain G in the model overshoots the desired value g. Since an overshoot is not observed in animals (figure 1), this provides constraints on the parameters. The parameter q in the learning rule for the vestibular nucleus (node N, gain D), determines the proportion of learning from Purkinje cell inputs compared to learning from climbing fiber inputs. When $q = 1$, only Purkinje cell inputs drive the adaptation at node N; if $q = 0$, learning at N occurs solely from climbing fiber inputs. These two inputs have quite different effects on learning as shown in figure 5. Asymptotically, P goes to 0, and D goes to g if $q = 1$; and P can only differ from 0 if $q = 0$. The gain has an overshoot for any value of q different than 0, as shown in figure 6. Nevertheless, its amplitude is only significant for a limited extent in the parameter space of q and r (graph of figure 6). The overshoot is reduced with a smaller q and a larger r. One possibility is that q is chosen close to 0 and $r \gg 1$, that is $\eta_A \gg \eta_D$. These conditions were used to choose parameter values in the simulations (figure 4).

6 DISCUSSION AND CONCLUSION

The VOR model analyzed here is a static model without time delays and multiple time scales. We are currently studying how these factors affect the time course of learning in a dynamical model of the VOR and smooth pursuit.

In our model, learning occurs in the dark if $P \neq 0$, which has not been observed in animals. One way to avoid learning in the dark when P is firing would be to gate the learning by a visual input, such as that provided by climbing fibers.

The responses of vestibular afferents to head motion can be classified into two categories: phase-tonic and tonic. In this model, only the tonic afferents were represented. Both afferent types encode head velocity, while the phasic-tonic responds to head acceleration as well. The steady state VOR gain can also be changed by altering the relative proportions of phasic and tonic afferents to the Purkinje cells (Lisberger and Sejnowski, 1992). We are currently investigating learning rules for which this occurs.

The model predicts that adaptation in the cerebellum is faster than in the vestibular nucleus, and that learning in the vestibular nucleus is mostly driven by the climbing fiber error signals.

The model shows how the dynamics of the whole system can lead to long-term adaptation

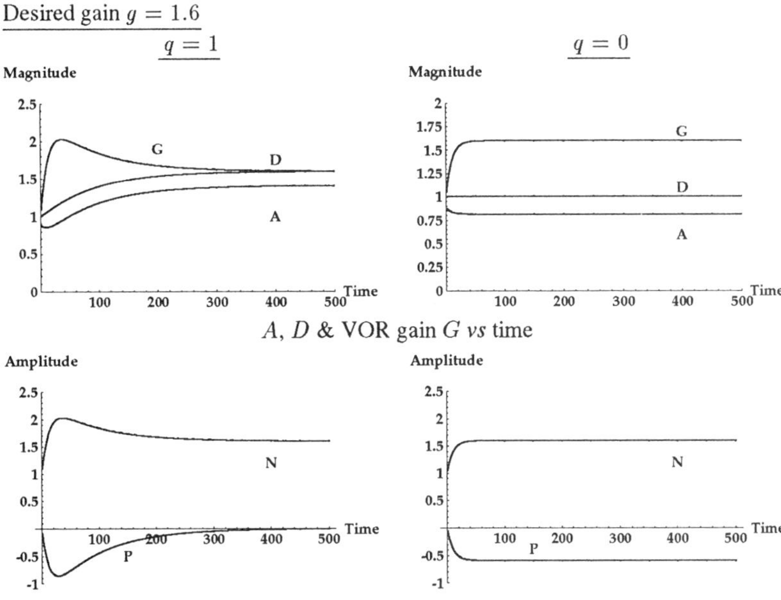

Figure 5: **Effect of q on learning curves for gain increase.** Left: $q = 1$ leads to an overshoot in the VOR gain G above the desired gain. D increases up to the desired gain, P starts from 0 and asymptotically goes back to 0; both indicate that learning is totally transferred from P to N. Right: With $q = 0$, there is no overshoot in the VOR gain, but since A decreases to a constant value and D only increases very slightly, learning is not transfered. Consequently, P firing rate stays constant after an initial drop.

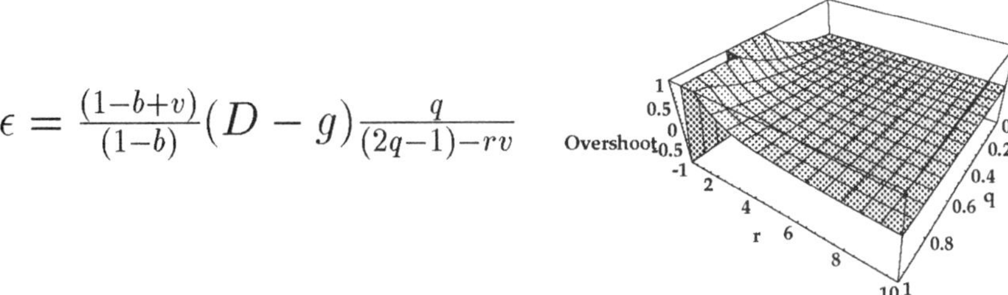

Figure 6: **Overshoot ϵ of the VOR gain G as a function of q and r.** The parameter q is the proportion of learning to node N (vestibular nucleus), coming from the P node (cerebellum) compared to learning from climbing fibers. The parameter r is the ratio of the learning rates η_A and η_D. No overshoot is seen in animals, which restricts the parameters space of q and r for the model to be valid. Note that the overshoot diverges for some parameter values.

which differs from what may be expected from the local learning rules at the synapses because of differences in time scales and shifts of activity in the system during learning. This may reconcile apparently contradictory evidence between local learning rules observed *in vitro* (Ito,1970) and the long-term adaptation seen *in vivo* in animals (Miles and Lisberger,1981).

Acknowledgments

O.C. was supported by NSERC during this research.

References

Albus, J. S. (1971). A theory of cerebellar function. *Math. Biosci.*, 10:25–61.

Arnold, D. B. and Robinson, D. A. (1992). A neural network model of the vestibulo-ocular reflex using a local synaptic learning rule. *Phil. Trans. R. Soc. Lond. B*, 337:327–330.

Fujita, M. (1982). Simulations of adaptive modification of the vestibulo-ocular reflex with an adaptive filter model of the cerebellum. *Biological Cybernetics*, 45:207–214.

Galiana, H. L. (1986). A new approach to understanding adaptive visual-vestibular interactions in the central nervous system. *Journal of Neurophysiology*, 55:349–374.

Ito, M. (1970). Neurophysiological aspects of the cerebellar motor control system. *Int.J.Neurol.*, 7:162–176.

Ito, M., Sakurai, M., and Tongroach, P. (1982). Climbing fibre induced depression of both mossy fibre responsiveness and glutamate sensitivity of cerebellar purkinje cells. *J. Physiol. Lond.*, 324:113–134.

Kawato, M. and Gomi, H. (1992). The cerebellum and VOR/OKR learning models. *Trends in Neuroscience*, 15:445–453.

Lisberger, S. G. (1988). The neural basis for learning of simple motor skills. *Science*, 242:728–735.

Lisberger, S. G. (1992). Neural basis for motor learning in the vestibulo-ocular reflex of primates:IV. The sites of learning. In preparation.

Lisberger, S. G. and Sejnowski, T. J. (1992). Computational analysis suggests a new hypothesis for motor learning in the vestibulo-ocular reflex. Technical Report 9201, INC, Univ. of California, San Diego.

Marr, D. (1969). A theory of cerebellar cortex. *J. Physiol.*, 202:437–470.

Melvill Jones, G. M. (1991). *The Vestibular Contribution*, volume 8 of *Vision and Visual Dysfunction*, chapter 2, pages 293–303. CRC Press, Inc., Boston. General Editor: J. R. Cronly-Dillon.

Miles, F. A. and Eighmy, B. B. (1980). Long-term adaptive changes in primate vestibulo-ocular reflex.I. Behavioural observations. *Journal of Neurophysiology*, 43:1406–1425.

Miles, F. A. and Lisberger, S. G. (1981). Plasticity in the vestibulo-ocular reflex: A new hypothesis. *Ann. Rev. Neurosci.*, 4:273–299.

Quinn, K. J., Baker, J., and Peterson, B. (1992). Simulation of cerebellar-vestibular interactions during VOR adaptation. In *Program 22nd Annual Meeting*. Society for Neuroscience.

Quinn, K. J., Schmajuk, N., Jain, A., Baker, J. F., and Peterson, B. W. (1992). Vestibuloocular reflex arc analysis using an experimentally constrained network. *Biological Cybernetics*, 67:113–122.

Viola, P. A., Lisberger, S. G., and Sejnowski, T. J. (1992). Recurrent eye tracking network using a distributed representation of image motion. In Moody, J. E., Hansen, S. J., and Lippman, R. P., editors, *Advances in Neural Information Processing Systems 4*, San Mateo. IEEE, Morgan Kaufmann Publishers.

Using Aperiodic Reinforcement for Directed Self-Organization During Development

PR Montague P Dayan SJ Nowlan A Pouget TJ Sejnowski
CNL, The Salk Institute
10010 North Torrey Pines Rd.
La Jolla, CA 92037, USA
read@helmholtz.sdsc.edu

Abstract

We present a local learning rule in which Hebbian learning is conditional on an incorrect prediction of a reinforcement signal. We propose a biological interpretation of such a framework and display its utility through examples in which the reinforcement signal is cast as the delivery of a neuromodulator to its target. Three examples are presented which illustrate how this framework can be applied to the development of the oculomotor system.

1 INTRODUCTION

Activity-dependent accounts of the self-organization of the vertebrate brain have relied ubiquitously on correlational (mainly Hebbian) rules to drive synaptic learning. In the brain, a major problem for any such unsupervised rule is that many different kinds of correlations exist at approximately the same time scales and each is effectively noise to the next. For example, relationships within and between the retinae among variables such as color, motion, and topography may mask one another and disrupt their appropriate segregation at the level of the thalamus or cortex.

It is known, however, that many of these variables can be segregrated both within and between cortical areas suggesting that certain sets of correlated inputs are somehow separated from the temporal noise of other inputs. Some form of supervised learning appears to be required. Unfortunately, **detailed supervision and**

selection in a brain region is not a feasible mechanism for the vertebrate brain. The question thus arises: What kind of biological mechanism or signal could selectively bias synaptic learning toward a particular subset of correlations ? One answer lies in the possible role played by diffuse neuromodulatory systems.

It is known that multiple diffuse modulatory systems are involved in the self-organization of cortical structures (*eg* Bear and Singer, 1986) and some of them appear to deliver reward and/or salience signals to the cortex and other structures to influence learning in the adult. Recent data (Ljunberg, *et al*, 1992) suggest that this latter influence is qualitatively similar to that predicted by Sutton and Barto's (1981,1987) classical conditioning theory. These systems innervate large expanses of cortical and subcortical turf through extensive axonal projections that originate in midbrain and basal forebrain nuclei and deliver such compounds as dopamine, serotonin, norepinephrine, and acetylcholine to their targets. The small number of neurons comprising these subcortical nuclei relative to the extent of the territory their axons innervate suggests that the nuclei are reporting scalar signals to their target structures.

In this paper, these facts are synthesized into a single framework which relates the development of brain structures and conditioning in adult brains. We postulate a modification to Hebbian accounts of self-organization: Hebbian learning is conditional on a incorrect prediction of future delivered reinforcement from a diffuse neuromodulatory system. This reinforcement signal can be derived both from externally driven contingencies such as proprioception from eye movements as well as from internal pathways leading from cortical areas to subcortical nuclei.

The next section presents our framework and proposes a specific model for how predictions about future reinforcement could be made in the vertebrate brain utilizing the firing in a diffuse neuromodulatory system (figure 1). Using this model we illustrate the framework with three examples suggesting how mappings in the oculomotor system may develop. The first example shows how eye movement commands could become appropriately calibrated in the absence of visual experience (figure 3). The second example demonstrates the development of a mapping from a selected visual target to an eye movement which acquires the target. The third example describes how our framework could permit the development and alignment of multimodal maps (visual and auditory) in the superior colliculus. In this example, the transformation of auditory signals from head-centered to eye-centered coordinates results implicitly from the development of the mapping from parietal cortex onto the colliculus.

2 THEORY

We consider two classes of reinforcement learning (RL) rule: static and dynamic.

2.1 Static reinforcement learning

The simplest learning rule that incorporates a reinforcement signal is:

$$\Delta w_t = \alpha x_t y_t r_t \tag{1}$$

where, all at times t, w_t is a connection weight, x_t an input measure, y_t an output measure, r_t a reinforcement measure, and α is the learning rate.

In this case, r can be driven by either external events in the world or by cortical projections (internal events) and it picks out those correlations between x and y about which the system learns. Learning is shut down if nothing occurs that is independently judged to be significant, *i.e.* events for which r is 0.

2.2 Dynamic Reinforcement learning - learning driven by prediction error

A more informative way to utilize reinforcement signals is to incorporate some form of prediction. The predictive form of RL, called temporal difference learning (TD, Sutton and Barto, 1981,1987), specifies weight changes according to:

$$\Delta w_t = \alpha x_t[(r_{t+1} + V_{t+1}) - V_t] \quad (2)$$

where r_{t+1} is the reward delivered in the next instant in time $t+1$. V is called a value function and its value at any time t is an estimate of the future reward. This framework is closely related to dynamic programming (Barto *et al*, 1989) and a body of theory has been built around it. The prediction error $[(r_{t+1} + V_{t+1}) - V_t]$, measures the degree to which the prediction of future reward V_t is higher or lower than the combination of the actual future reward r_{t+1} and the expectation of reward from time $t+1$ onward (V_{t+1}).

To place dynamic RL in a biological context, we start with a simple Hebbian rule but make learning contingent on this prediction error. Learning therefore slows as the predictions about future rewards get better. In contrast with static RL, in a TD account the value of r *per se* is not important, only whether the system is able to predict or anticipate the the future value of r. Therefore the weight changes are:

$$\Delta w_t = \alpha x_t y_t[(r_{t+1} + V_{t+1}) - V_t] \quad (3)$$

including a measure of post-synaptic response, y_t.

3 MAKING PREDICTIONS IN THE BRAIN

In our account of RL in the brain, the cortex is the structure that makes predictions of future reinforcement. This reinforcement is envisioned as the output of subcortical nuclei which deliver various neuromodulators to the cortex that permit Hebbian learning. Experiments have shown that various of these nuclei, which have access to cortical representations of complex sensory input, are necessary for instrumental and classical conditioning to occur (Ljunberg *et al.*, 1992).

Figure 1 shows one TD scenario in which a pattern of activity in a region of cortex makes a prediction about future expected reinforcement. At time t, the prediction of future reward V_t is viewed as an excitatory drive from the cortex onto one or more subcortical nuclei (pathway B). The high degree of convergence in B ensures that this drive predicts only a scalar output of the nucleus R. Consider a pattern of activity onto layer II which provides excitatory drive to R and concomitantly causes some output, say a movement, at time $t+1$. This movement provides a separate source of excitatory drive r_{t+1} to the same nucleus through independent

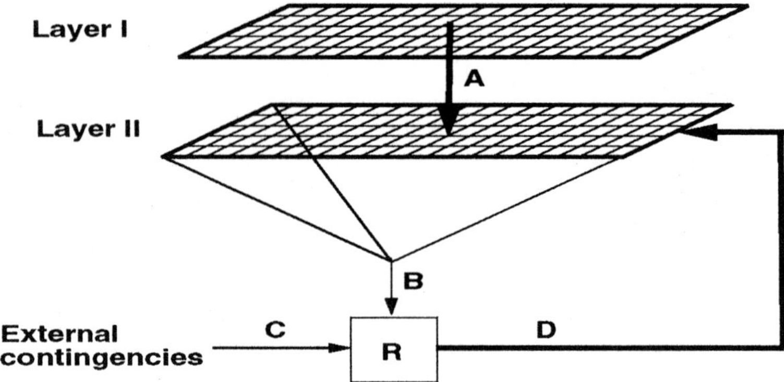

Figure 1: **Making predictions about future reinforcement.** Layer I is an array of units that projects topographically onto layer II. **(A)** Weights from I onto II develop according to equation 3 and represent the value function V_t. **(B)** The weights from II onto **R** are fixed. The prediction of future reward by the weights onto II is a scalar because the highly convergent excitatory drive from II to the reinforcement nucleus **(R)** effectively sums the input. **(C)** External events in the world provide independent excitatory drive to the reinforcement nucleus. **(D)** Scalar signal which results from the output firing of **R** and is broadcast throughout layer II. This activity delivers to layer II the neuromodulator required for Hebbian learning. The output firing of **R** is controlled by temporal changes in its excitatory input and habituates to constant or slowly varying input. This makes for learning in layer II according to equation 3 (see text).

connections conveying information from sensory structures such as stretch receptors (pathway C). Hence, at time $t + 1$, the excitatory input to R is the sum of the 'immediate reward' r_{t+1} and the new prediction of future reward V_{t+1}. If the reinforcement nucleus is driven primarily by changes in its input over some time window, then the difference between the excitatory drive at time t and $t + 1$, *ie* $[(r_{t+1} + V_{t+1}) - V_t]$ is what its output reflects.

The output is distributed throughout a region of cortex (pathway D) and permits Hebbian weight changes at the individual connections which determine the value function V_t. The example hinges on two assumptions: 1) Hebbian learning in the cortex is contingent upon delivery of the neuromodulator, and 2) the reinforcement nucleus is sensitive to temporal changes in its input and otherwise habituates to constant or slowly varying input.

Initially, before the system is capable of predicting future delivery of reinforcement correctly, the arrival of r_{t+1} causes a large learning signal because the prediction error $[(r_{t+1} + V_{t+1}) - V_t]$ is large. This error drives weight changes at synaptic connections with correlated pre- and postsynaptic elements until the predictions come to approximate the actual future delivered reinforcement. Once these predictions become accurate, learning abates. At that point, the system has learned about whatever contingencies are currently controlling reinforcement delivery. For the case in which the delivery of reinforcement is not controlled by any predictable contingencies, Hebbian learning can still occur if the fluctuations of the prediction error have a positive mean.

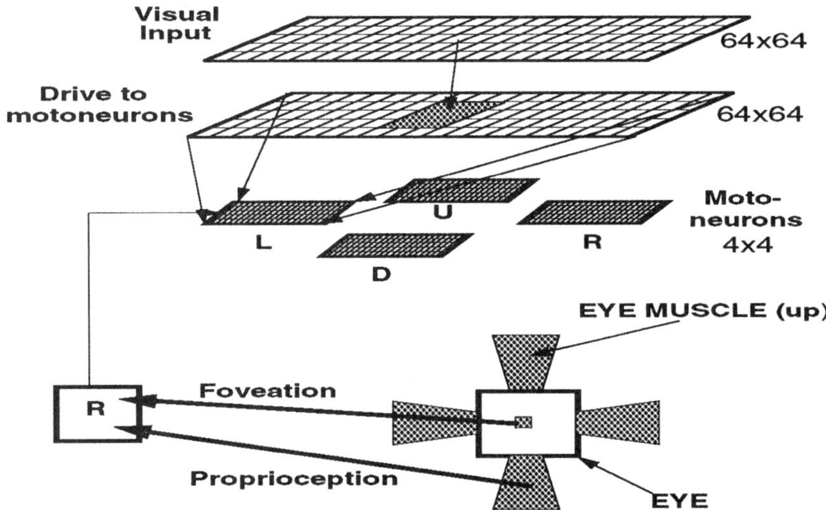

Figure 2: Upper layer is a 64 by 64 input array with 3 by 3 center-surround filters at each position which projects topographically onto the middle layer. The middle layer projects randomly to four 4 X 4 motoneuron layers which code for an equilibrium eye position signal, for example, through setting equilibrium muscle tensions in the 4 muscles. Reinforcement signals originate from either eye movement (muscle 'stretch') or foveation. The eye is moved according to $h = (r - l)g, v = (u - d)g$ where r,l,u,d are respectively the average activities on the right, left, up, down motoneuron layers and g is a fixed gain parameter. h and v are linearly combined to give the eye position.

In the presence of multiple *statistically independent sources of control* of the reinforcement signal (pathways onto R), the system can separately 'learn away' the contingencies for each of these sources. This passage of control of reinforcement delivery can allow the development of connections in a region to be staged. Hence, control of reinforcement can be passed between contingencies without supervision. In this manner, a few nuclei can be used to deliver information globally about many different circumstances. We illustrate this point below with development of a sensorimotor mapping.

4 EXAMPLES

4.1 Learning to calibrate without sensory experience

Figure 2 illustrates the architecture for the next two examples. Briefly, cortical layers drive four 'motor' layers of units which each provide an equilibrium command to one of four extraocular muscles. The mapping from the cortical layers onto these four layers is random and sparse (15%-35% connectivity) and is plastic according to the learning rule described above. Two external events control the delivery of reinforcement: eye movement and foveation of high contrast objects in the visual input. The minimum eye movement necessary to cause a reinforcement is a change of two pixels in any direction (see figure 3).

We begin by demonstrating how an unbalanced mapping onto the motoneuron

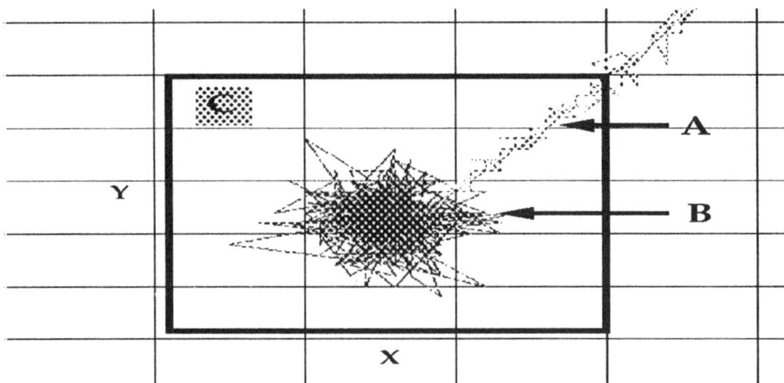

Figure 3: **Learning to calibrate eye movement commands.** This example illustrates how a reinforcement signal could help to organize an appropriate balance in the sensorimotor mapping **before** visual experience. The dark bounding box represents the 64x64 pixel working area over which an 8x8 fovea can move. **A** Foveal position during the first 400 cycles of learning. The architecture is as in figure 2, but the weights onto the right/left and up/down pairs are not balanced. Random activity in the layer providing the drive to the motoneurons initially drives the eye to an extreme position at the upper right. From this position, no movement of the eye can occur and thus no reinforcement can be delivered from the proprioceptive feedback causing all the weights to begin to decrease. With time, the weights onto the motoneurons become balanced and the eye moves. **B** Foveal position after 400 cycles of learning and after increasing the gain g to 10 times its initial value. After the weights onto antagonistic muscles become balanced, the net excursions of the eye are small thus requiring an increase in g in order to allow the eye to explore its working range. **C** Size of foveal region relative the working range of the eye. The fovea covered an 8x8 region of the working area of the eye and the learning rate α was varied from 0.08 to 0.25 without changing the result.

layers can be automatically calibrated in the absence of visual experience. Imagine that the weights onto the right/left and up/down pairs are initially unbalanced, as might happen if one or more muscles are weak or the effective drives to each muscle are unequal. Figure 3, which shows the position of the fovea during learning, indicates that the initially unbalanced weights cause the eye to move immediately to an extreme position (figure 3, A).

Since the reinforcement is controlled only by eye movement and foveation and neither is occurring in this state, r_{t+1} is roughly 0. This is despite the (randomly generated) activity in the motoneurons continually making predictions that reinforcement from eye-movement should be being delivered. Therefore all the weights begin to decrease, with those mediating the unbalanced condition decreasing the fastest, until balance is achieved (see path A). Once the eye reaches equilibrium, further random noise will cause no mean net eye movement since the mappings onto each of the four motoneuron layers are balanced. The larger amplitude eye movements shown in the center of figure 3 (labeled B) are the result of increasing the gain g (figure 2).

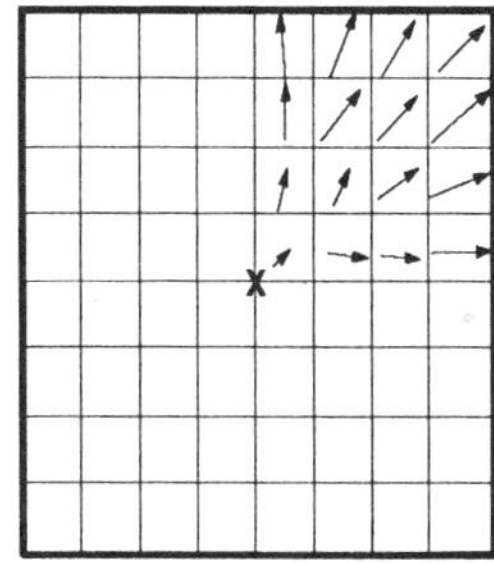

Figure 4: **Development of foveation map.** The map after 2000 learning cycles shows the approximate eye movement vector from stimulation of each position in the visual field. Lengths were normalized to the size of the largest movement. The undisplayed quadrants were qualitatively similar. Note that this scheme does not account for activity or contrast differences in the input and assumes that these have already been normalized. Learning rate = 0.12. Connectivity from the middle layer to the motoneurons was 35% and was randomized. Unlike the previous example, the weights onto the four layers of motoneurons were initially balanced.

4.2 Learning a foveation map with sensory experience

Although reinforcement would be delivered by foveation as well as successful eye-movements, the former would be expected to be a comparatively rare event. Once equilibrium is achieved, however, the reinforcement that comes from eye movements is fully predicted by the prior activity of the motoneurons, and so other contingencies, in this case foveation, grab control of the delivery of reinforcement. The resulting TD signals now provide information about the link between visual input on the top layer of figure 2 and the resulting command, and the system learns how to foveate correctly. Figure 4 shows the motor map that has developed after 2000 learning cycles. In the current example, the weights onto the four layers of motoneurons initially were balancedand the gain g was 10 times larger than before calibration (see figure 3). This learning currently assumes that some cortical area selects the salient targets.

4.3 Learning to align separate mappings

In the primate superior colliculus, it is known that cells can respond to multiple modalities including auditory input which defines a head centered coordinate system. Auditory receptive fields shift their position in the colliculus with changing eye position suggesting the existence of a mechanism which maintains the registration between auditory and visual maps (Jay and Sparks, 1984). Our framework suggests a developmental explanation of these findings in terms of an activity-dependent self-organizing principle.

Consider an intermediate layer, modeling the parietal cortex, which receives signals representing eye position (proprioception), retinal position of a visual target (selected visual input), and head position of an auditory target and which projects onto the superior colliculus. This can be visualized using figure 2 with parietal cortex as the top layer and the colliculus as the drive to the motoneurons. As before (figure 2), assume that foveation of a target, whether auditory or visual, delivers reinforcement and that learning in this layer and the colliculus follows equation 3. In a manner analagous to the example in figure 4, those *combinations* of retinal, eye position, and head centered signals in this parietal layer which predict a foveating eye movement are selected by this learning rule. Hence, as before, the weights from this layer onto the colliculus make predictions about future reinforcement. In figure 4, a foveation map develops which codes for eye movements in absolute coordinates relative to some equilibrium position of the eye. In the current example, such a foveation map would be inappropriate since it requires persistent activity in the collicular layer to maintain a fixed eye position. Instead, the collicular to motoneuron mapping must represent changes in the balance between antagonistic muscles with some other system coding for current eye position.

Why would such an initial architecture, acting under the aegis of the learning rule expressed in equation 3, develop the collicular mappings observed in experiments? Those combinations of signals in the parietal layer that correctly predict foveation have their connections onto the collicular layer stabilized. In the current representation, foveation of a target will occur if the correct *change* in firing between antagonistic motoneurons occurs. After learning slows, the parietal layer is left with cells whose visual and auditory responses are modulated by eye position signals. In the collicular layer, the visual responses of a cell are not modulated by eye position signals while the head-centered auditory responses are modulated by eye position.

The reasons for these differences in the colliculus layer and parietal layer are implicit in the new motoneuron model and the way the equation 3 polices learning. The collicular layer is driven by combinations of the three signals and the learning rule enforces a common frame of reference for these combinations because foveation of the target is the only source of reinforcement. Consider, for example, a visual target on a region of retina for two different eye positions. The change in the balance between right and left muscles required to foveate such a retinal target is the same for each eye position hence the projection from the parietal to collicular layer develops so that the influence of eye position for a fixed retinal target is eliminated. The influence of eye position for an auditory target remains, however, because successful foveation of an auditory target requires different regions of the collicular map to be active as a function of eye position.

These examples illustrate how diffuse modulatory systems in the midbrain and basal forebrain can be employed in single framework to guide activity-dependent map development in the vertebrate brain. This framework gives a natural role to such diffuse system for both development and conditioning in the adult brain and illustrates how external contingencies can be incorporated into cortical representations through these crude scalar signals.

References

[1] Barto, AG, Sutton, RS & Watkins, CJCH (1989). *Learning and Sequential Decision Making*. Technical Report 89-95, Computer and Information Science, University of Massachusetts, Amherst, MA.

[2] Bear, MF & Singer, W (1986). Modulation of visual cortical plasticity by acetylcholine and noradrenaline. *Nature*, **320**, 172-176.

[3] Jay, MF & Sparks, DL (1984). Auditory receptive fields in primate superior colliculus shift with changes in eye position. *Nature*, **309**, 345-347.

[4] Ljunberg, T, Apicella, P & Schultz, W (1992). Responses of monkey dopamine neurons during learning of behavioral reactions. *Journal of Neurophysiology*, **67**(1), 145-163.

[5] Sutton, RS (1988). Learning to predict by the methods of temporal difference. *Machine Learning*, **3**, pp 9-44.

[6] Sutton, RS & Barto, AG (1981). Toward a modern theory of adaptive networks: Expectation and prediction. *Psychological Review*, **88** 2, pp 135-170.

[7] Sutton, RS & Barto, AG (1987). A temporal-difference model of classical conditioning. *Proceedings of the Ninth Annual Conference of the Cognitive Science Society*. Seattle, WA.

How Oscillatory Neuronal Responses Reflect Bistability and Switching of the Hidden Assembly Dynamics

K. Pawelzik, H.-U. Bauer[†], J. Deppisch, and T. Geisel
Institut für Theoretische Physik and SFB 185 Nichtlineare Dynamik
Universität Frankfurt, Robert-Mayer-Str. 8-10, D-6000 Frankfurt/M. 11, FRG
[†]temporary adress:CNS-Program, Caltech 216-76, Pasadena
email: klaus@chaos.uni-frankfurt.dbp.de

Abstract

A switching between apparently coherent (oscillatory) and stochastic episodes of activity has been observed in responses from cat and monkey visual cortex. We describe the dynamics of these phenomena in two parallel approaches, a phenomenological and a rather microscopic one. On the one hand we analyze neuronal responses in terms of a hidden state model (HSM). The parameters of this model are extracted directly from experimental spike trains. They characterize the underlying dynamics as well as the coupling of individual neurons to the network. This phenomenological model thus provides a new framework for the experimental analysis of network dynamics. The application of this method to multi unit activities from the visual cortex of the cat substantiates the existence of oscillatory and stochastic states and quantifies the switching behaviour in the assembly dynamics. On the other hand we start from the single spiking neuron and derive a master equation for the time evolution of the assembly state which we represent by a phase density. This phase density dynamics (PDD) exhibits costability of two attractors, a limit cycle, and a fixed point when synaptic interaction is nonlinear. External fluctuations can switch the bistable system from one state to the other. Finally we show, that the two approaches are mutually consistent and therefore both explain the detailed time structure in the data.

1 INTRODUCTION

A few years ago, oscillatory and synchronous neuronal activity was discovered in cat visual cortex [1-3]. These experiments backed earlier considerations about synchrony in neuronal activity as a mechanism to bind features, e.g., of an object in a visual scene [4]. They triggered broad experimental and theoretical investigations of detailed neuronal dynamics as a means for information processing and, in particular, for feature binding. Many theoretical contributions tried to reproduce and explain aspects of the experimentally observed phenomena [5]. Motivated by the experiments, the models where particularly designed to exhibit spatial synchronization of permanent oscillatory responses upon stimulation by a common, connected stimulus like a bar. Most models consist of elements which exhibit a limit cycle after a simple Hopf bifurcation.

The experimental data, however, contain many details which the present models do not yet completely incorporate. One of these details is the coexistence of regular and irregular episodes in the data, which interchange in an apparently stochastic manner. This interchange can be observed in the signals from a single electrode [6] as well as in the time-resolved correlation of the signals from two electrodes [7]. In this contribution we show, that the observed time structure reflects a switching in the dynamics of the underlying neuronal system. This will be demonstrated by two complementary approaches:

On the one hand we present a new method for a quantitative analysis of the dynamical system underlying the measured spike trains. Our approach gives a quantitative description of the dynamical phenomena and furthermore explains the relation between the collective excitation in the network which is not accessible experimentally (i.e. hidden) and the contributions of the single observed neurons in terms of transition probability functions. These probabilities are the parameters of our Ansatz and can be estimated directly from multi unit activities (MUA) using the Baum-Welch-algorithm. Especially for the data from cat visual cortex we find that indeed there are two states dominating the dynamics of collective excitation, namely a state of repeated excitation and a state in which the observed neurons fire independently and stochastically.

On the other hand using simple statistical considerations we derive a description for a local neuronal subpopulation which exhibits bistability. The dynamics of the subpopulation can either rest on a fixed point - corresponding to the irregular firing patterns - or can follow a limit cycle - corresponding to the oscillatory firing patterns. The subpopulation can alternate between both states under the influence of noise in the external excitation. It turns out that the dynamics of this formal model reproduces the observed local cortical signals in much detail.

2 Excitability of Neurons and Neuronal Assemblies

An abstract model of a neuron under external excitation e is given by its threshold dynamics. The state of the neuron is represented by its phase ϕ^s, which is the time passed by since the last action potential ($\phi^s = 0$). The threshold Θ is high directly after a spike and falls off in time and the neuron can fire again when e exceeds Θ. In case of noise or internal stochasticity, an excitability description of the dynamics of the neuron is more adequate. It gives the probability P_f to fire again in dependence of the state ϕ^s with $P_f(\phi^s) = \sigma(e - \Theta(\phi^s))$ and σ some sigmoid function. A monotonously falling threshold Θ then corresponds to a monotonously increasing excitability P_f. Such a description neglects any memory in the neuron going beyond the last spike. In particular this means for an isolated neuron, that P_f can be easily calculated from the inter-spike interval histogram (ISIH) P_h using the relation $P_h(t) = P_f(t) \cdot (1 - \int_o^t P_h(t')dt')$. In that case also the autocorrelation function can be calculated from $P_h(t)$ via $\hat{C}(\tau) = P_h(\tau) + \int_0^\tau P_h(\tau)\hat{C}(\tau - t)dt$.

The excitability formulation sketched above is not valid for a neuron which is embedded in a neuronal assembly. However, we may use this Ansatz of a renewal process to describe the activation dynamics of the whole assembly (see section 5). The phase $\phi^b = 0$ here corresponds to the state of synchronous activity of many neurons in the assembly, which we call *burst* for convenience. Since the dynamics of the network can differ from the dynamics of the elements we expect the function $P_f^b(\phi^b)$ which now describes the burst excitability of the whole assembly to be different from the spike excitability $P_f(\phi_s)$ of the single neuron.

A simple example for this is a system of integrate and fire neurons in which oscillatory and irregular phases emerge under fixed stimulus conditions([8, 9] and section 5). Contrary to the excitability of the single refractory element the burst excitability P_f^b of the system has a maximum at $\phi^b = T$ which expresses the increased probability to burst again after the typical oscillation period T, i.e. the maximum represents a state o of oscillation. The assembly, however, can miss to burst around $\phi^b = T$ with a probability $p_{o \to s}$ and switch into a second state s in which the probability $p_{s \to o}$ to burst again is reduced to a constant level. The switching probabilities $p_{o \to s}$ and $p_{s \to o}$ can be easily calculated from P_f^b. In this way the shape of P_f^b distinguishes a system with an oscillatory state from a system which is purely refractory but which nevertheless can still have strong modulations in the autocorrelogram [13].

3 Hidden states and stochastic observables

The single neuron in an assembly, however, need not be strictly coupled to the state of the assembly, i.e. a neuron may also spike for $\phi^b > 0$ and it may not take part in a burst. This stochastic coupling to an underlying process suffices to destroy the equivalence of P_h and the autocorrelogram $C(\tau) = < s(t)s(t + \tau) >_t$ of the spike train $s(t) \in \{0, 1\}$ (Fig 1). We therefore include the probability $P_{obs}(\phi^b)$ to observe a spike when the assembly is in the state ϕ^b into our description (Fig. 2). The unlikely case where the spike represents the burst corresponds to the choice $P_{obs} = \delta_{\phi^b,0}$.

4 Application to Experimental Data

While our approach is quite general, we here concentrate on the measurements of Gray et al. [2] in cat visual cortex. Because our hidden state model has the structure of a hidden Markov model we can obtain all the parameters $P_{obs}(\phi)$ and

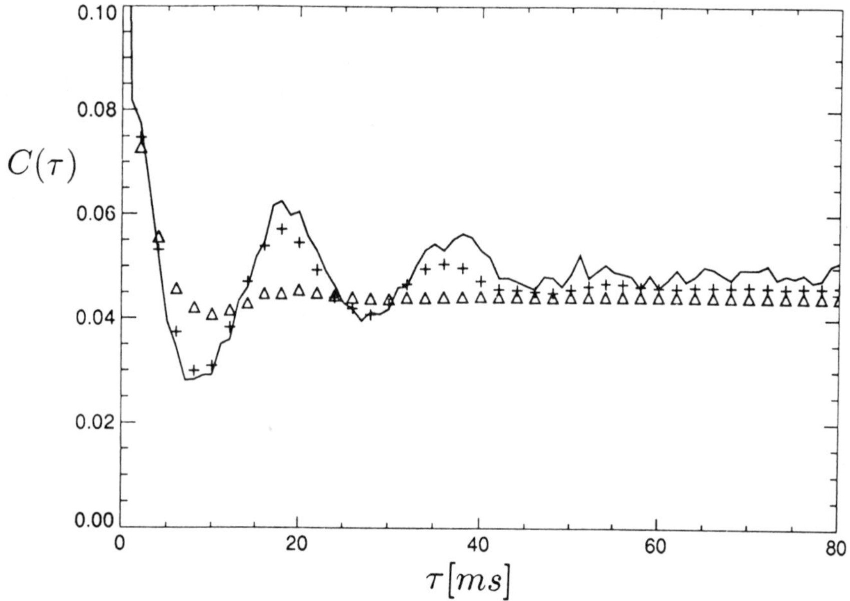

Figure 1: Correlogram of multi unit activities from cat visual cortex (line). Correlaograms predicted from the ISIH ($\triangle$) and from the hidden state model ($+$).

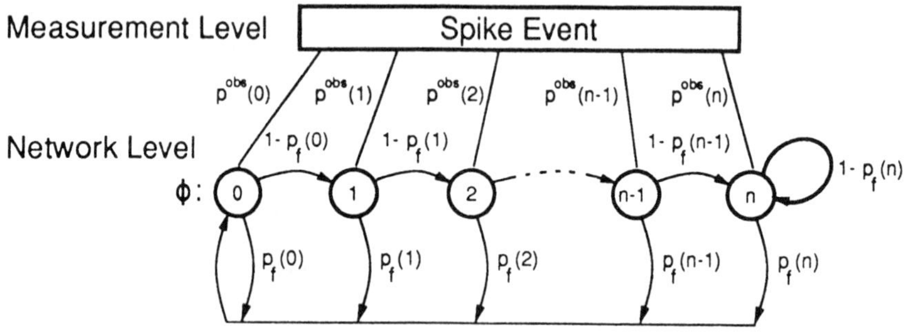

Figure 2: The hidden state model. While $P_f^b(\phi^b)$ governs the dynamics of assembly states ϕ^b, $P_{obs}(\phi^b)$ represents the probability to observe a spike of a single neuron.

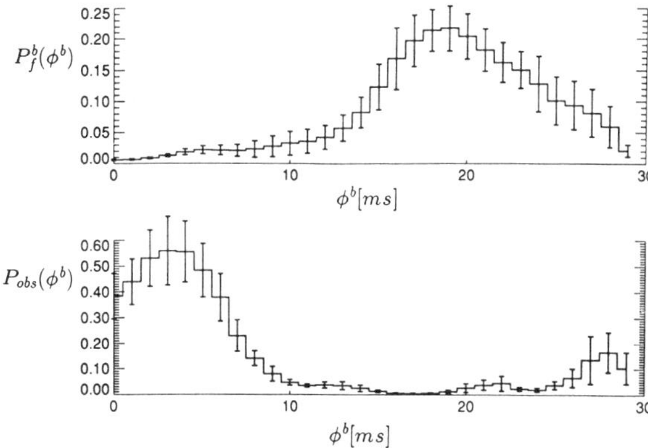

Figure 3: Network excitability P^b_f and single neuron contribution P_{obs} estimated from experimental spike trains (A17, cat).

$P^b_f(\phi)$ directly from the multi unit activities using the well known Baum-Welch algorithm[10]. The results can be seen in Fig. 3. The excitability shows a typical peak around the main period at $T = 19ms$, which indicates a state of oscillation. For larger phases we see a reduced excitability which reveals a state of stochastic activity ($P_{obs}(\phi^b > T) > 0$). The spike observation probability $P_{obs}(\phi)$ is peaked near the burst and is about constant elsewhere. This means that we can characterize the data by a stochastic switching between two dynamical states in the underlying system. Because of the stochastic coupling of the single neuron to the assembly state this can only hardly be observed directly. The switching probabilities between either states calculated from P^b_f coincide with results from other methods [11].

From the excitability P^b_f and the spike probabilities P_{obs} we now obtain the autocorrelation function $\hat{C}(\tau) = \int_\phi \int_{\phi'} P_{obs}(\phi')\mathbf{M}(\phi', \phi)^\tau P_{obs}(\phi)\rho(\phi)d\phi' d\phi$, with $\mathbf{M}$ being the transition matrix of the Markov model (see also below). The result is compared to the true autocorrelation $C(\tau)$ in Fig. 1. The excellent agreement confirms our simple Ansatz of a renewal process for the hidden burst dynamics of the assembly.

5 Bistability and Switching in Networks of Spiking Neurons

The above results indicate that the dynamics of a cortical assembly includes bistability rather than a simple Hopf bifurcation. In order to understand how this bistability emerges in a network we go one step back and derive a model for a neuronal subpopulation on the basis of spiking neurons. We assume again that the internal state of the neuron is given by the threshold function Θ depending on the time since the last spike event and that the excitability of the neuron can be described by a

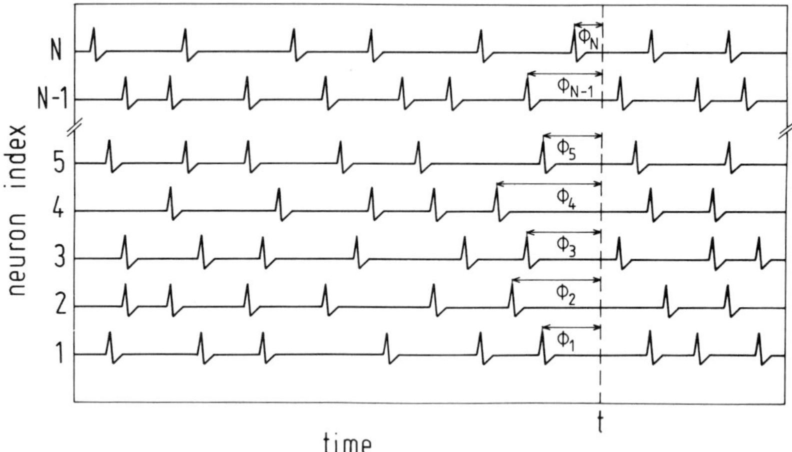

Figure 4: Illustration of assembly state representation by a phase density.

firing probability P_f. In a network, however, the input to the neuron has external contributions i_{ext} as well as from within i_{int} i.e.

$$P_f(\phi,t) \quad = \quad \mathrm{sigm}\left(w_{ext}i_{ext}(t) + w_{int}i_{int}(t) - \Theta(\phi)\right).$$

For a more formal treatment of the dynamics of such a network we characterize the assembly state by a phase density $\tilde{\rho}(\phi,t)$ which gives the relative amount of neurons in the assembly which are in phase ϕ at time t (Fig 4).

Discretizing the internal phases ϕ, we transform $\tilde{\rho}(\phi,t)$ to $\vec{\rho}(j)$, a vector whose components i give the probability to be in phase $\phi_i \in [(i-1)\Delta t, i\Delta t]$ at time $t_j = j\Delta t$. The number T of components is chosen large enough to ensure that $p_f(T,j) = P_f(T\Delta t, j\Delta t)$ does not change any more. This vector evolves in time according to

$$\vec{\rho}(j+1) = \mathbf{M}(j)\vec{\rho}(j) \tag{1}$$

with

$$\mathbf{M}(j) = \begin{pmatrix} 0 & p_f(1,j) & p_f(2,j) & \cdots & p_f(T{-}1,j) & p_f(T,j) \\ 1 & 0 & 0 & & & \\ 0 & 1{-}p_f(1,j) & 0 & \cdots & 0 & \\ & & 1{-}p_f(2,j) & \ddots & \vdots & \\ & \vdots & & & 0 & 0 \\ & 0 & \cdots & & 1{-}p_f(T{-}1,j) & 1{-}p_f(T,j) \end{pmatrix},$$

beeing a matrix that incorporates the effects of firing (reset) via the firing probability $p_f(i,j)$.

It remains to define the lateral interaction in the subpopulation. Clearly only the fraction of neurons that fire can interact, therefore we have

$$i_{int} \quad = \quad g(\vec{\rho}_0).$$

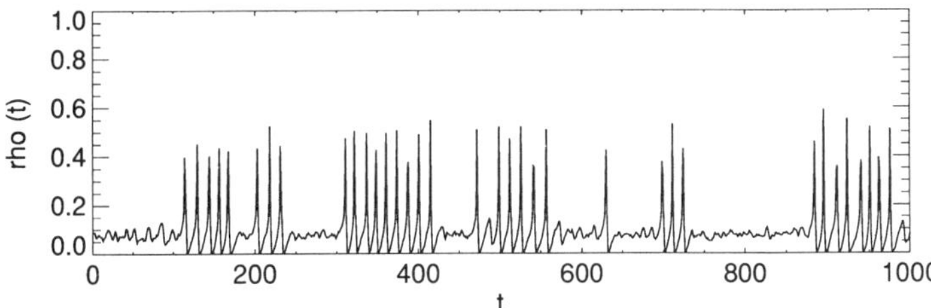

Figure 5: Switching in the assembly dynamics under external fluctuations. Note that ρ_0 denotes the time dependent firing rate.

Numerically iterating the dynamics (1) we find, that the distribution can evolve in two distinct ways, depending on the lateral interaction function g and the initialization. First $\vec{\rho}$ can relax to a fixed point, corresponding to a constant fraction of the neurons firing at a particular time. On the level of an individual neuron, this corresponds to a stochastic firing characteristics, and in the measurements this state corresponds to the irregular periods. Secondly the distribution can evolve according to a limit cycle, with a rather large fraction of the neurons in a narrow band of phases i.e. the neurons are synchronous. We find parameter combinations w_{ext}, w_{int} where both states coexist, i.e. we find bistability, if the interaction function is nonlinear, like $g(x) \propto x^2$ or $g(x) \propto x^4$. Nonlinearities of this kind can be brought about by a different type of preferred synapses with a nonlinear transmission characteristic (like an NMDA-receptor synapse) for the corticocortical projections, as compared to the thalamocortical projections. At this point we only want to make the point that our simple model system can exhibit bistability under reasonable assumptions. In the bistable regime some initializations of $\vec{\rho}$ lead to the oscillatory state, some to the stochastic state. Adding some noise to the external input the system can also switch between the two states(Fig. 5). In this way our simple local model can capture the switching phenomenon which is inherent in the experimental data [12].

6 Summary and Synthesis

We presented two complementary approaches to the dynamics of neuronal subpopulations, a phenomenological one which captures the time structure in measured spike trains and a neuronal one which provides a formal description of the dynamics of assemblies of spiking neurons. In the phenomenological approach we introduced the hidden state model which revealed that the system underlying the multi unit activities from the cat switches between states of oscillatory and stochastic activity. The analysis of the phase density dynamics showed, that bistability and switching emerges in networks of spiking neurons when the neuronal interaction is nonlinear. It remains to show that these approaches are also quantitatively consistent, i.e. that they are two sides of the same medal. Instead of a formal proof we only remark here that the parameters of the HSM can be extracted directly from the dynamics of the PDD under external noise. For this purpose one only needs to evaluate the interburst interval distribution from which P_f^b can be calculated. P_{obs} is easily estimated as the average shape of $\rho_0(t)$ between successive bursts. We find, that already this procedure gives HSMs which accurately reproduce the correlation function of the full firing dynamics $\rho_0(t)$. This means that the HSM captures relevant aspects of the assembly dynamics including the relation between the network dynamics and the contributions of single neurons.

References

[1] Gray C.M., Singer W., *Stimulus-Specific Neuronal Oscillations in Cat Visual Cortex: a Cortical Functional Unit*, Soc.Neurosci.Abstr. 13.404.3 (1989).

[2] Gray C.M., König P., Engel A.K., and Singer W., *Oscillatory Responses in Cat Visual Cortex Exhibit Inter-Columnar Synchronization which Reflects Global Stimulus Properties* Nature **338**, pp. 334-337 (1989).

[3] Eckhorn R., Bauer R., Jordan W., Brosch M., Kruse W., Munk M., and Reitboeck H.J., *Coherent Oscillations: a Mechanism of Feature Linking in the Visual Cortex?*, Biol. Cyb. **60**, pp121-130 (1988).

[4] C. v.d.Malsburg *The Correlation Theory of Brain Function* Internal Report 81-2, Max-Planck-Institute for Biophysical Chemistry, Göttingen, F.R.G. (1981).

[5] Schuster H.G. (Ed.), Nonlinear Dynamics and Neuronal Networks, VCH Weinheim, Heidelberg (1991)

[6] Pawelzik K., Bauer H.-U., Geisel T. *Switching between predictable and unpredictable states in data from cat visual cortex*, talk at CNS San Francisco 1992, to appear in the CNS Proceedings.

[7] Gray C.M., Engel A.K., König P., Singer W., *Temporal Properties of Synchronous Oscillatory Interactions in Cat Striate Cortex*, in: Nonlinear Dynamics and Neuronal Networks, Ed. H.G. Schuster, VCH Weinheim, pp. 27-55 (1991)

[8] Deppisch J., Bauer H.-U., Schillen T., König P., Pawelzik K., Geisel T., *Stochastic and Oscillatory Burst Activities*, accepted for ICANN'92, Brighton, UK. (1992).

[9] Deppisch J., Bauer H.-U., Schillen T., König P., Pawelzik K., Geisel T., *Alternating Oscillatory and Stochastic States in a Network of Spiking Neurons*, submitted to Biol.Cyb. (1992).

[10] Rabiner, L.R., *A Tutorial on Hidden-Markov Models and Selected Applications in Speech Recognition* Proc. IEEE **77**, 2 pp. 257-286 (1989).

[11] Bauer H.-U., Deppisch J., Geisel T., Pawelzik K., in preparation.

[12] Bauer H.U., Pawelzik K., *Alternating Oscillatory and Stochastic Dynamics in a Model for a Neuronal Assembly*, Physica D, submitted.

[13] Schuster H.G., Koch C., *Burst Synchronization Without Frequency-Locking in a Completely Solvable Network Model*, in Moody J.E., Hanson S.J., Lippmann R.P. (Eds.), Neural Information Processing Systems 4, p. 117, Morgan Kauffmann (1992).

Topography and Ocular Dominance with Positive Correlations

Geoffrey J. Goodhill
University of Edinburgh
Centre for Cognitive Science
2 Buccleuch Place
Edinburgh EH8 9LW
SCOTLAND
gjg@cns.ed.ac.uk

Abstract

A new computational model that addresses the formation of both topography and ocular dominance is presented. This is motivated by experimental evidence that these phenomena may be subserved by the same mechanisms. An important aspect of this model is that ocular dominance segregation can occur when input activity is both distributed, and positively correlated between the eyes. This allows investigation of the dependence of the pattern of ocular dominance stripes on the degree of correlation between the eyes: it is found that increasing correlation leads to narrower stripes. Experiments are suggested to test whether such behaviour occurs in the natural system.

1 INTRODUCTION

The development of topographic and interdigitated mappings in the nervous system has been much studied experimentally, especially in the visual system (e.g. [8, 15]). Here, each eye projects in a topographic manner to more central brain structures: i.e. neighbouring points in the eye map to neighbouring points in the brain. In addition, when fibres from the two eyes invade the same target structure, a competitive interaction often appears to take place such that eventually postsynaptic cells receive inputs from only one eye or the other, in a pattern of interdigitating "ocular dominance" stripes.

These phenomena have received a great deal of theoretical attention: several models have been proposed, each based on a different variant of a Hebb-type rule (e.g. [16, 17, 14, 13]). However, there are two aspects of the experimental data which previous models have not satisfactorily accounted for.

Firstly, experimental manipulations in the frog and goldfish have shown that when fibres from a second eye invade a region of brain which is normally innervated by only one eye, ocular dominance stripes can be formed (e.g. [2]). This suggests that ocular dominance may be a byproduct of the expression of the rules for topographic map formation, and does not require additional mechanisms [1]. However, previous models of topography have required additional implausible assumptions to account for ocular dominance (e.g. [16, 11], [17, 10]), while previous models of ocular dominance (e.g. [14]) have not simultaneously addressed the development of topography.

Secondly, the simulation results presented for most previous models of ocular dominance have used only localized rather than distributed patterns of input activity (e.g. [11]), or zero or negative correlations in activity between the two eyes (e.g. [3]). It is clear that, in reality, between-eye correlations have a *minimum* value of zero (which might be achieved for instance in the case of strabismus), and in general these correlations will be positive after eye-opening. In the cat for instance, the majority of ocular dominance segregation occurs anatomically three to six weeks after birth, whereas eye opening occurs at postnatal day 7-10.

Here I present a new model that accounts for (a) both topography and ocular dominance with the same mechanisms, and (b) ocular dominance segregation and receptive field refinement for input patterns which are both distributed, and positively correlated between the eyes.

2 OUTLINE OF THE MODEL

The model is formulated at a general enough level to be applicable to both the retinocortical and the retinotectal systems. It consists of two two dimensional sheets of input units (indexed by r) connected to one two-dimensional sheet of output units (indexed by c) by fibres with variable synaptic weights w_{cr}. It is assumed in the retinocortical case that the topography of the retina is essentially unchanged by the lateral geniculate nucleus (LGN) on its way to the cortex, and in addition, the effects of retinal and LGN processing are taken together. Thus for simplicity we refer to the input layers of the model as being retinae and the output layer as being the cortex. An earlier version of the model appeared in [4], and a fuller description can be found in [5].

Both retina and cortex are arranged in square arrays. All weights and unit activities are positive. Lateral interactions exist in the cortical sheet of a circular center-surround excitation/inhibition form, although these are not modeled explicitly. Initially there is total connectivity of random strengths between retinal and cortical units, apart from a small bias that specifies an orientation for the map. At each time step, a pattern of activity is presented by setting the activities a_r of retinal units. Each cortical unit c calculates its total input x_c according to a linear summation rule:

$$x_c = \sum_r w_{cr} a_r$$

We use assumptions similar to [9] concerning the effect of inhibitory lateral connections, to obtain the learning rule:

$$w_{cr} = w_{cr} + \alpha a_r s(c, g)$$

α is a small positive constant, g is the cortical unit with the largest input x_g, and s is the function that specifies how the activities of units c near to g decrease with distance from g. We assume s to be a gaussian function of the Euclidean distance between units in the cortical sheet, with standard deviation σ_c.

Inputs to the model are random dot patterns with short range spatial correlation introduced by convolution with a blurring function. Locally correlated patterns of activity were generated by assigning the value 0 or 1 to each pixel in each eye with a probability of 50%, and then convolving each eye with a gaussian function of standard deviation σ_r. Between-eye correlations were produced in the following way. Once each retina has been convolved individually with a gaussian function, activity a_j of each unit j in each retina is replaced with $ha_j + (1-h)a'_j$, where a'_j is the activity of the corresponding unit to j in the other eye, and h specifies the similarity between the two eyes. Thus by varying h it is possible to vary the degree of correlation between the eyes: if $h = 0$ they are uncorrelated, and if $h = 0.5$ they are perfectly correlated (i.e. the pattern of activity is identical in the two eyes).

The correlations existing in the biological system will clearly be more complicated than this. However, the simple correlational structure described above aims to capture the *key* features of the biological system: on average, cells in each retina are correlated to an extent that decreases with distance between cells, and (after eye opening) corresponding positions in the two eyes are also on the average somewhat correlated.

The sum of the weights for each postsynaptic unit is maintained at a constant fixed value. However, whereas this constraint is most usually enforced by dividing each weight by the sum of the weights for that postsynaptic unit ("divisive" normalization), it is enforced in this model by subtracting a constant amount from each weight ("subtractive" normalization), as in [13].

3 RESULTS

Typical results for the case of two positively correlated eyes are shown in figure 1. Gradually receptive fields refine over the course of development, and cortical units eventually lose connections from one or the other eye (figure 1(a-c)). After a large number of input patterns have been presented, cortical units are almost entirely monocular, and units dominant for the left and right eyes are laid out in a pattern of alternating stripes (figure 1(c)). In addition, maps from the two eyes are in register and topographic (figure 1(d-f)). The map of cortical receptive fields

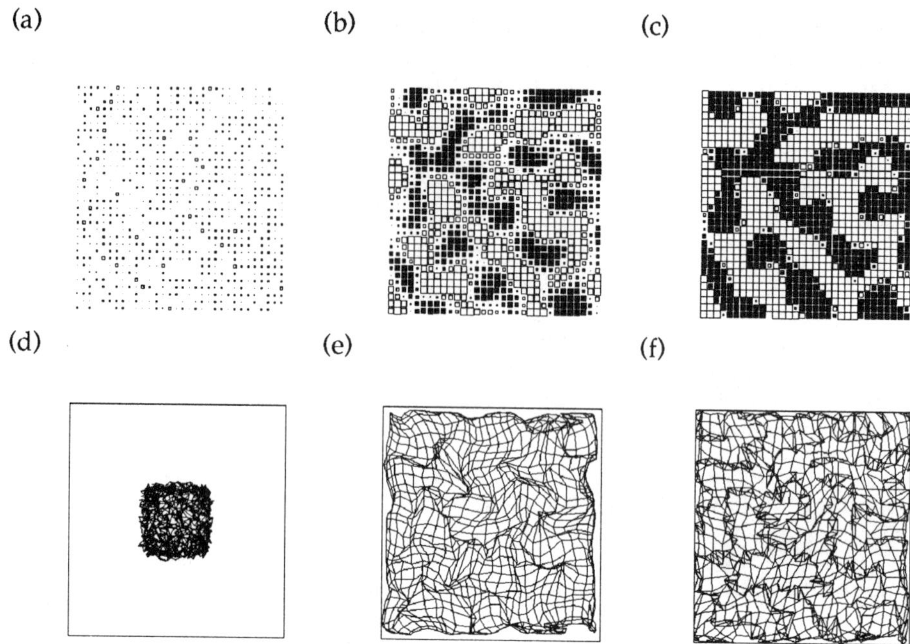

Figure 1: Typical results for two eyes. (a-c) show the ocular dominance of cortical units after 0, 50,000, and 350,000 iterations respectively. Each cortical unit is represented by a square with colour showing the eye for which it is dominant (black for right eye, white for left eye), and size showing the degree to which it is dominant. (d-f) represent cortical topography. Here the centre of mass of weights for each cortical unit is averaged over both eyes, imagining the retinae to be lying atop one another, and neighbouring units are connected by lines to form a grid. This type of picture reveals where the map is folded to take into account that the cortex must represent both eyes. It can be seen that discontinuities in terms of folds tend to follow stripe boundaries: first particular positions in one eye are represented, and then the cortex "doubles back" as its ocularity changes in order to represent corresponding positions in the other eye.

Figure 2: The receptive fields of cortical units, showing topography and eye preference. Units are coloured white if they are strongly dominant for the left eye, black if they are strongly dominant for the right eye, and grey if they are primarily binocular. "Strongly dominant" is taken to mean that at least 80% of the total weight available to a cortical unit is concentrated in one eye. Within each unit is a representation of its receptive field: there is a 16 by 16 grid within each cortical unit with each grid point representing a retinal unit, and the size of the box at each grid point encodes the strength of the connection between each retinal unit and the cortical unit. For binocular (grey) units, the larger of the two corresponding weights in the two eyes is drawn at each position, coloured white or black according to which eye that weight belongs. It can be seen that neighbouring positions in each eye tend to be represented by neighbouring cortical units, apart from discontinuities across stripe boundaries. For instance, the bottom right corner of the right retina is represented by the bottom right cortical unit, but the bottom left corner of the right retina is represented by cortical unit (3,3) (counting along and up from the bottom left corner of the cortex), since unit (1,1) represents the left retina.

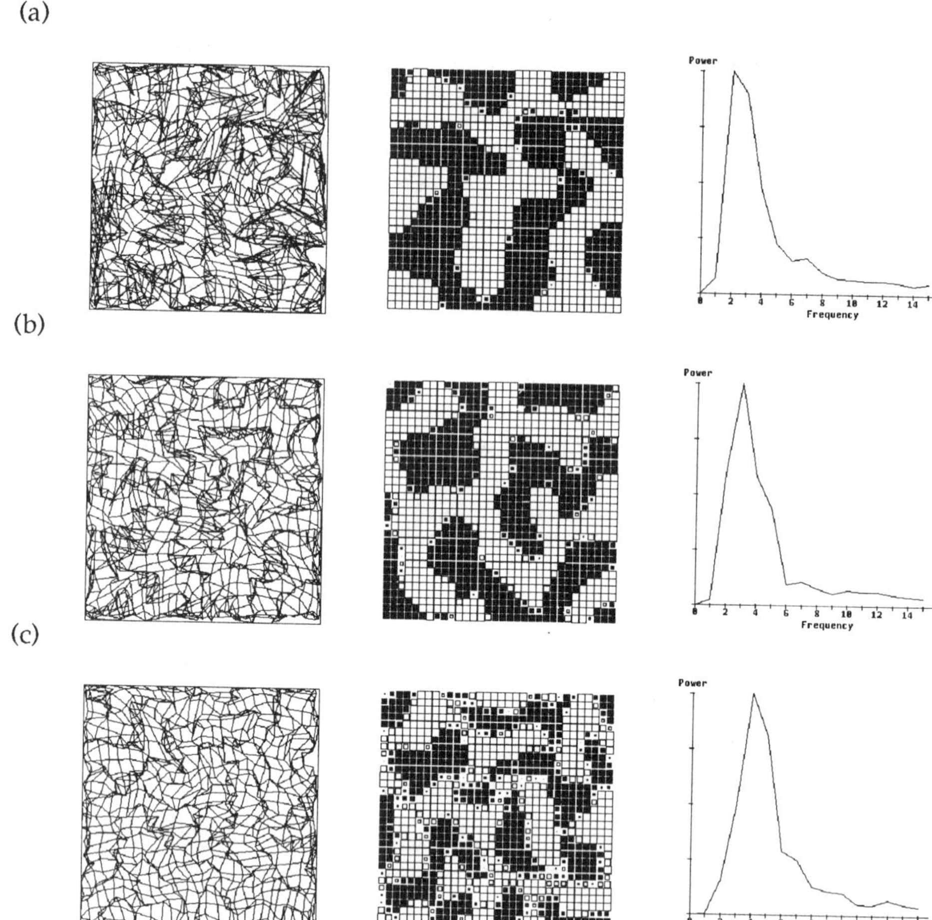

Figure 3: Effect on stripe width of the degree of correlation between the two eyes. Shown from left to right are the cortical topography averaged over both eyes, the stripe pattern, and the power spectrum of the fourier transform for each case. (a) $h = 0.0$ (b) $h = 0.1$ (c) $h = 0.2$. Note that stripe width tends to decrease as h increases, and also that the topography becomes smoother.

(figure 2) confirms that, as described for the natural system [8], there is a smooth progression of retinal position represented across a stripe, followed by a doubling back at stripe boundaries for the cortex to "pick up where it left off" in the other eye.

An important aspect of the model is that the effect on stripe width of the strength of correlation between the two eyes can be investigated, which has not been done in previous models. Figure 3 shows a series of results for the model, from which it can be seen that stronger between-eye correlations lead to narrower stripes. It is interesting to note that a similar relationship is seen in the elastic net model of topography and ocular dominance [6], even though this is formulated on a rather different mathematical basis to the model presented here.

4 DISCUSSION

It has sometimes been argued that it is not necessary to also consider the development of topography in models for ocular dominance, since in the cat for instance, topography develops first, and is established before ocular dominance segregation occurs. However, non-simultaneity of development does not imply different mechanisms. As a theoretical example, in the elastic net model [6], minimisation by gradient descent of a particular objective function produces two clear stages of development: first topography formation, then ocular dominance segregation. A similar (though less marked) effect can be seen with the present model in figure 1: the rough form of the map is established before ocular dominance segregation is complete.

Interest in the contribution to map formation and eye-specific segregation of pre-visual activity in the retina has been re-awakened recently by the finding that spontaneous retinal activity takes the form of waves sweeping across the retina in a random direction [12]. Although this finding has in turn generated a wave of theoretical activity, it is important to note that the theoretical principles of how correlated activity can guide map formation have been fairly well worked out since the 1970's [16, 11]. Discovery of the precise form that these correlations take does not invalidate earlier modelling studies.

Finally, the results for the model presented in figure 3 raise the question of whether stronger between-eye correlations lead to narrower stripes in the natural system. Perhaps the simplest way to test this experimentally would be to look for changes in stripe width in the cat after artificially induced strabismus, which severely reduces the correlations between the two eyes. Although the effect of strabismus on the degree of monocularity of cortical cells has been extensively investigated (e.g. [7]), the effect on stripe width has not been examined. Such experiments would shed light on the extent to which the periodicity of ocular dominance stripes is determined by environmental as opposed to innate factors.

Acknowledgements

This work was funded by an SERC postgraduate studentship, and an MRC/JCI postdoctoral training fellowship. I thank Harry Barrow for advice relating to this work, and David Willshaw and David Price for helpful comments on an earlier draft of this paper.

References

[1] Constantine-Paton, M. (1983). Position and proximity in the development of maps and stripes. *Trends Neurosci.* **6**, 32-36.

[2] Constantine-Paton, M. & Law, M.I. (1978). Eye-specific termination bands in tecta of three-eyed frogs. *Science*, **202**, 639-641.

[3] Cowan, J.D. & Friedman, A.E. (1991). Studies of a model for the development and regeneration of eye-brain maps. In D.S. Touretzky, ed, *Advances in Neural Information Processing Systems*, **III**, 3-10.

[4] Goodhill, G.J. (1991). Topography and ocular dominance can arise from distributed patterns of activity. *International Joint Conference on Neural Networks, Seattle, July 1991*, **II**, 623-627.

[5] Goodhill, G.J. (1991). *Correlations, Competition and Optimality: Modelling the Development of Topography and Ocular Dominance.* PhD Thesis, Sussex University.

[6] Goodhill, G.J. & Willshaw, D.J. (1990). Application of the elastic net algorithm to the formation of ocular dominance stripes. *Network*, **1**, 41-59.

[7] Hubel, D.H. & Wiesel, T.N. (1965). Binocular interaction in striate cortex of kittens reared with artificial squint. *Journal of Neurophysiology*, **28**, 1041-1059.

[8] Hubel, D.H. & Wiesel, T.N. (1977). Functional architecture of the macaque monkey visual cortex. *Proc. R. Soc. Lond. B*, **198**, 1-59.

[9] Kohonen, T. (1988). Self-organization and associative memory (3rd Edition). Springer, Berlin.

[10] Malsburg, C. von der (1979). Development of ocularity domains and growth behaviour of axon terminals. *Biol. Cybern.*, **32**, 49-62.

[11] Malsburg, C. von der & Willshaw, D.J. (1976). A mechanism for producing continuous neural mappings: ocularity dominance stripes and ordered retino-tectal projections. *Exp. Brain. Res. Supplementum 1*, 463-469.

[12] Meister, M., Wong, R.O.L., Baylor, D.A. & Shatz, C.J. (1991). Synchronous bursts of action potentials in ganglion cells of the developing mammalian retina. *Science*, **252**, 939-943.

[13] Miller, K.D., Keller, J.B. & Stryker, M.P. (1989). Ocular dominance column development: Analysis and simulation. *Science*, **245**, 605-615.

[14] Swindale, N.V. (1980). A model for the formation of ocular dominance stripes. *Proc. R. Soc. Lond. B*, **208**, 243-264.

[15] Udin, S.B. & Fawcett, J.W. (1988). Formation of topographic maps. *Ann. Rev. Neurosci.*, **11**, 289-327.

[16] Willshaw, D.J. & Malsburg, C. von der (1976). How patterned neural connections can be set up by self-organization. *Proc. R. Soc. Lond. B*, **194**, 431-445.

[17] Willshaw, D.J. & Malsburg, C. von der (1979). A marker induction mechanism for the establishment of ordered neural mappings: its application to the retinotectal problem. *Phil. Trans. Roy. Soc. B*, **287**, 203-243.

Statistical and Dynamical Interpretation of ISIH Data from Periodically Stimulated Sensory Neurons

John K. Douglass and Frank Moss
Department of Biology and Department of Physics
University of Missouri at St. Louis
St. Louis, MO 63121

Andre Longtin
Department of Physics
University of Ottawa
Ottawa, Ontario, Canada K1N 6N5

Abstract

We interpret the time interval data obtained from periodically stimulated sensory neurons in terms of two simple dynamical systems driven by noise with an embedded weak periodic function called the signal: 1) a bistable system defined by two potential wells separated by a barrier, and 2) a FitzHugh-Nagumo system. The implementation is by analog simulation: electronic circuits which mimic the dynamics. For a given signal frequency, our simulators have only two adjustable parameters, the signal and noise intensities. We show that experimental data obtained from the periodically stimulated mechanoreceptor in the crayfish tailfan can be accurately approximated by these simulations. Finally, we discuss *stochastic resonance* in the two models.

1 INTRODUCTION

It is well known that sensory information is transmitted to the brain using a code which must be based on the time intervals between neural firing events or the mean firing rate. However, in any collection of such data, and even when the sensory system is stimulated with a periodic signal, statistical analyses have shown that a significant fraction of the intervals are random, having no coherent relationship to the stimulus. We call this component the "noise". It is clear that coherent and incoherent subsets of such data must be separated. Moreover, the noise intensity depends upon the stimulus intensity in a nonlinear manner through, for example, efferent connections in the visual system (Kaplan and Barlow, 1980) and is often much larger (sometimes several orders of magnitude larger!) than can be accounted for by equilibrium statistical mechanics (Denk and Webb, 1992). Evidence that the noise in networks of neurons can dynamically alter the properties of the membrane potential and time constants has also been accumulated (Kaplan and Barlow, 1976; Treutlein and Schulten, 1985; Bernander, Koch and Douglas, 1992). Recently, based on comparisons of interspike interval histograms (ISIH's) obtained from passive analog simulations of simple bistable systems, with those from auditory neurons, it was suggested that the noise intensity may play a critical role in the ability of the living system to sense the stimulus intensity (Longtin, Bulsara and Moss, 1991). In this work, it is shown that in the simulations, ISIH's are reproduced provided that noise is added to a weak signal, i.e. one that cannot cause firing by itself. All of these processes are essentially nonlinear, and they indicate the ultimate futility of simply measuring the "background spontaneous rate" and later subtracting it from spike rates obtained with a stimulus applied. Indeed, they raise serious doubts regarding the applicability of any *linear* transform theory to neural problems.

In this paper, we investigate the possibility that the noise can enhance the ability of a sensory neuron to transmit information about periodic stimuli. The present study relies on two objects, the ISIH and the power spectrum, both familiar measurements in electrophysiology. These are obtained from analog simulations of two simple dynamical systems, 1) the overdamped motion of a particle in a bistable, quartic potential; and 2) the FitzHugh-Nagumo model. The results of these simulations are compared with those from experiments on the mechanoreceptor in the tailfan of the crayfish *Procambarus clarkii*.

2 THE ANALOG SIMULATOR

Previously, we made detailed comparisons of ISIH's obtained from a variety of sensory modalities (Longtin, Bulsara and Moss, 1991) with those measured on the bistable system,

$$\dot{x} = x - x^3 + \xi(t) + \epsilon \sin(\omega t) \tag{1}$$

where ϵ is the stimulus intensity, and ξ is a quasi white, Gaussian noise, defined by $\langle \xi(t)\xi(s) \rangle = (D/\tau)\exp(-|t-s|/\tau)$ with D the noise intensity and τ a (dimensionless) noise correlation time. Quasi white means that the actual noise correlation time is at least one order of magnitude smaller than the integrator time constant (the "clock" by which the simulator measures time). It was shown that the neurophysiological data could be satisfactorily matched by data from the simulation by adjusting *either* the noise intensity *or* the stimulus intensity provided that the other quantity had a value not very different from the height of the potential barrier. Moreover, bistable dynamical systems of the type represented by Eq. (1) (and many others as well) have been frequently used to demonstrate *stochastic resonance* (SR), an essentially **nonlinear** process whereby the signal-to-noise ratio (SNR) of a weak signal can be enhanced by the noise. Below we show that SR can be demonstrated in a typical excitable system of the type often used to model sensory neurons. This raises a tantalizing question: *can SR be discovered as a naturally occurring phenomenon in living systems?* More information can be found in a recent review and workshop proceedings (Moss, 1993; Chialvo and Apkarian, 1993; Longtin, 1993).

There is, however, a significant difference between the dynamics represented by Eq. (1) and the more usual neuron models which are excitable systems. A simple example of the latter is the FitzHugh-Nagumo (FN) model, the ISIH's of which have recently been studied (Longtin, 1993). The FN model is an excitable system controlled by a bifurcation parameter. When the voltage variable is perturbed past a certain boundary, a large excursion, identified with a neural firing event, occurs. Thus a *deterministic* refractory period is built into the model as the time required for the execution of a single firing event. By contrast, in the bistable system, a firing event is represented by the transition from well A to well B. Before another firing can occur, the system must be reset by a reverse transition from B to A, which is essentially stochastic. The bistable system thus exhibits *a statistical distribution* of refractory periods. The FN system is not bistable, but, depending on the value of the bifurcation parameter, it can be either periodically firing (oscillating) or residing on a fixed point. The FN model used here is defined by (Longtin, 1993),

$$\dot{v} = v(v - 0.5)(1 - v) - w + \xi(t), \quad (2)$$

$$\dot{w} = v - w - [b + \epsilon \sin(\omega t)], \quad (3)$$

where v is the fast variable (action potential) to which the noise ξ is added, w is the recovery variable to which the signal is added, and b is the bifurcation parameter. The range of behaviors is given by: b >0.65, fixed point and $b \geq 0.65$, oscillating. We operate far into the fixed point regime at $b = 0.9$, so that bursts of sustained oscillations do not occur. Thus single spikes at more-or-less random times but with some coherence with the signal are generated. A schematic diagram of the analog simulator is shown in Fig. 1. The simulator is constructed of standard electronic chips: voltage multipliers (X) and operational

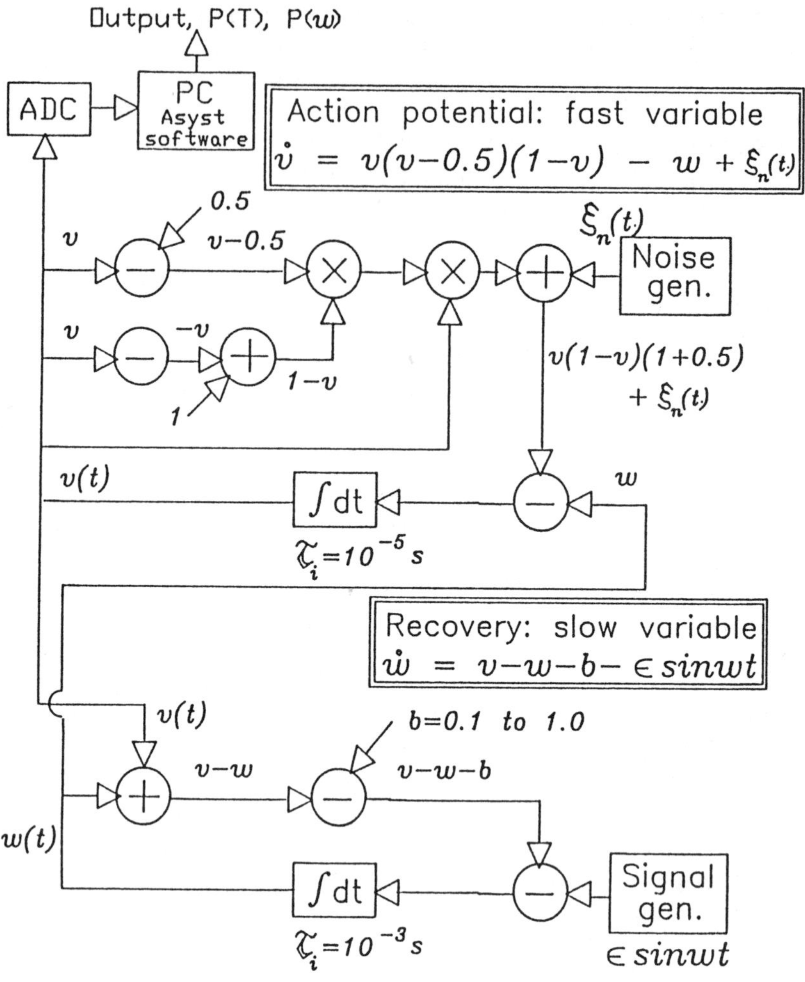

Fig.1 Analog simulator of FitzHugh-Nagumo model. The characteristic response times are determined by the integrator time constants as shown. The noise correlation time was $\tau_n = 10^{-5}$ s.

amplifier summers (±). The fast variable, $v(t)$, was digitized and analyzed for the ISIH and the power spectrum by the PC shown. Note that the noise correlation time, 10^{-5} s, is equal to the fast variable integrator time constant and is much larger than the slow variable time constant. This noise is, therefore, colored. Analog simulator designs, nonlinear experiments and colored noise have recently been reviewed (Moss and McClintock, 1989). Below we compare data from this simulator with electrophysiological data from the crayfish.

3 EXPERIMENTS WITH CRAYFISH MECHANORECEPTOR CELLS

Single hair mechanoreceptor cells of the crayfish tailfan represent a simple and robust system lacking known efferents. A simple system is necessary, since we are searching for a specific dynamical behavior which might be masked in a more complex physiology. In this system, small motions of the hairs (as small as a few tens of nanometers) are transduced into spike trains which travel up the sensory neuron to the caudal ganglion. These neurons show a range of spontaneous firing rates (internal noise). In this experiment, a neuron with a relatively high internal noise was chosen. Other experiments and more details are described elsewhere (Bulsara, Douglass and Moss, 1993). The preparation consisted of a piece of the tailfan from which the sensory nerve bundle and ganglion were exposed surgically. This appendage was sinusoidally moved through the saline solution by an electromagnetic transducer. Extracellular recordings from an identified hair cell were made using standard methods. The preparations typically persisted in good physiological condition for 8 to 12 hours. An example ISIH is shown in the upper panel of Fig. 2. The stimulus period was, $T_0 = 14\ ms$. Note the peak sequence at the integer multiples of T_0 (Longtin, *et al*, 1991). This ISIH was measured in about 15 minutes for which about $8K$ spikes were obtained. An ISIH obtained from the FN simulator in the same time and including about the same number of spikes is shown in the lower panel. The similarity demonstrates that neurophysiological ISIH's can easily be mimicked with FN models as well as with bistable models. Our model is also able to reproduce non renewal effects (data not shown) which occur at high frequency and/or low stimulus or noise intensity, and for which the first peak in the ISIH is *not* the one of maximum amplitude.

We turn now to the question of whether SR, based on the power spectrum, can be demonstrated in such excitable systems. The power spectrum typically shows a sharp peak due to the signal at frequency ω_0, riding on a broad noise background. An example, measured on the FN simulator, is shown in the left panel in Fig. 3. This spectrum was obtained for a constant signal intensity set just above threshold and for the stated external noise intensity. The SNR, in decibels, is defined as the ratio of the strength $S(\omega)$ of the signal feature to the noise amplitude, $N(\omega)$, measured at the base of the signal feature: SNR = 10 $\log_{10} S/N$. The panel on the right of Fig. 3 shows the SNR's obtained from a large number of such power spectra, each measured for a different noise intensity. Clearly there is an optimal noise intensity which maximizes the SNR. This is, to our knowledge, the first demonstration of SR based on the power spectra in an excitable system. Just as for the bistable systems (Moss, 1993), when the external noise intensity is too low, the signal is not "sampled" frequently enough and the SNR is low. By contrast, when the noise intensity is too

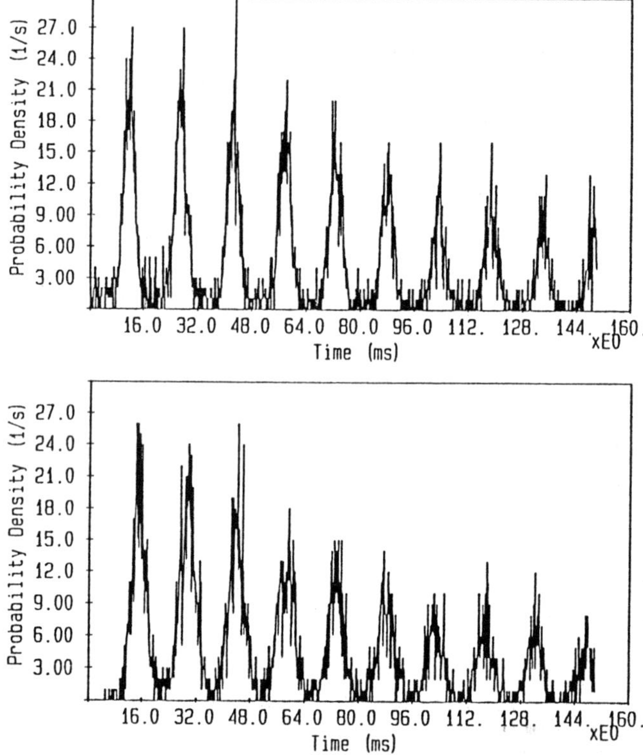

Fig. 2. ISIH's obtained from the crayfish stimulated at 68.6 Hz (upper); and the FN simulator driven at the same frequency with $b = 0.9$, $V_{noise} = 0.022\ V_{rms}$, and $V_{sig} = 0.53\ V_{rms}$ (lower).

high, the signal becomes randomized. The occurrence of a maximum in the SNR is thus motivated. SR has also been studied using well residence time probability densities, which are analogous to the physiological ISIH's (Longtin, *el al*, 1991), and was further studied in the FN system (Longtin, 1993). In these cases, it is observed that the individual peak heights pass through maxima as the noise intensity is varied, thus demonstrating SR, similar to that shown in Fig. 3, based on the ISIH (or residence time probability density).

4 DISCUSSION

We have shown that physiological measurements such as the familiar ISIH patterns obtained from periodically stimulated sensory neurons can be easily mimicked by analog simulations of simple noisy systems, in particular bistable sys-

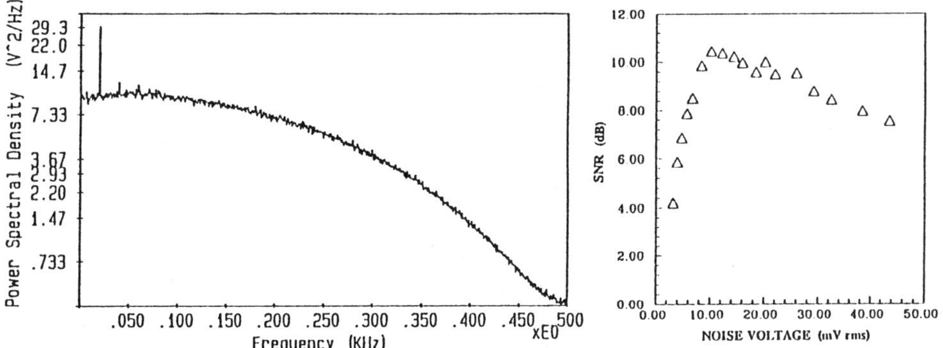

Fig. 3. A power spectrum from the FN simulator stimulated by a 20 Hz signal for $b = 0.9$, $\epsilon = 0.25\ V$ and $V_{noise} = 0.021\ V_{rms}$ (left). The SNR's versus noise voltage measured in the FN system showing SR at $V_{noise} \simeq 10\ mV_{rms}$ (right). Similar SR results based on the ISIH have been obtained by Longtin (1993) and by Chialvo and Apkarian (1993).

tems for which the refractory period is strictly stochastic and excitable systems for which the refractory period is deterministic. Further, we have shown that SR, based on SNR's obtained from the power spectrum, can be demonstrated for the FitzHugh-Nagumo model. It is worth emphasizing that these results are possible only because the systems are inherently nonlinear. The signal alone is too weak to cause firing events in either the bistable or the excitable models. Thus these results suggest that biological systems may be able to detect weak stimuli in the presence of background noise which they could not otherwise detect. Careful behavioral studies will be necessary to decide this question, however, a recent and interesting psychophysics experiment using human interpretations of ambiguous figures, presented in sequences with both coherent and random components points directly to this possibility (Chialvo and Apkarian, 1993).

Acknowledgements

This work was supported by the Office of Naval Research grant N00014-92-J-1235 and by NSERC (Canada).

References

Bernander, Ö, Koch, C. and Douglas R. (1992) Network activity determines spatio-temporal integration in single cells, in *Advances in Neural Information Processing Systems 3*; R. Lippman, J. Moody and D. Touretzky, editors; Morgan Kaufmann, San Mateo, CA. 43-50

Bulsara, A., Douglass, J. and Moss, F. (1993) Nonlinear Resonance: Noise-assisted information processing in physical and neurophysiological systems. Nav. Res. Rev. in press.

Chialvo, D. and Apkarian, V. (1993) Modulated noisy biological dynamics: three examples; in *Proceedings of the NATO ARW on Stochastic Resonance in Physics and Biology*, edited by F. Moss, A. Bulsara, and M. F. Shlesinger, J. Stat. Phys. **70**, forthcoming

Denk, W. and Webb, W. (1992) Forward and reverse transduction at the limit of sensitivity studied by correlating electrical and mechanical fluctuations in frog saccular hair cells. Hear. Res. **60**, 89-102.

Kaplan, E. and Barlow, R. (1976) Energy, quanta and *Limulus* vision. Vision Res. **16**, 745-751

Kaplan, E. and Barlow, R. (1980) Circadian clock in *Limulus* brain increases response and decreases noise of retinal photoreceptors. Nature **286**, 393

Longtin, A. (1993) Stochastic resonance in neuron models, in *Proceedings of the NATO ARW on Stochastic Resonance in Physics and Biology*, edited by F. Moss, A. Bulsara, and M. F. Shlesinger, J. Stat. Phys. **70**, forthcoming

Longtin, *A*, Bulsara, *A* and Moss F. (1991) Time interval sequences in bistable systems and the noise-induced transmission of information by sensory neurons. Phys. Rev. Lett. **67**, 656-659

Moss, F. (1993) Stochastic resonance: from the ice ages to the monkey's ear; in, *Some Problems in Statistical Physics*, edited by G. H. Weiss, SIAM, Philadelphia, in press

Moss, F. and McClintock, P.V.E. editors (1989) *Noise in Nonlinear Dynamical Systems, Vols. 1 - 3*, Cambridge University Press.

Treutlein, H. and Schulten, K. (1985) Noise induced limit cycles of the Bonhoeffer-Van der Pol model of neural pulses. Ber. Bunsenges. Phys. Chem. **89**, 710.

Spiral Waves in Integrate–and–Fire Neural Networks

John G. Milton
Department of Neurology
The University of Chicago
Chicago, IL 60637

Po Hsiang Chu
Department of Computer Science
DePaul University
Chicago, IL 60614

Jack D. Cowan
Department of Mathematics
The University of Chicago
Chicago, IL 60637

Abstract

The formation of propagating spiral waves is studied in a randomly connected neural network composed of integrate–and–fire neurons with recovery period and excitatory connections using computer simulations. Network activity is initiated by periodic stimulation at a single point. The results suggest that spiral waves can arise in such a network via a sub–critical Hopf bifurcation.

1 Introduction

In neural networks activity propagates through populations, or layers, of neurons. This propagation can be monitored as an evolution of spatial patterns of activity. Thirty years ago, computer simulations on the spread of activity through 2–D randomly connected networks demonstrated that a variety of complex spatio–temporal patterns can be generated including target waves and spirals (Beurle, 1956, 1962; Farley and Clark, 1961; Farley, 1965). The networks studied by these investigators correspond to inhomogeneous excitable media in which the probability of interneuronal connectivity decreases exponentially with distance. Although travelling spiral waves can readily be formed in excitable media by the introduction of non–uniform initial conditions (e.g. Winfree, 1987), this approach is not suitable for the study and classification of the dynamics associated with the onset of spiral wave formation. Here we show that spiral waves can "spontaneously" arise from target waves in a neural network in which activity is initiated by periodic stimulation at a single point. In particular, the onset of spiral wave formation appears to occur via a sub–critical Hopf bifurcation.

2 Methods

Computer simulations were used to simulate the propagation of activity from a centrally placed source in a neural network containing 100 × 100 neurons arranged on a square lattice with excitatory interactions. At $t = 0$ all neurons were at rest except the source. There were free boundary conditions and all simulations were performed on a SUN SPARC 1+ computer.

The network was constructed by assuming that the probability, λ, of interneuronal connectivity was an exponential decreasing function of distance, i.e.

$$\lambda = \beta \exp(-\alpha |r|)$$

where $\alpha = 0.6, \beta = 1.5$ are constants and $|r|$ is the euclidean interneuronal distance (on average each neuron makes 24 connections and ~ 1.3 connections per neuron, i.e. multiple connections occur). Once the connectivity was determined it remained fixed throughout the simulation.

The dynamics of each neuron were represented by an integrate–and–fire model possessing a "leaky" membrane potential and an absolute (1 time step) and relative refractory or recovery period as described previously (Beurle, 1962; Farley, 1965; Farley and Clark, 1961): the membrane and threshold decay constants were, respectively, $k_m = 0.3\ \text{msec}^{-1}$, $k_\theta = 0.03\ \text{msec}^{-1}$. The time step of the network was taken as 1 msec and it was assumed that during this time a neuron transmits excitation to all other neurons connected to it.

3 Results

We illustrate the dynamics of a particular network as a function of the magnitude of the excitatory interneuronal excitation, E, when all other parameters are fixed. When $E < 0.2$ no activity propagates from the central source. For $0.2 \leq E < 0.58$ target waves regularly emanate from the centrally placed source (Figure 1a). For $E \geq 0.58$ the activity patterns, once established, persisted even when the source was turned off. Complex spiral waves occurred when $0.58 \leq E < 0.63$ (Figures 1b–1d). In these cases spiral meandering, spiral tip break–up and the formation of new spirals (some with multiple arms) occur continuously. Eventually the spirals tend to migrate out of the network. For $E \geq 0.63$ only disorganized spatial patterns occurred without clearly distinguishable wave fronts, except initially (Figures 1e–f).

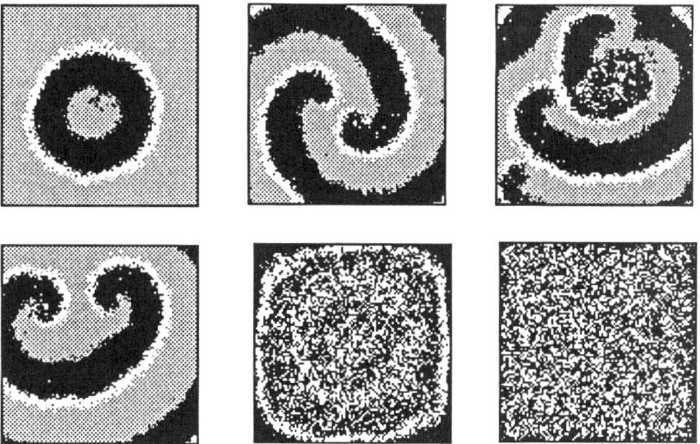

Figure 1: Representative examples of the spatial pattern of neural activity as a function of E:(a) $E = 0.45$, (b – e) $E = 0.58$ and (f) $E = 0.72$. Color code: gray = quiescent, white = activated, black = relatively refractory. See text for details.

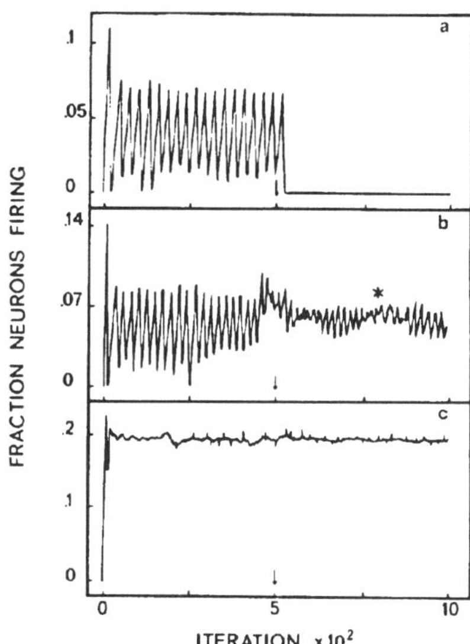

Figure 2: Plot of the fraction of neurons firing per unit time for different values of E: (a) 0.45, (b) 0.58, and (c) 0.72. At t = 0 all neurons except the central source are quiescent. At t = 500 (indicated by ↓) the source is shut off. The region indicated by (∗) corresponds to an epoch in which spiral tip breakup occurs.

The temporal dynamics of the network can be examined by plotting the fraction F of neurons that fire as a function of time. As E is increased through target waves (Figure 2a) to spiral waves (Figure 2b) to disorganized patterns (Figure 2c), the fluctuations in F become less regular, the mean value increases and the amplitude decreases. On closer inspection it can be seen that during spiral wave propagation (Figure 2b) the time series for F undergoes amplitude modulation as reported previously (Farley, 1965). The interval of low amplitude, very irregular fluctuations in F ($*$ in Figure 2b) corresponds to a period of spiral tip breakup (Figure 1c).

The appearance of spiral waves is typically preceded by 20–30 target waves. The formation of a spiral wave appears to occur in two steps. First there is an increase in the minimum value of F which begins at $t \sim 420$ and more abruptly occurs at $t \sim 460$ (Figure 2b). The target waves first become asymmetric and then activity propagates from the source region without the more centrally located neurons first entering the quisecent state (Figure 3c). At this time the spatially coherent wave front of the target waves becomes replaced by a disordered noncoherent distribution of active and refractory neurons. Secondly, the dispersed network activity begins to coalesce (Figures 3c and 3d) until at $t \sim 536$ the first identifiable spiral occurs (Figure 3e).

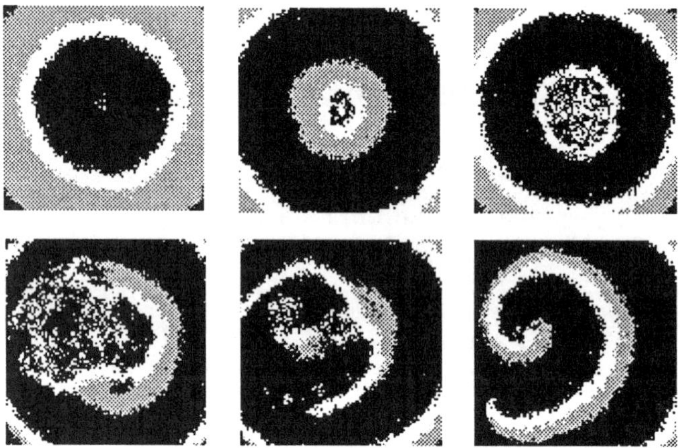

Figure 3: The fraction of neurons firing per unit time, for differing values of generation time t: (a) 175, (b) 345, (c) 465, (d) 503 (e) 536, and (f) 749. At t = 0 all neurons except the central source are quiescent.

It was found that only 4 out of 20 networks constructed with the same α, β produced spiral waves for $E = 0.58$ with periodic central point stimulation (simulations, in some cases, ran up to 50,000 generations). However, for all 20 networks, spiral waves could be obtained by the use of non-uniform initial conditions. Moreover, for those networks in which spiral waves occurred, the generation at which they formed differed. These observations emphasize that small fluctuations in the local connectivity of neurons likely play a major role in governing the dynamics of the network.

4 Discussion

Self-maintaining spiral waves can arise in an inhomogeneous neural network with uniform initial conditions. Initially well-formed target waves emanate periodically from the centrally placed source. Eventually, provided that E is in a critical range (Figures 1 & 3), the target waves may break up and be replaced by spiral waves. The necessary conditions for spiral wave formation are that: 1) the network be sufficiently tightly connected (Farley, 1965; Farley and Clark, 1961) and 2) the probability of interneuronal connectivity should decrease with distance (unpublished observations). As the network is made more tightly connected the probability that self-maintained activity arises increases provided that E is in the appropriate range (unpublished observations). These criteria are not sufficient to ensure that self-maintained activity, including spiral waves, will form in a given realization of the neural network. It has previously been shown that partially formed spiral-like waves can arise from periodic point stimulation in a model excitable media in which the inhomogeneity arises from a dispersion of refractory times, k_θ^{-1} (Kaplan, et al, 1988).

Integrate-and-fire neural networks have two stable states: a state in which all neurons are at rest, another associated with spiral waves. Target waves represent a transient response to perturbations away from the stable rest state. Since the neurons have memory (i.e. there is a relative refractory state with $k_\theta << k_m$), the mean threshold and membrane potential of the network evolve with time. As a consequence the mean fraction of firing neurons slowly increases (Figure 2b). Our simulations suggest that at some point, provided that the connectivity of the network is suitable, the rest state suddenly becomes unstable and is replaced by a stable spiral wave. This exchange of stability is typical of a sub-critical Hopf bifurcation.

Although complex, but organized, spatio-temporal patterns of spreading activity can readily be generated by a randomly connected neural network, the significance of these phenomena, if any, is not presently clear. On the one hand it is not difficult to imagine that these spatio-temporal dynamics could be related to phenomena ranging from the generation of the EEG, to the spread of epileptic and migraine related activity and the transmission of visual images in the cortex to the formation of patterns and learning by artificial neural networks. On the other hand, the occurence of such phenomena in artificial neural nets could conceivably hinder efficient learning, for example, by slowing convergence. Continued study of the properties of these networks will clearly be necessary before these issues can be resolved.

Acknowledgements

The authors acknowledge useful discussions with Drs. G. B. Ermentrout, L. Glass and D. Kaplan and financial support from the National Institutes of Health (JM), the Brain Research Foundation (JDC, JM), and the Office of Naval Research (JDC).

References

R. L. Beurle. (1956) Properties of a mass of cells capable of regenerating pulses. *Phil. Trans. Roy. Soc. Lond.* **240 B**, 55–94.

R. L. Beurle. (1962) Functional organization in random networks. In *Principles of Self–Organization*, H. v. Foerster and G. W. Zopf, eds., pp 291–314. New York, Pergamon Press.

B. G. Farley. (1965) A neuronal network model and the "slow potentials" of electrophysiology. *Comp. in Biomed. Res.* **2**, 265–294.

B. G. Farley & W. A. Clark. (1961) Activity in networks of neuron–like elements. In *Information Theory*, C. Cherry, ed., pp 242–251. Washington, Butterworths.

D. T. Kaplan, J. M.Smith,B. E. H. Saxberg & R. J. Cohen. (1988) Nonlinear dynamics in cardiac conduction. *Math. Biosci.* **90**, 19–48.

A. T. Winfree. (1987) *When Time Breaks Down*, Princeton University Press, Princeton, N.J.

Parameterising Feature Sensitive Cell Formation in Linsker Networks in the Auditory System

Lance C. Walton
University of Kent at Canterbury
Canterbury
Kent
England

David L. Bisset
University of Kent at Canterbury
Canterbury
Kent
England

Abstract

This paper examines and extends the work of Linsker (1986) on self organising feature detectors. Linsker concentrates on the visual processing system, but infers that the weak assumptions made will allow the model to be used in the processing of other sensory information. This claim is examined here, with special attention paid to the auditory system, where there is much lower connectivity and therefore more statistical variability. On-line training is utilised, to obtain an idea of training times. These are then compared to the time available to pre-natal mammals for the formation of feature sensitive cells.

1 INTRODUCTION

Within the last thirty years, a great deal of research has been carried out in an attempt to understand the development of cells in the pathways between the sensory apparatus and the cortex in mammals. For example, theories for the development of feature detectors were forwarded by Nass and Cooper (1975), by Grossberg (1976) and more recently Obermayer et al (1990).

Hubel and Wiesel (1961) established the existence of several different types of feature sensitive cell in the visual cortex of cats. Various subsequent experiments have shown that a considerable amount of development takes place before birth (i.e. without environmental input). This must either be dependent on a genetic predispostion for individual cells to develop in an appropriate way without external influence, or some low level rules sufficient to create the required cell morphologies in the presence of random action potentials.

Although there is a great deal of *a priori* information concerning axon growth and synapse arborisation (governed by chemical means in the brain), it is difficult to conceive of a biological system that could use genetic information to directly manipulate the spatial information about the pre-synaptic target with respect to the axon with which the synapse is made. However, there is considerable random activity in the sensory apparatus that could be used to effect synaptic development.

Various authors have constructed models that deal with different aspects of self-organisation of this kind and some have pointed out the value of these types of cells in pattern classification problems (Grossberg 1976), but either the biological plausibility of these models is questionable, or the subject of pre-natal development is not addressed (i.e. without environmental input).

In this paper, the networks of Linsker (1986) will be examined. Although these networks have been analysed quite extensively by Linsker, and also by Mackay and Miller (1990), the biological aspects of parameter ranges and choices have only been touched upon. It is our aim in this paper, to add further detail in this area by examining the one-dimensional case which represents the auditory pathways.

2 LINSKER NETWORKS

The network is based on a Multi Layer Perceptron, with feed forward connections in all layers, and lateral connections (inhibition and excitation) in higher layers. The neural outputs are sums of the weighted inputs, and the weights develop according to a constrained Hebbian Rule. Each layer is lettered for reference starting from A and subsequent layers are lettered B,C,D etc. The superscript M will be used to refer to an arbitrary layer, and L is used to refer to the previous layer. Each layer has a set of parameters which are the same for all neurons in that layer. Connectivity is random but is based on a Gaussian density distribution ($exp(-r^2/r_M^2)$), where r_M is the arbor radius for layer M.

Each layer is a rectangular array of neurons (or vector of neurons for the one dimensional case). The layers are assumed to be large enough so that edge effects are not important or do not occur. Layers develop one at a time starting from the B layer. The A layer is an input layer, which is divided into boxes, within each of which activity is uniform. This is biologically realistic, since sensory neurons fan out to a number of cells (an average of 10 in the cochlea) each of which only take input from one sensory cell. Hence the input layer for the network acts like a layer of tonotopically organised neurons.

3 NETWORK DEVELOPMENT

The output of a neuron in layer M is given by

$$F_n^{M\pi} = R_a + R_b.\sum_j c_{nj} F_{pre(nj)}^{L\pi} \tag{1}$$

Where,

π indexes a pattern presentation,

The subscript n is used to index the M layer neurons,

R_a, R_b are layer parameters,

$F_{pre(nj)}^{L\pi}$ is the output of the L layer neuron which is pre-synaptic to the j'th input of the n'th M layer neuron.

The synaptic weights develop according to a constrained Hebbian learning rule,

$$(\triangle c_{ni})^\pi = k_a + k_b.(F_n^{M\pi} - F_0^M).(F_{pre(ni)}^{L\pi} - F_0^L) \tag{2}$$

Where,

$(\triangle c_{ni})^\pi$ is the change in the i'th weight of neuron n,

k_a, k_b, F_0^M, F_0^L are layer parameters.

Synaptic weights are constrained to lie within the range $(n_{em} - 1, n_{em})$. (In this work, $n_{em} = 0.5$)

Linsker (1986a) derives an Ensemble Averaged Development equation which shows how development depends on the parameters, and how correlations develop between spatially proximate neurons in layers beyond the first. In so doing, the number of parameters is reduced from five per layer to two per layer, and therefore the equation is a very useful aid in understanding the self-organising nature of this model. The development equation is

$$\dot{c_{ni}} = K_1 + K_2.\bar{c_n} + \frac{\sum_j Q_{pre(ni).pre(nj)}^L . c_{nj}}{N_M} \tag{3}$$

$$Q_{ij}^L \equiv \frac{< (F_i^{L\pi} - \bar{F^L}).(F_j^{L\pi} - \bar{F^L}) >}{f_0^2} \tag{4}$$

Where,

N_M is the number of synaptic connections to an M layer neuron,

$\bar{F^L}$ is the average output activity in the L layer,

$$K_1 = \frac{k_a + k_b.(R_a - F_0^M).(\bar{F^L} - F_0^L)}{N_M k_b R_b f_0^2} \tag{5}$$

$$K_2 = \frac{\bar{F^L}.(\bar{F^L} - F_0^L)}{f_0^2} \tag{6}$$

f_0^2 is a unit of activity used to normalise the two point correlation function Q_{ij}^L. In this work f_0^2 is chosen to set $Q_{ii}^L = 1$

Angle brackets denote an average taken over the ensemble of input patterns.

4 MORPHOLOGICAL REGIMES

From equation 3, an expression can be found for the average weight value $\bar{c}$ in a layer, and therefore certain properties of the system can be described. Although Mackay and Miller (1990) have described the regimes with the aid of eigenvalues and eigenfunctions, there is a much simpler method which will provide the same information.

For an all-excitatory (AE) layer, the average weight value is equal to n_{em}. Since all weights are equal to n_{em}, the summation in equation 3 can be re-written $n_{em}.\sum_j Q^L_{pre(ni).pre(nj)} = n_{em}.N_M.\bar{q}$, where $\bar{q} = \frac{r_B}{2.N_C.\sqrt{r_C^2+r_B^2}}$.

A similar expression can be found for all-inhibitory (AI) layers, and therefore the $K_1 - K_2$ plane can be sub-divided into three regions which will yield AE cells, AI cells, and mixed-mode cells (see figure 1).

The plane can be divided further for the mixed-mode cell type in the C layer. On-center and off-center cells develop close to the AE and AI boundaries respectively. Mackay and Miller have shown why these cells develop and have placed a theoretical lower bound on $\bar{c}$ which agrees with experimental data. However, in so doing the effect of the intercept on the K_2 axis was deemed small, due to a large number of synaptic connections. This approximation depends upon the large number of connections between the B and C layers. In the auditory case, the number of connections is smaller, and it is possible that this assumption no longer holds.

From equation 3, it can be seen that movement into the On-Centre region from the AE region, causes the value of $\sum_j Q^L_{pre(ni).pre(nj)}.c_{nj}$ to decrease. This has the effect of moving the intercept of the constant $\bar{c}$ line from $K_2 = \bar{q}$ towards $K_2 = 0$. K_2 finally reaches 0 when $\bar{c} = 0$, and then begins to move back towards $\bar{q}$ as the AI regime is approached.

This has two potentially important effects. Firstly, it means that the tolerance of K_2 varies with K_1; for a particular value of K_1, there are upper and lower limits on the value of K_2 which will allow maturation of on-center cells. This range of values (i.e. the difference between the limits) varies in a linear way with K_1, but the ratio of the range to a value of K_2 which is within the range (i.e. the center value) is not linear with K_1. Here, tolerance is defined as that ratio. Secondly, there is a region of negative K_2 where the nature of the cell morphology which will be produced is unknown.

It is therefore important that K_2 should be larger than this value in order to produce On-Center or Off-Center cells reliably. Mackay and Miller use $|K_2| \to \infty$ in their analysis. Unfortunately, this would require the fundamental network parameter $F_0^L \to \infty$ from equation 6, and therefore is an unsuitable choice. It is reasonable to assume that F_0^L is of the same order as $\bar{F^L}$, and hence an order for K_2 can be established. For a concrete example, assume inputs are binary (giving $Q^L_{ii} = 0.25$) and $F_0^L = \bar{F^L} \times 1.2$, this will ensure $K_2 < 0$ (equation 6) while adhering to the assumption made above. Equation 6 now gives the order for $K_2 = 0.2$.

To find the value of $\bar{q}$, which will place a lower bound on $|K_2|$, a particular system should be chosen. The auditory system is chosen here.

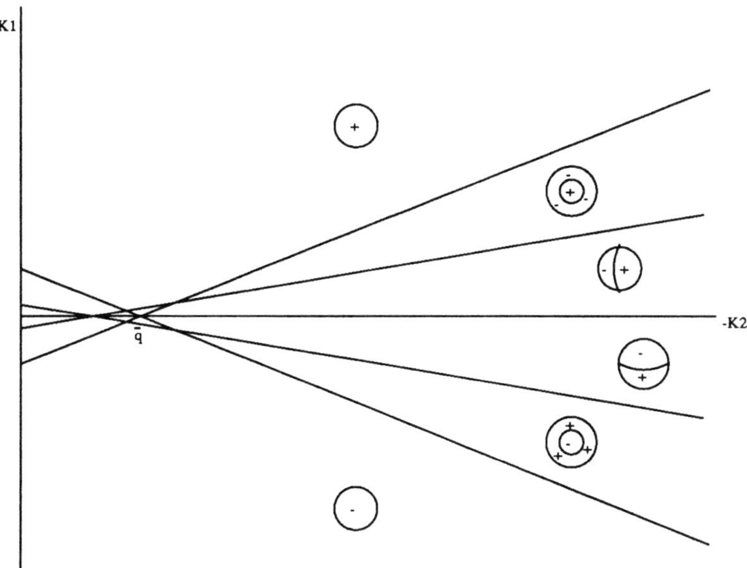

Figure 1: Graph of Morphological Regions for C Layer

There are approximately 3000 inner hair cells in the cochlea, each of which fans out to an average of 10 neurons (which sets our box size $\rho = 10$). These neurons take input from only one hair cell. The anteroventral cochlea nucleus takes input from this layer of cells, with a fan in $N_B \approx 50$ (c.f. the value of $N_B = 1000$ in Linsker (1986a)). The assumption is made that the three sections of the cochlea nucleus each contain approximately the same number of cells. With this smaller number of connections, the correlation function for this layer is somewhat coarser, and does not follow the theoretical curve for the continuum limit so well.

In addition, the on-center cells found in the posteroventral cochlea nucleus and the dorsal nucleus have centres with a tuning curve response Q of about 2.5 which corresponds to about 2000 B layer cells. If it is assumed that the surround of the cell is half the width of the core, then there is a total $r_C \approx 3000$ neurons. Simulations here use $N_C = 100$ which is a realistic number of connections in the context of a one-dimensional network.

In general, the arbor radius increases as layers become closer to the cortex. From Linsker, $r_C/r_B = 3$. r_B is therefore equal to 1000. This yields the average number of connections to a given B cell from a particular A box being approximately unity, which agrees well with the condition expressed by Linsker.

Using the expression above, $\bar{q}$ can be calculated as approximately 1.5×10^{-3}. This value is certainly insignificant with respect to the value of $K_2 = 0.2$ quoted earlier, and therefore any effects due to the summation term in equation 3 can be ignored in the calculation of $\bar{c}$ for this system. This means that the original approximation still holds even in this low connectivity case.

5 SIMULATION RESULTS

A network was trained using the connectivity stated above to give various values of $\bar{c}$ with $K_2 = 0.2$. To obtain an idea of the total number of presentations that were required to train the network, without any artifacts that might be produced as a result of batch training, the original network equations were used. In all of these simulations, $R_a, F_0^M = 0$ so that the value of K_1 could be easily controlled.

The findings were that the maximum value of k_b was about 10^{-3} which required 2.5 million pattern presentations to mature the network. With this value, on-center cells with an average weight value less than about 0.3 would not mature. However as the value of k_b was decreased (keeping K_1 constant), the value of $\bar{c}$ could be made lower, at the expense of more pattern presentations. The figures obtained for the maturation of feature sensitive cells are extremely biologically realistic in the light of the number of pattern presentations available to an average mammal. For example, the foetal cat has sufficient time for about 25 million presentations (assuming 10 presentations per second).

6 CONCLUSION

We have shown that the class of network developed by Linsker is extendable to the auditory system where the number and density of synapses is considerably smaller than in the visual case. It has also been shown that the time for layer maturation by this method is sufficiently short even for mammals with a relatively short gestation period, and therefore should also be sufficient in mammals with longer foetal development times. We conclude that the model is therefore a good representation of feature detector development in the pre-natal mammal.

References

Grossberg S. (1976) - On the Development of Feature Detectors in the Visual Cortex with Applications to Learning and Reaction Diffusion Systems, *Biological Cybernetics 21*, 145 - 159

Grossberg S. (1976) - Adaptive Pattern Classification and Universal Recoding : 1 Parallel Development and Coding of Neural Feature Detectors, *Biological Cybernetics 23*, 121 - 134

Hubel D. H. and Wiesel T. N. (1961) - Receptive Fields, Binocular Interaction and Functional Architechture in the Cat's Visual Cortex, *Journal of Physiology, 160*, 106 - 154

Kalil R. E. (1989) - Synapse Formation In The Developing Brain, *Scientific American, December 1989*, 38 - 45

Klinke R. (1986) - Physiology of Hearing, In Schmidt R. W. (ed.), *Fundamentals of Sensory Physiology*, 199 - 223

MacKay D. J. C. and Miller K. D. (1990) - Analysis of Linsker's Simulations of Hebbian Rules, *Neural Computation, 2*, 173 - 187

von der Malsburg C. (1979) - Development of Ocularity Domains and Growth

Behaviour of Axon Terminals, *Biological Cybernetics, 32*, 49 - 62

Linsker R. (1986a) - From Basic Network Principles To Neural Architecture : Emergence Of Spatial-Opponent Cells, *Proceedings of the National Academy of Sciences (USA), 83*, 7508 - 7512

Linsker R. (1986b) - From Basic Network Principles To Neural Architecture : Emergence of Orientation-Selective Cells, *Proceedings of the National Academy of Sciences (USA), 83*, 8390 - 8394

Linsker R. (1986c) - From Basic Network Principles To Neural Architecture : Emergence of Orientation-Columns, *Proceedings of the National Academy of Sciences (USA), 83*, 8779 - 8783

Nass M. M. and Cooper L. N. (1975) - A Theory for the Development of Feature Detecting Cells in the Visual Cortex, *Biological Cybernetics, 19*, 1 - 18

Obermayer K. Ritter H. and Schulten K. (1990) - Development and Spatial Structure of Cortical Feature Maps: A Model Study *NIPS, 3*, 11 - 17

Sloman A. (1989) - On Designing a Visual System (Towards a Gibsonian Computational Model of Vision) *Journal of Experimental and Theoretical Artificial Intelligence, 1*, 289 - 337

Tanaka S. (1990) - Interaction among Ocularity, Retinotopy and On-Center/Off Center Pathways During Development *NIPS, 3*, 18 - 25

A Recurrent Neural Network for Generation of Ocular Saccades

Lina L.E. Massone
Department of Physiology
Department of Electrical Engineering and Computer Science
Northwestern University
303 E. Chicago Avenue, Chicago, Il 60611

Abstract

This paper presents a neural network able to control saccadic movements. The input to the network is a specification of a stimulation site on the collicular motor map. The output is the time course of the eye position in the orbit (horizontal and vertical angles). The units in the network exhibit a one-to-one correspondance with neurons in the intermediate layer of the superior colliculus (collicular motor map), in the brainstem and with oculomotor neurons. Simulations carried out with this network demonstrate its ability to reproduce in a straightforward fashion many experimental observations.

1. INTRODUCTION

It is known that the superior colliculus (SC) plays an important role in the control of eye movements (Schiller et al. 1980). Electrophysiological studies (Cynader and Berman 1972, Robinson 1972) showed that the intermediate layer of SC is topographically organized into a motor map. The location of active neurons in this area was found to be related to the oculomotor error (i.e. how far the eyes are from the target) and their firing rate to saccade velocity (Roher et al. 1987, Berthoz et al. 1987). Neurons in the rostral area of the motor map, the so-called fixation neurons, tend to become active when the eyes are on target (Munoz and Wurtz 1992) and they can provide a gating mechanism to arrest the movement (Guitton 1992). SC sends signals to the brainstem whose circuitry translates them into commands to the oculomotor neurons that innervate the eye muscles (Robinson 1981).

This paper presents a recurrent neural network that performs a spatio-temporal transformation from a stimulation site on the collicular motor map and an eye movement. The units in the network correspond to neurons in the intermediate layer of the colliculus, neurons in the brainstem and to oculomotor neurons.

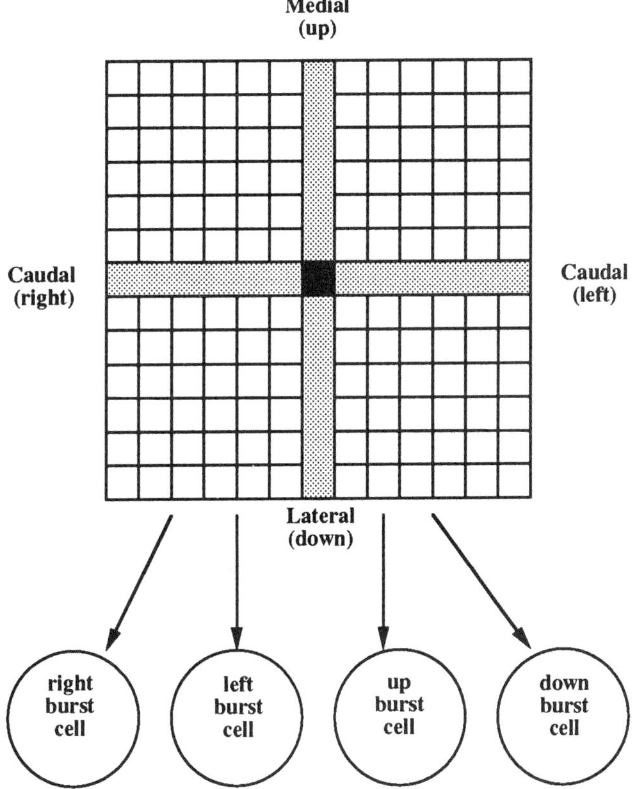

Figure 1: An array of units that represents the collicular motor map. The dark square represents the fixation area. The units in the array project to four units that represent burst cells devoted to process rightward, leftward, upward and downward saccades.

The network was built entirely on anatomical and physiological observations. Specifically, the following assumptions were used: (1) The activity on the collicular motor map shifts towards the fixation area during movement (Munoz et al. 1991, Droulez and Berthoz 1991). (2) The output of the superior colliculus is a vectorial velocity signal that is the sum of the contributions from each active collicular neuron. (3) Such signal is decomposed into horizontal velocity and vertical velocity by a topographic and graded connectivity pattern from SC to the burst cells in the brainstem. (4) The computation performed from the burst-cells level down to the actual eye movement is carried out according to the push-pull arrangement proposed by Robinson (1981). (5) The activity on the collicular motor map is shifted by signals that represent the eye velocity. Efferent copies of the horizontal and vertical eye velocities are fed back onto the collicular map in order to implement the activity shift.

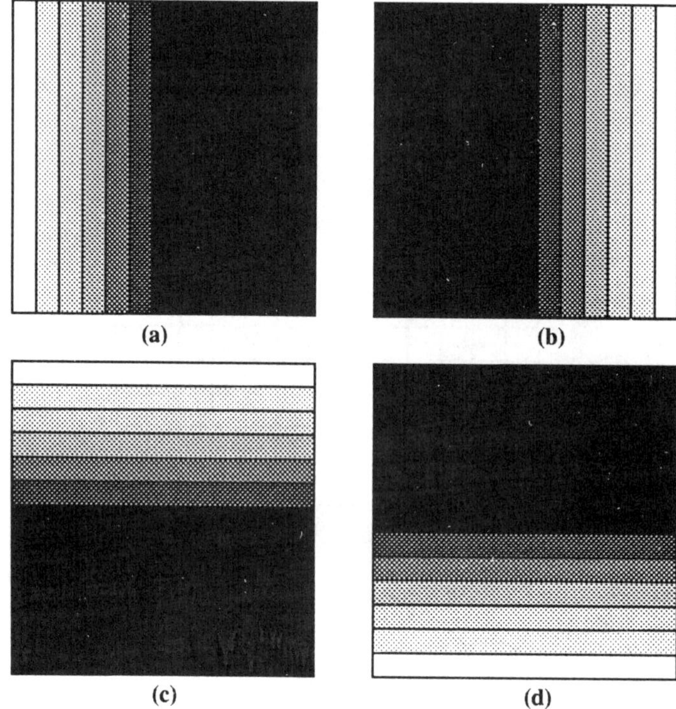

Figure 2: The topographic and graded pattern of connectivity from the collicular array to the four burst cells. Black means no connection, brighter colors represent larger weight values. (a) To the right cell. (b) To the left cell. (c) To the up cell. (d) To the down cell.

Simulations conducted with such a system (Massone submitted) demonstrated the network's ability to reproduce a number of experimental observations. Namely the network can: (1) Spontaneously produce oblique saccades whose curvature varies with the ratio between the horizontal and vertical components of the motor error.(2) Automatically hold the eye position in the orbit at the end of a saccade by exploiting the internal dynamic of the network. (3) Continuously produce efferent copies of the movements without the need for reset signals. (4) Account for the outcome of the lidocaine experiment (Lee et al. 1988) without assuming a population averaging mechanism.

Section 2 describes the network architecture. A more detailed description of the network, it mechanisms and physiological ground as well as a number of simulation results can be found in Massone (submitted).

2. THE NETWORK

The network input layer is a bidimensional array of linear units that represent neurons in the collicular motor map. The array is topographically arranged as shown in Figure 1. Activity along the caudal axis produces horizontal saccades in a contralateral fashion, activity along the medio-lateral axis produces vertical saccades, activity in the rest of the array produces oblique saccades. The dark square in the center (rostral area) represents the fixation area. The units in this array project to four logistic units that represent two pairs of burst cells, one pair devoted to control horizontal movements, one pair devoted to control vertical movements. The pattern of connectivity between the collicular array and the units that represent the burst cells is qualitatively shown in Figure 2. The value of the weights of such connections increases exponentially when one moves from the center towards the periphery of the array. The fixation area projects to four other units that represent the so-called omnipause neurons. These units send a gating signal to the burst-cells units and are responsible for arresting the movement when the eyes are on target. i.e. when the activity in the input array reaches the center. Each pair of burst-cells units project to the network shown in Figure 3. This network is a computational version of the push-pull arrangement proposed by Robinson (1981). The bottom part of the network represents the oculomotor plant, the top part represents the brainstem circuitry and the oculomotor neurons. The weights in the bottom part of the network were derived by splitting into two equations the differential equation proposed by Robinson (1981) to describe the behavior of the oculomotor plant under a combined motorneuron input R.

$$R_1 = k\theta_1 + r\,\frac{d\theta_1}{dt}$$

$$R_2 = k\theta_2 + r\,\frac{d\theta_2}{dt}$$

R1 and R2 are the firing rates of the agonist and antagonist motorneurons, $\theta 1$ and $\theta 2$ are the components of the eye position due to motions in opposite directions (e.g. left and right), k is the eye stiffness and r is the eye viscosity.

The weights in the top part of the network were analytically computed from the weights in the bottom part of the network by imposing the following constraints: (1) The difference between $\theta 1$ and $\theta 2$ must produce the correct θ. (2) The output of the neural integrators must be an efferent copy of the eye movement. (3) The output of the motorneurons must hold the eye at the current orbital position when the burst-cells units are shut off by the gating action of the omnipause cells. Efferent copies of the horizontal and vertical eye velocities were computed by differentiating the output of the neural

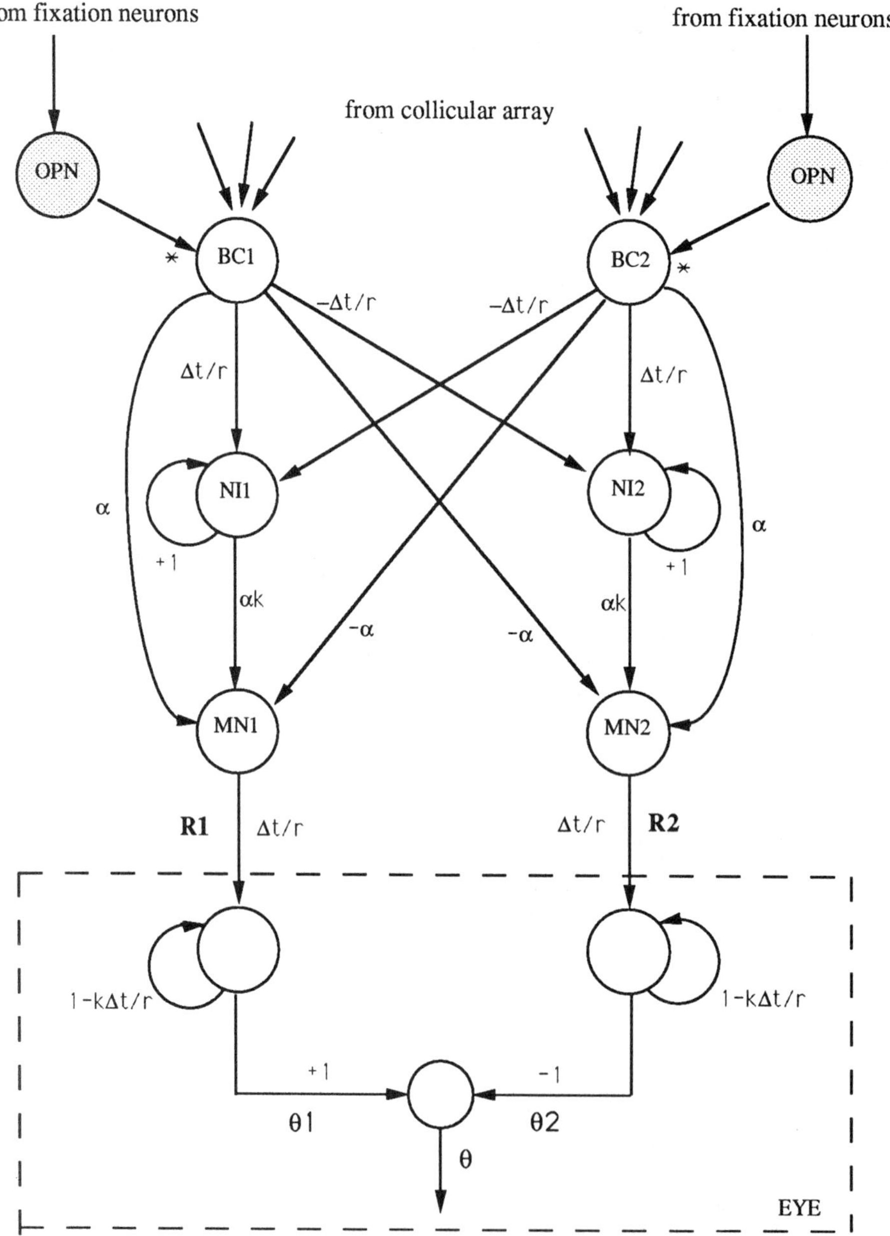

Figure 3: The recurrent network used to control eye movements in one direction, e.g. horizontal. An identical network is required to control vertical movements. OPN: omnipause neurons. BC1, BC2: burst cells. NI1, NI2: neural integrators. MN1, MN2: motor neurons. The architecture is based on Robinson's push-pull arrangement. k=4.0, r=0.95, α=0.5, Δt=1 msec.

integrators. These signals were recurrently fed back onto the input array and made the activity in the array shift towards the fixation area. This architecture assumes that the output of the collicular array represents saccade velocity. The network is started by selecting one unit in the input array, i.e. a "stimulation" site. When the unit is selected, a square area centered at that unit becomes active with a gaussian activity profile (Ottes et al. 1986, Munoz and Guitton 1991). At the time the input units are activated the eye starts moving and, as a consequence of the velocity feedback the activity on the input array starts shifting. The movement is arrested when the fixation area becomes activated. The activity of all units in the network represents neurons firing rates and is expressed in spikes/second.

Figure 4 shows the response of the network when the collicular array is stimulated at two sites sequentially. Each site causes an oblique saccade with unequal components. Stimulation number 1 brings the eye up and to the right, stimulation number 2 brings the eye back to the initial position. Fixation is maintained for a while inbetween stimulations and at the end of the two movements. The resulting trajectories in the movement plane (vertical angle versus horizontal angle) demonstrate the ability of the network to (i) maintain the eye position in the orbit when the burst cells activation is set to zero by the gating action of the omnipause neurons, (ii) produce curved trajectories with opposite curvatures when the eye moves back and forth between the same two angular positions. None of the units in the network is ever reset between saccades; because of the push-pull arrangement, when the activity of one neural integrator increases, the activity of the antagonist integrator decreases. This mechanism ensures that their activity does not grow indefinetely.

3. CONCLUSIONS

In this paper I presented an anatomically and physiologically inspired network able to control saccadic movements and to reproduce the outcome of some experimental observations. The results of simulations carried out with this network can be found in Massone (submitted). This work is currently being extended to (i) modeling the activity shift phenomenon as the relaxation of a dynamical system to its equilibrium configuration rather than as a feedback-driven mechanism, (ii) studying the role of the collicular output signals in the calibration and accuracy of arm movements (Massone 1992).

Acknowledgements

This work was supported by the National Science Foundation, grant BCS-9113455 to the author.

References

Berthoz A., Grantyn A., Droulez J. (1987) Some collicular neurons code saccadic eye velocity, *Neuroscience Letters*, 72, 289-294.

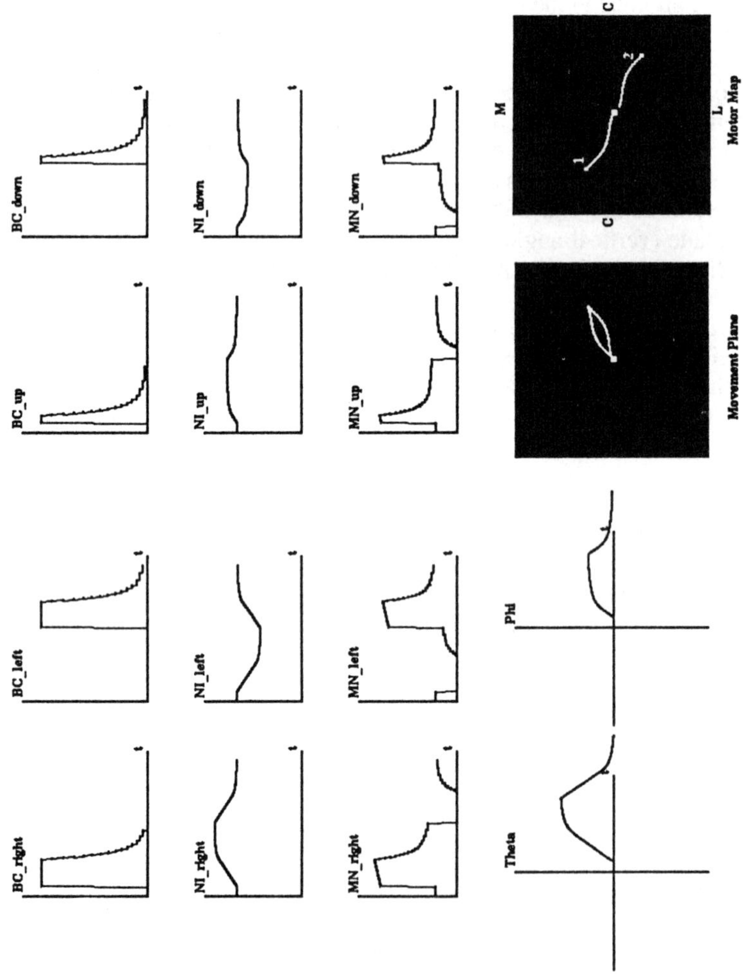

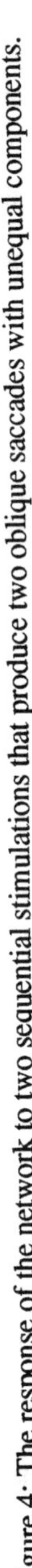
Figure 4: The response of the network to two sequential stimulations that produce two oblique saccades with unequal components.

Cynader M., Berman N. (1972) Receptive-field organization of monkey superior colliculus, *Journal of Neurophysiology*, 35, 187-201.

Droulez J., Berthoz A. (1991) The concept of dynamic memory in sensorimotor control, in *Motor Control Concepts and Issues*, Humphrey D.R. and Freund H.J. Eds., J. Whiley and Sons, 137-161.

Guitton D. (1992) Control of eye-head coordination during orienting gaze shifts, *Trends in Neuroscience*, 15(5), 174-179.

Lee C., Roher W.H., Sparks D.L. (1988) Population coding of saccadic eye movements by neurons in the superior colliculus, *Nature*, 332, 357-360.

Massone L. E. (1992) A biologically-inspired architecture for reactive motor control, in *Neural Networks for Control*, G. Beckey and K. Goldberg Eds., Kluwer Academic Publishers, 1992.

Massone L.E. (submitted) A velocity-based model for control of ocular saccades, *Neural Computation*.

Munoz D.P., Pellisson D., Guitton D. (1991) Movement of Neural Activity on the Superior Colliculus Motor Map during Gaze Shifts, *Science*, 251, 1358-1360.

Munoz D.P., Guitton D. (1991) Gaze control by the tecto-reticulo-spinal system in the head-free cat. II. Sustained discharges coding gaze position error, *Journal of Neurophysiology*, 66, 1624-1641.

Munoz D.P., Wurtz R.H. (1992) Role of the rostral superior colliculus in active visual fixation and execution of express saccades, *Journal of Neurophysiology*, 67, 1000-1002.

Ottes F.P., Van Gisbergen J.A.M., Eggermont J.J. (1986) Visuomotor fields of the superior colliculus: a quantitative model, *Vision Research*, 26, 857-873.

Robinson D.A. (1972) Eye movements evoked by collicular stimulation in the alert monkey, *Vision Research*, 12, 1795-1808.

Robinson D.A. (1981) Control of eye movements, in *Handbook of Physiology - The Nervous System II*, V.B. Brooks Ed., 1275-1320.

Roher W.H., White J.M., Sparks D.L. (1987) Saccade-related burst cells in the superior colliculus: relationship of activity with saccade velocity, *Society of Neuroscience Abstracts*, 13, 1092.

A Formal Model of the Insect Olfactory Macroglomerulus: Simulations and Analytical Results.

Christiane Linster
David Marsan
ESPCI, Laboratoire d'Electronique
10, Rue Vauquelin
75005 Paris, France

Claudine Masson
Laboratoire de Neurobiologie Comparée des Invertébrées
INRA/CNRS (URA 1190)
91140 Bures sur Yvette, France

Michel Kerszberg
Institut Pasteur
CNRS (URA 1284)
Neurobiologie Moléculaire
25, Rue du Dr. Roux
75015 Paris, France

Gérard Dreyfus
Léon Personnaz
ESPCI, Laboratoire d'Electronique
10, Rue Vauquelin
75005 Paris, France

Abstract

It is known from biological data that the response patterns of interneurons in the olfactory macroglomerulus (MGC) of insects are of central importance for the coding of the olfactory signal. We propose an analytically tractable model of the MGC which allows us to relate the distribution of response patterns to the architecture of the network.

1. Introduction

The processing of pheromone odors in the antennal lobe of several insect species relies on a number of response patterns of the antennal lobe neurons in reaction to stimulation with pheromone components and blends. Antennal lobe interneurons receive input from different receptor types, and relay this input to antennal lobe projection neurons via excitatory as well as inhibitory synapses. The diversity of the responses of the interneurons and projection neurons as well the long response latencies of these neurons to pheromone stimulation or electrical stimulation of the antenna, suggest a polysynaptic pathway between the receptor neurons and these projection neurons (for a review see (Kaissling, 1990; Masson and Mustaparta, 1990)).

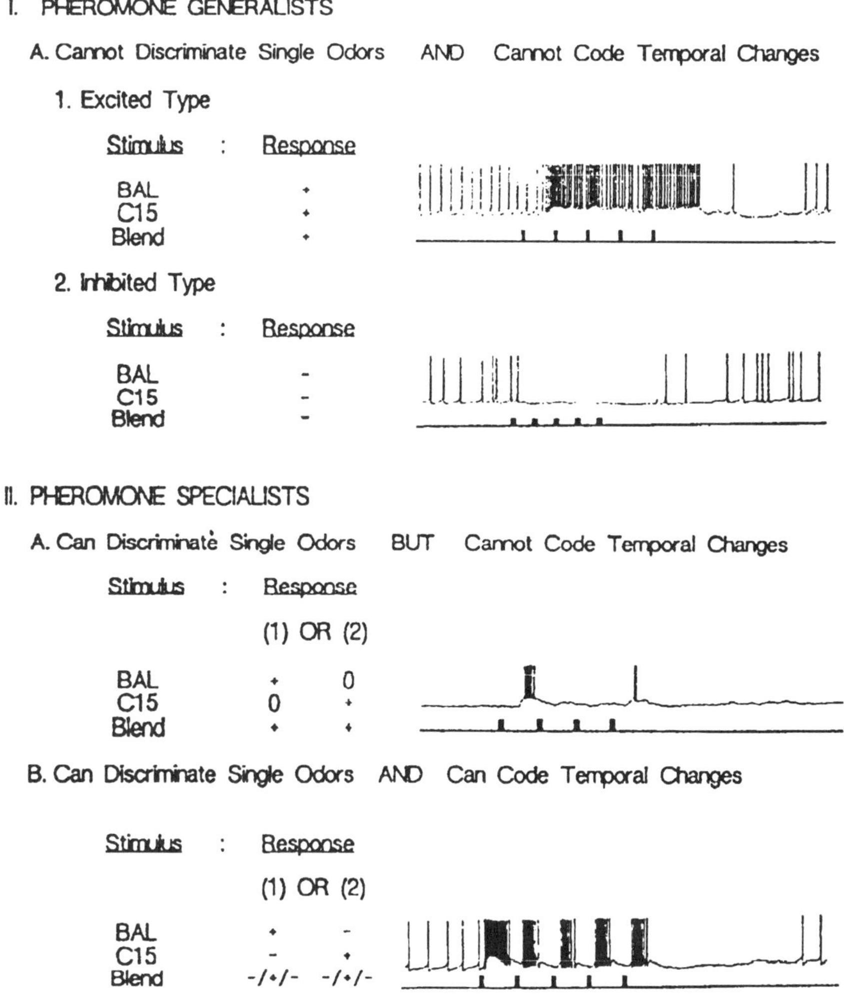

Figure 1: With courtesy of John Hildebrand, by permission from Oxford University Press, from: Christensen, Mustaparta and Hildebrand: Discrimination of sex pheromone blends in the olfactory system of the moth, Chemical Senses, Vol 14, no 3, pp 463-477, 1989.

In the MGC of *Manduca sexta*, antennal lobe interneurons respond in various ways to antennal stimulation with single pheromone components or the blend: pheromone generalists respond by either excitation or inhibition to both components and the blend: they cannot discriminate the components; pheromone specialists respond (i) to one component but not to the other by either excitation or inhibition, (ii) with different response patterns to the presence of the single components or the blend, namely with excitation to one component, with inhibition to the other component and with a mixed response to the blend. These neurons can also follow pulsed stimulation up to a cut-off frequency (Figure 1).

A model of the MGC (Linster et al, 1993), based on biological data (anatomical and physiological) has demonstrated that the full diversity of response patterns can be reproduced with a random architecture using very simple ingredients such as spiking neurons governed by a first order differential equation, and synapses modeled as simple delay lines. In a model with uniform distributions of afferent, inhibitory and excitatory synapses, the distribution of the response patterns depends on the following network parameters: the percentage of afferent, inhibitory and excitatory synapses, the ratio of the average excitation of any interneuron to its spiking threshold, and the amount of feedback in the network.

In the present paper, we show that the behavior of such a model can be described by a statistical approach, allowing us to search through parameter space and to make predictions about the biological system without exhaustive simulations. We compare the results obtained with simulation of the network model to the results obtained analytically by the statistical approach, and we show that the approximations made for the statistical descriptions are valid.

2. Simulations and comparison to biological data

In (Linster et al, 1993), we have used a simple neuron model: all neurons are spiking neurons, governed by a first order differential equation, with a membrane time constant and a probabilistic threshold Θ. The time constant represents the decay time of the membrane potential of the neuron. The output of each neuron consists of an all-or-none action potential with unit amplitude that is generated when the membrane potential of the cell crosses a threshold, whose cumulative distribution function is a continuous and bounded probabilistic function of the membrane potential. All sources of delay and signal transformation from the presynaptic neuron to its postsynaptic site are modeled by a synaptic time delay. These delays are chosen in a random distribution (gaussian), with a longer mean value for inhibitory synapses than for excitatory synapses. We model two main populations of olfactory neurons: *receptor neurons* which are sensitive to the main pheromone component (called A) or to the minor pheromone component (called B) project uniformly onto the network of *interneurons*; two types of interneurons (excitatory and inhibitory) exist: each interneuron is allowed to make one synapse with any other interneuron.

The model exhibits several behaviors that agree with biological data, and it allows us to state several predictive hypotheses about the processing of the pheromone blend. We observe two broad classes of interneurons: selective (to one odor component) and non-selective neurons (in comparison to Figure 1). Selective neurons and non-selective neurons exhibit a variety of response patterns, which fall into three classes: inhibitory, excitatory and mixed (Figure 2). Such a classification has indeed been proposed for olfactory antennal lobe neurons (local interneurons and projection neurons) in the specialist olfactory system in *Manduca* (Christensen and Hildebrand, 1987) and for the *cockroach* (Burrows et al, 1982; Boeckh and Ernst, 1987).

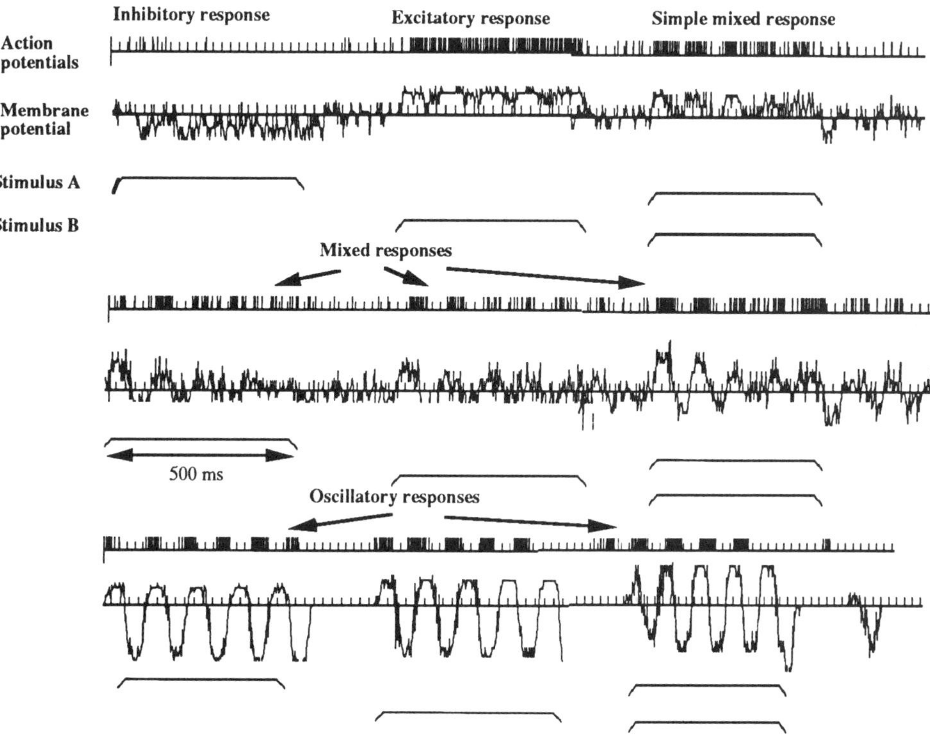

Figure 2: Response patterns of interneurons in the model presented, in response to stimulation with single components A and B, and with a blend with equal component concentrations. Receptor neurons fire at maximum frequency during the stimulations. The interneuron in the upper row is inhibited by stimulus A, excited by stimulus B, and has a mixed response (excitation followed by inhibition) to the blend: in reference to Figure 1, this is a pheromone specialist receiving mixed input from both types of receptor neurons. These types of simple and mixed responses can be observed in the model at low connectivity, where the average excitation received by an interneuron is low compared to its spiking threshold. The neuron in the middle row responds with similar mixed responses to stimuli A, B and A+B. The neuron in the lower row responds to all stimuli with the same oscillatory response, here the average excitation received by an interneuron approaches or exceeds the spiking threshold of the neurons. Network parameters: 15 receptor neurons; 35 interneurons; 40% excitatory interneurons; 60% inhibitory interneurons; afferent connectivity 10%; membrane time constant 25 ms; mean inhibitory synaptic delays 100 ms; mean excitatory synaptic delays 25 ms, spiking threshold 4.0, synaptic weights +1 and -1.

In our model, as well as in biological systems (Christensen and Hildebrand 1988, Christensen et al., 1989) we observe a number of local interneurons that cannot follow pulsed stimulation beyond a neuron-specific cut-off frequency. This frequency depends on the neuron response pattern and on the duration of the interstimulus interval.
Therefore, the type of response pattern is of central importance for the coding of the olfactory signal. Thus, in order to be able to relate the coding capabilities of a (model or biological) network to its architecture, we have investigated the distribution of response patterns both analytically and by simulations.

3. Analytical approach

In order to investigate these questions in a more rigorous way, some of us (C.L., D.M., G.D., L.P.) have designed a simplified, analytically tractable model.
We define two layers of interneurons: those which receive direct afferent input from the receptor neurons (layer 1), and those which receive only input from other interneurons (layer 2). In order to predict the response pattern of any interneuron as a function of the network parameters, we make the following assumptions: (i) statistically, all interneurons within a given layer receive the same synaptic input, (ii) the effect of feedback loops from layer 2 can be neglected, (iii) the response patterns have the same distribution for stimulations either by the blend or by pure components. Assumption (i) is correct because of the uniform distribution of synapses in the network of interneurons. Assumption (ii) is valid at low connectivity: if the average amount of excitation received by an interneuron is low as compared to its spiking threshold, its firing probability is low; therefore, the effect of the excitation from the receptors is vanishingly small beyond two interneurons: we thus neglect the effect of signals sent from layer 2. Thus, feedback is present within layer 1, and layer 2 receives only feedforward connections. Assumption (iii) is plausible if we suppose that the natural pheromone blend is more relevant for the system than the single components of the blend. We further assume in the analytical approach (as in the simulations) that the synaptic delays are longer on the average for inhibitory synapses than for excitatory synapses .
An interneuron can thus respond with four types of patterns: *non-response,* which means that it does not have a presynaptic neuron (this response pattern can only occur in layer 2, at low connectivity); *excitation*, meaning that an interneuron receives only afferent input from receptor neurons or from excitatory interneurons; *inhibition*, meaning that an interneuron receives only input from inhibitory interneurons (this can occur in layer 2 only); and *mixed responses,* covering all other combinations of presynaptic input.
We consider a network of $N + N_r$ neurons, N (number of interneurons) and N_r (number of receptor neurons) being random variables, $N + N_r$ being fixed. We define the probability n_i that a neuron is an inhibitory interneuron, and the probability n_e that it is an excitatory interneuron. Any interneuron has a probability c to make one synapse (with synaptic weight +1 or -1) with any other interneuron and a probability $(1 - c)$ not to make a synapse with this interneuron; c_r is the afferent connectivity: any receptor neuron has a probability c_r to connect once to any interneuron, and a probability $(1 - c_r)$ not to connect to this interneuron. Then $n_a = 1 - (1 - c_r)^{N_r}$ is the probability that an interneuron belongs to layer 1, and the number of interneurons in layer 1 obeys a binomial distribution with expectation value $N\ n_a$ and variance $N\ n_a (1 - n_a)$. In the following, the fixed number of interneurons in layer 1 will be taken equal to its expectation value. Similarly, the number of interneurons in layer 2 is taken to be $N\ (1 - n_a)$.

Because of the assumptions made above, in both layers, we take into account for each interneuron the $N\, n_a\, c$ synapses from presynaptic neurons of layer1. In layer 1, these neurons respond with excitatory or mixed responses. $P_e^1 = n_e n_a N c$ is the probability that an interneuron in layer 1 responds with an excitation, and $P_m^1 = 1 - n_e n_a N c$ is the probability that an interneuron in layer 1 receives mixed synaptic input.

In layer 2, we have to consider two cases: (i) at low connectivity, if $N c n_a < 1$, $P_0^2 = 1 - N c n_a$ is the probability that an interneuron of layer 2 does not receive a synapse, thus does not respond to stimulation, $P_e^2 = N c n_a n_e$ is the probability that a neuron in layer 2 responds with excitation, $P_i^2 = N c n_a n_i$ is the probability that an interneuron responds with inhibition; (ii) at higher connectivity, $N c n_a > 1$, $P_0^2 = 0$, $P_e^2 = n_e n_a N c$ and $P_i^2 = n_i n_a N c$. In both cases (i) and (ii), the probability that an interneuron in layer 2 has a mixed response pattern is $P_m^2 = 1 - P_0^2 - P_e^2 - P_i^2$.

Thus, an interneuron in the model responds with excitation with probability $P_e = n_a P_e^1 + (1 - n_a) P_e^2$, with inhibition with probability $P_i = n_a P_i^1 + (1 - n_a) P_i^2$ and has a mixed response with probability $P_m = n_a P_m^1 + (1 - n_a) P_m^2$.

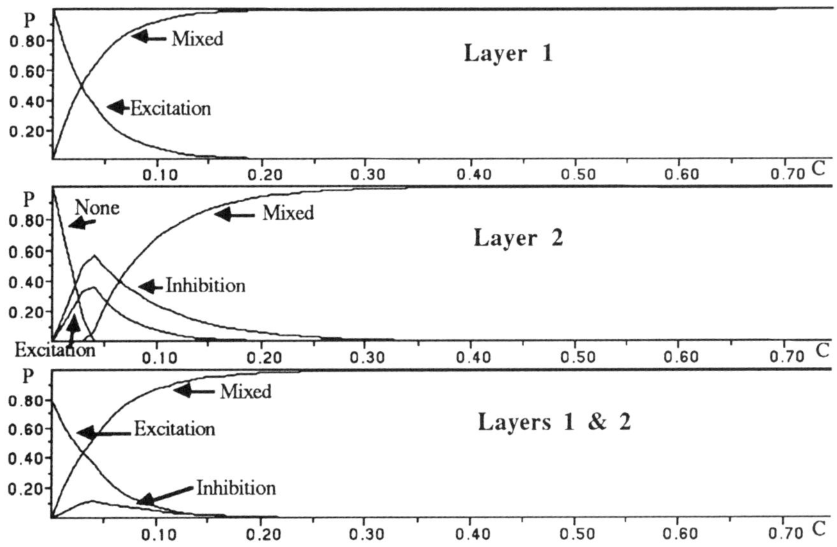

Figure 4: Analytically derived distribution of the response patterns in a typical network (35 interneurons, 15 receptor neurons, 40% excitation, 60% inhibition, spiking threshold 4.0); the curves show the percentage of interneurons in the model which respond with a given pattern, as a function of the connectivity c. In this case, the average excitation an interneuron receives from other interneurons is 3.15 at c=0.3.

Figure 4 shows the distribution of the response patterns computed analytically for a typical set of parameters. In order to perform comparisons between computed pattern distributions and pattern distributions obtained from simulations with the model, we designed an automatic classifier for the response patterns, based on the perceptron learning rule and the pocket algorithm (Gallant 1986). The classifier is trained to classify the responses of individual interneurons, based on their membrane potential, into 5 typical response classes: non-response, pure excitation, pure inhibition, simple mixed response and oscillatory responses. Figure 5 shows the simulation results for the same set of parameters as for Figure 4. The agreement between the two curves shows that the approximations which we have made in order to describe the analytical model are valid.

Figure 6 shows how the mixed responses in the simulations divide into simple mixed and oscillatory responses. When the validity limit of the approximations made in the analytical approach is reached, all neurons fire at maximum frequency and the network oscillates. Therefore, the analytical model describes satisfactorily the whole range of connectivity in which the pattern distribution does not reduce to oscillations. The oscillation frequency is determined by the mean synaptic delays and by the membrane time constants; more detailed results on the oscillatory behavior will be published in a future paper.

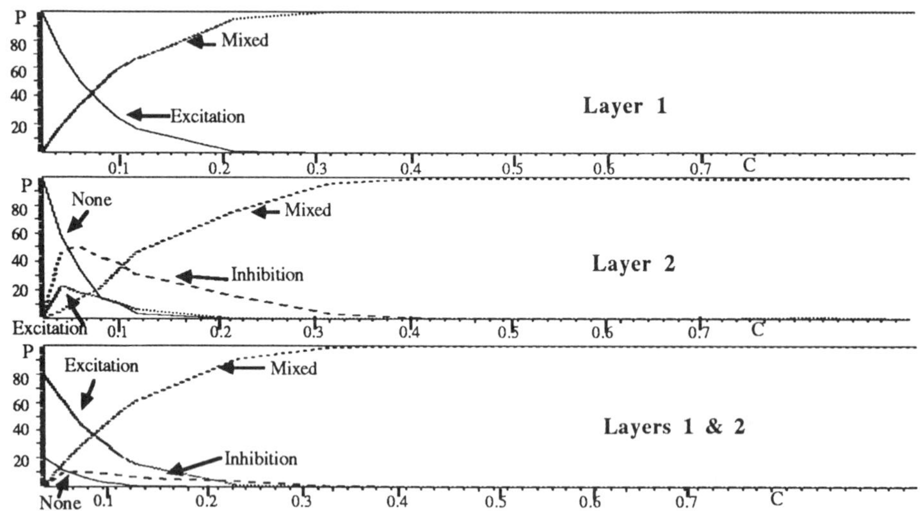

Figure 5: Distribution of the response patterns obtained from simulations of the model with the set of parameters described above. The curves show the percentages of interneurons that respond with a given pattern, as a function of connectivity c. For each value of c, 100 simulation runs with three different stimulation inputs have been averaged.

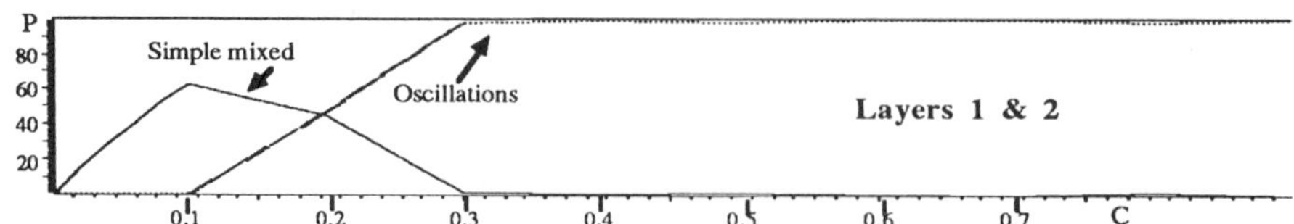

Figure 6: Distribution of simple mixed and oscillatory responses in the simulation model. With the set of parameters chosen, condition $n_e\, c \approx \Theta$ is satisfied for $c \approx 0.3$.

4. Conclusion

In the olfactory system of insects and mammals, a number of response patterns are observed, which are of central importance for the coding of the olfactory signal. In the present paper, we show that, under some constraints, an analytical model can predict the existence and the distribution of these response patterns. We further show that the transition between non-oscillatory and oscillatory regimes is governed by a single parameter (n_e c / Θ). It is thus possible, to explore the parameter space without exhaustive simulations, and to relate the coding capabilities of a model or biological network to its architecture.

Acknowledgements
This work was supported in part by a grant from Ministère de la Recherche et de la Technologie (Sciences de la Cognition). C. Linster has been supported by a research grant (BFR91/051) from the Ministère des Affaires Culturelles, Grand-Duché de Luxembourg.

References

Boeckh, J. and Ernst, K.D. (1987). Contribution of single unit analysis in insects to an understanding of olfactory function. *J. Comp. Physiolo.* A161:549-565.

Burrows, M., Boeckh, J., Esslen, J. (1982). Physiological and Morphological Properties of Interneurons in the Deutocerebrum of Male Cockroaches which respond to Female Pheromone. *J. Comp. Physiolo.* 145:447-457.

Christensen, T.A., Hildebrand, J.G. (1987). Functions, Organization, and Physiology of the Olfactory Pathways in the Lepidoteran Brain. *In Arthropod Brain: its Evolution, Development, Structure and Functions,* A.P. Gupta, (ed), John Wiley & Sons.

Christensen, T.A., Hildebrand, J.G. (1988). Frequency coding by central olfactory neurons in the spinx moth Manduca sexta. *Chemical Senses* 13 (1):123-130.

Christensen, T.A., Mustaparta, H., Hildebrand, J.G. (1989). Discrimination of sex pheromone blends in the olfactory system of the moth. *Chemical Senses* 14 (3):463-477.

Kaissling, K-E., Kramer, E. (1990). Sensory basis of pheromone-mediated orientation in moths. *Verh. Dtsch. Zoolo. Ges.* 83:109-131.

Linster, C., Masson, C., Kerszberg, M., Personnaz, L., Dreyfus, G. (1993). Computational Diversity in a Formal Model of the Insect Olfactory Macroglomerulus. *Neural Computation* 5:239-252.

Masson, C., Mustaparta, H. (1990). Chemical Information Processing in the Olfactory System of Insects. *Physiol. Reviews* 70 (1):199-245.

An Information-Theoretic Approach to Deciphering the Hippocampal Code

William E. Skaggs **Bruce L. McNaughton** **Katalin M. Gothard**

Etan J. Markus
Center for Neural Systems, Memory, and Aging
344 Life Sciences North
University of Arizona
Tucson AZ 85724
bill@nsma.arizona.edu

Abstract

Information theory is used to derive a simple formula for the amount of information conveyed by the firing rate of a neuron about any experimentally measured variable or combination of variables (e.g. running speed, head direction, location of the animal, etc.). The derivation treats the cell as a communication channel whose input is the measured variable and whose output is the cell's spike train. Applying the formula, we find systematic differences in the information content of hippocampal "place cells" in different experimental conditions.

1 INTRODUCTION

Almost any neuron will respond to some manipulation or other by changing its firing rate, and this change in firing can convey information to downstream neurons. The aim of this article is to introduce a very simple formula for the average rate at which a cell conveys information in this way, and to show how the formula is helpful in the study of the firing properties of cells in the rat hippocampus. This is by no means the first application of information theory to the study of neural coding; see especially Richmond and Optican (1990). The thing that particularly distinguishes our approach is its simplemindedness.

To get the basic idea, imagine we are recording the activity of a neuron in the brain of a rat, while the rat is wandering around randomly on a circular platform. Suppose we observe that the cell fires only when the rat is on the left half of the platform, and that it fires at a constant rate everywhere on the left half; and suppose that on the whole the rat spends half of its time on the left half of the platform. In this case, if we are prevented from seeing where the rat is, but are informed that the neuron has just this very moment fired a spike, we obtain thereby one bit of information about the current location of the rat. Suppose we have a second cell, which fires only in the southwest quarter of the platform; in this case a spike would give us two bits of information. If there were in addition a small amount of background firing, the information would be slightly less than two bits. And so on.

Going back to the cell that fires everywhere on the left half of the platform, suppose that when it is active, it fires at a mean rate of 10 spikes per second. Since it is active half the time, it fires at an overall mean rate of 5 spikes per second. Since a spike conveys one bit of information about the rat's location, the cell's spike train conveys information at an average rate of 5 bits per second. This does not mean that if the cell is observed for one second, on average 5 bits will be obtained—rather it means that if the cell is observed for a sufficiently short time interval Δt, on average $5\Delta t$ bits will be obtained. In 20 milliseconds, for example, the expected information conveyed by the cell about the location of the rat will be very nearly 0.1 bits. The longer the time interval over which the cell is observed, the more redundancy in the spike train, and hence the farther below $5\Delta t$ the total information falls.

The formula that leads to these numbers is

$$I = \int_x \lambda(x) \log_2 \frac{\lambda(x)}{\lambda} p(x) dx, \tag{1}$$

where I is the information rate of the cell in bits per second, x is spatial location, $p(x)$ is the probability density for the rat being at location x, $\lambda(x)$ is the mean firing rate when the rat is at location x, and $\lambda = \int_x \lambda(x)p(x)dx$ is the overall mean firing rate of the cell. The derivation of this formula appears in the final section. (To our knowledge the formula, though very simple, has not previously been published.)

Note that, as far as the formula is concerned, there is nothing special about spatial location: the formula can equally well be used to define the rate at which a cell conveys information about *any* aspect of the rat's state, or any combination of aspects. The only mathematical requirement[1] is that the rat's state x and the spike train of the cell both be stationary random variables, so that the probability density $p(x)$ and the expected firing rate $\lambda(x)$ are well-defined.

The information rate given by formula (1) is measured in bits per second. If it is divided by the overall mean firing rate λ of the cell (expressed in spikes per second), then a different kind of information rate is obtained, in units of bits per spike—let us call it the *information per spike*. This is a measure of the *specificity* of the cell: the more "grandmotherish" the cell, the more information per spike. For a population

[1]Other than obvious requirements of integrability that are sure to be fulfilled in natural situations.

of cells, then, a highly distributed representation equates to little information per spike.

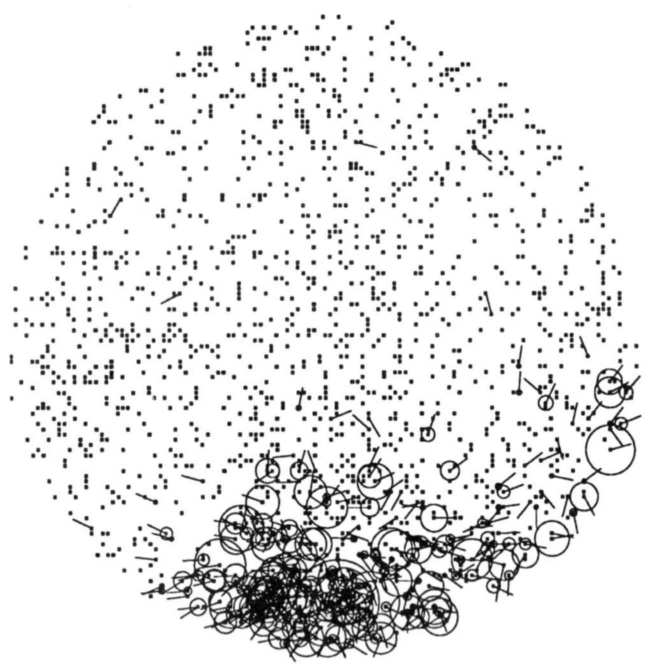

Figure 1: "Spot plot" of the activity of a single pyramidal cell in the hippocampus of a rat, recorded while the rat foraged for food pellets inside a small cylinder. The dots show locations visited by the rat, and the circles show points where the cell fired—large circles mean that several spikes occurred within a short time. The lines indicate which direction the rat was facing when the cell fired. The plot represents 29 minutes of data, during which the cell fired at an overall mean rate of 1.319 Hz.

Consider, as an example, a typical "place cell" (actually an especially nice place cell) from the CA1 layer of the hippocampus of a rat—Figure 1 shows a "spot plot" of the activity of the cell as the rat moves around inside a 76 cm diameter cylinder with high, opaque walls, foraging for randomly scattered food pellets. This cell, like most pyramidal cells in CA1, fires at a relatively high rate (above 10 Hz) when the rat is in a specific small portion of the environment—the "place field" of the cell—but at a much lower rate elsewhere. Different cells have place fields in different locations; there are no systematic rules for their arrangement, except that there may be a tendency for neighboring cells to have nearby place fields. The activity of place cells is known to be related to more than just place: in some circumstances it is sensitive to the direction the rat is facing, and it can also be modulated by running speed, alertness, or other aspects of behavioral state. The dependence on head direction has given rise to a certain amount of controversy, because in some types of environment it is very strong, while in others it is virtually absent.

Table 1 gives statistics for the amount of information conveyed by this cell about spatial location, head direction, running speed, and combinations of these variables. Note that the information conveyed about spatial location *and* head direction is hardly more than the information conveyed about spatial location alone—the difference is well within the error bounds of the calculation. Thus this cell has no detectable directionality. This seems to be typical of cells recorded in unstructured environments.

Table 1: Information conveyed by the cell whose activity is plotted in Figure 1.

VARIABLES	INFO	INFO PER SPIKE
Location	2.40 bits/sec	1.82 bits
Head Direction	0.48 bits/sec	0.37 bits
Running Speed	0.03 bits/sec	0.02 bits
Location *and* Head Direction	2.53 bits/sec	1.92 bits
Location *and* Running Speed	2.36 bits/sec	1.79 bits

The information-rate measure may be helpful in understanding the computations performed by neural populations. Consider an example. Cells in the CA3 and CA1 regions of the rat hippocampal formation have long been known to convey information about a rat's spatial location (this is discussed in more detail below). Data from our lab suggest that, in a given environment, an average CA3 cell conveys something in the neighborhood of 0.1 bits per second about the rat's position—some cells convey a good deal more information than this, but many are virtually silent. Cells in CA1 receive most of their input from cells in CA3; each gets on the order of 10,000 such inputs. Question: How long must the integration time of a CA1 cell be in order for it to form a good estimate of the rat's location? Answer: With 10,000 inputs, each conveying on average 0.1 bits per second, the cell receives information at a rate of 1000 bits per second, or 1 bit per millisecond, so in 5–10 msec the cell receives enough information to form a moderately precise estimate of location.

2 APPLICATIONS

We now very briefly describe two experimental studies that have found differences in the spatial information content of rat hippocampal activity under different conditions. The methods used for recording the cells are described in detail in McNaughton *et al* (1989)—to summarize, the cells were recorded with stereotrodes, which are twisted pairs of electrodes, separated by about 15 microns at the tips, that pick up the extracellular electric fields generated when cells fire. A single stereotrode can detect the activity of as many as six or seven distinct hippocampal cells; spikes from different cells can be separated on the basis of their amplitudes on the two electrodes, as well as other differences in wave shape. The location of the rat was tracked using arrays of LEDs attached to their heads and a video camera on the ceiling. Spatial firing rate maps for each cell were constructed using an adaptive binning technique designed to minimize error (Skaggs and McNaughton, *submitted*), and information rates were calculated using these firing rate maps. As a control, the spike train was randomly time-shifted relative to the sequence of locations; this was done 100 times, and the cell was deemed to have significant spatial dependence if its information rate was more than 2.29 standard deviations above the mean of the 100 control information rates.

2.1 EXPERIMENT: PROXIMAL VERSUS DISTAL VISUAL CUES

In this study (a preliminary account of which appears in Gothard *et al* (1992)), the activity of place cells was recorded successively in two environments, the first a 76 cm diameter cylinder with four patterned cue-cards on the high, opaque gray wall, the second a cylinder of the same shape, but with a low, transparent plexiglass wall and four patterned cue-cards on the distant black walls of the recording room. The two environments thus had the same shape, and from any given point were visually quite similar; the difference is that in one all of the visual cues were proximal to the rat, while in the other many of them were distal.

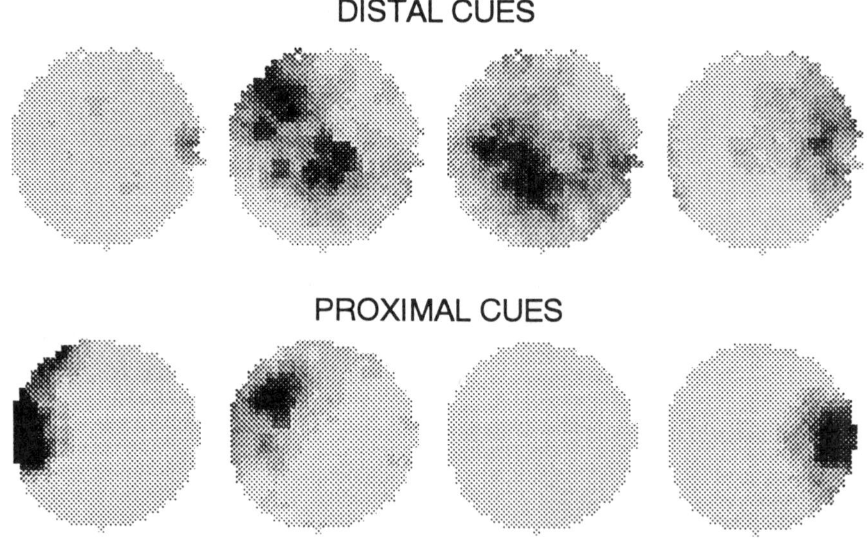

Figure 2: Firing rate maps of four simultaneously recorded cells, in the distal cue environment (top) and proximal cue environment (bottom). The scale is identical for all plots; black $\geq$ 5 Hz.

Fifty cells were recorded with robust place-dependent firing in one or the other cylinder. There was no discernable relationship between place fields in the two environments—a cell having a place field in the proximal cue environment might be nearly silent in the distal cue environment, and even if it did fire, its place field would be in a different location. (Figure 2 shows firing rate maps for four of the cells.) A substantially higher fraction of the cells had place fields in the proximal cue environment, and overall the average information per second was almost 50% higher in the proximal cue environment. For the cells possessing fields, the information per spike was significantly higher in the proximal cue environment, meaning that place fields were more compact.

These results indicate that in the proximal cue environment, spatial location is represented by the hippocampal population more precisely, and by a larger pool of cells, than in the distal cue environment. The most likely explanation is that, at least in the absence of local cues, the configuration of visual landmarks controls the activity of the place cell population.

2.2 EXPERIMENT: LIGHT VERSUS DARK

Visual cues have a great deal of influence on place fields, but they are not the only important factor; in fact, some hippocampal cells maintain place fields even in complete darkness (McNaughton *et al.*, 1989b; Quirk *et al.*, 1990). This experiment (Markus *et al.*, 1992) was designed to examine how lack of visual cues changes the properties of place fields. Rats traversed an eight-arm radial maze for chocolate milk reward, with the room lights being turned on and off on alternate trials. (A trial consisted of one visit to each of the eight arms of the maze.) Figure 3 shows firing rate maps for four simultaneously recorded cells.

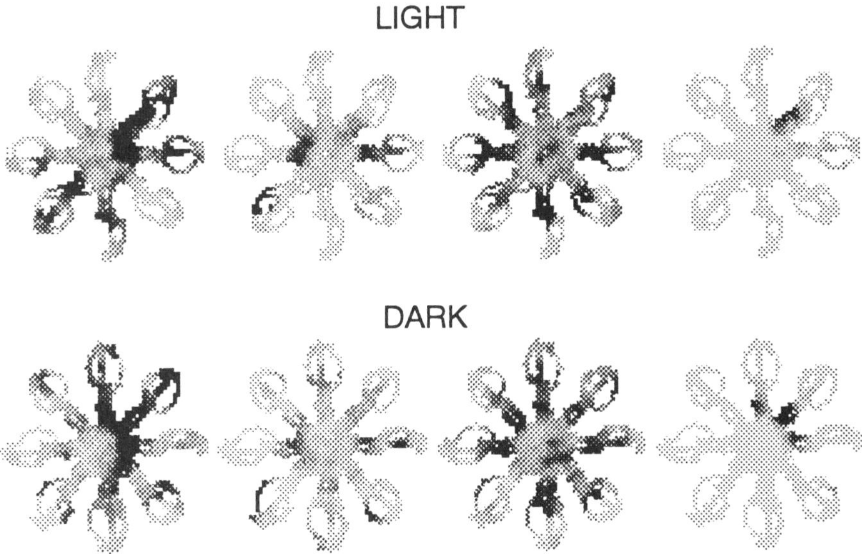

Figure 3: Firing rate maps of four simultaneously recorded cells, with room lights turned on (top) and off (bottom). The scale is identical for all plots; black ≥ 5 Hz. (The loops at the ends of the arms are caused by the rat turning around there.)

The most salient effect was that a much larger fraction of cells showed significant spatially selective firing in the light than in the dark: 35% as opposed to 20%. However, the average information per second decreased only by 15% in the dark as compared to the light, from 0.326 bits per second in the light to 0.278 bits per second in the dark. (These are overestimates of the population averages, because cells silent in both light and dark were not included in the sample.)

Interestingly, the drop in information content from light to dark seemed to be much smaller than the drop from proximal cues to distal cues in the previous experiment. A major difference between the two experiments is that, in the eight-arm maze, tactile cues potentially give a great deal of information about spatial location, but in a cylinder they serve only to distinguish the center from the wall. While it is dangerous to compare the two experiments, which differed methodologically in several ways, the results suggest that tactile cues can have a very strong influence on hippocampal firing, at least when visual cues are absent.

3 THEORY

The information-rate formula (1) is derived by considering a neuron as a "channel" (in the information-theoretic sense) whose input is the spatial location of the rat, and whose output is the spike train. During a sufficiently short time interval the spike train is effectively a binary random variable (i.e. the only possibilities are to spike once or not at all), and the probability of spiking is determined by the spatial location. The event of spiking may be indicated by a random variable S whose value is 1 if the cell spikes and 0 otherwise. If the environment is partitioned into a set of nonoverlapping bins, then spatial location may be represented by an integer-valued random variable X giving the index of the currently occupied bin.

In information theory, the information conveyed by a discrete random variable X about another discrete random variable Y, which is identical to the mutual information of X and Y, is given by

$$I(Y|X) = \sum_{i,j} p(y_i|x_j) \log_2 \frac{p(y_i|x_j)}{p(y_i)} p(x_j),$$

where x_j and y_i are the possible values of X and Y, and $p()$ is probability.

If λ_j is the mean firing rate when the rat is in bin j, then the probability of a spike during a brief time interval Δt is

$$P(S{=}1|X{=}j) = \lambda_j \Delta t.$$

Also, the overall probability of a spike is

$$P(S{=}1) = \lambda \Delta t,$$

where

$$\lambda = \sum_j \lambda_j p_j,$$

with $p_j = P(X{=}j)$.

After these expressions are plugged in to the equation for $I(Y|X)$ above, it is a matter of straightforward algebra, using power series expansions of logarithms and keeping only lower order terms, to derive a discrete approximation of equation (1).

4 DISCUSSION

In many situations, neurons must decide whether to fire on the basis of relatively brief samples of input, often 100 milliseconds or less. A cell cannot get much information from a single input in such a short time, so to achieve precision it needs to integrate many inputs. Formula (1) provides a measure of how much information a single input conveys about a given variable in such a brief time interval.

The formula can be applied to any type of cell that uses firing rate to convey information. The only requirement is to have enough data to get good, stable estimates of firing rates. In practice, for a hippocampal cell having a mean firing rate of around 0.5 Hz in an environment, twenty minutes of data is adequate for measuring position-dependence; and for a "theta cell" (an interneuron, firing at a considerably higher rate), very clean measurements are possible.

We have used the measure in the study of hippocampal place cells, but it might actually work better for some other types. The problem with place cells is that they fire at low overall rates, so it is time-consuming to get an adequate sample. Cortical pyramidal cells often have mean rates at least ten times faster, so it ought to be easier to get accurate numbers for them. The information measure might naturally be applied to study, for example, the changes in information content of visual cortical cells as a visual stimulus is blurred or dimmed.

Supported by NIMH grant MH46823

References

Gothard, K. M., Skaggs, W. E., McNaughton, B. L., Barnes, C. A., and Youngs, S. P. (1992). Place field specificity depends on proximity of visual cues. *Soc Neurosci Abstr*, **18**:1216. 508.10.

Markus, E. J., Barnes, C. A., McNaughton, B. L., Gladden, V., Abel, T. W., and Skaggs, W. E. (1992). Decrease in the information content of hippocampal ca1 cell spatial firing patterns in the dark. *Soc Neuroscience Abstr*, **18**:1216. 508.12.

McNaughton, B. L., Leonard, B., and Chen, L. (1989b). Cortical-hippocampal interactions and cognitive mapping: A hypothesis based on reintegration of the parietal and inferotemporal pathways for visual processing. *Psychobiology*, **17**:230–235.

McNaughton, B. L., Barnes, C. A., Meltzer, J., and Sutherland, R. J. (1989a). Hippocampal granule cells are necessary for normal spatial learning but not for spatially selective pyramidal cell discharge. *Exp Brain Res*, **76**:485–496.

Quirk, G. J., Muller, R. U., and Kubie, J. L. (1990). The firing of hippocampal place cells in the dark depends on the rat's previous experience. *J Neurosc*
10:2008–2017.

Richmond, B. J. and Optican, L. M. (1990). Temporal encoding of two-dime patterns by single units in primate primary visual cortex: Ii informat mission. *J Neurophysiol*, **64**:370–380.

AUTHOR INDEX

KEYWORD INDEX